KU-102-200

Consumer and Trading Standards:
Law and Practice

WITHDRAWN

LIVERPOOL JOHN MOORES UNIVERSITY
Aldham Robarts L.R.C.
Tel: 0151 - 231- 3179

LIVERPOOL JMU LIBRARY

3 1111 01510 4498

WITHDRAWN

Consumer and Trading Standards: Law and Practice

Fifth Edition

Bryan Lewin, MBE
DCA, DMS, FCTSI

Jonathan Kirk, QC
LLB (Hons), Barrister-at-law
Member of the Honourable Society of Lincoln's Inn

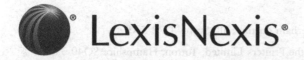

Published by LexisNexis

LexisNexis
Regus
Terrace Floor
Castlemead
Lower Castle Street
Bristol BS1 3AG

Whilst the publishers and the author have taken every care in preparing the material included in this work, any statements made as to the legal or other implications of particular transactions are made in good faith purely for general guidance and cannot be regarded as a substitute for professional advice. Consequently, no liability can be accepted for loss or expense incurred as a result of relying in particular circumstances on statements made in this work.

© RELX (UK) Limited, trading as LexisNexis 2017

All rights reserved. No part of this publication may be reproduced, stored in a retrieval system, or transmitted in any way or by any means, including photocopying or recording, without the written permission of the copyright holder, application for which should be addressed to the publisher.

Crown Copyright material is reproduced with kind permission of the Controller of Her Majesty's Stationery Office.

British Library Cataloguing-in-Publication Data

A catalogue record for this book is available from the British Library.

ISBN 978 1 78473 259 2

Typeset by Letterpart Limited, Caterham on the Hill, Surrey CR3 5XL

Printed in Great Britain by Hobbs the Printers Limited, Totton, Hampshire SO40 3WX

CONTRIBUTORS

Advertising
Anna Medvinskaia, LLB (Hons), LLM
(Cantab), Barrister

Age-restricted Products
Nadia Silver, BA (Hons), MA, Barrister

Animal Health and Welfare
John Chaplin MCTSI, DCATS, Chair
National Animal Health and Welfare
Panel

Civil Enforcement
David Altaras, MA (Oxon), Barrister

Consumer Credit
Daniel Brayley, MA (Cantab), Barrister
Fred Philpott, LLB (Hons), Barrister
Ruth Bala, BA (Hons), Barrister

Consumer Rights
Peter Stonely, MCTSI, MICA

Criminal Enforcement
Jonathan Spicer, MA (Cantab), Barrister
Miles Bennett, LLB (Hons), Barrister
Lee Reynolds, LLB (Hons), Barrister

Environmental
Robin Kingham, BA (Oxon), Barrister

Food Standards and Information
Adam Pearson, LLB (Nott), Barrister
Sue Powell, LLB (Hons), DTS, MCTSI

Fraud and Money Laundering
John Vincent, DTS, DMS, MCTSI
Cameron Crowe, BA (Hons), Barrister

General Matters
Peter Mellett, LLB (Hons), Solicitor

Information
Michael Coley, LLB (Lond), Barrister
Ben Mills, BA (Hons), Barrister

Intellectual Property
Kevin Barry, LLB (Hons), Barrister

Metrology and Hallmarking
Lee Finch, LLB (Hons), LLM, Barrister

Northern Ireland
Jim Frazer LLB, DCATS, MCTSI

Prices
Wendy Potts BA DCA CTSP MCTSI

Product Safety
Christine Heemskerk, BSC (Econ), DTS,
DMS, Chair CTSI 2012-13, 2015-16
Richard Roberts, BA (Oxon), Barrister

Scotland
Neil Coltart, Bsc, LLB, DTS, ILM,
MAPEA, MCTSI

Travel
Thomas Samuels, MA (Oxon), Barrister

Unfair Commercial Practices
Jonathan Goulding, LLB (Hons),
Barrister
Jason Freeman, MA (Cantab), Barrister

Unfair Contract Terms
Jason Freeman, MA (Cantab), Barrister

Unfair Trading
Alison Lambert, LLB, Barrister
Alison Hollis, LLB, Barrister

Wales
Timothy Keohane DBA, DTS, FCTSI,
MICA

First Edition
Ben Gumpert, MA (Cantab), Barrister

FOREWORD TO THE FIFTH EDITION

I am honoured to have been asked to write the foreword for the fifth edition of *Consumer and Trading Standards: Law and Practice*, more affectionately known as the 'Pink Book' and which is by now, I am sure, a staple diet of all UK Trading Standards practitioners and consumer lawyers.

Those that know me will know consumer protection is at the heart of all I do and I firmly believe that empowered consumers and reputable businesses contribute to a vibrant economy. The Chartered Trading Standards Institute's ('CTSI') aspiration therefore, that every UK citizen lives and works in a safe, healthy and fair trading environment, sits comfortably with this.

However, as an Institute, we face an uphill struggle to deliver on this vision when resources within the Trading Standards profession continue to diminish, as evidenced by the most recent refresh of the CTSI workforce survey; and austerity measures continue to bite, with no foreseen let-up in sight while the UK prepares its exit from the EU.

It is perhaps therefore no coincidence that UK consumers, as end users and beneficiaries of the Trading Standards service, are seeing the impact of such austere measures as a result of the diminution of resources in their local Trading Standard authorities. At the time of writing, by way of example, the media are reporting that MPs are debating the effect that scamming has on the most vulnerable consumers; data released from the Food Standards Agency revealed 4,000 major breaches of animal welfare laws at UK abattoirs in the last two years; a large mobile phone company has had to recall their latest phones because they have caught fire due to battery problems and the London Fire Brigade has urged consumers to stop using tumble dryers that are subject to product recall or safety notices following a recent fire in a tower block.

All of these instances highlight the fact that any one of us can be susceptible to detriment, of one sort or another, at a particular moment in time and how we rely therefore, on the invaluable work that Trading Standards professionals do when protecting us. Trading Standards have never been faint hearted and with a determination and a 'can-do' attitude, continually strive within their resources to find ways to protect consumers and honest business; the introduction of 'Friends Against Scams' being a case in point.

This brings me back to the Pink Book, which is just one such invaluable tool in the armoury of those involved in consumer protection and which can be relied upon to provide a definitive guide and clear analysis on the application and interpretation of a myriad of laws and regulations pertinent to the work undertaken. It is, to my knowledge, the only publication which brings together both civil and criminal laws in one place.

I wholeheartedly congratulate those that contribute to this book and for playing their part in protecting our consumers, business and the UK economy as a whole.

Carol Brady MBE, FCTSI
Chair, Chartered Trading Standards Institute Board

PREFACE TO THE FIFTH EDITION

It would be an understatement to say that in 2016 there has been change in the legal and regulatory landscape. In the 16 years since the first edition, we repeatedly commented on the shift away from domestic legislation to a 'European revolution in consumer and trading standards'. We concluded in last year's edition that virtually all of the consumer laws protecting UK citizens now have their origin in Pan-European measures.

Then, out of the red, white and blue, came Brexit.

We do not really understand where Brexit will ultimately take the UK. However, the political debate surrounding the referendum did not suggest that EU consumer protection laws were at the forefront of the complaint made against our EU membership. At the time of writing the Government had promised a *Great Repeal Bill* bringing an end to the European Communities Act 1972, with all laws being brought under the control of the British Parliament and courts. The High Court ruled in November 2016 that it was Parliament, rather than a politician using prerogative power, that must trigger the treaty process of leaving.

Ultimately, it seems to us that existing EU consumer law in force in the UK *is likely* to remain in place until it is amended, revoked or repealed by Parliament. Equally, the surviving body of CJEU case law and jurisprudence *is likely* to continue as persuasive authority, even if it no longer binds our courts.

Turning to the Pink Book, we have radically updated this Fifth Edition. A new chapter on Prices, perhaps the most significant issue for consumers, includes the 2016 Pricing Practices Guide that has been some years in the CTSI's design. A new Advertising chapter focusses on the contemporary importance of advertising standards. There is also now a detailed chapter on Travel coinciding with statutory change in Oct 2016 aligning that sector under the consumer rights umbrella. Finally, we have provided a new chapter on Information, to reflect the onerous data protection responsibilities now faced by public bodies.

As ever we are immensely grateful for the role played by our growing team of contributing editors, who provide real sectoral expertise, allowing the Pink Book to thrive in providing common-sense practical guidance. We must also acknowledge the fantastic support we have received from our publishing editors, Tony Hawitt and Claire Banyard. They have quietly transformed the presentation of this fifth edition and we are indebted to their skill and professionalism.

Lucy Florence Kirk (9) and Sophie Matilda Kirk (6 'but nearly 7') have reached an age where they have little interest in the Pink Book or the colour of its cover. If only we could find a way to include a little more on the topics of Hannah Montana or Taylor Swift, their interest might be rekindled. Bryan continues to be inspired by the efforts and achievements of his five grandchildren – Finbar, Orla, Joseph, Elsa and Nellie – and their parents.

We have agreed that all royalties from the publication of *Consumer and Trading Standards: Law and Practice* (Fifth Edition) will again be donated to Meningitis Now and the British Heart Foundation.

The law is stated as at 5 November 2016.

Jonathan and Bryan

PREFACE TO THE FOURTH EDITION

In the second edition of this book, in 2011, we commented on a European revolution in consumer and trading standards regulation. The same can be said of the fourth edition, although this time the shift in domestic legislation has also been seismic.

The Consumer Rights Act 2015 has radically transformed the media's perception of this area. Although some of these rights were already available, the public's awareness of a trader's statutory obligations is undoubtedly spreading at pace. Enforcement powers have been consolidated and improved. Civil enforcement by public bodies has been bolstered by a raft of new 'enhanced' remedies.

The Consumer Rights Directive has also been implemented in the UK since the last edition of this book. Powerful new consumer rights concerning information and cancellation are yet to make it fully into the public consciousness. But they will provide stout protection for consumers in the rapidly growing area of internet sales. There are new rights that can be used by consumers in the civil courts when traders have engaged in unfair commercial practices.

For us, this has meant a number of structural changes in this edition. We have consolidated the general principles and universal enforcement powers into a chapter on criminal enforcement. There is also a brand new chapter on consumer rights, which considers the obligations set out in the directive and also those concerning consumer contracts in Part 1 of the 2015 Act.

The remainder of the chapters have also been thoroughly updated and we remain enormously grateful to our team of specialist contributors. We thank them once again for their tireless professionalism.

Time has passed quickly since our last edition in 2013 and Lucy Florence (now 8) and Sophie Matilda (now 'nearly 6') no longer regard pink as their favourite colour for its cover. But it is now far too late to change it. The fourth edition is, we are afraid, doomed to its existence as the most garish and gaudy title in a legal library.

We would finally like to dedicate this book again to our families. In particular, Bryan would like to thank his five grandchildren – Finbar, Orla, Joseph, Elsa and Nellie for inspiring him with their own achievements and their ever-increasing bundle of talents.

We have agreed that all royalties from the publication of Consumer and Trading Standards: Law and Practice (Fourth Edition) will again be donated to Meningitis Now and the British Heart Foundation.

Unless otherwise identified, the law is stated as at 1 October 2015.

Jonathan and Bryan

PREFACE TO THE THIRD EDITION

The consumer enforcement landscape has changed forever since the last edition of this work. The Office of Fair Trading will soon be abolished, its strategic consumer protection responsibilities taken on by a National Trading Standards Board more closely linked to the realities of local authority enforcement. We bid farewell to Consumer Focus. We await the contribution that Citizens Advice is asked to make in its brand new role as a public educator of consumers bemused by the impenetrable complexity of laws designed to protect them. During all this radical change the inexorable march of European law continues unhalted.

A new Consumer Rights Act is not likely until late 2014, but, in anticipation of it introducing a civil right to consumer redress, we have increased our focus on civil rights. There are new chapters on Civil Enforcement, Unfair Contract Terms, Consumer Credit and Fraud. The increasing influence of European Union law is reflected in a new chapter on European Construction and a comprehensive review of the developing European case law in other areas.

Consumer law is best described as a collection of principles that pervade many diverse areas of consumer protection. Our chapter headings reveal the extent of that difference, covering such matters as finance and intellectual property to age-restricted sales, food and animal welfare. These areas are increasingly complicated by ever growing thickets of regulation and guidance emanating weekly from London and Brussels.

It is for this reason that, in this third edition, we have increased the contribution from specialist editors, who, as the leaders in their field, are well placed to provide erudite analysis. We remain immensely grateful for their effort and apologise for our demands on their time.

Any attempt to change the colour of the book from its current lurid pink was vigorously opposed by Lucy Florence and Sophie Matilda Kirk (now 5 and 3). For a quiet life, perhaps quieter life, it remains very much the Pink Book.

Bryan has attempted to apply practical considerations to many of this work's legislative concepts, despite the delightful counter attractions and distractions of his (now) five grandchildren (Nellie being the latest addition).

We have agreed that all royalties from the publication of Consumer and Trading Standards: Law and Practice (Third Edition) will again be donated to Meningitis Now and the British Heart Foundation.

We have attempted to state the law as at 1 May 2013.

Bryan and Jonathan

PREFACE TO THE SECOND EDITION

Over the last decade consumer law has undergone a revolution of a distinctly European type. The bedrock of trading law for 40 years, the Trade Descriptions Act 1968, has passed; to be replaced with shiny new regulation in the form of the CPUTR. Very soon the vast majority of UK trading law will have its origin in Brussels and Luxembourg. This will inevitably require domestic consumer law practitioners to understand and embrace the new concepts a European dimension brings. We hope that in completing our Second Edition we have gone some way to assisting practitioners to meet this new challenge.

In this edition we have introduced new chapters on product safety, food safety, the environment and animal welfare. We welcome Neil Coltart as our Scotland editor, which has enabled us to extend the geographical coverage of the book North of the Border. We are also immensely grateful to our team of contributing editors who have each brought to us their specialist knowledge and experience.

The editors would also like to express thanks to David Hedger, Angus Mackay, Samantha Diamond, Paul Maylunn, Carol Gamble (from Northamptonshire County Council TS) and Jenny Mainwaring (from Birmingham City Council TS) for their assistance in reviewing the text.

If an explanation is sought for why the cover of this book is bright pink, we can only thank Jonathan's two daughters, Lucy Florence and Sophie Matilda Kirk, for their advice. Occasionally even experienced barristers don't quite get the answers they want from the questions that they ask!

We have agreed that all royalties from the publication of Trading Standards: Law and Practice (Second Edition) will be donated to Meningitis Now (a charity that Bryan's family has actively supported since the death of his 17 year-old niece Stacey) and the British Heart Foundation.

We would finally like to dedicate the book to our families. Bryan would particularly like to give credit to his four grandchildren – Finbar, Orla, Joseph and Elsa – whose own academic achievements have provided a constant source of inspiration.

Bryan and Jonathan

CONTENTS

TABLE OF CASES

References are to paragraph numbers.

TABLE OF STATUTES

References are to paragraph numbers.

TABLE OF STATUTORY INSTRUMENTS

References are to paragraph numbers.

TABLE OF EUROPEAN LEGISLATION

References are to paragraph numbers.

TABLE OF ABBREVIATIONS

ASBA 2003	Anti-social Behaviour Act 2003
ASBO	Anti-social Behaviour Order
ATOL	Air Travel Organisers' Licensing
AWA 2006	Animal Welfare Act 2006
BBFC	British Board of Film Classification
BEIS	Department of Business, Energy and Industrial Strategy
BERR	Department for Business, Enterprise and Regulatory Reform
BIS	Department for Business, Innovation and Skills
BPR	Business Protection from Misleading Marketing Regulations 2008
BRDO	Better Regulation Delivery Office
CA 2006	Companies Act 2006
CCA 1974	Consumer Credit Act 1974
CHIS	Covert Human Intelligence Sources
CJA 1988	Criminal Justice Act 1988
CMA	Competition and Markets Authority
CPA 1987	Consumer Protection Act 1987
CPDA	Copyright, Designs and Patents Act 1988
CPR	Civil Procedure Rules 1998
CPUTR	Consumer Protection from Unfair Trading Regulations 2008
CRA 2015	Consumer Rights Act 2015
CTSI	Chartered Trading Standards Institute
CYPA 1933	Children and Young Persons Act 1933
DARD	Department of Agriculture and Rural Development
DEA 2010	Digital Economy Act 2010
DEFRA	Department for Environment Food and Rural Affairs
DETI	Department of Enterprise, Trade and Investment
DfE	Department for the Economy
EA 2002	Enterprise Act 2002
ECHR	European Convention for the Protection of Human Rights and Fundamental Freedoms
ECR 2002	Electronic Commerce (EC Directive) Regulations 2002
EIR 2011	Energy Information Regulations 2011
ETSD	European Technical Standards Directive
EU	European Union

FA 2006	Fraud Act 2006
FCA	Financial Conduct Authority
FMSA 2000	Financial Services and Markets Act 2000
FSA	Financial Services Authority
FSA 1990	Food Safety Act 1990
GFR 2004	General Food Regulations 2004
GSPR	General Product Safety Regulations 2005
HSE	Health and Safety Executive
LA 2003	Licensing Act 2003
LBRO	Local Better Regulation Office
LLP	Limited Liability Partnership
MCAD	Misleading and Comparative Advertising Directive
MID	Directive 2004/22/EC of the European Parliament and of the Council on measuring instruments (Measuring Instruments Directive)
NAWI Directive	Council Directive 90/384/EEC relating to non-automatic weighing instruments
NTS	National Trading Standards
Ofcom	Office of Communications
OFT	Office of Fair Trading
OSPA 1995	Olympic Symbol etc (Protection) Act 1995
PACE	Police and Criminal Evidence Act 1984
PERR 2003	Packaging (Essential Requirements) Regulations 2003
PMO 2004	Price Marking Order 2004
POCA 2002	Proceeds of Crime Act 2002
RESA	Regulatory Enforcement and Sanctions Act 2008
RIPA	Regulation of Investigatory Powers Act 2000
RIPSA	Regulation of Investigatory Powers (Scotland) Act 2000
SECCI	Standard European Consumer Credit Information
TDA	Trade Descriptions Act 1968
UCPD	European Unfair Commercial Practices Directive
UGSA 1971	Unsolicited Goods and Services Act 1971
UTCCR	Unfair Terms in Consumer Contracts Regulations 1994
VRA 1984	Video Recordings Act 1984
WEEE 2006	Waste Electronic and Electrical Equipment Regulations 2006
WMA 1985	Weights and Measures Act 1985

CHAPTER 1

INTRODUCTION AND GENERAL MATTERS

CONTENTS

INTRODUCTION

1.1 The origins of Inspectors of Weights and Measures in the United Kingdom can be traced to Magna Carta.

> **Magna Carta Clause 35**
>
> 'Let there be one measure of wine throughout the whole kingdom, and one measure of ale; and one measure of corn; and one width of cloth.'

However, even before the 'consumerism' period which brought in the Trade Descriptions Act 1968, the Fair Trading Act 1973, the Consumer Credit Act 1974 and a host of similar legislative developments, the role of many local authority weights and measures departments had already been extended into administering a myriad of laws regulating such diverse areas as transactions in food, fertilisers, feeding stuffs and poisons.

1.2 Whilst modern-day trading standards services still have as their main objectives consumer protection and fair-trading the areas which they have become either obliged or expected to enforce have increased both in size and complexity. Trading standards services and their employees are expected to be experts in (almost) everything. Copyright, trade marks and counterfeit goods investigations are now part of the staple diet of trading standards officers' work. The Consumer Protection from Unfair Trading Regulations 2008 ('CPUTR') have forced investigators and prosecutors to embrace both a legal language and jurisprudential approach which is new and unfamiliar to many. The reality is that the work of trading standards services now impacts on nearly all aspects of consumer and businesses daily lives.

1.3 Before the last century the predominant interest of weights and measures inspectors was largely to ensure that customers buying essentials were not cheated by unscrupulous merchants and latterly to ensure that dangerous goods were stored safely. For example, by the thirteenth century there were local Assizes of Bread and Ale who inspected the quality and quantity of these common items. Bread had to be weighed against the King's Standard pound and if a brewer or baker was found to have given a short measure they could be fined, put in the pillory or flogged. Bread was such an essential item of the British diet that its price was controlled from the twelfth century until 1815.

1.4 An important function of inspectors was to ensure that scales used by merchants were accurate. For example the Weights and Measures Act 1889 legislated that every scale used for selling in trade had to be stamped and verified. However, there was still great inconsistency in practice because of local custom and inspectors found it difficult to enforce standard measures when faced with a local unit. For example the 'Scotch pint' of milk was actually half a gallon.

1.5 In the early twentieth century, inspectors spent a considerable amount of time lobbying the government to legislate against the practice of merchants including the wrapper in the weight of packets of tea for example. Some commentators have noted that it was estimated in 1908 that some £1million was spent buying paper rather than tea. In the second part of the twentieth century a perennial problem was the practice of 'clocking' second hand cars by dishonest second-hand car traders and numerous prosecutions were brought against such traders. The fraudulent practice has been reduced by the DVLA compiling data of mileage of cars on a transfer of ownership but regrettably still continues today.

1.6 The increased regulation faced by businesses small and large caused concern within the business community and there was extensive press commentary about how the burdens of red tape were causing a drag on enterprise. This fed into the political process and resulted in the Regulatory Enforcement and Sanctions Act 2008 which had the objective of ensuring that sanctions sought against business were proportionate to the offence committed and sought to provide consistency of decision making by the Primary Authority scheme, which is of considerable importance and discussed in greater detail below.

1.7 The list of legislation designed to protect consumers seems to grow on a daily basis and the tide, at present, seems to suggest that the speed of change will not abate in the foreseeable future.

Wales

1.8 Currently, laws made by the National Assembly for Wales, which are, ostensibly, only applicable to Wales, still form part of the law of England and Wales. This is because England and Wales – unlike Scotland and Northern Ireland – share a single legal jurisdiction. Following a referendum in March 2011, the National Assembly for Wales was granted further powers to make laws known as Assembly Bills. Acts may include subordinate legislation. The National Assembly's approach to legislation is that it is made bilingually rather than made first in English and then translated into Welsh.

1.9 The 20 areas in which the National Assembly has competence to make laws are listed in Sch 7 to the Government of Wales Act 2006. They include:

- animal health and welfare;
- consumer protection, including the sale and supply of goods to consumers, consumer guarantees, hire purchase, trade descriptions, advertising and price indications, apart from in relation to food (including packaging and other materials which come into contact with food), agricultural and horticultural products, animals and animal products, seeds, fertilisers and pesticides (and things treated by virtue of any enactment as pesticides);
- food and food products: food safety (including packaging and other materials which come into contact with food); protection of interests of consumers in relation to food.

1.10 The first major piece of regulatory legislation, using the new powers, was the Food Hygiene Rating (Wales) Act 2013 which, when it comes into operation, will see Wales become the first country in the UK to introduce a mandatory scheme requiring food businesses to openly display their hygiene rating. However, the National Assembly had previously introduced Wales-only laws in a variety of areas such as sunbeds (under the Sunbeds (Regulation) Act 2010), charges for single use carrier bags (under the Climate Change Act 2008) and prohibiting the use of collars designed to administer an electric shock on cats and dogs (under the Animal Welfare Act 2006).

1.11 The Wales Bill was introduced into the House of Commons on 7 June 2016. It amends the Government of Wales Act 2006 and makes provision about the functions of the Welsh Ministers giving effect to the Government's policy of establishing a 'reserved powers' model for devolution to Wales.

Scotland

1.12 Although the majority of offences in Scotland are common law (for example there is no Theft Act) most of the offences reported to trading standards services have a statutory basis. Many of these offences derive from legislation that applies across the United Kingdom; however, it is important to note that the processes and evidential rules are quite different in Scotland. An illustration of this can be seen in a passage from *Hamilton v HMA*[1] in relation to the Trade Descriptions Act 1968 (TDA):

> 'No analogy can usefully be drawn as to what may be the correct application of the wording of section 19(1) to Scottish procedure for what may happen South of the border.'

1.13 Perhaps the best known evidential rule in Scotland is the requirement for corroboration, this requirement was classically set out in *Morton v HMA*:[2]

> 'No person can be convicted of a crime or a statutory offence except where the legislature otherwise directs, unless there is evidence of at least two witnesses implicating the person accused with the commission of the crime or offence with which he is charged. This rule has proved an invaluable safeguard in the practice of our criminal courts against unjust convictions and it is a rule from which the courts ought not to depart.'

1.14 Nowadays this statement might perhaps be better read as 'at least two independent sources' given the development of forensic science and the reliance on documentary evidence in many cases. The consequence of this evidential rule is that not only the offence but every essential fact in relation to it requires to be corroborated.

---

1   1997 SLT 31 per Lord Justice General Hope at pp 34G–34H.
2   1938 JC 50 per Lord Justice Clerk Aitchison.

1.15 The terms of reference of the 2011 Review of Scottish Law and Practice – the *Carloway Review* – required it to consider issues relating to the right of access to legal advice, police questioning of suspects, the operation of the current system of detention, evidence (including corroboration and adverse inference) and issues arising from the Criminal Procedure (Legal Assistance, Detention and Appeals) (Scotland) Act 2010. On the issue of corroboration, the Review was 'in no doubt that the requirement of corroboration should be entirely abolished for all categories of crime'. In December 2012 the Scottish Government sought views, in a public consultation, on additional safeguards required following the removal of the requirement for corroboration.

1.16 The successful prosecution of an accused will always rely on the care with which the investigation is carried out and the subsequent report to the Procurator Fiscal. This means that anyone investigating offences must be sure that they have followed the correct procedures and recorded their compliance. Some investigations may require the use of covert surveillance techniques such as directed surveillance or the use of covert human intelligence sources, the proper use of these is regulated by the Regulation of Investigatory Powers (Scotland) Act 2000. The Act requires that these techniques are only used when it is proportionate and necessary for the purposes of preventing or detecting crime or preventing disorder, in the interests of public safety or for the purpose of protecting public health.

1.17 Each local authority will have adopted processes that allow for these covert techniques to be considered and if appropriate authorised. The admissibility of any evidence gathered using these covert techniques relies on the investigating officer following these procedures so it is vital that they are followed and compliance with them properly recorded. If the investigation requires it the Regulation of Investigatory Powers Act 2000 outlines the requirements for acquiring communications data.

1.18 Another significant difference in the criminal justice process is the fact that all prosecutions in Scotland are dealt with through the Crown Office and Procurator Fiscal's Service. The majority of trading standards cases are prosecuted by Procurators Fiscal, for the area in which the offence has allegedly taken place, although cases heard in the High Court of Justiciary will be prosecuted by Advocates Depute.

1.19 Once a report, alleging that offence/s have been committed, has been submitted for consideration by the Procurator Fiscal, they determine whether or not the report should be accepted and, if so, in which court and whether under summary or solemn procedure. In a formal sense it is the Procurator Fiscal who directs investigations although in most cases that are dealt with by trading standards services the investigating officer will have presented a report covering all the necessary evidential elements.

1.20 In assessing whether or not to proceed to prosecution the Procurator Fiscal will consider a number of matters. Most obviously whether the alleged offence is known in the law of Scotland, whether there is sufficient evidence to prove a crime has taken place and who committed it, whether there is a reasonable prospect of securing a conviction and, perhaps most importantly, whether the prosecution is in the public interest?

1.21 The Criminal Procedure (Scotland) Act 1995 covers a large number of procedural matters including the submission of documentary evidence, however in most instances a witness will be required to speak to any evidence that is being led and indeed except in the instance of expert evidence, two witnesses will be required.

1.22 Although the majority of the offences reported to the Procurator Fiscal by trading standards services will be tried under summary procedure, where they are conducted under solemn procedure the jury will consist of 15 members. There are a number of other differences in Scotland, including the vocabulary of the criminal justice process and perhaps, most famously, there are three verdicts in Scottish Courts including 'not proven'.

1.23 The Scottish Parliament is able to make laws – see s 29 of the Scotland Act 1998 – but this section limits the competence of the Scottish Parliament to do so. Section 29(2) of the Scotland Act 1998 provides that a provision is outside the legislative competence of the Scottish Parliament if certain criteria apply – one of which is that a provision is outside that competence if it would form part of the law of any country or territory other than Scotland. This provision, therefore, prevents the Scottish Parliament from legislating matters affecting the law in England, Wales or elsewhere.

Northern Ireland

1.24 When the Northern Ireland Executive was formed under Devolution in 1998, it gave, through its Programme for Government, a commitment to publish a Consumer Strategy for Northern Ireland. Underpinning that strategy was an agreed policy position requiring that consumers and law-abiding businesses in Northern Ireland should be afforded a level of protection which was at least on a par with that enjoyed by their counterparts in England, Scotland and Wales.

1.25 Among the devolved administrations, only in Northern Ireland is consumer protection a transferred (or devolved) function. In Northern Ireland, trading standards, in contrast to Great Britain's local authority model, is a *central government* function, and, as a consequence, a national service. The Trading Standards Service comprises some 50 staff with headquarters in Belfast and regional offices in Londonderry, Ballymena, Armagh and Enniskillen, covering the North, East, South and West of the country respectively. The Service is now positioned as a business area within the Department for the

Economy (DfE).[3] The staff are civil servants and like their 'mainstream' departmental colleagues, accountable to the Minister for the Economy.

1.26 The Service's enforcement agenda has, therefore, been shaped largely by legislation covering areas such as trade descriptions (though the 1968 Act has now been repealed and replaced by a successor regime dealing with unfair commercial practices); weights and measures; fair trading; unfair terms in consumer contracts; consumer credit; hallmarking; estate agency; property misdescriptions; prices and price marking; trade marks and timeshare.

1.27 Trading Standards Officers in Northern Ireland, however, unlike many of their counterparts in Great Britain, have no rights of audience in any courts and, as a result, all of the Service's prosecutions are processed by Northern Ireland's Public Prosecution Service ('PPS') which is part of the Department of the Director of Public Prosecutions. Cases are sent to the PPS from the Trading Standards Service with a recommendation for the commencement of legal proceedings, and, if proceedings are directed, the case will be prosecuted by a PPS official or, more commonly, counsel instructed by the PPS.

1.28 The PPS, in contrast to, for example, the Crown Prosecution Service in Great Britain, has no investigative function. It acts solely to direct (or not) on the evidence compiled by the Trading Standards Service, and to process the investigation through to a hearing, and to an appeal if required. The Trading Standards Officer's role in court – in most cases the magistrates court – is to assist the prosecutor and to act as a witness for DfE, in whose name all trading standards cases are taken.

1.29 The Trading Standards function in Northern Ireland is positioned in notable contrast to Great Britain, within the same central government structure as DfE's other consumer affairs functions. The Northern Ireland Government's functions, therefore, relating to enforcement: advice; intervention: outreach: marketing: policy, legislation, and sponsorship of the Northern Ireland Consumer Council, are all positioned (and accommodated) together within DfE's Consumer Affairs Branch.

1.30 Along with the Northern Ireland Executive's desire to maintain parity of consumer protection with Great Britain, the UK-wide transposition of European Instruments has had the effect of not merely harmonising the consumer protection provisions across the European Union, but in addition, has significantly reinforced the commonality of the consumer protection framework within the United Kingdom. Although there may be equivalence, or even mirroring, of protection, there will be inevitably be minor differences in the section or article numbers referencing the particular provision. Drafting nuances and preferences should, therefore, be represented accurately in, for example, drafting summonses, informations or other legal instruments. There are also in existence, an admittedly small number of instances where, in the

---

3   It was formerly a part of the Department for Enterprise, Trade and Investment ('DETI').

transposition of a Directive into Northern Ireland-specific law, drafting 'anomalies' have resulted in an inexact match with the Great Britain instrument that was serving as the relevant template.

Local weights and measures authorities

1.31   There are now a wide variety of criminal offences and civil infringements that apply across the spectrum of commercial practices. Although legislation is principally concerned with the protection of consumers, some of the statutes enshrine the rights and interests of traders and their intellectual property. The responsibility for enforcing this criminal legislation is usually the statutory duty of 'local weights and measures authorities' through their trading standards service.

1.32   'Local weights and measures authorities' are defined in s 69 of the Weights and Measures Act 1985:

> **69 Local weights and measures authorities**
>
> (1) In England, the local weights and measures authority shall be –
>
> (a)   for each non-metropolitan county, metropolitan district and London borough, the council of that county, district or borough,
>
> (b)   for the City of London and the Inner and Middle Temples, the Common Council of the City of London, and
>
> (c)   for the Isles of Scilly, the Council of the Isles of Scilly.
>
> (2) In Wales, the local weights and measures authority for each county shall be the county council and for each county borough shall be the county borough council.
>
> (3) In Scotland, the local weights and measures authority for the area of each council constituted under section 2 of the Local Government etc. (Scotland) Act 1994 shall be the council for that area.

1.33   There are now over 200 local authorities exercising trading standards functions. They have duties and responsibilities for enforcing a wide range of national and European laws through both criminal and civil law processes. In addition to regulatory activities, most services provide advice, information and education to consumers and businesses in order to make them aware of their rights and obligations – although there are no powers, as such, to intervene or negotiate on behalf of consumers in disputes.

CONSUMER LAW INSTITUTIONS

Government

1.34   The majority of legislation enforced by Trading Standards (from July 2016) falls under the Department for Business, Energy and Industrial Strategy ('BEIS') which was formed by the merger of the Department for Business, Innovation and Skills (BIS) and the Department of Energy and Climate Change

('DECC'). BIS was itself created by the merger of the Department of Business, Enterprise and Regulatory Reform and the Department of Innovation, Universities and Skills in 2009.

1.35 The BEIS legislation primarily comprises areas concerned with fair trading, product safety, weights and measures, prices, consumer credit, estate agents, package travel, timeshare, video recordings and intellectual property. BEIS does not have a responsibility towards areas such as age restricted sales, food and animal health. Environmental matters – covering waste, energy and climate change were previously spread across a number of Departments. For example, the Single Use Carrier Bags Charges (England) Order 2015 was the responsibility of the Department for the Environment, Food and Rural Affairs ('Defra').

1.36 No government minister has a remit specifically dedicated to consumer matters. Margot James MP was appointed as the Minister for Small Business, Consumers, and Corporate Responsibility, a Parliamentary under Secretary of State, at the BEIS in July 2016. This post has responsibility for a wide range of issues including consumer and competition (including energy retail markets and competition law) deregulation and regulatory reform. The Government's wide-ranging reforms to the consumer, competition and credit regimes which started in 2011 were completed by March 2014 and resulted in the establishment of a number of new or revamped organisations, changed responsibilities and a Consumer Protection Partnership.

The Competition and Markets Authority

1.37 The Competition and Markets Authority (CMA), which was established under the Enterprise and Regulatory Reform Act 2013, came into being in shadow form in October 2013 and took on its full powers from April 2014 taking over many of the functions of the Competition Commission and the Office of Fair Trading (OFT). The CMA is an independent non-ministerial department. The OFT, which had responsibility for both protecting consumers and promoting competition, was a non-ministerial department. It was established under the Fair Trading Act 1973 and ceased to exist on 31 March 2014.

Citizens Advice

1.38 From April 2012 a Citizens Advice consumer service took over from the OFT-run Consumer Direct. This contact centre service provided free, practical advice on a range of consumer matters, including information on consumer rights and practical guidance on individual problems and how to gain redress. Citizens Advice has also undertaken consumer advocacy responsibilities for representing consumers' interest in areas such as gas, electricity and postal services as well as unregulated sectors. Consumer Futures, which was formerly Consumer Focus, and represented consumers across regulated markets, was abolished in April 2014, with all its functions transferred to other bodies

(Citizens Advice, Citizens Advice Scotland and General Consumer Council for Northern Ireland). Citizens Advice also took responsibility from the OFT for the national coordination of consumer education in Great Britain.

The Financial Conduct Authority

1.39 The Financial Services Act 2012 'abolished' the Financial Services Authority, renaming it as the Financial Conduct Authority (FCA). The FCA regulates the financial services industry in the UK. In 2014, the FCA took over the OFT's regulatory responsibility for the consumer credit industry. The OFT's anti-money laundering powers and responsibilities passed to the FCA in respect of consumer credit financial institutions, and to HMRC, in respect of estate agents. The Prudential Regulation Authority (PRA) is a part of the Bank of England and responsible for the prudential regulation and supervision of banks, building societies, credit unions, insurers and major investment firms.

The National Trading Standards Estate Agency Team

1.40 The OFT's functions and powers to prohibit or warn estate agents, and to authorise estate agents redress schemes, under the Estate Agents Act 1979, were transferred in 2014 to Powys County Council, as 'the lead enforcement authority'.

Consumer Protection Partnership

1.41 The Consumer Protection Partnership (CPP), formerly known as the Strategic Intelligence, Prevention and Enforcement Partnership (SIPEP) was formed in April 2012 and includes the National Trading Standards Board, Trading Standards Scotland, the Department for Enterprise, Trade and Investment Northern Ireland, the Financial Conduct Authority, the Chartered Trading Standards Institute, Consumer Council for Northern Ireland, and the Citizens Advice Service. Its purpose is to identify areas of where there is a risk that consumer will face harm and where action is not already in place, agree actions to tackle the issues as necessary. The third report on the Partnership's work to date and planned future activities was published in April 2016.

Local authority advisory bodies

1.42 Local Authorities Coordination of Trading Standards ('LACOTS') was originally established in 1978 with the aim of supporting and attempting to ensure that uniform enforcement was conducted by Trading Standards departments. LACOTS subsequently expanded to cover other areas such as food safety, gambling, civil registration and a number of other enforcement functions and, as a result, changed its title to Local Authorities Coordinators of Regulatory Services ('LACORS'). LACORS was renamed Local Government Regulation ('LGR') in 2010 but was disbanded a year later by the Local Government Association.

Better regulation bodies

1.43 The Local Better Regulation Office ('LBRO') was established in 2007, initially set up as a private company limited by guarantee. LBRO became an executive non-departmental public body and given a range of statutory duties and powers (including the operation of the Primary Authority scheme) under the Regulatory Enforcement and Sanctions Act 2008. LBRO was dissolved in April 2012, and its functions taken over by the Better Regulation Delivery Office ('BRDO'). BRDO was then incorporated into a new structure in April 2016, combining with the National Measurement and Regulation Office, known as Regulatory Delivery ('RD'), which is now part of the Department for Business, Energy and Industrial Strategy.

National Measurement and Regulation Office

1.44 The National Measurement and Regulation Office ('NMRO') combined with BRDO to create a new Regulatory Delivery ('RD') directorate 1 April 2016. It had previously been known as the National Weights and Measures Laboratory and, then the National Measurement Office. RD also has policy (legislative) responsibility for the hallmarking of precious metal articles The British Hallmarking Council, established and governed by the Hallmarking Act 1973, is an Executive Non-Departmental Public Body established the Hallmarking Act 1973. The Council is funded by the UK's four Assay Offices.

Chartered Trading Standards Institute

1.45 In 2013 the Chartered Trading Standards Institute ('CTSI') took over the OFT's role in providing (most) business information to retailers. The CMA retains primary responsibility for business education on the unfair contract terms. The OFT-managed consumer code approval scheme was succeeded by a self-funding model established by the CTSI as from April 2013.

National Trading Standards

1.46 National Trading Standards was set up in 2012 by the Government as part of changes to the consumer protection landscape. It brings together representatives of Trading Standards from England and Wales to prioritise, fund and coordinate national and regional enforcement cases. With effect from April 2013, the NTS took over some coordination and database-management functions previously undertaken by the OFT.

Designated enforcers

1.47 Under the Enterprise Act 2002 a designated enforcer is any public or private body in the UK which the Secretary of State designates in a Statutory Instrument, having identified that the person or body has the protection of the collective interests of consumers as one of its purposes. The following bodies are designated: the Civil Aviation Authority, the Financial Conduct Authority,

Ofcom, Ofwat, the Gas and Electricity Markets Authority (Ofgem), the Information Commissioner's Office, the Office of Road and Rail, the Consumer's Association (Which?) and the Northern Ireland Authority for Utility Regulation.

Food

1.48 The Food Standards Agency ('FSA') is an independent Government department established by the Food Standards Act 1999. In 2010 Machinery of Government changes resulted in the Department of Health ('DoH') taking over nutrition policy in England but in Scotland and Northern Ireland the FSA stayed in control. Responsibility for nutrition policy in Wales lies with the Welsh Government. The DoH and Department for Environment, Food and Rural Affairs ('Defra') took over food labelling policy in England, where this does not relate to food safety or nutrition, but the FSA continued to be in charge of labelling policy matters in Wales, Scotland and Northern Ireland.

1.49 In 2015 Food Standards Scotland (FSS) replaced the FSA in Scotland. FSS was established by the Food (Scotland) Act 2015 as a non-ministerial office, part of the Scottish Administration, alongside, but separate from, the Scottish Government The FSA maintains overall responsibility for food safety and food hygiene for the remainder of the UK. The FSA in Wales is based in Cardiff and the FSA in Northern Ireland is based in Belfast. The Welsh Food Advisory Committee and the Northern Ireland Food Advisory Committee provide advice or information to the FSA about matters connected with its functions, including, in particular, matters affecting or otherwise relating to Wales and Northern Ireland, respectively.

1.50 The FSA's National Food Crime Unit (NFCU) works with partners to protect consumers from serious criminal activity that impacts on the safety or authenticity of food.

PRIMARY AUTHORITY

Regulatory Delivery

1.51 Part 1 of the Regulatory Enforcement and Sanctions Act 2008 ('RESA') provided for the establishment of the Local Better Regulation Office ('LBRO') and made provision about its objectives and functions. LBRO was initially set up as a private company limited by guarantee and became an executive non-departmental public body with statutory powers, accountable to the Department for Business, Innovation and Skills ('BIS') in October 2008. LBRO's area of responsibility covers environmental health, trading standards, fire safety and licensing.

1.52 In February 2011 the Government announced that, subject to Parliamentary approval and the outcome of a consultation on plans for streamlined regulation, LBRO would be replaced by a new organisation within

BIS. LBRO was dissolved on 1 April 2012, and its functions taken over by the Better Regulation Delivery Office (BRDO). The BRDO was based within BIS and aimed to give 'the business voice' a more prominent platform in the delivery of regulation, working towards a simpler regulatory regime. BRDO were incorporated into a new structure in April 2016, known as Regulatory Delivery (RD), which is now part of the Department for Business, Energy and Industrial Strategy. RD aims to bring policy expertise and practical experience together to ensure that regulation is effectively delivered to reduce burdens on business, save public money and properly protect consumers and communities.

1.53 In the remainder of this section relating to Primary Authority, all references are to RD.

RD in Scotland

1.54 RD's functions under Part 1 do not apply in Scotland – Parts 2, 3 and 4 apply in Scotland in respect of matters that are reserved. The Regulatory Reform (Scotland) Act 2014 creates a legal framework for implementation of Primary Authority arrangements relating to the Devolved Regulatory responsibilities of Local Authorities in Scotland.[4]

1.55 Where RD exercises its functions in relation to matters which are the responsibility of Welsh Ministers, provision is made for RD to consult or seek the consent of Welsh Ministers – similarly, there are also specific procedures in Parts 2, 3 and 4 in respect of matters in which the Welsh Ministers exercise functions.

Co-ordination of regulatory enforcement

Home and lead authority

1.56 Non-statutory home and lead authority agreements have existed for many years between local authority regulators and business enterprises, most commonly those with multi-site operations. For trading standards and food safety matters the authority is generally referred to as the home authority, whereas, for health and safety matters, it is referred to as the lead authority. The home or lead authority is often, but not necessarily, the local authority where the company's head office is based. Home or lead authorities carry out a number of roles, for example providing advice and guidance to assist compliance and acting as a contact point for other local authorities.

Primary Authority

1.57 Part 2 of RESA establishes a Primary Authority Scheme (PA Scheme) for any business that trades across council boundaries with the aim of securing

---

4   A Scottish Government consultation, seeking views on the proposed scope of a primary authority scheme in Scotland and how it would operate in practice, had a closing date for responses of 25 June 2015.

co-ordination and consistency of regulatory enforcement by local authorities. Theoretically, the scheme was introduced to address many of the concerns expressed regarding local authority regulatory enforcement, including inconsistent advice, wasted resources, duplication of effort and the absence of an effective dispute resolution mechanism when two local authorities cannot agree on a regulatory approach. The provisions of Part 2 of RESA will be replaced by Part 3 of Enterprise Act 2016 (EA 2016), when it comes into force.

1.58 The Primary Authority is a local authority registered by RD as having responsibility for giving specialist advice and guidance on trading standards, environmental health, and some fire safety functions to a particular business that is subject to regulation by more than one local authority.

1.59 Where there is a registered Primary Authority, any other local authority (known as an 'enforcing authority' for the purposes of the scheme) that proposes to take enforcement action against the business must contact the Primary Authority first (it should be noted that the enforcing authority does not have to obtain the *consent* of the Primary Authority). However, if the Primary Authority believes that the proposed action is inconsistent with advice or guidance that it has previously given, it can prevent the action being taken. RD provides a referrals system to resolve differences of opinion between an enforcing authority and a Primary Authority over a proposed enforcement action.

1.60 The PA Scheme only applies to local authority functions which relate to matters which are devolved or not transferred. The Co-ordination of Regulatory Enforcement (Regulatory Functions in Scotland and Northern Ireland) Order 2009[5] specifies regulatory functions exercisable by local authorities in Scotland and Northern Ireland to which Part 2 applies.

1.61 The Co-ordination of Regulatory Enforcement (Enforcement Action) Order 2009[6] specifies the actions which are to be regarded as enforcement action for the purposes of the primary authority scheme. This Order also prescribes circumstances in which the enforcing authority does not have to notify the primary authority before it takes enforcement action. The Co-ordination of Regulatory Enforcement (Procedure for References to LBRO) Order 2009[7] prescribes that applications for consent to a reference and any representations made to RD in relation to a reference must be made in writing. This Order also prescribes a number of associated administrative matters.

1.62 When exercising a regulatory function specified by the Legislative and Regulatory Reform (Regulatory Functions) Order 2007,[8] local authorities, and their officers, must also have regard to the Principles of Good Regulation and the Regulators' Code, which came into force as a statutory Code of Practice in

---

5   SI 2009/669.
6   SI 2009/665 (as amended).
7   SI 2009/670.
8   SI 2007/3354.

April 2014.[9] Section 21 of the Legislative and Regulatory Reform Act 2006 sets out the five principles – regulatory activities should be carried out in a way that is transparent, accountable, proportionate, and consistent and should be targeted only at cases in which action is needed.

1.63 Section 22 of the Legislative and Regulatory Reform Act 2006 provides for the issuing of a code of practice, with s 23 providing detail on the issuing and revision of a code of practice. The Legislative and Regulatory Reform (Regulatory Functions) (Amendment) Order 2009[10] extends the duty to have regard to the Regulator's Code to local authorities in Scotland, Wales and Northern Ireland in respect of specified functions which are reserved, not devolved or not transferred. In addition, it extends the duty to have regard to the Regulators' Code to those who regulate private businesses and third sector operators carrying out 'public sector' functions for or on behalf of the public sector.

Dispute resolution between local authorities

1.64 The PA Scheme was established under Part 2 of the Regulatory Enforcement and Sanctions Act 2008 (RESA). The PA Scheme's policy is to promote efficient regulation by providing consistent advice from a Primary Authority. If a business operates in multiple local authority areas it can nominate a single authority to deal with its regulatory obligations. Under s 25 of RESA, a Primary Authority may be nominated to carry out this activity. Under s 27 of RESA, the Primary Authority has the function of:

'(a) giving advice and guidance to the regulated person in relation to the relevant function;
(b) giving advice and guidance to other local authorities with the relevant function as to how they should exercise it in relation to the regulated person.'

1.65 At Sch 3 to RESA is a list of relevant Acts concerning which the Primary Authority can give guidance to the regulated person. These include the Consumer Protection Act 1987, Environment Act 1995, Food Safety Act 1990 and Public Health Act 1936 to name but a few of the relevant enactments. Plainly a Primary Authority will be careful to give advice to a regulated person only on legislation which it is authorised to do so and found at Sch 3 to RESA. To achieve the policy, under s 28(1) of RESA an Enforcing Authority must notify the Primary Authority in advance before taking enforcement action against the Regulated Person. 'Enforcement Action' is defined as 'any action which relates to securing compliance with any ... requirement or condition in the event of breach (or putative breach) of a ... requirement or condition.'[11]

1.66 The Primary Authority then has to decide whether the proposed action is inconsistent with advice it has previously given to the Regulated Person. If it is,

---

9   Replacing the Regulators' Compliance Code.
10   SI 2009/2981.
11   RESA, s 28(5)(a).

it *may* direct the Enforcing Authority not to take the proposed enforcement action (s 28(2) of RESA). Pursuant to s 28(7) of RESA, Sch 4 to RESA provides a framework for resolving differences of opinion between a Primary Authority and Enforcement Authority concerning proposed enforcement actions. The matter can be referred to the Secretary of State to determine the dispute by either the Primary Authority, Enforcing Authority or Regulated Person. RD is responsible for this process. The Regulated Person may make a reference to RD but this would probably be an unusual case, and most references would be expected to have been made by either the Primary Authority or Enforcing Authority who cannot agree on whether an enforcement action can be taken.

1.67 The procedure for referring a dispute to RD is contained within Sch 4 to RESA, the Co-ordination of Regulatory Enforcement (Procedure for References to LBRO) Order 2009[12] and the References to BRDO for Determination: Policy and Procedure document issued by RD. During the procedure and up to its determination the Enforcing Authority cannot take the enforcement action. RD first considers whether to grant consent for the reference to proceed. If it does not, the matter is determined. There is no statutory (or case-law) authority on what informs RD in making its decision on whether to grant consent. However, guidance can be found in paragraph 7.1 of the Policy and Procedure document that provides as follows:

'A report will be prepared on each application for the Chief Executive. The report will consider the following and may include a recommendation as to whether consent should be granted:

a)   Whether the application is complete and properly made;
b)   Whether the subject of the application is an appropriate question for BRDO to determine;
c)   Whether multiple applications have been received in respect of the same question;
d)   Whether related applications have been received;
e)   Where the primary authority is the applicant, whether BRDO is satisfied that the primary authority has provided sufficient and appropriate reasons for making the application; and
f)   Whether all of the information required for the determination process has been made available to BRDO.'

1.68 Therefore, in a typical case, it would be expected that RD will consent to a reference. It would not do so for the reasons given above so, for example, if the question had already been referred by another party or, if it considered that the question was frivolous and vexatious. If consent is granted, RD will make a decision generally within 28 days of the reference being made to it (para 6(1) Sch 4 to RESA). The speed of decision making is important to ensure that the PA Scheme is seen by all stakeholders to operate efficiently and to give effect to the primary purpose of RESA.

---

[12]   SI 2009/670.

1.69 In determining a reference, RD will consider whether:

(1) the proposed enforcement action is inconsistent with Primary Authority Advice given by the Primary Authority;

(2) the Primary Authority's advice was correct; and

(3) the Primary Authority advice was properly given by the Primary Authority.

1.70

If RD determines that any one of the criteria is not satisfied then it will consent to the proposed enforcement action because in effect the protection afforded to the Regulated Person by s 28(2) of RESA is no longer effective because of its determination, otherwise it will direct the enforcing authority not to take the proposed enforcement action (see para 3(2), Sch 4 to RESA). RD will notify the parties in writing of its determination and make any relevant directions as soon as reasonably practical. It is likely to publish its determination on its website as guidance for other local authorities and to ensure that they are aware of the decision.

1.71 The Primary Authority, Enforcing Authority and Regulated Person must bear their own legal costs in respect of the reference procedure to RD. In general, RD will bear its own costs unless the Regulated Person makes the reference to it and it is in RD's discretion to recover those costs. The factors it considers relevant to exercising the discretion to recover costs include the outcome of the reference, the parties' conduct during the reference, the complexity of the dispute and the circumstances of the regulated person.

1.72 There is no statutory appeal from a decision of RD under the Schedule 4 appeal procedure. However, challenges may be made by judicial review on the application of public law principles. There has been only one reference to RD under Sch 4 to RESA to date, although it can be expected that more challenges will be made in the future.

1.73 In *R (Kingston Upon Hull CC) v BRDO, Newcastle CC, Greggs plc*[13] a judicial review challenge was made by Kingston upon Hull City Council to primary authority advice given by Newcastle City Council to Greggs Plc regarding the latter's obligations to provide toilets in its bakery shops. Newcastle had advised Greggs that it did not need to provide toilets where there were ten or less seats in a store. The High Court agreed that the advice was unlawful and quashed the decision of the BRDO to affirm it. Kerr J set out he considered that the PA scheme should operate by reference to the facts of the case:

'How then should Hull reconcile its retention of section 20 functions in relation to Greggs' branches in Hull, with its obvious, although unstated, obligation to take

---

[13] [2016] PTSR 967; [2016] CTLC 63; [2016] ACD 94.

account of Newcastle's advice about how to exercise those same functions? The interaction of statutory functions leads to the following division. I will use the facts of this case as an example of how the scheme should operate, in this case and in other cases.

First, it is for Newcastle to give advice and guidance to Hull, as it did. In doing so, it must get the law right; see above. It is crucial that it does so because the law must be the same for everyone in the relevant market, to avoid unlawful distortion of competition. You cannot have one law for Greggs and another for its competitors. That proposition alone is sufficient to defeat the objection founded on immateriality.

Secondly, in advising and giving guidance on the exercise of discretionary powers, Newcastle may suggest what weight should be given to particular factors. These may include matters such as the number of seats and the proportions of take away and sit down customers. Those discretionary matters must be clearly separated from, and seen to be separated from, statements of what the law is. For the reasons I have already given, that is not a matter that is merely cosmetic or immaterial. It is fundamental.

Third, the advice and guidance must obviously be taken very seriously by Hull. In practice, it is advice that should be followed unless there is a good reason not to do so, because otherwise either the primary authority (here, Newcastle) or the regulated person (here, Greggs) can, albeit ultimately subject to the consent of the BDRO, stop the enforcement action by using the section 28 and Schedule 4 machinery.'[14]

Permission to appeal was given to both the Secretary of State and to Greggs plc in this case. That appeal will be heard in 2017.

Relationship between the home and primary authority schemes

1.74 Home authority relationships may continue to operate or to be established in situations when a business does not have a primary authority partnership in place (for example, if a business chooses not to enter into a partnership or is legally unable to have one), but where there remains a clear need for regulatory activity in relation to that business to be co-ordinated.

1.75 On 20 February 2012, a shared vision for the home authority scheme and how it can work with its primary authority counterpart was developed by the regulatory bodies – RD, the Chartered Trading Standards Institute (CTSI) and the Chartered Institute of Environmental Health (CIEH). This framework document supports a Joint Statement of Commitment signed in June 2011 by the same three bodies, who also agreed to a document entitled *Towards a Unified Vision for Primary Authority and Home Authority* in September 2011. It is designed to ensure that no overlap or duplication exists between home and primary authority schemes and that there is improving coherence between them

---

[14] Paras 70–75.

– whilst also recognising that there are differences in their respective objectives. The Chartered Trading Standards Institute now hosts the Home Authority database.

Primary Authority – further developments

1.76 The Local Better Regulation Office (Dissolution and Transfer of Functions, Etc) Order 2012 amended RESA in a number of respects including repeal of BRDO's power, under s 7 of RESA, to direct local authorities to comply with guidance issued under s 6 of RESA. However, it should be noted that the power to issue guidance to local authorities (which transfers to the Secretary of State from LBRO) and the requirement that local authorities must have regard to that guidance, are retained.

1.77 The Enterprise and Regulatory Reform Act 2013 contains two sections which amend RESA. Firstly, the Act includes amendment provisions to Part 2 of RESA which broaden the eligibility requirements for the Primary Authority Scheme. From October 2013 franchises, group companies and other businesses that have a shared approach to compliance (eg through a sector-led certification scheme) are now eligible for Primary Authority partnerships.

1.78 In April 2014 changes were made in respect of some of the categories and areas included in Primary Authority, bringing into scope the Welsh regulations on single use carrier bag charging, alcohol in relation to age-restricted sales and a new fire safety category. In addition, Statutory Guidance relating to Primary Authority was published in September 2013 to provide support to local authorities in relation to their Primary Authority partnerships. This Guidance was produced under s 22(3) and s 33 of RESA 2008.

1.79 The Enterprise and Regulatory Reform Act 2013 made amendments to inspection plans, drawn up under s 30 of RESA which mean that enforcing authorities may not deviate from an inspection plan unless the Primary Authority has been given written notification of the deviation and given its written consent. Additionally, enforcing authorities must provide feedback to the Primary Authority where this is required in the inspection plan.

1.80 In September 2015, RD issued a discussion paper, setting out plans for further extension and simplification of Primary Authority. Changes were incorporated into the Enterprise Act, which received Royal Assent in May 2016 and which includes measures to make it easier for small businesses to access the scheme, following commitments made by the Business Secretary in May 2015. Part 3 of the Enterprise Act 2016 substitutes Part 2 of RESA and extends the provisions relating to Primary Authority – a summary of the provisions is given below.

1.81 Additionally, RD proposes to extend the Primary Authority scheme to other areas of legislation, in order to enable other regulators to participate and to ensure regulators recognise the advice issued in other nations. This is particularly important in relation to Scotland, where a consultation was undertaken at the beginning of 2015 on setting up a Primary Authority scheme and how this will work in practice. No further progress has been made on this to date, although the Regulatory Reform (Scotland) Act, which received Royal Assent in February 2014, created a legal framework for the implementation of Primary Authority in Scotland.

Enterprise Act 2016

1.82 The measures in Part 3 of Enterprise Act 2016 (EA 2016), when they come into force, will extend the application of the Primary Authority scheme and will enable the Secretary of State to make legislation that will bring regulators other than local authorities within the scope of the scheme. The Government's policy objectives for these measures were as follows:

- simplifying the scheme to make it easier for small businesses and pre-starts to form Primary Authority partnerships, including businesses not trading over local authority boundaries;
- simplifying access for co-ordinated partnerships by allowing the co-ordinated partnerships to sign up businesses on behalf of the businesses;
- providing powers to allow national regulators to enter into Primary Authority partnerships alongside local authorities and issue advice to businesses;
- technical changes to simplify how the scheme operates.

1.83 Part 3 of EA 2016 (which consists of ss 20 and 21) substitutes Part 2 of the Regulatory Enforcement and Sanctions Act 2008 (RESA), dealing with the coordination of regulatory enforcement. While much of the Primary Authority scheme remains the same, the Government have chosen to replace the legislative provisions, rather than simply amend them, for ease of comprehension.

1.84 The new Part 2 of RESA will enable the Secretary of State to prescribe in secondary legislation qualifying regulators other than local authorities that may be a primary authority, regulators that may provide support to primary authorities, and regulators that will be required to act consistently with primary authority advice. It provides that persons who carry on an activity in the area of only one qualifying regulator and those who do not yet carry on an activity are also in the scope of the Primary Authority scheme. It enables members of regulated groups to access the Primary Authority scheme via a co-ordinator and establishes the powers and duties of persons who act as a co-ordinator. This Part applies to England, Wales, Scotland and Northern Ireland. In relation to Scotland, Part 2 of RESA will continue to apply only to reserved matters. In relation to Northern Ireland, it will continue to apply only to matters that are not transferred.

CHAPTER 2

INTERPRETATION OF CONSUMER LAW

INTRODUCTION

2.1 Virtually all consumer protection laws in the UK are to be found in statutes and delegated legislation. The interpretation of these provisions can be complex, with layers of regulation that typically implement European Union ('EU') laws sometimes drafted in unfamiliar terms. The interpretation of domestic measures implementing EU law usually requires consideration of both domestic and EU law principles of interpretation.

2.2 It is inevitably difficult to analyse the correct approach to the interpretation of EU laws following the Brexit vote in June 2016. At the time of writing, the Government had promised a *Great Repeal Bill*, to repeal the European Communities Act 1972 and bring all UK laws under the control of the British Parliament and courts. It seems likely that existing EU law which has been brought into force in the UK will remain in place until it is amended, revoked or repealed by Parliament. It also seems likely that, in construing those measures, the courts will continue to consider the EU law upon which it is based and the judgments and jurisprudence of the Court of Justice of the EU. For those reasons we have continued to devote attention to the construction of EU law, which currently provides the basis of a substantial part of domestic consumer protection laws.

2.3 We have focused on the principles of statutory construction that we consider likely to be most helpful to practitioners in this area. It should be emphasised that we provide only an overview of those principles that are most relevant. For a more detailed analysis you should consider the general textbooks on the subject of statutory interpretation. In our analysis, we have distilled the relevant principles into two categories.

(a) The general principles of statutory interpretation that are primarily derived from the common law and other linguistic canons of construction.

(b) Interpretative rules derived from statute, including the interpretative obligations under s 3 of the Human Rights Act 1998 and, for the time being, the absolute obligation under s 2 of the European Communities Act 1972.

2.4 In this chapter the analysis of statutory construction applies only to England and Wales. The parts concerning EU law are, however, equally applicable in Scotland and Northern Ireland. The words 'construction' and 'interpretation' are used synonymously throughout the chapter.

GENERAL PRINCIPLES OF STATUTORY INTERPRETATION

Parliamentary intention

2.5 The primary purpose of statutory interpretation is to ascertain the intention of the legislature as expressed in a statutory provision. In *Regina (Spath Holme Ltd) v Secretary of State for the Environment*, Lord Nicholls of Birkenhead set out the process by which Parliamentary intention should be ascertained:

> 'Statutory interpretation is an exercise which requires the court to identify the meaning borne by the words in question in the particular context. The task of the court is often said to be to ascertain the intention of Parliament expressed in the language under consideration. This is correct and may be helpful, so long as it is remembered that the 'intention of Parliament' is an objective concept, not subjective. The phrase is a shorthand reference to the intention which the court reasonably imputes to Parliament in respect of the language used. It is not the subjective intention of the minister or other persons who promoted the legislation. Nor is it the subjective intention of the draftsman, or of individual members or even of a majority of individual members of either House. These individuals will often have widely varying intentions. Their understanding of the legislation and the words used may be impressively complete or woefully inadequate. Thus, when courts say that such-and-such a meaning 'cannot be what Parliament intended', they are saying only that the words under consideration cannot reasonably be taken as used by Parliament with that meaning.'[1]

2.6 In ascertaining Parliamentary intention an important constitutional principle must be observed. Those who are subject to the law ought to be able to read and understand those laws, without having to look into the process by which they were made. Lord Diplock expressed this aspect of the rule of law in *Fothergill v Monarch Airlines Ltd*:[2]

> 'The source to which Parliament must have intended the citizen to refer is the language of the Act itself. These are the words which Parliament has itself approved as accurately expressing its intentions. If the meaning of those words is clear and unambiguous and does not lead to a result that is manifestly absurd or unreasonable, it would be a confidence trick by Parliament and destructive of all legal certainty if the private citizen could not rely upon that meaning but was required to search through all that had happened before and in the course of the legislative process in order to see whether there was anything to be found from which it could be inferred that Parliament's real intention had not been accurately expressed by the actual words that Parliament had adopted to communicate it to those affected by the legislation.'

---

[1] [2001] 2 AC 349, at 398–9.
[2] *Fothergill v Monarch Airlines Ltd* [1981] AC 251, 279–280.

Plain meaning

2.7   The starting point for interpreting the words used in a statutory provision is that generally a court should follow the natural or ordinary meaning of the language used, its plain meaning. In *Pinner v Everett*, Lord Reid expressed this as:

> 'In determining the meaning of any word or phrase in a statue the first question to ask always is what is the natural or ordinary meaning of that word or phrase in its context in the statute. It is only when that meaning leads to some result which cannot reasonably be supposed to have been the intention of the legislature that it is proper to look for some other possible meaning of the word or phrase.'[3]

2.8   Evidence is generally not admissible about the meaning of an ordinary word,[4] although may be admissible in relation to other more specialist terms.[5] The citation of a 'well known and authoritative' dictionary meaning is permissible, although the court remains free to arrive at its own conclusion.

2.9   This approach to interpretation, although sometimes distinguished from purposive interpretation, is better viewed as a reflection of the general principle that statutory interpretation is always the process of ascertaining the legislator's intention. That intention can most easily be identified by a consideration of the natural or ordinary meaning of the words that Parliament has chosen to use.

2.10   There are numerous reasons that can be given for a court to depart from the plain meaning of a statutory provision. In recent times, the most commonly cited reasons include:

- The ordinary and natural meaning might lead to an absurd result,[6] or one not intended by Parliament.[7]

- The language used is ambiguous or obscure, for example it is capable of more than one grammatical meaning.

- The ordinary and natural meaning would lead to a result that is incompatible with an established common law principle of interpretation.

- The ordinary and natural meaning is incompatible with a statutory obligation, such as s 3 of the Human Rights Act 1998 or s 2 of the European Communities Act 1972.

---

3   [1969] 1 WLR 1266 at 1273.
4   *Marquis of Camden v IRC* [1914] 1 KB 641v.
5   *Blankley v Godley* [1952] 1 All ER 436.
6   Lord Wensleydale's 'golden rule', *River Wear Comrs v Adamson* (1877) 2 App Cas 743 at 764 HL.
7   For example, *Stock v Frank Jones (Tipton) Ltd* [1978] 1 All ER 948 HL, per Lord Simon of Glaidsdale.

Established common law principles

2.11 There is a vast number of presumptions that have developed through the common law about how legislation should be interpreted by the courts. Many of these have their justification in public policies, such as the protection of a citizen's rights. Although there have been attempts to codify these principles to strict rules, they are probably best analysed as merely assumptions that can reasonably be attributed to the intention of Parliament when enacting legislation. For example, Parliament would not ordinarily intend to deprive a person of their liberty by criminal sanction without expressly saying so. It follows that these interpretative principles are rarely, if ever, immutable and may be displaced by the circumstances, context or express language in a piece of legislation. There are many such principles to be found in the textbooks on statutory interpretation, however, we have referred only to those that are most likely to be of use to consumer law practitioners.

Presumption against doubtful penalisation

2.12 It is to be presumed that a provision is not intended to have penal consequences unless that purpose is unambiguous and clearly stated. The presumption dates back to the rule of law set out in Magna Carta 1215, that a person must not be imprisoned or stripped of rights without lawful judgment or by the law of the land.

2.13 The Court of Appeal has recently stated the principle to be that an obscure provision should be 'construed narrowly' because of its potentially penal consequences.[8] The principle exists even though there are potentially circumstances where it will be outweighed by other factors.[9]

2.14 The presumption is particularly strong in cases where imprisonment is a potential outcome. In *R v Hallstrom ex parte W (No 2)* it was stated that there is a 'canon of construction that Parliament is presumed not to enact legislation which interferes with the liberty of the subject without making it clear that this was its intention'.[10] However, the principle is not confined to criminal sanction and extends to any laws that inflict 'hardship or deprivation of any kind on a person'.[11] It has been applied, for example, in relation the deprivation of property rights without compensation (see below).[12]

2.15 In many consumer protection measures, the criminal offence is clearly set out together with the applicable sentence. An area of difficulty may be the drafting of charges for general provisions that define the criminal offence by reference to the breach of a standard not set out in the statute. For example,

---

8 Per Dyson LJ, *Aggasi v Robinson (Inspector of Taxes)* [2005] EWCA Civ 1507, [2006] 1 All ER 900 at [56].
9 *R v Dowds* [2012] EWCA Crim 281 at [37–8].
10 [1986] QB 1090 per McCullough J at [1104].
11 *Bennion on Stautory Interpretation* (6th edn), referring to Bennion in *Halsbury's Laws*.
12 *AG v Horner* (1884) 14 QBD 245 at 257; *Bond v Nottingham Corpn* [1940] Ch 429 at 435.

s 12(1) of the Consumer Protection Act 1987 creates an offence of supplying goods that contravene a safety regulation. In such cases it will be important that the offence is drafted clearly by focussing on its ingredients, setting out in simple terms the nature of the alleged contravention.

Presumption in favour of property rights

2.16   There is a general principle of interpretation that the property rights and other economic interests of private persons should be respected. This principle is similar to the presumption against doubtful penalisation in that it assumes that Parliament intends to protect a citizen's economic rights, unless Parliament's intention to interfere is unambiguous and clearly stated. It is also to be assumed that Parliament would not ordinarily intend to deprive a citizen of property without adequate compensation. An Act should not be construed to prejudice established private rights under contracts,[13] or title to property unless it is clearly intended to do so. This presumption is now reflected in the ECHR qualified right to the peaceful enjoyment of possessions.[14]

Presumption of positive effect

2.17   There is a general rule of statutory construction that it is better for a measure to be given effect rather than be considered void. This is really an application of the courts heeding the intention of Parliament that laws should be given effect. In *R (Hasani) v Blackfriars Crown Court*, Hooper LJ stated that it was a 'well-known rule of statutory interpretation that, if it is possible, the provisions of an Act must be construed so as to give them a sensible meaning'.[15]

Statutory materials

2.18   It follows from the principle that citizens should be able to know their law by reading it, that any approach to statutory interpretation must be cautious when using statutory material that is 'external' to the plain meaning of the words in a provision. In *R (Spath Holme Ltd) v Secretary of State for the Environment*, it was accepted that the courts were not 'confined to looking solely at the language in question in its context within the statute' and might consider the context and background. However, Lord Nicholls made it clear that:

> 'External aids differ significantly from internal aids. Unlike internal aids, external aids are not found within the statute in which Parliament has expressed its intention in the words in question. This difference is of constitutional importance.

---

13   *Allen v Thorn Electrical Industries* [1968] 1 QB 487.
14   ECHR Protocol, Art 1. 'No one shall be deprived of his possessions except in the public interest and subject to the conditions. Every natural or legal person is entitled to the peaceful enjoyment of his possessions. No one shall be deprived of his possessions except in the public interest and subject to the conditions provided for by law and by the general principles of international law.'
15   [2005] EWHC 3016, [2006] 1 All ER 817 [14].

Citizens, with the assistance of their advisers, are intended to be able to understand parliamentary enactments, so that they can regulate their conduct accordingly. They should be able to rely upon what they read in an Act of Parliament .... courts should ... approach the use of external aids with circumspection. Judges frequently turn to external aids for confirmation of views reached without their assistance. That is unobjectionable. But the constitutional implications point to a need for courts to be slow to permit external aids to displace meanings which are otherwise clear and unambiguous and not productive of absurdity.'[16]

Headings, cross headings and side-notes

2.19 The heading in a statutory provision may be used as a tool for interpretation, but only insofar as the heading provides a reliable guide to the material to which it is attached.[17] It must be remembered that a heading, by its nature, is only likely to represent a brief summary of the relevant sections. It is not as important as the wording of the provision itself. A cross-heading may also indicate the scope of the sections that follow it, however caution should be adopted in relation to sections that have since been amended.[18] Side-notes are no longer used in Acts of the UK Parliament. In older statutes where side-notes still appear, it is permissible to use[19] sidenotes to construe the legislation with some caution. In *DPP v Schildkamp*, Lord Reid stated:

'The question which has arisen in this case is whether and to what extent it is permissible to give weight to punctuation, cross-headings and side-notes to sections in the Act .... it may be more realistic to accept the Act as printed as being the product of the whole legislative process, and to give due weight to everything found in the printed Act. I say more realistic because in very many cases the provision before the court was never even mentioned in debate in either House, and it may be that its wording was never closely scrutinised by any member of either House. In such a case it is not very meaningful to say that the words of the Act represent the intention of Parliament but that punctuation, cross-headings and side-notes do not .... I would not object to taking all these matters into account, provided that we realise that they cannot have equal weight with the words of the Act. Punctuation can be of some assistance in construction. A cross-heading ought to indicate the scope of the sections which follow it but there is always a possibility that the scope of one of these sections may have been widened by amendment. But a side-note is a poor guide to the scope of a section, for it can do no more than indicate the main subject with which the section deals.'[20]

Explanatory notes

2.20 Most statutory provisions are now accompanied by a set of explanatory notes. In complex regulatory provisions, these notes are often valuable in determining the purpose of the legislation. Explanatory notes are usually prepared by the Government department responsible for the legislation. They

---

16 [2001] 2 AC 349, at 398–9.
17 *DPP v Schildkamp* [1971] AC 1 at 10.
18 *DPP v Schildkamp* [1971] AC 1, per Lord Reid.
19 *Stephens v Cuckfield RDC* [1960] 2 QB 373 at 383.
20 *DPP v Schildkamp* [1971] AC 1, per Lord Reid.

do not form part of a Bill or draft statutory instrument during its passage through Parliament and are not, consequently, endorsed by Parliament. It follows that they cannot be amended by Parliament. In *R (Westminster City Council) v National Asylum Support Service*, Lord Steyn observed:

> 'The notes are intended to be neutral in political tone: they aim to explain the effect of the text and not to justify it. The purpose is to help the reader to get his bearings and to ease the task of assimilating the law.'[21]

2.21 It is not necessary to show ambiguity before an explanatory note is used. They are admissible aids to construction as long as they 'cast light on the objective setting or contextual scene of the statute, and the mischief at which it is aimed'.[22]

Green papers, white papers and other reports

2.22 Green papers are consultation documents produced by the Government with the aim of generating feedback. They sometimes include different legislative options and are often the first step in the legislative process. White papers are policy documents produced by the Government setting out proposals for future legislation in a more concrete form. White papers sometimes include a draft version of a planned Bill, but remain consultative in nature. Where this type of Parliamentary material is useful to explain a legislative project, it may be relied on by the court when considering the resulting legislation.[23]

2.23 Reports made by the Law Commission and other committees of inquiry, such as a Royal Commission or parliamentary select committee, are to be considered a part of the enacting history of any Act that is based upon the report. Such a report can be cited and taken into consideration by a court when interpreting the Act's statutory provisions.[24]

Hansard

2.24 The rule in *Pepper v Hart*[25] is a rule of practice that permits the use of certain parliamentary materials to aid the interpretation of a statute. Where the legal meaning of an enactment is *ambiguous* or *obscure, or its literal meaning leads to an absurdity*, a court may have regard to any statement on the Bill for the Act containing the enactment, as set out in the official report or record of debates. The record may only be used if:

- it is clear;

---

21   [2002] UKHL 38; [2002] 4 All ER 654; [2002] 1 WLR 2956 para [2–6].
22   National Asylum Support Service, per Lord Steyn, para [6]; see also *R v Montila* [2004] UKHL 50 [35] and *Flora v Wakom (Heathrow) Ltd* [2006] EWCA Civ 1103 [14]–[18].
23   *Duke v GEC Reliance Ltd* [1988] AC 618 at 641.
24   *Black-Clawson International Ltd v Papierwerke Waldhof-Aschaffenburg AG* [1975] AC 591 at 647.
25   *Pepper (Inspector of Taxes) v Hart* [1993] AC 593, [1992] 1 All ER 42 HL.

- was made by or on behalf of the minister or other person who was the promoter of the Bill;[26] and
- discloses the legislative intention underlying the statutory provision.

2.25 Although the rule was stated strictly in *Pepper v Hart*, in modern appellate advocacy it would appear that greater flexibility is applied in practice, with Hansard material regularly considered without applying the letter of the limitation.[27] This can be founded on the basis that *Pepper v Hart* is merely a rule of practice rather than an absolute rule of law. It is also arguable that a court has a residuary inherent jurisdiction to consider such material when required, even though it would not meet the strict criteria set out in *Pepper v Hart*.

Executive guidance

2.26 Government departments and agencies often give guidance on the meaning of legislation after it has been enacted. This is sometimes provided as a consequence of a statutory duty.[28] On other occasions it is designed to provide practical advice. In *Governors of the Peabody Trust v Reeve* the High Court considered the OFT Guidance on unfair terms in tenancy agreements. It was stated that:

> 'Although the court is in no sense bound by the guidance provided by the Office of Fair Trading … that guidance does give landlords helpful common-sense indications of what is likely to be considered to be fair and should be carefully taken into account when drafting a variation clause in a tenancy agreement.'[29]

2.27 The cardinal principle when considering such guidance, in the context of statutory interpretation, is that it remains the constitutional responsibility of the courts to determine the legal meaning of a statutory provision. It is only a court that has the role of authoritatively interpreting legislation as far as it is necessary to do in deciding a case. Executive, investigative and prosecution agencies offering guidance on the construction of legislation remain subject to the determination of a court. In *Regina v London Transport Executive, ex parte Greater London Council*, Kerr LJ stated the principle:

> 'The interpretation of the intention of Parliament as expressed in our statutes is a matter for the courts. Once the meaning of an Act of Parliament has been authoritatively interpreted …. that interpretation is the law, unless and until it is thereafter changed by Parliament.'[30]

---

[26] See *R v Secretary of State for Foreign and Commonwealth Affairs, ex parte Rees-Mogg* [1994] 1 All ER 457 DC.
[27] See for example *R v Warwickshire CC ex parte Johnson* [1993] AC 583, 592.
[28] For example, s 30A of the Regulatory Enforcement and Sanctions Act 2008 (as amended).
[29] [2008] EWHC 1432 (Ch) [2009] L & TR 6.
[30] [1983] QB 484 at 490.

2.28   The weight that should be given to guidance will depend on the circumstances in which it is given. In *R (Ali) v Newham LBC*,[31] Parker J stated that:

> 'the weight that should be given to particular guidance depends upon the specific context in which the guidance has been produced. In particular (without intending to create an exhaustive list) I believe that it is necessary to give due regard to the authorship of the guidance, the quality and intensity of the work done in the production of the guidance, the extent to which the (possibly competing) interests of those who are likely to be affected by the guidance have been recognised and weighed, the importance of any more general public policy that the guidance has sought to promote, and the express terms of the guidance itself.'

LINGUISTIC CANONS OF CONSTRUCTION

2.29   The linguistic canons of construction apply equally to statutory provisions as they would to any text.

Consistent use of terms

2.30   The use of a particular word in a statute is presumed to be consistent throughout, unless the context otherwise requires. This can be important when analysing specific provisions in the context of an Act, however, care should be taken with statutes that cover a variety of different legislative topics. This rule applies in relation to delegated legislation as a consequence of s 11 of the Interpretation Act 1978.

Associated words principle

2.31   It is a contextual canon of construction that words should be construed by reference to associated words, unless the context requires otherwise, *noscitur a sociis*. The *noscitur a sociis* principle is that words should not be read in isolation and take colour from those that surround them. For example, in the phrase 'crane, winch, hoist or block and tackle', the word 'crane' plainly does not refer to a large bird. The principle is not confined to words in the same string or sentence and may extend to other passages within the text.[32]

2.32   In *Bourne (Inspector of Taxes) v Norwich Crematorium Ltd*, the principle was stated by the High Court as:

> 'English words derive colour from those which surround them. Sentences are not mere collections of words to be taken out of the sentence, defined separately by reference to the dictionary or decided cases, and then put back into the sentence with the meaning which you have assigned to them as separate words.'[33]

---

31   [2012] EWHC 2970 (Admin) (30 October 2012).
32   *City Index Ltd v Leslie* [1992] QB 98.
33   [1967] 1 WLR 691, per Stamp J at 696.

2.33 In *Miller v FA Sadd & Son Ltd*[34] the High Court considered s 6 of the Trade Descriptions Act 1968 (now repealed), which extended the meaning of 'offering to supply' goods to include 'having goods in [the trader's] possession for supply'. The defendant had contracted to supply schools with foodstuffs at a particular price, but later delivered the goods together with an invoice for a false price that was higher than agreed. The Prosecution argued that the defendant was deemed to have offered to supply goods with a false trade description because the goods were in the defendant's possession for supply, together with the false invoice, before being delivered.

2.34 The High Court rejected this interpretation of s 6 on the basis that the words 'in his possession for supply' must be read alongside (*'sui generis'*) 'exposing' for supply. It followed that a trader could not offer for supply goods that had already been the subject of a concluded contractual agreement. This is perhaps an example of a court using a canon of linguistic construction to avoid following the literal meaning of a phrase.

Restricting wide words, *ejusdem generis*

2.35 The *ejusdem generis* principle is really a specific application of the associative words principle. It suggests that in a string of words, a general or wide word should have its meaning restricted to the genus or class of the narrower words in the string, unless the context requires otherwise. For example, the meaning of 'other items' in the phrase 'watches, clocks, timers, chronometers and other items' is likely to be restricted to items of the same class or type as the others.

2.36 In *Westminster CC v Ray Alan (Manshops)* the High Court considered the word 'facilities' in s 14(1) of the Trade Descriptions Act 1968 (now repealed) which penalised false statements as to the nature of 'any services, accommodation or facilities'. It found that the word 'facilities' was limited by reference to the words 'service' and 'accommodation' and therefore did not include a closing down sale of goods.

2.37 The principle is most applied when the more general word is used at the end of a list, but may also apply when the wider word is within[35] the list or string of narrower words. The principle is, however, unlikely to have any application where the general word is first and then followed by a string of narrower words.[36]

---

[34]   [1981] 3 All ER 265 at 269.
[35]   *Scales v Pickering* (1828) 4 Bing 448; *Shaw v Ruddin* (1858) 9 Ir CLR 214.
[36]   *Wellsted's Will Trusts* [1949] Ch 296 at 318.

STATUTORY RULES OF INTERPRETATION

The Interpretation Act 1978

2.38 The Interpretation Act 1978 sets out various general rules for interpreting statutory materials. The following definitions are of particular relevance to consumer law practitioners.

Interpretation Act 1978

5 Definitions

In any Act, unless the contrary intention appears, words and expressions listed in schedule 1 to this Act are be construed according to that schedule.

Schedule 1

"Month" means calendar month...

"Person" includes a body of persons corporate or unincorporated...

"Statutory maximum", with reference to a fine or penalty on summary conviction for an offence-

- (a)   in relation to England and Wales, means the prescribed sum within the meaning of section 32 of the Magistrates' Courts Act 1980;
- (b)   in relation to Scotland, means the prescribed sum within the meaning of [section 225(8) of the Criminal Procedure (Scotland) Act 1995]; and
- (c)   in relation to Northern Ireland, means the prescribed sum within the meaning of Article 4 of the Fines and Penalties (Northern Ireland) Order 1984....

"Writing" includes typing, printing, lithography, photography, and any other modes of representing reproducing words in a visible form, and expressions referring to writing are construed accordingly.

Construction of certain expressions relating to offences

In relation to England and Wales—

- (a)   *"indictable offence"* means an offence which, if committed by an adult, is triable on indictment, whether it is exclusively so triable or triable either way;
- (b)   *"summary offence"* means an offence which, if committed by an adult, is triable only summarily;
- (c)   *"offence triable either way"* means an offence ....which, if committed by an adult, is triable either on indictment or summarily;

and the terms *"indictable"*, *"summary"* and *"triable either way"*, in their application to offences, are to be construed accordingly.

In the above definitions references to the way or ways in which an offence is triable are to be construed without regard to the effect, if any, ...on the mode of trial in a particular case.

6 Gender and number

In any Act, unless the contrary intention appears—

- (a)   words importing the masculine gender include the feminine;

(b)　words importing the feminine gender include the masculine;

(c)　words in the singular include the plural and words in the plural include the singular.

7 References to service by post.

Where an Act authorises or requires any document to be served by post (whether the expression "serve" or the expression "give" or "send" or any other expression is used) then, unless the contrary intention appears, the service is deemed to be effected by properly addressing, pre-paying and posting a letter containing the document and, unless the contrary is proved, to have been effected at the time at which the letter would be delivered in the ordinary course of post.

8 References to distance

In the measurement of any distance for the purposes of an Act, that distance shall, unless the contrary intention appears, be measured in a straight line on a horizontal plane.

9 References to time of day

Subject to section 3 of the Summer Time Act 1972 (construction of references to points of time during the period of summer time), whenever an expression of time occurs in an Act, the time referred to shall, unless it is otherwise specifically stated, be held to be Greenwich mean time.

Territorial jurisdiction

2.39 Unless the contrary intention appears, it is presumed that an Act of Parliament extends to the whole of the UK,[37] but not to any territory outside the UK.[38] The presumption applies equally to delegated legislation, which has the same territorial effect as the parent provision under which the it was made.

Territorial limits are defined in Sch 1 of the Interpretation Act 1978:

"England" means, subject to any alteration of boundaries under Part IV of the Local Government Act 1972, the area consisting of the counties established by section 1 of that Act, Greater London and the Isles of Scilly.

"Wales" means the combined area of the counties which were created by section 20 of the Local Government Act 1972, as originally enacted, but subject to any alteration made under section 73 of that Act (consequential alteration of boundary following alteration of watercourse).

"United Kingdom" means Great Britain and Northern Ireland.

"British Islands" means the United Kingdom, the Channel Islands and the Isle of Man.

2.40 Territorial jurisdiction for criminal offences is covered in Chapter 3, Criminal Enforcement.

---

[37]　*Bennion on Statutory Interpretation* (6th edn), p 314.

[38]　*King v Director of the Serious Fraud Office* [2009] 1 WLR 718, 725.

Delegated legislation

2.41 Consumer protection laws are often introduced in the form of secondary, or delegated, legislation. This allows Parliament to pass framework legislation, allowing the more detailed regulation to be introduced by Government departments, usually in the form of orders, regulations and rules under the Statutory Instruments Act 1946. The term 'statutory instrument' applies to all 'orders, rules, regulations or other subordinate legislation'.[39] Subordinate legislation is introduced in a variety of forms,[40] largely governed by convention. However, there is no hierarchy of subordinate legislation. In consumer protection measures, the most common are *regulations* and *orders*. Each clause of an order is referred to as an 'article'; in regulations each clause is referred to as a 'regulation'. Clauses within the schedules to both are referred to as 'paragraphs'. It is conventional to refer to the revocation of a statutory instruments, whereas statutes are 'repealed'.

2.42 The ambit and scope of a statutory instrument is limited to the power conferred by the delegating statute (the 'parent provision').[41] Subordinate legislation that goes beyond the scope of the parent provision is vulnerable to a finding that it is *ultra vires* (beyond power). Expressions used in the Act conferring power to make subordinate legislation have a consistent meaning in the subordinate legislation.

The Interpretation Act 1978

11 Construction of subordinate legislation

> Where an Act confers power to make subordinate legislation, expressions used in that legislation have, unless the contrary intention appears, the meaning which they bear in the Act.

2.43 It was historically considered that any disobedience of subordinate legislation was an indictable misdemeanour at common law.[42] An offence occurred even if the criminality was not expressly set out in the delegated legislation or parent statute. It seems highly unlikely that such a rule exists today.[43]

---

[39] Statutory Instruments Act 1946, s 1.

[40] 'Orders in Council, orders, rules, regulations, schemes, warrants, byelaws and other instruments made or to be made under any Act.' Interpretation Act 1978, s 21.

[41] See for example *R v Secretary of State the Home Department, ex parte Leech* (No 2) [1994] QB 198; *Raymond v Honey* [1983] 1 AC 1, per Lord Wilberforce.

[42] *R v Walker* (1875) LR 10 QB 355; *R v Hall* [1891] 1 QB 747 at 765; *Willingale v Norris* [1909] 1 KB at 64 DC.

[43] See *R v Horseferry Road Magistrates' Court, ex parte Independent Broadcasting Authority* [1987] QB 54 DC, where it was said that disobedience of a statute was not of itself an offence and in modern times, no more than a rule of construction.

Human rights

2.44

3 Interpretation of legislation

(1) So far as it is possible to do so, primary legislation and subordinate legislation must be read and given effect in a way which is compatible with the Convention rights.

(2) This section—

(a)   applies to primary legislation and subordinate legislation whenever enacted;

(b)   does not affect the validity, continuing operation or enforcement of any incompatible primary legislation; and

(c)   does not affect the validity, continuing operation or enforcement of any incompatible subordinate legislation if (disregarding any possibility of revocation) primary legislation prevents removal of the incompatibility.

2.45 It is beyond the scope of this chapter to consider the interpretative obligations required by s 3 of the Human Rights Act 1998 and the European Convention on Human Rights. A comprehensive guide to these obligations is to be found in *Lester, Pannick & Herberg: Human Rights Law and Practice*.

EUROPEAN UNION LAWS

2.46

European Communities Act 1972, section 2(1)-(2) and 3

2 General implementation of Treaties

(1) All such rights, powers, liabilities, obligations and restrictions from time to time created or arising by or under the Treaties, and all such remedies and procedures from time to time provided for by or under the Treaties, as in accordance with the Treaties are without further enactment to be given legal effect or used in the United Kingdom shall be recognised and available in law, and be enforced, allowed and followed accordingly; and the expression "enforceable EU right" and similar expressions shall be read as referring to one to which this subsection applies.

2.47 A useful starting point for the interpretative principles that apply to the UK courts is the European Communities Act 1972. The Act requires that judicial notice be taken of EU treaties, the EU's *Official Journal* and any decision or expression of opinion by the CJEU 'or any court attached thereto' and that national courts and tribunals make their decisions 'in accordance with the principles laid down by and any relevant decision of the [CJEU] or any court attached thereto'.[44] The Act also impliedly repealed all legislation that

---

[44]   European Communities Act 1972, s 3.

was inconsistent with EU law while requiring all subsequent legislation to be interpreted in light of, and in accordance with, the requirements of EU law.[45]

2.48 The duty contained in s 3 of the 1972 Act must be read in conjunction with the CJEU jurisprudence on Art 4(3) TEU, which imposes an obligation on Member States 'to ensure fulfilment of the obligations arising out of the Treaties or resulting from the acts of Union'. The CJEU has made it clear that the Art 4(3) duties are binding on all the authorities of the Member State, including its courts. In *Marks & Spencer v Commissioners of Customs and Excise*,[46] the CJEU indicated that the duties of the Member States go well beyond the implementation of Directives:

> 'Individuals are ... entitled to rely before national courts, against the state, on the [unconditional and sufficiently precise] provisions of a directive ... not only where the directive has not been implemented or has been implemented incorrectly, but also where the national measures correctly implementing the directive are not being applied in such a way as to achieve the result sought by it.'

2.49 The CJEU has ruled that national courts are under an obligation to 'apply EU law in its entirety and to protect rights which it confers on individuals, dis-applying, if necessary, any contrary provision of domestic law'.[47] It is important to note that incompatibility with EU law does not render the national provision void *ab initio*; the national court is simply under a procedural duty to dis-apply the rule insofar as it is incompatible with the protection of the EU law rights of the litigating parties.

2.50 Article 4(3) imposes a duty on the authorities of Member States to interpret and apply national law in accordance with the requirements of EU law. The leading authority on this obligation is *von Colson*, in which the CJEU ruled that national courts, as organs of the Member State responsible for the fulfilment of EU obligations, are required to interpret domestic legislation which implements EU law in light of the wording and purpose of the relevant directive.[48] In its subsequent ruling in *Marleasing*,[49] the CJEU extended the *von Colson* principle to include those national provisions which did not implement EU law:

> 'In applying national law, whether the provisions in question were adopted before or after the directive, the national court called upon to interpret it is required to do so, so far as possible, in the light of the wording and the purpose of the directive in order to achieve the result pursued by the latter.'

---

[45] See *Thorburn v Sunderland Council* [2003] QB 151, at 186.
[46] Case C-62/00 [2002] ECR I-6325, para 27.
[47] Joined cases C-444/09 & C-456/09 *Gavieiro Gavieiro and another v Conselleria de Educacion e Ordenacion Universitaria de la Xunta de Galicia* [2011] IRLR 504, paras 72–73.
[48] Case 14/83 *Von Colson v Land Nordhein-Westfalen* [1984] ECR 1891, paras 26–28.
[49] Case C-106/89 *Marleasing SA v La Comercial International de Alimentacion SA* [1990] ECR I-4153, at 4159; see also Case C-334/92 *Wagner Miret* [1993] ECR I-6911.

2.51 *Marleasing* also makes it clear that the duty of consistent interpretation allows the terms of an EU Directive to be enforced indirectly in so-called 'horizontal' situations, ie as against private individuals.

PURPOSIVE INTERPRETATION

2.52 The CJEU's approach to statutory interpretation is rather different to that of English courts. As noted by the late Bingham J in *Customs and Excise Commissioners v Samex ApS*:[50]

> '[t]he interpretation of Community instruments involves very often not the process familiar to common lawyers of laboriously extracting the meaning from words used but the more creative process of supplying flesh to a spare and loosely constructed skeleton.'

2.53 Thus, the CJEU seeks to reveal and advance the purpose of the particular provision and in so doing does not consider itself bound by the provision's precise wording.[51] This is understandable when EU law is drafted in general terms and in pursuit of broad aims and purposes. Accordingly, the CJEU approach to interpretation 'involves placing the provision in question in its context and interpreting it in relation to the broader scheme of which it forms a part'.[52] This is why, whilst the preamble of a particular EU legislative measure has no binding legal force, it is often resorted to as providing the context within which the particular provision is to be read.[53]

2.54 In the *CILFIT* judgment,[54] the CJEU noted that one of the features that needed to be borne in mind in the process of interpretation of EU law is the multilingual nature of EU law; EU law is drafted in several languages with each version being equally authentic. There is an overriding imperative for uniform interpretation across the Union and the CJEU will seek to interpret the provision in question in accordance with the different language versions. Divergences between language versions are resolved by reference to the provision's purpose and the general scheme of the rules of which it forms part.[55] The Court's 'teleological' approach to interpretation is not dissimilar to the common law 'purposive approach'. However, whilst the purposive approach is only resorted to in common law systems where provision is ambiguous or lacks clarity, the CJEU sees such an approach as a primary interpretative tool.

---

50   *Customs and Excise Commissioners v Samex ApS* [1983] 3 CMLR 194 (QBD), at 211.
51   See, for instance, Sir Patrick Neill *The European Court of Justice: a case study in judicial activism* (European Policy Forum, 1995) 47.
52   J Millet 'Rules of Interpretation of EEC Legislation' (1989) 11 *Statute Law Review* 163.
53   See, for instance, Case C-562/08 *Muller Fleisch GmbH v Land Baden-Wurttemberg* [2010] ECR I-1391, para 40, Case C-134/08 *Tyson Parketthandel* [2009] ECR I-2875, para 16.
54   In this regard, see Case 283/81 *CILFIT v Ministry of Health* [1982] ECR 3415, paras 17–20.
55   Case 30/77 *Bouchereau* [1977] ECR 1999, para 14.

2.55 In the first English case to consider the CPUTR in any detail, *OFT v Purely Creative,* the High Court reminded practitioners that the canons of construction of EU law are of paramount importance when interpreting legislation with an EU basis. This is of particular significance when the legislation has implemented a Directive that is expressly designed to harmonise laws throughout the Member States (such as the UCPD).

No binding precedents

2.56 A further important difference in approach between common law systems and that of the CJEU is the absence of the doctrine of binding precedent at EU level,[56] albeit in practice the CJEU rarely departs from principles laid down in its previous cases, often repeating passages verbatim. The absence of an explicit doctrine of binding precedent has a number of consequences.[57] It means, first of all, that the national courts remain entitled to refer questions previously dealt with by the CJEU to it a second time.[58] Secondly, the distinction between the *ratio* of a judgment of the CJEU and *obiter* remarks is not recognised in EU law. The entirety of the judgment is seen as an expression of the will of the Court. Finally, the absence of a formal doctrine of binding precedent means that the CJEU does not always indicate whether it is developing, distinguishing, departing from or altogether overruling its previous decisions,[59] causing occasional confusion on the part of practitioners.

Minimum and maximum harmonisation

2.57 Article 114 was used to harmonise national laws in the context and functioning of the internal market, enabling the EU to choose the relevant standards that become applicable across the Union.[60] There has been a proliferation of harmonised standards in the past few decades, with EU measures affecting such things as doorstep selling,[61] the labelling of foodstuffs[62] and the safety of toys.[63]

---

[56]   This is not to say that the judgments of the CJEU do not constitute a 'source of law'. Indeed, in Case C-224/01 *Kobler* [2003] ECR I-10239 the Court has held that a 'manifest breach' of its case law by a national authority of a Member State may render the Member State liable in damages to an injured party (para 56).

[57]   Aidan O'Neill QC *EU Law for UK Lawyers* (Hart Publishing, 2011), at pp 48–53.

[58]   See, for instance, Case C-91/92 *Dori v Recreb* [1994] ECR I-3325.

[59]   See, for instance, Case C-368/95 *Familiapress v Bauer Verlag* [1997] ECR I-3689, which failed to make any reference to its previous ruling which pointed the other way (Joined Cases 60 and 61/84 *Cinetheque SA and Others v Federation Nationale des Cinemas Français* [1985] ECR 2605). The CJEU has only expressly overruled its decisions in a small number of cases. See, for instance, Case C-267, 268/91 *Criminal Proceedings against Keck and Mithouard* [1993] ECR I-6097.

[60]   Weatherill *EU Consumer Law and Policy* (Elgar European Law, 2005) at p 2.

[61]   Directive 85/577/EEC to protect the consumer in respect of contracts negotiated away from business premises (OJ [1985] L 372/31.

[62]   Directive 2000/13 on labelling, presentation and advertising of foodstuffs (OJ [2000] L 109/29), and more recently the Food Information Regulation.

[63]   Directive 88/378 on the safety of toys (OJ [1988] L 187/1).

2.58 Minimum harmonisation measures act as minimum standards. Member States are allowed to maintain or introduce more stringent rules than those contained in the EU measure.[64] For instance, in *Buet*,[65] the CJEU upheld the French ban on doorstep selling, which gave consumers more protection than that laid down by the Doorstep Selling Directive, on the ground that the Union measure was one of minimum harmonisation. Hence, on the minimum harmonisation model, the EU measure acts as a floor below which national legislation cannot fall.

2.59 Maximum harmonisation, on the other hand, prevents Member States from maintaining or adopting measures that are more restrictive than the harmonising measure.[66] The *Plus*[67] and *Total*[68] cases under the UCPD illustrate this point. In both cases, Member States had unilaterally introduced blanket bans on commercial practices that were not listed in Annex I to the UCPD, which sets out the practices that are prohibited in all circumstances. The CJEU held that because the UCPD was a measure of maximum harmonisation, Member States were pre-empted from adopting more restrictive measures. If a practice was not in the Annex, then it had to be assessed individually in the light of the general clauses. The blanket bans were therefore found to be illegal. Under the maximum harmonisation model the harmonising measure acts as both floor and ceiling. This is not to say that any act on the part of the Member State which goes further than the maximum harmonising measure is necessarily illegal. In such instances of 'gold plating'[69] it becomes necessary to assess the reach of the Directive in question; 'gold plating' will only breach EU law if the national measure overlaps with the Directive and goes beyond it.

Sector-specific legislation

2.60 Wide-reaching harmonisation measures are often accompanied by a caveat: where sector-specific EU legislation is in place and its provisions overlap with the general provisions of the harmonising measure, the sector-specific legislation shall take precedence. For instance, Art 3(4) UCPD states:

> "In the case of conflict between the provisions of this Directive and other Community rules regulating specific aspects of unfair commercial practices, the latter shall prevail and apply to those specific aspects."

---

[64] For an example of a minimum harmonisation measure, see Directive 93/13 on unfair terms in consumer contracts ([1993] OJ L 95/29).

[65] Case 382/87 *Buet v Ministère Public* [1989] ECR 1235.

[66] See, for instance, Case C-44/01 *Hartlauer* [2003] ECR I-3095 on Directive 84/450 on misleading advertising.

[67] Joint cases C-261/07 and C-299/07 *VTB-VAB NV v Total Belgium NV and Galatea BVBA v Sanoma Magazines Belgium NV* [2010] All ER (EC) 694.

[68] Case C-304/08 *Zentrale zur Bekämpfung unlauteren Wettbewerbs eV v Plus Warenhandelsgesellschaft mbH* [2011] All ER (EC) 338.

[69] The term 'gold plating' is used to describe the process whereby a Member State goes beyond an EU harmonising measure. It has been defined by the European Commission as the act of 'transposition of EU legislation, which goes beyond what is required by that legislation, while staying within legality. If not illegal, 'gold plating' is usually presented as a bad practice because it imposes costs that could have been avoided'.

2.61 Recital 10 of the Preamble provides as follows:

> 'It is necessary to ensure that the relationship between this Directive and existing Community law is coherent, particularly where detailed provisions on unfair commercial practices apply to specific sectors ... This Directive accordingly applies only in so far as there are no specific Community law provisions regulating specific aspects of unfair commercial practices, such as information requirements and rules on the way the information is presented to the consumer. It provides protection for consumers where there is no specific sectoral legislation at Community level and prohibits traders from creating a false impression of the nature of products ...'

2.62 It will be interesting to see what significance the courts attribute to the word 'conflict' in Art 3(4). A broad view of Art 3(4) would suggest that where a specific sectoral measure applies to the commercial practice in question, it ousts the application of the UCPD. It could therefore be said that rather than meaning 'incompatibility', it could be argued that the word 'conflict' is used in the same way as in the 'conflict of laws', where the question is which system of laws applies to a given dispute. This appears to accord with the Commission Guidance on the Directive:[70]

> 'Where sectoral legislation is in place and its provisions overlap with the Directive's general provisions, the corresponding provisions of the *lex specialis* will prevail ... Often, such conflicts arise from the fact that the *lex specialis* contains more detailed precontractual information requirements, or stricter rules on the way the information is presented to consumers (see Recital 10 of the Directive).'

Time periods under EU law

2.63

> **EC Regulation 1182/71 determining the rules applicable to periods, dates and time limits**
>
> **Article 4**
>
> 1. Subject to the provisions of this Article, the provisions of Article 3 shall, with the exception of paragraphs 4 and 5, apply to the times and periods of entry into force, taking effect, application, expiry of validity, termination of effect or cessation of application of acts of the Council or Commission or of any provisions of such acts.
>
> **Article 3**
>
> 4. Where the last day of a period expressed otherwise than in hours is a public holiday, Sunday or Saturday, the period shall end with the expiry of the last hour of the following working day.

2.64 This provision may be important when construing provisions that implement EU law, such as the Consumer Contracts (Information, Cancellation

---

and Additional Charges) Regulations 2013, which provides for 14-day cancellation periods, see Chapter 5, Consumer Rights.

Definition of consumer

2.65 European directives[71] generally define a consumer to be any natural person who is acting for purposes which are outside his trade, business, craft or profession. The definition of consumer in UK legislation has been modified to include the words 'wholly or mainly' in recent enactments.[72]

2.66 Consumer Rights Act 2015, s 76(2) and s 2(3):

> 'consumer' means an individual acting for purposes that are wholly or mainly outside that individual's trade, business, craft or profession.

2.67 A consumer is an individual, not a legal entity, such as a company.[73] The courts look to the substance of a transaction. An individual who purchased a house to live in using an investment company was found to be a consumer. However, the result would have been different if the purchase had been for investment purposes.[74] In claims under the CRA 2015, a trader who claims an individual is *not* a consumer must prove it.[75]

2.68 There are three types of situation in which it is not always easy to assess whether an individual is acting outside their trade, business, craft or profession: where a business use is in the future or the past, where the individual is engaged in an activity which may be profitable, and where the purposes of the contract are a mixture of business and consumer.

2.69 The courts have set out some general principles to be applied.

- The focus must be on the person's role in the context of *that* contract, rather than their general situation. A person may be a consumer for some transactions and 'an economic operator' in others. The nature and aim of the contract, and all its facts, must be considered.[76]

---

[71] Article 2 of the UCPD/CRA.
[72] CCR 2013, The CPUTR, substituted by the Consumer Protection (Amendment) Regulations 2014, SI 2014/870, reg 2(3) and CRA 2015.
[73] CJEU *Cape v Idealservice* (C-541/99) at paras 15–16.
[74] *Heifer International Inc v Christiansen* [2008] Bus LR D49 at para 250. See also *R&B Customs Brokers Co Ltd v United Dominions Trust Ltd* [1988] 1 All ER 847.
[75] See for example CRA 2015, s 76(3).
[76] *Dentalkit* at para 16. See also CJEU *Costea* (C110/14) at para 20: an individual's personal technical skill or ability (eg if they are a lawyer) does not mean they are not a consumer if they enter a contract for non-business purposes (paras 26–27). It is also not relevant that a loan is secured on their business premises (para 28), since the consumer is presumed to be the weaker party when acting in a personal capacity.

- 'contracts concluded for the purpose of satisfying an individual's **own needs in terms of private consumption** come under the provisions designed to protect the consumer as the party deemed to be the weaker party economically'.[77]

- 'consumption' equates to 'enjoyment' or 'use of' the product.[78]

- Where an individual acts 'in such a way as to give the other party to the contract the legitimate impression that he was active for the purposes of his business' he may forfeit his consumer protection.[79]

Future and past business purpose

2.70   In *Benincasa v Dentalkit Srl*,[80] the CJEU considered a jurisdictional argument about an individual who made purchases intended for use in a future dentistry business, which ultimately never traded. It held that the fact that the business purpose lies in the future does not divest the contract of its trade or professional character.[81]

2.71   Similarly in *Turner & Co (GB) Ltd v Abi* the High Court found that a person selling their shares in the business that they ran was not a consumer:[82]

> 'Owning and running printing companies was his business. It was how he made his living. This contract was made for the purposes of that business. This was not, to use the words of the European Court of Justice, something for his family or personal use. It was a business decision made in the course of running the business through which he earned his living. I do not think it right to import into that factual analysis concepts of English company law differentiating the business of the company from the business of its owners.'

Profit making activities

2.72   The mere fact that an individual hopes to profit from a transaction does not necessarily remove their consumer status.[83] There are many squarely consumer transactions which aim to generate money, such as ISA investments or private pensions. The view of the European Commission is that such a person is not automatically to be viewed as a trader. Account must be taken of

---

[77]   *Dentalkit* at para 17. See also *Standard Bank London Ltd v Apostolakis (No 1)* [2002] CLC 933.

[78]   *Standard Bank London Ltd v Apostolakis (No 1)* [2002] CLC 933. See also the decision in *Turner and Co (GB) Ltd v Abi* [2010] EWHC 2078 (QB) at para 41.

[79]   *Gruber v BayWa AG* (C-464–01) at para 54. See also *Overy v PayPal* [2012] EWHC 2659 QB at para 169.

[80]   [1998] All ER (EC) 135, [1997] ECR I-3767.

[81]   *Dentalkit* at para 17.

[82]   *Turner and Co (GB) Ltd v Abi* [2010] EWHC 2078 (QB). The judge ruled at para 42 that the approach taken in *Turner* is consistent with that of the CJEU in *France v Di Pinto* [1993] 1 CMLR 399 where it held that a person selling their business is not a consumer in that transaction. This appears to be at odds with the older decision *Davies v Sumner* [1984] 1 WLR 1301, which focussed almost exclusively on the need for regularity before a person is to be regarded as a trader.

[83]   *Standard Bank London Ltd v Apostolakis (No 1)* [2002] CLC 933.

the extent to which they have a profit seeking motive, the number, amount and frequency of transactions, the seller's sales turnover and whether they purchase products in order to resell them.[84]

2.73 It may be important to consider:

- The regularity of the transactions.[85]
- The scale of the transaction, bearing in mind that even very large transactions have been held still to be consumer contracts.[86]
- Whether they in fact derive their living from it – whether it is a business that they carry on.[87]
- Whether it in fact relates to their main business.[88]
- Whether they bring expertise to the transaction.[89]
- Whether the transaction is part of a lifestyle choice, savings scheme or driven by personal circumstances.[90]

Mixed purpose contracts

2.74 The CRA 2015, in defining a consumer as someone acting for purposes that are 'wholly or mainly' outside their business, has extended protection beyond that which existed previously. The leading case was *Gruber v BayWa AG*,[91] concerning an Austrian farmer who purchased roof tiles from a German supplier for a building which contained not only his home, but also premises he used for his business. He brought a claim alleging the tiles were defective in the Austrian courts, relying on his status as a consumer under Art 15 of the Brussels Regulation. In that case, the CJEU held that an individual would only be protected if the business purpose *was* 'so limited as to be negligible in the overall context of the supply. The fact that the private element is predominant

---

[84] Commission Guidance [COM (2016) 320] para 2.1. See also Commission Communication *A European Agenda for the Collaborative Economy* [COM (2016) 356] para 2.3.
[85] See *R&B Customs Brokers Co Ltd v United Dominions Trust Ltd* [1988] 1 All ER 847.
[86] *Spreadex v Cochrane* [2012] EWHC 1290 (Comm).
[87] See *FSA v Asset LI Inc* [2013] EWHC 178 (Ch) at para 127, purchasers of plots of land as investments were consumers. However, see also *Allied Irish Bank Plc v Higgins and Ors* [2010] IEHC 219.
[88] *Maple Leaf Macro Volatility Master Fund and Another v Rouvroy and Another* [2009] 1 Lloyd's Rep 475 at para 209.
[89] *Ghandour v Arab Bank (Switzerland)* [2008] ILPr 35. However, this must now be treated with caution given the CJEU's ruling in *Costea* (C110/14) at para 20.
[90] *The Office of Fair Trading v Foxtons* [2009] EWHC 291 (Ch) at para 28. See also *Smith and Smith v Mortgage Express* [2007] CTLC 134- purchaser of buy-to-let property a consumer, and *Parker v NFU Mutual Insurance Society Ltd* [2012] EWHC 2156 (Comm), where property was let out but the UTCCR still applied.
[91] C-464–01, [2006] QB 204.

is irrelevant in that respect.'[92] Under the CRA 2015 the burden of proof is, however, on the trader to establish that the consumer purpose is not predominant.[93]

Definition of trader

2.75 The term *'trader'* is now used in most[94] EU consumer protection directives. This is reflected in the CRA 2015 which sought to align key terms in the implementation of EU consumer legislation in the UK.[95] The basic definition of trader focuses on the 'purpose' for which a person[96] is acting.

> CRA 2015, s 2(2)
>
> (2) 'Trader' means a person acting for purposes relating to that person's trade, business, craft or profession, whether acting personally or through another person acting in the trader's name or on the trader's behalf.

2.76 In *R (Khatun) v Newham LBC*[97] the Court of Appeal considered whether a local authority was acting for purposes relating to its 'trade, business or profession' when letting property to a homeless person under a statutory duty, for the purposes of the unfair terms legislation. A broad construction of 'trader' was applied to include, 'every entity engaged in an economic activity, regardless of the legal status of the entity and the way in which it is financed'. It was appropriate to ask whether the entity 'is engaged in activity which could, at least in principle, be carried out by a private undertaking in order to make profits'.

2.77 The term 'trader' is to be given a similarly broad construction for the purposes of the CPUTR, which implements the Unfair Commercial Practices Directive ('UCPD') in the UK, see Chapter 7 Unfair Commercial Practices. In the *BKK Mobil Oil Case*[98] the CJEU stated that the drafting of 'trader' in the UCPD had 'conferred a particularly broad meaning on the term'. In *Surrey Trading Standards v Scottish and Southern Energy PLC*[99] the Court of Appeal

---

[92] See also *Evans v Cherry Tree Finance* [2008] EWCA Civ 331 and [2007] EWHC 3523 (Ch) at paras 48–49 and 52. Applied in *Alfred Overy v Paypal Europe* [2012] EWHC 2659 (QB).

[93] See CRA 2015, s 76(3).

[94] An exception is the unfair terms directive (93/13/EEC) which uses the term 'seller or supplier' defined in Article 2(c) as 'acting for purposes relating to his trade, business or profession, whether publicly owned or privately owned'.

[95] For example, the Consumer Contracts (Information, Cancellation and Additional Charges) Regulations 2013, the Alternative Dispute Resolution for Consumer Disputes (Competent Authorities and Information) Regulations 2015 and the Consumer Protection from Unfair Trading Regulations 2008.

[96] 'Person' includes a body of persons corporate or unincorporated, Interpretation Act 1978, Sch 1.

[97] [2005] QB 37, [2004] 3 WLR 417, [2004] HLR 29, [2004] L & TR 18.

[98] *BP Mobile Oil Körperschaft des öffentlichen Rechts v Zentrale zur Bekämpfung unlauteren Wettbewerbs eV* Case C-59/12.

[99] [2012] EWCA Crim 539.

(Criminal Division) also gave a broad construction to the concept of 'trader' placed in the context of the 'commercial practices' definition under the UCPD. Davis LJ stated that:

> 'It is important to bear in mind that 'trader', for the purpose of (CPUTR), extends to any person who in relation to a commercial practice is acting for purposes relating to his business. The words 'any', 'in relation to', 'acting' and 'relating to' are all words of width and elasticity.'

2.78 EU Guidance[100] on the meaning of trader in the UCPD states that:

> 'Whether a seller qualifies as a "trader" or a consumer must be assessed on a case-by-case basis. Different criteria could be relevant, such as:
>
> – whether the seller has a profit-seeking motive, including the fact that he/she might have received remuneration or other compensation for acting on behalf of a given trader;
> – the number, amount and frequency of transactions;
> – the seller's sales turnover;
> – whether the seller purchases products in order to resell them.'

Agents, representatives and employees

2.79 The agent or representative of a trader will usually be acting for the purposes of trade, business, craft or a profession. However, the question of whether that agent or representative is also a 'trader' will depend on the particular provision concerned. There is a difference between the definition of 'trader' in the UCPD and in other EU consumer protection measures that are primarily concerned with the legal effect of a contractual relationship,[101] such as consumer contract information and cancellation. In the UCPD the definition of 'trader' expressly extends both to traders 'and anyone acting in the name or on behalf of the trader' (emphasis added). It follows that a trader's agent or representative is also bound, as a trader, not to engage in unfair commercial practices against consumers. This makes obvious policy sense as many such bad practices are committed by a principal trader's agents or representatives, for example, self-employed door-to-door salesmen.

2.80 The position is different for provisions focussing on contractual relationships, such as those implemented as a consequence of the EU Consumer Rights Directive.[102] These provisions do not expressly make the trader's agent or representative responsible for compliance with the relevant regulatory obligation. However, they do make the trader responsible for those obligations

---

[100] *Guidance on the implementation /application of directive 2005/29/EC on unfair commercial practices.*

[101] The CRA 2015, the Consumer Contracts (Information, Cancellation and Additional Charges) Regulations 2013; The Alternative Dispute Resolution for Consumer Disputes (Competent Authorities and Information) Regulations 2015.

[102] The CRA 2015 and the Consumer Contracts (Information, Cancellation and Additional Charges) Regulations 2013.

'whether acting personally or through another person acting in the trader's name or on the trader's behalf'. This reflects the contractual nature of the obligations concerned in these provisions. It plainly makes sense for the party contracting with a consumer, rather than an agent or representative, to be fixed with regulatory obligations affecting the contract, such as its cancellation. Of course this does not mean that a trader's agent or representative will never have regulatory obligations under this type of consumer protection provision. Their responsibility will simply depend on whether they themselves engage in the particular practice covered, for example, do they themselves contract.

2.81 This distinction is also relevant when considering the liability of a trader's employee as a 'trader'. In implementing the UCPD, the CPUTR expressly defined 'trader' additionally to include those acting 'in the name of or on behalf of a trader'. As the primary purpose of the UCPD is consumer protection, it seems likely that this creates liability for the employees of a trader. For example, it would not be logical for the UCPD liability of a door-to-door salesman to depend on whether he was engaged as an employee or self-employed agent. That is not to say that it will always be proportionate to bring proceedings against the employee of a trader. In many circumstances that may be disproportionate, however, the question is likely to be one of enforcement discretion, rather than actual liability.

2.82 An employee is unlikely, however, to be responsible for the obligations of a trader under the EU measures focussing on contractual obligations, for the same reason that agents and representatives ordinarily are not. Equally, the employees of a trader are not liable to pay consumer redress for unfair commercial practices under Part 4A of the CPUTR, even if they are criminally liable for them.[103]

Public bodies

2.83 It is now clear that most[104] UK consumer protection measures will apply to public authorities, to the extent that they engage in the practices covered by them. For example, the CRA 2015 expressly states that 'business' includes the activities of public authorities.[105]

> **CRA 2015, s 2(7)**
>
> (7) "Business" includes the activities of any government department or local or public authority.

---

[103] See CPUTR, reg 2.

[104] An exception is the Alternative Dispute Resolution for Consumer Disputes (Competent Authorities and Information) Regulations 2015.

[105] See also CPUTR, reg 2 and Consumer Contracts (Information, Cancellation and Additional Charges) Regulations 2013, reg 5.

Charities

2.84 It is very likely that charities and other not-for-profit organisations, such as NGOs, mutuals and cooperatives, will also be considered traders if they engage in the commercial practices covered by EU consumer protection laws. It is likely that the courts will apply the broad test used in *Khatun* and ask whether the activity could, in principle, be undertaken by a private body for profit. The fact that an organisation is structured as 'non-profit' is therefore likely to be immaterial to the assessment of whether it qualifies as a trader. These EU directives typically state expressly that a particular sector is excluded from the ambit of the measure. For example, the Consumer Rights Directive expressly excludes certain social services and healthcare provision.[106] There are no such express exclusions for charities or other not-for-profit organisations.

---

[106] CRD 2011/83/EC, Art 3(3).

CHAPTER 3

CRIMINAL ENFORCEMENT

CONTENTS

INTRODUCTION

3.1   Consumer law often provides criminal sanction for its breach. However, the number of criminal prosecutions taken annually has been decreasing for a number of years. For example, around 300 cases under the Consumer Protection from Unfair Trading Regulations 2008[1] ('CPUTR') reach the courts each year whereas the number taken under the legislation that the CPUTR replaced was three times that figure. However, it is also true to say that more cases are being dealt with by the Crown Court, indicating that local authorities have actively embraced the Macrory philosophy that 'criminal prosecution and the criminal courts ... should largely be preserved for the truly egregious offenders'.[2] It will also be interesting to see whether s 85(1) of the Legal Aid, Sentencing and Punishment of Offenders Act 2012 ('LASPO'), which introduced unlimited fines in the Magistrates' Court, will have the desired effect of reducing the number of cases sent to the Crown Court.

3.2   A central and fundamental criticism highlighted by the Macrory Review was the allegedly heavy reliance placed on criminal prosecution by regulators as a primary, core sanctioning tool. The Regulatory Enforcement and Sanctions Act 2008 ('RESA', see Chapter 1) provided a framework of civil sanctions in areas where criminal sanctions exist, although the Government was not convinced that this regime would be effective in consumer law. Recently enacted legislative controls on letting agents and secondary ticketing, in the Consumer Rights Act 2015, only provide for civil sanctions. Further, the revised food law enforcement regime now means that legislation will (generally) provide for civil, not criminal, sanctions.

3.3   Criminal prosecutions will, however, be considered by many local authorities to be an appropriate and proportionate response against those who flout the law or act irresponsibly. Particularly given that there is a range of out-of-court disposals that may also be employed. This will especially be the case in relation to cases that involve intentional, repeated or reckless acts and those concerned with fraud or public safety.

Strict liability

3.4   It is common to find that criminal offences designed to protect consumers are of strict or absolute liability, in that they do not require proof of a mental element such as intention or recklessness (*mens rea*). They are therefore an exception to the criminal law principle that a deed will not make a man guilty unless his mind is guilty.[3]

3.5   In applying this principle to 'truly criminal' offences the courts have shown a reluctance to impose criminal liability without proof of *mens rea*, even

---

[1]   SI 2008/1277.
[2]   The Macrory Review of Regulatory Penalties, 28 November 2006.
[3]   The principle found in the Latin maxim, *actus non facit reum nisi mens sit rea*.

when a statute does not expressly require its proof. In the seminal case on strict liability, *Sweet v Parsley*, Lord Reid stated that:

> '[i]n the absence of a clear indication in the Act that an offence is intended to be an absolute offence, it is necessary to go outside the Act and examine all relevant circumstances in order to establish that this must have been the intention of Parliament.'[4]

Regulatory offences of strict liability

3.6   The *Sweet v Parsley* principle does not apply, however, when Parliament is presumed to have intended that the offence should not require proof of a *mens rea*. Lord Reid made reference to regulatory offences when he stated that '[i]t has long been the practice to recognise absolute offences in this class of quasi criminal acts, and one can safely assume that, when Parliament is passing new legislation dealing with this class of offences, its silence as to mens rea means that the old practice is to apply'.

3.7   This is likely to be the position for most consumer and trading standards provisions that have created criminal liability. These regulatory offences generally follow a typical pattern of strict liability ingredients of the offence that the prosecution must prove to the criminal standard, which is counterbalanced with a defence that must be proven by the defendant to the civil standard. It would be difficult to argue that Parliament did not intend this class of offence to be of strict liability when such regulatory provisions have commonly been enforced in that way by the courts over decades.

3.8   The Trade Descriptions Act 1968 ('TDA') was the statutory predecessor to the CPUTR (see Chapter 7 Unfair Commercial Practices) and the main mechanism through which trading offences were prosecuted for 40 years. Although the TDA (now largely repealed) contained some quasi-*mens rea* offences, in *Wings v Ellis*[5] Lord Scarman said that 'it is not a truly criminal statute. Its purpose is not the enforcement of the criminal law but the maintenance of trading standards. Trading standards, not criminal behaviour, are its concern.'

3.9   The rationale for the imposition of strict liability has been explained on the basis that such offences are not '*truly criminal*' or when it is proportionate to an '*issue of social concern*'.[6] Although this might explain the different treatment of relatively minor offences, it is much harder to describe serious imprisonable regulatory offences in those terms. The justification of strict

---

4   [1970] AC 132 at p 149; see also *Gammon (Hong Kong) Ltd v A-G of Hong Kong* [1985] AC 1 PC; *Wings v Ellis* [1985] AC 272 HL.
5   [1985] 1 AC 272.
6   In the Privy Council case of *Gammon (Hong Kong) Ltd v A-G of Hong Kong* [1985] AC 1 Lord Scarman found justification for strict liability 'where the statute is concerned with an issue of social concern' and 'the creation of strict liability will be effective to promote the objects of the statute by encouraging greater vigilance to prevent the commission of the prohibited act'.

liability for such offences was perhaps better explained by the Court of Appeal in *R v Jackson [2007]*, in relation to the offence of 'low flying' under s 51 of the Air Forces Act 1955. The Court there found the offence to be of strict liability despite it carrying a maximum penalty of imprisonment. Hooper LJ stated that:

> 'The rationales behind the creation of such offences is generally that they cover conduct which of itself is potentially dangerous to other members of the public and accordingly the public interest overrides the need to prove knowledge on the part of the alleged offender that he was in fact committing an offence or did the act complained of with any particular *mens rea*. Guilt is to be found in the commission of the act -no particular frame of mind has to be established before guilt is established. This reflects the fact that some conduct -often not truly criminal in the way most people would understand that expression- carries with it such grave risk of endangering pubic safety or is so heavily the cause of public concern, that it can properly be punished without the need for the establishment of any degree of *mens rea*.'[7]

Corporate liability

3.10   Where a statute creates an offence for a 'person', that expression includes companies.[8] Where a corporation is charged with a criminal offence, different rules apply in relation to its representation and the procedure by which it can enter a plea. In the magistrates' court, the procedure is governed by s 46 and Sch 3 of the Magistrates' Court Act 1980.[9] The procedure for entering a plea on behalf of a company in the Crown Court is set out in s 33 of the Criminal Justice Act 1925.

3.11   The Criminal Procedure Rules 2015 state that:

> **46.1 Functions of representatives and supporters**
>
> (1) Under these Rules, anything that a party may or must do may be done—
>
> . . .
>
> (b) by a person with the corporation's written authority, where that party is a corporation;

Companies in liquidation

3.12   Before a court proceeds in the absence of a plea entered by a corporation it is important to ascertain whether the company is in liquidation, because the leave of the High Court will be needed. In *R v Dickson*,[10] a company in

---

7   Per Hooper LJ [2007] 1 WLR 1035 at 1040.
8   Interpretation Act 1978, Sch 1, '"Person" includes a body of persons corporate or unincorporate'.
9   A representative of the company is defined by reference to s 33(6) of the Criminal Justice Act 1925.
10   [1991] BCC 719.

liquidation was prosecuted to conviction without the leave of the High Court.[11] However, the argument that this invalidated the conviction of the director under the directors' liability provision of the TDA (s 20) was rejected.

Corporate liability for offences of strict liability

3.13 The circumstances in which a company is liable for the acts of its employees will depend upon the nature of the offence. A distinction can be drawn, however, between offences that require a *mens rea* (a particular mental state) to be proven and those that do not. For a *strict liability* offence, a company will be criminally liable when the *actus reus* of the offence can properly be attributed to it. In *Mousell Bros v London and North Western Railway*,[12] Lord Atkin stated:

> 'I think that the authorities ... make it plain that while prima facie a principal is not to be made criminally responsible for the acts of his servants, yet the legislature may prohibit an act or enforce a duty in such words as to make the prohibition or the duty absolute; in which case the principal is liable if the act is in fact done by his servants. To ascertain whether a particular Act of Parliament has that effect or not, regard must be had to the object of the statute, the words used, the nature of the duty laid down, the person upon whom it is imposed, the person by whom it would in ordinary circumstances be performed, and the person upon whom the penalty is imposed ... When a penalty is imposed for the breach of the duty, it is reasonable to infer that the penalty is imposed for a default of the person by whom the duty would ordinarily be performed.'

3.14 In construing a statute to ascertain whether it creates vicarious liability for a company, the verb used to create the offence will usually be significant. For example 'selling' or 'supplying' goods is an activity that can reasonably be attributed to a company, even though actually undertaken by its employees.[13] In the consumer and trading standards offences of strict liability it will rarely be difficult to attribute to a company criminal liability for the acts of its employees.

Corporate liability for offences with a mental element

3.15 The corporate liability for offences that involve proof of a mental element (*mens rea*) was discussed in *Tesco Supermarkets Ltd v Nattrass*.[14] Lord Reid considered the nature of a corporate 'personality' stating:[15]

> 'A living person has a mind which can have knowledge or intention or be negligent and he has hands to carry out his intentions. A corporation has none of these; it

---

11 The Insolvency Act 1986 requires leave to be given before proceedings are commenced against a company in administration, or which is the subject of a winding up order or where a provisional liquidator has been appointed.
12 [1917] 2 KB 836, DC at pp 845–846.
13 See for example *Coppen v Moore (No 2)* [1898] 2 QB 306.
14 [1971] 2 All ER 127, [1972] AC 153.
15 At pp 131–132.

must act through living persons, though not always one or the same person. Then the person who acts is not speaking or acting for the company. He is acting as the company and his mind, which directs his acts, is the mind of the company. There is no question of the company being vicariously liable. He is not acting as a servant, representative, agent or delegate. He is an embodiment of the company or, one could say, he hears and speaks through the persona of the company, within his appropriate sphere, and his mind is the mind of the company. If it is a guilty mind then that is the guilt of the company. It must be a question of law whether, once the facts have been ascertained, a person in doing particular things is to be regarded as the company or merely as the company's servant or agent. In that case any liability of the company can only be a statutory or vicarious liability ...

Normally the board of directors, the managing director and perhaps other superior officers of a company carry out the functions of management and speak and act as the company.'

3.16 A company will only be guilty of an offence requiring proof of a *mens rea*, if the *mens rea* can be attributed to someone who is the directing mind or will of the company. In *R v Andrews Weatherfoil Ltd* it was said that a company was not criminally responsible for the actions of every '*high executive*' or '*agent acting on behalf of the company*'.[16]

3.17 In *St Regis Paper Company Ltd v The Crown*,[17] a prosecution under the Pollution Prevention and Control (England and Wales) Regulations 2000, the Court of Appeal rejected the argument that the intentional actions of the company's technical manager could be attributed to the company. For the purposes of this specific regulation the question therefore was: '*Was the technical manager in actual control of the relevant operations of the company and not responsible to another person or under that other person's orders?*' The test set out in *Tesco Supermarkets Ltd v Nattrass* was to be followed. The Court held that there was no real sense in which it could be said that the company had delegated its responsibilities under the Regulations to the technical manager. Although he was required to submit the necessary records, that was far removed from the type of delegation necessary to be established. It was emphasised that the extent of delegation is a matter of fact for the jury.

Possible exceptions

3.18 This general application of the rule in *Tesco Supermarkets v Nattrass* has been considered in several cases where the courts have sought to avoid a restrictive approach that might allow companies unfairly to escape responsibility, where the employee with the requisite *men rea* was not strictly part of the company's directing mind and will.

---

[16]   56 Cr App R 31 CA; see also *Leonard's Carrying Co v Asiatic Petroleum Co* [1915] AC 705 and *Bolton (Engineering) Co v Graham* [1957] 1 QB 159.

[17]   [2011] EWCA Crim 2527.

3.19 In *Meridian Global Funds Management Asia Ltd v Securities Commission*[18] the chief investment officer of a New Zealand investment management company had used company managed funds to acquire public shares without giving the required notice. The failure to give the notice was a breach of a financial regulation duty, but was not itself a criminal offence. The investment had been made with the company's authority but the company directors did not know about it. The New Zealand Court of Appeal had found the company responsible on the basis that the chief investment officer had been a part of the company's directing mind and will.

3.20 The Privy Council, however, considered that the company could be attributed with the knowledge of the chief investment officer even if he was not a part of the company's directing mind and will. It upheld the decision on the basis that there would be cases where the ordinary rule of attribution to a company would defeat the statutory intention that a company should be responsible for the breach. It was necessary in those cases to apply a special rule of attribution. Lord Hoffmann stated that:

> 'In such a case, the court must fashion a special rule of attribution for the particular substantive rule. This is always a matter of interpretation: given that it was intended to apply to a company, how was it intended to apply? Whose act (or knowledge, or state of mind) was *for this purpose* intended to count as the act etc. of the company? One finds the answer to this question by applying the usual canons of interpretation, taking into account the language of the rule (if it is a statute) and its content and policy.'

3.21 In *Information Commissioner v Islington LBC*[19] a local authority was prosecuted for an offence of recklessly using data contrary to s 5(5) of the Data Protection Act 1998. The offence was committed by *using* data after the expiry of a data protection registration. The conviction was upheld on the basis that the authority's controlling minds had been reckless in failing to register for data protection and that its other employees had thereafter used the data. There was, however, no evidence that any single person had used data whilst actually having the requisite *mens rea* of recklessness.

3.22 In *Linnett v Metropolitan Police Commissioner*,[20] the conviction of a licensee for 'knowingly permitting disorderly conduct' was upheld, despite him being unaware of it. The rationale of the decision is that the licensee had a special statutory duty to keep an orderly public house which he had delegated to his servant. In those circumstances, the knowledge required by the offence would be imputed to him. It is unlikely that *Linnett* is authority for a general proposition of law and it is probably confined to offences under the Licensing Acts.[21]

---

[18] [1995] 3 WLR 413 [1995] 2 AC 500.
[19] [2003] LGR 38, DC.
[20] [1946] KB 290, DC.
[21] In *Vane v Yiannopoullos* [1965] AC 486, the House of Lords doubted any general application of the doctrine. However, in relation to licensing offences, it has since been applied in *R v Winson* [1969] 1 QB 371 and *Howker v Robinson* [1973] 1 QB 178, DC.

3.23 The danger of applying a single inflexible rule of corporate liability in every circumstance is illustrated by *Bilta (UK) Ltd (In liquidation) v Nazir* in the context of civil insolvency proceedings. The Supreme Court in *Bilta* considered a series of case[22] involving actions by liquidators against directors accused of fraudulent conduct. In simple terms, if the wrongdoing of the directors could be attributed to the company, the individual directors might have a legal defence to the liquidator's action. The reasoning in the judgments in *Bilta* is different, however, for understandable reasons the Supreme Court ruled against the directors. Lord Neuberger PSC stated:

> 'whether or not it is appropriate to attribute an action by, or a state of mind of, a company director ... must depend on the nature and factual context of the claim in question.'[23]

Directors' liability

3.24 Consumer and trading standards offences are often based upon individual transactions and consequently the conduct (*actus reus*) that constitutes the offence will be committed by a junior employee within a business. In many cases it is unsatisfactory that those truly responsible for the wrongdoing can hide behind the company 'corporate veil' and most trading standards offences also provide a penal sanction against those persons, charged with functions of management, who can be shown to have been responsible for the commission of a relevant offence by the corporate body (directors' liability).

3.25 In a prosecution using a directors' liability provision it is normal and desirable (although not a mandatory requirement) for the company to be a defendant in the same proceedings. If the company is not also prosecuted it will still be necessary for the prosecution to prove that the company would have been found guilty of the offence.

3.26 The provision that has generated most case-law is s 20(1) TDA which has now been largely replaced by the CPUTR and in particular regulation 15.[24]

CPUTR, reg 15

Offences committed by bodies of persons

15(1) Where an offence under these Regulations committed by a body corporate is proved –

    (a)   to have been committed with the consent or connivance of an officer of the body, or

    (b)   to be attributable to any neglect on his part, the officer as well as the body corporate is guilty of the offence and liable to be proceeded against and punished accordingly.

---

[22] Including *Stone & Rolls Ltd v Moore Stephens* [2009] AC 1391; [2009] 3 WLR 455 and *Safeway Stores Ltd v Twigger* [2010] EWCA Civ 1472; [2011] 2 All ER 841.

[23] Para 9 [1015] UKSC 23, [2015] 2 WLR 1168.

[24] SI 2008/1277.

(2) In paragraph (1) a reference to an officer of a body corporate includes a reference to –

    (a)   a director, manager, secretary or other similar officer; and

    (b)   a person purporting to act as a director, manager, secretary or other similar officer.

(3) Where an offence under these Regulations committed by a Scottish partnership is proved –

    (a)   to have been committed with the consent or connivance of a partner, or

    (b)   to be attributable to any neglect on his part, the partner as well as the partnership is guilty of the offence and liable to be proceeded against and punished accordingly.

(4) In paragraph (3) a reference to a partner includes a person purporting to act as a partner.

3.27 Directors' liability provisions can usually be found in most consumer and trading standards legislation that imposes criminal liability.[25] The burden of proving the liability of a director or manager under these provisions is on the prosecution to the criminal standard of proof although evidence can be inferred in appropriate cases.[26] The definition of a company director or company secretary is now governed by the Companies Act 2006 ('CA 2006') and will usually be a matter of public record.

3.28 In *Motor Depot Ltd v Kingston-Upon-Hull City Council*[27] a motor trading company and its managing director were guilty of various offences, including matters under the CPUTR, where they had published misleading advertisements. In relation to the personal liability of the managing director, it was alleged that each offence 'was committed with your consent, connivance or wilful neglect as a Director of Motor Depot Limited by reason of Regulation 15'. In fact, the case against him was advanced on the basis of neglect rather than consent or connivance. Furthermore, although the summonses referred to wilful neglect, it was appreciated that that was wrong and that the relevant test was merely neglect. No point was taken on that error in the summonses. Elias LJ observed:

> 'In cases like this, it is unlikely in practice that there would be direct evidence as to where exactly the duty lies and to identify who has taken responsibility within an organisation for drafting or checking or placing the advertisements.'

---

[25]   For example, s 169 of the Consumer Credit Act 1974; s 82 of the Weights and Measures Act 1985; s 40(2) of the Consumer Protection Act 1987; s 36 of the Food Safety Act 1990; s 101(5) of the Trade Marks Act 1994; s 110 of the Copyrights, Designs and Patents Act 1988. If the CA 2006 is a precedent for future legislation these provisions may be simplified. Section 1255 of CA 2006 merely refers to '… an officer of the body, or a person purporting to act in any such capacity'.

[26]   See for example, *Motor Depot Ltd v Kingston-Upon-Hull City Council* [2012] EWHC 3257 (Admin) and *R v X Ltd* [2013] EWCA Crim 818.

[27]   [2012] EWHC 3257 (Admin).

3.29   In *R v T*[28] the Court of Appeal rejected the argument that a charge was bad for duplicity because it included both an offence against the company and another against the director.[29] The charges were not duplicitous. Indeed, under the directors' liability provision, it was necessary to prove that the company was itself guilty of the offence.

3.30   It is unlikely that charging, 'consent, connivance or neglect' in a single charge would make a count bad for duplicity. It is likely that the three elements (principally relating to *mens rea*) are merely different modes through which one offence is committed.[30] In *Southend Borough Council v White*, the Divisional Court observed that a remedy, where there was insufficient proof of the director's neglect, would have been 'for the justices to allow the amendment of the information so as to include consent or connivance'.[31]

3.31   It is important to remember that directors' liability provisions do not create freestanding, separate offences. They simply enable a prosecution to be brought against a manager, director etc for the same offence as the company. For the importance of getting the drafting of any charges correct (although in this case it was not fatal) see *R v Michael Wilson*.[32]

Managerial roles

3.32   The scope of this type of provision in relation to managerial roles that are less formally defined was considered in *R v Boal*[33] where an assistant general manager was in charge of a well-known London bookshop whilst the manager was on holiday. He had been given no training in management and was prosecuted under s 23 of the Fire Precautions Act 1971. In quashing his conviction the Divisional Court reviewed a number of previous decisions and concluded that the defendant would only fall within the provision if he had, 'the management of the whole affairs of the company', and was 'entrusted with power to transact the whole affairs of the company' and was 'managing in a governing role the affairs of the company itself'. Simon Brown J went on to say:

---

28   [2005] EWCA Crim 3511.
29   The indictment was worded: 'Statement of offence. Applying a false trade description to goods contrary to s 1(1)(a) and s 20 of the Trade Descriptions Act 1968. Particulars of offence [TL] Limited on or before 23 August 2003 in the course of a trade or business applied to goods, namely a BMW motor vehicle registration mark V38 MGJ, a false trade description by means of the vehicle odometer reading of 66,066 miles, whereas the said vehicle had travelled not less than 127,000 miles. The said offence was committed with the consent and connivance of or was attributable to the neglect of [MJT] a Director of the said Company who, by virtue of s 20 of the Trade Descriptions Act 1968, is guilty of the said offence.'
30   In the way that 'knowledge or suspicion' in money laundering charges under the Proceeds of Crime Act 2002 is simply the *mens rea* of the single offence.
31   Similarly in *R v P*, the information which alleged that the director's offence was due to his 'consent and/or, connivance and/or neglect' was not challenged despite the court's focus on the difference between consent or connivance and neglect.
32   [2013] EWCA Crim 1780.
33   [1992] 1 QB, applied *R v Sadighpour* [2012] EWCA Crim 2669.

'The intended scope of section 23 is, we accept, to fix with criminal liability only those who are in a position of real authority, the decision-makers within the company who have both the power and responsibility to decide corporate policy and strategy. It is to catch those responsible for putting proper procedures in place; it is not meant to strike at underlings.'

3.33 The phrase 'any person who was purporting to act in any such capacity' overcomes the difficulty experienced in *Dean v Hiesler*[34] where the defendant was not a validly-appointed director in accordance with the provisions of the Companies Act 1929 but performed some of the duties of a director and even described himself as a director.

Consent or connivance

3.34 In considering 'consent' or 'connivance' it should be appreciated that 'neglect' requires a lower level of *mens rea* and therefore proof of 'consent' or 'connivance' will often be an unnecessary hurdle. Idiosyncratically the directors' liability provision that has been considered most by the courts (s 20 TDA) refers to 'consent *and* connivance'[35] in contrast to most other legislative provisions (including reg 15 of the CPUTR) that refer to them in the alternative, 'consent or connivance'. Both words were considered in *Huckerby v Elliott*[36] in proceedings concerning a similar statutory provision.[37] It was stated that:

'The learned stipendiary ... dealt with consent and said: 'It would seem that where a director consents to the commission of an offence by his company, he is well aware of what is going on and agrees to it.' I agree with the stipendiary ... The stipendiary went on: 'Where he connives at the offence committed by the company he is equally well aware of what is going on but his agreement is tacit, not actively encouraging what happens but letting it continue and saying nothing about it.' ... I do not disagree with that.'

3.35 For the purposes of consent, a director must be proved to know the material facts which constitute the offence, however it not necessary to show that the director knew that this was contrary to the law. In *AG's ref (No 1 of 1995)* the Court of Appeal considered the meaning of director's consent in the context of a company carrying on a deposit taking business without Bank of England authorisation, for the offence under s 3(1) of the Banking Act 1987. The Court of Appeal found that where consent is alleged the defendant has to be proved to know the material facts which constitute the offence by the body corporate and to have agreed to its conduct of the business on the basis of those facts. Ignorance of the law and its requirements was no defence. Lord Taylor of Gosforth CJ said:

'A director who knows that acts which can only be performed by the company if it is licensed by the bank are being performed when in fact no licence exists and who

---

34 [1942] 2 All ER 340.
35 This is widely considered to have been a draftsman's error.
36 [1970] 1 All ER 189.
37 Section 305(3) of the Customs and Excise Act 1952.

consents to that performance is guilty of the offence charged. The fact that he does not know it is an offence to perform them without a licence, ie, ignorance of the law, is no defence ... [the] suggestion that the director must actively have addressed his mind to the question of licences is wholly unreal. If the two directors, who were wholly responsible for the company's business activity, were ignorant of the need for a licence it can readily be inferred that they knew they did not have one. The concept of a director who is ignorant of the law requiring a licence, focusing his mind on the question of whether he has or has not obtained one is wholly academic. Had anyone approached the defendant directors and asked: "Have you a licence or authorisation from the Bank of England?" the ready answer would have been "No," probably supplemented by "I did not know I needed one." There would have been no need for a search, an inquiry or a focusing of the mind. Since the question had not occurred to them they would know that the company did not have one. The ignorance of the law on the point necessarily must in the context of this case point to the knowledge that the company is operating unlicensed.'[38]

3.36 The consent or connivance of a director may be proven by inference where the offence is directed towards the result to be achieved by the company. In *R v Chargot*, the House of Lords considered a directors' liability provision in the Health and Safety at Work etc Act 1974. Lord Hope stated that:

'consent can be established by inference as well as by proof of an express agreement. The state of mind that the words 'connivance' and 'neglect' contemplate is one that may also be established by inference. [These offences] are directed to the result that must be achieved by the body corporate. Where it is shown that the body corporate failed to achieve or prevent the result that those sections contemplate, it will be a relatively short step for the inference to be drawn that there was connivance or neglect on his part if the circumstances under which the risk arose were under the direction or control of the officer. The more remote his area of responsibility is from those circumstances, the harder it will be to draw that inference.'[39]

3.37 In *R v Hutchins and Charalambous*, the Court of appeal endorsed the language used by both Lord Taylor in *AG's ref (No 1 of 1995)* and Lord Hope and *R v Chargot*. Rix LJ went on to say that:

'it is emphasised that circumstances vary from case to case and that, in truth, no fixed rule can be laid down about what the prosecution must prove in order to establish consent, connivance or neglect. It is explained that in certain circumstances more detailed evidence might be required to fix a manager or director with the necessary knowledge. It is also emphasised that the strategy of provisions of this kind – and we emphasise that the wording in relation to consent, connivance and neglect is to be found in common form in statutes of this kind – is to provide a sanction against persons charged with functions of management.'[40]

---

38 [1996] 1 WLR 970, p 980.
39 Per Lord Hope at para 34 in *R v Chargot Limited (trading as Contract Services)* [2008] UKHL 73, [2009] 1 WLR 1.
40 [2011] EWCA Crim 1056.

Neglect

3.38 In *Re Hughes, Rea & Black*[41] it was said that '... neglect, in its legal connotation, implies failure to perform a duty of which the person knows or ought to know'. (Emphasis added)

3.39 There is support for the contention that a director of a company cannot be said to be neglectful if he fails to enquire about certain matters which he knows are dealt with by a fellow director or senior manager. In *Huckerby v Elliott*[42] it was stated:

> '... amongst other things it is perfectly proper for a director to leave matters to another director or to an official of the company, and that he is under no obligation to test the accuracy of anything that he is told by such a person, or even to make certain that he is complying with the law. It was pointed out that business cannot be conducted otherwise than on principles of trust, and accordingly as it seems to me ... the appellant left matters concerning the licences to her co-director ... who was the secretary of the company and fully acquainted with the business. One asks oneself this: Has she any reason to distrust [him] or to feel that he was not carrying out his duty? One finds that she had on the evidence produced no reason to distrust him.'

3.40 In *Lewin v Bland*[43] the managing director of a car selling company wrote to a customer enclosing a falsely-compiled replacement service book. He had not looked at the book before sending it out, but relied on a senior employee to have completed it correctly. He was subsequently acquitted of the offence of applying a false trade description, committed by the company on the basis of his neglect. In rejecting the prosecutor's appeal the Divisional Court said:

> 'There is nothing peculiar about the circumstances of this case which would mean that the managing director of what cannot be a small company should check the work of his senior staff... He was entitled to delegate work to his senior staff and could expect that work to be completed in accordance with the instructions given.'

3.41 In *R v P*[44] neglect was considered in the context of a health and safety prosecution of a company director. Latham LJ observed:

> 'the question, at the end of the day, will always be, where there is no actual knowledge of the state of facts, whether nonetheless the officer in question of the company should have, by reason of the surrounding circumstances, been put on enquiry so as to require him to have taken steps to determine whether or not the appropriate safety procedures were in place.'[45]

---

[41] [1943] Ch 296.
[42] Following Romer J in *Re City Equitable Fire Insurance Co Ltd* [1925] Ch 407 which related the provision of gaming premises without an appropriate licence and an offence under s 305(3) of the Customs and Excise Act 1952.
[43] (1984) 148 JP 69.
[44] [2007] EWCA Crim 1937.
[45] See also *Wotherspoon v HM Advocate* [1978] AC 74.

3.42 In *Hirschler v Birch*[46] the defendant, a director of a vehicle parts company, purchasing high level brake lights on the continent, was warned that they were no longer lawful in some countries and likely soon to be banned in others. A fellow director, who was understood by the defendant to be carrying out inquiries on the subject, told the defendant that they were legal in the UK. This was incorrect and the fellow director had not made diligent inquiries on the point. The lights were then imported and sold under the false description that they were fit for use in Britain. Charged with neglect, the defendant was convicted by the magistrates on the basis that he had failed to ensure that an authoritative answer on the lawfulness of the lights had been obtained. The Divisional Court upheld this verdict on the basis that the issue of neglect was one of fact and that there was evidence on which the magistrates were entitled to find neglect because the defendant was on notice as to the question of the legality of the lights.[47]

3.43 In *R v Hutchins and Charalambous*,[48] (see above) a prosecution under s 23 of the Private Security Industry Act 2001, the Court of Appeal held, applying the test set out by Lord Taylor in *Re Attorney General's Reference (No 1 of 1995)*[49] that what had to be proved was that H knew that unlicensed guards were being or would be deployed by X, and that he had agreed to X's conduct of its business on the basis of those facts. The prosecution did not have to prove specific knowledge of each individual offence. That was shown by the broadness of the terms 'consent, connivance and neglect' in s 23. It was impossible on the facts of the case to say that H had not consented to, or at least connived in the deployment of unlicensed guards. If directors had to be shown to be aware of specific deployments, that would allow them to shut their eyes to the management of their companies. The nature of regulatory statutes such as the 2001 Act, with the provisions for secondary liability by directors and managers, was to ensure that they were held to proper standards of supervision. The size of the company and the distance of directors from the coal face of individual acts should not, where there was consent, connivance or neglect, afford directors with a 'necessary knowledge' defence.

Causal liability

3.44 Consumer protection statutes and regulations usually include a provision making a person liable for causing another to commit an offence. These provisions are also known as 'bypass' provisions because the directly liable party can be bypassed in favour of prosecuting the person who has caused the offence to be committed.

3.45 Reg 16 of the CPUTR is typical of a provision creating causal liability.

---

[46]   [1988] BTLC 27, (1986) 151 JP 396.
[47]   For a further case where an offence was held to be attributable to neglect on the part of a director see *Crickitt v Kursaal Casino Ltd (No 2)* [1968] 1 All ER 189, (1969) 113 Sol Jo 1001.
[48]   [2011] EWCA Crim 1056.
[49]   [1996] 1 WLR 970.

Offence due to the default of another person

16(1) This regulation applies where a person 'X' –

(a)   commits an offence under regulation 9, 10, 11 or 12, or

(b)   would have committed an offence under those regulations but for a defence under regulation 17 or 18,

and the commission of the offence, or of what would have been an offence but for X being able to rely on a defence under regulation 17 or 18,[50] is due to the act or default of some other person 'Y'.

(2) Where this regulation applies Y is guilty of the offence, subject to regulations 17 and 18, whether or not Y is a trader and whether or not Y's act or default is a commercial practice.

(3) Y may be charged with and convicted.

3.46 The prosecutor must be able to show a causal connection between the offences committed. In *Tarleton v Nattrass*,[51] the defendants had entered a car for auction on 10 September, but had specifically not guaranteed the stated mileage. They were convicted, under s 23 of the TDA, the conviction being based upon the commission of an offence by the auctioneers on 2 November in offering the car for sale with what was, in fact, a false mileage. The Divisional Court held that, where it could not be said with certainty that the defendants had committed an offence on 10 September (since they had specifically not guaranteed the stated mileage) a conviction based upon the later commission of an offence by the auctioneers could not be sustained. On the facts found the offence committed by the auctioneers was unrelated to any act or default of the defendants two months earlier.[52]

3.47 It is not necessary to prove that the person causing an offence to be committed is a trader. Under the TDA the conviction of a private person knowingly selling a 'clocked' car to a dealer who then committed an offence when selling the car on was upheld in *Olgeirsson v Kitching*.[53]

3.48 In *Padgett Brothers (A-Z) Ltd v Coventry City Council*,[54] it was said that causal liability 'does not require that the relevant act should be solely due to the acts or default of the importer but merely that they are due, in part, to that.'

---

[50]   Under the TDA in *Coupe v Guyett* [1973] 2 All ER 1058 it was held that the fact that A may have a due diligence defence does not prevent him being regarded as having committed the offence for the purposes of the prosecution of B.

[51]   [1973] 3 All ER 99.

[52]   See also *Cottee v Douglas Seaton (Used Cars) Limited* [1972] 3 All ER 750; [1972] 1 WLR 1408; *Naish v Gore* [1971] 3 All ER 737 and *Richmond Upon Thames LB v Motor Sales (Hounslow) Ltd* [1971] RTR 116.

[53]   [1986] 1 All ER 746.

[54]   (1998) 162 JP 673.

General accessory liability

3.49 The general criminal law provides that criminal offences may be committed either by a principal or by secondary party.

3.50 Under s 8 of the Accessories and Abettors Act 1861 and s 44 of the Magistrates Court Act 1980 aiders, abettors, counsellors and procurers are liable to be charged, tried and sentenced as if they were principals.

3.51 It is not necessary to prove presence at the location where an offence is committed and a company, which cannot physically be present, may be convicted as a secondary party.[55]

3.52 Even for offences of strict liability, a secondary party must know the essential nature of what is being done in order to be found guilty. In *Johnson v Youden* it was stated by the Court of Appeal (Lord Goddard CJ) that:

> 'Before a person can be convicted of aiding and abetting the commission of an offence he must at least know the essential matters which constitute that offence. He need not actually know that an offence has been committed because he may not know that the facts constitute an offence and ignorance of the law is not a defence. If a person knows all the facts and is assisting another person to do certain things, and it turns out that the doing of those things constitutes an offence, the person who is assisting is guilty of aiding and abetting that offence.'[56]

3.53 The general criminal liability of accessories has also been substantially supplemented by the provisions in Part 2 of the Serious Crime Act 2007 on encouraging or assisting crime.

The due diligence defence

3.54 As a counterbalance to the strict liability regime of most regulatory offences, there is often an important safeguard in the form of the statutory 'due diligence' defence. Examples of this defence can be found in Reg 17 of the Consumer Protection from Unfair Trading Regulations 2008 ('CPUTR'), s 24 Trade Descriptions Act 1968 (which has attracted a large amount of case-law and academic commentary), the Consumer Credit Act 1974, the Consumer Protection Act 1987 and the Food Safety Act 1990.

3.55 The statutory wording is not consistent but, generally, the defence provides that the person charged has a defence if he can prove (or show) that he took all reasonable precautions (or steps) and exercised all due diligence to avoid the commission of the offence by himself (or by a person under his control).

---

[55] *Provincial Motor Cab Company v Dunning* [1909] 2 KB 599.
[56] *Johnson v Youden* [1950] 1 KB 544, per Lord Goddard CJ; approved in *Churchill v Walton* [1967] 2 AC 224 and *Maxwell v DPP for Northern Ireland* (1979) 68 Cr App R 128 HL.

3.56 Regulation 17 of CPUTR provides a typical example of a due diligence defence.

17 Due diligence defence

(1) In any proceedings against a person for an offence under regulation 9, 10, 11 or 12 it is a defence for that person to prove –

    (a)   that the commission of the offence was due to –
        (i)   a mistake;
        (ii)   reliance on information supplied to him by another person;
        (iii)   the act or default of another person;
        (iv)   an accident; or
        (v)   another cause beyond his control; and
    (b)   that he took all reasonable precautions and exercised all due diligence to avoid the commission of such an offence by himself or any person under his control.

(2) A person shall not be entitled to rely on the defence provided by paragraph (1) by reason of the matters referred to in paragraph (ii) or (iii) of paragraph (1)(a) without leave of the court unless –

    (a)   he has served on the prosecutor a notice in writing giving such information identifying or assisting in the identification of that other person as was in his possession; and
    (b)   the notice is served on the prosecutor at least seven clear days before the date of the hearing.

3.57 Regulation 17 provides a defence where the defendant can show that the offence was caused by a mistake, or reliance on information supplied to him, or the act or default of any other person, or an accident, or some other cause beyond his control *and* that he took all reasonable precautions *and* exercised all due diligence to avoid the offence. When due diligence defences are litigated, it is often the case that the prosecution will emphasise the words *'and'* and *'all'*, whereas the defence will emphasise the word *'reasonable'*.

3.58 In *Tesco Supermarkets Ltd v Nattrass*[57] Lord Diplock commented (in relation to s 24(1)(b) of the TDA 1968) as follows:

> 'What amounts to ... the exercise of due diligence ... depends on all the circumstances of the business carried on by the principal. It is a question of fact for the justices.'[58]

3.59 Having established the cause of the offence the defendant must go on to prove that he took all reasonable precautions *and* exercised all due diligence.

3.60 Particular problems may arise in cases involving very large businesses where the company cannot undertake the detailed supervision of all employees

---

[57] [1972] AC 153, 197.
[58] See also *Cambridgeshire CC v Kama* where the Divisional Court considered that the failure to maintain a refusals book for underage sales could be a significant failing on the part of a trader.

and delegates supervisory duties to more senior employees. The remarks of Lord Diplock in the *Nattrass* case are of assistance:

'If the principal has taken all reasonable precautions in the selection and training of servants to perform supervisory duties and has laid down an effective system of supervision and used due diligence to see that it is observed, he is entitled to rely on a default by a superior servant in his supervisory duties as a defence under section 24(1).'

3.61 The *Nattrass* decision has been considered by the Court of Appeal in *R v St Regis Paper Mill Co Ltd*.[59] It was held, in relation to reg 32(1)(g) of the Pollution Prevention and Control (England and Wales) Regulations 2000, that the *mens rea* of an employee should only be attributed to a company where the 'directing will and mind' could be said to be controlled, wholly or partly, by the employee in question. For example, if the employee was a managing director or senior company officer.

3.62 If the prosecution is unable to identify a reasonable precaution that was not taken, it is unlikely that the due diligence defence could be negated. Conversely, a reasonable precaution, identified and implemented after the discovery of an offence, does not necessarily disclose a failure to take all reasonable precautions to avoid the commission of the offence.[60] In *Sherratt v Gerald's The American Jewellers Ltd*[61] a watch described as a 'Diver's Watch' was engraved 'waterproof'. On taking it home the purchaser put the watch in a bowl of water. After an hour it had filled with water and stopped. In the Divisional Court Parker LCJ stated:

'Paragraphs (a) and (b) in s 24(1) have both got to be proved on a balance of probabilities, the burden being on the defendants. That they took no precautions at all is clear; they relied solely on their previous dealings with the wholesalers. ... To succeed here, they must show on a balance of probabilities that although no precautions were taken, there were no reasonable precautions that could be taken. ... There is clearly an obligation to take reasonable precautions if there are any precautions which are reasonable that can be taken ... The elementary precaution which would have prevented this offence from being committed was to dip the watch in a bowl of water as the purchaser did.'

3.63 Complete inaction on the part of a defendant is unlikely to provide a basis for a due diligence defence. In *Stainthorpe v Bailey*[62] the Divisional Court stated that:

'the fact is in reality [the defendant] did nothing. In those circumstances ... appreciating that the burden of proof was on the defendant, there really was no

---

[59]   [2011] CTLC 291.
[60]   *Enfield London Borough Council v Argos Ltd* [2008] EWHC 2597 (Admin).
[61]   (1970) 68 LGR 256.
[62]   [1980] RTR 7 per Michael Davies J.

evidence on which the justices could possibly find that [the defendant] did take all reasonable precautions and exercised all due diligence to avoid the commission of an offence.'

3.64 In *London Borough of Croydon v Pinch a Pound (UK) Ltd*[63] the Divisional Court reminded lower courts that the test should be applied in the ordinary language used in the relevant statutory provision. Roderick Evans J stated:

'The defence made available by the Act is couched in ordinary language; the words used are readily understood. For my part, I consider that it will only rarely be necessary for a court to formulate the test in anything other than the language used in the statute.'

3.65 The due diligence defences that run through consumer and trading standards law generally are similar, although not identical. The due diligence defence under the TDA, s 24, has now largely been replaced by reg 17 of CPUTR. It is likely that the case-law under the TDA will be equally applicable to the new law and will provide helpful guidance for many of the due diligence defences.

Burden and standard of proof

3.66 The defendant seeking to rely upon the due diligence defence must prove it to the civil standard of proof, that is to say to establish that it is more likely than not that a particular fact exists.[64] The mere assertion of reliance upon such a defence without evidence to support it does not require the prosecution to counter the defence.[65] The burden of proof is on the defendant in respect of *both*:

(a)   the primary fact to be proved; *and*
(b)   the requirement of due or reasonable diligence.[66]

3.67 The due diligence defence imposes a legal burden on the defendant, rather than merely an evidential burden.[67]

Reverse burdens and the ECHR

3.68 The courts have considered the compatibility of reverse burdens in criminal offences with Art 6(2) of the European Convention for the Protection of Human Rights ('ECHR'). In some cases the courts have accepted the argument that a reverse burden may be incompatible with the presumption of

---

[63]   [2010] EWHC 3283 (Admin).
[64]   *R v Carr-Briant* [1943] KB 607.
[65]   *Amos v Melcon (Frozen Foods) Ltd* (1985) 149 JP 712.
[66]   *Wandsworth Borough Council v Fontana* (1984) 148 JP 196.
[67]   An evidential burden is one that only requires the defendant to adduce sufficient evidence fit for the consideration of a jury.

innocence. In *R v DPP ex parte Kebilene*[68] the House of Lords said that Art 6(2) is not a blanket ban against reverse burdens for criminal charges but that reverse burdens must be confined within reasonable limits.[69]

3.69 Article 6(2) has been used since *Kebilene* to 'read down' legal burdens imposed on defendants in criminal cases and replace them with evidential burdens.[70] Following the decision of the House of Lords in is *R v Johnstone*,[71] however, that is unlikely to apply to the due diligence defence in a consumer or trading standards case.[72]

3.70 In *R v Johnstone* the House of Lords considered s 92(5) of the Trade Marks Act 1994, which provides a defence if the defendant can show he *'believed on reasonable grounds'* that usage was not a trade mark infringement. The legal burden imposed was found to be justified and proportionate[73] because it concerned matters within a defendant's own knowledge[74] and the legal burden was necessary in the interests of consumers and traders, to restrain widespread fraudulent trading in counterfeit goods.[75]

3.71 The rationale of *Johnstone* was repeated by a five judge Court of Appeal in *Attorney General's Reference (No 1 of 2004)*.[76]

Alternative elements of the defence

3.72 There are five alternative causes for the commission of the offence which the defendant may rely upon. The case-law identified below was mainly

---

68   [2000] 2 AC 326, HL.
69   Following the ECHR case-law and in particular *Salabiaku v France* 13 EHHR 379.
70   See *R v Lambert* [2002] 2 AC 545, HL (the knowledge burden in ss 28(2) and (3) of the Misuse of Drugs Act 1971), *R v Webster* [2010] EWCA Crim 2819 (Corruption Acts 1889 and 1916), *DPP v Wright, R (Scott, Heard and Summersgill) v Taunton Deane Magistrates' Court* [2009] EWHC 105 (Admin) (s 1 of the Hunting Act 2004); *Sheldrake v DPP, AG's Ref (No 4 of 2000)* [2005] 1 AC 264, HL.
71   [2003] 1 WLR 1736. The court in *Johnstone* considered another TMA case on reverse burdens *R v S (Trade mark defence)* [2002] EWCA Crim 25584.
72   See also *Attorney General Reference (No 1 of 2004)* [2004] 1 WLR 2111, [2005] 4 All ER 457, [2004] 2 Cr App R 27 [2004] EWCA Crim 1025 where it was stated that the 'Courts should strongly discourage the citation of authority to them other than the decision of the House of Lords in *Johnstone* and this guidance. *Johnstone* is at present the latest word on the subject'.
73   The opinion was expressly stated to be unnecessary to decide the appeal. But there had been conflicting statements in the Court of Appeal Lord Nichols stated: 'In the events which have happened this issue does not call for decision in the present case. But the House should not leave the law on this point in its present state, with differing views expressed by the Court of Appeal.'
74   Per Lord Nichols: 'The section 92(5) defence relates to facts within the accused person's own knowledge: his state of mind, and the reasons why he held the belief in question. His sources of supply are known to him.'
75   Per Lord Nicholls: 'Counterfeiting is fraudulent trading. It is a serious contemporary problem. Counterfeiting has adverse economic effects on genuine trade. It also has adverse effects on consumers, in terms of quality of goods and, sometimes, on the health or safety of consumers.'
76   [2004] 1 WLR 2111, [2005] 4 All ER 457, [2004] 2 Cr App R 27.

generated in relation to s 24 of the TDA, but is likely to be applicable generally when considered the merits of a due diligence defence:

(a) **Mistake.** The mistake must be that of the defendant and not of another person.[77] When the defendant is a company, the defence is not made out unless the employee making the mistake is a director, manager, secretary or other similar officer. In *Butler v Keenway Supermarkets*[78] a junior clerk made a genuine mistake in the pricing of goods. The Divisional Court ruled that she could not advance the defence, which was confined to the category of persons listed in s 20 of the TDA. It is clear from this case that the company could have advanced the defence of 'act or default of another person' rather 'mistake'.

(b) **Reliance on information supplied.** Many commentators have remarked that, despite the statute's silence on the point, reliance cannot be placed on this limb of the defence unless the information is shown to come from a reliable source. The authors suggest that the correct analysis may be that there is no such restriction upon the nature of the information relied upon, but that reliance on information from an unreliable source would obviously fall foul of the due diligence test. Where a defendant claimed reliance on an MOT certificate to show the condition of a vehicle the defence failed since the certificate clearly stated that it should not be relied upon for this purpose.[79]

(c) **The act or default of another person.** Where the defendant is a company, the fact that the 'other person' is an employee of the company (as where a company sold a mislabelled turkey through the failure of the manager of one of a chain of shops to read his instructions) does not prevent the company from relying on the statutory defence.[80] On the other hand it is not sufficient simply to name all the persons who might be to blame (for instance all the assistants present in the relevant branch of a chain of shops at the relevant time). The defendant must establish that they have done everything possible to establish the identity of the person to blame: *McGuire v Sittingbourne Co-operative Society Ltd.*[81] Lord Widgery CJ stated:

> 'I think it is important to emphasise ... that the onus cast upon the defendant under s 24 is not thus easily satisfied. The defendant has to prove on a balance of probabilities that the offence was due to the act or default of another, and that he, the defendant, took all reasonable precautions. The Justices should not accept either of those propositions unless the defendant has carefully examined and investigated the circumstances and done his best to show the justices how the offence was committed and why. Only then, in my judgment, will the onus be discharged and will it be open to the justices to say that the defence under s 24 is made out.'

---

[77] *Birkenhead and District Co-op v Roberts* [1970] 3 All ER 391.
[78] [1974] Crim LR 560.
[79] *Barker v Hargreaves* [1981] RTR 197.
[80] *Beckett v Kingston Bros (Butchers) Ltd* [1970] 1 QB 606.
[81] (1976) 140 JP 306, DC.

(d) **Accident.** There is scant authority on the meaning of this word within the context of the either reg 17 or s 24 of the TDA. It does not feature in other modern examples of the due diligence defence.[82] It may be that it is appropriate to read it in conjunction with the words *'some other cause beyond his control'*, since it is difficult to imagine an accident which would qualify to trigger the defence if it were in fact within the defendant's control.

(e) **Some other cause beyond his control.** In a prosecution under the Weights and Measures Act 1963, which provides a similarly worded statutory defence, it was held that the unanticipated and intermittent malfunction of a machine involved in the filling process of packaged crisps could be a cause beyond the defendant's control.[83] The unexpected illness of an employee has been held to be a cause beyond the defendant's control, although the defence failed on the due diligence test.[84]

Established systems

3.73 In cases where the defendant proves that he applied an established system of regulation he may advance the 'reliance upon information defence'. In *Hurley v Martinez*[85] the defendant had relied upon European Regulations in relation to the provision of information about wine. The Divisional Court held that the offence was due to reliance by the defendant on information supplied to him and that the requirement of due diligence was made out, notwithstanding the absence of specific checks by the defendant.

Sampling

3.74 Many due diligence cases revolve around the issues of sampling, essentially whether the sample taken was adequate. This topic is also covered in Chapter 14, Product Safety. In *Taylor v Lawrence Fraser (Bristol) Ltd*[86] the defendant supplied toys which were painted with a substance containing lead in excess of the proportions permitted by the Toys (Safety) Regulations 1974 and the defence was that the manufacturers had given the defendants a written guarantee that the toys were in compliance with the regulations and invited trading standards officers to take samples for analysis. The Divisional Court found that the defendant had not exercised all due diligence, since they could themselves have taken samples and had the paint analysed, but had failed to do so.

3.75 In *Garrett v Boots Chemists Ltd*[87] the defendant sold pencils with a higher lead content than permitted by the Pencils and Graphic Instruments

---

82 See, for example, s 139 of the Licensing Act 2003.
83 *Bibby-Cheshire v Golden Wonder* [1972] 3 All ER 738.
84 *Marshall v Herbert* [1963] Crim LR 506.
85 (1990) 154 JP 821 and *Carrick District Council v Taunton Vale Meat Traders Ltd* (1994) 158 JP 347.
86 (1977) 121 Sol Jo 757.
87 (Unreported) 16 July 1980.

(Safety) Regulations 1974. The defence was that in informing their suppliers of the existence of the regulations and requiring, as a condition of their order, that pencils supplied comply with the regulations, the defendants had taken all reasonable precautions. The Divisional Court found that, what was unreasonable for a village shop, was not necessarily so for a concern the size of Boots, and that the failure to take random samples of the pencils supplied meant that the defence must fail.

3.76 In *Hicks v SD Sullam Ltd*[88] the defendant was prosecuted under s 23 of TDA as the person 'due to whose act or default' British Home Stores committed an offence by supplying a light bulb which was described as 'safe'. The defendant had bought a large number of bulbs in the Far East and had tested none of those supplied to BHS. They had no sampling procedure for safety testing and had not obtained independent testing within the UK. They had arranged for testing to be carried out in the Far East, with satisfactory results. Since the emergence of the problem they had instituted a sampling procedure. The Divisional Court held that the absence of a testing procedure at the relevant time and the failure to obtain independent tests within the UK meant that the defence of due diligence was not made out, despite the evidence of the testing abroad.

3.77 In *Rotherham Metropolitan Borough Council Rayson (UK) Ltd*[89] a defendant who imported crayons as part of a business which employed 18 people and had a turnover (in 1986) of £4 million was prosecuted under the TDA as the person 'due to whose act or default' the retailer's offence in selling the crayons had been committed. The crayons were described on the packet as 'poisonless'. One of the crayons in a packet sold by a retailer contained excess amounts of toxic material under the relevant regulations. The defendants had provided the manufacturers with the requirements for the crayons to comply with the regulations and believed that sampling and analysis was taking place, on the basis that only adverse findings would be reported. In this country the system was that a single packet from the 7 to 10 thousand imported annually would be selected at random for analysis, this sample being found to comply with the regulations. The Divisional Court held that the system of reporting only adverse findings did not amount to due diligence and nor did the system of sampling just one of many thousands of packets in the UK.

3.78 In *P and M Supplies (Essex) Ltd v Devon County Council*[90] the defendant employed 65 to 80 staff with a turnover of £8 million and was responsible for the sale of a toy, manufactured in and imported from China, which failed to conform with safety regulations. The defendant had gone to some lengths to ensure compliance with the regulations, sending a director to the factory to check the methods of manufacture, random in-house testing on approximately 0.5% of all of the toys in a system set up in consultation with the trading standards authority, and external testing by the public analyst at a

---

[88] (1983) 91 ITSA MR 122.
[89] (1989) 153 JP 37.
[90] (Unreported) 1991, ref CO/249/90.

cost of £13,000. The Magistrates rejected a defence of due diligence based on these facts and the decision was upheld by the Divisional Court. Aside from reservations about the care with which the tests were undertaken the Divisional Court said that in such cases the burden was on the defence to provide statistical evidence as to what should be done by a reasonable trader by way of testing.

3.79 A general blanket condition in contractual terms that all goods supplied would conform with all requirements imposed by any statute or statutory regulation did not 'come within a mile of establishing or being able to comply with the provisions' in *Riley v Webb*[91] – Watkins LJ saying:

> 'It seems to me to be a minimum requirement, if sampling has not been undertaken, for the establishment of the defence ... that the sellers of the goods receive from the suppliers a positive assurance that they conform to the specific regulations which govern the sale of them.'

Written notice to the prosecutor

3.80 Section 24(2) requires the defendant to give written notice to the prosecutor if he is seeking to rely upon a s 24(1) defence and to assert that the cause of the offence was the act or default of another person or that he relied on information supplied by another person. No notice is required, it seems, if the cause of the offence is said to be mistake, accident or some other cause beyond the defendant's control.

3.81 The written notice must be given at least 7 clear days before the hearing. It must contain such information as is in the defendant's possession which will identify or assist in the identification of the other person. In *McGuire v Sittingbourne Co-operative Society Ltd*[92] it was held that the defendant had a duty to make reasonable inquiries to establish the identity of the other person. Watkins J stated that:

> 'It seems to me that it is incumbent upon the person who serves such a notice to have at least made some reasonable inquiry to establish the identity of the person who is going to be referred to in the course of the hearing of the informations so that at least the field of choice can be limited at the notice stage in cases where no single person can be identified.'

ENFORCEMENT POWERS

Introduction

3.82 The use of local authority powers to enter homes and businesses has been a contentious public issue for many years. Between 2006 and 2010 the Conservative peer, Lord Selsdon, introduced five Private Member's Bills that

---

[91]   (1987) 151 JP 372.
[92]   (1976) 140 JP 306, DC.

broadly sought to ensure that an official, whether of government or of another organisation, would not be able to enter somebody's property and seize or search without permission or without a court order. The Protection of Freedoms Act 2012 led to a mandatory review of powers of entry under various pieces of legislation and the introduction of a Code of Practice governing powers of entry and associated powers.

3.83 Schedule 5 of the Consumer Rights Act 2015 (CRA 2015) has introduced a generic set of investigatory powers, to replace the powers existing in around 60 different statutes or statutory instruments. This part of the chapter reviews the investigatory powers available to enforcers with a particular focus on the generic set within Schedule 5. It should be borne in mind that the investigatory powers under Schedule 5 only apply to enforcers as defined within the Schedule and for the purposes of enforcing legislation specified in the schedule. Separate powers still apply, for example, to alcohol and tobacco sales, food and feedstuffs, animal health and welfare and other non-BEIS[93] related subjects.

Evidence gathering

3.84 In England and Wales, the provisions of the Criminal Procedure and Investigations Act 1996, and its Code of Practice, are applicable to local authority officers (whether investigators, officers in charge of investigations or disclosure officers). Such officers must at all times:

> 'have regard to any relevant provision of a code which would apply if the investigation were conducted by police officers.' (CPIA 1996, s 26)

3.85 In particular, responsibilities for recording and retaining material are important. Officers must record any information which they consider may be relevant to an investigation, ie that it has some bearing on *any* offence under investigation, any person being investigated, or on the surrounding circumstances of the case, unless it is incapable of having any impact on the case. In *Leatherland v Powys County Council*[94] the Divisional Court quashed convictions where trading standards officers were found to be in breach of their obligations under the Act and the Code of Practice in an animal welfare investigation.

3.86 Local authority enforcement officers in England and Wales should also, 'have regard to any relevant provision' of Codes of Practice made under s 67(9) of the Police and Criminal Evidence Act 1984 ('PACE') because they are 'Persons other than police officers who are charged with the duty of investigating offences'. The requirement to have regard to relevant provisions does not equate to local authority officers, such as trading standards/ environmental health etc officers, or other non-police investigators, being obliged to comply with the provisions of the CPIA or PACE Codes.

---

[93] Department of Business, Energy and Industrial Strategy (formerly known as BIS – Business, Innovation and Skills).
[94] [2007] EWHC 148 (Admin).

3.87 Local authority officers who conduct investigations in collaboration with police officers need to be aware of the provisions relating to the lawful arrest of a suspected person under PACE. The revisions to PACE Code G, which came into effect on 12 November 2012, should be particularly noted in their application to s 24(5)(e) PACE (ie the circumstances where it is necessary to arrest a person in order 'to allow the prompt and effective investigation of the offence or of the conduct of the person in question').

3.88 However, there is an increasing frequency, generally, for challenges to be made regarding the execution of warrants to enter premises and the carrying out of connected enforcement activities. These have resulted, in cases where there has been a failure to comply with statutory requirements, in the entry, search and seizure being held to be unlawful, the material obtained being ordered to be returned and damages being awarded for trespass to property.

3.89 Examples of challenges in relation to the activities of local authorities may be found in *R (on the application of Helidon Vuciterni and Alsat UK Ltd) v Brent Magistrates' Court and Brent and Harrow Trading Standards Service,*[95] *R (on the application of Dulai and others) v Chelmsford Magistrates' Court and another*[96] and *R (Ahmed) v York Magistrates' Court and City of York Council.*[97] See also *R (on the application of RSPCA) v Colchester Magistrates' Court.*[98]

3.90 The evidence gathering methods explored above invariably give rise to issues of retention, disclosure and destruction of exhibits and material. In summary, the current CPIA regime, regarding prosecution disclosure of unused material before trial, proceeds in stages but involves a single objective test.

3.91 The prosecutor:

- has an initial duty to disclose prosecution material not previously disclosed that might reasonably be considered capable of undermining the case for the prosecution against the defendant or of assisting the case for the defendant – if there is no such material, then has a duty to give the defendant a written statement to that effect; and then

- has a continuing duty to disclose any such material:
  (i)   whenever there is any, until the court reaches its verdict or the prosecutor decides not to proceed with the case; and
  (ii)   in particular, after the service of the defence statement.

3.92 Issues of disclosure remain problematic. For example in *R v Joof,*[99] Hooper LJ said:

---

95   [2012] EWCA 2140 (Admin).
96   [2012] EWHC 1055 (Admin).
97   [2012] EWHC 3636 (Admin).
98   [2015] EWHC 1418.
99   [2012] EWCA Crim 1475.

'This is a very bad case of non-disclosure. It is to be hoped that the appropriate measures will be taken against those responsible for what appears to us to be a serious perversion of the course of justice, if those measures have not already been taken. It is to be hoped that lessons will be learnt from this shocking episode.'

Covert surveillance

3.93 The use of covert surveillance techniques for test purchasing or other functions carried out by local authorities was not regulated by statute before the enactment of Human Rights Act 1998 and the Regulation of Investigatory Powers Act 2000 ('RIPA'). In Scotland the use of covert surveillance falls under the Regulation of Investigatory Powers (Scotland) Act 2000 ('RIPSA'). However, abuse of process principles had developed at common law and evidential rules under the general exclusionary provision in s 78 of PACE.

3.94 The House of Lords considered many of these authorities in *R v Looseley and Attorney General's Reference (No 3 of 2000)*.[100] Several general principles can be distilled from the case-law:

- there is no defence of entrapment known to English law but it may be ground for mitigating sentence;
- the courts have to perform a balancing exercise and, if they conclude that the conduct of an undercover officer was so unworthy or shameful that it was an affront to the public conscience to allow a trial to proceed, or if it rendered a fair trial impossible, they will stay the proceedings;
- it would be unfair and an abuse of process if a person had been incited or pressurised by an undercover officer into committing a crime that he would not otherwise have committed;
- it would not be objectionable if an undercover officer, behaving as an ordinary member of the public would, gave a person an unexceptional opportunity to commit a crime, and that person freely took advantage of the opportunity;
- when exercising the judicial discretion of whether to exclude evidence of an undercover officer, some (but not an exhaustive list) of the factors to be taken into account are:
  - Was the officer acting as agent provocateur in the sense that he was enticing the defendant to commit an offence that he would not otherwise have committed?
  - What was the nature of any entrapment?
  - Does the evidence consist of admissions to a completed offence, or does it consist of the actual commission of an offence?
  - How active or passive was the officer's role in obtaining the evidence?
  - Is there an unassailable record of what happened, or is it strongly corroborated?
  - Has the officer abused his undercover role to ask questions which

---

[100] [2001] UKHL 53.

ought properly to have been asked in accordance with the PACE Codes of Practice (in Scotland the question is one of fairness to the accused and not one governed by PACE)?

3.95   RIPA regulates the use of a number of covert investigatory techniques, not all of which are available to local authorities. The three types of technique available to local authorities are:

(a)   the acquisition and disclosure of communications data (such as telephone billing information or subscriber details);

(b)   directed surveillance (covert surveillance of individuals in public places); and

(c)   covert human intelligence sources (CHIS) (such as the deployment of undercover officers).

3.96   In Scotland RIPSA regulates this conduct – except for the acquisition and disclosure of communications data in which case RIPA applies.

3.97   Local authority officers considering the deployment of covert enforcement activities should consider and have regard to the statutory Codes of Practice and the Procedures and Guidance document published in December 2014 by the Office of Surveillance Commissioners (OSC). In July 2010 the Home Secretary announced a review of investigatory powers conducted by Lord MacDonald. On the use of RIPA by local authorities the review concluded:

> 'On RIPA, the government will deliver the Coalition commitment to prevent local authorities from using these powers unless it is to prevent serious crime and has been authorised by a magistrate.'

3.98   The Review's recommendations were given statutory effect through the Protection of Freedoms Act 2012 and the Regulation of Investigatory Powers (Directed Surveillance and Covert Human Intelligence Sources) (Amendment) Order 2012. In summary, changes to use of RIPA by local authorities – which came into effect on 1 November 2012 – require:

- additional judicial approval for all RIPA authorisations (ie the use of directed surveillance, CHIS and the acquisition and disclosure of communications data); and

- directed surveillance to be confined to cases where the offence under investigation carries a maximum custodial sentence of 6 months or more (unless they relate to investigations into underage sales of alcohol and tobacco, which now includes nicotine-inhaling products).

3.99   The procedure, where the application is made in a criminal case, is set out in the Criminal Procedure Rules 2015[101] and, where the application is not

---

[101]   Section 6 – in force from 5 October 2015.

made in a criminal case, in the Magistrates' Courts (Regulation of Investigatory Powers) Rules 2012. Applicants should also note the 'Home Office Guidance to local authorities in England and Wales on the judicial approval process for RIPA and the crime threshold for directed surveillance'.

3.100 The regime in Scotland, with the exception of access to communications data, is unchanged.

Powers under the Consumer Rights Act 2015

3.101 Schedule 5 to the CRA 2015 introduces a consolidated set of investigatory powers which aim to be clear for both enforcers and businesses alike. The revised powers are modelled on the powers under the Consumer Protection from Unfair Trading Regulations 2008,[102] but with some differences. The consolidated powers only relate to what can broadly be described as consumer legislation: they do not apply, for example, to investigatory powers in relation to food or animal health and welfare.[103] Further, some certain specific powers contained in product safety and weights and measures legislation are retained and not included within the generic set of powers.[104]

3.102 Section 77 of the CRA 2015 blandly announces that Sch 5 'has effect'. The investigatory powers were brought into force from 27 May 2015 as regards the enforcement of duties of letting agents and secondary ticketing under Chapter 3 Part 3[105] and Chapter 5 Part 3[106] of the Act respectively. The remainder of the provisions were brought into force in October 2015.[107] BIS produced guidance regarding investigatory powers in May 2015: 'Investigatory Powers of Law Enforcers – Guidance for businesses on the Consumer Rights Act 2015'.[108]

Who can use the investigatory powers to enforce?

3.103 Paragraph 2 of the Schedule defines an enforcer as being either a domestic enforcer, an EU enforcer, a public designated enforcer or an unfair

---

[102] SI 2008/1277.
[103] Although Sch 5, para 12 does provide the Secretary of State with the power to extend the list of legislation to which Sch 5 applies.
[104] See, for example, reg 22(4) of the General Product Safety Regulations 2005, SI 2005/1803 for the power to ask for documentation, such as the product information file, to check compliance or details of the supplier, where the enforcer has reasonable suspicion that the goods have not been placed on the market since they were manufactured or imported; Furniture and Furnishings (Fire) (Safety) Regulations 1988, SI 1988/1324 and under the Weights and Measures Act 1985, ss 38–41. (see guidance p 27).
[105] Consumer Rights Act 2015 (Commencement) (England) Order 2015, SI 2015/965.
[106] Consumer Rights Act 2015 (Commencement No 1) Order 2015, SI 2015/1333.
[107] By the Consumer Rights Act 2015 (Commencement No 3, Transitional Provisions, Savings and Consequential Amendments) Order 2015, SI 2015/1630.
[108] At the time of writing, this was not available on the gov.uk website but can be found at: https://broadcast.tslinkonline.co.uk/docimages/273312/Trading%20standards%20visits%20 and%20inspections_BIS_INVESTIGATORY_POWERS_GUIDANCE_OCT15.pdf.

contract terms enforcer.[109] This chapter pertains to criminal enforcement and focusses on domestic enforcers. These are listed as being:

Sch 5, para 3

(1) In this Schedule 'domestic enforcer' means –

- (a)   the Competition and Markets Authority,
- (b)   a local weights and measures authority in Great Britain,
- (c)   a district council in England,
- (d)   the Department of Enterprise, Trade and Investment in Northern Ireland,
- (e)   a district council in Northern Ireland,
- (f)   the Secretary of State,
- (g)   the Gas and Electricity Markets Authority,
- (h)   the British Hallmarking Council,
- (i)   an assay office within the meaning of the Hallmarking Act 1973, or
- (j)   any other person to whom the duty in subsection (1) of section 27 of the Consumer Protection Act 1987 (duty to enforce safety provisions) applies by virtue of regulations under subsection (2) of that section.[110]

Delegation of powers

3.104   The powers described in Sch 5 refer to an enforcer or an officer of an enforcer. Paragraph 7 defines what is meant by an officer:

(1) In this Schedule 'officer', in relation to an enforcer, means –

- (a)   an inspector appointed by the enforcer to exercise powers under this Schedule, or authorised to do so,
- (b)   an officer of the enforcer appointed by the enforcer to exercise powers under this Schedule, or authorised to do so,
- (c)   an employee of the enforcer (other than an inspector or officer) appointed by the enforcer to exercise powers under this Schedule, or authorised to do so, or
- (d)   a person (other than an inspector, officer or employee of the enforcer) authorised by the enforcer to exercise powers under this Schedule.

(2) But references in this Schedule to an officer in relation to a particular power only cover a person within sub-paragraph (1) if and to the extent that the person has been appointed or authorised to exercise that power.

The enforcer's legislation

3.105

Sch 5, para 9(1):

9(1) In this Schedule 'the enforcer's legislation', in relation to a domestic enforcer, means –

- (a)   legislation or notices which, by virtue of a provision listed in paragraph 10, the domestic enforcer has a duty or power to enforce, and

---

[109] Paragraph 2(2).
[110] Sch 5, para 3(1).

(b)   where the domestic enforcer is listed in an entry in the first column of the table in paragraph 11, the legislation listed in the corresponding entry in the second column of that table.

(2) References in this Schedule to a breach of or compliance with the enforcer's legislation include a breach of or compliance with a notice issued under—

(a)   the enforcer's legislation, or
(b)   legislation under which the enforcer's legislation is made.

The consolidated powers in the CRA 2015 will apply to the legislative provisions listed in paragraphs 10 and 11. Under paragraph 12 the Secretary of State has power to amend the list. There have already been several amendments.[111] In summary, the enforcer's legislation primarily comprises areas concerned with fair trading, product safety, weights and measures, prices, consumer credit, estate agents, package travel, timeshare, video recordings and intellectual property.

Using the powers

3.106 Powers under Part 3 of the Schedule (powers in relation to production of information) may be used by each of the enforcers in the circumstances prescribed within that Part.

3.107 The powers under Part 4 of Sch 5 are only available to domestic enforcers for the purposes detailed in para 19. Domestic enforcers may exercise any power in paras 21 to 26 (test purchasing, observing the carrying on of a business, entering premises without a warrant, inspecting products, testing equipment) and in paras 31 to 34 (power to break open containers, power to enter premises with a warrant, power to require persons on premises to provide assistance) for the purposes of ascertaining compliance with the enforcer's legislation.[112]

3.108 Paragraph 35 provides interpretation for phrases used in Part 4 of the Schedule, as follows:

'goods' has the meaning given by section 2(8);[113]
'occupier', in relation to premises, means any person an officer of an enforcer reasonably suspects to be the occupier of the premises;
'premises' includes any stall, vehicle, vessel or aircraft;
'product' means—
    (a) goods,
    (b) a service,
    (c) digital content, as defined in section 2(9),[114]

---

[111] See for example the Consumer Rights Act 2015 (Commencement No 3, Transitional Provisions, Savings and Consequential Amendments) Order 2015, the Consumer Rights Act 2015 (Consequential Amendments) Order 2015.

[112] Paragraph 19(2).

[113] Section 2(8) – 'Goods' means any tangible moveable items, but that includes water, gas and electricity if and only if they are put up for supply in a limited volume or set quantity.

[114] Section 2(9) – 'Digital content' means data which are produced and supplied in digital form.

(d) immovable property, or

(e) rights or obligations.

Territorial jurisdiction for investigatory powers

3.109 Traditionally trading standards departments investigated and prosecuted cases within their own area and it was not always clear whether they required authorisation to work across boundaries. Paragraphs 44–46 of Sch 5 to the CRA 2015 provide for local authority trading standards services and enforcers in District Councils in Northern Ireland to investigate breaches and take criminal proceedings outside their local authority area. Trading Standards departments in Scotland do not take legal proceedings as these are brought by the Procurator Fiscal.

3.110 In summary:

- A local weights and measures authority in England or Wales may exercise CRA 2015, Sch 5 investigatory powers and may bring proceedings for a consumer law offence allegedly committed in a part of England or Wales which is outside that authority's area.

- A district council in England may exercise may exercise CRA 2015, Sch 5 investigatory powers and may bring proceedings for a consumer law offence allegedly committed in a part of England which is outside that authority's area.

- A local weights and measures authority in Scotland may exercise CRA 2015, Sch 5 investigatory powers in a part of Scotland which is outside that authority's area.

- A district council in Northern Ireland may exercise CRA 2015, Sch 5 investigatory powers and may bring proceedings for a consumer law offence allegedly committed in a part of Northern Ireland which is outside that council's district.

3.111 The BIS guidance notes:

'Enforcers operating across their local authority boundaries are encouraged to liaise with enforcers in the relevant local authorities and Primary authorities when considering operating outside their local area. This will help to avoid any likelihood of duplication of enforcement activities.'

3.112 These provisions will better enable national trading standards teams such as Scambusters, National Trading Standards Scams Team and the National Trading Standards e-crime team to work within local authorities but also across local authority boundaries.

Production of information

3.113 Part 3 of Sch 5 contains the powers in relation to the production of information. These powers are broadly similar to and replace those under

Part 8 of the Enterprise Act 2002[115] *but now apply to both civil and criminal consumer law enforcement.* Paragraph 13 of the Schedule details the purposes for which the powers may be used by domestic enforcers, EU enforcers, public designated enforcers and unfair contract terms enforcers.

3.114 A domestic enforcer may exercise the powers in Part 3 for the purpose of ascertaining whether there has been a breach of the enforcers' legislation,[116] but may only use the power to require the production of information for that purpose where an officer of an enforcer reasonably suspects a breach of the legislation, although this does not apply when the enforcer is acting as a market surveillance authority.

3.115 In *Lancashire County Council v Buchanan*[117] a trading standards officer used powers under the Property Misdescriptions Act 1991 to require the production of documents relating to an estate agent's business. The estate agent, Buchanan, had already provided a considerable amount of information and refused to provide any more. He was charged with the obstruction offence under the Act. The issue was whether the officer had reasonable grounds to suspect that an offence had been committed under the Act and so had power to require production of the documents. In a decision upheld by the Administrative Court, it was determined that on the basis of the information that was in the officer's possession, the officer had no reasonable grounds for suspecting an offence had been committed.

3.116 Paragraph 14 simply states that an enforcer or an officer thereof, may give notice to a person requiring the person to provide the enforcer with information specified in the notice. Exercise of this power may mean that the enforcer does not need to visit the person's premises. Paragraph 15 sets out the procedure by which this is to be done. The notice must be in writing and specify the purpose for which the information is required. The notice may specify the time within which and the manner in which the person to whom it is given must comply with it and the form in which the information is to be provided. The notice may require the creation of documents, or documents of a given description in the notice and the provision of the same to the enforcer or an officer of the enforcer. Such notice cannot require a person to produce documents which would be subject to legal professional privilege.

3.117 Paragraph 16 provides for enforcement of the notice. Where there is a failure to comply the enforcer may apply to the Court for enforcement under para 16. If the court considers that the person has failed to comply with the notice, it may make an order requiring the person to do anything that the court thinks is reasonable for the person to do, for any of the purposes for which the notice was given, to ensure the notice is complied with. Either the person failing

---

[115] CRA 2015, Sch 6, paras 68–71.
[116] Paragraph 13.
[117] [2007] EWHC 3194 (Admin).

to comply or an official of a company, partnership or unincorporated association failing to comply may be required by the Court to meet the costs or expenses of the application.[118]

3.118 There are limitations on the use of information[119] provided so as to preserve the right against self-incrimination. Paragraph 17 makes clear that in criminal proceedings against that person the prosecution may not adduce evidence or ask questions relating to that information. The rule does not apply where by or on behalf of the person providing the information it is adduced as evidence or a question is asked relating to it. Moreover, the restriction on use does not apply where a person is facing proceedings for the obstruction offence under para 36 or a perjury offence under s 5 of the Perjury Act 1911 (false statutory declarations).

Test purchasing

3.119 'Covert' sampling techniques (or test purchasing), have been part of the tools used to determine compliance with food and weights and measures laws for nearly 150 years. As Lord Nicholls said in *R v Looseley and Attorney General's Reference (No 3 of 2000)*:[120]

> 'Indeed, conduct of this nature by officials is sometimes expressly authorised by Act of Parliament. The statute creating an offence may authorise officials to make test purchases, as in section 27 of the Trade Descriptions Act 1968.'

3.120 The modern equivalent powers to test purchase are found under para 21 of Sch 5 to the CRA 2015. In our view, the vast majority of test purchasing operations are not likely to result in the obtaining of private information about any person (under s 26(2) RIPA – s 1(2)(b) RIPSA) or to establish or maintain a personal or other relationship with the seller (under s 26(8) RIPA – s 1(8)(b) RIPSA) so a RIPA/RIPSA authorisation is not required. There will be circumstances when one should be considered and, ultimately, the responsibility for authorising (or not authorising) a test-purchasing operation is that of the Authorising Officer.

Children used in test purchases

3.121 In *London Borough of Ealing v Woolworths*,[121] the Divisional Court considered a case involving the use of children to make test purchases. An 11-year-old boy had been used in a trading standards test purchase of an 18

---

[118] Paragraph 15(4), (5). An official is defined in para 16(6) as being a director, manager, secretary or other similar officer for a company, a member in the case of a limited liability partnership, a partner in the case of a partnership and as regards an unincorporated association, a person in management or control of its affairs.

[119] Including information contained in a document created pursuant to a notice under Paragraph 14.

[120] [2001] UKHL 53.

[121] [1995] Crim LR 58.

category video film at the respondent's shop.[122] The boy had simply bought the video and the sales assistant had made no inquiry of his age. The justices hearing the case at first instance accepted a submission that the evidence be excluded for entrapment under s 78 (of PACE) because the defendant had been induced to make the sale when otherwise no such sale would have taken place. The Divisional Court robustly overturned that decision:

> 'If the process employed, which we understand to be a common practice up and down the country, were to fall foul of s 78, it would in my judgment emasculate the enforcement of a sensible piece of legislation which, as earlier indicated, was passed for the express purpose of protecting young people such as the boy employed for the test purchase in this case from being exposed to undesirable influences. I do not accept that what happened was in any sense an entrapment of the respondents, or that the boy acted as an agent provocateur, nor incidentally, did he commit any offence in purchasing the video. He did not incite, aid or abet the commission of an offence by Woolworths. By purchasing the video he was simply playing a part in the situation which rendered Woolworths culpable. Had there been any element of persuasion of the sales girl by the customer, then perhaps different considerations would have prevailed.'

3.122 In *Wm Morrisons Supermarkets plc v Reading BC*[123] a test purchase of cigarettes had been made by a child on behalf of the local authority. The Divisional Court rejected the appellant's argument that there had not been a 'transaction of sale' for the purposes of s 7(1)(a) of the Children and Young Persons Act 1933. It was irrelevant whether property had passed to the young person or, as a result of his entering into the transaction, to someone else. What mattered was that the child or young person entered into a contract for the sale of tobacco and that property passed under that contract.

3.123 It should be noted that the OSC Procedures and Guidance document, in relation to 'Test Purchase of sales to juveniles', states 'intelligence must be sufficient to prevent "fishing trips"'. Also the non-statutory Age Restricted Products Code of Practice – issued by the Better Regulation Delivery Office in January 2013 and updated in April 2014 – contains a part (paras 13–18) which 'addresses the use of test purchasing by young people as a tactic for conducting spot checks on compliance'.

Power to test purchase under the Consumer Rights Act 2015

3.124 The power to test purchase products for the purpose of ascertaining compliance with the enforcer's legislation is found in Sch 5, para 21 to the CRA 2015. This power and the power under para 22 to observe the carrying on of a business are akin to the officer acting in the manner of a consumer and in neither case is the officer exercising a power of entry for which a notice or warrant requirement applies.

---

[122] Section 11(1) of the Video Recordings Act 1984 made it an offence to supply the video to a person under the age of 18.

[123] [2012] EWHC 1358 (Admin), [2012] PTSR 1643, [2012] 2 Cr App R 16, (2012) 176 JP 388, [2012] CTLC 33.

21 Power to purchase products

(1) An officer of an enforcer may –

(a)   make a purchase of a product, or
(b)   enter into an agreement to secure the provision of a product.

(2) For the purposes of exercising the power in sub-paragraph (1), an officer may –

(a)   at any reasonable time, enter premises to which the public has access (whether or not the public has access at that time), and
(b)   inspect any product on the premises which the public may inspect.

(3) The power of entry in sub-paragraph (2) may be exercised without first giving notice or obtaining a warrant.

3.125   The BIS guidance suggests that a reasonable time will generally be taken to mean when a business is open for trade but enforcers will need to take account of what is reasonable in the circumstances and for that particular business sector. The definition in Sch 5, para 7(1)(d) means that, for example, a volunteer, non-employee of a local authority, authorised by the authority to exercise the power of test purchasing under para 20, is an 'officer'.

Power to observe

3.126

22 Power to observe carrying on of business etc

(1) An officer of an enforcer may enter premises to which the public has access in order to observe the carrying on of a business on those premises.

(2) The power in sub-paragraph (1) may be exercised at any reasonable time (whether or not the public has access at that time).

(3) The power of entry in sub-paragraph (1) may be exercised without first giving notice or obtaining a warrant.

3.127   The BIS guidance[124] suggests that the power to observe the carrying on of a business for the purpose of ascertaining compliance with the enforcer's legislation might be used when the business is new to an area or where the enforcer has little intelligence about the business in question. Similar considerations will apply as under Paragraph 21 as to what constitutes a reasonable time.

Powers of entry

3.128 The Protection of Freedoms Act 2012 flowed from a Coalition Government declared intent to roll back state intrusion and protect civil liberties. The Act required the review of existing powers of entry and associated powers[125] with a view to:

- repealing them if they are considered to be either unnecessary or inappropriate by the relevant Minister;[126] or

- adding safeguards such as restrictions as to the times at which the power may be exercised or a requirement for the power of entry to be subject to an authorisation;[127] or

- rewriting them by, for example, consolidating a number of powers of entry exercisable for similar purposes or by a defined category of state officials.[128]

3.129 The Home Office-coordinated review identified 1,237 separate powers of entry – 749 in primary legislation; 478 in secondary legislation. The Government proposals will leave a total of 91 – with 231 further powers having additional 'safeguards'. Provision is also made in the Act[129] for the exercise of powers of entry and associated powers (which have not been devolved) to be subject to a code of practice. The Code of Practice came into force as from 6 April 2015.[130] The Code 'provides guidance and sets out considerations that apply before, during and after powers of entry and associated powers are exercised including those circumstances where entry is exercised with the consent of an occupier. The purpose of the Code is to ensure greater consistency in the exercise of powers of entry and greater clarity for those affected by them while upholding effective enforcement.'

3.130 'Relevant persons'[131] must have regard to the code when exercising any functions to which the code relates.[132] Not doing so does not create criminal or civil liability for the individual, but it is admissible as evidence in proceedings.[133] Authorities should ensure that all relevant persons are familiar with this Code of Practice.[134]

---

125 Section 42.
126 Section 39.
127 Section 40.
128 Section 41.
129 Section 47.
130 The Protection of Freedoms Act 2012 (Code of Practice for Powers of Entry and Description of Relevant Persons) Order 2015.
131 Defined in The Protection of Freedoms Act 2012 (Code of Practice for Powers of Entry and Description of Relevant Persons) Order 2015 as being any person who is exercising a power of entry or associated power which is not devolved and not subject to another code of practice.
132 Section 51(1).
133 Section 51(2), (3).
134 Code, para 24.

3.131 The Code mandates the provision of reasonable notice (usually not less than 48 hours or as specified in the relevant legislation), to the landowner or occupier affected by the power of entry. Notice should be considered even where it not required under the relevant legislation, unless to do so would frustrate the purpose of the entry. The Code recognises that there may be a need for unannounced inspections, such that the provision of notice would defeat the purpose of the entry and also that it may not always be practicable to provide notice. The powers of entry under Sch 5 to the CRA 2015, reflect the Code of Practice in terms of the provision of notice but it should be noted that the provisions regarding the notice requirements etc in the Act take precedence over those in the Code.

3.132 The Code also requires the consideration of the number of people needed to affect the entry[135] and where entry without consent or warrant is permitted by legislation, whether the object of the entry could be achieved by less intrusive means.[136] The Code also provides guidance on the conduct of authorised persons exercising powers of entry both during and after the entry and the records which should be maintained.

Powers of entry and the obtaining of warrants

3.133 Various pieces of consumer and trading standards legislation provide officers of enforcing authorities with powers of entry onto premises (dwellings and non-dwellings) either with or without a warrant. Many of these powers have now been consolidated into the generic set of investigatory powers under Sch 5 to the CRA 2015. Within these consolidated powers, officers have the power to enter premises which are not used as dwellings. This power may only be used on provision of 48 hours' notice, unless prescribed conditions are met. The power of entry to premises with a warrant may only be made after the magistrate hearing the application has been satisfied on receiving written evidence on oath that prescribed conditions have been met. In recent times the exercise of powers of entry, particularly where warrants have been required, has generated considerable case-law which provides guidance on how the Courts should approach such applications.

3.134 Officers should first consider whether a warrant is necessary or consider whether notice of entry is required under the legislation governing the power of entry. In *Hargreaves v Brecknock and Radnorshire Magistrates' Court and Powys County Council Trading Standards Department*,[137] an application was made to obtain a warrant for entry to premises which were not a dwelling citing both reg 21 (power of entry without a warrant) and reg 22 (power of entry with a warrant) of CPUTR 2008. The Court observed, 'no warrants were

---

[135] Code, para 9.
[136] Code, para 11.
[137] [2015] EWHC 1803 (Admin).

necessary in this case because neither of the premises concerned was used exclusively as a dwelling. We have concluded that everything was done within the scope of Regulation 21(1)'.[138]

3.135 In *R (Redknapp) v Commissioner of the City of London Police*[139] Latham LJ noted:

'The obtaining of a search warrant is never to be treated as a formality. It authorises the invasion of a person's home. All the material necessary to justify the grant of a warrant should be contained in the information provided on the form. If the magistrate ... does require any further information in order to satisfy himself that the warrant is justified, a note should be made of the additional information so that there is a proper record of the full basis upon which the warrant has been granted.'[140]

3.136 Notwithstanding the fact that reg 21(1) plainly gave the Trading Standards authority power of entry, the Court in *Hargreaves* went on to consider the warrant that was issued and in particular whether the Court could satisfy itself that the conditions for the granting of a warrant had been met. On quashing the warrant, the Court observed:

'What was required was a clear statement in writing that condition A was relied on and the basis upon which it was said that the condition was met. It should have been made plain to the Magistrate that he had first to be satisfied as to Condition A[141] before going on to the second stage of the decision. We are not confident that Condition A was referred to in terms by anyone. It is not on the form (save as part of the Regulation), it is not in the notes and it is not referred to by the Magistrate in his decision.'

3.137 The application for a warrant carries with it the duty of full and frank disclosure. In *R (on the application of Vuciterni) v Brent Magistrates Court*,[142] Davis LJ stated:

'it must never be forgotten that the granting of a warrant (no less than the making of a search and seize, or Anton Piller, order) is a most extreme and invasive kind of order, not to be granted without great caution and dependent on appropriate full and accurate disclosure by the applicant.'

3.138 In this case a warrant was obtained under CPUTR, reg 22 (power of entry with a warrant) from the magistrates' court on the basis that the supply in the UK of satellite television decoder cards meant for the Albanian market was likely to constitute an offence under s 297A of the Copyright, Designs and

---

[138] Per Thirlwall J at para 42.
[139] [2009] 1 WLR 2096.
[140] Per Latham LJ at para 13.
[141] Condition A stated 'that there are on the premises goods or documents which a duly authorised officer [.] has power to inspect and that there evidence is likely to disclose evidence of a breach of these Regulations'.
[142] [2012] EWHC 2140 (Admin), [2012] CTLC 171.

Patents Act 1988 as well as the banned practice of stating or otherwise creating the impression that a product could be legally sold when it could not, contrary to Sch 1, para 9 of the CPUTR.

3.139 The Administrative Court quashed the warrants by reason of material non-disclosure (see paras 24, 29, 34–35 and 38 of the judgment). At the time of the warrants being issued it could not have been fairly represented to the magistrates' court that it was 'likely' that the supplying of such cards would constitute an offence under s 297A given the significant doubts raised about this by the Advocate-General in *QC Leisure* and *Murphy* (by the time of the Administrative Court hearing the CJEU had ruled definitively that it was not an offence).[143]

3.140 In *Vuciterni* the Court had to consider whether the powers of entry under CPUTR impliedly carried a power to search. In finding that they did the Court commented:

> 'The powers to enter (and inspect) therefore plainly carry with them a power to search, as a matter of sensible construction.'[144]

3.141 Parliament did not take the opportunity to make this plain when drafting the generic set of powers under the CRA 2015, however the decision in *Vuciterni* is likely to remain good law for the powers of entry under Sch 5.

3.142 In *Hargreaves* the Court ruled that enforcement officer's making a video recording of an entry and search was not unlawful.

> 'In filming events the officers were not exercising a power ... They were making a record of the execution of the warrant ... we consider it would be a proportionate interference with the Article 8 right to respect for private life were the record to be made and retained for the purposes of and the duration of criminal proceedings (subject to any appeals).'[145]

Powers of entry under the CRA 2015

Entry without a warrant (Sch 5, para 21)

3.143 Paragraph 23(1) of Sch 5, provides:

> An officer of an enforcer may enter premises at any reasonable time.

The power under para 23 does not include entry to premises which are used wholly or mainly as a dwelling.[146]

---

[143] CJEU Cases C-403/03 and C-429–03.
[144] Per Davies LJ.
[145] Per Thirlwall J at paras 40, 41.
[146] Paragraph 23(2).

3.144 In the case of a routine inspection, the power of entry may only be exercised if a notice has been given to the occupier of the premises[147] unless the occupier waives the requirement to give notice.[148] There is no requirement that the waiver of notice be in writing, but clearly, as the BIS Guidance observes, as a matter of best practice a written communication of waiver (demonstrating understanding of the right to notice which is being waived) should be obtained from the trader and retained by the officer.

3.145 Paragraph 23(4) provides the formal requirements of the notice which are:

(a) The notice is in writing and given by an officer of the enforcer;

(b) The notice sets out why the entry is necessary and indicates the nature of the offence of obstruction (under paragraph 36), and

(c) That there are at least two working days between the date of the receipt of the notice and the date of entry.

3.146 The phrase 'routine inspection' is defined under Paragraph 23(6):

(6) In this paragraph 'routine inspection' means an exercise of the power in sub-paragraph (1) other than where –

(a) the power is exercised by an officer of a domestic enforcer who reasonably suspects a breach of the enforcer's legislation,

(b) the officer reasonably considers that to give notice in accordance with sub-paragraph (3) would defeat the purpose of the entry,

(c) it is not reasonably practicable in all the circumstances to give notice in accordance with that sub-paragraph, in particular because the officer reasonably suspects that there is an imminent risk to public health or safety, or

(d) the enforcer is a market surveillance authority within the meaning of Article 2(18) of the Regulation on Accreditation and Market Surveillance and the entry is for the purpose of market surveillance within the meaning of Article 2(17) of that Regulation.

3.147 Aside from waiver by the trader or occupier of premises, there remain four situations where notice need not be given. The most common exceptions likely to be used are the suspicion of the breach of the enforcer's legislation and the defeating of the purpose of the entry. What will amount to suspicion that there has been a breach of the enforcer's legislation? In *Hussien v Chong Fook Kam*,[149] Lord Devlin stated:

'Suspicion in its ordinary meaning is a state of conjecture or surmise where proof is lacking: "I suspect but I cannot prove". Suspicion arises at or near the starting point of an investigation of which the obtaining of prima facie proof is the end.'[150]

---

147 Paragraph 23(3).
148 Paragraph 23(5).
149 [1970] AC 942.
150 At 948.

3.148 This passage was approved by Lord Steyn in *O'Hara v Chief Constable of the Royal Ulster Constabulary*,[151] where it was said:

> '(1) In order to have a reasonable suspicion the constable need not have evidence amounting to a prima facie case. Ex hypothesi one is considering a preliminary stage of the investigation and information from an informer or a tip-off from a member of the public may be enough: Hussien v Chong Fook Kam [1970] A.C. 942, 949. (2) Hearsay information may therefore afford a constable reasonable grounds to arrest. Such information may come from other officers: Hussien's case, ibid.'

3.149 What amounts to reasonable suspicion will turn on the facts and circumstances of each case and can include intelligence material provided by others such as police or other local authorities.

3.150 Notice is not required where the officer reasonably considers that the giving of notice would defeat the purpose of entry. The most obvious reason why the giving of notice would defeat the purpose of the entry would be that evidence demonstrating a breach of the enforcer's legislation would be concealed, removed or destroyed. For example, an officer may be aware that counterfeit alcohol is being sold within an area, but uses this exception not to give notice as the likelihood would be that the counterfeit alcohol would be removed from the premises when the inspection takes place.

3.151 Where entry is effected other than in the circumstances of a routine inspection, the officer must provide the occupier with a document setting out why the entry is necessary and the nature of the obstruction offence under para 36, but this is not necessary where not practicable to do so.[152] On any entry to premises under para 23, an officer must provide to an occupier evidence of identity and authorisation, but this is not necessary where not practicable to do so.[153]

Power to enter premises with a warrant

3.152 Paragraph 32 provides for the power of entry into premises with a warrant whilst para 33 addresses the exercise of entry under the warrant.

32 Power to enter premises with warrant

(1) A justice of the peace may issue a warrant authorising an officer of an enforcer to enter premises if satisfied, on written information on oath given by such an officer, that there are reasonable grounds for believing that –

    (a)   condition A or B is met, and
    (b)   condition C, D or E is met.

(2) Condition A is that on the premises there are –

---

[151] [1997] AC 286.
[152] Paragraph 23(7), (9).
[153] Paragraph 23(8), (9).

(a) products which an officer of the enforcer has power to inspect under paragraph 25, or

(b) documents which an officer of the enforcer could require a person to produce under paragraph 27.

(3) Condition B is that, on the premises –

(a) in the case of a domestic enforcer, there has been or is about to be a breach of the enforcer's legislation,

(b) in the case of an EU enforcer, there has been or is about to be a Community infringement as defined in section 212 of the Enterprise Act 2002, or

(c) in the case of an EU enforcer, there has been a failure to comply with a measure specified in paragraph 20(3)(b), (c) or (d).

(4) Condition C is that –

(a) access to the premises has been or is likely to be refused, and

(b) notice of the enforcer's intention to apply for a warrant under this paragraph has been given to the occupier of the premises.

(5) Condition D is that it is likely that products or documents on the premises would be concealed or interfered with if notice of entry on the premises were given to the occupier of the premises.

(6) Condition E is that –

(a) the premises are unoccupied, or

(b) the occupier of the premises is absent, and it might defeat the purpose of the entry to wait for the occupier's return.

(7) In the application of this paragraph to Scotland –

(a) the reference in sub-paragraph (1) to a justice of the peace is to be read as a reference to a sheriff, and

(b) the reference in that sub-paragraph to information on oath is to be read as a reference to evidence on oath.

(8) In the application of this paragraph to Northern Ireland –

(a) the reference in sub-paragraph (1) to a justice of the peace is to be read as a reference to a lay magistrate, and

(b) the reference in that sub-paragraph to written information is to be read as a reference to a written complaint.

3.153 This power of entry extends further than the power under para 23 in that it also applies to domestic premises. This is not specified within the legislation but it follows from the absence of a provision such as that contained in para 23(2) (relating to premises which are used wholly or mainly as a dwelling) and the decision in *R (Vuciterni) v Brent Magistrates' Court*,[154] where the Court of Appeal made clear that the power under reg 22 of CPUTR (which is in similar terms to the para 32 power) applies to any premises.[155]

---

[154] [2012] EWHC 2140 (Admin), [2012] CTLC 171.
[155] Per Davies LJ at para 46.

3.154 A warrant for entry can be obtained where there are two conditions met. First, there must be reasonable grounds for believing that either:

(a)   there are products or documents on the premises which the officer would have power to inspect under para 25, or could require production of under para 27; OR

(b)   that there has been or there is about to be a breach of the domestic enforcers legislation.[156]

3.155 Secondly, the Court must be satisfied that there are reasonable grounds for believing one of the following:

(a)   that notice of the intention to apply for the warrant has been given to the occupier and access to the premises has been or is likely to be refused;

(b)   that products or documents on the premises would be concealed or interfered with if notice were given;

(c)   the premises are unoccupied or the occupier is absent and it might defeat the purpose of the entry to wait for the occupier's return.

3.156 The obtaining of a warrant for entry under para 32 reproduces the procedural requirements of reg 22 of the CPUTR 2008 in similar terms. However, Condition A no longer requires that inspection of the goods/documents is likely to disclose evidence of a breach and the wording of Condition D in CPUTR 2008 was (merely) that an application for admission, or the giving of a notice of intention to apply for a warrant, 'would defeat the object of the entry'.

3.157 Paragraph 33 reads as follows:

> **33 Entry to premises under warrant**
>
> (1) A warrant under paragraph 32 authorises an officer of the enforcer to enter the premises at any reasonable time, using reasonable force if necessary.
>
> (2) A warrant under that paragraph ceases to have effect at the end of the period of one month beginning with the day it is issued.
>
> (3) An officer entering premises under a warrant under paragraph 32 may be accompanied by such persons, and may take onto the premises such equipment, as the officer thinks necessary.
>
> (4) If the premises are occupied when the officer enters them, the officer must produce the warrant for inspection to an occupier of the premises.
>
> (5) Sub-paragraph (6) applies if the premises are unoccupied or the occupier is temporarily absent.
>
> (6) On leaving the premises the officer must –

---

[156] This paragraph should be contrasted with para 23(6)(b), where entry can be exercised by a domestic enforcer who 'reasonably suspects a breach of the enforcer's legislation' and not as in para 32 where there 'has been or is about to be a breach of the enforcer's legislation'.

> (a)   leave a notice on the premises stating that the premises have been entered under a warrant under paragraph 32, and
>
> (b)   leave the premises as effectively secured against trespassers as the officer found them.

3.158   As to para 33(3), Powers of Entry Code of Practice, para 9 is relevant:

'9.1 Relevant persons should consider the number of persons needed for the exercise of powers of entry and associated powers to be carried out effectively. The number of persons present should reflect what is reasonable and proportionate in the circumstances.'

Power to require assistance from person on premises

3.159   Where a domestic enforcer has exercised a power of entry under para 23 or 32 for the purposes of enforcing the Weights and Measures (Packaged Goods) Regulations 2006,[157] the officer may require any person on the premises to provide such assistance or information as the officer reasonably considers necessary. In particular, the officer may require any person on the premises to provide information in their possession about the name and address of packer or importer of goods found on the premises.

Powers of search and seizure generally

3.160   Powers of seizure were extended under Part 2 of the Criminal Justice and Police Act 2001 in relation to legislation within Sch 1 to that Act, which includes consumer and trading standards legislation. The CRA 2015 amends that Schedule to take account of the generic set of powers under Sch 5.[158] In general terms s 50 of the Act provides powers for officers lawfully on premises to seize items in order that may be sifted and searched to see whether they are relevant and to seize items which may contain information which would fall within the scope of their entry. This would therefore enable an officer to seize an item containing digital content for example a computer or mobile phone, for the purpose of ascertaining the contents of the item. Schedule 1 to the Act is amended to include the powers under paras 27(1)(b), 28(1) and 29(1) of Sch 5 to the CRA 2015.

Powers available on entry under CRA 2015, Sch 5

3.161   The powers under paras 25–31 of the Schedule only apply where an enforcer has entered under a power of entry under Paragraph 23 or with a warrant under Paragraph 32.[159] These powers are not free-standing – they are dependent on, and consequential to, entry onto premises through the use of CRA 2015 powers, not entry by consent.

---

[157]   SI 2006/659, or its Northern Irish equivalent Weights and Measures (Packaged Goods) Regulations (Northern Ireland) 2011, SR 2011/331.
[158]   Consumer Rights Act 2015, Sch 6, para 65.
[159]   Paragraph 24.

3.162 In *R (on the application of Helidon Vuciterni and Alsat UK Limited) v Brent Magistrates' Court and Brent and Harrow Trading Standards Service*[160] the defendant submitted that the power to enter premises and to inspect goods under CPUTR 2008 did not, in either case, sanction a search. Davies LJ:

> 'The powers given under Regulation 21(1)(a)–(d) and under Regulation 22(2)(a) and (b) are disjunctive and separate. It is impossible to see how they could be effectively exercised if a power to search is not available: is an enforcement officer, having lawfully obtained entry, confined to standing in the hallway and looking around, by way of 'inspection', for what he can (or cannot) see? Plainly not. The powers conferred necessarily connote a power to, for example, search a desk or cabinet to see if there are relevant documents which may be required to be copied, if a breach has reasonably been suspected; they connote that an enforcement officer may, for example, go into backrooms and store rooms to see if there are goods that should be seized or detained, if there is reasonable cause to believe (not just suspect) a breach; and likewise may search for containers or vending machines. The powers to enter (and inspect) therefore plainly carry with them a power to search, as a matter of sensible construction. It must also not be overlooked that in this area of consumer protection very often thoroughly unscrupulous and disreputable people may be involved (I am again talking generally, not necessarily by reference to this case) and appropriately robust powers are to be expected to be available.'

Power to inspect products

3.163 Under para 25 an officer of a domestic enforcer has the power to inspect any product on the premises[161] and to examine any procedure connected with the production of a product for the purpose of ascertaining compliance with the enforcer's legislation. The power to examine any procedure is, specifically, also available to an officer acting pursuant to the duty in s 27(1) of the Consumer Protection Act 1987 or reg 10(1) of the General Product Safety Regulations 2005.[162] Officers acting pursuant to the duty in reg 10(1) of the Weights and Measures (Packaged Goods) Regulations 2006[163] may inspect records or evidence of the kind referred to in those Regulations.[164] This power is available to Northern Irish officers acting under the equivalent regulations.[165] Further under para 26(7), (8), there are powers for domestic enforcers acting under duties[166] in the Electromagnetic Compatibility Regulations 2006[167] to inspect any apparatus or fixed installation or to examine any procedure connected with the production of apparatus.

---

[160] [2012] EWCA 2140 (Admin).
[161] Paragraph 25(1).
[162] SI 2005/1803.
[163] SI 2006/659.
[164] At reg 5(2) or 9(1) or 9(3).
[165] Weights and Measures (Packaged Goods) (Northern Ireland) Regulations 2011, SR 2011/331.
[166] Reg 37(1)(a)(ii) or (b)(ii).
[167] SI 2006/3418.

Power to test equipment

3.164 Paragraph 26 provides for the power for domestic enforcers to test weighing or measuring equipment for the purpose of ascertaining compliance with relevant legislation.

(1) An officer of a domestic enforcer may test any weighing or measuring equipment –

    (a)   which is, or which the officer has reasonable cause to believe may be, used for trade or in the possession of any person or on any premises for such use, or

    (b)   which has been, or which the officer has reasonable cause to believe to have been, passed by an approved verifier, or by a person purporting to act as such a verifier, as fit for such use.

(2) Expressions used in sub-paragraph (1) have the same meaning –

    (a)   as in the Weights and Measures Act 1985, in the case of a domestic enforcer in Great Britain;

    (b)   as in the Weights and Measures (Northern Ireland) Order 1981 (SI 1981/231 (NI 10)), in the case of a domestic enforcer in Northern Ireland.

(3) The powers in sub-paragraph (4) are available to an officer of a domestic enforcer acting pursuant to –

    (a)   the duty in regulation 10(1) of the Weights and Measures (Packaged Goods) Regulations 2006 (SI 2006/659) ('the 2006 Regulations'), or

    (b)   the duty in regulation 10(1) of the Weights and Measures (Packaged Goods) Regulations (Northern Ireland) 2011 (SR 2011/331) ('the 2011 Regulations').

(4) The officer may test any equipment which the officer has reasonable cause to believe is used in –

    (a)   making up packages (as defined in regulation 2) in the United Kingdom, or

    (b)   carrying out a check mentioned in paragraphs (1) and (3) of regulation 9.

(5) The references in sub-paragraph (4) to regulations are to regulations in the 2006 Regulations in the case of a domestic enforcer in Great Britain or the 2011 Regulations in the case of a domestic enforcer in Northern Ireland.

Power to require the production of documents

3.165 Paragraph 27 provides for the power for an officer, who reasonably suspects a breach of the enforcer's legislation, to require any trader to produce documents and to take copies of them in order to ascertain compliance with the enforcer's legislation. However, where the documents are required as evidence in proceedings or to be held by statute or for market surveillance purposes, the officer can require the documents to be produced etc even when they do not have suspicion of a breach.

27 Power to require the production of documents

(1) The officer may, at any reasonable time –

    (a)   require a trader occupying the premises, or a person on the premises acting on behalf of such a trader, to produce any documents relating to the trader's business to which the trader has access, and

    (b)   take copies of, or of any entry in, any such document.

(2) The power in sub-paragraph (1) is available regardless of whether –

    (a)   the purpose for which the documents are required relates to the trader or some other person, or

    (b)   the proceedings referred to in paragraph 19(3)(b) or 20(4)(b) could be taken against the trader or some other person.

(3) That power includes power to require the person to give an explanation of the documents.

(4) Where a document required to be produced under sub-paragraph (1) contains information recorded electronically, the power in that subparagraph includes power to require the production of a copy of the document in a form in which it can easily be taken away and in which it is visible and legible.

(5) This paragraph does not permit an officer to require a person to create a document other than as described in sub-paragraph (4).

(6) This paragraph does not permit an officer to require a person to produce any document which the person would be entitled to refuse to produce—

    (a)   in proceedings in the High Court on the grounds of legal professional privilege, or

    (b)   in proceedings in the Court of Session on the grounds of confidentiality of communications.

(7) In sub-paragraph (6) 'communications' means –

    (a)   communications between a professional legal adviser and the adviser's client, or

    (b)   communications made in connection with or in contemplation of legal proceedings or for the purposes of those proceedings.

(8) In this paragraph 'trader' has the same meaning as in Part 1 of this Act.

3.166 Paragraph 19(3) and (4) prescribe when this power may be used by a domestic enforcer:

19(3) A domestic enforcer may exercise the power in paragraph 27 (power to require the production of documents) for either of the following purposes –

    (a)   subject to sub-paragraph (4), to ascertain compliance with the enforcer's legislation;

    (b)   to ascertain whether the documents may be required as evidence in proceedings for a breach of, or under, the enforcer's legislation.

(4) A domestic enforcer may exercise the power in paragraph 27 for the purpose mentioned in sub-paragraph (3)(a) only if an officer of the enforcer reasonably suspects a breach of the enforcer's legislation, unless –

(a)   the power is being exercised in relation to a document that the trader is required to keep by virtue of a provision of the enforcer's legislation, or

(b)   the enforcer is a market surveillance authority within the meaning of Article 2(18) of the Regulation on Accreditation and Market Surveillance and the power is exercised for the purpose of market surveillance within the meaning of Article 2(17) of that Regulation.

Power to seize and detain goods

3.167 Paragraph 28 provides for the power to seize and detain goods. Paragraph 19(5) prescribes that a domestic enforcer may exercise this power in relation to:

(a)   goods which an officer of the enforcer reasonably suspects may disclose (by means of testing or otherwise) a breach of the enforcer's legislation,

(b)   goods which an officer of the enforcer reasonably suspects are liable to forfeiture under that legislation, and

(c)   goods which an officer of the enforcer reasonably suspects may be required as evidence in proceedings for a breach of, or under, that legislation.

28 Power to seize and detain goods

(1) The officer may seize and detain goods other than documents (for which see paragraph 29).

(2) An officer seizing goods under this paragraph from premises which are occupied must produce evidence of the officer's identity and authority to an occupier of the premises before seizing them.

(3) The officer need not comply with sub-paragraph (2) if it is not reasonably practicable to do so.

(4) An officer seizing goods under this paragraph must take reasonable steps to –

(a)   inform the person from whom they are seized that they have been seized, and

(b)   provide that person with a written record of what has been seized.

(5) If, under this paragraph, an officer seizes any goods from a vending machine, the duty in sub-paragraph (4) also applies in relation to –

(a)   the person whose name and address are on the vending machine as the owner of the machine, or

(b)   if there is no such name and address on the machine, the occupier of the premises on which the machine stands or to which it is fixed.

(6) In determining the steps to be taken under sub-paragraph (4), an officer exercising a power under this paragraph in England and Wales or Northern Ireland must have regard to any relevant provision about the seizure of property made by –

(a)   a code of practice under section 66 of the Police and Criminal Evidence Act 1984, or

(b)   a code of practice under Article 65 of the Police and Criminal Evidence (Northern Ireland) Order 1989 (SI 1989/1341 (NI 12)), (as the case may be).

(7) Goods seized under this paragraph (except goods seized for a purpose mentioned in paragraph 19(5)(b)) may not be detained –

(a)   for a period of more than 3 months beginning with the day on which they were seized, or

(b)   where the goods are reasonably required to be detained for a longer period by the enforcer for a purpose for which they were seized, for longer than they are required for that purpose.

3.168 Note that the following provisions apply to the power under para 28:

- Paragraph 31: Power to break open container etc.

- Access to seized goods – Paragraph 38 applies where anything seized by an officer of an enforcer is detained by the enforcer.

- Notice of testing of goods – Paragraph 39 applies where goods seized by an officer of a domestic enforcer under Paragraph 28 are submitted to a test.

Power to seize documents

3.169 Paragraph 29 provides the power to seize documents required as evidence and is drafted in similar terms to the power under para 28 for the seizure of goods. Paragraph 19(6) states that a domestic enforcer may exercise the power under para 29 in relation to documents which an officer of the enforcer reasonably suspects may be required as evidence:

(a)   in proceedings for a breach of the enforcer's legislation, or

(b)   in proceedings under the enforcer's legislation.

3.170 Paragraph 29(1) permits an officer to seize and detain documents and there is a requirement to produce to an occupier of the premises evidence of the officer identity and authority[168] (unless it is not reasonably practicable to do so).[169] Further with due account of relevant codes of practice under s 66 of PACE (or its Northern Irish equivalent), the officer must take reasonable steps to inform the person from whom the documents have been seized about the seizure and provide that person with a written record of what has been seized. Documents cannot be seized where legal professional privilege applies (or where the person before the Court of Session would be entitled to refuse to produce on the grounds of confidentiality of communications). As with detained goods under para 28, documents may not be detained for longer than 3 months or in the alternative for no longer period than they are reasonably required to be detained by the enforcer for the purposes of the proceedings for which they are seized.

---

[168] Paragraph 29(2).
[169] Paragraph 29(3).

3.171 Note that the following provisions apply to the power under para 28:

* Paragraph 31: Power to break open container etc.
* Access to seized documents – Paragraph 38 applies where anything seized by an officer of an enforcer is detained by the enforcer.

Decommissioning or switching off fixed installations

3.172 Paragraph 30 provides the power to an officer of a domestic enforcer acting pursuant to the duty in reg 37(1)(a)(ii) or (b)(ii) of the Electromagnetic Compatibility Regulations 2006[170] to decommission or switch off any fixed installation (as defined in those regulations) or part of such an installation. Paragraph 19(7) states that this power may be used where an officer of the enforcer reasonably suspects a breach of the regulations and also for the purpose of ascertaining or otherwise whether there has been a breach (whether by means of testing or otherwise.)

Power to break open containers

3.173 Paragraph 31 provides the power to break open any 'container' (which has an extensive meaning), where a person fails to comply with a request from an officer to do so, where it is for the purpose of exercising a power under paras 28–30 and where it is reasonably necessary for the purpose of ascertaining compliance with the enforcer's legislation.

(1) The officer may, for the purpose of exercising any of the powers in paragraphs 28 to 30, require a person with authority to do so to –

    (a)   break open any container,
    (b)   open any vending machine, or
    (c)   access any electronic device in which information may be stored or from which it may be accessed.

(2) Where a requirement under sub-paragraph (1) has not been complied with, the officer may, for the purpose of exercising any of the powers in paragraphs 28 to 30 –

    (a)   break open the container,
    (b)   open the vending machine, or
    (c)   access the electronic device.

(3) Sub-paragraph (1) or (2) applies if and to the extent that the exercise of the power in that sub-paragraph is reasonably necessary for the purposes for which that power may be exercised.

(4) In this paragraph 'container' means anything in which goods may be stored.

---

[170] SI 2006/3418.

Offences connected with enforcement

3.174 Part 5 of the Schedule details provisions supplementary to Parts 3 and 4. The first two paragraphs detail offences. The offence of obstruction is created by para 36:

36 Offence of obstruction

(1) A person commits an offence if the person –

(a)   intentionally obstructs an enforcer or an officer of an enforcer who is exercising or seeking to exercise a power under Part 4 of this Schedule in accordance with that Part,

(b)   intentionally fails to comply with a requirement properly imposed by an enforcer or an officer of an enforcer under Part 4 of this Schedule, or

(c)   without reasonable cause fails to give an enforcer or an officer of an enforcer any other assistance or information which the enforcer or officer reasonably requires of the person for a purpose for which the enforcer or officer may exercise a power under Part 4 of this Schedule.

(2) A person commits an offence if, in giving information of a kind referred to in sub-paragraph (1)(c), the person –

(a)   makes a statement which the person knows is false or misleading in a material respect, or

(b)   recklessly makes a statement which is false or misleading in a material respect.

(3) A person who is guilty of an offence under sub-paragraph (1) or (2) is liable on summary conviction to a fine not exceeding level 3 on the standard scale.

(4) Nothing in this paragraph requires a person to answer any question or give any information if to do so might incriminate that person.

3.175 Under para 37 a person commits an offence if he is not an officer of an enforcer and purports to act as such using powers under Part 3 or Part 4 of Sch 5. This offence is punishable on summary conviction with a fine.

Keeping documents and goods

3.176 Paragraphs 38 to 42 provide for the duties in relation to goods or documents seized or detained. Under para 38, provision is given for a person who had custody or control of goods or documents seized under Part 4 powers to be allowed supervised access to the thing seized when they request permission to do so. A person must be allowed supervised access to something seized for the purpose of photographing or copying it or have it photographed or copied for them.[171] Such right does not exist where an officer has reasonable grounds for believing that to do so would prejudice the investigation for the

---

[171] Paragraphs 38(3), (4) – if photographed or copied for them this must be supplied within a reasonable time.

purposes of which it was seized.[172] Paragraph 38 is a new provision, not based on any previous consumer law legislation, but reflects provisions contained in PACE Code B.

3.177 Paragraph 39 provides for the notice to be given where goods have been purchased under para 21 (test purchases) and are subsequently tested which lead to proceedings being brought for a breach of the enforcers legislation or a notice being served by the enforcer preventing a person from doing anything.[173] This also applies to good seized under para 28.[174] The enforcer must inform the relevant person of the results of the test[175] and, where reasonably practicable to do so, allow the person to have the goods tested. Relevant persons are defined as being the owners of vending machines from which goods were purchased or the occupier of premises where the machine stands[176] (for the purposes of being told the results of test) or those same persons and persons who are either parties to proceedings or who have an interest in the goods (for the purposes of being able to have the goods tested).

3.178 Under para 40, where goods or documents have been seized under Part 4 of the Schedule, a person with an interest in the goods or documents may apply to a magistrates' court in England, Wales and Northern Ireland or the Sheriff in Scotland for an order requiring them to be released. The Court or Sheriff may only order release if satisfied that one of two conditions are met. The conditions are:

(6) Condition A is that –

    (a)   no proceedings have been brought –
        (i)   for an offence as the result of the investigation in the course of which the goods or documents were seized, or
        (ii)   for the forfeiture of the goods or documents or (in the case of seized documents) any goods to which the documents relate, and
    (b)   the period of 6 months beginning with the date the goods or documents were seized has expired.

(7) Condition B is that –

    (a)   proceedings of a kind mentioned in sub-paragraph (6)(a) have been brought, and
    (b)   those proceedings have been concluded without the goods or documents being forfeited.

3.179 A right of appeal from a magistrates' court decision lies to the Crown Court in England and Wales or the county court in Northern Ireland.

---

[172] Paragraph 38(5).
[173] Paragraph 39(1).
[174] Paragraph 39(2).
[175] Paragraph 39(3).
[176] For the purposes of being informed of the result of the test.

3.180 Paragraph 40 is based on s 33 of the Consumer Protection Act 1987 (which applied to goods seized and detained in respect of product safety contraventions) but now has much wider application.

3.181 Where a domestic enforcer has seized goods under para 28 which the enforcer reasonably suspects may disclose (by means of testing or otherwise) a breach of the enforcer's legislation,[177] then by virtue of para 41(2) the enforcer must pay compensation to any person with an interest in the goods in respect of any loss or damage caused by the detention. This is subject to the following condition:

> (3) The condition that is relevant to a domestic enforcer is that –
>
> (a)   the goods have not disclosed a breach of the enforcer's legislation, and
> (b)   the power to seize and detain the goods was not exercised as a result of any neglect or default of the person seeking the compensation.

3.182 Compensation is determined by means of arbitration.[178]

CRIMINAL PROSECUTIONS

Introduction

3.183 Although there are various methods by which legislation can be enforced, the duty of enforcement frequently entails the prosecution of offences through the criminal courts. In Scotland all criminal prosecutions are conducted through the Crown Office and Procurator Fiscal Office.

3.184 There was once thought to be a potential difficulty with an enforcement authority prosecuting cases in which there had been police involvement: *R v Ealing Justices ex parte Dixon*.[179] However the case of *R v Croydon Justices ex p Holmberg*[180] approved such a course after an operation involving collaboration between a trading standards department and the police.

3.185 The Court of Appeal in *Scopelight Ltd & Others v Chief of Police for Northumbria*,[181] went further still. It found that prohibiting the use in private prosecutions of property seized and retained by the police would 'substantially … erode' the role of private prosecutions. Consequently, a decision whether detention is necessary in each case should made in light of its individual facts and circumstances, including the identity and motive of the prosecutor.

---

[177]   As per para 19(5)(a).
[178]   Paragraph 41(5).
[179]   [1990] 2 QB 91, DC.
[180]   (1992) 157 JP 277, CO/1391/1, QBD.
[181]   [2009] EWCA Civ 1156.

Territorial jurisdiction

3.186 In determining territorial jurisdiction for criminal offences, it is important to establish where the offence was actually committed. This may not be the same as the location of the defendant. The courts have traditionally asked the question whether the 'essence' or 'gist'[182] of the offence occurred within the jurisdiction, sometimes known as the 'last act' rule.[183] However, the modern approach is to ask where a 'substantial measure' of the activities constituting a crime took place.[184]

3.187 In our opinion the courts are likely to consider that a 'substantial measure' of an offence was committed within the UK jurisdiction, if the victim was a consumer in the UK at the time it occurred. This is likely to be the position even if the offence was committed remotely by somebody outside the jurisdiction, for example using the internet or acting through an agent.[185] The rationale for this is the consumer protection nature of these offences. They are primarily designed to protect UK consumers and it seems unlikely that Parliament would have intended that purpose to be jurisdictionally frustrated because a trader was selling to, or otherwise dealing with, UK consumers from abroad.

3.188 Specific provisions apply to offences committed on board a UK Ship[186] or UK aircraft in flight.[187]

The right to bring a criminal prosecution

3.189 The Prosecution of Offences Act 1985 specifically preserves the right, in England and Wales, of a private citizen to bring a criminal prosecution.[188] There will usually be a right for a private citizen to bring a private prosecution for the criminal offences concerning consumer and trading standards.

3.190 For example, any person can bring a prosecution under the CPUTR. In *House of Cars Ltd v Derby Car and Van Contracts Ltd*[189] a private prosecution under the CPUTR was brought after the OFT and the relevant local authority had declined to do so. However, there are exceptions[190] and the terms of the criminal provision should be considered carefully before any private prosecution is commenced.

---

[182] *R v Harden* [1963] 1 QB 8 46 Cr App R 90.
[183] *R v Manning* [1998] 2 Cr App R 461 CA.
[184] *R v Smith (Wallace Duncan) (no 4)* [2004] 2 Cr App R 17 CA.
[185] See also *R v Baxter* [1972] QB 1; Cr App R 214 on agency.
[186] Merchant Shipping Act 1995, ss 280–282.
[187] Civil Aviation Act 1982, s 92.
[188] Section 6(1).
[189] [2012] CTLC 62.
[190] Certain provisions, however, do not permit private prosecutions such as the Weights and Measures Act 1985, s 83(1).

LIVERPOOL JOHN MOORES UNIVERSITY
LEARNING SERVICES

3.191 The powers of entry and other rights to facilitate the gathering of evidence may not, however, be exercised by a private prosecutor, but only by a duly appointed officer. In *Media Protection Services Ltd v Crawford*[191] it was found that the laying of an information is a reserved legal activity under the Legal Services Act 2007 and can only be undertaken by a private prosecutor himself, or by a person authorised to carry out such a reserved legal activity.

3.192 Section 230 of the Enterprise Act 2002 requires local weights and measures authorities to give notice to the CMA of intended prosecutions, a summary of the evidence relied upon and their outcome, after they are finally determined. Paragraph 101 of Sch 2 CPUTR amends the Enterprise Act 2002 (Part 8 Notice to OFT of Intended Prosecution Specified Enactments, Revocation and Transitional Provision) Order 2003 to include intended prosecutions under the CPUTR. Proceedings are not invalid by reason only of the failure of the authority to comply with s 230.

Enforcement policies

3.193 In *R v Glen Adaway*[192] the Court of Appeal emphasised the importance of regulators considering the terms of their own enforcement policy before embarking on a criminal prosecution. The extent to which this will amount to an abuse of process, however, was doubted in *R v Golding*[193] where Tracey LJ said:

> 'In the absence of oppression or misconduct the decision to prosecute is for the prosecutor and an erroneous failure to apply policy or guidance will not affect the position. The task of the Crown Court, and this court if the matter goes to appeal, is to deal with the case on the merits. If the failure to adhere to policy guidance means that there is an insufficiency of evidence, then the remedy is in the court's hands.'[194]

3.194 Part 2 of the Legislative and Regulatory Reform Act 2006 introduced statutory force for a Regulator's Code based on the principles set out in section 21. The Regulators' Code replaced the Regulators' Compliance Code and came into force in 2014. Nearly all non-economic regulators, including local authorities and fire and rescue services, need to have regard to the Code when developing standards, policies or procedures that either guide their regulatory activities with businesses or apply to other regulators.

3.195 The Code contains the following principles (which persons exercising regulatory functions must have regard to, under s 21 of the Act):

---

[191] [2012] EWHC 2373 (Admin), [2013] 1 WLR 1068.
[192] [2004] EWCA Crim 2831, [2005] LLR 142.
[193] [2014] EWCA Crim 889.
[194] The court also referred to *R v A* [2012] EWCA Crim 434 (para 79-87 per Judge LCJ and *R (Barons Pub Company Limited) v Staines Magistrates' Court* [2013] EWHC 898 (Admin).

(i)   regulators should carry out their activities in a way that supports those they regulate to comply and grow;

(ii)   regulators should provide simple and straightforward ways to communication with those they regulate;

(iii) regulators should base their regulatory activities on risk;

(iv) regulators should share information about compliance and risk;

(v)   regulators should ensure clear information, guidance and advice is available to help those they regulate meet their responsibilities to comply; and

(vi) regulators should ensure that their approach to their regulatory activities is transparent.

3.196 In particular, the Regulators' Code provides:

'6.2 Regulators' published service standards should include clear information on:

...

     d) their enforcement policy, explaining how they respond to non-compliance;

6.4 Regulators should have mechanisms in place to ensure that their officers act in accordance with their published service standards, including their enforcement policy.'

'2.3 Regulators should provide an impartial and clearly explained route to appeal against a regulatory decision or a failure to act in accordance with this Code. Individual officers of the regulator who took the decision or action against which the appeal is being made should not be involved in considering the appeal. This route to appeal should be publicised to those who are regulated.'

Local authority borders

3.197 In relation to the bringing of either criminal or civil proceedings in the name of a local authority s 222 of the Local Government Act 1972 provides:

222. Power of local authorities to prosecute or defend legal proceedings

(1) Where a local authority consider it expedient for the promotion or protection of the interests of the inhabitants of their area –

    (a)   they may prosecute or defend or appear in any legal proceedings and, in the case of civil proceedings, may institute them in their own name, and

    (b)   they may, in their own name, make representations in the interests of the inhabitants at any public inquiry held by or on behalf of any Minister or public body under any enactment.

3.198 A *Consultation on consolidating and modernising consumer law enforcement powers* by the Department for Business Innovation and Skills ('BIS'), launched in March 2012, commented that 'the current law enabling Trading Standards Services to work across local authority boundaries is open to different interpretations. The result is uncertainty and administrative costs for enforcers.' BIS believed that 'Trading Standards Services probably already have the power to investigate and bring proceedings outside their own local authority area (except in Scotland). However, this is not clear to all parties.'

3.199   As set out earlier, paras 44–46 of Sch 5 to the CRA 2015 provide for criminal proceedings to be instituted for consumer law offences allegedly committed outside of the local authority's area, in England, Wales and Northern Ireland. In summary:

- A local weights and measures authority in England or Wales may bring proceedings for a consumer law offence allegedly committed in a part of England or Wales which is outside that authority's area.

- A district council in England may bring proceedings for a consumer law offence allegedly committed in a part of England which is outside that authority's area.

- A district council in Northern Ireland may bring proceedings for a consumer law offence allegedly committed in a part of Northern Ireland which is outside that council's district.

3.200   Under s 101 of the Local Government Act 1972 a local authority may arrange for the discharge of any of its functions by another local authority and, in *R (on the application of Donnachie) v Cardiff Magistrates' Court*[195] – a case brought under the Trade Descriptions Act 1968 – the Court observed that, in future, it would be wise for a local authority to enter into s 101 agreements with other local authorities before laying informations alleging offences committed outside of its administrative area.[196] This may still be prudent for offences committed under legislation not covered by CRA 2015.

Crown immunity

3.201   No statute binds the Crown unless its provisions specifically state that this is the case. (See for example, s 11, Corporate Manslaughter and Corporate Homicide Act 2007.) The Post Office, the few remaining nationalised industries, and local authorities[197] do not enjoy this immunity. Hospitals have been held to benefit from crown immunity[198] but the applicability of those decisions to today's more devolved management structure may be questioned.

Time limits

3.202   Many of the consumer and trading standards criminal sanctions are subject to strict time limits that must be scrupulously observed. The rationale for this temporal limitation is 'designed to achieve two important consequences.

---

[195]   [2009] EWHC 489 (Admin).
[196]   See also *Brighton & Hove v Woolworths Plc* [2002] EWHC 2565 (Admin).
[197]   *Re M* [1994] 1 AC, 377, per Lord Templeman at 395.
[198]   *Nottingham Area No 1 Hospital Management Committee v Owen* [1958] 1 QB 50, [1957] 3 All ER 358; *Pfizer Corporation v Ministry of Health* [1965] AC 512, [1965] 1 All ER 450.

The first is to provide protection to the citizen who may have committed a criminal offence, and the second is to bring about in the authority having responsibility for the prosecution, an efficient and timely investigation of the offence'.[199]

3.203

The start of the time limit

3.203 Regulatory time limit provisions are typically drafted by reference to two different time periods. A shorter period that runs from prosecution discovery, together with a longstop period that is typically three years from the commission of the offence. For example, the limitation period under reg 14(1) of the CPUTR states that no criminal prosecution for an offence may be commenced more than three years from the commission of the offence or more than one year after its discovery by the prosecutor, whichever is the earlier.

3.204 A distinction needs to be drawn between offences framed by reference to the date of 'discovery of the offence by the prosecutor'[200] or to the 'date on which evidence which the prosecutor thinks is sufficient to justify the proceedings comes to his knowledge'.[201] The distinction between the tests of *offence discovery* and *evidential sufficiency* is important in two respects. Firstly, *evidential sufficiency* may not occur until after the offence is discovered. For example, it may be clear that an offence has been committed, however, the perpetrator may not yet have been identified. Secondly, the evidential sufficiency test suggests a role that can only be performed by a lawyer or other individual with legal training.[202] This may affect the identification of the prosecutor for the purposes of the time limit. By contrast, it is likely that an offence can be discovered by an individual without such legal training. It follows from both of these points that the time limit for an *offence discovery* provision may start well before *evidential sufficiency* has occurred.

Discovery of the offence provisions

3.205 The *discovery* of the offence by the prosecutor means that 'all the facts material to found the relevant charge were disclosed to the appropriate officer' per McNeill J in *Brooks v Club Continental*.[203] The fact that it takes more than the permitted period of time to gather evidence to support the facts which have been made known to the prosecutor does not permit the laying of an

---

[199] *Tesco Stores Limited v London Borough of Harrow* [2003] EWHC 2919 Admin, per Newman J (para 25).

[200] For example, CPUTR, reg 14(1) and GPSR, reg 41.

[201] For example, s 31 of the Animal Welfare Act 2006.

[202] *Letherbarrow v Warwickshire County Council* [2014] EWHC 4820 (Admin).

[203] [1981] TrL126 DC See also *R v Thames Metropolitan Stipendiary Magistrate, ex parte Hackney LB* (1994) 158 JP 305, *Tesco Stores Ltd v LB of Harrow* [2003] EWHC 2919 (Admin), 167 JP 657.

information outside the permitted time period.[204] It has also been stated that an offence is 'discovered' if there are facts known by the prosecutor which, objectively considered, would have led the prosecuting authority to conclude that there were reasonable grounds to conclude that an offence had been committed by an identifiable person.[205]

3.206 In *R (Donnachie) v Cardiff Magistrates' Court*[206] the High Court considered the time limit under section 19 of the Trade Descriptions Act 1968 ('TDA'), which is materially the same as other *discovery of the offence* provisions. The court found that it was the local authority that was the prosecutor for the purposes of the time limit, not the person laying the information. Discovery of the offence had occurred when the local authority's officials had knowledge sufficient to found a reasonable belief that an offence had been committed.

3.207 In *Tesco Stores Ltd v Harrow LBC*,[207] a report was made by a consumer that bread rolls containing a piece of metal wire had been purchased from a supermarket. The complainant left a message for an environmental health officer to contact him. On the same day an environmental health officer spoke to the complainant's wife, who confirmed that her husband had complained about the bread rolls. Four days later the investigating officer spoke directly with the complainant and took possession of the contaminated bread rolls. The High Court held that the offence was discovered when the message had been left by the complainant, rather than 4 days later when the investigator spoke directly with him.

Evidential sufficiency provisions

3.208 The identification of the prosecutor in offences premised on evidential sufficiency will necessarily require greater focus on the individual responsible and capable of making that decision. It is the individual with responsibility for deciding whether a prosecution should go forward whose thoughts and beliefs are relevant. In *Letherbarrow v Warwickshire County Council*[208] a prosecution was challenged on the basis of time limits by reference to the state of knowledge of the prosecuting body as a whole. Bean LJ rejected the challenge stating that:

> 'although the prosecutor in the case as a whole is the collective body (here, the County Council), it is the individual with responsibility for deciding whether a prosecution should go forward whose thoughts and beliefs are relevant.'

---

[204] *R v Beaconsfield Justices, ex p Johnson Sons Ltd* (1985) 149 JP 535, *Newham LBC v Cooperative Retail Services Ltd* (1984) 149 JP 421.
[205] *Tesco Stores Ltd v Harrow LBC* [2003] EWHC 2919 (Admin), (2003) 167 JP 657.
[206] [2007] EWHC 1846 (Admin), [2007] 1 WLR 385.
[207] [2003] EWHC 2919 (Admin), (2003) 167 JP 657.
[208] [2014] EWHC 4820 (Admin); see also *Riley v CPS* [2016] EWHC 2531 at para 9-17.

3.209 This evidential sufficiency test should not, however, be used as an excuse to shuffle papers between departments. In *RSPCA v Johnson*[209] Pill LJ stated:

'It is right that prosecutors are not entitled to shuffle papers between officers or sit on information so as to extend a time limit. There is, however, a degree of judgment involved in bringing a prosecution, and knowledge, in my judgment, involves an opportunity for those with appropriate skills to consider whether there is sufficient information to justify a prosecution ... I cannot extract from *Donnachie* any principle of law that time begins to run as soon as some employee of the prosecuting organisation has information. On the other hand, the principle stated by Kennedy LJ in *Morgans v DPP* [1999] 1WLR 968, is, with respect, sound. The prosecuting authority is not entitled, by passing papers from hand to hand and failing to address the issue, to delay the running of time.'

Commencement of a prosecution

3.210 The commencement of a prosecution normally takes place when the information alleging the offence is received at the offices of the Clerk to the Justices for the relevant area.[210] The person who lays the information is the prosecutor.[211] A prosecution may also take place when the prosecutor causes an amendment to be made to an existing information or indictment after the time limit for bringing a prosecution has expired. This is permissible even when the amendment involves the introduction of a new offence. As long as the offence is founded on the same facts or misdoing, and there is no substantive injustice, such amendments are often allowed by the courts. The outcome of cases will, however, be fact specific.[212]

3.211 In *R v Newcastle Magistrates, ex p Poundstretcher*[213] an amendment was allowed to allege a more serious offence. Originally the defendant had faced an information under reg 7 of the General Safety Product Regulations 1994 in relation to the supply of felt tip pen caps that provided insufficient air flow and were therefore a danger to children. This was later amended outside the 12-month time limit to allege a breach of the Toys (Safety) Regulations 1995. Even though the potential fine was greater under the latter Regulations the Divisional Court held, on appeal, that there was no reason to interfere with the magistrates' decision. The offences were similar in character and *Poundstretcher* had not been prejudiced in its defence. However, in *R v Shaw*[214] the High Court allowed the defendant's appeal against the decision of the magistrates' court to amend an information outside of the 6-month time

---

[209] [2009] EWHC 2702 (Admin).
[210] *R v Dartford Justices, ex p Dhesi, R v Manchester Stipendiary Magistrate, ex p Hill, R v Edmonton Justices ex p Hughes* [1983] 1 AC 328.
[211] *R v Shrewsbury Magistrates' Court ex p Simon Dudley Ltd* (1995) [1996] CCLR 22, CO 3277 94.
[212] *R v Newcastle upon Tyne Justices, ex p John Bryce (Contractors)* [1976] 1 WLR 517, *R v Pain* (1986) 82 Cr App R 141, *R v Scunthorpe Justices, ex parte McPhee* (1998) 162 JP 635, *R v Newcastle Magistrates' Court, ex p Poundstretcher Ltd* [1998] COD 256, *Shaw v DPP* [2007] EWHC 207 (Admin).
[213] [1998] COD 256.
[214] [2007] EWHC 207 (Admin), [2007] 171 JP 254.

limit, from an offence concerning the custody of a dog punishable only by a fine to one that was punishable by imprisonment. It was held that, whilst the misdoing was the same, the fact that the new offence rendered the defendant liable to imprisonment rather than a fine was not in the interests of justice.

3.212 The case of *R v Pain*[215] demonstrates that a prosecutor must take care not to seek amendment out of time to an offence which, although substantially on the same facts, is of a substantially different nature. The case involved a plot to manufacture and market counterfeit perfume. The case had originally been indicted as a conspiracy to defraud. When that allegation was found to be bad the Crown Court allowed an application by the prosecution to amend, out of time, and allege offences under the TDA. The Court of Appeal allowed the appeals holding that, although the facts upon which the counts of conspiracy to defraud were substantially the same facts as the counts of conspiracy to commit offences under the TDA, a prosecution alleging conspiracy to defraud could not properly be described as a prosecution for offences under the TDA. However, the rationale behind the decision was doubted in *Poundstretcher* on the basis that, in *Pain*, the Crown Court had effectively, and wrongly, permitted the institution of fresh proceedings after an indictment had been quashed rather than by way of amendment of existing proceedings.

3.213 The statutory time limits will also apply where a summons has been issued within time, but against an incorrect defendant, for example, in relation to separate legal entities within the same corporate group.[216]

3.214 In Scotland, the reference to the date of discovery by the prosecutor is construed as a reference to the date on which evidence sufficient in the opinion of the Lord Advocate to warrant proceedings came to his knowledge.

Certificates

3.215 Many time limits offences also include a rebuttable statutory presumption if the prosecutor produces a certificate of the time the offence was discovered. Although there is usually no statutory requirement that the prosecutor must serve such a certificate,[217] in *Burwell v DPP*[218] it was stated that a prosecutor can only avail himself of the benefits of such a certificate if the certificate complies fully with the requirements of the relevant section.[219] In *Lamont-Perkins v RSPCA*[220] Wyn Williams J stated that:

> 'This case has highlighted the need for all prosecutors to take great care when certifying a date under statutory provisions which have the effect of extending the

---

[215] (1986) 82 Cr App R 141.
[216] *Sainsbury's Supermarkets Ltd v HM Courts Service (South West Region, Devon and Cornwall Area)* [2006] EWHC 1749 (Admin).
[217] *Browning v Lewes Crown Court and RSPCA* [2012] EWHC 1003 (Admin).
[218] [2009] EWHC 1069 (Admin) under the Computer Misuse Act 1990.
[219] See also *RSPCA v Ian James King and Kathleen Patricia King* [2010] EWHC 637 (Admin).
[220] [2012] EWHC 1002 (Admin).

time limit for bringing criminal proceedings. A prosecutor is exercising a crucial function when certifying such a date and it is incumbent upon the prosecutor to ensure the accuracy of the date.'

3.216 In Scotland a certificate signed by the Lord Advocate or on his behalf and stating the date on which evidence came to his knowledge is conclusive evidence of that fact and other presumptions and deeming provisions apply to this process.

Legal identity

3.217 In any prosecution it is of fundamental importance that the correct defendant is identified. The failure to do so has caused significant problems in consumer and trading cases, which are usually the subject of restrictive time limits.

3.218 Most offences permit the prosecution of a 'person', which includes 'any body of persons corporate or unincorporated'.[221] It follows that individuals, companies and other traders can usually be prosecuted. However, the courts have repeatedly refused applications to amend proceedings to permit a different legal identity to be substituted.

3.219 In *Marco (Croydon) Ltd v Metropolitan Police Commissioner*[222] a company hired out builder's skips and left one unlit on the highway at night. A cyclist rode into it and was killed. The skip company responsible was called 'Marco (Croydon) Limited' but traded as 'A & J Bull Containers'. A prosecution was commenced against 'A & J Bull Limited', a different company. The Divisional Court ruled that it had been wrong for the magistrates to permit the information to be amended to identify the correct company.[223]

3.220 *R v Greater Manchester Justices ex p Aldi GmbH & Co KG*[224] involved allegations of mispricing offences under s 20 of the Consumer Protection Act 1987 at a supermarket. The prosecutor had incorrectly named the wholesale company in a group as the defendant, rather than the retail company. The High Court again rejected the argument that the information could be amended to substitute the retail company.

3.221 In *Sainsbury's Supermarkets Limited v HM Courts Service*[225] the information was laid against 'J Sainsburys plc (trading as Sainsburys Supermarket Ltd)'. Although the actual company name was similar, neither 'J

---

[221] Interpretation Act 1978, Sch 1.

[222] [1983] Crim LR 395.

[223] See also *Essence Bars (London) Ltd v Wimbledon Magistrates' Court and Royal Borough of Kingston upon Thames* [2014] EWHC 4334 (Admin).

[224] (1994) 159 JP 727.

[225] *Sainsbury's Supermarkets Limited v HM Courts Service (South West Region, Devon and Cornwall Area) and Plymouth City Council (Interested Party): J Sainsbury Plc v HM Courts Service (South West Region, Devon and Cornwall Area) and Plymouth City Council* [2006] EWHC 1749 (Admin).

Sainsburys plc' nor 'Sainsburys Supermarket Ltd' existed as a company. It was held to be impermissible to amend the information to substitute the company as the defendant.[226]

3.222 There is, however, a distinction between cases where the wrong corporate defendant is prosecuted and those where the correct individual actually attends court in reply to a summons that incorrectly names him. If the individual attends court after receiving a summons, knowing that it was intended for him, the defective information may be amended where there is no significant prejudice.[227]

CAUTIONS

3.223 This section is not applicable to Scotland.

3.224 In June 2005 Part 1 of Home Office circular 30/2005 ('Cautioning of Adult Offenders') replaced circular 18/1994. It used the term 'Simple Caution' for the first time – 'to distinguish it from a Conditional Caution', which was to have been the subject for Part 2 of this circular. Home Office Circular 16/2008 for Simple Cautioning was replaced on 8 April 2013 by the Ministry of Justice's *Simple Caution for Adult Offender guidance*. In *R (on the application of Stratton) v Chief Constable of Thames Valley Police*[228] the decision to administer a simple caution was overturned where the full implications of accepting the caution had not been made clear to the suspect and she had therefore not been able to give informed consent, in accordance with the guidance.

3.225 When deciding if a simple caution is appropriate, the following criteria must be satisfied –

• the person must have made a clear, reliable and PACE-compliant admission of the offence, either verbally or in writing. In *R (on the application of Rupert Wyman) v The Chief Constable of Hampshire Constabulary*[229] it was held that there was no admission which would justify the claimant being formally cautioned for the alleged offence and the caution was ordered to be quashed. Under no circumstances should suspects be pressed, or induced in any way to admit offences in order to receive a simple caution as an alternative to being charged – see *R v Commissioner of Police of the Metropolis ex p Thompson*;[230]

---

[226] See also *British Airways Board v Taylor* [1976] 1 All ER 65 HL where the House of Lords found that there was no legal basis on which the Board could be liable for an offence committed by BOAC even though the Board had subsequently taken over BOAC's business.

[227] *Allan v Wiseman* [1975] RTR 217.

[228] [2013] EWHC 1561 (Admin).

[229] [2006] EWHC 1904 (Admin).

[230] [1996] 1 WLR 1519.

- there must be a realistic prospect of conviction if the person were to be prosecuted;
- it must be in the public interest to use a simple caution as the means of disposal;
- a simple caution must be appropriate to the offence and the offender.

3.226 A simple caution will not be appropriate where a person has raised a defence or if has refused to accept it. The significance of the admission of guilt in agreeing to accept a simple caution must be fully and clearly explained to the offender before they are cautioned. Repeat cautioning may be acceptable in circumstances where there has been a sufficient lapse of time to suggest that a previous caution has had a significant deterrent effect (2 years or more) and if the current offence is trivial or unrelated to any previous offences, or as part of a mixed disposal.

3.227 Offenders and their legal representatives may be entitled to seek and have disclosure of the evidence before the offender agrees to accept a caution. In *DPP v Ara*,[231] it was held, on the facts, that disclosure of an interview to a defendant's solicitor was necessary in order to enable informed advice to be given as to whether a caution was agreed. However, Rose LJ made it clear '*... that this does not mean that there is a general obligation on the police to disclose material prior to charge.*'

3.228 Where (i) disclosure is sought and refused, and (ii) consequently a caution is declined because the recipient has been unable to take proper legal advice, and (iii) a subsequent prosecution is instituted to comply with time limits, the case may be (and has at first instance) been stayed as an abuse of process.

3.229 Section 17 of the Criminal Justice and Courts Act 2015 *places restrictions on the circumstances in which simple cautions may be used*. In essence, the more serious the offence, the greater the restrictions. It also places restrictions on the use of simple cautions for repeat offending. The application of these restrictions does not extend to offences where local authorities may consider issuing a simple caution.

3.230 Part 3 of the Criminal Justice Act 2003 makes provision for conditional cautions to be available as a means of dealing with offenders in certain circumstances, as an alternative to prosecution. Conditional cautions may only be given by an authorised person, defined as a constable; a person designated as an investigating officer under s 38 of the Police Reform Act 2002; or a person authorised for the purpose by a relevant Prosecutor. A 'person authorised for the purposes' does not include a trading standards officer, a trading standards enforcement officer, nor a local authority.

---

[231] [2001] 4 All ER 559.

FINES

3.231 A standard scale of fines for summary offences is contained in s 37(2) of the Criminal Justice Act 1982 (as amended) for England and Wales, s 225 of the Criminal Procedure (Scotland) Act 1995 for Scotland and in Art 5 of the Fines and Penalties (Northern Ireland) Order 1984 for Northern Ireland.

3.232 Section 85(1) of the Legal Aid, Sentencing and Punishment of Offenders Act 2012 ('LASPO'), which applies to England and Wales, provides that a relevant offence which is punishable on summary conviction by a fine or maximum fine of £5,000 or more (however expressed) becomes punishable on summary conviction by a fine of any amount. An offence is relevant if, immediately before the commencement of s 85(1), it was a common law offence or it is contained in an Act or an instrument made under an Act (whether or not the offence is in force at that time). Therefore an offence where the penalty is expressed as eg 'a fine not exceeding level 5 on the standard scale' or 'a fine not exceeding the statutory maximum' is now punishable on summary conviction by a fine of any amount. This provision came into force on 12 March 2015[232] for offences committed on or after that date.[233]

3.233 The Legal Aid, Sentencing and Punishment of Offenders Act 2012 (Fines on Summary Conviction) Regulations 2015, which also came into force on 12 March 2015, make provision in relation to fines and maximum fines which may be imposed on summary conviction, for the purpose of implementing LASPO s 85. In particular, Parts 1 and 2 of Sch 4 contain amendments to legislation where the penalty for an offence, punishable on summary conviction, is expressed as a fine or maximum fine in a numerical amount of £5,000 or more. Examples include ss 9 and 10 of the Video Recordings Act 1984 and s 32 of the Animal Welfare Act 2006 where, in each instance, 'a fine' is substituted for 'a fine not exceeding £20,000'.

POST-CONVICTION ORDERS

3.234 This section is not relevant to procedures in Scotland.

3.235 The Code for Crown Prosecutors (January 2013), in relation to the selection of charges, states that prosecutors should select charges, *inter alia*, which give the court adequate powers to sentence and impose appropriate post-conviction orders.

3.236 Essentially the types of order that will be relevant to trading standards cases fall into three area:

- relating to financial matters – such as compensation, confiscation, costs;

---

[232] The Legal Aid, Sentencing and Punishment of Offenders Act 2012 (Commencement No 11) Order 2015 brought LASPO, s 85(1), (2) and (4) into force.

[233] LASPO, s 85(4)(a).

- relating to property – such as deprivation, forfeiture;
- relating to the offender – such as anti-social behaviour orders, driving bans and company director disqualifications.

Financial orders

3.237 Sections 13 and 97 (Scotland) of the Proceeds of Crime Act 2002 ('POCA 2002') require the court to have regard to a confiscation order before deciding whether to impose a fine or other order involving payment by a defendant (such as costs) *except* for a compensation order.

Compensation

3.238 Sections 130–134 of the Powers of Criminal Courts (Sentencing) Act 2000 ('PCCSA 2000') provide for a court to make a compensation order, requiring the convicted person to pay compensation for any personal injury, loss or damage resulting from the offence that the person was convicted for, or any other offence which is taken into consideration by the court in determining sentence, instead of or in addition to dealing with him in any other way. An order should only be made where 'the sum claimed by way of compensation is either agreed or proved'.

3.239 The Legal Aid, Sentencing and Punishment of Offenders Act 2012 imposes an express duty (rather than the current power) to consider making compensation orders where victims have suffered harm or loss.

3.240 Section 40(1) of the Magistrates' Courts Act 1980 prescribes the maximum amount that a magistrates' court can order. The Crime and Courts Act 2013 amends s 131 of the PCCSA 2000 to provide that the previous £5,000 limit will only apply in the case of a compensation order imposed on an offender under the age of 18. The effect of the amendment is that there is no limit on the value of a single compensation order handed down to an adult offender by a magistrates' court. This applies to offences committed on or after 11 December 2013.

3.241 The Crown Court has an unlimited power to fine, but should have regard to the means of the offender. The court may make the order whether or not the prosecution apply for it but must give its reasons if it does not do so if an application is made.

3.242 In Scotland ss 249–253 of the Criminal Procedure (Scotland) Act 1995 provide for the granting of compensation orders, how they will be determined and enforced. In summary proceedings the Sheriff may make an order up to the prescribed sum and in solemn proceedings the level of compensation is unlimited.

3.243 In *R v Patrick Connors*[234] the defendant pleaded guilty to two offences – one of aggressive commercial practice contrary to reg 11 CPUTR and the second of fraud. The two offences concerned different householders. He was ordered to pay compensation orders of £16,400 and £1,000. He appealed against the compensation order in respect of the first offence only – contending that it should be £6,500. Mitting J:

> 'As we have stated in our analysis of the transactions, the complainant got paving which had to be taken up, re-decoration which had to be re-done and had paid for a drain that was neither necessary nor installed. The total damage to him therefore was not the £16,400 in respect of which the compensation order was made, but £19,000. A compensation order in that sum could well have been made.'

3.244 The appeal was dismissed.

Recovering the proceeds of criminal activity

3.245 Many of the offences enforced by trading standards authorities are committed with the purpose of financial gain. Where an offender has benefitted from criminal activity, the Proceeds of Crime Act 2002 ('POCA 2002') may be applicable.

3.246 POCA 2002 (and the provisions of its predecessors the Criminal Justice Act 1988 and the Drug Trafficking Act 1994) has been the source of much appellate argument in the Court of Appeal, House of Lords and latterly the Supreme Court. This has interpreted the provisions of the Act and the way applications should be brought. This part of the chapter serves as an overview of the basic confiscation provisions following conviction with particular regard to the issues faced by trading standards authorities.

3.247 Application for the recovery of proceeds of crime can be made under POCA 2002, s 6 and applies to criminal activity taking place after 24 March 2003.[235] In *R v Boughton-Fox* the Court of Appeal quashed a confiscation order under POCA for an indictment alleging offending between 1 March 2003 and 1 June 2008.[236] Consideration of orders under the Act should take place long before a conviction is obtained. Enforcing authorities need to be alert to the risk that defendants will conceal or dissipate their assets before a confiscation order is made.

---

[234] [2012] EWCA Crim 2106.
[235] Proceeds of Crime Act 2002 (Commencement No 5, Transitional Provisions, Savings and Amendment) Order 2003/333. For offences prior to this date the provisions of the Criminal Justice Act 1988 are likely to apply but readers should consider specialist texts on the subject.
[236] *R v Boughton-Fox* [2014] EWCA Crim 227. However, there was no obstacle 'in principle' why it should not be replaced by an order under POCA's predecessor, the Criminal Justice Act 1988.

Production orders

3.248 Information held by banks or other financial institutions will generally not be provided to investigators other than by order of the Court. Section 345 of the POCA 2002 (production orders) sets out the procedure for investigators to obtain information held by third parties generally. A production order is an order made by a judge of the Crown Court, requiring a person specified in the order to deliver up documents to an appropriate officer to take away or to permit that officer to have access to the material.

3.249 In a trading standards context, production orders are likely to be obtained where there is either a confiscation investigation or a money laundering investigation.[237] A confiscation investigation is an investigation into whether a person has benefitted from his criminal conduct or into the extent or whereabouts of his benefit from criminal conduct.[238]

3.250 Application is made to the Crown Court by an 'appropriate officer' (defined under the Act as including accredited financial investigators).[239] The application must state that a person specified in the application is subject to a confiscation investigation or a money laundering investigation. The application must also state:

(a)   that the order is sought for the purposes of the investigation;

(b)   the order is sought in relation to material, or material of a description, specified in the application;

(c)   a person specified in the application appears to be in possession or control of the material.

3.251 The application would normally give 7 days for the production of documents but the Court has power to shorten this.[240] The Court should only depart from the 7-day period where there are good evidential grounds for doing so.[241]

3.252 The requirements for making a production order are detailed in Section 346.

> (2) There must be reasonable grounds for suspecting that –
>
> > (a)   in the case of a confiscation investigation, the person the application for the order specifies as being subject to the investigation has benefited from his criminal conduct;

---

[237]   A money laundering investigation is an investigation into whether a money laundering offence has been committed.

[238]   Section 341(1) Proceeds of Crime Act 2002. Note that on a date to be appointed this section is amended by Section 38 of the Serious Crime Act 2015 to add the following, '(c) the extent or whereabouts of realisable property available for satisfying a confiscation order made in respect of him.'

[239]   Section 378.

[240]   Section 345(5).

[241]   *R (Chatwani) v National Crime Agency* [2015] EWHC 1284.

....

    (c)   in the case of a money laundering investigation, the person the application for the order specifies as being subject to the investigation has committed a money laundering offence;

...

(3) There must be reasonable grounds for believing that the person the application specifies as appearing to be in possession or control of the material so specified is in possession or control of it.

(4) There must be reasonable grounds for believing that the material is likely to be of substantial value (whether or not by itself) to the investigation for the purposes of which the order is sought.

(5) There must be reasonable grounds for believing that it is in the public interest for the material to be produced or for access to it to be given, having regard to –

    (a)   the benefit likely to accrue to the investigation if the material is obtained;
    (b)   the circumstances under which the person the application specifies as appearing to be in possession or control of the material holds it.

3.253 Where relevant material is held on a computer, then the order should be read as producing the material in a visible and legible form which the officer can take away.[242] Orders can be made in relation to material held by government departments.[243] The order cannot compel the production of material which is subject to legal privilege.[244]

Restraint orders

3.254 In certain cases it is necessary to apply to the Court to prevent a suspect from hiding or dissipating assets to avoid them being the subject of an order under POCA 2002. This is found under ss 40 and 41 of the Act. The legislative steer behind these provisions is provided in s 69(2) of the Act:

(a)   The power must be exercised with a view to the value for the time being of realisable property being made available (by the property's realisation) for satisfying any confiscation order that has been or may be made against the defendant;

(b)   must be exercised, in a case where a confiscation order has not been made, with a view to securing that there is no diminution in the value of realisable property.

3.255 By s 40(1) of POCA 2002, the Crown Court may exercise the powers conferred by s 41 if any of one of five conditions is satisfied. In the context of this work, the first two conditions are germane:

    (2) The first condition is that –

---

[242] Section 349.
[243] Section 350.
[244] Section 348.

(a)   a criminal investigation has been started in England and Wales with regard to an offence, and

(b)   there are reasonable grounds to suspect[245] that the alleged offender has benefited from his criminal conduct.

(3) The second condition is that –

(a)   proceedings for an offence have been started in England and Wales and not concluded, and

(b)   there is reasonable cause to believe that the defendant has benefited from his criminal conduct.

(7) The second condition is not satisfied if the court believes that –

(a)   there has been undue delay in continuing the proceedings, or

(b)   the prosecutor does not intend to proceed.

3.256 Where the conditions are satisfied the Court may make an order (a restraint order) under s 41 prohibiting any specified person from dealing with any realisable property held by him.[246] A restraint order may provide that it applies to all realisable property held by the specified person whether or not the property is described in the order and may provide that it applies to realisable property transferred to the specified person after the order is made.[247]

3.257 A restraint order may make provision for reasonable living expenses and legal expenses and make provision for the purpose of enabling any person to carry on any trade, business, profession or occupation.

3.258 Aside from the statutory provisions, the Prosecutor must consider that there is a real risk of dissipation of assets before the making of the order. In *Jennings v Crown Prosecution Service*[248] Longmore LJ observed:

'Fear of dissipation of assets is the reason for seeking a restraint order. Such fear must, in fact, exist before an order should be applied for. But in a case where dishonesty is charged, there will usually be reason to fear that assets will be dissipated. I do not therefore consider it necessary for the prosecutor to state in terms that he fears assets will be dissipated merely because he or she thinks there is a good arguable case of dishonesty. As my Lord has said, the risk of dissipation will generally speak for itself. Nevertheless prosecutors must be alive to the possibility that there may be no risk in fact. If no asset dissipation has occurred over a long period, particularly after a defendant has been charged, the prosecutor should explain why asset dissipation is now feared at the date of application for the order when it was not feared before.'[249]

3.259 In making applications prosecutors have a duty of full and frank disclosure. *In Jennings v CPS*, Laws LJ stated:

---

[245] Note this provision is amended as from 1 June 2015 by virtue of s 11 of the Serious Crime Act 2015, which replaced reasonable to cause to believe with suspicion.

[246] Section 41(1).

[247] Section 41(2).

[248] [2006] 1 WLR 182.

[249] At para 61.

'Thus the court has imposed a duty on the shoulders of the Crown to make disclosure of material facts, if it seeks a restraint order without notice, just as a claimant in a private civil suit must do if he seeks a freezing order without notice.'

3.260 In *Ashford v Southampton City Council*[250] the Court observed the importance of providing sufficient court time to consider applications for restraint orders. Moreover the Court of Appeal approved the comments of Hooper LJ in *R v Windsor*:[251]

'Without being too prescriptive, it is vital that the judge is given material on which he can reach the conclusion himself that there is reasonable cause.'

3.261 In *Ashford* the Court concluded that the judge was being asked to accept that the investigators had concluded that there was reasonable cause (under s 40(2)), rather than being presented with evidence sufficient to reach his own conclusion to that effect.[252] It should be borne in mind that when having regard to case-law on restraint orders, that the older cases will be based on the first condition as being a 'reasonable cause to believe' and not the 'reasonable grounds to suspect' which is the standard as from 1 June 2015.

Confiscation following conviction

3.262 The criminal confiscation provisions for England and Wales fall under Part 2 of POCA 2002. The court must proceed[253] under s 6 of the Act where there has been a conviction (or the defendant has been sent to the Crown Court for confiscation[254] and asked the court to proceed under s 6) or the Court believes that it is appropriate to do so). The steps that the court has to take under s 6 are as follows:[255]

(4) The court must proceed as follows –

    (a)   it must decide whether the defendant has a criminal lifestyle;

    (b)   if it decides that he has a criminal lifestyle it must decide whether he has benefited from his general criminal conduct;

    (c)   if it decides that he does not have a criminal lifestyle it must decide whether he has benefited from his particular criminal conduct.

(5) If the court decides under subsection (4)(b) or (c) that the defendant has benefited from the conduct referred to it must –

    (a)   decide the recoverable amount, and

    (b)   make an order (a confiscation order) requiring him to pay that amount.

---

[250] [2014] EWCA 1244.

[251] [2011] EWCA Crim 143.

[252] At para 31.

[253] Section 14: The court may postpone determination under Section 6 but still proceed to sentence the defendant.

[254] Under Section 70, a defendant convicted by a magistrates' court can be committed to the Crown Court for proceedings under Part 2 of POCA.

[255] Section 6(4).

3.263 The reference to 'criminal lifestyle' imports extended benefit provisions: looking at offending beyond the predicate offences. Criminal lifestyle is defined in s 75 of the Act.

> The condition is that the offence (or any of the offences) concerned satisfies any of these tests –
>
> (a)   it is specified in Schedule 2;[256]
> (b)   it constitutes conduct forming part of a course of criminal activity;[257]
> (c)   it is an offence committed over a period of at least six months and the defendant has benefited from the conduct which constitutes the offence.

3.264 The defendant having a criminal lifestyle is the trigger for the court to be able to look at the defendant's general criminal conduct[258] and it mandates the court to make the following assumptions:[259]

(1)   that any property transferred to him after the relevant day[260] was obtained by him as a result of his general criminal conduct and at the earliest time he appears to have held it;

(2)   that any property held by him at any time after the date of conviction was obtained by him through his general criminal conduct and at the earliest time he appears to have held it;

(3)   that any expenditure incurred by the defendant at any time after the relevant day was met from property obtained by him as a result of his general criminal conduct;

(4)   that for the purpose of valuing any property obtained by the defendant he obtained it free of any interests in it.

3.265 The court must not make the required assumption in relation to particular property or expenditure, if the assumption is either shown to be incorrect or there would be a serious risk of injustice if the assumption were made.[261] If the defendant is not regarded as having a criminal lifestyle then the court will consider the benefit obtained from his particular criminal conduct[262] which in broad terms is the conduct which constituted the offences of which he was convicted. A person is deemed to benefit from conduct if he obtains

---

[256] These include intellectual property and money laundering offences.

[257] Conduct forms part of a course of criminal activity if the defendant has benefited from the conduct and: (a) in the proceedings in which he was convicted he was convicted of three or more other offences, each of three or more of them constituting conduct from which he has benefited, or (b) in the period of 6 years ending with the day when those proceedings were started (or, if there is more than one such day, the earliest day) he was convicted on at least two separate occasions of an offence constituting conduct from which he has benefited.

[258] Section 76(2).

[259] Section 10.

[260] Section 10(8) the relevant day is the first day of the period of 6 years ending with the day that proceedings for the offences concerned were started against him, or where there are two or more proceedings started on different days the earlier of those days.

[261] Section 10(6).

[262] Section 76(3).

property as a result of or in connection with the criminal conduct.[263] If a person benefits from conduct his benefit is the value of the property obtained.[264]

3.266   The operation of these provisions has given rise to a considerable body of case-law. In *R v May*[265] the House of Lords outlined the principles to be followed (per Lord Bingham):

'(1)   The legislation is intended to deprive defendants of the benefit they have gained from relevant criminal conduct, whether or not they have retained such benefit, within the limits of their available means. It does not provide for confiscation in the sense understood by schoolchildren and others, but nor does it operate by way of fine. The benefit gained is the total value of the property or advantage obtained, not the defendant's net profit after deduction of expenses or any amounts payable to co-conspirators.

(2)   The court should proceed by asking the three questions posed above: (i) Has the defendant (D) benefited from relevant criminal conduct? (ii) If so, what is the value of the benefit D has so obtained? (iii) What sum is recoverable from D? Where issues of criminal life style arise the questions must be modified. These are separate questions calling for separate answers, and the questions and answers must not be elided.

(3)   In addressing these questions the court must first establish the facts as best it can on the material available, relying as appropriate on the statutory assumptions. In very many cases the factual findings made will be decisive.

(4)   In addressing the questions the court should focus very closely on the language of the statutory provision in question in the context of the statute and in the light of any statutory definition. The language used is not arcane or obscure and any judicial gloss or exegesis should be viewed with caution. Guidance should ordinarily be sought in the statutory language rather than in the proliferating case-law.

(5)   In determining, under the 2002 Act, whether D has obtained property or a pecuniary advantage and, if so, the value of any property or advantage so obtained, the court should (subject to any relevant statutory definition) apply ordinary common law principles to the facts as found. The exercise of this jurisdiction involves no departure from familiar rules governing entitlement and ownership. While the answering of the third question calls for inquiry into the financial resources of D at the date of the determination, the answering of the first two questions plainly calls for a historical inquiry into past transactions.

(6)   D ordinarily obtains property if in law he owns it, whether alone or jointly, which will ordinarily connote a power of disposition or control, as where a person directs a payment or conveyance of property to someone else. He ordinarily obtains a pecuniary advantage if (among other things) he evades a liability to which he is personally subject. Mere couriers or custodians or other very minor contributors to an offence, rewarded by a specific fee and having no interest in the property or the proceeds of sale, are unlikely to be found to have obtained that property. It may be otherwise with money launderers.'

---

[263] Section 76(4).
[264] Section 76(7).
[265] [2008] UKHL 28.

Determining benefit in regulatory cases

3.267 In *Sumal and Sons (Properties) Limited v The Crown (London Borough of Newham)*, Davis LJ observed:

> 'Whether what may be styled a regulatory offence can, when committed, give rise to the availability of a confiscation order will depend on the terms of the statute or regulations creating the offence, read with the terms of the 2002 Act and set in the context of the facts of the case.'[266]

3.268 This was considered further in *R v McDowell and Singh*[267] appeals were made against confiscation orders in what had been referred to as 'regulatory offences'. Pitchford LJ remarked:

> 'It is not sufficient to treat "regulatory" offences as creating a single category of offence to which POCA is uniformly applied ... the question whether benefit has been obtained from criminal conduct must first depend upon an analysis of the terms of the statute that creates the offence and, by that means, upon an identification of the criminal conduct admitted or proved. It may be that ... the wider statutory context of the offence will assist to answer the critical question: what is the conduct made criminal by the statute – is it the activity itself or is it the failure to register, or obtain a licence for, the activity? In our judgment, there is a narrow but critical distinction to be made between an offence that prohibits and makes criminal the very activity admitted by the offender or proved against him (as in *del Basso*[268]) and an offence comprised in the failure to obtain a licence to carry out an activity otherwise lawful (as in *Sumal*[269]).'

3.269 *McDowell* was an arms trader. He flouted prohibitions on trading in arms under the Trade in Goods (Control) Order 2003.[270] The wording of the order prohibited various acts done in pursuance of trade in arms. The order creates an exception from those prohibitions by the permission to act with a licence. In the absence of the licence the trading is unlawful and *McDowell* was found to have benefited from his criminal conduct and could be the subject of an order under POCA 2002. Singh was a scrap metal dealer, who had failed to register his scrap metal dealing activity as required under the Scrap Metal Dealers Act 1964. The court found the failure to register was criminal activity but that the trading carried out was otherwise lawful and so should not be subject to the confiscation provisions of POCA 2002. It is submitted that the distinction in such cases is a fine one and will require close analysis of the legislation creating the offence.

3.270 In *R v Palmer*[271] the defendant had been convicted of engaging in licensable activity otherwise than in accord with a licence contrary to s 3 of the

---

[266] At para 30.
[267] [2015] EWCA Crim 173.
[268] *R v del Basso* [2010] EWCA Crim 1119; [2011] 1 Cr App R (S) 41.
[269] *Sumal and Sons (Properties) Limited v The Crown (London Borough of Newham)* [2012] EWCA Crim 1840; [2013] 1 WLR 2078.
[270] SI 2003/2765.
[271] [2016] EWCA 1049.

Private Security Industry Act 2001 ('PSIA'). The Crown appealed the decision of the Crown Court judge not to make a confiscation order. Paying close analysis to the terms of the statute and considering the judgment in *McDowell and Singh*, the Court considered that s 3 of the PSIA created and defined a prohibited act and criminalised the activity of engagement in licensable conduct, not simply failing to obtain a licence.

3.271   See also *R v Moss*[272] where a confiscation order imposed following pleas of guilty to record keeping offences under the Cattle Identification Regulations 2007 and the Animal By-Products Regulations 2005 was quashed.

Establishing the value of the benefit obtained

3.272   In many cases the value of the benefit obtained by the defendant from criminal conduct is readily ascertainable from the property obtained or pecuniary advantage that has been gained. Particular issues arise when determining benefit in the context of a business. In *R v Waya*[273] the Supreme Court acknowledged in its majority opinion that a legitimate, and proportionate confiscation order may, inter alia, have the effect of requiring a defendant to pay the whole of a sum which he has obtained by crime without enabling to set off expenses of the crime:

> 'These propositions are not difficult to understand. To embark upon an accounting exercise in which the defendant is entitled to set off the cost of committing his crime would be to treat his criminal enterprise as if it were a legitimate business and confiscation a form of business taxation. To treat (for example) a bribe paid to an official to look the other way, whether at home or abroad, as reducing the proceeds of crime would be offensive, as well as frequently impossible of accurate determination. To attempt to inquire into the financial dealings of criminals as between themselves would usually be equally impracticable and would lay the process of confiscation wide open to simple avoidance. Although these propositions involve the possibility of removing from the defendant by way of confiscation order a sum larger than may in fact represent his net proceeds of crime, they are consistent with the statute's objective and represent proportionate means of achieving it.'[274]

3.273   In *Hampshire County Council v Beazley*, the Court had gone on to consider the decision in *Waya*, explaining that 'a business which is founded entirely on the infringement of other people's property rights, and is a criminal offence, will inevitably attract the consequence of confiscation of the proceeds' and 'it will certainly remove their gross takings from [the] business'.[275] The Court confirmed the approach in *Waya* stating:

> 'There is nothing remotely disproportionate about removing from this unlawful business the proceeds which it has generated. It is not in any way analogous to the

---

[272]   [2015] EWCA Crim 713.
[273]   [2013] 1 AC 294.
[274]   At para 26.
[275]   At para 17.

kind of double recovery situation contemplated explicitly in *Waya*. The judgment in *Waya* specifically endorses the longstanding approval to the difference for confiscation purposes between gross proceeds on the one hand, which are the measure of benefit, and profit on the other, which is not. That is explicit in paragraph 26. There may be some other special cases in which a confiscation order can properly be described as disproportionate, but the fact that it is based on gross proceeds of crime is not one of them. Nor is there anything in this case which could possibly justify the description 'disproportionate', whether under *Waya* or otherwise.'

3.274 In *R v Scott King*[276] the defendant who was a used car salesman was convicted of various offences under the Consumer Protection from Unfair Trading Regulations 2008. He had been selling cars purporting to be a private seller to avoid providing a warranty. The defendant appealed the making of a confiscation order based on gross turnover valued at £109,970 which did not therefore take account of the purchase cost of the vehicles that he had sold, which had rendered him a profit of just £11,140. Having considered the previous authorities, Fulford LJ observed:[277]

'The authorities reveal there is a clear distinction to be drawn between cases in which the goods or services are provided by way of a lawful contract (or when payment is properly paid for legitimate services) but the transaction is tainted by associated illegality (eg the overcharging in *Shabir* or the bribery in *Sale*), and cases in which the entire undertaking is unlawful (eg a business which is conducted illegally, as in *Beazley*). When making a confiscation order, the court will need to consider, amongst other things, the difference between these two types of cases. It is to be stressed, however, that this divide is not necessarily determinative because cases differ to a great extent, but it is a relevant factor to be taken into account when deciding whether to make an order that reflects the gross takings of the business ....

If the transaction is inherently unlawful because of the manner in which it is conducted, that finding militates in favour of making an order that is directed at the gross takings of the business.'

3.275 The Court then determined that in the case of *King* the gross turnover approach had been appropriate, observing that the business was one which had been founded on illegality and that the result was severe but not disproportionate.[278] This approach was followed in *R v Rory J Holbrook Limited*[279] involving breaches of the Environmental Protection Act 1990 and other environmental regulations.

3.276 The Supreme Court had cause to consider this point afresh in *R v Harvey*[280] and in particular the inclusion of sums received by way of VAT being included within the overall turnover as part of the defendant's benefit.

---

[276] [2014] 2 Cr App R (S) 2014.
[277] At paras 32, 33.
[278] At paras 33, 34.
[279] [2015] EWCA Crim 1908.
[280] [2016] 2 WLR 37.

Affirming the general principle under POCA that VAT received should be included within the figure for benefit as being property obtained, the Court then turned to consider the issue of proportionality and Article 1 Protocol 1 of European Convention on Human Rights.

> '33 This court considered A1P1 in *Waya* at paras 28-33, where it was made clear that, where the proceeds of crime are returned to the loser, it would be disproportionate to treat such proceeds as part of the "benefit obtained" by a defendant as it would amount to "a financial penalty" or "an additional punitive sanction", which should not be imposed through the medium of POCA. Lord Hughes is right in para 71 to say that recognition of the disproportionality of treating property restored to the victim as property "obtained" for the purpose of POCA is not directly in point as it does not concern double recovery. However, given that VAT is effectively collected by a taxpayer as explained above, the two situations are quite similar; furthermore, as Lord Mance points out, the policy behind the principle discussed in *Waya*, paras 28-34 is in part that a defendant who makes good a liability to pay or restore should not be worse off than one who does not…
>
> For these reasons, we are of the view that, although it would be appropriate under the terms of POCA as traditionally interpreted, it would be disproportionate, at least when VAT output tax has been accounted for to HMRC (either by remittance or by its being set off against input tax), to make a confiscation order calculated on the basis that that tax, or a sum equivalent to it, has been "obtained" by the defendant for the purposes of POCA".[281]

3.277   This decision, as noted by Lord Toulson, will involve consideration of the accounting for VAT by a defendant and involves, 'just the sort of accountancy exercise against which the courts have taken a firm stand from the outset'. Practitioners and Crown Court Judges will have to determine how best to approach the calculation of benefit in the light of the majority reasoning of the Supreme Court in similar cases.

3.278   Care should be taken to pierce the corporate veil only in cases where it is appropriate to do so. In *R v Boyle Transport (Northern Ireland) Limited*[282] Davis LJ noted:

> '…even where a company mixed up in relevant wrong doing is solely owned and solely controlled by the (criminal) defendant that does not of itself always necessitate a conclusion in a confiscation case that it is an alter ego company, whose turnover and assets are to be equated with being the property of the defendant himself.'

3.279   The Court rejected the treating of a company's turnover as the benefit of the defendant's in the case involving infringement of driver's hours. See also *R v Jacqueline Powell*[283] in a case where the corporate veil was not pierced where environmental offences had been committed.

---

[281] At paras 34–36.
[282] [2016] 4 WLR 63.
[283] [2016] EWCA 1043.

Determining the recoverable amount

3.280 Once it has been established that the defendant has benefitted from his criminal conduct, the Court has to determine what falls to be recovered from the defendant and then order the payment of that amount.[284] Following the decision in *R v Waya*, the payment of the recoverable amount 'applies only if, or to the extent that, it would not be disproportionate to require the defendant to pay the recoverable amount.'[285]

Costs

3.281 Under s 18 of the Prosecution of Offences Act 1985 (POA) – which does not apply to Scotland – where a person is convicted of an offence before a Crown Court or magistrates' court, the court may make such order as to the costs to be paid by the accused to the prosecutor as it considers just and reasonable.

3.282 A local authority is unable to recover its costs in criminal proceedings from central funds (see s 16, POA). The Practice Direction on Costs in Criminal Proceedings [2013] EWCA Crim 1632 provides:

> '2.6.1 There is no power to order the payment of costs out of Central Funds of any prosecutor who is a public authority, a person acting on behalf of a public authority, or acting as an official appointed by a public authority as defined in the Act.'

3.283 Changes to costs that can be obtained from central funds by defendants, including preventing a corporate defendant from obtaining costs from central funds for proceedings commenced after 12 October 2012, may mean that there will be increased costs applications against local authorities in the event of acquittals.

Post-conviction orders relating to property

Deprivation

3.284 The following provision does not apply in Scotland.

Section 143 of the PCCSA 2000 contains the following:

> **143 Powers to deprive offender of property used etc for purposes of crime**
>
> (1) Where a person is convicted of an offence and the court by or before which he is convicted is satisfied that any property which has been lawfully seized from him, or which was in his possession or under his control at the time when he was apprehended for the offence or when a summons in respect of it was issued –

---

[284] Section 6(5).
[285] Amended by Serious Crime Act 2015, Sch 4, para 19.

(a) has been used for the purpose of committing, or facilitating the commission of, any offence, or

(b) was intended by him to be used for that purpose,

the court may (subject to subsection (5) below) make an order under this section in respect of that property.

...

(5) In considering whether to make an order under this section in respect of any property, a court shall have regard –

(a) to the value of the property; and

(b) to the likely financial and other effects on the offender of the making of the order (taken together with any other order that the court contemplates making).

Forfeiture

3.285 Specific provisions exist under trade mark, copyright, video recordings and weights and measures legislation for the forfeiture of items and reference should be made to those sections of this book for details of the relevant provisions.

Post-conviction orders relating to the offender

3.286 In Scotland there are different provisions and applications would be a matter for the Procurators Fiscal/Crown Office.

Criminal behaviour orders

3.287 Criminal behaviour orders ('CBOs') are made under the Anti-social Behaviour, Crime and Policing Act 2014 and replace, in effect, Anti-social Behaviour Orders ('ASBO'), which were made under the Crime and Disorder Act 1998.[286] A CBO can only be made on the application of the prosecutor following conviction of an offence. The court may make a CBO against the offender if two conditions are met: (i) the court must be satisfied, beyond reasonable doubt, that the offender has engaged in behaviour that caused or was likely to cause harassment, alarm or distress to any person and (ii) the court considers that making the order will help in preventing the offender from engaging in such behaviour. Various provisions of the Anti-social Behaviour, Crime and Policing Act 2014 were brought into force on 20 October 2014 including those relating to CBOs. The Home Office has issued relevant guidance: *Anti-social Behaviour, Crime and Policing Act 2014: Reform of anti-social behaviour powers. Statutory guidance for frontline professionals.*

---

[286] In Scotland the Anti-social Behaviour etc (Scotland) Act 2004.

Disqualification from driving

3.288 A court by or before which a person is convicted of an offence may, instead of or in addition to dealing with him in any other way, order him to be disqualified, for such period as it thinks fit, for holding or obtaining a driving licence (s 146, PCCSA 2000).

3.289 Although the power to disqualify an offender from driving is not limited to any particular offence and it was not necessary that the conviction should be connected in any way with the use of a motor vehicle, the court cannot impose a period of disqualification arbitrarily and there must be a sufficient reason for the disqualification – *R v Cliff*.[287]

3.290 In *R v Taylor*[288] the defendant was sentenced to 18 months' imprisonment in respect of offences involving counterfeit CDs, DVDs and MP3 discs. He was also disqualified from driving for 18 months under s 146 of the PCCSA 2000. The Court of Appeal did not think it appropriate to interfere with the sentence of imprisonment but were '… more troubled by the order for disqualification from driving. Since the appellant was in the habit of travelling to car boot fairs to sell these goods we can understand why the judge took that step, but the effect of the order will be to prevent him from driving for a period of 9 months after his release from prison and that will seriously interfere with his ability to earn his living and rehabilitate himself. In our view an order for disqualification was inappropriate in this case.'

Company director disqualification

3.291 Under the Company Directors Disqualification Act 1986 ('CDDA 1986') the court may make a disqualification order against a person where he is convicted of an indictable offence (whether on indictment or summarily) in connection with the promotion, formation, *management,* liquidation or striking off of a company, or with the receivership of a company's property or with his being an administrative receiver of a company. The maximum period of disqualification is 15 years in the Crown Court and 5 years when imposed in the magistrates' courts. Part 4 of the Deregulation Act 2015 – Disqualification of unfit directors of insolvent companies – amends CDDA 1986, amongst other matters, to enable the Secretary of State or the official receiver to request information relevant to a person's conduct as a director of a company that has been insolvent directly from any person, including from officers of the company themselves.

3.292 As amended by the Insolvency Act 2000, the CDDA 1986 gives the Secretary of State power to accept an undertaking from any person that, for a specified period, that person must not:

---

[287] [2004] EWCA Crim 3139.
[288] [2006] EWCA Crim 2503.

(a)   without the leave of the court, be a director of a company, act as a receiver of a company's property or in any way take part in the promotion, formation or management of a company; and

(b)   act as an insolvency practitioner.

3.293   In *R v Rafi Asghar Sheikh and Sami Asghar Sheikh*[289] the defendants were convicted of intellectual property crimes and sentenced to 6 years' imprisonment. In each case the judge made a disqualification order under CDDA 1986 for a period of 10 years. (The brothers were tried alongside their father, Khalid Asghar Sheikh, who was convicted of conspiracy to acquire criminal property and sentenced to 4 years' imprisonment, was also disqualified for a period of 10 years.) The defendants appealed (only) against the disqualification order. Treacy J stated:

> 'Given all the circumstances, we are not persuaded that the judge fell into error ...
> The term of disqualification imposed was severe but, in our judgment, deservedly so.'

CHAPTER 4

CIVIL ENFORCEMENT

CONTENTS

INTRODUCTION

4.1   Modern regulatory legislation often empowers the court to make an order regulating a person's activities and rendering any disobedience a contempt of court. As an alternative to criminal law enforcement of consumer legislation, Part 8 of the Enterprise Act 2002 ('EA 2002'), entitled 'Enforcement of Certain Consumer Legislation', provides a civil remedy by way of an enforcement order. Such an order should indicate the nature of the conduct which constitutes the domestic or community infringement or is likely to constitute such an infringement and direct the trader not to continue or repeat the conduct; not to engage in such conduct in the course of his business or another business; and not to consent to or connive in the carrying out of such conduct by a body corporate with which he has a special relationship.[1] Since the usual civil law remedies for breach of an order of the court apply to a breach of an enforcement order, Part 8 EA 2002 can provide an effective remedy for the enforcement of consumer legislation in the appropriate case.

4.2   In November 2012 the Department for Business, Innovation and Skills ('BIS') published a consultation paper on extending the range of remedies available to courts when public enforcers apply to them for enforcement orders under Part 8 EA 2002. Part 3 of the Consumer Rights Act 2015 ('CRA 2015') introduces new powers for public enforcers to seek:

- Redress for consumers who have been disadvantaged by breaches of consumer law.

- Remedies from traders who have breached consumer law to improve their compliance and reduce the likelihood of future breaches.

- Remedies to give consumers more information so they can exercise greater choice and help improve the functioning of the market for consumers and other businesses.

Origin of Part 8 of the EA 2002

4.3   For many years, consumer protection in the UK was achieved through criminal prosecution, particularly through the use of the Trade Descriptions Act 1968. Later, new pieces of legislation, for example the Fair Trading Act 1973, provided for injunctive type relief, but it was not until the introduction of the Stop Now Orders ('EC Directive') Regulations 2001 that there was a comprehensive approach allowing civil enforcement as a clear alternative to criminal enforcement. Part 8 of the EA 2002 was brought into force on 20 June 2003. It followed the short lived 'Stop Now' regime, which lasted from June 2001 until June 2003 and which need not now be considered in any detail. Part 8 has grown in importance with the introduction of the Consumer Protection from Unfair Trading Regulations 2008 ('CPUTR'), to the extent that almost all CPUTR infringements can be dealt with now under

---

[1]   EA 2002, s 217.

Part 8. That is not to say that Part 8 is limited to CPUTR infringements. As will become clear later in this Chapter, the procedure can be used over a wide spectrum of consumer infractions.

4.4 Part 8 of the EA 2002 sought to bring fully into UK law the provisions of Directive 98/27/EC of the European Parliament and of the Council of 19 May 1998 on injunctions[2] for the protection of consumers' interests ('the Injunctions Directive'). The Injunctions Directive was amended and largely re-cast in 2009 as Directive 2009/22/EC ('the 2009 Directive'). References below are to the Injunctions Directive with cross-references to the 2009 Directive where appropriate.

4.5 Since many of the concepts used in the provisions of Part 8 of the EA 2002 are in large part derived from the Injunctions Directive, they must at present[3] be construed in the light of the wording and purpose of that Directive in accordance with the principles laid down by the European Court of Justice in *Marleasing SA v La Comercial de Alimentación SA*.[4]

Recitals

4.6 The recitals to the Directive are of interest and can be important as an aid to the purposive construction of the Articles.[5] Recital (2)[6] notes:

> (2) Whereas current mechanisms available both at national and at Community level for ensuring compliance with those Directives[7] do not always allow infringements harmful to the collective interests of consumers to be terminated in good time; whereas collective interests mean interests which do not include the cumulation of interests of individuals who have been harmed by an infringement; whereas this is without prejudice to individual actions brought by individuals who have been harmed by an infringement.

4.7 In an interesting discussion, Lord Drummond-Young in *OFT v MB Designs (Scotland) Ltd*,[8] concluded in relation to the definition of 'collective interests' that the English translation was 'poorly expressed'. Having considered the French version, he proposed the alternative wording: 'by collective interests, one means interests which are not a *mere* accumulation of the interests of individuals to whom harm has been caused by an infringement' (emphasis added).

---

2   In the context of EA 2002, Part 8 'injunctions' have become 'Enforcement Orders'.
3   It is premature to consider the extent to which Brexit will affect this principle.
4   [1990] ECR I-4153, at paras 7–9 and 14.
5   Article 253 of the Treaty Establishing the European Community is the legislative source of the requirement that the reasons for the adoption of a legal act must be recited within the act: legal acts 'shall state the reasons on which they are based'.
6   Recital 3 of the 2009 Directive.
7   Namely those listed in the Annex to the Directive laying down rules with regard to the protection of consumers' interests. They are reflected in part in Sch 13 to the EA 2002: see further below.
8   [2005] SLT 691 at [13].

4.8   Recitals (13) and (14)[9] address the issue of consultation, relevant in the context of Part 8 EA 2002:

(13) Whereas Member States should be able to require that a prior consultation be undertaken by the party that intends to bring an action for an injunction, in order to give the defendant an opportunity to bring the contested infringement to an end; whereas Member States should be able to require that this prior consultation take place jointly with an independent public body designated by those Member States;

(14) Whereas, where the Member States have established that there should be prior consultation, a deadline of two weeks after the request for consultation is received should be set after which, should the cessation of the infringement not be achieved, the applicant shall be entitled to bring an action before the competent court or administrative authority without any further delay.

Articles[10]

4.9   Article 1 of the Directive defines its scope in the following terms:

The purpose of this Directive is to approximate the laws, regulations and administrative provisions of the Member States relating to actions for an injunction referred to in Article 2 aimed at the protection of the collective interests of consumers included in the Directives listed in the Annex, with a view to ensuring the smooth functioning of the internal market.

4.10   According to the Scottish judge, Lord Drummond-Young, the function of the Directive is therefore procedural rather than substantive.[11]

4.11   Article 2 of the Directive – Actions for an injunction – provides as follows:

Member States shall designate the courts or administrative authorities competent to rule on proceedings commenced by qualified entities within the meaning of Article 3 seeking:

- an order with all due expediency, where appropriate by way of summary procedure, requiring the cessation or prohibition of any infringement;
- where appropriate, measures such as the publication of the decision, in full or in part, in such form as deemed adequate and/or the publication of a corrective statement with a view to eliminating the continuing effects of the infringement;
- insofar as the legal system of the Member State concerned so permits, an order against the losing defendant for payments into the public purse or to any beneficiary designated in or under national legislation, in the event of failure to comply with the decision within a time-limit specified by the courts or administrative authorities, of a fixed amount for each day's delay or any other amount provided for in national legislation, with a view to ensuring compliance with the decisions.

---

[9]   Recitals 14 and 15 of the 2009 Directive.
[10]   The numbering of the Articles is identical in both Directives.
[11]   See *OFT v MB Designs (Scotland) Ltd* [2005] SLT 691 at [10].

4.12 The Directive, read together with recital (2), clearly anticipates that both an enforcer and the court will act with 'all due expediency' in seeking an enforcement order 'requiring the cessation or prohibition of any infringement'.[12] The need for expedition in bringing an infringement to an end also informs the relatively short period required for consultation. As regards a summary procedure 'where appropriate', the EA 2002 empowers the court to make an interim enforcement order. The Directive contemplates financial penalties in order to ensure compliance. It may be that in the future the Courts will take advantage of the compliance category of enhanced consumer measures set out in the CRA 2015 to include within the order financial penalties for non-compliance.[13]

4.13 Article 3 deals with 'Entities qualified to bring an action' and is discussed later in this chapter under the heading of 'Enforcers'.

4.14 Article 4 deals with 'Intra-Community infringements' and provides for a qualified entity of one Member State to take injunctive action in the courts of another Member State:

> 'Each member state shall take the measures necessary to ensure that, in the event of an infringement originating in that member state, any qualified entity from another member state where the interests protected by that qualified entity are affected by the infringement, may seize the court or administrative authority referred to in Article 2.'

This Article is also discussed in more detail later in this chapter.

4.15 Article 5 deals with 'Prior Consultation':

> Member States may introduce or maintain in force provisions whereby the party that intends to seek an injunction can only start this procedure after it has tried to achieve the cessation of the infringement in consultation with either the defendant or with both the defendant and a qualified entity within the meaning of Article 3(a) of the Member State in which the injunction is sought. It shall be for the Member State to decide whether the party seeking the injunction must consult the qualified entity. If the cessation of the infringement is not achieved within two weeks after the request for consultation is received, the party concerned may bring an action for an injunction without any further delay.

4.16 Note the reference to the 2-week period for consultation, a reflection of recitals (13) and (14). The Directive does not anticipate open-ended consultation between enforcer and trader in order to achieve a cessation of the infringement. If the infringement continues after 2 weeks, the enforcer may apply for an enforcement order 'without any further delay'.[14]

---

[12]   In the words of recital (2), the infringement should be 'terminated in good time'.
[13]   EA 2002, s 219A inserted by para 8 of Sch 7 to the CRA 2015.
[14]   Note however the 28-day period provided in certain circumstances by the EA 2002, s 214(4)(a) and (4A) inserted by para 5 of Sch 7 to the CRA 2015.

4.17 Article 6 provides for reporting on the application of the Directive to the European Parliament and the Council.

4.18 That the Directive establishes the minimum requirements, rather than the maximum is demonstrated by Art 7:

> This Directive shall not prevent Member States from adopting or maintaining in force provisions designed to grant qualified entities and any other person concerned more extensive rights to bring action at national level.

CRITERIA FOR SEEKING AN ENFORCEMENT ORDER

4.19 In order to obtain an enforcement order, very broadly three criteria need to be satisfied:

(i)   the trader has engaged, or is engaging, in conduct which constitutes a domestic or a Community infringement, or is likely to engage in conduct which constitutes a Community infringement;[15]

(ii) there is, or has been, or is likely to be, harm to the collective interests of consumers in the UK;

(iii) there has been appropriate Consultation that has failed to bring about the cessation of the conduct about which complaint is made or the need to consult has been waived.

4.20 Before those criteria are considered further, it is convenient first to consider who may enforce the provisions of Part 8 of the EA 2002.

Enforcers

Injunctions Directive

4.21 Article 2.1 of the Injunctions Directive requires Member States to 'designate the courts or administrative authorities competent to rule on proceedings commenced by qualified entities'.

4.22 'Qualified entities' are defined by Art 3 as:

> any body or organisation which, being properly constituted according to the law of a Member State, has a legitimate interest in ensuring that the provisions referred to in Article 1[16] are complied with, in particular:
>
> > (a)   one or more independent public bodies, specifically responsible for protecting the interests referred to in Article 1, in Member States in which such bodies exist and/or
> >
> > (b)   organisations whose purpose is to protect the interests referred to in Article 1, in accordance with the criteria laid down by their national law.

---

[15]   EA 2002, s 215.

[16]   Those are the Directives for the protection of consumers listed in the Annex, which are reflected in part in Sch 13 to the EA 2002.

General enforcers

4.23 By s 213(1) of the EA 2002, the following are specifically designated as 'general enforcers', namely the Competition and Markets Authority ('the CMA');[17] every local weights and measures authority in Great Britain;[18] and the Department of Enterprise, Trade and Investment in Northern Ireland. A general enforcer may make an application for an enforcement order in respect of any infringement.[19]

Designated enforcers

4.24 By s 213(2) of the EA 2002, the Secretary of State may by order designate any person or body as a 'designated enforcer' provided that he thinks that person or body has as one of its purposes the protection of the collective interests of consumers, and he is satisfied that it is independent. If the person or body proposed to be designated is not a public body, it must conform to criteria laid down by the Secretary of State by order.[20] A designated enforcer may make an application for an enforcement order in respect of an infringement to which his designation relates.[21]

4.25 The Secretary of State has made a number of orders pursuant to s 213:

- Enterprise Act 2002 (Part 8 Designated Enforcers: Criteria for Designation, Designation of Public Bodies as Designated Enforcers and Transitional Provisions) Order 2003, SI 2003/1399. The name of the Order speaks for itself. A number of **public** bodies were designated in respect of all infringements, namely the Civil Aviation Authority, the Director General of Electricity Supply for Northern Ireland, the Director General of Gas for Northern Ireland, the Office of Communications, the Water Services Regulation Authority, the Gas and Electricity Markets Authority, the Information Commissioner and the Rail Regulator;

- Enterprise Act 2002 (Part 8) (Designation of the Consumers' Association) Order 2005, SI 2005/917, in respect of all infringements;

- Enterprise Act 2002 (Part 8) (Designation of the Financial Conduct Authority as a Designated Enforcer) Order 2013, SI 2013/478, in respect of all infringements.

---

[17] The CMA replaced the OFT following its abolition by the Enterprise and Regulatory Reform Act 2013: see ss 25 and 26 of that Act.

[18] See the Weights and Measures Act 1985, s 69 – in effect trading standards departments of local authorities.

[19] EA 2002, s 215(2).

[20] EA 2002, s 213(4). The Secretary of State's criteria are to be found in the Enterprise Act 2002 (Part 8 Designated Enforcers: Criteria for Designation, Designation of Public Bodies as Designated Enforcers and Transitional Provisions) Order 2003, SI 2003/1399.

[21] EA 2002, s 215(3).

Community enforcers

4.26 By s 213(5) of the EA 2002:

> A Community enforcer is a qualified entity for the purposes of the Injunctions Directive –
>
> (a) which is for the time being specified in the list published in the Official Journal of the European Communities in pursuance of Article 4.3 of that Directive,[22] but
>
> (b) which is not a general enforcer, a designated enforcer or a CPC enforcer.

4.27 This provision was required in order to bring Art 4[23] of the Injunctions Directive into force in UK law. Community enforcers are entities from *other* EU States that are listed in the Official Journal of the European Communities under Art 4.3 and are entitled to make applications for enforcement orders in the UK courts in respect of Community infringements[24] that originate in the UK but produce effects in that particular Member State.[25] For example, if defective products were sold by mail order in the UK and delivered to consumers in Germany, a German qualified entity could apply for an enforcement order in the UK courts as a 'Community enforcer'.

4.28 Similarly, under the Injunctions Directive, a UK qualified entity can seek injunctive relief in the courts of another Member State where the infringement originates in that Member State but affects UK citizens. Thus, by s 221(2) of the EA 2002, a general enforcer and a designated enforcer, which is a public body, are both empowered to take proceedings in EEA States[26] other than the UK for the cessation or prohibition of a Community infringement.

4.29 Section 221(4) of the EA 2002 provides for cooperation between general enforcers, designated enforcers and CFC enforcers on the one hand and Community enforcers on the other hand for the purpose of assisting the UK enforcer taking proceedings in the EEA State or assisting the Community enforcer taking proceedings in the UK.

---

[22] The list, which is of the qualified entities of the various Member States, can be found at http://eur-lex.europa.eu/LexUriServ/LexUriServ.do?uri=OJ:C:2012:097:0001:0045:EN:PDF. The UK has 11 entries. All are either general or designated enforcers and so do not qualify as 'Community enforcers' within the meaning of the EA 2002.

[23] Entitled 'Intra-Community Infringements'.

[24] EA 2002, s 215(4).

[25] One of the purposes of the Injunctions Directive was to address the situation where the infringement of consumer legislation occurred in one Member State but its effects were felt in another Member State. In those circumstances, the qualified entity of the second State should be empowered to take injunction proceedings in the first State: see recitals (3), (6) and (11).

[26] An EEA State is a State which is a contracting party to the Agreement on the European Economic Area signed at Oporto on 2 May 1992 as adjusted by the Protocol signed at Brussels on 17 March 1993: EA 2002, s 221(5).

Consumer Protection Cooperation ('CPC') enforcers

4.30 Section 213(5A) of the EA 2002 lists 'CPC enforcers', namely bodies designated under Art 4(1) or (2) of Regulation (EC) No 2006/2004 of the European Parliament and of the Council of 27 October 2004 on cooperation between national authorities responsible for the enforcement of consumer protection laws as amended by the Unfair Commercial Practices Directive ('the CPC Regulation').[27] The bodies listed in s 213(5A) of the EA 2002 are the CMA; the Civil Aviation Authority; the Financial Conduct Authority; the Secretary of State for Health; the Department of Health, Social Services and Public Safety in Northern Ireland; the Office of Communications; the Department of Enterprise, Trade and Investment in Northern Ireland; every local weights and measures authority in Great Britain; an enforcement authority within the meaning of s 120(15) of the Communications Act 2003 (regulation of premium rate services);[28] and the Information Commissioner. A CPC enforcer may make an application for an enforcement order in respect of a Community infringement.[29]

4.31 Section 213(5A) was inserted by the Enterprise Act 2002 (Amendment) Regulations 2006, SI 2006/3363. The note to the Regulations explains that the CPC Regulation creates a network of enforcers responsible for taking action to stamp out cross-border infringements of the EC consumer protection legislation set out in the Annex to the Regulation and that Art 4(6), which prescribes the powers which enforcers under the CPC Regulation must have, requires further implementation. The note continues that, although Part 8 of the EA 2002 confers some of the enforcement powers referred to in the CPC Regulation on certain bodies in relation to most (but not all) of the EC consumer protection legislation to which the CPC Regulation applies, the amendment of Part 8 was necessary to ensure that the powers set out in Art 4(6) of the CPC Regulation could be exercised in accordance with its terms. The additional powers are largely in relation to search and seizure.

Dual enforcers

4.32 Some bodies are designated as more than one type of enforcer. Where that occurs, the body in question may act as the particular type of enforcer appropriate to the circumstances.[30]

---

[27] This Directive is again concerned with intra-Community infringements.
[28] See para 4 of Sch 7 to the CRA 2015.
[29] EA 2002, s 215(4A).
[30] EA 2002, s 235B.

Public bodies and private designated enforcers under the CRA 2015

4.33 The new enhanced consumer measures[31] set out in the CRA 2015 will only be available where the enforcer is a public body. A power is included in the Act to extend the use of the measures to private designated enforcers provided the following conditions are met:[32]

- The enforcer is specified for the purposes of this section by order made by the Secretary of State.[33]

- The enhanced consumer measures do not directly benefit the enforcer or an associated undertaking.

4.34 Enhanced consumer measures which directly benefit an enforcer or an associated undertaking include, in particular, measures which:

(a) require a person to pay money to the enforcer or associated undertaking;

(b) require a person to participate in a scheme which is designed to recommend persons supplying or seeking to supply goods or services to consumers and which is administered by the enforcer or associated undertaking; or

(c) would give the enforcer or associated undertaking a commercial advantage over any of its competitors.[34]

Infringements

4.35 The core power in Part 8 of the EA 2002 is to seek an enforcement order from the court to stop breaches or infringements of specific consumer protection legislation. Those are as follows:

Domestic infringements

4.36 By s 211 of the EA 2002:

(1) A domestic infringement is an act or omission which –

(a) is done or made by a person in the course of a business,

(b) falls within subsection (2), and

(c) harms the collective interests of consumers.

(1A) But an act or omission which satisfies the conditions in subsection (1) is a domestic infringement only if at least one of the following is satisfied –

(a) the person supplying (or seeking to supply) goods or services has a place of business in the United Kingdom, or

---

[31] Explained in detail below.

[32] EA 2002, s 219C as added by para 8 of Sch 7 to the CRA 2015.

[33] At the time of writing, no orders have been made. The Secretary of State must be satisfied that the criteria set out in EA 2002, s 219C(6) and (7) are met.

[34] EA 2002, s 219C(5).

(b)   the goods or services are supplied (or sought to be supplied) to or for a person in the United Kingdom (see section 232).[35]

(2) An act or omission falls within this subsection if it is of a description specified by the Secretary of State by order and consists of any of the following –

(a)   a contravention of an enactment which imposes a duty, prohibition or restriction enforceable by criminal proceedings;

(b)   an act done or omission made in breach of contract;

(c)   an act done or omission made in breach of a non-contractual duty owed to a person by virtue of an enactment or rule of law and enforceable by civil proceedings;

(d)   an act or omission in respect of which an enactment provides for a remedy or sanction enforceable by civil proceedings;

(e)   an act done or omission made by a person supplying or seeking to supply goods or services as a result of which an agreement or security relating to the supply is void or unenforceable to any extent;

(f)   an act or omission by which a person supplying or seeking to supply goods or services purports or attempts to exercise a right or remedy relating to the supply in circumstances where the exercise of the right or remedy is restricted or excluded under or by virtue of an enactment;

(g)   an act or omission by which a person supplying or seeking to supply goods or services purports or attempts to avoid (to any extent) liability relating to the supply in circumstances where such avoidance is restricted or prevented under an enactment.

4.37   The Secretary of State has made orders under s 211. Schedule 1 to the Enterprise Act 2002 (Part 8 Domestic Infringements) Order 2003, SI 2003/1593 as amended by the CPUTR, lists specified domestic infringements. The schedule consists of three parts:

- Part 1: legislation of the UK Parliament. This is a list of 33 specific Acts including, for example, the Consumer Credit Act 1974, the Estate Agents Act 1979, the Misrepresentation Act 1967 and the Unfair Contract Terms Act 1977.

- Part 2: Northern Ireland legislation. This is a list of 11 Acts of Northern Ireland.

- Part 3: entitled 'Rules of Law', which reads as follows:

> 'An act done or omission made in breach of contract for the supply of goods or services to a consumer.
>
> An act done or omission made in breach of a duty of care owed to a consumer under the law of tort or delict of negligence.'

4.38   Given that many consumer protection issues involve a breach of contract, the contract law provision can be used either alone or in conjunction with other provisions.

---

[35]   CRA 2015, Sch 7, para 3(3).

4.39   The reference to the tort or delict of negligence requires a breach of duty of care, for example negligently manufacturing sub-standard consumer goods.

Community infringements

4.40   By s 212 of the EA 2002:

> (1) A Community infringement is an act or omission which harms the collective interests of consumers and which –
>
> > (a)   contravenes a listed Directive as given effect by the laws, regulations or administrative provisions of an EEA State,
> > (b)   contravenes such laws, regulations or administrative provisions which provide additional permitted protections,
> > (c)   contravenes a listed Regulation, or
> > (d)   contravenes any laws, regulations or administrative provisions of an EEA State which give effect to a listed Regulation.
>
> (2) The laws, regulations or administrative provisions of an EEA State which give effect to a listed Directive provide additional permitted protections if –
>
> > (a)   they provide protection for consumers which is in addition to the minimum protection required by the Directive concerned, and
> > (b)   such additional protection is permitted by that Directive.
>
> (3) The Secretary of State may by order specify for the purposes of this section the law in the United Kingdom which –
>
> > (a)   gives effect to the listed Directives;
> > (b)   provides additional permitted protections, or
> > (c)   gives effect to a listed Regulation.

4.41   By s 210 of the EA 2002:

> (7) A Directive is a listed Directive –
>
> > (a)   if it is a Directive of the Council of the European Union or of the European Parliament and of the Council, and
> > (b)   if it is specified in Schedule 13 or to the extent that any of its provisions is so specified.
>
> (7A) A Regulation is a listed Regulation –
>
> > (a)   if it is a Regulation of the Council of the European Union or of the European Parliament and of the Council, and
> > (b)   if it is specified in Schedule 13 or to the extent that any of its provisions is so specified.

4.42   Thus, for listed Directives and Regulations, Sch 13 to the EA 2002, as amended, must first be consulted.

4.43   Part 1 of the Schedule lists 14 complete Directives and Regulations, namely those in respect of contracts negotiated away from business premises;[36]

---

[36]   Council Directive 85/577/EEC of 20 December 1985.

on package travel, package holidays and package tours;[37] on unfair terms in consumer contracts;[38] on the protection of consumers in respect of distance contracts;[39] on consumer protection in the indication of the prices of products offered to consumers;[40] on certain aspects of the sale of consumer goods and associated guarantees;[41] on electronic commerce;[42] concerning the distance marketing of consumer financial services;[43] establishing common rules on compensation and assistance to air passengers in the event of denied boarding and of cancellation or long delay of flights;[44] concerning unfair business-to-consumer commercial practices in the internal market;[45] on services in the internal market;[46] on credit agreements for consumers;[47] on the protection of consumers in respect of certain aspects of timeshare, long-term holiday product, resale and exchange contracts;[48] and on consumer rights.[49]

4.44 By contrast, Part 2 of the Schedule lists parts only of six named Directives, namely Arts 10–21 on the co-ordination of certain provisions laid down by law, regulation or administrative action in Member States concerning the pursuit of television broadcasting activities;[50] Arts 86–100 on the Community Code relating to medicinal products for human use;[51] Art 13 on privacy and electronic communications;[52] Art 13 on alternative dispute resolution for consumer disputes[53]; Art 14 on online dispute resolution for consumer disputes;[54] and Art 10(4) on interchange fees for card-based payment transactions.[55]

4.45 The Secretary of State has made orders under s 212(3) specifying the UK law which has given effect to a listed Directive or Regulation, namely:

---

[37] Council Directive 90/314/EEC of 13 June 1990.
[38] Council Directive 93/13/EEC of 5 April 1993.
[39] Directive 97/7/EC of the European Parliament and of the Council of 20 May 1997.
[40] Directive 98/6/EC of the European Parliament and of the Council of 16 February 1998.
[41] Directive 1999/44/EC of the European Parliament and of the Council of 25 May 1999.
[42] Directive 2000/31/EC of the European Parliament and of the Council of 8 June 2000.
[43] Directive 2002/65/EC of the European Parliament and of the Council of 23 September 2002.
[44] Regulation (EC) No 261/2004 of the European Parliament and of the Council of 11 February 2004.
[45] Directive 2005/29/EC of the European Parliament and of the Council of 11 May 2005. This is the important UCPD given force by the CPUTR.
[46] Directive 2006/123/EC of the European Parliament and of the Council of 12 December 2006.
[47] Directive 2008/48/EC of the European Parliament and of the Council of 23 April 2008.
[48] Directive 2008/122/EC of the European Parliament and of the Council of 14 January 2009.
[49] Directive 2011/83/EU of the European Parliament and of the Council of 25 October 2011.
[50] Council Directive 89/552/EEC of 3 October 1989.
[51] Directive 2001/83/EC of the European Parliament and of the Council of 6 November 2001.
[52] Directive 2002/58/EC of the European Parliament and of the Council of 12 July 2002.
[53] Directive 2013/11/EU of the European Parliament and of the Council of 21 May 2013. Art 14 of this Directive will be added to Part 2 of Sch 13 when reg 6 of the Alternative Dispute Resolution for Consumer Disputes (Amendment) Regulations 2015, SI 2015/1392 is brought into force.
[54] Regulation (EU) No 524/2013 of the European Parliament and of the Council of 21 May 2013.
[55] Regulation (EU) 2015/751 of the European Parliament and of the Council of 29 April 2015.

- The Schedule to the Enterprise Act 2002 (Part 8 Community Infringements Specified UK Laws) Order 2003, SI 2003/1374, as amended, which lists 15 Directives or parts of Directives which have been given effect by a UK law. Thus, for example Directive 2005/29/EC of the European Parliament and of the Council of 11 May 2005 concerning unfair business-to-consumer commercial practices in the internal market is specified as having been given effect by the CPUTR.

- The Enterprise Act 2002 (Part 8 Community Infringements Specified UK Laws) Order 2006, SI 2006/3372 lists a further one Directive and one Regulation which have been given effect by UK law.

- The Enterprise Act 2002 (Part 8 EU Infringements) Order 2014, SI 2014/2908 lists Directive 2011/83/EU of the European Parliament and of the Council of 25 October 2011 on consumer rights as having been given effect by the Consumer Contracts (Information, Cancellation and Additional Charges) Regulations 2013, SI 2013/3134 and certain regulations of the Consumer Rights (Payment Surcharges) Regulations 2012, SI 2012/3110.

4.46   When seeking undertakings or enforcement orders, there is no need to plead domestic and community infringements in separate documents. However, given the wider scope of community infringements, it may make sense to separate them in the same document under subheadings. Thus, the Particulars of Claim should clearly indicate which breaches are domestic infringements, which are Community infringements and which are both. In undertakings, enforcement orders and undertakings to the court there should be a similar degree of separation to ensure consistency of presentation.

Number of breaches

4.47   Under the old Fair Trading Act 1973,[56] it was necessary for an Enforcer to prove 'a course of conduct' before the court could grant an order. In subsequent legislation, that phrase was replaced with the single word 'conduct'. Is that change significant?

4.48   Whether a single infringement or breach of the law is enough to warrant seeking an enforcement order was explored in *Office of Fair Trading v Vance Miller*[57] where Arden LJ, disagreeing with the Scottish judgment of Lord Drummond-Young[58] said:[59]

'However, I would not for my part agree with Lord Drummond-Young's conclusion ... that "[m]ore than one instance of a defective supply is required before there can be a breach" of an order pursuant to the provisions of the Enterprise Act 2002 now providing for stop orders. It must depend on the facts. A Community infringement is committed when harm is caused to the collective

---

[56]   See ss 34 and 37.
[57]   [2009] EWCA Civ 34.
[58]   In *OFT v MB Designs (Scotland) Ltd* [2005] SLT 69.
[59]   At [44].

interests of consumers. It is possible that a single supply might be enough, as where a supplier puts on to the market a large consignment of a beverage stated to be a healthy drink for a baby that is wholly unsuitable for this purpose. For this reason, I do not consider that the expression "Community infringement" requires a course of conduct.'

4.49 Later,[60] she said that a Community Infringement 'could in appropriate circumstances be a single act, or several separate acts. They need not be connected in the same way that a course of conduct consists of a series of connected acts, but if they are connected that will be evidence from which the court can conclude that there is damage to the collective interests of consumers.'

4.50 In the same case, Sedley LJ said:[61]

'In my judgment, while the material provisions do not demand proof of a course of conduct, they do envisage something more than a simple breach of contract. This legislation does not seek to supplant or supplement individual consumers' private law rights; it seeks to protect the body of consumers from commercial malpractice. Accordingly, as it seems to me, infringement envisages a situation such that (at least in a case such as the present) the public cannot safely or confidently deal with the alleged infringer. There is nothing to prevent such a situation arising from a single event.'

4.51 The enforcer may need to decide whether a single infringement is sufficient to establish harm to the collective interest of consumers, which is the statutory requirement. As Arden LJ observed, a single infringement may still have a massive impact on consumers.

4.52 The number and nature of the infringements may also be a relevant consideration in determining whether there is a risk that they will continue unless enforcement action is taken. In the same case, Arden LJ said:[62]

'In my judgment, the findings of fact made by the judge on the nine cases show that there were serial episodes of significantly defective supplies of goods. These episodes were not just harmful to the customers concerned, but, by virtue of the risk of repetition, these episodes were also harmful to the collective interests of consumers generally. The judge found that they were not isolated or unconnected incidents. In his judgment they established a consistent pattern of failure to comply with contractual obligations. I do not consider that it is necessary for the court to investigate the level of complaints received by competitors in the industry nor does the limited number of breaches of contract that were proved, when set against the volume of sales, mean that there was no Community infringement.'

4.53 In that case, it was held that the evidence of nine complaints (which evidenced infringements) was enough, even when set against the 80,000 kitchens sold over 4 years.

---

[60] At [52].
[61] At [68].
[62] At [51].

Consumers

4.54 The legislation covered by Part 8 of the EA 2002 is aimed at the protection of 'consumers', as defined in s 210 of the Act.

4.55 In relation to domestic infringements, a consumer is an individual in respect of whom two conditions are satisfied. First, goods or services are supplied or are sought to be supplied to the individual in the course of a business carried on by the person making the supply. Second, the individual must receive or seek to receive the goods or services otherwise than in the course of a business.[63]

4.56 In relation to Community infringements, a consumer is a person who is so defined for the purposes of the Injunctions Directive and the listed Directive or Regulation with which the action is concerned. There is no definition of a consumer as such in the Injunctions Directive. The listed Directives and Regulations provide, generally speaking, that a consumer is a natural person who acts for purposes outside his trade, business or profession. Thus, for example, Art 2(a) of Directive 2005/29/EC concerning unfair business-to-consumer commercial practices in the internal market defines a consumer as 'any natural person who, in commercial practices covered by this Directive, is acting for purposes which are outside his trade, business, craft or profession'.

4.57 In short, in both cases a consumer may be described as an individual who is not acting in a trading or professional capacity.[64]

Harm to the collective interests of consumers

4.58 The meaning of 'harms the collective interests of consumers' was considered in *OFT v MB Designs (Scotland) Ltd*[65] by Lord Drummond-Young in the Court of Session. MB Designs argued that their actions could not be said to be harmful to the collective interests of consumers in the UK because they operated only in a relatively small geographical area. The judge rejected the argument. The concept of 'harm to the collective interests of consumers' was not based upon percentages of the population, geography or any statistical concept. There was collective harm when there was an infringement and there was potential risk to purchasers of the defective goods or services. The notion of collective interests of consumers indicates that there must be some harm or risk of harm to the public generally, or more precisely to members of the public who may buy the particular goods or service in question.

4.59 The following extracts appear from the judgment:

'... it is necessary that ... contravention should harm the collective interests of consumers. The latter expression is of fundamental importance; it makes clear that

---

[63]   EA 2002, s 210(2)–(4).
[64]   See *OFT v MB Designs (Scotland) Ltd* [2005] SLT 69 at [2].
[65]   [2005] SLT 69.

Part 8 is not concerned with individual breaches of contract or breaches of statutory provisions on the part of traders, but is rather concerned with the enforcement of general standards of trading.'[66]

'... the expression "collective interests" is not something wholly separate from the interests of individual consumers who have been harmed by infringements. "Collective interests" include those interests, but amount to something more than the mere aggregation of those interests. That makes perfectly good sense; it means that the adjective "collective" denotes the generality of consumers, considered as a body, but at the same time recognizes that the interests of individual consumers are part of those collective interests, and that harm to the collective interests will normally be inferred from a number of instances of harm to individual interests.'[67]

'The notion of the collective interests of consumers, therefore, indicates that there must be harm or a risk of harm to the public generally, or more precisely to members of the public who may buy the particular goods or services in question.'[68]

'The collective interests of consumers, by contrast, are concerned not with the contractual rights of individual consumers but with general trading standards, and in particular with the general standard of goods or services supplied by a particular trader. Part 8 of the 2002 Act is designed to enforce such trading standards. In my opinion a statutory provision of this nature has two important features. First, it is not designed to ensure that no defective product or service is ever supplied; it is rather designed to ensure that the incidence of defective products or services is kept at a low level, and that in cases where a defective product or service is supplied reasonable steps are taken to put matters right. The occasional instance where defective goods or services are supplied cannot be said to harm the collective interests of consumers; it is only when there is an accumulation of a number of such instances that the collective interests can be said to be engaged. Secondly, Part 8 is intended to deal with the overall incidence of defects in a trader's products or services, and it is immaterial for this purpose what the particular defects may be. It is accordingly immaterial that the defects may vary widely in their nature. The existence of a wide range of defects will often be an indication of poor management or poor quality control, and the function of consumer protection legislation is to protect against poor management or quality control just as much as poor fitting or poor manufacturing processes.'[69]

4.60 The concept of harm to the collective interests of consumers was considered further in *OFT v Vance Miller*[70] in which the Court of Appeal (Civil Division) essentially agreed with the earlier Scottish decision. The *Miller* case determined that it might be possible for collective harm to be made out by a single breach.

---

[66] At [1].
[67] At [13].
[68] At [14].
[69] At [14].
[70] [2009] EWCA Civ 34.

Consultation

4.61 This is an area of Part 8 of the EA 2002 which causes problems for both enforcers and traders alike. Consultation is not defined in the EA 2002. Section 214(1) of the EA 2002 simply provides that enforcers must engage in 'appropriate consultation' before applying to the court for an enforcement order, unless it is one of those rare case when the CMA thinks that an application for an enforcement order should be made without delay.[71] Absent appropriate consultation, the court has no power to make an enforcement order, save in those limited cases in which the CMA has dispensed with it. Consultation must be with the trader and, if the CMA is not the enforcer, with the CMA.

4.62 Some assistance as to the meaning of consultation can be gained by considering:

(a) when an enforcer should embark upon consultation;

(b) what consultation seeks to achieve; and

(c) how long consultation should last.

When should an enforcer embark upon consultation?

4.63 The short answer is that he should do so when satisfied that the trader has engaged, or is engaging in, conduct which constitutes a domestic or a Community infringement, or is likely to engage in conduct which constitutes a Community infringement. In other words, consultation must be seen as the last step before an application for an enforcement order is made. It should follow, not precede, investigation into the infringement.

What does consultation seek to achieve?

4.64 Recital (13) of the Injunctions Directive makes it clear that the sole purpose of consultation is 'to give the defendant an opportunity to bring the contested infringement to an end'. It is to that purpose that the consultation discussions should be directed.

4.65 To similar effect is s 214(2) of the EA 2002:

> Appropriate consultation is consultation for the purpose of –
>
> (a) achieving the cessation of the infringement in a case where an infringement is occurring;
>
> (b) ensuring that there will be no repetition of the infringement in a case where the infringement has occurred;
>
> (c) ensuring that there will be no repetition of the infringement in a case where the cessation of the infringement is achieved under paragraph (a);

---

[71] EA 2002, s 214(3).

(d)   ensuring that the infringement does not take place in the case of a
       Community infringement which the enforcer believes is likely to take
       place.

How long should consultation last?

4.66 Consultation is meant to be a summary, rather than a long drawn out,
process. That much is clear from the Injunctions Directive and is confirmed by
s 214(4) of the EA 2002. In the case of an application for an enforcement order,
there is no obligation to continue consultation for more than 14 days after
receipt of the request for consultation or, in the case of an application for an
interim enforcement order, for more than 7 days after its receipt. It may be
appropriate in some special circumstances to have a longer period of
consultation during which attempts are made to persuade the trader to change
his conduct. However, that ought to be the exception rather than the rule.

4.67 Paragraph 5 of Sch 7 to the CRA 2015 amends s 214 of the EA 2002 by
the addition of a further sub-section (4A) which extends the period of
consultation to 28 days in a case where the person against whom the
enforcement order would be made is a member of, or is represented by, a
representative body, and that body operates a consumer code which has been
approved by –

(a)   an enforcer, other than a designated enforcer which is not a public body,

(b)   a body which represents an enforcer mentioned in paragraph (a),

(c)   a group of enforcers mentioned in paragraph (a), or

(d)   a community interest company whose objects include the approval of
       consumer codes.

4.68 'Consumer code' is defined as 'a code of practice or other document
(however described) intended, with a view to safeguarding or promoting the
interests of consumers, to regulate by any means the conduct of persons
engaged in the supply of goods or services to consumers (or the conduct of their
employees or representatives)'.

4.69 'Representative body' is defined as 'an organisation established to
represent the interests of two or more businesses in a particular sector or area,
and for this purpose "business" has the meaning it bears in section 210'.[72]

Consultation procedure

4.70 The Enterprise Act 2002 (Part 8 Request for Consultation) Order 2003,
SI 2003/1375 covers how the initial request for consultation should be made. It
deals with:

---

[72]   EA 2002, s 214(4B).

- method of communication: by postal, electronic or personal service;[73]
- the address for service;[74]
- the person to whom an initial request for consultation should be addressed;[75] and
- the deemed date of receipt of the request.[76]

4.71 It is suggested that the letter initiating consultation should:

- tell the trader in the clearest terms that the letter is instituting consultation pursuant to Part 8 of the EA 2002. Something along the following lines might be appropriate:

    'You should treat this letter as a request for consultation pursuant to section 214 of the Enterprise Act 2002 and The Enterprise Act 2002 (Part 8 Request for Consultation) Order 2003.'

    'By virtue of section 214(4) (a) of the Act, the need for consultation will cease to apply 14 days after receipt of this letter. I would therefore be grateful to receive a substantive response from you by no later than 5pm on [...], failing which this Authority will apply to the High Court for an Enforcement Order without further notice.'

- detail the infringements or breaches that are alleged, so as to enable the trader to know the nature of the case against him. That should be done with as much precision as possible, always remembering that the particulars of the breaches can subsequently be used when drafting the pleadings;
- specify the changes in the trader's conduct or practices that the authority requires in order to achieve the cessation of the infringement and to prevent its recurrence or, in the case of a Community infringement, to ensure that the anticipated infringement does not occur. It is useful to append to the letter draft undertakings to be signed by the trader covering those changes;
- explain the enforcer's powers in the event that the trader declines to change his conduct;
- always offer further reasonable discussion;
- specify when the duty to consult will end.

4.72 The precise form of words in the request will need to be adjusted according to the nature of the trader, local policies and individual preference. The appropriateness of consultation is linked closely to the size and nature of the trader's organisation. A sole trader is responsible for everything that happens in his business. A local manager of a national chain may well break the

---

[73] Article 4.
[74] Article 5.
[75] Article 6.
[76] Article 7.

law but consultation solely with him is not likely to satisfy the need for appropriate consultation with the corporation. Discovering at an early stage the trader's organisational structure will help in deciding how consultation should be handled.

4.73 Three further points are worth making. First, given the stage of the enforcement process, it is probably unnecessary to enter into any prolonged argument as to whether an infringement has occurred or is likely to occur or recur. The enforcer will already be satisfied about those matters, otherwise he would not have commenced consultation. Second, it should always be remembered that consultation is an *attempt* to achieve cessation. Success, while desirable, cannot always be achieved. An enforcer should not spend an inordinate amount of time and valuable resources in trying to achieve a positive response where such a result is unlikely. Third, it is not the enforcer's job to run or re-model the trader's business.

Dispensing with consultation

4.74 Where a matter of extreme urgency arises and there is no time to engage with the trader or engagement is seen as pointless, the enforcer should ask the CMA for a waiver under s 214(3) of the EA 2002 and make an application to court without further delay. There needs to be a clear and immediate danger of serious consumer harm followed by a prompt application to court. Even where there is some urgency, it is usually best to attempt to engage with the trader, if at all possible.

Undertakings to the enforcer

4.75 By virtue of the provisions of s 219(1) of the EA 2002, an enforcer, if he has power to make an application for an enforcement order, may accept an undertaking from the trader.

4.76 The concept of an 'undertaking' is familiar to all lawyers practising in the civil courts. It means simply 'a promise'. While an undertaking to the court has all the force of an injunction or order of the court, this is a different legal concept, namely a statutory undertaking given to the enforcer. Breach of an undertaking given to the court is punishable as a contempt of court. Failure to comply with an undertaking given to an enforcer has no immediate sanction. However, following any breach, the enforcer may make an application to the court for an enforcement order or for an interim enforcement order and it is suggested that, in those circumstances, the court is likely to grant such an order without the need for much, if any, additional evidence.[77]

4.77 An undertaking may be accepted from any trader who the enforcer believes has engaged or is engaging in conduct which constitutes an

---

[77] By the EA 2002, s 217(4) the court must have regard to whether the trader has failed to comply with an undertaking given to the enforcer.

infringement or is likely to engage in conduct which constitutes a Community infringement.[78] Thus, like the duty to consult, the power to accept an undertaking should be exercised at the end of the investigative process, when the enforcer is satisfied that an infringement has occurred or is occurring or, in the case of a Community infringement, is likely to occur.

4.78 There is no duty on the enforcer to accept an undertaking if one is offered. He has an absolute discretion whether or not to do so. However, if, during or after the consultation period, the trader agrees (or promises) to refrain from the infringing or potentially infringing conduct, it seems unlikely that an enforcer would then seek an enforcement order from the court. If an undertaking were to be offered but refused and if the enforcer then applied to the court for an enforcement order, which was granted in substantially the same terms as the undertaking offered by the trader, the enforcer would find himself at risk of an adverse costs' order. If no undertaking is given, then the only avenue open to the enforcer for redress is the court. There should therefore be an expectation on the part of the enforcer that, if undertakings are refused, then an application to court will be made promptly.

4.79 The undertaking is that the trader will not continue or repeat the conduct,[79] of which complaint is made, will not engage in such conduct in the course of his business or another business, and will not consent to, or connive in, the carrying out of such conduct by a body corporate with which he has a special relationship.[80] It is preferable for the trader's undertaking to cover all three limbs (where applicable) but it is probably sufficient if it covers any one of them.

4.80 Paragraph 7 of Sch 7 to the CRA 2015 introduces new sub-sections into s 219 of the EA 2002, which provide that the person giving an undertaking may include a further undertaking to take enhanced consumer measures within the period specified in the undertaking and to provide information or documents to the enforcer to enable the enforcer to determine if the person is taking those measures. Such an undertaking can be given only to a public body unless a private designated enforcer has satisfied the conditions set out in s 219C.[81]

4.81 There is no formality required by the EA 2002. In theory, an undertaking could be given orally, although issues of proof might then arise. Again, in theory, there is no reason why an exchange of correspondence between enforcer and trader should not amount to an undertaking, if, on its proper construction, the correspondence amounts to an agreement or promise on the part of the trader to refrain from doing that which the statute requires him to refrain from doing. However, a degree of formality is probably preferable. It is suggested that a written document should be prepared by the enforcer identifying the

---

[78] EA 2002, s 219(3).
[79] That limb does not apply in the case of future conduct likely to amount to a Community infringement: see EA 2002, s 219(5).
[80] EA 2002, s 219(4).
[81] See above.

infringing, or potentially infringing, conduct and setting out the trader's agreement to refrain from continuing or repeating such conduct. The trader should then be invited to sign the document.

4.82 Earlier editions of this book suggested that possible difficulties could arise when the enforcer wished to require some positive steps to be taken by the trader and it was suggested that the solution might be for the trader to undertake to refrain from the infringing conduct unless he took the positive steps required. However, it is now considered that such difficulties are unlikely to arise, given the provisions in the CRA 2015 relating to enhanced consumer measures.[82] One such measure, falling within the compliance category, is directed at preventing or reducing the risk of the occurrence or repetition of the impugned conduct. That provision, it is submitted, would enable an enforcer to accept an undertaking requiring the trader to take the positive steps required by the enforcer.

INFORMATION GATHERING POWERS

4.83 Originally, ss 224 to 227F of the EA 2002 under the rubric 'information' set out the information gathering powers available to enforcers. Those sections have now been entirely repealed.[83] A new s 223A headed 'Investigatory Powers' has been inserted into the EA 2002. It reads:

> For the investigatory powers available to enforcers for the purposes of enforcers' functions under this Part, see Schedule 5 of the Consumer Rights Act 2015.[84]

Notices

CMA

4.84 Paragraphs 13 and 14 of Sch 5 to the CRA 2015, enable the CMA and other enforcers to give notice to a person requiring that person to provide the enforcer with the information specified in the notice.

4.85 The power of the CMA would be exercisable:

(a) to enable the Authority to exercise or to consider whether to exercise any function it has under Part 8 of the EA 2002;

(b) to enable a private designated enforcer to consider whether to exercise any function it has under that Part;

(c) to enable a Community enforcer to consider whether to exercise any function it has under that Part;

(d) to ascertain whether a person has complied with or is complying with an enforcement order or an interim enforcement order;

---

[82] See further below.
[83] CRA 2015, Sch 6, paras 67–77.
[84] CRA 2015, Sch 6, para 78.

(e)   to ascertain whether a person has complied with or is complying with an undertaking given under s 217(9), 218(10) or 219 of the EA 2002.

Other enforcers

4.86   The power of a public designated enforcer, a local weights and measures authority in Great Britain, the Department of Enterprise, Trade and Investment in Northern Ireland or an EU enforcer other than the CMA would be exercisable:

(a)   to enable that enforcer to exercise or to consider whether to exercise any function it has under Part 8 of the EA 2002;

(b)   to ascertain whether a person has complied with or is complying with an enforcement order or an interim enforcement order made on the application of that enforcer;

(c)   to ascertain whether a person has complied with or is complying with an undertaking given under s 217(9) or 218(10) of the EA 2002 following such an application;

(d)   to ascertain whether a person has complied with or is complying with an undertaking given to that enforcer under s 219 of that Act.

4.87   An 'EU enforcer' is defined[85] as the CMA, a local weights and measures authority in Great Britain, the Department of Enterprise, Trade and Investment in Northern Ireland, the FCA, the CAA, the Secretary of State, the Department of Health, Social Services and Public Safety in Northern Ireland, the Office of Communications, an enforcement authority within the meaning of s 120(15) of the Communications Act 2003 (regulation of premium rate services) and the Information Commissioner.

Form

4.88   Under para 15 of Sch 5 to the CRA 2015, the following provisions as to the form of the notice apply:

(1) The notice ... must be in writing and specify the purpose for which the information is required.

(2) If the purpose is to enable a person to exercise or to consider whether to exercise a function, the notice must specify the function concerned.

(3) The notice may specify –

    (a)   the time within which and the manner in which the person to whom it is given must comply with it;

    (b)   the form in which information must be provided.

(4) The notice may require –

---

[85]   CRA 2015, Sch 5, para 4.

(a) the creation of documents, or documents of a description, specified in the notice;

(b) the provision of those documents to the enforcer.

4.89 There is a saving provision which excuses a person from providing any information or creating any document which he would be entitled to refuse to provide or produce:

(a) in proceedings in the High Court on the grounds of legal professional privilege; or

(b) in proceedings in the Court of Session on the grounds of confidentiality of communications.[86]

4.90 A typical notice might read:

'NOTICE

This is a Notice given under paragraphs 14 and 15 of Schedule 5 to the Consumer Rights Act 2015.

X County Council ('the Council'), being a local weights and measures authority in Great Britain, requires you to provide it with the information and the documents specified in this Notice within seven days of receipt of this Notice. The information should be given in writing addressed to: [name and address of officer]

The Council requires the specified information for the purposes of determining whether or not it should exercise any of the following functions that it has under the Act against you, namely:

• Engage in appropriate consultation pursuant to section 214 of the Enterprise Act 2002 ('the Act').
• Apply for an Enforcement Order pursuant to section 215 of the Act.
• Accept undertakings pursuant to section 219 of the Act.

Information Required

Please specify in writing _____ [set out precisely the information required]

Please produce the following documents _____.

Note: you need not provide any information or produce any document which you would be entitled to refuse to provide or produce in proceedings in the High Court on the grounds of legal professional privilege.

You should be aware that failure to comply with this notice may lead to the council making an application to the court seeking an order compelling your compliance. Should such an application be necessary you may be required to meet all, or part, of the costs or expenses incurred by the council in that application.'

---

[86] CRA 2015, Sch 5, para 15(6).

The person to be served

4.91 In order to exercise or to consider whether to exercise the specified functions set out in paragraph 13 or to ascertain the specified matters set out in paragraph 13, the enforcer may serve a notice on any person, not just the trader who is the subject of the enquiry. For example, if the enforcer was concerned to discover details of a trader's bank account, his bank could be served with a notice seeking appropriate information, including the production of his bank statements.[87]

Enforcement

4.92 The only means of enforcing the notice is to apply to the court for an order.[88] If the court is satisfied that the person on whom the notice was served has failed to comply with it, the court may require that person to do anything the court thinks it is reasonable for him to do for any of the purposes for which the notice was given to ensure that the notice is complied with.[89] The court has power to order the person in default or, if that person is a company, partnership or unincorporated association, an official who is responsible for the failure, to pay the costs or expenses of the application.

Further powers

4.93 Part 4 of Sch 5 to the CRA 2015 is entitled 'Further Powers Exercisable by Domestic Enforcers and EU Enforcers'. As far as the present Chapter is concerned, the further powers exercisable by EU enforcers[90] are important.

4.94 The further powers given to an EU enforcer are:

(1) Under para 21, the power to purchase products (which includes a power to inspect any product).

(2) Under para 22, the power to enter premises to which the public has access in order to observe the carrying on of a business on those premises.

(3) Under para 23, the power to enter premises[91] without a warrant at any reasonable time.

    In the case of a routine inspection, the officer must give two days' notice in writing of his intention to enter, setting out why the entry is necessary and indicating the offence of obstruction.

    If the officer reasonably considers that to give notice would defeat the purpose of the entry or that it is not reasonably practicable in all the circumstances to give notice, in particular because the officer reasonably suspects that there is an imminent risk to public health or safety, then he

---

[87]   Such statements would not be protected by legal professional privilege.

[88]   CRA 2015, Sch 5, para 16.

[89]   CRA 2015, Sch 5, para 16(2) and (3).

[90]   As defined in para 4 of Sch 5 to the CRA 2015 above.

[91]   As with the former power under the EA 2002, no authority is given to enter premises used wholly or mainly as a dwelling.

has power to enter without prior notice but must produce a document to anyone on the premises setting out why entry is necessary and explaining the offence of obstruction.

The powers available to an enforcer, once he has lawfully obtained entry into premises, arguably include the power to search for goods and documents.[92]

(4) Under para 25, the power to inspect any product on the premises (including the power to examine any procedure connected with the production of a product).

(5) Under para 31, for the purpose of exercising the powers to seize and detain goods and documents,[93] the power to require a person with authority to do so to break open any container, open any vending machine, or access any electronic device in which information may be stored or from which it may be accessed. If the person fails to comply, the officer has the power to take any of those steps himself.

'Document' is widely defined as including 'information recorded in any form'.[94] Thus, information electronically recorded and stored would fall within that definition.

(6) Under para 32, the power to enter premises[95] with a warrant issued by a justice of the peace.[96]

The warrant[97] may be issued if the justice of the peace considers that there are reasonable grounds for believing that:

- there are, on the premises, products which an officer of the enforcer has power to inspect or documents which an officer of the enforcer could require a person to produce; or
- there has been or is about to be a Community infringement or there has been a failure to comply with an enforcement order, an interim enforcement order or an undertaking given to the court;

and either

- access to the premises has been or is likely to be refused, and notice of the enforcer's intention to apply for a warrant has been given to the occupier of the premises; or
- it is likely that products or documents on the premises would be concealed or interfered with if notice of entry on the premises were given to the occupier of the premises; or

---

[92] See *R (on the application of Vuciterni) v Brent Magistrates' Court* [2012] EWHC 2140 (Admin) at [48].
[93] Under paras 28 or 29 – see below.
[94] CRA 2015, Sch 5, para 8.
[95] Note that in this case, 'premises' does not exclude a dwelling.
[96] Sheriff in Scotland and lay magistrate in Northern Ireland.
[97] 'It must never be forgotten that the granting of a warrant is a most extreme and invasive kind of order, not to be granted without great caution and dependent on appropriate full and accurate disclosure by the applicant': see *R (on the application of Vuciterni) v Brent Magistrates' Court* [2012] EWHC 2140 (Admin) at [35]. The warrant may be quashed on an application for judicial review.

- the premises are unoccupied, or the occupier of the premises is absent, and it might defeat the purpose of the entry to wait for the occupier's return.

All the material necessary to justify the grant of the warrant should be contained in the information provided on the application form, which must identify which of the conditions specified in para 32 is being relied on by the applicant. If the magistrate requires any further information in order to be satisfied that the issue of a warrant is justified, a note should be made of additional information provided orally, so that there exists a proper record of the full basis upon which the warrant has been granted. Where further documents were considered that also had to be recorded.[98]

(7) Under para 33, where a warrant has been issued under the previous paragraph, the power to enter the premises at any reasonable time, using reasonable force if necessary.

(8) Under para 34, where an officer has entered premises with or without a warrant, the power to require any person on the premises to provide such assistance or information as the officer reasonably considers necessary.

The powers given under (1)–(8) above may be exercised by an EU enforcer for any purpose relating to the functions that the enforcer has under Part 8 of the EA 2002 in its capacity as a CPC enforcer provided that the enforcer reasonably suspects:

(a) that there has been, or is likely to be, a Community infringement;

(b) a failure to comply with an enforcement order or an interim enforcement order made on the application of that enforcer;

(c) a failure to comply with an undertaking given to the court; or

(d) a failure to comply with an undertaking given to that enforcer.[99]

(9) Under para 27, the power, at any reasonable time, to require a trader occupying the premises or a person on the premises acting on behalf of such a trader, to produce any documents relating to the trader's business to which the trader has access, and to take copies of, or of any entry in, any such document.

That power includes power to require the person to give an explanation of the documents.

There is a saving in respect of anything which the person could refuse to produce on grounds of legal professional privilege or confidentiality of communications.

The power given under (9) above may be exercised by an EU enforcer for any purpose relating to the functions that the enforcer has under Part 8 of the EA 2002 in its capacity as a CPC enforcer provided that the enforcer reasonably suspects:

(a) that there has been, or is likely to be, a Community infringement,

(b) a failure to comply with an enforcement order or an interim enforcement order made on the application of that enforcer,

(c) a failure to comply with an undertaking given to the court or

---

[98] *R (Redknapp) v Commissioner of the City of London Police* [2009] 1 WLR 2091; *Hargreaves v Brecknock and Radnorshire Magistrates Court* [2015] Crim LR 999.

[99] CRA 2015, Sch 5, para 20(2) and (3).

(d)   a failure to comply with an undertaking given to that enforcer.

Alternatively, it may be exercised in order to ascertain whether the documents may be required as evidence in proceedings under Part 8 of the EA 2002.[100]

(10) Under para 28, the power to seize and detain goods other than documents.

The power given under (10) above may be exercised by an EU enforcer in relation to goods which the officer reasonably suspects may disclose (by means of testing or otherwise) a Community infringement or a failure to comply an enforcement order, an interim enforcement order or an undertaking given to the court or to the enforcer; or may be required as evidence in proceedings under Part 8 of the Enterprise Act 2002.[101]

(11) Under para 29, the power to seize and detain documents.

There is a saving in respect of anything which the person could refuse to produce on grounds of legal professional privilege or confidentiality of communications.

The power given under (11) above may be exercised by an EU enforcer in relation to documents which an officer of the enforcer reasonably suspects may be required as evidence in proceedings under Part 8 of the EA 2002.[102]

(12) Under para 45, there is also the express power for a local authority to bring civil proceedings in relation to infringements occurring outside the local authority's area.

TOWARDS AN ENFORCEMENT NOTICE

Consultation

4.95 Unless the CMA has dispensed with the need for consultation, an enforcer cannot apply for an enforcement order until appropriate consultation has been undertaken with the trader and, as originally drafted, with the CMA. However, as a result of the Public Bodies (The Office of Fair Trading Transfer of Consumer Advice Scheme Function and Modification of Enforcement Functions) Order 2013, SI 2013/783, Part 8 enforcers, other than the CMA are no longer required to consult with the CMA before they make an application for an enforcement order. Instead, those enforcers are required to notify the CMA that they are making an application. No application for an enforcement notice (or an interim enforcement notice) may be made until 14 days (or seven days) after the giving of such notice.[103]

---

[100] CRA 2015, Sch 5, para 20(4).
[101] CRA 2015, Sch 5, para 20(5).
[102] CRA 2015, Sch 5, para 20(6).
[103] EA 2002, s 214(1).

Which court?

England and Wales

4.96 Courts having jurisdiction are the High Court or the county court[104] if the person against whom the order is sought carries on business or has a place of business in England and Wales.[105]

4.97 It is suggested that proceedings should be commenced in the Chancery Division of the High Court for serious cases and in the county court for less serious cases.

Scotland

4.98 Courts having jurisdiction in Scotland are the Court of Session or the sheriff if the person against whom the order is sought carries on business or has a place of business in Scotland.[106]

4.99 Again, it is suggested that proceedings should be commenced in the Court of Session for serious cases and before the sheriff for less serious cases.

Northern Ireland

4.100 Courts having jurisdiction in Northern Ireland are the High Court or a county court if the person against whom the order is sought carries on business or has a place of business in Northern Ireland.

Parties

Claimant

4.101 The enforcer, rather than the investigating officer, will be the claimant. Thus, for example, a local authority trading standards officer, investigating an infringement on behalf of his authority, will institute proceedings in the name of that authority, not in his own name. The officer should ensure that he is authorised to commence proceedings in the name of his authority.

4.102 If an application for an enforcement order is made by a Community enforcer, the court may examine whether the purpose[107] of the enforcer justifies its making the application. If the court concludes that there is no such justification, then it may refuse the application on that ground alone.[108]

---

[104] Part 2 of the Crime and Courts Act 2013 amended the County Courts Act 1984 by establishing in England and Wales a court called 'the county court' for the purposes of exercising the jurisdiction and powers previously conferred on the several individual county courts.

[105] EA 2002, s 215(5).

[106] EA 2002, s 215(5).

[107] The purpose of the enforcer is to be construed by reference to the Injunctions Directive: see s EA 2002, s 215(8).

[108] EA 2002, s 215(6) and (7).

4.103 If the application is made by an enforcer other than the CMA, then that enforcer must notify the CMA of the result of the application.[109]

Defendant

4.104 The trader, who may be a sole trader or a limited company, should be the defendant. Part 8 makes specific provision for bodies corporate, including limited liability companies. It is obvious that the separate legal personality of such bodies could be used as a device to evade the requirements of the EA 2002. Consequently Part 8 allows corporate personality to be disregarded, by permitting enforcement orders to be made against persons such as directors and controlling shareholders who consent to or connive in conduct that amounts to a domestic or Community infringement.[110] Thus, if the trader is a limited company, consideration should be given to joining a natural person, such as the company's director, as a defendant instead of, or in addition to, the company.

4.105 Under the heading 'accessories', s 222 of the EA 2002 provides that, if the conduct that constitutes the infringement takes place with the consent or connivance of a person who has a special relationship with the body corporate, the consent or connivance is also conduct which constitutes the infringement. It is suggested that 'consent' means nothing more than 'approval'. Thus, consent could be established by proving that the person positively authorised the infringing conduct or, knowing of it, failed to take any steps to prevent it in circumstances where he should have taken such steps. It is suggested that 'connivance' could be established by proving some involvement, responsibility, collusion or participation in the infringing conduct.

4.106 Section 222 provides that:

> (3) A person has a special relationship with a body corporate if he is –
>
> (a) a controller of the body corporate, or
> (b) a director, manager, secretary or other similar officer of the body corporate or a person purporting to act in such a capacity.
>
> (4) A person is a controller of a body corporate if –
>
> (a) the directors of the body corporate or of another body corporate which is its controller are accustomed to act in accordance with the person's directions or instructions, or
> (b) either alone or with an associate or associates[111] he is entitled to exercise or control the exercise of one third or more of the voting power at any general meeting of the body corporate or of another body corporate which is its controller.

4.107 There is inevitably a director or other 'controller' who is the directing mind of the company and the person who ultimately controls the manner in which the trading is carried on. As a general rule, that person should be made a

---

[109] EA 2002, s 215(9).
[110] Per Lord Drummond-Young in *OFT v MB Designs (Scotland) Ltd* [2005] SLT 69 at [8].
[111] For definitions of 'associates' see EA 2002, s 222(10)–(13).

defendant, either alone or with the corporate body. An order may be made against an accessory even if no order is made against the body corporate. Similarly, the accessory may give an undertaking either to the enforcer or to the court, even though no such undertaking is taken from the body corporate.[112] Thus, it is quite acceptable to pursue enforcement action against an accessory alone without also taking action against the corporate body with which he has a special relationship.

4.108 There are a number of reasons why accessories should be named as defendants:

- it is worth remembering that enforcement orders against, or undertakings from, the corporate body alone will be worthless if the company is subsequently wound up;
- in most cases, it is the accessories that are ultimately responsible for the infringing conduct and often, unless restrained, they will continue to repeat the conduct under other corporate guises. Many traders engage in what is commonly known as 'phoenixing' as a tactic in order to avoid enforcement action.

4.109 Section 223 deals with the case where defendant is a body corporate which is a member of a group of interconnected bodies corporate. In that case, the court is empowered to order that its order is binding upon all of the members of the group.

The CMA

4.110 Note the power of the CMA under s 216 of the EA 2002 to direct that any application for an enforcement order must be made by the CMA itself or by such other enforcer as it directs.

Interim relief

4.111 Even before a claim form has been issued, an enforcer may apply to the court for interim relief in the form of an interim enforcement order.

Interim enforcement order

4.112 Section 218 of the EA 2002 empowers the court to make an interim enforcement order provided four conditions are satisfied:

(a) it is alleged that the defendants are engaged in conduct which constitutes a domestic or Community infringement or are likely to engage in conduct which constitutes a Community infringement;

(b) if the application had been an application for an enforcement order it is likely that it would have been granted;

---

[112] See EA 2002, s 222(5)–(7).

(c) it is expedient that the conduct is prohibited or prevented (as the case may be) immediately;

(d) if no notice of the application has been given to the person named in the application, it is appropriate to make an interim enforcement order without notice.

4.113 The first condition speaks for itself and is unlikely to cause difficulties. It is sufficient that the enforcer is making the necessary allegation.

4.114 As to the second condition, two points can be made:

* given that the court is dealing with a paper application for interim relief where the evidence has not been tested by cross-examination, it manifestly cannot embark on a full trial of the issues. It is suggested that the approach of the court should be as follows: is it more likely than not that, on the evidence presently before the court, a final enforcement order would be made;[113]

* in the absence of specific references either to the 'serious issue to be tried' or to the 'balance of convenience' tests used in applications for interim injunctions,[114] it is probably preferable to approach the grant of an interim enforcement order without reference to those authorities that deal with the grant of interim injunction.[115]

4.115 The third condition requires the enforcer to establish some urgency in the matter – for example, because of the serious and immediate harm being caused or likely to be caused to consumers. The other side of the coin is that, if there has been delay in enforcement action on the part of the enforcer, an interim enforcement order is unlikely to be granted.

4.116 The fourth condition is considered in further detail in the following section. However, it is suggested that, if the court is not satisfied that the application should have been made without notice, then, rather than dismissing it, the court may decide to adjourn the hearing to enable proper notice to be given.

Procedure[116]

4.117 An interim enforcement order can be granted at any time before the grant of a final enforcement order.[117] It can be granted before the claim form has been issued. As a general rule, notice of the hearing should be given to the

---

[113] See *OFT v MB Designs (Scotland) Ltd* [2005] SLT 69 at [21].

[114] See *American Cyanamid Co v Ethicon Ltd* [1975] AC 396, particularly per Lord Diplock at 406–409.

[115] A similar view appears to have been taken by Lord Drummond-Young in *OFT v MB Designs (Scotland) Ltd* [2005] SLT 69 at [20].

[116] Any procedural issues not covered by the statute should be answered by reference to Parts 23 and 25 of the Civil Procedure Rules 1998 ('the CPR').

[117] EA 2002, s 218(5).

trader.[118] However, an application can be made without notice. Helpful guidance as to when an application can be made without notice is given in the Chancery Guide February 2016('the CG'). Paragraph 16.4 suggests that there are four classes of case that are exceptions to the general requirement to give notice. Three are relevant to an interim enforcement notice:

'(a) where the giving of notice might frustrate the order;
(b) where there is such urgency that it is truly not possible to give the requisite notice. Even in such a case, however, the applicant should give the respondent informally as much notice of the application as is possible;
(c) where the applicant cannot identify the respondent by name but only by description.'

4.118 An application must be lodged with the court (and served on the defendant, if notice is given). Practice Form N244[119] should be used, either alone or in conjunction with a witness statement. The application:

- must state why the application is being made. The facts of the case, as they are understood by the investigating officer, should be set out in full (preferably in a witness statement). It is on the basis of that evidence that the court will decide whether 'if the application had been an application for an enforcement order it is likely that it would have been granted';

- must make the fullest disclosure. In other words, those facts adverse to the application as well as those in its favour must be given. That is particularly important when the application is made without notice. Section 218(6) of the EA 2002 expressly provides:

    'An application for an interim enforcement order must refer to all matters –

    (a) which are known to the applicant, and
    (b) which are material to the question whether or not the application is granted.'

- if the application is made without notice, must explain why no notice has been given;[120]

- should set out the order that the enforcer is asking the court to make. It is usual to attach a draft order to the application form;

- if a claim form has not yet been issued, draft particulars of claim can (and probably should, if there is sufficient time to draft them) be exhibited to the witness statement.

---

[118] Normally three clear days' notice to the other party is required but in an emergency or for other good reason the application can be made without giving the full 3 days' notice. In the Chancery Division, permission to serve on short notice may be obtained on application without notice to the interim applications judge: see para 16.9 of Chancery Guide, as amended.
[119] All practice forms can be downloaded from www.justice.gov.uk/courts/procedure-rules/civil/forms.
[120] EA 2002, s 218(7).

4.119 A subsequent application may be made by the enforcer or the trader to vary or discharge the order.[121]

Order

4.120 The court has a discretion whether or not to grant an interim enforcement order. It is suggested that the greater the urgency and potential harm to consumers, the more likely that the court will grant an order.

4.121 An interim enforcement order must:

(a) indicate the nature of the alleged conduct; and

(b) direct the person not to continue or to repeat the conduct;[122] not to engage in such conduct in the course of his business or another business; and not to consent to or connive in the carrying out of such conduct by a body corporate with which he has a special relationship.[123]

4.122 However, if the order is made against an accessory alone, instead of paragraph (b) above, the order must direct the person not to continue or repeat the conduct;[124] in the course of any business carried on by him, not to engage in conduct such as that which constitutes the infringement committed by the body corporate; and not consent to or connive in the carrying out of such conduct by another body corporate with which he has a special relationship.[125]

4.123 An interim enforcement order will be expressed to last either until a specified date or until further order of the court or until the date of the full hearing. If the interim order was made without notice, it will usually contain a provision that the order will last for a limited period only – usually not more than 7 days. The enforcer will be then be required to give the trader notice of his intention to apply to the court at the expiration of that period for the order to be continued. In the meantime the trader will be entitled to apply, though generally only after giving notice to the enforcer, for the order to be varied or discharged.

Undertaking

4.124 Instead of making an order, the court may accept an undertaking from the trader in the terms of paragraph (b) above or alternatively an undertaking that he will take such steps as the court believes will secure his compliance with that paragraph.[126] Breach of an undertaking given to the court potentially has

---

[121] EA 2002, s 218(8).

[122] Unless the allegation is that the trader is likely to engage in conduct which constitutes a Community infringement, in which case the inclusion of this clause is meaningless and should be omitted.

[123] EA 2002, s 218(2) and (3).

[124] See fn 121 above.

[125] EA 2002, s 222(9).

[126] EA 2002, s 218(10).

more serious consequences than breach of an undertaking given to an enforcer. In the former case, the trader will be in contempt of court and liable to imprisonment, a fine or sequestration of his assets.[127]

Penal notice

4.125 The interim enforcement order and the undertaking should be endorsed with a penal notice in Form N77 explaining the consequence of disobedience.

Cross undertaking as to damages

4.126 Normally an applicant for an interim injunction is required to give the court a cross undertaking as to damages, generally in something like the following terms:

> And upon [the Claimant] undertaking to comply with any order that this court may make, if the court later finds that the order for an interim injunction has caused loss to [the defendant] and decides that [the defendant] should be compensated for that loss.

4.127 Leaving aside the question whether, as a matter of principle, it should ever be right to order cross-undertakings in the case of an interim enforcement order, it is now settled law that a public authority seeking to enforce the law in the interests of the public generally, often in pursuance of a public duty to do so, and enjoying only the resources which have been assigned to it for its functions, generally does not have to give such an undertaking.[128]

Costs schedule

4.128 This being an interlocutory application and unlikely to last more than one day, each side should serve on the other a written statement of its costs not less than 24 hours before the date fixed for the hearing.[129] At the conclusion of the hearing, the judge will decide what costs order to make and may summarily assess those costs on the basis of the written statement of costs before him.

Particulars of claim

4.129 The first step in proceedings is to issue a claim form.[130] Particulars of claim can, and preferably should, be served with the claim form. If not, they may be served separately 14 days after service of the claim form.[131]

---

[127] Contempt of court is dealt with below.
[128] See *Kirklees Metropolitan BC v Wickes Building Supplies Ltd* [1993] AC 227 and *FSA v Barclays Bank Ltd* [2013] UKSC 11.
[129] See subsection 9 of CPR, Practice Direction 44. The statement of costs should follow as closely as possible Form N260.
[130] See generally Part 7 of the CPR: practice form N1 must be used.
[131] See CPR, r 7.4.

4.130 The particulars of claim must include a concise statement of the facts on which the claimant relies and such other matters as may be set out in a Practice Direction.[132] In the case of an application for an enforcement order, the particulars of claim should include details of the infringement or infringements alleged and conclude with a request for the grant of an enforcement order, specifying the terms of the order sought.

Defence

4.131 CPR, r 16.5 provides:

(1) In his defence, the defendant must state –

(a)   which of the allegations in the particulars of claim he denies;
(b)   which allegations he is unable to admit or deny, but which he requires the claimant to prove; and
(c)   which allegations he admits.

(2) Where the defendant denies an allegation –

(a)   he must state his reasons for doing so; and
(b)   if he intends to put forward a different version of events from that given by the claimant, he must state his own version.

Reply

4.132 The claimant may serve a reply to the defence if he wishes to allege facts in answer to the defence which were not included in his particulars of claim.

Further interlocutory steps

4.133 Once pleadings are closed, there are further interlocutory steps that must or could be taken. They include:

- Directions as to the course of hearing. Although a case management conference may be held at any time during the course of the proceedings, it is usually held at an early stage when directions will be given such as, for example, a timetable and orders for the exchange of witness statements, for disclosure and for expert evidence.[133]

- The filing and exchange of cost budgets, following which a costs management conference may be convened and a costs management order made.[134] Once a costs management order has been made the court, when assessing costs on the standard basis, will have regard to the receiving

---

[132] See CPR, r 16.4. Para 8.2 of Practice Direction 16 – Statements of Case – requires, *inter alia*, that details be given of any allegation of fraud, the fact of any illegality, details of any misrepresentation, notice or knowledge of a fact and details of wilful default.

[133] See CPR, r 3.1 for the court's general powers of management and r 3.1A in the case of an unrepresented party.

[134] See CPR, rr 3.12–3.18 for Costs Management.

party's last approved or agreed budget for each phase of the proceedings and will not depart from it unless satisfied that there is good reason to do so.

- Applications for interim or interlocutory orders.[135]
- Disclosure and inspection of documents. The recent amendments to the CPR on disclosure alter considerably the extent of disclosure.[136]
- Exchange of witness statements, each verified by a statement of truth.[137]
- Obtaining the Court's permission to call expert evidence.[138]

Evidence from consumers

4.134 Is it essential that one or more consumers be called to testify? The short answer, it is suggested, is no.

In *OFT v MB Designs (Scotland) Ltd*[139] Lord Drummond-Young said:[140]

> 'In relation to the evidence, harm to the collective interests of consumers will normally be inferred from an accumulation of individual instances. Evidence relating to those individual instances will generally be provided, however, by officials of the relevant enforcer, such as the present petitioner, or officials in the trading standards departments of local authorities. That is appropriate because it is the collective interests that are relevant, and the individual instances are only adminicles of evidence that go to establish harm to the collective interests.'

4.135 The latter passage is of some practical importance. It is unnecessary in every instance for the enforcer to take numerous statements from individual dissatisfied consumers with a view to presenting them at the hearing. It is sufficient for the enforcer to present the evidence of harm to the collective interests of consumers in whatever manner seems most appropriate in the circumstances. That may be from his own and his colleagues' observations; from consumer complaints whether made orally or in writing; or from the direct evidence of the consumers themselves.

4.136 It is instructive to consider the evidence presented in the *MB Designs* case, the sufficiency of which was confirmed by Lord Drummond-Young. It took the form of two affidavits, although (certainly in England) it could have taken the form of two witness statements. One was from an officer of the OFT's Consumer Regulation Enforcement Division and one was from a Divisional Trading Standards Officer of South Lanarkshire Council. Those affidavits were backed up by documentation relating to individual complaints about defective products or services supplied by the trader. It appeared from the

---

135 See CPR, Part 23 for general rules about applications and Part 25 for applications for interim remedies.
136 See CPR, Part 31 and in particular CPR, r 31.5.
137 See CPR, Part 32.
138 See CPR, Part 35.
139 [2005] SLT 69.
140 At [15].

documentation that some of the complaints were investigated by independent third parties appointed or recommended by the Consumer and Trading Standards Department of South Lanarkshire Council and found to be justified; others were investigated by tradesmen or surveyors instructed by the householder concerned, or were backed up with photographs. The judge concluded:[141]

'In my opinion the fact that a significant number of complaints have been investigated or documented in this manner is important, because obviously ill-founded complaints are possible. In the present case, I am satisfied that the investigation of complaints relied on by the petitioner relates to a sufficiently large proportion to establish that those complaints are for the most part well-founded.'

It is significant that, in that particular case, no consumers gave evidence.

Factual claim

4.137 If an application for an enforcement order or an interim enforcement order is made in respect of a Community infringement involving a contravention of the Unfair Commercial Practices Directive (2005/29/EC) and if the trader has made a factual claim as part of his commercial practice,[142] the court has power to order the trader to provide evidence as to the accuracy of that claim. If he fails to do so or if he provides inadequate evidence, the court is entitled to infer that the claim was inaccurate.[143] That is a useful provision to be used, for example, to verify claims in a trader's advertising or promotional material.

The order

The statutory provisions

4.138 By s 217 of the EA 2002 (as amended by para 6 of Sch 7 to the CRA 2015):

(1) This section applies if an application for an enforcement order is made under section 215 and the court finds that the person named in the application has engaged in conduct which constitutes the infringement.

(2) This section also applies if such an application is made in relation to a Community infringement and the court finds that the person named in the application is likely to engage in conduct which constitutes the infringement.

(3) If this section applies the court may make an enforcement order against the person.

(4) In considering whether to make an enforcement order the court must have regard to whether the person named in the application –

---

[141] At [15].
[142] As defined in reg 2 of CPUTR.
[143] EA 2002, s 218A.

(a) has given an undertaking under section 219 in respect of conduct such as is mentioned in subsection (3) of that section;

(b) has failed to comply with the undertaking.

(5) An enforcement order must –

(a) indicate the nature of the conduct to which the finding under subsection (1) or (2) relates, and

(b) direct the person to comply with subsection (6).

(6) A person complies with this subsection if he –

(a) does not continue or repeat the conduct;

(b) does not engage in such conduct in the course of his business or another business;

(c) does not consent to or connive in the carrying out of such conduct by a body corporate with which he has a special relationship (within the meaning of section 222(3).

(7) But subsection (6) (a) does not apply in the case of a finding under subsection (2).

(8) An enforcement order may require a person against whom the order is made to publish in such form and manner and to such extent as the court thinks appropriate for the purpose of eliminating any continuing effects of the infringement –

(a) the order;

(b) a corrective statement.

(9) If the court makes a finding under subsection (1) or (2) it may accept an undertaking by the person –

(a) to comply with subsection (6), or

(b) to take steps which the court believes will secure that he complies with subsection (6).

(10) An undertaking under subsection (9) may include a further undertaking by the person to publish in such form and manner and to such extent as the court thinks appropriate for the purpose of eliminating any continuing effects of the infringement –

(a) the terms of the undertaking;

(b) a corrective statement.

(10A) An enforcement order may require a person against whom the order is made to take enhanced consumer measures (defined in section 219A) within a period specified by the court.

(10B) An undertaking under subsection (9) may include a further undertaking by the person to take enhanced consumer measures within a period specified in the undertaking.

(10C) Subsections (10A) and (10B) are subject to section 219C in a case where the application for the enforcement order was made by a designated enforcer which is not a public body.

(10D) Where a person is required by an enforcement order or an undertaking under this section to take enhanced consumer measures, the order or undertaking may include requirements as to the provision of information or documents to the court by the person in order that the court may determine if the person is taking those measures.

(11) If the court –

    (a)   makes a finding under subsection (1) or (2), and

    (b)   accepts an undertaking under subsection (9),

it must not make an enforcement order in respect of the infringement to which the undertaking relates.

(12) An enforcement order made by a court in one part of the United Kingdom has effect in any other part of the United Kingdom as if made by a court in that part.

4.139 Thus, if the court is satisfied that the person named in the application has engaged in conduct which constitutes the infringement or, in the case of a Community infringement, that the person named in the application is likely to engage in conduct which constitutes the infringement, it may grant an enforcement order. In other words, the court has a discretion whether or not to grant the order. In *OFT v Purely Creative Ltd*,[144] Briggs J said:

> 'Although the court's power to make an enforcement order is plainly discretionary, the Act gives no further guidance to the court beyond that set out in section 217(4) as to the matters which the court should take into account when deciding whether or not, and if so how, to exercise that discretion.'

4.140 Section 217(4) of the EA 2002 refers to the court's obligation to take into account whether the trader has given an undertaking to the enforcer and whether he has failed to comply with it.

The nature of the order

4.141 An enforcement order must (whether or not enhanced consumer measures are also imposed):

(a)   indicate the nature of the alleged conduct; and

(b)   direct the person not to continue or to repeat the conduct;[145] not to engage in such conduct in the course of his business or another business; and not to consent to or connive in the carrying out of such conduct by a body corporate with which he has a special relationship.[146]

4.142 However, if the order is made against an accessory alone, instead of paragraph (b) above, the order must direct the person not to continue or repeat the conduct; in the course of any business carried on by him, not to engage in

---

[144] [2011] EWHC 106 (Ch) at [25].

[145] Unless the allegation is that the trader is likely to engage in conduct which constitutes a Community infringement, in which case the inclusion of this clause is meaningless and should be omitted: see EA 2002, s 217(7).

[146] EA 2002, s 217(5) and (6).

conduct such as that which constitutes the infringement committed by the body corporate; and not consent to or connive in the carrying out of such conduct by another body corporate with which he has a special relationship.[147]

Enhanced consumer measures[148]

What are enhanced consumer measures?

4.143 Sections 219A–219C of the EA 2002[149] deal with enhanced consumer measures, which are intended to widen the scope of the measures that a court can impose and to permit the court on a case by case basis to determine the best way of dealing with a breach of the law. They apply only in relation to conduct which occurs, or which is likely to occur, after 1 October 2015 (the commencement of s 79 of the CRA 2015).[150] Section 219A(1) of the EA 2002 identifies three categories of enhanced consumer measures, namely:

- the redress category;
- the compliance category;
- the choice category.

The redress category

4.144 By s 219A(2) of the EA 2002, the measures in the redress category are:

> (a) measures offering compensation or other redress to consumers who have suffered loss as a result of the conduct which has given rise to the enforcement order or undertaking,
>
> (b) where the conduct referred to in paragraph (a) relates to a contract, measures offering such consumers the option to terminate (but not vary) that contract,
>
> (c) where such consumers cannot be identified, or cannot be identified without disproportionate cost to the subject of the enforcement order or undertaking, measures intended to be in the collective interests of consumers.

4.145 The redress category enables the court to make provision for compensation to consumers who have suffered loss as a result of the actions of a trader in breach of consumer law. Since the consumers will not be before the court as parties to the action, the order of the court should be directed at the trader ordering him to offer a quantified or quantifiable sum by way of compensation to those consumers who have suffered loss, for example, by purchasing certain products. It is submitted that the court will need to consider at least the following questions. Have consumers suffered loss as a result of the trader's infringement? How much loss have they suffered? How will consumers

---

[147] EA 2002, s 222(9).
[148] There is a useful guide published by the BIS in May 2015 entitled 'Enhanced Consumer Measures – Guidance for Enforcers of Consumer Law'.
[149] Added by CRA 2015, Sch 7, para 8.
[150] SI 2015/1630, para 3(e).

who have suffered loss be identified? How will consumers be contacted? How and when will the redress be paid? How will the measure be policed?

4.146 The court also has the option of permitting consumers to terminate a contract. For example, a consumer might have been misled as to the price of an annual subscription for certain services. They were advertised at one price but, after the consumer entered into the contract, the small print enabled the trader to debit more than the advertised price from the consumer's bank account. This measure allows the Court to offer the consumer the option to terminate the contract and, if he accepts that offer, to order that the contract be terminated. That approach would not preclude the court from also making provision for compensation.

4.147 The redress category allows the court to impose measures that are in the 'collective interest of consumers'. In circumstances where a trader has caused consumers loss, but it is impossible to identify some or all of the consumers who have been affected, the court could, for example, order the trader to pay the equivalent of the loss suffered to a consumer charity. Using measures that are in 'the collective interest of consumers' might also be appropriate when it is disproportionate for the trader to contact all the consumers who may have suffered loss, as might be the case where a large number of consumers suffered a small amount of loss.

The compliance category

4.148 By s 219A(3) of the EA 2002:

> The measures in the compliance category are measures intended to prevent or reduce the risk of the occurrence or repetition of the conduct to which the enforcement order or undertaking relates (including measures with that purpose which may have the effect of improving compliance with consumer law more generally).

4.149 A list of possible measures is not included in the legislation, but the BIS Guidance suggests such measures as a business having to sign up to the Primary Authority Scheme; having to appoint a compliance officer; having to update internal processes to ensure there is no repeat of the breach; or having to improve the training the business gives to its staff to ensure that there is no repeat of the breach.[151]

The choice category

4.150 By s 219A(4) of the EA 2002:

> The measures in the choice category are measures intended to enable consumers to choose more effectively between persons supplying or seeking to supply goods or services.

---

[151] See p 24 of the BIS Guidance 'Enhanced Consumer Measures – Guidance for Enforcers of Consumer Law'.

4.151   The assumption underlying this provision is that consumers, when exercising choice in a competitive market, are entitled to know something of a trader's history of compliance with consumer law. The choice category gives the court the flexibility to order the business to give consumers such information. This could include a business having to advertise on its website, in the press, on social media or in store its breach of the law and the steps taken to correct the breach and to prevent future breaches.

When can enhanced consumer measures be imposed?

4.152   There is an overarching discretion in the court to include such enhanced consumer measures as it considers just and reasonable.[152] However, in exercising its discretion, the court is bound to consider whether the proposed measures are proportionate, taking into account:

(a)   the likely benefit of the measures to consumers.

(b)   the costs likely to be incurred by the subject of the enforcement order or undertaking, such costs being the cost of the measures and the reasonable administrative costs associated with taking the measures, and

(c)   the likely cost to consumers of obtaining the benefit of the measures.[153]

4.153   Moreover, a court may only include enhanced consumer measures in the redress category:

(a)   in a case where the infringement has caused loss to consumers; and

(b)   if the court is satisfied that the cost of such measures (excluding the administrative costs associated with taking the measures) to the subject of the enforcement order or undertaking is unlikely to be more than the sum of the losses suffered by consumers as a result of the conduct which has given rise to the enforcement order or undertaking.[154]

Publication

4.154   In addition, the court can order the trader to publish the order, together with a corrective statement, in such form and manner and to such extent as the court thinks appropriate for the purpose of eliminating any continuing effects of the infringement.[155] Such publication is not an enhanced consumer measure.[156]

---

[152]   EA 2002, s 219B(1).

[153]   EA 2002, s 219B(2) and (3).

[154]   EA 2002, s 219B(4), (5) and (9).

[155]   EA 2002, s 217(8); see also Art 21(b) of the Injunctions Directive from which this provision is derived.

[156]   EA 2002, s 219A(5).

Undertaking

4.155 Instead of, but not in addition to, making an order, s 217(9) of the EA 2002 empowers the court to accept an undertaking from the trader to comply with subs (6), or to take steps which the court believes will secure that he complies with subs (6). That subsection requires the trader not to continue or to repeat the conduct complained of, not to engage in such conduct in the course of his business or another business, and not to consent to or connive in the carrying out of such conduct by a body corporate with which he has a special relationship. The undertaking may include a further undertaking by the person to take enhanced consumer measures within a period specified in the undertaking.[157] Additionally, the undertaking may include a further undertaking to publish the terms of the undertaking, together with a corrective statement, in such form and manner and to such extent as the court thinks appropriate for the purpose of eliminating any continuing effects of the infringement.[158]

Terms of the order

4.156 Under English law, an injunction whether interim or final, must state with precision what the defendant must or must not do if he is to avoid the peril of imprisonment for contempt of court.[159] A similar rule applies to interdicts in Scotland.[160]

4.157 Does the same rule apply to enforcement orders? In *OFT v MB Designs (Scotland) Ltd*[161] Lord Drummond-Young thought not:

'Where a trading standard is to be enforced, however, I am of opinion that the same degree of precision is not necessary; nor indeed does it appear possible. The critical point is that the enforcement of provisions such as Part 8 is not designed to ensure that no defective goods or services are ever supplied; it is rather designed to compel traders to achieve an acceptably low incidence of defects, and to rectify such defects as appear. Any court order of that nature must involve some degree of vagueness about the permissible incidence of defects. The order may also bear some degree of imprecision as to the nature of the defects that are prohibited. This is because the function of trading standards legislation is to minimize defects of every sort, and in cases where management or quality control is poor such defects may take many forms. For that reason I do not think it necessary that the court's order should specify the precise nature of the defects that are covered by it; it is rather designed to cover defects of every sort. Consequently it is not necessary that such an order should be directed against specific acts that are said to be in contravention of Part 8.'[162]

---

[157] EA 2002, s 217(10B and D).
[158] EA 2002, s 217(10).
[159] See *Lawrence David Ltd v Ashton* [1989] ICR 123, per Balcombe LJ and *CEF Holdings Ltd v Mundey* [2012] FSR 35 per Silber J at [43] and [51], but see the planning case of *Kettering Borough Council v Perkins* [1999] JPL 166, where the court adopted a less rigorous approach.
[160] See *Webster v Lord Advocate* [1985] SC 173.
[161] [2005] SLT 69.
[162] At [15].

4.158 The Judge was of the view that rules of domestic law should not generally be imported into the construction of Part 8, which was essentially inspired by the Injunctions Directive. Sections 217 and 218 were designed to enforce European legislation. Consequently the interpretation of Part 8 should aim at ensuring a uniform approach throughout the European Union. That interpretation should not be constrained by the detailed rules of procedure of any domestic legal system. Part 8 should rather be construed in a manner calculated to give effect to its underlying purposes, in particular the purposes disclosed in the Injunctions Directive.[163]

4.159 Lord Drummond–Young's views were partially, although not fully, endorsed by the Court of Appeal in *OFT v Vance Miller*.[164] Having been referred to the Scottish case, Arden LJ said:[165]

> 'As I see it, in England and Wales the order similarly need not apply only to specific acts and some degree of generality is acceptable, though, in respectful disagreement with Lord Drummond-Young, who thought that a considerable degree of generality was acceptable, I would be reluctant to say more than that "some" degree of generality is permitted. The court should see that what is prohibited is as clearly described as the circumstances permit, taking into account the need to give fair warning to the defendant of the acts that might constitute a breach.'

4.160 The situation, at least in England, would appear to be that:

- the rules of domestic law regarding injunctions should not be imported into Part 8 proceedings for an enforcement order;
- the specificity required for the wording of injunctions does not necessarily apply to the wording of an enforcement order;
- nevertheless, breach of an enforcement order is contempt of court and exposes the defendant to penal sanctions;
- in the circumstances, although some degree of generality is permissible, the prohibited conduct should be described 'as clearly as the circumstances permit'.

Penal notice

4.161 The enforcement order and the undertaking should be endorsed with a penal notice in Form N77 explaining the consequence of disobedience.

---

[163] At [16].
[164] [2009] EWCA Civ 34.
[165] At [46].

Breach

4.162 Breach of an enforcement notice, an interim enforcement notice or an undertaking given to the court renders the defendant in contempt of court and liable to imprisonment, a fine or sequestration of his assets.

4.163 Section 220(2) of the EA 2002 provides that any CPC enforcer has the same right to apply to the court in respect of a failure to comply with the order or undertaking as the enforcer who made the application for the order.

Contempt proceedings

4.164 Disobedience of an order of the court is punishable. Against an individual, the most severe sanction is a sentence of imprisonment exercised by an order of committal.[166] Against a limited company, it is sequestration exercised by a writ of sequestration.[167] The court may, as an alternative to committal or sequestration, impose a fine.[168] Sentencing for contempt has two purposes: first, punishment for breach of the order because court orders must not be flouted; and secondly, securing compliance with the order in the future. It should always be remembered that contempt must be proved to the criminal standard – in other words, the court must be sure that there was a contempt.

4.165 The procedure to be followed in order to establish liability for contempt is set out in CPR Part 81, which applies to proceedings both in the High Court and in the county court.[169] Section II of Part 81 deals with 'Committal for breach of a judgment, order or undertaking to do or abstain from doing an act'.

4.166 CPR, r 81.4(1) provides that where a person required by a judgment or order to do an act does not do it within the time fixed by the judgment or order; or disobeys a judgment or order not to do an act, the judgment or order may be enforced by an order for committal. If the person in contempt is a company, the committal order may be made against any director or other officer of the company.[170] Section II of CPR 81 applies to undertakings given by a party as it applies to judgments or orders.[171]

---

[166] The maximum term is one of two years: see Contempt of Court Act 1981, s 14(1).

[167] The writ is addressed to not less than four people named in the writ known as commissioners or sequestrators and directs them to sequestrate (seize) the property of the individual or company in contempt until the contempt is purged.

[168] There is no limit to the amount of the fine. The Contempt of Court Act 1981, s 14(2) does not apply to the County Court, which, by virtue of sub-section (4A) is treated as a superior court.

[169] County Courts Act 1984, s 38(1) gives the county court power to make any order which could be made by the High Court if the proceedings were in the High Court.

[170] CPR, r 81.4(3). Enforcement against the property of the company or its directors is by a writ of sequestration which can be issued only by the High Court. Section 7 of Part 81 deals with writs of sequestration. Rules 81.20–81.26 mirror the rules in 81.4–81.10 and are therefore not repeated here. However, enforcement by sequestration requires the permission of the court: CPR, r 81.20(1).

[171] CPR, r 81.4(4).

4.167   As a general rule, a judgment or order may not be enforced unless a copy has been personally served on the defendant.[172] Similarly, a copy of the defendant's undertaking must be delivered to him either by handing it to him before he leaves the court or by posting a copy to him or his solicitor.[173] Accordingly, on any application for committal proof of the service of the judgment or order or delivery of the undertaking should be given by the applicant.

4.168   CPR, r 81.10(1) provides that a committal application should be made by an application notice under CPR Part 23 in the proceedings in which the judgment or order was made or the undertaking given.[174] The application notice must contain a penal notice similar to the one found in Annex 3 of Practice Direction 81. Precision is vital in contempt proceedings. CPR, r 81.10(3) requires the application notice:

(a)   To set out **in full** the grounds upon which the application is made and to **identify** each alleged act of contempt including, if known, the date of each of the alleged acts.

      Some draftsmen like to set out the breaches in tabular form thus:

Order	Breach	Date
'Do not sell any goods not marked ....'	Sold goods not marked ...	27 June 2015

(b)   To be supported by one or more **affidavits** containing all the evidence relied upon.

4.169   The application notice and the supporting evidence must be served personally on the respondent.[175] Again, proof of service should be given to the court. A committal application for breach of a solicitor's undertaking cannot be made without first obtaining permission of the court pursuant to CPR, r 81.11.

4.170   Section VIII of CPR Part 81 deals with 'General rules about committal applications, orders for committal and writs of sequestration'. The basic rule is that, unless the court otherwise permits, the applicant is confined to those breaches set out in his application notice and to the evidence served in support.[176] This rule serves to emphasise the need for accuracy and completeness when drafting the application notice and the supporting evidence. The respondent is under no obligation to reply to the application notice or to file evidence. Whether or not he does so, he is entitled to give oral evidence and,

---

[172]   CPR, r 81. 5 and 81.6. The court may dispense with proof of personal service if satisfied, inter alia that the defendant was present when the judgment or order was given or made: CPR, r 81.8.

[173]   CPR, r 81.7

[174]   Reference should also be made to Practice Direction 81, paras 8–16.

[175]   CPR, r 81.10(4).

[176]   CPR, r 81.28(1).

with the permission of the court, to call witnesses.[177] A court making the committal order may also order that its execution be suspended for such period or on such terms or conditions as it may specify.[178] This power is often exercised. CPR, rr 81.31 and 81.32 deal with the discharge of a person in custody.[179]

4.171 Two cases can illustrate the exercise of contempt proceedings and the range of sentences. In *OFT v Vance Miller*,[180] the first instance judge was faced with an application to commit Mr Miller in respect of nine breaches of an order prohibiting the sale of goods not conforming to the contractual description or not being of satisfactory quality and prohibiting late delivery of goods. There had been earlier committal proceedings. On that occasion, following a hearing at which Mr Miller had been unrepresented, the judge sentenced Mr Miller to a custodial sentence of nine months. Subsequently, there was a successful application from Mr Miller to purge his contempt.

4.172 In his sentencing remarks in respect of the present application, the judge referred to 'the convoluted tale' which Mr Miller had told about the involvement of others as being 'simply incredible'; he held that the breaches were neither casual nor accidental; and he noted the fact that this was Mr Miller's second appearance for contempt of the same order of the court. As against that, he found that the last complaint had been about two years earlier; there was evidence of a significant and continuing reduction in complaints; there was a recent report that he had commissioned from management consultants; and there was evidence that apologies had been given to the complainants. However, the judge concluded that it was a serious case and he ordered that Mr Miller be committed for contempt for six months but suspended the sentence for two years and ordered it not to be enforced if Mr Miller complied with the original order. The judge further imposed a fine on Mr Miller of the sum of £90,000,[181] and ordered Mr Miller to pay a contribution towards the OFT's costs in the sum of £30,000. On appeal by Mr Miller, the Court of Appeal upheld the sentence, finding that it was not manifestly excessive.

4.173 In *Phillimore v Surrey County Council*,[182] Mr Phillimore was a second hand car dealer. There was an injunction against him which restrained him, inter alia, from providing consumers with goods that did not corresponded with their description; selling goods which were not of satisfactory quality; applying a false description to goods or supplying goods to which a false trade

---

[177] CPR, r 81.28(2)
[178] CPR, r 81.29.
[179] See *Swindon Borough Council v Webb* [2016] EWCA Civ 152, where the discharge of the defendant from custody went horribly wrong.
[180] [2009] EWCA Civ 34.
[181] £10,000 for each complaint. The judge found that the business was making an annual profit of some £200,000. The financial resources of the respondent will always be relevant to the quantum of the fine.
[182] [2010] EWCA Civ 61.

description had been applied; selling or offering to supply a vehicle or trailer in an unroadworthy condition; and suppling vehicles that were in an unsafe condition.

4.174 The first instance judge found that Mr Phillimore had been acting dishonestly as a second-hand car dealer. He had deliberately failed to give his own name and address on business documents, so that customers would find it difficult to pursue him personally by way of legal proceedings when their cars were found to be defective. He had continued to give false descriptions about the vehicles he had sold, as to the mileage, or as to the validity, or extent, of warranties he said he was providing. He had continued to sell cars which he must have known had serious defects. He decided that Mr Phillimore should be committed to prison for nine months.

4.175 On appeal, the Court of Appeal upheld the sentence. Stanley Burnton LJ said: 'This was a substantial sentence. In my judgment it was well within the range of sentences open to the judge, having regard to the fact that, first, these were repeated breaches of an injunction. Secondly, they must have been deliberate and dishonest breaches of the injunction. Thirdly, the victims were persons who could little afford the losses they suffered as a result of dealing with Mr Phillimore. Fourthly, the breaches were not simply breaches that would lead to financial loss on the part of his victims but could lead to injury or indeed loss of life as, for example, might have occurred when a wheel came off one of the vehicles that he had sold.'

4.176 In the case of a breach of an undertaking given to the court, rather than treat the defaulting party as being in contempt, the court has the option of making an enforcement order or an interim enforcement order, but may not accept a further undertaking.[183]

Costs

General

4.177 All litigation, whether it be civil or criminal, carries with it exposure to costs.[184] Cases have to be investigated, prepared and fought. It is understood that one of the concerns of enforcers is the risk of being subject to an adverse costs' order should a Part 8 case be lost. Regrettably, there is no way of obviating that risk. On the other hand, the trader is exposed to the same risk. It is that risk that frequently persuades him to settle the action, by giving acceptable undertakings to the enforcer or to the court.

4.178 It is sensible for the enforcer to bring the issue of costs to the attention of the trader at an early stage perhaps in the letter initiating consultation. The letter could include the following passage:

---

[183] EA 2002, s 220(4).
[184] Although it is hoped that the recent amendments to the CPR will have some effect on controlling the quantum of costs.

A response to these issues is required by 5pm on [...]. Should a substantive response or undertaking not be received within that time, I will assume that you are not prepared to comply with the requests made in this letter and my authority will commence court proceedings against you without further notice. In such circumstances, you may be ordered to pay the costs of the court proceedings.

Discretion

4.179 The power to award costs 'of and incidental'[185] to civil proceedings is derived from s 51 of the Senior Courts Act 1981. The award of costs and the quantum of costs are in the discretion of the court.

4.180 The general rule is that costs follow the event.[186] In the case of an application for an enforcement order, the 'event' is the grant of, or refusal to grant, an enforcement order. Thus the winner is generally entitled to an order that the loser pays his reasonable and proportionate costs.[187] Note the reference to 'reasonable and proportionate costs'. It is rare for the totality of the winning party's costs to be paid by the losing party. There is usually a shortfall between the costs actually incurred by a party and those recoverable from the other party.

4.181 However, the discretion exists to depart from the general rule that costs follow the event. CPR, r 44.2(4) and (5) provide:

(4) In deciding what order (if any) to make about costs, the court must have regard to all the circumstances, including –

    (a)   the conduct of all the parties;

    (b)   whether a party has succeeded on part of its case, even if that party has not been wholly successful; and

    (c)   any admissible offer to settle[188] made by a party which is drawn to the court's attention ...

(5) The conduct of the parties includes –

    (a)   conduct before, as well as during, the proceedings ...;

    (b)   whether it was reasonable for a party to raise, pursue or contest a particular allegation or issue;

    (c)   the manner in which a party has pursued or defended its case or a particular allegation or issue; and

    (d)   whether a claimant who has succeeded in the claim, in whole or in part, exaggerated its claim.

4.182 In *Straker v Tudor Rose*[189] Lord Justice Waller gave helpful guidance on the correct approach:

---

[185] *Re Gibson's Settlement Trusts* [1981] Ch 179 at 186, Sir Robert Megarry V-C pointed out that the costs 'incidental to' proceedings go beyond those 'of' the proceedings.

[186] See CPR, r 44.2(2)(a): 'The general rule is that the unsuccessful party will be ordered to pay the costs of the successful party.'

[187] See CPR, rr 44.3(2) and (5) and 44.4.

[188] It is suggested that 'an offer to settle' would include an offer of an undertaking to the enforcer.

[189] [2007] EWCA Civ 368.

(a)   Is it appropriate to make an order for costs?

(b)   If so, the general rule is that the unsuccessful party will pay the costs of the successful party.

(c)   Identify the successful party.

(d)   Consider whether there are reasons for departing from the general rule in whole or in part. If so the judge should make clear findings of the factors justifying costs not following the event.

Recoverable costs

4.183 Assuming that an order for costs has been made, what costs are recoverable? The short answer is that the court has a discretion to award any reasonable and proportionate costs of and incidental to the proceedings.

4.184 Costs normally fall into two categories:

(a)   expenses of a type which solicitors frequently incur when acting on behalf of clients (such as counsel's fees, court fees, witness expenses etc). These are known as 'disbursements';

(b)   the fees which a solicitor charges to his client. These are known as 'solicitors' charges' or 'profit costs'.

4.185 Costs incurred before the commencement of proceedings may be properly recoverable if those costs were reasonably incurred in order to obtain material that was, or would have been but for the settlement of the proceedings, of use and service in the claim.[190]

4.186 In criminal cases, it has been accepted that, on the basis of s 18(1) of the Prosecution of Offences Act 1985, the costs of the prosecution may include the costs of the prosecuting authority in carrying out investigations with a view to the prosecution of the defendant.[191] It is suggested that the same is not true in civil cases. In general, the work of a party's employees in investigating, formulating and prosecuting a claim by legal proceedings does not qualify for an order for the payment of the costs of and incidental to those proceedings. The exception is where the employees undertake work that would otherwise have been undertaken by an outside expert.[192] It is suggested that, although arguable, it is unlikely that a court would find that a local authority's trading standards officers were performing work that would otherwise have to be done or could lawfully be done by an outside expert.

---

[190] See *Admiral Management Services Ltd v Para-Protect Europe Ltd* [2002] 1 WLR 2722 at [25].

[191] See *R v Associated Octel Company Ltd (Costs)* [1997] 1 Cr App R (S) 435.

[192] See *Admiral Management Services Ltd v Para-Protect Europe Ltd* [2002] 1 WLR 2722; *Sisu Capital Fund Ltd v Tucker (Costs)* [2005] EWHC 2321 (Ch); and *Grant v Ralls* [2016] EWHC 1812 (Ch).

CHAPTER 5

CONSUMER RIGHTS

CONTENTS

INTRODUCTION

5.1   The enactment of the Consumer Rights Act ('CRA 2015') now provides a focus on the rights of consumers, which has developed primarily from the influence of European Union ('EU') law. However, the EU Consumer Rights Directive 2011/83/EU (the 'CRD') should not of itself be considered a radical measure that introduced many new European rights for consumers. Most of the rights it provides for were already in existence in EU law and although the CRD does strengthen consumer protection it is perhaps best described as a consolidation of existing consumer rights.

5.2   The CRD consolidates the EU directives on doorstep selling 85/577/EEC (the 'Doorstep Selling Directive') and distance sales 97/7/EC ('the Distance Sales Directive'). Under Art 4, however, the CRD now provides for full harmonisation rather than the previous minimal harmonisation. This means that Member States must implement the CRD fully and may not legislate in excess of the CRD's consumer protection measures in the areas that it covers. Guidance on the CRD has been provided by the European Commission Directorate-General for Justice and Consumers (the 'DG Guidance').[1]

5.3   In the UK the CRD has primarily[2] been implemented by the Consumer Contracts (Information, Cancellation and Additional Charges) Regulations 2013[3] (the 'CCR 2013'), which revoke the domestic regulations on doorstep[4] and distance selling.[5] These provisions will continue to apply, however, to contracts entered into before 13 June 2014. Part of the CRD was implemented, ahead of time, by the Consumer Rights (Payment Surcharges) Regulations 2012[6] which came into force on 6 April 2013.

5.4   UK consumer law on the sale of goods and services had long been considered to be unnecessarily complex and in need of clarification and simplification. Part 1 of the CRA 2015 has sought to do that by setting out a single set of rights and remedies that apply to the supply of goods, services and, for the first time, digital content to consumers. It came into effect on 1 October 2015 for contracts entered into from that date onwards. The CRA 2015 also implements certain parts of the CRD in its consolidation of the contractual rules[7] replacing provisions previously found in the CCR 2013.

5.5   The Consumer Protection from Unfair Trading Regulations 2008 ('CPUTR') have also been amended to provide for a new consumer right to

---

[1]   http://ec.europa.eu/consumers/consumer_rights/rights-contracts/directive/index_en.htm.

[2]   CRD, Art 27 (inertia selling) has been implemented by amendment of the CPUTR, reg 27M.

[3]   SI 2013/3134. CCR 2013 were amended by the Consumer Contracts (Amendment) Regulations 2015, SI 1629/2015.

[4]   Cancellation of Contracts made in a Consumer's Home or Place of Work etc Regulations 2008, SI 2008/1816.

[5]   Consumer Protection (Distance Selling) Regulations 2000, SI 2000/2334.

[6]   SI 2013/3110.

[7]   Sections 11, 12, 36, 37 and 50 (information requirements), s 28 (default rules for the delivery of goods) and s 29 (passing of risk in goods).

obtain civil redress when a trader has engaged in an unfair commercial practice (see Chapter 7). The new Part 4A of the CPUTR will permit consumers to base civil claims on commercial practices by traders that are misleading actions or aggressive practices. At the same time as the CRA 2015 came into effect, consumers were provided with a statutory alternative route to resolve a complaint using alternative dispute resolution (ADR) in the Alternative Dispute Resolution for Consumer Disputes (Competent Authorities and Information) Regulations 2015.

5.6   The Provision of Services Regulations 2009 ('PoSR 2009') implement an EU Directive aiming to remove barriers to accessing services across the EEA. Many of these provisions are repeated in the CCR 2013 and ADR Regulations. It should also be noted that many statutory rights for consumers are afforded by the Consumer Credit Act 1974 and related provisions. These are covered in Chapter 18 Consumer Credit. There are additionally specific rights to redress under the Package Travel, Package Holidays and Package Tours Regulations 1992 (see Chapter 15, Travel). The future rights of consumers will also be addressed by the current Law Commission consultations in relation to Bills of Sale and Consumer Prepayment on Retailer Insolvency.

INFORMATION AND CANCELLATION

5.7   The CCR 2013 primarily sets out the regime under which consumers are provided with the right to specified pre-contract information when contracting with traders, and also to a 14 days' right to cancel certain contracts without reason. It applies throughout the UK with minor modifications for Scotland[8] and Northern Ireland.[9]

5.8   The CCR 2013 is a relatively complex regulation and unhelpfully includes a variety of unclear definitions and exclusions, which perhaps reflect its origin in EU directives. The language used is a combination of EU law concepts and other terms that are more familiar to domestic regulation. In construing EU provisions it is important to consider the purpose of the EU legislation. In relation to cancellation rights that purpose has already been considered by the courts under both the doorstep and distance selling directives.

5.9   In *Robertson v Swift* the UK Supreme Court considered the Doorstep Selling Directive. Lord Kerr stated that:

> 'since the overall purpose of the Directive is to enhance consumer protection, that overarching principle must guide interpretation of the relevant national legislation.'[10]

---

8   CCR 2013, regs 20(2)(b) Due diligence notices, 22(3) Directors' liability, 23(3) Duty to enforce, 24(6) Powers and 45(1) Orders.
9   CCR 2013, regs 6(1)(a) NI Gambling legislation, 7(5)(c) NI health service, 23(1)(b) Duty to enforce and 44(3)(b) Complaints to DETI.
10   [2014] UKSC 50, [2014] 1 WLR 3438 at para 22. See also *Veedfald v Arhus Amtskommune*

5.10 It is likely that this consumer protection focus will also be made when construing domestic legislation implemented as a consequence of the CRD. The rationale for cancellation rights for doorstep sales is founded on the pressure that consumers feel when they are sold to directly in their home. It has been said that the objective of a cooling-off period is 'to protect the consumer from the element of surprise inherent in doorstep selling'.[11] In *Martin Martin*,[12] the ECJ observed that:

> 'the special feature of those contracts is that as a rule it is the trader who initiates the contract negotiations, and the consumer has not prepared for such door-to-door selling by, inter alia, comparing the price and quality of the different offers available.'[13]

5.11 In *Cox v Woodlands Manor Care Home* [2015] the Court of Appeal (Civil Division) stated that the:

> 'mischief at which [the Consumer Contracts Regulations] are aimed is that consumers in their homes may feel pressured into making a decision which they would not have made if they had an opportunity to reflect in the absence of a trader.'[14]

5.12 The rationale for consumer cancellation rights in distance contracts was explained in *Messner v Firma Stefan Krüger*, where the ECJ referred to recital 14 of the Distance Selling Directive:

> 'the right of withdrawal is designed to protect the consumer in the particular situation of mail-order sales, in which he 'is not able actually to see the product or ascertain the nature of the service provided before concluding the contract'. The right of withdrawal is therefore intended to offset the disadvantage for the consumer resulting from a distance contract by granting him an appropriate period for reflection during which he can examine and test the goods acquired.'[15]

SCOPE OF THE CCR 2013

5.13 Certain common contractual arrangements are excluded from the ambit of the CCR 2013 altogether. Under reg 6(1) the CCR 2013 obligations expressly do not apply to contracts for gambling,[16] financial services,[17] land,[18]

C-203/99 [2003] 1 CMLR 41 (at para 15) on the general principle that exceptions to consumer protection measures should be construed narrowly.

11   *Crailsheimer Volksbank* C-229/04 [2005] ECR I-9273, ECJ.

12   *Martin Martin v EDP Editores SL* C-227/08 [2010] 2 CMLR 27.

13   See also *Hamilton v Volksbank Filder eG* C-412/06 [2008] 2 CMLR 46, *Heininger v Bayerische Hypo- und Vereinsbank AG* C-481/99 [2003] 2 CMLR 42 and *E-Friz GmbH v Von der Heyden* C-215/08 [2010] 3 CMLR 23.

14   *Cox v Woodlands Manor Care Home* [2015] CTLC 53 Court of Appeal (Civil Division) per Underhill LJ.

15   C-489/07 [2009] ECR I-7315 at para 20.

16   CCR 2013, reg 6(1)(a) 'gaming, betting and participating in a lottery within the meaning of the Gambling Act 2005' 'or participating in a lottery which forms part of the National Lottery within the meaning of the National Lottery etc. Act 1993' Consumer Contracts (Amendment)

residential rentals,[19] new buildings,[20] regular rounds-men,[21] package travel[22] and timeshare.[23] Under reg 6(2) the CCR 2013 also do not apply to contracts concluded by vending machines,[24] by telephone for a telephone service[25] or contracts under which goods are sold by way of execution or otherwise by authority of law, such as the sale of goods after a court order.

CCR 2013 DEFINITIONS

5.14 It is important to consider the definitions in regs 4 and 5, which also limit the application of the CCR 2013. In particular, the CCR 2013 obligations apply only to contracts between a 'trader' and 'consumer' (reg 4). The rights available to a consumer will also depend upon whether the contract is a 'distance contract', 'off-premises contract' or 'on premises contract' (reg 5).

Consumer and trader

5.15 The definitions of 'consumer' and 'trader' are found in reg 4 of the CCR 2013. These definitions are the same in the CRA 2015 (s 2) and under the Consumer Protection from Unfair Trading Regulations ('CPUTR'),[26] where they have been the subject of consideration by the courts. The definition of consumer and trader are now considered in Chapter 2, Interpreting Consumer Law.

Distance contracts

5.16 The definition of a distance contract in reg 5 states:

> '"distance contract" means a contract concluded between a trader and a consumer under an organised distance sales or service-provision scheme without the

---

Regulations 2015, SI 2015/1629; in Northern Ireland the Betting, Gaming, Lotteries and Amusements (Northern Ireland) Order 1985, SI 1985/1204.

[17] CCR 2013, reg 6(1)(b) 'services of a banking, credit, insurance, personal pension, investment or payment nature'. Although these contracts are subject to regs 38(4) (ancillary contracts) and 40(3) (additional payments).

[18] CCR 2013, reg 6(1)(c) 'for the creation of immovable property or of rights in immovable property'.

[19] CCR 2013, reg 6(1)(d) 'rental of accommodation for residential purposes'.

[20] CCR 2013, reg 6(1)(e) 'for the construction of new buildings, or the construction of substantially new buildings by the conversion of existing buildings'.

[21] CCR 2013, reg 6(1)(f) 'for the supply of foodstuffs, beverages or other goods intended for current consumption in the household and which are supplied by a trader on frequent and regular rounds to the consumer's home, residence or workplace'.

[22] CCR 2013, reg 6(1)(g) 'within the scope of the Package Travel Directive 90/314/EEC'.

[23] CCR 2013, reg 6(1)(h) 'within the scope of the Timeshare Directive 2008/122/EC'.

[24] CCR 2013, reg 6(2)(a) 'concluded by means of automatic vending machines or automated commercial premises'.

[25] CCR 2013, reg 6(2)(b) 'concluded with a telecommunications operator through a public telephone for the use of the telephone' and (c) 'concluded for the use of one single connection, by telephone, internet or fax, established by a consumer'.

[26] Save for the burden of proof in CRA 2015, s 2(4).

simultaneous physical presence of the trader and the consumer, with the exclusive use of one or more means of distance communication up to and including the time at which the contract is concluded.'

5.17 This is a slightly different definition of distance contract to the one found in the Consumer Protection (Distance Selling) Regulations 2000,[27] which was itself a copy of the definition in Art 2(1) of the Distance Selling Directive. The definition of distance contract is perhaps not as clear as it might be. However, some assistance may be found in the recitals to the CRD. Recital 37 of the CRD refers to distance sales in the following way:

'Since in the case of distance sales, the consumer is not able to see the goods before concluding the contract, he should have a right of withdrawal.'

5.18 This reflects the central purpose of the protection afforded to consumers in this area. The growth in consumers purchasing goods at a distance, particularly using the internet, has meant that many more goods, services and digital content are sold by description. The distance selling provisions in the CRD essentially protect consumers against the mischief of traders that supply products that do not subsequently correspond to their description or are otherwise defective.

5.19 Recital 20 of the CRD provides a number of examples of distance communications, 'mail order, Internet, telephone or fax'. These examples are not exhaustive but suggest a type of transaction that is not immediately fulfilled. The Distance Selling Directive (97/7/EC) previously provided in Annex 1 an indicative list of the 'means of distance communication'. This included a wide variety of methods through which sales could be made at a distance.[28]

5.20 Recital 20 also provides that the definition should:

'cover situations where the consumer visits the business premises merely for the purpose of gathering information about the goods or services and subsequently negotiates and concludes the contract at a distance. By contrast, a contract which is negotiated at the business premises of the trader and finally concluded by means of distance communication should not be considered a distance contract. Neither should a contract initiated by means of distance communication, but finally concluded at the business premises of the trader be considered a distance contract. Similarly, the concept of distance contract should not include reservations made by a consumer through a means of distance communications to request the provision

---

[27] SI 2000/2334, reg 3(1): '"distance contract" means any contract concerning goods or services concluded between a supplier and a consumer under an organised distance sales or service provision scheme run by the supplier who, for the purpose of the contract, makes exclusive use of one or more means of distance communication up to and including the moment at which the contract is concluded'.

[28] Unaddressed printed matter; addressed printed matter; standard letter; press advertising with order form; catalogue; telephone with human intervention; telephone without human intervention (automatic calling machine, audiotext); radio; videophone (telephone with screen); videotex (microcomputer and television screen) with keyboard or touch screen; electronic mail; facsimile machine (fax) and television (teleshopping) (Art 2(4) and Annex I).

of a service from a professional, such as in the case of a consumer phoning to request an appointment with a hairdresser.'

5.21   In the European Commission DG Guidance it is stated that the 'Directive only applies to distance contracts concluded under an organised distance sales or service-provision scheme. For example, if a trader only exceptionally concludes a contract with a consumer by email or telephone, after being contacted by the consumer, such a contract should not be considered a distance contract under the Directive.'[29]

Business premises

5.22

> **CCR 2013 Reg 5**
>
> '"business premises" in relation to a trader means –
>
> (a)   any immovable retail premises where the activity of the trader is carried out on a permanent basis, or
> (b)   any movable retail premises where the activity of the trader is carried out on a usual basis;'

The CCR 2013 does not provide any further definition of 'retail premises' or what is meant by the 'activity of the trader being carried out on a usual basis'. However, recital 22 of the CRD states that

> '**Business premises** should include premises in whatever form (such as shops, stalls or lorries) which serve as a permanent or usual place of business for the trader. Market stalls and fair stands should be treated as business premises if they fulfill this condition. Retail premises where the trader carries out his activity on a seasonal basis, for instance during the tourist season at a ski or beach resort, should be considered as business premises as the trader carries out his activity in those premises on a usual basis. Spaces accessible to the public, such as streets, shopping malls, beaches, sports facilities and public transport, which the trader uses on an exceptional basis for his business activities as well as private homes or workplaces should not be regarded as business premises.'

5.23   In *Travel-Vac*[30] the meaning of 'business premises' for the purposes of the Doorstep Selling Directive 85/577/EEC was considered by the ECJ, which found that:

> 'As regards the question whether the contract was concluded away from the trader's business premises, it must be observed that this concept refers to premises in which the trader usually carries on his business and which are clearly identified as premises for sales to the public.'

5.24   In the European Commission's DG Guidance it is stated that:

---

[29]   EC DG Guidance, p 30.
[30]   *Travel Vac SL v Snachis* C-423/97 [1999] 2 CMLR 1111.

'if the trader uses spaces accessible to the public, such as streets, shopping malls, beaches, sports facilities and public transport on an exceptional basis, i.e., once or occasionally and for a short duration in a given location, the contracts concluded with consumers are likely to be off-premises contracts.'[31]

Off-premises contract

5.25

> **CCR 2013 reg 5**
>
> '"off-premises contract" means a contract between a trader and a consumer which is any of these –
> (a)   a contract concluded in the simultaneous physical presence of the trader and the consumer, in a place which is not the business premises of the trader;
> (b)   a contract for which an offer was made by the consumer in the simultaneous physical presence of the trader and the consumer, in a place which is not the business premises of the trader;
> (c)   a contract concluded on the business premises of the trader or through any means of distance communication immediately after the consumer was personally and individually addressed in a place which is not the business premises of the trader in the simultaneous physical presence of the trader and the consumer;
> (d)   a contract concluded during an excursion organised by the trader with the aim or effect of promoting and selling goods or services to the consumer.'

The definition in reg 5 is broader than its predecessor[32] because it includes venues that are not the trader's business premises, rather than merely contracts concluded in a consumer's home. The definition also now includes the situation where a trader makes an offer to a consumer away from his business premises, but the contract is concluded on business premises or at a distance. An example of how this might apply is given in the European Commission's DG Guidance:

> 'The trader's representative approaches the particular consumer in the street with an offer for a subscription to a monthly magazine and the contract is immediately signed on the trader's nearby business premises.'[33]

5.26   The concept of an excursion has also been changed to apply to one organised by a trader to promote or sell goods or services to the consumer. This appears to be a different approach to the one adopted in the *Travel Vac* case. It implies that the consumer is being taken on some kind of journey rather than, as in *Travel Vac*, the trader being on a journey away from their trading base. The European Commission's DG Guidance states:

---

[31]   At p 14.
[32]   The Cancellation of Contracts made in a Consumer's Home or Place of Work etc. Regulations 2008, SI 2008/1816.
[33]   At p 15.

'The notion of "excursion" includes journeys that involve sightseeing or other leisure-related activities rather than just transport to the place where the sale takes place. In applying this notion, it should not matter whether the trader selling the transport during an excursion organises the transport himself or has made arrangements with a transport company.'[34]

On-premises contract

5.27

> **CCR 2013 Reg 5**
>
> '"on-premises contract" means a contract between a trader and a consumer which is neither a distance contract nor an off-premises contract.'

Durable medium

5.28

> **CCR 2013 Reg 5**
>
> '"durable medium" means paper or email, or any other medium that—
> (a)   allows information to be addressed personally to the recipient,
> (b)   enables the recipient to store the information in a way accessible for future reference for a period that is long enough for the purposes of the information, and
> (c)   allows the unchanged reproduction of the information stored;'

Recital 23 of the CRD states that:

> 'Durable media should enable the consumer to store the information for as long as it is necessary for him to protect his interests stemming from his relationship with the trader. Such media should include in particular paper, USB sticks, CD-ROMs, DVDs, memory cards or the hard disks of computers as well as emails.'

5.29   In *Content Services Ltd*[35] the ECJ rejected the argument that the mere provision of information on a website amounted to a 'durable medium' under the Distance Selling Directive. It was stated that:

> 'a business practice consisting of making the information referred to in that provision accessible to the consumer only via a hyperlink on a website of the undertaking concerned does not meet the requirements of that provision, since that information is neither "given" by that undertaking nor "received" by the consumer, within the meaning of that provision, and a website such as that at issue in the main proceedings cannot be regarded as a "durable medium".'

---

[34]   See p 16.
[35]   *Content Services Ltd v Bundesarbeitskammer* (C-49/11) [2012] 3 CMLR 34.

PRE-CONTRACT INFORMATION

5.30 The requirements in Part 2 (Chapter 1) of the CCR 2013 for traders to provide consumers with pre-contract information only apply to on-premises contracts (reg 10), off-premises contracts (reg 11) and distance sales (regs 13 and 14) within the scope of the regulations. Save for criminal proceedings under reg 19, it is for the trader to prove that he has complied with the requirements as to provision of information.[36]

5.31 There are several exceptions to the application of the information requirements set out in reg 7 for medicinal products, healthcare products and passenger transport services. The most significant exception, however, is that the consumer information requirements do not apply to 'off-premises contracts under which the payment to be made by the consumer is not more than £42'.[37] This is also an express exception for the provision of cancellation rights under Part 3 of the CCR 2013. Information will be made available 'only if the consumer can reasonably be expected to know how to access it'.[38]

Information for on-premises contracts

5.32 The information requirements for on-premises contracts are set out in Sch 1 and must be provided in a 'clear and comprehensible manner'.[39] Required information given by the trader is treated as included as a term of the contract and any subsequent change (whether before entering the contract or later) is not legally effective unless 'expressly agreed between the consumer and trader'.[40] The same position is reached in relation to the 'supply of digital content other than for a price paid by the consumer' as a consequence of the amendments in the Consumer Contracts (Amendment) Regulations 2015.[41]

> **CCR 2013 Schedule 1**
>
> *Information relating to on-premises contracts*
>
> The information referred to in regulation 9(1) is—
>
> (a) the main characteristics of the goods or services, to the extent appropriate to the medium of communication and to the goods or services;
>
> (b) the identity of the trader (such as the trader's trading name), the geographical address at which the trader is established and the trader's telephone number;

---

[36] CCR 2013, reg 17.
[37] CCR 2013, reg 7(2).
[38] CCR 2013, reg 8.
[39] CCR 2013, reg 9(1).
[40] Now found in s 12 (goods), s 37 (contracts for digital content for a price) and CRA 2015, s 50(3)–(5) which restricted CCR 2013, reg 9(3) and omitted reg 9(4).
[41] Reg 4.

(c)   the total price of the goods or services inclusive of taxes, or where the
       nature of the goods or services is such that the price cannot reasonably
       be calculated in advance, the manner in which the price is to be
       calculated;

(d)   where applicable, all additional delivery charges or, where those charges
       cannot reasonably be calculated in advance, the fact that such additional
       charges may be payable;

(e)   where applicable, the arrangements for payment, delivery, performance,
       and the time by which the trader undertakes to deliver the goods or to
       perform the service;

(f)   where applicable, the trader's complaint handling policy;

(g)   in the case of a sales contract, a reminder that the trader is under a legal
       duty to supply goods that are in conformity with the contract;

(h)   where applicable, the existence and the conditions of after-sales services
       and commercial guarantees;

(i)   the duration of the contract, where applicable, or, if the contract is of
       indeterminate duration or is to be extended automatically, the conditions
       for terminating the contract;

(j)   where applicable, the functionality, including applicable technical
       protection measures, of digital content;

(k)   where applicable, any relevant compatibility of digital content with
       hardware and software that the trader is aware of or can reasonably be
       expected to have been aware of.

Day-to-day transactions

5.33 Under reg 9(2) these requirements do not apply to 'day to day'
transactions that are 'performed immediately at the time when the contract is
entered into'. This exception is taken directly from Art 5(3) of the CRD for
on-premises contracts 'which involve day-to-day transactions and which are
performed immediately at the time of their conclusion'.

5.34 In the European Commission DG Guidance it is stated that:

> 'By their nature, these transactions are likely to be for low cost items ... Examples
> of such possible day-to-day services are: shoe cleaning services provided on the
> street and cinema services where the ticket is purchased (i.e., where the contract is
> concluded) immediately before the film is watched.'[42]

Information for off-premises contracts

5.35 The information requirements for off-premises and distance contracts are
set out in Sch 2 (see below) and must be provided in a 'clear and
comprehensible manner'.[43] If it is applicable, the cancellation form must be
given as set out in Sch 3 (Part B). Sch 3 Part A provides model instructions on
cancellation which a trader may use to meet the requirements of paras (l), (m)
and (n) of Sch 2.[44] For off-premises contracts, the information and any

---

[42]   EC DG Guidance, p 20.
[43]   CCR 2013, regs 10(1) and 13(1).
[44]   CCR 2013, reg 10(3).

cancellation form must be given in writing or other durable medium[45] (if the consumer agrees to this) and must be legible.[46]

5.36 Required information given by the trader is treated as included as a term of the contract and any subsequent change (whether before entering the contract or later) is not legally effective unless 'expressly agreed between the consumer and trader'.[47] The same position is reached in relation to the 'supply of digital content other than for a price paid by the consumer' as a consequence of the amendments in the Consumer Contracts (Amendment) Regulations 2015.[48]

5.37 A copy or confirmation of the off-premises contract must be given to the consumer in accordance with reg 12. Regulation 11 modifies the information requirements where a consumer has requested a trader to carry out an immediate repair or maintenance contract and the payment by the consumer is not more than £170.

Information for distance contracts

5.38 The information requirements for distance contracts are set out in Sch 2 (see below) and must give 'or make available'[49] information to the consumer in a 'clear and comprehensible manner' 'in a way appropriate to the means of distance communication.'[50] If applicable, the model cancellation form must be given as set out in Sch 3 (Part B). Sch 3 Part A provides model instructions on cancellation which a trader may use to meet the requirements of paras (l), (m) and (n) of Sch 2.[51]

5.39 Required information under reg 13 given by the trader is treated as having been included as a term of the contract and any subsequent change (whether before entering the contract or later) is not legally effective unless 'expressly agreed between the consumer and trader'.[52] The same position is reached in relation to the 'supply of digital content other than for a price paid by the consumer' as a consequences of the amendments in the Consumer Contracts (Amendment) Regulations 2015.[53]

5.40 Under reg 13 the obligation to provide the required information in a durable form does not apply, although there is a legibility requirement for any

---

[45] Defined in reg 5.

[46] CCR 2013, reg 10(2).

[47] Now found in s 12 (goods), s 37 (contracts for digital content for a price) and CRA 2015, s 50(3)–(5) which restricted CCR 2013, reg 10(5) and omitted reg 10(6).

[48] Reg 5.

[49] See reg 8: 'if the consumer can reasonably be expected to know how to access it'.

[50] CCR 2013, reg 13(1).

[51] CCR 2013, reg 13(3).

[52] Now found in s 12 (goods), s 37 (contracts for digital content for a price) and CRA 2015, s 50(3)–(5) which restricted CCR 2013, reg 10(5) and omitted reg 10(6).

[53] Reg 6.

information that is provided on a durable medium.[54] However, confirmation of the contract must be given to the consumer under reg 16 on a durable medium and must include all of the Sch 2 information. Confirmation must be provided within a reasonable time after the conclusion of the contract and, in any event, no later than delivery of goods or performance of a service.[55] If a trader makes a telephone call to a consumer with a view to concluding a distance contract, at the beginning of the conversation he must disclose his identity, any person he acts for and the commercial purpose of the call (reg 15).

Contracts concluded by electronic means

5.41 There are additional requirements in reg 14 for distance contracts concluded by electronic means, if the contract places the consumer under an obligation to pay. 'Concluded by electronic means' is not further defined in either the CCR 2013 or the CRD.[56] However the explanation for this provision in recital 39 refers only to 'distance contracts concluded through websites'. It would seem plain therefore that any internet purchase would ordinarily fall within the definition. The European Commission DG Guidance suggests that the term ought to be construed by reference to the definition in the Electronic Commerce Directive 98/34/EC, where:

> '"by electronic means" means that the service is sent initially and received at its destination by means of electronic equipment for the processing (including digital compression) and storage of data, and entirely transmitted, conveyed and received by wire, by radio, by optical means or by other electromagnetic means.'[57]

This would suggest that the definition would exclude traders selling by mail order or by telephone (see reg 15 below), although there may be an issue in relation to modern internet telephones.

5.42 If the contract places the consumer under an obligation to pay, the consumer must be made aware 'in a clear and prominent manner, and directly before the consumer places the order' of the information requirements in Sch 2(a) (the main characteristics), (f) (total price), (g) (additional delivery charges), (h) (costs per billing period), (s) (contract duration) and (t) (minimum duration of the contract). These information requirements in Sch 2 are highlighted in bold text below. In addition, the consumer must explicitly acknowledge that their order implies an obligation to pay. If the order entails (which it normally does) clicking on a link, or similar function, the trader must ensure that the link is labelled as 'order with obligation to pay' or a similar wording that indicates that placing the order entails an obligation to pay the trader, EC Guidance suggests 'buy now' or 'pay now'.[58]

---

[54] CCR 2013, reg 13(2).
[55] Reg 16(4).
[56] See CRD, Art 8.
[57] Art 1(2).
[58] See p 32 of the European Commission DG Guidance.

Schedule 2

5.43

CCR 2013 Schedule 2

Information relating to distance and off-premises contracts

(a) **the main characteristics of the goods or services, to the extent appropriate to the medium of communication and to the goods or services;**[59]

(b) the identity of the trader (such as the trader's trading name);

(c) the geographical address at which the trader is established and, where available, the trader's telephone number, fax number and e-mail address, to enable the consumer to contact the trader quickly and communicate efficiently;

(d) where the trader is acting on behalf of another trader, the geographical address and identity of that other trader;

(e) if different from the address provided in accordance with paragraph (c), the geographical address of the place of business of the trader, and, where the trader acts on behalf of another trader, the geographical address of the place of business of that other trader, where the consumer can address any complaints;

(f) **the total price of the goods or services inclusive of taxes, or where the nature of the goods or services is such that the price cannot reasonably be calculated in advance, the manner in which the price is to be calculated,**

(g) where applicable, all additional delivery charges and any other costs or, where those charges cannot reasonably be calculated in advance, the fact that such additional charges may be payable;

(h) **in the case of a contract of indeterminate duration or a contract containing a subscription, the total costs per billing period or (where such contracts are charged at a fixed rate) the total monthly costs;**

(i) the cost of using the means of distance communication for the conclusion of the contract where that cost is calculated other than at the basic rate;

(j) the arrangements for payment, delivery, performance, and the time by which the trader undertakes to deliver the goods or to perform the services;

(k) where applicable, the trader's complaint handling policy;

(l) where a right to cancel exists, the conditions, time limit and procedures for exercising that right in accordance with regulations 27 to 38;

(m) where applicable, that the consumer will have to bear the cost of returning the goods in case of cancellation and, for distance contracts, if the goods, by their nature, cannot normally be returned by post, the cost of returning the goods;

(n) that, if the consumer exercises the right to cancel after having made a request in accordance with regulation 36(1), the consumer is to be liable to pay the trader reasonable costs in accordance with regulation 36(4);

---

[59] Bold emphasis added for the reg 14 information requirements for contracts concluded by electronic means.

(o) where under regulation 28, 36 or 37 there is no right to cancel or the right to cancel may be lost, the information that the consumer will not benefit from a right to cancel, or the circumstances under which the consumer loses the right to cancel;

(p) in the case of a sales contract, a reminder that the trader is under a legal duty to supply goods that are in conformity with the contract;

(q) where applicable, the existence and the conditions of after-sale customer assistance, after-sales services and commercial guarantees;

(r) the existence of relevant codes of conduct, as defined in regulation 5(3)(b) of the Consumer Protection from Unfair Trading Regulations 2008, and how copies of them can be obtained, where applicable;

(s) **the duration of the contract, where applicable, or, if the contract is of indeterminate duration or is to be extended automatically, the conditions for terminating the contract;**

(t) **where applicable, the minimum duration of the consumer's obligations under the contract;**

(u) where applicable, the existence and the conditions of deposits or other financial guarantees to be paid or provided by the consumer at the request of the trader;

(v) where applicable, the functionality, including applicable technical protection measures, of digital content;

(w) where applicable, any relevant compatibility of digital content with hardware and software that the trader is aware of or can reasonably be expected to have been aware of;

(x) where applicable, the possibility of having recourse to an out-of-court complaint and redress mechanism, to which the trader is subject, and the methods for having access to it.

Note: In the case of a public auction, the information listed in paragraphs (b) to (e) may be replaced with the equivalent details for the auctioneer.

Failure to provide required information

5.44 The consequence of a failure to comply with the consumer information requirements in Part 2 of CCR 2013 is set out in reg 18. The contract is treated as having a term that the trader has complied with his information duties under regs 9–14 and 16. It follows that the failure will usually amount to a breach of contract and the remedies open to a consumer will depend on the nature and gravity of the breach. The drafting of the CCR 2013 follows the CRD in its use of the words, 'before a consumer is bound'.[60] This is likely to refer only to the timing of the trader's duty to provide the information.[61] It is unlikely to mean that the consumer is not contractually bound under the terms of the contract as a consequence of any failure, however minor, of the duty to provide information. It has to be observed, however, that using the word 'bound' in this way is rather unclear.

---

[60] CCR 2013, regs 9(1), 10(1) and reg 13(1).
[61] This is also the view expressed in the BIS Guidance (December 2013) on implementing the CCR 2013.

5.45 A consumer's cancellation rights for off-premises contracts and distance sales will be preserved until the information requirements are remedied, for a maximum of 12 months (see reg 31 below). Every contract that Part 3 applies to is deemed[62] to contain a term that the trader has complied with the contract information requirements in regs 10–14 and 16 (for on-premises, off-premises and distance sales). It follows that a failure to provide the information is likely to amount to a breach of contract with the associated remedies.

5.46 Ordinarily a trader may recover from a consumer the diminution in value caused by unreasonable handling of delivered goods. However, this does not apply if the trader has failed to provide the consumer with required information about the right to cancel under para (l) of Sch 2.[63] A consumer is usually responsible for the cost of returning goods to a trader after a contract has been cancelled. However, if a trader has failed to provide the consumer with the required information about the consumer bearing the cost of returning goods under para (m) of Sch 2, the trader will be responsible for those costs (reg 35(6)). A consumer will also bear no cost for the supply of a service during the cancellation period if the trader failed to provide required Sch 2 information about cancellation rights and periods.[64]

CANCELLATION RIGHTS

5.47 The origin of cancellation rights in consumer contracts can be found in the Doorstep Selling Directive 85/577/EEC[65] and the Distance Selling Directive 97/7/EC.[66] Both of these Directives were implemented domestically by statutory instrument.[67]

5.48 Part 3 of the CCR 2013 provides consumers with cancellation rights for off-premises and distance contracts only. The CRD extended the cancellation period to 14 calendar days for both off-premises and distance contracts. This was implemented in Part 2 of the CCR 2013.

The right to cancel or withdraw

5.49 In determining whether a consumer has a right to cancel a contract it is important to consider five questions.

(a)   Does the CCR 2013 apply at all?

---

[62]   Reg 18.
[63]   CCR 2013, reg 34(11).
[64]   Sch 2, paras (l) and (m).
[65]   Council Directive 85/577/EEC to protect the consumer in respect of contracts negotiated away from business premises.
[66]   Directive 97/7/EC on the protection of consumers in respect of distance contracts.
[67]   Cancellation of Contracts made in a Consumer's Home or Place of Work etc Regulations 2008, SI 2008/1816 and the Consumer Protection (Distance Selling) Regulations 2000, SI 2000/2334 as amended by SI 2005/269.

(b)   Is the contract an 'off-premises contract' or a 'distance contract'?

(c)   Does the contract fall within any of the Part 3 exceptions?

(d)   Did the consumer cancel within the cancellation period or extended default cancellation period?

(e)   What is the effect of cancellation?

Withdrawing an offer and cancellation

5.50 The CCR 2013 refers both to 'cancellation' of a contract and also to a consumer's right to 'withdraw an offer'. Withdrawal covers the position when a consumer has made an offer, but that offer has not yet been accepted by the trader. In that situation there is no contractual agreement until the trader has accepted the offer. The CCR 2013 provides the same right to sever the relationship with a trader for a consumer withdrawing an offer as it does for a consumer cancelling a contract, regs 31 to 34.

Exercising the right to cancel or withdraw

5.51 Regulation 29 of the CCR 2013 provides a general right to cancel[68] a distance or off-premises contract at any time in the 14 days' cancellation period 'without giving any reason, and without incurring any liability'. The right is, however, subject to the four circumstances set out at regs 34 to 36. There are also numerous exceptions, which are discussed below.

5.52 A consumer wishing to withdraw from an offer, or cancel, may do so by informing the trader. This may be done either by using the form set out in part B of Sch 3, or by making any other 'clear statement setting out the decision to cancel the contract'.[69] The evidential burden is upon the consumer to show that the contract was cancelled during the cancellation period.[70] Regulation 32(5) incorporates the contractual postal rule such that a consumer who sends a letter, or other communication, to the trader will be treated as having cancelled the contract at the time at which the communication is sent, rather than when it is received by the trader.

The cancellation period

5.53 The cancellation period starts when the contract is made and its end date is defined in reg 30, depending upon the type of contract that has been entered into. This is summarised in the table below.

---

[68]   Or withdraw from an offer.
[69]   Reg 32.
[70]   Reg 32(6).

Type of contract	Cancellation period
A service contract	14 days after the day on which the contract was made
The supply of digital content not supplied on a tangible medium	14 days after the day on which the contract was made
A sales contract (goods or goods and services) *but see below*	14 days after the day on which the goods come into the physical possession of the consumer or the person that she asks you to deliver the goods to
A sales contract consisting of an order for multiple goods which are delivered on different days	14 days after the day on which the last of the goods come into the physical possession of the consumer or the person that she asks you to deliver the goods to
A sales contract consisting of an order for multiple lots or pieces which are delivered on different days	14 days after the day on which the last of the lots or pieces come into the physical possession of the consumer or the person that she asks you to deliver the goods to
A sales contract for regular delivery of goods during a period of longer than one day	14 days after the day on which the first of the goods come into the physical possession of the consumer or the person that she asks you to deliver the goods to

The cancellation period is extended, however, if the trader has breached the information requirements in Part 2 of the CCR 2013 (reg 31). The cancellation period continues to run until 14 days after the information failure is remedied by the trader, up to a maximum of 12 months. Note should also be taken of EC Regulation 1182/71,[71] which extends the last day of the cancellation period, if it falls on a Saturday, Sunday or Bank Holiday, to the next working day (see Chapter 2, para **2.63**).

Cancelling service contracts

5.54 A trader cannot supply a service during the cancellation period unless the consumer has made an express request that has also been recorded in a durable medium, in the case of an off-premises contract.[72] If such a request has been made and properly recorded, the consumer ceases to have the right to cancel[73] a service contract after it has been fully performed, if the service began with the consumer's acknowledgment that the right to cancel would be lost.[74]

---

[71] Regulation determining the rules and applicable periods, dates and time limits – see Art 3.4.
[72] CCR 2013, reg 36(1).
[73] Other than supply of water, gas electricity or district heating, reg 36(2).
[74] CCR 2013, reg 36(2).

Digital content not on a tangible medium

5.55 Regulation 36 of the CCR 2013 provides for an express exception to the right to cancel for the supply of digital content not on a tangible medium and the consumer consents. This is directed towards digital content that is supplied in an intangible form. Examples of this include software, mobile phone apps, books, music, film or ringtones that are downloaded or streamed, but not supplied in any tangible form. For the exception to apply the consumer must have given express *consent* and *acknowledged* that the consumer's right to cancel will be lost. The consumer will then cease to have the right to cancel if the supply of the digital content has begun *after* the consent and acknowledgment.[75]

Part 3 cancellation exceptions

5.56 Regulations 27 and 28 provide for a number of express exceptions to the right to cancel under Part 3 of the CCR 2013. These are summarised in the table below.

Regulation	Description	Exception
27(2)(a)	Medicines	Prescription medicinal products 'by administration by a prescriber'
27(2)(b)	Health products	Products supplied by a health care professional as part of the health service
27(2)(c)	Transport	Passenger transport services
27(4)	Less than £42	Off-premises contracts where the consumer pays less than £42
28(1)(a)	Financial markets	Price dependent on fluctuations in the financial market within cancellation period and not controllable by the trader
28(1)(b)	Bespoke goods	Supply of goods made to the consumer's specification or are clearly personalised
28(1)(c)	Perishables	Supply of goods liable to deteriorate or expire rapidly
28(1)(d)	Alcohol on market price	Alcoholic beverages, where value dependent on fluctuations in the market not controllable by the trader
28(1)(e)	Urgent repairs	Urgent repairs or maintenance, where consumer specifically requested a visit from the trader. But see reg 28(2) for services and goods 'in addition'
28(1)(f)	Newspapers	Newspapers, periodicals and magazines, with the exception of subscriptions

---

[75] CCR 2013, reg 37(1) and (2).

Regulation	Description	Exception
28(1)(g)	Public auctions	Contracts concluded at public auction (reg 5 – transparent, competitive bidding procedure run by an auctioneer where consumers are given the possibility to attend in person, and the successful bidder is bound to purchase)
28(1)(h)	Contracts for a specific time	Services where a specific date or period for performance is contracted: Transport of goods Vehicle rental service Catering or services related to leisure activities
28(3)(a)	Unhygienic returns	Sealed products that have been unsealed after delivery and are therefore unsuitable to return for health protection or hygiene reasons
28(3)(b)	Sealed recordings	Sealed audio recordings, video recordings or computer software unsealed after delivery
28(3)(c)	Mixed goods	Goods have become mixed inseparably with other items after delivery

Bespoke goods

5.57 Regulation 28(1)(b) of the CCR 2013 states that the cancellation provisions in Part 3 do not apply to 'the supply of goods that are made to the consumer's specifications or are clearly personalised'. Goods are defined as 'any tangible moveable items'. This is not further defined in the CCR 2013; however, Art 2(4) of the CRD provides a definition of 'goods made to the consumer's specifications' as 'non-pre-fabricated goods made on the basis of an individual choice or decision by the consumer'. Recital 49 of the CRD also states that the 'right of withdrawal should neither apply to goods made to the consumer's specifications or which are clearly personalised such as tailor-made curtains'.

5.58 The European Commission DG Guidance suggests that the exception should be 'interpreted narrowly'.

'So, this exception should cover, for example:

- goods, for which the consumer has provided specifications, such as measurements for furniture or the size of a fabric;
- goods, for which the consumer has requested specific personalised features, such as a particular design for a car that is made to order or a specific component for a computer, which has to be individually procured for that particular order and which was not part of the trader's general offer to the public;
- address labels with the consumer's contact information or T-shirts with a personalised print.

Specification/personalisation in this context should be taken to mean that the goods are, in principle, unique and produced according to the individual wishes and requirements stated by the consumer and agreed with the trader.

In contrast, where the consumer simply makes up the goods by picking from the standard (pre-set) options provided by the trader, such as colour or additional equipment in a car, or makes up a set of furniture on the basis of standard elements, it should not be possible to speak of either "specification" or "personalization" in the narrow sense of this provision.'

5.59 The BIS *Implementing Guidance to the Consumer Contracts Regulations*[76] states that an:

'item made up following a consumer order does not necessarily make it a bespoke item which is exempt from cancellation rights. An item, for example a sofa or computer, can be assembled following an order but the component parts may be made up of parts offered from a standard range. So, for instance, a sofa where the consumer chooses a fabric and colour from a range on offer will not be bespoke for the purposes of these Regulations. However, if the consumer asks the trader to source a special finish and which is not in the range generally offered by the trader, that is likely to be a bespoke item.'

5.60 The Guidance from both the European Commission and BIS suggests that the exception should be construed narrowly. The reference in the CRD to 'non-pre-fabricated goods' suggests that goods assembled from pre-fabricated component parts are less likely to fall within the exception if they are ordinarily available as part of the trader's range. It is likely that a distinction will be drawn between goods that are rendered unique when made up according to a consumer's specification and those that are merely the selection of options that a trader routinely makes available to consumers. Although this distinction may be difficult to draw for products with a vast array of options that are not assembled from pre-fabricated components.

5.61 A possible rationale for the bespoke goods exception is that it may be difficult for a trader to re-sell goods after they have been personalised or customised in accordance with an individual consumer's specification. The ability of a trader to resell goods may be a factor in determining whether the exception applies. It follows that it may be important to ascertain whether the assembly process is reversible.

Effect of cancellation or withdrawal

5.62 A contract that is effectively cancelled will end the contractual obligations of both parties to perform the contract. The same applies if the consumer withdraws an offer to enter into a distance or off-premises contract.[77]

---

[76] BIS Implementing Guidance, December 2013.
[77] Reg 33.

5.63 Under reg 38 ancillary contracts are automatically terminated as a consequence of cancellation or withdrawal.[78] 'Ancillary contract' is defined as one 'by which the consumer acquires goods or services relating to the main contract, where those goods or services are provided' by the trader or a 'third party on the basis of an arrangement between the third party and the trader'.[79]

Return of goods

5.64 In a sales contract the trader must collect goods that have been delivered to a consumer if he has offered to collect them, or (in the case of an off-premises contract) the goods have been delivered to the consumer's home and cannot 'by their nature, normally be returned by post' (reg 35(1)). Otherwise it is the consumer's responsibility to return[80] the goods to the trader without undue delay, and in any event not later than 14 days after cancellation.[81]

Reimbursement

5.65 The trader must generally reimburse all payments that have been made by a consumer. No fee may be charged for the reimbursement and it should be made using the same means of payment, unless the consumer has agreed otherwise.[82] Reimbursement must be made without undue delay and no later than 14 days after the trader receives the goods back[83] or has cancelled the contract.[84] This general right to reimbursement is, however, subject to four exceptions in regs 34–36.

Non-standard delivery charges

5.66 The trader must reimburse any payment that the consumer has made for delivery, unless the consumer expressly chose a more expensive delivery service 'costing more than the least expensive common and generally acceptable kind of delivery offered by the trader'.[85] If the consumer has chosen such a more expensive non-standard delivery service, the trader need only reimburse him the amount the trader charges for his standard delivery service.[86]

Value diminished by handling

5.67 In a sales contract the trader may make a deduction from the amount to be reimbursed to a consumer if the value of the goods is diminished because of

---

[78] Reg 38(2). The trader has the responsibility of informing any 'other trader with whom the consumer has an ancillary contract'.
[79] Reg 38(3).
[80] Reg 35(2) by sending them back or handing them over. Reg 35(3) deals with the appropriate address.
[81] Reg 35(4).
[82] CCR 2013, reg 34(7) and (8).
[83] CCR 2013, reg 34(5)(b) or has supplied evidence of having sent the goods back.
[84] See regs 34(4)–(6).
[85] CCR 2013, reg 34(2).
[86] CCR 2013, reg 34(3).

a consumer's handling 'beyond what is necessary to establish the nature, characteristics and functioning of the goods'.[87] This is further defined as handling that 'goes beyond the sort of handling that might reasonably be allowed in a shop'.[88]

5.68 The reduction made can amount to the entire contract price for the goods and can be deducted from the amount already paid by the consumer. However, if that is insufficient to pay for the diminution in value the consumer can be required to pay the amount to the trader.[89] The provisions permitting a trader to recover the diminution in value do not apply if the trader has failed to provide the consumer with required information about the right to cancel under para (l) of Sch 2.[90]

Cost of returning goods

5.69 In a sales contract the consumer must bear the direct cost of returning goods to the trader after cancellation. This is limited strictly to the actual cost of returning the goods and the consumer is not required to pay any additional amounts.[91] The consumer must pay the costs of returning the goods unless the trader has agreed to bear those costs or has failed to provide the consumer with required information about the consumer bearing such costs under para (m) of Sch 2.[92] The contractual term is statutorily implied that the trader must bear the costs of return when he has failed to provide that information.

Services provided during the cancellation period

5.70 If a trader legitimately[93] starts to perform a service during the cancellation period, but the consumer cancels before the service has been fully performed, the trader may recover a proportion of the total price he would have charged for the full coverage of the contract.[94] The recoverable amount is proportionate to the total price agreed unless that was 'excessive', in which case the market value is substituted.[95] A consumer will bear no cost for the supply of a service during the cancellation period of the trader failed to provide the Sch 2 information about cancellation rights and periods[96] or the service was not supplied in response to a consumer request recorded in a durable medium.[97]

---

[87] CCR 2013, reg 34(9).
[88] CCR 2013, reg 34(12).
[89] Under CCR 2013, reg 34(10)(b).
[90] CCR 2013, reg 34(11).
[91] CCR 2013, reg 6.
[92] CCR 2013, reg 35(5)(b).
[93] A trader cannot supply a service during the cancellation period unless the consumer has made an express request that has also been recorded, in the case of an off-premises contract in a durable medium, CCR 2013, reg 36(1).
[94] CCR 2013, reg 36(4).
[95] CCR 2013, reg 36(5)(b) market value 'calculated by comparing prices for equivalent services supplied by other traders'.
[96] Sch 2, paras (l) and (m).
[97] CCR 2013, reg 36(6).

Criminal offence

5.71

> **CCR 2013 Reg 19**
>
> *Offence relating to the failure to give notice of the right to cancel*
>
> **19**(1) A trader is guilty of an offence if the trader enters into an off-premises contract to which regulation 10 applies but fails to give the consumer the information listed in paragraph (l), (m) or (n) of Schedule 2 in accordance with that regulation.

This provision provides for criminal liability for a trader that fails, in an off-premises contract, to give a consumer notice of his cancellation rights. The remainder of the provisions in the CCR 2013 do not of themselves carry criminal sanction, although reg 6(3)(b) of CPUTR (misleading omissions in relation to Community obligations) should be considered in this context, see Chapter 7, Unfair Commercial Practices.

5.72 Enforcement of the CCR 2013 falls upon local weights and measures authorities and DETI in Northern Ireland.[98] In England and Wales proceedings for this offence can only be instituted by or on behalf of an enforcement authority.

5.73 The offence is also subject to a directors' liability provision (reg 22), a causal liability provision (reg 21) and a due diligence defence (reg 20). These types of provision are dealt with in greater detail in Chapter 3, Criminal Enforcement.

Sentencing

5.74 The offence is triable summarily and punishable by a fine.[99] As a consequence of s 85(1) of the Legal Aid, Sentencing and Punishment of Offenders Act 2012 the maximum fine is now not limited for offences committed on or after 12 March 2015. At the time of writing there were no appellate authorities on the levels of fines for offences under reg 19 of the CCR 2013.

5.75 It should be remembered, however, that the failure to notify a consumer of their cancellation rights might also generate criminal liability under the CPUTR, see Chapter 7 on Unfair Commercial Practices. In *R v Garfoot* and *Wilsher*,[100] a charge contrary to reg 8 of the CPUTR (contravening professional diligence) was brought where no cancellation rights were explained or communicated.[101]

---

[98]   CCR 2013, reg 23.
[99]   CCR 2013, reg 19(1).
[100]   [2011] EWCA Crim 2043.
[101]   In *R v Lewis Thomas Gilbertson* [2009] EWCA Crim 1715 the defendant pleaded guilty to two

CCR 2013 – OTHER MATTERS

5.76 Some provisions of the regulation have been moved to CRA 2015, in particular:

(a) Regulation 42 – time for delivery of goods – now CRA 2015, s 28.
(b) Regulation 43 – passing of risk – now CRA 2015, s 29.

Basic rate help-lines

5.77 Traders selling goods to consumers must have a basic rate telephone line available if they offer a telephone contact. This may be in addition to a premium rate number, or the sole contact number, but the requirement is that the consumer must be able to pay a basic rate – the same as a geographical, mobile or freephone number. This applies to any consumer contact 'in relation to contracts entered into with the trader'.[102] This is wider than simply having a customer service line and will also apply to calls for advice about what has been purchased or for amending a contract that has already been entered into – for example amending a flight booking. Consumers have the right to claim back any charge that exceeds the basic rate.[103]

Civil enforcement

5.78 The CCR 2013 places a duty upon an 'enforcement authority'[104] to consider any complaint regarding its contravention unless the complaint is frivolous or vexatious, or another enforcement authority has notified the CMA that it agrees to consider the complaint. Regulation 45 enables an enforcement authority to apply for an injunction, or in Scotland an interdict or order of specific implement, against any person who appears to be responsible for contravention of the CCR 2013. The CMA must be notified of any undertaking or court action.[105] The CCR 2013 is also prescribed as a community infringement for the purposes of the Enterprise Act 2002 (see Chapter 4, Civil Enforcement).[106]

PAYMENT SURCHARGES

5.79 The Consumer Rights (Payment Surcharges) Regulations 2012 (CR(PS) Regs) implement Art 19 of Directive 2011/83/EU of the European Parliament

---

misleading omission offences under CPUTR, reg 10 for failing to inform householders of their right to withdraw from a contract made after an unsolicited visit.

[102] CCR 2013, reg 41(1).
[103] CCR 2013, reg 41(2).
[104] A local weights and measures authority in Great Britain and the Department of Enterprise, Trade and Investment in Northern Ireland – reg 44(3).
[105] See reg 45.
[106] SI 2014/2908.

and Council on consumer rights. Laid before Parliament in December 2012, they came into force on 6 April 2013 and apply only to contracts entered into on or after that date (reg 1).

Purpose of the legislation

5.80   The central provision is at reg 4 which provides:

> **Excessive charges prohibited**
>
> A trader must not charge consumers, in respect of the use of a given means of payment, fees that exceed the cost borne by the trader for the use of that means.

That wording copies exactly the wording set out at Art 19 of the CRD.

5.81   The March 2013 Guidance on the CR(PS) Regs published by the Department for Business Innovation and Skills[107] ('BIS') comments that the policy objectives of the legislation are to:

> ' – increase price transparency, enhancing consumers' ability to choose effectively between different products and services; and
>
> – make payment surcharges cost reflective, steering consumers to the most efficient payment method,
>
> and thereby to remove barriers to effective competition both for the products and services being purchased and between payment methods.'

The Guidance anticipates that the CR(PS) Regs will be used in conjunction with the CPUTR to ensure surcharges are fair and transparent.

5.82   The CR(PS) Regs do not to prohibit payment surcharges in their entirety, but rather aim to ensure that such charges are limited to the costs borne by the trader, ie to ensure that such charges are not used as a 'back-door' method of generating profit for the trader. The BIS Guidance suggests that charges will not be caught by the legislation if the charge levied is the same no matter what method of payment is used because, in such a case, 'the charge would be part of the overall headline payment, and consumers would need to compare the overall price with what another trader charges.'

5.83   The CR(PS) Regs do not provide any further definition of 'means of payment', 'fee' or 'costs borne by the trader'. The BIS Guidance comments as follows:

> 'Means of payment clearly include (but are not limited to) cash, cheques, prepaid cards, charge cards, credit transfers and direct debits. As the technology relating to payments develops, any new methods of paying will also be subject to the prohibition.

---

[107] Now the Department for Business, Energy and Industrial Strategy.

...

"Fees" in the Department's view, include a payment surcharge payable other than in cash. This would be very unusual, but it is possible for example that a payment surcharge might be discharged using a voucher. The prohibition on the above cost surcharge would apply in the normal way.

...

The Department considers that under the Regulations and the Directive only the particular direct costs to a trader that are exclusively attributable to using a particular means of payment could be recoverable through a payment surcharge. A cost which is to indirect, such that an equivalent cost would have been incurred anyway for other means of payment, cannot properly be characterized as a cost "for" the use of the relevant means of payment.

The Department does not consider that indirect costs, such as general administrative overheads or staff training, should be included ...'

Scope of the CR(PS) Regs

5.84 The CR(PS) Regs apply to business-to-consumer contracts only. The legislation uses the terms 'trader' and 'consumer', which are both defined within reg 2 in the familiar way and are considered in more detail in Chapter 7, Unfair Commercial Practices and Chapter 8, Unfair Contract Terms.

5.85 Pursuant to reg 5(1), they apply to the extent that the payment in question relates to a contract 'is a sales or service contract, or a contract ... for the supply of water, gas, electricity, district heating or digital content' (reg 5(1)(a)) and 'is not an excluded contract' (reg 5(1)(b)). A specific list of 'excluded' contracts is set out at reg 5(2)(a)–(m) which, notably, includes contracts:

- for social services (reg 5(2)(a));
- for health services provided by health professionals (as defined by Art 3(f) of Directive 2011/24/EU on the application of patents' rights in cross-border healthcare) to patients (reg 5(2)(b));
- for services of a 'banking, credit, insurance, personal pension, investment or payment nature (reg 5(2)(d));
- relating to property including the creation of immovable property, rental of residential property and for the construction of new buildings or substantially new buildings by the conversion of existing buildings (reg 5(2)(e)–(g));
- for the supply of foodstuffs, beverages or other goods intended for current consumption in the household, and which are supplied by a trader on frequent and regular rounds to the consumer's home, residence or workplace (reg 5(2)(i)).

Enforcement

5.86 The CR(PS) Regs provide two methods of enforcement. The first, under reg 8, is by way of civil injunction against an offending trader in proceedings brought by an enforcement authority (being a local weights and measures authority in Great Britain and the Department for the Economy in Northern Ireland[108]). Such proceedings may be brought by an enforcement authority upon consideration of any complaint made to it about a contravention of reg 4.

5.87 Under reg 7, enforcement authorities are under an obligation to consider such complaints unless they appear to be 'frivolous or vexatious' (reg 7(1)(a)) or 'another enforcement authority has notified the OFT that it agrees to consider the complaint' (reg 7(1)(b)). If an enforcement authority has notified the OFT that it agrees to consider a complaint, it then comes under a duty to do so (reg 7(2)) and must decide whether or not to make an application under reg 8 and give reasons for its decision (reg 7(3)).

5.88 Alternatively, the CR(PS) Regs provide consumers with a direct right of redress against traders. Regulation 10 provides:

> **Consumer's right of redress**
>
> Where a trader charges a fee in contravention of regulation 4 –
>
> (a) any provision of a contract requiring the consumer to pay the fee is unenforceable to the extent of the excess charged; and
>
> (b) the contract for the purposes of which payment is made is to be treated as providing for the excess to be repaid to the consumer.

5.89 Accordingly, consumers who consider they may have been subject to a charge in contravention of reg 4 have a right to have any sum paid over and above the 'cost borne by the trader' refunded to them and might commence proceedings in the county court for the same.

SUPPLY OF GOODS, SERVICES AND DIGITAL CONTENT

Introduction

5.90 It has long been considered that UK law on the sale of goods and services was unnecessarily complex and in need of clarification and simplification. Part 1 of the CRA 2015 seeks to remedy that issue for the supply of goods, and services by consolidating the provisions as they apply to consumers. It also sets out, for the first time, rights and remedies for consumers who are supplied with digital content. It applies to contracts (whether written, oral or implied) for the supply of goods, services or digital content by a trader to a consumer. It came into effect on 1 October 2015 for contracts entered into from that date onwards.

---

[108] Formerly the Department of Enterprise, Trade and Industry ('DETI').

5.91 Part 1 of the CRA 2015 consolidates the main provisions in Sale of Goods Act 1979 ('SOGA 1979') and the main statutory provisions relating to the supply of services to consumers.[109] The focus of this legislation was to imply terms into consumer contracts to ensure that goods and services provided by a trader were of the agreed quality and description. This legislation will still be applicable, however, for contracts between traders or between consumers

5.92 A stated aim of the legislation was to make consumer rights 'more accessible to consumers, business and their advisers'.[110] It would improve consumer contract law if the disparate rules provisions could be brought together into a single provision that subjected all consumer supply contracts to the same rights and remedies. It was also suggested that this should be achieved using simpler language, avoiding specialist legal language such as the previous reference to 'implied terms'.

5.93 Part 1 of the CRA 2015 applies throughout the UK with slight modifications to reflect the different legal system in Scotland.[111]

5.94 The following is a summary of the law in an area that is complex. The legislation should be considered carefully together with the substantial body of case law that was built up around the previous law.

Mixed contracts

5.95 An important aspect of Part 1 of the CRA 2015 is its application to mixed contracts that involve some combination of the sale of goods, services or digital content. For example, the supply and installation of a central heating system is likely to involve goods (the boiler, radiators etc.) a service (the installation) and also digital content (the programmer). The CRA makes it clear[112] that each of the three chapters on goods, services and digital content may apply to a mixed contract. It follows that a consumer can take advantage of the applicable rights under each chapter if the contract involves any relevant element.

Definitions

Consumer and trader

5.96 The definitions of 'consumer' and 'trader'[113] are found in s 2 of the CRA 2015. These definitions are the same in the unfair terms provisions and under the Consumer Protection from Unfair Trading Regulations ('CPUTR'), where

---

[109] Supply of Goods (Implied Terms) Act 1973; Supply of Goods and Services Act 1982; Sale and Supply of Goods Act 1994; Sale and Supply of Goods to Consumers Regulations 2002.

[110] 'Consolidation and Simplification of UK Consumer Law 2010.' Commissioned by BIS.

[111] CRA 2015, ss 3(3)(e) and 48(3) (gratuitous contracts); s 27 (Consignation); s 30(8)–(10) Guarantees; s 46 (remedies for damage to a digital device) and s 58 (Powers of the court).

[112] CRA 2015, s 1(3)–(5).

[113] CRA 2015, s 2(7) 'Business' includes the activities of any government department or local or public authority.

they have been the subject of consideration by the courts. The definition of consumer and trader are now considered in Chapter 2, Interpreting Consumer Law.

5.97 Under s 2(4) of the CRA 2015 the evidential burden of proving that an individual is not a consumer is placed upon the trader.

Goods

5.98

> CRA 2015, s 2(8)
>
> "Goods" means any tangible moveable items, but that includes water, gas and electricity if and only if they are put up for supply in a limited volume or set quantity.

This new definition reflects that found in the 1999 Directive on certain aspects of the law of the sale of consumer goods and associated guarantees (Sale of Consumer Goods and Associated Consumer Guarantees Directive).[114]

Public auctions

5.99 The purchase of second hand goods at public auction, where individuals have the opportunity to attend in person, is treated as an exception to some of the rights afforded to a consumer in an ordinary sales contract. This exception has its origin in the Sale of Consumer Goods and Associated Consumer Guarantees Directive.[115] The rights that still apply relate to pre-contract information, delivery and risk.[116]

Supply of goods

Introduction

5.100 Chapter 2 of the CRA 2015 consolidates the law in relation to the sale and supply of goods by traders to consumers. It seeks to simplify the law and provide consistent remedies for goods supplied under different contract types such as sale, conditional sale, transfer, hire or hire purchase. It introduces a near absolute right for consumers to reject sub-standard goods within the first 30 days and claim a full refund. It also limits the number of repairs or replacements that a trader can offer before consumers can choose to demand their money back.

---

[114] 99/44/EC.
[115] 99/44/EC.
[116] Pre-contract information, CRA 2015, s 11(4) and (5) and s 12; delivery, s 28 and risk, s 29.

Goods contracts covered by Chapter 2

5.101 The goods contracts covered by Chapter 2 are set out in CRA 2015, ss 3 to 8. In addition to a sales contract, Chapter 2 applies to a contract for hire (s 6), hire purchase (s 7) and the transfer of goods (s 9). Section 5 defines a sales contract as one under which the 'trader transfers or agrees to transfer ownership of goods' to a consumer, who 'pays or agrees to pay the price'.[117] Conditional sales contracts[118] and contracts for goods to be manufactured in the future are also covered within the definition.[119]

5.102 Contracts for a 'trader to supply coins or notes (money) to consumers for use as currency' are excluded, although this will not be the case if money is supplied for another purpose such as a collector's item. Contracts for goods sold by execution or authority of law are not covered, such as goods sold under legal authority to pay off a debt. Chapter 2 also does not apply to contracts intended to operate as a mortgage, pledge, charge or other security. In Scotland it does not apply to a gratuitous contract.[120]

Rights for the supply of goods

The core rights

5.103 Part 2 of the CRA 2015 is designed to simplify and clarify the implied terms that were previously found in ss 12 to 15 of SOGA 1979. Section 14 clarifies the position when a consumer buys goods by reference to a model seen or examined. Sections 15 and 16 provide additional rights in relation to installation and goods with digital content.

Satisfactory quality

5.104

> **CRA 2015, s 9 Goods to be of satisfactory quality**
>
> (1) Every contract to supply goods is to be treated as including a term that the quality of the goods is satisfactory.
>
> (2) The quality of goods is satisfactory if they meet the standard that a reasonable person would consider satisfactory, taking account of –
>
> > (a)   any description of the goods,
> > (b)   the price or other consideration for the goods (if relevant), and
> > (c)   all the other relevant circumstances (see subsection (5)).
>
> (3) The quality of goods includes their state and condition; and the following aspects (among others) are in appropriate cases aspects of the quality of goods –

---

[117] Section 5(2) deals with goods.
[118] CRA 2015, s 5(3).
[119] CRA 2015, s 5(2).
[120] CRA 2015, s 3(3) also (d) in England, Wales and Northern Ireland contracts by deed where the only consideration is the presumed consideration imported by the deed.

(a)   fitness for all the purposes for which goods of that kind are usually supplied;

(b)   appearance and finish;

(c)   freedom from minor defects;

(d)   safety;

(e)   durability.

(4) The term mentioned in subsection (1) does not cover anything which makes the quality of the goods unsatisfactory –

(a)   which is specifically drawn to the consumer's attention before the contract is made,

(b)   where the consumer examines the goods before the contract is made, which that examination ought to reveal, or

(c)   in the case of a contract to supply goods by sample, which would have been apparent on a reasonable examination of the sample.

(5) The relevant circumstances mentioned in subsection (2)(c) include any public statement about the specific characteristics of the goods made by the trader, the producer or any representative of the trader or the producer.

(6) That includes, in particular, any public statement made in advertising or labelling.

(7) But a public statement is not a relevant circumstance for the purposes of subsection (2)(c) if the trader shows that –

(a)   when the contract was made, the trader was not, and could not reasonably have been, aware of the statement,

(b)   before the contract was made, the statement had been publicly withdrawn or, to the extent that it contained anything which was incorrect or misleading, it had been publicly corrected, or

(c)   the consumer's decision to contract for the goods could not have been influenced by the statement.

(8) In a contract to supply goods a term about the quality of the goods may be treated as included as a matter of custom.

(9) See section 19 for a consumer's rights if the trader is in breach of a term that this section requires to be treated as included in a contract.

The implied term that goods should be of satisfactory quality is derived from the requirement in the Sale of Goods Act 1893 that goods should be of 'merchantable quality'. This remained the position in SOGA 1979 until 1994 when the standard was amended to the more accessible definition of 'satisfactory quality'.[121] CRA 2015, s 9 also requires that goods sold to consumers be of satisfactory quality and is almost identical to s 14(2) of SOGA 1979.[122] It follows that authorities on s 14 will remain relevant.

5.105   The duty to supply goods that are of satisfactory quality is strict. A trader cannot argue that he has taken all possible care or that he had not seen

---

[121]   Sale and Supply of Goods Act 1994, s 1.

[122]   As it was amended by the Sale and Supply of Goods Act 1994.

the goods.[123] The responsibility is the trader's and, as against the consumer, he cannot rely on undertakings given by his own supplier.[124] The burden of proof under s 9 remains on the consumer to the civil standard. However, if a consumer can show that goods were not of satisfactory quality during the first 6 months after delivery, there is a statutory presumption that they were not of satisfactory quality when delivered.[125]

5.106 It is important to recognise that the price at which goods are sold is relevant to the standard that a reasonable person would consider satisfactory.[126] It is plain that this standard might be very different for goods sold brand new, second hand[127] or as scrap. In the Scottish case of *Thain v Anniesland Trade Centre* a second-hand car that developed a faulty gearbox within 2 weeks of purchase was found to have been of satisfactory quality because of its relatively low price.[128]

5.107 The requirement to consider 'all the other relevant circumstances' in s 9(2)(c) reflects the common sense notion that the 'standard that a reasonable person would consider satisfactory' must not be approached artificially without consideration of relevant circumstances. In a case under s 14 of SOGA 1979, *Bramhill v Edwards,* the Court of Appeal made clear that, 'although the test is objective, the reasonable buyer must be attributed with knowledge of all relevant background facts.'[129]

5.108 The requirement that goods be free of 'minor defects' reflects the approach taken in *Rogers v Parish (Scarborough) Ltd*,[130] which was decided before s 14 of SOGA 1979 was amended to include that term. That case involved a defective Range Rover motorcar that had been sold new. Mustill LJ stated that it was 'not merely the buyer's purpose of driving the car from one place to another, but of doing so with an appropriate degree of comfort, ease of handling and reliability and, one may add, of pride in the vehicle's outward and interior purpose'.

5.109 In *Clegg v Andersson (trading as Nordic Marine)*,[131] Mr and Mrs Clegg had bought a brand new yacht for £236,000. The yacht had been supplied with

---

[123] *Grant v Australian Knitting Mills Ltd* [1936] 1 AC 85.
[124] *Young & Marten Ltd v McManus Childs Ltd* [1969] 1 AC 454.
[125] CRA 2015, s 19(14) and (15).
[126] CRA 2015, s 9(2)(b).
[127] See eg, *Bartlett v Sydney Marcus Ltd* [1965] 1 WLR 1013.
[128] 1997 SLT (Sh Ct) 102, 1997 SCLR 991 in the Glasgow Sheriff Court – consumer purchase of a second-hand motorcar with an automatic gear box that had done 80,000 miles and was sold by a trader for £2,995. The consumer had declined a 3-month warranty that was on offer. After about two weeks' use of the car the consumer noticed an intermittent droning noise, the source of which was a faulty gearbox. However, it was not economic to replace the gearbox. The trader had offered the consumer a number of alternative cars as a replacement but none was acceptable to her and she insisted that the gearbox should be replaced.
[129] *Bramhall v Edwards* [2004] EWCA Civ 403 (the sale of a motor home between consumers).
[130] [1987] QB 933.
[131] [2003] EWCA Civ 320, [2003] 1 All ER (Comm) 721, per Hale LJ.

a keel, designed for stability, that was too heavy. The supplier offered to correct the defect for free. The Court of Appeal rejected the argument that the boat was of satisfactory quality. Hale LJ stated:

> 'In some cases, such as a high priced quality product, the customer may be entitled to expect that it is free from even minor defects, in other words perfect or nearly so.'

5.110 *Lamarra v Capital Bank plc*[132] concerned the hire and subsequent purchase of a brand new luxury motor car that had been sold with a number of defects,[133] but also a trader warranty. The consumer was entitled to reject the car despite the warranty covering those defects. Although satisfactory quality did not imply perfection in the goods concerned, the Scottish Court of Session found that the warranty was not a justification for the supply of goods that were of unsatisfactory quality. It was held that, while 'the words "all the other relevant circumstances" are potentially of wide scope ... in the context, they must be seen as referring only to circumstances actually bearing upon the quality of the goods in question'.[134]

5.111 The implied term of satisfactory quality is excluded for faults that are pointed out to a consumer, that should have been apparent from the consumer's examination of the goods, or which have been apparent from a consumer's reasonable examination of a sample.[135] The Act does not require a consumer to examine goods for faults; the test is whether the examination that they did carry out would have revealed that particular defect.

Fit for particular purpose

5.112

> **CRA 2015, s 10 Goods to be fit for particular purpose**
>
> (1) Subsection (3) applies to a contract to supply goods if before the contract is made the consumer makes known to the trader (expressly or by implication) any particular purpose for which the consumer is contracting for the goods.
>
> (2) Subsection (3) also applies to a contract to supply goods if –
>
> > (a) the goods were previously sold by a credit-broker to the trader,
> >
> > (b) in the case of a sales contract or contract for transfer of goods, the consideration or part of it is a sum payable by instalments, and
> >
> > (c) before the contract is made, the consumer makes known to the credit-broker (expressly or by implication) any particular purpose for which the consumer is contracting for the goods.

---

[132] [2006] CSIH 49, 2007 SC 95.

[133] Front wheels incorrectly balanced causing excessive tyre wear; road speed related noise; scratch on the ashtray cover; misalignment of the glove box and poorly finished paintwork on parts of the roof.

[134] Per Lord Osbourne at para 62.

[135] CRA 2015, s 59(4); see also *R & B Customs Brokers v United Dominions Trust* [1988] 1 WLR 321.

(3) The contract is to be treated as including a term that the goods are reasonably fit for that purpose, whether or not that is a purpose for which goods of that kind are usually supplied.

(4) Subsection (3) does not apply if the circumstances show that the consumer does not rely, or it is unreasonable for the consumer to rely, on the skill or judgment of the trader or credit-broker.

(5) In a contract to supply goods a term about the fitness of the goods for a particular purpose may be treated as included as a matter of custom.

This provision is very similar to s 14(3) of SOGA 1979 and it follows that case law concerning that provision is likely to be relevant. The use of the words, 'expressly or by implication', suggest that the surrounding circumstances of a contractual relationship are likely to be considered when determining the particular purpose.

5.113 In *Ashington Piggeries v Christopher Hill Ltd*[136] the House of Lords framed the test as *what could reasonably be foreseen* as the particular purpose. An illustration of this can be found in *Griffiths v Peter Conway Ltd* where the purchaser of a tweed coat developed a skin condition because of her unusually sensitive skin. The seller was not liable as the coat would not have harmed a normal person and the purchaser had not herself realised that she had such a skin condition.[137]

5.114 There are various examples of consumer goods that the courts have found were not fit for a particular purpose, including *Godley v Perry*[138] (broken plastic catapult); *Priest v Last*[139] (bursting hot water bottle); *Grant v Australian Knitting Mills Ltd*[140] (irritating underwear); *R & B Customs Brokers Ltd v United Dominions Trust Ltd*[141] (car that leaked); *Spencer v Claude Rye Vehicles*[142] (overheating motorcar); *Jackson v Chrysler Acceptances Ltd*[143] (car for holiday) and *Finch Motors Ltd v Quin (No 2)* (car for towing a boat).

5.115 In *Lambert v Lewis*[144] the House of Lords considered a defective trailer coupling that had led to a fatal accident. Lord Roskill stated in relation to the implied term concerning fitness for purpose that it was:

'a continuing warranty that the goods will continue to be fit for that purpose for a reasonable time after delivery, so long as they remain in the same apparent state as that in which they were delivered, apart from normal wear and tear. What is a reasonable time will depend upon the nature of the goods.'

---

[136] [1972] AC 441.
[137] [1939] 1 All ER 685, see also *Salter v Finning Ltd* [1997] AC 473.
[138] [1960] 1 WLR 9.
[139] [1903] 2 KB 148.
[140] [1936] AC 85.
[141] [1988] 1 WLR 321.
[142] *The Guardian*, 19 December 1972.
[143] [1978] RTR 474.
[144] [1982] AC 225, at 226.

Goods to be as described

5.116

> **CRA 2015, s 11 Goods to be as described**
>
> (1) Every contract to supply goods by description is to be treated as including a term that the goods will match the description.
>
> (2) If the supply is by sample as well as by description, it is not sufficient that the bulk of the goods matches the sample if the goods do not also match the description.
>
> (3) A supply of goods is not prevented from being a supply by description just because –
>
> > (a)   the goods are exposed for supply, and
> > (b)   they are selected by the consumer.
>
> (4) Any information that is provided by the trader about the goods and is information mentioned in paragraph (a) of Schedule 1 or 2 to the Consumer Contracts (Information, Cancellation and Additional Charges) Regulations 2013 (SI 2013/3134) (main characteristics of goods) is to be treated as included as a term of the contract.
>
> (5) A change to any of that information, made before entering into the contract or later, is not effective unless expressly agreed between the consumer and the trader.
>
> (6) See section 2(5) and (6) for the application of subsections (4) and (5) where goods are sold at public auction.[145]

This provision is similar to SOGA 1979, s 13 but now refers to the information obligation in the CCR 2013 to provide information about the 'main characteristics of the goods'. A failure to do so will amount to a breach of a core term and will provide consumers with the same range of remedies available for other breaches of a core term. The same remedies are not available, however, in relation to the other CCR 2013 information obligations.

Goods to match a sample

5.117

> **CRA 2015, s 13 Goods to match a sample**
>
> (1) This section applies to a contract to supply goods by reference to a sample of the goods that is seen or examined by the consumer before the contract is made.
>
> (2) Every contract to which this section applies is to be treated as including a term that –
>
> > (a)   the goods will match the sample except to the extent that any differences between the sample and the goods are brought to the consumer's attention before the contract is made, and
> > (b)   the goods will be free from any defect that makes their quality unsatisfactory and that would not be apparent on a reasonable

---

[145] Section 11(7) is identical to s 9(9) above.

examination of the sample.[146]

Goods to match model seen or examined

5.118

> **CRA 2015, s 14 Goods to match a model seen or examined**
>
> (1) This section applies to a contract to supply goods by reference to a model of the goods that is seen or examined by the consumer before entering into the contract.
>
> (2) Every contract to which this section applies is to be treated as including a term that the goods will match the model except to the extent that any differences between the model and the goods are brought to the consumer's attention before the consumer enters into the contract.[147]

Other rights

Installation as part of conformity of the goods

5.119

> **CRA 2015, s 15 Installation as part of conformity of the goods with the contract**
>
> (1) Goods do not conform to a contract to supply goods if –
>
> (a)   installation of the goods forms part of the contract,
> (b)   the goods are installed by the trader or under the trader's responsibility, and
> (c)   the goods are installed incorrectly
>
> (2) Every contract to which this section applies is to be treated as including a term that the goods will match the model except to the extent that any differences between the model and the goods are brought to the consumer's attention before the consumer enters into the contract.[148]

Although new, this term reflects a requirement of the Sale of Consumer Goods and Associated Consumer Guarantees Directive. Logically this term does not entitle a consumer to exercise a short-term right to reject goods that are not installed properly.

5.120   This illustrates how different terms will apply to the same situation in a mixed contract, with overlapping but, sometimes, different remedies. As an example, a newly installed patio door that does not lock could breach this term but could also not be of satisfactory quality (s 9), or might constitute a failure to use reasonable care and skill in the provision of a service (s 49).

---

[146]   Section 13(3) is identical to s 9(9) above.
[147]   Section 14(3) is identical to s 9(9) above.
[148]   Section 14(3) is identical to s 9(9) above.

Digital content within goods must conform

5.121

> **CRA 2015, s 16 Goods not conforming if digital content does not conform**
>
> (1) Goods (whether or not they conform otherwise to a contract to supply goods) do not conform to it if -
>
>   (a)   the goods are an item that includes digital content, and
>   (b)   the digital content does not conform to the contract to that content (for which see section 42(1).
>
> (2) See section 19 for the effect of goods not conforming to the contract.

Unlike the CCR 2013, the CRA 2015 deals with both tangible and intangible digital content.

Pre-contract information

5.122 Section 12 provides that pre-contract information that a trader is required to give a consumer under the CCR 2013, other than the main characteristics of the goods (see s 11), should be a contractual term.

The right to supply

5.123 Section 17 provides a contractual term that a trader has the right to supply the goods. It also repeats the SOGA 1979 term[149] that a consumer should have 'quiet possession' of the goods in that the consumer's possession of the goods will not be disturbed by the trader.[150]

Delivery and risk

5.124 Section 28 of the CRA 2015 provides for a contractual term that the trader must deliver goods to a consumer unless they have agreed otherwise. Where there has been no agreement about when the goods will be delivered there is included a term that they must be delivered 'without undue delay' and in any event 'not more than 30 days' after the contract was entered into.

5.125 Section 28 also provides for when a trader does not deliver goods at the agreed time. A consumer may treat the contract 'as at an end' if the trader has refused to deliver goods, the consumer has specified that the time for delivery is essential or it is essential having regard to the relevant circumstances.[151] The trader must then reimburse all payments to a consumer without undue delay.[152]

5.126 Section 29 provides for a term that the goods remain at the trader's risk until they 'come into the physical possession' of the consumer.[153] However, this

---

[149] SOGA 1979, s 12(2)(b).
[150] CRA 2015, s 17(6)–(7).
[151] CRA 2015, s 28(5) and (6), see also s 28(7) and (8) for specified periods for delivery.
[152] CRA 2015, s 28(9).
[153] CRA 2015, s 29(2) or a person identified by the consumer to take possession of the goods.

does not apply if the goods are delivered to a carrier that is commissioned by the consumer and not provided as an option by the trader.[154] Sections 28 and 29 are identical to regs 42 and 43 of the CCR 2013 which were revoked for contracts entered into after 1 October 2015.[155] Section 26 additionally provides rules in relation to contracts for instalment deliveries.

Delivery of the wrong quantity

5.127 Under s 25 a consumer has the right to reject goods if the trader delivers a quantity less than was agreed. If he accepts them, however, he must pay for them at the contract rate.[156] If the trader delivers more than the agreed quantity the consumer may reject all of the goods or just the excess. Although there would not appear to be any specific right in s 28 for a consumer to accept a larger amount, he must pay for the larger amount at the contract rate if he keeps it.[157] In order to reject goods under s 25 the consumer must indicate to the trader that he is rejecting the goods so that 'it is clear enough to be understood by the trader'.

Remedies – sale of goods

Overview of the new remedies

5.128 A major change that the CRA 2015 sought to introduce was a single, coherent set of remedies in accordance with those required by the Sale of Consumer Goods and Associated Consumer Guarantees Directive.[158] A purpose of the CRA 2015 was to make the language more accessible to consumers and businesses and consequently words such as 'breach' 'rescission' or 'acceptance' are not used.

5.129 The main statutory remedies in ss 19–24 arise when goods do not conform to any of the core standards,[159] installation standard,[160] or included digital content does not conform to the core standards in Chapter 3 (Digital content).[161] These new rights are additional to other legal rights or common law contractual remedies available to a consumer.[162]

5.130 In summary, the effect of the new provisions is that a consumer will usually[163] have the right to reject goods that do not conform during the first 30 days after receipt and claim a full refund (the 'short term right to reject'). The consumer also has the alterative right to claim a free repair or replacement,

---

[154] CRA 2015, s 29(3).
[155] The Consumer Contracts (Amendment) Regulations 2015, SI 2015/1629.
[156] CRA 2015, s 25(10).
[157] CRA 2015, s 25(2) and (3).
[158] The Sale of Goods Act was amended by the Sale of Supply of Goods to Consumers Regulations 2002, SI 2002/3045.
[159] CRA 2015, s 19(3).
[160] CRA 2015, s 15.
[161] CRA 2015, s 16.
[162] CRA 2015, s 19(9)–(11).
[163] Not in the case of defective installation under CRA 2015, s 15.

which continues after the expiry of the 30 days. If the consumer has exercised this right[164] and the goods still do not conform, the consumer may then choose between a price reduction and the final right to reject. If the consumer chooses the final right to reject the goods, in the first 6 months he will ordinarily be entitled to a full refund (except in the case of motor vehicles). If he rejects the goods after six months, a deduction for the usage of the goods may be made from the consumer's refund.

5.131 There is a rebuttable presumption that goods which do not conform during the first 6 months, did not conform on the day they were delivered to the consumer.[165] This, reverse burden of proof, is not available if a consumer is exercising their short-term right to reject. Those rights in the CRA 2015 that are not specifically time limited are subject only to the periods set out in the ordinary rules of limitation for civil proceedings.

Short-term right to reject

5.132 The short-term right to reject applies for a breach of the core rights and s 16 digital content, but not in relation to a breach of s 15 installation. It applies during the first 30 days after the consumer has taken possession or ownership of the goods and they have been delivered and installed if appropriate.[166] A shorter period may apply for perishable goods, although what this might be is not defined.[167] If the consumer asks or agrees to the trader repairing or replacing the goods, the period stops running during the waiting time. When the trader provides repaired or replaced goods the short term right to reject continues for at least 7 days, or more if the original expiry date is later.[168]

Effects of rejection generally

5.133 The contract is treated at an end when a consumer rejects goods under s 20 by indicating clearly[169] that he is 'rejecting the goods and treating the contract at an end'. This applies both to the short term and final right to reject goods. Under s 19 there is also the right to partial rejection of goods so that the consumer may reject 'some or all' of the goods.

5.134 On rejection the trader then has a duty to refund the consumer in accordance with the provisions in s 20(9) to (19). If a consumer has paid in money he is entitled to be repaid in the same amount using the same means of payment. The right is qualified where the consumer has not paid in money and it is not possible to return what he has used to pay in its original state, although this problem may be resolved by a claim in damages.[170] After the consumer has

---

[164] Or it is impossible or unfeasible to do so, CRA 2015, s 23(4).
[165] CRA 2015, s 19(14) and (15).
[166] CRA 2015, s 22(3), although the consumer may reject at an earlier stage (s 22(5)).
[167] CRA 2015, s 22(4).
[168] CRA 2015, s 22(6), (7) and (8).
[169] Clear enough to be understood by the trader, CRA 2015, s 20(6).
[170] CRA 2015, s 20(18) and (19).

rejected the goods he also has a duty to 'make the goods available for collection by the trader' or, where the consumer has agreed, to return them to the trader. However, in either case the trader must bear any reasonable costs incurred by the consumer, unless they are returning the goods to where they originally took possession of them.[171]

Right to repair or replacement

5.135 The statutory right to a repair or a replacement under s 23 is available from the time that a consumer receives the goods and is not subject to any time limit other than the ordinary limitation period for civil proceedings. The right is available when goods do not conform to any of the core standards,[172] installation standard,[173] or included digital content does not conform to the core standards in Chapter 3 (Digital content).[174] If a consumer exercises this right the trader must repair or replace the goods for free within a reasonable time and without significant inconvenience to the consumer.[175] A consumer who requires or agrees to the repair of goods cannot require the trader to replace them, or exercise the short-term right to reject (if still within the initial 30-day period), without giving the trader a reasonable time to repair them.[176]

5.136 Unlike the initial short-term right to reject, there is an element of proportionality built into this right. Section 23(3) states that a consumer cannot ask a trader for a repair or a replacement if that remedy is impossible or disproportionate to the other remedy. This is assessed upon the basis of the price of the goods, the significance of the other remedy and whether the alternative remedy can be delivered without causing the consumer significant inconvenience.[177] The assessment of what is a reasonable time or significant inconvenience should take account of the nature of the goods and the purpose for which were acquired.[178] A consumer must ordinarily have required the trader to repair or replace goods before he can exercise his right to a price reduction or the final right to reject under s 24. However, he need only exercise the right once and need not do so if repair or replacement is impossible or disproportionate.[179]

Price reduction or the final right to reject

5.137 Section 24 provides for the right to a price reduction or a final right to reject. The remedies are alternatives and the consumer must therefore choose between them. Under s 24(5) a consumer can only use either remedy if one of three separate circumstances occurs.

---

[171] CRA 2015, s 20(7)(b) and (8).
[172] CRA 2015, s 19(3).
[173] CRA 2015, s 15.
[174] CRA 2015, s 16.
[175] CRA 2015, s 23(3).
[176] CRA 2015, s 23(6) and conversely if the consumer requires a replacement he cannot require repair or exercise the short term right to reject, CRA 2015, s 23(7).
[177] CRA 2015, s 23(4).
[178] CRA 2015, s 23(5).
[179] CRA 2015, s 23(3) to (5).

- The first is that the goods still do not conform after 'one repair or one replacement'.[180] Not conforming in this context means the failure of the goods to comply with the core standards, the standards for installation[181] or digital content[182] or generally failing to comply with 'requirements that are stated in the contract'.[183]

- The second is that the consumer cannot require the trader to replace or repair the goods because that is impossible or disproportionate.[184]

- The third is that the consumer has already required the trader to repair or replace the goods but the trader has failed to do so 'within a reasonable time and without significant inconvenience to the consumer.'[185]

5.138 If any one of those three circumstances apply then the consumer is entitled to choose between the right to a price reduction and the final right to reject. The right to a price reduction is the right to a refund of 'an appropriate amount' from what the consumer has already 'paid, or otherwise transferred'.[186] As under s 20 the right may be qualified where the consumer has not paid in money.[187] If a consumer chooses to exercise the final right to reject the goods the provisions in s 20 apply and the consumer is entitled to a refund.

Final right to reject – deduction for usage

5.139 The consumer is entitled to a refund if the final right to reject is exercised. This is subject to a reduction to take account of the consumer's use of the goods in the period since they were delivered.[188] However, no deduction for usage can be made if the final right to reject is exercised during the first 6 months,[189] save in the case of a motor vehicle.[190]

Pre-contract information

5.140 A consumer has the right to recover any costs[191] that have been incurred as a result of any breach of terms that import[192] pre-contract information.[193]

---

[180] As defined by CRA 2015, s 24(6) and (7).
[181] CRA 2015, s 15.
[182] CRA 2015, s 16.
[183] CRA 2015, s 19(1).
[184] For the purposes of CRA 2015, s 23(3).
[185] For the purposes of CRA 2015, s 23(2)(a).
[186] CRA 2015, s 24(1).
[187] CRA 2015, s 24(3) and (4).
[188] CRA 2015, s 24(8).
[189] Defined in CRA 2015, s 24(11).
[190] CRA 2015, s 24(10) and this exception may be supplemented by statutory instrument (s 24(10)(b)). A 'motor' vehicle' is defined in s 24(12) and (13).
[191] CRA 2015, s 19(5).
[192] Required by the CCR 2013, regs 9, 10 and 13.
[193] CRA 2015, s 12.

Right to supply

5.141 A consumer will have the right to reject goods if there is a breach of s 17(1) because the trader did not have the legal right to supply the goods to the consumer. This right is not time limited other than by the ordinary rules of limitation for civil proceedings.

Summary table

5.142 The remedies under Chapter 1 of the CRA 2015 for contracts for the sale of goods are summarised in the following table.

Type of breach	Remedy
s 9 goods to be of satisfactory quality; s 10 goods to be fit for a particular purpose; s 11 goods to be as described by the trader; s 13 goods to match a sample; s 14 goods to match a model; s 16 included digital content to conform with standards in Chapter 3 (Digital content)	The short term right to reject, under s 20 The right to a repair or replacement, under s 23 The right to a price reduction or the final right to reject, under s 24
s 15 Goods incorrectly installed by the trader where installation is a part of the contract	The right to a repair or replacement under s 23 The right to a price reduction or final right to reject, under s 24
s 12 inclusion of certain pre-contract information as terms of the contract	The right to recover any costs incurred by the consumer as a result of the failure to provide certain pre-contract information, up to the price paid, under s 19(5)
s 17 the trader has the right to supply the goods	The right to reject, under s 19(6)
s 28 late delivery of goods	The right to be reimbursed of all payments made under the contract without undue delay, under s 28(9)

Exclusion of liability not permitted

5.143 A term that excludes or restricts any of the supply of goods rights is not binding on a consumer to the extent that it excludes or restricts a right or remedy, applies restrictive or onerous conditions, allows the trader to put a consumer pursuing such a right or remedy at a disadvantage, or excluding rules of evidence or procedure.[194] Unfair contract terms are dealt with in Chapter 8.

---

[194] CRA 2015, s 31(1) and (2).

Services

Introduction

5.144 Chapter 4 provides for rights and remedies in contracts where a trader supplies a service to a consumer. It sets out four basic contractual rights and provides for the remedies on breach that a consumer is entitled to request and the trader must offer. The two key remedies are the right for a trader to re-perform the service or where that is not possible or feasible to make a reduction in the price paid.

5.145 Chapter 4 does not apply to contracts for employment or apprenticeship (s 48(2)) or to a gratuitous contract in Scotland.

5.146 It should be noted that the Provision of Services Regulations 2009[195] also creates regulatory obligations in relation to services (see below). In particular reg 12 requires that the provider of a service must respond to complaints as quickly as possible and make best efforts to find a satisfactory solution. These provisions can be enforced under Part 8 of the Enterprise Act 2002 (see Chapter 4, Civil Enforcement).

Standards for services

5.147 Section 49 provides for a term the trader will perform the service with reasonable care and skill. This follows the similar term in s 13 of the Supply of Goods and Services Act 1982. Section 50 provides a new right that 'anything that is said or written to the consumer by or on behalf of the trader about the trader or service' is a term of the contract' if the consumer takes it into account when deciding whether to enter into the contract or making any subsequent decision about the service. This is, however, subject to any qualifications made by the trader at the time and any agreed changes.[196] Pre-contract information required for on-premises, off-premises and distance contracts[197] is also treated as a contractual term. Section 51 provides that where a contract does not fix the price to be paid, it will include a term that the 'consumer must pay a reasonable price for the service, and no more'. Section 52 makes similar provision for contracts that 'do not fix the time for the service to be performed' by providing an implied term that the trader 'must perform the service within a reasonable time'.

5.148 These standard terms do not affect any other 'enactment or rule of law' that imposes a stricter duty on the trader, or 'defines or restricts the rights, duties or liabilities' arising.[198] Section 57 prevents the exclusion or restriction of liabilities created under these consumer rights.

---

[195] SI 2009/2999 implementing the Services Directive 2006/123/EC.
[196] CRA 2015, s 50(2).
[197] CCR 2013, regs 9, 10 and 13.
[198] CRA 2015, s 53.

Remedies – services

5.149 The remedies provided for in Chapter 4 are additional to any rights available to a consumer in general contract law.[199] The key right in relation to services is to require the trader to repeat performance to the extent that is necessary to comply with the ss 49 and 51 terms, in relation to reasonable care and skill and in accordance with the information provided by the trader. The right is phrased 'perform the service again to the extent necessary to complete its performance in conformity with the contract',[200] which suggests that the trader is not required to redo the work completely, but put right those faults in the original performance sufficiently to make it conform.

5.150 The right to repeat performance, to an extent, limits the right of a consumer to an immediate price reduction for breaches of ss 49 and 50. Where there is a right to repeat performance, a price reduction under s 56 may only be obtained when repeat performance is impossible[201] or the trader is in breach of the requirement to do the repeat work 'within a reasonable time and without inconvenience to the consumer'.[202]

5.151 The remedies in Chapter 4 in relation to contracts for services are summarised in the table below.

Type of breach	Remedy
s 49 service to be performed with reasonable care and skill s 50 information relating to the performance of the service that s50 requires to be a term of the contract	The right to require repeat performance, under s 55. The right to a price reduction, under s 56, but only after repeat performance has become impossible or has not been provided within a reasonable time or without significant inconvenience to the consumer
s 50 information relating to the trader that s 50 requires to be a term of the contract	The right to a price reduction, under s 56. There is no right to repeat performance
s 52 Performance within a reasonable time	The right to a price reduction, under s 56. There is no right to repeat performance
s 51 Reasonable price to be paid for a service in the absence of a price being fixed	No special remedy under Chapter 4

---

[199] CRA 2015, s 54(6) and (7).
[200] CRA 2015, s 55(1).
[201] CRA 2015, s 55(3) 'if completing performance of the service in conformity with the contract is impossible'.
[202] CRA 2015, s 55(2) and (4).

Digital content

Introduction

5.152 Chapter 3 of Part 1 of CRA 2015 seeks to clarify the treatment of digital content as between the different standards that had applied for goods and services. The legal rights of consumers were not clear when digital content proved defective or otherwise unsatisfactory. The new legislation is based on the premise that digital content ought to be treated the same as physical goods 'so far as that is possible'.[203]

Meaning of digital content

5.153 Digital content is defined as 'data which are produced and supplied in digital form'.[204] This will include a wide variety of digital products such as computer software, mobile phone apps, books, music, film or ringtones that are downloaded or streamed. It will apply to tangible goods that contain data in a digital form such as a compact disc, Blue-ray or DVD. It will also apply to goods that have parts that include data in a digital form such as a mobile phone, television, car, computer or washing machine.

5.154 The provisions in s 1 of the CRA 2015 concerning mixed contracts are particularly important in the content of the contracts for the supply of digital content, which will often have elements that are covered by the provisions concerning goods, services and digital content. For example, the supply of a mail order DVD computer game will consist of a contract for its supply (a service) of a DVD (goods) with digital content. Under Part 1 of the CRA 2015 all of the provisions covering each of the three elements of the contract will apply.[205]

5.155 A trader does not supply digital content, however, merely because the trader 'supplies a service by which digital content reaches the consumer'.[206] This distinction is not particularly clear; however, it is referred to in the BIS Guidance on Digital Content where it is stated that:

> 'Digital content is not to be confused with the ways by which digital content or goods and services are chosen, purchased, supplied or transmitted. If a trader sells products online using a website, the use of the website to sell those products is not digital content, it is just a virtual shopping place. The supply, for example, of a mobile telephone contract (calls, texts and data) is not digital content. It is a service for customers to use.'

---

[203] R Bradgate (2010) 'Consumer rights in digital products' (report prepared for BIS).
[204] CRA 2015, s 2(9).
[205] CRA 2015, s 1(3)–(5).
[206] CRA 2015, s 33(4).

Free digital content

5.156 The rights in Chapter 3 apply if the digital content is supplied 'for a price paid by the consumer'[207] such that completely free digital content falls outside its ambit. However, digital content that is supplied 'free' with other goods or services that a consumer pays for are covered if the digital content is 'not generally available' to consumers unless they pay for it, or other goods or services.

Standards for digital content

5.157 Under Part 3 statutory terms are implied (although the legislation avoids using this word) into a consumer contract for the supply of digital content. These terms broadly mirror those in Part 1 for the sale of goods and will in practice overlap with each other.

The core rights

5.158 Section 34 provides a contractual term that digital content be of satisfactory quality, which may include a consideration of public statements made about the product by the trader, the producer[208] or their representatives. Section 35 provides a contractual term that the digital content be fit for a particular purpose that the consumer has made known to the trader expressly or by implication. Save for these two provisions there are no other implied terms about the quality of the digital content or its fitness for purpose, although these may plainly be specified as express terms of the contract.[209]

5.159 Section 36 provides a contractual term that digital content will match any description given by the trader to the consumer. If a consumer examines a trial version pre-contract, it is insufficient that the digital content that is subsequently obtained matches the trial version, if it does not also match the description given.

Information

5.160 Section 37 provides that certain pre-contract information that a trader is required to give a consumer under the CCR 2013 (see above) should be a contractual term.[210]

---

[207] CRA 2015, s 33(1).
[208] CRA 2015, s 59: 'producer', in relation to goods or digital content, means: (a) the manufacturer, (b) the importer into the European Economic Area, or (c) any person who purports to be a producer by placing the person's name, trade mark or other distinctive sign on the goods or using it in connection with the digital content.
[209] CRA 2015, s 38.
[210] All the pre-contract information, save for – in an on-premise contract (reg 9) paras (a), (j) or (k) of Sch 1, and for off-premises contracts (reg 10) and distance sales (reg 13) paras (a), (v) and (w) of Sch 2.

Right to supply

5.161   Section 41 provides a contractual term that a trader has the right to supply any digital content. This is directed towards traders that breach intellectual property rights by selling digital content that they do not own or have the legal right to supply to consumers.

Remedies – digital content

5.162   Chapter 3 creates similar remedies when the statutory implied terms for digital content are breached as Chapter 1 does in relation to the sale of goods. The remedies are expressly stated to be in addition to a consumer's existing right to bring a civil claim in contract or tort.[211] However, the provisions do not permit double recovery.

5.163   There is a statutory presumption that a contract for digital content did not confirm when it was first supplied, if it does not conform at any time during the first six months after its supply. Although this can be rebutted if the trader can establish that the digital content did conform, or that the presumption is incompatible with nature of the digital content or how it fails to conform.[212]

5.164   The remedies are summarised in the table below.

Type of breach	Remedy
s 34 (satisfactory quality); s 35 (fit for a particular purpose); or s 36 (as described)	The right to a repair or a replacement, under s 43. The right to a price reduction up to the full amount of the price, under s 44. The right to remedies under Part 1 if goods include digital content, under s 16
s 37 the requirement in the CCR 2013 to provide certain pre-contract information	The right to recover any costs incurred by the consumer as a result of the failure to provide the pre-contract information, up to the price paid, under s 42(4)
s 41 the requirement that a trader has the right to supply the digital content to the consumer	The right to a refund, under s 45
s 46 digital content supplied by a trader to a consumer has caused damage to the consumer's own device or other digital content and the damage would not have occurred had the trader exercised reasonable care and skill	The right to require the trader to repair the damage or compensate the consumer, under s 46(2) The right to bring a civil claim to enforce the right, under s 46(7)

---

[211]   CRA 2015, s 42(7).
[212]   CRA 2015, s 42(9) and (10).

CIVIL REDRESS FOR UNFAIR COMMERCIAL PRACTICES

5.165 The Consumer Protection from Unfair Trading Regulations ('CPUTR') implement the EU Unfair Commercial Practices Directive. The CPUTR can be enforced by designated enforcers such as local authorities and the OFT in the civil courts using Part 8 of the Enterprise Act 2002. In *McGuffick v The Royal Bank of Scotland plc*[213] the High Court held that an individual had no locus to enforce the CPUTR or any cause of action for their breach.[214]

5.166 The absence of any private civil redress for breaches of the CPUTR was the subject of a joint report by the Law Commission and the Scottish Law Commission in March 2012.[215] The report recommended a new statutory right of redress for a consumer against a trader. The Law Commission's recommendation was implemented in part by the Consumer Protection (Amendment) Regulations 2014,[216] which added a new Part 4A to the CPUTR.

5.167 Under Part 4A, consumers now have a right to civil redress against traders depending on the nature of their complaint. Redress is, however, limited to cases involving misleading or aggressive commercial practices. The Law Commission also recommended that the civil right should be extended to the Sch 1 banned practices; however, this was not implemented. The concepts of misleading actions and aggressive commercial practices are dealt with in detail in Chapter 7, Unfair Commercial Practices.

The rights

5.168 Consumers now have the right to unwind the contract, a discount or damages when a trader has engaged in misleading actions or aggressive commercial practices under CPUTR. These civil rights apply only to contracts entered into, or payments made, on or after 1 October 2014. The inclusion of payments made after 1 October 2014 broadens the timeframe for application of the new rights such that Part 4A will in fact cover many longstanding arrangements.

5.169 The existing general provision on damages for misrepresentation under s 2 of the Misrepresentation Act 1967 has been restricted if the consumer now has a right to redress under Part 4A of CPUTR.[217]

---

[213] [2009] EWHC 2386 (Comm).
[214] Per Flaux J, it 'is quite clear that the United Kingdom government deliberately excluded any civil law remedies from the Regulations'.
[215] The Law Commission and the Scottish Law Commission Joint Report on 'Consumer Redress For Misleading and Aggressive Practices' March 2012.
[216] SI 2014/870.
[217] Misrepresentation Act 1967, s 2(4): 'This section does not entitle a person to be paid damages in respect of a misrepresentation if the person has a right to redress under Part 4A ... in respect of the conduct constituting the misrepresentation.'

When do the rights apply

5.170 The rights under Part 4A apply any time there is:

(a) a sale to, purchase from, or payment made by a consumer; and

(b) a 'prohibited practice' by either:
  (i) a trader; or
  (ii) a producer (if the trader was or should have been aware of the prohibited practice); and

(c) the prohibited practice was a 'significant factor' in the consumer's transactional decision.

5.171 What amounts to a 'significant factor' is not further defined and will plainly be a fact sensitive question. Part 4A does not apply to contracts for immovable property (other than assured tenancies or leases for holiday accommodation) or financial services (other than restricted use credit agreements not secured on land).

The prohibited practice

5.172 Regulation 27B limits the prohibited practices to:

(a) misleading actions under reg 5; and

(b) aggressive commercial practices of coercion, undue influence, and harassment under reg 7.

The other unfair commercial practices, such as contravening professional diligence, misleading omissions, and banned practices in Sch 1 do not entitle a consumer to redress under Part 4A.

5.173 Regulation 27C clarifies that, except for a 'relevant lease', the reference to a 'product' does not include immoveable property. With certain exceptions, a 'relevant lease' is an assured tenancy or a holiday let. Regulation 27D clarifies that 'product' does not include a service provided in the course of carrying on a regulated activity within the meaning of s 22 of the Financial Services and Markets Act 2000, other than a service consisting of the provision of credit under an agreement which is a restricted-use credit agreement within para (a) or (b) of the definition of that term in Art 60L(1) of the Financial Services and Markets Act 2000 (Regulated Activities) Order 2001.[218]

The right to unwind

5.174 Under reg 27E, a consumer has the right to unwind a business to consumer contract if the consumer indicates to the trader that the consumer rejects the product, and does so within a period of 90 days and at a time when the product is capable of being rejected.

---

[218] With the exception of a mortgage.

5.175 A product remains capable of being rejected only if the goods have not been fully consumed, the service has not been fully performed, the digital content has not been fully consumed, the lease has not expired, or the right has not been fully exercised.

5.176 Regulation 27F provides that the effect of unwinding such a contract is that:

(a) The contract comes to an end so that the consumer and the trader are released from their obligations under it.

(b) The trader has a duty to give the consumer a refund.

(c) If the contract was wholly or partly for the sale or supply of goods the consumer must make the goods available for collection by the trader.

5.177 The provisions as to a refund are as follows:

- To the extent that the consumer paid any money under the contract, he is entitled to receive back the same amount of money. If, however, the contract was for the sale or supply of a product on a regular or continuous basis, and the consumer rejected the product after one month, he is only entitled to receive back the amount (if any) found by deducting the market price of the product at the time of rejection from the amount the consumer paid for it, unless it is inappropriate to do so having regard to the behaviour of the person who engaged in the prohibited practice, and the impact of the practice on the consumer. Where the product supplied up to the time when the consumer rejected it consists wholly or partly of goods, their market price is only to be taken into account to the extent that they have been consumed.

- To the extent that the consumer transferred anything else under the contract, he is entitled to receive back the same amount as that transferred. If the consumer transferred under the contract something for which the same amount of the same thing cannot be substituted the consumer is entitled to receive back in its original state whatever the consumer transferred, or if it cannot be given back in its original state, the consumer is entitled to be paid its market price as at the time when the product was rejected.

5.178 Regulation 27G provides that, in the case of a consumer to business contract, the consumer has the right to treat the contract as at an end so that the trader and the consumer are released from their obligations under it. The consumer also has a right to the return of the goods, but must repay to the trader the amount (if any) that the trader has paid for the goods. If the goods cannot be returned in the same condition, the consumer is entitled to be refunded any difference between the amount the trader paid and the amount the goods were worth.

5.179 Regulation 27H provides that consumers have a right to unwind a consumer payment which they were not required to make and to receive that money back from the trader.

The right to a discount

5.180 Regulation 27I deals with the right to a discount under a business to consumer contract where the consumer has made one or more payments for the product to the trader or one or more payments under the contract have not been made, and the consumer has not exercised the right to unwind the contract.

5.181 If the consumer has made one or more payments, he has the right to receive back from the trader the relevant percentage of the payment or payments. The relevant percentages are as follows:

(a)   if the prohibited practice is more than minor, 25%;

(b)   if the prohibited practice is significant, 50%;

(c)   if the prohibited practice is serious, 75%; and

(d)   if the prohibited practice is very serious, 100%.

5.182 The seriousness of the prohibited practice is assessed by reference to the behaviour of the trader, the impact of the practice on the consumer and the time which has elapsed since the prohibited practice took place. If one or more payments have not been made, the consumer has the right to reduce by the relevant percentage as many of those payments as is appropriate having regard to the seriousness of the prohibited practice.

5.183 If the amount payable for the product under the contract exceeds £5,000 and the market price of the product, at the time that the consumer entered into the contract, was lower than the amount payable for it under the contract, the relevant percentage is the percentage difference between the market price of the product and the amount payable for it under the contract. Exercising the right to the discount has no effect on any other rights and liabilities under the contract.

The right to damages

5.184 A consumer has a right to damages if he or she has:

(a)   incurred financial loss; or

(b)   suffered alarm, distress, physical inconvenience, or discomfort.

5.185 However, it should be noted that 'financial loss' does not include the difference in market value of the product between the point of sale and the exercise of the right to damages (reg 27J(3)). Traders are protected by the requirement that the damage be reasonably foreseeable (reg 27J(4)) and a due diligence defence (reg 27J(5)).

Proceedings

5.186 Under Regulation 27K, consumers can bring civil proceedings to enforce their rights to unwind, to a discount or to damages. It is suggested that the county court is likely to be the most appropriate forum to bring such an action in England and Wales: and the Sheriff's Court in Scotland. The limitation period is six years. Regulation 27L makes clear that the new rights to redress do not affect existing causes of action which consumers may have in respect of the same conduct save that they cannot recover twice for the same loss.

Consumer transaction	Right to redress
Business to consumer contract	The right to unwind (reg 27F) The right to a discount (reg 27I) The right to damages (reg 27J)
Consumer to business contract	The right to unwind (reg 27G) The right to damages (reg 27J)
Consumer payment for product within reg 2(1A) and (1B)	The right to unwind (reg 27H) The right to damages (reg 27J)
Consumer payment for any other type of product	The right to damages

TRADER GUARANTEES AND WARRANTIES

5.187 The product guarantees that traders themselves provide to consumers purchasing goods ('trader guarantees') can be of real value to consumers because they will often provide an easy remedy without the need to resort to a legal claim. However, they have also proven to be contentious. This is primarily because traders sometimes treat their time-limited guarantee as the only right that a consumer has when a product is defective or otherwise unsatisfactory. If the trader guarantee has expired many consumers wrongly believe that they have no right to a repair or replacement. In some cases this will not be their legal position with consumer rights often extending long after a trader's own guarantee period. There has also been concern about the sale of extended warranties that are of poor value and provide little benefit beyond a consumer's existing statutory rights.

5.188 In response to those concerns limited consumer protection is now provided in relation to both trader guarantees and extended warranties for electrical goods. Although it has to be said that neither of these two measures remedy the central problem that, generally, consumers simply do not understand their statutory rights in this area.

Guarantees under CRA, s 30

5.189 Section 30 of the CRA 2015 implements Art 6 (Guarantees) of the Sale of Consumer Goods and Associated Guarantees Directive 1999/44/EC (the 'CSD'). It replaces reg 15 of the Sale and Supply of Goods Regulations 2002, which are revoked by CRA 2015.[219] The requirements of s 30 are limited to the information and transparent presentation of a guarantee to consumers by a trader. It concerns guarantees given voluntarily by the trader and does not bind the trader to any particular contractual arrangement or specify a minimum length for a guarantee.

5.190 Section 30 applies to goods[220] that are the subject of a trader's guarantee. Guarantee is defined in s 30(2) as:

> '"Guarantee" here means an undertaking to the consumer given without extra charge by a person acting in the course of the person's business (the "guarantor") that, if the goods do not meet the specifications set out in the guarantee statement or in any associated advertising—
> (a) the consumer will be reimbursed for the price paid for the goods, or
> (b) the goods will be repaired, replaced or handled in any way.'

5.191 The contents of the guarantee and the essential particulars for making claims under it are required to be set out in plain and intelligible language. This must include the name and address of the guarantor and the guarantee's territorial scope. It must state that a consumer's statutory rights are not affected and it must be written in English if the goods are offered in the UK. Under s 30(6) a trader must make a guarantee available and accessible to a consumer in writing within a reasonable time after the consumer has requested it.

5.192 Article 6(1) of the CSD also requires that guarantees should be legally binding against the guarantor. Article 6(2) makes it clear that the validity of the guarantee should not be affected by the failure of the guarantor to comply with the Art 6 information and transparency provisions that are implemented by s 30 of the CRA 2015 (above). Section 30(3) states that a guarantee takes effect, at the time the goods are delivered, as a contractual obligation owed by the guarantor to the consumer.

5.193 Section 30(8)–(10) also provides a power for an enforcer to obtain injunctive relief against a trader for breach of the guarantee obligations, which can only be taken by the CMA, a local weights and measures authority in Great Britain or DETI.

---

[219] SI 2002/3045 revoked by CRA 2015, Sch 1, para 53.
[220] Defined in CRA 2015, s 2 as 'any tangible moveable items, but that includes water, gas and electricity if and only if they are put up for supply in a limited volume or set quantity.'

Extended warranties on electrical goods

5.194 The Supply of Extended Warranties on Domestic Electrical Goods Order 2005[221] (the '2005 Order') was introduced following an OFT report[222] about the lack of competition in the sale by retailers of extended warranties on electrical appliances. It was reported that there were few warranty providers other than large electrical retailers that took advantage of a near monopoly and their 'point of sale advantage'. Consumers did not shop around and the warranties were often not good value. Consumers were also provided with insufficient information with some retailers unfairly emphasising the potential for goods to develop faults.

5.195 The 2005 Order applies only to domestic electrical goods, defined as 'a product designed to be connected to an electricity supply or powered by batteries and used for domestic purposes, but does not include watches, jewellery or fixed installations (other than integrated appliances)'.[223] It does not apply to distance sales or off-premises contracts under the CCR 2013.[224]

5.196 The provider of an extended warranty to a consumer has the obligation to display its price and duration in a manner that is clear, legible and also makes clear that its purchase is optional. A provider must provide information about a consumer's cancellation rights, termination rights and the fact that the extended warranty does not need to be purchased at the same time as the electrical goods.[225] There are further consumer information obligations in relation to advertising.[226]

5.197 The 2005 Order seeks to alleviate the pressure placed on consumers at the point of sale by giving them 30 days to decide whether they will accept the offer of an extended warranty. It is now unlawful for a provider only to offer the warranty at the point of sale so that a consumer has to make the decision immediately.[227] The 2005 Order also gives consumers the right to cancel an extended warranty during the first 45 days after its purchase.[228] After that time the consumer continues to have the right to cancel the warranty throughout the period it covers and to receive a pro rata refund.[229] The provider must also inform the consumer of these rights, in writing, at least 20 days before the 45-day period expires.[230] The CMA is given power to direct providers in relation to compliance with the 2005 Order.[231]

---

[221] SI 2005/37 made under the Fair Trading Act 1973.
[222] OFT July 2002, Extended Warranties on Domestic Electrical Goods.
[223] 2005 Order, Art 1(3).
[224] 2005 Order, Art 2 as amended by the CCR 2013, Sch 4, para 5.
[225] 2005 Order, Art 3.
[226] 2005 Order, Arts 4–6.
[227] 2005 Order, Art 7.
[228] 2005 Order, Art 8(1)(a) as long as a claim has not been made under the extended warranty.
[229] 2005 Order, Art 8(1)(b) regardless of whether a valid claim has been made under the extended warranty.
[230] 2005 Order, Art 8(1)(c).
[231] 2005 Order, Art 10.

Limitation and trader guarantees

5.198 It is important to understand that the period for which a trader guarantees goods is subject to a consumer's other contractual rights, which will often allow for claims beyond the trader's own guarantee period. Article 5(1) of the CSD provides that a consumer should be entitled to a free repair or replacement of goods where the lack of conformity becomes apparent within 2 years of delivery to the consumer. Several retailers have recently adopted this 24 months' period to limit their own consumer guarantees. However, this period is a minimum guarantee under the CSD and Art 5(1) is without prejudice to the right of Member States to permit longer periods.

5.199 In England and Wales[232] the limitation periods for civil litigation are primarily set by the Limitation Act 1980 ('LA 1980'). The supply of a defective or unsatisfactory product to a consumer is likely to make a trader liable for breach of contract[233] in a civil claim. This will particularly be the case following the introduction of the new sale of goods, services and digital content provisions in CRA 2015 (see above), which imply statutory contractual terms in relation to products supplied and give consumers specific remedies when those terms are breached.

5.200 Under s 5 of the LA 1980 an action in contract[234] 'shall not be brought after the expiration of 6 years from the date on which the cause of action accrued'. In a simple[235] sale of goods case the cause of action is likely to accrue at the time the product is delivered to, or obtained by, the consumer.[236] Although this may be extended when there has been fraud, concealment or mistake for the purpose of s 32 of the LA 1980. It follows that a consumer will frequently have the right to bring a civil claim in contract against a trader if a product becomes defective or unsatisfactory during the six years following its delivery. The success of such a claim will depend upon whether there has in fact been a breach of the implied statutory terms; however, this right may well endure far longer than the trader's own guarantee or warranty.

RIGHT TO USE UNSOLICITED GOODS

Introduction

5.201 There has been legislation in the UK concerning unsolicited goods for over 40 years.[237] These measures were designed to combat an unwelcome growth in the practice of 'inertia selling', which involved unsolicited goods

---

[232] LA 1980, s 41(4).

[233] It may also generate other liability, for example in the tort of negligence.

[234] The Latent Damage Act 1980 is unlikely to apply to actions in contract, *Iron Trades Mutual Assurance v JK Buckenham* [1990] 1 All ER 808.

[235] Caution should be adopted before applying this limitation period in relation to modern transactions, particularly where products are updated after their delivery.

[236] *Battley v Faulkner* (1820) 3 B & Ald 288, applied in *Lynn v Bamber* [1930] 2 KB 72 at 74.

[237] The Unsolicited Goods and Services Act 1971.

being sent to consumers on a speculative basis. Typically, goods would be sent to a random consumer as an offer, with an option to return the goods within a specified period, or failing that an obligation to pay for them. A consumer who did neither would frequently be subjected to demands for payment and threats of legal action.

Inertia selling

5.202 The domestic legislation on unsolicited goods has been replaced by an EU provision which provides for an outright ban on the commercial practice of 'inertia selling'. This is criminalised as a commercial practice banned by para 29 of Sch 1 to the CPUTR, which are dealt with in detail in Chapter 7, Unfair Commercial Practices. This applies when a trader demands from a consumer 'immediate or deferred payment for or the return or safekeeping of products supplied by the trader, but not solicited by the consumer'. 'Product' is defined broadly in reg 2 of CPUTR and includes both goods and services. 'Unsolicited' is not defined in CPUTR, however, it is likely to be construed to mean 'sent or supplied without any prior request made by or on behalf of the recipient', as it was in the Unsolicited Goods and Services Act 1971.[238]

5.203 The provisions in CPUTR have now been amended by CCR 2013, as a consequence of the CRD. Regulation 27A of CPUTR now makes further provision in relation to inertia selling.

> **CPUTR, reg 27A Inertia selling**
>
> (1) This regulation applies where a trader engages in the unfair commercial practice described in paragraph 29 of Schedule 1 (inertia selling).
>
> (2) The consumer is exempted from any obligation to provide consideration for the products supplied by the trader.
>
> (3) The absence of a response from the consumer following the supply does not constitute consent to the provision of consideration for, or the return or safekeeping of, the products.
>
> (4) In the case of an unsolicited supply of goods, the consumer may, as between the consumer and the trader, use, deal with or dispose of the goods as if they were an unconditional gift to the consumer.

5.204 The legal effect of this provision is to transfer property in the unsolicited products to a consumer as a gift. The consumer is under no obligation to pay for the goods and may use or dispose of the goods as if the consumer owned them. It would appear that the right can be exercised by the consumer from the point at which the trader makes a demand for payment, demands the return of goods or demands that a consumer keeps goods safe.

5.205 The drafting of these provisions does not have the clarity of the previous domestic legislation. There appears to be no clear distinction between a trader

---

[238] Section 25(6) (now repealed).

acting deliberately, taking advantage of consumers, and a trader who sends goods to a consumer mistakenly and merely demands that the consumer returns them or keeps them safe. The risk of consumers abusing the provision is, however, subject to the qualification that it implements EU law and must be construed purposively.

ALTERNATIVE AND ONLINE DISPUTE RESOLUTION

Alternative dispute resolution

5.206 Alternative dispute resolution ('ADR') is a method of resolving disputes between consumers and traders that avoids going to court. The common forms of ADR are mediation or conciliation and adjudication or arbitration. Conciliation or mediation involves an independent third party helping the disputing parties to come to a mutually acceptable outcome, a mediator is likely to take a more active role in bringing the two parties together. Adjudication or arbitration is where an independent third party considers the facts and takes a decision that is often binding on one or both parties.

5.207 The Alternative Dispute Resolution Directive (2013/11/EU) (the 'ADR Directive') has been implemented[239] in the UK by the Alternative Dispute Resolution for Consumer Disputes (Competent Authorities and Information) Regulations 2015 (the 'ADR Regulations').[240] The ADR Regulations came fully into force on 1 October 2015 and apply to disputes relating to contracts entered into on, or after, 9 July 2015. The aim of the ADR Directive is set out in Art 1 as:

> 'ensuring that consumers can, on a voluntary basis, submit complaints against traders to entities offering independent, impartial, transparent, effective, fast and fair alternative dispute resolution procedures.'

5.208 The primary obligation in the ADR Directive is upon Member States to 'facilitate access by consumers to ADR procedures' and to 'ensure that disputes covered by this Directive and which involve a trader established on their respective territories can be submitted to an ADR entity which complies with the requirements set out in this Directive' (Art 5(1)). The disputes that the ADR Directive applies to are 'domestic and cross-border disputes concerning contractual obligations stemming from sales contracts or service contracts between a trader established in the Union and a consumer resident in the Union' (Art 2(1)).

5.209 The ADR Directive does not apply to a trader's own complaint-handling systems or direct negotiations with a consumer. It does not apply to claims by a

---

[239] Member States were required to implement the requirements of the ADR Directive into national law by 9 July 2015.

[240] As amended by the Alternative Dispute Resolution for Consumer Disputes (Amendment) Regulations 2015.

trader against a consumer or any attempt by a judge to settle a dispute in the course of a judicial proceeding. It will not apply to health services, medicinal products, medical devices or to public providers of further or higher education (see Art 2(2) generally).

5.210 The ADR Directive provides the framework for the operation of an authorised ADR by including standards in relation to expertise, independence and impartiality (Art 6), fairness (Art 7), effectiveness (Art 8) and transparency (Art 9). These requirements have been implemented in Part 2 of the ADR Regulations.

5.211 Regulation 19 of the ADR Regulations requires traders to provide information to consumers where the trader is obliged to use ADR services by any enactment or the rules of a trade association. In those circumstances the trader must provide the name and website address of the ADR entity on his website and his general terms and conditions.

ADR Regulation 19(2)

(2) Where a trader has exhausted its internal complaint handling procedure when considering a complaint from a consumer relating to a sales contract or a service contract, the trader must inform the consumer, on a durable medium—

(a)   that the trader cannot settle the complaint with the consumer;

(b)   of the name and website address of an ADR entity which would be competent to deal with the complaint, should the consumer wish to use alternative dispute resolution; and

(c)   whether the trader is obliged, or prepared, to submit to an alternative dispute resolution procedure operated by that ADR entity.

5.212 Regulation 19(2) is the key requirement for a business selling to consumers, that does not belong to a professional body or trade association that obliges them to use and accept the rulings of an ADR scheme. These unattached businesses must simply tell the consumer that they cannot settle their complaint, give them the name of an ADR scheme (which they may or may not be signed up to) and finally they must tell the consumer whether they are prepared to submit to the ADR procedure themselves. Breaches of the information requirements in Art 13 of the ADR Directive (reg 19 of the ADR Regulations 2015) are enforceable as community infringements under Part 8 of the Enterprise Act 2002[241] (see Chapter 4, Civil Enforcement).

5.213 The Chartered Trading Standards Institute ('CTSI') has been appointed to carry out the function of approving ADR entities along with competent authorities for the regulated sectors – energy, transport, financial services, legal, and communications. CTSI also has the duty, on behalf of the Secretary of State, of keeping the EU up to date with all certified ADR bodies details. The EU website listing all certified ADR bodies can be accessed through the CTSI

---

website. At end of July 2016 there were 40 UK certified ADR bodies ranging from some sector specific bodies to some general ADR schemes.

Online dispute resolution

5.214 The EU Regulation on online dispute resolution for consumer disputes (524/2013) (the 'ODR Regulation') came into force[242] on 15 February 2016. The ODR Regulation obliges the EU Commission to establish an online dispute resolution ('ODR') platform for online cross-border disputes. This is designed to facilitate ADR for disputes between consumers and traders in different Member States using a certified ADR provider.[243] Member States are required to designate an ODR contact point to assist consumers with disputes submitted using the ODR Platform.

5.215 Most provisions of the ODR Regulation are therefore concerned with the functions of the ODR Platform and do not require implementation into domestic UK law. However, Art 14 of the ODR Regulation does create information requirements for online traders, which are required to 'provide on their websites an electronic link to the ODR platform' that is 'easily accessible for consumers'.

5.216 Under Art 14(2) online traders that are 'committed or obliged to use one or more ADR entities to resolve disputes with consumers' must inform consumers 'about the existence of the ODR platform' and the possibility of using it to resolve their disputes. All online traders, whether or not committed or obliged to use an ADR process, must provide an electronic link to the ODR platform on their websites and in email offers.[244] Breaches of the information requirements in Art 14 of the ODR Regulation will be enforceable as community infringements under Part 8 of the Enterprise Act 2002 (see Chapter 4, Civil Enforcement).

THE PROVISION OF SERVICES REGULATIONS 2009

Purpose and scope

5.217 The Provision of Services Regulations 2009 ('POSR 2009') came into force on 28 December 2009, implementing the EU Services Directive.[245] The aim of the Directive is to further open the internal market for services, allowing service providers to trade across the EU without unjustifiable barriers to doing so. Part 2 places duties on service providers regarding the information that they

---

[242] Although the requirements relating to the creation of an ODR contact point applied on 9 July 2015.

[243] The EU Implementing Regulation 2015/1051 relating to the ODR Platform was published in the Official Journal on 2 July 2015.

[244] ec.europa.eu/odr

[245] 2006/123/EC.

must provide and how they must deal with complaints. Regulation 30 prevents the use of discriminatory provisions with regard to the place of residence of the recipient of the service.

5.218 POSR 2009 applies to providers of a 'service', which is defined as, 'any self-employed economic activity normally provided for remuneration'.[246] POSR 2009 is not confined to consumer protection and applies to any 'recipients' of a regulated service. A 'recipient' is defined as a professional or non-professional person who uses or wishes to use the service.[247] It is therefore important, when considering the requirements of the regulations, to remember that this covers both actual and potential customers, as well as trade and consumer recipients. Breaches of the POSR 2009 will be enforceable as community infringements under Part 8 of the Enterprise Act 2002 (see Chapter 4, Civil Enforcement).

5.219 The POSR 2009 covers all service providers, unless they fall within the exemptions in reg 2(1) which are listed in the table below.

Regulation	Description	Exception
2(2)(a)	Financial services	Such as banking, credit, insurance and re-insurance, occupational or personal pensions, securities, investment funds, payments and investment advice, including the services listed in Annex 1 to Directive 2006/48/EC[248]
2(2)(b)	Electronic communication services and networks	Including associated facilities and services covered by: Directive 2002/19/EC[249] Directive 2002/20/EC[250] Directive 2002/21/EC[251] Directive 2002/22/EC[252] Directive 2002/58/EC[253]
2(2)(c)	Transport services	Services in the field of transport, including port services
2(2)(d)	Temporary work agencies	Services of temporary work agencies, which includes any employment business as defined in s 13(3) of the Employment Agencies Act 1973

---

[246] POSR 2009, reg 2(1).
[247] POSR 2009, reg 4.
[248] Relating to the taking up and pursuit of the business of credit institutions.
[249] Access to, and interconnection of, electronic communications networks and associated facilities.
[250] The authorisation of electronic communications networks and services.
[251] A common regulatory framework for electronic communications networks and services.
[252] Universal service and users' rights relating to electronic communications networks and services.
[253] Processing of personal data and the protection of privacy in the electronic communications sector.

Regulation	Description	Exception
2(2)(e)	Healthcare services	Healthcare services, whether or not they are provided via healthcare facilities and regardless of the ways in which they are organised and financed at national level or whether they are public or private
2(2)(f)	Audiovisual services	Including cinematographic services, whatever their mode of production, distribution and transmission, and radio broadcasting
2(2)(g)	Gambling activities	Activities which involve wagering a stake with pecuniary value in games of chance, including lotteries, gambling in casinos and betting transactions
2(2)(h)	Official authority	Activities which are connected with the exercise of official authority
2(2)(i)	Social services	Relating to social housing, childcare and support of families and persons permanently or temporarily in need which are provided by the State, by providers mandated by the State or by charities recognised as such by the State
2(2)(j)	Private security services	Private security services
2(2)(k)	Notaries of bailiffs	Services provided by notaries or bailiff, if or to the extent that they are appointed by an official act of government to provide those services

Duty to provide information

5.220 The information set out below must be provided in a clear and ambiguous manner and in a good time before the conclusion of the contract. If there is no written contract, the information must be provided before the service is provided.[254] It is to be noted that there is some duplication of the information required by POSR 2009 with other legislation such as CCR 2013 and the ADR Regulations.

Duty to make contact details available

5.221 Service providers must make their contact details available to enable all recipients of their service to contact them regarding a complaint or to request information regarding their service.[255]

The contact details must include:

(a)   a postal address, fax number or e-mail address;

---

[254] POSR 2009, reg 11.
[255] POSR 2009, reg 7(1).

(b)   a telephone number; and

(c)   where the service provider has an official address, that address.[256]

Regulation 7 is silent upon how this information should be provided, but guidance provided by BIS,[257] suggests that one of the methods listed in reg 8 could be used.

Other information to be made available

5.222

POSR 2009 Regulation 8(1)

(1) The provider of a service must make the following information available to a recipient of the service—

(a)   the provider's name;

(b)   the provider's legal status and form;

(c)   the geographic address at which the provider is established and details by which the provider may be contacted rapidly and communicated with directly (including, where the provider may be contacted and communicated with by electronic means, the details of how the provider may be so contacted and communicated with);

(d)   where the provider is registered in a trade or other similar public register, the name of the register and the provider's registration number or equivalent means of identification in that register;

(e)   where the activity is subject to an authorisation scheme in the United Kingdom, the particulars of the relevant competent authority or the electronic facility referred to in regulation 38;

(f)   where the activity is subject in another EEA state to a scheme equivalent to an authorisation scheme, the particulars of the authority involved or the single point of contact in that state;

(g)   where the provider exercises an activity which is subject to VAT, the identification number referred to in Article 22(1) of the Sixth Council Directive 77/88/EEC of 17 May 1977 on the harmonization of the laws of the member states relating to turnover taxes – Common system of value added tax: uniform basis of assessment;

(h)   where the provider is carrying on a regulated profession, any professional body or similar institution with which the provider is registered, the professional title and the EEA state in which that title is granted;

(i)   the general terms and conditions, if any, used by the provider;

(j)   the existence of contractual terms, if any, used by the provider concerning the competent courts or the law applicable to the contract;

(k)   the existence of any after-sales guarantee not imposed by law;

(l)   the price of the service, where a price is pre-determined by the provider for a given type of service;

(m)   the main features of the service, if not already apparent from the context;

---

[256] An address which a person is required by law to register, notify or maintain for the purpose of receiving notices or other communications. POSR 2009, reg 7(3).

[257] BIS 'Guidance for Business on the Provision of Services Regulations', October 2009.

(n)   where the provider is subject to a requirement to hold any professional liability insurance or guarantee, information about the insurance or guarantee and in particular –
(i) the contact details of the insurer or guarantor, and
(ii)   the territorial coverage of the insurance or guarantee.

5.223   This information can be made available by four means:

- supplied at the provider's initiative;
- made easily accessible to the recipient at the place where the service is provided or where the contract for the service is concluded;
- made easily accessible to the recipient electronically by means of an address supplied by the provider;
- including it in any information document (which gives a detailed description of the service) that has been supplied by the provider to the recipient.[258]

Information to be supplied on request etc.

5.224   Regulation 9 of the PSOR requires additional information to be supplied upon request from a recipient (an actual or potential customer):

- the price of the service, how it will be calculated or a sufficiently detailed estimate – unless the price of the service is pre-determined;
- if a regulated professional – the rules applicable to the profession and how they can be accessed;
- information about other activities undertaken by the provider, which are directly linked to the service in question, and the measures taken to avoid any conflict of interest;
- any codes of conduct that the provider is subject to and an electronic link to access these.

The information regarding other related activities and how conflicts of interest are avoided must be given in any documents that the provide supplies which contain a detailed description of the service.

Information about dispute resolution

5.225   Service providers who are subject of a code of conduct, trade association or professional body that provides access to an ADR procedure must inform the recipient of this and how to access it. They must also mention this in any information document that gives a detailed description of the service. This requirement is now also found in the ADR Regulations (see above).

---

[258] POSR 2009, reg 8(2).

Complaints

5.226 Regulation 12 requires service providers to respond to complaints, from recipients of their service, as quickly as possible and to make their best efforts to find a satisfactory solution (unless the complaint is vexatious).

Restriction on discriminatory provisions

5.227 Service providers cannot include discriminatory provisions, in the general conditions of access to their service, which are based upon the place of residence of recipients who are individuals. This will not apply to differences in conditions of access that are directly justified by objective criteria.[259] What might be considered to be 'objective criteria' is not defined but BIS Guidance[260]suggests that these should be objective reasons, based upon the service provider's individual circumstances, and could include:

- additional costs because of the distance involved, or the technical characteristics of the provision of the service;
- differing market conditions, such as higher or lower demand influenced by seasonality, different holiday periods or pricing by competitors;
- extra risks linked to rules differing between EEA states;
- the absence of sufficient intellectual property rights in a particular territory.

The guidance also advises that an outright refusal to provide a service will be more difficult to justify than adapting conditions, for example charging a higher price to cover additional costs.

---

[259] POSR 2009, reg 30(2) and (3).
[260] BIS 'Guidance for Business on the Provision of Services Regulations', October 2009.

CHAPTER 6

INFORMATION

CONTENTS

INTRODUCTION

6.1   We live in an age where a general culture of greater transparency and improved access to information is emerging, particularly where that information is held by public bodies. The Information Commissioner's Office ('ICO') is an executive non-departmental public body and independent regulatory office which upholds information rights in the public interest, promoting openness by public bodies and data privacy for individuals. The ICO's goal is to achieve a society in which:

- All organisations which collect and use personal information do so responsibly, securely and fairly.
- All public authorities are open and transparent, providing people with access to official information as a matter of course.
- People are aware of their information rights and are confident in using them.
- People understand how their personal information is used and are able to take steps to protect themselves from its misuse.

6.2   The ICO has specific responsibilities set out in the Data Protection Act 1998, the Freedom of Information Act 2000, Environmental Information Regulations 2004 and Privacy and Electronic Communications Regulations 2003. It is not possible to provide a comprehensive discourse of all provisions relating to the acquisition and dissemination of information in a work of this nature and the narrower focus is therefore on the legislation which enable enforcers to disclose information to others – consumers, traders and other enforcers – or which enforcers may use to obtain information in order to carry out their functions.

THE ENTERPRISE ACT 2002

6.3   Part 9 of the Enterprise Act 2002 (EA 2002) introduced restrictions against public authority disclosure of material obtained in connection with certain statutory consumer and competition functions. Since the Part 9 regime was introduced it has surprisingly never been substantively litigated in the higher courts to any significant degree. The disclosure regime was designed to reflect the 'Government strategy of widening and harmonising the gateways through which information can be disclosed in the UK and overseas and at the same time introduce appropriate safeguards in respect of permitted disclosure of information'.

6.4   Therefore, Part 9 establishes a set of rigid requirements which have to be met before public authorities can disclose specified information within the United Kingdom or overseas. The importance of complying with these rules is reflected by the fact that criminal offences, attracting sentences of imprisonment, can be committed if the rules are contravened. Although at first glance the rules are strict, the exceptions are wide and Part 9 is unlikely to prevent enforcers doing anything that they might reasonably want to for the further protection of the public. The rules created by Part 9 should not be taken to be a complete self-contained code for disclosure. For example, they do not affect a public authority's duties to comply with the requirements of the Data Protection Act 1998 or the Freedom of Information Act 2000.

Specified information

6.5 The core of Part 9 applies to the disclosure of 'specified information' which is held by a public authority and which relates to the affairs of an individual or of an undertaking. It applies equally to information that has come to the public authority before or after the commencement of the Act. It is therefore deliberately wide ranging in its scope. If a public authority has any other information, the disclosure restrictions in this Part will not apply.

6.6   Specified information is defined in s 238.

238 Information

(1) Information is specified information if it comes to a public authority in connection with the exercise of any function it has under or by virtue of –

(a)   Part 1 (The Office of Fair Trading), 3 (Mergers), 4 (Market Investigations), 6 (Cartel Offences), 7 (Miscellaneous Competition Provisions) or 8 (Enforcement of certain Consumer Legislation);

(b)   an enactment specified in Schedule 14;

(c)   such subordinate legislation as the Secretary of State may by order specify for the purposes of this subsection. (The Orders which have been made pursuant to this section are set out in the footnote below.)

Section 238(1)(a): Part 8

6.7   Part 8 gives enforcers strong powers to obtain court orders against businesses that do not comply with their legal obligations to consumers. These powers include the obtaining of enforcement orders or undertakings, designed to stop businesses from continuing with conduct that harms the collective interests of consumers, along with powers to search premises and retain evidence. The investigatory powers available to enforcers for the purposes of their functions under Part 8 are now contained in Sch 5 to the Consumer Rights Act 2015.[1]

Section 238(1)(b): an enactment specified in Sch 14

6.8   This schedule sets out the Acts under which any information obtained by a public authority in connection with the exercise of any statutory function will be 'specified information' for the purposes of Part 9. It includes both primary

---

[1]   See, in particular, paras 13–18 – 'Powers in relation to the production of information' – and para 27 – 'Power to require the production of documents'.

and secondary legislation and Scottish and Northern Ireland legislation. Schedule 14 currently contains 21 Acts, which are listed in the footnote below.[2]

Public authority

6.9   Public authority is defined by s 238(3) of the Act and s 6(3) of the Human Rights Act 1998. The definition in s 6(3) of the Human Rights Act 1998 does not provide a precise definition for what constitutes 'functions of a public nature'. This has been left to the courts to refine. The House of Lords considered the general approach to this in the case of *YL v Birmingham City Council*.[3] In that case they concluded that s 6 of the Human Rights Act 1998 was designed to be given a 'generously wide scope'. They went on to conclude that there was 'no single test of universal application to determine whether a function [was] of a public nature'. However, they held that there were a number of general propositions which were relevant to determining whether a person's functions were 'functions of a public nature'. These propositions reflected the analysis of Lord Nicholls in the case of *Aston Cantlow and Wilmcote with Billesley Parochial Church Council v Wallbank*[4] and are as follows:

- Is the nature of the function public or private?
- What is the role of the State in relation to the function in question?[5]
- What is the extent and nature of any statutory power or duty in relation to the function in question? The absence of any statutory intervention will tend to indicate parliamentary recognition that the function in question is private.
- To what extent does the state, directly or indirectly, regulate, supervise and inspect the performance of the function in question, and impose criminal penalties on those who fall below publicly promulgated standards in performing it?

---

[2]   Parts 1, 3, 4, 5, 6, 7, 8 and 11 of the Fair Trading Act 1973; Trade Descriptions Act 1968; Hallmarking Act 1973; Prices Act 1974; Consumer Credit Act 1974; Customs and Excise Management Act 1979; Estate Agents Act 1979; Competition Act 1980; Video Recordings Act 1984; Consumer Protection Act 1987; Consumer Protection (Northern Ireland) Order 1987, SI 1987/2049 (NI 20); Copyright, Designs and Patents Act 1988; Property Misdescriptions Act 1991; Clean Air Act 1993; Value Added Tax Act 1994; Trade Marks Act 1994; Competition Act 1998; Chapter 3 of Part 10 and Chapter 2 of Part 18 of the Financial Services and Markets Act 2000 or an order made under section 95 of that Act; Fireworks Act 2003; Compensation Act 2006; Consumers, Estate Agents and Redress Act 2007.

[3]   [2008] 1 AC 95.

[4]   [2004] 1 AC 546.

[5]   *XL v Birmingham City Council* [2008] 1 AC 95 at p 105: 'It is also relevant to consider the role and responsibility of the state in relation to the subject matter in question. In some fields the involvement of the state is long-standing and governmental in a strict sense: one might instance defence or the running of prisons. In other fields, such as sport or the arts, the involvement of the state is more recent and more remote. It is relevant to consider the nature and extent of the public interest in the function in question.'

- What risk is there that an improper exercise of the function might violate a convention right?

- Does the State ultimately fund the function? The greater the state's involvement in making payment for the function in question, the greater (other things being equal) is its assumption of responsibility.

6.10 Conversely the court considered that 'it will not ordinarily matter whether the body in question is amenable to judicial review. Section (6)(3)(b) extends the definition of public authority to cover bodies which are not public authorities but certain of whose functions are of a public nature, and it is therefore likely to include bodies which are not amenable to judicial review.'[6] The court also made it clear that the list of considerations were neither comprehensive nor exhaustive and that cases would effectively have to be dealt with on a case by case basis. For example, there will be entities that have both a public and a private function, in which case they would only be a pubic authority for the purposes of its public function. An entity akin to a consumer watchdog is likely to fall into this category.

The general restriction

6.11 Specified information is subject to the general restriction set out in s 237. If a person discloses information in breach of it, they commit a criminal offence (s 245).

237 General restriction

(1) This section applies to specified information which relates to –

    (a)   the affairs of an individual;
    (b)   any business of an undertaking.

(2) Such information must not be disclosed –

    (a)   during the lifetime of the individual, or
    (b)   while the undertaking continues in existence,

unless the disclosure is permitted under this Part.

(3) But subsection (2) does not prevent the disclosure of any information if the information has on an earlier occasion been disclosed to the public in circumstances which do not contravene –

    (a)   that subsection;
    (b)   any other enactment or rule of law prohibiting or restricting the disclosure of the information.

(4) Nothing in this Part authorises a disclosure of information which contravenes the Data Protection Act 1998.

(5) Nothing in this Part affects the Competition Appeal Tribunal.[7]

---

6   *XL v Birmingham City Council* [2008] 1 AC 95, p 105.
7   For an example of how this exclusion operates, see *Albion Water Limited, Albion Water Group Limited v Water Services Regulation* Authority [2008] CAT 3, where on an application for

(6) This Part (except section 244) does not affect any power or duty to disclose information which exists apart from this Part.

Exceptions to the general restriction under EA 2002, s 237

Information already in the public domain

6.12 The general provision set out above effectively states that, if the information has previously been made public in circumstances which do not contravene s 237(2) or any other enactment or rule of law, then it may be further disclosed (s 273(3)). The reason that this is not included as a separate gateway is that, if it has already been properly and publicly disclosed, then clearly there is no need to look for a gateway through which to disclose it again.

6.13 This is an important and wide ranging exception to the rule. Consider for example the effect of the Civil Procedure Rules Part 5.4C:

> **Civil Procedure Rules Part 5.4C**
>
> (1) The general rule is that a person who is not a party to proceedings may obtain from the court records a copy of –
>
> (a)   statement of case, but not any documents filed with or attached to the statement of case, or intended by the party whose statement it is to be served with it;
>
> (b)   a judgment or order given or made in public (whether made at a hearing or without a hearing), subject to paragraph (1B).

6.14 This rule permits a third party, unconnected to the proceedings, to apply for copies of the statements of case, any rulings that have been given, or judgments that have been made public. So, for instance, if an application for an enforcement order under s 215 (or s 218 for interim orders) has been filed at court, any member of the public will be able to gain access to the statement of case in which contain the details of the allegations. Therefore, as a general rule, the Part 9 disclosure rules will cease to apply to any specified information that is included within that documentation once it is filed with a court.

Existing power or duty to disclose

6.15 In the case of *Dumfries and Galloway Council v Dunion, Scottish Information Commissioner*[8] the court had to consider the tension between the

---

disclosure of certain redacted information, the Tribunal considered that some of it had to be disclosed because it was relevant and necessary to the issues to be determined. By virtue of s 237(5) of the EA 2002, the restrictions on disclosure of confidential information did not apply to the Tribunal. See also *Umbro Holdings Ltd v Office of Fair Trading (Application for Leniency: Confidentiality)* [2003] CAT 2, for a useful example of where, although the OFT did not disclose what it considered to be confidential information, the Competition Appeal Tribunal took the view that they themselves would have to disclose that information as part of their decision.

8   [2008] CSIH 12.

restrictions in Part 9 and the disclosure requirements in other legislation. Although this is a Scottish jurisdiction case, its consideration of the interplay between Part 9 EA 2002 and the Freedom of Information (Scotland) Act 2002 (FOISA) is instructive as the provisions of FOISA are very similar to those in the Freedom of Information Act 2000. In that case the court concluded that the FOISA did not justify the disclosure of information in s 237 EA 2002. A review of that decision assists in understanding how s 237(6) is likely to be construed.

6.16 Section 1(1) of FOISA provides: 'A person who requests information from a Scottish public authority which holds it is entitled to be given it by the authority.' In Part 2 FOISA, ss 25–41 set out various categories of information which is exempt provided that the information falls within the description applicable to the category in question and the conditions specified in relation to that category are satisfied. Section 26, which relates to prohibitions on disclosure, provides inter alia:

> 'Information is exempt information if its disclosure by a Scottish public authority (otherwise than under this Act) –
>
> (a) is prohibited by or under an enactment; ...'

6.17 The court had to consider the meaning in s 237(6) EA 2002, of the phrase 'does not affect any power or duty to disclose information which exists apart from Part 9' along with the meaning, in s 26 of FOISA, of the words 'information is exempt information if its disclosure ... (otherwise than under the Act) is *inter alia* prohibited by or under an enactment, such as the Enterprise Act'.[9] In that case, the local council had determined that the information requested by the applicant was exempt absolutely because disclosure was prohibited by Part 9 EA 2002. The Commissioner had then held that it was not so exempt, by reason of s 237(6) of the EA 2002. As regards s 237(6), the court held that:

> 'Part 9 does not "affect" any power or duty of disclosure which "exists apart from this Part". In our opinion, contrary to the approach of the Commissioner, these words have a twofold connotation. First, the source of the power or duty in question must be found elsewhere than in Part 9. Second, exercise of the power or performance of the duty must not be inconsistent with the prohibitions or restrictions imposed by the provisions of Part 9.'[10]

6.18 To illustrate this point they provided a number of examples as follows:

> '[19] Information as to an individual's private life may be "specified information" within the meaning of section 238 but will not necessarily be information relating to the "affairs" of that person within the meaning of section 237. Whether it is so or not, the duty of non-disclosure under the Data Protection Act 1998 is consistent with the provisions of Part 9 and is not "affected" by section 237.

---

9   Judgment para 9.
10   Judgment para 18.

[20] Again, where information is "specified information" within the meaning of section 238, but does not relate to the affairs of an individual or any business of an undertaking within the meaning of section 237, section 237 does not constitute a "prohibition" against disclosure for the purposes of section 26 of FOISA. Consequently (except, it seems, in one possible respect) the powers and duties of a public authority under FOISA in relation to disclosure (or non-disclosure) of information are not "affected" by Part 9. (The possible exception relates to section 244 of the Enterprise Act ...).'

6.19 Applying that reasoning the court concluded that:

'where specified information falls within section 237(1), section 237(2) expressly prohibits disclosure of that information. In that event, exercise of a power or performance of a duty under FOISA to disclose that information would be inconsistent with the provisions of Part 9. It is necessarily affected by the prohibition in section 237(2). Consequently, in our opinion, such a power or duty cannot be said to "exist apart from" Part 9.'[11]

6.20 They therefore held that the Commissioner had erred in law in holding that s 237(6) of the EA 2002 allowed disclosure of the information sought by the applicant in that case.

Permitted disclosure – the six gateways

6.21 If the information does not come within the exceptions to the general restriction set out above, then it will need to go through one of the six gateways before it can be disclosed. All of the gateways are also subject to the public interest test in s 244.

Consent (s 239)

6.22 If a public authority obtains the consent of the individual concerned, or the consent of the person carrying on the business of the undertaking to which the information relates, then they can disclose the information in question. If the information was obtained by the authority from a person who had the information lawfully, and the authority knows the identity of that person, then the consent of that person is also required. Plainly therefore, if the information in question has been provided by an anonymous source, their consent would not be required.

6.23 If the undertaking is a company, consent may be given by a director, secretary or other officer of the company. If it is a partnership, by a partner and, if it is an unincorporated body or association, then consent can be given by a person concerned in the management or control of that undertaking. It is important therefore, that the correct person is identified and it would be prudent to ensure that any consent is obtained in writing.

---

[11] Judgment para 23.

Community obligations (s 240)

6.24 This section simply states that, Part 9 does not prohibit the disclosure of information if the disclosure is required for the purpose of a European Union obligation. Examples of community obligations include Treaty articles, European Directives, Regulations and Decisions which are binding on those to whom they are addressed.

Statutory functions (s 241)

6.25 Under s 241(1) a public authority may disclose information if it is done to facilitate the exercise of any of its functions it has under, or by virtue of, the EA 2002 or indeed any other enactment. The word 'enactment' includes a reference to an enactment contained in an Act of the Scottish Parliament, Northern Ireland legislation and subordinate legislation (s 241(5)). It therefore extends to relevant functions that arise under statutory instruments.

6.26 Equally, under s 241(3) a public authority may disclose information to any other person for the purpose of facilitating the exercise by that person of any function they have under or by virtue of the EA 2002, an enactment specified in Sch 15 or any subordinate legislation specified for the purposes of this subsection. So, for example, under this section, one public authority could disclose information to another. The word 'function' in this context has been held to connote 'an act or activity susceptible of being facilitated by disclosure of information', but it cannot be said that disclosure of information itself 'facilitates' disclosure of information.[12]

Civil proceedings (s 241A)

6.27 Section 241A of the EA 2002 was added by the Enterprise Act 2002 (Disclosure of Information for Civil Proceedings etc) Order 2007. It permits the disclosure of prescribed information if it is for the purpose of or in connection with, actual or prospective civil proceedings. But it is only in respect of civil proceedings which relate to or arise out of:

- a legal right or obligation of a consumer;
- the infringement of an intellectual property right;
- passing off or the misuse of a trade secret.

6.28 It also permits disclosure for the purpose of obtaining legal advice in relation to any such proceedings or if it is for the purpose of establishing, enforcing or defending legal rights that are or may be the subject of any such proceedings. This would seem to extend the scope of the section to include the establishment of consumer rights, which may potentially lead to civil litigation

---

[12] *Dumfries and Galloway Council v Dunion, Scottish Information Commissioner* [2008] CSIH 12.

by a consumer and is therefore, arguably, an extremely important tool in the protection of consumers and their rights generally.

Criminal proceedings (s 242)

6.29 This section follows the approach taken in other legislation such as the Data Protection Act 1998, namely, that the duties of public authorities should not unduly frustrate the proper process of criminal proceedings. Section 242 allows a public authority to disclose specified information to any person so long as it is in connection with the investigation of a criminal offence in any part of the United Kingdom, or for the purpose of any criminal proceedings. In either case, information can also be disclosed for the purposes of deciding whether to start or end such proceedings.

6.30 Perhaps for obvious reasons, the ambit of this section is very wide. But there is a safeguard in this provision and it is that a public authority must not disclose the information unless it is satisfied that doing so is proportionate to what is sought to be achieved by it (s 242(3)). The requirement for the public authority to actively consider the aims to be achieved by the proposed disclosure should ensure that global, wide ranging disclosures, are not routinely made. This is perhaps particularly important given that the range of criminal offences to which the section applies is not limited in any way.

Overseas disclosures (s 243)

6.31 Section 243 sets out a restrictive regime relating to the disclosure of information to overseas authorities. Under subsection (3) certain classes of information cannot be disclosed overseas at all. These include information obtained in a merger or market investigation along with other commercially sensitive information. Outside of this specific limitation, disclosure can only generally be made if it facilitates the investigation, enforcement or bringing of criminal proceedings, or of civil proceedings relating to competition or consumer matters.

The general public interest test (s 244)

6.32 Once the relevant gateway has been identified and the various requirements of it have been met, before any disclosure takes place, the public authority making the decision must have proper regard to the considerations set out in s 244.

244 Specified information: considerations relevant to disclosure

(1) public authority must have regard to the following considerations before disclosing any specified information (within the meaning of section 238(1),

(2) The first consideration is the need to exclude from disclosure (so far as practicable) any information whose disclosure the authority thinks is contrary to the public interest,

(3) The second consideration is the need to exclude from disclosure (so far as practicable) –

(a)   commercial information whose disclosure the authority thinks might significantly harm the legitimate business interests of the undertaking to which it relates; or

(b)   information relating to the private affairs of an individual whose disclosure the authority thinks might significantly harm the individual's interests,

(4) The third consideration is the extent to which the disclosure of the information mentioned in subsection (3)(a) or (b) is necessary for the purpose for which the authority is permitted to make the disclosure.

6.33   Of course, the application of these principles will be very fact specific and focussed consideration will need to be given to their effect on a case by case basis. If the view is that the information in question meets the relevant requirements in s 244, then disclosure can be made. For a recent example of how those considerations have applied in practice see *Ryanair Holdings Plc v Competition Commission*[13] where the Commission righty refused to disclose to Ryanair the names and evidence of other airlines which they had taken into account when deciding whether Ryanair's minority shareholding in a rival airline had resulted in a substantial lessening of competition.

Steps to disclosure

6.34   In analysing whether disclosure is restricted under Part 9 five questions can be asked:

(1)   Is the information specified information? Has it come to a public authority in connection with the exercise of a function referred to in s 238?
      If the answer is 'no' the Part 9 regime does not apply.
      If the answer is 'yes' then consider question (2).

(2)   Has the information already been lawfully disclosed to the public?
      If the answer is 'yes' the information falls within the exception provided by s 237(3) and the Part 9 regime does not apply.
      If the answer is 'no' then consider question (3).

(3)   Is there an existing 'power or duty to disclose the information'?
      If the answer is 'yes' then disclosure need not be justified under the gateways, however, the public interest test (question (5)) must still be applied.
      If the answer is 'no' then consider question (4).

(4)   Does the information fall to be disclosed under any of the six gateways?
      (a)   Has the necessary consent been obtained (s 239)?
      (b)   Is there an EU obligation that applies (s 240)?
      (c)   Does disclosure facilitate a statutory function (s 241)?
      (d)   Is the information required for civil proceedings and, if so, are the requirements of s 241A met?

---

[13]   [2015] EWCA Civ 83.

LIVERPOOL JOHN MOORES UNIVERSITY
LEARNING SERVICES

(e)   Is the information required for criminal proceedings (s 242)?

(f)   Is the disclosure to a public authority overseas and, if so, are all the conditions in s 243 met?

If the answer is 'no' then the information cannot be disclosed.

(5)   Does disclosure meet the public interest test in s 244?

> If the answer is 'no' the information cannot be disclosed. If 'yes' then it can.

Offences (s 245)

6.35   There are three circumstances relating to the disclosure of information under Part 9 in which criminal offences can be committed and they are all offences of strict liability. The first offence is committed if a person discloses specified information during the lifetime of the relevant individual or undertaking which is not otherwise permitted by Part 9. The second offence is committed if a disclosure is made to an overseas recipient where the Secretary of State has directed that no such disclosure should be made.[14] The third offence is committed if, when in receipt of disclosure, the receiver uses the information for a purpose which is not permitted under Part 9.

THE DATA PROTECTION ACT 1998

6.36   The Data Protection Act 1998 (DPA) regulates the manner in which personal data is held and processed. It applies to both public and private bodies. It is chiefly concerned with:

- safeguarding personal data held by the persons to whom it applies (eg by setting out in what circumstances and for what reasons data may be processed, and imposing a duty of non-disclosure);

- affording persons whose personal data are being processed the right to know what data are held in respect of them; and

- a remedy where data are processed improperly.

Key concepts and definitions

6.37   The DPA is concerned with the processing of data by data controllers and the principles which data controllers must apply in processing those data. The Act distinguishes between personal data and sensitive personal data. The main definitions are provided in s 1(1) of the DPA as follows:

> **1 Basic interpretative provisions**
>
> (1) In this Act, unless the context otherwise requires –
>
> "data" means information which –

---

[14]   See s 243(4).

(a) is being processed by means of equipment operating automatically in response to instructions given for that purpose,

(b) is recorded with the intention that it should be processed by means of such equipment,

(c) is recorded as part of a relevant filing system or with the intention that it should form part of a relevant filing system,

(d) does not fall within paragraph (a), (b) or (c) but forms part of an accessible record as defined by section 68; or

(e) is recorded information held by a public authority and does not fall within any of paragraphs (a) to (d);

"data controller" means, subject to subsection (4), a person who (either alone or jointly or in common with other persons) determines the purposes for which and the manner in which any personal data are, or are to be, processed;

"data processor", in relation to personal data, means any person (other than an employee of the data controller) who processes the data on behalf of the data controller;

"data subject" means an individual who is the subject of personal data;

"personal data" means data which relate to a living individual who can be identified –

(a) from those data, or

(b) from those data and other information which is in the possession of, or is likely to come into the possession of, the data controller,

and includes any expression of opinion about the individual and any indication of the intentions of the data controller or any other person in respect of the individual;

"processing", in relation to information or data, means obtaining, recording or holding the information or data or carrying out any operation or set of operations on the information or data, including –

(a) organisation, adaptation or alteration of the information or data,

(b) retrieval, consultation or use of the information or data,

(c) disclosure of the information or data by transmission, dissemination or otherwise making available, or

(d) alignment, combination, blocking, erasure or destruction of the information or data;

"public authority" means a public authority as defined by the Freedom of Information Act 2000 or a Scottish public authority as defined by the Freedom of Information (Scotland) Act 2002;

"relevant filing system" means any set of information relating to individuals to the extent that, although the information is not processed by means of equipment operating automatically in response to instructions given for that purpose, the set is structured, either by reference to individuals or by reference to criteria relating to individuals, in such a way that specific information relating to a particular individual is readily accessible.

6.38 Sensitive personal data is defined in s 2 of the DPA as follows:

2 Sensitive personal data

In this Act "sensitive personal data" means personal data consisting of information as to –

(a)   the racial or ethnic origin of the data subject,

(b)   his political opinions,

(c)   his religious beliefs or other beliefs of a similar nature,

(d)   whether he is a member of a trade union (within the meaning of the Trade Union and Labour Relations (Consolidation) Act 1992),

(e)   his physical or mental health or condition,

(f)   his sexual life,

(g)   the commission or alleged commission by him of any offence, or

(h)   any proceedings for any offence committed or alleged to have been committed by him, the disposal of such proceedings or the sentence of any court in such proceedings.

The data protection principles

6.39   The data protection principles are set out in Part I of Sch 1 to the DPA and are as follows:

(1) Personal data shall be processed fairly and lawfully and, in particular, shall not be processed unless –

(a)   at least one of the conditions in Schedule 2 is met, and

(b)   in the case of sensitive personal data, at least one of the conditions in Schedule 3 is also met.

(2) Personal data shall be obtained only for one or more specified and lawful purposes, and shall not be further processed in any manner incompatible with that purpose or those purposes.

(3) Personal data shall be adequate, relevant and not excessive in relation to the purpose or purposes for which they are processed.

(4) Personal data shall be accurate and, where necessary, kept up to date.

(5) Personal data processed for any purpose or purposes shall not be kept for longer than is necessary for that purpose or those purposes.

(6) Personal data shall be processed in accordance with the rights of data subjects under this Act.

(7) Appropriate technical and organisational measures shall be taken against unauthorised or unlawful processing of personal data and against accidental loss or destruction of, or damage to, personal data.

(8) Personal data shall not be transferred to a country or territory outside the European Economic Area unless that country or territory ensures an adequate level of protection for the rights and freedoms of data subjects in relation to the processing of personal data.

6.40   Schedule 2 to the DPA contains the conditions which must be met in order for personal data to be processed. In addition, Sch 3 to the DPA contains further conditions which are relevant in cases concerning sensitive personal data. In such cases, at least one of the conditions in Sch 3 must be present in addition to at least one of the conditions in Sch 2 in order for sensitive personal data to be processed. Part II of Sch 1 contains guidance relevant for determining whether the principles in Part I of Sch 1 are met. Section 4(4) of the DPA states that it is the duty of a data controller to comply with the data protection principles in relation to all personal data with respect to which he is the data controller. The duty contained in s 4(4) of the DPA is qualified by s 27(1) of the DPA, which provides for certain forms of data to be exempt from that duty.

Rights of data subjects and others

6.41 Provisions concerning the rights of subjects and other persons are to be found in Part II of the DPA. The key rights are the right of access, the right to prevent processing, and the right to apply for rectification, erasure, blocking, and destruction.

The right of access (s 7)

6.42 The basic rights of access are contained in s 7(1) of the DPA:

7 Right of access to personal data

(1) Subject to the following provisions of this section and to sections 8, 9 and 9A, an individual is entitled –

(a) to be informed by any data controller whether personal data of which that individual is the data subject are being processed by or on behalf of that data controller,

(b) if that is the case, to be given by the data controller a description of –
(i) the personal data of which that individual is the data subject,
(ii) the purposes for which they are being or are to be processed, and
(iii) the recipients or classes of recipients to whom they are or may be disclosed,

(c) to have communicated to him in an intelligible form –
(i) the information constituting any personal data of which that individual is the data subject, and
(ii) any information available to the data controller as to the source of those data, and

(d) where the processing by automatic means of personal data of which that individual is the data subject for the purpose of evaluating matters relating to him such as, for example, his performance at work, his creditworthiness, his reliability or his conduct, has constituted or is likely to constitute the sole basis for any decision significantly affecting him, to be informed by the data controller of the logic involved in that decision-taking.

6.43 A data controller is only obliged to supply any of the information in s 7(1) of the DPA if the request is made in writing, and he may charge a fee (s 7(2) of the DPA). If, in order to satisfy himself of the identity of the person making the request and locate the information sought, a data controller reasonably requires further information and informs the person making the request of that fact, he is not bound to comply with the request until the information is received. Sections 7(4)–(6) of the DPA deal with the factors to be taken into consideration in cases where there is a danger of revealing another person's personal data in responding to a request under s 7(1) of the DPA. Under s 7(8) of the DPA, requests under s 7(1) must be complied with promptly, and in any case not later than 40 days from receipt of the request (or receipt of the fee and/or further information required where applicable).

Right to prevent processing likely to cause damage or distress (s 10)

6.44   Section 10(1) of the DPA allows an individual to give written notice requiring a data controller to stop (or not to begin) processing data on the grounds such processing is likely to cause substantial damage or substantial distress to him or to another, and that damage or distress is or would be unwarranted. The notice must specify the reasons for claiming the grounds for prevention of processing are made out. Where any of the factors in paras 1–4 of Sch 2 to the DPA are present, the right does not arise (s 10(2) of the DPA). If a s 10 request is made, a data controller has 21 days in which to serve notice to the effect that he has complied, or will comply, with it; or that he regards it as unjustified (s 10(3) of the DPA).

Right to prevent processing for purposes of direct marketing (s 11)

6.45   This section allows for a similar procedure to s 10 of the DPA above. However there are no qualifications mirroring the provisions in ss 10(2) and (3): on receipt of written notice, the data controller must comply within the time specified in the notice.

Rectification, blocking, erasure and destruction (s 14)

6.46   These are remedies available on application to the High Court or county court in respect of data which are inaccurate.

Exemptions

6.47   The list of exemptions is to be found at Part IV of the DPA. The list covers a wide range of forms of data and circumstances, to reflect the broad application of the Act. In a Trading Standards context, the main exemptions are likely to be crime and taxation (s 29), information available to the public under enactment (s 34), and disclosures required by law or made in connection with legal proceedings etc (s 35). In addition to the specific provisions cited in relation to certain exemptions, Part IV of the DPA makes reference to 'the subject access provisions' and 'the non-disclosure provisions'. These are defined in s 27 of the DPA as follows:

27 Preliminary

(1) References in any of the data protection principles or any provision of Parts II and III to personal data or to the processing of personal data do not include references to data or processing which by virtue of this Part are exempt from that principle or other provision.

(2) In this Part "the subject information provisions" means –

(a)   the first data protection principle to the extent to which it requires compliance with paragraph 2 of Part II of Schedule 1, and
(b)   section 7.

(3) In this Part "the non-disclosure provisions" means the provisions specified in subsection (4) to the extent to which they are inconsistent with the disclosure in question.

(4) The provisions referred to in subsection (3) are –

(a)   the first data protection principle, except to the extent to which it requires compliance with the conditions in Schedules 2 and 3,
(b)   the second, third, fourth and fifth data protection principles, and
(c)   sections 10 and 14(1) to (3).

(5) Except as provided by this Part, the subject information provisions shall have effect notwithstanding any enactment or rule of law prohibiting or restricting the disclosure, or authorising the withholding, of information.

Crime and taxation (s 29)

6.48 This section will be relevant to Trading Standards authorities in circumstances where they are engaged in investigating and prosecuting criminal offences. The section sets out a framework for exemption from duties which would otherwise apply (eg non-disclosure) where such an exemption is required in order to ensure that an investigation or prosecution is not prejudiced. In a Trading Standards context, the relevant parts of the section are as follows:

29 Crime and taxation

(1) Personal data processed for any of the following purposes –

(a)   the prevention or detection of crime,
(b)   the apprehension or prosecution of offenders, or
(c)   the assessment or collection of any tax or duty or of any imposition of a similar nature,

are exempt from the first data protection principle (except to the extent to which it requires compliance with the conditions in Schedules 2 and 3) and section 7 in any case to the extent to which the application of those provisions to the data would be likely to prejudice any of the matters mentioned in this subsection.

(2) Personal data which –

(a)   are processed for the purpose of discharging statutory functions, and
(b)   consist of information obtained for such a purpose from a person who had it in his possession for any of the purposes mentioned in subsection (1),

are exempt from the subject information provisions to the same extent as personal data processed for any of the purposes mentioned in that subsection.

(3) Personal data are exempt from the non-disclosure provisions in any case in which –

   (a)   the disclosure is for any of the purposes mentioned in subsection (1), and
   (b)   the application of those provisions in relation to the disclosure would be likely to prejudice any of the matters mentioned in that subsection.

6.49   Section 29(1) of the DPA sets out the purposes for which the data in question must be processed in order to qualify for the exemption. It is the purpose for which the data are being processed, not the nature of the data or the organisation doing the processing, which triggers the exemption. Accordingly, a company investigating (for example) infringements of its Intellectual Property rights with a view to bringing a private prosecution or passing the evidence to a prosecuting authority will come within the exemption.

6.50   Section 29 of the DPA does not provide a blanket exemption in relation to all data processed for one of the purposes in s 29(1) of the DPA. The test is whether the normal application of the DPA would be likely to prejudice the purposes set out in s 29(1) of the DPA. Anybody seeking to rely on s 29 of the DPA should be able to identify the prejudice in question and establish a causal link between that prejudice likely to occur and the exemption not being implemented. The question of likelihood was considered in *R (Lord) v SSHD*[15] in which it was held that it required a degree of probability where there is a very significant and weighty chance to prejudice to the identified public interests'. For a recent example of where the use of this provision was successfully challenged see *Guriev v Community Safety Development (UK) Ltd*[16] where the defendant failed to establish that either a crime or a privilege exemption applied in respect of a subject access request under s 7 of the Data Protection Act 1998.

6.51   Even where the s 29 exemption applies, a condition under Sch 2, and, in cases involving sensitive personal data, a further condition under Sch 3, must be present in order for the data to be processed. Where processing is being done for purposes of crime prevention it is likely that the conditions at para 5 of Sch 2 DPA and para 7 of Sch 3 of the DPA will apply:

Schedule 2

Conditions relevant for purposes of the first principle: processing of any personal data

...

5. The processing is necessary –

   (a)   for the administration of justice,

---

[15]   [2003] EWHC 2073 (Admin).
[16]   [2016] EWHC 643.

(aa)   for the exercise of any functions of either House of Parliament,

(b)   for the exercise of any functions conferred on any person by or under any enactment,

(c)   for the exercise of any functions of the Crown, a Minister of the Crown or a government department, or

(d)   for the exercise of any other functions of a public nature exercised in the public interest by any person.

Schedule 3

Conditions relevant for purposes of the first principle: processing of sensitive personal data

...

7. The processing is necessary –

(a)   for the administration of justice,
(aa)   for the exercise of any functions of either House of Parliament,

(b)   for the exercise of any functions conferred on any person by or under any enactment,

(c)   for the exercise of any functions of the Crown, a Minister of the Crown or a government department.

6.52 Section 29(2) of the DPA extends the exemption to bodies which have obtained personal data in pursuance of their statutory functions (i e not for the purposes set out in s 29(1)), but would prejudice the s 29(1) purposes were they to disclose them in accordance with the subject information provisions. Section 29(3) allows for disclosure by a data controller for any of the s 29(1) purposes. It is an enabling provision, not a mandatory one. Thus, it allows the data controller in question to make a disclosure (for example to an investigating officer) without falling foul of the DPA; however, it does not compel such a disclosure to be made. Like the other provisions in this section, it is dependent on one of the s 29(1) purposes being prejudiced.

Information available by or under enactment (s 34)

6.53 This section simply excludes from certain provisions of the DPA data which a data controller is obliged to make available to the public.

34 Information available to the public by or under enactment

Personal data are exempt from –

(a) the subject information provisions,

(b) the fourth data protection principle and section 14(1) to (3), and

(c) the non-disclosure provisions,

if the data consist of information which the data controller is obliged by or under any enactment other than an enactment contained in the Freedom of Information Act 2000 to make available to the public, whether by publishing it, by making it available for inspection, or otherwise and whether gratuitously or on payment of a fee.

Disclosures required by law (s 35)

6.54   This section deals with disclosures which are required by law or made in connection with legal proceedings. The former are covered by s 35(1) of the DPA, where the test is that the disclosure is 'required'. The latter are covered by s 35(2) of the DPA, where the test is one of necessity.

> **35 Disclosures required by law or made in connection with legal proceedings etc**
>
> (1) Personal data are exempt from the non-disclosure provisions where the disclosure is required by or under any enactment, by any rule of law or by the order of a court.
>
> (2) Personal data are exempt from the non-disclosure provisions where the disclosure is necessary –
>
> > (a)   for the purpose of, or in connection with, any legal proceedings (including prospective legal proceedings), or
> > (b)   for the purpose of obtaining legal advice,
>
> or is otherwise necessary for the purposes of establishing, exercising or defending legal rights.

6.55   This section allows for disclosures which would otherwise fall within the non-disclosure provisions to be made where they are required by law or a court order or are necessary for any of the s 35(2) purposes. Like s 29(3) of the DPA, this is an enabling provision, not a mandatory one (although in many cases, the underlying court order or enactment may have mandatory effect). Where non-disclosure would amount to a contempt of court or a breach of the law, the decision to disclose will be clear-cut. Where s 35(2) is relied on, the test of necessity must be met in order for the exemption to apply. If the exemption does apply, the data controller in question then has a discretion over whether to make the disclosure or not.

Enforcement

6.56   The enforcement provisions are contained in Part V of the DPA. This part allows for the Information Commissioner to issue enforcement notices, assessment notices, and information notices where there is non-compliance with the provisions of the DPA. In addition, the Commissioner has the power under s 55A of the DPA to impose monetary penalties.

THE FREEDOM OF INFORMATION ACT 2000

6.57   In contrast to the DPA, the purpose of the Freedom of Information Act 2000 (FOIA) is to provide a framework for the release of information held by public bodies. The overall scheme of the Act and the reasons it was considered necessary were set out in the 1997 White Paper *Your Right to Know*. The premise behind the Act is to provide for more open government. This is accomplished by mandating the publication of certain information as well as allowing for requests for information to be made by the public.

General right of access

6.58 The general right of access to information is contained in s 1 of the FOIA, which reads as follows:

1 General right of access to information held by public authorities

(1) Any person making a request for information to a public authority is entitled –

(a) to be informed in writing by the public authority whether it holds information of the description specified in the request, and

(b) if that is the case, to have that information communicated to him.

(2) Subsection (1) has effect subject to the following provisions of this section and to the provisions of sections 2, 9, 12 and 14.

(3) Where a public authority –

(a) reasonably requires further information in order to identify and locate the information requested, and

(b) has informed the applicant of that requirement,

(c) the authority is not obliged to comply with subsection (1) unless it is supplied with that further information.

(4) The information –

(a) in respect of which the applicant is to be informed under subsection (1)(a), or

(b) which is to be communicated under subsection (1)(b),

is the information in question held at the time when the request is received, except that account may be taken of any amendment or deletion made between that time and the time when the information is to be communicated under subsection (1)(b), being an amendment or deletion that would have been made regardless of the receipt of the request.

(5) A public authority is to be taken to have complied with subsection (1)(a) in relation to any information if it has communicated the information to the applicant in accordance with subsection (1)(b).

(6) In this Act, the duty of a public authority to comply with subsection (1)(a) is referred to as "the duty to confirm or deny".

Information

6.59 Per s 84 of the FOIA, information is defined as 'information which is recorded in any form'. It is not limited to documentary information, and extends to media such as audio or visual recordings. It is also not limited to formal or official items, and can include drafts, notes, and internal communications. However, s 1(1)(b) only contains an obligation for the communication of information, not the provision of the original document within which that information is contained. In order to fall within the definition at s 84 of the FOIA, the information must be recorded. If it is not recorded, there is no obligation on the public authority in question to create a record or obtain information in response to a request. Further, the obligation to provide the information in s 1(1)(b) of the FOIA only arises if the information is held by the public authority.

Public authorities

6.60 The provisions of FOIA are only engaged in respect of information held by public authorities. Schedule 1 to the FOIA sets out a list of bodies which are considered public authorities for the purposes of FOIA. Section 4 of the FOIA empowers the Secretary of State to add bodies to, or remove them from, Sch 1. In relation to additions, s 4 of the FOIA provides as follows:

4 Amendment of Schedule 1

(1) The Secretary of State may by order amend Schedule 1 by adding to that Schedule a reference to any body or the holder of any office which (in either case) is not for the time being listed in that Schedule but as respects which both the first and the second conditions below are satisfied.

(2) The first condition is that the body or office –

(a) is established by virtue of Her Majesty's prerogative or by an enactment or by subordinate legislation, or

(b) is established in any other way by a Minister of the Crown in his capacity as Minister, by a government department or by the Welsh Ministers, the First Minister for Wales or the Counsel General to the Welsh Assembly Government.

(3) The second condition is –

(a) in the case of a body, that the body is wholly or partly constituted by appointment made by the Crown, by a Minister of the Crown, by a government department or by the Welsh Ministers, the First Minister for Wales or the Counsel General to the Welsh Assembly Government, or

(b) in the case of an office, that appointments to the office are made by the Crown, by a Minister of the Crown, by a government department or by the Welsh Ministers, the First Minister for Wales or the Counsel General to the Welsh Assembly Government.

Section 4(5) of the FOIA deals with removal and provides that a body may be removed from Sch 1 if the first and/or second conditions above cease to apply, or if the body in question ceases to exist.

Request and response

6.61 To be considered a 'request for information' within the meaning of the Act, a request must be made in writing, state the name of the applicant and an address for correspondence, and describe the information requested (s 8(1) of the FOIA). Once a request for information has been received by a public authority, it must comply with s 1(1) of the FOIA promptly, and in any event, not later than the twentieth working day following receipt of the request (s 10(1) of the FOIA). The authority may charge a fee in order to provide a response, in which case, it must serve a fees notice on the applicant within the compliance period set out at s 10(1) above (s 9(1) of the FOIA). Where this is done, the authority is under no obligation to provide a response unless the fee has been paid within three months of the fees notice being served (s 9(2) of the FOIA). In cases where a fee is charged, time for compliance starts to run from receipt of the fee (s 10(2) of the FOIA). The maximum fee which may be charged is set out at reg 6 of the Freedom of Information and Data Protection (Appropriate Limit and Fees) Regulations 2004:

Maximum fee for complying with section 1(1) of the 2000 Act

6 –

(1) Any fee to be charged under section 9 of the 2000 Act by a public authority to whom a request for information is made is not to exceed the maximum determined by the public authority in accordance with this regulation.

(2) Subject to paragraph (4), the maximum fee is a sum equivalent to the total costs the public authority reasonably expects to incur in relation to the request in –

    (a)   informing the person making the request whether it holds the information, and

    (b)   communicating the information to the person making the request.

(3) Costs which may be taken into account by a public authority for the purposes of this regulation include, but are not limited to, the costs of –

    (a)   complying with any obligation under section 11(1) of the 2000 Act as to the means or form of communicating the information,

    (b)   reproducing any document containing the information, and

    (c)   postage and other forms of transmitting the information.

(4) But a public authority may not take into account for the purposes of this regulation any costs which are attributable to the time which persons undertaking activities mentioned in paragraph (2) on behalf of the authority are expected to spend on those activities.

Qualifications to the general right of access

6.62 The general right of access is qualified by ss 2, 9, 12, and 14 of the FOIA.[17]

Exempt information (s 2)

6.63 Section 2 of the FOIA provides for certain classes of information (which are set out at Part II of the Act) to be treated as exempt information. These are dealt with below.

---

17 FOIA, s 1(2).

Fees (s 9)

6.64   Section 9 of the FOIA provides that compliance with s 1(1) of the FOIA may be subject to a fee being paid. For the provisions relating to the payment of fees and the timescales which apply in such cases, see above.

Exceeding the appropriate limit (s 12)

6.65   Section 12 of the FOIA removes the obligation to comply with s 1(1) of the FOIA if the authority in question estimates that the cost of doing so would exceed the appropriate limit:

> **12 Exemption where cost of compliance exceeds appropriate limit**
>
> (1) Section 1(1) does not oblige a public authority to comply with a request for information if the authority estimates that the cost of complying with the request would exceed the appropriate limit.
>
> (2) Subsection (1) does not exempt the public authority from its obligation to comply with paragraph (a) of section 1(1) unless the estimated cost of complying with that paragraph alone would exceed the appropriate limit.
>
> (3) In subsections (1) and (2) "the appropriate limit" means such amount as may be prescribed, and different amounts may be prescribed in relation to different cases.
>
> (4) The Secretary of State may by regulations provide that, in such circumstances as may be prescribed, where two or more requests for information are made to a public authority –
>
> (a)   by one person, or
> (b)   by different persons who appear to the public authority to be acting in concert or in pursuance of a campaign,
>
> the estimated cost of complying with any of the requests is to be taken to be the estimated total cost of complying with all of them.
>
> (5) The Secretary of State may by regulations make provision for the purposes of this section as to the costs to be estimated and as to the manner in which they are to be estimated.

6.66   The appropriate limit is set by reg 3 of the Freedom of Information and Data Protection (Appropriate Limit and Fees) Regulations 2004, and is £600 in the case of a public authority listed in Part I of Sch 1 of the FOIA, and £450 in the case of all other public authorities (including local authorities, which are listed under Part II of Sch 1 of the FOIA). It is important to note that the duties under ss 1(1)(a) and 1(1)(b) of the FOIA are distinct: if an authority proposes to refuse to comply with s 1(1)(a) (the duty to confirm or deny), it must be because the cost of confirming or denying alone exceeds the appropriate limit (s 12(2) of the FOIA). If the cost of confirming that an authority holds the information sought does not exceed the appropriate limit, but the overall cost of confirming and disclosing does, then the authority is still obliged to confirm, but not to disclose.

6.67 The provisions for estimating the cost of complying with s 1(1) of the FOIA are contained in reg 4 of the Freedom of Information and Data Protection (Appropriate Limit and Fees) Regulations 2004:

Estimating the cost of complying with a request – general

4 –

...

(3) In a case in which this regulation has effect, a public authority may, for the purpose of its estimate, take account only of the costs it reasonably expects to incur in relation to the request in–

    (a)   determining whether it holds the information,

    (b)   locating the information, or a document which may contain the information,

    (c)   retrieving the information, or a document which may contain the information, and

    (d)   extracting the information from a document containing it.

(4) To the extent to which any of the costs which a public authority takes into account are attributable to the time which persons undertaking any of the activities mentioned in para (3) on behalf of the authority are expected to spend on those activities, those costs are to be estimated at a rate of £25 per person per hour.

6.68 Section 12(4) of the FOIA and reg 5 of the Freedom of Information and Data Protection (Appropriate Limit and Fees) Regulations 2004 deal with estimating the cost of compliance in cases where two or more requests for information are made by the same person or by different persons appearing to the authority to be acting on concert or in pursuance of a campaign. In such cases, if the requests relate, to any extent, to the same or similar information AND are received within any period of 60 consecutive working days, the estimated cost of complying with any request is to be taken as the cost of complying with all of them.

Vexatious and repeated requests (s 14)

6.69 Section 14 FOIA deals with vexatious and repeated requests and reads as follows:

14 Vexatious or repeated requests

(1) Section 1(1) does not oblige a public authority to comply with a request for information if the request is vexatious.

(2) Where a public authority has previously complied with a request for information which was made by any person, it is not obliged to comply with a subsequent identical or substantially similar request from that person unless a reasonable interval has elapsed between compliance with the previous request and the making of the current request.

6.70 In determining what is to be considered a 'reasonable interval' in the case of a repeated request, the ICO's guidance acknowledges that there can be no definitive answer, but two important factors which should be taken into account are: the likelihood that the information will differ significantly from that provided in response to the previous request and the amount of time that has passed (where it is unlikely that the information will differ in any significant way) since the authority complied with the previous request.

Exempt information

6.71 Section 2 of the FOIA reads as follows:

> **2 Effect of the exemptions in Part II**
>
> (1) Where any provision of Part II states that the duty to confirm or deny does not arise in relation to any information, the effect of the provision is that where either –
>
> (a)   the provision confers absolute exemption, or
> (B)   in all the circumstances of the case, the public interest in maintaining the exclusion of the duty to confirm or deny outweighs the public interest in disclosing whether the public authority holds the information,
>
> section 1(1)(a) does not apply.
>
> (2) In respect of any information which is exempt information by virtue of any provision of Part II, section 1(1)(b) does not apply if or to the extent that –
>
> (a)   the information is exempt information by virtue of a provision conferring absolute exemption, or
> (b)   in all the circumstances of the case, the public interest in maintaining the exemption outweighs the public interest in disclosing the information.
>
> (3) For the purposes of this section, the following provisions of Part II (and no others) are to be regarded as conferring absolute exemption –
>
> (a)   section 21,
> (b)   section 23,
> (c)   section 32,
> (d)   section 34,
> (e)   section 36 so far as relating to information held by the House of Commons or the House of Lords,
> (ea)   in section 37, paras (a) to (ab) of subsection (1), and subsection (2) so far as relating to those paras,
> (f)   in section 40 –
> (i)   subsection (1), and
> (ii)   subsection (2) so far as relating to cases where the first condition referred to in that subsection is satisfied by virtue of subsection (3)(a)(i) or (b) of that section,
> (g)   section 41, and
> (h)   section 44.

6.72 Section 2 of the FOIA provides for certain classes of information to be considered 'exempt information'. This removes or qualifies an authority's obligations under s 1(1) of the FOIA in respect of such information. The relevant classes of information, and the particular considerations pertaining to them, are listed at Part II of the Act. Section 2 of the FOIA designates certain classes of information as being the object of absolute exemption. Where absolute exemption applies, the obligations under s 1(1)(a) and (b) are dis-applied. In the case of exempt information to which absolute exemption does not apply, the s 1(1) obligations will be disapplied if the public interest in doing so outweighs the public interest in complying with the obligations. For local authorities, the relevant classes of exempt information are likely to be investigations and proceedings conducted by public authorities (s 30 of the FOIA), law enforcement (s 31 of the FOIA), and prohibitions on disclosure (s 44 of the FOIA).

Investigations and proceedings conducted by public authorities (s 30)

6.73 The exemption under s 30 of the DPA may be claimed by a public authority which has a duty or a power to investigate whether a person has committed a criminal offence. The scope of the exemption will depend on whether the authority in question has a duty or a power to investigate, and whether the authority can investigate, bring proceedings, or both. The relevant part of the section reads:

30 Investigations and proceedings conducted by public authorities

(1) Information held by a public authority is exempt information if it has at any time been held by the authority for the purposes of –

(a) any investigation which the public authority has a duty to conduct with a view to it being ascertained –
(i) whether a person should be charged with an offence, or
(ii) whether a person charged with an offence is guilty of it,
(b) any investigation which is conducted by the authority and in the circumstances may lead to a decision by the authority to institute criminal proceedings which the authority has power to conduct, or
(c) any criminal proceedings which the authority has power to conduct.

(2) Information held by a public authority is exempt information if –

(a) it was obtained or recorded by the authority for the purposes of its functions relating to –
(i) investigations falling within subsection (1)(a) or (b),
(ii) criminal proceedings which the authority has power to conduct,
(iii) investigations (other than investigations falling within subsection (1)(a) or (b)) which are conducted by the authority for any of the purposes specified in section 31(2) and either by virtue of Her Majesty's prerogative or by virtue of powers conferred by or under any enactment, or
(iv) civil proceedings which are brought by or on behalf of the authority and arise out of such investigations, and
(b) it relates to the obtaining of information from confidential sources.

(3) The duty to confirm or deny does not arise in relation to information which is (or if it were held by the public authority would be) exempt information by virtue of subsection (1) or (2).

6.74 The exemption in s 30 of the DPA is class-based: if a piece of information falls into one of the classes described in the section, it will be exempt from the usual duties under FOIA. It is not necessary to establish any prejudice. The exemption under s 30(1)(a) can only be claimed in cases where the authority in question has a duty (as opposed to a power) to investigate. The investigation must also be one relating to a criminal charge as opposed to purely civil sanctions. The wording of s 30(1)(a)(i) makes it clear that a charge need not in fact result from the investigation in question, but it must at least be capable of resulting. The exemption under s 30(1)(b) covers authorities with a power to investigate. However, in order for this exemption to apply, the authority in question must not only have the power to investigate, but also to conduct proceedings. Like s 30(1)(a), this section is concerned only with criminal matters, and applies whether or not proceedings are ultimately conducted.

6.75 What amounts to an investigation was considered in *Wynn v Information Commissioner and the Serious Fraud Office*.[18] In that case, the SFO had carried out a vetting procedure it described as the 'pre-investigative stage'. At that stage, it was determined that no charges should be laid. The claimant sought to argue that as a result, no investigation had taken place and the s 30 exemption did not apply. The Tribunal held that notwithstanding that the SFO's internal terminology distinguished between the pre-investigative stage and "the 'investigative' stage, involving the exercise of powers afforded to the SFO ... in the Tribunal's clear judgement, the fact that the SFO may use such labels does not in any way conceal the reality that there was ... an investigation falling squarely within section 30(1).'

6.76 While ss 30(1)(a) and (b) relate to investigations, s 30(1)(c) covers all proceedings an authority has a power to conduct. This allows the exemption to cover proceedings regardless of whether the authority conducting them has also conducted the investigation. Section 30(2) is concerned with the protection of confidential sources. For that section to apply, the information in question must have been obtained or recorded within the scope of s 30(2)(a)(i)–(iv) AND relate to the obtaining of information from confidential sources. For the list of purposes specified in s 31(2) of the FOIA, referred to in s 30(2)(a)(iii) of the FOIA, see the section on law enforcement below.

6.77 Section 30 does not confer absolute exemption, and so the public interest test will apply to any exemptions claimed under this section. Examples of how the Tribunal has applied the public interest test include:

> *Toms v Information Commissioner:*[19] '[freedom of information] should not undermine the investigation, prosecution or prevention of crime, or the bringing of

---

[18]   EA/2011/0084 7 September 2012.
[19]   EA/2005/0027 19 June 2006.

civil or criminal proceedings by public bodies. The investigation and prosecution of crime involve a number of essential requirements. These include the need to avoid prejudicing effective law enforcement, the need to protect witnesses and informers, the need to maintain the independence of the judicial and prosecution processes, and the need to preserve the criminal court as the sole forum for determining guilt.'

Digby-Cameron v the Information Commissioner and Bedfordshire Police and Hertfordshire Police:[20] "in assessing where the public interest balance lies in section 30(1) case relevant matters are therefore likely to include (a) the stage a particular investigation or prosecution has reached, (b) whether and to what extent the information is already in the public domain, (c) the significance or sensitivity of the information requested and (d) whether there is any evidence that an investigation or prosecution has not been carried out properly which may be disclosed by the information."'

Law enforcement (s 31)

6.78 Information which is not caught by s 30 of the FOIA may be caught by s 31 of the FOIA, which is drafted somewhat more broadly:

31 Law enforcement

(1) Information which is not exempt information by virtue of section 30 is exempt information if its disclosure under this Act would, or would be likely to, prejudice
–

    (a)   the prevention or detection of crime,

    (b)   the apprehension or prosecution of offenders,

    (c)   the administration of justice,

    (d)   the assessment or collection of any tax or duty or of any imposition of a similar nature,

    (e)   the operation of the immigration controls,

    (f)   the maintenance of security and good order in prisons or in other institutions where persons are lawfully detained,

    (g)   the exercise by any public authority of its functions for any of the purposes specified in subsection (2),

    (h)   any civil proceedings which are brought by or on behalf of a public authority and arise out of an investigation conducted, for any of the purposes specified in subsection (2), by or on behalf of the authority by virtue of Her Majesty's prerogative or by virtue of powers conferred by or under an enactment, or

    (i)   any inquiry held under the Fatal Accidents and Sudden Deaths Inquiries (Scotland) Act 1976 to the extent that the inquiry arises out of an investigation conducted, for any of the purposes specified in subsection (2), by or on behalf of the authority by virtue of Her Majesty's prerogative or by virtue of powers conferred by or under an enactment.

(2) The purposes referred to in subsection (1)(g) to (i) are –

    (a)   the purpose of ascertaining whether any person has failed to comply with the law,

---

[20]   EA/2008/0023 and 0025 26 January 2009.

(b)   the purpose of ascertaining whether any person is responsible for any conduct which is improper,

(c)   the purpose of ascertaining whether circumstances which would justify regulatory action in pursuance of any enactment exist or may arise,

(d)   the purpose of ascertaining a person's fitness or competence in relation to the management of bodies corporate or in relation to any profession or other activity which he is, or seeks to become, authorised to carry on,

(e)   the purpose of ascertaining the cause of an accident,

(f)   the purpose of protecting charities against misconduct or mismanagement (whether by trustees or other persons) in their administration,

(g)   the purpose of protecting the property of charities from loss or misapplication,

(h)   the purpose of recovering the property of charities,

(i)   the purpose of securing the health, safety and welfare of persons at work, and

(j)   the purpose of protecting persons other than persons at work against risk to health or safety arising out of or in connection with the actions of persons at work.

(3) The duty to confirm or deny does not arise if, or to the extent that, compliance with section 1(1)(a) would, or would be likely to, prejudice any of the matters mentioned in subsection (1).

6.79 While s 30 of the FOIA is class-based, s 31 of the FOIA is prejudice-based. This means that any person seeking to rely on the exemption will need to identify the specific prejudice to the relevant purpose under s 31(1) of the FOIA and a causal link between the normal application of FOIA and that prejudice.

6.80 Like s 30 of the FOIA, s 31 of the FOIA does not confer absolute exemption, and is subject to the public interest test.

Prohibitions on disclosure (s 44)

6.81 Section 44 of the FOIA creates an exemption in the case of information the disclosure of which is prohibited by law extraneous to FOIA. The section confers absolute exemption.

44 Prohibitions on disclosure

(1) Information is exempt information if its disclosure (otherwise than under this Act) by the public authority holding it –

(a)   is prohibited by or under any enactment,

(b)   is incompatible with any EU obligation, or

(c)   would constitute or be punishable as a contempt of court.

(2) The duty to confirm or deny does not arise if the confirmation or denial that would have to be given to comply with section 1(1)(a) would (apart from this Act) fall within any of paras (a) to (c) of subsection (1).

Enforcement

Decision notices

6.82 Under s 50 of the FOIA, any person may apply to the Information Commissioner for a decision on whether a public authority has dealt with a request for information in accordance with the provisions of the Act. A decision will not be made until any complaints procedure provided by the authority in question has been exhausted. Section 50(2) sets out the further grounds for the Commissioner to refuse to make a decision, namely that there has been undue delay in making the complaint, the complaint is frivolous or vexatious, or the complaint has been withdrawn. If the Commissioner refuses to make a decision, he must serve notice to that effect on the complainant stating his grounds for refusing. If a decision is made, a decision notice setting out the decision is to be served on the complainant and the authority (s 50(3) of the FOIA). If the Commissioner decides that the authority has failed to carry out its obligations under ss 1(1), 11, or 17, he must specify in the decision notice the steps which must be taken in order to secure compliance and the period within which those steps must be taken (s 50(4) of the FOIA).

Information notices

6.83 Section 51 of the FOIA provides that where the Commissioner has been asked to make a decision under s 50 of the FOIA or (regardless of whether there has been a request for a decision) he reasonably requires information for the purpose of ascertaining whether an authority has complied with Part I of the Act or the codes of practice, he may serve an information notice on the authority in question. The information notice must specify the information which the Commissioner requires the authority to provide. Where a request for a decision has been made under s 50 of the FOIA, the information notice must contain a statement to that effect. Where the information notice is issued in order to determine compliance with Part I of the FOIA or the codes of practice, the notice must state that the Commissioner regards the information specified in the notice as relevant for the determination of such compliance (s 51(2) of the FOIA. Section 51(5) of the FOIA contains an exclusion for legally-privileged information.

Enforcement notices

6.84 Section 52 of the FOIA provides that if the Commissioner is satisfied that an authority has failed to comply with its obligations under Part I of the FOIA, he may serve an enforcement notice. An enforcement notice will require the authority to take steps to ensure compliance, and will set a period within which those steps must be taken. An enforcement notice must contain a statement of the requirements of Part I of the FOIA with which the Commissioner is satisfied the authority has failed to comply.

Failure to comply with notices

6.85   Where an authority has failed to comply with a decision notice requiring it to take action, an information notice, or an enforcement notice, the Commissioner may certify such a failure to the High Court, which then has the power to deal with the non-compliance as if it were a contempt of court (s 54 of the FOIA).

Powers of entry and inspection

6.86   The Commissioner may apply for a warrant in order to enforce compliance. The provisions relating to warrants and powers of entry and inspection are set out at Sch 3 to the FOIA. An application for a warrant may be made to a Circuit Judge or a District Judge (Magistrates' Courts).

Appeals

6.87   Section 53 of the FOIA provides that there is a right of appeal by a complainant or an authority against decision notices made under s 50 of the FOIA, and by an authority against information and enforcement notices issued under ss 51 and 52 of the FOIA. Appeals lie to the General Regulatory Chamber of the First-Tier Tribunal, and are governed by The Tribunal Procedure (First-Tier Tribunal) (General Regulatory Chamber) Rules 2009). Where a decision or notice requires that an authority take any action, the period within which that action must be completed may not be within the period in which an appeal may be brought, and where an appeal is brought, no step which is required by the decision or notice need be taken until the appeal is determined or withdrawn (ss 50(6), 51(4), and 52(3) of the FOIA respectively). The time limit for lodging an appeal is 28 days from the date the notice or decision being appealed was sent to the appellant (Rule 22(1)(b) of The Tribunal Procedure (First-Tier Tribunal) (General Regulatory Chamber) Rules 2009).

6.88   There are two grounds of appeal under s 58 of the FOIA, these are:

- that the notice against which the appeal is brought is not in accordance with the law;
- to the extent that the notice involved an exercise of discretion by the Commissioner, he should have exercised his discretion differently.

6.89   Where the tribunal allows an appeal, it may substitute any other notice which could have been made by the Commissioner. Section 58(2) provides that the tribunal is entitled to review any finding of fact on which a notice is based. An appeal from a decision of the First-Tier Tribunal lies to the Upper Tribunal. An appeal from a decision of the Upper Tribunal is a second appeal, and so must be made to the Court of Appeal and must satisfy the second appeals test, namely that the appeal would raise one important point of principle or practice, or that there is some other compelling reason to hear the appeal.

THE ENVIRONMENTAL INFORMATION REGULATIONS 2004

6.90 The Environmental Information Regulations 2004 ('EIR') implement Council Directive 2003/4/EC and provide freedom of access to environmental information held by UK public authorities (except in relation to Scottish public authorities – see the Environmental Information (Scotland) Regulations 2004).

6.91 The extensive meaning given to 'public authorities' in reg 2(2) includes government departments, local authorities, the NHS, police forces and universities. The Regulations also cover some other bodies that do public work that affects the environment.

6.92 The EIR enable information to be accessed in two ways:

- public authorities must make environmental information available proactively;
- a public authority that holds environmental information must generally make it available on request, as soon as possible and no later than 20 working days after the date of receipt of the request. A public authority may charge applicants a reasonable amount for making the information available (subject to certain restrictions).

6.93 Information may only be withheld if an exception to disclosure applies and the public interest in not disclosing the information outweighs the public interest in disclosure. Enforcement powers are given to the Information Commissioner.

THE PRIVACY AND ELECTRONIC COMMUNICATIONS (EC DIRECTIVE) REGULATIONS 2003

6.94 The Privacy and Electronic Communications (EC Directive) Regulations 2003 (PECR) govern the sending of electronic messages to members of the public for marketing purposes. PECR sets out the circumstances in which such messages may and may not be sent by various media, and provides for the maintenance of registers of persons who do not consent to receiving such communications.

Direct marketing

6.95 Regulations 19–22 of the PECR deal with the use of automatic calling systems, fax machines, unsolicited (or 'cold') calls, and e-mail for direct marketing purposes.

Automated calling systems (reg 19)

6.96 Regulation 19 of the PECR prohibits the use of automated calling systems for direct marketing purposes, save in circumstances where a subscriber has given his consent to be so contacted persons making or instigating the calls do not prevent presentation of calling line identity on the called line. Regulation 19(3) covers subscribers who do not themselves cause transmissions to be made from automated calling systems, but permit their lines to be used for that purpose.

19 Use of automated calling systems

(1) A person shall neither transmit, nor instigate the transmission of, communications comprising recorded matter for direct marketing purposes by means of an automated calling or communication system except in the circumstances referred to in paragraph (2).

(2) Those circumstances are where –

   (a)   the called line is that of a subscriber who has previously notified the caller that for the time being he consents to such communications being sent by, or at the instigation of, the caller on that line; and

   (b)   the person transmitting, or instigating the transmission of, such communications –

      (i)   does not prevent presentation of the identity of the calling line on the called line; or

      (ii)   presents the identity of a line on which he can be contacted.

(3) A subscriber shall not permit his line to be used in contravention of para (1).

(4) For the purposes of this regulation, an automated calling system is a system which is capable of –

   (a)   automatically initiating a sequence of calls to more than one destination in accordance with instructions stored in that system; and

   (b)   transmitting sounds which are not live speech for reception by persons at some or all of the destinations so called.

Fax (reg 20)

6.97 The provisions of reg 20 of the PECR are somewhat more complicated than those of reg 19 of the PECR. In the case of recipients who are individuals, use of fax machines for direct marketing is prohibited, save with consent. However, in the case of corporate recipients, the prohibition applies once the recipient has notified the caller that such communications should not be sent.

6.98 Regulation 25 of the PECR provides for a register to be kept of persons who do not consent to being contacted by fax for direct marketing purposes, and for all subscribers (whether individual or corporate), inclusion on the register raises the prohibition on using fax for direct marketing. However, where a recipient has been on the register for under 28 days at the time of the communication being made, no contravention will occur. Additionally, any person on the register may notify a caller that they consent to direct marketing by fax, and no contravention will occur until that consent is withdrawn.

20 Use of facsimile machines for direct marketing purposes

(1) A person shall neither transmit, nor instigate the transmission of, unsolicited communications for direct marketing purposes by means of a facsimile machine where the called line is that of –

(a)   an individual subscriber, except in the circumstances referred to in para (2);

(b)   a corporate subscriber who has previously notified the caller that such communications should not be sent on that line; or

(c)   a subscriber and the number allocated to that line is listed in the register kept under regulation 25.

(2) The circumstances referred to in para (1)(a) are that the individual subscriber has previously notified the caller that he consents for the time being to such communications being sent by, or at the instigation of, the caller.

(3) A subscriber shall not permit his line to be used in contravention of para (1).

(4) A person shall not be held to have contravened para (1)(c) where the number allocated to the called line has been listed on the register for less than 28 days preceding that on which the communication is made.

(5) Where a subscriber who has caused a number allocated to a line of his to be listed in the register kept under regulation 25 has notified a caller that he does not, for the time being, object to such communications being sent on that line by that caller, such communications may be sent by that caller on that line, notwithstanding that the number allocated to that line is listed in the said register.

(6) Where a subscriber has given a caller notification pursuant to para (5) in relation to a line of his –

(a)   the subscriber shall be free to withdraw that notification at any time, and

(b)   where such notification is withdrawn, the caller shall not send such communications on that line.

(7) The provisions of this regulation are without prejudice to the provisions of regulation 19.

Calls for direct marketing purposes (reg 21)

6.99   In the case of calls for direct marketing purposes, there is no distinction between individual and corporate recipients. The conditions for the prohibition to apply are that either the recipient has notified the caller that direct marketing calls should not be made or the recipient is listed in a register of persons who do not consent to receiving unsolicited calls for direct marketing purposes. As in the case of reg 20 above, there is a 28-day grace period from a recipient being listed on the register during which calls may be made without a contravention occurring, and a person on the register may notify a caller that he consents to direct marketing by way of unsolicited calls, and no contravention will occur until that consent is withdrawn. In addition, the persons making or instigating such calls (whether solicited or unsolicited) must not prevent presentation of calling line identity on the called line.

21 Calls for direct marketing purposes

(A1) A person shall neither use, nor instigate the use of, a public electronic communications service for the purposes of making calls (whether solicited or unsolicited) for direct marketing purposes except where that person –

> (a)   does not prevent presentation of the identity of the calling line on the called line; or
>
> (b)   presents the identity of a line on which he can be contacted

(1) A person shall neither use, nor instigate the use of, a public electronic communications service for the purposes of making unsolicited calls for direct marketing purposes where –

> (a)   the called line is that of a subscriber who has previously notified the caller that such calls should not for the time being be made on that line; or
>
> (b)   the number allocated to a subscriber in respect of the called line is one listed in the register kept under regulation 26.

(2) A subscriber shall not permit his line to be used in contravention of para (1).

(3) A person shall not be held to have contravened para (1)(b) where the number allocated to the called line has been listed on the register for less than 28 days preceding that on which the call is made.

(4) Where a subscriber who has caused a number allocated to a line of his to be listed in the register kept under regulation 26 has notified a caller that he does not, for the time being, object to such calls being made on that line by that caller, such calls may be made by that caller on that line, notwithstanding that the number allocated to that line is listed in the said register.

(5) Where a subscriber has given a caller notification pursuant to para (4) in relation to a line of his –

> (a)   the subscriber shall be free to withdraw that notification at any time, and
>
> (b)   where such notification is withdrawn, the caller shall not make such calls on that line.

6.100   The Privacy and Electronic Communications (EC Directive) (Amendment) Regulations 2016, which came into force 16 May 2016, amended regs 19 (in relation to automated calling systems) and 21 (in relation to calls for direct marketing purposes) PECR to require that persons making or instigating calls for direct marketing purposes do not prevent presentation of calling line identity on the called line. In addition, they expanded the scope of reg 21 to include solicited calls, where it previously covered only unsolicited calls.

Email (regs 22–23)

6.101   In the case of email, there are only two circumstances in which direct marketing may take place: the first is with the consent of the recipient; the second is where the requirements of reg 22(3) (which are cumulative) are met.

Regulation 23 of the PECR prohibits the use of e-mail for direct marketing where the identity of the person on whose behalf the e-mail in question has been sent is disguised or concealed, or where there is no address provided to which a request that the e-mail contact should cease may be sent.

22 Use of electronic mail for direct marketing purposes

(1) This regulation applies to the transmission of unsolicited communications by means of electronic mail to individual subscribers.

(2) Except in the circumstances referred to in para (3), a person shall neither transmit, nor instigate the transmission of, unsolicited communications for the purposes of direct marketing by means of electronic mail unless the recipient of the electronic mail has previously notified the sender that he consents for the time being to such communications being sent by, or at the instigation of, the sender.

(3) A person may send or instigate the sending of electronic mail for the purposes of direct marketing where –

   (a)   that person has obtained the contact details of the recipient of that electronic mail in the course of the sale or negotiations for the sale of a product or service to that recipient;
   (b)   the direct marketing is in respect of that person's similar products and services only; and
   (c)   the recipient has been given a simple means of refusing (free of charge except for the costs of the transmission of the refusal) the use of his contact details for the purposes of such direct marketing, at the time that the details were initially collected, and, where he did not initially refuse the use of the details, at the time of each subsequent communication.

(4) A subscriber shall not permit his line to be used in contravention of para (2).

23 Use of electronic mail for direct marketing purposes where the identity or address of the sender is concealed

A person shall neither transmit, nor instigate the transmission of, a communication for the purposes of direct marketing by means of electronic mail –

   (a)   where the identity of the person on whose behalf the communication has been sent has been disguised or concealed; or
   (b)   where a valid address to which the recipient of the communication may send a request that such communications cease has not been provided.

Enforcement

Compensation (reg 30)

6.102 Enforcement of the PECR is covered by regs 30–32. Regulation 30 provides a right to compensation for any person who has suffered damage by virtue of a contravention of any of the regulations under the PECR. Regulation 30(2) provides a defence that the person in contravention took reasonable care to comply with the regulations.

30 Proceedings for compensation for failure to comply with requirements of the Regulations

(1) A person who suffers damage by reason of any contravention of any of the requirements of these Regulations by any other person shall be entitled to bring proceedings for compensation from that other person for that damage.

(2) In proceedings brought against a person by virtue of this regulation it shall be a defence to prove that he had taken such care as in all the circumstances was reasonably required to comply with the relevant requirement.

(3) The provisions of this regulation are without prejudice to those of regulation 31.

Enforcement by the Information Commissioner (regs 31 and 32)

6.103 In addition to the private right to compensation for non-compliance with the Regulations, the Commissioner has jurisdiction to take enforcement action. Regulation 31 extends the enforcement provisions contained in Part V and Schs 6 and 9 of the DPA (*ante*) to cover non-compliance with the PECR. That regime is modified by Sch 1 to the PECR. Many of the modifications in that schedule deal with changing the language of the DPA to reflect that of the PECR or omitting irrelevant matters. The key substantive differences are as follows:

- when deciding whether to serve an enforcement notice (s 40 of the DPA) the Commissioner shall consider whether the contravention has caused damage (as opposed to damage or distress);
- a request to the Commissioner for an assessment of compliance (s 42 of the DPA) cannot be made under the PECR;
- ss 43(1) and (2) on information notices are modified to remove references to notices issued as a result of a s 42 request;
- special information notices are not available under the PECR.

6.104 Regulation 32 of the PECR provides that the Commissioner's enforcement functions may be exercised on a request by OFCOM, an aggrieved person, or of his own motion. In October 2016 DCMS announced a proposed amendment to the PECR which would make directors of companies which act in contravention of the regulations personally liable for monetary penalty notices. The amendment is expected to come into force in the spring of 2017.

OTHER LEGISLATION

Acquisition of information

6.105 Examples of other legislative provisions which enable local authorities to obtain information are given below.

6.106 The Road Vehicles (Registration and Licensing) Regulations 2002 enables the Driver and Vehicle Licensing Agency to disclosure vehicle registration and licensing particulars to a local authority for enforcement purposes.

27(1) The Secretary of State may make any particulars contained in the register available for use –

(a) by a local authority for any purpose connected with the investigation of an offence or of a decriminalised parking contravention;

...

(e) by any person who can show to the satisfaction of the Secretary of State that he has reasonable cause for wanting the particulars to be made available to him.

(2) Particulars may be provided to such a person as is mentioned in paragraph (1)(e) on payment of such fee, if any, of such amount as appears to the Secretary of State reasonable in the circumstances of the case.

6.107 The Postal Services Act 2011 (Disclosure of Information) Order 2012 prescribes bodies or other persons, enactments and circumstances and purposes which are exempt from the general prohibition in the Postal Services Act 2011 on disclosure of information obtained by virtue of the exercise of regulatory functions under Part 3 of that Act.

6.108 A local weights and measures authority is a prescribed body and each of the following is a prescribed enactment for the purposes of s 56(2)(d) or (f) of the Act:

- Trade Descriptions Act 1968.
- Fair Trading Act 1973.
- Consumer Credit Act 1974.
- Estate Agents Act 1979.
- Consumer Protection Act 1987; the Regulation of Investigatory Powers Act 2000.
- Business Protection from Misleading Marketing Regulations 2008.
- Consumer Protection from Unfair Trading Regulations 2008.

Disclosure of information

The Regulation of Investigatory Powers Act 2000

6.109 Each public authority must ensure that arrangements are in place for the secure handling, storage and destruction of material obtained through the use of surveillance. Authorising officers, through their relevant Data Controller, must ensure compliance with the appropriate data protection requirements under the Data Protection Act 1998 and any relevant codes.

6.110 There have been a number of recent developments as to how public body information disclosure and information sharing between regulators can be improved, enabling services to work more closely together to deliver better outcomes for business and communities. They include:

- 'Local Government Transparency', issued under s 2 of the Local Government, Planning and Land Act 1980, sets out information which must be published and information that is recommended for publication. See also the Openness of Local Government Bodies Regulations 2014 which were made under the Local Audit and Accountability Act 2014 and make provision to allow members of the public to report and commentate on public meetings of local government bodies in England. They also require written records to be kept of certain decisions taken by officers of these bodies.

- Data Sharing Code of Practice published by the Information Commissioner.

- 'Overcoming cultural barriers to information sharing within regulatory services' published by the Centre of Excellence for Information Sharing and commissioned by the Better Regulation Delivery Office.

CHAPTER 7

UNFAIR COMMERCIAL PRACTICES

INTRODUCTION

7.1 The Consumer Protection from Unfair Trading Regulations 2008[1] ('CPUTR') came into force on 26 May 2008. The CPUTR replaced most of the criminal offences in the Trade Descriptions Act 1968 and numerous other trading law provisions with a set of new criminal offences based on unfair commercial practices. The same unfair commercial practices now also form the basis for injunctive relief under the Enterprise Act 2002 and the new consumer rights to civil redress. The scope of the CPUTR is considerably broader than the legislation it replaced. The distinction between goods and services has been swept away and the new legislation also applies to immovable property, intangible property and financial services.

7.2 The CPUTR's history can be traced back to the public consultation undertaken by the European Commission in 2001 on fair trading.[2] In 2005, this consultation resulted in the European Unfair Commercial Practices Directive ('UCPD');[3] which was implemented into UK law in the form of the CPUTR. The CPUTR is therefore Directive-based law and its purpose, as set out in Art 1 of the UCPD, is to 'contribute to the proper functioning of the internal market and achieve a high level of consumer protection'.[4]

7.3 At the same time the Business Protection from Misleading Marketing Regulations 2008[5] ('BPR') came into force to implement the European Directive on Misleading and Comparative Advertising.[6] This Directive-based law regulates business-to-business commercial practices and has similar aims to the UCPD.

7.4 The UCPD is a maximum harmonisation Directive designed to secure harmonisation of consumer law throughout the EU[7] and has introduced a general concept of unfair commercial practices, which is applicable throughout the Member States of the EU. This consumer policy goal now needs to be read together with the other principles set out in the European Union's Charter of Fundamental Rights. The Charter was conditionally adopted by the United Kingdom in December 2009 in the Lisbon Treaty. Although its application is confined to EU law, the Charter repeats the obligation of Member States to provide a high level of consumer protection (Art 38). However, it potentially counterbalances this with a requirement that citizens are given freedom to conduct a business (Art 16).

---

[1]   SI 2008/1277.
[2]   Green Paper on European Union Consumer Protection, COM (2001) 531.
[3]   Directive 2005/29/EC of the European Parliament and of the Council of 11 May 2005 concerning unfair business-to-consumer commercial practices in the internal market (OJ L149, 11.6.2005, p 22).
[4]   See also Directive 2005/29/EC, Recital (1) of the preamble.
[5]   SI 2008/1276.
[6]   2006/114/EC.
[7]   Art 4 of the UCPD.

7.5   In the UK the CPUTR is often enforced using the criminal law; however, it is also enforceable under Part 4A of CPUTR and Part 8 of the Enterprise Act 2002 in the civil courts. The key principles concerning construction and the main concepts are common to both the criminal and civil jurisdictions in the UK. The BPR is considered in Chapter 11, Advertising. The Consumer Protection (Amendment) Regulations 2014 created rights to redress that are enforceable by consumers in relation to contracts entered into, or payments made, on or after 1 October 2014, where certain provisions of the CPUTR are infringed.

APPROACH TO CONSTRUCTION OF THE CPUTR

7.6   There will always be a tendency for UK regulatory lawyers to focus on the construction of terms using domestic case law and tools of interpretation. Although this may well provide useful assistance in certain cases, it must be remembered that the CPUTR implemented a maximum harmonisation Directive.[8] In *Office of Fair Trading v Purely Creative*, Briggs J described the process of interpreting the CPUTR:[9]

> 'Domestic regulations designed to implement EU Directives, and in particular maximum harmonisation Directives, must be construed as far as possible so as to implement the purposes and provisions of the Directive. The interpretation of words and phrases is neither a matter of grammars nor dictionaries, nor even a matter of the use of those phrases (or of the underlying concepts) in national law. If similar words and phrases are used in the Directive itself, then they must be interpreted both in the Directive and in the implementing regulations by means of a process of interpretation which is independent of the Member State's national law and, for that matter, independent of any other Member State's national law. For that purpose the primary recourse of the national court is to the jurisprudence of the ECJ. The national court may also obtain assistance from, but is not bound by, guidance issued by the Commission, and by the decisions of other national courts as to the meaning of the relevant Directive.'

7.7   The court was also critical of the OFT's attempt to use differences in the implementation of the UCPD in other Member States as a method of construing the CPUTR.[10]

> 'In my judgment recourse to differences of implementation of a Directive intended to have uniform effect throughout the EU is likely to prove a time-consuming and ultimately fruitless exercise.'

---

[8]   See Chapter 2, Interpretation of Consumer Law, for construction of EU-based legislation.
[9]   [2011] EWHC 106 (Ch), [2011] CTLC 45.
[10]   An attempt had been made to rely on the Irish Regulations implementing para 31 of Annex 1 to the UCPD.

7.8   On appeal, the Court of Appeal (Civil Division) found that, although it agreed with this statement of practice, such national differences might be relevant to a decision to refer a case to the Court of Justice of the European Union (CJEU):

> 'But the different approaches of Member States may well be important to the exercise of this court's discretion whether to refer questions of interpretation of the Directive to the Court of Justice of the European Union.'[11]

The approach of the Court of Appeal to this issue was confirmed when the *Purely Creative* case was later considered by the CJEU.[12]

7.9   The use of case law from other Member States is dealt with in greater detail in Chapter 2, Interpretation of Consumer Law. It is suggested that, although the case law of other Member States is not binding, it can be useful in assisting in the construction of the Directive by providing representative examples. Some summaries of cases from other EU Member States referred to in this chapter are available from the EU/UCPD database.[13] The current Commission guidance on the meaning of the UCPD was published on 25 May 2016.[14]

PROVISIONS REVOKED BY THE CPUTR

7.10   The CPUTR replaced most of the criminal offences in the Trade Descriptions Act 1968 ('TDA'), which itself replaced the various Merchandise Marks Acts passed between 1887 and 1953. The CPUTR does, however, retain a number of key liability concepts found in the TDA (for example liability of directors). The body of TDA case law remains relevant when considering these concepts. Schedule 2 of the CPUTR sets out the amendments to existing legislation. These amendments are too voluminous to set out comprehensively, however the main criminal sanctions that are revoked are as follows:

(a)   under the TDA:
- prohibition of false trade descriptions under s 1(1);
- trade descriptions used in advertisements under s 5;
- offer to supply under s 6;
- false representations concerning services under ss 13–15;

(b)   the misleading pricing indication offences under ss 20–26 of the Consumer Protection Act 1987;[15]

---

[11]   [2011] EWCA Civ 920, [2012] CTLC 40.

[12]   *Purely Creative Ltd v Office of Fair Trading* (C-428/11) European Court of Justice (Sixth Chamber), 18 October 2012 [2013] 1 CMLR 35.

[13]   See https://webgate.ec.europa.eu/ucp. However, please note that this database has not been kept up to date, and so is not comprehensive.

[14]   See http://ec.europa.eu/justice/consumer-marketing/files/ucp_guidance_en.pdf.

[15]   Which additionally resulted in legislation made under s 26 – the Price Indications (Method of

(c) the Fair Trading Act 1973 offences under ss 29–33;[16]

(d) the Mock Auctions Act 1961;

(e) the false advertisements offence in s 46 of the Consumer Credit Act 1974;

(f) the misrepresentation offence under s 29 of the Weights and Measures Act 1985;

(g) the Control of Misleading Advertisements Regulations 1988, SI 1988/915, and the amending SI 2000/914 and 2003/3183;

(h) the unlawful harassment of debtors offence under s 40 of the Administration of Justice Act 1970 is confined to situations not covered by the CPUTR (for example transactions that do not involve consumers).

Additionally the Property Misdescriptions Act 1991 has now been repealed and the cases that had previously been brought under its provisions will now be dealt with under CPUTR.

THE APPLICATION OF THE CPUTR

Jurisdiction

7.11 The CPUTR were made pursuant to powers in s 2(2) of the European Communities Act 1972, which allows (by order in council) the implementation of, 'any EU obligation of the United Kingdom ... or of enabling any rights enjoyed or to be enjoyed by the United Kingdom.' The traditional presumption under domestic law was that, unless there is an express statutory exception, criminal sanction will usually only extend to acts committed within the jurisdiction.[17]

7.12 Under the TDA, the courts had already expressed a willingness to extend the geographical jurisdiction of consumer offences. For example, the TDA was construed to catch descriptions or statements made in travel brochures about holidays abroad, provided that they were read within the UK.[18] By analogy to the TDA, this is very likely to remain the position under the CPUTR. The modern view of geographical jurisdiction is that, in the absence of express geographical limitation, it should be ascertained by a consideration of the intention of the legislator.[19] Under s 2(2) this can only be by reference to the intention and purpose behind the original European provision. It may be observed that it was plainly a purpose of the UCPD to provide uniform

---

Payment) Regulations 1991 and the Price Indications (Resale of Tickets) Regulations 1994 – ceasing to have effect, although a specific saving was made for the Price Indications (Bureaux de Change) (No 2) Regulations 1992.

[16] The saving for Orders made under the Fair Trading Act 1973, contained in the Enterprise Act 2002, also ceased to have effect – and, by this means, the Consumer Transactions (Restrictions on Statements) Order 1976 and the Business Advertisements (Disclosure) Order 1977 were also repealed).

[17] See eg *Board of Trade v Owen* [1957] AC 602 per Lord Tucker at 625.

[18] *R v Thompson Holidays* [1974] QB 592.

[19] *Treacy v DPP* [1971] AC 537, per Lord Diplock.

protection to consumers throughout the European Union. In the same way, a trader who is outside the EU may infringe the UCPD if they direct their activities towards consumers in any state in the EU and also the CPUTR if directed towards consumers in the UK.

7.13 The position in respect of the law applying to civil liability under the Enterprise Act 2002 (and for breach of the redress provisions of the CPUTR) is governed by the Rome II Regulation on non-contractual obligations, which applies the law of the country where the collective interests of consumers are affected, wherever the trader is located.[20] If the business or the affected consumer is within the UK, there is unlikely to be any successful argument against domestic enforcement; the definition of commercial practice under the CPUTR is broad enough to encompass almost every aspect of consumer trading.

7.14 There remains a question of whether the CPUTR may potentially be available for criminal offences when both the consumer, and the relevant business, is outside the United Kingdom. For example, if an offence was committed against a UK consumer whilst abroad, could the CPUTR be used to prosecute the UK consumer's grievance in the UK courts? This might mirror the jurisdictional position for an EU consumer enforcing his civil contractual rights.[21] However, it seems most unlikely that the enforcement authorities would be able to enforce offences outside the UK. There is no express power to do so and it is unlikely that the courts would construe the CPUTR to allow the domestic prosecution of offences when the circumstances have little or no connection with the United Kingdom. The courts are unlikely to have an appetite for entertaining criminal prosecutions with only a tangential connection to the UK. The most convenient forum for resolving such questions is inevitably the EU country in which the offence occurred. The disadvantage and cost to a defendant of being tried for a consumer offence abroad are likely to be seen as disproportionate, potentially generating abuse of process applications.

7.15 The CPUTR will also cover offences by persons if they were committed:

(a)   on board a United Kingdom ship;[22]

(b)   on offshore installations;[23]

(c)   on board a British controlled aircraft or hovercraft while in flight.[24]

---

[20]   Art 6(1) of the Rome II Regulation 864/2007.

[21]   See the Contracts (Applicable Law) Act 1990.

[22]   Merchant Shipping Act, ss 686 and 687 as contained in the Merchant Shipping (Registration etc) Act 1993, Sch 4, para 62.

[23]   Installations covered by the Oil and Gas Enterprise Act 1982, s 22.

[24]   Civil Aviation Act 1982, s 92.

Maximum harmonisation

7.16 The UCPD is a maximum harmonisation directive. This means first of all that its provisions must be implemented in the Member States, which are not permitted to cut down the scope of protection, for example by granting immunity to certain traders.[25] Member States are expected to implement it purposively but must not exceed its provisions (except for financial services and immovable property). This is provided for in Art 4 which states:

> 'Member States shall neither restrict the freedom to provide services nor restrict the free movement of goods for reasons falling within the field approximated by this Directive.'[26]

7.17 The CPUTR has been implemented in the UK in such a way that it is, for the most part, a virtual word-for-word copy of the UCPD. This is the first step to ensuring that the objectives of the Directive are attained. The courts must also ensure that they interpret the Directive in this way. A Member State cannot adopt stricter rules even if the aim is to achieve a higher level of consumer protection. In *Zentrale zur bekampfung unlauteren Wettbewerbs eV v Plus Warenhandelsgesellschaft mbH*[27] the CJEU found that German law had done just this and fell foul of Art 4 because it prohibited promotions where entry to a lottery was on condition of buying goods. This particular case concerned a retailer of lingerie which invited consumers to buy goods in order to obtain free entry into a lottery. The CJEU found that the German law did not have regard to the Directive, under which this practice would not be unfair, and that the law was contrary to Art 4 by implementing a more restrictive national measure.

7.18 Similarly, in *VTB-VAB NV v Total Belgium*[28] a Belgian law prohibiting combined offers was found by the CJEU to contravene Art 4. In that case, Total had offered a limited free breakdown service to Total Club cardholders with every purchase of a minimum amount of fuel. The Belgian law outlawing such a practice exceeded the provisions of the Directive which would only have required its assessment for fairness.

7.19 The European Commission first report on the application of the UCPD[29] refers to other cases where the CJEU has ruled that national provisions are incompatible with the Directive. In *Telekomunikacja Polska*,[30] another national prohibition on combined offers was found to be incompatible. This concerned a telecom company which had made the conclusion of a contract for the

---

[25] See C-421/12 *Commission v Belgium* paras 42–48.
[26] Directive 2005/29/EC.
[27] *Zentrale zur Bekampfung unlauteren Wettbewerbs eV v Plus Warenhandelsgesellschaft mbH* (C-304/08) European Court of Justice (First Chamber) [2011] 1 All ER (Comm) 658.
[28] *VTB-VAB NV v Total Belgium NV* (C-261/07) European Court of Justice (First Chamber) [2010] All ER (EC) 694.
[29] European Commission Report First Report on the application of Directive 2005/29/EC COM(2013)139 final (para 31).
[30] C-522/08, *Telekommunikacja Polska SA w Warszawie v Prezes Urzędu Komunikacji Elektronicznej* [2010] ECR I-02079.

provision of broadband internet access services contingent on the conclusion of a contract for telephone services. *Wamo*[31] and *Inno*[32] were cases where prohibitions had been made on the announcement of price reductions during the period preceding sales, in so far as the provision in question sought to protect the economic interests of consumers. The provisions were not prohibitions contained in Annex 1 to the UCPD and therefore would be required to be assessed for fairness by the national court. In *Kock*[33] an Austrian trader had announced a 'total clearance' of the products in his shop without applying for an administrative authorisation, as required by national law. The CJEU ruled that a commercial practice not covered by Annex 1 of the Directive cannot be prohibited on the sole ground that the practice had not been the subject of prior authorisation by the competent administrative authority, without an assessment of the unfairness of the practice in question set out in Arts 5 to 9 of the UCPD.

7.20 However, in *Citroen Benlux NV v Federatie voor Verzekerings en Financiele Tussenpersonen*,[34] the CJEU held that a national restriction on combined offers did not contravene Art 4 as at least one component of the offer was a financial service in respect of which the UCPD applies only a minimum harmonisation standard (see Art 3(9)). So long as one component was a financial service, the exception applied and Member States were permitted to impose requirements that were more restrictive or prescriptive than those set out in the Directive. Member States are also permitted to apply more prescriptive protections where there is scope to do so under a *lex specialis* (specific law) provision.[35] However in other respects the UCPD continues to apply, as a safety net, so that mere compliance with a *lex specialis* provision, such as that found in the Consumer Rights Directive, may not guarantee compliance with UCPD.[36]

7.21 In addition, Member States may pass legislation that impacts on the commercial operations of traders, where the purpose of the legislation is not consumer protection, for example a restriction on Sunday trading aiming to protect small businesses.[37] *Pelckmans Turnhout NV*[38] concerned the compatibility of a Belgian provision with the Directive. The Belgian law prohibited a trader from opening his shop seven days a week, thereby requiring that he choose a weekly closing day for the shop. The ECJ considered that the provision only aimed to protect the interests of workers and employees in the distribution sector and was not intended to protect consumers. Finally, of

---

[31] C-288/10, *Wamo BVBA v JBC NV and Modemakers Fashion NV* [2011] ECR I-05835.
[32] C-126/11, *INNO NV v Unie van Zelfstandige Ondernemers VZW (UNIZO) and Others*, report not published at this time.
[33] C-206/11 *Georg Köck v Schutzverband gegen unlauteren Wettbewerb*, report not published at this time.
[34] C-265/12, [2014] 1 CMLR 26.
[35] Recital 15.
[36] Joined cases C-544/13 and C-545/13, para 82.
[37] C-483/12 *Pelckmans Turnhout* para 24; C-540/08 *Mediaprint* para 21.
[38] C-559/11, *Pelckmans Turnhout NV v Walter Van Gastel Balen NV and Others*, 4 October 2012, report not published at this time.

course Member States can extend the protection offered by the Directive into other, non-harmonised, areas (such as business to business transactions).

Overlap with other EU provisions

7.22 Article 3.4 of the UCPD (which is not directly transposed into the CPUTR) states that:

> 'In the case of conflict between the provisions of this Directive and other Community rules regulating specific aspects of unfair commercial practices, the latter shall prevail and apply to those specific aspects.'

7.23 On the one hand, there is the view that sectoral Directives prevail when they clearly cover a specific unfair commercial practice that could also be covered by the CPUTR. This means that if a sectoral Directive (eg the Package Travel Directive[39]) covers misleading information provided in respect of a package holiday then the CPUTR do not apply.[40] On the other hand, there is the view that where sectoral Directives provide for greater protection than the CPUTR then, by virtue of Art 3.4, they shall prevail. If the latter view is correct then there would be no impediment to using both Directives in respect of the same unfair commercial practice. It would seem from the CJEU case of *Abcur AB v Apoteket AB and Apoteket Farmaci AB*[41] that the latter view has been preferred, in a case concerning the overlap between the UCPD and the Medicines Directive.

7.24 This issue is considered in detail in Chapter 2, Interpretation of Consumer Law, but a useful aid to construction is Recital 10 to the UCPD which provides that:

> 'It is necessary to ensure that the relationship between this Directive and existing Community law is coherent, particularly where detailed provisions on unfair commercial practices apply to specific sectors ... This Directive accordingly applies only in so far as there are no specific Community law provisions regulating specific aspects of unfair commercial practices, such as information requirements and rules on the way information is presented to the consumer. It provides protection for consumers where there is no specific sectoral legislation at community level and prohibits traders from creating a false impression of the nature of products. This is particularly important for complex products with high levels of risk to consumers, such as certain financial services products. This Directive consequently complements the Community acquis, which is applicable to commercial practices harming consumers' economic interests.'

---

[39] Package Travel, Package Holidays and Package Tours Directive 90/314/EEC.
[40] This view was preferred by DJ Roger House sitting at Bournemouth Magistrates' Court on 17 April 2013, in dismissing CPUTR informations laid in a Package Travel Context, *Dorset County Council v Alpine Elements Ltd* (unreported).
[41] Joined cases C-544/13 and C-545/13.

The Crown

7.25 The Crown may not be criminally liable under the CPUTR (although individuals serving the Crown may be).[42] However, if the Crown were to act in breach of the CPUTR, action may be taken against it under Part 8 of the Enterprise Act 2002.[43] The crucial question is whether an emanation of the Crown is acting as a 'trader' under the UCPD, which is an autonomous concept, not to be restricted by national legal classifications.[44] Hospitals have been held to benefit from Crown immunity[45] but the applicability of those decisions to today's more devolved management structure may be questioned. Local authorities do not benefit from Crown immunity.[46]

Time limits

7.26 The limitation period under the CPUTR mirrors s 19 of the TDA. Under reg 14(1)(a) and (b), no criminal prosecution for an offence under the CPUTR may be commenced more than 3 years from the commission of the offence or more than 1 year after its discovery by the prosecutor, whichever is the earlier. If the prosecutor provides a certificate stating the date he discovered the offence, there is a rebuttable presumption of its correctness under the CPUTR.[47]

Time limit provisions are now covered in Chapter 3, Criminal Enforcement.

ENFORCERS

The duty to enforce

7.27 Regulation 19 of the CPUTR places a duty on every 'enforcement authority' to enforce the CPUTR. In Great Britain, this includes every 'Local weights and measures authority'.[48] In Northern Ireland, the authority having the duty of enforcement is now the Department for the Economy ('DfE'). For a weights and measures authority, the duty used to extend geographically to within its own area, but Sch 5 of the Consumer Rights Act 2015 ('CRA 2015') has removed this limitation in England and Wales.

7.28 This duty does not automatically mean that formal (civil or criminal) enforcement action will be taken in respect of each and every infringement, nor

---

[42]   CPUTR, reg 28.

[43]   Enterprise Act 2002, s 236.

[44]   C-59/12 *BKK Mobil* para 26.

[45]   *Nottingham Area No 1 Hospital Management Committee v Owen* [1958] 1 QB 50, *Pfizer Corporation v Ministry of Health* [1965] AC 512.

[46]   *Re M* [1994] 1 AC 377, per Lord Templeman at 395 (defining what is meant by the Crown).

[47]   CPUTR, reg 14(2).

[48]   Defined in CPUTR, reg 2 by reference to the Weights and Measures Act 1985, s 69. For non-metropolitan counties, the county council. For metropolitan districts, the district council. For London boroughs, the borough council. For Scottish areas, the area council.

does it impose any geographical restriction on the powers of officers. Instead the duty will oblige enforcers to take steps to promote compliance by the most appropriate means, in line with their enforcement priorities and consistent with available resources. This is the Government's view as expressed in its reply to the consultation on implementation of the Directive.[49]

7.29 It should also be noted that the duty of the OFT to enforce CPUTR has been replaced by a power for the CMA to do so.

Regulation 19(4) states:

> (4) 'In determining how to comply with its duty of enforcement every enforcement authority shall have regard to the desirability of encouraging control of unfair commercial practices by such established means as it considers appropriate having regard to all the circumstances of the particular case.'

7.30 Regulation 19(4) gives effect to Art 10 of the UCPD, which states that the Directive does not prevent Member States controlling unfair commercial practices using codes of conduct. Although this provision is new, similar wording was contained in the Control of Misleading Advertisements Regulations 1988. After the Government consulted on the appropriate enforcement regime for the implementation of the UCPD it concluded that the provision did not 'substantially alter the current enforcement regime, where the division of responsibilities between enforcers and self-regulatory bodies generally works extremely well'. The 'established means' that an enforcer might have regard to includes referral to a self-regulatory body, such as the Advertising Standards Authority.

The right to bring a criminal prosecution

7.31 The right to prosecute is not restricted to a member or officer of an enforcement authority. Any person can bring a prosecution under the CPUTR. In *House of Cars Ltd v Derby Car and Van Contracts Ltd*[50] a private prosecution under the CPUTR was brought after the OFT and the relevant local authority had declined to do so. The powers of entry and other rights contained within the CPUTR to facilitate the gathering of evidence may not, however, be exercised by a private prosecutor, but only by a duly appointed officer. In *Media Protection Services Ltd v Crawford*[51] it was found that the laying of an information is a reserved legal activity under the Legal Services Act 2007 and can only be undertaken by a private prosecutor himself, or by a person authorised to carry out such a reserved legal activity.

7.32 Section 230 of the Enterprise Act 2002 requires local weights and measures authorities to give notice to the CMA of intended prosecutions, a

---

[49] Government response to the Consultation Paper on Implementing the Unfair Commercial Practices Directive, DTI, December 2006.
[50] [2012] CTLC 62.
[51] [2012] EWHC 2373 (Admin), [2013] 1 WLR 1068.

summary of the evidence relied upon and their outcome, after they are finally determined. Proceedings are not invalid by reason only of the failure of the authority to comply with s 230.

PROSECUTIONS

7.33 Any person, other than the Crown, may be prosecuted for an offence under the CPUTR. This includes both individuals and bodies corporate. Regulation 15 (directors' liability), reg 16 (causal liability) and general criminal accessory liability are considered in detail in Chapter 3, Criminal Enforcement.

ENFORCEMENT POWERS

7.34 Schedule 5 to the CRA 2015 consolidates enforcement powers in trading standards investigations. Test purchases, the powers of entry, search and seizure and the criminal offences relating to obstruction are now dealt with in detail in Chapter 3, Criminal Enforcement.

PROHIBITIONS UNDER THE CPUTR

7.35 The prohibitions created by the CPUTR follow the European wording and the 'principles based' model provided by the UCPD. The CPUTR essentially uses the framework of the Directive to place into UK domestic legislation the five 'commercial practice' prohibitions, creating criminal offences in respect of each one. The five CPUTR prohibitions are also made amenable to injunctive relief under the civil jurisdiction of the Enterprise Act 2002.[52] The CPUTR sweeps away the developed concepts of 'false trade descriptions' under the TDA and 'misleading price indications' under the Consumer Protection Act 1987. The CPUTR does, however, retain some of the familiar modes of liability and defences that derive from the TDA and other domestic trading legislation.

7.36 The CPUTR creates five prohibitions which are all labelled as unfair commercial practices (reg 3). CPUTR also provides that it is a criminal offence[53] for a trader to engage in any of the prohibited unfair commercial practices.[54] The five prohibitions are as follows:

(a) Contravention of the requirements of professional diligence, reg 3(3) (made a criminal offence, where the requisite element of *mens rea* is proven, by reg 8).

---

[52]   See 441c above and Chapter 4, Civil Enforcement.
[53]   Except for CPUTR, Sch 1, paras 11 and 28 which are only amenable to civil action.
[54]   There are additional enforcement and obstruction offences under regs 21(1), 23(1) and 23(2) that are very similar to those seen in the TDA.

(b) A commercial practice that is a misleading action, reg 5 (made a criminal offence by reg 9).[55]

(c) A commercial practice that is a misleading omission, reg 6 (made a criminal offence by reg 10).

(d) A commercial practice that is an aggressive commercial practice, reg 7 (made a criminal offence by reg 11).

(e) Commercial practices which are in all circumstances considered unfair under Sch 1, paras 1–31 of the CPUTR (made a criminal offence by reg 12 except in respect of paras 11 and 28).

When prosecuted criminally, the prohibitions are triable either way, carrying a maximum sentence of 2 years' imprisonment and an unlimited fine when tried on indictment.[56] Following the entry into force of s 85 of the Legal Aid, Sentencing and Punishment of Offenders Act 2012, summary conviction is now punishable with an unlimited fine.

Key concepts

7.37 There are three concepts under the CPUTR that are central to the interpretation of the prohibitions:

(a) Commercial practice.
(b) Transactional decision.
(c) The average consumer.

Proof of a 'commercial practice' is an element of all five of the new prohibitions. 'Transactional decision'[57] and the 'average consumer' are elements of all of the prohibitions, save for the Sch 1 banned practices, under which it is only necessary to prove that a trader engaged in a 'commercial practice' of a type described in the 31 specific practices listed.

Commercial practice

7.38

CPUTR, reg 2

Interpretation

"commercial practice" means any act, omission, course of conduct, representation or commercial communication (including advertising and marketing) by a trader,

---

[55] However, note that while civil liability attaches to the misleading action of failing to comply with a code requirement, this is excluded from the scope of the reg 9 offence.

[56] CPUTR, reg 13.

[57] In the case of contravention of professional diligence, the threshold condition is 'materially distorts or is likely to materially distort the economic behaviour of the average consumer with regard to the product' CPUTR, reg 3(3)(b) rather than 'transactional decision'.

which is directly connected with the promotion, sale or supply of a product to or from consumers, whether occurring before, during or after a commercial transaction (if any) in relation to a product.

The scope of commercial practice

7.39   There are three main limitations in the definition of 'commercial practice'. Its scope is confined to the relationship between 'traders' and 'consumers' in respect of 'products'. These three concepts are further defined in reg 2. It is considered that the scheme of the CPUTR is best analysed by first considering the definition of 'commercial practice' and 'trader' together because their respective definitions include reference to each other. This chapter will first consider those concepts before considering who can be 'consumers' and what can be 'products'.

7.40   As a starting point, it is important to recognise that commercial practices are limited to those that might affect consumers and not those that only affect businesses. The definition of 'commercial practice' is purposely broad, including virtually any act or omission that might occur during the course of any consumer transaction. It is intended to cover everything that forms 'part of the commercial strategy of an operator'.[58] It may be a single act, being a specific instance (such as an advertisement, or a statement) not necessarily a modus operandi.[59] It does not depend on the conclusion of a contract or the exchange of money. It does not require the consumer to have acted to his detriment in any way. It may take place before, during, or after any transaction and would also include business practices where the business is buying a product from a consumer. But it does not require a transaction and might concern a mere advertisement.

7.41   The definition does not require any personal contact between the trader and consumer. It may concern products that are sold over the internet or by any other distance selling. It concerns all aspects of a consumer relationship including its advertising, marketing, and pricing. In *Deutsche Bank NV v Delta Lloyd Bank NV*,[60] a type of account was promoted through various mediums such as radio, a website, and leaflets. The radio advertisement did not mention that the interest rate was dependent on taking other products. It just said it was 'subject to conditions' and referred to a website or leaflets. The court held that the fact that a promotion of the product in one distribution channel is not misleading does not affect its potentially misleading character through another distribution channel, namely the radio. Each channel was found to be a 'commercial practice' and required to be assessed separately for compliance. In that case the condition of buying an additional product was material information needed by an average consumer to make an informed transactional decision.

---

[58]   C-206/11 *Georg Kock*, para 27.
[59]   C-388/13 *UPC* para 41.
[60]   Belgium, Commercial Court of Brussels, 2008.

7.42 The provision of information on a website was found to be a 'commercial practice' by Latvian Courts in *Consumer Protection Rights Centre v Air Baltic Corporation*[61] and *Consumer Protection Rights Centre v Fiji Travel Alma Tour Group*.[62] In the first case, an airline did not identify the final price of an air fare on its website. The trader argued that it was merely a technical issue relating to its website set-up. This was irrelevant and it was not necessary to demonstrate that consumers have actually used the site or entered into a contract. In the latter case, the court decided that it did not need to show detriment by establishing whether anyone had purchased a more expensive tour in order to find that a misleading advert was a commercial practice.

7.43 In the Austrian piano case, *Place of production of pianos*,[63] a guarantee, usually handed to a consumer after sale, stated that a piano was produced in Austria when it was produced in China. It was held that this misleading statement was a commercial practice even though it had been handed to a consumer after sale. This accords with the definition of 'commercial practice' in reg 2 which provides that it can take place after a commercial transaction, and with the comments of the Court of Criminal Appeal, who have held that the concept 'clearly applies' to sending of letters after a contract is concluded.[64]

One-off acts

7.44 Whether a one-off act can amount to a 'commercial practice' has been the subject of extended debate and litigation. However, recent decisions of the Court of Appeal and the CJEU have added some much needed clarification to the issue, and it is now beyond doubt that the fact that the 'action of the professional concerned took place only on one occasion and affected only one consumer is immaterial'.[65] The concept of commercial practice should, as the definition itself says, be taken to include individual acts and omissions. The CJEU in *UPC* considered the situation where a cable television operator in Hungary charged a customer for television service accidentally provided for 4 days following the termination of the contract. The domestic appeal court held that the company's conduct could not amount to a 'commercial practice' since it was not continuous. The CJEU heard the matter as a preliminary reference from the Hungarian Supreme Court. It held that, on the facts, the communication of erroneous information to a consumer (specifically, that the consumer's cable television service would be terminated on a certain day) could be classified as a 'commercial practice' even though the information only concerned a single consumer.

---

[61] 2009 E03 – REUD-54, Latvia Tribunal First Degree.
[62] 2010, A42774708, Latvia District Court.
[63] Austria Supreme Court, 2008, 4 Ob 42/08t.
[64] *R v Waters & Westminster Recliners Ltd* [2016] EWCA Crim 1112 at para 21.
[65] *Nemzeti Fogyasztóvédelmi Hatóság v UPC Magyarország Kft* C-388/13; [2015] CTLC 100 at para 41.

7.45 This decision is consistent with, but may go further than, UK case law, where in *R v X Ltd*[66] the Court of Appeal (Criminal Division) held that a commercial practice may be derived from a single incident affecting a sole consumer although it will depend on the circumstances. In that case, X Ltd sold a domestic CCTV security system to a 76-year-old customer who was alleged to be vulnerable and infirm. One of X Ltd's sales representatives had told the customer that burglaries in his postcode had risen by 46.2% in the previous 12 months, when in fact this was untrue. At trial, the defence succeeded in an application of no case to answer on the basis that the one-off communication of erroneous information to a sole consumer could not be a 'commercial practice'. On appeal, the court held that the concept of commercial practice could, depending on the circumstances, cover both a single incident and a pattern of repeated behaviour.[67] In particular the evidence of a single incident could be sufficient *'to infer that the same failure ran at every stage of the process from top to bottom'.*[68]

Traders

7.46

> **CPUTR, reg 2**
>
> **"trader"**
>> (a) means a person acting for purposes relating to that person's business, whether acting personally or through another person acting in the trader's name or on the trader's behalf, and
>> (b) except in Part 4A, includes a person acting in the name of or on behalf of a trader;
>
> **"business"** includes
>> (a) a trade, craft or profession, and
>> (b) the activities of any government department or local or public authority;

The five commercial practice offences (as set out in A to E above) can only be committed by a 'trader'. Reading the definitions of 'trader' and 'business' together, a trader is a person acting *for purposes relating to his trade, craft or profession*. It has 'a particularly broad meaning', encompassing any natural or legal person carrying out a 'gainful activity,' including public bodies engaging in activities that could in principle be carried out by the private sector.[69]

---

[66] [2013] EWCA Crim 818; [2013] CTLC 145.

[67] At para 22, Leveson LJ stated 'it is clear that a commercial practice can be derived from a single incident. It will depend on the circumstances'.

[68] At para 33 – Leveson LJ stressed that it should not be required of trading standards services, given their stretched resources, to find more complaints if one is sufficient.

[69] C-59/12 *BKK Mobil* para 41. This was a case that originated from Germany, *Betriebskrankenkasse(* Germany, Higher Regional Court, 2010, 13U 173/09) involving a compulsory health care provider set up under public law to administer health funds. The German court considered it to be a trader because it competed for consumers to pay in. The information on its website was not for social purposes, but instead for business purposes.

7.47 The broad definition of trader was recognised by the Court of Appeal (Criminal Division) in *R v Scottish and Southern Energy plc*[70] (SSE PLC), which was the first substantive criminal case to be heard at this level in respect of the CPUTR. The prosecution arose out of the doorstep selling of electricity and gas based on a sales script. The PLC and an individual salesman employed by a subsidiary company (the subsidiary) wholly owned by the PLC were defendants. The PLC was convicted of two misleading action offences under reg 5(2) CPUTR on the basis that:

'Its sales staff and agents were trained to deliver an Energy Script which in its overall presentation ... deceived or was likely to deceive the average consumer ... and thereby caused or was likely to cause the average consumer to take a transactional decision he would not have taken otherwise.'

7.48 All salesmen were employed by the subsidiary rather than the PLC, which also carried out the salesman's training. It was the subsidiary that was licensed to supply electricity because the PLC was only a holding company. The Court of Appeal found that the definition of 'trader' in reg 2(1) was broad in scope and should be construed purposively. It was possible for more than one trader to be guilty of a specific offence under the Regulations. It found that the mere fact that the subsidiary could be prosecuted as a trader did not mean that the PLC could not also be properly prosecuted for the same offence. At para 28, Davis LJ said:

'It is perfectly possible to have a prosecution of more than one person for the same alleged offence under the 2008 regulations. The very wide definition of "trader" and "commercial practice" demonstrates that: and that is also consistent with the provisions of regulation 16(2), which contemplates that both "X" and "Y" may be traders in relation to the same activity.'

7.49 In construing 'trader' together with 'commercial practice' the court noted the wide definition of both in the Regulations. Even though the PLC was correctly described as a 'non-trading holding company', that did not mean that it was incapable of being a trader within the meaning of the CPUTR. A key factor in the court's decision on this was that there was some evidence that training was carried out with the involvement of the PLC and under its ultimate supervision and control. Davis LJ stated:

'It is important to bear in mind that "trader", for the purposes of the 2008 Regulations, extends to any person who in relation to a commercial practice is acting for purposes relating to his business. The words "any", "in relation to", "acting" and "relating to" are all words with width and elasticity. As to the definition of "commercial practice" that is likewise broadly framed. It is amply sufficient to cover involvement in or supervision or control of training, in appropriate circumstances, as being directly connected with the promotion or sale or supply of a product; and it is also to be noted that the definition of "commercial practice" carefully avoids saying that the promotion or sale or supply has to be made by the trader itself.'

---

[70]   [2012] EWCA Crim 539, [2012] CTLC 1, (2012) 176 JP 241.

7.50 It can be hard to draw the line between a person engaged in trade and merely engaging in a hobby. Some guidance on this question may be found in *Reading BC v Younis*,[71] which drew on the older TDA case of *Davies v Sumner*.[72] To be liable as a trader a person must engage in the impugned activities with a *'degree of regularity'* such that they form part of the *'normal practice of a business'*. In a UK competition case, *Durkan Holdings v OFT*,[73] the Competition Appeal Tribunal concluded that if a group company gave strategic direction to subsidiaries and exerted its influence then it could be liable as a trader.

7.51 The definition of trader also includes anyone 'acting in the name of or on behalf of a trader'. It is arguable that this is broad enough to include an employee if he or she carries out an act or makes a representation on behalf of the employer in relation to a 'commercial practice'. The view of the European Commission is that the definition covers persons, including consumers, who act in the name of or on behalf of another trader, which could include intermediaries, such as online platforms.[74] It would include a media company that places advertisements on behalf of another trader,[75] review sites,[76] search engines, comparison sites, app stores, group buying sites etc.

7.52 Organisations pursuing charitable or ethical goals may qualify as traders when they engage in commercial activities towards consumers.[77] A charity shop selling goods such a mugs or t-shirts in a commercial capacity would likely be considered to be a trader. However, it is less likely that the mere solicitation for a donation would make a charity a trader, but if it is linked to some form of commercial practice then it could be; for example, when a donation is solicited by a third party paid to fundraise for the charity.

7.53 It is unlikely that a private members club would be a trader because transactions between it and its members would not be in the course of a 'person's business'. The situation is analogous to the case of *John v Matthews*,[78] when referring to the Trade Descriptions Act 1968, Lord Parker CJ said:

---

71 [2015] EWHC 3212.
72 [1984] 1 WLR 1301 (HL).
73 UK, Competition Appeal Tribunal, 2011, CAT 6.
74 Commission Staff Working Document Guidance on the Implementation/Application of Directive 2005/29/EC on Unfair Commercial Practices [COM(2016) 320] pp 31 and 119–124. This means that where an intermediary is taken to be a trader, they would not benefit from the defences provided in the E-Commerce Directive (2000/31/EC), since they would not be a 'mere' host. See also a French decision that a price comparison site, by ranking products in exchange for remuneration, was acting as a trader for UCPD purposes – Cass Com 4 Décembre 2012, 11-27729, *Publicité Sté Pewterpassion.com c/ Sté Leguide.com.*
75 Latvian court decision Administratīvās rajona tiesas spriedums lietā Nr. A420632710, 8 March 2012. See also CMA investigation into MyJar, Starcom and Tan Media https://www.gov.uk/cma-cases/online-endorsements-potential-non-disclosure
76 CMA investigation into trusted trader sites, https://www.gov.uk/cma-cases/review-sites-handling-of-negative-reviews.
77 Commission Guidance [COM(2016) 320].
78 [1970] 2 QB 443.

'The object of the 1968 Act surely is to protect the public, not a husband from his wife or a club from a member of the club.'

The rationale was that false descriptions in such circumstances would not be in the course of a trade or business. The mere use of the word 'club' in respect of a person or body having none of the features of a club, however, did not prevent the application the 1968 Act.[79] The definition of trader is further considered in Chapter 2, Interpretation of Consumer Law.

Consumers

7.54

> **CPUTR, reg 2**
>
> **"consumer"** means an individual acting for purposes that are wholly or mainly outside that individual's business;
>
> **"business"** includes a trade, craft or profession;

The focus of the CPUTR is consumer transactions. This is a marked departure from the position under the TDA. Under the TDA, liability extended to trade sales. Offences were not confined to trade descriptions given to consumers, such that an offence would be committed where the transaction was between a person acting in the course of a trade or business and another trader.

7.55 This is a significant difference between the CPUTR and its predecessors. A part of this lacuna is filled by the Business Protection from Misleading Marketing Regulations 2008 ('BPR') which were made at the same time as the CPUTR (see below at p 259). The BPR provide protection for businesses against misleading and unfair comparative advertising. Under the CPUTR, the definition of 'commercial practice' is concerned only with relationships that are 'directly connected with the promotion, sale or supply of a product to or from consumers'. It follows from this that there will be no 'commercial practice' if the relationship concerns, for example, the sale of a product to a person acting for the purposes of his business.

7.56 However, where the victim of a commercial practice is acting for purposes that are a mixture of private and business, the CPUTR will apply, as long as the consumer use is predominant. This is an extension of protection beyond that required by the UCPD, and implemented in some other states, where any professional use of goods or services, even if only to a limited degree, is likely to prevent it being that of a consumer.[80]

7.57 Other difficult situations include where an individual is engaging in activities before setting up their business, or after they have ceased trading, and where they are engaged in profit making activities that may fall short of full

---

[79]   *Cahalne v Croydon London Borough Council* (1985) 149 JP 561.
[80]   *BVAB De Keukiliere Gebroeders v KAAS* (Antwerp Court of Appeal 2009).

trade. This is likely to be particularly acute as an issue where individuals are engaging as suppliers in the collaborative economy. The view of the European Commission is that such a person is not automatically to be viewed as a trader. Account must be taken of the extent to which they have a profit seeking motive, the number, amount and frequency of transactions, the seller's sales turnover and whether they purchase products in order to resell them.[81]

7.58 The definition of 'consumer' is now considered in Chapter 2, Interpretation of Consumer Law.

Consumers and causal liability

7.59 Regulation 16 creates liability for those who cause traders to commit CPUTR offences. Under this mode of liability, the person causing the trader's offence may or may not be a trader himself. It follows that a trader that sold a falsely described motor car to another trader might be guilty (under reg 16) if that motor car was then sold on to a consumer. However, there is no CPUTR offence committed by either trader until a consumer becomes involved. Causal liability is covered in Chapter 3, Criminal Enforcement.

Product

7.60

> **CPUTR, reg 2**
>
> **"product"** means
>
> (a) goods,
> (b) a service,
> (c) digital content,
> (d) immovable property,
> (e) rights or obligations, or
> (f) a product of the kind mentioned in paragraphs (1A) and (1B), but the application of this definition to Part 4A is subject to regulations 27C and 27D;
>
> **"digital content"** means data which are produced and supplied in digital form'
>
> **"goods"** means any tangible moveable items, but that includes water, gas and electricity if and only if they are put up for sale in a limited volume or set quantity;'
>
> Reg 2(1A) "a trader ("T") who demands payment from a consumer ("C") in full or partial settlement of C's liabilities or purported liabilities to T is to be treated for the purposes of these Regulations as offering to supply a product to C.
>
> Reg 2(1B) In such a case the product that T offers to supply comprises the full or partial settlement of those liabilities or purported liabilities"

---

81 Commission Guidance [COM(2016) 320] para 2.1. See also Commission Communication *A European Agenda for the Collaborative Economy* [COM(2016) 356] para 2.3.

The definition of 'product' in the CPUTR is predominantly directly from the definition in Art 2 of the Unfair Commercial Practices Directive ('UCPD'), although the UK has clarified that the definition also includes digital content and 'liability management services' as set out in reg 2(1A) and (1B). The definition is wide and likely to cover all goods and services, including intangible products such as statutory rights. The CPUTR offences apply to both goods or services and therefore any combination of the two.

7.61 The BERR/OFT guidance to the CPUTR states that:[82]

'The CPRs use **"product"** to refer to goods and services in a wide sense, including immovable property, rights and obligations. The prohibitions apply to **commercial practices** relating to products in this wider sense. It is important to note this because the legislation they replace was in many cases narrower in scope, for instance applying to just goods or services. The Trade Descriptions Act 1968 applied to both goods and services but there were, different sets of rules applied to goods and to services. The CPRs apply in the same way to both goods and services, and also extend to intangible rights such as cancellation or cashback options.'

7.62 Where a product is supplied completely free of consideration, it is unlikely that the UCPD will apply.[83] However, relevant consideration could comprise consumer data, in the view of the European Commission.[84] The CPUTR clarify that they apply also where it is the consumer who supplies a product *to* the trader – this is to provide protection in the many circumstances where consumers risk being misled during the course of transactions where a trader is seeking to buy items from the consumer – see for example OFT undertakings obtained from traders purchasing consumers' gold, cars and houses.[85]

Goods

7.63 The definition of 'goods' has been a part of many domestic statutory provisions. In the Consumer Rights Act 2015 it is defined to include 'any tangible moveable items'.[86] The essence of the definition has been to draw a distinction between personal chattels (moveable, tangible articles of property) and interests in land.[87] The definition of 'goods' is not purposive. It does not connote any requirement that the goods be for future sale or supply, nor do they need to be owned by a trade or business.[88] In *Formula One Autocentres v Birmingham City Council*[89] a false representation was made that the servicing

---

[82] Department for Business Enterprise and Regulatory Reform Guidance on the UK Regulations.
[83] C-515/12 *4Finance UAB* para 24; C-391/12 *RLvS Verlagsgesellschaft mbH*.
[84] Commission Guidance [COM(2016) 320] pp 95–96.
[85] https://www.gov.uk/cma-cases/purchase-of-gold-by-post-unfair-contract-terms; and https://www.gov.uk/cma-cases/we-buy-any-car-unfair-practices-by-trader-offering-vehicle-buying-service.
[86] Section 2(8).
[87] The definition also excludes other interests in freehold and leasehold land (chattels real).
[88] *Fletcher v Sledmore* [1973] RTR 371.
[89] (1999) 163 JP 234.

of a motor car had been carried out effectively. The motor car was held to be 'goods' for the purpose of s 1 of the TDA. The importance of the case is that there was no anticipated transfer of ownership; the contract was simply one of bailment where the vehicle's owner allowed the motor car out of his possession for a short period.

Service

7.64 'Service' is not further defined in the CPUTR or in the UCPD. In *Newell v Hicks*[90] the Divisional Court defined the word 'service' for the purposes of the TDA as 'doing something for someone'. The CPUTR does not expressly exclude 'contracts of service' (employment contracts) from the ambit of 'product' in the way that they were excluded from the TDA.[91] The definition of 'commercial practice' does, however, include 'the supply of a [service] ... from a consumer'. It seems unlikely that the UCPD or CPUTR were ever intended to regulate employment contracts closely (see also Art 3.4 of the UCPD). It was directed at business to consumer transactions and there is a wealth of other European legislation governing employment situations and that sector generally.

Immovable property

7.65 Although the definition of product is straightforward in its application to a simple transaction concerning goods, it is more difficult when considering different forms of property or services over property. The difference between the European concept of 'product' and the British definition of 'goods' is potentially unclear. The background to this may be found in the UCPD itself, which suggests that a Member State, must implement the financial services and immovable property provisions that are already in the UCPD, but may also go further than the UCPD because of their inherent complexity:[92]

> 'Financial services and immovable property, by reason of their complexity and inherent serious risks, necessitate detailed requirements, including positive obligations on traders. For this reason, in the field of financial services and immovable property, this Directive is without prejudice to the right of Member States to go beyond its provisions to protect the economic interests of consumers.'

7.66 The UK did not provide any detailed requirements concerning financial services or immovable property in the CPUTR. But to comply with its treaty obligations the UK did adopt the definition of 'product' in the UCPD, presumably to avoid the suggestion that the Directive had not been properly implemented. The consequence of this rather muddled definition is not satisfactory and raises several practical questions.

---

[90]   Reported as *Newell v Taylor* (1983) 148 JP 308.
[91]   TDA, s 14(4).
[92]   And in Art 3 (scope): 'In relation to "financial services", as defined in Directive 2002/65/EC, and immovable property, Member States may impose requirements which are more restrictive or prescriptive than this Directive in the field which it approximates.'

Real property

7.67 The expression 'immovable property' is plainly capable of being a reference to real property. The expression appears in the UCPD, which refers to the definition in the European Timeshare Directive, which defines the term as follows:[93]

> '"immovable property" shall mean any building or part of a building for use as accommodation to which the right which is the subject of the contract relate.'

7.68 The main provisions of the TDA did not apply to real property because the s 1(1) offences (false trade descriptions) applied only to goods and the s 14 offences (false statements as to services) applied only to 'services, accommodation or facilities'. It is perhaps surprising that the CPUTR does not expressly deal with real property in the interpretation regulation in the manner of most domestic statutes. It seems unlikely that the words 'immovable property' were intended only to mean services over immovable property, such that it was confined to services such as building or refurbishing accommodation. If that was the correct interpretation of 'product' then the definition would read services 'over' or 'in connection' with immovable property.

7.69 It has become clear that the UCPD should be read so that 'product' includes real property. Parliament repealed the Property Misdescriptions Act 1991 in October 2013, explaining that the 1991 Act had been made redundant by the CPUTR. As a result:

(a) services in relation to 'immoveable property' are also likely to be considered a 'product', such that the CPUTR might apply to solicitors or estate agents involved in real property transactions.

(b) 'anything attached to land' is also a 'product', regardless of whether it is a fixture (a part of the land by its attachment to it)[94] or merely a chattel on the land.

Intangible property, rights and obligations

7.70 The definition of 'product' in the CPUTR includes the promotion, sale or supply of 'rights and obligations' to consumers. It is tolerably clear that this was intended by the UCPD to include incorporeal or intangible property such as financial products, which are referred to expressly. In the BERR/OFT guidance (see above) to the CPUTR it is stated that it applies to intangible rights such as cancellation or cash back options.

7.71 There is, however, no detailed guidance or limit to the rights and obligations that are covered in the CPUTR. The essence of intangible or incorporeal property is that it has a value but lacks any physical presence. This

---

[93] 94/47/EC (OJ L280, 29.10.1994, p 83).
[94] See KJ Gray and SF Gray, *Elements of Land Law* (OUP, 2009) 1246 *et seq* for the distinction.

is similar to the concept of 'pecuniary advantage' that the courts have grappled with in the context of the proceeds of crime. Pecuniary advantage has been construed to mean any financial advantage. It would include a chose in action (a bank account) or any financial product such as a pension or investment, but it also extends to the evasion of a debt or tax owed. It would include a consumer guarantee or any other valuable promise. The breadth of the expression 'product' has not yet been addressed by the courts. However, on a literal interpretation it is capable of covering a vast array of situations that were not regulated by the TDA and the other legislation the CPUTR replaced.

Demanding full or partial settlement of liabilities

7.72   The additions to the definition of product in reg 2(1A) and (1B) clarify that the CPUTR applies where the 'product' that the consumer takes is in one sense involuntary – such as where their vehicle is clamped, or they are subjected to debt collection or civil recovery.

Digital content

7.73   The CPUTR now clarify that digital content is within its scope. It was previously thought that digital content might be goods, when supplied through a tangible medium such as a CD ROM, but it was unclear what it was in law when supplied in purely digital form. This uncertainty has now been addressed by the Consumer Rights Act 2015 ('CRA 2015') provisions on digital content, and also by this amendment to the definition of product in the CPUTR.

Transactional decision

7.74

> **CPUTR, reg 2**
>
> **"transactional decision"** means any decision taken by a consumer, whether it is to act or to refrain from acting, concerning –
>
> (a)   whether, how and on what terms to purchase, make payment in whole or in part for, retain or dispose of a product; or
>
> (b)   whether, how and on what terms to exercise a contractual right in relation to a product;
>
> (but the application of this definition to regulations 5 and 7 as they apply for the purposes of Part 4A is subject to regulation 27B(2)).

The CPUTR introduces the concept of a 'transactional decision', which is part of all of the commercial practice offences except the reg 12 (banned practices) offence. This 'transactional decision' element essentially introduces an objective threshold test, that the average consumer might have acted, or not acted, because of the unfair commercial practice.

7.75   A 'transactional decision' is not confined merely to the decision to enter into a binding contract. It is extended to **any** decision the consumer might take about exercising contractual rights or ultimately retaining or disposing of the product. It follows that decisions as diverse as an initial visit to a trader's website, returning a defective product, exercising a guarantee, or suing under the terms of the contract are all potentially transactional decisions.

7.76   In *OFT v Purely Creative Ltd* the High Court found that a transactional decision was a causal decision equivalent to the English standard of the balance of probabilities:[95]

> 'The phrase "to take a transactional decision he would not have taken otherwise" suggests a *sine qua non* test, namely, whether but for the relevant misleading action or omission of the trader, the average consumer would have made a different transactional decision from that which he did make. This may not mean that the misleading act or omission was the sole cause of the average consumer's decision, but it appears to mean that those Regulations will not have been infringed if the court concludes that, but for the misleading act or omission, the average consumer would nonetheless have decided as he did.'

7.77   This potential breadth of 'transactional decision' is reflected in the 2010 Office of Fair Trading Report: *Online Targeting of Advertising and Prices*, where it is suggested) that in relation to the internet and electronic communications:[96]

> 'Both "commercial practice" and "transactional decision" are given a wide definition. In the context of an online environment, the OFT considers that "transactional decision" may include the decision to visit a trader's site in the first place, as opposed to that of its competitors, and the decision to click through to another page on a site to view further content.'[97]

7.78   In the *Trento*[98] case, a consumer complained that a supermarket advertisement was inaccurate because a laptop advertised at a promotional rate was not available in the store when he visited. A dispute arose as to whether the decision to enter the shop was itself a 'transactional decision' distinct from the decision to purchase the laptop. The CJEU held in a preliminary ruling that the concept of 'transactional decision' was broadly defined. The concept covered not only the decision as to whether or not to purchase the laptop, but also

---

[95]   [2011] EWHC 106 (Ch), [2011] CTLC 45.

[96]   At para 817, the report summarises the prohibition against unfair commercial practices in the CPUTR.

[97]   In *OFT v Purely Creative Ltd* [2011] EWHC 106 (Ch) Briggs J described the Commission's Guidance (contained in the Commissions Guidance on the Application/Implementation of Directive 2005/29/EC on Unfair Commercial Practices (SEC (2009) 1666)) that a decision such as stepping into a shop is a transactional decision as 'debatable' (para 68). The current Commission Guidance [COM(2016) 320] opines that decisions to travel to a sales outlet, to agree to a sales presentation and to click through a website may be transactional decisions (p 36).

[98]   *Trento Sviluppo srl and Centrale Adriatica Soc. Coop. arl v Autorita Garante della Concorrenza e del Mercato* C-281/12, [2014] CTLC 326.

related decisions. In this case, the decision to enter the shop was related to the decision to purchase the laptop and, as a result, was a 'transactional decision' within the meaning of the UCPD. The debate concerning whether the mere decision to step into a shop is a 'transactional decision' has now been emphatically resolved. In the *SSE PLC case* it was held that judge's direction to the jury where he said 'did it cause or was it likely to cause the average consumer to switch suppliers?' was amply sufficient and that to introduce a 'but for exposition' would have been an unnecessary elaboration.[99]

7.79   The CJEU held in *Konsumentombudsmannen v Ving Sverige AB*[100] that it is for the national court to decide whether the information is sufficient so that a consumer can make an informed transactional decision, however it seems from the later CJEU decision in *Canal Digital Danmark*, that certain information, notably pricing information, is so significant that it can be assumed that its omission will impact on transactional decision.[101] In *Nicht Einhaltung Lieferfrist II*[102] it was found that choosing which trader to purchase from can be a transactional decision even before a product is purchased. The *Air Baltic*[103] case further provided that the selection of a business to trade with, before actually buying a product, can be a transactional decision even if the consumer does not go on to buy. Further, in *Competition Authority v Vodaphone Magyarorszag Mobil*[104] corrections to untrue advertisements about airtime contracts were held to have been made too late, as the initial transactional decision had already been taken. Likewise, statements made after the commercial transaction has been completed may also affect transactional decisions.[105]

The average consumer

7.80

> **CPUTR, reg 2**
>
> "average consumer" shall be construed in accordance with paragraphs (2) to (6);
>
> (2) In determining the effect of a commercial practice on the average consumer where the practice reaches or is addressed to a consumer or consumers account shall be taken of the material characteristics of such an average consumer including his being reasonably well informed, reasonably observant and circumspect.
>
> (3) Paragraphs (4) and (5) set out the circumstances in which a reference to the average consumer shall be read as in addition referring to the average member of a particular group of consumers.

---

[99]   [2012] EWCA Crim 539, [2012] CTLC 1, paras 43-46.
[100] *Konsumentombudsmannen v Ving Sverige AB* (C-122/10) [2011] ECR I-3903.
[101] CJEU *Canal Digital Danmark* (C-611/14) paras 46-49.
[102] Germany Regional Court, 2009, 312 0 74/09.
[103] 2009 E03 – REUD-54, Latvia Tribunal First Degree.
[104] Hungary Competition Tribunal, 2010, Vj/149-041/2009.
[105] *R v X Ltd* [2013] [EWCA] Crim 818, para 25.

(4) In determining the effect of a commercial practice on the average consumer where the practice is directed to a particular group of consumers, a reference to the average consumer shall be read as referring to the average member of that group.

(5) In determining the effect of a commercial practice on the average consumer –

(a) where a clearly identifiable group of consumers is particularly vulnerable to the practice or the underlying product because of their mental or physical infirmity, age or credulity in a way which the trader could reasonably be expected to foresee, and

(b) where the practice is likely to materially distort the economic behaviour only of that group,

a reference to the average consumer shall be read as referring to the average member of that group.

(6) Paragraph (5) is without prejudice to the common and legitimate advertising practice of making exaggerated statements which are not meant to be taken literally.

"materially distort the economic behaviour" means in relation to an average consumer, appreciably to impair the average consumer's ability to make an informed decision thereby causing him to take a transactional decision that he would not have taken otherwise.

The CPUTR 'average consumer' is a central concept in the consumer protection that the new legislation provides. Although it is conceptually similar to the common law reasonable man test, it is derived from European jurisprudence and has a number of differences. In paras 18 and 19 of the preamble to the UCPD it was stated that:

'(18) It is appropriate to protect all consumers from unfair commercial practices; however the Court of Justice has found it necessary in adjudicating on advertising cases since the enactment of Directive 84/450/EEC to examine the effect on a notional, typical consumer. In line with the principle of proportionality, and to permit the effective application of the protections contained in it, this Directive takes as a benchmark the average consumer, who is reasonably well informed and reasonably observant and circumspect, taking into account social, cultural and linguistic factors, as interpreted by the Court of Justice, but also contains provisions aimed at preventing the exploitation of consumers whose characteristics make them particularly vulnerable to unfair commercial practices. Where a commercial practice is specifically aimed at a particular group of consumers, such as children, it is desirable that the impact of the commercial practice be assessed from the perspective of the average member of that group. It is therefore appropriate to include in the list of practices which are in all circumstances unfair a provision which, without imposing an outright ban on advertising directed at children, protects them from direct exhortations to purchase. The average consumer test is not a statistical test. National courts and authorities will have to exercise their own faculty of judgment, having regard to the case-law of the Court of Justice, to determine the typical reaction of the average consumer in a given case.

(19) Where certain characteristics such as age, physical or mental infirmity or credulity make consumers particularly susceptible to a commercial practice or to the underlying product and the economic behaviour only of such consumer is likely to be distorted by the practice in a way that the trader can reasonably foresee, it is appropriate to ensure that they are adequately protected by assessing the practice from the perspective of the average member of that group.'

7.81 The UCPD does not provide a complete definition of the average consumer other than this guidance. The CPUTR definition can be broken down into three parts:

(a)   the 'ordinary' **average consumer**, under reg 2(2);

(b)   **targeted groups** of consumers, under reg 2(4);

(b)   the **vulnerable consumer**, under reg 2(5).

The ordinary average consumer

7.82 Under reg 2(2), the CPUTR requires the court to consider the material characteristics of an average consumer, but makes specific reference to three particular characteristics: his being reasonably well informed, reasonably observant, and reasonably circumspect (these three characteristics have been considered above in relation to 'transactional decision'). The CPUTR essentially enshrines the notion that the average consumer in the United Kingdom is both intelligent and cautious.

7.83 The concept of the average consumer is one that has been derived from the jurisprudence of the European Court of Justice. In 1998, the ECJ gave judgment on a case referred to it by the German courts concerning misleading labelling of eggs – *Gut Springenheide GMBH v Oberkreisdirektor des Krieses Steinfurt*.[106] The ECJ referred with approval to the average consumer test and the line of authorities in which the test had been developed:[107]

'in order to determine whether the description, trade mark or promotional description or statement in question was liable to mislead the purchaser, the Court took into account the presumed expectations of an average consumer who is reasonably well-informed and reasonably observant and circumspect, without ordering an expert's report or commissioning a consumer research poll.'

7.84 The threshold test is objective and therefore the fact that a consumer has actually made a transactional decision based on the unfair practice will not be conclusive of the issue. The question is whether the average consumer would make the same decision. When assessing the effect of a commercial practice, the

---

[106]   C-210/96 *Gut Springenheide GmbH and Rudolf Tusky v Oberkreisdirektor des Kreises Steinfurt – Amt für Lebensmittelüberwachung* [1998] ECR I-04657.

[107]   Case C-362/88 *GB-INNO-BM* [1990] ECR I-667, Case C-238/89 *Pall* [1990] ECR I-4827, Case C-126/91 *Yves Rocher* [1993] ECR I-2361, Case C-315/92 *Verband Sozialer Wettbewerb* [1994] ECR I-317, Case C-456/93 *Langguth* [1995] ECR I-1737, and Case C-470/93 *Mars* [1995] ECR I-1923.

court must take into account that the average consumer is deemed (with the exception of the vulnerable consumer provisions) to have the characteristics of being reasonably well informed, observant, and circumspect. However, the court is willing to relax its approach in appropriate circumstances; for example, 'social, cultural or linguistic factors' of the Member States can be taken into account.[108] Similarly, in a case which concerned the doorstep sales of educational materials, the court had regard to the 'particularly vulnerable consumer' such as those who are 'behind with their education and are seeking to catch up'.[109]

7.85 The average consumer is therefore, by law, a reasonably intelligent and careful character when making a transactional decision. In *OFT v Purely Creative Ltd*,[110] Briggs J commented that the UCPD exists to protect consumers who take reasonable care of themselves, rather than the ignorant, the careless, or the over hasty consumer. The practical reality is, however, that consumers are often not well informed, observant, or circumspect when making purchases. This has been recognised by the CJEU when stressing that the consumer is taken to be the 'target and victim of unfair commercial practices.' He or she is intrinsically in a weaker position and must be considered economically weaker and less experienced in legal matters than the trader.[111] The CJEU has gone on to hold that due to this weakness, when assessing whether the average consumer has been misled, it is not in principle relevant that they could themselves check the veracity of the trader's claim, if it is otherwise misleading.[112]

7.86 There is a temptation to assume that purely by providing information a trader can avoid liability for misleading the average consumer. Being informed, observant, and circumspect does not mean the average consumer would read the whole of the text of relevant promotions.[113] It is a fact-intensive issue for the court to decide whether a misleading act or omission has caused a different transactional decision to be taken. However, a court is not limited to considering only the characteristics of being informed, observant, and circumspect. It can consider how consumers behave in relation to the commercial practice in question.

7.87 In *Competition Authority v Vodaphone Magyarorszag Mobil*[114] the headline price for a phone contract was untrue. Although later information corrected some of the claim before contracts were signed the first impression, particularly price, was important and it was untrue. The initial transactional decision had already been made.

---

[108] Case C-220/98 *Estée Lauder Cosmetics GmbH v Lancaster Group GmbH* [2000] ECR I-117.
[109] Case 382/87 *Ministère Public v Buet* [1989] ECR 1235, para 13.
[110] [2011] EWHC 106 (Ch), [2011] CTLC 45.
[111] C-59/12 *BKK Mobil*, para 36.
[112] C-388/13 *UPC*, paras 52–54.
[113] *Purely Creative*, para 66.
[114] Hungary Competition Tribunal, 2010, Vj/149–041/2009.

7.88 In *Nicht Einhaltung Lieferfrist II*,[115] the court found that a consumer selecting the trader to purchase from could be a transactional decision. Consumers expect an online shop where offers are updated regularly to have the items in stock and immediately available unless indicated otherwise. Consumers typically expect quick delivery from such online shops. To advertise and take orders for items which were not in stock, and not tell this to consumers, affected their transactional decisions.

7.89 In reg 2(2), the definition of the 'average consumer' is objective. It does not include any subjective element. This is in contrast to most domestic criminal law provisions that have at least some regard to the complainant's actual position and whether they have actually been deceived, cheated, or wronged in some other way.

7.90 Experience suggests that many consumers are cheated because they are commercially naïve or not well informed. It can be argued that under the CPUTR a naïve consumer who is duped is not protected under reg 2(2) if the reasonably observant or circumspect consumer would not have been duped. However, in *OFT v Purely Creative Ltd*[116] Briggs J drew similarities between the decisions made by the court in passing off cases and those under CPUTR. Where a trader sets out to deceive potential customers it will not be difficult for the court to infer that his deliberate deception has succeeded and affected the transactional decision of the average consumer. The court also rejected a submission that in the real world a regular recipient of a product would soon realise the subtle mischief behind the practice in question. The court said the test to be applied was not that of the habitual user of the product.

7.91 In *OFT v Ashbourne Management Services*,[117] under the UTCCR, when considering the position of the average consumer the court concluded that the business model was designed to take advantage of the naivety and experience of the average consumer using gym clubs at the lower end of the market. The defendant's standard form agreements contained a trap into which the average consumer was likely to fall. By recommending the use of contracts containing unfair terms, the company contravened the CPUTR.

7.92 Whilst it may be beneficial to introduce witnesses who have been misled by a commercial practice, (see statistical surveys below) the prosecutor need not find a complainant who has actually been wronged to prove a CPUTR offence. Courts will consider what decisions would have been made based upon the characteristics of the average consumer. Commercial naivety cannot be a material characteristic of the average consumer (see *Unilever v Materne Confilux*).[118] However, some typical behaviours, such as not closely reading

---

[115] *Nicht Einhaltung Lieferfrist II*, Regional Court 2009, 312 0 74/09.
[116] [2011] EWHC 106 (Ch), [2011] CTLC 45, para 118.
[117] [2011] EWHC 1237 (Ch), [2011] CTLC 237, para 173.
[118] Belgium Court of Appeal 2008 – the average consumer should be deemed to understand that claiming by words and pictures that 100mg of product contains the equivalent of 200mg of fruit should not be taken literally.

small print, appear to be characteristic of the average consumer.[119] If the impression created by a promotion is misleading to the average consumer paying average attention, then small print requiring meticulous analysis will not save it from being misleading.[120] The question is a matter of fact for each individual case and not appropriate for 'invariable and irrebuttable' presumptions of the type advanced by the trader in that case.[121]

Statistical surveys

7.93 The European jurisprudence about the average consumer encourages the court to conduct the exercise so far as possible without recourse to statistical or other expert evidence about typical consumer behaviour, or even the evidence of particular consumers.[122] Recital 18 of the UCPD provides that 'the average consumer test is not a statistical test. National Courts and authorities will have to exercise their own faculty of judgment, having regard to the case-law of the Court of Justice, to determine the typical reaction of the average consumer in a given case.' The assessment is a question of law, rather than fact.[123] A further rationale for this is recorded in the 2005 *OFT v Officers Club* judgment:[124]

> 'If the evidence is given by too few of them, their views will not be sufficiently representative of the entire range of such consumers; if a large number, intended to cover the full range, gives evidence, the adverse effect on the cost and duration of the trial may be disproportionate to the value of their evidence.'

7.94 This approach was supported in *OFT v Purely Creative Ltd*[125] and the *Austrian Supreme Court*.[126] The question of how the average consumer perceives an advertisement can be answered by the court when everyday experience and knowledge are sufficient to do so. However, this does not mean that real evidence of the effect the practice has on people is irrelevant – and this may be presented through expert or statistical evidence where appropriate. The approach in relation to the UCPD can be compared with the debate regarding the use of statistical surveys in the context of trademark infringement litigation.[127]

---

[119] The use of behavioural insights is likely to increase in litigation to assess the impact of practices on consumers – see the Commission Guidance [COM(2016) 320] p 42.

[120] Austria Supreme Court 2008, 4Ob 245/07v and France Supreme Court 2009, 09–83059 *Lionel and Societe ENDIS Telecom*.

[121] It does not follow that the trader must in all circumstances give complete disclosure: the average consumer may be taken to do some amount of their own research – see *BIS v PLT Anti-Marketing Ltd* [2015] EWCA Civ 76 paras 31–32.

[122] [2011] EWHC 106 (Ch), [2011] CTLC 45.

[123] See *Interflora v Marks & Spencer plc* [2014] EWCA Civ 1403, paras 113–115.

[124] [2005] EWHC 1080 (Ch), para 146.

[125] Briggs J: 'In accordance with European and English jurisprudence, the parties abstained (wisely in my judgment) from seeking to pursue their cases on that issue by reference either to expert evidence or statistical surveys', [2011] EWHC 1237 (Ch) at para 6.

[126] [2008] 4 Ob 42/08t.

[127] (1) *Interflora inc* (2) *Interflora British Unit v Marks and Spencer PLC* [2013] EWCA Civ 319, Official Transcript para 124.

A characteristic lacuna

7.95 The 'ordinary' average consumer definition under reg 2(2) makes no reference to characteristics such as age, infirmity, or mental and physical disability. It would appear that this is deliberate because reg 2(4) (targeted groups) and (5) (vulnerable consumers) are both directed towards specific groups or characteristics. However, these two provisions require proof of other elements before they are engaged (see below). If neither of these two provisions is engaged, it would appear that particular characteristics, such as age, infirmity, or mental or physical disability, cannot be considered when applying the test in reg 2(2). It is only the material characteristics of the average consumer that are relevant and the average consumer in reg 2(2) is not particularly young, old, infirm, or disabled.[128]

Regulation 2(4) and (5)

7.96 Under reg 2(3) the 'ordinary' average consumer test *must* be read as meaning the average member of a particular consumer group if either reg 2(4) (targeted groups) or 2(5) (vulnerable consumers) is engaged. The provision is worded mandatorily that the reg 2(2) test 'shall be read as **in addition** referring to the average member of a particular group of consumers'. The words 'in addition' are unlikely to create a two-pronged average consumer test that can be satisfied by *either* the reg 2(2) average consumer, or the alternative average consumer described by reg 2(4) or (5). The wording of reg 2(4) and (5) suggests that (if either provision is engaged) the reg 2(2) test should be modified by the addition of a further material characteristic: that he is an average member of the identified group of consumers.

7.97 Regulation 2(4) requires proof that the commercial practice has been, '*directed* to a particular group of consumers' before it is engaged. If it is engaged, it is the material characteristics of the average member of that particular group that must be considered. This is a subjective element that contrasts with reg 2(5), which asks only objective questions, principally about whether it was reasonably foreseeable that a clearly defined group was 'particularly vulnerable'.

Directed

7.98 The use of the verb 'direct' is likely to be considered a further element in the definition, such that reg 2(4) will not be engaged unless the trader has done something that demonstrates the product was **targeted** at a particular type of consumer. In *OFT v Purely Creative Ltd*[129] the court acknowledged that prize draw letters were sent to the names and addresses of consumers who had previously responded to one or more promotions. It was not, however, targeted

---

[128] However, see the approach taken in the German Oberlandesgericht Karlsrue (4 U 141/11) and by the Slovak Trade inspectorate (P/0359/07/2010) which found that the average consumer includes those with impaired eyesight, such that using a very small font could be misleading.

[129] [2011] EWHC 106 (Ch), para 84.

at any particular social or economic class. This appears to place a narrow interpretation of 'directed to a particular group of consumers' and arguments for a wider interpretation can be envisaged. This approach may be at variance with that taken in other EU states, such as Sweden, where in the case of advertisements for babies' nappies, the average consumer was taken to be 'parents with small children, not having any special knowledge about allergies.'[130]

Specialist knowledge

7.99 If the product was directed at a specialist group, should the average consumer be attributed with specialist knowledge that a member of that consumer group would ordinarily have? For example, a rock climbing product is obviously directed at rock climbing consumers. Clearly, the average member of that group is likely to have some rock climbing experience. Does the focus in reg 2(4) on the average member of the group exclude a consumer that is not average, for example the novice or beginner?

7.100 The level of understanding possessed by the average consumer will normally be determined by the courts by reference to everyday experience. Otherwise, factual disputes as to the average consumer's level of understanding will require expert evidence – particularly where the commercial practice is directed to an expert group of consumers.[131] If a beginner buys a falsely described rock climbing product, could it be argued that the average member of the targeted group of rock climbing consumers might not have done so because his experience and specialist knowledge would tell him that the description was misleading? The court must decide whether it can put itself in the position of the average member of rock climbers, without expert assistance, in order to decide the effect of the commercial practice on the transactional decisions of that group.

7.101 This issue is important in applying the CPUTR because the wording of reg 2(3) makes reg 2(4) mandatory if the product is directed at a particular group of consumers. It is a proposition that might leave consumers who are inexperienced in a particular area unprotected if a more experienced consumer, but still average for the group, would not have made such a transactional decision. This interpretation does not suit the purposive approach of the UCPD to provide a high level of protection for consumers. An argument that could be advanced is that the average member should not be given an artificial amount of knowledge by becoming the statistical 'average'. This is supported within the UCPD where it states that the average consumer test is not a statistical test. In the above example of rock climbing products, the concept of the 'average consumer' has narrowed from the general population to a sub-set of those interested in rock climbing. The court should apply the *transactional decision test* to the 'average consumer' of the new population. This may well alter the

---

[130] Decision of 4 July 2012 of the Marknadsdomstolen,
[131] Austria Supreme Court 2008, 4 Ob 42/08t.

degree to which the average consumer is expected to be informed, observant, or circumspect. However, it stops short of expecting the average consumer to possess the statistically 'average' rock climber's level of *specialist knowledge*.[132] A further argument about specialist knowledge is that beginners purchasing products in specialist areas might fall under the protection afforded to vulnerable consumers in reg 2(5), which includes consumers who are vulnerable because of their 'credulity' (see below).

Vulnerable consumers

7.102 Regulation 2(5) of the CPUTR is designed to provide consumer protection for vulnerable consumers. It does so by the mechanism of making the average consumer the average member of the vulnerable group of consumers (in the same way that reg 2(4) does for targeted consumers). Before reg 2(5) is engaged, however, it is necessary to prove 4 elements:

(a) there is a 'clearly identifiable group';

(b) the group is 'particularly vulnerable' to the commercial practice or underlying product because of its members' mental or physical infirmity, age, or credulity;[133]

(c) that particular vulnerability is reasonably foreseeable; and

(d) the commercial practice is, 'likely to distort' **only** the economic behaviour of the 'particularly vulnerable' group.

7.103 All of these elements are objective so that it does not matter whether the trader has actually directed the commercial practice at the particularly vulnerable group or whether the trader was actually aware that the group of consumers was particularly vulnerable to it. The language used in reg 2(5) has the effect (not necessarily intended) of creating several thresholds:

(a) the group of consumers must be *clearly* identifiable; and

(b) the group must be *particularly* vulnerable to the commercial practice or underlying product in a way that the trader could foresee; and

---

[132] However, it is legitimate to take into account the social, cultural and linguistic features of the consumers, which might mean that a practice which is misleading in one Member State is not elsewhere – such as where the misleading nature depends on the meaning of a word in one language, which it would not necessarily have in another – see C-220/98 *Estee Lauder* para 29. *Cf* the decision of the CJEU in C-75/15 concerning 'evocation' within the scope of protected geographical indication of spirit drinks. It was held that the national court is required to refer to the perception of the average consumer who is reasonably well informed, observant and circumspect, that concept being understood as concerning European consumers and not only consumers of the Member State in which the product giving rise to the evocation of the protected geographical indication is manufactured.

[133] It is important to note that Recital 19 states that this is not a closed list, and consumers may be vulnerable for further, unspecified, reasons. This wider scope appears to be favoured by the European Commission – Commission Guidance [COM(2016) 320] p 45, where reference is made to a Hungarian decision finding that consumers with a poor credit rating were to be treated as vulnerable (decision Vj-5/2011/73).

(c)   the commercial practice must be likely to distort *only* the economic behaviour of that vulnerable group; and

(d)   it must not fall within the common and legitimate advertising practice of making exaggerated statements that are not meant to be taken literally.

7.104 In drafting the CPUTR, the vulnerability of child consumers has obviously been important and reg 2(5) reflects that policy consideration. However, these thresholds seem unnecessary and capable of overcomplicating a relatively simple concept. The reason for requiring the group to be 'clearly' defined and 'particularly' vulnerable is not readily apparent. The language will undoubtedly generate legal argument about how clearly the group must be defined and how vulnerable it needs to be. Is a consumer group that is vulnerable, but not 'particularly' vulnerable, excluded? This begs the question whether the paragraph would not have been better drafted without the words 'clearly' and 'particularly'.

Only the vulnerable group

7.105 Equally, it is not obvious why there is a requirement that the commercial practice is likely to distort the economic behaviour of *'only'* the vulnerable group. If a product was likely to affect the economic behaviour of two distinct vulnerable groups, reg 2(5) would not appear to bite. Evidentially, it is potentially difficult to prove that only one group of consumers would be affected by a commercial practice. For example, products that are capable of misleading child consumers may well be capable of misleading consumers with mental impairment. Could it be argued that reg 2(5) does not apply since the commercial practice might mislead two different groups of vulnerable consumers?

7.106 It is not easy to find a linguistic construction of reg 2(5) that overcomes this problem of its literal meaning. It was plainly not an intended consequence in the UCPD, which refers to 'provisions aimed at preventing the exploitation of consumers whose characteristics make them particularly vulnerable to unfair commercial practices'. One possible route to overcoming this might be to use the direction of Briggs J:[134] that the interpretation is neither a matter of grammar or dictionaries but must be construed as far as is possible to implement the purposes and provisions of the Directive.

Credulity

7.107 Although the noun 'credulity' appears in the English version of the UCPD it is not a word that is in popular English usage. It means the disposition or willingness to believe easily or readily. A credulous consumer is one with a tendency to believe too readily. It is synonymous with the tendency to be naïve or gullible. Its etymology is derived from the Latin verb 'credo' (to believe) and 'credulous' (to believe easily).

---

[134] [2011] EWHC 106 (Ch), [2011] CTLC 45 at para 40.

CPUTR, reg 2

(6) Paragraph (5) is without prejudice to the common and legitimate advertising practice of making exaggerated statements which are not meant to be taken literally.

7.108 It is important to appreciate that reg 2(6) only applies to the vulnerable average consumer test in reg 2(5). It is not a general exclusion of all 'exaggerated statements which are not meant to be taken literally.' Such statements were generally excluded by the TDA. A statement that was too vague to be treated as definite or one that was obviously not to be taken seriously did not amount to a trade description. In the law of contract such statements are distinguished from contractual terms as mere puffs. However, the scope of the TDA exclusion went further than this. In *Cadbury v Halliday* the Divisional Court drew the distinction between s 2(1) of the TDA which embraced examples of physical characteristics, and other non-factual concepts upon which opinion could differ.[135]

7.109 Regulation 2(6) of the CPUTR is plainly not as broad as the rule was under the TDA. It only applies when considering the vulnerable average consumer. The main thrust of the CPUTR was to enhance consumer rights. This is illustrated by reg 4, which penalises commercial practices that are likely to deceive even if a statement is not actually incorrect. It follows that even opinions of a non-factual type are likely be covered by the CPUTR, subject to misleading the average consumer.

CONTRAVENING PROFESSIONAL DILIGENCE

7.110 **Contravening professional diligence** is made a prohibition by regs 3(3) and an offence by reg 8(1). The reg 17 due diligence defence is not available to a trader charged under reg 8, proof that a trader has contravened professional diligence inevitably means he has not exercised due diligence. The reg 18 (innocent publication defence) is also unavailable in a prosecution under reg 8.

CPUTR, reg 3(3)

Prohibition of unfair commercial practices

3(3) A commercial practice is unfair if –

    (a)   it contravenes the requirements of professional diligence; and
    (b)   it materially distorts or is likely to materially distort the economic behaviour of the average consumer with regard to the product.

CPUTR, reg 8(1)

Offences relating to unfair commercial practices

8(1) A trader is guilty of an offence if –

---

[135] [1975] 2 All ER 226, the description, 'extra value', was printed on chocolate bars.

(a)   he knowingly or recklessly engages in a commercial practice which contravenes the requirements of professional diligence under regulation 3(3)(a); and

(b)   the practice materially distorts or is likely to materially distort the economic behaviour of the average consumer with regard to the product under regulation 3(3)(b).

(2) For the purposes of paragraph (1)(a) a trader who engages in a commercial practice without regard to whether the practice contravenes the requirements of professional diligence shall be deemed recklessly to engage in the practice, whether or not the trader has reason for believing that the practice might contravene those requirements.

Mens rea for the criminal offence

7.111   Unlike the main offences under the TDA, the criminal offence requires proof of *mens rea*, that the offence was committed knowingly or recklessly. Recklessly is statutorily defined in reg 8(2) to include a trader that engaged in the practice 'without regard' to whether it contravened a requirement of professional diligence. This makes the recklessness test entirely objective such that it is not necessary to prove that the trader actually foresaw any risk that the commercial practice might contravene the requirements of professional diligence.

7.112   Regulation 8(2) is very similar to s 14(2)(b) of the TDA, which provided that a:

'statement made regardless of whether it is true or false shall be deemed to be made recklessly, whether or not the person making it had reasons for believing that it might be false.'

This was considered by the Divisional Court in *MFI Warehouses v Nattrass*[136] where the common law definition of recklessness was rejected.[137] Lord Widgery stated:[138]

'recklessly in the context of the 1968 Act does not involve dishonesty. Accordingly it is not necessary to prove that the statement was made with the degree of irresponsibility which is implied in the phrase 'careless whether it be true or false'. I think it suffices for present purposes if the prosecution can show that the advertiser **did not have regard to the truth or falsity** of his advertisement even if it cannot be shown that he was deliberately closing his eyes to the truth, or that he had any kind of dishonest mind.' (emphasis added)

---

[136] [1973] 1 WLR 307.

[137] The definition of 'total irresponsibility and a total lack of consideration whether the statement was true or false' per Lord Widgery CJ (taken from *Derry v Peek* (1889) 14 App Cas 337).

[138] At p 768, the Divisional Court rejected the construction of Parker J in *Sunair Holidays v Dodd* [1970] 2 All ER 410 at 411, that the test was the same as *Derry v Peek*, on the basis that the issue had not been fully argued.

7.113 The question is, did the defendant 'have regard' to whether the statement was true or false? In effect this creates a duty upon the maker of a statement to 'have regard' to its truth. What is meant by 'having regard' will depend upon the circumstances, however it will be insufficient to simply address one's mind to the issue of falsity. In *Nattrass* the company chairman had considered a statement before approving it, but had not thought through its implications sufficiently to appreciate that it could be misconstrued. The rationale of the judgment is that he ought to have given *reasonable consideration to whether the practice contravened the requirements of professional diligence* if he is not to be considered reckless.

7.114 In another TDA case, *Best Travel v Patterson*,[139] the defendant company had made a statement in a brochure that a particular hotel had various amenity rooms, which the company knew would not be available until a particular date. A customer made a booking at the hotel after the date when the rooms should have been available, and later found that they were not in fact available. It was held that the company's failure to inquire whether the rooms were available when they took the booking put them in the position that they did not know if the brochure statement was true. The statement had therefore been made recklessly.

Attributing recklessness

7.115 The nature of recklessness involves a consideration of the state of an individual's mind. Where recklessness is alleged against non-human corporate entities, a question arises as to whose state of mind must be proven. In the Divisional Court hearing of *Wings v Ellis* case, Mann J stated that:[140]

> 'a company cannot be guilty of an offence unless the specified state of mind was a state of mind of a person who is or forms part of the directing mind and will of the company.'

Although the House of Lords overturned the decision of the Divisional Court on its construction of s 14(1)(a) of the TDA, Lord Hailsham implicitly approved the judgment of Mann J on this issue.[141]

7.116 The rationale of Mann J's principle is that a company will not be vicariously responsible for the recklessness of those who do not form part of its directing mind and will. Whether a person forms part of the directing mind and will of a company will depend upon a construction of the responsibility that he holds within the company and his role in the decision making process. The issue

---

[139] (1987) 151 JP 619.
[140] [1984] 1 All ER 1046.
[141] At p 284E. *Cf* Parker LJ in *Yugotours v Wadsley* [1988] BTLC 300.

was indirectly traversed by the House of Lords in *Tesco Supermarkets Ltd v Nattrass*[142] where it was stated by Lord Reid:[143]

> 'Normally the board of directors, the managing director and perhaps other superior officers of a company carry out the functions of management and speak and act as the company. Their subordinates do not. They carry out orders from above and it can make no difference that they are given some measure of discretion. But the board of directors may delegate some part of their functions of management giving to their delegate full discretion to act independently of instructions from them. I see no difficulty holding that they have thereby put such a delegate in their place so that within the scope of the delegation he can act as the company.'

7.117 It is open to defendant companies to argue that they are not guilty of *mens rea* offences because the 'offender' was not part of the company's controlling mind. This proposition is supported by the TDA case, *Airtours v Shipley*,[144] where a false statement was made by the company's product manager in a holiday brochure. The company's appeal was allowed by the Divisional Court on the principal ground that the product manager was not a director or part of the directing mind of the company; he was merely 'a cog in the machine'. In *Airtours v Shipley,* McCowan LJ said:

> 'In *Yugotours Ltd v Wadsley* [(1989) 153 JP 345] ... Parker LJ ... said ... "I have no doubt myself that the company can properly be found to have been reckless, notwithstanding the absence of specific evidence of recklessness on the part of somebody who might properly be called part of the directing mind of the company." ... I find that perfectly acceptable if he meant no more than that a directing mind of the company must in the circumstances have been reckless, even if the particular directing mind cannot be identified. If, on the other hand, he was meaning to say that, an inferior employee being reckless, a directing mind can be vicariously liable therefore in an offence requiring *mens rea*, that would ... have been a radical departure from principle and authority.'

7.118 Similarly, in *British Airways Board v Taylor*[145] the House of Lords found that the Board was not liable to prosecution in respect of a statement made in a letter, since it had not authorised the writing of the letter. In both cases prosecution of the writer, rather than the company, would have succeeded. For authority to support the proposition that a poor system can found the basis for recklessness to be imputed to the company's controlling mind see *Sunworld Ltd v Hammersmith and Fulham London Borough Council.*[146]

---

[142] [1972] AC 153, [1971] 2 All ER 127, see also *Coupe v Guyett* [1973] 2 All ER 1058 a case dealing with an offence being committed under TDA, s 23, where such persons were described as the 'ruling officers'.
[143] At pp 132 or 171. See also Viscount Dilhorne at pp 145 or 187 and Lord Diplock at pp 155 or 199.
[144] (1994) 158 JP 835.
[145] [1976] 1 WLR 13.
[146] [2000] 1 WLR 2102 at 2109F–2110D.

7.119 Further support for the proposition that it is not always necessary to identify the particular controlling mind is found in *R v X Ltd*,[147] where Leveson LJ held that an inference could be drawn from the evidence that the way in which the company operated (which must have been through at least one of its controlling minds) demonstrated the requisite recklessness. As a result, it was not important that the prosecution could not prove the identity of a particular controlling mind.

Professional diligence

7.120

> **CPUTR, reg 2**
>
> **Interpretation**
>
> "**professional diligence**" means the standard of special skill and care which a trader may reasonably be expected to exercise towards consumers which is commensurate with either –
>
> (a)   honest market practice in the trader's field of activity, or
> (b)   the general principle of good faith in the trader's field of activity.

The definition of 'professional diligence' in the CPUTR replicates the definition set out in Art 2(h) of the UCPD. It is essentially defined by the 'reasonable expectation' that traders should behave honestly and in good faith. The concepts of 'honest market practice' and 'good faith' are not defined in the CPUTR, but assistance to their meaning can be found in case law and official guidance.

7.121 Honest market practice in the trader's field of activity is likely to mean no more than *market practices of reasonable and honest traders in that field of activity*. This will inevitably involve a consideration of how traders generally practice in the particular field. However, the fact that a commercial practice is widespread does not make it honest because there may be many dishonest traders in that field and it is not by their dishonest standards that the practice must be judged. In the OFT/BERR Guidance[148] the following direction is given which supports this view:

> 'Professional diligence is an objective standard which will vary according to the context. The word "special" is not intended to require more than would reasonably be expected of a trader in their field of activity. However, poor current practice that is widespread in an industry/sector cannot amount to an acceptable objective standard. That is because this is not what a reasonable person would expect from a trader who is acting in accordance with honest market practice or "good faith".'

---

[147] [2013] EWCA Crim 818; [2013] CTLC 145.
[148] OFT/BERR Guidance on the CPUTR (August 2008).

7.122 An authoritative exposition of the meaning of 'good faith' in the context of unfair terms was set out by Lord Bingham in *Director General of Fair Trading v First National Bank*[149] where he said:

> 'The requirement of good faith in this context is one of fair and open dealing. Openness requires that the terms should be expressed fully, clearly and legibly, containing no concealed pitfalls or traps. Appropriate prominence should be given to terms which might operate disadvantageously to the customer. Fair dealing requires that a supplier should not, whether deliberately or unconsciously, take advantage of the consumer's necessity, indigence, lack of experience, unfamiliarity with the subject matter of the contract, weak bargaining position or any other factor ... Good faith in this context is not an artificial or technical concept ... It looks to good standards of commercial morality and practice.'

7.123 What amounts to contravention of professional diligence has been considered in the UK and cases from other Member States. A good example is to be found in *OFT v Ashbourne Management Services Ltd*[150] where the High Court found that a gym provider's standard terms were unfair under the Unfair Terms in Consumer Contracts Regulations 1999. One such term provided for the gym receiving the whole of a minimum term subscription in the event of termination for whatever reason:

> 'in recommending the use of these agreements which are unfair ... and in seeking payment of subscriptions under them ... the defendants ... have not acted in accordance with the standard commensurate with honest market practice and have caused consumers to take transactional decision they would not otherwise have taken.' (per Kitchin J at para 227)

7.124 In *Competition Authority v Made in Italy, RVM, Vismara, Cascobene and X Moto*[151] a company produced and distributed motor cycle helmets for adults and children and made declarations on the helmets and in adverts that they were compliant with EU rules. It was not clear whether the helmets did or did not meet the rules, but there was a failure to verify and do all the checks as required under the rules. This was held to constitute a lack of professional diligence. The standard of special skill and care expected was high due to the product being a motor cycle helmet and also because the intended recipients included children and teenagers.

7.125 In *CHS Tour Services v Team 4 Travel*,[152] the CJEU held that there is no automatic infringement of the requirements of professional diligence if a commercial practice is categorised as a misleading commercial practice under Art 6 of the UCPD. As a result, the two tests for determining whether: (a) an act constitutes a misleading commercial practice, or (b) a failure to meet professional diligence, remain distinct.

---

[149] [2001] UKHL 52, [2002] 1 AC 481, para 17.
[150] [2011] EWHC 1237 (Ch), [2011] CTLC 237.
[151] Italy, Competition Tribunal, 2009, PS 1174.
[152] C-435/11, [2013] Bus LR 1302, [2014] 1 CMLR 38.

Standard of special skill and care

7.126   The professional diligence test also refers to the 'standard of special skill and care'. The word 'special' may be significant in understanding the scope of the professional diligence test. It has the potential to limit professional diligence to those commercial standards that are 'special' to the trader's field, rather than ordinary commercial standards of universal application to traders. Could it be argued that professional diligence was intended only to apply to specialist aspects of a trader's practice? For example, it will cover the standard of skill and care to be expected of a mechanic fitting a car part, but not to the way that he provides written invoices. The *Made in Italy* case, summarised above, discussed the special skill and care required in the making of motor cycle helmets particularly when young people are included as recipients of the product. *Competition Authority v Acea Ato SPA*[153] concerned the supply of water. A water company interrupted or cut off the water supply without warning customers. Due to the essential nature of the product, the Court held that the expected standards, and therefore the degree of expected professional diligence, were higher than for other traders. The failure to inform about the interruption to water supply contravened professional diligence.

7.127   A construction that avoids this narrowing of the scope of professional diligence might be to confine the word 'special' to merely the 'kind' or 'type' of skill and care associated with traders generally, rather than the skill and care that is special to the trader's particular field. On the other hand, it can be argued that *professional* diligence was intended to apply only to those specific professional duties and that there are several other offences that would cover unfair trading of a general nature. Against this narrow wording, several court decisions have tended to take a wider approach – including *R v X*, which held that poor customer service and dismissiveness when dealing with complaints could contravene professional diligence.[154] Likewise providing a service that is generally so poor as to require remedial work infringes this provision.[155] Requiring airline complainants to use a premium rate phone service has been held to be contrary to professional diligence by the Italian courts,[156] as has the practice of hiding a 'no insurance required' option among a list of potential countries of residence, so that consumers who do not want insurance find it hard to opt out of it.[157]

---

[153]   Italy, Competition Tribunal, 2009, PS166.
[154]   *R v X Ltd* [2013] EWCA Crim 818 paras 30–32.
[155]   *R v David Hamilton* [2015] EWCA Crim 278.
[156]   Decision of the Italian AGCM PS8378, *Ryanair*, 19 January 2015.
[157]   Decision of the Italian AGCM PS7275, *Ryanair*, 20 December 2013.

Distorting economic behaviour

7.128

CPUTR, reg 2

Interpretation

"materially distort the economic behaviour" means in relation to an average consumer, appreciably to impair the average consumer's ability to make an informed decision thereby causing him to take a transactional decision that he would not have taken otherwise.

The definitions of 'average consumer' and 'transactional decision' are considered above. The definition of 'materially distort the economic behaviour' can be separated into two parts:

(a) appreciably impairing the average consumer's ability to make an informed decision; and

(b) thereby causing him to take a transactional decision he would not have taken otherwise.

7.129 The adjective 'appreciable' means: capable of being estimated, measured, or perceived. The use of the word 'appreciably' creates a threshold test. Examples of what might be considered to be contraventions of professional diligence, which also materially distort economic behaviour, include:

• *Offering products at inflated prices to those you have sold alcohol.* Even if the test applied is the average drunken consumer, a commercial practice may still lack an operative deception, omission, or aggressive element for the purposes of regs 5, 6 or 7 of the CPUTR. It may, however, contravene the requirements of professional diligence. In such circumstances, the ability of the average drunken consumer to make an informed decision is plainly impaired.

• *A broker selling unfavourable life assurance to hospital patients immediately before medical operations.* Such a practice may lack the requisite undue influence (the application of pressure) for an aggressive commercial practice. However, it could contravene the requirements of professional diligence. The ability of the average patient to make an informed decision about life insurance will probably be impaired when they are just about to go under the surgeon's knife.

7.130 The 'appreciably impairing' test is also supplemented by the requirement that it be sufficient to cause a transactional decision. Under reg 8, the causal test is not whether the average consumer would take a different transactional decision as a consequence of the contravention of professional diligence. It is whether the impairment of his ability to make an informed decision would cause the average consumer to make a different decision. In applying this factually, the question is not whether the average consumer would take a different transactional decision because of the unfair commercial practice, but whether the impairment of the consumer's decision-making ability meant that a different decision was taken.

7.131 The concept of 'materially distorting economic behaviour' is taken directly from the UCPD. It is perhaps not the simplest way that this concept could be expressed. It combines several long and wordy definitions. In combination with the very wide definition of transactional decision, however, it amounts to little more than *whether the average consumer might have, in any way, relied upon the commercial practice as a consumer*. The language is unnecessarily clumsy, which may reflect a failure of the CPUTR's draftsmen to translate the UCPD effectively into plain English. In its present prolix form there is real scope for legal argument, as demonstrated by the two views set out above, that could have been avoided with a simple approach to language.

MISLEADING ACTIONS

7.132 Engaging in a commercial practice that is a misleading action is made an offence by regs 5 and 9.

> **CPUTR, reg 5**
>
> **Misleading actions**
>
> 5(1) A commercial practice is a misleading action if it satisfies the conditions in either paragraph (2) or paragraph (3).
>
> (2) A commercial practice satisfies the conditions of this paragraph –
>
> (a)   if it contains false information and is therefore untruthful in relation to any of the matters in paragraph (4) or if it or its overall presentation in any way deceives or is likely to deceive the average consumer in relation to any of the matters in that paragraph, even if the information is factually correct; and
>
> (b)   it causes or is likely to cause the average consumer to take a transactional decision he would not have taken otherwise.
>
> (3) A commercial practice satisfies the conditions of this paragraph if –
>
> (a)   it concerns any marketing of a product (including comparative advertising) which creates confusion with any products, trade marks, trade names or other distinguishing marks of a competitor; or
>
> (b)   it concerns any failure by a trader to comply with a commitment contained in a code of conduct which the trader has undertaken to comply with, if –
>
> (i)   the trader indicates in a commercial practice that he is bound by that code of conduct, and
>
> (ii)   the commitment is firm and capable of being verified and is not aspirational, and it causes or is likely to cause the average

consumer to take a transactional decision he would not have taken otherwise, taking account of its factual context and of all its features and circumstances.

CPUTR, reg 9

9 A trader is guilty of an offence if he engages in a commercial practice which is a misleading action under regulation 5 otherwise than by reason of the commercial practice satisfying the condition in regulation 5(3)(b).

Falsity

7.133 Regulation 5(2) applies to commercial practices that 'contain' false information or are likely to deceive even if the information is factually correct. It would appear from this that the offence is one of strict liability subject to the CPUTR defences (mirroring the TDA) that place the evidential burden of proof on the offender. The strict liability of the CPUTR offence is similar to s 1 of the TDA, albeit now covering both goods and services, which also did not require proof of a mental state.[158] It follows that the offence can be committed unknowingly. The test to be applied by the courts for a reg 5 offence is not the degree of falsity but whether the average consumer would have, in reliance, taken a different transactional decision based upon the false or deceptive information.[159] Where a trader misstates the consumer's legal rights – for example by including in their contracts terms which are unfair or otherwise unenforceable – this is likely to be a misleading action.[160]

Promises as to the future

7.134 The status of promises as to the future is likely to be the same under reg 5 CPUTR as it was under the TDA because the essential question remains one of falsity or deception. Under the TDA, promises that were genuinely made but not actually carried out were not false trade descriptions. In *Beckett v Cohen*, a builder failed to construct a building within an agreed period because he had run out of money. He was prosecuted under s 14(1) of the TDA, but it was held that the section had:[161]

> 'no application to statements which amount to a promise in regard to the future, and which therefore at the time they are made cannot have the character of being either true or false.'

However, in *British Airways Board v Taylor*[162] an airline confirmed a customer's reservation on a flight, but later overbooked the flight so that no

---

[158] *Swithland Motors v Peck* [1991] Crim LR 386 and *Alec Norman Garages v Phillips* (1984) 148 JP 741, *cf Cottee v Douglas Seaton (Used Cars)* [1972] 3 All ER 750, [1972] 1 WLR 1408.
[159] See *Motor Depot Ltd, Philip Wilkinson v Kingston Upon Hull City Council* [2012] EWHC 3257.
[160] *OFT v Ashbourne Management Services Ltd* [2011] EWHC 1237.
[161] [1973] 1 All ER 120, per Widgery LCJ.
[162] [1976] 1 WLR 13.

seat was available for him. The House of Lords held that there may be an implied statement of fact in a promise: 'A statement of intention may itself be a statement of fact and so capable of being true or false'.[163] These two TDA cases can be reconciled on the basis that, in *Beckett*, the maker of the statement intended to keep his promise when the statement was made. In *Taylor*, the airline had no intention of maintaining the customer's seat reservation because there was a policy of overbooking.

7.135 Where information is false, the fact that it is later corrected may not save it. In a German Federal Supreme Court case, a statement of a price for an espresso machine, on a price comparison site, was held to be misleading, when it did not represent the price that the seller would subsequently offer the item for, even though the price had been accurate three hours previously. A major part of the court's reasoning was that the consumer would be hooked in by the low price claim, and then fail to appreciate that the item might not be the cheapest when they got to the seller's own website.[164]

Deceived by its overall presentation

7.136 The second route by which the offence can be committed does not require the proof of actual falsity. It is sufficient that the 'overall presentation' of the commercial practice in any way 'deceives' or is likely to deceive the average consumer (in relation to a s 11 matter). The test is by reference to the average consumer and the use of the word 'deceives' (rather than 'deceived') makes it clear that it is objective. It will not therefore be sufficient to demonstrate that the individual complainant was deceived if the reasonably well informed, observant, and circumspect consumer would not have been deceived (unless the 'targeted consumer' or 'vulnerable consumer' provisions have been engaged under CPUTR reg 2(4) or (5)).

7.137 This is a marked broadening of the protection that was afforded to consumers under the TDA that focused on actual falsity. It reflects the European Community's expressed desire for a high level of consumer protection by tackling traders that operate at the fringes of falsity. This protection allows a prosecutor to consider offences for the aggregate combined effect of all relevant information which may not individually be misleading or satisfy the transactional decision test.

7.138 The provision could provide extra protection from misleading omissions not covered by reg 6.[165] The misleading omissions provision requires the material information to be that which is needed by the average consumer to take, according to context, an informed transactional decision. The omitted information must have been necessary to enable an informed transactional

---

[163] Ibid. Per Lord Wilberforce, p 17.

[164] Case I ZR 123/08 of 11 March 2010.

[165] See for example CJEU *Canal Digital Danmark* (C-611/14) paras 49 and 64, where the Court seems to have expressed a firmer view that omission of important pricing information would be a misleading action, than that it would be a misleading omission.

decision to be made.[166] This is not the same as being likely to cause the consumer to take a different transactional decision. No breach of reg 6 occurs where a promotion leaves out information which might assist or be relevant to an average consumer's transactional decision. However, if that promotion, by leaving out the information, was likely to deceive the average consumer and cause him to take a different transactional decision, then there is the potential for a breach of reg 5. Further, the limitations of space or time are likely to be irrelevant when considering if there has been a misleading action.[167]

7.139 It follows that there may be a misleading action even where the representations made are true.[168] Examples of deceptive, though literally true, practices from the UK and in other Member States include:

- describing a credit product as 'interest free' when there is a cost of credit;[169]

- advertising tickets for sale when the trader cannot guarantee to supply them;[170]

- describing a product as 'travel insurance' when it only covers booking refunds;[171]

- stating a storage capacity for an IT product, which it does not have in practice due to the presence of other software;[172]

- misleading phrases in marketing which a close examination of the mailing would show to be untrue;[173]

- 'up to' claims in respect of broadband speeds, which cannot be attained by most (that is 80%) of consumers;[174]

- including the price of holiday insurance in the total price of a product, when in fact the insurance policy was optional and not mandatory.[175]

The eleven matters

7.140 The reg 5(2) offence can only be committed if the deception is in relation to one of the eleven 'matters' identified in reg 5(4). Further definition of these eleven matters is found in reg 5(5), (6), and (7).

---

[166] [2011] EWHC 106 (Ch), para 74.
[167] CJEU *Canal Digital Danmark* (C-611/14) para 42.
[168] See *OFT v Purely Creative Ltd* [2011] EWHC 106.
[169] *Motor Depot & Wilkinson v Kingston upon Hull CC* [2012] EWHC 3257, para 33.
[170] *OFT v Andreas Gyrre & Euroteam* (High Court, July 2012 unreported).
[171] Italy – *AGCM v Ryanair* case PS7245 (17 February 2014).
[172] Italy – *AGCM v Samsung* case PS9678 (19 December 2014).
[173] Belgium – *Agence de Marketing Applique* Mons Court of Appeal 2011/RG/302.
[174] Denmark – Danish Consumer Ombudsman Marketing Guidelines.
[175] Czech Supreme Administrative Court Decision 1 As 59/2001-61 of 22 June 2011 *Blue Style sro v Czech Trade Inspectorate*.

5(4)	The eleven 'matters' that may be the subject of a deceptive commercial practice	
(a)	the existence or nature of the product;	
(b)	the main characteristics of the product	This is defined further in reg 5(5) which states 'The definition of 'main characteristics of the product' include:
		(a) availability of the product;
		(b) benefits of the product;
		(c) risks of the product;
		(d) execution of the product;
		(e) composition of the product;[176]
		(f) accessories of the product;
		(g) after-sale customer assistance concerning the product;
		(h) the handling of complaints about the product;
		(i) the method and date of manufacture of the product;
		(j) the method and date of provision of the product;
		(k) delivery of the product;
		(l) fitness for purpose of the product;
		(m) usage of the product;
		(n) quantity of the product;
		(o) specification of the product;
		(p) geographical or commercial origin of the product;[177]
		(q) results to be expected from use of the product; and
		(r) results and material features of tests or checks carried out on the product.'
(c)	the extent of the trader's commitments;	
(d)	the motives for the commercial practice;	
(e)	the nature of the sales process;	

---

[176] For example, describing furniture as made of 'textile leather' when in fact it does not include any leather – German cases Urteil Az. I-4 U 174/11 OLG Hamm 8 March 2012 and Urteil Az. 3 U 219/11 OLG Bamberg 21 March 2012.

[177] For example, strongly implying that a rum product is from Cuba, when it is in fact not – Court of Appeal of Paris 10 May 2012, *Societe Havana Club v SAS Etablissements* (ref 10/04016). See also Commission Interpretive Notice C-375/5 on indication of origin claims on products from Israel and the Occupied Palestinian Territories, which may be contrasted with the UK Supreme Court decision in *Richardson v DPP* [2014] UKSC 8.

(f)	any statement or symbol relating to direct or indirect sponsorship or approval of the trader or the product;	
(g)	the price or the manner in which the price is calculated;	
(h)	the existence of a specific price advantage;	
(i)	the need for a service, part, replacement or repair;	
(j)	the nature, attributes and rights of the trader;	This is defined further in para 5(6) which states that 'In paragraph (4)(j), the 'nature, attributes and rights' as far as concern the trader include the trader's:
		(a) identity;
		(b) assets;
		(c) qualification;
		(d) status;
		(e) approval;
		(f) affiliations or connections;
		(g) ownership of industrial, commercial or intellectual property rights;
		(h) awards and distinctions.'
(k)	The consumer's rights or the risks he may face.[178]	It should be noted that this is further defined in reg 5(7) which states that, 'In paragraph (4)(k) 'consumer's rights' include rights the consumer may have under ss 19 and 23 or 24 of the Consumer Rights Act 2015.

7.141 The eleven 'matters' identified in the CPUTR are deliberately broader than the list of essentially physical characteristics under s 2(1) of the TDA that were a requirement for an offence under s 1 of the TDA in relation to goods. It should also be noted that the list for (b) main characteristics of the product and (j) nature attributes and rights of the trader are prefixed by 'include'. This implies that the lists are non-exhaustive. Indeed, while there is no specific reference in any of the listed characteristics to the ecological credentials of a product, there have been numerous rulings and pages of guidance given on the application of the UCPD to so called 'green claims'.[179] They give, by choice of the words used, broad scope to the matters covered under reg 5(2). However, the matter should probably be included where, even though it is not directly mentioned, it goes to the main characteristic, nature, attribute, or right of the trader. Regulation 5 of the CPUTR applies to 'products' which includes goods

---

[178] A mere reference to the legal provision setting out the right of withdrawal may not be sufficient – see Prague City Court decision of 11 May 2015 *Bredley & Smith v Czech Trade Inspection Authority*. Likewise, offering a commercial guarantee which in fact duplicates the consumer's statutory protection was found to be misleading in Italy (decision PS7256 of the AGCM upheld on appeal – Consiglio di Stato N 05253.2015 Reg Prov Coll N 05096/2012 Reg Ric).

[179] See Commission Guidance [COM(2016) 320] s 5.1 on Environmental Claims for a comprehensive overview.

and services. It applies to prices[180] and, perhaps most significantly, to non-physical characteristics, such as motive.

Non-physical characteristics

7.142 The CPUTR has introduced several non-physical characteristics into the definition of a misleading act under reg 5, such as a trader's motive for a commercial practice and after sale customer assistance. Its statutory predecessor, the TDA, avoided characteristics that were not susceptible to clear proof, such as future promises or commercial motive. It is doubtful that real consideration was given to these less certain concepts when drafting the CPUTR, which is largely a copy out of the UCPD. It is, however, important as the UK has opted for criminal enforcement. Such subjective concepts are likely to give rise to difficulty in trading cases, particularly when applied to complex corporate organisations (see also reg 6 misleading omissions, failure to disclose commercial intent).

Prices

7.143 The CPUTR applies to prices.[181] The CPUTR revoked Part III of the Consumer Protection Act 1987 ('CPA 1987') which created the main criminal offences for misleading price indications.[182] Prices are now covered in Chapter 12.

Confusing marketing and non-compliance with codes of conduct

7.144 It is a misleading action, under reg 5(3)(a), to market a product in such a way as to create confusion with another trader's product, so that the average consumer takes a different transactional decision. It seems that this is likely to require the average consumer to consider the product is that of the other trader, and so may not cover instances of so called copycat packaging where the consumer is not so deceived as to purchase the wrong product. An example of confusing marketing could be sending out invoices that mimic the other trader's branding, thus creating the impression that a service was rendered by the trader responsible for the invoice.[183]

7.145 Although not criminalised, reg 5(3)(b) makes it unlawful for a trader to fail to comply with commitments in a code of conduct, which the trader has publicly indicated he is bound by, where that commitment is firm and capable

---

[180] In its original form, the TDA included prices (s 11). This was repealed and replaced by the Consumer Protection Act 1987, s 20 *et seq*. The pricing parts of the CPA 1987 were repealed by the CPUTR.

[181] CPUTR, regs 5(4)(g) and (h), 6(4)(d) and (e), Sch 1 paras 5, 6, 7, 15, 18 and 20.

[182] The CPA 1987 had in turn removed prices from the ambit of trade descriptions in the Trade Descriptions Act 1968.

[183] Swedish Market Court MD 2009:36, 19 November 2009. Another example was the use of yellow designs on the side of Gothenburg taxis, which mimicked the designs of another trader who had been providing taxi services in the Gothenburg area since 1922 (Swedish Market Court MD 2015:9, 11 June 2015).

of being verified. Such a misleading action may be enforced by civil action, and may form the basis for a claim for redress by the consumer.

7.146 A code of conduct is defined in reg 2(1) as an agreement or set of rules (which is not imposed by legal or administrative requirements), which defines the behaviour of traders who undertake to be bound by it in relation to one or more commercial practices or business sectors. Examples could be the Property Ombudsman Code for Letting Agents or one of the other CTSI approved codes. It is likely that the display of the relevant code logo would be sufficient to satisfy the public indication test.

MISLEADING OMISSIONS

7.147 Engaging in a commercial practice that is a misleading omission is made an offence by regs 6 and 10.

CPUTR, reg 6

Misleading omissions

6(1) A commercial practice is a misleading omission if, in its factual context, taking account of the matters in paragraph (2) –

    (a)   the commercial practice omits material information,

    (b)   the commercial practice hides material information,

    (c)   the commercial practice provides material information in a manner which is unclear, unintelligible, ambiguous or untimely, or

    (d)   the commercial practice fails to identify its commercial intent, unless this is already apparent from the context,

and as a result it causes or is likely to cause the average consumer to take a transactional decision he would not have taken otherwise.

(2) The matters referred to in paragraph (1) are –

    (a)   all the features and circumstances of the commercial practice;

    (b)   the limitations of the medium used to communicate the commercial practice (including limitations of space or time); and

    (c)   where the medium used to communicate the commercial practice imposes limitations of space or time, any measures taken by the trader to make the information available to consumers by other means.

(3) In paragraph (1) "material information" means –

    (a)   the information which the average consumer needs, according to the context, to take an informed transactional decision; and

    (b)   any information requirement which applies in relation to a commercial communication as a result of a Community obligation.

(4) Where a commercial practice is an invitation to purchase, the following information will be material if not already apparent from the context in addition to any other information which is material information under paragraph (3) –

(a) the main characteristics of the product, to the extent appropriate to the medium by which the invitation to purchase is communicated and the product;

(b) the identity of the trader, such as his trading name, and the identity of any other trader on whose behalf the trader is acting;

(c) the geographical address of the trader and the geographical address of any other trader on whose behalf the trader is acting;

(d) either –
  (i) the price, including any taxes; or
  (ii) where the nature of the product is such that the price cannot reasonably be calculated in advance, the manner in which the price is calculated;

(e) where appropriate, either –
  (i) all additional freight, delivery or postal charges; or
  (ii) where such charges cannot reasonably be calculated in advance, the fact that such charges may be payable;

(f) the following matters where they depart from the requirements of professional diligence –
  (i) arrangements for payment,
  (ii) arrangements for delivery,
  (iii) arrangements for performance,
  (iv) complaint handling policy;

(g) for products and transactions involving a right of withdrawal or cancellation, the existence of such a right.

CPUTR, reg 10

10 A trader is guilty of an offence if he engages in a commercial practice which is a misleading omission under regulation 6.

7.148 The criminal offence does not require proof of a *mens rea*, however it is subject to the defences set out in the Regulations. Consideration of a misleading omission is subject to the features and circumstances of the commercial practice. This includes limitations of space or time imposed by the medium used and, where there are such limitations, the measures taken to make the information available by other means. This has particular relevance to some electronic mediums. Traders may provide material information by other means where it is not possible to include it because of the 'intrinsic characteristics of the product'.[184]

Hiding

7.149 There is a clear distinction between omitting and hiding under reg 6. The verb to hide means to keep out of sight, to conceal, or to obscure. It follows that material information may have been included in the commercial practice but has been hidden. This is of particular importance if material information is buried amongst the small print of consumer contracts. The extent to which material information will be considered 'hidden' will depend upon the circumstances.

---

[184] CJEU *Canal Digital Danmark* (C-611/14), paras 62 and 63.

7.150 In *OFT v Purely Creative Ltd*[185] the court considered whether various pieces of information in prize promotions were omitted or hidden. In a prize award letter the small print stated that premium line telephone calls might take a maximum of 6 minutes at £1.50 per minute. It omitted to say that over 99% of all claims would take 2 seconds less than 6 minutes and, therefore, that almost all consumers would have to pay £8.95. The per minute charge was not hidden, but the actual cost was omitted. However, the actual cost was not misleadingly hidden since it was included in the small print. The small print was intelligible and the actual cost was identified by an asterisk that cross referred to the small print.

7.151 For an alternative promotion involving scratch cards, the court considered 'by a narrow margin' that the representative quantities of awards were not hidden in the very small print. Part of the consideration was the limitation on space available because of the scratch card format used. On the same basis, information on a cruise that was one of the awards was also not hidden. After having discovered that they had been awarded a cruise, the average consumer would take some trouble looking for the terms and conditions as they would not think an apparently free cruise would be entirely free of conditions.

7.152 Plainly some contracts are necessarily lengthy because detail is necessary in defining the contractual relationship. Important matters, particularly in relation to price or exclusions, should be communicated prominently in the commercial practice to avoid allegations that the matter has been hidden within the pages of the contract. For example, a telephone operator in Finland was found to mislead by omission because it presented the restrictions and conditions of an offer in small print and for only a very short time, in a TV advert. The Supreme Court of Finland held that nothing prevented it from presenting these important facts more clearly.[186] Likewise, a Hungarian trader was guilty of hiding information by informing consumers of their right of withdrawal by setting out the full text of the government decree. This contained conditions not applicable to the contract, and was not plain for consumers to understand.[187]

Unclear, unintelligible, ambiguous or untimely

7.153 The use of the words 'unclear, unintelligible, ambiguous or untimely' illustrate the breadth of the CPUTR. It is unlikely that the word 'unintelligible' adds very much to 'unclear' or 'ambiguous'. If a phrase cannot be understood it will also be unclear and ambiguous. However, is 'unintelligible' to be taken literally or purposively? A primary purpose behind the UCPD is to remove barriers to cross-border trade. In this open trading environment there could be promotions in part or totally in a foreign language to the consumer. The words themselves may be clear and unambiguous but they might be unintelligible to

---

[185] [2011] EWHC 106 (Ch).
[186] KKO 2011:65.
[187] Administrative Court of Gyor, Decision No K. 27.272/2014.

those who are not fluent in that language. The court would have to consider the abilities of the average consumer to whom the commercial practice reaches or is addressed. The CPUTR repeats the UCPD benchmark of the average consumer being reasonably well informed, observant, and circumspect but does not repeat 'taking into account social, cultural and linguistic factors'. As the CPUTR implements the UCPD, these factors will have to be considered where relevant. Traders willing to engage in cross-border trade will need to make their offers and terms of business clear to all intended customers and overcome any social, cultural, or linguistic barriers.

7.154 The use of the word 'untimely' is significant when combined with the broad definition of transactional decision. The failure of a trader to mention an important matter, before a *transactional decision* is taken, could be considered untimely if the omission concerns material information. Transactional decisions may include decisions made by a consumer before he finally pays or binds himself contractually. For example, it is common practice for many businesses selling goods or services (particularly internet traders) to introduce conditions or extra payments at the end of the transactional process. Visiting a website (or engaging in the process of making a purchase) can amount to a transactional decision, so extra charges or conditions may well be untimely if they are only mentioned at the end of the process.

Commercial intent

7.155 The requirement for traders to identify the commercial intent behind a particular practice has the potential to be significant for any business dealing with consumers. The obligation does not apply if the commercial intent is already apparent from the circumstances, however, UK traders frequently do not disclose what is really behind a specific practice. A recent example is the widespread publicity concerning the provision of boarding passes at airports shops, where the traders' main purpose was to avoid paying tax, rather than provide consumers with discounts. Another unlawful practice is that of hooking the consumer's interest by asking them to take part in a survey, or other presentation, as a prelude to being exposed to marketing.[188]

7.156 It is additionally necessary to prove that the trader's failure to identify the commercial intent caused, or was likely to cause, the average consumer to take a different transactional decision. This threshold is likely to be important in the application of this provision because it can be argued the undisclosed commercial intention behind a practice is unlikely to affect a consumer's

---

[188] See eg the Polish Office of Competition and Consumer Protection Decision No RPZ 6/2015, against a trader offering a free health check as part of an 'I care for my health' programme, when in fact the intention was to present products for sale. The practice of inviting consumers to take part in a 'lifestyle survey' (sometimes referred to as 'sugging') may also infringe reg 21 of the Privacy and Electronic Communications Regulations 2003, where conducted over the phone – see the recent ICO Enforcement Notice issued against Change and Save Ltd https://ico.org.uk/media/action-weve-taken/enforcement-notices/1624601/en-change-and-save-ltd-20160708.pdf

decision if there is clarity about the subject matter of the contract and its price. However, there may be situations where the consumer would prefer not to engage with a trader at all, if the commercial intent was disclosed – an example being where the purpose of a practice is to harvest consumer's personal data for marketing purposes, when this is not made clear.[189]

Material information

7.157 The Regulations set out three categories of 'material information'. The categories are broad and necessarily overlap:

(a) Under reg 6(3)(a), information the average consumer needs to make an informed transactional decision.

(b) Under reg 6(3)(b), any information requirement which applies in relation to a commercial communication as a result of a community obligation.

(c) Under reg 6(4), specific listed information when there is an 'invitation to purchase'.

Informed decision

7.158 A trader must provide all information the consumer needs to make an informed transactional decision. This is likely to be a very broad category of information. An informed decision equates to all relevant information for making a particular decision. When it is combined with the wide concept of a transactional decision, it amounts to any information that would have made a difference to the average consumer's decision making. This is not limited to the decision to purchase a product but extends to all transactional decisions.

7.159 The German Higher Regional Court has decided that an unexpected condition limiting a 'lowest price guarantee' to a €100 cap should have been in a printed advert. In order to take up the offer, consumers would have to go to the company website where the condition became clear. The court considered that merely referring consumers to the terms and conditions on a website would not prevent a misleading omission.[190] The average consumer would not expect such an exclusion and it therefore became material information needed in the consumer's first transactional decisions as to whether to look at the offer further. Similarly, a Spanish court found that limitations on an offer of saving 3% on purchases with a promoted credit card were material, and should have been included in the promotional leaflet and not just in the contract terms.[191] Likewise important limitations to insurance cover have been found to be misleadingly omitted when not included in the glossy advertising.[192] The CJEU

---

[189] See the OFT investigation into a company that offered a free psychic assessment as a means of acquiring personal information http://webarchive.nationalarchives.gov.uk/20140402142426/http:/www.oft.gov.uk/news-and-updates/press/2008/130-08

[190] Germany, Higher Regional Court 2009, 6U 26/09.

[191] Audiencia Provincial de Madrid Sentencia No 270/2014.

[192] Polish Office of Competition and Consumer Protection Decision No DKK 7/2014.

has held that pricing information is 'in principle, a determining factor in the consumer's mind, when it must make a transactional decision'.[193]

7.160 There is no reasonableness test in the reg 6 obligation to provide material information. The focus is on the consumer's rights to have all relevant information, regardless of whether it is reasonable to expect the particular trader to have provided it. This may prove an onerous burden for smaller traders selling complex products remote from their manufacture. There is a tension between whether material information might have been omitted or just provided in an untimely manner. During a purchase, there can be a number of transactional decisions and the material information relates to that which is needed by the consumer at the time of each decision. For a complex purchase, such as buying a house, the information needed at the start of the process may be very broad and include matters such as location, the number of bedrooms, and the price. As the purchase progresses, the information needed to make an informed decision is likely to narrow to specific matters, such as when the wiring was last checked and whether there have been any problems with neighbours. Rather than remaining silent on an issue, it may be prudent for a trader to be open to expressing, and recording, that they do not know or possess the information. A trader that has failed to provide relevant information may still fall back on the due diligence defence in reg 17. However, proving the defence retrospectively in relation to an omission is often not easy.

The concept of need

7.161 In *Secretary of State for Business, Innovation and Skills v PLT Anti-Marketing Ltd*,[194] the Court of Appeal considered the definition of 'material information' for the purposes of reg 6. In that case, the appellant company offered to register customers for a fee with telephone preference services in order to reduce cold calling. However, the company did not inform customers that the telephone preference service was offered independently free of charge to the public. Although the court declined to determine whether the company's practices were in breach of reg 6, it did give some guidance. In determining what is 'material information', the critical question is whether the average consumer *needs* to obtain that information from the trader. Information about alternative products will generally be available in the marketplace, but 'inward-facing' information about the trader's own product is likely to be only available from the trader. As a result, if the consumer could obtain the information by shopping around, then it is unlikely that the information was material. This is because shopping around for information about alternative products is characteristic of the reasonably well-informed, observant, and circumspect consumer. Furthermore, neither CPUTR nor the UCPD required a trader to disclose to consumers its mark-up or the cost of obtaining the product from a supplier.

---

[193] CJEU *Canal Digital Danmark* (C-611/14), para 55.
[194] [2015] EWCA Civ 76, [2015] CTLC 8.

7.162 In *Office of Fair Trading v Purely Creative* the High Court considered the extent of the information a consumer needed to make an informed transactional decision. Briggs J stated:[195]

'The starting point under English common law in relation to pre-contractual negotiations is *caveat emptor*. That may be qualified both by statute and even by the common law in relation to particular types of transaction, such as the obligation to disclose latent defects when negotiating a sale of land, and the obligation of utmost good faith on an applicant for insurance. Again, these English law concepts must be put on one side, not least because in systems of civil law widely used in Europe there exist general obligations of good faith in contractual relationships which have no parallel in the common law.

A literal reading of Regulation 6(3)(a) and its equivalent in Article 7.1 of the UCPD might suggest that something approaching an utmost good faith obligation is imposed in relation not merely to the consumer's decision whether to contract, but also to every transactional decision, such as, in the present case, a decision whether to respond to a promotion by post, text message or premium rate telephone call. Although qualified by the causation requirement to which I have referred, I regard that analysis as imposing an excessively high hurdle, and counsel did not suggest otherwise. It cannot have been the intention of the framers of the UCPD to require that level of disclosure, and to do so would indeed cause barriers to the free movement of goods and services beyond that necessary to achieve a high degree of consumer protection.

In my judgment the key to understanding this paragraph is the concept of "need". The question is not whether the omitted information would assist, or be relevant, but whether its provision is necessary to enable the average consumer to take an informed transactional decision.' [emphasis added]

7.163 The issue of need was explored further in considering the individual promotions in the case. The first transactional decision for the consumer was whether or not to respond to the prize draw letter they had been sent and, if so, whether to respond by premium rate phone line or by post. As the representative quantities of each award was presented to the consumer in the letter they did not need information on their chances of winning in order to decide whether to respond or not. What the consumer did need to know at this stage was the true cost of the premium rate phone call which in 99.9% of cases would be £8.95.

7.164 Other cases support the view that the true cost to consumers needs to be given up front. In a Dutch case[196] a telephone and internet package was promoted at a price of €20 a month. There was a €17 monthly cable network charge that was revealed on the website when signing up. The court found this information was needed by the consumer when they saw the advert or a consumer would consider they could have the whole package at a total cost of €20 a month.

---

[195] [2011] EWHC 106 (Ch), paras 73–74.
[196] *Tele2 Nederland v UPC Nederland*, Court of Appeal, IER 2010/60.

7.165   The offence has two main tests, the concept of need in order to take an informed decision and the second stage of affecting the transactional decision made by the consumer. However, having proved that the information is needed in order to take an informed decision, it is unlikely that the omission or hiding of that information would not affect the transactional decision of the average consumer.

7.166   In the BERR/OFT guidance[197] to the CPUTR it is stated that:

> '7.16 What information is required will depend on the circumstances, for example what the **product** concerned is, and where and how it is offered for sale. This may range from a very small amount of information for simple **products**, to more information for complex **products**.

> 7.17 The price of a **product** in most circumstances is material information. Therefore, failing to provide this in a timely fashion before a transactional decision is made is likely to amount to a misleading omission. For example, in restaurants, the prices of the food and drink available will usually need to be given to **consumers** before they order.

> 7.18 Material information includes any information which causes or is likely to cause the **average consumer** to take a different decision about the **product**.

7.167   Examples:

> A trader omits to mention that a contract has to run for a minimum period, or that the consumer has to go on making purchases in the future, this would probably be a material omission.

> A trader advertises mobile phones for sale. If the phones were second hand and/or had been reconditioned, this would be material information, which would need to be made clear to **consumers**.

> A trader operates a car park. If he fails to clearly display the price(s) of parking at a point before the consumer enters the car park and incurs a charge, this would be failing to provide material information.

> A trader sells audio visual equipment. He omits to inform the consumer that a particular product includes an analogue tuner, and the implications in the context of the switch from analogue to digital-only television. This is likely to be material information that the consumer needs to make an informed decision.'[198]

---

[197] Consumer Protection from Unfair Trading – Guidance on the UK Regulations implementing the Unfair Commercial Practices Directive.

[198] The European Commission are of the view that where a trader is aware that a product is designed to fail after a period of time (so called planned obsolescence) this could be material information – see Guidance [COM(2016) 320] s 3.4.8.

Community obligations

7.168 Under reg 6(3)(b) 'material information' also includes 'any information requirement which applies in relation to a commercial communication as a result of a community obligation'. A trader is obliged to provide a consumer with any information that is required by community law in relation to commercial communications. It follows that this is not limited to obligations about commercial communication with consumers.

7.169 The failure to advertise airplane ticket prices in accordance with the Air Services Regulations (a community obligation) constituted an unfair commercial practice.[199] The tribunal found it was irrelevant whether consumers had entered into a contract as a result. An advert that merely convinces a consumer to seek further details may be misleading, since the consumer has made a transactional decision to seek those details – even if he or she does not go on to buy a ticket.

7.170 It is not clear how much extra protection this requirement adds, as the failure to comply with a community obligation is likely to infringe the law that has introduced the obligation, however it may mean that the trader is exposed to a more significant penalty. For example, a failure to give notice of a consumer's cancellation right in a doorstep contract is punishable by a modest fine only, whereas as a CPUTR breach the trader could face prison or an unlimited fine.[200] Likewise, some community information requirements may not carry any other criminal penalty.[201]

Invitation to purchase

7.171 Under reg 6(3)(b), information is deemed to be material information when there is an 'invitation to purchase', which is defined by reg 2(1) (interpretation):

> "invitation to purchase" means a commercial communication which indicates characteristics of the product and the price in a way appropriate to the means of that commercial communication and thereby enables the consumer to make a purchase.[202]

7.172 In the OFT Guidance to the CPUTR it is stated that:

> '7.25 The following will normally be invitations to purchase where the product's price and characteristics are given:

---

[199] Latvia – *Consumer Protection Rights Centre v Air Baltic Corporation*, 2009 E03 – REUD-54, Latvia Tribunal First Degree.

[200] See *R v Michael Tolliday* [2015] EWCA Crim 603 for an example of a trader prosecuted under the CPUTR for failing to give notice of doorstep cancellation rights.

[201] An example could be the information requirements for distance contracts under the Consumer Contracts (Information, Cancellation and Additional Charges) Regulations 2013, SI 2013/ 3134.

[202] The concept of invitation to purchase is also relevant to the meaning of banned practices 5 and 6.

- an advertisement in a newspaper where part of the advertisement is an order form that can be sent to the trader
- an interactive TV advertisement through which orders can be directly placed
- a page or pages on a web site where consumers can place an order
- a menu in a restaurant from which consumers can place an order
- a text message promotion to which consumers can directly respond in order to purchase the promoted product
- a radio advertisement for a mobile phone ring tone, which provides a word and number to text in order that the consumer can purchase and pay for (via their phone bill) the jingle to be uploaded to their device.
- a price on a product in a shop.'

Deemed 'material information'

7.173 The CPUTR define an 'invitation to purchase' as a communication that indicates the characteristics of the product (including its price) and thereby enables a consumer to make a purchase. It will be up to the courts to decide what information about the product and the price is sufficient for a consumer to make a transactional decision. It is clear that the communication does not have to appear at the same time as, or in proximity to, the actual opportunity to make the purchase. This was made clear by the CJEU in the *Ving Sverige* case.[203] A general description of the product with a 'starting from' price is likely to be sufficient to make the commercial practice an invitation to purchase.[204] However, mere brand advertising would not constitute an invitation to purchase.[205]

7.174 When there is an 'invitation to purchase', all of the categories of information listed in reg 6(4)(a)–(g) are deemed to be material information (where they are applicable). The effect of the regulation is to make the reg 6(4) list of material information additional to the material information that cannot be omitted if a consumer needs it in order to take an informed transactional decision under reg 6(3). Omitting to provide the reg 6(4) listed information will not automatically be an offence, however, unless the failure to provide it would also cause a different transactional decision to have been taken as required by reg 6(1). However mere provision of this information may not be enough as a commercial practice may still be misleading even if the invitation to purchase listed information has been given in full.[206]

7.175 Especially important is the provision of fully inclusive pricing (ie, a price which includes all taxes and charges). In two Polish cases, consumers were misled where contracts did not explicitly state the remuneration including tax. The decision was that consumers presented with net value contracts may consider the price to be beneficial and as a result were likely to be deceived.

---

[203] *Konsumentombudsmannen v Ving Sverige AB* (C-122/10) [2011] ECR I-03903.
[204] The Commission Guidance suggests that a visual representation of the product could be sufficient (COM(2016) 320, p 50.
[205] See for example the Belgian decision of the Commercial Court of Antwerp *Federatie voor verzekerings en financiele tussenpersonen v ING Insurance Services* (29 May 2008).
[206] CJEU *Canal Digital Danmark* (C-611/14), para 71.

Price related information is a key condition enabling consumers to make an informed choice.[207] In the second case[208] a price given did not include VAT and was found to contravene the general obligation that all taxes should be included in all communications. Traders need also to be vigilant to include all additional charges. In another Polish case, a telecom operator failed to disclose an activation fee until after the contract was signed,[209] and in a Spanish case, an internet service provider wrongly failed to include network charges in its advertised prices.[210] Similarly in a German case, it was unlawful for a trader offering holiday flats to fail to indicate in the price such mandatory costs as cleaning, city taxes and additional service charges for booking.[211] The CJEU has ruled in the context of cable television contracts, that failing to give equal prominence to a 6 monthly charge (in addition to the monthly fee) was likely to be misleading.[212]

7.176 Where the nature or the product itself means that the price cannot be calculated in advance, then it must be stated how the price will be calculated. It is considered that this does not permit traders deliberately to create complex pricing, unless the complexity relates to the nature of the product. For example, an invitation to purchase minced meat in a butcher's shop may state the price on a per kilo basis, since by its nature the meat may be sold in many different quantities. By contrast the price of an airline ticket has no complexity which means it cannot be calculated in advance.

7.177 Sometimes there are optional extras. These do not need to be included in the price, as long as they are genuinely optional. For example, where an airline operated a charging structure whereby different payment cards attracted different charges, the OFT considered that it infringed the CPUTR to fail to include the cost of paying by debit card in the headline price, because this is the payment method most prevalent in the UK.[213] Likewise an airline cannot charge separately for hand luggage, but it may for checked luggage.[214]

7.178 This provision must now be read in conjunction with the information requirements set out in the Consumer Contracts Regulations 2013, which implement the consumer information obligations in the Consumer Rights Directive, and also the prohibition on additional charges for items going

---

[207] *Office of Competition and Consumer Protection v Grzegorz Daszkowski t/a ETNA*, Poland, 2010, RLO 9/2010.

[208] *Office of Competition and Consumer Protection v Eko-Park SA*, Poland, 2010, RWA 25/2010.

[209] Polish Office of Competition and Consumer Protection Decision No RBG 38/2014.

[210] Tribunal Superior de Justicia de Madrid, Sala de lo Contencioso Administrativo Seccion 10, No 112/2014.

[211] OLG Hamm, 06.06.2013, Az. I-4 U 22/13.

[212] CJEU *Canal Digital Danmark* (C-611/14).

[213] This is in contrast to the cost of paying by credit card, which the OFT considered to be genuinely optional, and so should be presented no more than 1 click away from the headline price, along with other genuinely optional add ons. See the investigation case page: http://webarchive.nationalarchives.gov.uk/20140402142426/http:/www.oft.gov.uk/OFTwork/consumer-enforcement/consumer-enforcement-completed/card-surcharges/

[214] C-487/12 *Vueling Airlines*.

beyond the trader's main contractual obligation. The information provisions in the 2013 Regulations are dealt with in Chapter 5, Consumer Rights.

AGGRESSIVE COMMERCIAL PRACTICES

7.179   Engaging in an aggressive commercial practice is made an offence by regs 7 and 11.

CPUTR, reg 7

Aggressive Commercial Practices

7(1) A commercial practice is aggressive if, in its factual context, taking account of all of its features and circumstances –

    (a)   it significantly impairs or is likely significantly to impair the average consumer's freedom of choice or conduct in relation to the product concerned through the use of harassment, coercion or undue influence; and

    (b)   it thereby causes or is likely to cause him to take a transactional decision he would not have taken otherwise.

(2) In determining whether a commercial practice uses harassment, coercion or undue influence account shall be taken of –

    (a)   its timing, location, nature or persistence;

    (b)   the use of threatening or abusive language or behaviour;

    (c)   the exploitation by the trader of any specific misfortune or circumstance of such gravity as to impair the consumer's judgment, of which the trader is aware, to influence the consumer's decision with regard to the product;

    (d)   any onerous or disproportionate non-contractual barrier imposed by the trader where a consumer wishes to exercise rights under the contract, including rights to terminate a contract or to switch to another product or another trader; and

    (e)   any threat to take any action which cannot legally be taken.

(3) In this regulation –

    (a)   "coercion" includes the use of physical force; and

    (b)   "undue influence" means exploiting a position of power in relation to the consumer so as to apply pressure, even without using or threatening to use physical force, in a way which significantly limits the consumer's ability to make an informed decision.

CPUTR, reg 11

11 A trader is guilty of an offence if he engages in a commercial practice which is aggressive under regulation 7.

The criminal offence

7.180   The reg 7 offence is one of strict liability, being defined by the effect of a commercial practice upon the average consumer rather than any necessary *mens rea*. Although the penalties for committing the offence are the same as for the other commercial practice offences, the label of an 'aggressive' commercial practice that can only be committed when the trader has used 'harassment', 'coercion', or 'undue influence' make it a more serious offence than those under regs 3, 5, and 6. The offence is subject to the defences set out in regs 17 and 18. The meaning of trader, commercial practice, average consumer, and transactional decision are considered above.

The threshold: 'significantly impaired'

7.181 The reg 7 offence includes a threshold that is absent from the reg 3, 5, and 6 offences. Before a reg 7 offence is committed there must be a **significant** impairment (or likely impairment) of the average consumer's freedom of choice or conduct. The CPUTR follows the wording of Art 8 of the UCPD such that a distinct threshold for aggressive commercial practice was deliberate. This is perhaps understandable when the nature of the offence is considered and the potential stigma associated with conviction for such an offence. It seems likely that to be an aggressive practice there should be some active conduct by the trader, which in fact limits the consumer's freedom of choice.[215] However, it seems likely that the threshold is not particularly high for a practice to qualify as aggressive – for example in Latvia the use of pre-ticked boxes has been ruled to be aggressive.[216] Sending a letter demanding payment where a consumer has exercised their right to cancel a doorstep contract may amount to an aggressive practice.[217]

Mandatory considerations

7.182 Regulation 7(2) (following Art 9 of the UCPD) sets out five factors that *must* be considered when deciding whether the commercial practice uses harassment, coercion, or undue influence.[218] These five factors set out features that one might commonly find in a genuinely aggressive commercial practice, such as threatening or abusive language. Although proof of one of the five factors is not an element of the offence, the absence of any of the reg 7(2) factors in the commercial practice may make an allegation under reg 7 difficult. This is because account must be taken of them when determining whether harassment, coercion, or undue influence is present.

Harassment

7.183 Harassment is not defined in the CPUTR, other than by reference to the five reg 7(2) factors. The term 'harassment' has a statutory definition in the Protection from Harassment Act 1997. The *actus reus* under the 1997 Act is 'pursuing a course of conduct ... which amounts to', 'alarming the person or

---

[215] Italian decision of the Consiliglio de Stato, Adunanza Plenaria – Sentenza 11 May 2012, n 14.
[216] CRPC Decision No.E03-PTU-K115-39 of 23 October 2013 against Air Baltic.
[217] *R v Waters & Westminster Recliners Ltd* [2016] EWCA Crim 1112 at para 31.
[218] The wording of reg 7(2) has omitted the words 'including the use of physical force' from Art 9 of the UCPD.

causing the person distress' 'on at least two occasions'.[219] However, a course of conduct will not amount to harassment if it 'was pursued under any enactment or rule of law' or 'in the particular circumstances the pursuit of the course of conduct was reasonable'.[220]

7.184 By excluding conduct amounting to a pursuit under a 'rule of law', the 1997 Act excludes the pursuit of contractual claims and debt.[221] The rationale of this is that the 1997 Act targeted the particular problems of human stalking, anti-social behaviour, and racial harassment. Under the CPUTR, however, the aggressive pursuit of lawful contractual debt etc is unlikely to be excluded. This is clearly indicated by the fact that threatening to take action that cannot lawfully be taken is only one of the five factors in determining whether harassment, coercion, or undue influence is present.

7.185 In *Lisa Maria Angela Ferguson v British Gas Trading Ltd*[222] the claimant successfully argued that British Gas's course of conduct amounted to unlawful harassment contrary to the Protection from Harassment Act 1997. Sedley LJ stated:

> 'Parliament's intention in passing the Protection from Harassment Act 1997 was to criminalise the kind of serious and persistent unwarranted threat which is alleged here, giving a right of civil action as a fallback. In this situation it ought not to be left to hardy individuals to put their savings and homes at risk by suing. *The primary responsibility should rest upon local public authorities which possess the means and the statutory powers to bring alleged harassers, however impersonal and powerful, before the local justices.*'

7.186 In *OFT v Ashbourne Management Services Ltd*[223] the threat to report customers to credit agencies had no basis because there were no credit agreements, let alone any breach of such agreements. Such threats were therefore aggressive commercial practices. Such conduct was harassment on the basis that there was a threat of action that could not lawfully be taken.[224]

Responsible trading practice

7.187 The concept of harassment in the context of commercial activity is problematic because the enforcement of contractual rights, and in particular debts owed by consumers, is inevitably persistent and necessarily robust. If it was not so, many debtors would simply not pay. There is perhaps a fine line between the reasonable but persistent pursuit of a reluctant debtor and harassment. The focus must surely be upon the reasonableness of the individual

---

[219] Reading ss 1 and 7 of the Protection from Harassment Act 1997 together.
[220] Ibid s 1(3).
[221] *Tuppen v Microsoft Corporation Ltd* (2000) *The Times*, 15 November.
[222] [2009] EWCA Civ 46, [2010] 1 WLR 785.
[223] [2011] EWHC 1237(Ch), [2011] CTLC 237.
[224] See also the Italian decision of the AGCM that sending a notice to appear before a judge, who lacked jurisdiction, and had not received any application from the trader, was aggressive (Decision PS8215 no 24117 of 12 December 2012).

trader's conduct. But that remains a rather grey area in which the line has to be drawn. The factors set out in reg 7(2) are too general to help with many cases and reasonableness (on its own) is an uncertain guide to a tribunal's consideration of a hard edged question. One possible solution would be to approach the question of reasonableness on the basis of good practice within the industry. To decide whether conduct amounted to harassment, for example, the question could be asked: *was it reasonable having regard to the practices generally adopted by responsible practitioners in that industry?* This approach would at least allow traders to avoid criminal liability by following responsible practice within their own industry.

Coercion

7.188 Coercion is not defined in the CPUTR other than by the express inclusion of 'the use of physical force.'[225] The ordinary meaning of 'coercion' is forcing a person to do something involuntarily by threats or intimidation. There is currently no guidance on its meaning from the CJEU. However, in the Polish case *Office of Competition and Consumer Protection v WEH Inwestycje sp*,[226] a debt recovery business sent uniform letters threatening legal action. These letters were sent ahead of the process and were not legally permissible at that stage. The letters were not easy to understand and the purpose was to convince them to repay the debt. It deprived the consumer of making an autonomous and reasonable decision regarding payment. The business was putting wilful pressure on the consumer and the letters were clearly written with the purpose of exerting pressure and using the consumer's inexperience and fear. The facts of this case certainly amounted to harassment. It might also be a marginal example of coercion, in that it involved using threats to force a consumer to act in a certain way. Another example of coercion could be where a trader makes it especially burdensome for customers to terminate their contracts, so that they become trapped in de facto automatic renewals.[227]

7.189 'Coercion' has been defined in other UK legislation. Under s 47 of the Criminal Justice Act 1925 (now repealed) it was a defence for a woman to prove that an offence (except murder or treason) was committed, 'in the presence of, and under the **coercion** of, the husband'. This defence was wider than duress because it did not require threats of death or serious injury. In *R v Shortland*[228] it amounted to the wife being 'overborne by the wishes of her husband' so that 'she was forced unwillingly to participate'.[229] Coercing is also used in s 40 of the Administration of Justice Act 1970 to define the offence of

---

[225] Reg 7(3)(b).
[226] 2010, RWR 32/2010, Poland, Office of Competition and Consumer Protection Delegature.
[227] Bulgarian Supreme Court decision of 3 November 2011 (15182/2011, VII d); Italian decisions PS1268 – TELE2 –ostruzionismo migrazione, Provv. n 20266 del 03/09/2009 (Bollettino n. 36/2009); PS1700 – Tiscali-ostruzionismo passaggio a TELECOM, Provv. n 20349 del 01/10/2009 (Bollettino n 40/2009).
[228] [1996] 1 Cr App R 116.
[229] See also *R v Cairns* [2003] 1 WLR 796, coercion does not require physical force or the threat of physical force.

unlawfully harassing a debtor. It is used in conjunction with various modes (harassment, threats, or false representations) to mean forcing a person to repay a debt.

Undue influence

7.190 'Undue influence' is defined in the CPUTR as 'exploiting a position of power in relation to the consumer so as to apply pressure, even without using or threatening to use physical force, in a way which significantly limits the consumer's ability to make an informed decision'.

7.191 The reference in reg 7(3)(b) to 'in relation to **the consumer**' and to 'significantly limiting **the consumer's** ability to make an informed decision' does not use to the 'average consumer' test that pervades the CPUTR. This is surprising because Art 8 of the UCPD suggests that the test for aggressive practices should be by reference to the average consumer. Regulation 7(3) appears to be a domestic gloss on the UCPD. It is not clear whether this was deliberate or an oversight such that reg 7(3)(b) should have been written 'in a way which would significantly limit the average consumer's ability to make an informed decision' if it was to be faithful to the UCPD.

7.192 The omission does now raise a question as to whether (when the allegation is purely one of undue influence) it is *also* necessary for the prosecution to prove that pressure was applied to an actual consumer (as well as the average consumer) so as to limit significantly his ability to make an informed decision. Put in the negative, would an allegation fail because the pressure did not have this effect on a particularly robust consumer, even though it would have had that effect on the average consumer? The answer to this question may depend upon how the courts construe the difference between the European UCPD and the CPUTR. However, on the literal reading of 'the consumer' in the reg 7(3)(b) of the CPUTR, it may well be necessary to show that the actual consumer's ability to make an informed decision was significantly limited.

7.193 In the German *Gravestone Case*[230] a letter advertising gravestones was sent to the deceased's relatives shortly after a death had taken place. It was held that this was an aggressive commercial practice taking advantage of the circumstances. It could be harassment or undue influence, but the relevant factor was the exploitation by the trader of any specific misfortune or circumstance of such gravity as to impair the consumer's judgement (CPUTR reg 7(2)(c)). A further example of undue influence could be accompanying a consumer to a cash machine to withdraw money,[231] or threatening to publish the consumer's name in a newspaper as a defaulter, in order to put pressure on them to pay a debt.[232]

---

[230] Germany, Higher Regional Court, 2009, 6U 90/08.
[231] See *R v Derek Montague* [2015] EWCA Crim 902 at para 7.
[232] Slovakian decision *Krajsky sud v Presove*, 27 October 2011, 2Co/116/2011.

Undue influence: threatening legal action

7.194 In cases where the trader has threatened to take legal action that he has no right to take (thereby falling within reg 7(2)(e)), undue influence may be easier to identify if it passes the threshold test. *Ashbourne* and *Inwestycje* are examples of cases where such a threat was made.

7.195 A more difficult question arises when a trader merely threatens legal action that he is entitled to take. It is possible that this could be construed as 'undue influence' if the threat is disproportionate or unjustified, particularly as the trader is often in a position of economic 'power' in relation to a consumer. The real question must be whether the trader's conduct significantly limits the consumer's ability to make an *informed* decision. The threat of legal action does not limit the consumer's ability to make an *informed* decision if it is both justified and does not mislead the consumer about his own rights.

Threshold condition

7.196 For an aggressive commercial practice it is also necessary to show that the impairment:

> 'thereby causes him or is likely to cause him to take a transactional decision he would not have taken otherwise' (reg 7(1)(b)).'

Unlawful harassment of debtors

7.197 Section 40 of the Administration of Justice Act 1970 (the unlawful harassment of debtors) remains in force after the introduction of the CPUTR, however, it does not now apply to anything that amounts to a commercial practice under the Regulations.[233] This is likely to confine its operation to non-consumer relationships.

> **Administration of Justice Act 1970**
>
> **40 Punishment for unlawful harassment of debtors**
>
> (1) A person commits an offence if, with the object of coercing another person to pay money claimed from the other as a debt due under a contract, he –
>
> > (a)   harasses the other with demands for payment which, in respect of their frequency or the manner or occasion of making any such demand, or of any threat or publicity by which any demand is accompanied, are calculated to subject him or members of his family or household to alarm, distress or humiliation;
> >
> > (b)   falsely represents, in relation to the money claimed, that criminal proceedings lie for failure to pay it;
> >
> > (c)   falsely represents himself to be authorised in some official capacity to claim or enforce payment; or

---

[233] Section 40(3A) as amended by the CPUTR.

(d)   utters a document falsely represented by him to have some official
        character or purporting to have some official character which he knows
        it has not.

(2) A person may be guilty of an offence by virtue of subsection (1)(a) above if he
concerts with others in the taking of such action as is described in that paragraph,
notwithstanding that his own course of conduct does not by itself amount to
harassment.

(3) Subsection (1)(a) above does not apply to anything done by a person which is
reasonable (and otherwise permissible in law) for the purpose –

(a)   of securing the discharge of an obligation due, or believed by him to be
        due, to himself or to persons for whom he acts, or protecting himself or
        them from future loss; or
(b)   of the enforcement of any liability by legal process.

(3A) Subsection (1) above does not apply to anything done by a person to another
in circumstances where what is done is a commercial practice within the meaning
of the CPUTR and the other is a consumer in relation to that practice.

(4) A person guilty of an offence under this section shall be liable on summary
conviction to a fine of not more than £100, and on a second or subsequent
conviction to a fine of not more than £400.

BANNED PRACTICES

7.198   The CPUTR create a series of banned practices that are to be regarded
as always unfair (reg 3(4)(d)). These are set out in Sch 1 of the CPUTR and
follow the wording of Annex 1 of the UCPD, save that items 1–23 are given the
sub heading 'Misleading Commercial Practices' and items 24–31 are headed
'Aggressive Commercial Practices' in the UCPD. The subheadings are missing
from the CPUTR. Engaging in a commercial practice that is a Sch 1 banned
practice is made an offence by reg 12 (except for paras 11 (advertorials) and 28
(children's advertising)).[234] The crucial difference between banned practices and
the other CPUTR unfair commercial practices is that they do not require proof
of a causative element such as the objective effect upon the average consumer. A
Sch 1 commercial practice will be unfair even if it would not cause the average
consumer to make a different transactional decision.

Mens rea

7.199   Most of the criminal offences created by Sch 1 are of strict liability and
the prosecution will bear the burden of proving each element of the offence to
the criminal standard. Each offence will need to be considered separately,
however, to determine its elements. For example, under reg 13, the prosecution
must prove that the trader promoted a product so as 'deliberately to mislead'.

---

[234] It is important to note that to be liable it must be proven that the trader is engaging in a
    'commercial practice'. Mere proof of the banned practice is insufficient – see C-391/12 *RL v S*
    para 35.

The courts are likely to construe such criminal sanctions to require proof of a *mens rea* (see the analysis of strict liability offences in Chapter 3, Criminal Enforcement).

Scope

7.200 The scope of Sch 1 is relatively broad for a measure that introduces substantial criminal sanctions using general words or phrases, many of which have not been carefully defined. The drafting of Sch 1 follows the UCPD and is sometimes unclear, but nonetheless the guidance from the CJEU is that these provisions must be read literally.[235]

7.201 Some of the difficulties in interpreting the banned practices may be illustrated by looking at paragraph 9, which makes it a criminal offence for a trader to state or otherwise create 'the impression that a product can legally be sold when it cannot.' There is no definition of what 'legally' means. Importantly, there is no distinction made between criminal, regulatory, tort, or contractual rules in relation to what can 'legally' be sold. When considered in this context the scope of the offence is potentially all encompassing. In *R (Vuciterni) v Brent Magistrates Court*[236] it was held that because it was not a criminal offence under s 297A of the Copyright, Designs and Patents Act 1988 to supply decoders in the UK that were meant for the Albanian market that search warrants should be quashed. Once it was decided that there was no underlying criminality, the High Court considered whether the alleged breach of para 9 of Sch 1 to the 2008 Regulations was enough on its own to justify the grant of the warrants. In disagreeing with this Davis LJ said at para 33:

> 'As presented to the District Judge, this case connoted – and was intended to connote – criminal illegality. I find that difficult. Absent s 297A of the 1988 Act, the underlying relevant allegation in its essentials comes down to the claimants selling in the UK decoder cards which they knew were only authorised to be sold in Albania and were only authorised to be for domestic use. That scenario might or might not give rise to a civil liability. But, as at present advised, I think it very debateable as a matter of interpretation whether the word "legally" (by reference to what is "sold") as used in paragraph 9 of Schedule 1 to the 2008 regulations – reflecting the corresponding provision in Annex 1 to Directive 2005/29/EC – extends to such civil wrong doing: the more so when, by Regulation 12, a criminal offence is capable of arising from breach of paragraph 9 of Schedule 1. As put to Mr. Mellor in argument, if a shop owner is subject to a restrictive covenant in his lease not to sell, for example, meat and he, in breach of such a covenant, knowingly proceeds to sell meat to customers is it really to be said that he is in breach of the 2008 Regulations, with a potential criminal sanction? Mr. Mellor himself was disinclined to say that he would be. To the extent that he then sought to say that in the present case the purported sales by Alsat were "nullities", and so – he asserted – within paragraph 9 of Schedule 1, I also found that difficult. On the face of it, and whatever the contractual restrictions purporting to apply, Alsat had property and title in the acquired decoder cards (they were, for example, not stolen

---

[235] C-428/11 *Purely Creative* paras 35, 43 and 45–46.
[236] [2012] EWHC 2140 (Admin), [2012] CTLC 171.

or counterfeit) and which on the face of it, it could transfer to buyers. At all events, nothing was addressed to the District Judge to indicate that, at the very least arguably, something other than criminality under the 2008 regulations might be involved.'

7.202 This leaves open the question of what type of illegality is required for civil injunctive relief. Should there be a different test dependent on whether or not the jurisdiction is civil or criminal? For its part, the European Commission sees two aspects to this prohibition – the situation referred to above where a trader cannot give good title, and secondly where the product may be marketed only under certain conditions or subject to certain restrictions.[237] An example of the second is where a package travel product is marketed by a trader who has not lodged a guarantee deposit, as required by the Package Travel Directive.[238]

CPUTR, Sch 1		Commentary
1	'Claiming to be a signatory to a code of conduct when the trader is not.' reg 2(1): 'code of conduct' means an agreement or set of rules (which is not imposed by legal or administrative requirements), which defines the behaviour of traders who undertake to be bound by it in relation to one or more commercial practices or business sectors.	This makes it automatically unfair to claim to be a signatory to a voluntary code of conduct for business, such as the rules set out by a trade organisation. Rules that are 'imposed by legal or administrative requirements' do not fall within the scope of Paragraph 1. It follows that it would exclude many professional codes of conduct (for example the Bar Code of Conduct) which are imposed by law. Many trade organisations require the trader to pay annual membership fees. The use of the word 'signatory' suggests that the trader's membership of such a scheme would need to be current. It is unlikely to be a defence that the trader was once a signatory to a particular code of conduct; or that he complied by its terms even though he had never been a signatory to it.
2	'Displaying a trust mark, quality mark or equivalent without having obtained the necessary authorisation.'	There is no definition of trust mark or quality mark within the CPUTR and it is broad enough to cover quality marks that are private without any legal basis. What amounts to the necessary authorisation will depend on the particular organisation and its rules.
3	'Claiming that a code of conduct has an endorsement from a public or other body which it does not have.'	This provision targets claims that a code of conduct has the approval by body, when it does not. 'Public or other body' is not defined in the CPUTR. The nature of a public body in law is relatively well understood, however the construction of 'other body' is not.

[237] European Commission Guidance [COM(2016) 320, s 4.1.
[238] Swedish decision of the Market Court 2009:17, *Consumer Ombudsman v Casa Nordica* 26 June 2009.

CPUTR, Sch 1		Commentary
		It remains questionable whether 'other body' might also include a private organisation. The language used in para 4 below is 'public or private body'. A question remains about whether it was intended that this would extend to a private company or individual; such as the claim that a code of conduct was approved by a particular company or famous individual.
4	'Claiming that a trader (including his commercial practices) or a product has been approved, endorsed or authorised by a public or private body when the trader, the commercial practices or the product have not or making such a claim without complying with the terms of the approval endorsement or authorisation.'	The example given in the BERR/OFT guidance to the CPUTR is a plumber claiming he is CORGI-registered when he is not (para 6.1). The expression 'public or private body' does not make it clear that the offence will be committed if the trader refers to an endorsement by an individual. It relates to where the rules lay down requirements to do with the status of the trader or quality of his products.[239]

5	'Making an invitation to purchase products at a specified price without disclosing the existence of any reasonable grounds the trader may have for believing that he will not be able to offer for supply, or to procure another trader to supply, those products or equivalent products at that price for a period that is, and in quantities that are, reasonable having regard to the product, the scale of advertising of the product and the price offered (bait advertising).' reg 2(1) 'invitation to purchase' means a commercial communication which indicates characteristics of the product and the price in a way appropriate to the means of that commercial communication and thereby enables the consumer to make a purchase.'	The elements of this offence are convoluted:
		
		(a) a trader;
		
		(b) made an invitation to purchase;
		
		(c) a product;
		
		(d) at a specified price;
		
		(e) without disclosing any reasonable grounds the trader may have for believing that he will not be able to:
		
		  (i) offer for supply or procure another trader to supply
		
		  (ii) those products or equivalent products
		
		  (iii) at that price;
		
		  (iv) for a period and in quantities that are reasonable having regard to the product, the scale of advertising and the price offered.
		
		The burden of proving all of these elements of the offence are upon the prosecution to the criminal standard. This compares unfavourably to the simpler Misleading Action offence under reg 5 (which includes the availability of the product – reg 5(5)(a)). The only real advantage to pursuing a para 5 offence is that the CPUTR defences are not available. This might be particularly important if the trader blames the unavailability of the product upon a supplier. The BERR/OFT Guidance to the CPUTR gives the following example of an offence under para 5:

---

[239] C-206/11 *Kock* para 39.

CPUTR, Sch 1		Commentary
		A camera firm advertises nationally using the line 'Digital cameras for £3'. They had only ever planned to have a very small number of such cameras available at that price. This would breach the CPRs because the number of cameras actually available for £3 would not be sufficient to meet the likely level of demand arising from the scale of the advertising and the trader knew this but failed to make clear in the advertisement that only limited numbers were available.
6	Making an invitation to purchase products at a specified price and then: (a) refusing to show the advertised item to consumers, (b) refusing to take orders for it or deliver it within a reasonable time, or (c) demonstrating a defective sample of it, with the intention of promoting a different product (bait and switch). See above for the definition of 'invitation to purchase'.	The BERR/OFT Guidance to the CPUTR gives the following example of an offence under para 6: *A trader advertises a television in his shop window for £300. When consumers ask him about it, he shows them a model which does not work properly, and then refers them to a different model of television. If the trader intentionally used this practice to promote a different model (for instance one offering a higher profit margin), it would breach the CPRs.*
7	'Falsely stating that a product will only be available for a very limited time, or that it will only be available on particular terms for a very limited time, in order to elicit an immediate decision and deprive consumers of sufficient opportunity or time to make an informed choice.'	The elements of the offence require the prosecution to prove a very specific dual *mens rea*. The false statement must be made 'in order' to: (a) elicit an immediate decision; **and** (b) deprive consumers of sufficient opportunity or time to make an informed choice. 'In order' most likely implies an element of intention.

CPUTR, Sch 1		Commentary
		The addition of a complex *mens rea* element will inevitably makes the para 7 offence more difficult to prove, particularly when the offence has been committed by a corporate identity. In most cases it will be simpler to prosecute using the reg 5 (misleading actions) or 6 (misleading omissions) offences. The BERR/OFT Guidance to the CPUTR gives the following example of an offence under para 7: '*A trader falsely tells a consumer that prices for new houses will be increased in 7 days' time, in order to pressurise him into making an immediate decision to buy.*' There is some discussion of the harm of having a practice of creating unnecessary time limits on sales in *Official Receiver v Wild*.[240]
8	'Undertaking to provide after-sales service to consumers with whom the trader has communicated prior to a transaction in a language which is not an official language of the EEA State where the trader is located and then making such service available only in another language without clearly disclosing this to the consumer before the consumer is committed to the transaction.'	The BERR/OFT Guidance to the CPUTR gives the following example of an offence under para 8: '*A trader based in the UK agrees to provide after-sales service to a consumer with whom he has been communicating in German. The trader then provides after-sales services only in English, without warning the consumer pre-contract that that would be the case. This would breach the CPRs.*'
9	'Stating or otherwise creating the impression that a product can legally be sold when it cannot.'	The BERR/OFT Guidance to the CPUTR gives the following example of an offence under para 9: '*A trader offers goods for sale in circumstances in which the consumer cannot legally become their owner by buying them from him, for instance because they have been stolen and he has no legal title to pass on. This would breach the CPRs.*' It is necessary for the prosecution to prove that the product in question cannot be legally sold. It is questionable whether this adds much to the existing law if the illegality is confined to criminal offences preventing sale; for example stolen property, where there are simple charges under the Theft Act that are preferable.

---

[240] [2012] EWHC 4279.

CPUTR, Sch 1		Commentary
		A more interesting potential application of para 9 is to cases where there has been the sale of a product that contravenes civil law, for example in breach of tortious or contractual duties. If para 9 is construed broadly it has the potential to criminalise vast areas of what would historically have been civil commercial dispute. See, however, the observations of Davis LJ in the *Brent Magistrates Court* case referred to in the discussion above on the scope of banned practices. It is likely that this prohibition should be restricted to situations where there is a statutory restriction on selling a product.[241]
10	'Presenting rights given to consumers in law as a distinctive feature of the trader's offer.'	The BERR/OFT Guidance to the CPUTR gives the following example of an offence under para 10: '*A stationer sells pens. He advertises on the following basis: 'Pens for sale. If they don't work I'll give you your money back or replace them. You won't find this offer elsewhere'. If the pen is faulty at the time of purchase the consumer would be entitled to a refund, repair or replacement under contract law. The trader's emphasis on the unique nature of his offer to refund or replace would breach the CPRs.*'
11	'Using editorial content in the media to promote a product where a trader has paid for the promotion without making that clear in the content or by images or sounds clearly identifiable by the consumer (advertorial).'	A breach of para 11 is expressly **not** a criminal offence under the CPUTR (see reg 11). The BERR/OFT Guidance to the CPUTR gives the following example of an offence under para 11: '*A magazine is paid by a holiday company for an advertising feature on their luxury Red Sea diving school. The magazine does not make it clear that this is a paid-for feature – for example by clearly labelling it 'Advertising Feature' or 'Advertorial'. This would breach the CPRs.*'
12	'Making a materially inaccurate claim concerning the nature and extent of the risk to the personal security of the consumer or his family if the consumer does not purchase the product.'	The expression 'materially inaccurate' is a different term to the other definitions of misleading statements in the CPUTR. It is not clear whether it will be construed any differently to the tests in reg 5 or 6. The claim must be in relation to 'personal security'. This is not a term that is defined in the CPUTR but is likely to be confined to claims concerning personal safety, for example protection from offences against the person, rather than a broader meaning to include any risk of personal injury.

---

[241] See European Commission Guidance [COM(2016) 320, s 4.1.

CPUTR, Sch 1		Commentary
		The BERR/OFT Guidance to the CUPTR gives the following example of an offence under para 12: *'A trader selling video door entry systems tells potential customers 'There have been a lot of doorstep muggings in your street recently. There is clearly a gang at work in this area, and you will probably be mugged on your doorstep too, before very long, unless you purchase one of my door entry systems now'. If the risk of doorstep mugging is materially exaggerated the statement would breach the CPRs.'*
13	'Promoting a product similar to a product made by a particular manufacturer in such a manner as deliberately to mislead the consumer into believing that the product is made by that same manufacturer when it is not.'	The expression 'deliberately to mislead' generates a *mens rea* that the defendant intended to mislead, not only intended to promote a product that did in fact mislead. The prosecution must prove this to the criminal standard. The BERR/OFT Guidance to the CPUTR gives the following example of an offence under para 13: *'A trader designs the packaging of shampoo A so that it very closely resembles that of shampoo B, an established brand of a competitor. If the similarity was introduced to deliberately mislead consumers into believing that shampoo A is made by the competitor (who makes shampoo B) – this would breach the CPRs.'*
14	'Establishing, operating or promoting a pyramid promotional scheme where a consumer gives consideration for the opportunity to receive compensation that is derived primarily from the introduction of other consumers into the scheme rather than from the sale or consumption of products.'	The BERR/OFT Guidance to the CPUTR gives the following example of an offence under para 14: *'A trader operates a holiday club which offers consumers, on payment of a membership fee, the opportunity of earning large amounts of money by recruiting other consumers to membership of the club. The other benefits of club membership are negligible compared to the potential rewards of earning commission for introducing new members. This practice would breach the CPRs.'*

CPUTR, Sch 1		Commentary
		The CJEU gave some guidance on this in *4finance UAB v Valstybine*.[242] It held that a scheme could only come within this paragraph if (1) the members of the scheme gave some financial consideration, but the amount of the consideration was irrelevant, and (2) there was a link between the consideration given by new members and the compensation received by existing members. In other words, most of the revenue does not come from real economic activity. Examples of unlawful pyramid schemes include three Italian decisions where the compensation was based on the number of new sales agents recruited,[243] the registration fee paid by new agents on joining,[244] and initial subscriptions to a programme of personal purchases.[245] See also a Polish decision against a scheme where new entrants had to make a cash donation to existing participants.[246] See also an OFT/CMA prosecution of a Bristol based pyramid scheme, involving cash payments by new joiners.[247] Further discussion of this banned practice is contained in the recently published Commission Guidance.[248]
15	'Claiming that the trader is about to cease trading or move premises when he is not.'	The BERR/OFT Guidance to the CPUTR gives the following example of an offence under para 15: *'A trader runs a clothes shop. He puts up a sign in the shop window stating: 'Closing down sale'. Unless the shop was genuinely closing down this would breach the CPRs.'*
16	'Claiming that products are able to facilitate winning in games of chance.'	'Games of chance' are not defined in the CPUTR. It is likely that the provision was designed to cover only those games that are purely games of chance, such as lotteries. It cannot have been intended to criminalise any product that claims to be able to facilitate winning in games that involve an element of both chance and skill, for example card games. The OFT Guidance to the CUPTR gives the following example of an offence under para 16: *'A trader advertises a computer program with the claim: 'This will help you win money on scratchcard lotteries'. This would breach the CPRs.'*

---

[242] C-515/12, [2014] Bus LR 574, [2014] 3 CMLR 33 at paras 20 and 34.
[243] AGCM PS6425 15 December 2010.
[244] AGCM PS4893 2 August 2012.
[245] AGCM PS7621 5 February 2014.
[246] Office of Competition and Consumer Protection decision No RKR 34/2014.
[247] https://www.gov.uk/cma-cases/prosecution-of-a-number-of-individuals-involved-in-an-alleged-unlawful-pyramid-scheme
[248] See Commission Guidance [COM(2016) 320] s 4.2.

CPUTR, Sch 1	Commentary
17	'Falsely claiming that a product is able to cure illnesses, dysfunction or malformations.'	This provision will require the prosecution to prove that the claim is false to the criminal standard. This could prove to be a complex exercise in many cases, requiring medical evidence to be adduced by the prosecution. 'Malformation' is not defined in the CPUTR but has a medical usage that equates to a deformity or an abnormal growth or structure. It is likely to be relevant to look at this prohibition in conjunction with other EU legislation on sales of medication.[249] Examples of cases brought in other EU states include a Polish ruling on claims that a massage armchair could cure spine and blood circulation problems,[250] and a Lithuanian case against a trader who claimed its products could reduce pain, improve sleep and decrease wrinkles, but could not substantiate its claims.[251]
		The BERR/OFT Guidance to the CPUTR gives the following example of an offence under para 17: *'A trader sells orthopaedic beds to the elderly with the advertisement 'Cure your backache once and for all with my special beds'. If untrue, his definitive statement about the curative effects of his product would breach the CPRs.'*
		The BERR/OFT Guidance goes on to say that: *'The court may order the trader to substantiate such a claim in proceedings.'*
		The CPUTR (reg 27) inserted s 218A (Unfair commercial practices: substantiation of claims) into the Enterprise Act 2002. Where an application for an enforcement order is made, the court, for the purposes of considering the application, may require the person named in the application to provide evidence as to the accuracy of any factual claim made as part of a commercial practice of that person if, taking into account the legitimate interests of that person and any other party to the proceedings, it appears appropriate in the circumstances. The court may consider that the factual claim is inaccurate if the person fails to provide such evidence or provides evidence as to the accuracy of the factual claim that the court considers inadequate.

---

[249] See Commission Guidance [COM(2016) 320] s 4.3 for a fuller discussion.
[250] Office for Competition and Consumer Protection Decision RPZ 2/2012, 13 March 2012,
[251] 2S-17 Lietuvos Respublikos konkurencijos taryba, 4 November 2011.

CPUTR, Sch 1		Commentary

18	'Passing on materially inaccurate information on market conditions or on the possibility of finding the product with the intention of inducing the consumer to acquire the product at conditions less favourable than normal market conditions.'	This is a convoluted provision. It requires the prosecution to prove to the criminal standard that the trader:
		
		(a) passed on;
		
		(b) materially inaccurate information on;
		
		   (i) market conditions; or
		
		   (ii) the possibility of finding a product
		
		(c) with the intention of inducing a customer to acquire the product at conditions less favourable than normal market conditions.
		
		The BERR/OFT Guidance to the CPUTR gives the following example of an offence under para 18:
		'An estate agent tells a consumer that he has recently sold several houses in the same area, just like the one the consumer is viewing, at a certain price. If this is not true and he is making the claim in order to persuade the consumer to buy at an inflated price, the estate agent would breach the CPRs.'

19	'Claiming in a commercial practice to offer a competition or prize promotion without awarding the prizes described or a reasonable equivalent.'	The BERR/OFT Guidance to the CPUTR gives the following example of an offence under para 19: *'A trader operates a scratch-card prize promotion with a top prize of £10,000. In fact, he does not print any cards that win this top prize (or does print the cards but does not make them available). As this would mean that no prizes of £10,000 could be awarded, this would breach the CPRs.'* A Czech court decision ruled against a practice where a trader gave the false impression that consumers could win a prize of a laptop, by participating in a lottery. However, no such prize could be won.[252]

---

[252] Prague City Court, 29 October 2014 *Golden Gate Marketing v Czech Trade Inspection Authority*.

CPUTR, Sch 1		Commentary
20	'Describing a product as 'gratis', 'free', 'without charge' or similar if the consumer has to pay anything other than the unavoidable cost of responding to the commercial practice and collecting or paying for delivery of the item.'	The BERR/OFT Guidance to the CPUTR gives the following example of an offence under para 20: *'A trader advertises a 'free' gift. He then tells consumers that in order to receive their 'free' gift they need to pay an extra fee. This would breach the CPRs.'* There has been considerable discussion of the application of this prohibition to combined offers. The view of the European Commission is that a combined offer is acceptable as long as the trader does not alter the price of the single item, or the quality of the product being offered. Further, where products are always sold in a combination, one part of that should not be marketed as 'free'.[253] Examples of practices found to have fallen foul of this prohibition include, offering a mobile phone for free as part of a subscription, but then increasing the monthly instalments,[254] offering credit as 'free' when the consumer has to purchase credit insurance to get the offered loan, offering a buy one get one free offer when the price of the paid for item had doubled,[255] claiming a social media service is free when in fact the trader's revenues are derived from analysing users' private data and selling targeted advertising space.[256] The EU CPC authorities also take the view that it could be contrary to this banned practice to describe an app based or online game as 'free' if in fact it is necessary to make in game purchases in order to play it as the consumer would reasonably expect.
21	'Including in marketing material an invoice or similar document seeking payment which gives the consumer the impression that he has already ordered the marketed product when he has not.'	The BERR/OFT Guidance to the CPUTR gives the following example of an offence under para 21: *'A trader sends letters to consumers with his marketing material which are or closely resemble invoices for a product that has not been ordered. This would breach the CPRs.'*

---

[253] Commission Guidance [COM(2016) 320] s 4.4.
[254] Swedish Market Court joint judgments Dnr B 2/11 and B 3/11 11 May 2012.
[255] 2S-27 Lietuvos Respublikos konkurencijos taryba 11 November 2010.
[256] Germany – *Verbraucherzentrale Bundesverband v Facebook* Landgericht Berlin Az. 160341/15. This case is similar to an Italian decision of the AGCM under Directive 84/450/EEC on misleading advertising, that it is unlawful to offer a service for free when in fact the condition is that the consumer's internet use will be tracked and they have to receive commercial communications – see PI2671.

CPUTR, Sch 1		Commentary
22	'Falsely claiming or creating the impression that the trader is not acting for purposes relating to his trade, business, craft or profession, or falsely representing oneself as a consumer.'	The BERR/OFT Guidance to the CPUTR gives the following example of an offence under para 22: *'A second-hand car dealership puts a used car on a nearby road and displays a handwritten advertisement reading 'One careful owner. Good family run-around. £2000 or nearest offer. Call Jack on 01234 56789'. The sign gives the impression that the seller is not selling as a trader, and hence this would breach the CPRs.'* In *R v Scott King*[257] the defendant advertised and sold 58 vehicles as a private seller, whereas the reality was that this formed part of his business activities. The reason that he did this was to avoid providing a guarantee or warranty. He was prosecuted for contravening paragraph 22, pleaded guilty and was sentenced to a community order and was made the subject of a confiscation order in the sum of £109,970. This practice is particularly relevant to the creation of online reviews, which a number of enforcement authorities have investigated. The CMA has taken civil enforcement action under Part 8 of the Enterprise Act against firms that create fake reviews, which purport to be from consumers.
23	'Creating the false impression that after-sales service in relation to a product is available in an EEA State other than the one in which the product is sold.'	A European Economic Area (EEA) State includes all European Members States and Norway, Iceland, and Liechtenstein.
24	'Creating the impression that the consumer cannot leave the premises until a contract is formed.'	There is an overlap in this offence with a reg 7 (aggressive commercial practice) offence. The BERR/OFT Guidance to the CPUTR gives the following example of an offence under para 24: *'A holiday company advertise sales presentations at hotels. During the presentations, intimidating doormen are posted at all the exits, creating the impression that the consumers cannot leave before buying. This would breach the CPRs.'*
25	'Conducting personal visits to the consumer's home ignoring the consumer's request to leave or not to return, except in circumstances and to the extent justified to enforce a contractual obligation.'	The BERR/OFT Guidance to the CPUTR gives the following example of an offence under para 25: *'A door to door salesman visits a consumer to sell her some cleaning products. She tells him she is not interested and asks him to leave. He is determined to try and get her to change her mind and continues his sales pitch on her doorstep. This would breach the CPRs.'* This practice also applies to collection of legitimate debts, since it prohibits visits which go beyond 'the extent justified' to enforce the debt.

---

[257] [2014] 2 Cr App R (S) 54.

CPUTR, Sch 1		Commentary
26	'Making persistent and unwanted solicitations by telephone, fax, email or other remote media except in circumstances and to the extent justified to enforce a contractual obligation.'	There may be an overlap with reg 7 aggressive commercial Practices. The BERR/OFT Guidance to the CPUTR gives the following example of an offence under para 26: *'A direct seller telephones consumers to sell them products, but does not record when consumers have explicitly asked to be removed from their contact lists. The trader calls back consumers several times, who have asked him not to. This would breach the CPRs.'* Note that a consumer who has signed up to the Telephone Preference Service is likely to be regarded as a consumer who does not want unsolicited telephone calls. The recent Commission Guidance[258] reiterates that this ban does not prohibit distance marketing per se, but rather persistent and unwanted solicitations. In an Austrian case an insurance adviser searched for reports of accidents and then sent letters to the victims offering advice. The Austrian Supreme Court ruled that sending a single letter to a person does not qualify as 'persistent and unwanted solicitations' within the meaning of paragraph 26.[259]
27	'Requiring a consumer who wishes to claim on an insurance policy to produce documents which could not reasonably be considered relevant as to whether the claim was valid, or failing systematically to respond to pertinent correspondence, in order to dissuade a consumer from exercising his contractual rights.'	The provision creates an offence for an insurance company that deters claims by requiring the production of irrelevant documents by claimants. The language used is clumsy and makes it unclear whether the second part of the provision 'failing systematically to respond' creates a more general offence that applies outside the insurance industry. In our view, it is likely to create two separate offences, the second of which is not confined to consumers making an insurance claim. This is based principally on the use of the words, 'requiring a consumer who wishes to claim on an insurance policy to ...', which cannot then be read grammatically with, 'failing systematically to respond ...'.

---

[258] Commission Guidance [COM(2016) 320] s 4.5.
[259] 4 Ob 174/09f, OGH (Oberster Gerichtshof), 19 January 2010.

CPUTR, Sch 1		Commentary
28	'Including in an advertisement a direct exhortation to children to buy advertised products or persuade their parents or other adults to buy advertised products for them.'	A breach of para 11 is expressly not a criminal offence under the CPUTR (see reg 11). This is a surprisingly broad prohibition. The plain English meaning of 'exhortation' is capable of including both the process of exhorting and persuading or encouraging. However, the broadness of this prohibition is tempered somewhat by the requirement that such exhortation be 'direct'. The prohibition extends to exhortations to buy which made in games, which are directed towards children, or are otherwise likely to appeal to children.[260] The Swedish Market Court found that 'buy more', 'buy here', 'upgrade now' and 'upgrade to superstar' (where each of these involved spending real money in a game) were direct exhortations to children.[261] The OFT previously gave guidance (since adopted by the CMA) on what practices might be more and less likely to comply with this provision.[262] The Commission Guidance[263] provides further discussion of this banned practice and states that the assessment of whether something falls foul of the provision must be carried out on a case-by-case basis.
		The BERR/OFT Guidance to the CPUTR gives the following example of an offence under para 28: '*Advertising a comic book for children stating "read about the adventures of Fluffy the Bunny in this new comic book each week – ask your mum to buy it from your local newsagents". This (telling children to ask their mothers) would breach the CPRs.*'
29	'Demanding immediate or deferred payment for or the return or safekeeping of products supplied by the trader, but not solicited by the consumer.	The BERR/OFT Guidance to the CPUTR gives the following example of an offence under para 29: '*A trader writes to consumers informing them of a new grease eradicating dishcloth which he is selling for £2.99. In the letter the trader encloses one of the cloths for the consumer to inspect and says that if the consumer does not return the cloth within 7 days then action will be taken to collect the £2.99. This would breach the CPRs.*'

[260] The EU CPC authorities took the view in their common position on this matter that the prohibition will apply if the trader could reasonably be expected to foresee that the game is likely to appeal to children.

[261] MD 2012:14, Marknadsdomstolen, 6 December 2012, *Stardoll*. This decision was relied on by the Norwegian Market Council, who ruled that encouraging Justin Bieber fane to purchase RIMI cards and concert tickets, was contrary to Practice 28.

[262] https://www.gov.uk/government/publications/principles-for-online-and-app-based-games

[263] Commission Guidance [COM(2016) 320] s 4.6.

CPUTR, Sch 1	Commentary
30	'Explicitly informing a consumer that if he does not buy the product or service, the trader's job or livelihood will be in jeopardy.'	It would appear that the offence is committed even if the consumer does not purchase the product. Whether or not the trader's claims are accurate is irrelevant.
31	'Creating the false impression that the consumer has already won, will win, or will on doing a particular act win, a prize or other equivalent benefit, when in fact either: (a) there is no prize or other equivalent benefit, or (b) taking any action in relation to claiming the prize or other equivalent benefit is subject to the consumer paying money or incurring a cost.'	There are two limbs to this provision – either there is no prize, or it will cost the consumer money to obtain the prize. An example of the first limb is where a trader stated in a letter to a consumer that he had won 18,000 euros, when in fact he had not.[264] The second limb was considered in *OFT v Purely Creative Ltd* [2011] EWHC 106 (Ch) where the OFT argued that the provision would be infringed if (regardless of the value of the prize) the process of claiming the prize involved the 'winner having to post a letter (other than a prepaid letter) or make a minimum charge telephone call or pay for a short bus journey to go and collect it from somewhere too far to reach by walking. This was rejected by the High Court on the basis that the critical requirement in para 31 was that a 'false impression was created.' The imposition of some clearly identified minimal cost was not sufficient to make out the prohibition. However, this was reversed by the CJEU (Case C-428/11, 18 October 2012), the first time that an Annex 1 prohibition had been considered by the CJEU. The court considered that all such practices are prohibited even when the cost imposed on the consumer is minimal (as in the case of a stamp) compared with the value of the prize, and regardless of whether the payment of such costs procures any benefits to the trader. The trader may not even invite the consumer to spend money, or offer any paid claim route, even if there is a free route available (para 50).[265] The BERR/OFT Guidance to the CPUTR gives the following example of an offence under para 31:

---

[264] Spain – *Audencia Provincial de Barcelona*, 26 June 2014, 323/2014.

[265] See also a Dutch case where consumers were told they were 100% guaranteed to receive an electronic product, when in fact they had to respond within two days and pay 19.99 euros for 'administration and transport costs.' This practice was held also to fall foul of banned practice 20. Case CA/NB/544/10 *Consumentenautoriteit*, 21 September 2010, Garant-o-Matic BV.

CPUTR, Sch 1	Commentary
	'*A trader sends letters to consumers which, at the top of the letter in large characters, state: 'You have won our top prize of £3,000. 'This is false – only the small print on the back of the letter mentions that the consumer must buy a product before being entered into a draw for the money. This would breach the CPRs.*' This guidance was provided before the *OFT v Purely Creative* decision. The recent Commission Guidance[266] further discusses this prohibition and some case law from member states. In relation to the first limb the Prague City Court found that a trader had created the false impression that consumers could win a prize by stating that everyone who participated in a specific lottery would have the chance to win a laptop computer when in reality no such computer could be won.[267] The Spanish *Audencia* case is also discussed.[268] Under the second limb the Netherlands Authority for Consumers and Markets considered the case of a mail order company that sent promotional advertising by post saying that a consumer was guaranteed to receive an electronic product free of charge. In fact, the consumer had to respond within 2 days and pay 19 Euros to cover costs. This was held to give consumer the false impression that they have already won a prize while requiring them to pay a fee and thus contravened paragraph 31.

THE PRIVATE RIGHT TO REDRESS

7.203 The Consumer Protection (Amendment) Regulations 2014 provide a private right of redress in respect of certain infringements, where the consumer has entered a contract or paid money after 1 October 2014. It is a civil right enforceable as a breach of contract (reg 27K).[269] It applies only to misleading actions and aggressive practices, and the practice must have an actual impact on the specific decisions the consumer makes, ie to enter a contract for the trader to supply a product to the consumer (or for the consumer to supply a product to the trader) or to make a payment to the trader (reg 27B).[270]

7.204 There are five steps necessary to prove to establish the right of redress:

(1)   The practice is within scope.

---

[266]   Commission Guidance [COM(2016) 320] s 4.7.

[267]   Prague City Court, 29 October 2014, *Golden Gate Marketing v Czech Trade Inspection Authority*.

[268]   See n 289 above.

[269]   It is considered that absent these provisions, consumers have no other private rights of redress under the CPRs – see *Abbot & Ors v RCI Europe* [2016] EWHC 2602 (Ch) para 56.

[270]   Where the consumer supplies an item in part exchange for a product from the trader, this is treated as a business to consumer supply.

(2) It is a misleading action or aggressive practice.

(3) It is carried out by a trader or with the trader's knowledge.

(4) It was a significant factor in causing the consumer making the complaint to take a specific transactional decision.

(5) It would have caused the average consumer to take the transactional decision.

7.205 Regulation 27A describes the scope of the redress right, including some exclusions (notably most immovable property and financial services). The requirement that the misleading action or aggressive practice must have a significant impact on the consumer's decision making is set out in reg 27A(6). It does not have to be the only or main cause, but it should be possible to describe how the practice changed the consumer's decision making, and what they would have done otherwise. The requirement to prove the impact on the average consumer is because this is necessary to prove the breach of the CPUTR in the first place. Depending on the circumstances, it may also be relevant to consider the impact on the average vulnerable or targeted consumer – if the complainant is within one of these categories.

The rights

7.206 Where the consumer establishes that they have a right to redress, these rights are the right to unwind the contract, the right to a discount and the right to damages. Bringing a claim under these provisions exhausts all other rights the consumer might otherwise have against the trader. In order to unwind a contract, the consumer must clearly indicate that the contract is at an end, and the effect is to release both parties from their obligations.

7.207 Where the trader has supplied goods to the consumer:

- The right is only available if the product remains capable of rejection –so not fully consumed or fully performed[271] – and if the consumer has not already exercised their right to a discount.

- The consumer must reject the product within 90 days of delivery or start of performance.

- Any goods must be made available for the trader to collect.

- The trader must refund the consumer any money, and restore any item the consumer has given them, in its original state, or by paying the market price if this is not possible.[272]

7.208 Where the consumer has supplied an item to the trader:

- The trader must return the goods, unless he is not able to, in which case he must pay the amount by which the market price exceeds the price he paid.

---

[271] Reg 27E.
[272] Reg 27F.

- The consumer must pay back any money they received.[273]

The right to a discount applies where the right to unwind is lost, or not used, and the contract continues to exist. For most contracts involving payments of less than £5,000, it requires an assessment of the seriousness of the practice in order to identify how much the consumer should be reimbursed. The position envisaged by the legislation is that reimbursement will be on a fixed scale of 25% if it is more than minor, 50% if significant, 75% if serious and 100% if very serious. The assessment of seriousness is based on a consideration of the behaviour of the trader, the impact on the consumer and the time elapsed since the practice took place.[274]

7.209   Where the contract price is above £5,000, and there is clear evidence of what the market price actually was, the discount must equate to whatever this difference is. So for example if a trader sold a consumer a mobility aid for £6,500, but in fact the market value of that mobility aid was only £3,000 (and there is clear evidence of this), then the right to a discount would be £3,500. If, however, there is not clear evidence of what the market price should be, then it would seem the normal rules would apply, and the discount could be up to 100%.

7.210   The right to damages applies in addition to the rights to unwind or get a refund. It applies where:

- the prohibited practice causes financial loss (beyond that incurred in entering the contract) or alarm, distress or physical inconvenience or discomfort; and
- this harm was reasonably foreseeable at the time of the practice; and
- the trader is unable to prove the due diligence defence set out in reg 27J(5).

Although not set out in the legislation, the government guidance on the right of redress expects these damages to be 'restrained and modest'.

DEFENCES UNDER THE CPUTR

7.211

> **CPUTR, regs 17, 18**
>
> **Due diligence defence**
>
> 17(1) In any proceedings against a person for an offence under regulation 9, 10, 11 or 12 it is a defence for that person to prove –
>
> (a)   that the commission of the offence was due to –

---

[273]   Reg 27G.
[274]   Reg 27I.

> (i) a mistake;
> (ii) reliance on information supplied to him by another person;
> (iii) the act or default of another person;
> (iv) an accident; or
> (v) another cause beyond his control; and
>
> (b) that he took all reasonable precautions and exercised all due diligence to avoid the commission of such an offence by himself or any person under his control.

(2) A person shall not be entitled to rely on the defence provided by paragraph (1) by reason of the matters referred to in paragraph (ii) or (iii) of paragraph (1)(a) without leave of the court unless –

> (a) he has served on the prosecutor a notice in writing giving such information identifying or assisting in the identification of that other person as was in his possession; and
> (b) the notice is served on the prosecutor at least seven clear days before the date of the hearing.

Innocent publication of advertisement defence

18 (1) In any proceedings against a person for an offence under regulation 9, 10, 11 or 12 committed by the publication of an advertisement it shall be a defence for a person to prove that –

> (a) he is a person whose business it is to publish or to arrange for the publication of advertisements;
> (b) he received the advertisement for publication in the ordinary course of business; and
> (c) he did not know and had no reason to suspect that its publication would amount to an offence under the regulation to which the proceedings relate.

(2) In paragraph (1) "advertisement" includes a catalogue, a circular and a price list.

The reg 17 defence is now considered in Chapter 3, Criminal Enforcement.

SENTENCING UNDER THE CPUTR

7.212 Regulation 13 of the CPUTR provides that:

> 13 'A person guilty of an offence under regulations 8, 9, 10, 11 or 12 shall be liable –
>
> (a) on summary conviction, to a fine not exceeding the statutory maximum; or
> (b) on conviction on indictment, to a fine or imprisonment for a term not exceeding two years or both.

It should be noted that the statutory limit on fines imposed after summary conviction was removed by s 85 of the Legal Aid, Sentencing and Punishment of Offenders Act 2012. Consequently, on summary conviction offenders now face an unlimited fine.

7.213   There will still be many cases that are suitable for summary disposal in the magistrates' courts. However, where a commercial practice has affected a large number of consumers, or where the behaviour was systemic, coercive, or dishonest, significant sentences can be expected from the Crown Court. There are no guidelines from the Sentencing Guidelines Council in relation to CPUTR offences, nor is there a guideline sentencing case from the Court of Appeal (Criminal Division). In *R v Stone*[275] it was held that the Sentencing Guidelines for Fraud should not be applied to sentencing under the CPUTR because the guidance was predicated upon dishonesty, which is not an essential ingredient for CPUTR. However, it is anticipated that (particularly in cases involving large corporate defendants) the courts will adopt a similar approach to that mandated in the sentencing guidelines on health and safety offences, corporate manslaughter, and food safety and hygiene offences.

7.214   The largest fine imposed under CPUTR is £1.2m by the Recorder of Guildford in *R v Scottish and Southern Energy PLC*.[276] The facts of this case are set out in the section above on 'scope of commercial practice'. This is a paradigm example of the level of punishment that might be expected for an unfair commercial practice that affected a large number of consumers. In this case, the judge imposed a sentence of this magnitude because the offending script had been used in doorstep sales presentations to 300,000 consumers.

7.215   In *Henry and Victor Mears*[277] the defendants were found guilty of eight offences under CPUTR following a 10-week trial at Bristol Crown Court in relation to the 'Lapland New Forest'. Both men were sentenced to 13 months' imprisonment and also disqualified for a period of 5 years under the Company Directors Disqualification Act 1986. The Mears were charged with misleading acts contrary to reg 9 and misleading omissions contrary to reg 10 on the grounds that they had allowed the company to give descriptions of various features of the attraction in its advertising material that were either not present at all or which fell far short of what was actually provided. Trading standards officers viewed the company's website, obtained advertising material from local shops, and visited the attraction itself. They considered that the descriptions given in the advertisements were misleading in various respects. This case went to the Court of Appeal (Criminal Division),[278] where the conviction was quashed as a result of jury irregularity.

7.216   In the case of *R v John Lawrence Connolly*[279] a director of a company called Homesure Home Improvements Ltd, which was in the business of replacement windows and doors, was sentenced to 5 months' imprisonment for two CPUTR offences, including a month's imprisonment for breaching a two year conditional discharge for a CPUTR offence. He was also disqualified for 5 years under the Company Directors Disqualification Act 1986. Both offences

---

[275]   *R v Stone* and *R v Moore* [2012] EWCA Civ 186.
[276]   [2012] CTLC 1.
[277]   Before HHJ Horton and a jury [2011] EWCA Crim 2651.
[278]   [2011] EWCA Crim 2651, (2011) 108(45) LSG 21.
[279]   [2012] EWCA Crim 477, Official Transcript.

involved the use of aggressive tactics during disputes over the quality of his company's jobs. In one instance, he had instructed the fitters to remove the windows unless the customer paid in full. The customer paid, feeling that he had no option. The judge in sentencing found that an incident involving an old age pensioner was an aggressive practice. The trader had demanded payment there and then and put fear into the customer by saying that, if payment was not made, the customer's home would be left without the door and fittings. A similar incident occurred involving a second victim. The tactic of 'pay up or shut up', as the judge described it, was a mean spirited and cruel way to conduct business. The judge, in concluding his sentencing remarks, said: 'This defendant … is unfit to be a director in my view and he was responsible for issuing the rather cruel instructions of removing the property. I am told that was on a misunderstanding. I don't think it was at all, it is just called bullying. "Pay up and shut up", that was the manner in which business was conducted by his employees on his direct instruction.' On appeal against sentence, Dobbs J said: 'Looking at the overall sentence and the mitigation, in our judgment, the sentence whilst tough and intentionally so cannot be said to be manifestly excessive. It follows therefore that this appeal against sentence must fail.'

7.217 In *R v Williams and Stagg*[280] the defendants were charged with offences relating to car clamping activities which involved the extortion of considerable sums of money from members of the public whose vehicles they had clamped by bullying and threatening behaviour. Williams also pleaded guilty to an offence under the CPUTR, contrary to reg 11 and was given a total sentence of 5 years and 6 months' imprisonment (including CPUTR offence, 1 year's imprisonment to be served concurrently). On appeal the sentence of 4 years for conspiracy was quashed, and in its place a sentence of 3 years' imprisonment imposed. However, the remaining sentences stood, including the one in respect of the CPUTR offence.

7.218 In a case prosecuted by the OFT, Colin Michael Ogle pleaded guilty to five charges under the CPUTR and eight charges under s 2 of the Fraud Act 2006 in relation to his business offering a 'mileage adjustment service'. Ogle also agreed to a further 19 offences being taken into consideration. The matter was committed to Swindon Crown Court[281] for sentence where Ogle was jailed for 9 months. The sentencing judge said:

> 'The second-hand car market affects us all. Mileage significantly affects the market. Consumers rely on mileage when making purchasing decisions. It is the second biggest purchase consumers make after property and for others it is the single biggest purchase. The clocking of cars corrupts the market and brings unjustified suspicion on honest traders.'

7.219 In the first private prosecution under the CPUTR (*House of Cars v Derby Car and Van Contracts Ltd*[282]), an internet car broker pleaded guilty to

---

[280] [2012] EWCA Crim 1483, [2013] 1 Cr App R (S) 70.
[281] His Honour Judge Ambrose.
[282] [2012] CTLC 62.

engaging in a commercial practice that was a misleading omission and was fined £500 and ordered to pay £3,000 in prosecution costs. The defendant sold cars to consumers but registered them initially in the name and address of a third party company in order to obtain a 'fleet car' discount from the car manufacturer. A consumer that purchased a car from the defendants would own and use the car from the outset, however the vehicle would not be DVLA registered in the consumer's name and address until a period of 4 to 6 months had elapsed. The defendant failed to warn purchasers that during this period they were at risk of being prosecuted for an offence under s 43C of the Vehicle Excise and Registration Act 1994 or that a claim made against a car insurance policy might be prejudiced by the commercial practice. The defendant argued that no offence was committed under s 43C and that the risk of insurance being prejudiced was notional. The judge indicated the future sentences would be much higher because the unlawfulness was now no longer novel.

7.220 In *R v Garfoot and Wilsher*[283] Henry Wilsher was a traveller who resided on a caravan park and ran a business, trading as H W Block Paving and Landscaping Specialists. Wilsher was concerned that, if he informed customers of the true business address, they would, prejudicially, not employ him, so he asked his employee, John Garfoot, if he could use his address for the business instead. Garfoot agreed. Flyers were produced bearing this false address and an unregistered pay-as-you-go phone number. Prosecutions were brought by Leicester City Trading Standards in connection with two separate transactions, where the complainants were an 85-year-old woman and (concerning Wilsher alone) a 75-year-old man. Garfoot pleaded guilty to three offences involving his single incident. He was sentenced to 6 months' imprisonment for an offence under reg 8 of CPUTR (in respect of the fact that no cancellation rights were explained or communicated); no separate penalty was passed in respect of two charges of fraud (dishonestly made representations as to the location of the business which gave a false impression as to its pedigree and reputation). The central figure responsible, Wilsher – who had previously been warned by trading standards officers in 2006 and 2007 – was sentenced to 10 months' imprisonment (to run concurrently) for two similar reg 8 matters. Again, no separate penalty was imposed in relation to a count of fraud (the false statement on the flyer). Both appealed against their sentences.

7.221 In Garfoot's case Treacy J said that, although the facts of the case warranted an immediate custodial sentence:

> 'we are persuaded that taking account of (his) position in the business and what can be viewed as his lesser role, together with his particular personal circumstances.'

On that basis Garfoot's sentence was reduced to 3 months. Wilsher's appeal had a different foundation. He did plead guilty, but only on the day fixed for his trial and only as set out in a basis of plea document. Treacy J said:

---

[283] [2011] EWCA Crim 2043, Official Transcript.

'the central complaint is that the judge took into account matters which were contrary to matters set out in a basis of plea document ... there is force in the complaint that the sentencing judge was not entitled to find that the works were "shoddy", there was considerable room for debate about him finding that the works were unnecessary but he was perfectly entitled to find that the victims were frail and vulnerable. We have to say that in our judgment insufficient attention was given by prosecuting counsel and the judge to the basis of plea document. There are elements of it which we would regard as unrealistic and elements of it which we consider would not have stood up to any sensible scrutiny. However, that was the basis upon which Mr Wilsher fell to be sentenced and the court having agreed to proceed on that basis should have adhered to the terms of that document.'

Accordingly Wilsher's sentence was reduced to 8 months.

7.222 The issue of compensation to be paid to victims of CPUTR offences was considered in *R v Patrick Connors*.[284] The Court of Appeal held that it was right in principle when assessing loss or damage in respect of compensation to take no account of any benefit conferred on the victim from any work carried out by the offender. An 81-year-old man had been aggressively persuaded to agree to a series of works to be carried out to his house. He was charged £16,400 and the Crown Court judge made a compensation order in that sum, which was upheld on appeal.

7.223 Another recent case provides a good example of the impact confiscation orders may have on traders that contravene the requirements of the CPUTR. In *R v Scott King*,[285] a trader sold motorcars on the false basis that he was selling privately, so as to avoid offering a warranty or guarantee. He pleaded guilty to falsely claiming that he was not acting in the course of business contrary to para 22 of Sch 1 of the CPUTR. The Court of Appeal upheld a confiscation order of over £109,000 (representing the turnover of the business) on the basis that it was not disproportionate. Three further cases have recently been considered by the Court of Appeal.

7.224 In *R v David Philip Hamilton*[286] a trader was sentenced to 12 weeks' imprisonment for contravening professional diligence. He pleaded guilty to a single offence which concerned incompetent building and brick work. He described himself as a good builder and competent brick layer, but the work he did was done very poorly and required to be put right. The Court of Appeal allowed his appeal by suspending the sentence for 12 months observing that whilst the conduct was criminal it did not involve overt bullying or aggression and fell short of being fraudulent.

7.225 The case of *R v Michael Tolliday*[287] concerned a defendant who had pleaded guilty to 11 counts of fraud and three offences under CPUTR. The fraud aspect of the case concerned serious misrepresentations which caused

---

[284] [2012] EWCA Crim 2106, Official Transcript.
[285] [2014] EWCA Crim 621.
[286] [2015] EWCA Crim 278.
[287] [2015] EWCA Crim 603.

significant loss to 11 different customers by reason of them not being supplied with the quality of kitchen promised and the failure of the defendant to carry out particular work. The total loss was £42,000. He was sentenced to 30 months' imprisonment for the fraud offences. The CPUTR offences concerned only two of the customers. Two counts involved the provision of an invoice with logos he was not entitled to use and the third involved a customer not being given written notice of their right to cancel their agreement. He was sentenced to 12 months' imprisonment for each of the three CPUTR offences consecutive to the fraud sentence giving a total of 42 months' imprisonment. The Court of Appeal allowed the appeal and said that if the CPUTR offences had stood alone they would not have crossed the custody threshold, but that the context of the repeated frauds could not be ignored. However, the Court held that 12 months' imprisonment for the CPUTR offences was manifestly excessive and that the sentences should have been three months' imprisonment on each to run concurrently with the 30 months' imprisonment for fraud.

7.226 In *R v Derek Montague*[288] the defendant was sentenced to 42 months' imprisonment after trial on each of four counts of fraud. He was also sentenced to concurrent prison terms of 12 months and 18 months' imprisonment respectively on two CPUTR offences. The case concerned a sole trader who over the course of seven months carried out works at the home of a 60-year-old vulnerable woman who lived alone. The quality of work done was poor and the total loss was £25,000. The two CPUTR offences concerned a professional diligence count and an aggressive commercial practice. The professional diligence matter concerned the appellant's failure to provide a written guarantee for the works being carried out. The aggressive commercial practice concerned the pernicious act of accompanying the victim to her bank where she withdrew £1,200 for work in respect of which he had already been paid £2,000. The Court of Appeal upheld the sentence and all its component parts stating that this was not just a case of overcharging, but involved the deliberate targeting of a vulnerable victim.

Sentences under the TDA

7.227 An important principle that emerged from the many sentencing cases under the TDA was that custodial sentences in trading cases should ordinarily be accompanied by a substantial fine. The rationale for this was that this type of offence will invariably be committed by a trader acting for financial gain. This is clearly illustrated by the leading authority of *R v Gupta*. It should be remembered, however, that these authorities were decided long before the confiscation of the proceeds of crime became mainstream criminal practice.

7.228 In *R v Gupta*[289] the appellant who was of previous good character, pleaded guilty, *inter alia*,[290] to a count of applying a false trade description to goods under s 1(1)(a) TDA. He was engaged in the second-hand car business

---

[288] [2015] EWCA Crim 902.
[289] (1985) 7 Cr App R (S) 172.
[290] There were several other deception offences for which he received concurrent sentences.

and advertised cars in newspapers without disclosing that he was a dealer. He sold an Austin Maxi motor car which had been 'clocked' from 77,000 miles down to 41,800 and claimed it had had only one previous owner; when it had in fact had three previous owners. The car was sold for an agreed price of £1,000 to a couple who were unaware that he was a second-hand car dealer. When trading standards officers visited him, he refused to discuss the matter at all. He was sentenced to **12 months' imprisonment** in the Crown Court. The Court of Appeal confirmed that sentence but, on account of the appellant's 'comparative youth' and previous good character, varied it partly, to allow 6 months to be suspended. Lawton LJ stated that the offence was one:

> 'which this appellant admitted he had with someone else, or so he said, knowingly committed. Dishonest second-hand car dealers frequently do put the clock back. All too often they claim that they did not know it had been put back and the owner from whom they bought it had put it back. That was not a defence available to this appellant. The problem for the courts, since the passing of the Trade Descriptions Act 1968, has been what kind of sentence should be imposed on second-hand car dealers who "clock" motor cars? This Court has no hesitation whatsoever in adjudging that this kind of fraud calls for a sentence of immediate loss of liberty. It is an offence which is all too prevalent from one end of England and Wales to the other and it is one of which dishonest second-hand car dealers make a great deal of money. It is a matter of observation of this Court reading newspapers, particularly local newspapers, that all too frequently dishonest second-hand car dealers get fined. This appellant had the impudence to suggest, in his application for notice of appeal against conviction, that he expected to get a substantial fine. Dishonest second-hand motor car dealers who "clock" vehicles should expect not to get a substantial fine but a sentence imposing immediate loss of liberty plus a substantial fine. It is very important in these cases that not only should dishonest second-hand car dealers be punished, in the sense of losing their liberty, but the very large profits which they make from this kind of behaviour should be taken away from them by way of substantial fines.'

CHAPTER 8

UNFAIR CONTRACT TERMS

INTRODUCTION

8.1 Initially regulation of unfair terms in the UK came principally from the Unfair Contract Terms Act 1977 ('UCTA'), which focuses on clauses that exclude or limit liability. In 1993 the European Council of Ministers passed the European Unfair Terms Directive 1993/13/EEC ('the Directive') which applies, with exceptions, to unfair terms of any type in consumer contracts. In 2015 Parliament brought these two regimes together, by re-implementing the Directive and extending its protections, in Part 2 and Schs 2 and 3 to the Consumer Rights Act 2015 ('the CRA 2015'). The Unfair Terms in Consumer Contracts Regulations 1999 (UTCCR), which previously implemented the Directive in the UK, was revoked.[1]

8.2 The CRA 2015 is now the principal provision by which the fairness of terms found in contracts between businesses and *consumers* should be assessed, and UCTA no longer has application to consumer contracts.[2]

The main changes

8.3 The CRA 2015 was drafted following two reports by the Law Commission that recommended reform, in particular to combine the UTCCR and UCTA regimes, and to clarify, and narrow, the main subject matter and price exemption.[3] The key changes to the UTCCR regime that CRA 2015 has brought are to bring notices and negotiated terms within scope, extending the grey list, and to narrow the core exemption so that to benefit from it terms must not only be transparent, but also be *prominent* and not be on the grey list. Terms which were blacklisted by UCTA remain prohibited by the CRA 2015.

THE CONSUMER RIGHTS ACT 2015, PART 2

8.4 The CRA 2015 applies to contracts concluded between a trader and a consumer, as well as notices that appear to affect rights, obligations or liabilities

---

1   The CRA 2015 came into force on 1 October 2015. The UTCCR came into force on 1 October 1999. This in turn replaced the UTCCR 1994 which came into force on 1 July 1995. The old legislation, and UCTA remain in force in respect of contracts entered into during their time of application see Consumer Rights Act 2015 (Commencement No 3, Transitional Provisions, Savings and Consequential Amendments) Order 2015, SI 2015/1630, Arts 6(1), (4) and (5). In respect of contracts which predate even the 1994 regulations, there would still appear to be scope for the requirements of the Directive to apply – see CJEU *Kasler* (C-26/13) at para 32, although this was doubted by the Supreme Court in *Arnold v Britton* [2015] UKSC 36 at para 93 (per Lord Carnwath, dissenting on the main issues).

2   UCTA does, however, continue to apply to business-to-business relationships and employment contracts, whether or not their terms are individually negotiated, and also when notices are used. It restricts exclusions of liability for negligence, and where standard form contracts are used, liability for breach of contract or substandard performance, applying a test of reasonableness. It prohibits exclusions of liability for death or personal injury. Part I of UCTA applies to England, Wales and Northern Ireland. Part II (ss 15 to 25) applies to Scotland.

3   Law Commission and Scottish Law Commission *Unfair Terms in Contracts: A Joint Consultation Paper* (2005) and *Unfair Terms in Consumer Contracts: Advice to the Department For Business, Innovation and Skills* (2013).

between a trader and a consumer. It is intended to give effect to the Directive, which has the aim of removing unfair terms from existing contracts, preventing their inclusion in future contracts, and deterring traders from attempting to use them in the first place.[4]

8.5 Apart from some limited exemptions, the CRA 2015 requires that terms and notices must be transparent,[5] and must be fair.[6] Consumers must not lose protection because they have agreed to a choice of law clauses.[7] Unfairness is defined, together with a list of terms that are presumed to be unfair.[8] A term that is unfair will not bind the consumer, however the contract will continue in existence if at all possible.[9] This obligation binds Member States and their courts, which must take steps to ensure that the consumer's rights are protected. In addition to the right of consumers to challenge unfair terms, the CRA 2015 provides a system of collective or pre-emptive challenge, under which a regulator may obtain orders against use of unfair terms.[10]

8.6 The Directive lays down the minimum level of consumer protection that the UK must ensure exists.[11] However, the UK has now consciously gone beyond the level of protection required. Accordingly, some case law which previously held terms to be out of scope or exempt from the fairness assessment is not necessarily to be relied on. It is important that the new tests in the CRA 2015 are applied, even though the central unfairness test remains the same.

Jurisdiction over unfair terms

8.7 The power to rule a term to be unfair is reserved to the national courts, who have a 'significant element of judgment to exercise in the light of the circumstances of each case'[12] the Court of Justice has competence only to construe the meaning of an article of the Directive.[13][14] Indications provided by the CJEU *must* be taken into account by the national court in order to assess whether a term is unfair.[15]

---

4   CJEU *Banco Espanol de Credito* (C-618/10) at paras 68–69, and 6th and 24th Recitals.
5   See the 20th Recital, Arts 4.2 and 5 and s 62.
6   See the 14th and 21st Recitals.
7   See the 22nd Recital, Art 6.2 and s 74.
8   See the 15th to 18th Recitals, Arts 3 and 41 and the Annex and ss 62, 63 and Sch 2.
9   See the 21st Recital, Art 6.1 and s 67.
10   See the 23rd and 24th Recitals, Arts 7 and 10 and CRA 2015, Sch 3.
11   See the Court of Appeal in *London Borough of Newham v Khatun* [2004] EWCA Civ 55 at para 56.
12   *Cavendish V El Makdessi, ParkingEye Ltd v Beavis* [2015] UKSC 67 para 105(1). Only the national court can decide whether a term is unfair in all the circumstances (CJEU *Pannon* (C-243/08) paras 42–43). Since the Treaty of Lisbon, the CJEU has been renamed the Court of Justice, as part of the Court of Justice for the European Union. For simplicity's sake we refer throughout to the CJEU.
13   CJEU *VB Penzugyi* (C-137/08) at para 37.
14   *OFT v Abbey National* [2009] UKSC 6 per Lord Walker at para 50. See also CJEU *Pannon* (C-243/08) at paras 42–43, CJEU *Caja de Ahorros* (C-484/08) at para 33.
15   *Nemzeti v Invitel* (C-472/10) at para 22.

8.8   Under the CRA 2015, s 71 UK courts have a duty to consider the fairness of terms in consumer contracts that are before them, and under s 70 and Sch 3, various regulators have power to ask the courts to rule on the fairness and transparency of terms.

Interpretation

8.9   In interpreting the Directive's requirements, it is important to bear in mind that it aims to have a wide application, where one party is acting in a trade, business or professional capacity. The CJEU has ruled it is particularly important that consumers should be protected where the contract relates to their essential needs, involves significant sums or is in a complex legal context, where the professional is likely to have a high degree of technical knowledge or the consumer is likely to find it difficult to judge the quality of the product provided.[16] The sources that may be used to interpret the Directive are numerous and include:

- the Treaty;
- the wording of the Directive and (importantly) its recitals;
- the European Policy programmes that led to the Directive;
- the draft directive and the opinions of the various committees;
- the Commission Explanatory Memorandum;
- the different language versions of the Directive;
- case law (especially that of the CJEU, but also Advocate General Opinions, and the case law and administrative decisions of other Member States);
- the current views of the European Commission and UK Government Departments.[17]

8.10   In construing the CRA 2015, it is important to bear in mind:[18]

- The Directive's purposes to improve the functioning of the European market place through fair standard contracts and to protect consumers.[19]

---

[16] CJEU *Asbeek Brusse v Jahani BV* (C-488/11) at paras 2932, ruling that tenancy contracts must fall within scope.

[17] See *London Borough of Newham v Khatun* [2004] EWCA Civ 55 at para 76, where the Court of Appeal stated that 'it is right that in its search for a purposive construction of the Directive, the court should consider all these materials'. See also CJEU *Asbeek Brusse v Jahani BV* (C-488/11) at para 26, where in considering the same issue, the CJEU considered how the intention of the legislator, and the aim of the Directive, is reflected in the different language versions. Contrary to the Court of Appeal's views in *Khatun*, it is not helpful to consider the use of similar concepts in other Directives, or even similar language in other Directives, since different Directives have different purposes – see CJEU *Kasler* (C-26/13) para 58 and CJEU *BEST Laser Sorters v Bert Peelaers* (C-657/11) para 51.

[18] *Director General of Fair Trading v First National Bank* [2001] UKHL 52 at paras 31–32.

[19] See also *London Borough of Newham v Khatun* [2004] EWCA Civ 55 at para 57.

- The core concepts and scope of the Directive must be given an autonomous and uniform interpretation through the EU.[20]

- The Directive is aimed at 'take it or leave it contracts'.

- The Directive treats consumers as presumptively weaker parties, and therefore in need of protection from abuses by stronger contracting parties.

- It is not possible to contract out of the CRA 2015.

Consumer protection

8.11 Consumer protection is the Directive's 'dominant purpose'.[21] Article 100a of the EC Treaty required the Commission to 'take as its base a high level of protection'.[22] Therefore it follows that the scope is broad, and there must be a clear rationale for excluding transactions involving consumers from its scope.[23] The Directive is premised on:[24]

> 'the idea that the consumer is in a weak position vis-à-vis the trader as regards both his bargaining power and his level of knowledge, which leads to the consumer agreeing to terms drawn up in advance by the trader without being able to influence the content of those terms.'[25]

8.12 A central purpose of the Directive is that unfair terms should not be binding on the consumer (Art 6.1).[26] This aims to 'replace the formal balance which the contract establishes between the parties with an effective balance which re-establishes equality between them'.[27] The imbalance that exists between the trader and the consumer may sometimes only be corrected by 'positive action unconnected with the actual parties to the contract'.[28] Articles 3 to 6 are intended to grant rights to consumers that they must be able to rely on before the courts.[29] A rationale behind this high level of protection is to enable consumers to shop with confidence, without fearing one-sided terms or unfair exclusion clauses. A trader cannot lawfully abuse its position of power.[30] This

---

20 CJEU *Kasler* (C-26/13) at paras 37–38.

21 There are, however, other, subsidiary, purposes which are discussed below, namely the single market, and competition objectives.

22 In *London Borough of Newham v Khatun* [2004] EWCA Civ 55 (paras 57 and 77), the court noted that Art 100a of the EC Treaty relates to measures which 'have as their object the establishment and functioning of the internal market'. This required that 'in drafting proposals concerning consumer protection with this objective in mind, the Commission will take a "high level of protection".' The court stated, 'thus the Directive has the twin purposes of advancing the internal market, and providing a high level of consumer protection'.

23 *London Borough of Newham v Khatun* [2004] EWCA Civ 55 at para 77.

24 CJEU *Perenicova* at para 27.

25 The CJEU has often repeated this purpose which was first developed in the case of *Oceano Groupo* (joined cases C-240/98, 241/98, 242/98, 243/98 and 244/98).

26 *Pannon* (C-243/08) at paras 21, 23.

27 CJEU *Nemzeti* at para 34.

28 CJEU *Asturcom v Nogueira* (C-40/08) at para 31.

29 CJEU *Commission v Sweden* (C-478/99) at paras 16–18, *Commission v Spain* (C-70/03), CJEU at para 15.

30 See the 5th, 6th, 8th and 9th Recitals.

aim is important in the furtherance of the other two objectives of the Directive, building the internal market and driving effective competition.

The single market

8.13 In *Commission v Sweden* the CJEU stated that the progressive establishment of the EU internal market is supported by confident consumers.[31] The Directive aims, at least partially, to harmonise consumer contract law throughout the EU, and increase consumer awareness of the laws governing contracts in other Member States. It is therefore inappropriate to define the Directive's scope by reference to English legal principles, no matter how well established or useful in the domestic context, because 'European legislation has to be read as a single corpus of law binding across the Member States'. Further, creating arbitrary distinctions in this way could lead to absurdities in the application of the Directive.[32] The concepts of the Directive, as reflected in the CRA 2015, must be given autonomous meaning, so that the Directive has uniform minimum application as far as possible.[33] The test of fairness must be applied by all Member States, no matter what their pre-existing law.[34] The measures and court proceedings Member States use to implement the Directive should not frustrate its purpose.[35] As stated in *Banco Espanol de Credito*:[36]

> 'The directive as a whole constitutes a measure which is essential to the tasks entrusted to the European Union and, in particular, to raising the standard of living and the quality of life throughout the EU.'

Freedom of competition and choice

8.14 The internal market helps businesses to trade throughout the EU, thus stimulating competition and increasing choice for consumers.[37] Harmonisation of EU contract law aims to give traders greater certainty and reduce the costs of doing business across borders. Disparities in the level of legal protection have the potential to distort competition.[38] Legal certainty means the Directive seeks

---

[31]   See the 1st to 6th Recitals of the Directive.

[32]   *London Borough of Newham v Khatun* [2004] EWCA Civ 55 at para 78. See also *Turner and Co (GB) Ltd v Abi* [2010] EWHC 2078 (QB) at para 42 where the judge emphasised, in considering the European jurisprudence on the definition of a consumer, that the Court of Justice 'has made clear that the concept must be given an autonomous interpretation. By "autonomous interpretation", I mean an interpretation not grounded in any national law, but which is of general application across the community'.

[33]   *Director General of Fair Trading v First National Bank* [2001] UKHL 52, per Lord Bingham at para 8 and per Lord Steyn at paras 31–32.

[34]   *Director General of Fair Trading v First National Bank* [2001] UKHL 52, per Lord Bingham at para 17.

[35]   *Banco Espanol de Credito* (C-618/10) at paras 55 and 69.

[36]   CJEU *Banco* (C-618/10) at para 67. See also CJEU *Asturcom v Nogueira* (C-40/08) at para 52.

[37]   See the 7th Recital. Unfair terms can give an unfair advantage to one trader over another, where they profit by tying consumers into lengthy contracts, preventing switching or increase their income through concealed terms. This hinders competition on quality of product and value for money.

[38]   See the 2nd Recital.

to preserve, rather than terminate contractual relations.[39] Freedom of choice means that contractual terms that relate to the main subject matter of the contract or to the adequacy of the price or remuneration face limited review because the consumer is deemed to be adequately protected by competition.[40]

APPLICATION OF THE CONSUMER RIGHTS ACT 2015

8.15

CRA, s 61

61 Contracts and notices covered by this Part

(1) This Part applies to a contract between a trader and a consumer.

(2) This does not include a contract of employment or apprenticeship.

(3) A contract to which this Part applies is referred to in this Part as a "consumer contract".

(4) This Part applies to a notice to the extent that it—

    (a)   relates to rights or obligations as between a trader and a consumer, or
    (b)   purports to exclude or restrict a trader's liability to a consumer.

(5) This does not include a notice relating to rights, obligations or liabilities as between an employer and an employee.

(6) It does not matter for the purposes of subsection (4) whether the notice is expressed to apply to a consumer, as long as it is reasonable to assume it is intended to be seen or heard by a consumer.

(7) A notice to which this Part applies is referred to in this Part as a "consumer notice".

(8) In this section "notice" includes an announcement, whether or not in writing, and any other communication or purported communication.

8.16 The CRA 2015 applies to terms in **contracts** or **notices**:

- involving **traders** and **consumers**;
- including secondary contracts, no matter who the contracting parties are, if these impact on a consumer contract;
- which do not reflect mandatory statutory or regulatory provisions; or
- the provisions or principles of international conventions to which the state or Community are party; and[41]

---

[39] CJEU *Perenicova* (C-453/10) at para 32 and AG's Opinion at paras 66–68.
[40] For a fuller discussion see CJEU *Caja de Ahorros* (C-484/08) AG's Opinion at paras 38–40. This also means that where the consumer has not actually been made properly aware of the term, as now explicitly required by the CRA 2015, it is difficult to maintain that they exercised 'freedom of contract' in any meaningful sense.
[41] See CJEU *Caja de Ahorros* (C-484/08) AG's Opinion at para 57.

• Are not in employment or apprenticeship contracts or notices.

Consumer

8.17 CRA 2015, s 76(2) and s 2(3):

> 'consumer' means an individual acting for purposes that are wholly or mainly outside that individual's trade, business, craft or profession.

The definition of consumer is now considered in Chapter 2, Interpretation of Consumer Law.

Trader

8.18 CRA 2015, s 76 and s 2(2):

> 'Trader' means a person acting for purposes relating to that person's trade, business, craft or profession, whether acting personally or through another person acting in the trader's name or on the trader's behalf.

The definition of trader is now considered in Chapter 2, Interpretation of Consumer Law.

Contract

8.19 The Directive is stated to apply to all contracts concluded after 31 December 1994.[42] The CRA 2015 applies to both written and oral contracts. It looks to the substance of the agreement, not the form.[43] The formation of a contract is not necessarily defined by the English law. The concept of a contract for the purposes of the Directive must be one that applies across the EU.[44] The CRA 2015 applies to contracts for land and to all tenancies, even though in the assignment of a tenancy there is no privity of contract between assignees, only privity of estate.[45]

8.20 The 10th Recital of the Directive sets out a number of obvious exclusions.

> 'contracts relating to employment, contracts relating to succession rights, contracts relating to rights under family law and contracts relating to the incorporation and organization of companies or partnership agreements.'

The CRA 2015 expressly excludes, by s 61(2), contracts of employment or apprenticeship.

---

[42] Art 10.1. It is unlikely to apply to contracts which were entered into before this date, although where a long lease is re-issued subsequently, the Directive's provisions will apply to the re-issued contract – see *Roundlistic Ltd v Jones & Seymour* [2016] UKUT 325 (LC) para 100.

[43] See the 11th Recital. It is not contingent on whether it is contained in one or many documents.

[44] *London Borough of Newham v Khatun* [2004] EWCA Civ 55 at para 78.

[45] See the CJEU in *Asbeek Brusse v Jahani BV* (C-488/11) at paras 29–32, holding that the Directive must apply to tenancies.

8.21 The CRA 2015 also brings within scope 'secondary contracts' – which are those which 'reduce the rights or remedies or increase the obligations of a person under another contract' ('the main contract').[46] It does not matter whether the secondary contract is itself a consumer contract, or made between the same persons as the main contract.[47] The effect of this is to bring within scope for example a contract that an individual might make in a trade capacity, if this has a material impact on a consumer contract which they or another consumer has entered into. The terms of such secondary contracts are also assessable for fairness.[48]

Term

8.22 Subject to the exclusions below, the CRA 2015 applies to all terms in consumer contracts, whether or not they are individually negotiated by the consumer.

8.23 In *Office of Fair Trading v Foxtons Ltd* in the High Court it was said that it was important 'to look at the substance, not the form, and therefore to focus on obligations not precise written terms'.[49]

> 'A "term" comprises all contractual provisions which give rise to a particular obligation, not withstanding these contractual provisions might be found in various clauses of the contractual documentation.'[50]

A 'term' may also be just part of a clause.[51]

8.24 In *Margaret Baybut v Eccle Riggs Country Park Ltd,*[52] it was held that implied terms may not be assessed for fairness because an unfair term could never be implied by operation of law or to give effect to the obvious common but unspoken intention of the parties. Neither does the test apply to effects caused by a rule of law.[53]

Notice

8.25 The CRA 2015 applies to a notice to the extent that it (a) 'relates to rights or obligations as between a trader and a consumer or (b) purports to exclude or restrict a trader's liability to a consumer'.[54] This includes any

---

[46] CRA 2015, s 72(1).
[47] CRA 2015, s 72(3).
[48] CRA 2015, s 72(2).
[49] *OFT v Foxtons Ltd* [2009] EWHC 1681 (Ch) at para 41.
[50] Andrew Smith J in *OFT v Abbey National* [2008] 2 All ER (Comm) 625 at para 431, a part of the judgment which was not appealed.
[51] *Bankers Insurance Company Ltd v South* [2003] EWHC 380 at para 35.
[52] Unreported, High Court, Manchester District Registry, 2 November 2006.
[53] *Direct Line Insurance v Khan* [2001] EWCA Civ 1794 at para 36.
[54] CRA 2015, s 61(4).

announcement, and any other communication, as long as it is reasonable to assume it is intended to be seen or heard by a consumer.[55]

8.26 The application to notices ensures that enforcement action can be taken against statements that are not incorporated into any contract, but which a trader may seek to invoke against a consumer. Examples include End User Licence Agreements, which may not be of contractual status, but define the terms on which the consumer contracts with a vendor of software.[56] Where a notice is incorporated into a contract, it is assessed for fairness as a Term.

Exclusions

8.27 CRA 2015, s 73 provides:

> **Disapplication of rules to mandatory terms and notices**
>
> 73(1) This Part does not apply to a term of a contract, or to a notice, to the extent that it reflects
>
> > (a) mandatory statutory or regulatory provisions [which includes rules which, according to law, apply between the parties on the basis that no other arrangements have been established],[57] or
> >
> > (b) the provisions or principles of an international convention to which the United Kingdom or the EU is a party.
>
> (2) In subsection (1) "mandatory statutory or regulatory provisions" includes rules which, according to law, apply between the parties on the basis that no other arrangements have been established.

Mandatory statutory provisions

8.28 Provisions that are mandatorily required by primary or secondary legislation fall within this exception. Section 73(2) has clarified that this concept also applies to rules which apply between the parties in the absence of other arrangements, for example terms implied by statute.[58] The rationale for this exception is the presumption that Member States will not require unfair terms to be included in contracts – in both the rules they create and the contracts they themselves enter into.[59] It is presumed that in drafting legislation, Member States 'struck a balance between all the rights and obligations of the parties' to the relevant contracts.[60]

8.29 In *Rochdale Borough Council v Dixon*, the statutory right for a local authority to collect water charges from council tenants was considered. The

---

[55] CRA 2015, s 61(6) and (8).
[56] See the CRA 2015 *Explanatory Notes* para 296.
[57] CRA 2015, s 73(2).
[58] This is consistent with the CJEU in *Barclays Bank v Sara Sancha Garcia* (C-280/13) at paras 39–42.
[59] Recitals 13 and 14. Member States are obliged not to contract with their citizens on unfair terms.
[60] CJEU *RWE Vertrieb AG v VBZ Nordrhein Westfalen* Case C-92/11 at para 28.

Court of Appeal stated that 'a term which is expressly authorised by a statutory power ... is unlikely to be unfair'.[61] However, this was not on its own conclusive. The court went on to consider a range of other factors that led to the conclusion that the term was fair. The Upper Tribunal (Lands Chamber) has applied this exemption where a landlord has a statutory obligation to grant a new lease on the same terms as a lease which predated the application of the Unfair Terms Directive –meaning that the terms of the new lease could not be assessed for fairness.[62]

8.30 Where a term merely reproduces a national legal provision (it is not mandatory), it does not fall within the exemption.[63] Likewise, where legislation sets out limitations on parties' conduct it should not be assumed that a term that does not exceed these limits is fair. For example, where statute sets a penalty interest rate ceiling, in particular where this is applicable not only to consumer contracts, this does not prevent assessment of fairness of a term setting the penalty interest rate in a consumer contract, even where this does not exceed the statutory limit.[64]

International conventions

8.31 Section 73(1) excludes the 'provisions or principles of an international convention to which the United Kingdom or the EU is a party'. The reason or this exclusion is again because it is presumed that states, when negotiating treaties, will not impose unfair terms on their citizens.

Employment contracts

8.32 The CRA 2015 does not apply to contracts of employment or apprenticeship, or notices which relate to rights, obligations or liabilities as between an employer and employee.[65] This is because these are governed by employment law.

Blacklisted terms

8.33 Some types of term are prohibited, and automatically unfair. They cannot be included in consumer contracts, and are not binding on the consumer. There are three types:

(1) Those blacklisted in goods, services and digital content contracts by Part 1 of the CRA 2015.

(2) Those blacklisted in all contracts by Part 2 of the CRA 2015.

(3) Those blacklisted by other legislation.

---

[61] [2011] EWCA Civ 1173 at para 68.
[62] *Roundlistic Ltd v Jones & Seymour* [2016] UKUT 325 (LC) para 101.
[63] CJEU *RWE Vertrieb AG v VBZ Nordrhein Westfalen* Case C-92/11 at paras 29–31.
[64] CJEU *Unicaja Banco v Rueda* (C-482/13) at paras 36–40.
[65] CRA 2015, s 61(2) and (5).

Exclusions of liability in goods, digital content and services contracts

8.34 Section 62(8) provides that certain exclusion of liability clauses need not be assessed for fairness in order not to bind consumers. These are exclusions of liability in goods (s 31), digital content (s 47) and services contracts (s 57) (covered in Part 1), and exclusions of liability for negligence (set out in s 65).

8.35 The Part 1 exclusions replicate and extend the protections previously afforded consumers by ss 6 and 7 of UCTA. In summary, a trader may not exclude from a goods contract their liability for goods not being of satisfactory quality, fit for purpose, or as described. Goods must conform to pre-contract information that the consumer has relied on, a sample or a model. Goods must be properly installed, and any digital content supplied must also conform to the contract. The trader must have the right to supply the goods and deliver them, and the goods remain at the trader's risk until they come into the physical possession of the consumer.

8.36 Digital content must be of satisfactory quality, fit for purpose, as described, and in conformity with pre-contract information that the consumer has relied on (see Chapter 5, Consumer Rights). The trader must have the right to supply it. A trader cannot exclude their liability under a service contract for performing it with reasonable care and skill, or for the inaccuracy of information they give that the consumer takes into account when deciding about the service. Unless otherwise agreed, the trader may charge only a reasonable price and must perform the service within a reasonable time. In all of these cases, terms are also not binding on consumers if they make the consumer's rights or remedies subject to onerous or restrictive conditions, allow the trader to put a person at a disadvantage as a result of pursuing a right, or exclude or restrict rules of evidence or procedure.[66]

Exclusion of negligence liability

8.37 Section 65(1) bars a trader from excluding or restricting liability for death or personal injury resulting from negligence.

Other terms that must be regarded as unfair

8.38 Section 63(6) blacklists any term that has the effect of requiring the consumer to bear the burden of proof with regard to compliance with any obligation under the Distance Marketing Directive. This is similar to other prohibitions found in a range of legislation which forbid traders from seeking to contract out of their obligations.[67]

---

[66] Part 1, ss 31(2), 47(2), 57(4).
[67] For example, reg 14B of the Alternative Dispute Resolution for Consumer Disputes (Competent Authorities and Information) Regulations 2015, SI 2015/542, which prohibits certain agreements to submit to ADR.

Jurisdiction of law terms

8.39

> **74 Contracts applying law of non-EEA State**
>
> (1) If—
>
> (a)   the law of a country or territory other than an EEA State is chosen by the parties to be applicable to a consumer contract, but
>
> (b)   the consumer contract has a close connection with the United Kingdom,
>
> this Part applies despite that choice.
>
> (2) For cases where the law applicable has not been chosen or the law of an EEA State is chosen, see Regulation (EC) No. 593/2008 of the European Parliament and of the Council of 17 June 2008 on the law applicable to contractual obligations.

The CRA 2015 applies when a contractual terms purports to select the law of a country outside the EEA as long as the contract '*has a close connection with the UK*'.[68] This is designed to protect consumers against the unfair use of foreign jurisdictional clauses to oust the laws of a Member State.[69] Such terms are unfair without the need for an assessment of fairness, and in this sense is similar to the jurisdiction clauses discussed elsewhere in this chapter. Any judgment entered against the consumer in the overseas jurisdiction should not be enforced against the consumer in the EU.

8.40   Section 74(2) makes clear that where the law of another EU Member State is chosen, or there is no choice of law clause at all, reference should be made to the Rome I Regulation. This means that it is in principle possible for a consumer to agree that the law of another EEA State should apply to the contract.[70] Where such a term is in the small print, and might be a surprise for the consumer however, it may still be unfair, particularly if the effect is to exclude mandatory protections that the consumer has under his own law.[71]

---

[68]   Section 74(1). The concept of 'close connection' was left deliberately vague so that it could be given a wide interpretation – CJEU *Commission v Spain* (C-70/03) at para 33. An example of where there was *not* a close connection is *Chopra v Bank of Singapore Ltd* [2015] EWHC 1549 at para 135 – contracts with a company based in Singapore, to open accounts in Singapore, in order to invest outside the EU (in particular Russia).

[69]   See the 6th and 22nd Recitals, CJEU *Commission v Spain* (C-70/03) at para 30.

[70]   CJEU *VFK v Amazon* (C-191/15) para 66.

[71]   CJEU *VFK v Amazon* (C-191/15) para 59 and Rome I Regulation, Art 6(2).

FAIRNESS

Transparency

8.41

> ### 68 Requirement for transparency
>
> 68(1) A trader must ensure that a written term of a consumer contract, or a consumer notice in writing, is transparent.
>
> (2) A consumer notice is transparent for the purposes of subsection (1) if it is expressed in plain and intelligible language and it is legible.
>
> 64(3) A term is transparent for the purposes of this Part if it is expressed in plain and intelligible language and (in the case of a written term) is legible.

The CRA 2015 requires that written terms and notices should be transparent. The trader is under an obligation to ensure they are in plain and intelligible language, and legible.[72] This goes much further than grammatical intelligibility: the average consumer must be able to foresee, on the basis of clear, intelligible criteria, the economic consequences for them that derive from the term.[73] The consumer should also be able clearly to understand the economic reasons for the term, and the term's relationship with other terms.[74] In making this assessment, the court must have regard to all the relevant facts including:

8.42

The Consumer's attributes

- The level of attention to be expected of the average consumer.[75]
- Whether the average consumer would actually understand the implications of the term, given the market and its practices.[76]

---

[72] Section 68 and Arts 4.2 and 5, see also Recital 20. For the trader's obligation see CJEU *RWE Vertrieb* (C-92/11) at para 43. Transparency is a broad requirement – CJEU *Kasler* (C-26/13) at para 72.

[73] CJEU *Matei v SC Volksbank* Romania (C-143/13) at paras 73–74. This seems to be a more rigorous test than set out in *OFT v Abbey National* [2008] EWHC 875 (Comm) at para 119 that the contractual terms must be 'sufficiently clear to enable the typical consumer to have a proper understanding of them for sensible and practical purposes.'

[74] CJEU *Kasler* (C-26/13) at para 60.

[75] CJEU *Matei v SC Volksbank* Romania (C-143/13) at para 75. The average consumer is reasonably well informed, and reasonably observant and circumspect. The consumer is not expected to have the same level of vigilance where concluding a contract that is ancillary to another – such as an insurance contract taken out with a loan (see CJEU *Van Hove v CNP Assurances* (C-96/14) at para 48). Generally UK courts have assumed that the average consumer is able 'to read the relevant documents and to seek to understand the contractual terms from that reading', but there is an acceptance that they do not in fact always read contracts. In *OFT v Ashbourne Management Services Ltd* [2011] EWHC 1237 (Ch) the average consumer was said to be 'a member of the public interested in using a gym club which is not a high end facility and who may be attracted by the relatively low monthly subscriptions' (para 155).

[76] CJEU *Kasler* (C-26/13) at para 74.

- The need for the consumer actually to be given the opportunity to examine all the terms of the contract, before concluding it.[77]
- A consumer should be able to understand what they are agreeing to.[78]

8.43

The quality of the contract and surrounding literature

- The average consumer's expectation that terms correspond to the overall purpose of the contract – and don't create surprising carve outs.[79]
- The term should not be *obscure* and it must not be *ambiguous*.[80]
- This requires transparency, flagging and explanation that the consumer can also *understand the effect of the term on his rights and obligations*.[81] The true effect of the contract should not be buried in the small print requiring 'some legal mining to bring it to the surface' – 'the typical consumer is not a miner for these purposes'.[82]
- The headings and layout used in the contract should facilitate, rather than obscure, understanding.[83]
- The promotional material and other information provided by the trader during the negotiations.

8.44

The language actually used

- Terms should not have broad and uncertain application.[84]
- The meaning of terms contained in general conditions must not depend 'on which of a number of possible divergent interpretations is placed on them'.[85]

---

[77] CJEU *RWE Vertrieb* (C-92/11) at paras 43–44.
[78] CJEU *Van Hove v CNP Assurances* (C-96/14) at paras 41 and 43. CJEU *Caja de Ahorros* (C-484/08) AG's Opinion at para 67. Where the consumer did not in fact understand the scope of a term, this is evidence that it was not transparent. See also *OFT v Abbey National* [2009] UKSC 6, per Lord Mance at para 113.
[79] CJEU *Van Hove v CNP Assurances* (C-96/14) at para 44.
[80] CJEU *Caja de Ahorros* (C-484/08) at para 38; also *Commission v Spain* (C-70/03), AG's Opinion at para 14.
[81] *OFT v Abbey National* [2008] EWHC 875 (Comm) at para 103. This formulation was affirmed and adopted also in *OFT v Foxtons Ltd* [2009] EWHC 1681 (Ch) at para 59.
[82] *OFT v Foxtons Ltd* [2009] EWHC 1681 (Ch) at para 74.
[83] CJEU *Matei v SC Volksbank* Romania (C-143/13) at para 77.
[84] Such terms prevent the consumer from predicting their application. For example, variation of an interest rate due to 'significant changes in the money market' does not allow the consumer to foresee when the rate may change: CJEU *Matei v SC Volksbank* Romania (C-143/13) at para 76. Other examples – the terms 'associated' and 'connected' persons are too vague, and 'their scope would puzzle even lawyers'. Terms that, when used in statute, require close definition are likely to be unintelligible if used in contracts. See *OFT v Foxtons Ltd* [2009] EWHC 1681 (Ch) at para 62.
[85] *Commission v Spain* (C-70/03), AG's Opinion at para 14.

- A phrase or word may have many uses in everyday parlance, and if so, the contract must make clear which of these is intended in the contract.

- Crucial information (especially that expressly required by EC law) must be given and be given correctly.

- Terms should not be contradictory. Where they are, the term most favourable to the consumer will prevail.[86]

- 'Just because a highly skilled lawyer can find (or contrive) some equivocation in a word, does not make the language lacking in plainness and intelligibility.'[87]

- The test is not one of 'absolute and pedantic rigour', and errors that are obvious do not make a term unintelligible.[88]

8.45 Other than this, the court is expected to construe the contract as it would usually do for any contractual dispute.[89]

> **69 Contract terms that may have different meanings**
>
> (1) If a term in a consumer contract, or a consumer notice, could have different meanings, the meaning that is most favourable to the consumer is to prevail.
>
> (2) Subsection (1) does not apply to the construction of a term or a notice in proceedings on an application for an injunction or interdict under paragraph 3 of Schedule 3.

8.46 If, following the normal principles of construction of contracts, a term in a contract or notice could have different meanings, the interpretation most favourable to the consumer must prevail (s 69(1)).[90] However, where a collective challenge is brought, the meaning *least* favourable to the consumer must be given.[91] A term that is not transparent is always assessable for fairness, but is not necessarily unfair.[92]

The core exemptions

8.47 CRA 2015, s 64 provides:

> 64(1) A term of a consumer contract may not be assessed for fairness under section 62 to the extent that

---

[86] *Peabody Trust Governors v Reeve* [2008] EWHC 1432 (Ch) at para 31.
[87] *OFT v Foxtons Ltd* [2009] EWHC 1681 (Ch) at para 63.
[88] *OFT v Foxtons Ltd* [2009] EWHC 1681 (Ch) at para 64.
[89] *Commission v Spain* (C-70/03), AG's Opinion at para 11.
[90] *Commission v Spain* (C-70/03), CJEU at paras 16–17. See also *AJ Building & Plastering Ltd v Turner* [2013] EWHC 484 at para 53, where it was held that 'there is not material difference between the principle of construction in reg 7(2) and the *contra proferentem* rule'. Both are used only where there is a case of 'genuine interpretative doubt or ambiguity'. See also *West v Ian Finlay & Assocs* [2014] EWCA Civ 316 at paras 30–32.
[91] CRA 2015, s 69(2).
[92] However, lack of transparency may be a reason why the term is used contrary to the requirements of good faith – *Evans v Cherry Tree Finance Ltd* [2007] EWHC 3523 (Ch) at para 61.

   (a)   it specifies the main subject matter of the contract, or

   (b)   the assessment is of the appropriateness of the price payable under the contract, by comparison with the goods, digital content or services supplied under it.

(2) Subsection (1) excludes a term from an assessment under section 62 only if it is transparent and prominent.

(3) A term is transparent for the purposes of this Part if it is expressed in plain and intelligible language and (in the case of a written term) is legible.

(4) A term is prominent for the purposes of this section if it is brought to the consumer's attention in such a way that an average consumer would be aware of the term.

(5) In subsection (4) "average consumer" means a consumer who is reasonably well-informed, observant and circumspect.

(6) This section does not apply to a term of a contract listed in Part 1 of Schedule 2.

8.48 Member States do not have to provide for this exemption in their legislation, but where they do, the exemption must be no broader than that set out in the Directive – which must be 'given an autonomous and uniform interpretation throughout the European Union'.[93]

8.49 The exclusion is narrow and must be strictly interpreted,[94] restricted only to the 'essential obligations' of contracts.[95] These could otherwise be referred to as the 'substance of the bargain', 'of central and indispensable importance' to the contract, as distinct from the ancillary 'incidental (if important) terms which surround them'. They represent what, objectively, both parties would view as the core bargain,[96] and what in fact is the substance of the bargain.[97] The exclusion does not apply to terms which set out secondary obligations, which apply only on breach of a primary obligation.[98] It is important to look at the substance and reality of the transaction, not at the form.[99] Although the

---

[93]   CJEU *Matei v SC Volksbank* Romania (C-143/13) at para 50.

[94]   CJEU *Matei v SC Volksbank* Romania (C-143/13) at para 49; OFT *v Abbey National* [2009] UKSC 6, per Lord Mance at para 104. *Director General of Fair Trading v First National Bank* [2001] UKHL 52, per Lord Bingham at para 12.

[95]   CJEU *Caja de Ahorros* (C-484/08) at para 34. These are likely to be the factors on which traders compete: CJEU *Caja de Ahorros* (C-484/08) AG's Opinion at para 40). There should be a functioning market based on competition in respect of price and efficiency (CJEU *Caja de Ahorros* (C-484/08) AG's Opinion at para 62).

[96]   *OFT v Abbey National* [2009] UKSC 6 per Lord Mance at para 113, *OFT v Foxtons Ltd* [2009] EWHC 1681 (Ch) at para 40 and paras 50–51 (what would the consumer expect instead of being surprised at?). The test does not however consider what the parties actually knew – *OFT v Abbey National* [2009] UKSC 6, per Lord Phillips at para 72.

[97]   Ie what enables the contract to function effectively, and what in fact does the consumer pay for what he receives: see *Foxtons v O'Reardon* [2011] EWHC 2946 (QB) at paras 60–61, *Smith v Mortgage Express* [2007] CTLC 134 at para 61.

[98]   *Cavendish V El Makdessi, ParkingEye Ltd v Beavis* [2015] UKSC 67 para 102 – and see also para 32 for discussion of the distinction between primary and secondary obligations.

[99]   *Bairstow Eves v Smith* [2004] EWHC 263 QB at paras 20 and 28. See also *Smith v Mortgage*

language of the contract is important in this regard, it is not conclusive.[100] The court must also look at the surrounding circumstances or contractual matrix, such as the market generally, the actual negotiation between the parties, and their assumptions, together with the actual package the consumer received, and what he pays for this.[101]

8.50 Where an element is defined as main subject matter or price by other legislation, it does not follow that it falls within the core exemption – because a purposive interpretation may require the other legislation to be construed more broadly than the Directive.[102] The fact that a term may have been individually negotiated is not a relevant criterion in assessing whether a term falls within the exclusion.[103] The CRA 2015 further constrains the scope of the exclusion by confirming that it does not apply to terms that are listed in the grey list.[104]

8.51 The exclusion applies only 'to the extent' that terms define the core bargain – so price terms for example may still be attacked for reasons other than the appropriateness of the price – for example the timing of payments, or if they apply in surprising circumstances, or if they have an unfair application to a section of consumers.[105]

Requirement for transparency and prominence

8.52 The Directive does not require consumer contracts to represent a 'good deal' for consumers.[106] This is because the Directive preserves freedom of choice and competition.[107] Accordingly, the definition of the 'main subject matter' and the 'appropriateness of price' are excluded from the fairness consideration only if they are *transparent* and *prominent*. Prominence requires that the term be 'brought to the consumer's attention',[108] which implies active flagging and up front presentation in glossy brochures as well as on the face of

---

Express [2007] CTLC 134 at para 20: 'the core terms of any agreement must be what in substance amounts to the core terms, however so described or not in the agreement'.

[100] The fact that an agreement has a subheading 'the main content of the agreement' does not mean these are 'core terms' *Smith v Mortgage Express* [2007] CTLC 134 at para 20.

[101] *Bairstow Eves v Smith* [2004] EWHC 263 QB at paras 27–28. Also *Smith v Mortgage Express* [2007] CTLC 134 at para 61.

[102] CJEU *Matei v SC Volksbank* Romania (C-143/13) paras 47–49: elements of the cost of credit that must be included in the APR of a loan might not be 'price' under the Directive, because APR is to be construed broadly, whereas the unfair terms core exemption is to be construed narrowly.

[103] CJEU *Kasler* (C-26/13) at para 47.

[104] Part 1 of Sch 2. This was also the decision of the CJEU in *Matei v SC Volksbank* Romania (C-143/13) at para 60. Those qualifications to the grey list set out in Part 2 of Sch 2 may still be 'core' terms.

[105] *OFT v Abbey National* [2009] UKSC 6 at paras 29 (per Lord Walker JSC), 57–61 and 78–80 (per Lord Phillips PSC), and 95 and 101 (per Lord Mance JSC).

[106] *OFT v Abbey National* [2009] UKSC 6 per Lord Walker at para 4 and *Director General of Fair Trading v First National Bank* [2001] UKHL 52 per Lord Rodger at para 64.

[107] *OFT v Abbey National* [2009] UKSC 6, per Lord Walker at para 44.

[108] Section 64(4).

the contract. The level of prominence is of an objective standard – it is such that 'the average consumer would be aware of the term'.[109]

Main subject matter

8.53 The main subject matter of a contract is what defines the 'very essence of the contractual relationship.' It is those terms that 'lay down the essential obligations of the contract and, as such, characterise it.' It is the substance of the obligation the trader – and consumer – have agreed to perform. It may be a single item or a multiplicity of items. In the case of a loan, it includes the debtor's obligation to repay.[110] In the case of a bank current account the main subject matter was the package of services supplied, including collection and payment of cheques, money transmission services ATM machines and provision of statements.[111] In the case of insurance, it is the promise to provide the insured, in the event of the risk materialising, with the service agreed when the contract was concluded.[112] Other subjects considered by the courts have included estate agent's duties, gym minimum membership periods, a yearly caravan pitch licence, an e-money payment service, and a disclaimer of what services a seller of land will not carry out.[113]

Price

8.54 The price is potentially 'any monetary price or remuneration payable under the contract'.[114] However the CJEU has now confirmed that in order to qualify, the trader should be providing an 'actual service which could constitute consideration for that charge' – the fact that a payment constitutes an an income stream for the trader, 'is in principle irrelevant' to the question of whether it is part of the 'price'.[115] A penalty cannot be redrafted to be part of the price.[116] Further, it is only the 'appropriateness' of the price that is excluded

---

[109] Section 64(4). The average consumer is defined as 'a consumer who is reasonably well informed, observant and circumspect' – s 64(5).

[110] CJEU *Matei v SC Volksbank* Romania (C-143/13) at para 54.

[111] *OFT v Abbey National* [2009] UKSC 6, per Lord Walker at paras 39–40, per Lord Phillips at para 53.

[112] CJEU *Van Hove v CNP Assurances* (C-96/14) at paras 34–35.

[113] See *Foxtons v O'Reardon* [2011] EWHC 2946 (QB) at paras 57 and 60; *OFT v Ashbourne Management Services Ltd* [2011] EWHC 1237 (Ch) at para 152; *Margaret Baybut v Eccle Riggs Country Park Ltd* (High Court, Manchester District Registry, 2 November 2006) at para 24; *Alfred Overy v Paypal (Europe) Ltd* [2012] EWHC 2659 (QB) at para 207; and *FSA v Asset LI Inc* [2013] EWHC 178 (Ch) at para 132.

[114] *OFT v Abbey National* [2009] UKSC 6, per Lord Walker at para 41.

[115] CJEU *Matei v SC Volksbank* Romania (C-143/13) at paras 70 and 68. See also CJEU *Kasler* (C-26/13) at para 58.

[116] *OFT v Abbey National* [2009] UKSC 6 per Lord Walker at para 43 (referring to *Bairstowe Eves v Smith* [2004] 263) and Lord Phillips at para 83.

from assessment – other aspects of the price may be assessed.[117] It is also possible to have a contract under which the consumer makes no payments at all.[118]

Part of the price

8.55 The following terms have been found to fall within or outside the definition of price:

- Sums that are an important part of the trader's charging structure, amounting to over 30% of their revenue stream.[119]
- Sums the trader relies on in order to be able profitably to provide the services on offer are likely to be price or remuneration.[120]
- Sums which the vast majority of consumers know about and expect to pay.[121]
- Bank charges made for various current account services, including interest forgone.[122]
- The price payable for early redemption of a 20-year mortgage within a fixed 3-year period, where the consumer enjoyed a discounted interest rate for the first 2 years.[123]

Not part of the price

8.56

- Interest payments in the event of default by the consumer in breach of contract.[124]
- Renewal commission paid by a landlord to a letting agent.[125]
- An early redemption charge on a loan.[126]
- Provision for the time of payment.[127]

---

[117] CJEU *Matei v SC Volksbank* Romania (C-143/13) at paras 56 and 63. CJEU *Caja de Ahorros* (C-484/08) AG's Opinion at para 70, fn 41.
[118] *OFT v Abbey National* [2009] UKSC 6, per Lord Mance at para 103.
[119] *OFT v Abbey National* [2009] UKSC 6, per Lord Walker at para 47.
[120] *OFT v Abbey National* [2009] UKSC 6 at para 88.
[121] *OFT v Abbey National* [2009] UKSC 6, per Lord Mance at para 105, see also *OFT v Foxtons Ltd* [2009] EWHC 1681 (Ch).
[122] *OFT v Abbey National* [2009] UKSC 6, per Lord Walker at para 42.
[123] *Smith v Mortgage Express* [2007] CTLC 134 at para 61.
[124] *Director General of Fair Trading v First National Bank* [2001] UKHL 52 paras 12, 34 and 43.
[125] *OFT v Foxtons Ltd* [2009] EWHC 1681 (Ch) at para 50. Also conceded by Chesterton Global Ltd in *Chesterton v Finney.*
[126] *Evans v Cherry Tree Finance Ltd* [2007] EWHC 3523 (Ch), although this point was not argued in this case.
[127] *Foxtons v O'Reardon* [2011] EWHC 2946 (QB) at para 56. Although on the facts in this case the clause in question was held to relate to the main subject matter of the contract.

- Price escalation clauses.[128]
- Any other mechanism for amending the price or a rate of interest, including a price indexation clause.[129]
- A sales commission where no selling service was provided.[130]
- A regular charge for converting the currency of a loan, due to the loan being tied to a foreign currency, where no foreign exchange service was actually supplied to the consumer – even though this formed part of the APR for a loan.[131]
- Terms falling within paras (d), (e), (f) and (l) in Sch 2 para 1.[132]
- Sums not necessary to profitable operation, but which are 'adventitious benefits'.[133]

The fairness test

8.57 Section 62(4) provides that a:

> 62(4) Term is unfair if, contrary to the requirement of good faith, it causes a significant imbalance in the parties' rights and obligations arising under the contract, to the detriment of the consumer.

8.58 Section 62(6) applies the same test to Notices. The courts in the UK have construed three aspects:

(1) Is there a significant imbalance in the parties' rights and obligations?

(2) Is this to the detriment of the consumer?

(3) Is the detriment in a manner, or to an extent, that is contrary to good faith?[134]

8.59 In *UK Housing Alliance (North West) Ltd v Francis* the Court of Appeal stated that:[135]

> 'the existence of an imbalance caused by the term was held [in First National Bank] not to be enough on its own despite argument that the imbalance of itself demonstrated the absence of good faith.'[136]

---

[128] *Bairstow Eves v Smith* [2004] EWHC 263 QB. See also *Director General of Fair Trading v First National Bank* [2001] UKHL 52 at para 34.

[129] CJEU *Nemzeti v Invitel* (C-472/10) at para 23; CJEU *Matei v SC Volksbank* Romania (C-143/13) at para 57; EFTA *Gunnar Engilbertsson v Islandsbanki* (E-25/13) at para 96.

[130] *OFT v Foxtons Ltd* [2009] EWHC 1681 (Ch).

[131] CJEU *Kasler* (C-26/13) at para 58.

[132] *OFT v Abbey National* [2009] UKSC 6, per Lord Walker at para 43.

[133] *OFT v Foxtons Ltd* [2009] EWHC 1681 (Ch) at para 85.

[134] Lord Bingham in *Director General of Fair Trading v First National Bank* [2001] UKHL 52 at para 17.

[135] *UK Housing Alliance (North West) Ltd v Francis* [2010] EWCA Civ 117 at para 21.

[136] See also *Cavendish V El Makdessi, ParkingEye Ltd v Beavis* [2015] UKSC 67 para 107 where the Supreme Court held that a term which created an imbalance was not unfair because it was not contrary to good faith.

8.60   Although the three limbs of the test are separate stages, it is plain that they are interlinked. In *First National Bank* Lord Steyn observed that there was 'a large area of overlap between the concepts of good faith and significant imbalance'.[137]

8.61   Section 62(5) adds that[138] the unfairness of a contractual term shall be assessed:

- taking into account the nature of the subject matter of the contract; and
- by reference to all the circumstances existing when the term was agreed; and
- to all the other terms of the contract or of any other contract on which it depends.

8.62   Indeed it is mandatory to take into account all of the terms of the contract, unless the term is being challenged by a regulator.[139]

8.63   Section 63(1) creates a presumption that terms falling within the indicative and non-exhaustive list of the terms in Part 1 of Sch 2 (the grey list) will be regarded as unfair.[140] Section 63(2) confirms that while those terms listed in Part 2 of Sch 2 are not presumed to be unfair, they may still be assessed for fairness.[141]

8.64   Some guiding principles as to whether a term is likely to be unfair are:[142]

- Compare the effect of the contract with the term, and the effect it would have without it.[143]
- Consider the effect of the inclusion of the term on the substance or core of the transaction.[144]
- Whether if it were drawn to his attention the consumer would be likely to be surprised by it.[145]

---

[137]   *Director General of Fair Trading v First National Bank* [2001] UKHL 52 at paras 36 and 17 respectively.

[138]   Section 62(7) applies comparable provisions to the assessment of notices.

[139]   CJEU *Banif Plus Bank Zrt v Csaba Csipai* (C-472/11) at paras 40–41, CJEU *Commission v Spain* (C-70/03) at para 16.

[140]   However, they are not necessarily unfair – *Cavendish V El Makdessi, ParkingEye Ltd v Beavis* [2015] UKSC 67 para 105.

[141]   Unless they are otherwise excluded from assessment as core provisions, or mandatory statutory terms.

[142]   And see the speech of Lord Millett in *First National Bank* for the core of this list.

[143]   See also *Mohamed Aziz v Caixa d'Estalvis* (C-415/11) at para 68 and *Cavendish V El Makdessi, ParkingEye Ltd v Beavis* [2015] UKSC 67 para 105(2).

[144]   In cases where the term is inconsistent with the main object and intent of the contract, this consideration may lead to a term not being incorporated into the contract at all, see *Alexander v West Bromwich Mortgage Company Ltd* [2016] EWCA Civ 496, para 46.

[145]   The CJEU has expressed this as asking whether the trader, dealing fairly and equitably with the consumer, could reasonably assume they would have agreed to the term in individual contract

- Whether the term, bearing in mind its significance, purpose and practical effect, is necessary to secure a legitimate objective of the trader.[146]

- Whether the term is a standard term, not merely in non-negotiable consumer contracts, but in commercial contracts freely negotiated between parties acting on level terms and at arm's length.[147]

- Whether, in such cases, the party adversely affected by the inclusion of the term or his lawyer might reasonably be expected to object to its inclusion or press for its deletion.[148]

- What, if any, protection the consumer has against the unfair application of the term.[149]

- The consequences of the term under the law applicable to the contract.[150]

- Any benefit to the consumer deriving from the term under challenge.[151]

All the circumstances of the contract

8.65 This has a wide definition, and includes all the surrounding circumstances including a telesales pitch.[152] Where the trader creates a sense of 'gravity' about the signing of the contract, this will not operate to make unfair terms fair.[153]

Time of the assessment

8.66 While the primary focus is on 'all the circumstances existing *when the contract was agreed*,' this does not rule out consideration of later events, such as how the term was enforced[154] or events that demonstrate how the term

---

negotiations – *Mohamed Aziz v Caixa d'Estalvis* (C-415/11) at para 69. Also *Cavendish V El Makdessi, ParkingEye Ltd v Beavis* [2015] UKSC 67, para 105(3).

[146] This may include benefits to the trader, indirectly to the consumer and to other interested parties, see *Cavendish V El Makdessi, ParkingEye Ltd v Beavis* [2015] UKSC 6,7 paras 105(4), 106 and 107 and *Mohamed Aziz v Caixa d'Estalvis* (C-415/11) at paras 71–74. This might include other rules of law which constrain the trader's application of the term – see *Parker v NFU Mutual Insurance Society Ltd* [2012] EWHC 2156 (Comm) & *Abbot & Ors v RCI Europe* [2016] EWHC 2602 (Ch) para 46.

[147] *FSA v Asset LI Inc* [2013] EWHC 178 (Ch) at para 138(i); *Munkenbeck & Marshall v Harold* [2005] EWHC 356 (TCC) at para 15. Also the Opinion of Advocate General Kokott in *Mohamed Aziz v Caixa d'Estalvis* (C-415/11) at para AG75.

[148] *Director General of Fair Trading v First National Bank* [2001] UKHL 52 at para 54.

[149] *Cavendish V El Makdessi, ParkingEye Ltd v Beavis* [2015] UKSC 67, paras 106 and 111 and AG's Opinion in *Mohamed Aziz v Caixa d'Estalvis* (C-415/11) at para AG75.

[150] CJEU *Freiburger* (C-237/02) at para 21.

[151] CJEU *Freiburger* (C-237/02) at paras 16 and 23.

[152] *FSA v Asset LI Inc* [2013] EWHC 178 (Ch) at para 134.

[153] *FSA v Asset LI Inc* [2013] EWHC 178 (Ch) at para 138(vi).

[154] *Du Plessis v Fontgary Leisure Parks Ltd* [2012] EWCA Civ 409 at para 52.

applies in fact.[155] It is also important to consider the likely effect of a term in the future.[156] However the trader's subsequent misuse of a fair term does not render it unfair.[157]

Circumstances existing when the contract was agreed

8.67 Section 62(5)(b) refers to all the circumstances existing when the contract was agreed. In *Tew v BoS*,[158] the High Court considered that the comparable wording in the UTCCR meant that circumstances such as the actual understanding of the individual consumers, and whether the transaction made sense for that consumer, were relevant: courts decide 'individual cases' rather than cases in the abstract. The whole notion of fairness 'involves the impact of matters on a person' and individual circumstances of the consumers (such as how well-heeled, well-informed, well-advised or open-eyed they were) could be relevant. The 'personal circumstances of each individual' had to be considered. This ruling is at odds with that in *Foxtons v O'Reardon*[159] where the High Court ruled that the personal circumstances of the consumers (in terms of vulnerability or ill health, or special requirements that they had) were not relevant to the fairness of terms requiring payment of commission to an estate agent.[160]

8.68 In a collective challenge, the courts have to consider the 'typical' circumstances existing when the contract was agreed.[161] This has been taken to include the typical sorts of consumers targeted by a trader, such those who are not financially experienced or sophisticated, and whom the trader discourages from seeking legal advice.[162]

Significant imbalance

8.69 In *Spreadex v Cochrane* it was said that this was about 'the balance between rights and obligations'.[163] However the imbalance is not assessed by weighing the rights and obligations of the parties in the contract as a whole, but simply in respect of the particular term under challenge – thus a term that obliges the consumer to pay a tax that the national law requires to be paid by the trader may create a significant imbalance, even though it is a relatively small sum in comparison to the transaction as a whole.[164]

---

[155] See *Clipper Ventures Plc v Boyde* Sheriff Principal's Judgment (Sheriffdom of Lothian and Borders) case A709/11 (24 December 2012).
[156] *Director General of Fair Trading v First National Bank* [2001] UKHL 52, per Lord Bingham at para 13 and per Lord Hope of Craighead at para 45.
[157] *Director General of Fair Trading v First National Bank* [2001] UKHL 52, per Lord Bingham at para 24.
[158] [2010] EWHC 203 (Ch) at para 21.
[159] [2011] EWHC 2946 (QB) at para 63.
[160] See also *Harrison v Shepherd Homes Ltd* [2011] EWHC 1811 (TCC).
[161] Lord Steyn in *The Director General of Fair Trading v First National Bank plc* at para 33.
[162] *FSA v Asset LI Inc* [2013] EWHC 178 (Ch) at para 136.
[163] *Spreadex v Cochrane* [2012] EWHC 1290 (Comm) at para 17.
[164] CJEU *Constructora Principado SA v Alvarez* (C-226/12) at paras 22–26 and 30.

8.70 'The term must be judged by reference to all situations in which it might potentially be applicable.'[165] The term must be considered in context: one which might at first blush appear unfair to the consumer might not cause an imbalance if its effect is mitigated by another term.[166]

8.71 The CJEU has held that it is particularly relevant to consider whether there are rules of national law that would apply, absent the term under challenge, and if so whether the term puts the consumer in a worse position. The court must also consider whether the consumer is able to use legal means to prevent the application of the term.[167] However mere formal equivalence between the parties may still give rise to a significant imbalance if this does not reflect the dependence of the consumer on the trader's product.[168]

8.72 The illustrative list of terms in Sch 2, Part 1 *may* be unfair, and those in Part 2 *may* be fair – but in either case, there must be an assessment of fairness.[169]

8.73 Factors that courts have taken into account include:

- What does the consumer get for the term that they are required to submit to? Is it reasonable?[170]

- What risks does the trader take in return for the term, judged at the time the contract was made?[171]

- Whether the term in fact reflects the commercial realities of the transaction.[172]

- Whether the term protects the trader's legitimate interests (such as where the trader has given a special discount on a loan for a fixed period of time, and protects their income by means of an early payment charge).[173]

---

[165] *Spreadex v Cochrane* [2012] EWHC 1290 (Comm) at para 19.

[166] *Director General of Fair Trading v First National Bank* [2001] UKHL 52, per Lord Bingham at para 17.

[167] CJEU *Mohamed Aziz v Caixa d'Esalvis de Catalunya* (C-415/11) at para 68. See also *Parker v NFU Mutual Insurance Society Ltd* [2012] EWHC 2156 (Comm).

[168] *Alfred Overy v Paypal (Europe) Ltd* [2012] EWHC 2659 (QB) at para 211.

[169] Section 63(1) and (2). CJEU *RWE Vertrieb AG v VBZ Nordrhein-Westfalen* (Case C-92/11) at paras 46–47.

[170] For example, in *Rochdale Borough Council v Dixon* [2011] EWCA Civ 1173, it was held to be entirely reasonable to require a tenant to pay for water charges as part of their rent, since they made use of the water, and it would be unfair to expect them to get water for free.

[171] See, eg *UK Housing Alliance (North West) Ltd v Francis* [2010] EWCA Civ 117 at para 27. Where the consumer has control over the risks in fact, it may be more appropriate for the trader to limit their liability if things go wrong – see *West v Ian Finlay & Assocs* [2014] EWCA Civ 316 at paras 53 and 59.

[172] See, eg in *Du Plessis v Fontgary Leisure Parks Ltd* [2012] EWCA Civ 409 the court considered that it was legitimate for owners of a caravan park to seek to re-grade the pitches, and accordingly to charge certain caravan owners proportionately more money (paras 36–37, 41 and 49).

[173] *Smith v Mortgage Express* [2007] CTLC 134 at para 63.

- Whether this legitimate interest could have been protected in a less harmful way, and if the term is drafted too broadly.[174]
- Whether the regulatory framework means that the term could not in fact be enforced as broadly as at first appears.[175]
- What other rules of law operate to restrain the trader's use of the term (such as a requirement to act with reasonable care and skill).[176]
- Where there is an insurable risk, it is generally expected that trader, rather than the consumer, would insure against it.[177]

8.74 Examples of terms which have been held to create a significant imbalance include:

- Making a consumer liable for all trades on a spread betting account, whether authorised or not.
- Terms where the trader assumes no obligations and the consumer has no rights.[178]
- Terms making the consumer liable to pay costs on an indemnity basis, plus interest in the event of a dispute, when there is no corresponding liability on the trader.[179]
- Terms which lock consumers into long gym contracts, in circumstances where this brings advantages to the gym, but does not significantly benefit the consumer – in particular where the consumer cannot terminate easily if their circumstances change.[180]
- Where a loan is granted at a high interest rate to a consumer in need of a swift loan.[181]
- Unfair renewal commission charged by a letting agent.[182]
- Terms which exclude important legal rights in new house build contracts.[183]
- Terms which require the consumer to pay an unknown future sum.[184]

---

[174] *Spreadex v Cochrane* [2012] EWHC 1290 (Comm) at para 19; *Alfred Overy v Paypal (Europe) Ltd* [2012] EWHC 2659 (QB) at para 210.
[175] *Parker v NFU Mutual Insurance Society Ltd* [2012] EWHC 2156 (Comm) at para 191.
[176] *Abbot & Ors v RCI Europe* [2016] EWHC 2602 (Ch) at para 46.
[177] *West v Ian Finlay & Assocs* [2014] EWCA Civ 316 at para 52.
[178] *Spreadex v Cochrane* [2012] EWHC 1290 (Comm) (para 17).
[179] *Munkenbeck & Marshall v Harold* [2005] EWHC 356 (TCC) at paras 12 and 15.
[180] In *OFT v Ashbourne Management Services Ltd* [2011] EWHC 1237 (Ch).
[181] *Evans v Cherry Tree Finance Ltd* [2007] EWHC 3523 (Ch) at paras 63–64.
[182] *OFT v Foxtons Ltd* [2009] EWHC 1681 (Ch) at paras 90–95. The commission was surprising, of a significant amount, and payable even where the agent did no work.
[183] *Harrison v Shepherd Homes Ltd* [2011] EWHC 1811 (TCC) at paras 107, 115 and 118. See also CJEU *Constructora Principado SA v Alvarez* (C-226/12) at para 28.
[184] CJEU *Constructora Principado SA v Alvarez* (C-226/12) at para 26.

- Terms which require an insured consumer promptly to pass information to their insurer, where the effect of not doing so is that they may forfeit all cover where the insurer suffers no prejudice.[185]

- Terms which permit a trader to terminate an e-payment service immediately and at will, or for grounds that are not serious.[186]

- Terms which exclude liability for statements of telesales staff.[187]

- A term which imposes a parking charge in excess of the consumer's liability to the landowner in tort for trespass.[188]

Detriment of the consumer

8.75 A term that clearly operates to the consumer's advantage will not fall foul of the UTCCR. Where the consumer has imposed the term either by their own choice or a choice made by their professional agent there appears to be a presumption that there is no detriment to the consumer. A trader has no duty to draw the consumer's attention to the pitfalls in terms which the trader is not offering.[189]

Good faith

8.76 In the Directive, Recital 16 states that in making an assessment of good faith, particular regard shall be had:

- to the strength of the bargaining positions of the parties;[190]

- to whether the consumer had an inducement to agree to the term; and

- to whether the goods or services were sold or supplied to the special order of the consumer.

8.77 Recital 16 adds that the requirement of good faith may be satisfied where the seller or supplier 'deals fairly and equitably with the other party whose

---

[185] *Bankers Insurance Company Ltd v South* [2003] EWHC 380 at para 34. However, see also *Parker v NFU Mutual Insurance Society Ltd* [2012] EWHC 2156 (Comm) at para 191.

[186] *Alfred Overy v Paypal (Europe) Ltd* [2012] EWHC 2659 (QB) at paras 211–213 and 226.

[187] *FSA v Asset LI Inc* [2013] EWHC 178 (Ch) at paras 135–138.

[188] *Cavendish V El Makdessi, ParkingEye Ltd v Beavis* [2015] UKSC 67, para 107, although in this case the term was not unfair, because it was not used contrary to good faith.

[189] *Mylcrist Builders Ltd v Mrs G Buck* [2008] EWHC 2172 (TCC) at para 51(7), and *Bryen and Langley Ltd v Martin Boston* [2004] EWHC 2450 at para 45; see also *Westminster Building Company Lt v Beckingham* [2004] EWHC 138 (TCC).

[190] In some circumstances, the parties may be of more or less equal strength – see for instance *West v Ian Finlay & Assocs* [2014] EWCA Civ 316 at paras 59–60, where the consumers, who were wealthy professionals, were held to be of 'savvy nature', and therefore in an equal bargaining position. Also *Khurana v Webster Construction Ltd* [2015] EWHC 758 (TCC) at para 53(1), where the consumers were professional persons owning a substantial property, whereas the trader was effectively a modest one man building company. In *Deutsche Bank (Suisse) SA v Gulzar Ahmed Khan* [2013] EWHC 482 (Comm) at para 380, millionaires who were legally advised, during extensive negotiations, conducted assertively by the consumers, to achieve significant terms in the trader's terms, were held not to have been taken advantage of. No lack of good faith was shown.

legitimate interests he has taken into account', which the CJEU has interpreted as including consideration of whether the trader 'could reasonably assume that the [reasonable] consumer would have agreed to such a term in individual contract negotiations'.[191] The UK Supreme Court has also emphasised the need to consider whether the trader has a legitimate interest in imposing the liability (although it is vital that the liability is no more severe than is necessary).[192] In *First National Bank* Lord Bingham described good faith as amounting to a requirement of 'fair and open dealing', which he treated as two separate, cumulative criteria. Good faith can never be viewed simply as a matter of being open about objectively imbalanced terms. There must also be consideration of whether the trader is acting fairly. Lord Steyn, described good faith as 'an objective criterion'. It is about whether the trader has dealt fairly and equitably. It is not a procedural requirement to do with the negotiating procedures.[193] Rather it looks also to the trader's motives and the effect of their conduct. It is a question of 'commercial morality'.

Openness

8.78

'[T]erms should be expressed fully, clearly and legibly, containing no concealed pitfalls or traps. Appropriate prominence should be given to terms which might operate disadvantageously to the consumer.'[194]

8.79   The sorts of contractual practices that have been held to lack openness include:

- A term that was only likely to be discovered by a person looking for it.[195]
- An onerous and surprising term contained only in the small print.[196]
- An important liability that was 'severely camouflaged' by lack of proper headings or signposting in a contract.[197]
- A surprising sales commission in the small print, where the consumer would be astonished to find this clause in the contract, and would feel they had been ambushed when it was invoked.[198]

---

[191]   *Mohamed Aziz v Caixa d'Esalvis de Catalunya* (C-415/11) at para 69, applied by the UK Supreme Court as the main factor of the good faith test in *Cavendish V El Makdessi, ParkingEye Ltd v Beavis* [2015] UKSC 67 para 105(3) and 108. The Supreme Court stressed that the test is whether the *reasonable* consumer would have agreed to the term, not the individual challenging the term.

[192]   *Cavendish V El Makdessi, ParkingEye Ltd v Beavis* [2015] UKSC 67 para 107, here the whole aim of the contract was to provide two hours' free parking for shoppers at a retail park, and in order for this system to work, it was imperative to incentivise those shoppers to leave on time.

[193]   *Director General of Fair Trading v First National Bank* [2001] UKHL 52 at para 36.

[194]   *Director General of Fair Trading v First National Bank* [2001] UKHL 52 at para 17; *Mylcrist Builders Ltd v Mrs G Buck* [2008] EWHC 2172 (TCC) at para 51(4)(a).

[195]   *OFT v Foxtons Ltd* [2009] EWHC 1681 (Ch).

[196]   *OFT v Foxtons Ltd* [2009] EWHC 1681 (Ch).

[197]   *OFT v Foxtons Ltd* [2009] EWHC 1681 (Ch) at para 98.

[198]   *OFT v Foxtons Ltd* [2009] EWHC 1681 (Ch) at paras 103–105.

- Where the risks of signing a contract with long and onerous liabilities were not spelled out to consumers (and so the term operated as a trap for consumers).[199]

- A surprising term fixing consumer liability found by a web link to a 49-page terms document.[200]

- Introducing a term into the contract after the consumer has already paid a deposit.[201]

8.80 By contrast, a term displayed on signs in a car park, imposing a liability to pay £85 for overstaying beyond two hours permitted free parking was held to be fair, the terms 'could not have been briefer, simpler or more prominently proclaimed', such that motorists 'could hardly avoid reading the notice.'[202]

Reading the small print

8.81 In *OFT v Foxtons Ltd*,[203] it was noted that the 'theory is that the typical consumer ... will read all the standard terms. But the practice is that even the circumspect one will be unlikely to do so with a great deal of attention'. The consumer expects the small print to contain points of detail to do with things that are not of everyday concern to the consumer. The consumer would not expect important obligations to be tucked away in the small print without prior flagging, notice or discussion.

8.82 Similarly, it has been held to be reasonable for consumers not to read contracts in the context of:

- A contract relating to 'a perfectly ordinary small suburban dwelling house' it was 'not at all surprising' that the full import of the agreement should be missed by the vendors. It was therefore not determinative that the vendors had failed to read the agreement carefully, and they were accordingly not bound by a surprising price escalation clause in an estate agency contract.[204]

- A RIBA standard form of agreement for the appointment of an architect, containing onerous costs provisions, that were not pointed out to the consumer, where it was held that 'even a commercial customer ... might well miss those two unusual and onerous clauses'.[205]

- An online contract, where it was held that ticking 'I Agree' to 'terms and conditions', which are closely typed and lengthy, is an entirely

---

[199] *OFT v Ashbourne Management Services Ltd* [2011] EWHC 1237 (Ch). See also *West v Ian Finlay & Assocs* [2014] EWCA Civ 316 at paras 56–58.

[200] In *Spreadex v Cochrane* [2012] EWHC 1290 (Comm) at para 21.

[201] *FSA v Asset LI Inc* [2013] EWHC 178 (Ch) paras 137–138. In particular when the sales pitch was contradicted by the term, and there is no compensation for loss of use of the money paid as a deposit.

[202] *Cavendish V El Makdessi, ParkingEye Ltd v Beavis* [2015] UKSC 67, para 108.

[203] [2009] EWHC 1681 (Ch) at para 92.

[204] *Bairstow Eves v Smith* [2004] EWHC 263 QB.

[205] *Munkenbeck & Marshall v Harold* [2005] EWHC 356 (TCC) at para 10.

inappropriate way to fix a consumer with surprising or onerous liabilities. It is likely therefore to be irrational for a trader to assume that the consumer would read, understand or appreciate the implications of terms set out in such documents. Surprising and onerous terms must be flagged in some other way.

8.83 The requirement of openness goes further than the doctrine of incorporation of terms under the common law as set out in *Interfoto Picture Library Ltd v Stiletto Visual Programmes Ltd* which is that the common law requires that reasonable steps are taken to draw the other party's attention to printed conditions, or they would not be part of the contract. Where one condition in a set of printed conditions is particularly onerous or unusual, the party enforcing must show it was fairly brought to the other's attention. If it is not, it will not become part of the contract.[206]

8.84 Generally 'the more unreasonable a clause is, the greater the notice which must be given of it. Some clauses ... would need to be printed in red ink on the face of the document with a red hand pointing to it, before the notice could be held to be sufficient'.[207] An example of a term not being incorporated into a consumer contract was where pinning a copy of the rules for a caravan park onto a notice board would not 'come anywhere near being sufficient notice to incorporate the terms into a contract'. There was no evidence that any consumer saw it, or that its existence was drawn to their attention before they paid their site fees, or at all.[208] Likewise, a small print term which is inconsistent with the main purpose of the contract (for example as set out in specifically agreed terms), is not to be treated as a term of the contract.[209] Ultimately if a term is not incorporated into a contract, however, it cannot bind a consumer. It can be assessed for fairness as a notice for enforcement purposes.

Fair dealing

8.85 '[A] supplier should not, whether deliberately or unconsciously, take advantage[210] of the consumer's necessity, indigence, lack of experience, unfamiliarity with the subject matter of the contract, weak bargaining position or any other factor listed in or analogous to those' in Recital 16. The supplier should deal fairly and equitably with the consumer.[211] A term that is fully

---

[206] [1988] 1 All ER 348 (CA) per Dillon LJ at 352.
[207] *Spurling v Bradshaw* [1956] 1 WLR 461 per Denning LJ at 466. It is for the trader to prove the term was incorporated – and the more unusual or onerous it is the harder this task is. See *Picardi v Cuniberti* [2002] EWCA 2923 QB at para 98.
[208] *Margaret Baybut v Eccle Riggs Country Park Ltd* (High Court, Manchester District Registry, 2 November 2006) (at para 10).
[209] *Alexander v West Bromwich Mortgage Company Ltd* [2016] EWCA Civ 496, paras 46–47. Here small print terms which permitted wide changes to a mortgage interest rate, which was set out in an offer document, were not incorporated.
[210] See *Rochdale Borough Council v Dixon* [2011] EWCA Civ 1173.
[211] *Director General of Fair Trading v First National Bank* [2001] UKHL 52 at para 17, *Mylcrist Builders Ltd v Mrs G Buck* [2008] EWHC 2172 (TCC), para 51(4)(b).

transparent may still be unfair if it takes advantage of the consumer's necessity or weak economic circumstances for instance.[212]

8.86 Traders should not take advantage of the fact that a consumer is not legally represented to slip unfair terms into their contracts. If a consumer would be surprised by the effect of the clause, and his notional lawyer would press for its deletion, this is indicative of a lack of fair dealing.[213] Where a term objectively serves a useful purpose, and gives real benefits to consumers who might nonetheless be adversely affected by it, it may well be fair, especially if the risk of falling foul of the term is wholly under the consumer's control. This is because the notional reasonable consumer, faced with the term in individual negotiations would be likely to have accepted it.[214] A term which is unfair in one contract, may be fair in another, where there is a fairer balancing of the interests of the parties overall.[215]

8.87 Fair dealing goes further than[216] the common law principle of an unconscionable bargain set out in *Multiservice Bookbinding Ltd v Marden*[217] under which a party will be freed from a term if it is an objectionable term imposed on them in a morally reprehensible manner. For example, where advantage is taken of a young, inexperienced or ignorant person to introduce a term which no sensible, well-advised person would have accepted.

Legal advice and process

8.88 Where a consumer is legally advised, unfair terms are not necessarily rendered fair.[218] However, in individual cases, specific legal advice on a term may prevent the consumer from showing that it is unfair, such as where:

- A wealthy individual was advised by lawyers who were able to influence the substance of the terms he was complaining about.[219]

- A transaction required the consumer to instruct a solicitor, who in fact made a careful report on the contract, drawing his specific attention to the consequences of the term, and the consumer would have the protection of

---

[212] *OFT v Ashbourne Management Services Ltd* [2011] EWHC 1237 (Ch).

[213] *OFT v Foxtons Ltd* [2009] EWHC 1681 (Ch).

[214] *Cavendish V El Makdessi, ParkingEye Ltd v Beavis* [2015] UKSC 67, paras 109 and 209. It is relevant also to consider whether the consumer is able to shop around for another supplier, and the relative strengths of the parties bargaining positions (paras 100 and 35).

[215] *Cavendish V El Makdessi, ParkingEye Ltd v Beavis* [2015] UKSC 67, para 211.

[216] An example of the breadth of the UTCCRs protection in contrast to the law on unconscionable bargain is provided by *Evans v Cherry Tree Finance* [2007] EWHC 3523 (Ch) at para 81, where it was held that a term was not unconscionable, not least because the consumer was legally represented. However, it was held that it was unfair.

[217] [1978] 2 All ER 489 at 502.

[218] *Evans v Cherry Tree Finance Ltd* [2007] EWHC 3523 (Ch) (at para 63) – where the term was so opaque that even the lawyer did not understand it.

[219] *Heifer International Inc v Christiansen* [2008] Bus LR D49.

the court in possession proceedings, which were required before the term under challenge would have effect.[220]

- A borrower was assisted by a solicitor and was dealing at arm's length with the lender of a buy to let mortgage.[221]

- The consumer, already in a dispute, was represented by solicitors, who provided advice on the merits of agreeing to submit the dispute to adjudication.[222]

8.89 By contrast, where the consumer's solicitor does not in fact point out the problems with a term, the trader is likely to be held to be acting contrary to good faith.[223] Where the term cannot have application without sanction of a court a term that potentially creates a significant imbalance may be less likely to be held to be unfair.[224]

THE GREY LIST

8.90

63 Contract terms which may or must be regarded as unfair

(1) Part 1 of Schedule 2 contains an indicative and non-exhaustive list of terms of consumer contracts that may be regarded as unfair for the purposes of this Part.

(2) Part 1 of Schedule 2 is subject to Part 2 of that Schedule; but a term listed in Part 2 of that Schedule may nevertheless be assessed for fairness under section 62 unless section 64 or 73 applies to it.

8.91 Part 1 of Sch 2 sets out a list ('the grey list') of the terms that are likely to be unfair. The list gives 'concrete form to the high level principles set out in' the fairness test.[225] The grey list also provides a base for the assessment of fairness, in considering the type of factors the court should take into account.[226] It is a 'check list of terms which must be regarded as potentially vulnerable to being unfair'[227] – and according ly terms listed there cannot benefit from the price or main subject matter exclusion.[228] The grey list is indicative but non-exhaustive. A term that appears in the list is not automatically unfair, in the same way that a term that does not appear in the list may nonetheless be regarded as unfair.[229] It is qualified by Part 2 to Sch 2, so that while these clarify that a term falling

---

[220] *UK Housing Alliance (North West) Ltd v Francis* [2010] EWCA Civ 117 at para 29. See also *Roundlistic Ltd v Jones & Seymour* [2016] UKUT 325 (LC) at para 105.
[221] *Smith v Mortgage Express* [2007] CTLC 134 at para 62, where there was held to be no lack of good faith.
[222] *Khurana v Webster Construction Ltd* [2015] EWHC 758 (TCC) at para 53(2).
[223] *Harrison v Shepherd Homes Ltd* [2011] EWHC 1811 (TCC) at para 113.
[224] *UK Housing Alliance (North West) Ltd v Francis* [2010] EWCA Civ 117 at para 24.
[225] See CJEU *Commission v Sweden* (C-478/99) AG's Opinion at paras 28–29.
[226] CJEU *Nemzeti v Invitel* (C-472/10) para 26.
[227] *Mylcrist Builders Ltd v Mrs G Buck* [2008] EWHC 2172 (TCC) at para 51(5).
[228] Section 64(6).
[229] CJEU *Freiburger* (C-237/02) at para 20. *Cavendish V El Makdessi, ParkingEye Ltd v Beavis* [2015] UKSC 67, para 105.

within their terms is not presumed to be unfair, it may still be unfair if it fails to meet the general 'requirements of good faith, balance and transparency'.[230] The CRA 2015 has added three new grey list terms – those in paras 5, 12 and 14.

8.92 The sorts of terms in the grey list can be described as relating to exclusions, one sided obligations or rights, compensation payable, lock-ins or auto rollovers, incorporation and variation of terms, dispute resolution, and assignment of rights.

SCHEDULE 2 Part 1

CONSUMER CONTRACT TERMS WHICH MAY BE REGARDED AS UNFAIR

A term which has the object or effect of –

1.   excluding or limiting the trader's liability in the event of the death of or personal injury to the consumer resulting from an act or omission of the trader. This does not include a term which is of no effect by virtue of section 65 (exclusion for negligence liability);

2.   inappropriately excluding or limiting the legal rights of the consumer in relation to the trader or another party in the event of total or partial non-performance or inadequate performance by the trader of any of the contractual obligations, including the option of offsetting a debt owed to the seller or supplier against any claim which the consumer may have against him;[231]

3.   making an agreement binding on the consumer in a case where the provision of services by the trader is subject to a condition whose realisation depends on the trader's will alone;

4.   permitting the trader to retain sums paid by the consumer where the consumer decides not to conclude or perform the contract, without providing for the consumer to receive compensation of an equivalent amount from the trader where the trader is the party cancelling the contract;

5.   requiring that, where the consumer decides not to conclude or perform the contract, the consumer must pay the trader a disproportionately high sum in compensation or for services which have not been supplied;

6.   requiring a consumer who fails to fulfil his obligations under the contract to pay a disproportionately high sum in compensation;

7.   authorising the trader to dissolve the contract on a discretionary basis where the same facility is not granted to the consumer, or permitting the trader to retain the sums paid for services not yet supplied by the trader where it is the trader who dissolves the contract;

8.   enabling the trader to terminate a contract of indeterminate duration without reasonable notice except where there are serious grounds for doing so. This is subject to paragraphs 21 (financial services) and 24 (sale of securities, foreign currency etc);[232]

---

[230]   CJEU *RWE Vertrieb AG v VBZ Nordrhein-Westfalen* (Case C-92/11) at paras 46–47. See also s 63(2), and *Peabody Trust Governors v Reeve* [2008] EWHC 1432 at para 49.
[231]   *Alfred Overy v Paypal (Europe) Ltd* [2012] EWHC 2659 (QB) at paras 259–260.
[232]   CJEU *Banco Popular Espanol* (C-537/12) at para 70.

9. automatically extending a contract of fixed duration where the consumer does not indicate otherwise, when the deadline fixed for the consumer to express his desire not to extend the contract is unreasonably early;

10. irrevocably binding the consumer to terms with which the consumer has had no real opportunity of becoming acquainted before the conclusion of the contract;

11. enabling the trader to alter the terms of the contract unilaterally without a valid reason which is specified in the contract. This is subject to paragraphs 22 (financial services), 23 (contracts which last indefinitely) and 24 (sale of securities, foreign currency etc);

12. permitting the trader to determine the characteristics of the subject matter of the contract after the consumer has become bound by it. This is subject to paragraph 23 (contracts which last indefinitely);

13. enabling the trader to alter unilaterally without a valid reason any characteristics of the goods, digital content or services to be provided;

14. giving the trader the discretion to decide the price payable under the contract after the consumer has become bound by it, where no price or method of determining the price is agreed when the consumer becomes bound. This is subject to paragraphs 23 (contracts which last indefinitely), 24 (sale of securities, foreign currency etc) and 25 (price index clauses);

15. permitting a trader to increase the price of goods, digital content or services without giving the consumer the right to cancel the contract if the final price is too high in relation to the price agreed when the contract was concluded. This is subject to paragraphs 24 (sale of securities, foreign currency etc) and 25 (price index clauses);

16. giving the trader the right to determine whether the goods, digital content or services supplied are in conformity with the contract, or giving the trader the exclusive right to interpret any term of the contract;

17. limiting the trader's obligation to respect commitments undertaken by the trader's agents or making the trader's commitments subject to compliance with a particular formality;[233]

18. obliging the consumer to fulfil all the consumer's obligations where the trader does not perform the trader's obligations;

19. allowing the trader to transfer the trader's rights and obligations under the contract, where this may reduce the guarantees for the consumer, without the consumer's agreement;

20. excluding or hindering the consumer's right to take legal action or exercise any other legal remedy, in particular by

(a) requiring the consumer to take disputes exclusively to arbitration not covered by legal provisions,

(b) unduly restricting the evidence available to the consumer, or

(c) imposing on the consumer a burden of proof which, according to the applicable law, should lie with another party to the contract.

Incorporation – concealed terms

8.93 Paragraph 10 refers to terms which have the object or effect of 'irrevocably binding the consumer to terms with which he had no real

---

[233] Entire agreement clauses, see *FSA v Asset LI Ltd* [2013] EWHC 178 (Ch).

opportunity of becoming acquainted before the conclusion of the contract'. Examples of such terms that have been held unfair include:

- A compulsory arbitration clause contained in a guarantee supplied to the consumer after they had already entered into a contract to purchase a new build house.[234]

- An obscure term connected with the early settlement of a loan, the effect of which had not been explained to the consumer.[235]

- A term making the consumer liable for all trades on their account, which was concealed in 49 pages of closely typed, complex paragraphs, and which the consumer accepted by clicking 'agree' on a website.[236]

Variation clauses

8.94 Paragraphs 11 to 15 of the grey list deal with variation of contracts. Terms which allow for variation of the terms, characteristics of the subject matter, or price cannot fall within the core exemption, and are generally likely to be unfair. All except para 13 (relating to changes to characteristics of the product) are qualified by paragraphs in Part 2 of Schedule 2, which recognises that the trader may have a legitimate interest in being able to vary the terms of service. However where a qualification applies, the term must still be assessed for fairness, unless it falls within the core exemption.[237]

8.95 The courts have laid down how variation terms should be assessed.[238]

- The reason for the variation and its method should be set out very clearly in the contract. Without this the term is likely to be unfair. It is not enough if consumers are simply informed of the variation during the life of the contract.

- The terms should be properly brought to the consumer's attention so that the consumer can examine them and appreciate the consequences. It is of 'fundamental importance' that the consumer can foresee on the basis of clear intelligible criteria, what amendments the supplier might make to the price.

- If the method of amendment is governed by mandatory statutory or regulatory provisions, or where these provisions give the consumer the right to terminate the contract, it is 'essential' that the supplier inform the consumer of these.

---

[234] *Zealander v Laing* (2000) 2 TCLR 724 at 728.
[235] *Evans v Cherry Tree Finance* [2007] EWHC 3523 (Ch) at para 66.
[236] *Spreadex v Cochrane* [2012] EWHC 1290 (Comm) para 21 – it was 'an entirely inadequate way' to make the consumer liable.
[237] *Peabody Trust Governors v Reeve* [2008] EWHC 1432 (Ch) at para 49; CJEU *RWE Vertrieb* (C-92/11) at paras 46–47.
[238] See in particular CJEU *Nemzeti v Invitel* (C-472/10) at paras 24–31 and CJEU *RWE Vertrieb AG v VBZ Nordrhein-Westfalen* (Case C-92/11) at paras 49–54.

- Where the trader exercises the right to vary, the consumer must be notified of this in good time, so that they can take the appropriate action.

- The consumer should have a right to terminate the contract, which must not be purely formal, but must be actually exercisable. The court must consider, 'whether the market concerned is competitive, the possible cost to the consumer of terminating the contract, the time between the notification and the coming into force of the new tariffs, the information provided at the time of the notification, and the cost to be borne and the time taken to change supplier'.[239] The consumer's right to cancel must be *more than illusory*. If, in the circumstances it is likely to be impracticable for the consumer to walk away then a trader's right to vary the contract is not likely to be balanced by a corresponding consumer's right to cancel.[240]

8.96 An example of an unfair term was a mortage interest variation term, permitting the bank to increase their interest to ensure the bank operates 'prudently, efficiently and competitively', where there is no obligation to reduce rates, and no provision for the borrower to exit the contract.[241] Where the contract contains a price indexation clause, this may be fair, but it is crucial that the consumer is given adequate information about its effect before concluding the contract.[242] In *Rochdale Borough Council v Dixon* it was found that a variation clause may be fair where it is set out in a statutory scheme and the variation worked in the best interests of the whole cohort of consumers. The variation must be consulted upon and consumers must have actually agreed to it.[243]

Long lock-in contracts

8.97 The new para 5 confirms that charging for services that are not in fact supplied cannot be a price term. This sort of term operates as a quasi-penalty, and its application is illustrated in *OFT v Ashbourne Management Services Ltd*,[244] where a term tying consumers to lengthy (1 to 3 year) gym contracts at 'low-end' gyms was found to be unfair. Consumers were attracted by low monthly subscriptions that were discounted from the rolling monthly membership. There was in fact little benefit to the consumer in this discount unless they remained a member for many months. The gyms were aware that many consumers stopped attending gyms after 2 or 3 months. The gyms did not highlight the risks to consumers of signing these contracts, which were, 'designed and calculated to take advantage of the naivety and inexperience of the average consumer using gym clubs at the lower end of the market'.[245]

---

[239] CJEU *RWE Vertrieb AG v VBZ Nordrhein-Westfalen* (Case C-92/11) at para 54.
[240] *Peabody Trust Governors v Reeve* [2008] EWHC 1432 (Ch) at para 57.
[241] *Firstplus Financial Group Plc v Murphy & Dye* (Woolwich County Court, 17 October 2013) at paras 15–18.
[242] EFTA *Gunnar Engilbertsson v Islandsbanki* (E-25/13) at para 141.
[243] *Rochdale Borough Council v Dixon* [2011] EWCA Civ 1173 at para 68. See also *Du Plessis v Fontgary Leisure Parks Ltd* [2012] EWCA Civ 409 at paras 47–54.
[244] [2011] EWHC 1237 (Ch).
[245] See paras 162–174.

Penalties

8.98 Paragraph 6 presumes terms to be unfair which require 'any consumer who fails to fulfil his obligation to pay a disproportionately high sum in compensation'. This is essentially to prevent a trader benefiting financially from the consumer's breach. This concept is wider than the common law rule that a secondary obligation is void, where it imposes detriment out of all proportion to the legitimate interest of the innocent party in the enforcement of the obligation.[246]

8.99 In assessing the imbalance created by a term, the cumulative effect of all the terms which could adversely affect the consumer must be assessed, whether or not they are actually invoked by the trader.[247] In general, when assessing unfairness, the courts have considered whether the consumer received a particular benefit in exchange, whether the sum in question is high compared to other market rates,[248] whether it has a surprising impact on the substance of the bargain, whether similar terms are commonly used elsewhere, and whether the term defends a legitimate primary obligation in a proportionate way.[249] It is also important to consider whether the rights of the trader, in the event of breach by the consumer, is proportionate to the breach, if it derogates from a rule of law, and whether the consumer has adequate and effective means under the law to remedy the matter – or whether in fact the term makes it harder for the consumer to exercise his rights.[250]

8.100 The courts will consider the reality of the situation, rather than the form, for example where a price escalation clause is used.[251] A requirement that a consumer pay an early repayment sum based on 6 months of repayments under an already expensive loan was held to be unfair as a disproportionately high sum in compensation.[252]

---

[246] See *Cavendish v El Makdessi, ParkingEye Ltd v Beavis* [2015] UKSC 67, paras 32 and 100 for a summary of the current law on penalties at Common Law, and paras 207 and 309 for the proposition that unfair terms is in principle wider than the rule against penalties. See also *Munkenbeck v Harold* [2005] EWHC 356 at para 16, sum that was not a penalty was still unfair.

[247] CJEU *Radlinger v Finway* (C-377/14), para 95.

[248] *Smith v Mortgage Express* [2007] CTLC 134 at paras 35 and 66–67.

[249] *Director General of Fair Trading v First National Bank* [2001] UKHL 52 at paras 20–24, per Lord Bingham and paras 55–56 per Lord Millett. See also *Parking Eye v Beavis* [2015] EWCA Civ 402 at paras 36–39 and *Cavendish v El Makdessi, ParkingEye Ltd v Beavis* [2015] UKSC 67, para 109.

[250] *Mohamed Aziz v Caixa d'Esalvis de Catalunya* (C-415/11) at paras 73–75 and *Cavendish v El Makdessi, ParkingEye Ltd v Beavis* [2015] UKSC 67, paras 108–111. In some situations it will be important for a penalty to make allowances for circumstances, such as to avoid penalising the disabled, or to build in a grace period before it kicks in, and to be appealable, see the dissenting judgment of Lord Toulson at paras 310–311 and the acknowledgement of the relevance of a binding Code of Practice which provided certain protections at paras 100 and 111 of the main judgment.

[251] *Bairstow Eves v Smith* [2004] EWHC 263 QB.

[252] *Evans v Cherry Tree Finance* [2007] EWHC 3523 (Ch) para 66.

DISPUTE RESOLUTION

8.101 In cases where the trader wishes to reserve the right of unilateral determination, the court must assess whether the term derogates from the rules that would otherwise apply, and whether this makes it more difficult for the consumer, given the procedural means at his disposal, to take legal action and exercise rights of defence.[253]

Jurisdiction and applicable law clauses

8.102 Where a consumer contract, with a close connection with the UK, is governed by the law of a non EEA state, s 74(1) nonetheless gives UK courts the power to rule that any of its terms are unfair. This could include ruling that the jurisdiction clause itself is unfair. The courts are generally suspicious of terms that require a consumer to submit to an overseas jurisdiction. This is consistent with the policy of the Brussels Regulation concerning the forum for civil litigation. In *Pannon* it was suggested that such a term is likely to be unfair.[254] In *Oceano Groupo* the CJEU appeared to go further suggesting that such a term is *necessarily* unfair[255] because:

- It may be too far for the consumer to travel to enter an appearance conveniently.

- If the dispute is for a small sum it may be disproportionately costly for the consumer to attend.

- This sort of term has the object or effect of excluding or hindering the consumer's right to take legal action, as set out in para 20 of the grey list.

- By contrast, this sort of term enables the trader to deal with all the litigation relating to his trade in one court, and makes it less onerous for him to enter an appearance.

8.103 In *Standard Bank London Ltd v Apostolakis (No 2)*,[256] the test in *Oceano Group* was applied to an investment contract entered into by a Greek consumer, under which disputes had to be settled in the courts of England and Wales. This was held to be unfair on the basis of the cost and inconvenience suffered by the consumer. The proceedings would be conducted in a language foreign to the consumer. The term also permitted the consumer to be sued in many different countries; however, the trader could only be sued in England. Finally, the impact of the jurisdiction clause was not carefully explained or even translated for the consumer.

8.104 This position is slightly different to applicable law clauses, which are effectively blacklisted by s 74(1) if the applicable law is that of a non EEA state, but where the law applied to the contract is that of another EEA state, it may

---

[253] *Mohamed Aziz v Caixa d'Estalvis* (C-415/11) para 75.
[254] *Pannon* (C-243/08) para 40.
[255] CJEU *Oceano Groupo* para 22 and CJEU *VB Penzugyi* (C-137/08), para 54.
[256] [2002] CLC 939 at paras 49–51.

still be fair, unless the term has the effect of depriving the consumer of statutory protections they would have enjoyed had their own law applied.[257] According to the CJEU such a choice of law clause will be unfair where it is not in plain intelligible language, or where the contract fails to inform the consumer of the mandatory statutory provisions that they still enjoy under their own law, notwithstanding the choice of law clause.[258] Such mandatory statutory provisions are all those which cannot be derogated from by agreement, and include provisions transposing the Unfair Terms Directive, which provide a higher standard of protection for the consumer.[259] It would appear from the CJEU decision that a merely general statement along the lines of 'statutory rights are not affected' would not be sufficient – the actual legal provisions must be set out.[260]

Arbitration clauses

8.105 Paragraph 20 is likely also to apply to arbitration clauses. Such clauses may also be unfair because the arbitration process may be expensive and disproportionate to the size of the sum in dispute, not be able to resolve all matters in dispute, and prevent the consumer from taking legal action.[261] Even where the fact that arbitration will apply to the contract is explained, and the consumer is given information on the likely consequences of this, the term may still be unfair.[262] Where an arbitration scheme is statutory it is not presumed to be unfair.[263]

8.106 There are two types of arbitration clause that are blacklisted by other legislation.

Regulation 14B of the Alternative Dispute Resolution for Consumer Disputes (Competent Authorities and Information) Regulations 2015[264] provides that an agreement to submit to ADR is not binding on the consumer if (a) it is concluded before the dispute materialised, and (b) it deprives the consumer of access to court.[265]

8.107 Section 91(1) of the Arbitration Act 1996 provides that:

---

[257] CJEU *VFK v Amazon* (C-191/15), paras 59 and 66.

[258] CJEU *VFK v Amazon* (C-191/15), paras 68 and 69.

[259] CJEU *VFK v Amazon* (C-191/15), paras 70 and 59.

[260] CJEU *VFK v Amazon* (C-191/15), para 69 and CJEU *Invitel* (C-472/10), para 29.

[261] See *Khurana v Webster Construction Ltd* [2015] EWHC 758 (TCC) at para 53(5).

[262] CJEU *Katalin Sebastyen* (C-342/13) at paras 34–36.

[263] See *Zealander v Laing* (2000) 2 TCLR 724 at 729 and *Mylcrist v Buck* at para 54. However, see also CJEU *Asturcom v Nogueira* (C-40/08) at paras 38, 46, 53.

[264] SI 2015/542.

[265] This does not cast doubt over the fairness of adjudication clauses – which may have been held to be fair, as in *Domsalla v Dyason* [2007] EWHC 1174 (TCC) at para 92, on the basis that they offer a 'rapid, cheap and temporary legal process which determines the parties' rights'.

'a term which constitutes an arbitration agreement is unfair for the purposes of the [CRA 2015 Part 2] so far as it relates to a claim for pecuniary remedy which does not exceed the amount specified by order for the purposes of this section.'[266]

8.108 That amount is currently £5,000, such that a clause that referred to arbitration any claim for less than that amount would be automatically unfair.[267] A clause referring a claim of greater than £5,000 may still be unfair.[268] If a consumer is represented by a competent agent, or otherwise requests an arbitration clause, it is unlikely to be unfair.[269] Likewise an agreement to submit to arbitration or adjudication *after* the dispute has arisen is not necessarily unfair.[270]

CONSEQUENCES OF UNFAIRNESS

8.109

62 Requirement for contract terms and notices to be fair

(1) An unfair term of a consumer contract is not binding on the consumer.

(2) An unfair consumer notice is not binding on the consumer.

(3) This does not prevent the consumer from relying on the term or notice if the consumer chooses to do so.

67 Effect of an unfair term on the rest of a contract

Where a term of a consumer contract is not binding on the consumer as a result of this Part, the contract continues, so far as practicable, to have effect in every other respect.

A term or notice that is held to be unfair is not binding on the consumer.[271] The consumer may rely on it if they so choose.[272] Traders remain bound by their

---

[266] SI 1999/2167 sets this at £5,000 as does the corresponding SI for Northern Ireland (SI 2005/219).

[267] In the High Court case of *Mylcrist Builders Ltd v Mrs G Buck* [2008] EWHC 2172 (TCC), it was held that the £5,000 includes VAT, on the basis that on its ordinary meaning 'a pecuniary remedy would relate to the whole of the monetary claim which would include VAT' (para 35).

[268] See *Mylcrist Builders Ltd v Mrs G Buck* [2008] EWHC 2172 (TCC) (see paras 54–59); *Zealander v Laing* (2000) 2 TCLR 724; and *Picardi v Cuniberti* [2002] EWHC 2923 QB at para 131.

[269] *Heifer International Inc v Christiansen* [2008] Bus LR D49; *Westminster Building Co Ltd v Beckingham* [2004] EWHC 138 (TCC).

[270] *Khurana v Webster Construction Ltd* [2015] EWHC 758 (TCC) at para 53. In this case parties already in dispute and advised by solicitors agreed to refer the matter to adjudication.

[271] CRA 2015, s 62(1) and (2). This is a fundamental objective of the Directive, and a duty on the Member States. See *Banco Espanol de Credito* (C-618/10) at paras 61–62. CJEU *Asbeek Brusse v Jahani BV* (C-488/11) at para 51 where a term is found to be unfair, the court must annul it. Compensation is not in itself sufficient remedy – CJEU *Banco Popular Espanol* (C-537/12) at para 56.

[272] CRA 2015, s 62(3). See CJEU *Sinues v Caixabank SA* (C-381/14) para 25.

contracts even if this causes them hardship.[273] The term must not be modified and the contract must continue in existence even if this creates disadvantages for the trader.[274] The Directive has a deterrent purpose and otherwise traders might be tempted to try their luck by including unfair terms, in the hope that the court modifies them.[275] In *Spreadex v Cochrane*,[276] it was observed that:

> 'Importantly the Regulations do not operate by precluding reliance on the contractual term in cases where it would be unfair to do so. Their proscription is absolute and binary: the term is either unfair and hence unenforceable, or not.'[277]

8.110 Equally, the contract should continue to bind the consumer if it is capable of so doing, absent the impugned term(s).[278] However, where the deletion of the term would expose the consumer to particularly unfavourable consequences (eg a loan gets called in at once), such that the dissuasive effect resulting from annulment of the term might be jeopardised, the court may substitute a provision from national law (and in the UK this might require implying a term).[279] Where a consumer has paid money under a term, subsequently found to be unfair, that money appears to be recoverable, as money paid under a mistake of law.[280] In *OFT v Ashbourne Management Services Ltd*,[281] it was held that including unfair terms in agreements and

---

[273] CRA 2015, s 67 – 'the contract continues, so far as practicable, to have effect in every other respect.'

[274] See CJEU *Asbeek Brusse v Jahani BV* (C-488/11) at para 59 – the court cannot reduce an unfair penalty sum, but must exclude it completely. It may be appropriate to sever only part of a clause –see *Bankers Insurance Company Ltd v South* [2003] EWHC 380 at para 35 – but the court must ensure it excludes all unfair terms and not merely some of them – CJEU *Radlinger v Finway* (C-377/14) para 100.

[275] *Banco Espanol de Credito* (C-618/10) at paras 64–66 and 69. This ruling must be borne in mind when reading the judgments in *OFT v Foxtons Ltd* [2009] EWCA Civ 288. It was suggested there that a judge could give an injunction to stop the use of a term in specific circumstances (see paras 73 and 98). It seems rather that if a term is found to be unfair, its use must be prohibited in all circumstances. It is only when the court considers the position of *similar* terms, that it may be possible to rule that such terms are only unfair in certain given circumstances (see the judgment of Waller LJ at para 49.

[276] [2012] EWHC 1290 (Comm) at para 19.

[277] See also the 7th recital and *Perenicova* (C-453/10) para 32 and AG's Opinion paras 66–68.

[278] CJEU *Perenicova* (C-453/10) at paras 31–32 and 34–36 – the fact that the consumer may benefit from the contract ending is not sufficient reason to terminate it.

[279] CJEU *Kasler* (C-26/13) at paras 81–84.

[280] This principle was set out in *Kleinwort Benson v Lincoln City Council* [1998] 1 All ER 513, and applied in an unfair terms context in *Chesterton v Finney* (Lambeth County Court). The High Court has also accepted this is the consequence of unfairness – see *Re Welcome Financial Services Ltd* [2015] EWHC 815 (Ch) at para 106. Such an outcome was also envisaged by the CJEU in *Alexandra Schulz* (C-359/11) at para 55, however the precise consequences of unfairness have not been harmonised at EU level, meaning that the remedy simply has to be no less favourable than under domestic law, and sufficiently effective – CJEU *Sinues v Caixabank SA* (C-381/14) para 32. This position appears likely to be further confirmed by the CJEU in Joined cases C-307/15 and C-308/15 *Palacios Martinez* and C-154/15 *Gutierrez Naranjo*. The AG's opinion has suggested that the question of repayment of money is a matter for Member States, and in principle, in extreme cases, a court could restrict the temporal effect of its judgment so that no money already paid over is returned.

[281] [2011] EWHC 1237 (Ch) at para 227.

enforcing them also amounted to an infringement of the CPUTR (see Chapter 7, Unfair Commercial Practices).

ASSESSMENT OF THE COURT'S OWN MOTION

8.111

71 Duty of court to consider fairness of term

(1) Subsection (2) applies to proceedings before a court which relate to a term of a consumer contract.

(2) The court must consider whether the term is fair even if none of the parties to the proceedings has raised that issue or indicated that it intends to raise it.

(3) But subsection (2) does not apply unless the court considers that it has before it sufficient legal and factual material to enable it to consider the fairness of the term.

A court must assess the fairness of terms even if no party raises the issue.[282] This is so even where the court is dealing with the matter on appeal, and unfairness was not raised in the court below.[283] The Directive seeks to re-establish substantive equality between the parties. A consumer is in a weaker bargaining position and may agree to terms he cannot influence.[284] That imbalance may need to be corrected by positive action. If a consumer was required to raise the issue of unfairness himself, in order for him to receive the protection the Directive intends, the aim of Art 6 would not be achieved, in particular because the consumer may not be able or willing to challenge the term.[285]

8.112   Where the court considers that a term is unfair, it should invite each of the parties to set out their views on the matter (in order to ensure each has the chance to be heard), but it should not need to wait for the consumer to request the term be declared invalid.[286]

---

[282]   CRA 2015, s 71(2) – subject to the court having the necessary legal and factual material before it to do so (s 71(3)). See CJEU *VB Penzugyi* (C-137/08) at paras 46–49. Courts must also construe legislation to give effect to the Directive (CJEU *Oceano Groupo* at para 32), and assess whether any limitation periods are so short as to render the exercise of consumer rights excessively difficult (CJEU *Asturcom v Nogueira* (C-40/08) at paras 41–42).

[283]   CJEU *Erika Joros v Aegon* (C-397/11).

[284]   The obligation to ensure consumers are not bound by unfair terms may extend to officials, such as notaries, who draft official contracts, meaning that they must advise the consumer as to any doubts he has over the fairness of the terms – CJEU *ERSTE Bank Hungary Zrt v Sugar* (C-32/14) paras 54–58). However, such officials are not obliged to refuse to enforce a potentially unfair term, where the consumer still has recourse to a court – CJEU *ERSTE Bank Hungary Zrt v Sugar* (C-32/14) paras 62–65.

[285]   *Pannon* (C-243/08) at paras 23, 28 and 32; *Mostaza Claro* (C-168/05) at para 39; CJEU *VB Penzugyi* (C-137/08) at paras 49–52; and *Banco Espanol de Credito* (C-618/10) at para 54.

[286]   CJEU *Banif Plus Bank Zrt v Csaba Csipai* (C-472/11) at paras 28–36.

PROCEDURAL RULES

8.113 Procedural rules that prevent the court from assessing fairness, where it has the legal and factual elements necessary to do so, or which otherwise prevent consumers from asserting that a term is unfair, are liable to undermine the effectiveness of the Directive, and so fall foul of EU law.[287]

8.114 In line with the principle of legal certainty, there is a very high threshold for courts to limit the temporal effect of their judgment so that it does not apply to existing contracts, or only applies after a period of time.[288] Similarly the existence of a Scheme of Arrangement made under the Companies Act 2006 does not require consumers who have been subjected to unfair penalties to claim as creditors under the Scheme – they are still able to claim restitution.[289]

8.115 Limitation periods may frustrate the purpose of the Directive if the consumer is time barred from asserting that terms are unfair when a contract is still enforceable by the trader.[290] Likewise, rules which require individual challenges to be stayed pending the outcome of a collective challenge, are liable to be unlawful.[291] However Member States remain free to organise their court processes as they wish, and are not required to create processes that make it especially cheap or easy for consumers (or consumer associations) to challenge terms.[292]

Injunctions

8.116 Section 70 and Sch 3 allow certain regulators[293] to obtain injunctions against any person appearing to be using, proposing or recommending use of a term or notice that is unfair, blacklisted under the CRA 2015, or not transparent.[294] The court may grant an injunction (or interdict in Scotland) against the term or notice under challenge, or against any term or notice of

---

[287] *Banco Espanol de Credito* (C-618/10) at paras 52–53; CJEU *BBVA SA v Pedro Penalva Lopez* (C-8/14) paras 39–41 – where a transitional provision that reasonably allowed consumers to raise an unfairness argument for the first time was struck down because it did not require those consumers to be notified individually of their right.

[288] CJEU *Alexandra Schulz* (C-359/11) at paras 54–64.

[289] *Re Welcome Financial Services Ltd* [2015] EWHC 815 (Ch) at para 106.This is consistent with the CJEU's position in *Radlinger v Finway* (C-377/14) paras 51–59, where consumers must in insolvency proceedings also be able to challenge unfair terms as a shield.

[290] CJEU *Cofidis v Fredout* (C-473/00) at paras 35–37. However, this does not permit actions to be raised indefinitely – limitation of actions can still apply, particularly if the consumer has not appealed a decision, because of the important principle of *res judicata* – CJEU *Asturcom v Nogueira* (C-40/08) at paras 36–37 and 47.

[291] CJEU *Sinues v Caixabank SA* (C-381/14) paras 27–39.

[292] As long as the principles of equivalence and effectiveness are satisfied – CJEU *Nora Baczo* (C-567/13) at paras 39–59; CJEU *Asociacion de Consumidores Independientes de Castilla y Leon* (C-413/12) at paras 30–45.

[293] Listed in Sch 3, para 8.

[294] See Sch 3, para 3. This does not oblige the courts to permit consumer associations or other enforcers to intervene as of right in individual challenges however – see CJEU *Pohotovost' s.r.o.* (C-470/12) at paras 53–57.

similar kind or with a similar effect.[295] It may be granted in very broad terms.[296] 'Use' of an unfair term covers not just including it in a contract, but also enforcing it in contracts already agreed with consumers.[297] 'Enforcing' includes any reliance on a term, such as demands for payment, letters invoking its existence, or any action, which refers to the unfair term.[298] The trader need not be the person who has actually entered into the contract with the consumer, but may be for example the contracting trader's agent, or another person invoking the term.[299] In addition to seeking an injunction, an enforcer is also entitled to obtain a declaration as to the unfairness of a term – which could be relied on by other persons.[300]

8.117 In order to bring a matter to court, the enforcer need not have received any complaints, and the terms need not even have been used in any actual contracts.[301]

Collective challenges

8.118 Regulator action (a 'collective challenge') is a more effective way of preventing the continuing use of unfair terms, and of changing contracting practice, than individual challenges.[302] In a collective challenge the unfair character of a term is assessed _in abstracto_ bearing in mind it may be incorporated in contracts that have not yet been concluded.[303]

8.119 Although the meaning of a contract must be given the most favourable interpretation to consumers in an individual challenge, this rule of interpretation does not apply in the context of a collective challenge.[304] The term under challenge must therefore be given the reading _least_ favourable to the consumer, since this has the effect of achieving a result that brings about the most favourable result for consumers as a whole.[305] The CJEU has held that this is a 'binding legislative provision which confers rights on consumers, and assists in determining the result which the Directive seeks to achieve'.[306]

---

[295] Sch 3, para 5(3). This includes interim injunction or interdict – Sch 3, para 9.
[296] Sch 3, para 5(1) and (2). The enforcement power is required to discharge the UK's obligations under the Directive – see _OFT v Foxtons Ltd_ [2009] EWCA Civ 288 at para 42.
[297] CJEU _Nemzeti v Invitel_ (C-472/10) at para 43. A challenge may also be brought against terms not yet in use – CJEU _Commission v Italy_ (C-372/99) at para 15 and _Oceano Groupo_ (C-240/98) at para 27.
[298] _OFT v Foxtons Ltd_ [2009] EWCA Civ 288 at para 47.
[299] _OFT v Ashbourne Management Services Ltd._
[300] _OFT v Foxtons Ltd_ [2009] EWCA Civ 288 at paras 59–61.
[301] Schedule 3, para 3(6), CJEU _Sinues v Caixabank SA_ (C-381/14) para 29.
[302] _Director General of Fair Trading v First National Bank_ [2001] UKHL 52, per Lord Steyn at para 33.
[303] CJEU _Commission v Spain_ (C-70/03) para 16.
[304] Art 5 and s 69(2).
[305] CJEU _Commission v Spain_ (C-70/03) para 16.
[306] CJEU _Commission v Spain_ (C-70/03) para 17.

8.120 It is not a defence to a collective challenge that the term could not be enforced due to a rule of law.[307] In a collective challenge, 'it is necessary to consider the position of typical parties when the contract is made'.[308] It is simply assumed that the consumer is in a much weaker bargaining position than a large trader contracting on its own standard form.[309]

8.121 A 'typical consumer' test may be useful in determining the factual basis on which a term's fairness should be assessed in the context of a collective challenge.[310] It has also been used to assess whether a term is in plain intelligible language.[311] However, the Supreme Court has disapproved of its use to identify the price or main subject matter for the purpose of the s 64 exception, finding it was an overly complex addition to what should be an objective test.[312]

8.122 The fact that a collective challenge is being brought must not prevent individual consumers from asserting their rights as individuals, sine this would contravene the principle of effectiveness.[313] An individual challenge may still be brought if a collective challenge has failed, although the consumer would need to demonstrate why his case was different, drawing on the individual circumstances of their situation.[314] Where a term is found to be unfair in a collective challenge, it is unfair for all purposes and in all circumstances.[315] This could have an impact on traders using the term, who are not before the

---

[307] Sch 3, para 5(4). As seen above, this factor may be relevant in an individual challenge.

[308] *Director General of Fair Trading v First National Bank* [2001] UKHL 52, per Lord Bingham at para 20. The court has to have regard to 'contemplated or typical relationships between parties' in order to assess any 'substantive unfairness' – per Lord Steyn at para 33.

[309] *Director General of Fair Trading v First National Bank* [2001] UKHL 52, per Lord Bingham at para 13. There will be little attention paid to factors relevant to individual situations, such as whether the consumer had an inducement to agree to the term, or whether the product was sold or supplied to the special order of the consumer.

[310] As in *OFT v Ashbourne Management Services Ltd* [2011] EWHC 1237 (Ch) at para 128.

[311] *OFT v Abbey National* [2008] EWHC 875 and *OFT v Foxtons Ltd* [2009] EWHC 1681 – where it was held that It does not attempt to understand the 'mindset, thinking or attributes' of a typical consumer (at para 34).

[312] *OFT v Abbey National* [2009] UKSC 6 per Lord Mance at paras 108 and 113.

[313] CJEU *Sinues v Caixabank SA* (C-381/14) para 36–40. This also means that individual challenges must not be stayed for administrative reasons to avoid overburdening the court system (para 42).

[314] CJEU *Sinues v Caixabank SA* (C-381/14) para 40, *OFT v Foxtons Ltd* [2009] EWCA Civ 288 at para 46.

[315] CJEU *Nemzeti v Invitel* (C-472/10) para 43, *Commission v Spain* (C-70/03), para 16. See also the AG's Opinion paras 12 and 13, where he states that where in a collective challenge, a term is found to be unfair, its continued use must be prevented. The CJEU therefore supports the position of Waller LJ in *OFT v Foxtons Ltd* [2009] EWCA Civ 288 at para 47, rather than that of Moore-Bick LJ at para 98. However, this does not prevent consumers from submitting to a term, if they wish – CJEU *Sinues v Caixabank SA* (C-381/14) para 25.

court.[316] It is also a finding that the term is and always has been unfair – which could lead to serious financial consequences for those traders who have been relying on it.[317]

8.123 Where an enforcer wishes to bring proceedings against a trader operating from elsewhere in the EEA, who is directing their activities towards UK consumers, the law that applies to this challenge will be determined under the Rome II Regulation on non-contractual obligations –this is because use of an unfair term is a harmful as a tortious act. Therefore the enforcer may act under Part 8 of the Enterprise Act 2002 or Schedule 3 of the Consumer Rights Act 2015.[318] However the law that applies to the assessment of the fairness of the term will be determined under the Rome I Regulation on contractual relations.[319] This is the same as where a challenge is brought by an individual. The result is that where a choice of law clause validly applies the law of another EEA state, the assessment of fairness may have to be made under the law of that state, rather than of the UK.

8.124 Schedule 3 should be read alongside the enforcement provisions in Part 8 of the Enterprise Act 2002 (see Chapter 4, Civil Enforcement), and the Enhanced Consumer measures in Sch 7 to the CRA 2015 (see Chapter 4, Civil Enforcement).

---

[316] CJEU *Nemzeti v Invitel* (C-472/10) para 38, *Director General of Fair Trading v First National Bank* [2001] UKHL 52 at para 9. This appears also to be contemplated by Sch 3, para 5(3)(b).
[317] CJEU *RWE Vertrieb v VBZ Nordrhein Westfalen* (C-92/11) para 58.
[318] CJEU *VFK v Amazon* (C-191/15), paras 39–48.
[319] CJEU *VFK v Amazon* (C-191/15), para 49.

CHAPTER 9

FRAUD AND MONEY LAUNDERING

CONTENTS

THE FRAUD ACT 2006

Introduction

9.1 In *Reddaway v Banham*,[1] Lord MacNaghten stated:

> 'Fraud is infinite in variety, sometimes it is audacious and unblushing; sometimes it pays a sort of homage to virtue, and then it is modest and retiring; it would be honesty itself if it could only afford it.'

9.2 English criminal law did not include a general offence of 'fraud' until the Fraud Act 2006 ('FA 2006') was introduced. The Act is mainly based on the Law Commission report on fraud, which concluded that the deception offences in the Theft Act 1968 were too specific, overlapping and outdated. In its post-legislative assessment of the FA 2006 published in June 2012 the Ministry of Justice stated: 'Our overall assessment of the Act is that it has been successful in achieving its initial objectives of modernising the former array of deception offences.'

The Act repealed the following Theft Act 1968 offences:

- s 15 (obtaining property by deception);
- s 15A (obtaining a money transfer by deception);
- s 16 (obtaining pecuniary advantage by deception);
- s 20(2) (procuring the execution of a valuable security by deception).

It also amended s 25 of the Theft Act 1968 (going equipped for burglary, theft or cheat) by removing references to 'cheat'. The FA 2006 came into force on 15 January 2007 in England, Wales and Northern Ireland.[2]

Scotland

9.3 The FA 2006 does not apply in Scotland, other than s 10, which increases the maximum sentence for fraudulent trading by a company to 10 years. However, Scotland has the common law crime of fraud, committed when someone achieves a practical result by a false pretence. A reasonable working definition of fraud in Scotland might be:

> 'Fraud consists of a false pretence made to another person in the knowledge of its falsity and with the intention that the other person should be deceived by it into acting in a way which s/he would not otherwise have acted, provided that the other person is so deceived and does act on account of it.'

A particular form of fraud in Scotland is 'Uttering' – which occurs where a forged document (or instrument) is passed off as real and has a prejudicial effect on another person.

---

[1] [1896] AC 199.
[2] Fraud Act 2006 (Commencement Order) 2006, SI 2006/3200.

Fraud offences

9.4   Under s 1 an offence is committed if a person acts dishonestly and breaches any of the three different ways of committing the offence of fraud: by false representation, by failing to disclose information or by abuse of position.

1 Fraud

(1) A person is guilty of fraud if he is in breach of any of the sections listed in subsection (2) (which provide for different ways of committing the offence).

(2) The sections are –

> (a)   section 2 (fraud by false representation),
> (b)   section 3 (fraud by failing to disclose information), and
> (c)   section 4 (fraud by abuse of position).

A person who is guilty of an offence under s 1 is liable:

(a)   on summary conviction, to imprisonment for a term not exceeding 12 months or to a fine (or to both);

(b)   on conviction on indictment, to imprisonment for a term not exceeding 10 years or to a fine (or to both).

Section 2 (fraud by false representation)

9.5

2 Fraud by false representation

(1) A person is in breach of this section if he –

> (a)   dishonestly makes a false representation, and
> (b)   intends, by making the representation –
> > (i)   to make a gain for himself or another, or
> > (ii)   to cause loss to another or to expose another to a risk of loss.

(2) A representation is false if –

> (a)   it is untrue or misleading, and
> (b)   the person making it knows that it is, or might be, untrue or misleading.

(3) "Representation" means any representation as to fact or law, including a representation as to the state of mind of –

> (a)   the person making the representation, or
> (b)   any other person.

(4) A representation may be express or implied.

(5) For the purposes of this section a representation may be regarded as made if it (or anything implying it) is submitted in any form to any system or device designed to receive, convey or respond to communications (with or without human intervention).

9.6   A representation is defined as false if it is untrue or misleading and the person making it knows that it is, *or might be*, untrue or misleading. It makes no difference if the representation is made to a machine or to a person. A representation may be express or implied; it can be stated in words or communicated by conduct or by omission. There is no limitation on the way in which the representation must be expressed. It could be written, spoken or posted on a website.

9.7   *R v Vig (Deekan)*[3] provides an example of an implied representation. The defendant gave driving lessons using a car with dual pedals and showed pupils documents suggesting he was insured as a driving instructor. He was not a qualified driving instructor and was convicted of fraud under s 2 FA 2006. In rejecting his appeal against conviction the Court of Appeal stated:

> '... in our judgment ... We do not accept that it had to be shown that the applicant represented himself specifically or expressly as [a driving instructor] only that the implicit representations which were proved amounted in substance to that.'

9.8   In *R v Greig*[4] the defendants had done gardening work at the home of a vulnerable elderly consumer who was easily confused. The value of the work was £300, however, the defendants had charged the consumer £6,850, which he paid in three cheques. The defendants were convicted of fraud by from the implicit representation that the amounts they had charged 'represented fair payment for gardening work'. The Court of Appeal upheld their convictions.

9.9   In *R v Silverman*,[5] it was said that the question of whether a trader has made a false representation in relation to quotations for work or services would always depend on the circumstances. Consumers often rely on tradesmen to act fairly and reasonably towards them. A false representation might be made if a grossly excessive price was charged when there was a relationship of trust between the consumer and tradesmen, even if no pressure to accept the price had been applied by the tradesman.

9.10   The representation must be made dishonestly. The definition of dishonesty was established in *R v Ghosh*.[6] In determining whether the accused had acted dishonestly the questions are:

(i)   whether the accused's actions had been dishonest according to the ordinary standards of reasonable and honest people; and, if so

(ii)   whether the accused himself had realised that his actions were, according to those standards, dishonest.

---

3   [2010] EWCA Crim 2245.
4   [2010] EWCA Crim 1183.
5   86 Cr App R 213, CA.
6   [1982] QB 1053.

A genuine belief by the accused that he was morally justified in acting as he did is no defence if he knew that ordinary people would consider such conduct to be dishonest. The Court of Appeal, in *R v Cornelius*[7] made clear that the decision in *Ghosh* remains good law.

9.11 In *R v Hayes*[8] it was made clear that the objective (first) limb of the test must not be modified to reflect the standards of a particular market or group of traders. However, the context in which a trader is working may be relevant to the subjective (second) limb of the test.

9.12 The person must make the representation with the intention of making a gain or causing loss or risk of loss to another. It is not necessary to prove an actual gain or loss. Section 5 defines 'gain' and 'loss' in the same way as s 34(2)(a) of the Theft Act 1968:

> **5 'Gain' and 'loss'**
>
> (2) 'Gain' and 'loss' –
>
> > (a) extend only to gain or loss in money or other property;
> >
> > (b) include any such gain or loss whether temporary or permanent;
>
> and 'property' means any property whether real or personal (including things in action and other intangible property).
>
> (3) 'Gain' includes a gain by keeping what one has, as well as a gain by getting what one does not have.
>
> (4) 'Loss' includes a loss by not getting what one might get, as well as a loss by parting with what one has.

9.13 It is a matter for the decision-maker, on the facts of each case, whether the causative link between the intention and the making of the false representation, required by the section, is established, *R v Gilbert (Stephanie Rae)*.[9] Unlike its predecessor, s 15 of the Theft Act 1968, it is no longer necessary to prove that any victim was actually deceived by the defendant's behaviour. In *R v Lee*[10] the defendant was an itinerant seller of misdescribed upholstered furniture who would say 'practically anything' to ensure a sale. The Court of Appeal rejected his appeal against conviction on the grounds that there was no evidence of reliance on his false statements.

9.14 A single offence under s 1 may sometimes be charged where numerous false representations are made. In *R v Downing*[11] the defendant pleaded guilty to one offence of fraud covering 47 false claims for payment. In *R (on the application of Burns) v Woolwich Crown Court*[12] the single offence involved persuading a 76-year-old man that his property was in urgent need of repair

---

7 [2012] EWCA Crim 500.
8 [2015] EWCA Crim 1944.
9 [2012] EWCA Crim 2392.
10 [2010] EWCA Crim 268.
11 [2010] EWCA Crim 739.
12 [2010] EWHC 129 (Admin).

and obtaining three banker's drafts totalling £140,000 from him. The offence was said to have taken place over 3 months and reflected the cumulative effect of false representations made on different occasions.

Section 3 (fraud by failing to disclose information)

9.15

> **3 Fraud by failing to disclose information**
>
> A person is in breach of this section if he –
>
> (a)   dishonestly fails to disclose to another person information which he is under a legal duty to disclose, and
> (b)   intends, by failing to disclose the information –
>   (i)   to make a gain for himself or another, or
>   (ii)   to cause loss to another or to expose another to a risk of loss.

The section is apparently not limited to *statutory or regulatory* disclosure obligations. A legal duty to disclose information may include duties under oral contracts as well as written contracts.

9.16   The Law Commission's Report on Fraud explained the concept of 'legal duty' in the following terms:

> '7.28 Such a duty may derive from statute (such as the provisions governing company prospectuses), from the fact that the transaction in question is one of the utmost good faith (such as a contract of insurance), from the express or implied terms of a contract, from the custom of a particular trade or market, or from the existence of a fiduciary relationship between the parties (such as that of agent and principal).

> 7.29 For this purpose there is a legal duty to disclose information not only if the defendant's failure to disclose it gives the victim a cause of action for damages, but also if the law gives the victim a right to set aside any change in his or her legal position to which he or she may consent as a result of the non-disclosure. For example, a person in a fiduciary position has a duty to disclose material information when entering into a contract with his or her beneficiary, in the sense that a failure to make such disclosure will entitle the beneficiary to rescind the contract and to reclaim any property transferred under it.'

9.17   In *R v Razoq (Adil)*,[13] Hallett LJ said:

> 'The Fraud Act contains no definition as to what constitutes a legal duty. The question is one of law for the judge who should then direct the jury that if they find certain facts proved they could conclude that a duty to disclose existed in all the circumstances.'

---

13   [2012] EWCA Crim 674.

9.18 It follows that the repeated non-provision of cancellation notices under the Consumer Contracts (Information, Cancellation and Additional Charges) Regulations 2013[14] may constitute a breach of s 3. A single failure to provide notice of cancellation rights now constitutes a criminal offence under reg 19 of the 2013 Regulations; however, the maximum sentence is limited to a fine.

Section 4 (fraud by abuse of position)

9.19

> **4 Fraud by abuse of position**
>
> (1) A person is in breach of this section if he –
>
> (a)   occupies a position in which he is expected to safeguard, or not to act against, the financial interests of another person,
>
> (b)   dishonestly abuses that position, and
>
> (c)   intends, by means of the abuse of that position –
>
>   (i)   to make a gain for himself or another, or
>
>   (ii)   to cause loss to another or to expose another to a risk of loss.
>
> (2) A person may be regarded as having abused his position even though his conduct consisted of an omission rather than an act.

Section 4 applies in situations where the defendant has been put in a privileged position, and by virtue of this position is expected to safeguard another's *financial* interests or not act against those interests.

9.20 There is no express requirement that a defendant must know that he is expected to safeguard or not to act against the financial interests of the other person, or to know that his act (or failure to act) constitutes such an abuse. 'Abuse' is not defined in the FA 2006. The current CPS Guidance on the FA 2006 gives as an example of the type of conduct that would give rise to a charge under FA 2006, s 4:

> 'a tradesman who helps an elderly person with odd jobs, gains influence over that person and removes money from their account.'

9.21 In considering how to frame a charge of fraud by abuse of position it may be appropriate to allege a 'general deficiency' of funds misappropriated over a period of time rather than specific financial transactions, see the case of *R v TJC*.[15]

---

14   SI 2013/3134.
15   (2015) EWCA Crim 1276.

Other offences
Articles used in fraud
9.22

> **6 Possession etc. of articles for use in frauds**
>
> (1) A person is guilty of an offence if he has in his possession or under his control any article for use in the course of or in connection with any fraud.
>
> **7 Making or supplying articles for use in frauds**
>
> (1) A person is guilty of an offence if he makes, adapts, supplies or offers to supply any article –
>
> (a) knowing that it is designed or adapted for use in the course of or in connection with fraud, or
> (b) intending it to be used to commit, or assist in the commission of, fraud.

Note that the offence in s 6 does not relate to an article 'made or adapted' for use in fraud (compared with s 7). The wording of s 6 follows s 25 of the Theft Act 1968 (although s 6 also applies to articles found in an offender's home). Case-law on s 25 is therefore likely to continue be relevant.

9.23 In *R v Ellames*,[16] the court said that:

> 'In our view, to establish an offence under s 25(1) the prosecution must prove that the defendant was in possession of the article, and intended the article to be used in the course of or in connection with some future burglary, theft or cheat. But it is not necessary to prove that he intended it to be used in the course of or in connection with any specific burglary, theft or cheat; it is enough to prove a general intention to use it for some burglary, theft or cheat; we think that this view is supported by the use of the word "any" in s 25(1). Nor, in our view, is it necessary to prove that the defendant intended to use it himself; it will be enough to prove that he had it with him with the intention that it should be used by someone else.'

9.24 In *R v Nimley (Emmanuel)*[17] the defendant was jailed for 6 months for illegally recording Hollywood movies at a cinema. He then distributed them using his iPhone on the day of their official release. He was charged under ss 6 and 7 of the FA 2006 and s 107(1)(e) Copyright, Designs and Patents Act 1988. The defendant uploaded the recordings to a file-sharing website where viewers could access the material free of charge. On appeal, his sentence was reduced to a 12-month community order and 120 hours of unpaid work.

9.25 In *R v Rasoul (Hana Kadir)*[18] the defendant was an Iraqi national who, in an attempt to gain permission to remain in the UK, attempted to have forged

---

[16] [1974] 3 All ER 130.
[17] [2010] EWCA Crim 2752.
[18] [2012] EWCA Crim 1248.

documents submitted on his behalf to the government. He pleaded guilty to the offence but appealed on the basis that, in fact, he had never had 'possession' of the relevant documents for the purposes of s 6. The appeal was dismissed on the basis that s 6 requires proof of possession *or control*.

9.26 In *R v Ryan*[19] the defendant was convicted of conspiracy to defraud and controlling an article for use in fraud. He was sentenced to a total of 30 months' imprisonment. One of the other four co-accused was convicted of conspiracy to defraud and sentenced to 51 weeks' imprisonment suspended for 2 years; three other co-accused were found not guilty or verdicts of not guilty were entered. Ryan, was the head of a fraudulent operation Car Clamping Securities which defrauded motorists by tampering with a pay and display machine, fitting it with a computer chip so although it accepted two pound coins and issued a ticket, no credit was given to the motorist. Motorists would leave their cars thinking they had paid the right amount only to return and discover their car had been taken to the company's compound in Ladywood where they usually had to pay over £300 to get it back.

9.27 It is also important to note, as per *R v Sakalaukas*[20] that '[a]ny article in s 6(1) meant any article the defendant had with him for the purpose or intention of using in the course of or in connection with any fraud' and use necessarily related to use in the future and *not* articles which had been used in the past.

Fraudulent trading

9.28 Fraudulent trading is effectively a general fraud offence. The Companies Act 2006 creates liability for a corporate defendant. The provision extends to Scotland. The FA 2006 creates a parallel offence for non-corporate traders such as sole traders and partnerships.

> **Companies Act 2006, s 993**
>
> **993 Offence of fraudulent trading**
>
> (1) If any business of a company is carried on with intent to defraud creditors of the company or creditors of any other person, or for any fraudulent purpose, every person who is knowingly a party to the carrying on of the business in that manner commits an offence.
>
> (2) This applies whether or not the company has been, or is in the course of being, wound up.

---

[19]   [2011] EWCA Crim 1425.
[20]   [2013] EWCA Crim 2278.

Fraud Act 2006, s 9

9 Participating in fraudulent business carried on by sole trader etc

(1) A person is guilty of an offence if he is knowingly a party to the carrying on of a business to which this section applies.

(2) This section applies to a business which is carried on –

> (a)   by a person who is outside the reach of [section 993 of the Companies Act 2006]; and
>
> (b)   with intent to defraud creditors of any person or for any other fraudulent purpose.

9.29 The term 'fraudulent purpose' connotes an intention to go 'beyond the bounds of what ordinary decent people engaged in business would regard as honest' – *R v Grantham*.[21] 'The words "defraud" and "fraudulent purpose" are words which connote actual dishonesty involving, according to current notions of fair trading among commercial men, real moral blame' – *Re Patrick and Lyon Ltd*.[22]

9.30 Dishonesty is an essential element of the offence. This may include 'blind eye knowledge', a firmly grounded suspicion that relevant facts exist and a deliberate decision to avoid confirming their existence: *Re Bank of Credit and Commerce International SA; Morris v State Bank of India*.[23]

9.31 Some helpful guidance on the application of s 9 is given in:

(a) Home Office Circular 42/2006 – 'section 9 is an "activity" offence, meaning that it captures a course of conduct, and is not limited to specific transactions ... An example of fraudulent trading would be a pattern of behaviour by a dishonest roof repairer who consistently inflated bills and charged for work he had not done'.

(b) the Crown Prosecution Service Legal Guidance – which includes: 'Prosecutors should consider charges under (s 9) where ... a business is being run for a fraudulent purpose, for example, rogue "cold calling" traders who regularly submit inflated bills to customers for shoddy work (and who often target the elderly or vulnerable)'.

9.32 In *R v Stansfield*[24] the director of a company called One Food Limited, was sentenced – with two others – to 27 months' imprisonment, after pleading guilty to an offence under s 993 of the Companies Act 2006 for fraudulent trading. In addition, he was disqualified under s 2 of the Company Directors Disqualification Act 1986 from acting as a director of a company for a period of 6 years. Refusing a renewed application for leave to appeal against sentence Stanley Burnton LJ said:

---

[21]   [1984] 3 All ER 166.
[22]   [1933] All ER 590.
[23]   [2003] BCC 735 Ch D.
[24]   [2010] EWCA Crim 528.

'This was a prolonged period of fraud. It was exacerbated not only by the deliberateness of the fraud, but by the involvement of staff, including (your) own wife, in what were frauds involving forgery and false accounting.'

9.33 In *R v Waring*[25] the defendant was sentenced to a total of 5 years' imprisonment in relation to 10 offences of fraudulent trading. Refusing leave to appeal the judge said:

'This was a long running fraudulent course of trading in which in effect you ran a scheme whereby largely bogus companies sent totally bogus invoices to other companies which were in a number of instances paid without challenge. By this means the prosecution says you profited to the tune of nearly £1 million. Your own estimate was £630,000 and the exact figure was a difficult one to ascertain. The fraudulent trading was fraudulent virtually from the beginning.'

9.34 In *R v Ventriglia (Walter)*[26] the defendant pleaded guilty under s 9, following a trading standards enquiry into letters sent by him to members of the public which included misleading information about the requirements for a valid will, along with an invitation to redraft for a fee. The sentence of 14 months' imprisonment was upheld on appeal.

9.35 In *R v Boakes*[27] the Court of Appeal upheld a sentence of ten years in relation to two counts of fraudulent trading, one under the Companies Act 1985 (the previous statute) and one under the Companies Act 2006. The Court commented that ten years' imprisonment for a large number of unpleasant offences against vulnerable people, taking away much or all of their savings, was not a day too long.

9.36 It should be noted that fraudulent trading is not included in the Definitive Sentencing Guidelines for Fraud, Bribery and Money Laundering Offences (see Sentencing below), although it may be appropriate to have some regard to them. This is no doubt due to the wide spectrum of mechanisms by which the offence can be committed. However, relevant factors to sentencing have been held to be:

- The value of the fraud;
- The manner in which it was committed;
- The period over which it was committed;
- The position of the offender and his measure of control within the company;
- Any abuse of trust;
- Any effect on public confidence in the integrity of commercial life;
- Any loss to investors;
- Any personal benefit.

---

[25] [2011] EWCA Crim 1567.
[26] [2011] EWCA Crim 2912.
[27] (2015) EWCA Crim 2288.

Directors' liability

9.37 Section 12 creates liability for directors etc, which is covered in Chapter 3, Criminal Enforcement.

Enforcement

9.38 There is no duty of enforcement or any powers for enforcement officers under the Act.

Sentencing

9.39 In October 2014 the Sentencing Council issued a Definitive Guideline for Fraud, Bribery and Money Laundering Offences. It applies to all individual offenders aged 18 and older and to organisations sentenced after 1 October 2014, regardless of the date of the offence. The Guidelines require the Court to assess the culpability and the harm. The level of culpability is determined by weighing up all the factors of the case to determine the offender's role, the extent to which the offending was planned and the sophistication with which it was carried out.

9.40 Harm is initially assessed by the actual, intended or risked loss as may arise from the offence. The court should then take into account the level of harm caused to the victim(s) or others to determine whether it warrants the sentence being moved up to the corresponding point in the next category or further up the range of the initial category. For example in relation to FA 2006, s 1 offences, one of the indicators of high impact is where the victim is particularly vulnerable (due to factors including but not limited to their age, financial circumstances, mental capacity). This can be particularly relevant in cases such as doorstep crime, which are often perpetrated against vulnerable people and where the non-financial harm caused is recognised by the courts frequently imposing longer sentences than under previous regimes. For an illustration of this point see *R v Montague*.[28]

9.41 The case of *R v Tolliday*[29] has been described as a 'textbook application of the sentencing guidelines for fraud' in the context of a trading standards investigation. The case is also noteworthy for the manner in which the Court of Appeal addressed the issue of consecutive over concurrent sentences for CPUTR offences related to the overarching fraud.

9.42 The prosecution should always consider obtaining a Victim Personal Statement ('VPS') in any fraud allegation. The VPS provides an opportunity for a victim to explain how the crime has affected them, physically, emotionally,

---

[28]   (2015) EWCA Crim 902.
[29]   (2015) EWCA Crim 603.

psychologically, financially or in any other way. The use of a VPS was considered in *R v Perkins, Bennett and Hall.*[30] It was stated that such statements:

> 'allow victims a more structured opportunity to explain how they have been affected by the crime or crimes of which they were victims. They provide a practical way of ensuring that the sentencing court will consider, in accordance with s143 CJA 2003, "any harm which the offence caused", reflecting on the evidence of the victim about the specific and personal impact of the offence or offences, or in the cases of homicide, on the family of the deceased. The statements may, albeit incidentally to the purposes of the sentencing court, identify a need for additional or specific support or protection for the victims of crime, to be considered at the end of the sentencing process. At the same time, the process does not create or constitute an opportunity for the victim of crime to suggest or discuss the type or level of sentence to be imposed. The distinction is important, and is sometimes misunderstood.'

9.43 There is now a practice direction on impact statements for businesses.[31] Where a victim is a business or enterprise, including charities but excluding public sector bodies, a nominated representative may make an impact statement.

CONSPIRACY (TO DEFRAUD)

9.44 There are now two types of conspiracy, statutory and the common law offence of conspiracy to defraud.

Statutory conspiracy

9.45

Criminal Law Act 1977, s 1

1 The offence of conspiracy

(1) Subject to the following provisions of this part of this Act, if a person agrees with any other person or persons that a course of conduct shall be pursued which, if the agreement is carried out in accordance with their intentions, either –

(a) will necessarily amount to or involve the commission of any offence or offences by one or more of the parties to the agreement, or

(b) would do so but for the existence of facts which render the commission of the offence or any of the offences impossible

he is guilty of conspiracy to commit the offence or offences in question.

---

[30] [2013] EWCA Crim 323.
[31] Criminal Practice Directions (Amendment No 1) [2013], EWCA Crim 2328.

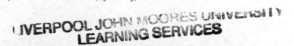
LIVERPOOL JOHN MOORES UNIVERSITY
LEARNING SERVICES

The penalties for conspiracy to commit an offence mirror the sentence of the statutory offence which was the object of the conspiracy. The time limit for the institution of legal proceedings also mirrors that of the statutory offence.

Common law conspiracy to defraud

9.46 The offence of conspiracy to defraud was preserved as a common law offence by s 5(2) Criminal Law Act 1977 (CLA 1977). Proceedings for the offence are indictable only. A conspiracy is an agreement between two or more persons to do an unlawful act or to do a lawful act by unlawful means. In addition to direct communication links, it may take the form of a 'wheel' or 'chain' where no contact is made (possible) between all members – there is no need to show that co-conspirators know the identity of the other conspirators, only that they knew there were other parties to the agreement. When the parties to the conspiracy enter into the agreement the offence of conspiracy is complete. It is not necessary for any action to be performed in pursuance of it (*R v Mulcahy*).[32]

9.47 In *R v Mehta*[33] It was stated:

'The authorities establish the following propositions: 1. A conspiracy requires that the parties to it have a common unlawful purpose or design. 2. A common design means a shared design. It is not the same as similar but separate designs. 3. In criminal law (as in civil law) there may be an umbrella agreement pursuant to which the parties enter into further agreements which may include parties who are not parties to the umbrella agreement.'

9.48 Following this, in *R v Shillam*[34] the Court said:

'Conspiracy requires a single joint design between the conspirators within the terms of the indictment ... it is always necessary that for two or more persons to be convicted of a single conspiracy each of them must be proved to have shared a common purpose or design.'

9.49 The offence has been successfully used by Trading Standards Services in a wide range of prosecutions in relation to, amongst others, doorstep crime, counterfeiting and rogue car dealing. However, prosecuting such offences *can* cause difficulties in terms of the drafting of charges, which will often be said to lack particularity, and the appropriateness of the charge at all. Legal arguments are frequently raised about whether a conspiracy charge is properly included on an indictment. As a general rule, where there is an effective and sufficient charge of a substantive offence, a charge of conspiracy is undesirable.[35]

---

[32] (1868) LR 3 HL 306.
[33] [2012] EWCA Crim 2824.
[34] [2013] EWCA Crim 160.
[35] *Verrier v DPP* [1967] 2 AC 195, HL; *R v Watts, The Times*, 14 April 1995, CA.

9.50 Consideration was given to abolishing the common law offence, following the introduction of the FA 2006. However, the Ministry of Justice in 2012 stated that:

'With regard to conspiracy to defraud, taking account of the comments and experience provided by the key prosecution practitioners, we have concluded that this offence continues to be an effective and essential tool in combating fraud. This is particularly pertinent where there are various levels of criminal activity involved and the court would not otherwise be aware of the full extent of criminality involved. Whilst it would be possible to consider codifying the common law offence in statute, the evidence strongly suggests that the current situation is working perfectly satisfactorily and therefore we have concluded that we should leave matters as they are.'

9.51 Conspiracy charges are perhaps most useful where the criminality of the agreement is more serious than the act itself.

MONEY LAUNDERING

9.52 The majority of trading standards investigations centre on offences perpetrated in order to make financial gain. Consequently, in many, if not most circumstances, those committing substantive offences are also committing offences against the money laundering provisions of the Proceeds of Crime Act 2002 ('POCA 2002').

9.53 Sections 327–329 of the Act (which extend to Scotland and Northern Ireland) create the principal money laundering offences, namely:

- concealing, disguising, converting, transferring or removing criminal property (s 327);
- entering into or becoming concerned in a money laundering arrangement (s 328);
- acquiring, using or possessing criminal property (s 329).

These offences came into force on 24 February 2003. All of the offences are either way and carry a maximum sentence of 14 years. Offences under s 327 and s 328 are listed in Schs 2 (England and Wales), 4 (Scotland) and 5 (Northern Ireland) to the Act and therefore attract the criminal lifestyle assumptions in confiscation proceedings.

9.54 There are no powers for trading standards officers under any of these provisions but, as with the Fraud Act 2006, trading standards departments are increasingly considering the use of money laundering offences. For example, in *R v Coyle*,[36] the defendant allowed his bank accounts to be used to launder money that had been defrauded by others from three elderly and vulnerable victims. He pleaded guilty to three counts of money laundering, one count of

---

[36] [2011] EWCA Crim 36.

transferring a criminal property and five counts of converting criminal property. His sentence, of 42 months' imprisonment imposed on each count, was reduced, on appeal, to 2½ years on each count.

9.55 Careful consideration must always be given before charging money laundering offences. Whilst acquisitive crime will almost always be accompanied by a money laundering offence common sense principles should be applied. In *R v GH*[37] Lord Toulson said that the 'courts should be willing to use their powers to discourage inappropriate use of the provisions of POCA 2002 to prosecute conduct which is sufficiently covered by substantive offences …'.

9.56 The appropriateness of using money laundering charges was considered further in the case of *R v Ogden*.[38] The Court of Appeal accepted that every person who buys illicit drugs, even for their own personal use, may in fact be guilty of conspiring to convert criminal property. However, the court commented that the spectre of the authorities charging in that way was unreal because 'good sense' would prevail.

Criminal property

9.57 Under POCA 2002, money laundering does not just relate to money, but instead to a concept of 'criminal property', that is that the property constitutes or represents a person's benefit from criminal conduct. The concept of criminal property is common to all of the money laundering offences and is central to each of them. It is defined, along with criminal conduct, in s 340.

> **Section 340 Interpretation**
>
> (1) This section applies for the purposes of this Part.
>
> (2) Criminal conduct is conduct which –
>
> > (a)   constitutes an offence in any part of the United Kingdom, or
> >
> > (b)   would constitute an offence in any part of the United Kingdom if it occurred there.
>
> (3) Property is criminal property if –
>
> > (a)   it constitutes a person's benefit from criminal conduct or it represents such a benefit (in whole or part and whether directly or indirectly), and
> >
> > (b)   the alleged offender knows or suspects that it constitutes or represents such a benefit.
>
> (4) It is immaterial –
>
> > (a)   who carried out the conduct;
> >
> > (b)   who benefited from it;
> >
> > (c)   whether the conduct occurred before or after the passing of this Act.

---

[37]   [2015] UKSC 24.
[38]   [2016] EWCA Crim 6.

(5) A person benefits from conduct if he obtains property as a result of or in connection with the conduct.

(6) If a person obtains a pecuniary advantage as a result of or in connection with conduct, he is to be taken to obtain as a result of or in connection with the conduct a sum of money equal to the value of the pecuniary advantage.

(7) References to property or a pecuniary advantage obtained in connection with conduct include references to property or a pecuniary advantage obtained in both that connection and some other.

(8) If a person benefits from conduct his benefit is the property obtained as a result of or in connection with the conduct.

(9) Property is all property wherever situated and includes –

  (a) money;
  (b) all forms of property, real or personal, heritable or moveable;
  (c) things in action and other intangible or incorporeal property.

(10) The following rules apply in relation to property –

  (a) property is obtained by a person if he obtains an interest in it;
  (b) references to an interest, in relation to land in England and Wales or Northern Ireland, are to any legal estate or equitable interest or power;
  (c) references to an interest, in relation to land in Scotland, are to any estate, interest, servitude or other heritable right in or over land, including a heritable security;
  (d) references to an interest, in relation to property other than land, include references to a right (including a right to possession).

9.58 An essential point to note is that, in seeking to prove that property is criminal property, the prosecution do not have to prove the exact offence from which it is derived. This is a significant change from previous legislation. In *R v Anwoir*[39] the court stated 'there are two ways in which the Crown can prove the property derives from crime, (a) by showing that it derives from conduct of a specific kind or kinds and that conduct of that kind or those kinds is unlawful, or (b) by evidence of the circumstances in which the property is handled which are such as to give rise to the irresistible inference that it can only be derived from crime'. This approach has been reinforced more recently in *R v Smith*.[40]

9.59 This point is illustrated by *R v F*[41] where two passengers at an airport had four suitcases in their possession. When asked if there was any money in the suitcases one of them said no and one said yes. The suitcases were actually found to contain in excess of one million pounds. At interview their answer was that they had been asked by a friend to carry the money. One of the defendants stated that he had done it two or three times before and had been paid for each trip. He did not know where the money was coming from but knew that it was wrong and only did it because he was on benefits and had financial problems.

---

[39] [2008] 2 Cr App R 36.
[40] [2015] EWCA Crim 333.
[41] [2009] Crim LR 45.

The Court of Appeal upheld their convictions, stating that there was no procedural unfairness just because the prosecution were unable to point to any particular criminality.

9.60   Failure to declare legitimately earned income, does not automatically convert legitimate profits into criminal property – see *R v Gabriel*,[42] where the defendant was charged with possession of criminal property (s 329) in respect of money which he had obtained from legitimate trading but which he had not declared for revenue or benefits purposes, although, of course, other offences may have been committed on the facts.

9.61   Each case must, however, be considered on its own facts. In *R v K(I)*[43] it was found that the failure to declare profits from dealing in legitimate goods might give rise to an offence if a *prima facie* case of cheating the Revenue was made out. The trader would have obtained a pecuniary advantage as a result of criminal conduct and by reason of s 340(6) would be taken to have obtained a sum of money equal to the amount of tax of which the Revenue had been deprived.

9.62   The prosecution must prove that the defendant 'knows or suspects' that the property constitutes or represents benefit from criminal conduct. The question of what is meant by the word 'suspect' was considered in *R v Da Silva*[44] where it was stated:

> 'the defendant must think that there is a possibility, which is more than fanciful, that the relevant facts exist. A vague feeling of unease would not suffice. But the statute does not require the suspicion to be "clear" or "firmly grounded and targeted on specific facts", or based upon "reasonable grounds".'

Concealing etc

9.63

Section 327 Concealing etc

(1) A person commits an offence if he –

    (a)   conceals criminal property;
    (b)   disguises criminal property;
    (c)   converts criminal property;
    (d)   transfers criminal property;
    (e)   removes criminal property from England and Wales or from Scotland or from Northern Ireland.

(2) But a person does not commit such an offence if –

---

[42]   [2007] 1 WLR 2272.
[43]   [2007] 2 Cr App R 10.
[44]   [2006] EWCA Crim 1654.

(a) he makes an authorised disclosure under section 338 and (if the disclosure is made before he does the act mentioned in subsection (1)) he has the appropriate consent;

(b) he intended to make such a disclosure but had a reasonable excuse for not doing so;

(c) the act he does is done in carrying out a function he has relating to the enforcement of any provision of this Act or of any other enactment relating to criminal conduct or benefit from criminal conduct.

(3) Concealing or disguising criminal property includes concealing or disguising its nature, source, location, disposition, movement or ownership or any rights with respect to it.

For an offence under s 327 to be committed, the property that is concealed, disguised, converted or transferred, must be criminal property at the time it is concealed, disguised, converted or transferred. If the property is not criminal property at the time the laundering act takes place, the offence is not committed (*R v Loizou*[45]).

9.64 In *R v Fazal* it was said that the meaning of 'converting' under POCA is not necessarily the same as the civil tort of conversion, but it cannot be far removed from its nature. Conversion in the civil law is a broad tort which is essentially concerned with the taking, receiving, retaining or parting with someone else's property.[46]

Arrangements

9.65

Section 328 Arrangements

(1) A person commits an offence if he enters into or becomes concerned in an arrangement which he knows or suspects facilitates (by whatever means) the acquisition, retention, use or control of criminal property by or on behalf of another person.

(2) But a person does not commit such an offence if –

(a) he makes an authorised disclosure under section 338 and (if the disclosure is made before he does the act mentioned in subsection (1)) he has the appropriate consent;

(b) he intended to make such a disclosure but had a reasonable excuse for not doing so;

(c) the act he does is done in carrying out a function he has relating to the enforcement of any provision of this Act or of any other enactment relating to criminal conduct or benefit from criminal conduct.

9.66 It is necessary for the arrangement to relate to property which has already become criminal property:

---

[45] [2005] 2 Cr App R 37.
[46] *R v Fazal* [2010] 1 Cr App R 6.

'As section 340(3)(b) makes clear, the mental element of the offence includes knowledge or suspicion on the part of the defendant that the property in question is criminal property, but that cannot be the case until it has been acquired by means of criminal conduct. In order for an offence under section 328 to be committed, therefore, the arrangement into which the defendant enters, or in which he becomes involved, must be one which facilitates the acquisition, retention, use or control by another of property which has already become criminal property at the time when it becomes operative. That requirement is not satisfied if the only arrangement into which he enters is one by which the property in question first acquires its criminal character.'[47]

9.67   In *R v Geary*[48] it was stated, when referring to ss 327, 328 and 329:

'In each case the natural meaning of the statutory language is that in each case the property in question must have become criminal property as a result of some conduct which occurred prior to the act which is alleged to constitute the offence, whether that be concealing, disguising, converting, transferring or removing it contrary to section 327 or entering into or becoming concerned in an arrangement which facilitates its acquisition, retention, use or control by another contrary to section 328.'

9.68   And in *R v Amir and Akhtar*[49] the question considered was whether property was 'criminal property for the purposes of section 328 only after some other offence has been committed, or is it to be characterised as criminal property because of the criminal objective which the arrangements were designed to achieve?' In allowing the appeal against conviction of the appellant who had knowingly submitted false mortgage applications, the court stated:

'They (ss 327, 328, 329) are all concerned in one way or another with dealing with criminal property. By section 340(3) that is property which in fact constitutes a person's benefit from criminal conduct or represents such a benefit and the offender knows or suspects that that is so. The definition does not embrace property which the accused intends to acquire by criminal conduct and the language of the statute is not capable of construing the definition in that way. Property is not criminal property because the wrongdoing intends that it should be so.'

9.69   This requirement for the property to constitute criminal property prior to the arrangement coming into operation for the commission of an offence under s 328 has been confirmed and clarified in *R v GH*.[50]

---

[47]   *Kensington International v Republic of Congo* [2008] 1 WLR 1144.
[48]   [2011] 1 Cr App R 8.
[49]   [2011] 1 Cr App R 37.
[50]   [2015] UKSC 24.

Acquisition, use and possession

9.70

Section 329 Acquisition, use and possession

(1) A person commits an offence if he –

  (a)   acquires criminal property;
  (b)   uses criminal property;
  (c)   has possession of criminal property.

(2) But a person does not commit such an offence if –

  (a)   he makes an authorised disclosure under section 338 and (if the disclosure is made before he does the act mentioned in subsection (1)) he has the appropriate consent;
  (b)   he intended to make such a disclosure but had a reasonable excuse for not doing so;
  (c)   he acquired or used or had possession of the property for adequate consideration;
  (d)   the act he does is done in carrying out a function he has relating to the enforcement of any provision of this Act or of any other enactment relating to criminal conduct or benefit from criminal conduct.

(3) For the purposes of this section –

  (a)   a person acquires property for inadequate consideration if the value of the consideration is significantly less than the value of the property;
  (b)   a person uses or has possession of property for inadequate consideration if the value of the consideration is significantly less than the value of the use or possession;
  (c)   the provision by a person of goods or services which he knows or suspects may help another to carry out criminal conduct is not consideration.

9.71 This section differs from the preceding ones in that it is not a Sch 2 'lifestyle' offence and there is an additional defence, namely if the person acquires, uses or has possession of criminal property for 'adequate consideration'. 'Inadequate' consideration is defined in sub-s 3. In *Hogan v DPP*[51] the defendant had scaffolding in his possession which was worth over £6,000 and for which he had paid £1,100 in cash. He did not have a receipt, did not get the surname or contact details of the seller and did not record the purchase in his business records. The court stated that in most cases there will be an evidential burden on the defence in relation to adequate consideration and that once raised it should be regarded as an element of the offence to be proved by the prosecution to the normal criminal standard. However, it is also clear that even if it can be shown that the property is criminal property, and, the suspect knew that goods were stolen, if he has given adequate consideration then he does not commit an offence under this section.

---

[51]   [2007] 1 WLR 2944.

Sentencing for money laundering

9.72 The Sentencing Council has issued a definitive guideline for the sentencing of offences contrary to ss 327 to 329 of POCA. The levels of culpability and harm should be assessed having regard to the following major factors:

- The value;
- The role played by the offender;
- Abuse of power or trust;
- Significant planning or sophisticated offence;
- Period of offending;
- Proximity to the underlying criminal act(s);
- The level of harm associated with the underlying offence.

Confiscation

9.73 Fraud and money laundering offences will often generate criminal confiscation proceedings under Part 2 of POCA. Criminal confiscation, restraint orders and the related investigatory powers for accredited financial investigators are now covered in Chapter 3, Criminal Enforcement.

CHAPTER 10

UNFAIR TRADING

CONTENTS

10.1 In this chapter we cover a wide variety of unfair trading legislation that falls outside the other main chapter areas. The chapter could perhaps best be described as a miscellany of other consumer protection laws and, for this reason, the topics are covered in alphabetical order.

BUSINESS NAMES

Introduction

10.2 The disclosure of business identities is a key part of consumer protection. If consumers cannot identify the correct legal identity of a trader, they may be unable to enforce their consumer rights. The Business Names Act 1985 has been repealed and replaced by the Companies Act 2006 and the Regulations made under it. Following a BIS consultation and response during the course of 2013, the Company, Limited Liability Partnership and Business Names (Sensitive Words and Expressions) Regulations 2014[1] ('SWER 2014') and Company, Limited Liability Partnership and Business (Names and Trading Disclosures) Regulations 2015[2] ('NTDR 2015') were introduced from 31 January 2015. These regulations revoke and consolidate various other secondary legislation, most notably the Companies (Trading Disclosure) Regulations 2008.

Companies

10.3 The Companies Act 2006 ('CA 2006') allowed for the repeal of the Business Names Act 1985 from 1 October 2008. In particular, the NTDR 2015 creates criminal liability for failure to properly disclose a company's identity. Regulations 20 to 29 set out disclosure obligations for a variety of circumstances. It broadly replicates the former Companies (Trading Disclosure) Regulations 2008 as follows:

> **Legibility of displays and disclosures**
>
> **20** Any display or disclosure of information required by this Part must be in characters that can be read with the naked eye.
>
> **Requirement to display registered name at registered office and inspection place**
>
> **21**(1) A company shall display its registered name at –
>
> > (a) its registered office; and
> > (b) any inspection place.
>
> (2) But paragraph (1) does not apply to any company which has at all times since its incorporation been dormant.
>
> (3) Paragraph (1) shall also not apply to the registered office or an inspection place of a company where –

---

[1]   SI 2014/3140.
[2]   SI 2015/17.

(a)   in respect of that company, a liquidator, administrator or administrative receiver has been appointed; and

(b)   the registered office or inspection place is also a place of business of that liquidator, administrator or administrative receiver.

Requirement to display registered name at other business locations

22(1) This regulation applies to a location other than a company's registered office or any inspection place.

(2) A company shall display its registered name at any such location at which it carries on business.

(3) But paragraph (2) shall not apply to a location which is primarily used for living accommodation.

(4) Paragraph (2) shall also not apply to any location at which business is carried on by a company where –

(a)   in respect of that company, a liquidator, administrator or administrative receiver has been appointed; and

(b)   the location is also a place of business of that liquidator, administrator or administrative receiver.

(5) Paragraph (2) shall also not apply to any location at which business is carried on by a company of which every director who is an individual is a relevant director.

(6) In this regulation –

(a)   "administrative receiver" has the meaning given –
(i) in England and Wales or Scotland, by section 251 of the Insolvency Act 1986, and
(ii) in Northern Ireland, by Article 5 of the Insolvency (Northern Ireland) Order 1989

(b)   "credit reference agency" has the meaning given in section 243(7) of the Act;

(c)   "protected information" has the meaning given in section 240 of the Act; and

(d)   "relevant director" means an individual in respect of whom the registrar is required by regulations made pursuant to section 243(4) of the Act to refrain from disclosing protected information to a credit reference agency.

Manner of display of registered name

23(1) This regulation applies where a company is required to display its registered name at any office, place or location.

(2) Where that office, place or location is shared by no more than five companies, the registered name –

(a)   shall be so positioned that it may be easily seen by any visitor to that office, place or location; and

(b)   shall be displayed continuously.

(3) Where any such office, place or location is shared by six or more companies, each such company must ensure that either –

(a) its registered name is displayed for at least fifteen continuous seconds at least once every three minutes; or

(b) its registered name is available for inspection on a register by any visitor to that office, place or location.

Registered name to appear on communications

24(1) Every company shall disclose its registered name on –

(a) its business letters, notices and other official publications;

(b) its bills of exchange, promissory notes, endorsements and order forms;

(c) cheques purporting to be signed by or on behalf of the company;

(d) orders for money, goods or services purporting to be signed by or on behalf of the company;

(e) its bills of parcels, invoices and other demands for payment, receipts and letters of credit;

(f) its applications for licences to carry on a trade or activity; and

(g) all other forms of its business correspondence and documentation.

(2) Every company shall disclose its registered name on its websites.

Further particulars to appear in business letters, order forms and websites

25(1) Every company shall disclose the particulars set out in paragraph (2) on –

(a) its business letters;

(b) its order forms; and

(c) its websites.

(2) The particulars are –

(a) the part of the United Kingdom in which the company is registered;

(b) the company's registered number;

(c) the address of the company's registered office;

(d) in the case of a limited company exempt from the obligation to use the word "limited" as part of its registered name under section 60 of the Act, the fact that it is a limited company;

(e) in the case of a community interest company which is not a public company, the fact that it is a limited company; and

(f) in the case of an investment company within the meaning of section 833 of the Act, the fact that it is such a company.

(3) If, in the case of a company having a share capital, there is a disclosure as to the amount of share capital on –

(a) its business letters;

(b) its order forms; or

(c) its websites,

that disclosure must be as to paid up share capital.

Disclosure of names of directors

26(1)Where a company's business letter includes the name of any director of that company, other than in the text or as a signatory, the letter must disclose the name of every director of that company.

(2) In paragraph (1), "name" has the following meanings –

(a)   in the case of a director who is an individual, "name" has the meaning given in section 163(2) of the Act; and

(b)   in the case of a director who is a body corporate or a firm that is a legal person under the law by which it is governed, "name" means corporate name or firm name.

Disclosures relating to registered office and inspection place

27(1) A company shall disclose –

(a)   the address of its registered office;
(b)   any inspection place; and
(c)   the type of company records which are kept at that office or place,

to any person it deals with in the course of business who makes a written request to the company for that information.

(2) The company shall send a written response to that person within five working days of the receipt of that request.

10.4   Under reg 28, a failure to comply with any of the requirements under regs 20 to 27 results in the commission of a criminal offence by the company and all officers in default. The offences are summary only and punishable by a fine not exceeding level 3 on the standard scale, and for continuing defaults, a daily sum not exceeding one-tenth of level 3 on the standard scale.

Directors' addresses

10.5   The Companies (Disclosure of Address) Regulations 2009 came into force on 1 October 2009.[3] It requires all companies to provide a service address for every director in their register of directors. The residential addresses of directors can be disclosed to a public authority (which includes a local authority) for the purpose of facilitating the carrying out by that specified public authority of a public function.[4]

Protected names

10.6   Sensitive words and expressions such as 'Queen', 'Council' or 'University' are protected against use in the commercial sector by the Sensitive Words and Expressions Regulations 2014[5] ('SWER 2014'). The relevant lists of words and expressions are set out in Parts 1 and 2 of Sch 1 to SWER 2014. Following a Government consultation in 2013, words and expressions that were previously restricted have been removed from the lists in Sch 1, such as 'board', 'national' and 'watchdog'.

---

3   SI 2009/214. Subsequently amended by the Companies (Disclosure of Address) (Amendment) Regulations 2010, SI 2010/2156.
4   Companies (Trading Disclosures) (Amendment) Regulations 2009, SI 2009/218 amend the Regulations by introducing two exceptions (one relating to insolvency, the other to protection for sensitive locations).
5   Company, Limited Liability Partnership and Business Names (Sensitive Words and Expressions) Regulations 2014, SI 2014/3140.

Public authorities

10.7 Section 54 of the CA 2006 requires that a company which wishes to use a name 'suggesting a connection' with a HM government, a local authority or a specified public authority must apply to the Secretary of State for approval. Schedule 4 to the NTDR 2015 sets out the public authorities which are specified for the purposes of s 54.

Misleading names

10.8 The Secretary of State has power[6] to direct a company to change a misleading name, regardless of how long the company has had the name. Before such a direction can be given (in writing) he must first be of the opinion that:

(a)   the name gives a misleading indication of the nature of the company's activities; and also

(b)   that the public are likely to suffer harm as a result.

If a company fails to comply with such direction an offence is committed by both the company and every officer of the company who is in default. However, there is a right of appeal for the company by which the decision can be set aside. A CA 2006, s 76 direction can also be made to an LLP. In addition, regulated consumer credit firms must not use business names which contravene the obligation to communicate with customers in a manner which is 'clear, fair and not misleading' under CONC 3.3.3R, as set out in the Financial Conduct Authority's Handbook.

Overseas companies

10.9 The Overseas Companies Regulations 2009[7] require overseas companies that trade in the UK to register at Companies House. Every company incorporated in a country outside the UK that operates its business in the UK through at least one establishment (that is to say either a branch or a place of business that is not a branch) and is not a UK-incorporated subsidiary company, must register its particulars with the Registrar of Companies. In addition, regs 12 to 15 of the NTDR 2015 set out certain provisions relating to the names of overseas companies registered in the UK.

Limited Liability Partnerships

10.10 A new corporate vehicle, the limited liability partnership ('LLP'), was created by the Limited Liability Partnerships Act 2000. LLPs have flexibility in relation to their internal arrangements in much the same way as conventional partnerships, but they are bodies corporate with limited liability, and are

---

6   Sections 1197 and 1198 of the Companies Act 2006.
7   SI 2009/1801.

accordingly subject to the provisions of CA 2006 Act by regs 14 and 15 of the Limited Liability Partnerships (Application of Companies Act 2006) Regulations 2009.[8] Regulation 11 of the NTDR 2015 also extends the restriction on names suggesting a connection with a public authority to LLPs.

Sole traders, partnerships etc

10.11 The disclosure requirements for non-corporate businesses are set out in Part 41 (ss 1192–1208) CA 2006 and came into force on 1 October 2009.[9] The key provisions relating to business names are set out below:

1200 Application of this Chapter

(1) This Chapter applies to an individual or partnership carrying on business in the United Kingdom under a business name. References in this Chapter to "a person to whom this Chapter applies" are to such an individual or partnership.

(2) For the purposes of this Chapter a "business name" means a name other than –

    (a)   in the case of an individual, his surname without any addition other than a permitted addition;

    (b)   in the case of a partnership –
        (i)   the surnames of all partners who are individuals, and
        (ii)   the corporate names of all partners who are bodies corporate,
    without any addition other than a permitted addition.

(3) The following are the permitted additions –

    (a)   in the case of an individual, his forename or initial;
    (b)   in the case of a partnership –
        (i)   the forenames of individual partners or the initials of those forenames, or
        (ii)   where two or more individual partners have the same surname, the addition of "s" at the end of that surname;
    (c)   in either case, an addition merely indicating that the business is carried on in succession to a former owner of the business.

1201 Information required to be disclosed

(1) The "information required by this Chapter" is –

    (a)   in the case of an individual, the individual's name;
    (b)   in the case of a partnership, the name of each member of the partnership;

and, in relation to each person so named, an address at which service of any document relating in any way to the business will be effective.

(2) If the individual or partnership has a place of business in the United Kingdom, the address must be in the United Kingdom.

---

[8]   SI 2009/1804.
[9]   However, note that the substituted s 1201 came into force on 28 December 2009 under the Companies Act 2006 (Substitution of Section 1201) Regulations 2009.

(3) If the individual or partnership does not have a place of business in the United Kingdom, the address must be an address at which service of documents can be effected by physical delivery and the delivery of documents is capable of being recorded by the obtaining of an acknowledgement of delivery.

1202 Disclosure required: business documents etc

(1) A person to whom this Chapter applies must state the information required by this Chapter, in legible characters, on all –

- (a) business letters,
- (b) written orders for goods or services to be supplied to the business,
- (c) invoices and receipts issued in the course of the business, and
- (d) written demands for payment of debts arising in the course of the business.

This subsection has effect subject to section 1203 (exemption for large partnerships if certain conditions met).

(2) A person to whom this Chapter applies must secure that the information required by this Chapter is immediately given, by written notice, to any person with whom anything is done or discussed in the course of the business and who asks for that information...

[*Section 1203 concerns the exemption for large partnerships if certain conditions are met.*]

1204 Disclosure required: business premises

(1) A person to whom this Chapter applies must, in any premises –

- (a) where the business is carried on, and
- (b) to which customers of the business or suppliers of goods or services to the business have access,

display in a prominent position, so that it may easily be read by such customers or suppliers, a notice containing the information required by this Chapter...

1205 Criminal consequences of failure to make required disclosure

(1) A person who without reasonable excuse fails to comply with the requirements of –

- (a) section 1202 (disclosure required: business documents etc), or
- (b) section 1204 (disclosure required: business premises),

commits an offence.

(2) Where an offence under this section is committed by a body corporate, an offence is also committed by every officer of the body who is in default.

(3) A person guilty of an offence under this section is liable on summary conviction to a fine not exceeding level 3 on the standard scale and, for continued contravention, a daily default fine not exceeding one-tenth of level 3 on the standard scale.

(4) References in this section to the requirements of section 1202 or 1204 include the requirements of regulations under that section.

CAT AND DOG FUR

10.12 The Cat and Dog Fur (Control of Import, Export and Placing on the Market) Regulations 2008[10] introduce criminal sanction for breach of an EC Regulation banning the commercial import, export and sale of cat and dog fur. Regulation 2 makes contravention of Art 3 of the EC Regulation a criminal offence, punishable on indictment with a maximum penalty of £75,000 and on summary conviction with an unlimited fine.[11] A duty[12] is imposed on local weights and measures authorities (in Great Britain) and district councils (in Northern Ireland) to enforce reg 2 but reg 3(2) excludes from this duty the enforcement of the Regulations within areas where the goods are under the supervision of Her Majesty's Revenue and Customs, in which areas enforcement will be the responsibility of Her Majesty's Revenue and Customs.

10.13 Regulation 3(3) provides:

Powers of investigation and enforcement

3(3) For the purposes of enforcing these Regulations, an officer may at any reasonable hour and on production, if required, of evidence that he is an officer –

    (a)   inspect any goods;
    (b)   enter any premises (including any place or vehicle) other than premises occupied only as a dwelling;
    (c)   purchase any goods for the purposes of inspection;
    (d)   examine any procedure connected with the production of any goods;
    (e)   require any person carrying on a business, or employed in connection with a business, to produce any records relating to the business;
    (f)   seize and detain any goods or records where there are reasonable grounds for believing that they may be –
        (i)   required as evidence in proceedings for an offence under regulation 2; or
        (ii)   (in relation to goods only) liable to be forfeited;
    (g)   take copies of, or of any entry in, any records produced by virtue of sub-paragraph (e) or seized by way of sub-paragraph (f);
    (h)   require any person having authority to do so to open any container; and
    (i)   where a requirement made under sub-paragraph (h) has not been complied with, open or break open any container.

10.14 Powers are granted to local weights and measures authorities (in England and Wales) and district councils (in Northern Ireland) to apply to court for forfeiture orders in respect of goods which contravene the reg 2 prohibition (reg 4). In Scotland, the Proceeds of Crime (Scotland) Act 1995 will apply following a conviction for a breach of the Regulations. Regulation 5 makes it a criminal offence for a person intentionally to obstruct or fail to co-operate with an officer exercising powers granted under reg 4. The penalty on summary conviction is a fine not exceeding level 3 on the standard scale.

---

[10]   SI 2008/2795.
[11]   Legal Aid, Sentencing and Punishment of Offenders Act 2012, s 85 for offences committed after 12 March 2015.
[12]   Reg 3(1).

CRYSTAL GLASS

10.15   The Crystal Glass (Descriptions) Regulations 1973[13] were made under the European Communities Act 1972. It is an offence under reg 3 for a person in the course of a trade or business, to supply or offer to supply in the United Kingdom, glass to which there is applied 'a description' (see reg 4), 'symbol' (see reg 5), 'trade mark, name or other inscription' (see reg 6) in contravention of the Regulations.

10.16   By virtue of reg 8, certain provisions of the Trade Description Act 1968 are applied (with necessary modifications) to the Regulations – ss 4, 5, 18, 19, 20, 23, 24, 25 and 26. Notwithstanding their repeal by the CPUTR, ss 5, 19(4)(b) and (c) and s 24(3) of the Trade Descriptions Act 1968 will continue to apply for the purposes of reg 8. The enforcement powers in Sch 5 to the CRA 2015 apply to the Regulations; see Chapter 3, Criminal Enforcement.

EDUCATIONAL DEGREES AND AWARDS

10.17   The vast majority of the provisions of the Education Reform Act 1988 ('ERA 1988') have now been repealed. However, a limited number of sections under Part II remain in force for the purpose of regulating, through criminal sanctions, the provision of education within the UK. The following deals only with the key remaining aspects of the ERA 1988.

10.18   Universities and some colleges in the UK are given the power to grant degrees under an Act of Parliament or by Royal Charter. There are over 150 institutions in the UK that are permitted to award a wide variety of degrees by the UK government and other institutions. These are known as 'recognised bodies'.[14] The degrees that recognised bodies grant are referred to as 'recognised UK degrees'.[15] It is only recognised bodies can award genuine UK degree. There are over 850 educational establishments – colleges and other organisations providing higher education, in full or part – within the UK, which do not grant degrees but run courses in preparation for a degree to be granted by a Recognised Body. These are known as 'Listed Bodies' and are defined in s 216.

10.19   In Northern Ireland, Art 3(1) of the Education (Unrecognised Degrees) (Northern Ireland) Order 1988 makes it an offence to grant, offer to grant or issue any invitation relating to certain degrees and awards. This does not apply to anything done in relation to a recognised award. A 'recognised award' means:

---

[13]   SI 1973/1952.
[14]   Defined in s 214(2).
[15]   In addition, the Secretary of State may, by Order, designate recognised awards – for example the Education (Recognised Awards) (Richmond The American International University in London) Order 2006.

(a) any award granted or to be granted by a university, college or other body which is authorised by Royal Charter or Act of Parliament to grant degrees; or

(b) any award granted or to be granted by any body for the time being permitted by any body falling within sub-paragraph (a) to act on its behalf in the granting of degrees.

10.20 The Education (Listed Bodies) (Northern Ireland) Order 2004, as amended, contains the list of the names of each body which is not a recognised body within Art 3(2)(a) or (b) of the 1988 Order but which either:

(a) provides any course which is in preparation for a degree to be granted by a recognised body and is approved by or on behalf of the recognised body; or

(b) is a constituent college, school, or hall or other institution of a university which is a recognised body.

Offence and related provisions

10.21 Section 214(1) of the Act provides:

> Unrecognised degrees
>
> (1) Any person who, in the course of business, grants, offers to grant or issues any invitation relating to any award –
>
> > (a) which may reasonably be taken to be an award granted or to be granted by a United Kingdom institution; and
> > (b) which either –
> > > (i) is described as a degree; or
> > > (ii) purports to confer on its holder the right to the title of bachelor, master or doctor and may reasonably be taken to be a degree;
>
> shall be guilty of an offence and liable on summary conviction to a fine not exceeding level 5 on the standard scale.

10.22 Section 214(1) above does not apply as respects anything done in relation to any 'recognised award' – which means a recognised UK degree (or such other award which has been designated by Order). It is not an offence for overseas organisations to offer their own awards in the UK, as long as they make it clear that they are not qualifications from a UK institution and that accreditation is from overseas and s 214(4)–(6) provide specific, but limited, statutory defences.

10.23 Section 214(7) permits the prosecution and conviction of any 'director, manager, secretary or other similar officer' of a company or 'any person who was purporting to act in such a capacity' where an offence under s 214 has been committed by the company 'with the consent and connivance' of that person or as a result of that person's neglect. Directors' liability is now covered in Chapter 3, Criminal Enforcement. Importantly, s 214(8) provides that proceedings for an offence under s 214 cannot be instituted in England and Wales, except by or on behalf of a local weights and measures authority or the chief officer of police for a police area.

Enforcement

10.24   Enforcement powers are now covered by Sch 5 of the CRA 2015; see Chapter 3, Criminal Enforcement. In Northern Ireland, it is the duty of the Department of Economic Development to enforce the provisions of Art 3 of the Education (Unrecognised Degrees) (Northern Ireland) Order 1988 and a duly authorised officer of the Department has similar powers to those described above.

ESTATE AGENTS

Introduction

10.25   The Estate Agents Act 1979 ('EA 1979') applies throughout the UK and regulates the work of those who are engaged in 'estate agency work' – referred in this chapter as 'estate agents'.

10.26   The EA 1979:

> 'was the culmination of many attempts begun as long ago as 1888 to regulate the activities of estate agents by legislation. During the 90 years before the Act was passed, public concern had been expressed that neither Parliament nor the profession itself had made provision for registration, for minimum standards of competence and for safeguards to protect clients against defaulting practitioners. In short, any person could adopt the title of, and act as, an "estate agent" though he had no specific qualification and the public had no assurance that he was skilled, competent or even honest. After many unsuccessful attempts by private members to introduce legislation to regulate estate agency practices, a Bill introduced by a private member Mr Bryan Davies in 1978 was adopted by the government to become the Estate Agents Act 1979. The Act did not introduce any system of registration but provided means by which an estate agent could be judged unfit to practice.'[16]
>
> Beldham LJ in *Antonelli v Secretary of State for Trade and Industry*
> (96/0015/D).

10.27   The main features of EA 1979 are that it:

* covers commercial, industrial and agricultural property as well as residential homes;

* applies to those engaged in 'estate agency work' (not necessarily 'estate agents' in the normal sense);

---

[16]   *Antonelli v Secretary of State for Trade and Industry* [1997] EWCA 2282, [1998] 1 All ER 1997, per Beldam LJ.

- creates a statutory framework whereby a failure to comply with its requirements may result in criminal proceedings, civil action or action by the lead enforcement authority (to warn or prohibit unfit persons from engaging in estate agency work);
- places obligations on estate agents to maintain proper financial arrangements and provide information;
- prohibits bankrupts from carrying on an estate agency business (but they may work for one).

10.28 EA 1979 imposes a 'negative licensing' regime in that there is no requirement to demonstrate any particular qualification or competence in order to set up as an 'estate agent' (in fact, the provision of the Act dealing with standards of competence (s 22) have not been brought into force – nor have others relating to insurance cover for clients' money, regulation of pre-contract deposits outside Scotland). Article 5 of the Public Bodies (Abolition of the National Consumer Council and Transfer of the Office of Fair Trading's Functions in relation to Estate Agents etc) Order 2014 transferred the functions of the OFT, in relation to the regulation of estate agents in the EA 1979, to Powys County Council, the 'lead enforcement authority'.

10.29 The National Trading Standards Estate Agency Team (NTSEAT), hosted by Powys County Council, as the 'lead enforcement authority', is responsible under the EA 1979 for:

- issuing banning or warning orders to businesses or individuals found to be unfit to engage in estate agency work in the UK;
- maintaining a public register of such banning or warning orders;
- approving and monitoring consumer redress schemes;
- providing specific advice and guidance to businesses and consumers about their rights and obligations.

The lead enforcement authority is also a Competent Authority in this sector for the purposes of the Alternative Dispute Resolution for Consumer Disputes (Competent Authorities and Information) Regulations 2015.

10.30 The Consumers, Estate Agents and Redress Act 2007 ('CEAR 2007') amended EA 1979 in a number of respects, including a requirement for residential estate agents to join an independent redress scheme, the provision of additional powers to enforcers and an increase of the grounds under which the lead enforcement authority can issue warning and prohibition orders.

Estate agency work

10.31 The meaning of 'estate agency work' is given in s 1 EA 1979. In practical terms, it means introducing to someone else a person who wishes to buy, sell or lease land or property, and being involved in negotiating the subsequent deal. The work must be in the course of business, whether as employer or employee, and as a result of instructions from a client. The land or property may be freehold or leasehold (or their Scottish equivalents) and may be commercial, industrial, agricultural or residential. Section 1 also details property-related work which is not covered by EA 1979 (for example 'things done ... in the course of his profession by a practising solicitor or a person employed by him or by an incorporated practice (within the meaning of the Solicitors (Scotland) Act 1980) or a person employed by it').

10.32   The Enterprise and Regulatory Reform Act 2013 amended s 1 EA 1979 by extending the exemption of 'estate agency work' to exclude businesses, such as private sales internet portals, which provide a means for prospective parties to a property transaction to make contact in response to an advertisement or property information. The exemption applies provided that such businesses do 'no other things which fall within subsection 1(1)', eg they do not otherwise participate in the transaction by advising, negotiating or providing other services.

Connected persons

10.33   The meaning of 'connected person', in relation to an estate agent, is given in the Estate Agents (Undesirable Practices) (No 2) Order 1991; it means any of the following:

    (a)   his employer or principal, or
    (b)   any employee or agent of his, or
    (c)   any associate of his or of any person mentioned in (a) and (b) above.

10.34   Section 32 EA 1979 sets out the meaning of 'associate'.

The combined effect of the Estate Agents (Undesirable Practices) (No 2) Order 1991 and s 2 is that the 'connected persons' of an estate agent are likely to be numerous – this is of critical importance, for example, when dealing with the 'personal interest' obligations in s 23.

Estate agent obligations

10.35   The obligations on estate agents are summarised below:

(i)   Open client account(s) to hold deposits; provide receipts for deposits with all the necessary details; keep records of money paid into and out of client accounts; arrange for an annual audit of client accounts; be able to produce the latest auditor's report on demand;[17] failure to comply is an offence.

(ii)   Pay interest on deposits if appropriate;[18] failure to comply is a trigger condition for a prohibition/warning order and may form the basis of a civil claim.

---

[17]   Section 14 – 'Keeping of clients' accounts' and the Estate Agents (Accounts) Regulations 1981.
[18]   Section 15 – 'Interest on clients' money' and the Estate Agents (Accounts) Regulations 1981.

(iii) Provide advance written information about fees and charges; make written statements of when fees become payable; provide written information about changes to fees and charges; give written definitions of terms in contracts or agreements; tell clients in writing if the estate agent or a connected person or another person will offer services to a potential buyer; explain the terms 'sole selling rights', 'sole agency' and 'ready, willing and able purchaser' if they are used;[19] failure to comply is a trigger condition for a prohibition/warning order and means that the contract is not enforceable without a court order.

(iv) Not to accept a pre-contract deposit in Scotland;[20] it is illegal to do so in Scotland.

(v) Tell all potential buyers in writing about any existing personal interest (including that of connected persons); tell clients in writing about possible future personal interests (including those of connected persons);[21] failure to comply is a trigger condition for a prohibition/warning order and but does render the estate agent liable to any criminal penalty or constitute ground for any civil claim.

(vi) Belong to an approved redress scheme.[22]

Redress schemes

10.36 CEAR 2007 amended EA 1979 to require that residential estate agents join an approved redress scheme that deals with complaints about the buying and selling of residential property. Estate agents that fail to join an approved scheme are subject to a £1,000 penalty charge, which can be repeated if necessary, and will ultimately be banned from carrying out estate agency work if they refuse to sign up.

Prohibition and warning orders

10.37 Section 3 EA 1979 provides power for the 'lead enforcement authority'[23] to make a prohibition order banning an estate agent person from doing any estate agency work at all, or of a description specified in the order, but only if it is satisfied that particular 'triggering' conditions have been met and that the person is unfit to engage in estate agency work. The triggering conditions which may lead to prohibition order are set out in s 3(1). The lead enforcement authority must be satisfied that the person:

- has 'committed' (but not necessarily been convicted of) a criminal offence:
    - involving fraud or other dishonesty or violence;

---

[19] Section 18 – 'Information to clients of prospective liabilities' and the Estate Agents (Provision of Information) Regulations 1991.

[20] Section 20 'Prohibition of pre-contract deposits in Scotland'.

[21] Section 21 – 'Transactions in which an estate agent has a personal interest' and the Estate Agents (Undesirable Practices) (No 2) Order 1991.

[22] Section 23A and Sch 3 'Redress schemes', the Estate Agents (Redress Scheme) Order 2008 and the Estate Agents (Redress Scheme) (Penalty Charge) Regulations 2008.

[23] Section 33(1) defines the 'lead enforcement authority' as Powys County Council.

- under s 23(4) EA 1979 ('Bankrupts not to engage in estate agency work');
- listed in the Estate Agents (Specified Offences) (No 2) Order 1991, as amended (for example regs 8–12 and 23 of the CPUTR);
- has committed discrimination in the course of estate agency work;
- has failed to comply with either an undertaking or an enforcement order – in respect of estate agency work – made under the Part 8 of the Enterprise Act 2002;
- has failed to comply with any obligation imposed by any of the following sections of EA 1979:
    - section 15 – Interest on clients' money;
    - section 18 – Information to clients of prospective liabilities;
    - section 19 – Regulation of pre-contract deposits outside Scotland (not in force);
    - section 20 – Prohibition of pre-contract deposits in Scotland;
    - section 21 – Transactions in which an estate agent has a personal interest;
- has failed to join an estate agents redress scheme approved by the lead enforcement authority (under s 23A EA 1979);
- has failed to comply with a requirement to provide information to the OFT under s 9 EA 1979 or to an enforcement authority under s 11(1A)(b) EA 1979;
- has engaged in a practice listed in the Estate Agents (Undesirable Practices) (No 2) (Order) 1991 – for example, failing to pass on an offer to the seller promptly and in writing (except where the client has indicated that he does not want particular types of offer to be passed on), or to misrepresent an offer.

10.38 Note that Sch 1 EA 1979 supplements the provisions outlined in the first two trigger points above – those relating to previous convictions (reworded by CEAR 2007; spent convictions may not be relied upon) and discrimination (this part was amended by the Equality Act 2010 (Consequential Amendments, Saving and Supplementary Provisions) Order 2010[24] to extend EA 1979 to apply not just to sex and race but to discrimination because of all the protected characteristics.) In basic terms, a warning order under s 4 EA 1979 can be made by the lead enforcement authority if it is satisfied that the person has engaged in any of the conduct or practices which would lead to prohibition order and that, if the person repeated this conduct or practice, the lead enforcement authority would consider him unfit and proceed to make a prohibition order. Sections 5–8 and Sch 2 of the EA 1979 make supplementary provisions for prohibition and warning orders, including the procedure for appeals and the maintenance of a register by the lead enforcement authority containing details of all orders made.

---

[24] SI 2010/2279.

10.39 In *Littlewood v Powys County Council*[25] it was held that the procedure, which Powys County Council currently propose to adopt in their consideration of whether or not to make prohibition orders in relation to either or both of the claimants, does not comply with the requirements of the EA 1979 and is unlawful. For the purposes of Sch 2 to the Act, where the making of an order under s 3, prohibiting an unfit person from acting as an estate agent had been delegated to an adjudicator, it was that adjudicator who personally had to hear oral representations from the person affected.

Offences

10.40 The main sanctions employed under EA 1979 are warning and prohibition orders but offences, which may be committed by estate agents, are, in summary form, where:

- a person fails without reasonable excuse to comply with a prohibition order – punishable on conviction on indictment or on summary conviction to a fine[26] on summary conviction;[27]
- the offence under EA 1979, s 9 has been repealed and replaced with the provisions of Part 3 of Sch 5 of the Consumer Rights Act 2015. Under para 14 an enforcer or an officer of an enforcer may give notice to a person requiring the person to provide the enforcer with the information specified in the notice. If the person fails to provide the information specified in the notice then the enforcer may make an application to the Court under para 16 for an order. An order may require the person to meet the costs or expenses of the application. Para 15 sets out the requirements to be followed for a notice under para 14;
- a person contravenes the provisions of EA 1979 or of the Estate Agents (Accounts) Regulations 1981 as to the manner in which clients' money is to be dealt with or accounts and records relating to such money are to be kept, or fails to produce an auditor's report when required to do so by those Regulations – punishable on summary conviction to a fine not exceeding level 4 on the standard scale.

Due diligence defence

10.41 Section 28(1) states:

(1) In any proceedings for an offence under this Act it shall be a defence for the person charged to prove that he took all reasonable precautions and exercised all due diligence to avoid the commission of an offence by himself or any person under his control.

---

[25] [2015] EWHC 2125 (Admin).
[26] Legal Aid, Sentencing and Punishment of Offenders Act 2012, s 85 for offences committed after 12 March 2015.
[27] Section 3(8).

Directors' liability

10.42   Section 28(2) states:

> (2) Where an offence under this Act committed by a body corporate is proved to
> have been committed with the consent or connivance of, or to be attributable to
> any neglect on the part of, any director, manager, secretary or other similar officer
> of the body corporate, or any person who was purporting to act in any such
> capacity, he as well as the body corporate shall be guilty of that offence and shall
> be liable to be proceeded against and punished accordingly.

10.43   The meanings of 'business associate' and 'controller', given in s 31, are
also relevant in the determination of liability in respect of corporate bodies and
partnerships. Directors' liability is covered in Chapter 3, Criminal Enforcement.

Enforcement

10.44   Investigatory powers are now contained in Sch 5 to the CRA 2015, see
Chapter 3, Criminal Enforcement.

FOOTWEAR COMPOSITION[28]

10.45   The Footwear Composition (Indication of Composition) Labelling
Regulations 1995 were made under the European Communities Act 1972. The
Regulations require the manufacturer or the responsible person (either the
manufacturer, the manufacturer's authorised representative or the person who
first supplies footwear in the Community) to ensure that footwear placed on the
market complies with certain labelling requirements (reg 4). The information
may be provided by way of pictogram or written indication (reg 5). Retailers
must ensure that footwear is labelled in accordance with the requirements of
the Regulations and that consumers are informed of the meaning of the
pictograms (reg 6). Under reg 8, failure to comply with the requirements of
reg 4 or 6 of the Regulations is an offence. An offence under reg 8 is triable
either way and subject to a fine.

10.46   By virtue of reg 10, certain provisions of the Trade Description Act 1968
are applied (with necessary modifications) to the Regulations – ss 19, 20, 23, 24
and 26. Notwithstanding their repeal by the Consumer Protection from Unfair
Trading Regulations 2008, ss 19(4)(b) and (c) and s 24(3) of the Trade
Descriptions Act 1968 will continue to apply for the purposes of reg 10. The
enforcement powers in Sch 5 to the CRA 2015 apply to the Regulations; see
Chapter 3, Criminal Enforcement. However, under reg 9, before taking
enforcement action, trading standards officers may serve a compliance notice
(as set out in Sch 3) to give an opportunity for footwear labelling to be brought
into line with the requirements of the Regulations – the provisions of the Trade

---

[28]   SI 1995/2489.

Descriptions Act 1968 'shall not be applied until such a notice has been so served and the person upon whom it has been served has failed to comply with its requirements.'

LEGAL ACTIVITIES

10.47 Section 14 of the Legal Services Act 2007 makes it an offence for a person who is not entitled to carry on 'a reserved legal activity' to carry out that activity. Section 16 provides that if an employer carries on 'a reserved legal activity' through a manager or employee who is not entitled to carry on that activity, the employer will commit an offence, even if the employer is so entitled, unless the employer has taken all reasonable precautions and exercised all due diligence to avoid committing the offence. Both offences are subject to imprisonment of 12 months and/or a fine and imprisonment of 2 years and/or an unlimited fine on conviction on indictment (ss 14(3) and 16(5)). Section 198 has the same effect as s 22A of the Solicitors Act 1974 (repealed as of 1 January 2010) and provides that a local weights and measures authority may institute proceedings for an offence under s 14 or under s 16 if the activity which it is alleged that the accused person was not entitled to carry on constitutes a specific type of 'reserved legal activity', namely 'reserved instrument activities' (which are defined in Sch 2).

10.48 Article 23 of the Solicitors (Northern Ireland) Order 1976 provides for an offence where an unqualified person, either directly or indirectly, prepares certain Northern Ireland instruments etc, in a manner equivalent to the reserved instrument activities described below. The Department of Economic Development 'may institute proceedings' for an offence under Art 23.

Schedule 2, para 5

5(1) 'Reserved instrument activities' means –

    (a)   preparing any instrument of transfer or charge for the purposes of the Land Registration Act 2002;

    (b)   making an application or lodging a document for registration under that Act;

    (c)   preparing any other instrument relating to real or personal estate for the purposes of the law of England and Wales or instrument relating to court proceedings in England and Wales.

(2) But 'reserved instrument activities' does not include the preparation of an instrument relating to any particular court proceedings if, immediately before the appointed day, no restriction was placed on the persons entitled to carry on that activity.

(3) In this paragraph 'instrument' includes a contract for the sale or other disposition of land (except a contract to grant a short lease), but does not include –

    (a)   a will or other testamentary instrument,

(b)   an agreement not intended to be executed as a deed, other than a contract that is included by virtue of the preceding provisions of this sub-paragraph,

(c)   a letter or power of attorney, or

(d)   a transfer of stock containing no trust or limitation of the transfer.

(4) In this paragraph a 'short lease' means a lease such as is referred to in section 54(2) of the Law of Property Act 1925 (short leases).

10.49   Section 198 also provides a 'weights and measures officer' (an officer of a local weights and measures authority who is authorised by the authority) with detailed powers to investigate offences under ss 14 and 16. Section 198(4)–(9) provides:

(4) A weights and measures officer who has reasonable cause to suspect that a relevant offence may have been committed may, at any reasonable time –

(a)   enter any premises which are not used solely as a dwelling;

(b)   require any officer, agent or other competent person on the premises who is, or may be, in possession of information relevant to an investigation of the suspected offence to provide such information;

(c)   require the production of any document which may be relevant to such an investigation;

(d)   take copies, or extracts, of any such documents;

(e)   seize and retain any document which the weights and measures officer has reason to believe may be required as evidence in proceedings for a relevant offence.

(5) Any person exercising a power given by subsection (4) must, if asked to do so, produce evidence that that person is a weights and measures officer.

(6) A justice of the peace may issue a warrant under this section if satisfied, on information on oath given by a weights and measures officer, that there is reasonable cause to believe that a relevant offence may have been committed and that –

(a)   entry to the premises concerned, or production of any documents which may be relevant to an investigation of the relevant offence, has been or is likely to be refused to a weights and measures officer, or

(b)   there is reasonable cause to believe that, if production of any such document were to be required by the weights and measures officer without a warrant having been issued under this section, the document would not be produced but would be removed from the premises or hidden, tampered with or destroyed.

(7) A warrant issued under this section must authorise the weights and measures officer accompanied, where that officer considers it appropriate, by a constable or other person –

(a)   to enter the premises specified in the information, using such force as is reasonably necessary, and

(b)   to exercise any of the powers given to the weights and measures officer by subsection (4).

(8) It is an offence for a person ("P") –

    (a)   intentionally to obstruct a weights and measures officer in the exercise of any power under this section;

    (b)   intentionally to fail to comply with any requirement properly imposed on P by a weights and measures officer in the exercise of any such power;

    (c)   to fail, without reasonable excuse, to give a weights and measures officer any assistance or information which the weights and measures officer may reasonably require of P for the purpose of exercising any such power; or

    (d)   in giving to a weights and measures officer any information which P has been required to give a weights and measures officer exercising any such power, to make any statement which P knows to be false or misleading in a material particular.

(9) A person who is guilty of an offence under subsection (8) is liable on summary conviction to a fine not exceeding level 3 on the standard scale.

(10) Nothing in this section is to be taken to require any person to answer any question put to that person by a weights and measures officer, or to give any information to such an officer, if to do so might incriminate that person.

There are two other areas where the provisions of the Legal Services Act 2007 may impact on the future operational activities of trading standards officers.

Will writing

10.50 On 13 February 2013, the Legal Services Board (LSB) concluded a two-year investigation by recommending to the Lord Chancellor that the list of reserved legal activities be amended to include will-writing activities, so that the significant risks consumers currently face when using these critical services is reduced. The LSB found comprehensive evidence that the market was working contrary to the statutory regulatory objectives outlined in the Legal Services Act 2007 and to the detriment of consumers and providers alike.

10.51 An example of the market working 'to the detriment of consumers' was illustrated in *R v Ventriglia*.[29] Jackson LJ commented:

> 'The fraud committed by the appellant was a particularly pernicious one because he was preying upon customers or clients in the later stages of life, who were obviously concerned about how their assets and their estate would be distributed after death. They were obviously concerned that their dependents and descendants should be provided for in a fair and proper way. In our view, this was a particularly unpleasant form of breach of trust, the character of which the judge rightly had in mind.'

Jackson LJ also hoped:

> '... that this judgment will receive some publicity in whatever journal may be published for and read by will writers. If such persons fraudulently prey upon the fears of vulnerable clients for their own personal gain, they can expect to get

---

[29] [2011] EWCA Crim 2912.

caught, because their letters may well go to the Trading Standards Office, and they can expect to receive substantial prison sentences.'

On 14 May 2013 it was announced that the Government and the Lord Chancellor had decided not to accept the recommendation of the Legal Services Board that will-writing activities should be made subject to regulation.

Scotland

10.52 Note that the majority of the Legal Services Act 2007 does not apply in Scotland (except ss 195, 196(1) and Sch 20) but that provisions regulating legal activities are contained in the Solicitors (Scotland) Act 1980 and the Legal Services (Scotland) Act 2010. In particular s 23 of the Solicitors (Scotland) Act 1980 provides an offence to practise without a practising certificate.

LETTING AGENTS

Introduction

10.53 The size of the private rented sector in England is rapidly increasing – up from 2.4m households in 2005 to 4.0m in 2012 – with around 1 million of these households moving every year. The majority of these moves include a letting agent, who is a person appointed by a landlord to find tenant or who is instructed by a prospective tenant who wants to find a property, or who is both. A report published by the Office of Fair Trading in February 2013 identified several consumer protection issues in the lettings market. Common complaints about lettings and property management in the private rented sector are around how agents handle the security and holding deposits, missed appointments, pressuring tenants to take tenancies, poor customer service, out of date and misleading adverts and opaque and variable fees. Many landlords also appoint an agent to manage their properties on their behalf with common complaints about how the property is managed being around repairs not being carried out in a timely manner or to a satisfactory standard, general customer service and notice and conduct of visits from agents.

10.54 There are a number of non-statutory measures aimed at raising standards, eg the DCLG guide for local authorities: *Improving the private rented sector and tackling bad practice: a guide for local authorities*, which was updated in March 2015. Also, *Guidance for lettings professionals on consumer protection law*, published by the Competition and Markets Authority in June 2014, is relevant to lettings professionals in England, Wales, Scotland and Northern Ireland (highlighting national variations in legislation) and is intended 'to complement existing industry schemes such as those operated by industry bodies and codes of conduct, which help lettings professionals keep up-to-date with changes to the law, achieve compliance, and provide good quality services to tenants and landlords'.

10.55 Since November 2013 the Committee of Advertising Practice (CAP) has required lettings agents and private landlords to make sure that fees are prominently displayed in advertisements alongside rental prices. CAP's guidance was triggered by an Advertising Standards Authority ruling against rental advertisements on an internet property portal. The Government has stated that it does not intend to introduce regulation in this sector, but there have been legislative developments in the areas of redress schemes and publication of fees.

Requirement to join a redress scheme

10.56 The Enterprise and Regulatory Reform Act 2013 ('ERRA 2013') introduced powers to require persons who engage in lettings agency work and property management work in respect of dwelling-houses in England to join an approved redress scheme or a government administered redress scheme. Section 83(1) provides for an Order-making power to require persons who engage in 'lettings agency work' to belong to such a scheme. Similar provision is made in s 84(1) in respect of persons who engage in 'property management work'. Section 85 enables the Secretary of State to make provision for enforcement.

10.57 The Redress Schemes for Lettings Agency Work and Property Management Work (Approval and Designation of Schemes) (England) Order 2013[30] (the 'Approval Order') sets out the procedure relating to applications for approval; the conditions a scheme must meet before the Secretary of State may approve the scheme or designate it as a government administered redress scheme; and for the procedure relating to the withdrawal of approval or designation from such schemes. Three redress schemes had been approved under the Approval Order – The Property Ombudsman; Ombudsman Services Property; and The Property Redress Scheme.

10.58 The Redress Schemes for Lettings Agency Work and Property Management Work (Requirement to Belong to a Scheme etc) (England) Order 2014[31] (the 'Requirement Order') makes it a legal requirement for a person engaged in letting agency work to be a member of a redress scheme 'for dealing with complaints' with effect from 1 October 2014. 'Lettings agency work', in s 83(7) ERRA 2013, essentially means things done by an agent in the course of a business in response to instructions from:

- a private rented sector landlord who wants to find a tenant; or
- a tenant who wants to find a property in the private rented sector.

There are, however, a number of areas which are not to be regarded as 'lettings agency work'.[32]

---

[30] SI 2013/3192.
[31] SI 2014/2359.
[32] Set out in ERRA 2013, s 83(8) and (9) and Art 4 of the Requirement Order.

Enforcement

10.59 Article 7 of the Requirement Order makes provision for enforcement by an enforcement authority, which is defined as 'a district council, a London Borough Council, the Common Council of the City of London in its capacity as a local authority, or the Council of the Isles of Scilly'. In practice, enforcement will be by local housing authorities.

10.60 Article 8 provides that an enforcement authorities may impose a monetary penalty of up to £5,000 (with a right of appeal to the First-tier Tribunal under Art 9) where it is satisfied, on the balance of probability, that someone is engaged in letting or management work and is required to be a member of a redress scheme, but has not joined. The Requirement Order also provides for procedures for the imposition and recovery of the monetary penalty.

Duty of Letting Agents to publicise fees etc

10.61 The provisions in Chapter 3 of Part 3 (ss 83–88) and Sch 9 to the Consumer Rights Act 2015 ('CRA 2015') provide a framework for requiring letting agents to publicise relevant fees and for enforcement. There are also requirements, for letting agents who are obliged by law to be a member of a redress scheme, for such persons to display details of that redress scheme, and, for certain agents who hold client money, to display a statement of whether or not they are a member of a client money protection scheme.

10.62 Enforcement of these duties will be by a local weights and measures authority in England and Wales.

10.63 Chapter 3 of Part 3 was brought into force on 27 May 2015 by the Consumer Rights Act 2015 (Commencement) (England) Order 2015.[33] The Order also brought into force on the same date the investigatory powers provisions (contained in s 77 and Sch 5 in relation to the enforcement of this area) and Sch 9 which deals with financial penalties. See Chapter 3, Criminal Enforcement for details of the investigatory powers provisions.

The duty

10.64 Section 83 provides:

> (1) A letting agent must, in accordance with this section, publicise details of the agent's relevant fees.
>
> (2) The agent must display a list of the fees –
>
> > (a) at each of the agent's premises at which the agent deals face-to-face with persons using or proposing to use services to which the fees relate, and
> >
> > (b) at a place in each of those premises at which the list is likely to be seen by such persons.

---

[33] SI 2015/965.

(3) The agent must publish a list of the fees on the agent's website (if it has a website).

(4) A list of fees displayed or published in accordance with subsection (2) or (3) must include –

   (a) a description of each fee that is sufficient to enable a person who is liable to pay it to understand the service or cost that is covered by the fee or the purpose for which it is imposed (as the case may be),

   (b) in the case of a fee which tenants are liable to pay, an indication of whether the fee relates to each dwelling-house or each tenant under a tenancy of the dwelling-house, and

   (c) the amount of each fee inclusive of any applicable tax or, where the amount of a fee cannot reasonably be determined in advance, a description of how that fee is calculated.

(5) Subsections (6) and (7) apply to a letting agent engaging in letting agency or property management work in relation to dwelling-houses in England.

(6) If the agent holds money on behalf of persons to whom the agent provides services as part of that work, the duty imposed on the agent by subsection (2) or (3) includes a duty to display or publish, with the list of fees, a statement of whether the agent is a member of a client money protection scheme.

(7) If the agent is required to be a member of a redress scheme for dealing with complaints in connection with that work, the duty imposed on the agent by subsection (2) or (3) includes a duty to display or publish, with the list of fees, a statement –

   (a) that indicates that the agent is a member of a redress scheme, and
   (b) that gives the name of the scheme.

(8) The appropriate national authority may by regulations specify –

   (a) other ways in which a letting agent must publicise details of the relevant fees charged by the agent or (where applicable) a statement within subsection (6) or (7);

   (b) the details that must be given of fees publicised in that way.

(9) In this section –

   "client money protection scheme" means a scheme which enables a person on whose behalf a letting agent holds money to be compensated if all or part of that money is not repaid to that person in circumstances where the scheme applies;
   "redress scheme" means a redress scheme for which provision is made by order under section 83 or 84 of the Enterprise and Regulatory Reform Act 2013.

Letting agents to which the duty to publicise fees applies

10.65 Section 84 specifies those who are covered by the duty and s 86 provides the meanings of 'Letting agency work and property management work'. The meaning of 'Letting agency work' follows that contained in s 83(7) ERRA 2013 and, similarly, describes activities which are not to be regarded as 'lettings agency work'. The broad definition of a letting agent includes members of the legal profession acting in a professional legal capacity on lettings-related work, for example if a landlord instructs a solicitor to draft a tenancy agreement. The Duty of Letting Agents to Publicise Fees etc. (Exclusion) (England) Regulations 2015[34] which came into force on 27 May 2015 exclude legal professionals from the requirement to publicise their fees etc when they engage only in legal activity within the meaning of s 12 Legal Services Act 2007.

10.66   Section 85 defines the 'relevant fees' which must be disclosed under s 83. A letting agent must include, in its list of fees, any fees which are payable to it by a landlord or a tenant in respect of letting agency or property management work or otherwise in connection with an assured tenancy of a dwelling-house (including a proposed assured tenancy). Guidance on the duty of letting agents to publicise fees etc can be found in Annex D to the DCLG guide for local authorities *Improving the private rented sector and tackling bad practice: a guide for local authorities*.

Redress information

10.67   Subsection 83(7) provides that, if the agent is required to be a member of a redress scheme under ERRA 2013, there is also a duty to display or publish, with the list of fees, a statement indicating that the agent is a member of a (named) redress scheme. Under sub-s 83(6), if the agent holds money on behalf of persons to whom the agent provides services as part of that work, there is also a duty to display or publish, with the list of fees, a statement of whether the agent is a member of a 'client money protection scheme' (which means a scheme that enables a person on whose behalf a letting agent holds money to be compensated if all or part of that money is not repaid to that person in circumstances where the scheme applies).

Enforcement

10.68   Section 87 provides for enforcement of the duties.

> 87(1) It is the duty of every local weights and measures authority in England and Wales to enforce the provisions of this Chapter in its area.

10.69   Section 87 provides for the imposition of a financial penalty of up to £5,000 on a letting agent who has breached a duty in s 83, subject to any statutory guidance issued and an appeals process. Schedule 9 provides for the procedure for, and appeals against, financial penalties.

Wales

10.70   The CRA 2015 provisions relating to letting agents apply only to England and Wales. Part 1 of the Housing (Wales) Act 2014 also relates to the Regulation of Private Rented Housing and includes provisions prohibiting letting and management without registration and licence. Part 1 includes a requirement for most landlords of dwellings let, or to be let, under domestic

---

[34]   SI 2015/951.

tenancies, to register with the relevant designated licensing authority. Similarly, persons engaged in letting or managing such dwellings, are required to obtain a licence from the relevant designated licensing authority.

Scotland

10.71 The law in Scotland was clarified in 2012 so that all tenant charges, other than rent and a refundable deposit, are illegal. Section 32 of the Private Rented Housing (Scotland) Act 2011 was brought into force by the Private Rented Housing (Scotland) Act 2011 (Commencement No 4) Order 2012,[35] amending the definition of 'premium' in s 90 of the Rent (Scotland) Act 1984 to make clear that it includes any service or administration fee or charge.

Mobile homes

10.72 The Mobile Homes Act 2013 (the 'MHA 2013') received Royal Assent on 26 March 2013. The MHA 2013 amends current legislation – in particular the Mobile Homes Act 1983 – and brings the licensing regime that applies to mobile home sites more closely in line with other local authority licensing regimes. The MHA 2013 also introduces new requirements about site rules, provides a framework for better transparency on pitch fee reviews and includes a power to enable the Secretary of State to introduce by way of secondary legislation a 'fit and proper' person requirement for managers of sites, although the latter provision is not yet in force.

10.73 The legal position in relation to Wales is unaltered by the Mobile Homes Act 2013 but, on 21 February 2013, a report published by the National Assembly for Wales Communities, Equality and Local Government Committee supported the general principles of a parallel Bill – the Regulated Mobile Homes Sites (Wales) Bill – to modernise the legal framework in Wales. The Bill – proposed by Peter Black AM – the first non-government Member Bill to come before the Assembly. The Mobile Homes (Wales) Act 2013 came into force on 1 October 2014. All mobile homes sites must have a site licence issued by the local authority on a park with relevant planning permission. Local authorities had 6 months from the MHA 2013 coming into force to revoke and relicense all sites and site owners have 12 months to make and lodge new site rules (by 1 October 2015). The MHA 2013 does not apply to holiday caravans.

10.74 The main features of the MHA 2013 are:

- site owners will be required to apply for a licence from their local authority to operate a site. The licence will last up to 5 years;
- site managers will need to pass a 'fit and proper person' test before being awarded a licence;
- site owners will no longer be able to block the sale of a mobile home. The mobile home owner will be free to sell their home to whomever they wish;

---

[35] SSI 2012/267.

- local authorities will be able to inspect sites and issue a fixed penalty notice to site owners if conditions on the site are not kept properly;

- in more serious instances, local authorities will be able to issue the site owners with a compliance notice to make sure that site conditions are upheld;

- pitch fees can only be increased in line with the Consumer Prices Index;

- site owners and residents will be able to appeal to the Residential Property Tribunal in certain circumstances.

10.75   The Caravans (Northern Ireland) Act 2011 introduced, for the first time in Northern Ireland, specific legislation controlling the dealings between caravan park owners and those renting holiday caravan pitches for more than 28 days.

PEDLARY AND STREET TRADING

Pedlary

10.76   In summary, a person must obtain a certificate from the police under the Pedlars Act 1871 (the 'PA 1871') in order to trade as a pedlar throughout the United Kingdom. The definition of a pedlar in the PA 1871, in essence, means that that the person must trade on the move, not from a static location, and carry their goods with him: see *Jones v Bath and North East Somerset Council*[36] (below). A pedlar is required on demand to show his certificate to the police, to a justice of the peace, to any person to whom he offers his goods for sale and to any person on whose private property the pedlar is found. It is an offence not to produce the certificate in these circumstances. The only manner in which a pedlar can be deprived of his certificate is by order of the court under s 16 of the PA 1871; there are no provisions for the police to seize, suspend or revoke certificates – see *R (on the application of Jones) v Chief Constable of Cheshire Police*.[37] A person may appeal against the refusal to grant a certificate by virtue of s 15.

Offences

10.77   The PA 1871 creates several offences. Under s 10 a pedlar to whom a certificate is granted must not lend, transfer or assign the same to another person. By s 11 no person may borrow or make use of a certificate granted to another and it is an offence under s 12 to make representations with a view to obtaining a certificate under the Act. All of these offences are punishable on summary conviction by a fine not exceeding level 1 on the standard scale. Any subsequent offence under s 12 is punishable by a maximum of six months' imprisonment. Any convictions under this Act must be indorsed on the certificate.

---

[36]   [2012] EWHC 1361 (Admin).
[37]   [2005] EWHC 2457 (Admin).

Street trading

10.78 The Local Government (Miscellaneous Provisions) Act 1982 (LG(MP)A) provides local authorities in England and Wales with the option of adopting powers to regulate street trading. Pedlars are exempt from the LG(MP)A. Those councils that adopt the LG(MP)A powers can designate streets in their area as prohibited, consent or license streets for street trading purposes. Councils can then require street traders to apply for licences in order to trade in designated streets and apply the consequent penalties for not being licensed for trading in those streets. Street trading for the purposes of the LG(MP)A is defined as the selling or exposing or offering for sale of any article (including a living thing) in a street. Thus, street trading under the LG(MP)A regulates the sale of goods only. Paragraph 4 of Sch 4 LG(MP)A allows Local Authorities to attach such conditions as they think reasonable to the licence.

10.79 In Scotland, the Civic Government (Scotland) Act 1982 gives local authorities powers to regulate street trading by requiring persons selling or offering to sell goods and services in a public place (whether from a kiosk, vehicle, moveable stall or otherwise) to hold a licence. See *McCluskey v North Lanarkshire Council*[38] where an appeal against a condition attached to a licence which prohibited trading within a distance of 250 m from all secondary schools between 8 am and 5 pm on any school day during term time was allowed on the basis that Parliament could not have intended local licensing authorities to have the implied power to attach a condition with such a significant effect on the commercial contracts of street traders, regardless of the aim of the condition.

10.80 The policy objectives of the Street Trading Act (Northern Ireland) 2001 are to enable district councils to control and regulate street trading in their districts in such a way as to prevent undue nuisance, interference and inconvenience to persons and vehicles. The Act includes measures to allow councils to control the activities of those trading without a licence or outside the conditions of their licence. The London Local Authorities (No 2) Act 1990 (as amended), which has been adopted by all 32 London boroughs, gives bespoke powers in respect of licensing, enforcement, seizure, retention and forfeiture of goods. Some local authorities have obtained private Acts of Parliament – for example, in 2013, Canterbury City Council, Leeds City Council, Nottingham City Council and Reading Borough Council. These Acts generally contain provisions to extend the regulation of street trading to the provisions of services, as well as trade in goods, and provide additional powers in relation to enforcement against illegal street trading (such as the imposition of fixed penalties and the seizure of goods).

---

[38] 2016 SLT (Sh Ct) 31.

Offences

10.81   Paragraph 10 of Schedule 4 of the LG(MP)A creates offences thus:

(1) A person who –

    (a)   engages in street trading in a prohibited street; or

    (b)   engages in street trading in a licence street or a consent street without being authorised to do so under this Schedule; or

    (c)   contravenes any of the principal terms of a street trading licence; or

    (d)   being authorised by a street trading consent to trade in a consent street, trades in that street –

        (i)   from a stationary van, cart, barrow or other vehicle; or

        (ii)   from a portable stall,

        without first having been granted permission to do so under paragraph 7(8) above; or

    (e)   contravenes a condition imposed under paragraph 7(9) above, shall be guilty of an offence.

(2) It shall be a defence for a person charged with an offence under sub-paragraph (1) above to prove that he took all reasonable precautions and exercised all due diligence to avoid commission of the offence.

(3) Any person who, in connection with an application for a street trading licence or for a street trading consent, makes a false statement which he knows to be false in any material respect, or which he does not believe to be true, shall be guilty of an offence.

(4) A person guilty of an offence under this paragraph shall be liable on summary conviction to a fine not exceeding level 3 on the standard scale.

10.82   In *Jones v Bath and North East Somerset Council*[39] the defendant was convicted of 'street trading' without a local authority licence under LG(MP)A. He unsuccessfully appealed on the basis of the statutory exception of being a person acting as a pedlar under the authority of a pedlar's certificate granted under the Pedlars Act 1871. It was undisputed that the defendant had parked his car in a nearby street from which he was able to replenish his stock (of umbrellas) during a day on which it was either raining or drizzling. Mitting J stated:

> '... absent any authority to the contrary, it seems to me that the definition of pedlar ... requires that the pedlar is both peripatetic and ambulatory ... In modern times someone who drives with his goods in his own van or car to a town or city to offer goods for sale, is not acting as a pedlar. He is not acting as a pedlar because he is not travelling there on foot. The requirement that he conducts his activities on foot applies both to travel and trade.'

Proposals for reform

10.83   The Department for Business, Enterprise and Regulatory Reform published a consultation document – 'Street Trading and Pedlar Laws – A joint

---

[39]   [2012] EWHC 1361 (Admin).

consultation on modernising Street Trading and Pedlar Legislation, and on draft guidance on the current regime' – on 6 November 2009, seeking views on the case for, and possible options for amending and modernising the law as it applies to the control of street trading and the certification of pedlars. However, it was subsequently recognised that new legislation, containing authorisation schemes (such as those applied to pedlars or street traders), would need to satisfy the requirements of the European Services Directive 2006/123/EC.

10.84 A joint consultation between the UK and Scottish governments and the Northern Ireland Executive – 'Street Trading and Pedlary Laws – Compliance with the European Services Directive' – was published in November 2012. The consultation sets out proposals and draft regulations to:

- repeal the Pedlars Act 1871 and 1881 in relation to the whole of the United Kingdom, in order to ensure compliance with the Directive;
- set-out a new definition of pedlary in Sch 4 to the LG(MP)A to provide a new legal basis for the exemption of pedlars from the national street trading regime; and
- amend 'national' street trading legislation for England and Wales and for Northern Ireland to ensure that the legislation complies fully with the requirements of the Directive

10.85 On 16 October 2014 the Government's response to the consultation on reform of the street trading regimes in England, Wales and Northern Ireland and the pedlary regime across the UK was announced. In summary, the Government intends to make the minimum changes required to bring the regime into compliance with the Services Directive:

- the Pedlars Acts will be retained. The certification process will be amended to remove a requirement for prior residency in an area and to make the required good character check an objective one that can be applied consistently across the UK;
- there will be no changes to the definition of pedlary or to the exemption in Sch 4 to the Local Government (Miscellaneous Provisions) Act 1982 ('LGMPA');
- other changes to Sch 4 of the LGMPA, necessary to bring the regime into compliance with the Services Directive, will be made. These concern the application process, the duration of licences and the grounds for refusing or revoking a licence or consent as well as consequential changes to other parts of the Schedule. Secondary legislation to effect these changes will be brought forward as soon as the Parliamentary timetable allows;
- no action will be taken in relation to two additional proposals in the consultation – for an additional power to designate streets for established traders only and for new discretionary grounds for refusing a licence based on the suitability of the street.

10.86 These changes mainly affect England, Wales and Scotland because Northern Ireland's separate street trading regime effectively negates the pedlary regime; however, Northern Ireland's Social Development Minister has since confirmed that changes will be made to the application procedures for street trading licences, which are granted by local councils and the type of street trading allowed. At the time of publication the Secretary of State had not published any Guidance on the application of the PA 1871.

SUNDAY TRADING
Introduction

10.87 The Sunday Trading Act 1994 (the 'STA 1994') was enacted to reform the complex rules in relation to Sunday trading. The STA 1994 does not apply to Scotland or Northern Ireland.

Offences

10.88 The principal offence created by the STA 1994 is one of unlawful Sunday trading.[40] Although the offence is summary only it carries a maximum penalty of an unlimited fine. There is no specified extended time period for prosecutions so the six-month time period for laying informations for summary offences must be observed.

10.89 The STA 1994, Sch 1, paras 2 and 7(1) provides:

2. Restrictions on Sunday opening of large shops

(1) Subject to sub-paragraphs (2) and (3) below, a large shop shall not be open on Sunday for the serving of retail customers.

(2) Sub-paragraph (1) above does not apply in relation to –

    (a)   any of the shops mentioned in paragraph 3(1) below, or
    (b)   any shop in respect of which a notice under paragraph 8(1) of Schedule 2
            to this Act (shops occupied by persons observing the Jewish Sabbath) has
            effect.

(3) Sub-paragraph (1) above does not apply in relation to the opening of a large shop during any continuous period of six hours on a Sunday beginning no earlier than 10 am and ending no later than 6 pm, but this sub-paragraph has effect subject to sub-paragraph (4) below.

(4) The exemption conferred by sub-paragraph (3) above does not apply where the Sunday is Easter Day.

(5) Nothing in this paragraph applies where the Sunday is Christmas Day (the opening of large shops on Christmas Day being prohibited by section 1 of the Christmas Day (Trading) Act 2004).

---

[40]   Schedule 1, para 7.

7. Offences

(1) If paragraph 2(1) above is contravened in relation to a shop, the occupier of the shop shall be liable on summary conviction to a fine.

Other offences

10.90 Other offences under the STA 1994:

- Schedule 1, para 7(2) creates an offence of failure to display a Sch 1, para 4 notice (a notice inside and outside a large shop detailing the permitted Sunday opening hours) which is punishable by a fine (maximum level 2 on the standard scale).
- Schedule 2, para 8(10) creates an offence of making a false statement in a notice of intention to keep a shop closed on the Jewish Sabbath. This is punishable by a fine (maximum level 5 on the standard scale).
- Schedule 3, para 9 creates an offence of the occupier of a large shop, loading or unloading on a Sunday morning before 9am, without local authority consent which is punishable by a fine (maximum level 3 on the standard scale).

8. Shops occupied by persons observing the Jewish Sabbath

(1) A person of the Jewish religion who is the occupier of a large shop may give to the local authority for the area in which the shop is situated a notice signed by him stating –

(a) that he is a person of the Jewish religion, and
(b) that he intends to keep the shop closed for the serving of customers on the Jewish Sabbath.

Defences

10.91

The half hour defence: Schedule 1, paragraph 8

Where a person is charged with having contravened paragraph 2(1) above, in relation to a large shop which was permitted to be open for the serving of retail customers on the Sunday in question, by reason of his having served a retail customer after the end of the period during which the shop is permitted to be open by virtue of paragraph 2(3) above, it shall be a defence to prove that the customer was in the shop before the end of that period and left not later than half an hour after the end of that period.

Offences due to the act or default of another: Schedule 2, paragraph 5

Where the commission by any person of an offence under this Act is due to the act or default of some other person, that other person shall be guilty of the offence, and a person may be charged with and convicted of the offence by virtue of this paragraph whether or not proceedings are taken against the first-mentioned person.

Offences by body corporates: Schedule 2, paragraph 6.

(1) Where an offence under this Act committed by a body corporate is proved to have been committed with the consent or connivance of, or to be attributable to any neglect on the part of, any director, manager, secretary or other similar officer of the body corporate, or any person who was purporting to act in any such capacity, he as well as the body corporate shall be guilty of the offence and shall be liable to be proceeded against and punished accordingly.

Defence of due diligence: Schedule 2, paragraph 7

(1) In any proceedings for an offence under this Act it shall, subject to sub-paragraph (2) below, be a defence for the person charged to prove that he took all reasonable precautions and exercised all due diligence to avoid the commission of the offence by himself or by a person under his control.

(2) If in any case the defence provided by sub-paragraph (1) above involves the allegation that the commission of the offence was due to the act or default of another person, the person charged shall not, without leave of the court, be entitled to rely on that defence unless, at least seven clear days before the hearing, he has served on the prosecutor a notice in writing giving such information identifying or assisting in the identification of that other person as was then in his possession.

The burden of proving this defence is on the defendant to the civil standard.

Definitions within the STA 1994

10.92   The definitions are provided in Schedule 1 of the STA 1994:

- 'shop' means any premises where there is carried on a trade or business consisting wholly or mainly of the sale of goods;
- 'large shop' means a shop which has a relevant floor area exceeding 280 square metres;
- 'relevant floor area', in relation to a shop, means the internal floor area of so much of the shop as consists of or is comprised in a building, but excluding any part of the shop which, throughout the week ending with the Sunday in question, is used neither for the serving of customers in connection with the sale of goods nor for the display of goods.

10.93   The definition of 'relevant floor area' is rather ambiguous and has been the subject of litigation. It is commercially advantageous for a shop to fall outside the definition of a 'large shop' and there has been some wrangling over the floor areas that can be legitimately excluded. The essence of the definition is the 'internal' floor area comprised in a building:

(a)   The internal floor area of part of a shop that has been temporarily closed should be included in the definition. A retailer cannot avoid the legislation by closing part of a 'large shop' on a Sunday, so that the remaining part that is open to the public is then smaller than 280 square metres. In

Haskins Garden Centres v East Dorset District Council,[41] the main building of the garden centre had been closed, leaving a smaller covered area open. The Divisional Court held that the shop was a 'large shop' despite the part of the building that was open having a floor area of less than 280 square metres. On the rationale of *Haskins*, if the relevant floor area of a shop is over 280 square metres during weekdays, the shop will be a 'large shop' on a Sunday.

(b) The external area of a shop, which is not 'internal floor area ... comprised in a building' shall be excluded from the definition. Areas that are not comprised within a building fall outside the definition, such that a garden centre consisting of a building with less than 280 square metres of floor space would fall outside the definition, even if it was built on 100 acres of land, as long as the land did not comprise of buildings with a floor space that would aggregate to greater than 280 square metres.

(c) Parts of the shop that are used for the sale of meals, refreshments or intoxicating liquor[42] are excluded. The area used for customer restaurant or food takeaway area, is therefore excluded from the relevant floor space.

(d) Areas that are not[43] used for 'serving customers in connection with the sale of goods' or for the 'display of goods' are excluded from the relevant floor area. Whereas an area used for the display of goods can be readily identified, the definition of an area used for serving customers is not as simple. It is tolerably clear that areas such as staff and customer amenity rooms would be excluded[44] It is less clear whether area used solely for the storage of goods are excluded from the definition. It depends upon whether a storage area is used for 'serving' customers. There is no definition of 'serving' in the STA 1994 and the ordinary meaning of the word includes attending to a customer and supplying him with goods.[45] There is no requirement that a serving area is one that the public have access to, and when a sales assistant goes to a storage area to collect requested goods, that is an area used for serving the customer that is connected with the sale of goods.[46]

'For the serving of retail customers'

10.94 A 'retail customer' is defined in the STA 1994 to mean, 'a person who purchases goods retail'; and a 'retail sale' means 'any sale other than a sale for use or resale in the course of a trade or business'.[47] The STA 1994 does not apply therefore to shops selling only to trade customers and to any businesses that supply only a service, rather than goods. The definition of 'shop' (wholly

---

41 [1998] NPC 75, DC.
42 Schedule 1, para 1 Interpretation of 'sale of goods'.
43 '... throughout the week ending with the Sunday in question'.
44 Staff rooms, staff canteens, staff or customer toilets, customer lounges, customer care facilities, playrooms etc.
45 OED definition of 'serving' includes 'supply goods to a customer'.
46 Schedule 1, para 1.
47 Schedule 1, para 1.

or mainly the sale of goods) prevents the STA 1994 applying to a business that principally supplies a service, which incidentally includes the supply of goods as a minor part of the service.

The paragraph 3 exemptions

10.95   The legislation does not apply to any of the shops referred to in para 3 of Sch 1[48] which are laid out below. In determining whether a shop falls within the definitions provided, consideration should be given to the nature of the trade or business that is carried on during the week.[49]

> 3. Exemptions
>
> (1) The shops referred to in paragraph 2(2)(a) above are –
>
> (a)   any shop which is at a farm and where the trade or business carried on consists wholly or mainly of the sale of produce from that farm,
>
> (b)   any shop where the trade or business carried on consists wholly or mainly of the sale of alcohol,
>
> (c)   any shop where the trade or business carried on consists wholly or mainly of the sale of any one or more of the following –
>
> > (i)   motor supplies and accessories, and
> >
> > (ii)   cycle supplies and accessories,
>
> (d)   any shop which –
>
> > (i)   is a registered pharmacy, and
> >
> > (ii)   is not open for the retail sale of any goods other than medicinal products, veterinary medicinal products and medical and surgical appliances,
>
> (e)   any shop at a designated airport which is situated in a part of the airport to which sub-paragraph (3) below applies,
>
> (f)   any shop in a railway station,
>
> (g)   any shop at a service area within the meaning of the Highways Act 1980,
>
> (h)   any petrol filling station,
>
> (j)   any shop which is not open for the retail sale of any goods other than food, stores or other necessaries required by any person for a vessel or aircraft on its arrival at, or immediately before its departure from, a port, harbour or airport, and
>
> (k)   any stand used for the retail sale of goods during the course of an exhibition.
>
> (2) In determining whether a shop falls within sub-paragraph (1)(a), (b) or (c) above, regard shall be had to the nature of the trade or business carried on there on weekdays as well as to the nature of the trade or business carried on there on Sunday.
>
> (3) This sub-paragraph applies to every part of a designated airport, except any part which is not ordinarily used by persons travelling by air to or from the airport.

---

[48]   Schedule 1, para 2(2)(a).
[49]   Schedule 1, para 3(2).

(4) In this paragraph *"designated airport"* means an airport designated for the purposes of this paragraph by an order made by the Secretary of State, as being an airport at which there appears to him to be a substantial amount of international passenger traffic.

Enforcement powers

10.96 Schedule 2, paras 3 (powers of entry) and 4 (obstruction of inspectors) of the STA 1994 have been repealed and replaced with powers in the Consumer Rights Act 2015. Schedule 1 contains the 'Restrictions on Sunday opening of large shops'. Schedule 3 contains the provisions regarding 'Loading and unloading at large shops on a Sunday morning' and Part II concerns 'Shops occupied by persons occupying the Jewish Sabbath'.

Investigatory powers are now covered in Chapter 3, Criminal Enforcement.

TEXTILE PRODUCTS

10.97 The Textile Products (Labelling and Fibre Composition) Regulations 2012[50] were made under the European Communities Act 1972. They came into force on 8 May 2012 and replace the Textile Products (Indications of Fibre Content) Regulations 1986 in their entirety. Products are excluded from the scope of the Regulations if they were placed on the market in the UK before 8 May 2012, remain available on the market in the UK until 9 November 2014 and complied with the 1986 Regulations as amended (reg 1)).

10.98 The Regulations require any person who makes a textile product[51] available on the market in the UK to ensure that their product meets the requirements set out in Regulation (EU) No 1007/2011 ('the EU Regulation'), as reproduced in Sch 2. These obligations relate to the labelling and marking of the fibre composition of such products. In particular, the EU Regulation, at Annex 1, sets out a list of textile fibre names and the fibre description to which they can be applied. For example, 'silk' may be applied only to 'fibre obtained exclusively from silk-secreting insects'.

10.99 It is an offence for any person to make a product available on the market in the UK in breach of the provisions of the EU Regulation listed at Sch 2 (reg 5(1)) unless they are either a person working in their home, to whom products are contracted out or an independent firm that carries out work from materials supplied without property being transferred for consideration (reg 5(2)(a)); or, a self-employed tailor making up customised products (reg 5(2)(b)). An offence under reg 5 is triable either way and subject to a fine. The Regulations provide for a due diligence defence (reg 10) and, subject to it, the person as a result of whose acts or omissions the offence was committed, will be guilty of that offence (reg 9). The Department of Business Innovation

---

[50] SI 2012/1102.
[51] As defined by Art 3(1)(a) of Regulation (EU) No 1007/2011.

and Skills[52] ('BIS') issued guidance notes to business on the Regulations in July 2012. Enforcement powers are now covered by Sch 5 of the CRA 2015; see Chapter 3, Criminal Enforcement.

TICKET RESELLING

Introduction

10.100 With few exceptions (such as the offence for an unauthorised person to sell or otherwise dispose of a ticket for a designated football match under the Criminal Justice and Public Order Act 1994) the law in the UK does not generally prohibit the re-sale of event tickets. Secondary ticket platforms may be simply described as a means by which individuals or businesses can re-sell tickets they have bought from 'authorised' sellers – often at a different price to the face value of the ticket.

Secondary ticketing

10.101 Chapter 5 of Part 3 and Sch 10 to the Consumer Rights Act 2015 ('CRA 2015') (ss 90–95) regulate online secondary ticketing marketplaces where tickets for sporting, recreational and cultural events are re-sold. They set out:

(i)   details of information to be provided when a ticket is offered for re-sale;

(ii)   certain protections that will apply to the re-sale of tickets;

(iii) the duty to report criminal activity; and

(iv)   the requirement for a review to be established to consider the consumer protection measures in relation to the secondary ticketing market;

(v)   provisions for enforcement by local weights and measures authorities and the imposition of financial penalties.

10.102 Chapter 5 of Part 3 was brought into force on 27 May 2015.[53] The Order also brought into force on the same date the investigatory powers provisions (contained in s 77 and Sch 5 in relation to the enforcement of this area) and Sch 10 which deals with financial penalties. See Chapter 3, Criminal Enforcement for details of the investigatory powers provisions. Consumer Rights Act: Secondary Ticketing Guidance for Business ('BIS Guidance') was published in May 2015.

Duty to provide information about tickets

10.103 Section 90 applies where a person re-sells a ticket for a recreational, sporting or cultural event in the United Kingdom through a 'secondary ticketing facility', which means 'an internet-based facility for the resale of tickets for

---

[52]   Now the Department of Business Energy and Industrial Strategy.

[53]   Consumer Rights Act 2015 (Commencement No 1) Order 2015, SI 2015/1333.

recreational, sporting or cultural events' (s 95). This includes both ordinary consumers selling on a ticket they no longer want and traders who operate as more frequent re-sellers of tickets. The buyer of the ticket must be given the information specified, where this is applicable to the ticket. The required information must be given in a clear and comprehensible manner, and before the buyer is bound by the contract for the sale of the ticket.

Prohibition on cancellation or blacklisting

10.104 Section 91, which applies in the same circumstances as s 90, provides that an event organiser cannot cancel a ticket merely because it is re-sold or offered for re-sale; nor may an organiser blacklist a person who re-sells or offers to re-sell a ticket. The BIS Guidance on s 91 states:

> 'This restriction (on cancellation and blacklisting) will always apply unless the event organiser has met two conditions:
>
> (i) It must have been clearly set out as a term of the contract under which the original buyer purchased the ticket from the event organiser that cancellation of the ticket and/or blacklisting of the seller may occur as a consequence of that ticket being resold or offered for resale.
>
> (ii) The term of the contract under which the original buyer purchased the ticket from the event organiser must not be unfair ... This is a significant requirement. Contract law ordinarily allows a purchaser to transfer to someone else what they have bought. Terms that prohibit resale are considered to be open to scrutiny for fairness and therefore must meet the principles of fair and open dealing, ensuring that their substance, expression and use respects consumers' legitimate interests. Those terms which are not fair cannot be enforced against a consumer.'

Duty to report criminal activity

10.105 Section 92 requires an operator of a secondary ticketing facility, who knows that a person has used or is using the facility in such a way that an offence has been or is being committed, and the offence relates to the re-sale of a ticket for a recreational, sporting or cultural event in the UK, to disclose certain matters to 'an appropriate person' (the police) and an organiser of the event. This would therefore apply to situations where, for example, the fraudulent sale of non-existent tickets is taking place.

Enforcement of Chapter 5

10.106 Section 93 provides:

> (1) A local weights and measures authority in Great Britain may enforce the provisions of this Chapter in its area.
>
> (2) The Department of Enterprise, Trade and Investment may enforce the provisions of this Chapter in Northern Ireland.
>
> (3) Each of the bodies referred to in subsections (1) and (2) is an "enforcement

authority" for the purposes of this Chapter.

10.107 An enforcement authority, if is satisfied on the balance of probabilities that a person has breached a duty or prohibition imposed by Chapter 5, may impose a financial penalty, not exceeding £5,000, on the person in respect of that breach (sub-s 93(4)) but a 'due diligence' defence applies in relation to a breach of either s 90 or 91 (sub-s 93(5)). Schedule 10 provides a procedure for, and appeals against, financial penalties.

TRADE DESCRIPTIONS

Introduction

10.108 The offence provisions of the Trade Descriptions Act 1968 ('TDA') were substantially repealed by the Consumer Protection from Unfair Trading Regulations 2008 ('CPUTR') but other provisions continue to apply to legislation such as the Hallmarking Act 1973, the Crystal Glass (Descriptions) Regulations 1973, the Textile Products (Indications of Fibre Content) Regulations 2012, and the Footwear (Indication of Composition) Labelling Regulations 1995.[54] A considerable body of case law has been established under the TDA; however, that has relevance to other legislation.

Territorial jurisdiction

10.109 The TDA is applicable throughout the United Kingdom.

Offences

10.110 The only remaining offences are contained in s 12 (False representations as to royal approval or award, etc) which is amended by the addition of s 12(3) and now states:

> **12 False representations as to royal approval or award, etc**
>
> (1) If any person, in the course of any trade or business, gives, by whatever means, any false indication, direct or indirect, that any goods or services supplied by him or any methods adopted by him are or are of a kind supplied to or approved by Her Majesty or any member of the Royal Family, he shall, subject to the provisions of this Act, be guilty of an offence.
>
> (2) If any person, in the course of any trade or business, uses, without the authority of Her Majesty, any device or emblem signifying the Queen's Award to Industry or anything so nearly resembling such a device or emblem as to be likely to deceive, he shall, subject to the provisions of this Act, be guilty of an offence.
>
> (3) A person shall not be guilty of an offence under subsection (1) or (2) by reason of doing anything that is a commercial practice unless the commercial practice is unfair.

---

[54] SI 2008/1277.

In this subsection "commercial practice" and "unfair" have the same meaning as in the Consumer Protection from Unfair Trading Regulations 2008.

10.111 When Royal Patronage is granted, for instance a Tradesmen's Warrant, the Royal Arms may be displayed in circumstances laid down in the Lord Chamberlain's Rules for holders of a Tradesmen's Warrant. However, they may not be used as a trade mark and should only be displayed for the duration of the grant of a Royal Warrant.

Defences

10.112 Section 24(1) provides a defence where the defendant can show that the offence was caused by a mistake, or reliance on information supplied to him, or the act or default of any other person, or an accident, or some other cause beyond his control *and* that he took all reasonable precautions *and* exercised all due diligence to avoid the offence. Section 25 provides a defence where the allegation is of an offence committed by the publication of an advertisement. It is a defence for the defendant to show that he is a person whose business is to publish or arrange for the publication of advertisements *and* that the advertisement in question was received in the ordinary course of business *and* that he did not know *and* had no reason to suspect that its publication would amount to an offence under the TDA. Statutory defences of this nature are considered in detail in Chapter 3, Criminal Enforcement.

Restrictions on proceedings

Time limits

10.113

19 Time limit for prosecutions

(1) No prosecution for an offence under this Act shall be commenced after the expiration of three years from the commission of the offence or one year from its discovery by the prosecutor, whichever is the earlier.

(2) Notwithstanding anything in section 127(1) of the Magistrates' Courts Act 1980, a magistrates' court may try an information for an offence under this Act if the information was laid at any time within twelve months from the commission of the offence.

(3) Notwithstanding anything in section 23 of the Summary Jurisdiction (Scotland) Act 1954 (limitation of time for proceedings in statutory offences) summary proceedings in Scotland for an offence under this section may be commenced at any time within twelve months from the time when the offence was committed, and subsection (2) of the said section 23 shall apply for the purposes of this subsection as it applies for the purposes of that section.

(4) Subsections (2) and (3) of this section do not apply where –

    (a)   the offence was committed by the making of an oral statement ...

In relation to Scotland it is worth noting the comments of Lord Justice General Hope in *Hamilton v HMA*:[55] 'No analogy can usefully be drawn as to what may be the correct application of the wording of s 19(1) to Scottish procedure for what may happen south of the border' and the fact that time limits for offences are also covered by the Criminal Procedure (Scotland) Act 1995. No prosecution for an offence under the TDA may be commenced more than 3 years from the commission of the offence or more than 1 year after its discovery by the prosecutor, whichever is the earlier.[56] The shorter time limit in the case of an offence allegedly committed by the making of an oral statement apparently provided by s 19(4) of the TDA has been held to be of no effect since the passing of the Magistrates' Courts Act 1980.[57] Time limits are considered in detail in Chapter 3, Criminal Enforcement.

10.114   Although s 19(4)(b) and (c) were repealed by CPUTR they continue to have effect for certain legislation made under the European Communities Act 1972.[58]

> 19(4) Subsections (2) and (3) of this section do not apply where –
>
> (b)   the offence was one of supplying goods to which a false trade description is applied, and the trade description was applied by an oral statement; or
>
> (c)   the offence was one where a false trade description is deemed to have been applied to goods by virtue of section 4(3) of this Act and the goods were supplied in pursuance of an oral request.

Prosecutions

10.115   Any person, other than the Crown, may be prosecuted for an offence under the Act. This includes both individuals and bodies corporate.

Directors' liability

10.116

> 20 Offences by corporations
>
> (1) Where an offence under this Act which has been committed by a body corporate is proved to have been committed with the consent and connivance of, or to be attributable to any neglect on the part of, any director, manager, secretary or other similar officer of the body corporate, or any person who was purporting to act in any such capacity, he as well as the body corporate shall be guilty of that offence and shall be liable to be proceeded against and punished accordingly.
>
> (2) In this section "director", in relation to any body corporate established by or under any enactment for the purpose of carrying on under national ownership any industry or part of an industry or undertaking, being a body corporate whose affairs are managed by the members thereof, means a member of that body

---

55   1997 SLT 31 at pp 34G–34H.
56   Section 19(1).
57   *R v Dacorum Magistrates ex p Michael Gardner* (1985) 149 JP 677 (transcript CO/1219/84).
58   CPUTR, Sch 3, para 2.

corporate.

The liability of directors etc is considered in detail in Chapter 3, Criminal Enforcement.

Causal liability

10.117

> **23 Offences due to fault of other person**
>
> Where the commission by any person of an offence under this Act is due to the act or default of some other person that other person shall be guilty of the offence, and a person may be charged with and convicted of the offence by virtue of this section whether or not proceedings are taken against the first-mentioned person.

Causal liability is considered in Chapter 3, Criminal Enforcement.

Duty to enforce

10.118 Section 26(1) of the TDA places a duty on every local 'weights and measures authority' to enforce within their area the provisions of the TDA but the section does not permit a local weights and measures authority in Scotland to institute proceedings for an offence.

Powers of enforcement officers

10.119 Enforcement powers are now covered by Sch 5 of the CRA 2015, see Chapter 3, Criminal Enforcement.

Sentencing

10.120 Section 18 of the TDA deals with maximum sentences for offences under s 12. On summary conviction, the maximum is a fine not exceeding the prescribed sum.[59] On indictment, the maximum penalty is a fine and/or 2 years' imprisonment. It follows that the Crown Court may impose a lesser community sentence if considered appropriate. Section 238 of the Criminal Procedure (Scotland) Act 1995 allows for the imposition of a community service order instead of a period of imprisonment.

---

[59] The 'prescribed sum' is now unlimited upon summary conviction in the Magistrates Court (Magistrates' Courts Act 1980, s.32(10); Legal Aid, Sentencing and Punishment of Offenders Act 2012, s 85).

UNSOLICITED PRODUCTS

Unsolicited goods

Introduction

10.121 The Unsolicited Goods and Services Act 1971 ('UGSA 1971') was enacted to combat an unwelcome growth in the trade practice of 'inertia selling', which involved unsolicited goods being sent to consumers on a speculative basis. Typically, goods would be sent to a random consumer as an offer, with an option to return the goods within a specified period, or failing that an obligation to pay for them. A consumer who did neither would frequently be subjected to demands for payment and threats of legal action. The rights of a recipient of unsolicited goods are now dealt with by reg 27M of the CPUTR (see Chapter 5, Consumer Rights). Criminal liability for a trader demanding immediate or deferred payment for, or the return or safekeeping of, unsolicited products to consumers is also covered by the CPUTR.

Offences

Business-to-business offences

10.122 Section 2 UGSA 1971 provides for business-to-business offences in relation to demands and threats regarding payment concerning unsolicited goods ('unsolicited' means, in relation to goods sent to any person, that they are sent without any prior request made by him or on his behalf). Section 2(1) makes it an offence for a person who, not having reasonable cause to believe there is a right to payment, in the course of any trade or business makes a demand for payment, or asserts a present or prospective right to payment, for what he knows are unsolicited goods sent to another person with a view to his acquiring them for the purposes of his trade or business.

10.123 In *Barking & Dagenham (LB of) v Jones* (1999/035/1) Brooke LJ observed:

> '... Without going into the matter at any length, it appears to me that an offence of demanding payment for unsolicited goods, if made over the telephone, is committed both at the place where the demand is made and in the place where the demand is received.'

10.124 A case brought under s 2(1) – *Eiman v London Borough of Waltham Forest*[60] – considered the issue as to whether a council worker, who, as a hobby, compiled and privately printed a book of verse in Urdu at his own expense – and sought payment for unsolicited copies – did so in the course of a trade or business. The Divisional Court did not interfere with the Crown Court's conclusion that the activity was in the course of business. Omerod LJ has opined that, in general, the word 'business' in statutes should be given its widest possible meaning so as to meet the mischief at which the legislation is aimed.

---

[60] (1982) 90 ITSA MR 204.

10.125 Section 2(2) makes it an offence for a person who, not having reasonable cause to believe there is a right to payment, in the course of any trade or business and with a view to obtaining any payment for what he knows are unsolicited goods sent to another person with a view to his acquiring them for the purposes of his trade or business:

(a) threatens to bring any legal proceedings; or

(b) places or causes to be placed the name of any person on a list of defaulters or debtors or threatens to do so; or

(c) invokes or causes to be invoked any other collection procedure or threatens to do so.

Business-to-consumer offences

10.126 The Consumer Protection (Distance Selling) Regulations 2000 provided for business-to-consumer offences in relation to demands and threats regarding payment concerning unsolicited goods and these were worded in similar terms to s 2 offences. However these provisions of the Regulations were revoked by the CPUTR.

10.127 Regulation 12 of the Consumer Protection from Unfair Trading Regulations 2008 provides that a trader is guilty of an offence if he engages in a commercial practice set out in any of paras 1–10, 12–27 and 29–31 of Sch 1 (Commercial practices which are in all circumstances considered unfair). The commercial practice in para 29 of Sch 1 is:

> Demanding immediate or deferred payment for or the return or safekeeping of products supplied by the trader, but not solicited by the consumer.

10.128 The detailed provisions of the CPUTR are set out in Chapter 7, Unfair Commercial Practices.

Reasonable cause to believe there is a right to payment

10.129 As the burden of proof on this issue has not been statutorily placed upon the defence, it is for the prosecution to discharge it to the criminal standard. Whether the sender has a reasonable cause to believe there is a right to payment is a question of fact. It is however, an objective question and it is submitted that a seller's mistaken understanding of his legal rights would not amount to a reasonable cause; which would be contrary to the policy of UGSA 1971.

10.130 A mistaken understanding of the facts, as opposed to the law, was considered in *Readers Digest Association v Pirie*[61] which concerned the billing for copies of a magazine sent to customers after they had cancelled their subscriptions by letter. A junior employee at the company had failed to enter the cancellations onto computer records and the bills had been sent out in error.

---

[61] 1973 SLT 170.

The High Court of Justiciary decided that it had not been proven that the company did not have a reasonable belief that there was a right to payment. Lord Kissen opined that there could be no breach, 'if the person in question had an honest belief which was based on circumstances which would lead an ordinary prudent man to the same conclusion'.

10.131 The rationale of the decision in *Readers Digest* was that the company had established a system that would ordinarily have prevented the unwarranted demands for payment. There had been nothing to indicate that the system was not functioning properly and liable to cause mistakes. It was therefore not unreasonable for the company to rely upon the accuracy of the system. The defender in *Readers Digest* was the company and the analysis must be on the basis of whether the company had reasonable cause to believe. The fact that a junior employee had no reasonable cause to believe the company had a right to payment was not enough to make the company liable. This approach reflects decisions in other trading standards areas about the nature of corporate liability when there is a mental element to the offence.

Territorial jurisdiction

10.132 The parts of UGSA 1971 relating to unsolicited goods apply to Great Britain.

Defences

10.133 There are no statutory defences to the offences in s 2 UGSA 1971.

Restrictions on proceedings

10.134 The offences in s 2 are summary only – there is therefore a 6-month time limit, from the time when the offence was committed (see s 127 Magistrates' Courts Act 1980). In Scotland, as the offences in s 2 can only be tried under summary procedure, the time limits are established under s 136 of the Criminal Procedure (Scotland) Act 1995 – within six months after the contravention occurred.

Prosecutions

10.135 The nature of the offences in s 2 mean that, for the most part, prosecutions will be brought against principals of businesses or corporate bodies.

10.136 Section 5 permits the prosecution and conviction of any 'director, manager, secretary or other similar officer' of a company or 'any person who was purporting to act in such a capacity' where an offence under the UGSA 1971 has been committed by the company 'with the consent and connivance' of that person or as a result of that person's neglect. Where the affairs of the body corporate are managed by its members, the provisions apply in relation to the acts and defaults of 'a member in connection with his functions of management as if he were a director of the body corporate'. Directors' liability is considered in detail in Chapter 3, Criminal Enforcement.

Sentencing

10.137 Under UGSA 1971, a person guilty of a s 2(1) offence is liable to a fine not exceeding level 4 on the standard scale and a person guilty of a s 2(2) offence is liable to an unlimited fine.[62]

Unsolicited directory entries

Introduction

10.138 Other than the provision relating to the non-application of UGSA 1971 prior to its commencement (s 3(4)), the entire provisions of the Act relating to unsolicited directory entries have been amended, at least once, since it was enacted. The provisions apply to charging for the inclusion in a directory of entry relating to a person or his trade or business. Unless the provisions of UGSA 1971 are complied with, a person has no liability to make any payment and is entitled to recover any payment made. The definition of 'directory' under s 3 has been considered in civil proceedings in *Re Supporting Link Alliance Ltd.*[63] There, annual business guides, in which the company had sold advertising space through cold calling, were held not to be 'directories' on the basis that the editorial content was not a list of people or things listed by reference to any category or in any order, alphabetical or otherwise.

10.139 Four methods of legitimately charging for a directory entry are specified s 3(1)(a)–(d) UGSA 1971:

(a) where there has been signed by the purchaser or on his behalf an order complying with s 3(3)(a); or

(b) where there has been signed by the purchaser or on his behalf a note complying with s 3(3)(b) of his agreement to the charge and before the note was signed, a copy of it was supplied, for retention by him, to him or a person acting on his behalf; or

(c) where there has been transmitted by the purchaser or a person acting on his behalf an electronic communication which includes a statement that the purchaser agrees to the charge and the relevant condition is satisfied in relation to that communication; or

(d) where the charge arises under a contract in relation to which the conditions set out in s 3B(1) – which relates to renewed and extended contracts – are met.

---

[62] Legal Aid, Sentencing and Punishment of Offenders Act 2012, s 85.
[63] [2004] 1 WLR 1549.

Territorial jurisdiction

10.140 The parts of UGSA 1971 relating to unsolicited directory entries apply to Great Britain.

Offence

10.141 Section 3(2) creates an offence in a case where a payment in respect of a charge would be recoverable from him in accordance with the terms of s 3(1), the person demands payment, or asserts a present or prospective right to payment, of the charge or any part of it, without knowing or having reasonable cause to believe that:

(a) the entry to which the charge relates was ordered in accordance with s 3(1)(a);

(b) a proper note of the agreement has been duly signed; or

(c) the requirements set out in s 3(1)(c) or (1)(d) above have been met.

Defences

10.142 There are no statutory defences to the offence in s 3(2).

Restrictions on proceedings

10.143 There are no time limit restrictions to the offence in s 3(2) as it is an either-way matter by virtue of s 3 of the Unsolicited Goods and Services (Amendment) Act 1975 and no time limits are contained in UGSA 1971.

Prosecutions

10.144 The nature of the offences in s 3(2) mean that, for the most part, prosecutions will be brought against principals of businesses or corporate bodies.

10.145 Section 5 of the Act permits the prosecution and conviction of any 'director, manager, secretary or other similar officer' of a company or 'any person who was purporting to act in such a capacity' where an offence under the Act has been committed by the company 'with the consent and connivance' of that person or as a result of that person's neglect. Where the affairs of the body corporate are managed by its members, the provisions apply in relation to the acts and defaults of 'a member in connection with his functions of management as if he were a director of the body corporate'. Directors' liability is considered in detail in Chapter 3, Criminal Enforcement.

Sentencing

10.146 Under UGSA 1971, a person guilty of a s 3(2) offence punishable on summary conviction is liable to an unlimited fine. By virtue of s 3(1) of the

Unsolicited Goods and Services (Amendment) Act 1975 an offence under s 3(2) may be prosecuted on indictment; and a person convicted shall be liable to a fine.

Unsolicited publications

10.147 Section 4 of UGSA 1971 provides:

4 Unsolicited publications

(1) A person shall be guilty of an offence if he sends or causes to be sent to another person any book, magazine or leaflet (or advertising material for any such publication) which he knows or ought reasonably to know is unsolicited and which describes or illustrates human sexual techniques.

(2) A person found guilty of an offence under this section shall be liable on summary conviction to a fine not exceeding level 5 on the standard scale.

(3) A prosecution for an offence under this section shall not in England and Wales be instituted except by, or with the consent of, the Director of Public Prosecutions.

10.148 In *DPP v Beate UHSE (UK) Ltd*[64] the defendant's contention was that no offence is committed under s 4 unless the advertising material itself describes or illustrates human sexual techniques. The advertising material in this case was for a catalogue that described or illustrated human sexual techniques but the advertising material itself did not give any such descriptions or illustrations. On appeal against conviction Widgery LCJ said:

'It is ... clearly within the mischief of this legislation that there should be a prohibition of advertising material ... even though [it] does not of itself contain a description or illustration of human sexual techniques ... On the construction urged by the defendant ... the reference to advertising material would be wholly unnecessary ... because, if such material itself illustrated the technique in question, it would in any event when so illustrating those techniques come within the opening words of s 4(1)).'

---

[64] [1974] 1 QB 158.

CHAPTER 11

ADVERTISING

CONTENTS

INTRODUCTION

11.1   Advertising in the United Kingdom is governed by a combination of regulation and self-regulation. Self-regulation in the advertising sector dates back to the 1960s, when the advertising industry rejected calls for an American-style Federal Trade Commission to regulate advertising by statute. An official report on Consumer Protection by the Molony Committee declared:

> 'We are satisfied that the wider problem of advertising ought to be, and can be, tackled by effectively applied voluntary controls. We stress, however, that our conclusion depends on the satisfactory working of the new scheme, and in particular on the continued quality and independence of the Authority at its pinnacle.'[1]

11.2   The Advertising Association formed the Committee of Advertising Practice ('CAP') in 1961 and the Advertising Standards Authority ('the ASA') came into existence the following year. The ASA was tasked with overseeing the implementation of the first Code of Advertising Practice in 1962, which only covered non-broadcast advertising. Since 2004, the ASA has also been in charge of regulating certain aspects of broadcast advertising, since the Office of Communications ('Ofcom'), the communications regulator, contracted out responsibility for handling and resolving complaints relating to certain TV and radio advertisements to the ASA.[2] The advertising industry set up the Advertising Standards Board of Finance ('ASBOF') in 1974, which was to secure funding for the ASA's activities through a levy. The ASA continues to be funded by the ASBOF levy today.

11.3   Legislation to tackle misleading advertising was introduced in 1988 in the form of the Control of Misleading Advertisements Regulations 1988 ('the 1988 Regulations'), which implemented the Directive on misleading advertising.[3] The Regulations retained the ASA's role as a non-statutory body, but enabled it, for the first time, to refer persistently non-compliant advertisers to the Director General of Fair Trading for legal action.

11.4   The 1988 Regulations have been superseded by the Consumer Protection from Unfair Trading Regulations 2008 ('CPUTR'), which implement the Unfair Commercial Practices Directive[4] ('UCPD'), and by the Business Protection from Misleading Marketing Regulations 2008 ('BPR'), which implement the Directive on misleading and comparative advertising[5] ('MCAD 2006'). The

---

[1]   Molony Committee, 'The Final report of the Committee on Consumer Protection', 1962. The Molony Committee had been set up in July, 1959, under Mr JT Molony to review existing consumer protection legislation.

[2]   Crucially, however, Ofcom has only contracted out powers relating to breaches of the Uk Broadcast Advertising Standards Code ('BCAP') and the relevant provisions of the Medicines (Advertising) Regulations 1994. Ofcom retains powers in relation to complaints relating to political advertising, unsuitable sponsorship, discrimination between advertisers and the scheduling of advertisements.

[3]   84/450/EEC.

[4]   2005/29/EC Directive concerning unfair business-to-consumer commercial practices.

[5]   2006/114/EC.

UCPD regulates unfair and misleading business-to-consumer commercial practices, whilst MCAD 2006 regulates business-to-business advertising, as well as laying down the conditions in which comparative advertising is permitted. The UCPD is a maximum harmonisation measure, which prevents Member States from maintaining or adopting rules that are more restrictive than those contained in it.[6] The MCAD 2006 is a maximum harmonisation measure in relation to comparative advertising, but a minimum harmonisation measure in relation to misleading advertising.[7]

CONSUMER PROTECTION FROM UNFAIR TRADING REGULATIONS 2008

11.5 The definition of 'commercial practice'[8] in the CPUTR is broad and does not require the conclusion of a transaction.[9] Accordingly, advertisements and website content that is directly connected with the promotion, sale or supply of a product to or from consumers fall within its remit. Whilst the CPUTR do cover comparative advertising (in the sense, eg that such can constitute a misleading action under reg 5[10] or a misleading omission under reg 6), the conditions for permissible comparative advertising are to be found in reg 4 of the BPR (see below).

11.6 The main CPUTR provisions that are of relevance to advertising are misleading actions (reg 5) and misleading omissions (reg 6). These provisions are deliberately broad and likely to cover most false or deceptive advertisements made to consumers. The CPUTR is covered in detail in Chapter 7.

11.7 In addition to these provisions, Schedule 1 of the CPUTR bans certain advertising practices outright. The provisions that are of particular importance are set out in the table below.

Provision of Schedule 1	Summary of provision
Para 5	Bait advertising[11]

---

[6] This is considered further in Chapter 2, Interpreting Consumer Law.

[7] Art 8(1) of the MCAD 2006.

[8] 'Commercial practice' is defined in reg 2(1) of the CPUTR as 'any act, omission, course of conduct, representation or commercial communication (including advertising and marketing) by a trader, which is directly connected with the promotion, sale or supply of a product to or from consumers, whether occurring before, during or after a commercial transaction (if any) in relation to a product'.

[9] See, for instance the CJEU case of *Trento Sviluppo srl and Centrale Adriatica Soc Coop arl v Autorita Garante della Concorrenza e del Mercato* (C-281/12) [2014] CTLC 326.

[10] See the express reference to comparative advertising in reg 5(3)(a).

[11] Making an invitation to purchase products at a specified price without disclosing the existence

Provision of Schedule 1	Summary of provision
Para 6	Bait and switch advertising[12]
Para 11	Using editorial content in the media to promote a product where a trader has paid for the promotion without making that clear in the content or by images or sounds clearly identifiable by the consumer (advertorial).
Para 17	Falsely claiming that a product is able to cure illnesses, dysfunction or malformations
Para 21	Including in marketing material an invoice or similar document seeking payment which gives the consumer the impression that he has already ordered the marketed product when he has not
Para 28	Including in an advertisement a direct exhortation to children to buy advertised products or persuade their parents or other adults to buy advertised products for them

BUSINESS PROTECTION FROM MISLEADING MARKETING REGULATIONS 2008

11.8 The BPR came into force on 26 May 2008 and implement MCAD 2006, which seeks to protect traders from misleading advertising and identifies the circumstances in which comparative advertising is permitted. MCAD 2006 replaced the Misleading and Comparative Advertising Directive ('MCAD 1984')[13] which sought to protect both traders and consumers from misleading advertising and which had been amended in 1997 to include comparative advertising.[14] MCAD 1984 was implemented by the Control of Misleading Advertising Regulations 1988 ('the 1988 Regulations'). Under the 1988 Regulations, now revoked, the OFT had the power to seek civil injunctions against publishers of misleading advertisements. The 1988 Regulations did not

---

of any reasonable grounds the trader may have for believing that he will not be able to offer for supply, or to procure another trader to supply, those products or equivalent products at that price for a period that is, and in quantities that are, reasonable having regard to the product, the scale of advertising of the product and the price offered.

[12] Making an invitation to purchase products at a specified price and then: (a) refusing to show the advertised item to consumers, (b) refusing to take orders for it or deliver it within a reasonable time, or (c) demonstrating a defective sample of it.

[13] Council Directive 84/450/EEC concerning misleading and comparative advertising.

[14] By Directive 97/55/EC.

provide for criminal sanctions and were used sparingly. In the UK, the emphasis in this area had previously been on self-regulation using non-statutory bodies such as the ASA.

11.9 The BPR provide for criminal sanctions and wider injunctive powers that can be exercised by any 'enforcement authority', which includes any weights and measures authority.[15] Although injunctive relief can only be sought by enforcement authorities, the offence of engaging in misleading advertising under reg 6 can be privately prosecuted.

11.10 The structure of the BPR closely resembles that of CPUTR:

- Regulation 7 sets out the applicable penalties (see CPUTR, reg 13).
- Regulation 8 provides for corporate liability (see CPUTR, reg 15).
- Regulation 9 covers causal liability (see CPUTR, reg 16).
- Regulation 10 sets the time limit for prosecutions (see CPUTR, reg 14).
- Regulation 11 provides the due diligence defence (see CPUTR, reg 17).
- Regulation 12 provides the innocent publication of an advertisement defence (see CPUTR, reg 18).
- Regulation 13 sets out the duty to enforce the BPR (equivalent to CPUTR, reg 19).

11.11 A weights and measures authority that wishes to bring a criminal prosecution under reg 6 of the BPR is required to notify the Competition and Markets Authority ('CMA') under reg 14.[16] This requirement is expressly stated to be directory rather than mandatory, however, and a failure to comply with it will not render the criminal proceedings invalid.[17] Investigatory powers are now covered by Sch 5 of the CRA 2015, see Chapter 3, Criminal Enforcement.

Misleading advertising

11.12 Regulation 3 prohibits misleading advertising against traders and provides as follows:

> **Business Protection from Misleading Marketing Regulations 2008, reg 3**
>
> **Prohibition of advertising which misleads traders**
>
> '3(1) Advertising which is misleading is prohibited.
>
> (2) Advertising is misleading which –

---

[15] Reg 2 defines 'enforcement authority' as the CMA, every local weights and measures authority, the Department of Enterprise, Trade and Investment Northern Ireland (now DfE, the Department for the Economy) and the Gas and Electricity Markets Authority.

[16] This does not apply in Scotland.

[17] Reg 14(3). This is equivalent to the requirement to notify the CMA of prosecutions under the CPUTR under the Enterprise Act 2002, s 230.

(a)   in any way, including its presentation, deceives or is likely to deceive the traders to whom it is addressed or whom it reaches; and by reason of its deceptive nature, is likely to affect their economic behaviour; or

(b)   for those reasons, injures or is likely to injure a competitor.

(3) In determining whether advertising is misleading, account shall be taken of all its features, and in particular of any information it contains concerning –

(a)   the characteristics of the product (as defined in paragraph (4));

(b)   the price or manner in which the price is calculated;

(c)   the conditions on which the product is supplied or provided; and

(d)   the nature, attributes and rights of the advertiser (as defined in paragraph (5)).

(4) In paragraph (3)(a) the "characteristics of the product" include –

(a)   availability of the product;

(b)   nature of the product;

(c)   execution of the product;

(d)   composition of the product;

(e)   method and date of manufacture of the product;

(f)   method and date of provision of the product;

(g)   fitness for purpose of the product;

(h)   uses of the product;

(i)   quantity of the product;

(j)   specification of the product;

(k)   geographical or commercial origin of the product;

(l)   results to be expected from use of the product; or

(m)   results and material features of tests or checks carried out on the product.

(5) In paragraph (3)(d) the "nature, attributes and rights" of the advertiser include the advertiser's –

(a)   identity;

(b)   assets;

(c)   qualifications;

(d)   ownership of industrial, commercial or intellectual property rights; or

(e)   awards and distinctions.'

Advertising

11.13 'Advertising' is defined in reg 2 as 'any form of representation which is made in connection with a trade, business, craft or profession in order to promote the supply or transfer of a product' and 'advertiser' is to be construed accordingly. This broad definition includes any representation that is made to promote the supply or transfer of a 'product'. Product is defined in the same way as it is in CPUTR and now includes immovable property, rights, and obligations. The term 'advertising' is likely to cover not only print, broadcast and billboard advertising, but also other marketing and promotional activities, such as details in catalogues or websites, descriptions on packaging and oral representations.[18]

---

[18]   This was the view taken by the Office of Fair Trading in its Guidance on the BPR, 'Business to

Misleading

11.14 'Misleading advertising' is defined in reg 3(2) as advertising that in any way, including its presentation, 'deceives or is likely to deceive the traders to whom it is addressed or whom it reaches' and by reason of its deceptive nature: (a) it is likely to affect the economic behaviour of those traders; or (b) it injures or is likely to injure a competitor.

11.15 There is no guidance in the legislation or the case-law relating to it as to what is meant by deceiving a trader. Some assistance can be derived from the definition given to the term 'trader' in the BPR:

'"trader" means any person who is acting for purposes relating to his trade, craft, business or profession **and anyone acting in the name of or on behalf of a trader**.'

(emphasis added).[19]

It would appear, therefore, that an advertisement could be misleading if it deceives or is likely to deceive an employee of the trader in question (eg the buyer of a retail chain). Even though there is no concept of an 'average trader', this is likely to be an objective test. Further, the wording of reg 3(2) would appear to suggest that the traders to be taken into account are not only those to whom the advertisement is addressed (ie the intended recipients), but also the traders reached by the advertisement, which may well include unintended recipients.

11.16 As specified in reg 3(3), in determining whether advertising is misleading, account shall be taken of all its features, and in particular of any information it contains concerning the characteristics of the product, the price or manner in which the price is calculated, the conditions on which the product is supplied or provided, and the nature, attributes and rights of the advertiser. The OFT Guidance on the BPR provided the following examples of advertising that could be deceptive:

- advertising that contained a false statement of fact – this may be possible to prove or disprove by evidence;
- advertising that concealed or left out important facts;
- advertising that promised to do something when there was no intention of carrying it out;
- advertising that created a false impression, even if everything stated in it was literally true.

---

business promotions and comparative advertisements – A quick guide to the Business Protection from Misleading Marketing Regulations 2008', 2009. No guidance on the BPR has yet been issued by the CMA.

[19] Reg 2(1).

11.17 The BPR definition of 'misleading' differs from that provided for misleading actions and misleading omissions in CPUTR.[20] In particular:

- Misleading actions and misleading omissions under CPUTR contain the threshold condition of causing or being likely to cause the average consumer to take a transactional decision he would not have taken otherwise. The BPR do make reference to affecting the economic behaviour of the traders to whom the advertisement is addressed or who it reaches, but the advertisement may be deemed to be misleading without having this effect – it may be sufficient to demonstrate that it injures or is likely to injure a competitor.

- The CPUTR require the distortion of a consumer's economic behaviour to be material; there does not appear to be a corresponding requirement in the BPR, although it is arguable that some *de minimis* test ought to be implied into the legislation.[21]

- The wording 'even if the information is factually correct' contained in reg 5(2)(b) of CPUTR (misleading actions) is omitted from the BPR. CPUTR and BPR were brought into force together and the omission of these words from the BPR might be taken to have been deliberate. It could be argued, therefore, that advertising could not be deceptive under the BPR if it is factually correct. Such a conclusion is likely to be contrary to the general purpose of the legislation, however. The BPR focus on the likelihood of deception, and they specifically identify the manner in which the advertising is presented as being capable of doing that. For instance, a newspaper advertisement might make a bold claim about a product that is only accurate when read together with a disclaimer. If the disclaimer were hidden in small print, the presentation of the advertisement would deceive – regardless of whether the information was factually accurate.

Affect a trader's economic behaviour

11.18 Affecting a trader's economic behaviour is left undefined by the BPR, but it is unlikely that this term can be equated with taking a transactional decision under CPUTR. The breadth of the CPUTR definition[22] was recently the subject of a CJEU ruling,[23] where it was held that even the decision to enter the shop was a 'transactional decision' within the meaning of the UCPD. The CJEU would be unlikely to adopt such a broad definition under the MCAD 2006: the MCAD 2006 is not a maximum harmonisation measure in relation to

---

[20]   Regs 5 and 6, respectively.

[21]   This is in contrast to the position under the Trade Descriptions Act 1968, s 1, where the materiality (or de minimis test) related to the falsity rather than the distortion of the economic behaviour. See, for instance, *Harrison v Freezemaster* (1972) 80 MR 75.

[22]   'Any decision taken by a consumer, whether it is to act or to refrain from acting, concerning ... whether, how and on what terms to purchase, make payment in whole or in part for, retain or dispose of a product; or ... whether, how and on what terms to exercise a contractual right in relation to a product ....'

[23]   *Trento Sviluppo srl and Centrale Adriatica Soc Coop arl v Autorita Garante della Concorrenza e del Mercato* (C-281/12) [2014] CTLC 326.

misleading advertising, in contrast to the UCPD, and its purpose is to protect businesses, as opposed to consumers. Accordingly, a lower level of protection would be expected and justified. It is likely that this condition will require proof that a trader entered into or chose not to enter into a binding contract as a result of the deceptive advertisement.

11.19 This appears to have been the view of the Office of Fair Trading, whose Guidance[24] stated that an advertisement 'will be likely to affect the economic behaviour of traders if, for example, it induces or is likely to induce them to part with money for what is being advertised'.

Injure a competitor

11.20 The offence will be committed if the deceptive advertisement does or is likely to 'injure a competitor'. In this context, it is probable that this will require proof that the deceptive advertisement does or is likely to cause a competitor economic or financial harm.[25] In its guidance on the BPR, the OFT provided the following example:

> 'a competitor may be injured as a result of traders being deceived by a misleading advertisement, for example, where an advertiser misleads traders into using their services when the trader actually intended to use the service of company X (a competitor), perhaps by confusing the trader into believing they were actually dealing with company X. This is likely to injure company X (the competitor) as company X loses out on business as a result of the misleading advertisement.'

Statutory defences

11.21 A trader engaging in advertising which is misleading under reg 3 is guilty of a criminal offence under reg 6 of the BPR, with the penalties for the offence set out in reg 7. The BPR include both a due diligence defence (reg 11) and an innocent publication defence (reg 12). The burden of proof for both rests with the defendant on the balance of probabilities. Due diligence is now covered in Chapter 3, Criminal Enforcement.

Injunctive relief

11.22 Injunctions to secure compliance with reg 3 can be brought under reg 15 by an enforcement authority if the authority considers that there has been or there is likely to be a breach. Under reg 15(3) an injunction can only be brought by a local weights and measures authority if it has complied with the CMA notice requirements. If more than one local weights and measures authority in

---

[24] Office of Fair Trading, 'Business to business promotions and comparative advertisements – A quick guide to the Business Protection from Misleading Marketing Regulations 2008', 2009. No guidance on the BPR has yet been issued by the CMA.

[25] For a pre-MCAD analysis of false statements leading to pecuniary loss, see *Emaco Ltd v Dyson Appliances Ltd* [1999] ETMR 903.

Great Britain is contemplating bringing proceedings the CMA may direct which enforcement authority is to bring the proceedings or decide that only the CMA may do so.[26]

11.23 In *Oldham Metropolitan Borough Council v Worldwide Marketing Solutions Ltd*[27] an application was made for an injunction against a company accused of engaging in misleading advertising in national telesales. It was argued that the local authority had no power to obtain an injunction because the company was no longer based in the local authority's area. The High Court rejected an argument that the injunction could not be 'expedient for the promotion or protection of the interests' of Oldham's inhabitants for the purposes of s 222 of the Local Government Act 1972. Phillips J stated that 'a local authority can properly take into account broader considerations of how to promote or protect the interests of its inhabitants, not limited to situations where unlawful activity is continuing or contemplated within its area'.

11.24 This issue is unlikely to be important following the entry into force of the CRA 2015, which now enables civil proceedings to be instituted by a local authority for consumer law breaches outside its area.[28] In *Croydon LBC v Hogarth*,[29] an enforcement authority successfully applied for an injunction for a breach of reg 3(2)(a) against a company sending out contracts disguised as invoices.

11.25 Under reg 16 of the BPR, an enforcement authority that considers that there has been or there is likely to be a breach of regs 3, 4 or 5 may resolve the matter by way of undertakings. Under reg 18, the court has the power to order publication of final injunctions and corrective statements.

Comparative advertising

11.26 'Comparative advertising' is defined broadly, in reg 2:

> **Business Protection From Misleading Marketing Regulations 2008**
>
> **Regulation 2 – Interpretation**
>
>> '"**comparative advertising**" means advertising which in any way, either explicitly or by implication, identifies a competitor or a product offered by a competitor.'

11.27 Comparative advertising is permitted, provided it cumulatively meets the conditions set out in reg 4(a)–(i).

---

[26]   Reg 17(1).
[27]   [2014] PTSR 1072.
[28]   CRA 2015, para 45 of Sch 5.
[29]   [2011] EWHC 1126 (QB), [2011] CTLC 34.

Business Protection from Misleading Advertising Regulations 2008, regs 4, 5

Comparative advertising

'4 Comparative advertising shall, as far as the comparison is concerned, be permitted only when the following conditions are met –

(a)   it is not misleading under regulation 3;

(b)   it is not a misleading action under regulation 5 of the Consumer Protection from Unfair Trading Regulations 2008 or a misleading omission under regulation 6 of those Regulations;

(c)   it compares products meeting the same needs or intended for the same purpose;

(d)   it objectively compares one or more material, relevant, verifiable and representative features of those products, which may include price;

(e)   it does not create confusion among traders –
       (i)   between the advertiser and a competitor, or
       (ii)   between the trade marks, trade names, other distinguishing marks or products of the advertiser and those of a competitor;

(f)   it does not discredit or denigrate the trade marks, trade names, other distinguishing marks, products, activities, or circumstances of a competitor;

(g)   for products with designation of origin, it relates in each case to products with the same designation;

(h)   it does not take unfair advantage of the reputation of a trade mark, trade name or other distinguishing marks of a competitor or of the designation of origin of competing products;

(i)   it does not present products as imitations or replicas of products bearing a protected trade mark or trade name.'

11.28 Regulation 4 implements Art 4 of MCAD 2006. The predecessor provision was Art 3a(1) of MCAD 1984 and was in materially the same terms. Accordingly, most of the leading CJEU cases on comparative advertising, which were under MCAD 1984, remain of relevance under MCAD 2006. These are discussed below.

11.29 The importance of comparative advertising is set out in the recitals to the MCAD 2006:

'(6) The completion of the internal market means a wide range of choice. Given that consumers and traders can and must make the best possible use of the internal market, and that advertising is a very important means of creating genuine outlets for all goods and services throughout the Community, the basic provisions governing the form and content of comparative advertising should be uniform and the conditions of the use of comparative advertising in the Member States should be harmonised. If these conditions are met, this will help demonstrate objectively the merits of the various comparable products. Comparative advertising can also stimulate competition between suppliers of goods and services to the consumer's advantage.

...

(8) Comparative advertising, when it compares material, relevant, verifiable and representative features and is not misleading, may be a legitimate means of informing consumers of their advantage. It is desirable to provide a broad concept of comparative advertising to cover all modes of comparative advertising.'

11.30 Recitals 14 and 15 clarify that for comparative advertising to be effective, the use of a competitor's trade mark may be indispensable and that such use is permissible provided it complies with the conditions laid down by MCAD 2006:

'(14) It may, however, be indispensable, in order to make comparative advertising effective, to identify the goods or services of a competitor, making reference to a trade mark or trade name of which the latter is the proprietor.

(15) Such use of another's trade mark, trade name or other distinguishing marks does not breach this exclusive right in cases where it complies with the conditions laid down by this Directive, the intended target being solely to distinguish between them and thus to highlight differences objectively.'

11.31 As the CJEU made clear in *L'Oréal SA v Bellure NV*[30] the purpose of the conditions in Art 4 (albeit the case refers to its predecessor, Art 3a) is:

'... to achieve a balance between the different interests which may be affected by allowing comparative advertising. Thus, it is apparent from a reading of recitals 2, 7 and 9 in the preamble to Directive 97/55 that the aim of Article 3a is to stimulate competition between suppliers of goods and services to the consumer's advantage, by allowing competitors to highlight objectively the merits of the various comparable products while, at the same time, prohibiting practices which may distort competition, be detrimental to competitors and have an adverse effect on consumer choice.'[31]

11.32 The leading authority on comparative advertising is the CJEU case of *Lidl SNC v Vierzon*.[32] Lidl objected to an advertisement published by competitor supermarket Vierzon comparing the prices of its products with those of Vierzon and stating that Vierzon's were 'the cheapest'. Lidl alleged that the comparative advertising was unlawful on the ground that it compared products which were different in quality and quantity. The CJEU found the comparison to be lawful and stated the following principles:

- The conditions listed in Art 3a of MCAD 1984 (now Art 4 of MCAD 2006) must be interpreted in the sense most favourable to permitting advertisements which objectively compare the characteristics of goods or

---

[30] Case C-487/07 *L'Oréal SA v Bellure NV* [2009] ECR I-5185, at para. 68. L'Oréal brought proceedings against a company that sold non-luxury perfumes in packaging that resembled that of well-known luxury brands. This company had compiled price comparison lists bearing L'Oréal's trademark.

[31] See also Case C-159/09 *Lidl SNC v Vierzon Distribution SA*, para 20.

[32] Case C-159/09 *Lidl SNC v Vierzon Distribution SA*.

services, whilst ensuring at the same time that comparative advertising is not used anti-competitively and unfairly or in a manner which affects the interests of consumers.[33]

- MCAD 1984 exhaustively harmonises the conditions under which comparative advertising is permitted. Such a harmonisation implies by its nature that the lawfulness of comparative advertising throughout the EU is to be assessed solely in the light of the criteria laid down by the EU legislature.[34]

- The conditions listed in Art 3a are cumulative and so each condition must be satisfied for the comparative advertising in question to be permitted.[35]

- If comparative advertising is to be permitted, the comparison must relate to goods or services which meet the same needs or are intended for the same purpose. That condition implies that the goods being compared must display a sufficient degree of interchangeability for consumers.[36] The angle from which the comparison is made (eg price) can have no bearing on whether two products meet the same needs or are intended for the same purpose within the meaning of Art 3a(1)(b).[37]

- It is for the national court to ascertain in the circumstances of each case, and bearing in mind the consumers to which the advertising is addressed, whether the advertising may be misleading.[38] In carrying out the requisite assessment, the national court must, first, take into account the perception of an average consumer of the products or services being advertised. It must also take account of all the relevant factors in the case, the information contained in the advertisement and, more generally, all its features.[39]

Misleading

11.33 The CJEU case-law under MCAD 1984 is of limited assistance on this point, as MCAD 1984 covered advertising that misled or was likely to mislead consumers as well as traders and defined 'misleading advertising' as:

> 'any advertising which in any way, including its presentation, deceives or is likely to deceive the persons to whom it is addressed or whom it reaches and which, by reason of its deceptive nature, is likely to affect their economic behaviour or which, for those reasons, injures or is likely to injure a competitor.'[40]

---

[33] Para 21, citing Case C-487/07 *L'Oréal SA v Bellure NV* [2009] ECR I-5185, para. 68.

[34] Para 22, citing Case C-44/01 *Pippig Augenoptik* [2003] ECR I-3095, para 44.

[35] Para 16, citing C-487/07 *L'Oréal SA v Bellure NV* [2009] ECR I-5185, para 67.

[36] Para 25, citing *Lidl Belgium GmbH & Co KG v Etablissementen Franz Colruyt NV* (C-356/04) [2007] Bus LR 492, para 26, and Case C-381/05 *De Landtsheer Emmanuel* [2007] ECR I-3115, para 44.

[37] Para 27.

[38] Para 46, citing Case C-356/04 *Lidl Belgium* [2006] ECR I-8501.

[39] Paras 47–48, citing *Lidl Belgium*, para 79.

[40] Art 2 of MCAD 1984. This definition has been retained in MCAD 2006, at Art 2, but it is

11.34   Two cases under MCAD 1984 are worth a mention nevertheless. In *Lidl Belgium*[41] Lidl objected to the advertisement of another supermarket chain, Colruyt, which compared some of Colruyt's prices with those charged at other supermarket chains, including Lidl. Lidl argued that this gave consumers the impression that Colruyt was always cheaper than its competitors. The CJEU made it clear that such advertising could be misleading if the advertisement:

'•   does not reveal that the comparison related only to such a sample and not to all the advertiser's products,
 •   does not identify the details of the comparison made or inform the persons to whom it is addressed of the information source where such identification is possible, or
 •   contains a collective reference to a range of amounts that may be saved by consumers who make their purchases from the advertiser rather than from his competitors without specifying individually the general level of the prices charged, respectively, by each of those competitors and the amount that consumers are liable to save by making their purchases from the advertiser rather than from each of the competitors.'

11.35   In *Lidl SNC v Vierzon*,[42] the CJEU stated, that advertisements that compared prices could be misleading if the national court were to find that:

*   A significant number of consumers may make the decision to buy in the mistaken belief that the selection of goods in the advertisement: (a) is representative of the general level of the advertiser's prices compared to those of his competitor, and (b) that the savings of the kind claimed by the advertisement could be made by regularly buying everyday consumer goods from the advertiser rather than from the competitor.

*   The decision to buy on the part of a significant number of consumers to whom the advertising is addressed may be made in the mistaken belief that all of the advertiser's products are cheaper than those of his competitor.[43]

*   The products compared are in fact objectively different and the differences are capable of significantly affecting the consumer's choice. If such differences are not disclosed, such advertising may be perceived by the average consumer as claiming, by implication, that the other characteristics of the products in question are equivalent.[44]

11.36   Whilst these cases apply a definition of 'misleading' that is out of date, they may nevertheless be of assistance in understanding the manner in which the conditions in reg 4 interact with each other. In particular, they make it clear that the question of whether the advertisement is misleading is linked to the question of interchangeability.

---

arguably of limited assistance given the new focus of the Directive, namely other traders. This is reflected in the BPR, which replace 'the persons to whom it is addressed' with 'the traders to whom it is addressed' in reg 3(2).
[41]   Case C-356/04 *Lidl Belgium* [2006] ECR I-8501.
[42]   Case C-159/09 *Lidl SNC v Vierzon Distribution SA*.
[43]   Para 50, citing *Lidl Belgium*, paras 83 and 84.
[44]   Paras 51–52.

Meeting the same needs or intended for the same purpose

11.37 As noted by the CJEU in *Lidl Belgium*, this condition implies that the goods being compared must display a sufficient degree of interchangeability for consumers.[45] The CJEU made it clear in *Lidl Vierzon* that this required an individual and specific assessment of products that are the subject of the comparison.[46] In *Lidl Vierzon*, the CJEU was specifically asked whether what is now Art 4 of MCAD 2006 precluded the comparison of products (in that case food) on the basis of price where the products differed on the basis of non-price elements. The CJEU concluded that it did not and that the question was one of fact and degree.[47] Accordingly, two products need not be identical in order to be regarded as comparable.

11.38 This issue recently fell to be determined by the High Court in *R (Sainsbury's Supermarkets Limited) v The Independent Reviewer of ASA Adjudications*.[48] Sainsbury's complained to the ASA regarding Tesco's 'Price Promise' advertisement, which claimed that customers would not 'lose out on big brands, fresh food or own-label' products to Tesco's competitors. Sainsbury's argued that Tesco's comparison failed to factor in a number of key non-price attributes, such as ethical and environmental characteristics and provenance. Its complaint was rejected by the ASA and the Independent Adjudicator. The Independent Adjudicator had concluded that whilst such characteristics could be material to many customers, it did not mean that the ASA was wrong to conclude that they were not material, essential or important to this particular comparison. The High Court was equally unsympathetic to Sainsbury's argument, dismissing it as unsustainable in light of *Lidl Vierzon*.[49]

Verifiability

11.39 The leading authority on verifiability is the CJEU case of *Lidl Belgium*, which established that:

> 'in order for the prices of the goods comprising a selection of products or the general level of the prices charged by a chain of stores in respect of its selection of comparable goods to be verifiable, it is a necessary precondition that, even though . . . the goods whose prices have been thus compared are not required to be expressly and exhaustively listed in the advertisement addressed to the consumer, they must nevertheless be capable of being individually and specifically identified

---

[45] *Lidl Belgium GmbH & Co KG v Etablissementen Franz Colruyt NV* (C-356/04) [2007] Bus LR 492, para 26. See also Case C-381/05 *De Landtsheer Emmanuel* [2007] ECR I-3115, para 44 and *Lidl Vierzon*, para 25. Further, the CJEU found, at para 27, that the angle from which the comparison is made (eg price) can have no bearing on whether two products meet the same needs or are intended for the same purpose within the meaning of Art 4.

[46] *Lidl Vierzon*, paras 29–30, 32–33.

[47] Paras 29 and 33.

[48] [2014] EWHC 3680 (Admin).

[49] At paras 153–154.

on the basis of the information contained in that advertisement. The prices of goods can necessarily only ever be verified if it is possible to identify the goods.'[50]

11.40 The CJEU observed that:

'[s]uch an obligation makes it possible, in accordance with the objective of consumer protection pursued by the [MCAD 1984], for the persons to whom an advertisement of that kind is addressed to be in a position to satisfy themselves that they have been correctly informed with regard to the purchases of basic consumables which they are prompted to make.'[51]

11.41 The advertiser is thus under an obligation to indicate, in particular for the attention of the persons to whom the advertisement is addressed, where and how they may readily examine the details of the comparison with a view to verifying their accuracy or having it verified. As the CJEU made clear, however, this:

'does not mean that the accuracy of the features compared must in all circumstances be capable of being verified by those to whom the advertising is addressed acting in person. It is sufficient for the details allowing such verification to be accessible to those persons ... in such a way that they may, as a general rule, carry out the desired verification themselves or, more exceptionally and if such verification demands a skill which they do not possess, have it carried out by a third party.'[52]

11.42 It could be argued that these passages, too, are of limited assistance. The Court expressly refers to the objective of MCAD 1984 as being one of consumer protection and this objective clearly formed an important part of the Court's reasoning. The objective of MCAD 2006 is different:

'The purpose of this Directive is to protect traders against misleading advertising and the unfair consequences thereof and to lay down the conditions under which comparative advertising is permitted.'[53]

Discrediting a competitor

11.43 In *Pippig Augenoptik v Hartlauer*[54] the CJEU was asked whether a price comparison entailed discrediting a competitor if the products were chosen in such a way as to obtain a price difference greater than the average price

---

[50] *Lidl Belgium GmbH & Co KG v Etablissementen Franz Colruyt NV* (C-356/04) [2007] Bus LR 492, para 61.

[51] *Lidl Belgium*, para 72.

[52] *Lidl Belgium*, para 73.

[53] MCAD 2006, Art 1. The objective of MCAD 1984 was stated to be: 'to protect consumers, persons carrying on a trade or business or practising a craft or profession and the interests of the public in general against misleading advertising and the unfair consequences thereof'. The scope of the Directive was later expanded to include the conditions under which comparative advertising would be permitted.

[54] Case C-44/01 *Pippig Augenoptik GmbH & Co. KG v Hartlauer Handelsgesellschaft mbH and Verlassenschaft nach dem verstorbenen Franz Josef Hartlauer.*

difference and/or the comparisons were repeated continuously, creating the impression that the competitor's prices were excessive. The CJEU had no hesitation in finding that it did not, noting that the 'comparison of rival offers, particularly as regards price, is of the very nature of comparative advertising'.[55]

11.44 The advertisement that was subject to British Airways' complaint in *British Airways plc v Ryanair Ltd* [2001] ETMR 24 is an example of what might be regarded as denigration.[56]

Taking unfair advantage

11.45 The CJEU has considered Art 4(f) (or its predecessor, Art 3a(1)(g) of MCAD 1984) in a number of cases:

- When assessing whether the condition laid down in Art 3a(1)(g) of MCAD 1984 (now Art 4(f) of MCAD 2006) has been satisfied, it is necessary to have regard to Recital 15 in the Preamble to Directive 97/55, which states that the use of a trade mark or distinguishing mark does not breach the right to the mark where it complies with the conditions laid down by Directive 84/450, the aim being solely to distinguish between the products and services of the advertiser and those of his competitor and thus to highlight differences objectively.[57]

- In *Siemens AG v VIPA*[58] the CJEU found that the use of a core element of the Siemens trade mark by a competitor (here, catalogue numbers) did not take unfair advantage of the reputation of the Siemens mark. The CJEU confirmed that the benefit of comparative advertising to consumers must necessarily be taken into account in answering whether the advertisement complies with Art 4(f). On the other hand, the benefit derived by an advertiser from comparative advertising cannot alone be determinative of its legality.[59]

- The expression 'takes unfair advantage' in Art 4(f) is to, in principle, be interpreted in the same way as in Art 5(2) of Directive 89/104.[60]

- In order to determine whether the use of a mark takes unfair advantage of the distinctive character or the repute of the mark, it is necessary to undertake a global assessment, taking into account all factors relevant to the circumstances of the case, which include:
  (i)   the strength of the mark's reputation;

---

[55]   Para 80.

[56]   This was the view taken by the editors of *Halsbury's Laws of England, Trade Marks and Trade Names*, Volume 97A (2014))/2, at 75. A Ryanair advertisement comparing Ryanair's prices to those of British Airways was featured beneath the headline 'EXPENSIVE BA——DS!', the word 'BA——DS!' being an allusion to the word 'BASTARDS'.

[57]   Case C-112/99 *Toshiba Europe* [2001] ECR I-7945, para 53.

[58]   Case C-59/05, *Siemens AG v VIPA Gesellschaft für Visualisierung und Prozeßautomatisierung mbH*.

[59]   Paras 24 and 25.

[60]   Case C-487/07, *L'Oréal SA v Bellure NV*. See also Case C-533/06 *O2 Holdings Ltd v Hutchison 3G Ltd* [2008] ECR I-4231.

(ii)   the degree of distinctive character of the mark;
(iii) the degree of similarity between the marks at issue;
(iv)   the nature and degree of proximity of the goods or services concerned; and
(v)   the likelihood of dilution or tarnishing of the mark.[61]

Comparative advertising and the law on trademarks

11.46   Comparative advertising often uses competitor trademarks without their consent. Accordingly, comparative advertising that fails to satisfy the requirements of reg 4 of BPR could expose the advertiser to trademark infringement proceedings under the Trade Marks Act 1994. The Trade Marks Act 1994 has a specific provision intended to relate to comparative advertising.[62] This provision does not add anything of substance to the other provisions of the Trade Marks Act 1994, however.

Pricing Practices Guide 2016

11.47   The CTSI published a new version on the Pricing Practices Guide ('PPG 2016') in 2016. It is covered in detail in Chapter 12, Prices. The PPG 2016 also gives guidance to traders when comparing their own prices to those of a competitor.

Comparison to a competitor's price

Comparisons that you make to a competitor's price must comply with both the requirements of the Regulations and the Business Protection from Misleading Marketing Regulations 2008. The price comparison must not be false or mislead consumers and they must be told any material information in a way that is clear, transparent and timely.

A fair comparison may be made between the price of a product you sell against the same product being sold by a competitor. Such comparisons can be helpful to consumers who are looking for the best price for that item or service.

You can also make comparisons with products which, whilst not identical, meet the same needs or are intended for the same purpose. You should set out any material differences between your product and the competitor's product clearly and transparently. This is unlikely to be achieved if material differences are not a prominent part of the presentation of the price comparison to consumers. You should not selectively focus on element(s) of a competitor's price that are unrepresentative and give an overall impression that is misleading.

The basis of any comparison you make against your competitor should be objective rather than subjective. The comparison must objectively compare one or more material, relevant, verifiable and representative feature of the product. You should consider providing simple mechanisms through which a consumer can verify the comparison, such as online, by email, telephone or in writing.

---

[61]   *Case C-487/07, L'Oréal SA v Bellure NV*, paras 44–45. See also *Specsavers International Healthcare Ltd v Asda Stores Ltd* [2012] ETMR 17.
[62]   Section 10(6).

If you operate in a particularly price sensitive sector, where prices frequently change, you should take care to ensure that your price comparison does not become misleading because your competitor's price has changed. You should monitor the position and take prompt action to withdraw claims if necessary.

You must not compare the price of your product against the price of a product with a designation of origin, for example a Cornish pasty,[63] unless your product has the same designation of origin.[64]

If you wish to make a comparison based on prices in specific locations, care needs to be taken to establish if there are local price variations. If the prices you wish to use are based on information made available centrally by your competitor, for example online, you should check for local variations.

You should not make general claims that give the overall impression that all of your products are cheaper, if that is only true for selected items. If you make a claim that your prices are generally lower, you should explain why it is a fair and suitable comparison, for example by telling consumers the basket of products chosen is based on a typical weekly shop.

It is important that you keep clear documentary records of any price comparisons that you have made against a competitor's price. You should identify your competitor, their product and the circumstances in which they offered the product at the price you are comparing against. In some instances, it may also be important to provide technical evidence to demonstrate that your product is not materially different.

In making a price comparison to the price of a competitor you must observe the following rules.

- You must not deliberately mislead consumers into believing that your product is made by a particular manufacturer, when it is not.[65]
- You must not create confusion between you and your competitor.
- You must not create confusion between your trademarks, trade names, other distinguishing marks, products and those of your competitor.
- You must not discredit or denigrate the trademark, trade name or other distinguishing mark, goods, services, activities or circumstances of a competitor.
- You must not take unfair advantage of the reputation of a trade mark, trade name or distinguishing mark of a competitor or of the designation of origin of competing products.
- You must not present products as imitations or replicas of products bearing a protected mark or trade name.

Code owners

11.48 Regulation 5 prohibits the promotion of misleading advertising or of non-compliant comparative advertising by a Code Owner in a code of conduct. A similar prohibition can be found in CPUTR, reg 4.

---

[63] Council Regulation (EC) No 510/2006 on Protected Geographical Indications and Protected Designations of Origin: Cornish Pasty 2007.
[64] Business Protection from Misleading Marketing Regulations 2008, reg 4(g).
[65] Consumer Protection from Unfair Trading Regulations 2008, Sch 1, para 13.

Business Protection from Misleading Marketing Regulations 2008, Regulation 5

Promotion of misleading advertising and comparative advertising which is not permitted

'5 A code owner shall not promote in a code of conduct –

(a) advertising which is misleading under regulation 3; or
(b) comparative advertising which is not permitted under regulation 4.'

11.49 'Code owner' is defined in reg 2.

Business Protection From Misleading Marketing Regulations 2008

Regulation 2 – Interpretation

'"code owner" means a trader or body responsible for –
(a) the formulation and revision of a code of conduct; or
(b) monitoring compliance with the code by those who have undertaken to be bound by it.'

Enforcement (regs 4 and 5)

11.50 There is no criminal sanction for breach of the comparative advertising requirements (reg 4) or for breach of the provision relating to codes of conduct (reg 5). It follows that there is no provision in the BPR for a private party to enforce regs 4 or 5. Breaches of these regs would therefore a qualified regulator to take injunctive action under reg 15.

THE ADVERTISING STANDARDS AUTHORITY

11.51 The Advertising Standards Authority ('ASA') was established in 1962 by the advertising industry, which came together in the 1961 to form the CAP[66] and produced the first edition of the British Code of Advertising Practice. The ASA was to act as the independent adjudicator under the newly-created Code, which covered non-broadcast advertising.[67] This continues to be the ASA's role today. Non-broadcast advertising is governed by the UK Code of Non-broadcast Advertising, Sales Promotion and Direct Marketing ('CAP Code'). All television and radio advertisements are required to comply with the UK Code of Broadcast Advertising ('BCAP Code'). The focus of this Chapter is on the CAP Code, but reference will be made to the BCAP Code, where relevant.

---

[66]   Today, CAP's membership comprises Advertising Association, Atvod Industry Forum, Cinema Advertising Association, Direct Marketing Association, Direct Selling Association, Incorporated Society of British Advertisers, Institute of Practitioners in Advertising, Institute of Promotional Marketing, Internet Advertising Bureau, Mobile Broadband Group, Mobile Marketing Association, News Media Association, Outsmart Out of Home, Professional Publishers Association, Proprietary Association of Great Britain, Royal Mail, Scottish Newspaper Society, Clearcast, Radiocentre.

[67]   The ASA's remit has subsequently been extended to cover broadcast advertising.

The CAP Code

11.52 The CAP Code is largely premised on statutory provisions and is intended accurately to reflect EU and domestic consumer protection legislation in respect of misleading and unfair advertising. In particular, it incorporates the requirements of CPUTR, BPR and Regulation (EC) No 1924/2006 on nutrition and health claims made on foods. It covers matters of general application to advertisers, such as misleading and comparative advertising, as well as sector- and audience-specific topics, such as advertising to children, environmental claims and claims relating to weight control and slimming.

11.53 The CAP Code makes it clear that context is key to its application:

> 'compliance with the Code is assessed according to the marketing communication's probable impact when taken as a whole and in context. That will depend on the medium in which the marketing communication appeared, the audience and its likely response, the nature of the product and any material distributed to consumers'.[68]

Rule 2 of the CAP Code provides that advertisements should reflect 'the spirit, not merely the letter, of the Code'. Accordingly, arguments of a purely technical nature are rarely successful before the ASA.

Scope

11.54 The Scope of the CAP Code is set out in the Code's introductory section. It covers:

- advertisements in newspapers, magazines, brochures, leaflets, circulars, mailings, e-mails, text transmissions, fax transmissions, catalogues, follow-up literature and other electronic or printed material;

- posters and other promotional media in public places, including moving images;

- cinema, video, DVD and Blu-ray advertisements;

- advertisements in non-broadcast electronic media, including online advertisements in paid-for space, paid-for search listings and preferential listings on price comparison sites;

- marketing databases containing consumers' personal information;

- sales promotions in non-broadcast media;

- advertorials;

- advertisements and other marketing communications by or from companies, organisations or sole traders on their own websites, or in other non-paid-for space online under their control, that are directly connected

---

[68] CAP Code, Part IV, para c.

with the supply or transfer of goods, services, opportunities and gifts, or which consist of direct solicitations of donations as part of their own fund-raising activities.[69]

11.55   The CAP Code also sets out the areas that fall outside its remit. These include (but are not limited to):

- broadcast advertisements (which are covered by the BCAP Code);
- the contents of premium-rate services (the responsibility of PhonepayPlus);
- marketing communications in foreign media, even if targeted at UK consumers;[70]
- claims addressed only to medical, dental, veterinary or allied practitioners, that relate to those practitioners' expertise;
- private correspondence, including correspondence between organisations and their customers about existing relationships or past purchases; and
- packages, wrappers, labels, tickets, timetables and price lists unless they advertise another product or a sales promotion or are visible in a marketing communication.

11.56   The CAP Code also makes it clear that if there is doubt as to whether a communication falls within the remit of the Code, the ASA will be more likely to apply the Code if the material complained about is in paid-for space.[71]

Key provisions

11.57   This section sets out the key provisions of the CAP Code and provides examples of recent ASA adjudications (the ASA now tends to refer to its adjudications as rulings). ASA's previous adjudications are not binding on it. They do, however, provide an indication of how the ASA is likely to reason should it be faced with a similar issue in the future.

Part 1 – Legal, decent, honest and truthful

11.58   A core principle of the CAP Code set out in rule 1 is that advertisements must be 'legal, decent, honest and truthful'. This includes the requirement that advertisements, as well as the products being advertised, be lawful. Relevant legislation is set out on the ASA website, although it is made clear that the list is not exhaustive.[72]

---

[69]   The Code's remit was extended beyond sales promotions and paid-for advertisements in March 2011, to cover marketing claims on company websites and in other third party space under their control, such as social media. See 'Scope of the Code', para 1(h).

[70]   If, however, the relevant authority in the country from which the advertisements originate does not operate a suitable cross-border complaint system, the ASA will take what action it can.

[71]   CAP Code, Scope of the Code, Part IV, para b.

[72]   Available at www.cap.org.uk/Advertising-Codes.

Part 2 – Recognition of marketing communications

11.59 This rule aims to ensure that advertising is clearly separated from editorial content, so that consumers do not confuse the two. The rules in Part 2 are premised on the requirements of the Electronic Commerce (EC Directive) Regulations 2002[73] and CPUTR.[74] Recent adjudications include:

- *Wallshield (UK) Ltd, 3 August 2016*: This adjudication concerned an envelope sent to recipients, which was completely blank and did not contain any text to alert recipients to the fact that it contained a marketing communication. The ASA concluded that the advertisement was not obviously identifiable as a marketing communication and was in breach of the CAP Code.
- *OfficeMax Australia Ltd, 11 May 2016*: A mailing, which stated 'Best Offers for Office Supplies. Office Supplies Offer' was laid out like an invoice. Small print stated, 'This is a solicitation for the order of goods, services or both and not a bill, invoice or statement of account due…' The ASA concluded that the mailing was not obviously identifiable as a marketing communication and so breached the CAP Code.

Part 3 – Misleading marketing communications

11.60 Misleading marketing communications are dealt with in Part 3 of the Code, which covers the following:

- Substantiation.
- Qualification.
- Exaggeration.
- Prohibited claims.
- Pricing claims (including the description of a product as 'free' and availability).
- Comparative advertising.
- Endorsements and testimonials.
- Guarantees and after-sales service.

11.61 The core rule is rule 3.1, which provides that marketing communications 'must not materially mislead or be likely to do so'.[75] Misleading by omission is dealt with in rule 3.3 (and expanded upon in rules 3.4 and 3.5).[76] The wording of these rules fails to fully reflect the wording of the legislation on which they are based, namely regs 5 and 6 of CPUTR and reg 3 of the BPR. In particular, rules 3.1 and 3.4 fail to incorporate the threshold condition contained in CPUTR, ie that the advertisement must cause or be likely to cause 'the average consumer to take a transactional decision he

---

[73] For example, r 2.2.
[74] For example, rr 2.3 and 2.4.
[75] An identical rule is contained in the BCAP Code, r 3.1.
[76] In the BCAP Code, the relevant rule is 3.2.

would not have taken otherwise' and ASA adjudications rarely make reference to it. It could be argued, therefore, that the CAP Code goes beyond the remit of CPUTR, which is significant given the maximum harmonisation nature the UCPD. The CAP Code does, however, make reference to the relevant test in Appendix 1.

11.62   Examples of recent adjudications include:

- *Power Leisure Bookmakers Ltd*, 6 July 2016. The ASA upheld a complaint under the BCAP Code about an advertisement that implied that an offer was available to 'everyone', when there were restrictions as to who could take advantage of it. Although the adjudication relates to broadcast advertising, it is likely to be a helpful guide as to how the ASA is likely to approach 'de minimis' arguments on absolute claims.
- *Hutchinson 3G UK's (trading as 3)*, 27 July 2016. A claim on 3's website regarding 'all you can eat data' was found to be misleading, as it failed to refer to any fair use or other limitations on the amount of data available as part of the offer.

Substantiation

11.63   Rule 3.7 requires marketers to 'hold documentary evidence to prove claims that consumers are likely to regard as objective and that are capable of objective substantiation'. The ASA may regard claims as misleading in the absence of adequate substantiation.[77]

11.64   This rule is premised on *inter alia* Art 12 of the UCPD,[78] which provides:

> 'Member States shall confer upon the courts or administrative authorities powers enabling them in the civil or administrative proceedings provided for in Article 11:
>
> (a)   to require the trader to furnish evidence as to the accuracy of factual claims in relation to a commercial practice if, taking into account the legitimate interest of the trader and any other party to the proceedings, such a requirement appears appropriate on the basis of the circumstances of the particular case; and
>
> (b)   to consider factual claims as inaccurate if the evidence demanded in accordance with (a) is not furnished or is deemed insufficient by the court or administrative authority.'

11.65   A recent example of an adjudication under rule 3.7 involved *ASDA Stores Ltd t/a ASDA* (3 Aug 2016). ASDA's website claimed that its 'Little Angels Supreme Protection' nappies were their 'most absorbent nappy ever'.

---

[77]   For the corresponding requirement in the BCAP Code, see r 3.9.
[78]   Implemented by the Enterprise Act 2002, s 218A. Art 7 of MCAD 2006 is in identical terms.

ASDA was unable to provide evidence to demonstrate that this was the case and so was found to have breached rule 3.7 of the CAP Code, as well as rule 3.1.

Disclaimers

11.66 Rule 3.9 requires marketing communications to 'state significant limitations and qualifications' and provides that 'Qualifications may clarify but must not contradict the claims that they qualify.' Accordingly, a potentially misleading claim cannot be remedied by a disclaimer or explanatory text in the small print. This principle is enshrined in CPUTR, which provides that information may be misleading 'if it or its overall presentation in any way deceives or is likely to deceive the average consumer ..., even if the information is factually correct'.[79] A recent example of the application of this Rule by the ASA is The Carphone Warehouse Ltd, 3 August 2016. The complaint challenged claims appearing on Carphone Warehouse's website which alleged that the retailer offered 'UK'S LOWEST PRICE' and 'AT THE BEST PRICE'. The ASA found that the small print at the bottom of the page was insufficient to counteract the overall impression created by the marketing communication in question.

Pricing claims

11.67 Pricing claims are dealt with in rules 3.17 to 3.32 (as well as in the rules governing comparative advertising, as to which please see below). Pricing claims are now covered in Chapter 12.

Comparative advertising

11.68 Comparative advertising is covered by rules 3.33 to 3.44, which broadly reflect the requirements of Art 4 of MCAD 2006, as well as reg 5(3)(a) of CPUTR (rule 3.36). The Rules cover comparisons with identifiable and unidentifiable competitors. An area that causes the most difficulty is the verifiability criterion in rule 3.35, which requires comparisons with identifiable competitors to 'objectively compare one or more material, relevant, verifiable and representative feature of those products, which may include price'. Accordingly, in addition to having substantiation to support any claims made, the CAP Code requires advertisers to ensure that consumers are able to verify the comparison themselves.

---

[79] Reg 5(2)(a). See also *Director General of Fair Trading v Blinkhorn* (1989, unreported), under the Control of Misleading Advertisements Regulations 1988, where Vinelott J stated: 'A document may be misleading, though literally everything in it is true, if the way in which what it says is presented carries with it implications and inferences which the ordinary reader would certainly draw.'

11.69   The CAP has published Advertising Guidance on this topic (updated 24 Sep 2015) which makes express reference to the CJEU case of *Lidl Belgium*.[80] The CAP provides the following guidance:

- Some comparisons are easy for consumers to verify (eg a comparison between two identical products sold by two different retailers could be checked by looking on their websites).

- Other comparisons (eg those that involve many products), could be more difficult.[81]

- The most straightforward way to ensure comparisons are verifiable is to direct readers to a website that contains a list of all the features (such as the products and prices) of the comparison, for example by including the claim 'prices can be verified on www.thiswebsite.co.uk/comparisons/date'.

- Marketers should be explicit about how readers can verify the comparison. The mere inclusion of a website or postal address without stating that readers can verify the comparison might be insufficient.

- It might not be sufficient for marketers to cite a third-party website (eg MySupermarket.com) in the case of grocery retailer price comparisons, without informing readers of the products used in the comparison.

Endorsements and testimonials

11.70   Endorsements and testimonials are addressed by rules 3.45 to 3.52 of the CAP Code and broadly reflect, inter alia, the prohibitions in Sch 1, paras 1 to 4 of CPUTR, which prohibit the following commercial practices:

- Claiming to be a signatory to a code of conduct when the trader is not.

- Displaying a trust mark, quality mark or equivalent without having obtained the necessary authorisation.

- Claiming that a code of conduct has an endorsement from a public or other body which it does not have.

- Claiming that a trader (including his commercial practices) or a product has been approved, endorsed or authorised by a public or private body when the trader, the commercial practices or the product have not or making such a claim without complying with the terms of the approval, endorsement or authorisation.

---

[80]   *Lidl Belgium GmbH & Co KG v Etablissementen Franz Colruyt NV* (C-356/04) [2007] Bus LR 492. The Advertising Guidance is available at www.cap.org.uk/Advice-Training-on-the-rules.

[81]   The Guidance provides the example *ASDA Stores Ltd*, 14 January 2009, where the ASA found the advertisement to be non-compliant on the basis that it gave no way for readers to verify the advertised savings. A further example given is Wren Kitchens Ltd, 30 January 2013. Wren's advertisement for kitchens provided only enough information to verify some aspects of the products being compared, and their respective prices. Whilst some further information could be found on the advertisers' competitors' website it could not be said that all the necessary information was available.

11.71 A recent adjudication, *ABC Counselling Services*, 3 Aug 2016, concerned directory entries for ABC Counselling Services claiming that the organisation, as well as one of its individual counsellors, was a member of the British Association for Counselling & Psychotherapy, when this was no longer the case. Unsurprisingly, the advertisement was found to fall foul of rules 3.50 and 3.51 of the CAP Code.

Guarantees and after-sales service

11.72 Claims relating to guarantees and after-sales services are governed by rules 3.53 to 3.57 of the CAP Code.[82]

ASA investigations procedure

11.73 The ASA acts on complaints.[83] It will not normally pursue complaints if the point at issue is subject to legal proceedings. Complaints must be made within three months of the advertisement's appearance (although extensions may be granted in exceptional circumstances) and should focus on no more than three of the most important issues (although more issues may be considered in exceptional circumstances). Complaints may be made by members of the public or by the advertiser's competitors. The ASA's 2015 Annual Report recorded that a vast majority (97%) of complaints that year were made by members of the public. Where the complainant is an individual member of the public, their identity will not be disclosed by the ASA without their permission.

11.74 Where a complaint is made by a competitor, the ASA requires the complainant to follow a number of 'Inter-Party Resolution steps'. The competitor complainant must raise its concerns with the advertiser in the first instance. The advertiser should then be given five working days to respond. Any subsequent complaint to the ASA must include the original letter setting out the competitor complainant's concerns and the advertiser's response, if any. The ASA makes it clear, however, that it may not always be appropriate to follow this procedure, but such occasions are deemed to be rare.[84]

11.75 Complainants who provide evidence in support of their complaints must consent to such evidence being shared with the advertiser. If the complainant fails to give consent if and when requested, the ASA Council will not take the

---

[82] Rules 3.56 and 3.57 broadly reflect the prohibitions contained in Sch 1, paras 8 and 23 of CPUTR. Undertaking to provide after-sales service to consumers with whom the trader has communicated prior to a transaction in a language which is not an official language of the EEA State where the trader is located and then making such service available only in another language without clearly disclosing this to the consumer before the consumer is committed to the transaction. Creating the false impression that after-sales service in relation to a product is available in an EEA State other than the one in which the product is sold.

[83] It may, however, initiate an investigation itself where: (a) it believes that there are potential breaches of the CAP Code based on complaints received; or (b) an apparent breach of the CAP Code has been identified by CAP during monitoring.

[84] 'Non-broadcast Complaint Handling Procedures', para 6.

evidence into account when making its adjudication. If consent is given, the
ASA passes on whatever information it deems (during its investigation) to be
relevant 'and needs to be disclosed' to the advertiser. The ASA website also
clarifies what is meant by 'evidence':

> 'For clarity, by "evidence" we mean documentary information supplied in addition
> to the point of complaint; it doesn't include a simple description of the
> circumstances that led the complainant to come to the ASA or an expression of the
> complainant's opinion or interpretation of a claim.'[85]

11.76   This revision to the ASA's procedures was introduced in February 2016.
Whilst it goes some way in achieving transparency, some would argue that it
does not go far enough. In particular, the ASA retains a wide discretion as to
whether to disclose evidence to the advertiser and whilst its procedures state
that the ASA will not take evidence that the complainant has refused to share
into account when making its adjudication, advertisers would perhaps rightly
be sceptical of this assurance.

11.77   On receipt of a complaint, the ASA may decide to:

• Take no further action (either because the complaint is unfounded or
  because it falls outside the ASA's remit). According to the ASA website,
  around 80% of the complaints received by the ASA do not raise any
  concerns and are responded to without the need to contact the
  advertiser.[86]

• Resolve the matter informally, usually after receiving assurances from the
  advertiser that the advertisement will be suitably amended or withdrawn.
  Such cases are not placed before the ASA Council and no adjudication is
  published.[87]

• Commence a formal investigation.

11.78   If the ASA proceeds to an investigation, its procedure[88] is as follows:

• An investigations executive is appointed, as the person in charge of the
  case and the point of contact for complainants and advertisers.

• A summary of the complaint is sent to the advertiser, inviting a written
  response. The ASA may also raise issues beyond those raised by the
  complainant.

• An advertiser is given five working days to respond in cases that involve
  harm, offence or social responsibility, and seven working days in all other
  cases. The ASA may grant an extension, but the grounds for requesting the

---

[85]   'Update to ASA procedures: Complainants' evidence', 11 February 2016.
[86]   www.asa.org.uk/Industry-advertisers/Complaint-about-your-ad.aspx.
[87]   The ASA does, however, publish on its website the names of those advertisers that have agreed
       to amend or withdraw advertisements without the need for a formal investigation.
[88]   The ASA's detailed complaints-handling procedure for non-broadcast advertising is set out on
       its website, 'Non-broadcast Complaint Handling Procedures' available at www.asa.org.uk/
       Industry-advertisers.

same must be set out in writing. Where the claim is capable of objective substantiation, the CAP Code requires the advertiser to submit documentary evidence to substantiate any such claims.

- On receipt of the response and any further written comments or clarification, the Investigations Executive prepares a draft recommendation. The draft recommendation is circulated to those named in the report, to other relevant parties if appropriate, and to the complainant for comments.[89]

- The recommendation is then placed before the ASA Council ('the Council')[90] In exceptional circumstances, advertisers are given the opportunity to provide written submissions (typically limited to 1000 words) directly to the Council. No provision is made for oral hearings.

- The Council is not bound by the recommendation. If it introduces an important argument or point of view to which the advertiser has not yet had a reasonable opportunity to respond, the ASA will 're-present' the case to the advertiser.

- Once the Council has reached a decision, the Investigations Executive sends a letter to the advertiser informing them of the Council's adjudication. If the Council finds that a breach of the Code has occurred, the decision letter details the remedial action that the advertiser is required to take.

- Adjudications are published on the ASA website[91] within 14 calendar days of the Council's decision and remain on the website for a period of five years. In exceptional circumstances, where the advertiser or complainant have indicated they intend to or have requested an Independent Review, the ASA has a discretion to suspend publication.

Challenging ASA adjudications

Independent Review of ASA adjudications

11.79 Council decisions are subject to review by an Independent Reviewer. The Independent Reviewer can only accept the request if one or both of the following conditions are satisfied:

- there is a substantial flaw in the Council's adjudication or the process by which that adjudication was made;

- additional relevant evidence becomes available that could not reasonably have been made available during the investigation.

---

[89] The ASA's 'Non-broadcast Complaint Handling Procedures' state the such comments should relate to 'the factual accuracy of the draft recommendation' and so would tend to suggest that legal representations are not invited at this stage.

[90] The Council is comprised of 13 people, appointed by the ASA Chairman, two-thirds of whom are independent of the advertising industry. ASA Council members serve three-year terms for a maximum of six years and are appointed following public advertisement.

[91] www.asa.org.uk.

Full terms of reference of the Independent Review procedure are set in the CAP Code and in the 'Non-broadcast Complaint Handling Procedures' document,[92] for non-broadcast advertisements, and in the BCAP Code for broadcast advertisements.

11.80   In summary:

- Requests for review may be made by the complainant or the advertiser. The request must be made in writing and must set out a full statement of the grounds for review in a single document; the Independent Reviewer should not be required to cross-refer to previous correspondence.

- The request must be sent within 21 calendar days of the date on the ASA's letter of notification of the formal adjudication or the Council decision that a complaint requires no additional investigation. The 21-day time limit may be waived by the Independent Reviewer in exceptional circumstances.

- Requests for review from the advertiser or from a non-public complainant must be signed by the Chairman, Chief Executive or equivalent office holder; requests made only by a solicitor or agency will not be accepted.

- Oral hearings or meetings with the Independent Reviewer will not be granted.

- Publication of an adjudication pending the review process will only be suspended in exceptional circumstances.[93]

- The Independent Reviewer can request that an adjudication be reconsidered by the Council, following a further investigation by the Reviewer or after the Council re-opens its investigation on the Reviewer's recommendation.

- The Independent Reviewer may invite the Council to reconsider its adjudication. However, the final decision as to whether to revise its decision in accordance with the Independent Reviewer's recommendation rests with the ASA Council.

Judicial review of ASA adjudications

11.81   Decisions made by the ASA are susceptible to judicial review. In *R v ASA Ex Parte Insurance Services*,[94] the Divisional Court confirmed that the ASA:

> '... is clearly exercising a public law function which, if the authority did not exist, would no doubt be exercised by the Director General of Fair Trading'.[95]

---

[92]   Paras 48–61, available at www.asa.org.uk/Industry-advertisers.

[93]   A request for the same must be received no later than 10am on the Friday that immediately precedes the notified publication date.

[94]   (1990) 2 Admin LR 77.

[95]   This is in contrast with the court's position on Clearcast, a body that clears advertisements for broadcast: *Diomed Direct Ltd v Clearcast Ltd*. Mr Justice Stewart found that Clearcast '...exercises no statutory/public law power; nor does it exercise any public law function. The

11.82 Both the decisions of the ASA Council and those of the Independent Reviewer can be challenged by way of judicial review. The normal practice is to seek to review both at once; an application to review the ASA Council decision without engaging with the Independent Review process exposes the claimant to arguments on the failure to exhaust existing remedies.[96] This formed one of the grounds for dismissing an advertiser's application for judicial review in *R (Debt Free Direct Ltd) v ASA*.[97] It is worth noting the strict time limits imposed by the Civil Procedure Rules 1998,[98] and the requirement to comply with them will need to be balanced against the risks of having the claim dismissed on alternative remedy grounds.

11.83 The courts will apply ordinary judicial review principles.[99] Whilst some questions are hard-edged questions of law (such as whether the ASA applied the correct legal test), others are susceptible to an assessment on irrationality grounds only.[100] Judicial review is a difficult remedy and it is perhaps unsurprising that challenges of ASA decisions by way of judicial review have only been successful in a handful of cases.

Unsuccessful judicial review challenges[101]

11.84 *R v Advertising Standards Authority Ltd Ex p Vernons Organisation Ltd*.[102] The court dismissed the advertiser's application for an order restraining publication of the ASA's decision pending determination of its application for judicial review. Accordingly, publication could take place notwithstanding the fact that there might be errors of law in the decision which might be reversed on review.[103] See also *R (Jamba GmbH) v ASA*[104] on this point.

---

      fact that private arrangements are used to secure public law objectives is insufficient.' Stewart J found that Clearcast simply assisted with broadcasters' functions and if a broadcaster decided not to approve an advertisement because of a risk of an adverse finding by the ASA due to a lack of BCAP compliance, then that decision would not be amenable to Judicial Review.

[96] The general principle was stated by Lord Scarman in *R v Inland Revenue Commissioners, Ex parte Preston* [1985] AC 835, at 852. See also *R v Epping and Harlow General Commissioners, Ex parte Goldstraw* [1983] 3 All ER 257, at 262. See [2007] EWHC 1337 (Admin) on this point.

[97] [2007] EWHC 1337 (Admin). Note, however, that the court did make it clear that the complaints put forward were suitable for resolution within the Independent Review procedure. It may be that some complaints are considered less suitable for the said procedure.

[98] Rule 54.5(1) of the CPR.

[99] For a recent example, see *R (on the application of Sainsbury's Supermarkets Ltd) v Independent Reviewer of Advertising Standards Authority Adjudications* [2015] ACD 23.

[100] *Associated Provincial Picture Houses Ltd v Wednesbury Corpn* [1948] 1 KB 223. A decision is Wednesbury unreasonable if it is so unreasonable that no reasonable person acting reasonably could have made it.

[101] See also *R (Debt Free Direct Ltd) v ASA* and *R (Sainsbury's Supermarkets Ltd) v Independent Reviewer of ASA Adjudications* discussed above.

[102] [1992] 1 WLR 1289.

[103] Vernons was successfully distinguished in *R v ASA ex parte Direct Line Financial Services Limited* [1998] COD 20.

[104] [2005] EWHC 2609 (Admin).

11.85 *R v ASA Ex p City Trading Limited.*[105] The advertiser's application for judicial review on Art 10 (freedom of speech) of the European Convention on Human Rights ('ECHR') grounds was dismissed, but it should be noted that this decision pre-dates the Human Rights Act 1998 ('HRA 1998'). For a post-HRA 1998 decision, please see *R v ASA ex parte Matthias Rath BV;*[106] where the court found that whilst the ASA Codes did not have direct statutory effect, they fell within the meaning of Art 10(2) of the ECHR and could therefore form the basis of a restriction on the advertiser's freedom of speech.

11.86 *R v ASA ex parte DSG Retail Limited.*[107] The High Court held that whilst decisions by the ASA were subject to judicial review, the court's role was supervisory such that it could only interfere on the grounds of irrationality, illegality or procedural impropriety.

11.87 *R v ASA ex parte Charles Robertson (Developments) Limited.*[108] The High Court adopted a light-touch approach, finding that the question of whether a column was an advertisement was for ASA to decide and the court would not intervene unless the decision was manifestly unreasonable. A similar approach was adopted in *R (Coys of Kensington Automobiles Ltd) v ASA,*[109] where it was found that the ASA's decision could not be impugned on irrationality grounds; it came from those with expertise within the advertising industry who understood the potential effects of misleading adverts.

11.88 *R (Smithkline Beecham Plc) v ASA.*[110] The court found that there was no real danger of bias on the part of the ASA, even though it had based its decision on the opinion of an ASA consultant who had previously made complaints regarding the products in the advertisement.

11.89 *Buxton v Advertising Standards Authority.*[111] The advertiser's arguments regarding alleged breaches of Art 6 of ECHR were dismissed. Whilst the Court accepted that Art 6 of ECHR was engaged, it found the ASA's processes to have been compliant with it.

Successful judicial review challenges

11.90 Whilst many have no doubt been brought, few applications for judicial review have been successful. The two reported cases that were successful concern procedural impropriety, rather than the substance of the ASA's decisions. An example of a successful challenge to an ASA adjudication is that of *R v ASA Ex Parte Insurance Services*[112] regarding the opportunity to comment on the draft recommendation and any other material put before the

---

[105] [1997] COD 202.
[106] [2001] EMLR 22.
[107] [1997] COD 232.
[108] [2000] EMLR 463.
[109] [2012] EWHC 902 (Admin).
[110] [2001] EMLR 23.
[111] [2002] EWHC 2433 (Admin).
[112] (1990) 2 Admin LR 77.

ASA Council. This case has not been followed in subsequent cases, howevr. A further example is *R v ASA ex parte Direct Line Financial Services Limited*,[113] where it was held that where a body acted in a judicial or quasi-judicial capacity, a duty existed to give all parties ample opportunity to make whatever representations would normally be appropriate in those circumstances.

Copy advice

11.91 The CAP provides copy advice, although the ASA website makes it clear that such advice is not binding on the ASA or CAP. It does clarify, however, that the ASA will check if copy advice was consulted as part of its investigation process. The adviser who dealt with the enquiry will then explain the potential problems that were identified and what recommendations were made for changes. If it is evident that the advertiser 'tried to avoid provoking complaints', the ASA will bear that in mind when reaching its decision.

Advertising guidance

11.92 The CAP also publishes 'Advertising Guidance' (previously known as 'Help Notes') on a host of areas to assist advertisers in complying with their obligations. Recent Advertising Guidance notes have covered matters such as:

- lowest price claims and promises;
- promotions with prizes;
- retailers' price comparisons;
- marketing of spiritual and psychic services;
- substantiation for health, beauty and slimming claims; and
- ticket pricing.

Again, the CAP makes it clear that its Advertising Guidance is not intended to bind the ASA in the event of a complaint about an advertisement that follows it.

Sanctions

11.93 The ASA does not have the power to impose fines or take legal action against non-compliant advertisers. It does have a number of sanctions at its disposal, however, some of which can have a significant impact on an advertiser's business.

Publication

11.94 ASA adjudications are published weekly on the ASA website. An adverse ASA adjudication normally comes with a direction to amend or withdraw the advertisement (or website content) in question and not to repeat

---

[113] [1998] COD 20.

it in its current form. Once published, adjudications remain on the ASA's website for a period of five years. The ASA also publishes a list of non-compliant advertisers (ie those who have continued to make non-compliant advertising claims on their websites, despite repeated requests to amend them) on its website.[114]

Ad alerts

11.95 The CAP can issue alerts to its members, including the media, advising them to consult the copy advice team before accepting advertisements for publication or, in some circumstances, to withhold their services (eg access to advertising space) from non-compliant advertisers. The alerts can be either general (relating to a general subject or a policy change that results from an ASA ruling) or specific (relating to individual advertisers). The alerts may cover an entire sector if the CAP perceives a widespread problem.

Withdrawal of trading privileges

11.96 An adverse ASA adjudication can result in CAP members revoking, withdrawing or temporarily withholding the non-compliant advertiser's recognition and trading privileges. The ASA website provides an example of the Royal Mail withdrawing its bulk mail discount, which can make running direct marketing campaigns prohibitively expensive. In severe cases of non-compliance, CAP members may expel traders from membership.

Pre-vetting

11.97 The ASA can require repeatedly non-compliant advertisers to have their marketing material vetted prior to publication. Advertising agencies (or other CAP members) are effectively ordered not to carry material to which the ASA objects unless it has been pre-vetted by it.[115] The pre-vetting can last for two years. French Connection was subject to the pre-vetting procedure in 2004, following an advertisement which stated 'Fcuk FM from Pnuk to Rcok and back. Non-stop Fnuk. Fcuk Fm'. This followed a series of adjudications deeming offensive the use of the 'FCUK' trademark where it was used to replace the common expletive.

11.98 The sanction of pre-vetting is a serious one, particularly in light of the fact that the ASA's decision-making procedures cannot be described as elaborate; there is no right to an oral hearing and the evidence submitted by the complainant is usually summarised rather than disclosed. This contrasts with the intricate procedures that must be followed if a regulator, eg the CMA, wishes to obtain an injunction against an advertiser under the Enterprise Act 2002.

---

[114] www.asa.org.uk/Rulings.
[115] The ASA provides the following example on its website: CAP's poster industry members can invoke mandatory pre-vetting for advertisers who have broken the CAP Code on grounds of taste and decency or social responsibility.

Referral to trading standards

11.99 The Control of Misleading Advertisements Regulations 1988, which implemented Directive 84/450/EEC on misleading advertising, provided the ASA with legal backing from the Office of Fair Trading ('OFT', now the Competition and Markets Authority). The ASA was thereby given the power to refer persistently non-compliant advertisers to the OFT for legal action. The Control of Misleading Advertisements Regulations 1988 have subsequently been replaced with CPUTR and the BPR and referrals have, since 2013, been made to Trading Standards, rather than the OFT. National Trading Standards has in turn contracted Camden Council's Trading Standards department to investigate, and if necessary act on, matters referred to it by the ASA.

11.100 The first example of such a referral, under predecessor legislation, dates back to 1988 and the case of Tobyward Ltd. The case concerned an advertisement for a slimming product made from guar gum, which the ASA had found to be misleading and therefore in breach of the CAP Code. The matter was referred to the Director General of Fair Trading, who obtained an injunction against Tobyward Ltd. In granting the injunction, Hoffman J observed:

> 'It is ... desirable and in accordance with the public interest ... that the courts should support the principle of self-regulation. I think that advertisers would be more inclined to accept the rulings of their self-regulatory bodies if it were generally known that in cases in which their procedures had been exhausted and the advertiser was still publishing an advertisement which appeared to the court to be *prima facie* misleading, an injunction would ordinarily be granted.'[116]

11.101 For a recent referral, please see the matter of Electronic Healing (a provider of complementary and alternative therapies and devices), which was prosecuted by the London Borough of Camden following a referral by the ASA. In 2015, 38% of referred advertisers had their websites taken down, 13% ceased trading altogether, and 8% amended their advertising to comply with the rules.[117] In relation to broadcast advertising, non-compliant advertisers are referred to Ofcom, as the ASA's co-regulatory partner for broadcast advertising.

---

[116] *Director General of Fair Trading v Tobyward Ltd* [1989] 1 WLR 517, at 522.
[117] ASA Annual Report 2015, p 14.

CHAPTER 12

PRICES

CONTENTS

INTRODUCTION

12.1   The regulation of prices can be found in various legislative provisions, some of which are general and others sector-based. Most of these domestic provisions are now derived from EU law directives. The legislation in this area can be categorised as follows:

(a)   Price marking obligations under the Price Marking Order 2004 ('PMO 2004').

(b)   Sectoral provisions for bureaux de change, package travel and consumer credit.

(c)   Misleading prices under the Consumer Protection from Unfair Trading Regulations 2008 ('CPUTR').

(d)   Pricing obligations derived from EU based consumer rights legislation.

12.2   The following table sets out the main pricing obligations and where they are covered in this work.

Statutory provision			Description	CTSLP Ref
Price Marking Order 2004	Art 4	Selling price	Obligation to indicate the selling price of goods	12.12
	Art 5	Unit price	Obligation to indicate the unit price of goods	12.14
	Arts 6, 7 & 8	Manner of price indication	Obligation to indicate the price in sterling, legibly etc	12.17
	Art 9	General price reductions	Obligation to indicate details of the reduction so it is prominently displayed, unambiguous, easily identifiable and clearly legible	12.19
Bureaux de Change (No. 2) Regulations 1992	Regs 5–8	Price indications about exchange rates	Regulation of the manner of price indications about exchange rates by bureaux de change	12.30

Statutory provision			Description	CTSLP Ref
Package Travel, Package Holidays and Package Tour Regulations 1992	Reg 4	Misleading indications about the package price	The descriptive matter concerning the price of a package must not contain any misleading information	15.14
	Reg 5	Legibility of the package price	The price of a package must be provided in a way that is legible, comprehensible and accurate	15.20
	Reg 11	Package price revisions	Regulation of terms that permit a variation of the price of a package after a contract has been agreed	15.36
Consumer Credit (Information) Regulations 2010	Sch 1	Information about the price	Information to be provided about the amount of credit, cash price, interest, total amount payable, AR etc	18.45
Consumer Rights Act 2015, Part 2 (unfair terms)	Part 2	Unfair terms	Fairness of an aspect of the price that falls outside the core exemption for adequacy	8.54
	Sch 2, part 1, para 6	Grey list: penalties	Requiring a consumer who fails to fulfil his obligations under the contract to pay a disproportionately high sum in compensation	8.90
	Sch 2, part 1, para 14	Grey list: unilateral price variation	Giving the trader the discretion to decide the price payable under the contract after the consumer has become bound by it, when no price or method of determining the price is agreed when the consumer becomes bound	8.90
	Sch 2, part 1, para 15	Grey list: price variation without right to cancel	Permitting a trader to increase the price without giving the consumer the right to cancel the contract if the final price is too high	8.90
Consumer Rights (Payment Surcharges Regulations) 2012	Reg 4	Excessive credit and debit card fees	Charging consumers a fee for using a credit card or debit card that exceeds the cost for providing that method of payment	5.80

Statutory provision			Description	CTSLP Ref
Consumer Contracts (Information, Cancellation and Additional Charges) Regulations 2013	Regs 10–14; Sch 1 & 2	Pre-contractual information	Obligation to provide pre-contractual information about the total price, delivery charges etc	5.30
	Reg 40	Default options on additional fees	Use a default option (such as a pre-ticked box on a website) in order to obtain a consumer's consent to an additional fee or charge	12.80
Consumer Protection from Unfair Trading Regulations 2008	Regs 3, 5, 6 and Sch 1	Unfair commercial practices	These provisions are set out below at para **12.37**. These regulations are covered in detail in Chapter 7, Unfair Commercial Practices	12.37

PRICE MARKING

Introduction

12.3 The Prices Act 1974 ('PA 1974') was introduced by Harold Wilson's Labour government as a method of controlling inflation. Its main purpose was to allow governmental control over the price of food and other staple products. The PA 1974 also sought to regulate the way that retailers displayed prices, which was seen as a way of reducing inflationary pressures by increasing public awareness of price differentials. The Act's wide powers have, however been largely repealed and its sole function now is to provide the basis for the Price Marking Order 2004,[1] which was made under s 4 of the PA 1974.

12.4 Other price marking orders made under the Prices Act 1974 – and other Acts – were repealed by the CPUTR, but there was an express saving for the Price Indications (Bureaux de Change) (No 2) Regulations 1992.[2]

THE PRICE MARKING ORDER 2004

12.5 The Price Marking Order 2004 ('PMO 2004')[3] came into force on 22 July 2004. It replaces the Price Marking Order 1999, which replaced the convoluted provisions of the Price Marking Order 1991. It implements the EU

---

[1]   SI 2004/102.
[2]   SI 1992/737 (made under the now-repealed s 26 of the Consumer Protection Act 1987).
[3]   SI 2004/102.

Price Indications Directive.[4] Equivalent provisions to PMO 2004 are contained in the Price Marking Order (Northern Ireland) 2004.

Application

12.6 The PA 1974 applies across the UK. The territorial extent of the PMO 2004 is not expressly limited, however, the Price Marking Order (Northern Ireland) in virtually identical terms also applies in Northern Ireland.[5] Both provisions are made pursuant to s 4 of the PA 1974 which provides for the making of orders about the price that food is sold at, and the manner that prices are displayed for, all goods. The PMO 2004 generally requires traders to indicate the selling price of all products offered for sale to consumers and, for specified products (such as fruit and vegetables sold from bulk), to indicate the unit price of the product. Importantly, PMO 2004 does not cover products which are supplied in the provision of a service and only regulates sales between traders and consumers. Another significant exception is that the obligation to indicate selling price or unit price does not apply to advertisements. Other exceptions are for sales by auction and sales of works of art or antiques.

12.7 In the *Citroën Commerce case*[6] the CJEU ruled on a complaint about the final price of a motor car in a newspaper advertisement (see below at para **12.68**). The case also addressed the relationship between the Price Indications Directive,[7] a sectoral provision, and the Unfair Commercial Practices Directive ('UCPD') which generally covers all unfair commercial practices. The CJEU was asked to consider both the Price Indications Directive and whether the advertisement also amounted to an unfair commercial practice. It declined to consider the latter on the basis of the sectoral conflict provision in Art 3(4) of the UCPD, which requires precedence to be given to a specific sectoral requirement in another EU measure. This is potentially an important development because it suggests that the CPUTR, which implements the UCPD, may not be the appropriate provision to use where there are specific obligations under the PMO 2004.

> **Price Marking Order 2004, Art 1**
>
> **Citation, commencement and interpretation**
>
> (2) In this Order –
>
>> "advertisement" means any form of advertisement which is made in order to promote the sale of a product but does not include any advertisement by means of which the trader intends to encourage a consumer to enter into a distance contract, a catalogue, a price list, a container or a label;

---

4   Directive 98/6/EC of the European Parliament and of the Council of 16 February 1998 on consumer protection in the indication of the prices of products offered to consumers.
5   SI 2004/368, a separate process for Northern Ireland is required by PA 1974, s 4(5).
6   *Citroën Commerce GMBH v Zentralvereinigung des Kraftfahrzeuggewerbes zur Aufrechterhaltung lauteren Wettbewerbs eV (ZLW)* Case C-476/14, 7 July 2016.
7   Directive 98/6/EC of the European Parliament and of the Council of 16 February 1998 on consumer protection in the indication of the prices of products offered to consumers.

"consumer" means any individual who buys a product for purposes that do not fall within the sphere of his commercial or professional activity;

"cosmetic products" means any substance or preparation intended to be placed in contact with an external part of the human body, or with the teeth, inside of the mouth or throat with a view exclusively or mainly to one or more of the following purposes: cleaning, perfuming, changing the appearance of, protecting, and keeping in good condition it or them or correcting body odour;

"distance contract" means any contract concerning products concluded between a trader and a consumer, by any means, without the simultaneous physical presence of the trader and the consumer;

"itinerant trader" means any trader who, as a pedestrian, or from a train, aircraft, vessel, vehicle, stall, barrow, or other mobile sales unit, offers products to consumers other than by means of pre-printed material;

"liquid medium" has the meaning given for the purposes of the second subparagraph of point 5 of Annex IX to Regulation (EU) No 1169/2011 of the European Parliament and of the Council on the provision of food information to consumers;

"make-up products" means cosmetic products solely intended temporarily to change the appearance of the face or nails, including (but not limited to) lipsticks, mascaras, eye shadows, blushers and concealers;

"net drained weight" means the weight of a solid food product when it is presented in a liquid medium;

"precious metal" means gold, silver or platinum, or any other metal to which by an order under section 17 of the Hallmarking Act 1973 the provisions of that Act are applied;

"products sold from bulk" means products which are not pre-packaged and are weighed or measured at the request of the consumer;

"relevant floor area" in relation to a shop means the internal floor area of the shop excluding any area not used for the retail sale of products or for the display of such products for retail sale;

"selling price" means the final price for a unit of a product, or a given quantity of a product, including VAT and all other taxes;

"shop" includes a store, kiosk and a franchise or concession within a shop;

"small shop" means any shop which has a "relevant floor area" not exceeding 280 square metres;

"standard of fineness" means any one of the standards of fineness specified in column (2) of paragraph 2 of Schedule 2 to the Hallmarking Act 1973;

"trader" means any person who sells or offers or exposes for sale products which fall within his commercial or professional activity;

"unit price" means the final price, including VAT and all other taxes, for one kilogram, one litre, one metre, one square metre or one cubic metre of a product, except (i) in respect of the products specified in Schedule 1, where unit price means the final price including VAT and all other taxes for the corresponding units of quantity set out in that Schedule; and (ii) in respect of products sold by number, where unit price means the final price including VAT and all other taxes for an individual item of the product.

Price Marking Order 2004, Art 3

Scope of application of the Order

3(1) This Order shall not apply –

(a) to products which are supplied in the course of the provision of a service; or

(b) to sales by auction or sales of works of art or antiques.

(2) The Electronic Commerce (EC Directive) Regulations 2002 shall apply to this Order notwithstanding Regulation 3(2) of those Regulations.

12.8 Article 3 defines the application of PMO 2004. The important exclusions are products supplied in the course of the provision of a service; and auction sales of art or antiques; both of which were excluded by the 1991 and 1999 Orders. It is important to note that delivery of a product does not constitute a service for this purpose. A product that can be bought without a service should also indicate its price. Goods manufactured to order do not have to be price marked unless there is only a limited number of choices available.

12.9 The PMO 2004 states that Electronic Commerce (EC Directive) Regulations 2002[8] ('ECR 2002') applies to the PMO 2004 despite the empowering statute (PA 1974) having been made almost 20 years before the Directive. The ECR 2002 are poorly drafted and slavishly follow a series of EC Directives. Definitions and concepts are overcomplicated and the language used offends against basic principles of plain English.

12.10 The ECR 2002 apply to those who provide 'information society services', which is defined by reference to Art 2(a) of the amended European Technical Standards Directive ('ETSD').[9] It is summarised in the recital to the ETSD and in the definitions set out in the ECR as:

'any service normally provided for remuneration, at a distance, by means of electronic equipment for the processing (including digital compression) and storage of data, and at the individual request of a recipient of a service.'

12.11 A list of areas that fall outside the definition of an ISS is set out at annex J of the amended ETSD. The definition is also augmented by the following:

'For the purposes of this definition:

"**at a distance**" means that the service is provided without the parties being simultaneously present,
"**by electronic means**" means that the service is sent initially and received at its destination by means of electronic equipment for the processing (including digital compression) and storage of data, and entirely transmitted, conveyed and received by wire, by radio, by optical means or by other electromagnetic means,
"**at the individual request of a recipient of services**" means that the service is provided through the transmission of data on individual request.'

---

[8] SI 2002/2013.

[9] 98/34/EC as amended by Directive 98/48/EC. The key definitions are provided by the amending Directive.

Obligation to indicate selling price

12.12

> Price Marking Order 2004, Art 4
>
> **Obligation to indicate selling price**
>
> 4(1) Subject to paragraph (2) of this article, where a trader indicates that any product is or may be for sale to a consumer, he shall indicate the selling price of that product in accordance with the provisions of this Order.
>
> (2) The requirement in paragraph (1) above shall not apply in respect of –
>
> > (a)　products sold from bulk; and
> >
> > (b)　an advertisement for a product.

Article 4 provides the general obligation for a trader to indicate the selling price on all goods for sale to a consumer,[10] in a manner prescribed by the other provisions of the Order.[11] Products that are not pre-packaged, but weighed or measured at the request of the consumer (sold from bulk) are excluded, in favour of an obligation simply to indicate the unit price.[12] An 'advertisement' for a product is also excluded from the obligation to indicate the price. 'Advertisement' is defined narrowly, however thereby reducing the scope of the exception. It excludes, 'any advertisement by means of which the trader intends to encourage a consumer to enter into a distance contract, a catalogue, a price list, a container or label',[13] such that the Order does apply to catalogues, price lists, containers and labels. In the *Citroën Commerce case*[14] the CJEU considered the meaning of 'final price' in Art 2(a) of the Price Indications Directive (see below at para **12.68**).

Internet advertising

12.13　PMO 2004 also applies to goods that are advertised for sale over the internet because advertisements encouraging 'distance contracts' are regulated. The definition of a 'distance contract' includes contracts formed 'by any means', without the simultaneous physical presence of the parties.

---

[10]　Defined as the final price including VAT and other taxes.
[11]　'Trader' and 'consumer' are defined in Art 1 (see above).
[12]　Article 5.
[13]　The categories should be read disjunctively.
[14]　*Citroën Commerce GMBH v Zentralvereinigung des Kraftfahrzeuggewerbes zur Aufrechterhaltung lauteren Wettbewerbs eV (ZLW)* Case C-476/14, 7 July 2016.

Unit prices

12.14

Price Marking Order 2004, Art 5

Obligation to indicate unit price

5(1) Subject to paragraph (2), (3) and (4) and article 9, where a trader indicates that any product is or may be for sale to a consumer, he shall indicate the unit price of that product in accordance with the provisions of this Order.

(2) The requirement in paragraph (1) only applies in respect of products sold from bulk or required by or under Parts IV or V of the Weights and Measures Act 1985 to be –

(a) marked with an indication of quantity; or
(b) made up in a quantity prescribed by or under that Act.

(3) The requirement in paragraph (1) shall not apply in relation to:

(a) any product which falls within Schedule 2;
(b) any product the unit price of which is identical to its selling price;
(c) bread made up in a prescribed quantity which is or may be for sale in a small shop, by an itinerant trader or from a vending machine; or
(d) any product which is pre-packaged in a constant quantity which is or may be for sale in a small shop, by an itinerant trader or from a vending machine.

(4) The requirement in paragraph (1) applies in relation to an advertisement for a product only where the selling price of the product is indicated in the advertisement.

SCHEDULE 2

Products in respect of which a trader is exempt from the requirement to unit price

1. Any product which is offered by traders to consumers by means of an advertisement which is –

(a) purely aural;
(b) broadcast on television;
(c) shown at a cinema; or
(d) inside a small shop.

2. Any product the price of which has been reduced from the usual price at which it is sold, on account of –

(a) its damaged condition; or
(b) the danger of its deterioration.

3. Any product which comprises an assortment of different items sold in a single package.

4. Any product the unit price of which is 0.0p as a result of article 12 (Decimal places and rounding of unit prices) of this Order.

Article 5 provides a simple rule that the unit price must be indicated on goods that are sold from bulk. The unit price is simply the total price[15] for a **metric** unit of the particular product. The obligation to indicate the unit price extends to goods that come within the Weights and Measures Act 1985 (see Chapter 17).[16] Advertisements for goods sold in bulk[17] do not need to indicate the unit price, unless the actual price is advertised. If the goods are of a type listed in Sch 1 of the Order, the obligation is to indicate the price for the quantity listed in the Schedule (see below).

12.15   In 2005 the then-Department for Trade and Industry ('DTI') (now Business, Energy and Industrial Strategy) issued a *Guidance Note on the Price Marking Order 2004*. Although no longer available, it included useful analysis. As to Art 5 it stated that:

> 'The standard units of quantity to be used for unit pricing purposes are one kilogram, litre, metre, square metre or cubic metre and the unit 'one' for goods sold by number. Some exceptions are allowed and the Order contains a list of products that must be unit priced using different units of quantity – usually 100g or 100ml. Similar products should use the same unit for unit pricing purposes to allow consumers to readily compare prices between them. In exceptional circumstances this may mean that a product required to show a unit price per kilogram, for example, could usefully show a further price per 100g.'

Goods that must indicate the price of a specified quantity

12.16   For the types of goods listed in Sch 1 of the Order, the price must be given for the metric amount listed in column 2 of the Schedule.[18]

Price Marking Order 2004, Art 14

Units of Quantity

14. For the purposes of Schedule 1, the figure denoting the relevant units of quantity in the second column of the table for the corresponding product in the first column of the table refers to a unit indicated by or under the Weights and Measures Act 1985 and unless specified otherwise:

(a)   grams where the product is sold by weight;

(b)   millilitres where the product is sold by volume; and

(c)   either grams or millilitres, as indicated by the manufacturer of the product, where the product may be sold by either weight or volume.

---

[15]   To include VAT and all other taxes.

[16]   The obligation applies to goods for which the Weights and Measures Act 1985 prescribes the selling quantity (for example beer), and goods which the Act simply requires the quantity to be indicated.

[17]   Or those under the Weights and Measures Act 1985.

[18]   For example, for herbs the metric amount is 10 grams, whereas for handcream the amount is 100 millilitres.

SCHEDULE 1
Relevant unit of quantity for specific products for the purpose of the definition of 'unit price'

PRODUCT	UNITS
Flavouring essences	10
Food colourings	10
Herbs	10
Make-up Products	10 (except where sold by number)
Seeds other than pea, bean, grass and wild bird seeds	10
Spices	10
Biscuits and shortbread	100 (except where sold by number)
Bread	100 (except where sold by number)
Breakfast cereal products	100 (except where required to be quantity marked by number)
Chocolate confectionery and sugar confectionery	100
Coffee	100
Cooked or ready-to-eat fish, seafoods and crustacea	100
Cooked or ready-to-eat meat including game and poultry	100
Cosmetic products other than make-up products	100
Cream and non-dairy alternatives to cream	100
Dips and spreads excluding edible fats	100
Dry sauce mixes	100
Fresh processed salad	100
Fruit juices, soft drinks	100
Handrolling and pipe tobacco	100
Ice cream and frozen desserts	100
Lubricating oils other than oils for internal combustion engines	100
Pickles	100
Pies, pasties, sausage rolls, puddings and flans indicating net quantity	100 (except where sold by number)
Potato crisps and similar products commonly known as snack foods	100
Preserves including honey	100
Ready to eat desserts	100
Sauces, edible oils	100
Soups	100
Tea and other beverages prepared with liquid	100

PRODUCT	UNITS
Waters, including spa waters and aerated waters	100
Wines, sparkling wine, liqueur wine, fortified wine	75 cl
Coal, where sold by the kilogram	50 kg
Ballast, where sold by the kilogram	1,000 kg

The manner of price indications

12.17

Price Marking Order 2004, Arts 6, 7 and 8

Manner of indication of selling price and unit price

6(1) The indication of selling price and unit price shall be in sterling.

(2) If a trader indicates his willingness to accept foreign currency in payment for a product, he shall, in addition to the required price indications in sterling –

    (a)   give an indication of the selling price and any unit price required for the product in the foreign currency in question together with any commission to be charged; or

    (b)   clearly identify the conversion rate on the basis of which the foreign currency price will be calculated together with any commission to be charged; and

indicate that such selling price, unit price or conversion rate as the case may be does not apply to transactions via a payment card to be applied to accounts denominated in currencies other than sterling, the conversion rate for which will be that applied by the relevant payment scheme which processes the transaction.

7(1) An indication of selling price, unit price, commission, conversion rate or a change in the rate or coverage of value added tax given in accordance with article 11 shall be –

    (a)   unambiguous, easily identifiable and clearly legible;

    (b)   subject to paragraph 2, given in proximity to –

        (i)   the product; or

        (ii)   in the case of distance contracts and advertisements, a visual or written description of the product; and

    (c)   so placed as to be available to consumers without the need for them to seek assistance from the trader or someone on his behalf in order to ascertain it.

(2) Paragraph (1)(b)(i) does not apply to an indication given in relation to any item of jewellery, item of precious metal, or watch displayed in a window of the premises where it is or may be for sale and the selling price of which is in excess of £3,000.

(3) The indication of any charges for postage, package or delivery of a product shall be unambiguous, easily identifiable and clearly legible.

(4) Where, in addition to a unit price, a price per quantity is indicated in relation to a supplementary indication of quantity the unit price shall predominate and the price per supplementary indication of quantity shall be expressed in characters no larger than the unit price.

(5) In paragraph (4) "supplementary indication of quantity" refers to an indication of quantity expressed in a unit of measurement other than a metric unit as authorised by section 8(5A) of the Weights and Measures Act 1985.

8 In the case of a pre-packaged solid food product presented in a liquid medium, the unit price shall refer to the net drained weight of the product. Where a unit price is also given with reference to the net weight of the product, it shall be clearly indicated which unit price relates to net drained weight and which to net weight.

The unit price by its definition must be expressed metrically. Like its predecessors, however, PMO 2004 expressly allows supplementary indications given in imperial measures. The restriction that is placed upon additional measurements is that the metric unit price should 'predominate' and imperial price per quantity should, 'be expressed in characters no larger than the unit price'.[19] The unit must also be authorised by s 8(5A) of the Weights and Measures Act 1985.

12.18 The DTI *Guidance Note* stated that:

'5. The Order requires that prices must be "unambiguous, easily identifiable and clearly legible" but it is not prescriptive about the way in which those requirements are met. It does, however, require that consumers should not have to ask for assistance in order to be able to see a price. Legibility of price indications in this context means legible to a consumer with normal sight. Traders are, however, reminded of their obligations under the Disability Discrimination Act 1995 and to take account of the special needs of the elderly and disabled groups. When considering the needs of those with less than perfect eyesight, traders are encouraged to take account of the Royal National Institute for the Blind's Clear Print Guidelines.

6. There is no requirement to price mark items individually. Prices can be shown on the goods themselves, on a ticket or notice on or near to them, or grouped together with other prices on a list or catalogue(s) in close proximity to them. If counter catalogues are used then there should be sufficient copies for consumers to refer to. Goods kept out of sight of the consumer are exempt from price marking until an indication is given that they are for sale.

7. Price indications given in the course of conducting a sale by telephone clearly cannot meet the Order's "legibility" requirement. However, such indications must be clearly audible and linked to the subject of the sales transaction if they are to meet the Order's requirements of "unambiguous, easily identifiable" and to be in keeping with the "proximity" requirement.'

---

[19] Article 7(4).

Price reduction indications

12.19

> Price Marking Order 2004, Art 9
>
> **Special provisions relating to general reductions**
>
> 9 Where a trader proposes to sell products to which this Order applies at less than the selling price or the unit price previously applicable and indicated in accordance with article 7(1), he may comply with the obligations specified in articles 4(1) (to indicate the selling price) and 5(1) (to indicate the unit price) by indicating by a general notice or any other visible means that the products are or may be for sale at a reduction, provided that the details of the reduction are prominently displayed, unambiguous, easily identifiable and clearly legible.

There is longstanding concern among consumer organisations about the practice of traders that advertise reductions in prices, that such reductions are genuine. All price indications must be (among other things) unambiguous under Art 7(1) PMO 2004. Under Art 9, a price reduction indication will only comply with PMO 2004 requirements if, 'details of the reduction are prominently displayed, unambiguous, easily identifiable and clearly legible'.

12.20 The DTI *Guidance Note* stated that:

> '8. Where a trader wants to reduce the price of products that are already priced as the Order requires he may indicate the final selling and/or unit price of the product by displaying a general notice (or by any other visible means) that the products are for sale at a reduction, provided that the details of the reduction are prominently displayed, unambiguous, easily identifiable and clearly legible.
>
> 9. In the case of products the selling price of which varies from day to day according to the price of the precious metals contained in them, the obligation to indicate the selling price may be complied with by indicating, in a manner which is unambiguous, easily identifiable and clearly legible, the weight, type and standard of fineness of each precious metal contained in the product, the price per unit of weight and any element of the selling price which is not referable to weight.'

Exceptions

12.21 There are several exceptions from the requirement to price mark. These were set out in the DTI *Guidance Note* (also subsequently adopted by certain local authority trading standards departments):

> 'a.   A unit price is not required when the selling and unit price of the product are identical.
>
> b.   The Order does not require advertisements to show a selling price but some advertisers might choose to include one. If they do, the advertisement must also show a unit price where one is normally required under the terms of the Order. However, selling and unit prices are always required (notwithstanding any other exemptions) when the advertisement is actually inviting consumers

to conclude a distance contract as opposed to merely seeking to encourage them to visit another retail outlet where prices will be displayed. Examples of advertisements that invite consumers to conclude a distance contract are mail order advertisements in newspapers and goods sold direct from the Internet or the media. Catalogues do not fall within the definition of advertisement and are required to show selling and unit prices as relevant.

c.   Where unit pricing would not be useful to the consumer or would be confusing, then an exemption from unit pricing only may be allowed. The exemption applies to:

    i.   Advertisements (as defined in the Order) with brief exposure times (eg radio and television) and advertisements in a small shop.

    ii.   Promotional offers where the price has been reduced because of the damaged condition of the product and/or the danger of its deterioration. In these cases the condition of the product renders comparisons with perfect equivalents less than useful.

    iii.   An assortment of different items sold in a single packet – where individual unit prices may be confusing and a single one misleading. This includes different items packaged together from which a mixture is to be prepared (eg a cake mix).

    iv.   Any product where the unit price (as a result of the provisions for decimal places and rounding of unit prices) would be 0.0p.

d.   Small shops, with an internal sales/display area not exceeding 280 square metres, itinerant traders and vending machines are all exempt from the requirement to unit price pre-packaged products in constant quantities. However, there is no exemption from the requirement to unit price products sold loose from bulk or pre-packaged in variable quantities. In measuring area for the purposes of the small shops exemption only that used for the retail sale or display of products should be included. Concessions operating within larger outlets should additionally be able to demonstrate that they are a separate business and may thus benefit from the exemption.

e.   Itinerant traders, includes barrows in shopping malls, and other movable premises and vehicles of all sorts. "Pitching" in markets is allowed by the Order but once the market trader has revealed the final price for which the goods will actually change hands then that price must be given in writing. Catalogues used by itinerant traders must be unit priced but where the trader uses his discretion to offer a selling price different from that shown in the catalogue then a new unit price does not have to be calculated.'

Offence

12.22 The offence, in para 5 of the Schedule to PA 1974, is one of contravening an Order made under s 4 PA 1974.

12.23 The offence is triable either way and penalties are limited to a fine.[20] In Scotland the level of the potential fine will depend on which court and under which process the case is heard.

---

[20]   Unlimited in the Crown Court, the prescribed limit in the magistrates' court.

Prices Act 1974, Schedule, para 5(1)

5(1) Any person who contravenes an order under section 4 of this Act shall be guilty of an offence and liable –

    (a)   on conviction on indictment, to a fine;

    (b)   on summary conviction, to a fine not exceeding the prescribed sum.

Causal liability

12.24 The provisions of s 23 of the Trade Descriptions Act 1968 (Offences due to the fault of other person) have effect in relation to offences under PA 1974.[21] Causal liability is considered generally in Chapter 3, Criminal Enforcement.

Liability of directors

12.25 Paragraph 13 of the Schedule to PA 1974 enables proceedings to be brought against a director or other senior employee of a company where the company is itself guilty of an offence and it can be shown that offence has been committed with the 'consent or connivance' of the person in question or as a result of his neglect. This provides essentially the same basis of liability for directors as is present in the majority of trading standards statutes. Directors' liability is considered generally in Chapter 3, Criminal Enforcement.

Restriction on proceedings

12.26 Proceedings for offences under PA 1974 can only be instituted by or on behalf of a local weights and measures authority, who have a duty to enforce the provisions of any Order made under the Act within its area.[22] This provision does not apply in Scotland (Sch 1, para 8(4)). In its application to Northern Ireland, Sch 1 provides that, for any reference to a local weights and measures authority, there shall be substituted a reference to the Department of Commerce for Northern Ireland.

Procedural requirements

12.27 Paragraph 8 of the Schedule to the PA 1974 creates a requirement, similar to the notice of intended prosecution under the Weights and Measures Act 1985. The requirements are that:

(a)   within 30 days of the date of the offence actually occurring (not the date that the offence is discovered by trading standards officers) (para 8(2)(a));

(b)   a written notice detailing that:

    (i)   the offender has infringed para 5 of the Schedule to PA 1974 and the related statutory instrument; and

    (ii) giving the date of offence; and

---

[21]   PA 1974, Sch 1, para 5(2).

[22]   Schedule 1, paras 8(1) and 6. An exception is made for Scotland where all prosecutions are undertaken by the Procurator Fiscal.

(iii) brief details of its nature (see the example below) (para 8(2)(a));

(c) should be served on the offender either in person or by post to his usual or last known residence or place of business in the United Kingdom, or a company's registered office (para 8(3)).

(d) proceedings must then be issued in within 3 months of the offence occurring.

Example of a PA 1974 Notice

12.28

> 'Notice of Prices Act 1974 offence
>
> Northshire County Council Trading Standards department hereby gives notice that:
>
> Sainco Supermarkets PLC on [date] committed an offence under paragraph 5 of the Schedule to the Prices Act 1974, and article 4 of the Price Marking Order 2004;
>
> in that they failed to indicate in writing the selling price on a bottle of lemonade which was for sale by retail at their Northshire supermarket.
>
> This notice is given this [date] pursuant to paragraph 8 of the Schedule to the Prices Act 1974.'

Defence

12.29 The due diligence defence in s 24 of the Trade Descriptions Act 1968 has effect in relation to offences under PA 1974 (s 5(2)). See Chapter 3, Criminal Enforcement for further details.

SECTORAL PROVISIONS

Bureaux de change

12.30 The Price Indications (Bureaux de Change) (No 2) Regulations 1992[23] came into force on 18 May 1992, save for regs 4(2) [travellers' cheques] and 5(3) [clarity of statements] which came into force a year later on 18 May 1993. The Regulations were made under s 26 of the Consumer Protection Act 1987 (CPA 1987). Although s 26 and the other pricing provisions of CPA 1987 were repealed by the CPUTR, the Regulations were expressly saved.[24] The Regulations apply throughout the UK.

---

[23] SI 1992/737. The No 2 Regulations immediately repealed the No 1 Regulations of 1992 which contained a printing error.

[24] CPUTR, Sch 3, paras 5 and 6.

12.31   The Regulations regulate the manner in which a person, operating as a bureau de change, gives an indication to consumers of the rate at which business may be done (an 'exchange rate indication') (reg 3). Such indications must state the terms on which transactions will be conducted and provide other specified information, including any commission or other charges. The exchange rate indications and related information must be given clearly and prominently and either legibly or audibly (reg 5). Special provision is made in relation to circumstances where a consumer requests information about the terms on which a particular transaction will be conducted (reg 4(4)) and for coin-operated machines (reg 7). The Regulations require that a receipt setting out the terms of the transaction must be provided to the consumer in all cases except that of a transaction conducted through a machine (reg 6). An exchange rate indication must be accurate and no suggestion may be made that it is not to be relied on (reg 8). The enforcement provisions in Sch 5 to the CRA 2015 apply. The defences and allied provisions contained in ss 24(2), 39 and 40 CPA 1987 are specifically applied to the Regulations by reg 9(2), see Chapter 3 Criminal Enforcement.

Package travel

12.32   The Package Travel, Package Holidays and Package Tour Regulations 1992 create various obligations in relation to price indications. The descriptive matter concerning the price of a package must not contain any misleading information (reg 4). The price of a package must be provided in a way that is legible, comprehensible and accurate (reg 5). These provisions also regulate the terms that permit a variation of the price of a package after a contract has been agreed (reg 11). They are covered in Chapter 15, Travel.

Consumer credit

12.33   The Consumer Credit (Information) Regulations 2010 regulate the way that pricing information about regulated consumer credit agreements must be provided. Schedule 1 of the Regulations provides detailed rules on how the cash price, interest, total amount payable, and APR must be indicated. These provisions are covered in Chapter 18, Consumer Credit.

MISLEADING PRICES

12.34   Statutory regulation of misleading prices dates back over half a century. In 1964 the abolition of retail price maintenance[25] allowed traders greater flexibility in the prices they charged and the reductions offered consumers. This era of discounting was the background to introduction of s 11 of the Trade Descriptions Act 1968 ('TDA 1968'), which first introduced a misleading price offence and required maintenance of a price for at least 28 days before a trader

---

[25]   The Resale Prices Act 1964.

could claim it had been reduced.[26] It was, however, widely recognised that the provision was insufficiently broad to cover the range of misleading pricing practices that developed during the 1970s and 1980s. Section 11 of the TDA 1968 was therefore repealed in the Consumer Protection Act 1987 ('CPA 1987'), which introduced a broader misleading prices offence.[27] The misleading prices part of the CPA 1987 was repealed when the Consumer Protection from Unfair Trading Regulations 2008 ('CPUTR') came into force in May 2008. The CPUTR and PMO 2004 are now the primary measures regulating unfair pricing practices.

Unfair pricing practices

12.35 The CPUTR are broad and likely to cover all forms of representation made about the price, or price promotion, of a product (goods and services) sold by traders to consumers. In particular, there is specific reference in the Regulations to:

- the price of a product;
- the manner in which the price is calculated;
- the existence of a specific price advantage.[28]

The CPUTR also prohibit misleading omissions. Information that is material to a consumer must not be omitted, hidden or presented in a manner which is unclear, unintelligible, ambiguous or untimely. The CPUTR impose a general obligation on traders not to contravene the requirements of professional diligence, which are defined by reference to the standard of skill and care that is commensurate with honest market practice or the general principle of good faith.

12.36 The relationship between the overlapping requirements of the PMO 2004 and the CPUTR was considered by the CJEU in the *Citroën Commerce case*,[29] in a ruling about the 'final price' of a motor car in a newspaper advertisement (see below at para **12.68**). Both provisions implement EU directives. In *Citroën* the CJEU was asked to consider both the Price Indications Directive and whether the advertisement also amounted to an unfair commercial practice. It declined to consider the latter on the basis of the sectoral conflict provision in Art 3(4) of the UCPD, which requires precedence to be given to a specific sectoral requirement in another EU measure. This is potentially an important development because it suggests that the CPUTR may not be the appropriate provision to use where the PMO 2004 applies.

---

[26] Section 11(3) of the Trade Descriptions Act 1968 (repealed in 1987).
[27] CPA 1987, s 20.
[28] Consumer Protection from Unfair Trading Regulations 2008, reg 5(4).
[29] *Citroën Commerce GMBH v Zentralvereinigung des Kraftfahrzeuggewerbes zur Aufrechterhaltung lauteren Wettbewerbs eV (ZLW)* Case C-476/14, 7 July 2016.

12.37 The provisions of the CPUTR that are likely to be relevant to pricing are summarised in the table below. They are covered in further detail in Chapter 7, Unfair Commercial Practices.

Statutory provision			Description	CTSLP Ref
Consumer Protection from Unfair Trading Regulations 2008	Reg 3	Contravening professional diligence	Contravening the requirements of professional diligence, defined by reference to the standard of skill and care that is commensurate with honest market practice or the general principle of good faith	7.110
	Reg 5	Misleading actions	False or misleading commercial practices concerning the price, its calculation or a price advantage	7.132
	Reg 6	Misleading omissions	Material information is omitted, hidden or provided in a manner that is unclear, unintelligible, ambiguous or untimely	7.147
	Sch 1, para 5	Bait advertising	Advertising products at a specific price without reason to believe that they will be available in reasonable quantities without making this clear in the promotion	7.202
	Sch 1, para 6	Bait and switch	Advertising a product at an attractive price to encourage interest and then discouraging its purchase in order to persuade the consumer to switch to something different	7.202
	Sch 1, para 7	Pressure selling	Falsely stating that a product will only be available at a particular price for a very limited amount of time in order to persuade the consumer to make an immediate decision and deny them the time or opportunity to make an informed choice	7.202
	Sch 1, para 15	Closing down sales	Claiming that you are about to cease trading or move premises when you are not	7.202
	Sch 1, para 20	Describing a product as 'free'	Describing a product as 'free' if the consumer has to pay anything other than the unavoidable cost of responding to the commercial practice and collecting or paying for delivery of the item	7.202

12.38 An important question when considering a pricing practice under CPUTR, reg 5 (misleading actions) is whether the price indication was 'misleading'. This is a now a broad question which is not confined to the indication itself, but takes into account all of the relevant circumstances. A pricing practice may be unfair if its overall presentation is likely to deceive consumers, even if the information contained is factually correct. The question must be assessed using the objective standard of the average consumer, which is modified to take into account the characteristics of targeted and vulnerable groups, see Chapter 7 Unfair Commercial Practices, para **7.102**.

The Pricing Practices Guide

12.39   The Pricing Practices Guide ('PPG') is executive guidance for traders on fair pricing practices.

History

12.40   The origin of the PPG can be found in the Consumer Protection Act 1987 ('CPA 1987'), which first introduced a general misleading prices offence.[30] Section 25 of the CPA 1987 also provided for a statutory code of practice on pricing, under which the Consumer Protection (Code of Practice for Traders on Price Indications) Approval Order 1988 was made ('the code of practice').

12.41   The code of practice was designed to give 'practical guidance' and promote 'desirable practices' by which traders could avoid making misleading price indications. A contravention did not of itself create liability. However, s 25 expressly made breach or compliance admissible in enforcement proceedings.[31]

12.42   In May 2008 the misleading price indications provisions of the CPA 1987 were replaced by CPUTR. BERR[32] published pricing guidance for traders to coincide with its introduction.[33] Although the 2008 publication reflected the new legislation, the practical guidance remained very similar to the code of practice. However, the 2008 Guidance was not issued statutorily under s 25, which was also repealed. The PPG was republished by BIS in November 2010.

12.43   In 2013 the CTSI was given the responsibility for updating the PPG as the previous guidance was widely regarded as being outmoded. The CTSI conducted a widespread consultation on misleading pricing and published an updated version of the PPG in November 2016.

---

[30]   CPA 1987, s 20.
[31]   In 2005 the code was updated and re-published under s 25: The Consumer Protection (Code of Practice for Traders on Price Indications) Approval Order 2005; In 2006 for Northern Ireland.
[32]   The Department of Business, Enterprise and Regulatory Reform, which was replaced by BIS in 2009.
[33]   http://www.berr.gov.uk/files/file46254.pdf – Guidance for traders on good practice on giving information about prices (May 2008).

Status of the PPG 2016

12.44 The Pricing Practices Guide 2016 ('PPG 2016') is expressly stated to provide practical guidance to traders rather than set out a strict and comprehensive regulatory code. Compliance with the guidance will not automatically determine liability. In the PPG 2016 introduction it is stated that:

> 'Regulators may refer to the guidance when making enforcement decisions about a trader's pricing practices. This guidance is not statutory guidance and a court is not bound to accept it. The decision whether any particular pricing practice is unlawful remains to be judged by all of the relevant circumstances. Only a court can determine whether a trader has breached the law in a specific case.' (PPG 2016)

12.45 Unlike the statutory code of practice issued under s 25 of the CPA 1987, there is no equivalent statutory provision providing that the PPG 2016 should automatically be admitted as evidence in criminal or civil court proceedings. Its admissibility in any particular case will depend on the factual circumstances and the ordinary principles of evidential admissibility. For example, the PPG 2016 may be of significant relevance in the consideration of a due diligence defence. When the PPG 2016 is relevant, the courts are likely to give significant weight to the guidance that it provides because of the specific context in which it has been produced.[34] The guidance was given by the CTSI following an extensive consultation process with business, public bodies and other consumer protection organisations.

12.46 The legal effect of executive guidance generally is covered further in Chapter 2, Interpretation of Consumer Law, para 2.26.

Misleading pricing practices

12.47 We have set out below relevant passages from the PPG 2016 together with any useful case law. There are currently few appellate authorities on misleading prices under the CPUTR. However, previous case law under s 20 of the Consumer Protection Act 1987 ('CPA 1987') is likely to be helpful as the focus of that provision was whether the price indication was 'misleading'. The assessment of that question was also by reference to the objective standard of the reasonable man.[35] That is broadly the same approach that reg 5 of CPUTR requires. The primary requirements of the PMO 2004 in relation to the indication of final price and price reductions (see above) are also relevant in relation this question.

12.48 We have also included certain illustrative decisions made by the Advertising Standards Authority ('ASA') and cases decided in other European Member States. The approach in these cases focuses on whether the pricing practice was misleading and reflects the general requirements of the CPUTR,

---

[34]   *R (Ali) v Newham LBC* [2012] EWHC 2970 (Admin) (30 October 2012).
[35]   CPA 1987, s 21(1) 'what those consumers might reasonably be inspected to infer'.

which implements an EU directive. However, they do not represent binding appellate authority and are useful only as an illustration of the type of pricing practices that have been considered misleading and unlawful.

Price comparisons

12.49 The Guidance in the PPG 2016 on reference pricing states:

Reference Pricing

Including a reference price in an offer can create a point which consumers use as a base for estimating the value of the product and might reduce the effort consumers put into shopping around and comparing prices. It follows that reference pricing calls for a high level of trust and integrity. It is unlikely that consumers will have made a record of the reference prices in order to determine for themselves whether the claimed price reduction is genuine.

Any specific price advantage claimed must not be misleading or unfair. It is important to be clear and not to make unfair price comparisons. If your proposed pricing practice explicitly or by implication indicates a saving against another price, you must be able to satisfy yourself that the quoted saving is genuine and is therefore not unfair. Ask yourself whether the average consumer would think that it is a fair comparison. Below is a non-exhaustive list of issues that should be considered when determining whether a price reduction is genuine.

1. How long was the product on sale at the higher price compared to the period for which the price comparison is made?
2. How many, where and what type of outlets will the price comparison be used in, compared to those at which the product was on sale at the higher price?
3. How recently was the higher price offered compared to when the price comparison is being made?
4. Where products are only in demand for short periods each year, are you making price comparisons with out-of-season reference prices?
5. Were significant sales made at the higher price prior to the price comparison being made or was there any reasonable expectation that consumers would purchase the product at the higher price?

Issues to be considered	More likely to comply	Less likely to comply
1. How long was the product on sale at the higher price compared to the period for which the price comparison is made?	The price comparison is made for a period that is the same or shorter than the period during which the higher price was offered.	The price comparison is made for a materially longer period than the higher price was offered.
2. How many, where and what type of outlets will the price comparison be used in, compared to those at which the product was on sale at the higher price?	The retailer makes a price comparison against a reference price that has been offered in the same store as the price comparison is made.	A retailer charges £3 in store A and £2 in store B and then claims 'Was £3 Now £1.50' in store B, referring to a reference price in a store where that price was never charged.

Issues to be considered	More likely to comply	Less likely to comply
3. How recently was the higher price offered compared to when the price comparison is being made	A travel agent refers to a selling price that was charged fewer than two months ago with no intervening prices and therefore gives a genuine indication of the current value of the holiday.	A website refers to previous selling prices that were charged many months ago and therefore no longer represent a genuine indication of the current value of the item.
4. Where products are only in demand for short periods each year, are you making price comparisons with out-of-season reference prices?	An online trader reduces its prices in order to generate sales where demand has fallen away when the sales season for a product has passed.	A trader offers the product at a higher price when the product is out-of-season and then lowers the price in time for the expected product demand.
5. Were significant sales made at the higher price prior to the price comparison being made or was there any reasonable expectation that consumers would purchase the product at the higher price?	The retailer can provide evidence to show significant sales at the higher price or that this was a realistic selling price for the product.	A retailer repeatedly uses a reference price knowing that it had not previously sold a significant number of units at that price.

Is your price promotion genuine?

It is important that price comparisons are genuine. Examples of price comparisons that may not be genuine include:

1. During the period that the product was sold at the higher price, different types of discount were offered, for example, multi-buy.
2. The higher price is not the last price that the product was sold at, for example there have been any intervening prices.
3. A series of price claims made against a reference price, where each subsequent claim does not offer a greater discount.

Examples of price comparisons that may not be genuine	More likely to comply	Less likely to comply
During the period that the product was sold at the higher price, different types of discount were offered, for example, multibuy.	An online retailer offers a product for sale with the price claim of 'Was £500 Now £350' for a month. For the preceding month the product was priced at £500 with no price promotions or other price reductions.	An online retailer offers a product for sale with the price claim of 'Was £500 Now £350' for a month. For the preceding month the product was priced at £500 with a volume promotion operating at the same time – Buy 2 get 10% Off.

Examples of price comparisons that may not be genuine	More likely to comply	Less likely to comply
The higher price was not the last price that the product was sold at, for example there have been intervening prices.	A sofa is offered for sale at £500 immediately before the price promotion 'Was £500 Now £350' is advertised.	A sofa is offered at £500 then reduced to £350 with no claim of saving. A number of weeks later the product is labelled as 'Was £500 Now £350'.
If a series of price claims are made against a reference price then each subsequent claim should offer a better discount.	A coat is offered at 'Was £150 Now £99' then a further reduction is made and the item is advertised as 'Was £150 Was £99 Now Half Price £75'.	A coat is offered at 'Was £150 Now Half Price £75' subsequently the same item is advertised as 'Was £150 Now £99'.

12.50 There are overlapping obligations under the PMO 2004 and CPUTR in relation to representations about price reductions. Where the PMO 2004 is applicable, reg 9 requires that the 'details of the reduction are prominently displayed, unambiguous, easily identifiable and clearly legible'. The relationship between the PMO 2004 and CPUTR is considered above at para **12.7**. In a case decided before the implementation of the CPUTR, *Office of Fair Trading v Officers Club Ltd*[36] the OFT brought civil enforcement proceedings against a chain of retail clothing stores that operated a '70% off' sales strategy. This involved a small number of items being marked at full price in a limited number of stores for 28 days and thereafter being sold in all stores at a 70% discount. There were advertisements placed in the store windows promoting and explaining the 70% discount scheme. The High Court found the advertised discounts to be misleading. Etherington J stated that:

> 'a customer would have regarded the notices as implicitly stating that the higher price was a genuine price as distinct from, and by contrast with, an artificial price ... it is a facet of a genuine price, in this context, that the seller honestly believes that the price is an appropriate sale price for the goods. I also agree ... that the notices carried the implied representation that significant quantities of the goods had actually been offered for sale at the higher price .... in this context, a "significant" quantity for sale at the higher price involves a comparison with the total number available for sale at any moment of time at the lower price: in other words, it involves a snapshot comparison at a particular moment in time between what had previously been offered for sale at the higher price and what at that later snapshot moment was offered for sale at the discounted price.'[37]

12.51 In *AG Stanley Ltd v Surrey CC*[38] a retailer sold an occasional table in its outlets for £7.99 for a period of 5.5 months. The price was then reduced to £4.99 for a 5-month period as part of a general promotion. During that 5-month period the retailer also advertised two shorter sales, a 13-day sale and a Christmas sale. At these two shorter sales a sign was displayed saying 'Sale,

---

[36] [2005] EWHC 1080 (Ch).
[37] Paras 157–9.
[38] (1995) 159 JP 691; (1995) 159 JPN 655.

round occasional table, now £4.99 was £7.99'. The retailer was convicted on the basis that these price comparisons were misleading. The High Court rejected its appeal on the basis that the notices contained a clear message that immediately prior to each of the shorter sales, the table had been on sale at a higher price, when in fact it had not.

12.52   The ASA ruling in *Sofa Sofa Ltd*[39] concerned a furniture retailer that advertised a sofa as 'Was £649, now £499'. A consumer complained that the higher price was not genuine because the sofa price had fluctuated and it had previously been sold at the lower price. The retailer was able to show that during the 10 months before the advertisement was published the sofa had been sold at £649 for a total of seven months (two periods of two months, and one of three months) and at £490 during two separate six-week sale periods. There was also evidence to show that a reasonable number of sofas were sold at £649 during each of the full price periods. The ASA did not uphold the complaint. It found that consumers would expect that £649 was the normal price. Despite the fluctuation in price, the higher price had been charged for the majority of the time and could be regarded as the normal price. The advertisement was not therefore found to be misleading.

12.53   In the *Wren Living ASA Ruling*[40] a furniture retailer claimed 'Now only £169 Was £378' for a nest of tables. A competitor complained that the higher price was not a genuine retail price. The product had been sold for approximately six months at the time the advertisement was seen. During that time it had been on sale for £378 at all of the retailer's 50 stores (including online) for 28 days in November 2013 and subsequently for 28 days at two stores from March to April 2013. The advert referred to this later period as the basis for the savings claim. The ASA considered that, although the qualification was likely to be seen by consumers, it did not override the general impression that £378 had been the usual selling price for the product. The product had been on sale for the lower price of £169 for five out of the last six months at all of the retailer's 50 stores and online, apart from at two stores, for a further 28 days. The ASA considered that consumers would understand from the claim 'Now only £169.00. Was £378.00 – Save £209.00' that £378 was the usual selling price for the product and that the sale price of £169 represented a genuine saving on the usual price. The ASA, ruling found that in fact the normal selling price of the product was £169 and it was misleading to refer to £378 as a 'Was' price.

12.54   The *Humber Imports Ltd ASA Ruling*[41] concerned a website advertised several garden benches with reductions such as 'Westminster Teak Bench Was £319 Now £169'. In smaller print below the listed products it was stated 'All Internet sale prices are based on the discount from our current showroom prices'. The complainant challenged whether the savings claims were misleading and could be substantiated. The retailer provided a video and photographs

---

[39]   A14 – 280247 December 2014

[40]   A14 – 268611 December 2014.

[41]   A15 – 308966 November 2015.

which they said demonstrated that they had a showroom on their premises. They also provided evidence of sales and a spreadsheet listing the higher showroom prices. The ASA found the price comparison to be misleading. The retailer had not provided any sales history for products sold over the internet. The showroom sales were insufficient to justify a comparison with the website prices. The retailer 'had not demonstrated that the "was" prices were the prices at which the benches were usually sold across all channels and in particular online'.

Recommended retail prices

12.55 Some guidance is provided in the PPG 2016 on the use of recommended retail prices.

> ### Recommended Retail Price (RRP)
>
> A recommended retail price ('RRP') is a price that a manufacturer or supplier has independently recommended. The use of RRPs is contentious – there have been calls to prohibit the practice completely. Traders must take extra care when using RRPs to ensure that they do not mislead consumers.
>
> When making comparisons to an RRP, you should clearly and prominently tell consumers that the higher price is an RRP, rather than a price that you have charged. The initials RRP have historically been used in the UK and its meaning is likely to be understood by most consumers. You should avoid using other abbreviations unless you can be sure that consumers will have a clear understanding of their meaning in the context of the sale.
>
> An RRP must not be false; it must not be created purely in order to present the appearance of a discount. An RRP must represent a genuine selling price. You should not recommend your own RRP or influence the price at which your third party supplier or manufacturer sets the RRP.
>
> Traders using RRPs should consider obtaining substantiation from their suppliers or manufacturers that the RRP represents a genuine selling price. The use of RRPs as a reference price without such substantiation leaves the business open to the risk that the RRP is not genuine and may be considered misleading.

12.56 In the Finnish case of *Consumer Ombudsman v Maskun Kalustetaio*[42] a furniture retailer advertised discounts for several months by reference to a higher price, as well as by reference to RRPs charged by other retailers. The Finnish court prohibited a discount that lasted longer than two months, as otherwise the price would become the normal price. The court also prohibited the promotion of the same discount for more than three months total in a year (in order to prevent 'yo-yo' pricing). The Market Court of Helsinki ruled that the trader should not discount from a price or an RRP that had not been charged at the shop in question.

12.57 This case should be considered with some caution to the extent that it suggests a general approach to RRPs. It is questionable whether a UK court

---

[42] Finnish Market Court of Helsinki 2009, MAO 655/09.

would be willing to impose such a rigid requirement that retailers should not discount from an RRP, unless they had themselves sold the product at the RRP in the same outlet. The use of an RRP is not a banned practice under Sch 1 of the CPUTR and a UK court is more likely to approach an RRP case by addressing whether, in the applicable circumstances, the pricing practice was misleading.

Comparison with prices in different circumstances

12.58   Some guidance is provided in the PPG 2016 on how to compare against prices in different circumstances.

> **Comparison with prices in different circumstances**
>
> It may be possible to make a fair price comparison against the price of a product that has been sold in different circumstances. However, it is very important that any material differences in the circumstances are communicated to consumers in a way that is transparent, fair and prominent. Features that differentiate the circumstances must be clear and not hidden in the small print. Any material information must be provided in a clear, intelligible, unambiguous and timely manner.
>
> The comparison must be readily understandable and relevant to the consumer that it is directed towards. The differences between the circumstances must still allow for a fair comparison to be made. The overall impression given to consumers must not be misleading even if the information provided is correct.
>
> Explanatory text (refer to guidance on Page **) may be useful to ensure that the pricing practice can be clearly understood by the average consumer, provided that it is provided in a clear, intelligible, unambiguous and timely manner.

Examples	More likely to comply	Less likely to comply
Comparing pricing models that are not like-for-like.	The website claims 'Save 50% on airport parking' and also states 'When you book in advance compared to the turn up and pay price' in a clear, intelligible, unambiguous and timely manner.	The website claims 'Save 50% on airport parking' with no further details of the basis of the claim of 50% savings.

Examples	More likely to comply	Less likely to comply
Comparing products in different conditions.	A car retailer advertises the price of a second hand car and claims a saving against the higher price of the car when new. The circumstances in which the higher price was offered are clearly stated alongside the claimed saving.	A car retailer advertises the price of a second hand car and claims a saving against the higher price of the car when new. The circumstances in which the higher price was actually offered are omitted to give misleading impression of a better discount.

12.59   In the *Available Car Ltd* ASA Ruling[43] a website contained listings for used cars, comparing their price to the price of a new car, using the words, 'When New £X – You Save £Y'. The 'When New' price was the price paid for the car when it was originally bought new and not the current price for an equivalent model. They trader argued it was important to draw attention to the significant depreciation in the price of cars after they were sold new. The listings also showed a photograph of the car, its year of registration and mileage. The ASA rejected a complaint that this was misleading because it compared the price of a second hand car to a new one. The information was presented sufficiently clearly for readers to understand the basis of the price comparison and to understand that the 'You Save' figure referred to the difference between the price of the car when originally new and the current market value of a used car.

12.60   Comparisons made with a competitor's price are covered in the PPG 2016 and fall under both CPUTR and the Business Protection from Misleading Marketing Regulations 2008. These types of claim are covered in Chapter 11, Advertising.

Representations that become misleading

12.61   The Guidance in the PPG 2016 on after-promotion and introductory pricing states:

> **After Promotion Price**
>
> You can make a comparison against a price that you will subsequently charge for a product. However, this type of pricing practice is likely to be considered unfair if the price is not subsequently increased to the advertised after-promotion price at the end of the promotional period or the reference price did not meet the guidance *[see the PPG guidance on reference pricing above]*.

---

[43]   A15 – 310623 December 2015.

Introductory Price

Traders must consider carefully the use of "new" or "introductory price" in price promotions. You should assess what consumers in your particular sector would consider as new and therefore how long the claim can be made before the new or introductory price becomes the normal selling price. The claim "new" could be used for a longer period where the product is rarely purchased, compared to a regularly purchased product.

This type of pricing practice is likely to be considered unfair if the price of the product is not in fact increased at the end of the promotional period.

12.62   *R v Warwickshire CC Ex p Johnson*[44] concerned a price-beating promise that was said to be misleading under s 20(1) of the CPA 1987. A retailer selling televisions displayed a notice stating 'We will beat any TV, Hi-Fi and Video price by £20 on the spot'. A consumer identified the price of a television sold by a local competitor of the retailer at £159.99. However, when the consumer sought to take advantage of the notice and purchase the television from the retailer for £20 less than this price, the shop manager refused. It was accepted that this was an error on the part of the manager. There was no evidence that it was the retailer's normal practice to refuse to honour the price promise. The House of Lords considered the following certified question set by the Divisional Court:

> 'Whether ... a statement, which in itself is not misleading on the face of it, can be rendered misleading by virtue of the fact that, even in the absence of evidence to show a general practice or intention to dishonour the offer contained therein, on one occasion the person making the statement declined to enter into a contract within the terms of the statement.'

12.63   The House of Lords found that the price promise was misleading, albeit allowing the appeal on a different ground, and endorsed the approach of the Divisional Court, which had found that 'The notice [was] a continuing offer and whether it is misleading or not can only be tested by somebody taking up the offer.' Lord Roskill stated that:

> 'To hold otherwise would be seriously to restrict the efficacy of this part of the consumer protection legislation. Seemingly innocent notices could be put up and then when such notices were followed by a refusal to honour them by a person acting in the course of his business no offence would be committed.'

12.64   The rationale of *Johnson* is that whether a representation is 'misleading' may be judged objectively on facts occurring after the representation was made, rather than the subjective intent of the person that originally made the indication. Although *Johnson* is a case decided under the now repealed s 20(1) of the CPA 1987, the test that the court applied was simply an analysis of whether the price indication was 'misleading'. In our opinion it follows that *Johnson* would be very likely to be determined in the same way under reg 5 of the CPUTR.

---

[44]   [1993] AC 583, [1993] 2 WLR 1.

12.65 In *DSG Retail Ltd v Oxfordshire County Council*[45] a retailer displayed a notice in one of its electrical stores which read, 'Price check price – we can't be beaten we guarantee to match any local price.' The retailer refused to reduce the price of a £300 music system to £190 to match a competitor. The retailer had always operated a price promise but excluded certain prices, such as mail-order prices. As a matter of policy, they had not included those conditions on the notice that was displayed. The retailer was convicted under s 20(1) of the CPA 1987 on the basis that the price indication was misleading. It was argued by the retailer on an appeal before the Divisional Court that there needed to be identified specified goods and a specific price before the indication could be regarded as misleading. This argument was rejected. Kennedy LJ referred to Lord Roskill's judgment in *Johnson*, stating that:

> 'the transaction, the interplay between the consumer and the store is the evidence by which, in any individual case, it is possible to test whether the notice is in fact misleading. But once it has been tested, it is then established, not that it was misleading from the moment that the test was made, but that it was misleading from the outset.'[46]

12.66 An important distinction of principle can be drawn between the cases of *Johnson* and *DSG Retail*. In *Johnson*, the price promise could not sensibly be regarded as misleading when it was made because there was no evidence that the retailer did not generally intend to honour it. It was only later that an individual error on the part of the manager rendered the original promise misleading. In effect, the House of Lords decided as a matter of policy that the later act deemed the original price indication to be misleading. By contrast, in *DSG Retail* there was a factual inference that the promise was misleading from the outset because the retailer applied general exceptions that were not disclosed to the consumer. It was a case where the practice itself was misleading and the later act was merely evidence of that misleading practice.[47]

Additional charges

12.67 The PPG 2016 guidance on additional charges draws a distinction between three types of additional charge, compulsory fixed charges, compulsory charges that vary and optional charges.

Additional charges

Examples of additional charges are:

- Fixed compulsory charges, which all consumers have to pay.
- Charges for a component of the product or service that is compulsory but where there is a range of possible charges for that compulsory component.

---

[45] [2001] EWHC Admin 253, [2001] 1 WLR 1765 (DC).

[46] Per Kennedy LJ, para 29.

[47] It is arguable that the Divisional court failed to appreciate this distinction in *Link Stores Ltd v Harrow London Borough Council* [2001] 1 WLR 1479 where a trader failed to honour a promise to refund the difference if the goods were sold cheaper within 7 days.

- Additional charges for an optional product or service.

Compulsory charges that are fixed

Additional charges should be included in the up-front price if they are compulsory. A failure to include compulsory charges in the up-front price may breach the Regulations.

Examples of compulsory charges:

- A non-optional administration fee that must be paid for a service.
- A compulsory cover charge at a restaurant.
- Mandatory insurance cover required for hiring a car.

Compulsory charges that may vary

Compulsory charges may vary in accordance with the consumer's choices or circumstances. Even if the charge may vary, it is still compulsory if the consumer must always pay something extra for it. For example, a delivery charge might depend on the consumer's location or the size/weight of the product.

Where a compulsory charge may vary, you should alert consumers to the charge at the outset. You should give information about how it will be calculated in a clear, intelligible, unambiguous and timely manner while still allowing the total cost to be easily and readily calculated by the average consumer before they have expended significant time or effort engaging in the sales process.

Examples of compulsory charges that vary:

- A charge for a component part of bespoke furniture that may vary according to the material used, such as the fabric chosen.
- A charge for delivery that is compulsory but varies according to location.

Optional charges

It is not necessary to include an **optional** charge within the up-front price. However, the charge must be genuinely optional. Charges that are, in reality, an unavoidable part of the main purchase are not optional. You should ask the question whether the average consumer would consider 'optional' to be a fair description of the charge. Where a charge is optional, it should still be presented to the consumer clearly.

Examples of optional charges

- When booking a flight, a charge for the option of hiring a car at the destination.
- When buying a product, a charge for gift wrapping.

12.68 It is important to appreciate that there are overlapping obligations under the PMO 2004 and CPUTR in relation to representations concerning the final price of a product. In the *Citroën Commerce case*[48] the CJEU ruled on a German complaint about a newspaper advertisement for a motor car. The advertisement represented the selling price of a motor car was €21,800. This

---

[48] *Citroën Commerce GMBH v Zentralvereinigung des Kraftfahrzeuggewerbes zur Aufrechterhaltung lauteren Wettbewerbs eV (ZLW)* Case C-476/14, 7 July 2016.

price was footnoted with the words 'Price plus transfer costs of €790' at the foot of the advertisement. This additional fixed fee was a mandatory charge for transferring the car between the manufacturer and dealership. It was not included in the €21,800 price. The CJEU considered the requirement in the Price Marking Directive[49] (implemented in the UK by the PMO 2004) to provide the selling price, defined in Art 2(a) to mean 'the final price for a unit of the product, or a given quantity of the product, including VAT and all other taxes.' The court found that 'having regard to all the features of that advertisement, in the eyes of the consumer it [set] out an offer concerning that vehicle.' The advertisement breached the obligation to give the final price:

> 'As a final price, the selling price must necessarily include the unavoidable and foreseeable components of the price, components that are necessarily payable by the consumer and constitute the pecuniary consideration for the acquisition of the product concerned.'

The CJEU distinguished the fixed cost of transferring a car between the manufacturer and dealer, from a charge for delivering the car to a place chosen by the consumer because such a delivery charge could not 'be regarded as an unavoidable and foreseeable component of the price'.

12.69 In *Toyota (GB) Ltd v North Yorkshire CC*[50] a newspaper advertisement suggested that the price for a particular model of car was £11,655. In very small print at the bottom of the advertisement it was noted that a compulsory delivery charge of £445 applied. The Divisional Court rejected the argument that this was not misleading. This case is likely to be decided in the same way under regs 5 or 6 of the CPUTR. In a Hungarian case, *Competition Authority v Vodaphone Magyarorzag Mobil*,[51] an airtime contract where the initial price was not the full price, although subsequent information gave details. The Hungarian Competition Court found the initial price is the most important element that consumers consider. The first impression is the most relevant and in this case it was untrue. In *OCCP v Eko-Park SA*[52] the court held that consumers are misled where contracts do not explicitly state the price including tax. When presented with an agreement that only gives net value, consumers may consider the price beneficial to them and be deceived as a result.

12.70 In the ASA ruling in *Bapchild Motoring World (Kent)*[53] the home page of a website for a car dealer featured a number of cars with their starting prices. These were linked to detailed product pages that also displayed the price of each model and other information. Text at the bottom of each page stated 'All cars sold are subject to a buyer's fee of £142.30'. The ASA upheld a complaint

---

[49] Directive 98/6/EC on consumer protection in the indication of the prices of products offered to consumers.
[50] Co/0110/98 Divisional Court 11 March 1998, 1998 WL 1043583.
[51] Hungary Competition Tribunal 2010, Vj/149–041/2009.
[52] Poland, Office of Competition and Consumer Protection Delegature 2010, RWA 25/2010.
[53] A15 – 314167 December 2015.

that the advertisement was misleading because it did not make the non-optional buyer's fee sufficiently clear. The fee should have been included in the headline price for the vehicles.

12.71 In the *Manchester Airport Group* ASA Ruling[54] the website for an airport included the claim 'By pre-booking your parking you could be SAVING UP TO 70%* ... *See terms & conditions'. The complainant was quoted pre-booking prices that were higher than the equivalent rates when parking was not pre-booked. The airport argued that the words 'could' and 'up to' in the claim made it clear that not every customer would achieve savings. They explained that booking for certain shorter periods might not benefit from the pre-book savings. Although the ASA accepted that the claim was conditional, it found the advertisement to be misleading because it omitted to say clearly that in some circumstances pre-booking was more expensive.

Small print

12.72 The guidance on the use of additional text in the PPG 2016 states:

> **Use of additional text**
>
> You must ensure that the presentation of your offer is transparent and clear. You should consider how consumers are likely to understand it, having regard to its overall presentation.
>
> In particular, you should consider the prominence and clarity of any additional text in comparison to the headline text or main message.
>
> You should ensure that the headline or prominent message is truthful, clear and consistent with other information you provide. It should not need explanatory text to make it comply, particularly if that text is not prominent.
>
> Consider how the offer is expressed – a simple offer can be communicated in straightforward terms using direct language. If your offer is more complex you should take care to ensure that it is presented in a way that consumers will fully understand.
>
> Additional information should not contradict the headline claim. It must be given in a clear, intelligible, unambiguous and timely manner. Including material information in the small print in a manner that is not clear and prominent may mean that you do not meet that requirement.
>
> Material information might be:
>
> - Qualifying statements, for example, "Wednesdays from 6pm".
> - Important conditions of the offer, for example, "minimum 2 diners".
> - Relevant exclusions, for example, "set menu only".
>
> If you operate a website or use other digital communication, you should use technology so that information is communicated to consumers in a way that is transparent and timely. Additional text that is likely to make a difference to the consumer's decision should be prominent and close to the price, headline or main

---

message. You should not delay telling consumers about additional charges or other material information when it is possible to do so from the outset. You should not design the buying process so that consumers are only told about additional charges after they have expended significant time or effort engaging in the process.

It may amount to an unfair practice if your technology requires that consumers take extra steps, such as clicking on a link or scrolling down a page, to obtain material information, such as additional costs. You should consider carefully whether it is possible to provide consumers with material information about the price and additional costs without the need to visit other webpages or to follow links.

12.73 The Dutch case of *Tele2 Nederland v UPC Nederland*[55] concerned a radio campaign for a telephone package at €20 with a reference to a website or phone line for more details. The offer was subject to a €17 per month cable subscription which was explained on the website or when consumers telephoned. In a poster advert for the same package the small print explained the cable subscription. In both situations the promotion was held to be misleading by the Netherlands Court of Appeal because the small print on the poster was overshadowed by the general advert.

12.74 The *GPS (Great Britain) Limited* ASA Ruling[56] concerned the headline of an email promoting a sale in the retailer's outlet stores stating 'Everything under the sun. It's all 40% off ... excluding sale items'. In smaller print at the end of the email it stated '40% off everything; Excluding Sale Items. Offer applies to select products as indicated at participating *** Outlet stores'. The retailer argued that the prominent qualification of the claims made it clear that the discount applied to everything except sale items. The ASA ruled that the advertisement was misleading because the exclusion of some clothes 'contradicted rather than clarified the nature of the offer, regardless of the prominence of the qualification'.

12.75 In the *Hutchinson 3G UK Ltd* ASA Ruling[57] a mobile telephone company advertised a mobile phone plan using a banner advertisement on mobile devices. It stated 'Scratching around for the best deal sucks. Get the Samsung Galaxy S6 at the UK's lowest price for a limited time only ... From £35 a month. No upfront cost'. This was qualified in a footnote saying that the price claim was based on the equivalent plans of six other competitors. The complainant found a plan the could be purchased elsewhere for less than £35 per month and challenged whether the claim 'UK's lowest price' was misleading. The retailer argued that the basis of the comparison had been made clear in the small print. The identified six competitors constituted over 95% of the market and the remainder of the market was so fragmented that it was not practical to check the pricing of other small independent retailers. The ASA found that the claim was misleading. It considered that consumers would

---

[55] Netherlands Court of Appeal, IER 2010/60.
[56] A15 – 302099 August 2015.
[57] A15 – 307500.

understand the claim 'the UK's lowest price' to mean that the phone and plan could not be purchased from any other retailer across the UK for less than £35, at the time they viewed the advert. The information in the footnote was not sufficient to counteract the overall impression that the claim related to all retailers.

Using the word 'free' in a promotion

12.76   The PPG 2016 guidance on using the word free in a price promotion. This reflects the banned practice in para 20 of Sch 1 CPUTR which prohibits 'Describing a product as "gratis", "free", "without charge" or similar if the consumer has to pay anything other than the unavoidable cost of responding to the commercial practice and collecting or paying for delivery of the item'.

> **Use of 'Free'**
>
> You must not use the term 'free', or similar phrases, unless the consumer pays nothing other than the unavoidable cost of responding to the commercial practice and collecting or paying for delivery of the item.[58]
>
> In promotions where an item is described as 'free' traders should be able to show:
>
> - that the free item is genuinely additional to or separable from what is being sold;
> - if the consumer complies with the terms of the promotion, the free item will be supplied alongside what the consumer is paying for;
> - the stand-alone price of what is being sold is clear and is the same with or without the free item.
>
> Receiving the free product can be conditional on the purchase of a product provided this is made clear. For example:
>
> - The claim 'Free Wall-Chart When You Buy Thursday's Paper' is legitimate if the paper is sold without a wall-chart on other days for the same price.
> - A claim of 'Free Travel Insurance For Customers Who Book Their Holiday Online' is legitimate if customers who book the same journey by telephone are offered the same price but not offered free insurance.
>
> The item must, however, be truly free. The cost of the free item should not be recovered by reducing quality or composition or inflating the price of the product that is to be paid for. You should not describe a part of any package as 'free' if it is already included in the package price.
>
> You should not exaggerate the value of any free product or service to persuade consumers to make qualifying purchases.
>
> You should not describe a service as free, if it is not free for consumers that choose not to enter into an agreement with you after receiving the service. For example, you should not use the terms "free valuation" or "free call-out" if there is a one-off charge for a consumer that decides not to proceed with a subsequent purchase or agreement.

---

[58]   Schedule 1, para 20.

Volume offers

12.77 It is common to find volume offers in UK supermarkets. They are essentially price promotions that aim to demonstrate good value by reference to the volume, weight or amount of the product purchased, or the purchase of a combination of different products. Examples of volume offers include **multi-buys**, such as the ubiquitous *buy-one-get-one-free* offer; **combination offers**, where a discount is given for buying a combination of products such as a meal deal; **linked offers**, where a free or discounted product is offered for buying something else; **extra value offers**, such as 50% free. In April 2015, the Consumers' Association (Which?) made a super-complaint to the CMA on misleading and opaque pricing practices in the grocery market. This included substantial criticism about misleading volume offers. In July 2015, the CMA responded to the super-complaint and noted that it had found examples of pricing and promotional practices that had the potential to mislead consumers. However, the CMA concluded that the breaches were not occurring in large numbers and that retailers were generally taking compliance seriously.

> **Volume Offers**
>
> You should not use this type of price promotion unless the consumer is genuinely getting better value because of the offer. Care must be taken to ensure that any volume offer is not made to be unfair because better value was offered before the volume promotion or for the same product elsewhere in your business.
>
> The risk of these price promotions being unfair is increased if they are not easy to understand. You must ensure that the price promotion provides all of the material information that the consumer needs to understand it and that this information is provided in a clear, intelligible, unambiguous and timely manner. You should not take advantage of the fact that many consumers will not calculate for themselves whether your price promotion actually offers better value. For example, the price of a combination offer should be cheaper than the total cost of buying the same items separately.
>
> Pre-printed value claims on pack such as "Bigger Pack – Better Value" should be objectively accurate and justifiable.
>
> Care should be taken that general notices such as 'Up to half price sale' or 'From 50% off' are not misleading because they do not reflect the reality of the offer. You should only make such a claim if the maximum reduction quoted applies to a significant proportion of the range of products that are included in the sale.
>
> A prominent general claim of a maximum discount such as this, should represent the true overall picture of the price promotion. The 'up to' and 'from' claims are essential to the understanding of the pricing practice so should be shown clearly and prominently.

'Up to' and 'from' claims

12.78 Guidance is provided on the 'Up to' and 'from' claims in the PPG 2016. This reflects the general requirement the overall impression of a pricing practice should not be misleading under reg 5 of the CPUTR. The reference to 'significant proportion' in the guidance has its origin in the language used by Etherington J in *OFT v Officers Club*[59] (see above).

'Up to' and 'from' claims

Care should be taken that general notices such as 'Up to half price sale' or 'From 50% off' are not misleading because they do not reflect the reality of the offer. You should only make such a claim if the maximum reduction quoted applies to a significant proportion of the range of products that are included in the promotion.

A prominent general claim of a maximum discount such as this, should represent the true overall picture of the price promotion. The 'up to' and 'from' claims are essential to the understanding of the pricing practice so should be shown clearly and prominently.

Subscriptions

12.79

Subscriptions

If your agreement with a consumer requires that repeat payments are made, such as a monthly subscription, the extent of the consumer's financial commitment should be set out clearly and prominently from the outset and the consumer's express consent to these additional payments secured before they are charged. You must not mislead consumers about the extent of their future commitment in order to secure an agreement. If you initially offer a product that is free or heavily discounted, you should inform consumers clearly and prominently of any additional payment obligations that will be incurred, including the duration of any contract.

In the *Canal Digital case*,[60] the CJEU considered a television commercial for a Danish satellite television service. A monthly subscription fee of kr.99 was payable for the service. However, an additional card charge of kr.389 was also payable every six months. In the advertisement the monthly subscription fee predominated. The six-monthly card fee was not mentioned in the commercial's voiceover and referred to in less conspicuous text. The CJEU found that the practice of dividing the price into components and highlighting only one part was a misleading omission. At para 64 it was stated:

> 'where a trader has opted to state the price for a subscription so that the consumer must pay both a monthly charge and a six-monthly charge, that practice must be regarded as a misleading omission if the price of the monthly charge is particularly highlighted in the marketing, whilst the six-monthly charge is omitted entirely or presented only in a less conspicuous manner, if such failure causes the consumer to take a transactional decision that he would not have taken otherwise.'

---

[59]   [2005] EWHC 1080 (Ch).
[60]   *Canal Digital Danmark A/S* C-611/14 (judgment 26/10/16).

Default options

12.80 The practice of using default options, common for website transactions, to charge an additional fee was prohibited by reg 40 of the Consumer Contracts (information, Cancellation and Additional Charges) Regulations 2013 ('CCR 2013').

Additional payments under a contract

40(1) Under a contract between a trader and a consumer, no payment is payable in addition to the remuneration agreed for the trader's main obligation unless, before the consumer became bound by the contract, the trader obtained the consumer's express consent.

(2) There is no express consent (if there would otherwise be) for the purposes of this paragraph if consent is inferred from the consumer not changing a default option (such as a pre-ticked box on a website).

(3) This regulation does not apply if the trader's main obligation is to supply services within regulation 6(1)(b), but in any other case it applies even if an additional payment is for such services.

(4) Where a trader receives an additional payment which, under this regulation, is not payable under a contract, the contract is to be treated as providing for the trader to reimburse the payment to the consumer.

CHAPTER 13

INTELLECTUAL PROPERTY

CONTENTS

INTRODUCTION

13.1

'Intellectual property rights underpin investment in research and manufacturing, reward innovation in design and branding, and support creativity of all types.

But these crucial IP rights are undermined and devalued on all fronts by infringement, whether by the wholesale sharing of digital content through myriad file sharing and streaming websites, deliberate copying of patent or design protected products, or the importation and sale of counterfeit goods on a massive scale.

The harm that this infringement causes is hard to measure, but it is also hard to understate. Infringement of IP rights is not just an economic matter, although it does cause financial loss to legitimate business, and to the exchequer. The harms caused by IP infringement go much further, to the heart of communities and the wellbeing of UK citizens. Unsafe counterfeit goods can pose serious risks to safety.

The prevalence of IP crime such as counterfeiting is closely associated with other serious criminality, and where entire markets are devoted to counterfeits, the chilling effect on legitimate traders can result in entire communities suffering from a lack of investment and the chance to thrive economically.

Infringement of IP rights online also causes harm to consumers, with close links between illegitimate websites and the spread of malware and other cybercrime. The extensive copying and distribution of infringing material also undermines the ability of our world leading creative industries to invest in new content, reducing the payback for creators, and damaging the long term cultural wealth of the nation.'[1]

13.2   IP crime is widespread and can be found everywhere from the internet to traditional markets. It is big business: it is estimated that approximately 10% of global trade is in counterfeit goods.[2] IP crime in the UK takes place 'on a vast scale reaching into every part of society' and 'enforcement of IP rights is a complex matter'.[3] In 2011 almost half of the UK's £137 billion annual investment in tangible assets was in intellectual property.[4] It is very difficult to accurately assess the level of IP crime, however all commentators agree that it causes huge financial loss to UK rights owners. A recent estimate is that losses to the UK economy in terms profits and taxes are in the region of £1.3 billion per year, and the National Crime Agency recognises the threat IP Crime poses to the UK economic growth is such that it has been made a 'priority' for its

---

[1]   Baroness Neville-Rolfe, DBE, CMG Minister for Intellectual Property in the Foreword to *'Protecting creativity, supporting innovation: IP enforcement 2020'*, the government's strategy for tackling intellectual property infringement, which was published in May 2016.

[2]   IP Crime Group Annual Report 2013–2014, p 4.

[3]   IP Crime Group Annual Report 2011–2012, p 2.

[4]   IPO report 'Prevention and Cure – The UK IP Crime Strategy 2011' Foreword by Baroness Wilcox.

Economic Crime Command.[5] IP Criminality continues to evolve as criminals find new ways to exploit opportunities.

13.3 Enforcement agencies have consequently been driven to attempt to find smarter ways to catch them. The cost is not exclusively economic: IP crime endangers consumers as well as cheating them, with a thriving market in counterfeit pharmaceuticals, car and aero parts, food and drink, as well as the more commonplace fake sportswear and pirated DVDs. The scale of IP crime continues to increase, often facilitated by the technological advances, such as the ubiquity of internet use and the increasing use of social media sites to transact consumer trades, which have transformed the commercial and consumer landscapes over the past decade. The internet continues to be a major facilitator of IP Crime, and platforms such as social media have presented criminals with new and expanding markets to exploit for the sale of counterfeit goods and infringing material.[6] Research indicates that during 2013–14 the sale of counterfeit goods via social media rose 15%, whereas the rise in sales via online auction sites rose by just 2%.[7] However although the online sale of counterfeit items remains a significant problem, it has not increased significantly from 2013/14 after a significant increase in recent years.[8]

13.4 IP is covered by many areas of both common and statute law which are not featured in this work – for example, patents, passing off and breach of confidence. The areas that are considered primarily relate to those parts of trade mark, copyright and (to a limited degree) design law which local authority trading standards departments are most likely to be involved. There were major developments in relation to design and patent law with the enactment of the Intellectual Property Act 2014.

TRADE MARKS ACT 1994

Introduction

13.5 The EU legal framework on trade marks encompasses the Trade Mark Directive (89/104), which was codified in 2008 (2008/95), together with the Trade Mark Regulation (40/94) which was codified in 2009 (207/2009) and which established the Community Trade Mark and the Office for Harmonisation in the Internal Market (OHIM). The Trade Marks Act 1994 ('TMA') replaced previous trade mark law and implemented EC Directive 89/104. Details of a European trade mark reform package were published in December 2015. They comprise:

- a new Trade Mark Regulation (2015/2424) which amends Regulation 207/2009 and entered into force on 23 March 2016; and

5   IP Crime Group Annual Report 2013–2014, p 3.
6   IP Crime Report 2013–2014, p 4.
7   IP Crime Report 2013–2014, p 4.
8   IP Crime Group Annual Report 2014–2015, p 6.

- a new Trade Mark Directive (2015/2436) which repeals Directive 2008/95 with effect from 15 January 2019. Member States therefore have until 14 January 2019 to transpose the provisions of the new Directive into their national laws.

13.6 The European Union Trade Mark Regulations 2016, which came into force 6 April 2016, amend ss 51 and 52 of the TMA and the Community Trade Mark Regulations 2006, to reflect, *amongst other matters*, changes in terminology made by new Regulation 2015/2424. Examples include:

- references to 'Community' are replaced by 'European Union';
- 'Community trade mark' is renamed 'European Union trade mark';
- the Office for Harmonisation in the Internal Market (OHIM) becomes European Union Intellectual Property Office (EUIPO).

Offences

13.7 Sections 92–101 TMA create offences and provide associated provisions concerning the unauthorised use of registered trade marks in relation to goods. The Act places a duty of policing those offences upon local authorities and provides powers of enforcement. Action against unauthorised use of trade marks (whether registered or unregistered) in relation to services (and for unregistered marks in relation to goods) may be considered under the Consumer Protection from Unfair Trading Regulations 2008,[9] which implemented the Unfair Commercial Practices Directive into UK law. Two provisions of the Regulations have specific application in this context:

- By virtue of regs 5(3) and 9 of the Regulations, a trader is guilty of an offence if he engages in a commercial practice which concerns any marketing of a product (including comparative advertising) which creates confusion with any products, trade marks, trade names or other distinguishing marks of a competitor; and it causes or is likely to cause the average consumer to take a transactional decision he would not have taken otherwise, taking account of its factual context and of all its features and circumstances.

- Under reg 12 of, and Sch 1, para 13 to the Regulations, a trader is guilty of an offence if he engages in a commercial practice of promoting a product similar to a product made by a particular manufacturer in such a manner as deliberately to mislead the consumer into believing that the product is made by that same manufacturer when it is not.

13.8 In 2014 the Government conducted a Review of the enforcement provisions of the Consumer Protection from Unfair Trading Regulations 2008 in respect of copycat packaging – seeking views on the case for granting businesses a civil injunctive power. The Ministerial Statement, accompanying

---

[9]   SI 2008/1277.

the outcome of the Review[10] stated: 'Following the review, I conclude there is little clear evidence that the use of similar packaging is causing any significant consumer detriment or hindering competition or innovation. There would be risks of unintended consequences if we changed the status quo, given the uncertainty around the evidence and the effects of the change, particularly in respect of the litigation that would result, and on enforcement. More generally, it would be difficult to reconcile granting this enforcement power with the Government's deregulatory objectives.'

Territorial jurisdiction

13.9 Section 108 provides that the Act extends to England and Wales, Scotland and Northern Ireland. Section 103 provides for the particular meaning of words used in the Act in its application to Scotland.

Offences

13.10 Section 92(1)–(3) sets out the offences in relation to a registered trade mark (in respect of goods, materials and articles).

92 Unauthorised use of trade mark, &c. in relation to goods

(1) A person commits an offence who with a view to gain for himself or another, or with intent to cause loss to another, and without the consent of the proprietor –

(a)   applies to goods or their packaging a sign identical to, or likely to be mistaken for, a registered trade mark, or

(b)   sells or lets for hire, offers or exposes for sale or hire or distributes goods which bear, or the packaging of which bears, such a sign, or

(c)   has in his possession, custody or control in the course of a business any such goods with a view to the doing of anything, by himself or another, which would be an offence under paragraph (b).

(2) A person commits an offence who with a view to gain for himself or another, or with intent to cause loss to another, and without the consent of the proprietor –

(a)   applies a sign identical to, or likely to be mistaken for, a registered trade mark to material intended to be used –
(i)   for labelling or packaging goods,
(ii)   as a business paper in relation to goods, or
(iii)   for advertising goods, or

(b)   uses in the course of a business material bearing such a sign for labelling or packaging goods, as a business paper in relation to goods, or for advertising goods, or

(c)   has in his possession, custody or control in the course of a business any such material with a view to the doing of anything, by himself or another, which would be an offence under paragraph (b).

(3) A person commits an offence who with a view to gain for himself or another, or with intent to cause loss to another, and without the consent of the proprietor –

---

[10]   Published on 13 October 2015.

(a)   makes an article specifically designed or adapted for making copies of a sign identical to, or likely to be mistaken for, a registered trade mark, or

(b)   has such an article in his possession, custody or control in the course of a business,

knowing or having reason to believe that it has been, or is to be, used to produce goods, or material for labelling or packaging goods, as a business paper in relation to goods, or for advertising goods.

13.11 Although only the offences in s 92 have specific enforcement responsibilities attached to them, there are other criminal offences under the TMA including:

- section 84 – unregistered person being described as a 'registered trade mark agent';
- section 94 – making of a false entry in the register of trade marks;
- section 95 – falsely representing that a mark is a registered trade mark (either by means of the word 'registered' or any other word or symbol);
- section 99 – unauthorised use of Royal arms.

There are a number of common ingredients of s 92 offences which are examined below.

Mens rea

13.12 Although the offences under s 92 require that, to be convicted, a defendant must have either a view to gain for himself or another, or an intent to cause loss to another, it is not necessary to prove knowledge of, or intent to infringe, a registered trade mark and thus the offence is one of 'near absolute liability' – see *Torbay Council v Satnam Singh*[11] and *R v Keane*.[12] The words '... with a view to gain for himself or another, or with intent to cause loss to another' appear in the Theft Act 1968 and the meaning given for the purposes of that Act (s 34(2)(a)) is:

'... 'gain' and 'loss' are to be construed as extending only to gain or loss in money or other property, but as extending to any such gain or loss whether temporary or permanent; and

(i)   'gain' includes a gain by keeping what one has, as well as gain by getting what one has not; and

(ii)   'loss' includes a loss by not getting what one might get, as well as a loss by parting with what one has ....'

13.13 In *R v Zaman*[13] the Court of Appeal considered whether the words 'with a view to' have the same meaning as 'with intent to' in s 92 – it concluded, dismissing the appeal, that they do not. The Court of Appeal agreed

---

with the prosecution that the phrase 'with a view to' should simply mean what the defendant has in his contemplation as something that might realistically occur.

Registered Trade Marks

13.14 All the offences under s 92 are concerned with the abuse of 'signs identical to, or likely to be mistaken for, a registered trade mark'. It was confirmed in *R v Boulter*[14] that these heads of liability are distinct. Section 1 defines a trade mark as meaning 'any sign capable of being represented graphically which is capable of distinguishing goods or services of one undertaking from those of other undertakings'.[15] Such a sign may consist of words, names, designs, letters, numerals or the shape of goods or their packaging. Simple colours *are not* capable of being signs: so found the Court of Appeal in overturning the decision of the High Court in the case *Société des Produits Nestlé SA v Cadbury UK Ltd.*[16] In that case the court ruled that a colour – in this case a particular shade of purple – could not, without further definition of application and use in and of itself constitute 'a sign' that was 'represented graphically'. Section 63 provides for the keeping of a Register of Trademarks and for the supply of certified or uncertified copies, or extracts, of entries in the register.

13.15 An invisible sign is capable of infringing a registered trade mark if it becomes visible on a computer screen: *Reed Executive plc v Reed Business Information Ltd.*[17] It follows from this decision that a sign within the electronic data on an article, such as a DVD or piece of software, could be a sufficient basis for liability under the Act.

13.16 An offence may be committed in respect of goods not covered by the trade mark's registration. Section 92(4) provides that an offence is committed not only where the goods are goods in respect of which the trade mark is registered, but also where the trade mark has a reputation in the United Kingdom and the use of the sign takes or would take unfair advantage of, or is or would be detrimental to, the distinctive character or the repute of the trade mark. This not a defence provision – proof that the mark has a reputation etc rests with the prosecutor.

13.17 The prosecutor must therefore prove that, on the date of the commission of the alleged offence, the trade mark:

* was registered for the goods in question (or that the circumstances fall within s 92(4)); and

* the registration had been published (see s 9(3)(b)).

---

14 (2009) ETMR 6.

15 Note that, with effect from September 2017, under the new Directive, 2015/2436, the requirement for graphic representability will be removed.

16 [2013] EWCA Civ 1174.

17 [2002] EWHC 101; see also [2004] EWCA Civ 159.

The equivalent provision for civil liability under s 10(2) requires a likelihood of confusion on the part of the public. It is arguable that the criminal test of 'likely to be mistaken for' creates a higher threshold, but there is little guidance in the case-law on the issue.

The sign and the goods

13.18 It will be a necessary part of proving any offence under s 92 that the sign in question was identical to, or likely to be mistaken for, a registered trade mark. The question is whether the sign (not the item) is likely to be mistaken for that of the registered trade mark proprietor – see *Kensington and Chelsea RLBC v O'Callaghan*,[18] where the magistrates erroneously found that there was no case to answer because they were 'not satisfied that either the watches in themselves or the circumstances in which they were offered for sale provided any, other than minimal, evidence that watches were likely to be mistaken for Gucci watches'.

Without consent

13.19 All of the offences under s 92 stipulate that the use of the trade mark in question is without the consent of the proprietor of the trade mark. In *Houghton v Liverpool City Council*[19] the question arose as to whether it was incumbent on the prosecution to adduce positive evidence that the proprietor of the trade mark did not consent to the defendant's activities. Laws LJ said:

> 'It is a matter, like so many matters of fact, that may be the subject of proper inferences by the court, never forgetting that the criminal standard of proof applies. In this case ... the inference is most plainly to be drawn.'

In Scotland, some Procurators Fiscal have expected the registered trade mark owner to provide evidence that they have informed sellers of the infringement.

In the course of a business

13.20 By virtue of s 103, the words 'business' and 'trade' may be regarded as synonymous. In *R v Johnstone and others*[20] Tuckey LJ said:

> 'This is not a narrow definition, the use of a mark "... even on a single article to be sold or hired out for reward will normally amount to use of the mark 'in the use of trade'" as will its use on orders, invoices, advertisements, brochures and the like ...'

13.21 It is ostensibly a requirement, for certain offences under s 92, that the offender be acting 'in the course of a business'. However, the combined effect of the decision of the Court of Appeal in *R v Johnstone* (not overturned by the

---

18   [1997] COD 164 CO-2753–96.
19   (1999) *The Independent*, 22 November.
20   [2002] EWCA Crim 194.

House of Lords and followed in subsequent cases) and the defence in s 92(5) is that those who commit criminal offences under s 92 can only be convicted where there is civil infringement. Since there can be no civil infringement unless the activity under s 10 occurs 'in the course of trade', successful prosecutions of s 92 offences can therefore only occur where the offender is acting in the course of a trade/business. This causes no injustice – as Lord Nicholls said in *R v Johnstone*:[21]

> '... it is hard to think of a realistic example of conduct which would attract criminal liability and yet be excluded from civil liability because it would not be "in the course of trade".'

In possession

13.22 Sections 92(1)(c), 92(2)(c) and 92(3)(b) are offences involving the 'possession custody or control' of particular goods, materials and articles. Possession by an agent will be covered by these provisions – see, for example, *Essex Trading Standards v Singh*.[22]

13.23 In *R v Kousar (Rukhsana)*[23] the wife of a market trader appealed against her conviction under s 92(1)(c) in circumstances where trading standards officers searched their home address and found a large quantity of counterfeit items. The prosecution's case was that she was aware of the counterfeit goods because they were stored in the family home and on this basis it could be said that she also was in possession of them. Quashing the conviction, David Clarke J said[24]:

> 'The Crown had to prove that her possession of the goods was possession in the course of a business and it seems to us that, if they could not establish that she was involved in the business as a participant, whether paid or otherwise, in the business of dealing with these goods, then they could not establish that element of their case. Thus, even if, contrary to our view, her so-called ability or right to control the goods was sufficient to render her in possession of them, this still did not suffice to establish that further element of these offences. Our conclusion, therefore, is that this appellant in truth did not have a case to answer and the learned Recorder fell into error in ruling that she did.'

13.24 In *R v Harpreet Singh*,[25] D was convicted of TMA offences, including s 92(1)(c) and sentenced to 6 months' imprisonment suspended for 2 years, with 120 hours unpaid work. He assisted a stallholder in selling goods, but took no part in replenishing stock and did not concern himself with its legitimacy. He admitted that he was aware that 'loads of people at [the event] were selling fake goods'. He was of previous good character. His appeal against sentence was dismissed: it was a serious offence passing the custody threshold.

---

21   [2003] 1 WLR 1736.
22   [2009] EWHC 520 (Admin).
23   [2009] EWCA Crim 139.
24   At para 19.
25   [2012] EWCA Crim 1855.

Use as a trade mark

13.25 In *R v Johnstone*[26] Lord Nicholls said:

'... section 92 is to be interpreted as applying only when the offending sign is used as an indication of trade origin. This is one of the ingredients of each of the offences created by section 92. It must therefore be proved by the prosecution. Whether a sign is so used is a question of fact in each case.'

Cases since *Johnstone* have shown that an indication to the immediate purchaser that the product is a replica does not of itself exclude a conclusion that the sign in question was indicative of trade origin (*CPS v Gary Robert Morgan*[27]) – since the essential function of a trade mark is to guarantee the identity of origin of the marked goods or services to the consumer or end user – and that there is no defence even where material bearing the trade marks was of such poor quality that no one could think that its trade origin was that of the trade mark owner (*R v Boulter*[28]).

Section 92(2) and (3)

13.26 Section 92(2) and (3) substantially mirror s 92(1) in form, however they are concerned with the creation, possession and application of labelling, packaging or promotional material which infringe registered trademarks, or the means of producing the same, rather than being concerned with the counterfeit goods themselves.

13.27 Where copies of a registered trademark have been electronically stored on a computer or other electronic storage device, in circumstances where it is apparent that it has been used, or is intended to be used, to apply the trademark to unauthorised labels or packaging the person in control of the machine risks falling foul of one or other of these sections – provided that the relevant elements of *mens rea* are also present. Given the ubiquitous nature of computers and linked printers, this is an increasingly important matter in relation to seizure and forfeiture of computer equipment. The fact that the computer may also have been used, or that it was intended to be used, for other, lawful, purposes, is irrelevant as the section does not require that the illegal purpose need be an exclusive one.

Defences

13.28 Section 92(5) provides a statutory defence:

(5) It is a defence for a person charged with an offence under this section to show that he believed on reasonable grounds that the use of the sign in the manner in which it was used, or was to be used, was not an infringement of the registered trade mark.

---

26   [2003] 1 WLR 1736.
27   [2006] EWCA Crim 1742.
28   [2008] EWCA Crim 2375.

13.29 Section s 92(5) requires the accused to prove his defence on the balance of probabilities: see *R v Johnstone*.[29] The statutory defence has been considered in a number of cases – see, in particular, *R v McCrudden*,[30] *West Sussex County Council v Habib Kahraman*,[31] *Essex Trading Standards v Singh*[32] and *Stockton on Tees Borough Council v Dawn Frost*.[33] They support the view that the section affords a positive and specific defence and does not provide a defence of mere good faith. In *R v Malik*[34] Rix LJ concurred with this concept: '... in *McCrudden* ... Laws LJ was quite right to say that there was no general defence of good faith in section 92(5) ...' However, the Court of Appeal allowed the defendant's appeal on the facts of this case, which involved a shop selling counterfeit vodka:[35]

> 'it is very hard for this court to say ... that purchases from a long-term reputable supplier, which can be proved by records in the form of invoices, purchases of apparently genuine stock at full price, are not evidence capable of providing a defence for the jury's consideration.'

Restrictions on proceedings

13.30 There is no statutory time limit for s 92 offences.

In Scotland, s 96 (supplementary provisions as to summary proceedings in Scotland) provides:

96 Supplementary provisions as to summary proceedings in Scotland

(1) Notwithstanding anything in section 136 of the Criminal Procedure (Scotland) Act 1995, summary proceedings in Scotland for an offence under this Act may be begun at any time within six months after the date on which evidence sufficient in the Lord Advocate's opinion to justify the proceedings came to his knowledge.

For this purpose a certificate of the Lord Advocate as to the date on which such evidence came to his knowledge is conclusive evidence.

(2) For the purposes of subsection (1) and of any other provision of this Act as to the time within which summary proceedings for an offence may be brought, proceedings in Scotland shall be deemed to be begun on the date on which a warrant to apprehend or to cite the accused is granted, if such warrant is executed without undue delay.

---

29 [2002] EWCA Crim 194.
30 [2005] EWCA 4662.
31 [2006] EWHC 1703 (Admin).
32 [2009] EWHC 520 (Admin).
33 [2010] EWHC 1304 (Admin).
34 [2011] EWCA Crim 1107.
35 At para 17.

Cases such as *Burwell v DPP*[36] and *RSPCA v Ian James King and Kathleen Patricia King*[37] underline the importance of a prosecutor, who wishes to avail himself of the benefits of such a certificate, fully complying with the statutory requirements.

Prosecutions

13.31 Any person (whether an individual or a body corporate), other than the Crown or its servants or agents, can be prosecuted under the Act.

Partnerships

13.32 Under s 101 partnerships must be prosecuted in the name of the firm and not that of the partners and any fine imposed following the partnership's conviction must be paid out of partnership assets. Where a partnership is guilty of an offence under the Act, every partner, other than a partner who is proved (on the balance of probabilities) to have been ignorant of or to have attempted to prevent the commission of the offence, is also guilty of the offence and liable to be proceeded against and punished.

13.33 In *R v Wakefield and Purseglove*[38] the defendants contended that the section under which the prosecution purported to proceed – s 101(4) – requires there to have been a conviction of the partnership before the partners themselves can have liability. Since there was no longer any partnership (at the time of the hearing – the partnership had been dissolved after the offences were committed), it was argued that the defendants could not be prosecuted as individuals. The Court of Appeal considered that the argument was misconceived – the subsection does not require there to have been a conviction of the partnership, merely that the court be satisfied that the partnership is guilty of an offence. The appeals were dismissed.

Directors' liability

13.34 Section 101(5) permits the prosecution and conviction of any 'director, manager, secretary or other similar officer' of a company or 'any person who was purporting to act in such a capacity' where an offence under the Act has been committed by the company 'with the consent and connivance' of that person or as a result of that person's neglect. It is good practice (though not strictly necessary) to include the company as a defendant in the same proceedings as the person prosecuted under s 101(5), as it will be necessary to prove that the company could have been found guilty of the offence even if it is not a defendant. Directors' liability provisions are considered in Chapter 3, Criminal Enforcement.

---

[36]   [2009] EWHC 1069 (Admin).
[37]   [2010] EWHC 637 (Admin).
[38]   [2004] EWCA Crim 2278.

Duty to enforce

13.35 Section 93 of the Trade Marks Act 1994 Act provides that:

93 Enforcement function of local weights and measures authority

(1) It is the duty of every local weights and measures authority to enforce within their area the provisions of section 92 (unauthorised use of trade mark, &c. in relation to goods)'

(5) Nothing in this section shall be construed as authorising a local weights and measures authority to bring proceedings in Scotland for an offence.

Although the right to prosecute offences under the Act is not restricted to a member or officer of an enforcement authority, powers are only exercisable by specified persons; see *Media Protection Services Ltd v Crawford*.[39]

13.36 The Copyright, etc and Trade Marks (Offences and Enforcement) Act 2002 rationalised legal provisions relating to copyright and trade marks in a number of areas including police search and seizure powers, and continues to supplement the Trade Marks Act 1994. Section 92A enables a search warrant to be issued to a constable to enter and search premises where there are reasonable grounds for believing:

(a) that an offence under s 92 has been or is about to be committed in any premises; and

(b) that evidence that such an offence has been or is about to be committed is in those premises.

Enforcement powers for officers of local weights and measures authorities and DETI are now covered by Sch 5 to the CRA 2015, see Chapter 3, Criminal Enforcement.

Sentencing

13.37 Section 92(6), as amended by the Legal Aid, Sentencing and Punishment of Offenders Act 2012 (Fines on Summary Conviction) Regulations 2015,[40] which came into force on 12 March 2015, provides:

(6) A person guilty of an offence under this section is liable –

(a) on summary conviction to imprisonment for a term not exceeding six months or a fine, or both;

(b) on conviction on indictment to a fine or imprisonment for a term not exceeding ten years, or both.

13.38 Offences under s 92 are triable either way. The Sentencing Guidelines Council's 'Magistrates' Court Sentencing Guidelines' includes guidance in

---

[39] [2012] EWHC 2373 (Admin).
[40] SI 2015/664.

relation to s 92.[41] The Guidelines indicate that where an offence arises from a serious case involving a high number of counterfeit items or involvement in a wider operation then magistrates should consider sending the case to the Crown Court for sentence. Offenders who occupied a central role in large scale operations should be sent to the Crown Court. Factors indicating a higher level of seriousness include: a high degree of professionalism; high profit levels; and the exposure of purchasers to risk of harm. Mistake or ignorance as to the provenance of goods may indicate a lower level of culpability.

13.39   There have been many appeals in relation to sentencing for offences under s 92, however the general principle, enunciated in *R v Erskine; R v Williams*[42] – that appeals against conviction and sentence could be heard without an excessive citation of earlier, largely factual decisions which did no more than illustrate or restate a principle – should be noted.

13.40   The scale of the enterprise is often a very significant factor in sentencing such cases. In *R v Brayford*[43] the defendant was sentenced to 2 years' imprisonment, upheld on appeal, in relation to the importation into the United Kingdom from China of 25,000 kilograms of washing powder and 2,875 flat pack boxes into which the powder was to be filled. The boxes unlawfully bore the trademark 'Persil'. In *R v Reilly*[44] – where the defendant sold counterfeit cigarettes from his home address – his sentence of 49 days' imprisonment was quashed and a conditional discharge for 2 years was substituted. In *R v Guest (Maxwell)*[45] the defendant's sentence was reduced from 6 to 4 months' imprisonment on appeal, for 10 offences under s 92. He sold computers with counterfeit Microsoft software loaded onto them worth £3,000. In *R v Sarbjit Singh*[46] the defendant pleaded guilty to a total of 17 offences contrary to s 92(3)(b) and s 92(1)(a). His offending involved running, together with others, a large scale, sophisticated counterfeiting operation from a screen printing factory and his sentence of 11 months' imprisonment was upheld. In *R v Khan*[47] four defendants pleaded guilty to conspiracy to commit TMA offences arising from the conduct of a company involved in selling counterfeit items of clothing and footwear from two Birmingham shops. They successfully appealed against their sentences which ranged from 2 years' imprisonment to a community order. In his judgment, reducing the sentences, Sweeney J helpfully summarised the factors which commonly arise when sentencing in such case:

> 'As to the authorities, there is plainly no guideline case as such ... However, they do make clear that when considering sentence in a case of this type the court must take into account, amongst other things, that: (1) offences of this type are difficult, time consuming and expensive to detect; (2) they undermine reputable companies

---

41   Guidelines effective from 4 August 2008, and current as of the 12th Update, issued 1 October 2014, see p 105.
42   [2009] EWCA Crim 1425.
43   [2010] EWCA Crim 2329.
44   [2010] EWCA Crim 2534.
45   [2013] EWCA Crim 1437.
46   [2014] EWCA Crim 1803.
47   [2013] EWCA Crim 802.

who are entitled to be protected; (3) the court should consider how professional the offending was; (4) there should be an estimation of the likely or actual profit; (5) the need for an element of deterrence must be borne in mind ...'

The length of the custodial sentences were reduced by between one-quarter and almost one-half.

13.41 The Court of Appeal has acknowledged that intellectual property offences, such as those under s 92 of the Act, '... are difficult to detect, that investigations are time-consuming and that cases of this sort are very expensive to bring to court' (Lloyd Jones J, endorsing the observations of the trial judge, in *R v Lee*.[48] These remarks were further endorsed by Sweeney J in *R v Khan*[49]) and that the '... nature of these offences is such that not only do they involve the deception of innocent members of the public, but also such activities impact upon the reputation and profits of legitimate, reputable companies and can in its most extreme form affect the employment prospects of people working or wishing to work for such reputable companies.' (Davies J in *R v Edwards (Mark)*).[50]

Forfeiture

13.42 Section 97 provides that where goods, materials or articles – which are connected with 'relevant' offences – come into the possession of any person in connection with the investigation or prosecution of a relevant offence, that person may apply for a forfeiture order. The application may be made as part of proceedings or by way of complaint. In Scotland s 98 provides that an order for forfeiture may be made following conviction or on an application by the Procurator Fiscal made in the manner specified in s 134 of the Criminal Procedure (Scotland) Act 1995.

13.43 The court must be satisfied that a 'relevant offence' has been committed in respect of the goods etc, or a representative sample of them. It may order that the goods etc are to be destroyed or impose conditions for them to be re-manufactured. A decision of the Magistrates' Court in relation to such forfeiture is subject to appeal by 'any person aggrieved' – who need not have been a party to any original proceedings.[51] Forfeiture proceedings brought under s 97, and any appeal by an aggrieved person to the Crown Court against an order made under that section, are civil proceedings in character, and therefore the Brussels Convention 1968 applies to them.[52]

---

[48] [2010] EWCA Crim 268.
[49] *R v Khan (Yasar)* [2013] EWCA Crim 802.
[50] [2008] EWCA Crim 2705.
[51] Section 97(5).
[52] *R v Harrow Crown Court, ex parte UNIC Centre Sarl* [2000] 1 WLR 2112.

Proceeds of crime

13.44 The Proceeds of Crime Act 2002 ('POCA 2002') sets out a procedure for a confiscation order to be made against offenders. The criminal lifestyle tests under the Act have particular relevance to IP crime. A person has a criminal lifestyle if he satisfies one or more of the tests set out in the Act – and the first test is that he is convicted of an offence specified in Sch 2 (England and Wales), Sch 4 (Scotland) or Sch 5 (Northern Ireland) (which includes the Copyright, Designs and Patents Act 1988 ss 107(1) (2), 198(1) and 297A and s 92(1), (2) or (3) of the Trade Marks Act 1994).

13.45 The Act has been used increasingly in relation to intellectual property offences, with enforcement agencies, industry bodies and private enterprises finding that significant confiscation orders can act as a 'strong deterrent' to involvement in IP crime.[53] In one notable example Victor Tin Yau Cheng pleaded guilty in 2003 to Trade Marks Act 1994 offences and was fined £200 but his confiscation order was £334,793.61 and failure to pay would result in a 5-year prison term. In *R v Priestley*,[54] the confiscation order was £2,290,907.52. Local authority IP crime cases considered by the appellate courts where confiscation orders have been made (from England and Wales – the process differs in Scotland) include *Birmingham City Council v Solinder Ram*,[55] *R v Jhalman Singh*[56] (in the latter case the amount of the confiscation order was £585,422.63), *R v Banti Sohal*,[57] *R v William Kenneth Ross*,[58] and *R v Kamran Hameed Ghori*.[59]

13.46 In the case of *R v Beazley*[60] the defendants were a husband and wife who operated a business selling counterfeit branded car wheel trims, and were convicted of unauthorised use of a trade mark contrary to s 92(1) of the Trade Marks Act 1994. Confiscation proceedings were commenced against them on the basis that they had been convicted of a 'criminal lifestyle' offence. At first instance in the Crown Court the Recorder stayed confiscation proceedings as an abuse of the process of the court and oppressive of the prosecution to proceed to confiscation on such a basis. His ruling was made principally on the basis that he considered that it would be stretching the term 'criminal lifestyle' beyond the meaning intended by Parliament to apply it to the defendants in the particular circumstances of the case, where their culpability was relatively low, and they had otherwise been running a largely legitimate business. On appeal it was held that there had been no abuse of process by the prosecution. In his judgment Hughes LJ found that it was not oppressive to apply the POCA confiscation regime to defendants convicted of Trade Mark Act 1994 offences in such circumstances. Trade mark offences are lifestyle, repeat offences, which

---

53 See IPO IP Crime Annual Report 2011–2012, p 62.
54 [2004] EWCA Crim 2237.
55 [2007] EWCA Crim 3084.
56 [2008] EWCA Crim 243.
57 [2012] EWCA Crim 471.
58 [2012] EWCA Crim 750.
59 [2012] EWCA Crim 1115.
60 [2013] EWCA Crim 567.

cause real damage to those entitled to the profits of a trade mark and deprive the manufacturers of the legitimate fruits of the research and development of their product. It was generation of criminal proceeds as a result of the offences which was at the heart of the matter rather than a fine measure of the degree of culpability. The stay on proceedings was quashed and the matter was remitted back to the Crown Court for the confiscation proceedings to proceed.

13.47   In *R v Jie Yu and Elaine Lin*[61] the appellants were a married couple who had pleaded guilty to TMA offences involving the sale of counterfeit goods and appealed against confiscation orders which had been made against each of them in the sum of £768,508. It was held that the judge had not erred in her calculation of the 'available' amount when making the confiscation order; the defendants had failed to establish that there should be a discount from the available amount for expenses they had incurred. Their appeals were dismissed.

13.48   The case of *R (on the application of Virgin Media Ltd) v Zinga (Munaf Ahmed)*[62] provides useful guidance in relation to confiscation proceedings where the case has been brought by a private prosecutor, or there has been a financial arrangement reached between a private prosecutor and a public enforcer.[63]

COPYRIGHT, DESIGNS AND PATENTS ACT 1988

Introduction

13.49   The Copyright, Designs and Patents Act 1988 ('CDPA 1988') is a piece of legislation of which only small portions are concerned with criminal offences. The bulk of its provisions bear upon the commercial interests of those involved in the world of technical innovation and intellectual property. As will be seen the duty of enforcement on local authorities, and powers of enforcement, relate only to ss 107 and 198 and the focus of this commentary is in relation to those sections.

13.50   Digital IP crime – the infringement of copyright of content that is stored in electronic form – has dramatically changed the landscape in relation to copyright offending. Technological advances have made it increasingly easy to make unauthorised copies of protected material and to allow expansive access to it. Illegal copying and sharing of material now takes place on a vast scale. The borderless nature of the internet and the extremely widespread participation by individuals in such behaviour exacerbate difficulties faced in detecting breaches and enforcing owners' rights. Digital IP crime represents the most significant challenge facing copyright owners and enforcement agencies in this field today. The law continues to scramble to catch up with technological developments.

---

61   [2015] EWCA Crim 1076.
62   [2014] EWCA Crim 52.
63   See digest of Zinga under 'Enforcement of IP rights: criminal v civil' later in this chapter.

13.51   On 9 December 2015, as part of its strategy to harmonise national copyright regimes across the EU and reflect the digital age, the EC published:

- a 'Communication on the modernisation of the European copyright framework' (which sets out the main political objectives and areas of action as well as the timeline, based on a step-by-step approach);

- a draft 'Regulation on ensuring the cross-border portability of online content services' (which aims at ensuring that consumers who buy or subscribe to films, sport broadcasts, music, e-books and games can access them when they travel in other EU countries); and

- a 'Consultation on the enforcement of IP rights within the EU' (which aims at modernising the copyright framework, focusing on allowing for wider online availability of content across the EU, adapting exceptions and limitations to the digital world, and achieving a well-functioning copyright market place).

Territorial jurisdiction

13.52   The relevant parts of CDPA 1988 (covering s 107 (and associated sections) and s 198 (and associated sections)) extend to England and Wales, Scotland and Northern Ireland by virtue of ss 157 and 207 of the Act.

Offences

13.53   Section 107 of CDPA 1988 creates criminal offences relating to activities such as making, selling and distributing articles which infringe copyright without the licence of the copyright owner and s 198 provides for similar, but not identical, criminal liability in relation to illicit recordings. All the offences under ss 107 and 198 are *mens rea* offences – for example under s 107(1) the person must know or have reason to believe that the article is an infringing copy of a copyright work. The majority of the offences under these two sections require that there be a commercial dimension to the person's infringement of copyright. This is *not* the case with all of the offences however.[64]

13.54   Other criminal offences that are contained in CDPA 1988 include s 296ZB – to knowingly circumvent technological protection measures, or to supply software, equipment or services for that purpose (commonly referred to as 'chipping') – and s 297A – relating to unauthorised decoders. It should be noted that s 72 of the CDPA – free public showing or playing of broadcast – now only provides a defence against infringement (in the showing or playing of a broadcast) of the rights in a broadcast *per se*, and will not extend to any film rights in the broadcast.[65] The situation in respect of any other underlying rights remains unchanged.

---

[64]   See, eg, s 107(2A)(b).
[65]   Copyright (Free Public Showing or Playing) (Amendment) Regulations 2016 which came into force 15 June 2016.

13.55 There is no duty of enforcement or powers for local authority officers in relation to these offences. Nevertheless, it has become an increasingly commercially sensitive area and there have been a number of prosecutions, involving trading standards, concerning the sale and importation of 'modchips' (devices which enable counterfeit games to be played on consoles despite the protective measures taken by manufacturers to prevent such activity) – see for example *R v Higgs*,[66] *R v Gilham*[67] and *Nintendo Company Ltd and another v Playables Ltd and another*.[68]

13.56 In the case of *R (on the application of Helidon Vuciterni and Alsat UK Limited) v Brent Magistrates' Court and Brent and Harrow Trading Standards Service*[69] the defendant sold allegedly illegal Albanian decoder cards through his business Alsat UK Ltd (the case was principally brought under CPRs but it was alleged that there had been a breach of CDPA 1988, s 297A). It was held on appeal to the Divisional Court that foreign decoder devices used outside the permitted geographical area were not 'unauthorised decoders' within s 297A. The case was also significant as the court remarked to the effect that it was not necessarily unlawful for proceedings to be indemnified by a private party, though it may be of concern if the prosecution was only brought at the behest of and funded by a powerful, wealthy corporation. The unsatisfactory state of the law in relation to illegal downloading of media outlets content was summed up by Coulson J in his judgment in *R (on the application of Redcar Cleveland BC) v Dady*[70] when he remarked that:

> 'It would, I think, be difficult to leave this case without expressing surprise and disquiet that the combination of UK and European case law on this topic has got into such a muddle. It is to be hoped that Parliament can amend the relevant statutory provisions to bring them in line with market (mal) practices.'

13.57

107 Criminal liability for making or dealing with infringing articles, &c

(1) A person commits an offence who, without the licence of the copyright owner –

- (a) makes for sale or hire, or
- (b) imports into the United Kingdom otherwise than for his private and domestic use, or
- (c) possesses in the course of a business with a view to committing any act infringing the copyright, or
- (d) in the course of a business –
  - (i) sells or lets for hire, or
  - (ii) offers or exposes for sale or hire, or
  - (iii) exhibits in public, or

---

[66] [2008] EWCA Crim 1324.
[67] [2009] EWCA Crim 2293.
[68] [2010] EWHC 1932 (Ch).
[69] [2012] EWHC 2140 (Admin).
[70] [2013] EWCA 475 (QB).

(iv)   distributes, or

(e)   distributes otherwise than in the course of a business to such an extent as to affect prejudicially the owner of the copyright,

an article which is, and which he knows or has reason to believe is, an infringing copy of a copyright work.

(2) A person commits an offence who –

(a)   makes an article specifically designed or adapted for making copies of a particular copyright work, or

(b)   has such an article in his possession,

knowing or having reason to believe that it is to be used to make infringing copies for sale or hire or for use in the course of a business.

(2A) A person who infringes copyright in a work by communicating the work to the public –

(a)   in the course of a business, or

(b)   otherwise than in the course of a business to such an extent as to affect prejudicially the owner of the copyright,

commits an offence if he knows or has reason to believe that, by doing so, he is infringing copyright in that work.

(3) Where copyright is infringed (otherwise than by reception of a communication to the public) –

(a)   by the public performance of a literary, dramatic or musical work, or

(b)   by the playing or showing in public of a sound recording or film,

any person who caused the work to be so performed, played or shown is guilty of an offence if he knew or had reason to believe that copyright would be infringed.

. . .

(6) Sections 104 to 106 (presumptions as to various matters connected with copyright) do not apply to proceedings for an offence under this section; but without prejudice to their application in proceedings for an order under section 108 below.

198 Criminal liability for making, dealing with or using illicit recordings

(1) A person commits an offence who without sufficient consent –

(a)   makes for sale or hire, or

(b)   imports into the United Kingdom otherwise than for his private and domestic use, or

(c)   possesses in the course of a business with a view to committing any act infringing the rights conferred by this Part, or

(d)   in the course of a business –
(i) sells or lets for hire, or
(ii) offers or exposes for sale or hire, or
(iii) distributes,

a recording which is, and which he knows or has reason to believe is, an illicit recording.

(1A) A person who infringes a performer's making available right –

    (a)   in the course of a business, or

    (b)   otherwise than in the course of a business to such an extent as to affect prejudicially the owner of the making available right,

commits an offence if he knows or has reason to believe that, by doing so, he is infringing the making available right in the recording.

(2) A person commits an offence who causes a recording of a performance made without sufficient consent to be –

    (a)   shown or played in public, or

    (b)   communicated to the public

thereby infringing any of the rights conferred by this Chapter, if he knows or has reason to believe that those rights are thereby infringed.

Copyright

13.58 Copyright is based on the rights of the author, artist, creator or composer to prevent another person from copying an original – it protects the form in which ideas are expressed rather than the ideas themselves to prevent unfair advantage being taken of a person's creative efforts. Definitions of 'copyright' and 'copyright work' are to be found in s 1 of the Act. Copyright is a property right and legal protection exists only for the following descriptions of work: original literary, dramatic, musical or artistic works, databases, sound recordings, films, broadcasts, and the typographical arrangement of published editions. The Copyright (Computer Programs) Regulations 1992[71] extended the rules covering literary works to include computer programs. Section 1(2) defines a copyright work as a work of any of the preceding descriptions in which copyright subsists. Part 6 of the Enterprise and Regulatory Reform Act 2013 ('ERRA')[72] has enacted important enabling provisions which mark a decisive step towards greater state intervention in the copyright sphere.

Copyright infringement

13.59 Under s 27 an article is an 'infringing copy' if its making constituted an infringement of the copyright of the work in question. Copyright infringement – under civil law – may be either primary or secondary. Primary infringement is direct infringement – doing or authorising an act restricted to the owner of the copyright ('restricted act'). The owner of the copyright in a work has the exclusive right to do the acts set out in ss 17–21 in the United Kingdom, for example: copying the work; issuing or communicating copies of the work to the public; or performing, showing or playing the work in public. Secondary infringements (set out in ss 22–26) are indirect and cover activities such as importing, possessing or dealing with infringing copy. The principal difference between the two types of infringement is the mental element – for secondary infringement, it must be shown that the infringer '... knows or has reason to believe [that the article] is an infringing copy of the work'.

---

[71] SI 1992/3233.

[72] 'ERRA' received Royal Assent on 25 April 2013. See 'Commentary' below for detail regarding relevant provisions ss 74–78.

13.60   In *Allen v Redshaw*[73] it was alleged that artistic works arising from the children's television show 'Button Moon' had been infringed by copying them onto mugs, t-shirts and other merchandise. It decided that there was no defence of parody to a claim of copyright infringement and passing off where there had been a substantial reproduction of a copyright work or works.

Acts that do not infringe copyright

13.61   Chapter III of the Act deals with acts permitted in relation to copyright works. 'Fair dealing' is a term used to describe acts which are permitted to a certain degree (normally copies of parts of a work) without infringing copyright. These acts include: s 28A – making of temporary copies (excludes computer programs and databases); s 29 – non-commercial research and private study; s 30 – criticism, review and news reporting; s 31 – incidental inclusion of copyright material, for example in an artistic work. The detail of certain of these provisions has been subject to recent amendment by a series of 2014 Regulations.[74]

Registration

13.62   Copyright is an automatic right and arises whenever an individual or company creates a work. There is no central source of reference to determine the authorship, ownership or duration of copyright in a particular work and there is no requirement, or provision, relating to the formal registration of copyright. Sections 104–106 (as amended by the various 2014 Regulations) provide for certain presumptions to apply in respect of literary, dramatic, musical and artistic works, sound recordings, films and works subject to Crown copyright but these sections do not apply to proceedings for an offence under s 107. Sections 104–106 do apply in proceedings for a forfeiture order under s 108.

Duration of copyright

13.63   The terms of protection or duration of copyright vary depending on the type of copyright work and are set out in ss 12–15A.[75]

Illicit recordings

13.64   The rights contained in the Act are largely related to the 'recording' of 'performances'. The meaning of 'illicit recording' is given in s 197 and includes a recording of the whole or any substantial part of a performance made,

---

[73]   [2013] WL 2110623 a decision at first instance in Patents County Court.

[74]   See: Copyright (Public Administration) Regulations 2014; Copyright and Rights in Performances (Personal Copies for Private Use) Regulations 2014; Copyright and Rights in Performances (Quotation and Parody) Regulations 2014; Copyright and Rights in Performances (Disability) Regulations 2014; Copyright and Rights in Performances (Research, Education, Libraries and Archives) Regulations 2014.

[75]   The implementation of provisions under ERRA 2013 may have a bearing on the duration of copyright in certain circumstances.

otherwise than for private purposes, without the performer's consent. The Act provides for the duration of performers' rights – see s 191.[76]

Without licence/consent

13.65 Section 101 of the Magistrates' Courts Act 1980 may be applied to 'without the licence of the copyright owner' (s 107) and 'without sufficient consent' (s 198) – the onus is on the accused to show that he had such licence or consent, or that one of the exceptions set out in the various 2014 Regulations applies.[77] In *Musa v Le Maitre*,[78] an industry investigator was considered as being an expert witness in the field of copyright infringement of films. The Divisional Court held that magistrates would be fully justified in inferring from his evidence that relevant copies were infringing copies and agreed with the prosecutor's 'well founded' submission, that it was not necessary for the prosecution '... to go as far as calling from distant parts the makers of the original films or, indeed, the current owner of the copyright'. Stephen Brown LJ:

> '... I can see no practical difficulty to prevent a prosecutor from inviting a defendant to make an admission of fact as to first publication. An obstructive attitude might result in substantial costs. In any event it is unlikely to require the evidence of the actual maker or the holder of the copyright.'

It should be noted that, in Scotland, s 257 of the Criminal Procedure (Scotland) Act 1995 requires the prosecutor and the accused to identify facts which are agreed and secure agreement about these.

Orphan works

13.66 Implementing what has become an increasingly important element of the long standing recommendations made under the 'Hargreaves Review',[79] the Copyright and Rights in Performances (Certain Permitted Uses of Orphan Works) Regulations 2014[80] and Copyright and Rights in Performances (Licensing of Orphan Works) Regulations 2014[81] came into force on 29 October 2014. Orphan works are works which are of a nature which renders them subject to protection by copyright, but where one or more right holders cannot be identified or the right holder(s), even if identified, cannot be located. In such circumstances permission to reproduce the works cannot be obtained in the usual way. Under the new scheme, a licence can be granted by the IPO so that such works can be reproduced without infringing copyright, while protecting the rights of owners so they can be remunerated if they come forward at a later date.[82]

---

[76] See Copyright and Rights in Performances (Personal Copies for Private Use) Regulations 2014.
[77] See Regulations listed under fn 77 above.
[78] (1987) FSR 272.
[79] *Digital Opportunity – a review of Intellectual Property and Growth*, available at www.ipo.gov.uk/ipreview-finalreport.pdf.
[80] SI 2014/2861.
[81] SI 2014/2863.
[82] The Regulations require an annual report to be completed. During the passage of the Enterprise

Defences

13.67   There are no statutory defences relating to ss 107 and 198.

Restrictions on proceedings

13.68   The offences in s 107(1)(c), (d)(i), (ii) and (iii) and s 198(1)(c), (d)(i) and (ii) are summary-only matters and are subject to a 6-month time limit. The other offences in ss 107 and s 198 are triable either way and are not subject to any statutory time limit.

Prosecutions

13.69   Any person (whether an individual or a body corporate), other than the Crown or its servants or agents, can be prosecuted under the Act.

Directors' liability

13.70   Sections 110 and 202 are Directors' liability provisions (see Chapter 3, Criminal Enforcement).

13.71   In *Thames & Hudson Ltd v Design and Artists Copyright Society Ltd* (1994)[83] – where proceedings were brought under ss 107 and 110 – it was said that Parliament had elected to provide that breach of copyright could in certain circumstances constitute an offence and that where such an offence was committed by a body corporate, the directors who connived at such commission were themselves guilty of an offence. No qualification appeared in the statute limiting the types of offender capable of committing the offence to 'pirates'.

Duty to enforce

13.72   By virtue of ss 107A and 198A, inserted by s 165 of the Criminal Justice and Public Order Act 1994, it is the duty of local weights and measures authorities, to enforce ss 107 and 198 respectively.

Powers of enforcement officers

13.73   Enforcement powers for officers of local weights and measures authorities and DETI are now covered by Sch 5 to the CRA 2015, see Chapter 3, Criminal Enforcement. Sections 109 and 200 enable a search warrant to be issued to a constable to enter and search premises where there are reasonable grounds for believing:

---

and Regulatory Reform Act 2013 and the Regulations in 2014, the Minister for Intellectual Property also committed to a review of the orphan works licensing scheme after 12 months. A review – *Orphan works: Review of the first twelve months* – met both of these requirements. From 2016, data on the orphan works scheme will be included in the IPO Annual Report.

[83]   [1995] FSR 153.

(a) that an offence under s 107 or 198 has been or is about to be committed in any premises; and

(b) that evidence that such an offence has been or is about to be committed is in those premises.

Sections 100 and 196 provide for a right of seizure and detention of infringing copies/illicit recordings, by the copyright owner/a person having performer's or recording rights or by authorised persons, from premises to which the public have access, provided:

- notice of the time and place of the proposed seizure is given to a local police station before anything is seized;

- the seizure is not made from a person at a permanent or regular place of business of his;

- force is not used;

- a notice in prescribed form (see Copyright and Rights in Performances (Notice of Seizure) Order 1989[84]) is left at the place where the seizure occurs.

Sentencing

13.74 Following amendments, most recently by the Legal Aid, Sentencing and Punishment of Offenders Act 2012 (Fines on Summary Conviction) Regulations 2015,[85] which came into force on 12 March 2015, s 107(4) provides:

(4) A person guilty of an offence under subsection (1)(a), (b), (d)(iv) or (e) is liable –

    (a) on summary conviction to imprisonment for a term not exceeding six months or a fine, or both;

    (b) on conviction on indictment to a fine or imprisonment for a term not exceeding ten years, or both.

(4A) A person guilty of an offence under subsection (2A) is liable –

    (a) on summary conviction to imprisonment for a term not exceeding three months or a fine, or both;

    (b) on conviction on indictment to a fine or imprisonment for a term not exceeding two years, or both.

(5) A person guilty of any other offence under this section is liable on summary conviction to imprisonment for a term not exceeding three months or a fine not exceeding level 5 on the standard scale, or both.

13.75 Following amendments, most recently by the Legal Aid, Sentencing and Punishment of Offenders Act 2012 (Fines on Summary Conviction) Regulations 2015, which came into force on 12 March 2015, s 198(5) provides:

---

[84] SI 1989/1006.
[85] SI 2015/664.

(5) A person guilty of an offence under subsection (1)(a), (b) or (d)(iii) is liable –

    (a)   on summary conviction to imprisonment for a term not exceeding six months or a fine or both;

    (b)   on conviction on indictment to a fine or imprisonment for a term not exceeding ten years, or both.

(5A) A person guilty of an offence under subsection (1A) is liable

    (a)   on summary conviction to imprisonment for a term not exceeding three months or a fine, or both;

    (b)   on conviction on indictment to a fine or imprisonment for a term not exceeding two years, or both.

(6) A person guilty of any other offence under this section is liable on summary conviction to a fine not exceeding level 5 on the standard scale or imprisonment for a term not exceeding six months, or both.

13.76 Copyright offences have not been covered by the Sentencing Guidelines Council. In *R v Carter*[86] – an appeal against a sentence of 9 months' imprisonment, on each of two counts under s 107, suspended for 2 years – it was said that counterfeiting of video tapes was a serious offence and to distribute pirated copies of film was, in effect, to steal, from the copyright's true owner, property for which he had to pay money in order to possess. The IPO have more recently published an interesting study of the criminal sanctions for copyright infringement available under the CDPA 1988 entitled 'Penalty Fair'.[87] The object of the study was to establish whether such sanctions were currently proportionate and correct. Overall the study concluded that:

> 'While there is no proof that higher sentences would act as a deterrent to online copyright crime, there is evidence to suggest that increasing the maximum sanction could be important in facilitating investigation and prosecution, now that there is a better foundation of civil cases on which courts can make decisions (in the absence of criminal case law precedents).'[88]

13.77 In July 2015 the Government consulted on increasing the maximum custodial sentence for criminal online copyright infringement offences from two to ten years. Following the consultation, the Government stated, in January 2016, that it intended to introduce to Parliament 'at the earliest available legislative opportunity' re-drafted offence provisions in relation to ss 107(2A) and 198(1A) of the CDPA, in addition to increasing the maximum custodial sentence to ten years in ss 107(4A) and 198(5A) of the CDPA.

13.78 *R v Umar Shahzad*[89] is a sentencing case involving an offence under CDPA 1988, s 296ZB(1)(c)(iv). The defendant was convicted on two counts of attempting to handle stolen goods and of possessing a device designed to circumvent effective technological measures contrary to s 296ZB(1)(c)(iv). The

---

[86]   (1992) 13 Cr App R (S) 576.
[87]   This report was published by the IPO on 4 March 2015.
[88]   'Penalty Fair?' p 5.
[89]   [2013] EWCA Crim 389.

CDPA charge against him arose from possession of electronic storage devices, including a micro-SD card reader containing 113 pirated games. He was sentenced to a 15-month sentence which was made up of 9 months' imprisonment concurrent on each of the handling charges and 6 months' imprisonment consecutive on CDPA charge. His appeal against the sentence was dismissed.

Forfeiture

13.79 Sections 108 and 199 empower a court to order infringing copies/illicit recordings to be 'delivered up' as a result of criminal proceedings. The court can make an order for the delivery up of these goods and articles to the copyright owner or such other person as the court may direct. Provision is made for appeals to be made against these orders.

13.80 After delivery up – either under s 108 or as a result of an application by the owner of the copyright under s 99 or equivalent for illicit copies – the goods/articles must be retained, pending a court decision on the making of an order for forfeiture or destruction. Goods and articles which have been seized and detained under s 100 may also be made the subject of a forfeiture order under s 114 – and similar provisions for seizures, under s 196, exist in s 204.

13.81 Sections 114A and 204A provides that where infringing copies or illicit recordings – which are connected with 'relevant' offences – come into the possession of any person, that person may apply for a forfeiture order. The application may be made as part of proceedings or by way of complaint. The equivalent provisions for Scotland are contained in ss 114B and 204B.

REGISTERED DESIGNS

13.82 Design law has been primarily governed in the UK by the Registered Designs Act 1949, as amended ('RDA 1949'). A 'design' in this context refers to the *appearance* of the whole or a part of a product resulting from the features of, and in particular, the lines, contours, colours, shape, texture or materials of the product or its ornamentation.[90] A design can be protected by a UK (or EU) registered design right to the extent that it is:

- *new* – a design shall be considered to be new if no identical design has been made available to the public; *and*
- *has individual character*. In this respect:

> ' . . . in order for a design to be considered to have individual character, the overall impression which that design produces on the informed user must be different from that produced on such a user by one or more earlier designs taken individually and viewed as a whole, not by an amalgam of various features of earlier designs'

---

[90] RDA 1949, s 1(2).

(see the CJEU case of *Karen Millen Fashions Ltd v Dunnes Stores, Dunnes Stores (Limerick) Ltd*[91]).

Intellectual Property Act 2014

13.83 The Intellectual Property Act 2014 ('IPA 2014') has brought sweeping changes to the law in this area. IPA 2014 was designed to modernise IP law and to enhance support for UK businesses in seeking to protect their IP rights both in the UK and abroad. The majority of the provisions of the IPA came into force on 1 October 2014.[92] For present purposes the most significant element of the Act is s 13, which, by way of amendments to the Registered Design Act 1949, introduced a new criminal offence of intentionally copying a UK or EU registered design. This now gives registered designs the same level of protection as copyright and trade marks. The offence requires that the relevant acts were done in the course of a business.

13.84 The new offence can be committed in one of two ways. First, intentionally copying a registered design under s 35ZA(1) of the RDA 1948 is made out if a person, in the course of a business, has intentionally copied a design; without the consent of its owner; whilst knowing (or having reason to believe) that the design is registered. The intentional copying must also result in making a product which is exactly like the design in question, or at least where a design has only been very slightly altered: 'with features that differ only in immaterial details'.[93] Second, the offence can also be committed by secondary use of a copied design: under s 35ZA(3) it is an offence for a person to knowingly use such an intentionally copied design in the course of business to profit from that copying. This includes using, marketing, importing, exporting, or stocking the design for one of those purposes.

13.85 The relevant acts must be carried out with intent. Accidental use of a copied registered design does not amount to an offence under this section. It is a defence for a person to show that they reasonably believed that the registration of the design was invalid;[94] or that the person either did not infringe the right in the design, or reasonably believed that the person did not do so.[95] Reference to 'using a product in the course of business' does not include circumstances where it has been used for a purpose which is merely incidental to the carrying on of the business (for example: where a copied design of a coffee machine is used to supply drinks to staff, rather than to customers). The offences apply to any intentional copying, or use of such copied designed that take place after 1 October 2014, and then only to designs which were registered at the time of the offence.

---

[91]   Case C-345/13, [2014] Bus LR 756.
[92]   Intellectual Property Act 2014 (Commencement No 3 and Transitional Provisions) Order 2014, SI 2014/2330.
[93]   RDA 1949, s 35ZA(1)(a)(ii).
[94]   RDA 1949, s 35ZA(4).
[95]   RDA 1949, s 35ZA(5).

13.86 A person convicted of an offence under s 35ZA is liable to (a) on conviction on indictment to imprisonment up to 10 years or a fine or both; or (b) on summary conviction in England and Wales to imprisonment for up to 6 months or a fine or both (12 months in Scotland).[96]

13.87 Prosecutions under the new provisions can be brought by Trading Standards, or by rights holders privately. There is no duty of enforcement placed on local authorities by the IPA 2014. The investigatory powers available to a local weights and measures authority or DETI in Northern Ireland for the purposes of the enforcement of s 35ZA, are contained in Sch 5 to the Consumer Rights Act 2015. This mirrors the position for s 93(2) of the Trade Marks Act 1994 and ss 107A and 198A of CDPA 1988. It is not anticipated that the new offence will lead to a flood of prosecutions; the Impact Assessment for the introduction of the offence estimated it was likely to provide the basis for around six prosecution cases per annum in the UK.

13.88 Powers of forfeiture are attached to the offences[97] – upon conviction, or upon satisfying the court that an offence under s 35ZA has been committed, application may be made for the forfeiture of relevant products or 'relevant articles' – articles which have been specifically designed or adapted for making relevant copies.

IPA 2014, s 13 Offence of unauthorised copying etc. of design in course of business

After section 35 of the Registered Designs Act 1949 insert –

'**35ZA Offence of unauthorised copying etc. of design in course of business**

(1) A person commits an offence if –

    (a)   in the course of a business, the person intentionally copies a registered design so as to make a product –
        (i)   exactly to that design, or
        (ii)   with features that differ only in from that design, and
    (b)   the person does so –
        (i)   knowing, or having reason to believe, that the design is a registered design, and
        (ii)   without the consent of the registered proprietor of the design.

(2) Subsection (3) applies in relation to a product where a registered design has been intentionally copied so as to make the product –

    (a)   exactly to the design, or
    (b)   with features that differ only in immaterial details from the design.

(3) A person commits an offence if –

    (a)   in the course of a business, the person offers, puts on the market, imports, exports or uses the product, or stocks it for one or more of those purposes,

---

[96]   RDA 1949, s 35ZA(8).
[97]   RDA 1949, s 35ZC.

(b)   the person does so without the consent of the registered proprietor of the
design, and

(c)   the person does so knowing, or having reason to believe, that –

(i)   a design has been intentionally copied without the consent of the
registered proprietor so as to make the product exactly to the
design or with features that differ only in immaterial details from
the design, and

(ii)   the design is a registered design.

(4) It is a defence for a person charged with an offence under this section to show
that the person reasonably believed that the registration of the design was invalid.

(5) It is also a defence for a person charged with an offence under this section to
show that the person –

(a)   did not infringe the right in the design, or

(b)   reasonably believed that the person did not do so.

(6) The reference in subsection (3) to using a product in the course of a business
does not include a reference to using it for a purpose which is merely incidental to
the carrying on of the business.

(7) In this section 'registered design' includes a registered Community design; and
a reference to the registered proprietor is, in the case of a registered Community
design, to be read as a reference to the holder.

(8) A person guilty of an offence under this section is liable –

(a)   on conviction on indictment, to imprisonment for a term not exceeding
ten years or to a fine or to both;

(b)   on summary conviction in England and Wales or Northern Ireland, to
imprisonment for a term not exceeding six months or to a fine or to
both;

(c)   on summary conviction in Scotland, to imprisonment for a term not
exceeding 12 months or to a fine or to both.

Design Opinions Service

13.89   IPA 2014, s 11 introduced through the addition of s 28A to the RDA
1948 the potential of the creation of a Design Opinions Service. It vests in the
Secretary of State the power to provide in Regulations for a non-binding
opinions service for designs, similar to that which already exists for patents. On
19 March 2015, the IPO launched a consultation seeking views on the detailed
implementing Regulations for the Design Opinions Service. The consultation
closed on 15 May 2015 and the outcome was not known at the time of writing.

Commentary

13.90   With the introduction of IPA 2014 and related regulations the UK
finally saw some long overdue radical reform of IP law. This has been viewed as
a practical, commercial and economic necessity in response to fast-changing
circumstances, particularly arising from rapid, game-changing technological

advances. The Digital Britain White Paper[98] had proposed amendments to UK copyright legislation – especially relating to the illicit use of peer-to-peer (P2P) file-sharing technology and the continuing global legal issues in this area. The Digital Economy Act 2010 subsequently sought to address certain issues arising from rapid technological developments including online infringement of copyright, liability of internet service providers, internet domain registries, copyright and performers' property rights penalties and public lending rights. Although s 56 of the Deregulation Act 2015 repeals ss 17 and 18 of the Digital Economy Act 2010 (which confer power on the Secretary of State to make regulations about the granting by courts of injunctions requiring the blocking of websites that infringe copyright) the courts have been willing to grant website blocking order under both s 37(1) of the Senior Courts Act 1981[99] and also under s 97A of CPDA 1988.[100]

13.91 In November 2010 the Prime Minister announced an independent review of how the Intellectual Property framework supports growth and innovation. The review – *Digital Opportunity – A review of Intellectual Property and Growth*[101] – reported to Government in May 2011 ('The Hargreaves Review'). The key recommendations, so far as copyright is concerned, included:

- The UK should have a 'Digital Copyright Exchange': a digital market place where licences in copyright content can be readily bought and sold, a form of online copyright shop. This has yet to be implemented.

- The Government should legislate to permit access to 'orphan works', where the owner cannot be traced. For example some copyrighted works remain locked away and unused because their authors either aren't known or can't be traced to give permission for use. In the worst cases, where one owner cannot be located – just one out of hundreds contained in a film or TV programme – they can effectively hold the interests of others to ransom as it becomes a criminal offence to exploit that work commercially. This has now been implemeted, with the advent of the Copyright and Rights in Performances (Certain Permitted Uses of Orphan Works) Regulations 2014[102] and Copyright and Rights in Performances (Licensing of Orphan Works) Regulations 2014.

- Updating what it is lawful to copy. This includes copying for private purposes (such as shifting music from a laptop to an mp3 player) and copying which does not conflict with the core aims of copyright – for example, digital copying of medical and other journals for computerised analysis in research. For example an academic working on malaria cannot draw on previous research through data mining because they cannot get

---

[98]   Published in June 2009.
[99]   *AG and Others v British Sky Broadcasting Ltd and Others* [2014] EWHC 2254 (Ch).
[100] *1967 Ltd and others v British Sky Broadcasting Ltd and Others* [2014] EWHC 3444 (Ch).
[101] Available at www.ipo.gov.uk/ipreview-finalreport.pdf.
[102] SI 2014/2861.

permission to copy the datasets they need to mine. The 2014 regulations go some considerable way to addresing these issues.

- The Government's IP policy decisions need to be more closely based on economic evidence and should pay more attention to the impact on non-rights holders and consumers. There has been real progress in this sphere. There has been genuine 'top down' recoginition of the impact of IP law and policy in these regards.

- Changes to the Intellectual Property Office's ('IPO') powers to enable it to help the IP framework adapt to future economic and technological change. Change in this respect has so far not been as swift or as radical as was hoped for.

13.92 The Government broadly accepted the proposals in its response (published in August 2011) and launched a Copyright Consultation. The final part of the Government's response to that Consultation was published in December 2012: 'Modernising Copyright: a modern, robust and flexible framework'. Within that response the Government proposes changes to the framework for 'copyright exceptions', including their intention to 'introduce greater freedoms in copyright law to allow third parties to use copyright works for a variety of economically and/or socially valuable purposes without the need to seek permission from copyright owners'. Reassurance is offered that 'protections for the interests of copyright owners and creators are built in to the revised framework'. Steps to implement changes based on the Hargreaves recommendations are finally beginning to gain momentum.

13.93 The Enterprise and Regulatory Reform Act 2013 ('ERRA') received Royal Assent on 25 April 2013. It ushers in a period of significant change to the law in the area of IP and copyright. Part 6 of the Act, ss 74–78, concern IP. Sections 75–78 are now in force, s 74 partially in force. These are principally enabling provisions, and have been followed by implementing statutory instruments and regulations. The sections of the Act concerning IP include, controversially, endowing the Secretary of State with the power to make changes to copyright exception by Order.[103] The Law Society had voiced concerns that the ramifications of creating new copyright exceptions is sufficiently commercially important that changes to them should be subject to the full scrutiny of primary legislation. Bodies representing, among others, professional photographers have expressed outrage at the latitude that the Act allows for the use of orphan works, and complain that they grant a licence to wealthy corporate entities to commandeer original work to their own commercial ends without recompensing the rightful owner of the work. This demonstrates the difficulties faced in seeking to balance the societal interests of modernising and liberalising the law of IP and copyright, against the legitimate economic concerns of trademark and copyright holders.

---

[103] Section 76.

13.94 The following is a summary of the most significant elements of the Act:

- Section 74 (only partially in force as of 4 September 2015): Envisages the repeal of s 52 of the Copyright, Designs and Patents Act 1988 so as to provide full copyright protection for the period of the author's life plus 70 years where an item has been mass produced (ie more than 50 copies have been made). This is likely to have a significant impact on the market for replicas of iconic designs – for example in the furniture market. It also creates a power to amend exceptions for copyright and rights in performances without affecting the existing criminal penalties regime.

- Section 76: Amended s 170 of the Copyright, Designs and Patents Act 1988 to give the Secretary of State the power to reduce the duration of copyright in existing works which are unpublished, pseudonymous or anonymous.

- Section 77: Made a series of amendments to Copyright, Designs and Patents Act 1988 to allow (through regulations: leading to the introduction of Copyright and Rights in Performances (Certain Permitted Uses of Orphan Works) Regulations 2014[104] and Copyright and Rights in Performances (Licensing of Orphan Works) Regulations 2014) for the introduction of systems for the licensing of 'orphan works' (for both commercial and non-commercial purposes) provided that a user can demonstrate that they had conducted a 'diligent search' for the owner of the orphan work before using it. It also provides for the authorisation of voluntary extended collective licensing schemes. This part also inserts a new Schedule into the Act which conferred power on the Secretary of State to require a licensing body to adopt a code of practice under certain circumstances, and which makes provision regarding licensing of performers' rights.

- Sections 75 and 78: Made provision for the implementation of EU Directive 2011/77/EU under the European Communities Act 1972, whilst retaining the current levels of penalty for infringement of copyright.

13.95 The tension between consumer privacy and the rights of copyright holders in the internet age, and the difficulties faced in pitching the level of regulation at the correct level, is demonstrated by the draft Code published by Ofcom in June 2012[105] concerned with ISP's responsibilities in relation to copyright infringement by their customers. Under s 124D of the Communications Act 2003 (as inserted by the Digital Economy Act 2010), Ofcom has a duty to issue a code for the purpose of regulating the initial obligations of ISPs to send notifications and provide copyright infringement lists to copyright owners on request. The code will initially cover the largest ISPs who together account for more than 93% of the retail broadband market in the UK. The draft code requires ISPs to send letters to customers, at least a

---

[104] SI 2014/2861.
[105] Consultation in relation to the Code closed in July 2012. It was anticipated that the Code be laid before Parliament by the end of January 2013; however, it has still not been laid at the time of writing in November 2016.

month apart, informing them when their account is connected to reports of suspected online copyright infringement. If a customer receives three letters or more within a 12-month period, anonymous information may be provided on request to copyright owners showing them which infringement reports are linked to that customer's account. The copyright owner may then seek a court order requiring the ISP to reveal the identity of the customer, with a view to taking legal action for infringement under the Copyright, Designs and Patent Act 1988. Further progress on implementation has been long awaited.[106]

OLYMPIC SYMBOL ETC (PROTECTION) ACT 1995

Introduction

13.96   Various words, terms, logos that are connected with the Olympic or Paralympic movementare protected by law to prevent an unauthorised association between people, goods or services and the movement or the Games.

13.97   The Olympic Symbol etc (Protection) Act 1995 ('OSPA 1995') provides for offences, in similar terms to the Trade Marks Act 1994, where 'a controlled representation' is applied.

13.98   Other marks associated with the Olympics and Paralympics are legally protected by a combination of registered trademarks, copyright, registered community designs, and common law.

Territorial jurisdiction

13.99   The Act has application throughout the UK.

Offences

13.100   The offences in the Act are contained in s 8(1)–(3) and mirror those in s 92(1)–(3) of the Trade Marks Act 1994.

> **8 Offences in relation to goods.**
>
> (1) A person shall be guilty of an offence if with a view to gain for himself or another, or with intent to cause loss to another, and without the consent of the proprietor, he –
>
> > (a)   applies a controlled representation to goods or their packaging,
> >
> > (b)   sells or lets for hire, offers or exposes for sale or hire or distributes goods which bear, or the packaging of which bears, such a representation, or
> >
> > (c)   has in his possession, custody or control in the course of a business any such goods with a view to the doing of anything, by himself or another, which would be an offence under paragraph (b) above.

---

[106] OFCOM reiterated their commitment to implementation in this sphere in their Annual Plan 2013/14 published 28 March 2013, but still no firm schedule for such implementation has been set.

(2) A person shall be guilty of an offence if with a view to gain for himself or another, or with intent to cause loss to another, and without the consent of the proprietor, he –

> (a) applies a controlled representation to material intended to be used –
>> (i) for labelling or packaging goods,
>> (ii) as a business paper in relation to goods, or
>> (iii) for advertising goods,
> (b) uses in the course of a business material bearing such a representation for labelling or packaging goods, as a business paper in relation to goods, or for advertising goods, or
> (c) has in his possession, custody or control in the course of a business any such material with a view to the doing of anything, by himself or another, which would be an offence under paragraph (b) above.

(3) A person shall be guilty of an offence if with a view to gain for himself or another, or with intent to cause loss to another, and without the consent of the proprietor, he –

> (a) makes an article specifically designed or adapted for making copies of a controlled representation, or
> (b) has such an article in his possession, custody or control in the course of a business, knowing or having reason to believe that it has been, or is to be, used to produce goods, or material for labelling or packaging goods, as a business paper in relation to goods, or for advertising goods.

13.101 A 'controlled representation' has the meaning given by s 3(1) – it is a representation of:

- the Olympic symbol (the symbol of the International Olympic Committee, consisting of five interlocking rings) or the Paralympic symbol (the symbol of the International Paralympic Committee which consists of three 'agitos'); or

- the Olympic motto ('Citius, altius, fortius') or the Paralympic motto ('Spirit in Motion'); or

- a protected word (Olympic, Olympian, Olympiad, Paralympic, Paralympian, Paralympiad their plurals, translations and anything similar to them); or

- a representation of something so similar to the Olympic symbol or the Olympic motto as to be likely to create in the public mind an association with it (such as 'Olympix').

References to the Olympic motto or a protected word include the motto or word in translation into any language.

Defences

13.102 Section 8(4) of the Act provides a statutory defence:

> (4) It shall be a defence for a person charged with an offence under this section to show that he believed on reasonable grounds that the use of the representation in the manner in which it was used, or was to be used, was not an infringement of

the Olympics association right.

13.103 The defence under s 8(4) is comparable to s 92(5) of the Trade Marks Act 1994, which has been considered in a number of cases that support the view that the section affords a positive and specific defence and does not provide a defence of good faith.

13.104 A person infringes the Olympics association right – subject to the Act's provisions, in particular, s 4(1)–(10) of the Act – if in the course of trade he uses 'a controlled representation' or a word so similar to a protected word as to be likely to create in the public mind an association with the Olympic Games or the Olympic movement (s 3) and this is done without the consent of 'the proprietor'. The provisions of the Act apply in relation to the Paralympics association right as they apply to the Olympics association right (so a reference to the Olympic Games, the Olympic motto, the Olympic movement and the Olympic symbol are treated as a reference to the Paralympic Games, the Paralympic motto, the Paralympic movement and the Paralympic symbol respectively).

13.105 For the purposes of s 3:

> ... a person uses a controlled representation if, in particular, he –
>
> (a)   affixes it to goods or the packaging thereof,
> (b)   incorporates it in a flag or banner,
> (c)   offers or exposes for sale, puts on the market or stocks for those purposes goods which bear it or whose packaging bears it,
> (d)   imports or exports goods which bear it or whose packaging bears it,
> (e)   offers or supplies services under a sign which consists of or contains it, or
> (f)   uses it on business papers or in advertising.

13.106 It will be seen that infringement under s 3 could only occur where the use is the course of trade – therefore, as with offences under s 92 of the Trade Marks Act 1994, those who commit criminal offences under s 8 can only be convicted where there is civil infringement and where the offender is acting in the course of a trade/business (by virtue of s 18 these terms are synonymous).

Restrictions on proceedings

13.107 There is no statutory time limit for s 8 offences. However, the provisions of s 9 of the Act, relating to Scotland should be noted.

> **9 Supplementary provisions as to summary proceedings in Scotland.**
>
> (1) Notwithstanding anything in section 136 of the Criminal Procedure (Scotland) Act 1995 section 331 of the Criminal Procedure (Scotland) Act 1975, summary proceedings in Scotland for an offence under this Act may be begun at any time within six months after the date on which evidence sufficient in the Lord Advocate's opinion to justify the proceedings came to his knowledge.
>
> (2) For the purposes of subsection (1) above –

(a) a certificate of the Lord Advocate as to the date mentioned in that subsection shall be conclusive evidence, and

(b) proceedings in Scotland shall be deemed to be begun on the date on which a warrant to apprehend or to cite the accused is granted, if such warrant is executed without undue delay.

Prosecutions

13.108 Any person (whether an individual or a body corporate), other than the Crown or its servants or agents, can be prosecuted under the Act. Section 10 of the Act provides that s 101 of the Trade Marks Act 1994 applies to offences under the Act.

Partnerships

13.109 Under s 101 of the Trade Marks Act 1994 partnerships must be prosecuted in the name of the firm and not that of the partners and any fine imposed following the partnership's conviction must be paid out of partnership assets. Where a partnership is guilty of an offence, every partner, other than a partner who is proved (on the balance of probabilities) to have been ignorant of or to have attempted to prevent the commission of the offence, is also guilty of the offence and liable to be proceeded against and punished.

Directors' liability

13.110 Section 101(5) of the Trade Marks Act 1994 contains a Director's liability provision (see Chapter 3, Criminal Enforcement).

Duty to enforce

13.111 Whilst not placing a duty of enforcement, as such, s 8A(1) of the Act provides that: 'A local weights and measures authority may enforce within their area the provisions of section 8.'

Powers of enforcement officers

13.112 The investigatory powers now available to a local weights and measures authority or the DETI for the purposes of the powers in s 8A, are contained in Sch 5 to the Consumer Rights Act 2015.

> **8A Enforcement by trading standards authority**
>
> (4) Nothing in this section shall be construed as authorising a local weights and measures authority to bring proceedings in Scotland for an offence.

Section 8B of the Act provides:

> (2) A constable in Scotland may arrest without warrant a person who the constable reasonably believes is committing or has committed an offence under section 8 of the Olympic Symbol etc. (Protection) Act 1995.

(3) Subsection (2) is without prejudice to any power of arrest which is otherwise exercisable by a constable in Scotland.

Sentencing

13.113 The penalties for s 8 offences, which were increased during a specified period for the London Olympic Games and Paralympic Games, are:

(a) on summary conviction, to a fine; and

(b) on conviction on indictment, to a fine.

13.114 The Act also provides for powers of forfeiture.

11 Forfeiture: England and Wales or Northern Ireland.

(1) Section 97 of the Trade Marks Act 1994 (which makes provision about the forfeiture of certain goods, material or articles which come into the possession of any person in connection with the investigation or prosecution of a relevant offence) shall also have effect with the following modifications.

(2) In subsection (1) (which describes the goods, material or articles concerned) –

    (a)   in paragraph (a), for 'sign identical to or likely to be mistaken for a registered trade mark' there shall be substituted 'representation within paragraph (a) or (b) of section 3(1) of the Olympic Symbol etc. (Protection) Act 1995', and

    (b)   in paragraphs (b) and (c), for 'sign' there shall be substituted 'representation'.

(3) In subsection (7)(a) (power of court to direct release instead of destruction on condition that offending sign erased etc.) for 'sign' there shall be substituted 'representation'.

(4) In subsection (8) (which defines 'relevant offence') for 'section 92 above (unauthorised use of trade mark etc. in relation to goods)' there shall be substituted 'section 8 of the Olympic Symbol etc. (Protection) Act 1995'.

12 Forfeiture: Scotland.

(1) Section 98 of the Trade Marks Act 1994 (which makes provision about the forfeiture of certain goods, material or articles on application by the procurator-fiscal or where a person is convicted of a relevant offence) shall also have effect with the following modifications.

(2) In subsection (1) (which describes the goods, material or articles concerned) –

    (a)   in paragraph (a), for 'sign identical to or likely to be mistaken for a registered trade mark' there shall be substituted 'representation within paragraph (a) or (b) of section 3(1) of the Olympic Symbol etc. (Protection) Act 1995', and

    (b)   in paragraphs (b) and (c), for 'sign' there shall be substituted 'representation'.

(3) In subsection (13) (power of court to direct release instead of destruction on condition that offending sign erased etc.) for 'sign' there shall be substituted 'representation'.

(4) In subsection (14), in the definition of 'relevant offence', for 'section 92 (unauthorised use of trade mark, &c. in relation to goods)' there shall be substituted 'section 8 of the Olympic Symbol etc. (Protection) Act 1995'.

ENFORCEMENT OF IP RIGHTS: CRIMINAL V CIVIL

Introduction

13.115

'The ability of holders of IP rights to enforce their rights through the courts in a particular jurisdiction is vital to that country's attractiveness to overseas investment. The UK sees its own IP enforcement system, whether civil or criminal, as crucial to its own economic future.'[107]

Criminal and civil liability for IP infringements will often arise in parallel from the same set of facts: counterfeiting of goods, and pirating copyrighted material are examples of such scenarios. The use of aggressive and misleading business practices, and failure to preserve the integrity and security of data are other, less obvious, areas where such dual liability arises.

13.116 Rights holders will therefore frequently have the following, often overlapping, options:

- pursue a civil claim;
- complain to the relevant enforcement authority in the hope that they bring criminal proceedings;
- bring a private prosecution pursuant to s 6(1) of the Prosecution of Offences Act 1985; or
- a combination of the above.

13.117 An interesting example of a case where a combination of civil and criminal proceedings were brought was in *Football Association Premier League Ltd v QC Leisure* (C-403/08)[108] and *Murphy v Media Protection Services Ltd* (C-429/08),[109] where the actions were against a pub landlady in Portsmouth who was found to have screened Premier League football matches using a foreign decoder card, contrary to s 298 of the CPDA. The Grand Chamber of the CJEU subsequently considered references in both cases together. Parallel proceedings should be approached with caution as they often

---

[107] IPO Report 'Prevention and Cure – The UK IP Crime Strategy 2011'. Foreword by Baroness Wilcox.

[108] [2011] FSR 1.

[109] [2012] FSR 1.

raise difficult procedural issues and require careful oversight. A number of the most commonplace issues are addressed below.

Control

13.118 A claimant in civil proceedings retains substantial control over proceedings, for example in relation to disclosure of material and the pace of litigation. Where the relevant enforcement authority proceeds with a criminal investigation and prosecution in a particular case, a rights holder with a vested interest has no power to influence the course of proceedings. This highlights a significant potential advantage to affected rights holders launching private prosecutions: control over proceedings. This is of course subject to the DPP's discretion to step in and take over such proceedings, and if deemed appropriate, to then bring them to a close.

13.119 Public funding of criminal enforcement agencies has been under constant, and brutal downward pressure, and despite it being widely acknowledged that the overall level of IP crime has increased, actual prosecutions and cautions for trade mark and copyright offences have seen a reduction over the last measured period.[110] It was accepted in the recent IP Crime Group reports by the IPO that IP rights holders are playing a more important role in enforcement due to 'the pressures on public sector spending cuts'. In this environment the opportunity for rights holders to choose whether, and when, to initiate private prosecutions to protect their interests has become increasingly attractive. Though traditionally industry rights groups have been more proactive in pursuing private prosecutions (the film and music industries are prime examples), this is beginning to change as individual companies recognise that launching private prosecutions may be in their individual commercial interest.

Complexity

13.120 Not all cases will be suitable for trial in the criminal courts.[111] Copyright cases in particular may involve the consideration of complex questions concerning technical factual matters, and the proper application of the relevant law to them. *R v Gilham*[112] is an example of a case which concerned the precise use made of complicated electronic devices. Criminal proceedings were brought against the defendant arising from his dealings in 'modchips'. On appeal it was found that the trial judge in the crown court, faced with a highly technical interaction of law and fact, failed to properly direct the jury (the conviction was nevertheless upheld). Similar potential difficulties led Stanley Burnton LJ in *R v Higgs*[113] to recommend that such cases should be tried in the civil courts before specialist judges:

---

[110] See IP Crime Group Annual Report 2011–12, p 3.
[111] See Sharp and Smith, 'The interplay between civil and criminal IP litigation in the UK' (2012) 7(8) *Journal of Intellectual Property Law & Practice*.
[112] [2009] EWCA Crim 2293.
[113] [2008] FSR 34.

'They can be tried so much more efficiently in terms of cost and time than before a jury, and questions of law can if necessary be determined on appeal on the basis of clear findings of fact. In appropriate cases, the Court will grant injunctive relief, and a breach of an injunction will lead to punishment for contempt of court.'

Investigatory powers

13.121 The full range of investigatory powers outlined above, and those under the Police and Criminal Evidence Act 1984, are only available to the police or prosecuting authorities. If the police have investigated, but the CPS or Trading Standards are unwilling to prosecute, then a person considering a private prosecution – in the interests of preserving access to potentially useful material – should contact the police or prosecution authority before any material is returned to its owner. In deciding whether or not to retain such material, Leveson LJ set out factors to be considered in *Scopelight Ltd v Chief Constable of Northumbria Police & FACT*,[114] para 53:

'... the identity and motive of the potential prosecutor; the gravity of the allegation along with the reasoning behind the negative decision of the CPS and thus the extent to which, in this case, the public have a legitimate interest in the criminal prosecution of this conduct; the police view of the significance of what has been retained; and any material fact concerning the proposed defendant. All this falls to be considered so that a balanced decision can be reached upon whether retention is necessary "in all the circumstances". Such a decision would be capable of challenge on traditional public law grounds.'

Privilege against self-incrimination

13.122 Derogations have been made from the general right of privilege against self-incrimination. One of the most significant by s 72 of the Senior Courts Act 1981 which provides that a person shall not be excused from answering questions or complying with an order in relation to proceedings for infringement of IP rights, where such an answer or compliance may tend to expose that person to proceedings for a related criminal offence. Very helpful guidance in relation to the meaning of 'intellectual property' in this context was given by the Court of Appeal in two linked cases arising from 'Phone Hacking' litigation: *Coogan v News Group Newspapers Ltd & Glenn Mulcaire, Phillips v the same*.[115]

Disclosure and collateral use of material

13.123 Running parallel proceedings often raises complicated issues in relation to disclosure, and the use which can be made of material received.

---

[114] [2010] QB 438.
[115] [2012] 2 All ER 74, see interesting commentary on this point in Sharp and Smith, 'The interplay between civil and criminal IP litigation in the UK' (2012) 7(8) *JIPL & Practice*.

13.124 A claimant in civil proceedings can rely on legal professional privilege or litigation advice privilege to restrict the range of material which must be disclosed. However, material generated by a rights holder pursuing a private prosecution may not automatically attract privilege in the same way, and may in certain circumstances therefore have to be disclosed to the accused. Great care must therefore be taken in relation to the generation and disclosure of documents during both the preparation and running of private prosecutions.

13.125 Similarly, where parallel proceedings are contemplated, or embarked upon, careful consideration must be given to the disclosure and use which may be made of documents generated or disclosed in the civil proceedings, by those involved in the criminal proceedings, and vice versa. The law relating to the use in collateral proceedings of evidence obtained in the civil courts is governed by r 31.22 of the CPR.[116] The consent of the relevant court can be sought for material to be disclosed or used in parallel proceedings, and is often granted. The senior courts have not always taken a very consistent approach on this issue, see *Marlwood Commercial Inc v Kozeny*[117] and *SITA UK Group Holdings Ltd v Serruys*.[118] Section 17 of the Criminal Procedure and Investigations Act 1996 prohibits a defendant's collateral use of unused material disclosed by the prosecution. However, the prosecution can disclose such material to a third party where it is in the interests of justice to do so. Part 9 of the Enterprise Act 2002 places restrictions on disclosure for the purposes of civil and criminal proceedings (see Chapter 6, Information). However, s 241A of the Enterprise Act 2002 and the Enterprise Act 2002 (Disclosure of Information for Civil Proceedings etc.) Order 2007 apply particularly to disclosure concerning intellectual property matters.

Cost

13.126 Plainly, allowing a prosecuting authority to bear the cost of investigation and prosecution is the cheapest route – however, rights holders are increasingly frustrated at the relatively low priority accorded to infringements of their rights by the publicly funded prosecution authorities. Civil action will usually be the most expensive option, although the Patents Court has introduced a small claims track for the protection of all IP rights for damages of less than £5,000. Like the small claims track of the County Court, it will consist of an informal hearing without legal representation, therefore ensuring proportionate costs in the case. It is now possible for judges in the Patents Court to issue non-binding preliminary opinions on the merits of a particular case (see *Weight Watchers Ltd v Love Bites Ltd*[119] and *Fayus v Flying Trade*[120]) which will provide a useful tool in early settlement and therefore in cost

---

[116] See also Practice Direction to CPR Part 25 concerning undertakings not to use material obtained under a civil search order or freezing injunction in other (civil or criminal) proceedings.

[117] [2004] 3 All ER 648.

[118] [2009] EWHC 869 (QB).

[119] [2012] EWPCC 43.

[120] [2012] EWPCC 11.

reduction. The cost of private prosecutions depends very much on the scale of the proceedings, however when compared to the quickly escalating costs incurred in comparable civil actions, private prosecutions can be relatively cost effective; it is worth noting that the costs of the prosecution can be recovered from convicted defendants.

Agreements between a private prosecutor and a public enforcer

13.127   The case of *R (on the application of Virgin Media Ltd) v Zinga (Munaf Ahmed)*[121] was an important decision concerning issues that may arise where a private prosecutor seeks to bring confiscation proceedings, and the propriety of partnerships, and financial agreements, between private prosecutors and public enforcers such as the police. In *Zinga* the criminal prosecution was brought by Virgin Media Ltd against the defendants for selling equipment and software which enabled customers to obtain Virgin's media services without payment. Virgin agreed to donate 25% of any sums recovered under a compensation order to the police. The Court of Appeal confirmed that private prosecutors were entitled to pursue confiscation under POCA; and the agreement that Virgin would donate a proportion of any sum recovered under a confiscation order to the police did not, in the circumstances of the case, amount to an abuse of process.

13.128   The court remarked that there had been a pattern of increasing private prosecutions, including cases which presented potential conflicts of interest from the interrelationship between the public interest/public bodies, and the private prosecutor.[122] The court emphasised that further guidance from the Home Office should be forthcoming. It is clear from the ruling that parties potentially embarking on prosecutions of this kind must be careful to behave with the upmost probity and openness throughout proceedings in so far as any private/public agreements are concerned.

13.129   Regard must also be had to the guidance given in *R v Hounsham (Robin Edward)*[123] if any such financial arrangements under the Police Act 1996, s 93(1) are reached. In *R (on the application of Helidon Vuciterni and Alsat UK Limited) v Brent Magistrates' Court and Brent and Harrow Trading Standards Service*[124] the court remarked to the effect that it was not necessarily unlawful for proceedings to be indemnified by a private party, though it may be of concern if the prosecution was *only* brought at behest of and funded by powerful, wealthy corporation. Prosecutors must ensure that they can justify the cases they bring as being in the public interest.

---

[121]   [2014] EWCA Crim 52.
[122]   See paras 55–63.
[123]   [2005] EWCA Crim 1366.
[124]   [2012] EWCA 2140 (Admin).

CHAPTER 14

PRODUCT SAFETY

CONTENTS

INTRODUCTION

14.1

> Every day of our lives we consume, use, or simply come into contact with countless different products. We should be able to assume that those products are safe. Not absolutely safe – that remains unattainable. Nor safe at unbearable cost to industry – that would put innovation at risk. But as safe as is reasonable to expect.

Department of Trade and Industry – Guide to the Consumer Protection Act 1987 – revised November 2001.

14.2 As a Member State of the European Union, in the UK product safety is governed by a wider framework. This new regulatory framework (more often called the 'New Legislative Framework') has the objective of strengthening the effectiveness of the Union's legislation on product safety. All UK product safety work is now determined by this framework. It is an *'integrated industrial policy for the globalisation era'* consisting of three strands:

- Regulation 765/2008/EC on accreditation and market surveillance ('RAMS');
- Decision 768/2008/EC establishing a common framework for the marketing of products, that is sector-specific legislation;
- General Product Safety Directive 2001/95/EC ('GPSD').

14.3 RAMS places obligations on Member States to carry out market surveillance and have appropriate measures in place. 'Market surveillance' means the activities carried out and measures taken by public authorities to ensure that products comply with the requirements set out in the relevant Community harmonisation legislation and do not endanger health, safety or any other aspect of public interest protection.

14.4 The GPSD is implemented in the UK by the General Product Safety Regulations 2005 ('GPSR'), which are addressed in more detail below. Following public consultation on the revision of the GPSD, the Commission proposed on 13 February 2013 a new set of rules consisting of a proposal for a Regulation on Consumer Product Safety and a proposal for a Regulation for Market Surveillance of Product, as well as non-legislative documents. These are being discussed in the European Parliament and the Council of the EU.

14.5 The Decision outlines the framework that all future Directives must meet to ensure the safety of community harmonised products. It should be noted that there is now a working relationship between the GPSD and RAMS. The GPSD first introduced requirements on the organisation and performance of market surveillance for health and safety aspects of (non-food) consumer products – now with RAMS there are two horizontal pieces of community law containing requirements for market surveillance. The GPSD will still ensure a high level of consumer protection with general obligations for producers and distributors, market surveillance for products already placed on the EU market under its scope, and a system of rapid exchange of information and action, RAPEX. The Guidelines on the application of the GPSD and RAMS give an application hierarchy as set out below, but it is envisaged that in the future the safety requirements will be contained in sector specific legislation or the GPSD, leaving the enforcement measures to RAMS alone.

Risks	Risk to health and safety of consumers	Other risks (health and safety at the workplace, environment security)
Serious	GPSD (Arts 6–18) RAMS (Arts 16–26)	RAMS (Arts 16–26)
Non-serious	GPSD (Arts 6–18) RAMS (Arts 16–26)	RAMS (Arts 16–26)

14.6 Much of the legislation concerning product safety, therefore, derives from European Directives and Regulations such as that relating to cosmetics, toys, aerosols and electrical appliances – but there still exists some national legislation in areas such as furniture, nightwear flammability and plugs and sockets. This chapter outlines the principal legislation that aims to ensure products are safe to use and which creates criminal consequences for those who contravene its provisions. The legislative framework is set out under the following three headings:

- Consumer Protection Act 1987 ('CPA 1987');
- European Communities Act 1972;
- General Product Safety Regulations 2005 ('GPSR').

14.7 This structure was described by Bingham LCJ in *R v Liverpool City Council, Ex parte Baby Products Association and Another*[1] in the following manner:

'It is apparent that these provisions comprise a detailed and carefully-crafted code designed, on the one hand, to promote the very important objective of protecting the public against unsafe consumer products and, on the other, to give fair protection to the business interests of manufacturers and suppliers.'

14.8 The European Commission has made a similar statement, reflecting these aims:

'Market surveillance plays a crucial role in the field of consumer product safety as even the best rules are worth little if they are not enforced properly. That is why effective market surveillance is so important; not only to protect consumers from unsafe products but also to ensure a level playing field for reputable businesses.'

---

[1] (CO/3733/99).

CONSUMER PROTECTION ACT 1987

Introduction

14.9 The CPA 1987 is the last in a series of statutes designed to ensure the safety of consumer goods in the UK.

14.10 Part I of the CPA 1987 has the effect of implementing the product liability Directive[2] and provides for civil liability where any damage is caused wholly or partly by a defect in a product. This has been extended to cover food sold in its raw state, 'primary agricultural products and game'.[3]

14.11 Part II of the Act consolidated previous consumer safety laws and introduced a general safety requirement. this was subsequently repealed and has largely been replaced by the GPSR. The CPA 1987 provides regulation-making powers for the Secretary of State concerning the safety of specific products. Selling or offering for sale those products in breach of any provisions made under Part II is an offence. The CPA 1987 also introduced new powers to local authorities to issue suspension notices and to apply for forfeiture orders whether or not a person has been convicted of an offence in relation to them. The powers of enforcement in the CPA 1987 have been amended by the Consumer Rights Act 2015 ('CRA 2015').

Application and jurisdiction

14.12 The CPA 1987 applies throughout Great Britain. Section 11(1) provides for the making of 'safety regulations', which are the key provisions of Part II of the Act. In broad terms, goods must be safe, unsafe goods must not be made available to persons generally or to particular classes of person and appropriate information must be, and inappropriate information must not be, provided. The meaning of 'safe' is given in s 19(1) and (2). Section 11(2) lists the types of provisions that the 'safety regulations' may contain. Some Regulations are jointly made under s 11 and the European Communities Act 1972 – eg the Toys (Safety) Regulations 2011. The Consumer Protection Act 1987 (Commencement No 1) Order 1987[4] made provision for regulations made under previous legislation, including the Consumer Protection Act 1961, to be treated as though they had been made under s 11.

14.13 Much domestic legislation has been repealed as a result of the government's Red Tape Challenge, which led to the implementation of the Product Safety (Revocation) Regulations 2012 and the Product Safety Amendment and Revocation Regulations 2012. However, despite the

---

2   Council Directive 85/374/EEC on the approximation of the laws, regulations and administrative provisions of the Member States concerning liability for defective products.

3   Directive 1999/34/EC implemented in England and Wales by the Consumer Protection Act 1987 (Product Liability) (Modification) Order 2000, SI 2000/2771 and in Scotland by the Consumer Protection Act 1987 (Product Liability) (Modification) (Scotland) Order 2001, SSI 2001/265.

4   SI 1987/1680.

government rhetoric with regard to easing burdens on business, the products concerned still fall within the jurisdiction of general product safety. For example, restrictions on the use of cords in children's clothing are now found in BS EN 14682:2014 'Safety of children's clothing. Cords and drawstrings on children's clothing. Specifications'. Another example is that asbestos products are now controlled via REACH (see later) rather than domestic legislation. A brief summary of the remaining regulations made, or deemed to have been made, under s 11 is given below:

UK secondary legislation

Oil Heaters (Safety) Regulations 1977[5]

14.14 Controls on domestic oil heaters that must also have warnings against various hazards and specifies construction and mechanical requirements.

Filament Lamps for Vehicles (Safety) Regulations 1982[6]

14.15 Prohibits the supply of lamps for motor vehicles unless they bear the ECE Approval mark.

Nightwear (Safety) Regulations 1985[7]

14.16

- Children's nightdresses and dressing gowns must comply with flammability requirements.
- Pyjamas, babies garments and bath robes and adult nightwear must be labelled:

KEEP AWAY FROM FIRE

or

LOW FLAMMABILITY TO BS 5722

Action may also be taken under the GPSR since flammability performance requirements for children's nightwear introduced by the European standard: BS EN 14878 *Textiles – Burning behaviour of children's nightwear – Specification.*

---

[5]   SI 1977/167.
[6]   SI 1982/444.
[7]   SI 1985/2043.

Furniture and Furnishings (Fire) (Safety) Regulations 1988[8]

14.17 Applies to new and second-hand furniture which contains upholstery intended for private use in a dwelling. All new furniture must carry a display label at the point of sale:

- prominent position;
- clearly visible.

All new furniture must carry a permanent label either full or short which is securely attached on any external surface. Upholstery (except mattresses, bed bases, pillows and cushions) must pass the cigarette test specified in BS 5852: Part 1 1979. Filling material and fillings in all furniture (except pillows and cushions with a primary cover which passes the relevant ignitability test) must pass the relevant ignitability test. Permanent covers on, and loose and stretch covers for all furniture (except mattresses, bed bases, pillows, cushions and baby nests) must pass the match test unless (in the case of permanent covers) an interliner is fitted. Manufacturers and importers must keep records for 5 years from date of supply:

- results of any relevant test that has been carried out;
- how the test results relate to particular pieces of furniture;
- how records are related to the information given on labels, batch numbers or other marks.

14.18 In *Northumberland County Council v PR Manufacturing Ltd (t/a Paul Rosco)*[9] the prosecution's methods of testing garden chair cushions, which, it was alleged, did not satisfy the requirements of the Furniture and Fittings (Fire) (Safety) Regulations 1988 were attacked by the defendant as flawed. The defendant relied on subsequent tests on different cushions. The magistrates preferred the defendant's test as the more accurate and dismissed the charges. The appeal was allowed, the not guilty verdict was ordered to be set aside and the matter will be remitted to a differently constituted Bench for a new trial. Beatson J said:

> 'It is inconsistent and an error of law to conclude that the prosecution's test satisfied the 1988 Regulations and the British Standards and that the Respondent had not complied with regulation 6(2)(b) but that the result of the test could not be relied upon in order to bring in a guilty verdict in respect of the charges brought under section 12(1) of the Consumer Protection Act.'

---

8   SI 1988/1324.
9   [2004] EWHC 112 (Admin).

Food Imitations (Safety) Regulations 1989[10]

14.19 Prohibits supply etc of manufactured goods which are ordinarily intended for private use and are not food but which:

(a) have a form, odour, colour, appearance, packaging, labelling, volume or size which is likely to cause persons, in particular, children to confuse them with food and in consequence to place them in their mouths or suck them or swallow them; and

(b) where such action as is mentioned in (a) above is taken in relation to them, may cause death or personal injury.

Motor Vehicle Tyres (Safety) Regulations 1994[11]

14.20 New tyres must be marked with an approval notice in accordance with ECE Regulation 30. Retread tyres must conform to an approved type, the carcass must be no more than 7 years old, be permanently marked to enable identification of the original manufacturer and be marked RETREAD. Part worn tyres must not have cuts, internal lumps and bulges, exposed ply, penetration damage when fully inflated and have 2mm grooves. Should be marked PART WORN and bear an approval mark, speed category and load capacity. Both retreads and part worn tyres, if repaired, must be properly repaired.

Plugs and Sockets etc (Safety) Regulations 1994[12]

14.21 Standard plug must:

- contain a BS 1362 fuse;
- comply with BS 1363 (have insulation on live and neutral pins) or equivalent level of safety;
- be approved by notified body.

All other electrical devices must comply with relevant standards:

Round-pin plugs, sockets or adaptors	BS 546
2-pin reversible plugs or shaver sockets	BS 4573
Fuses intended for standard plugs	BS 1362
Cartridge fuses (up to 5A) for round-pin plugs	BS 646
Adaptors	BS 5733

---

[10] SI 1989/1291.
[11] SI 1994/3117.
[12] SI 1994/1768.

14.22   Electrical Appliances must be fitted with:

- BS 1363 plug which has a fuse of the correct rating made to BS 1362;
- non-UK plug complying with IEC 884–1 which is enclosed by a conversion plug which can only be removed with a tool.

14.23   Standard plug or conversion plug must be:

- marked with or bear a label legibly marked with words, marks or abbreviations of name and reference number of the approving organisation eg BEAB, ASTA, BSI;
- be marked with or accompanied by a notice in English which gives information on safe usage;
- must not give false information re approval.

N-Nitrosamines and N-Nitrostable Substances in Elastomer Rubber Teats and Dummies (Safety) Regulations 1995[13]

14.24   Teats and dummies shall not, after saliva test, release 0.1 mg/kg of N-nitrosamines or N-Nitrostable substances.

Road Vehicles (Brake Linings) Safety Regulations 1999[14]

14.25   Prohibition on supply/fitting of brake linings which contain asbestos to a vehicle.

Except for fitting to a vehicle first used before 1 January 1973 and clearly marked:

'ILLEGAL TO FIT TO POST – 1972 VEHICLES'

Fireworks Regulations 2004[15]

14.26

- Prohibits supply of an excessively loud category 3 firework.
- Prohibits retail supply of > 50 kg unless require certain information and person buying shows licence or registration certificate.
- Prohibits supply between certain dates unless the person holds an all year round licence.
- Provides for a statutory notice re selling to under 18 years.

---

[13]   SI 1995/1012.
[14]   SI 1999/2978.
[15]   SI 2004/1836.

The duty of enforcement is transferred in relation to some aspects of these Regulations from weights and measures authorities to other enforcers. For the Fireworks (Scotland) Regulations 2004, it is transferred to the police.

Aerosol Dispensers Regulations 2009[16]

14.27 Prohibits the supply etc of relevant aerosol dispensers which are not marked with the 'compliance mark' to show compliance with Directive and construction requirements.

Pedal Bicycles (Safety) Regulations 2010[17]

14.28 Provide that new bicycles either assembled or unassembled which have a saddle height of 635 mm must have:

- a bell;
- correctly adjusted brakes;
- reflectors front and rear wheels and pedals;
- lights or reflectors front and rear.

The construction requirements are covered by GPSR using BS EN ISO 4210.

'New Approach' Regulations

14.29 The following Regulations implement European 'New Approach' Directives but are made under the CPA 1987 – the offences, powers etc are therefore under the Act as opposed to the other 'New Approach' statutory instruments, which are made under the European Communities Act 1972, where such matters are self-contained. These are so called 'CE marking' regulations.

Electrical Equipment (Safety) Regulations 1994[18]

14.30 The Regulations implement Council Directive 73/23/EEC – the Low Voltage Directive (LVD) as modified. Only electrical equipment which does not jeopardise the safety of people, domestic animals and property shall be placed on the market. Regulation 14 – prohibition on supply – provides that no person shall supply any electrical equipment in respect of which the requirements of regs 5(1) (safe, constructed in accordance with principal elements of the safety objectives) and 9(1) (affixing of CE marking) are not satisfied.

---

[16] SI 2009/2824.
[17] SI 2010/198.
[18] SI 1994/3260.

Gas Appliances (Safety) Regulations 1995[19]

14.31   The Regulations implement Council Directive 90/396/EEC relating to appliances burning gaseous fuels and provide that:

- No manufacturer etc shall supply an appliance which does not satisfy essential safety requirements.

- No person shall supply an appliance which when normally used is not safe.

- No person shall supply an appliance to which the CE mark has not been affixed.

- No manufacturer or his authorised representative established in the Community shall supply an appliance or a fitting in respect of which there is not in force at that time an EC type-examination certificate and an EC declaration of conformity to type.

Medical Devices Regulations 2002[20]

14.32   Implements three European Community Directives: Council Directive 90/385/EEC on the approximation of the laws of the Member States relating to active implantable medical devices, Council Directive 93/42/EEC concerning medical devices,[21] and Directive 98/79/EC of the European Parliament and of the Council on *in vitro* diagnostic medical devices[22] ('the Medical Devices Directives'). Each weights and measures authority shall enforce concurrently with the Secretary of State that part of the regulations (Part 11) that relate to consumer goods. Enforcement in relation to non-consumer devices falls to the Medical and Healthcare products Regulatory Agency.

Toys (Safety) Regulations 2011[23]

14.33   The Toy Safety Directive 2009/48/EC was one of the first to be aligned into the new framework and has been transposed into the UK by the Toys Safety Regulations 2011.[24] Subject to certain exceptions (eg playground equipment intended for public use), 'Toys are products designed or intended (whether or not exclusively) for use in play by children under 14 years old'. In *PMS International Group plc v North East Lincolnshire Council; In the Pink Ltd v Same*[25] the prosecution argued that a stationery set, which included small safety scissors, a small stapler, pens and a craft knife and other objects – the packaging of which displayed a 'CE' mark – was a toy and failed to meet the warning requirements and safety standards of the Toys (Safety) Regulations 1995. The defendants disputed that it was a toy and their appeal

---

[19]   SI 1995/1629.
[20]   SI 2002/618.
[21]   OJ L169, 12.7.1993, p 1.
[22]   OJ L331, 7.12.1998, p 1.
[23]   SI 2011/1881.
[24]   OJ L170, 30.6.2009, p 1.
[25]   [2005] EWHC 1111 (Admin).

against the justices' decision that it was a toy was dismissed. The justices had properly directed themselves – per Beatson J:

> 'It was ... open to the justices to find that the product was designed or clearly intended for use in play, having regard to the objective characteristics of the product, including appearance and presentation.'

14.34 The 2011 Regulations place an obligation on manufacturers/importers to only supply toys which comply with essential safety requirements, consisting of general and particular requirements. Users and third parties must be protected when toys are used as intended or in a foreseeable way, bearing in mind the normal behaviour of children. The particular risks cover:

- physical and mechanical properties;
- flammability;
- chemical properties;
- electrical properties;
- hygiene;
- radioactivity.

14.35 Before a product is placed on the market the manufacturer must compile the technical file, which makes it possible to assess whether the toy complies with the requirements of the Directive and the Declaration of conformity. A Declaration of conformity must be drawn up in at least one of the official languages of the community. Both sets of documents can be kept electronically and must:

- be kept for 10 years;
- be made available for inspection within a reasonable time;
- be held by the importer, the manufacturer or their representative if they have no community presence.

14.36 Manufacturers also have an obligation to have procedures in place to ensure toys comply with the essential safety requirements. Importers have an obligation to ensure that this has been done and to produce the documentation when required. Distributors have an obligation to verify that the toy bears the correct labelling. Both manufacturers and importers have an obligation to monitor the safety of toys by carrying out sample testing of marketed toys and investigating any complaints. It could be said that in complying with the obligations required under this new framework an economic operator is acting with all due diligence and so the traditional statutory defence is redundant.

Offences

14.37 A breach of the 'safety regulations' is not an offence in itself (s 11(4) – Safety regulations shall not provide for any contravention of the regulations to be an offence). Section 12 provides for offences where there is a contravention or non-compliance or a failure to provide information in accordance with requirements of the 'safety regulations'.

12 Offences against the safety regulations

(1) Where safety regulations prohibit a person from supplying or offering or agreeing to supply any goods or from exposing or possessing any goods for supply, that person shall be guilty of an offence if he contravenes the prohibition.

(2) Where safety regulations require a person who makes or processes any goods in the course of carrying on a business –

(a) to carry out a particular test or use a particular procedure in connection with the making or processing of the goods with a view to ascertaining whether the goods satisfy any requirements of such regulations; or

(b) to deal or not to deal in a particular way with a quantity of the goods of which the whole or part does not satisfy such a test or does not satisfy standards connected with such a procedure,

that person shall be guilty of an offence if he does not comply with the requirement.

(3) If a person contravenes a provision of safety regulations which prohibits or requires the provision, by means of a mark or otherwise, of information of a particular kind in relation to goods, he shall be guilty of an offence.

(4) Where safety regulations require any person to give information to another for the purpose of enabling that other to exercise any function, that person shall be guilty of an offence if –

(a) he fails without reasonable cause to comply with the requirement; or

(b) in giving the information which is required of him –

(i) he makes any statement which he knows is false in a material particular; or

(ii) he recklessly makes any statement which is false in a material particular.

14.38 Under s 13(1)(a), the Secretary of State may serve a notice on any person prohibiting him from supplying, offering to supply, exposing for supply, or possessing for supply, any relevant goods which are considered unsafe, except with the consent of the Secretary of State and in accordance with the conditions (if any) on which the consent is given. Under s 13(1)(b) the Secretary of State may require a supplier to publish, at his own expense, a warning about any relevant goods which the Secretary of State considers are unsafe. It is an offence under s 13(4) for a person to contravene a prohibition notice or a notice to warn.

14.39 An enforcement authority may serve a suspension notice on any person who they have grounds to suspect is contravening any safety provision under s 14. This has the effect of prohibiting the person on whom the notice is served from supplying the goods, offering to supply them, agreeing to supply them or exposing them for supply for up to 6 months. A suspension notice may also require the person on whom it is served to keep the enforcement authority informed on the whereabouts of all the goods in question. Any person who contravenes a suspension notice is guilty of an offence under s 14(6).

Supply

14.40 Section 46 extensively sets out the meaning of the word 'supply'. Section 46(1) states:

46 Meaning of "supply"

(1) Subject to the following provisions of this section, references in this Act to supplying goods shall be construed as references to doing any of the following, whether as principal or agent, that is to say—

    (a)   selling, hiring out or lending the goods;

    (b)   entering into a hire-purchase agreement to furnish the goods;

    (c)   the performance of any contract for work and materials to furnish the goods;

    (d)   providing the goods in exchange for any consideration other than money;

    (e)   providing the goods in or in connection with the performance of any statutory function; or

    (f)   giving the goods as a prize or otherwise making a gift of the goods;

and, in relation to gas or water, those references shall be construed as including references to providing the service by which the gas or water is made available for use.

(2) For the purposes of any reference in this Act to supplying goods, where a person ("the ostensible supplier") supplies goods to another person ("the customer") under a hire-purchase agreement, conditional sale agreement or credit-sale agreement or under an agreement for the hiring of goods (other than a hire-purchase agreement) and the ostensible supplier—

    (a)   carries on the business of financing the provision of goods for others by means of such agreements; and

    (b)   in the course of that business acquired his interest in the goods supplied to the customer as a means of financing the provision of them for the customer by a further person ("the effective supplier"),

the effective supplier and not the ostensible supplier shall be treated as supplying the goods to the customer.

(3) Subject to subsection (4) below, the performance of any contract by the erection of any building or structure on any land or by the carrying out of any other building works shall be treated for the purposes of this Act as a supply of goods in so far as, but only in so far as, it involves the provision of any goods to any person by means of their incorporation into the building, structure or works.

(4) Except for the purposes of, and in relation to, notices to warn, references in this Act to supplying goods shall not include references to supplying goods comprised in land where the supply is effected by the creation or disposal of an interest in the land.

(5) Except in Part I of this Act references in this Act to a person's supplying goods shall be confined to references to that person's supplying goods in the course of a

business of his, but for the purposes of this subsection it shall be immaterial whether the business is a business of dealing in the goods.

(6) For the purposes of subsection (5) above goods shall not be treated as supplied in the course of a business if they are supplied, in pursuance of an obligation arising under or in connection with the insurance of the goods, to the person with whom they were insured.

(7) Except for the purposes of, and in relation to, prohibition notices or suspension notices, references in Part 2 or Part 4 of this Act to supplying goods shall not include—

    (a)   references to supplying goods where the person supplied carries on a business of buying goods of the same description as those goods and repairing or reconditioning them;

    (b)   references to supplying goods by a sale of articles as scrap (that is to say, for the value of materials included in the articles rather than for the value of the articles themselves).

(8) Where any goods have at any time been supplied by being hired out or lent to any person, neither a continuation or renewal of the hire or loan (whether on the same or different terms) nor any transaction for the transfer after that time of any interest in the goods to the person to whom they were hired or lent shall be treated for the purposes of this Act as a further supply of the goods to that person.

(9) A ship, aircraft or motor vehicle shall not be treated for the purposes of this Act as supplied to any person by reason only that services consisting in the carriage of goods or passengers in that ship, aircraft or vehicle, or in its use for any other purpose, are provided to that person in pursuance of an agreement relating to the use of the ship, aircraft or vehicle for a particular period or for particular voyages, flights or journeys.

14.41   The general definition in s 46(1) of the CPA 1987 is qualified by s 46(2)–(9). In particular, s 46(5) limits the definition of supply to a 'person's supplying goods in the course of a business of his'. The meaning of this phrase was considered by the House of Lords in the price mis-descriptions case of *R v Warwickshire County Council Ex parte Johnson*[26] where Lord Roskill stated that, 'the words "in the course of any business of his" must mean any business of which the defendant is either the owner or in which he has a controlling interest'.

14.42   Generally the meaning of 'supply' excludes buying goods for repair or recondition and supplying goods as scrap.[27] Where any goods have at any time been supplied by being hired out or lent to any person, neither a continuation or renewal of the hire or loan nor any transaction for the transfer after that time of any interest in the goods to the person shall be treated for the purpose of the Act as a further supply.[28]

---

26   [1993] AC 583.
27   Section 46(7).
28   Section 46(8).

14.43 In *Drummond-Rees v Dorset County Council*[29] the defendant was a landlord, prosecuted under the Act for supplying the equipment in breach of the Low Voltage Electrical Supply (Safety) Regulations 1989. Per Hooper J: 'When the landlord lets property, in circumstances similar to those in this case, then the goods which are in the premises and being left there for the use of the tenant are either being hired out or lent' – (s 46(1)(a) of the Act).

Due diligence

14.44 The due diligence defence set out in s 39(1) applies to the offences in s 12(1), (2), (3), 13(4) and 14(6). The defence is made out if the defendant can show that he took all reasonable steps and exercised all due diligence to avoid committing the offence. Broadly speaking, 'all reasonable steps' will involve setting up a system and safeguards to prevent the offence. Such safeguards may be risk assessment, quality assurance controls and sampling plans. 'All due diligence' is making sure that the system is operated properly.

14.45 In *Balding v Lew-Ways Ltd*[30] the defendant's s 39(1) defence relied on certificates, which showed that the offending toy complied with the relevant British Standard. The British Standard, however, was less stringent than the Regulations dealing with toy safety at that time and the certificates did not purport to deal with whether there had been compliance with the Regulations. Per Pill LJ:

> 'The standard to be applied is that laid down by regulations made under the authority of Parliament ... It is not taking [all reasonable] steps or exercising [all due] diligence to show that you have complied with some other standard, however reputable the organisation which has proclaimed that standard ... The company were not entitled to assume that British Standards complied with the requirements laid down by Parliament.'

Due diligence is also covered in Chapter 3, Criminal Enforcement.

Notice

14.46 Section 39(2) states:

> (2) Where in any proceedings against any person for such an offence the defence provided by subsection (1) above involves an allegation that the commission of the offence was due –
>
> (a)   to the act or default of another; or
> (b)   to reliance on information given by another,
>
> that person shall not, without the leave of the court, be entitled to rely on the defence unless, not less than seven clear days before the hearing of the proceedings, he has served a notice ... on the person bringing the proceedings.

---

[29]   (1998) 162 JP 651.
[30]   (1995) 159 JP 541.

14.47   The purpose of the notice period is to allow the prosecutor opportunity to investigate this aspect of the defence before trial. Leave is discretionary and the central question is whether it is fair to proceed when the prosecutor has not had 7 days to investigate the information. If the information has been available to the prosecutor for some time before the hearing, for example in a defence interview or statement, leave is less likely to be given. Companies may avail themselves of this statutory defence. In *Tesco Supermarkets Ltd v Nattrass*[31] it was held that an employee who is not part of the directing mind of the company, can be 'another person'.

Sampling

14.48   Most of the 'due diligence' case-law revolves around sampling and testing – whether what was undertaken was adequate and demonstrated what is expected of suppliers, ie retailers, wholesalers, manufacturers and importers. This will be a question determined by magistrates. In *Powys County Council v David Halsall International Ltd*[32] – concerning packs of caps which failed BS7114, contrary to the Fireworks (Safety) Regulations 1997 – it was held that it was a question of fact and degree for the magistrates to satisfy themselves that the in-house sampling and testing was sufficient to meet BS7114.

14.49   The size of the organisation and the extent of the operation will affect the level of precautions and diligence that may be reasonably expected. In *Garrett v Boots The Chemists Ltd*[33] Lane LCJ said: 'What might be reasonable for a large retailer might not be reasonable for the village shop.' However the smaller trader still has to do the maximum that can be expected of them, having regard to their size and resources. In *Sherratt v Gerald's The American Jewellers Ltd*[34] – a non-safety matter – failure to take an elementary precaution, which would have prevented the offence from being committed, was fatal to the defence being pleaded successfully. A general blanket condition in contractual terms that all goods supplied would conform with all requirements imposed by any statute or statutory regulation did not 'come within a mile of establishing or being able to comply with the provisions' in *Riley v Webb*[35] – Watkins LJ saying:

> 'It seems to me to be a minimum requirement, if sampling has not been undertaken, for the establishment of the defence ... that the sellers of the goods receive from the suppliers a positive assurance that they conform to the specific regulations which govern the sale of them.'

14.50   For importers more is required. In *London Borough of Sutton v David Halsall plc*[36] Kennedy LJ said (in relation to s 39(1)):

---

[31]   [1972] AC 153.
[32]   [2006] EWHC 613.
[33]   (1980) 88 ITSA MR 238.
[34]   (1970) 68 LGR 256.
[35]   (1987) 151 JP 372.
[36]   (1995) 159 JP 431.

'An importer ... may be able to satisfy the burden of proof if, for example, the importer buys from an established manufacturer who he has reason to trust, who is aware of his requirements, and in particular of the safety requirements laid down by English law, and if the importer then subjects the goods to sampling. The sampling should however itself be properly organised random sampling, with a sufficient number of samples being properly tested to indicate compliance with the specifications. ... If the tests were not equivalent [to the British Standard] then it really follows, as the night the day, that [the defendants] have not done all that was reasonably practicable and exercised due diligence to ensure that these goods complied with the flammability test. ... There simply was no evidence ... that in relation to consignments two, three and four, an appropriate number of samples had been taken, and there was no evidence ... that in fact the testing which was done was sufficient in that it complied with or was better than the tests laid down by British Standards.'

14.51 In *Taylor v Lawrence Fraser (Bristol) Ltd*[37] the defendant carried out no checks or sampling. Widgery LCJ said:

'I draw particular attention to the practice apparently of (the defendant) of relying on assurances of some kind from their suppliers to satisfy the regulations then in force. Although every case depends on its own facts, I should think there are very few cases of this kind where reliance on certificates by itself is to be treated as sufficient when there is a possibility of professional sampling ...'

14.52 In this case, the defendant's premises were opposite those of the trading standards department, whose officers, by invitation, took occasional samples – but Peter Pain J said: '(The defendant) can hardly be heard to say that, simply because they have fair and proper relations with the enforcing authority, they can therefore in some way shuffle off on to the enforcing authority their responsibility for taking precautions.' In *Hicks v Sullam Ltd*[38] the defendant company's claim to have taken all reasonable precautions – having relied on their Hong Kong agent's verbal assurance about the quality of the goods which they imported – was rejected in the absence of random sampling by them or their supplier, 'or anything of that kind'. A similar view was taken in *Rotherham MBC v Rayson (UK) Ltd*[39] where the method of reporting back only adverse analysis through agents did not prove such tests were taking place (the company merely assumed that analyses in Hong Kong were all proving favourable) and sampling in the UK of one packet in respect of an importation of a batch of 10,000 dozen crayons was found not to indicate the taking of the standard of care required.

14.53 Finally, when attempting to justify satisfactory sampling levels in order to establish a defence, the burden is on the defendant to show that his testing system was sufficient for both the type and number of goods involved and that this system was carried out scrupulously. The defendants in *P & M Supplies*

---

[37] (1977) 121 Sol Jo 757.
[38] (1983) 147 JP 493.
[39] (1989) 153 JP 37.

(Essex) Ltd v Devon County Council[40] – a case where there was in-house testing levels of allegedly 0.49% and the testing of 18 toys out of 76,960 by an external analyst – failed to produce evidence necessary as to whether that degree of sampling was adequate. Due diligence and sampling are also covered in Chapter 3, Criminal Enforcement.

Time limits

14.54   As a general rule, the offences under the Act are summary-only – there is therefore a 6 months' time limit, from the time when the offence was committed (see s 127 Magistrates' Courts Act 1980). In Scotland, as the offences can only be tried under summary procedure, the time limits are established under s 136 of the Criminal Procedure (Scotland) Act 1995 – within 6 months after the contravention occurred.

14.55   However, it is essential to refer to individual Regulations to determine precise time limits. For example:

Toys (Safety) Regulations 2011 – No proceedings for an offence under these Regulations shall be commenced after the earlier of:

(a)   the end of the period of 3 years beginning with the date of the commission of the offence; or
(b)   the end of the period of 1 year beginning with the date of the discovery of the offence by the prosecutor.

Pedal Bicycles (Safety) Regulations 2010 – A magistrates' court in England and Wales may try an information if it is laid within 12 months from the time when the offence was committed.

14.56   Summary proceedings for an offence may be brought in Scotland at any time within 12 months from the time when the offence was committed. Time limits are covered generally in Chapter 3, Criminal Enforcement.

Prosecutions

Causal liability

14.57   By virtue of s 40(1) where the prosecution can show that A has committed an offence under ss 12(1), (2) or (3), 13(4) or 14(6) and that the offence has been committed because of the act or default of B in the course of any business of his, then B shall be guilty of the offence and may be proceeded against and convicted even if A is not proceeded against.

---

40   (1992) 156 JP 328.

14.58 In *Padgett Brothers (A-Z) Ltd v Coventry City Council*,[41] concerning a similar provision contained in the General Product Safety Regulations 1994, Schiemann LJ said:

> 'The fact that the goods were in the retailer's hands and were not safe was due, amongst other causes, to the default of the importer [the defendant in this case]. The regulation does not require that the relevant act should be solely due to the acts or default of the importer but merely that they are due, in part, to that.'

14.59 In proceedings partly brought under s 40(1), involving furniture not complying with fire safety standards (whilst purporting to do so), the defendant submitted that it would be an abuse of process for him to be tried for substantially the same allegations in respect of which he had already been acquitted (in Cardiff). The magistrates accepted that argument and stayed the proceedings. However, on appeal – *North Yorkshire Trading Standards Service v Coleman*[42] – it was held not to be an abuse of process for a defendant to be prosecuted in different courts for similar offences (in fact, Burton J expressed his view that it would be difficult to support the conclusions reached by the magistrates in Cardiff).

14.60 The UK agent for a German company – which supplied a painted child's toy hammer bench that contained unacceptably high levels of lead and chromium – was convicted of an offence brought under s 40(1) in *Scott Kenworthy (t/a K-Play International) v North Tyneside Borough Council*.[43] However, the retailer could only be guilty of an offence under reg 13 of the Toys (Safety) Regulations 1995 if the toy 'jeopardised the safety or health of users or third parties when used as intended or in a foreseeable way, bearing in mind the normal behaviour of children' but the magistrates heard no evidence to this effect. On appeal the agent's conviction was quashed – Maurice Kay LJ said:

> '... any conviction of him could only be parasitic on the guilt of (the retailer) ... Her guilt could not be established simply on the basis of non-compliance with the general safety requirements.'

Causal liability is now covered generally in Chapter 3, Criminal Enforcement.

Directors' liability

14.61 Section 40(2) permits the prosecution and conviction of any director, manager, secretary or other similar officer or any person who was purporting to act in any such capacity, where an offence has been committed by the company with the consent or connivance of, or is found to be attributable to any neglect on the part of that person. Directors' liability is now covered generally in Chapter 3, Criminal Enforcement.

---

[41] (1998) 162 JP 673.
[42] (2002) 166 JP 76.
[43] [2007] EWHC 434.

Enforcement powers

14.62 Under s 27, it is the duty of every weights and measures authority in Great Britain to enforce within their area 'the safety provisions' (any provision of safety regulations, a prohibition notice or a suspension notice). Nothing in s 27 authorises any weights and measures authority to bring proceedings in Scotland for an offence.

14.63 In *Brighton and Hove City Council v Woolworths plc*[44] it was held that s 14(1) does not limit the power a local authority to issue a suspension notice only in respect of its area – the notice had countrywide effect. However, in the further judgment of Field J the local authority had no power to prosecute in its own right breaches of the suspension notice which occurred outside its area because:

> 'such a prosecution could not ex hypothesi be expedient for the promotion or protection of the interests of the inhabitants of its area as required by section 222(1) of the Local Government Act 1972.'

14.64 Although it is arguable that this opinion of Field J was not the correct test, since it is for the local authority to make this judgment, not the court – see *London Borough of Barking & Dagenham v Jones*[45] and *Mole Valley District Council v Smith*[46] – in subsequent legislation such as General Product Safety Regulations 2005[47] and the Pyrotechnic Articles Safety Regulations 2015 2015[48] it specifically states that a local authority shall have the power to investigate and prosecute for an alleged contravention of any provision imposed in the regulations which was committed outside its area in any part of England and Wales.

14.65 This has been further clarified within Sch 5 to the CRA 2015 – a local weights and measures authority in England or Wales may exercise powers in a part of England or Wales which is outside that authority's area. A local weights and measures authority in Scotland may exercise powers in a part of Scotland which is outside that authority's area. The investigatory powers available to an officer for the purposes of the duty imposed by subsection (1), are now found in Sch 5 to the CRA 2015; see Chapter 3, Criminal Enforcement.

14.66 The requirement to give notice of intention to carry out a routine inspection or to have reasonable suspicion to require the production of information does not apply if the enforcer is a market surveillance authority within the meaning of Art 2(18) of RAMS and the power is exercised for the purpose of market surveillance within the meaning of Art 2(17) of that Regulation. It follows that officers will be exempt from giving notice, under the

---

44   [2002] EWHC 2565 (Admin).
45   (1999/035/1).
46   [1992] 24 HLR 442.
47   SI 2005/1803.
48   SI 2010/1554.

CRA 2015, when they are undertaking market surveillance activity (inspections, audits, investigations, sampling, advising etc) and there is a corresponding duty to enforce EU harmonised legislation. A notice is required, however, for domestic UK legislation.

14.67 It is useful to note that the power within the CPA 1987 to inspect, seize and detain goods that have not yet been placed on the market – ie at the port or airport prior to customs clearance or at an enhanced remote transit shed – without the need for suspicion of any contravention of any regulation is still in force.

14.68 Under s 16 an enforcement authority in England and Wales or Northern Ireland may apply for an order to a magistrates' court for an order that goods be forfeited or destroyed on the grounds that there has been a contravention in relation to the goods of a safety provision. Such orders may also be made in Scotland by a sheriff under s 17. Suppliers can appeal to a magistrates' court against forfeiture (and suspension) of goods. In certain circumstances enforcement authorities are liable to pay compensation for losses to a supplier against whom enforcement action has been taken, if there has been no contravention of a safety provision.

14.69 There are no powers to warn the public of unsafe products beyond those in the statutory code. In *R v Liverpool City Council, ex parte Baby Products Association and Another,*[49] it was held, that a particular press release issued by a local authority, without statutory power to do so, was contrary to law as it deprived those affected of their rights and safeguards under the Act. Following the *Liverpool* case – in June 2000 – the Department of Trade and Industry issued guidance to Chief Trading Standards Officers on powers of enforcement authorities to issue press releases relating to product safety. In summary, this guidance confirms that press releases may be used to draw attention to formal enforcement action (including circumstances where a suspension notice has been served '… irrespective of whether the supplier in question is appealing against the suspension notice'). It would also be acceptable to issue stand-alone press releases where the supplier agrees to this course of action or where the intention/effect does not lead to the suspension of the supply of the goods.

14.70 This has been superseded by the duty under reg 39 of the General Product Safety Regulations 2005 where an authority shall, in general, make available to the public information on risks to consumer health and safety posed by a product:

- nature of risk;
- product identification;
- measures taken in respect of risk.

---

[49] (CO/3733/99).

Sentencing

14.71   A person guilty of an offence under s 12(1), (2), (3) and (4) is liable on summary conviction to imprisonment for a term not exceeding 6 months or to an unlimited fine or to both. A person guilty of an offence under s 13(4) or s 14(6) is liable on summary conviction to imprisonment for a term not exceeding 3 months or to an unlimited fine or to both.

Mutual recognition

14.72   EU Regulation on Mutual Recognition of Non-Harmonised Goods (EC 764/2008) is a directly applicable European regulation made to ensure that there are no artificial barriers to European trade. The Regulation only applies to the 'non-harmonised' field of goods (such as the current laws on nightwear and furniture flammability, which are UK-specific) not in sectors where the EU has adopted harmonising legislation (such as the Toys, Low Voltage and Cosmetics Directives).

14.73   Mutual recognition means that products that are lawfully marketed in one EU Member State must be allowed to be marketed in all Member States. The type of enforcement action which will engage the Regulation would include issuing suspension notices under s 14. The Department for Business has issued the Mutual Recognition Guide. Enforcement and notification guide for Local Authorities in relation to Regulation 764/2008 which includes:

> 'The Regulation will only apply to a small proportion of the enforcement activities of most Local Authority consumer protection officers. Where the Regulation does apply, it will often make little difference to the ultimate outcome, and compliance with it may amount to much the same thing in procedural terms as following existing good practice. But since failure to comply with the Regulation has serious consequences, it is important to follow its provisions very precisely when they do apply.'

EUROPEAN COMMUNITIES ACT 1972

Introduction

14.74   'New Approach' Directives set out the broad essential requirements (on safety, for example – but they apply in other legislative areas) which must be met before products may be placed on the market in the UK or anywhere else in the European Community. The implementation of these Directives in the UK is made through 'New Approach – CE marking regulations' ('The New Approach Regulations') which are made under s 2(2) of the European Communities Act 1972.

14.75   European harmonised standards provide the detailed technical information enabling manufacturers to meet the essential requirements. Products which meet the essential requirements are required to display the CE marking as described in the particular Directive, which means that the products can be sold anywhere in the Community/EEA. Products made to harmonised European Standards enjoy a presumption of conformity with the essential requirements of the Directives.

14.76 The New Approach Regulations place a duty on any 'responsible person' who places products on the market to comply with certain requirements. These requirements are that the products must satisfy certain essential safety or health and safety requirements which are applicable to that class or type of product, the appropriate conformity assessment procedures must have been carried out including the drawing up of technical files and a declaration of conformity, CE marking must have been correctly affixed and the products must not compromise the safety of individuals – and sometimes domestic animals or property – when properly maintained and used. Contravention of these duties is an offence under the individual New Approach Regulations and provision is made for liability of persons other than the principal offender and directors and managers of corporate bodies.

The New Approach Regulations

14.77

- Simple Pressure Vessels (Safety) Regulations 1991;[50]
- Pressure Equipment Regulations 1999;[51]
- Radio Equipment and Telecommunications Terminal Equipment Regulations 2000;[52]
- Personal Protective Equipment Regulations 2002;[53]
- Recreational Craft Regulations 2004;[54]
- Electromagnetic Compatibility Regulations 2006;[55]
- Supply of Machinery (Safety) Regulations 2008;[56]
- Pyrotechnic Articles (Safety) Regulations 2015.[57]

See also the Regulations implementing 'New Approach' Directives, relating to medical devices, electrical safety, gas safety and toys, which are made under the CPA 1987.

---

[50] SI 1991/2749.
[51] SI 1999/2001.
[52] SI 2000/730.
[53] SI 2002/1144.
[54] SI 2004/1464.
[55] SI 2006/3418.
[56] SI 2008/1597.
[57] SI 2015/1553.

Pyrotechnic Articles (Safety) Regulations 2015[58]

14.78 The Regulations implement EC Pyrotechnic Articles Directive 2013/29/EU[59] and place an obligation on manufacturers/importers to only supply fireworks which comply with essential safety requirements. There are also labelling requirements and obligations on distributors to only supply fireworks which bear a valid CE mark etc. The provisions relating to sales to young persons are contained in Chapter 16, Age Restricted Products. The categories for fireworks are:

(a) category F1: fireworks which present a very low hazard and negligible noise level and which are intended for use in confined areas, including fireworks which are intended for use inside domestic buildings;

(b) category F2: fireworks which present a low hazard and low noise level and which are intended for outdoor use in confined areas;

(c) category F3: fireworks which present a medium hazard, which are intended for outdoor use in large open areas and whose noise level is not harmful to human health;

(d) category F4: fireworks which present a high hazard, which are intended for use only by persons with specialist knowledge (commonly known as fireworks for professional use) and whose noise level is not harmful to human health.

The market surveillance and enforcement duty in reg 54(1) requires local authorities to carry out regular inspections in relation to category F1, F2 or F3 fireworks following entry into the EU and at storage sites. Enforcement powers are found in Sch 7.

Definitions

14.79 Certain definitions – such as 'placing on the market', 'transposed harmonised standard' and 'responsible person – are important in the context of the New Approach Regulations and their meaning is given in the New Approach Regulations themselves and/or is defined in the Commission Notice, the 'Blue Guide' on the implementation of EU products rules.[60]

14.80 For the purposes of EU harmonisation legislation, a product is placed on the market when it is made available for the first time on the Union market. The manufacturer and the importer are the only economic operators who place products on the market. When a manufacturer or an importer supplies a product to a distributor or an end-user for the first time, the operation is always labelled in legal terms as 'placing on the market'. Any subsequent operation, for instance, from a distributor to distributor or from a distributor to an end-user is defined as making available.

---

[58] SI 2015/1553.
[59] OJ L154, 14.6.2007, p 1.
[60] 2016/C 272/01.

14.81 In particular it is worth noting that 'placing on the market' refers to each individual product, not type of product, so occurs each time any product is placed on the market by any economic operator. Consequently, even though a product model or type has been supplied before new Union harmonisation legislation laying down new mandatory requirements entered into force, individual units of the same model or type, which are placed on the market after the new requirements have become applicable, must comply with these new requirements.

Fulfilment houses

14.82 A new business model has emerged involving on–line sellers based outside the EU offering products to EU customers using a fulfilment house company ('FHC'). Products are generally warehoused by the FHC, which is located within the EU to guarantee swift delivery to EU consumers. The FHC will merely distribute products, at the direction of the seller. The FHC does not own or engage in selling the product, either itself or as an agent. The contractual relationship between the seller and UK consumer will not ordinarily involve the FHC.

14.83 The FHC's limited role is essentially to distribute the product for the non-EU seller. On this basis, it is important to distinguish the position of an FHC from traders that engage in the process of selling a product to consumers, either as principal or agent. The criminal liability of an FHC in relation to the UK product safety framework is likely to depend on the offence alleged. The CPA 1987, s 12 offences relating to the contravention of a safety regulation (for example plugs and sockets, electrical equipment, and toys) are contingent on their 'supply' (see above). 'Supply' is defined in s 46 to include 'selling' as principal or agent.

14.84 An FHC is unlikely to engage in 'selling' the product to a consumer where it does not own the product, advertise it for sale, enter into a contract of sale with the consumer or otherwise engage in selling it. However other EU Directives and regulations such as for machinery, cosmetic products and chemicals introduce the concept of placing on the market or making available on the market. For example, under the Cosmetic Product Regulation[61] 'distributor' means any natural or legal person in the supply chain, other than the manufacturer or the importer, who makes a cosmetic product available on the Community market. The FHC would fit within this definition. The regulation goes on to say that:

> 'A cosmetic product made available on the market shall be safe for human health ....'

14.85 The Blue Guide also states that products stored in such fulfilment houses are considered to have been supplied for distribution, consumption or

---

[61] EU 1223/2009.

use in the EU market and thus placed on the EU market. When an online operator uses a fulfilment house, by shipping the products to the fulfilment house in the EU the products are in the distribution phase of the supply chain. When made available on the market, products must be in compliance with the Union harmonisation legislation applicable at the time of placing on the market.

14.86 Finally, there is the distinction between the enforcement provisions in the CPR 1987 and the GPSR. Regulation 2 of the GPSR extends the meaning of supply to include 'making a product available, in the context of providing a service, for use by consumers'. So the GPSR could potentially be used to prosecute an FHC, in appropriate circumstances, on the basis that it was a 'distributor' as suggested in the Blue Guide that had breached its duty of care under reg 8. The FHC's duty of care is likely to be breached if it knowingly distributes dangerous products or ought to have known that it was distributing dangerous products.

Duty of enforcement

14.87 Local weights and measures authorities in Great Britain have a duty to enforce the New Approach Regulations – in whole or in association with other regulators – within their areas.

Powers

14.88 Each set of New Approach Regulations provides for powers of enforcement – in relation to a number of Regulations, ss 14, 15, 28–35, 37, 38, 44 and 47 of the CPA 1987 apply.

Time limits

14.89 In general terms, the New Approach Regulations require that, in relation to an offence committed under the New Approach Regulations or under s 12 of the CPA 1987 in relation to a contravention of the New Approach Regulations, the information is laid (in the case of England and Wales) within 12 months from the time when the offence is committed, and (in Scotland) summary proceedings for such an offence may be begun at any time within 12 months from the time when the offence is committed.

14.90 The above provisions do not apply to the following three New Approach Regulations:

Simple Pressure Vessels (Safety) Regulations 1991 and Supply of Machinery (Safety) Regulations 2008

14.91 The time limit for offences under the above New Approach Regulations is derived from s 34 of the Health and Safety at Work etc Act 1974 so that summary proceedings for an offence may be commenced at any time within 6 months from the date on which there comes to the knowledge of a responsible enforcing authority evidence sufficient in the opinion of that authority to justify a prosecution for that offence. In Scotland, summary proceedings for an offence may be commenced at any time within 6 months from the date on which evidence, sufficient in the opinion of the enforcing authority to justify a report to the Lord Advocate with a view to consideration of the question of prosecution, comes to the knowledge of the authority – and s 331(3) of the Criminal Procedure (Scotland) Act 1975 has effect.

Electromagnetic Compatibility Regulations 2006

14.92 Notwithstanding s 127 of the Magistrates' Courts Act 1980 and s 136 of the Criminal Procedure (Scotland) Act 1995, proceedings for an offence under these New Approach Regulations may be commenced at any time within 3 years from the date of the offence, or one year from the date on which there comes to the knowledge of the prosecutor evidence sufficient to justify a prosecution for that offence, whichever is the earlier.

Technical documentation

14.93 All the New Approach Regulations have technical documentation requirements. Each are specific but in the main a manufacturer must retain for at least 10 years from the date on which the last product was manufactured.

Penalties

14.94 Persons guilty of an offence under the New Approach Regulations are liable on summary conviction to:

(a) imprisonment for a term not exceeding 3 months; or

(b) an unlimited fine,

or both.

Defence of due diligence

14.95 This defence appears in all the New Approach Regulations It is expressed in similar terms to that outlined previously under s 39 of the CPA 1987. Due diligence defences are now covered in Chapter 3, Criminal Enforcement.

Compliance notice

14.96 Except where, in the opinion of an enforcement authority, a product may endanger the safety of persons and, where appropriate, domestic animals or property, where an enforcement authority has reasonable grounds for suspecting that the CE marking has been affixed to the product, or its packaging, and in relation to which any provision of the regulations has not been complied with, it may serve notice in writing on the responsible person, and no other action may be taken, and no proceedings may be brought in respect of that product, until such notice has been given and the person to whom it is given has failed to comply with its requirements. This would be used in such instances as not keeping a technical file, not issuing a declaration of conformity etc. Enforcement action can only be taken in respect of the alleged non-compliance if such a notice has been issued and not acted upon within the time specified in the notice.

Duty of enforcement authority to inform Secretary of State of action taken

14.97 Where an enforcement authority takes action to prohibit or restrict the placing (eg issuing a suspension notice or compliance notice) on the market of any product to which the regulations apply which bears the CE marking they must inform the Secretary of State of the action taken and the reasons for it with a view to this information being passed by the Secretary of State to the Commission.

The Tobacco and Related Products Regulations 2016

14.98 Made under the European Communities Act 1972 these Regulations implement the Tobacco Products Directive.[62] The regulations deal with the labelling of tobacco products. They require tobacco products for smoking to carry a health warning label including a colour photograph on the front and back surfaces and a general warning and information message on other surfaces. They also deal with emissions and additives, setting maximum tar, nicotine and carbon dioxide levels for cigarettes and prohibit cigarettes and hand rolling tobacco with a characterising flavour, certain additives and tobacco for oral use.

14.99 Producers of tobacco products, including herbal products and electronic cigarettes are required to submit ingredients, emissions, sales data and market research information to the Secretary of State. For electronic cigarettes the regulations stipulate safety and quality standards, including a leak-proof refill mechanism and tamper-proof packaging, and the need for consistent nicotine delivery. They limit tank and refill container volume, and nicotine solution concentration. They also restrict marketing, require the provision of product information and stipulate that products cannot be sold to under 18s. The Medicines and Healthcare Regulatory Authority is the designated 'competent authority' monitoring compliance, with local Trading Standards authorities enforcing compliance. Responsibility to comply lies with producers (those who manufacture or import e-cigarette products or solutions). Retailers must remove non-compliant stock from sale by 20 May 2017.

---

[62]   2014/40/EU, which revoke and replace the Tobacco for Oral Use (Safety) Regulations 1992, SI 1992/3134 and the Tobacco Products (Manufacture, Presentation and Sale) (Safety) Regulations 2002, SI 2002/3041.

14.100 There is a duty on each weights and measures authority in Great Britain and each district council in Northern Ireland to enforce these Regulations within their area and they are to be enforced as if they were safety regulations within the meaning of the Consumer Protection Act 1987. Persons guilty of an offence under these Regulations are liable on summary conviction to:

(a) imprisonment for a term not exceeding 3 months; or

(b) an unlimited fine,

or both.

Directly applicable European Regulations

14.101 There is a growing tendency for Europe to produce directly applicable European Regulations rather than directives. These require no transposition as they are directly applicable across all Member States. Local weights and measures authorities have a duty to enforce the following.

REACH

14.102 The Registration, Evaluation, Authorisation and Restriction of Chemicals Regulation[63] prohibits and restricts, among other requirements, the use of certain chemicals in articles for consumer use such as phthalates in toys and child care articles, azo dyes in toys and textiles and di-methyl fumerate in leather goods. It is enforced in the UK via the REACH Enforcement Regulations 2008[64] which contain the duties, powers and offences. There is no statutory defence.

Classification, Labelling and Packaging Regulations

14.103 The Classification, Labelling and Packaging Regulation[65] lays down requirements for the classification, packaging and labelling of dangerous chemicals such as the requirement for child resistant packaging and tactile devices. It is enforced in the UK via the Biocidal Products and Chemicals (Appointment of Authorities and Enforcement) Regulations 2013.[66]

Regulation (EU) No 305/2011 laying down harmonised conditions for the marketing of construction products

14.104 This EU regulation outlines the basic requirements for construction products and manufacturer/importer/distributor obligations. These include conformity assessment procedures, declaration of performance and CE

---

63 EC Regulation 1907/2006.
64 SI 2008/2852.
65 EC Regulation 1272/2008.
66 SI 2013/1506.

marking. They are enforced in the UK via the Construction Products Regulations 2013. These regulations impose duties, grant powers including the issue of a suspension and recall notice, and create offences.

Marketing of Construction Products Regulations

14.105   The EU Regulation on the marketing of construction products[67] sets out harmonised basic requirements for construction products and the obligations of manufacturers, importers and distributors. These include conformity assessment procedures, declaration of performance and CE marking. They are enforced in the UK via the Construction Products Regulations 2013.[68] These regulations impose duties, grant powers including the issue of a suspension and recall notice, and create offences.

Cosmetic Products Regulations

14.106   The Cosmetic Products Regulation[69] protects public health by prohibiting the use of certain substances in cosmetics and imposing restrictions on the use of others. The Cosmetic Products Notification Portal ('CPNP') is the IT tool for the new notification procedure under this regulation. The responsible person, who is responsible for the safety assessment, is required to notify the European Commission of each product placed on the market in detail (there are also separate requirements for products containing nanomaterials). There are also labelling requirements, a prohibition on animal testing and the requirement to produce a product information package. The EU regulation is enforced in the UK via the Cosmetic Products Enforcement Regulations 2013[70] which create offences and allow for a due diligence defence. Enforcement powers are found within the CRA 2015; see Chapter 3, Criminal Enforcement.

GENERAL PRODUCT SAFETY REGULATIONS 2005

Introduction

14.107   The General Product Safety Regulations 2005[71] ('GPSR') – made under s 2(2) of the European Communities Act 1972 – implement Directive 2001/95/EC[72] The GPSR apply to the supply of new and second-hand consumer products, excluding second-hand products supplied as a product to be repaired or reconditioned prior to being used, provided the supplier clearly informs the person to whom he supplies the product to that effect (reg 4).

---

67   EU Regulation 305/2011.
68   SI 2013/1387.
69   EC Regulation 1223/2009.
70   SI 2013/1478.
71   SI 2005/1803.
72   OJ L 11, 15.1.2002, p 4.

14.108 The Regulations primarily aim to do the following:

- specify that products placed on the market or supplied by producers and distributors must be safe;
- define a safe product;
- impose obligations on producers and distributors consistent with marketing safe products;
- lay down a framework for assessing safety;
- require and empower enforcement authorities to take action necessary to protect consumers from unsafe products.

Relationship with other Regulations

14.109 Regulation 3(2) states:

> (2) Where a product is subject to specific safety requirements imposed by rules of Community law other than the GPS Directive, these Regulations shall apply only to the aspects and risks or category of risks not covered by those requirements. This means that:
>
> (a) the definition of "safe product" and "dangerous product" in regulation 2 and regulations 5 and 6 shall not apply to such a product in so far as concerns the risks or category of risks covered by the specific rules, and
> (b) the remainder of these Regulations shall apply except where there are specific provisions governing the aspects covered by those regulations with the same objective.

In September 2009 the Department for Business, Innovation and Skills published *Guidance on the interaction between the General Product Safety Regulations 2005 and national safety regulations*. The Conclusion of this document states:

> '16. The GPSR therefore act as a safety net to prevent the placing on the market of dangerous products within its scope:
>
> (a) where there are no specific safety regulations in place covering those products,
> (b) those products do not comply with national safety regulations; or
> (c) which, even if they do comply with national safety regulations, are nevertheless considered to be dangerous.
>
> 17. As such, they operate in parallel to relevant national safety regulations and can be used as an alternative means of enforcement.'

14.110 In *Caerphilly County Borough Council v Stripp*[73] the defendant was prosecuted under reg 13(b) of the General Product Safety Regulations 1994 for offering to supply a second-hand car which, it was said, was a dangerous product. The magistrates accepted the defendant's submission that the

---

[73] [2001] 2 CMLR 5 (CO/609/00).

prosecution was an abuse of process, on the basis that reg 3(c) stated that those regulations did not apply to any product where there are specific provisions in rules of Community law governing all aspects of the safety of the product. The magistrates found that s 75 of the Road Traffic Act 1988 was such a specific provision governing all aspects of the safety of second-hand vehicles. The prosecutor appealed. Per Butterfield J:

> '... regulation 13(b) is available legislation under which to bring a prosecution in respect of a dangerous product, namely a second-hand motor vehicle, if that is thought appropriate by the local authority or other prosecuting agency.'

14.111 In another case involving this point, *R v Newcastle Upon Tyne Magistrates' Court ex p Poundstretcher Ltd*,[74] a prosecution under reg 13 of the General Product Safety Regulations 1994 was brought for supplying a dangerous product. The defendant suggested that, having regard in particular to reg 3(c), the prosecution should have been brought under the Toys (Safety) Regulations 1995 which specifically deal with the risk from suffocation and which give effect to an EEC Council Directive. Whilst not accepting that argument, the prosecutor successfully applied to amend the information to allege an offence under the 1995 Regulations. Under the Toys (Safety) Regulations 1995 an information must be laid within 12 months of the date of offence. By the time of the application to amend, 12 months had elapsed. The defendant sought judicial review of the decision to amend. Per Dyson J (Bingham LCJ agreeing): 'The decision in this case was very far from being plainly wrong.'

14.112 The issue before the Administrative Court in *Essex County Council v PMS International Group Plc*[75] actually related to procedural matters under the Criminal Procedure Rules and Practice Direction. However, the legal argument that took place before the magistrates concerned whether it was open to Essex County Council to proceed under the GPSR when proceedings under the Furniture and Furnishings (Fire) (Safety) Regulations 1988 were available to it. The magistrate held that the prosecution under the provisions of the GPSR was prevented by virtue of the provisions of reg 3(1) ('Each provision of these Regulations applies to a product in so far as there are no specific provisions with the same objective in rules of Community law governing the safety of the product other than the GPS Directive') due to the fact that there was a specific provision governing flammability of cushions contained in the Furniture and Furnishings Fire Safety Regulations 1988.

Key general concepts

14.113 The GPSR provide a number of definitions of the key concepts of the legislation and the offences created.

---

[74] (CO/3282/97).
[75] [2012] EWHC 1500 (Admin).

Product

14.114 Regulation 2 provides for interpretation and gives the following definition:

> (2) "Product" for the purposes of the Regulations means a product which is intended for consumers or likely, under reasonably foreseeable conditions, to be used by consumers even if not intended for them and which is supplied or made available, whether for consideration or not, in the course of a commercial activity and whether it is new, used or reconditioned and includes a product that is supplied or made available to consumers for their own use in the context of providing a service. "Product" does not include equipment used by service providers themselves to supply a service to consumers, in particular equipment on which consumers ride or travel which is operated by a service provider.

14.115 This pithy definition can be summarised as all goods that are or could be placed on the market, or supplied or made available, including in the course of providing a service, to consumers for their private use. The fact that the definition includes products that are not intended for consumers means that products that were originally designed and intended for professional use will still be subject to the GPSR if it is reasonably foreseeable that they will migrate to the consumer market. Producers and distributors must, therefore, be very careful in considering the likelihood of their product, intended for professionals, ending up in the consumer market *and* ensuring that the product is accompanied by sufficient labelling and instruction as to the risks, or inappropriateness of consumer use. If the product is unlikely to ever be considered safe for the consumer market then steps must be taken to ensure the marketing and supply of the product is strictly controlled. Clear markings provide an unambiguous guide for the enforcement authorities about whether a product is intended for professional use or consumer use, and whether the risks to consumers are sufficiently covered so as to meet the general safety requirements.

Supply

14.116 Assistance is again provided by reg 2, where the following meaning is given: 'Supply' in relation to a product includes making it available, in the context of providing a service, for use by consumers. The meaning of supply clearly goes further than that above. The Regulations expressly refer to producers and distributors and the meaning of supply must therefore be seen in that context. Producers make the product and place it on the market for distributors, the first stage of the supply. Distributors, having received the product from the producers, then supply the products to the consumers thereafter, the second stage of the supply. In addition, supply extends to the hire and making a product available for use by consumers in the course of providing a service, an express departure from the previous regulations.

14.117   The following are, however, key features of the GPSR:

- They only apply to commercial supply ie in the course of a business or a trade.
- Each time a product is made available that constitutes a separate supply.
- Preparatory acts of agreeing to supply and possessing any product for supply are caught by the Regulations.
- They do not apply to products used in the workplace by workers.
- They do not apply to products which are exported, or intended to be exported to a country outside the European Community.
- They do not apply to products used or intended only for display at exhibitions or trade fairs.

14.118   The following are examples of how a product can be supplied for the purposes of the Regulations:

- selling, leasing, hiring it out or lending it;
- entering into a hire purchase or other credit agreement for it;
- exchanging it for any consideration other than money;
- giving it as a prize or otherwise making a gift; and
- providing it in the course of the delivery of a service.

14.119   The above examples are self-explanatory with the exception of the previously absent provision of a product in the course of the delivery of a service. The explanatory memorandum to the Regulations prepared by the Department for Trade and Industry provides a useful example of this particular supply of a product:

> 'A person books into a hotel room that provides a hairdryer for use by the guest. These Regulations apply to that hairdryer as it is provided to the consumer in the course of delivering a service, namely the hotel room. By contrast, a hairdryer used in a hairdresser's by the professional hairdresser at work rather than by the consumer is not covered by the Regulations.'

Meaning of a safe product

14.120   Regulation 2 defines a safe product as follows:

> (2) "safe product" means a product which, under normal or reasonably foreseeable conditions of use including duration and, where applicable, putting into service, installation and maintenance requirements, does not present any risk or only the minimum risks compatible with the product's use, considered to be acceptable and consistent with a high level of protection for the safety and health of persons. In determining the foregoing, the following shall be taken into account in particular –

(a)   the characteristics of the product, including its composition, packaging, instructions for assembly and, where applicable, instructions for installation and maintenance,

(b)   the effect of the product on other products, where it is reasonably foreseeable that it will be used with other products,

(c)   the presentation of the product, the labelling, any warnings and instructions for its use and disposal and any other indication or information regarding the product, and

(d)   the categories of consumers at risk when using the product, in particular children and the elderly.

14.121   Reasonable or foreseeable use will include misuse – commonly using a product other than how it is intended. For example, a screwdriver is designed to withstand turning stresses, however, the normal consumer when looking to open a can of paint will often use a handy screwdriver as a lever – therefore to be safe a screwdriver should also withstand such stress as is foreseeable from a consumer's wider use (in this case opening a can of paint). It is important to note that the mere possibility or feasibility of obtaining higher levels of safety or the availability of other products presenting a lesser degree of risk shall not constitute grounds for considering a product to be a dangerous product.[76]

Standards of safety

14.122   The assessment of whether a product is safe is manifestly the key consideration in cases arising out of this legislation. As is clear from earlier in this chapter, products are subject to national safety regulations made under s 11 of the CPA 1987, which detail standards required for those particular products (eg the Aerosol Dispensers Regulations 2009). Frequently, these national regulations reflect EC provisions. However, in the absence of European Community provisions governing the safety of a product, the product will be deemed safe if it conforms to the specific rules of national law so long as those rules cover the specific risk under consideration. A product will also be presumed safe, in the absence of the above, if it conforms to a voluntary national standard that gives effect to a European standard that has had its references published in the Official Journal of the European Union, but only so far as the risks are covered by that standard.

14.123   Where, however, neither a specific regulation nor national safety law applies, safety will be assessed according to reg 6(3):

... the conformity of a product to the general safety requirement shall be assessed taking into account –

(a)   any voluntary national standard of the United Kingdom giving effect to a European standard, other than one referred to in paragraph (2),

(b)   other national standards drawn up in the United Kingdom,

(c)   recommendations of the European Commission setting guidelines on product safety assessment,

(d)   product safety codes of good practice in the sector concerned,

---

[76]   Defined in reg 2 of the Regulations as a product other than a safe product.

(e)   the state of the art and technology, and

(f)   reasonable consumer expectations concerning safety.

14.124 This important aspect of the GPSD involves Commission decisions. The safety of many consumer products that fall under the General Product Safety Regulations is assessed in accordance with the hierarchy of standards. There have been many recent decisions by the Commission as a result of failing safety requirements leading to injuries and even fatalities due to a lack of such standards. Obviously when designing products for vulnerable consumers such as children, extra hazards need to be addressed and extra precautions need to be taken. To assist manufacturers of these products the Commission has mandated a large range of harmonised standards for products, in particular those which are for children's use and care – such as bunk beds, cots, prams and pushchairs. Recent examples of mandates also include looped cords in blinds and reduced ignition propensity cigarettes.

14.125 Compliance with one or more of the above will not, however, necessarily mean that the product is automatically a safe product. Indeed, the Regulations give specific consent to enforcement authorities to take appropriate measures where there is evidence that despite such conformity the product is dangerous.[77]

Application

14.126 The GPSR apply to all UK suppliers of products. However, suppliers for the purposes of the GPSR may be either 'producers' or 'distributors', but both have particular meanings in the context of the GPSR. It should not be assumed that the words have the meaning attributed by everyday usage. In addition, where it can be shown that an offence has been committed with the aid or consent of, or is attributable to any neglect on the part of any director, manager, secretary or other similar officer of a company, such persons (in addition to the company in question) may also be proceeded against.[78]

Producers

14.127 Regulation 2 states that 'producer' means:

(a)   the manufacturer of a product, when he is established in a Member State and any other person presenting himself as the manufacturer by affixing to the product his name, trade mark or other distinctive mark, or the person who reconditions the product;

(b)   when the manufacturer is not established in a Member State –

(i)   if he has a representative established in a Member State, the representative,

(ii)   in any other case, the importer of the product from a state that is not a Member State into a Member State;

(c)   other professionals in the supply chain, insofar as their activities may

---

[77]   Regulation 6(4) of the Regulations.

[78]   Regulation 31(2).

affect the safety properties of a product.

14.128 A 'producer' for the purposes of the Regulations, therefore, is not simply the manufacturer. It will include any professional in the supply chain whose activities affect the safety of the product. For example:

> A person based in the UK who imports a product manufactured in China will be the producer for the purposes of the Regulations.

> A person based in France who modifies a product manufactured in the UK will be a producer for the purposes of the Regulations, as well as the original UK manufacturer. A question will then arise as to what point in the chain the safety risk arose.

If the relevant person's activity did not affect the safety properties of the product, the original producer will continue to be responsible for its safety.

Distributors

14.129 Regulation 2 states that 'distributor' means a professional in the supply chain whose activity does not affect the safety properties of the product. This can include wholesalers, retailers, agents and auctioneers[79] and also includes a person who makes a product available for the use of a consumer in the course of delivering a service.

Obligations, offences and penalties

The general safety requirement

14.130 The general obligation is on producers to supply only products that are safe.

Regulation 5 imposes the general safety requirement on producers:

> **General safety requirement**

> 5(1) No producer shall place a product on the market unless the product is a safe product.

> (2) No producer shall offer or agree to place a product on the market or expose or possess a product for placing on the market unless the product is a safe product.

> (3) No producer shall offer or agree to supply a product or expose or possess a product for supply unless the product is safe.

> (4) No producer shall supply a product unless the product is a safe product.

A person who contravenes reg 5 is guilty of an offence and liable on conviction on indictment to imprisonment for a term not exceeding 12 months or to an

---

[79] Auctioneers are excluded from the Regulations if they are merely acting under instructions in conducting the sale. In those circumstances, it is the owner of the product who is the seller.

unlimited fine or to both, or on summary conviction to imprisonment for a
term not exceeding 3 months or to an unlimited fine or to both (reg 20(1)).

Producer obligations

14.131 The GPSR express obligations in addition to the general safety
requirement on both producers and distributors alike. Regulation 7 sets out the
following in relation to obligations of producers:

> **Other obligations of producers**
>
> 7(1) Within the limits of his activities, a producer shall provide consumers with
> the relevant information to enable them –
>
> (a)   to assess the risks inherent in a product throughout the normal or
>   reasonably foreseeable period of its use, where such risks are not
>   immediately obvious without adequate warnings, and
> (b)   to take precautions against those risks.
>
> (2) The presence of warnings does not exempt any person from compliance with
> the other requirements of these Regulations.
>
> (3) Within the limits of his activities, a producer shall adopt measures
> commensurate with the characteristics of the products which he supplies to enable
> him to –
>
> (a)   be informed of the risks which the products might pose, and
> (b)   take appropriate action including, where necessary to avoid such risks,
>   withdrawal, adequately and effectively warning consumers as to the risks
>   or, as a last resort, recall.
>
> (4) The measures referred to in paragraph (3) include –
>
> (a)   except where it is not reasonable to do so, an indication by means of the
>   product or its packaging of –
>   (i)   the name and address of the producer, and
>   (ii)   the product reference or where applicable the batch of products to
>   which it belongs; and
> (b)   where and to the extent that it is reasonable to do so –
>   (i)   sample testing of marketed products,
>   (ii)   investigating and if necessary keeping a register of complaints
>   concerning the safety of the product, and
>   (iii) keeping distributors informed of the results of such monitoring
>   where a product presents a risk or may present a risk.

14.132 A person who contravenes reg 7(1), (3) (by failing to take any of the
measures specified in reg 7(4)) is guilty of an offence and liable on summary
conviction to imprisonment for a term not exceeding 3 months or to an
unlimited fine or to both (reg 20(2)). Producers, it can be seen, must ensure that
consumers are provided with all relevant information and warnings, and that
they maintain a high level of information about possible risks. However,
common sense dictates that the diversity of products and the risks they pose
reflects on the extent of action expected and required of producers and

distributors alike. Some products are inherently more dangerous than others and producers or distributors are only required to act within the limits of their activities.

Distributor obligations

14.133 Regulation 8 of the Regulations sets out the following in relation to obligations of distributors:

Obligations of distributors

8(1) A distributor shall act with due care in order to help ensure compliance with the applicable safety requirements and in particular he –

(a) shall not expose or possess for supply or offer or agree to supply, or supply, a product to any person which he knows or should have presumed, on the basis of the information in his possession and as a professional, is a dangerous product; and

(b) shall, within the limits of his activities, participate in monitoring the safety of a product placed on the market, in particular by –
   (i) passing on information on the risks posed by the product,
   (ii) keeping the documentation necessary for tracing the origin of the product,
   (iii) producing the documentation necessary for tracing the origin of the product, and cooperating in action taken by a producer or an enforcement authority to avoid the risks.

(2) Within the limits of his activities, a distributor shall take measures enabling him to cooperate efficiently in the action referred to in paragraph (1)(b)(iii).

14.134 A person who contravenes reg 8(1)(a) is guilty of an offence and liable on conviction on indictment to imprisonment for a term not exceeding 12 months or to an unlimited fine or to both, or on summary conviction to imprisonment for a term not exceeding 3 months or to an unlimited fine or to both (reg 20(1)). A person who contravenes reg 8(1)(b)(i), (ii) or (iii) is guilty of an offence and liable on summary conviction to imprisonment for a term not exceeding 3 months or to an unlimited fine or to both.

Obligations of producers and distributors

14.135 Regulation 9 of the Regulations imposes obligations on both producers and distributors:

Obligations of producers and distributors

9(1) Subject to paragraph (2), where a producer or a distributor knows that a product he has placed on the market or supplied poses risks to the consumer that are incompatible with the general safety requirement, he shall forthwith notify an enforcement authority in writing of that information and –

(a) the action taken to prevent risk to the consumer; and

(b)   where the product is being or has been marketed or otherwise supplied to consumers outside the United Kingdom, of the identity of each Member State in which, to the best of his knowledge, it is being or has been so marketed or supplied.

(2) Paragraph (1) shall not apply –

(a)   in the case of a second-hand product supplied as an antique or as a product to be repaired or reconditioned prior to being used, provided the supplier clearly informed the person to whom he supplied the product to that effect,

(b)   in conditions concerning isolated circumstances or products.

(3) In the event of a serious risk the notification under paragraph (1) shall include the following –

(a)   information enabling a precise identification of the product or batch of products in question,

(b)   a full description of the risks that the product presents,

(c)   all available information relevant for tracing the product, and

(d)   a description of the action undertaken to prevent risks to the consumer.

(4) Within the limits of his activities, a person who is a producer or a distributor shall co-operate with an enforcement authority (at the enforcement authority's request) in action taken to avoid the risks posed by a product which he supplies or has supplied. Every enforcement authority shall maintain procedures for such co-operation, including procedures for dialogue with the producers and distributors concerned on issues related to product safety.

14.136 Such notifications should also be transmitted to the enforcement authorities of all Member States in which they believe the product has been marketed. If the product poses a serious risk, the notification becomes a RAPEX (Community Rapid Alert System for non-food consumer products) notification; otherwise it is a safeguard notification. The obligation is to notify the authorities, in writing, if producers or distributors discover that they have placed an unsafe product on the market, and what action they have taken to remove the risk posed. This notification should be done 'forthwith' and is a very important step in ensuring the safety of consumers by taking the appropriate corrective action as soon as possible. The provisions of reg 9 do not apply:

(a)   in the case of a second-hand product supplied as an antique or as a product to be repaired or reconditioned prior to being used, provided the supplier clearly informed the person to whom he supplied the product to that effect,

(b)   in conditions concerning isolated circumstances or products.

A person who contravenes reg 9(1) is guilty of an offence and liable on summary conviction to imprisonment for a term not exceeding 3 months or to an unlimited fine or to both (reg 20(1)).

14.137 A producer or distributor who does not give notice to an enforcement authority under reg 9(1) in respect of a product he has placed on the market or supplied commits an offence where it is proved that he ought to have known that the product poses risks to consumers that are incompatible with the general safety requirement and he shall be liable on summary conviction to imprisonment for a term not exceeding 3 months or to an unlimited fine or to both (reg 20(2)).

14.138 For those cases that go to trial, prosecutors should be aware of evidential limitations about notification statements. Regulation 44 sets out the following:

Evidence in proceedings for offence relating to regulation 9(1)

44(1) This regulation applies where a person has given a notification to an enforcement authority pursuant to regulation 9(1).

(2) No evidence relating to that statement may be adduced and no question relating to it may be asked by the prosecution in any criminal proceedings (other than proceedings in which that person is charged with an offence under regulation 20 for a contravention of regulation 9(1), unless evidence relating to it is adduced, or a question relating to it asked, in the proceedings by or on behalf of that person.

Causal and directors' liability

14.139 Regulation 31 states:

Liability of person other than principal offender

(1) Where the commission by a person of an offence under these Regulations is due to an act or default committed by some other person in the course of a commercial activity of his, the other person shall be guilty of the offence and may be proceeded against and punished by virtue of this paragraph whether or not proceedings are taken against the first-mentioned person.

(2) Where a body corporate is guilty of an offence under these Regulations (including where it is so guilty by virtue of paragraph (1)) in respect of any act or default which is shown to have been committed with the consent or connivance of, or to be attributable to any neglect on the part of, any director, manager, secretary or other similar officer of the body corporate or any person who was purporting to act in any such capacity he, as well as the body corporate, shall be guilty of that offence and shall be liable to be proceeded against and punished accordingly.

(3) Where the affairs of a body corporate are managed by its members, paragraph (2) shall apply in relation to the acts and defaults of a member in connection with his functions of management as if he were a director of the body corporate.

(4) Where a Scottish partnership is guilty of an offence under these Regulations (including where it is so guilty by virtue of paragraph (1)) in respect of any act or default which is shown to have been committed with the consent or connivance of, or to be attributable to any neglect on the part of, a partner in the partnership, he, as well as the partnership, shall be guilty of that offence and shall be liable to

be proceeded against and punished accordingly.

14.140 Causal and directors' liability provisions are covered in Chapter 3, Criminal Enforcement.

Defences

14.141 A defence of due diligence (expressed in similar terms to s 39 of the CPA 1987) is available in relation to all offences under the GPSR by virtue of reg 29:

Defence of due diligence

29(1) Subject to the following provisions of this regulation, in proceedings against a person for an offence under these Regulations it shall be a defence for that person to show that he took all reasonable steps and exercised all due diligence to avoid committing the offence.

(2) Where in any proceedings against any person for such an offence the defence provided by paragraph (1) involves an allegation that the commission of the offence was due –

(a) to the act or default of another, or

(b) to reliance on information given by another,

that person shall not, without the leave of the court, be entitled to rely on the defence unless, not less than seven clear days before, in England, Wales and Northern Ireland, the hearing of the proceedings or, in Scotland, the trial diet, he has served a notice under paragraph (3) on the person bringing the proceedings.

(3) A notice under this paragraph shall give such information identifying or assisting in the identification of the person who –

(a) committed the act or default, or

(b) gave the information,

as is in the possession of the person serving the notice at the time he serves it.

(4) A person may not rely on the defence provided by paragraph (1) by reason of his reliance on information supplied by another, unless he shows that it was reasonable in all the circumstances to have relied on the information, having regard in particular –

(a) to the steps which he took, and those which might reasonably have been taken, for the purpose of verifying the information; and

(b) to whether he had any reason to disbelieve the information.

14.142 Due diligence defences are dealt with generally in Chapter 3, Criminal Enforcement. A specific defence applies in respect of the prosecution of a person for the supply, offer or agreement to supply or exposure or possession for supply of second hand products supplied as antiques (reg 30). Regulations 30(2) and (3) state:

(2) It shall be a defence for that person to show that the terms on which he supplied the product or agreed or offered to supply the product or, in the case of a product which he exposed or possessed for supply, the terms on which he intended

to supply the product, contemplated the acquisition of an interest in the product by the person supplied or to be supplied.

(3) Paragraph (2) applies only if the producer or distributor clearly informed the person to whom he supplied the product, or offered or agreed to supply the product or, in the case of a product which he exposed or possessed for supply, he intended to so inform that person, that the product is an antique.

Enforcement

14.143 Primary enforcement of the Regulations falls to local authorities through local trading standards authorities in England, Wales and Scotland, and in Northern Ireland District Council Environmental Health Officers (reg 10). Certain products, however, require enforcement by both Local Authorities and the Health and Safety Executive ('HSE') working cooperatively. This will be required where the product in question is one that is either designed for dual purpose (ie for consumers and professionals), or where it is a product that has migrated to the consumer market. Note that reg 10(5) states:

(5) An enforcement authority shall in enforcing these Regulations act in a manner proportionate to the seriousness of the risk and shall take due account of the precautionary principle. In this context, it shall encourage and promote voluntary action by producers and distributors. Notwithstanding the foregoing, an enforcement authority may take any action under these Regulations urgently and without first encouraging and promoting voluntary action if a product poses a serious risk.

14.144 Enforcement powers are now found under Sch 5 to the CRA 2015 (see Chapter 3, Criminal Enforcement).

Time limits

14.145 The GPSR require that any prosecution must be brought within 3 years from the commission of the offence, or 12 months from the discovery of the offence by the prosecutor, whichever is the sooner.[80] The normal 6-month time limit in relation to summary only offences contained in s 127 of the Magistrates' Courts Act 1980 is expressly distinguished. And, notwithstanding s 136 of the Criminal Procedure (Scotland) Act 1995, summary proceedings in Scotland for an offence under the GPSR may be commenced within 3 years from the date of the offence or within one year from the discovery of the offence by the prosecutor whichever is the earlier. In *R v Thames Magistrates' Court ex p Academy International plc*[81] – it was held that the same time limit applied for the causal liability 'by-pass' offence (now contained in reg 31 (Liability of person other than principal offender)) as for the primary offence. Time limits are now covered generally in Chapter 3, Criminal Enforcement.

---

[80] Regulation 41.
[81] (CO/293/99).

Other measures

14.146 Enforcement authorities have access to a range of measures in regs 11–19 which can be employed to remove risk to consumer safety where producers and distributors have not fulfilled their obligations under the GPSR – these comprise 'safety notices' (which means a suspension notice, a requirement to mark, a requirement to warn, a withdrawal notice or a recall notice) and forfeiture. Generally, it is assumed that where the producer or distributor is already taking the action necessary to remove the risk to consumers it will not be necessary for the enforcement authorities to serve a safety notice.

Safety notices

Suspension notices[82]

14.147   These notices temporarily ban the placing on the market or the supply of a product while tests are undertaken to determine compliance with the Regulations. They can be issued when an authority has reasonable grounds for suspecting that there has been a contravention.

Requirement to mark

14.148   These notices allow an authority to make the marketing of a product subject to prior conditions, thereby making it safe or marked with warnings as to the risks. This is a very powerful tool and could be used in circumstances where a product is safe in some hands but not in others, eg a laser pointer for use by a lecturer is safe but not in the hands of teenagers shining it at the pilot of a helicopter. Such a notice could be issued on a retailer to ensure they do not sell laser pointers to under 18s for example. Additionally, a requirement to mark notice can be used on a car forecourt where second-hand cars have been examined and found to be unsafe – such a notice could be served on the trader requiring them not to supply the vehicles unless they have a valid MOT certificate.

Requirement to warn[83]

14.149   These powers allow an authority to insist on a product being marked with suitable warnings where it could pose risks in certain conditions, or require that specific warnings are given to certain at risk individuals (eg the elderly or children). For example, where an air freshener is found to contain a known allergen a requirement to warn notice could be issued to ensure that users of the air fresheners are alerted to the presence of the allergen.

Withdrawal notices[84]

14.150   Authorities can issue a notice to permanently prevent a person from further supplying a product that is believed to be dangerous or from placing it

---

[82]   Regulation 11.
[83]   Regulation 12 and 13.
[84]   Regulation 14.

on the market if it has not yet been placed. This notice would effectively remove the product from the entire supply chain. Again, this notice can only be served if the authority has reasonable grounds for believing that a product is dangerous.

Recall notices[85]

14.151 This requires a person on whom it is served to take such steps as are identified in the notice to organise the return of the product, deemed upon reasonable grounds to be dangerous by an authority, from consumers. The notice may be temporarily suspended if an appeal is to be launched. All safety notices may be subject to an appeal made before the end of the period of 21 days beginning on the day the notice was served.

Implementation of Commission decisions

14.152 Regulation 35 of the GPSR provides for the implementation of Commission decisions in respect of products that pose serious risks. In 2009 the Department for Business issued a Direction under reg 35(2) to all local authorities relating to the Commission decision (which has since been renewed) ensuring that only child-resistant lighters are supplied to consumers and that no novelty lighters are supplied to consumers.

Forfeiture

Forfeiture and destruction

14.153 Under reg 18 an enforcement authority in England and Wales or Northern Ireland may apply for an order for the forfeiture of a product on the grounds that the product is a dangerous product. Equivalent provision for a forfeiture order, by a sheriff, in Scotland is contained in reg 19. Both sections contain provisions for appeal against the decision to impose a forfeiture order.

The Psychoactive Substances Act 2016

14.154 The Psychoactive Substances Act 2016 ('PSA 2016') came into force across the United Kingdom on 26 May 2016. The Act is intended to restrict the production, sale and supply of a class of psychoactive substances often previously referred to as 'legal highs'. The background to the legislation is that new psychoactive substances were produced for the market more quickly than Government could regulate them, whether by classifying them as controlled substances or otherwise. According to the European Monitoring Centre for Drugs and Drug Addiction, 101 new substances were identified in the European Union in 2014, up from 24 in 2009. According to a Select Committee Report on the Psychoactive Substances Bill, the UK had the highest usage of any country in Europe.

---

[85] Regulation 15.

14.155   The PSA 2016 is based on a piece of Irish legislation, the Criminal Justice (Psychoactive Substances) Act 2010. The Irish Act was not without its critics. To bring a prosecution the authorities had to prove that a substance has a psychoactive effect, usually by way of scientific evidence. This proved difficult to obtain. By 2015 there had been only four successful prosecutions in five years. Similar problems may arise with the PSA 2016 because it works in a similar way. Since the PSA 2016 came into force, a substance does not need to be classified in a particular way by the government for its production or supply to be controlled.

14.156   The Act doesn't replace the Misuse of Drugs Act 1971, so laws around existing illegal (controlled) drugs will remain the same. Temporary Class Drug Orders (TCDOs) can still be applied and the Human Medicines Regulations 2012 will remain the same. However, the Intoxicating Substances Supply Act 1985 has been repealed.

Definition of 'psychoactive substances'

14.157   The key definition of 'psychoactive substance' is provided in s 2 of the PSA 2016:

> 2 Meaning of "psychoactive substance" etc
>
> (1) In this Act "psychoactive substance" means any substance which—
>
> (a)   is capable of producing a psychoactive effect in a person who consumes it, and
>
> (b)   is not an exempted substance (see section 3).
>
> (2) For the purposes of this Act a substance produces a psychoactive effect in a person if, by stimulating or depressing the person's central nervous system, it affects the person's mental functioning or emotional state; and references to a substance's psychoactive effects are to be read accordingly.
>
> (3) For the purposes of this Act a person consumes a substance if the person causes or allows the substance, or fumes given off by the substance, to enter the person's body in any way.

14.158   Therefore the central issue in deciding whether a substance is caught by the PSA 2016 is what effect, if any, its consumption is capable of having on the central nervous system. The Explanatory Notes to the PSA 2016 elaborate on the s 2 definition: 'by speeding up or slowing down activity on the central nervous system, psychoactive substances cause an alteration in the individual's state of consciousness by producing a range of effects including, but not limited to: hallucinations; changes in alertness, perception of time and space, mood or empathy with others; and drowsiness.'

14.159   Prior to the coming into force of the Act concerns were raised in various quarters that the definition of 'psychoactive substances' was too broad. This is particularly so given that an effect on a person's 'emotional state' can be caught, if triggered by stimulation of the central nervous system. It remains to be seen how workable it will be in practice and how narrowly or broadly the courts will interpret the definition. Section 3 of the PSA 2016 provides that any substances listed in Schedule 1 will be 'exempted substances' for the purposes of the Act. The Secretary of State can by regulations add or vary any description of substance, or remove substances previously added by regulations.

14.160 Schedule 1 currently lists controlled drugs (within the meaning of the Misuse of Drugs Act 1971), medicinal products, alcohol, nicotine and tobacco products, caffeine and food. In the course of a prosecution the burden of proving that a substance is not an exempt substance will probably fall on the prosecution; the Act is silent on the issue.

14.161 The listed exemptions are potentially broad because they include medicines and other substances with complex definitions. Difficulties in identifying a clear meaning of 'medicinal products', for example, is highlighted by case a decided by the CJEU, C-358/13, D (12 June 2014). This concerned the interpretation of the term 'medicinal product' within the meaning of Art 1(2)(b) of Directive 2001/83/EC. Two German defendants had been charged with selling herb mixtures containing, inter alia, synthetic cannabinoids, which, at the material time, did not fall under the German law on narcotic drugs. The CJEU decided that legal highs were not medicines, but the reasoning behind the decision (paras 38 to 50 of the judgment) was not entirely clear or easy to apply in future cases.

14.162 One area of controversy during the passage of the Psychoactive Substances Bill through Parliament was whether alkyl nitrates ('poppers') would be caught by the definition of psychoactive substances. The issue was referred to the Advisory Council on the Misuse of Drugs (ACMD), who came to the view that they would not, on the basis that alkyl nitrates do not *directly* stimulate or depress the central nervous system. However, the s 2 definition as drafted does not distinguish between direct and indirect effects. It remains to be seen whether the ACMD's view on indirect effect will be followed by the courts, should the issue arise. It may be that in due course alkyl nitrates need to be added to the list of exempt substances.

14.163 According to the Explanatory Notes with the PSA 2016, nitrous oxide is authorised by EU legislation for use as a propellant, for example, to administer whipped cream given that it will leave traces in the cream and, as such, would not constitute a prohibited ingredient when used in this way. But the consumption of nitrous oxide gas from a canister for its psychoactive effect would not fall within the food exemption and therefore would constitute a psychoactive substance under the Act.

Identification of psychoactive substances

14.164 When an unknown substance is seized it will need to be tested to determine what it is, and whether it is a 'psychoactive substance' within the meaning of the PSA 2016. If the substance is already known to have the required effect on the central nervous system then this should not be a problem.

In the case of novel substances however reliable evidence will need to be produced that they have such an effect.

14.165 The government has acknowledged this issue in a Forensic Strategy published in relation to the PSA 2016. The strategy sets out guidance for Forensic Service Providers (FSPs), law enforcement agencies, prosecuting agencies and expert witnesses to support the operation of the PSA 2016. It recognises that unlike the regime established under the Misuse of Drugs Act 1971, the PSA 2016 'covers substances by virtue of their psychoactive properties, rather than the identity of the drug or its chemical structure. Consequently, there is a requirement for a new forensic capability'. The Home Office has established a programme of in-vitro testing (ie testing outside the body, such as in a test tube). A commercial supplier has been contracted to perform testing 'for a range of Certified Drug Reference Standards (CDRS) of substances detected in the UK'. CDRSs are pure samples of drugs which are used to identify seized substances by their chemical structure. If a seized sample matches a psychoactive CDRS, this will provide evidence that it is a psychoactive substance within the meaning of the Act.

14.166 The problems however are likely to arise when novel substances are seized and sent for testing, and do not match any known CDRS. It will then be incumbent upon the testing service to carry out scientific tests which can be used by a prosecuting authority to prove, beyond reasonable doubt, that the substances are capable of having the required psychoactive effect. The ACMD provided guidance to the Home Office on how to establish its in-vitro testing programme. It has noted that although biochemical tests can show a substance is *likely* to have a psychoactive effect, proving psychoactivity via this method to the standard required for a conviction cannot be guaranteed.

14.167 It therefore remains to be seen, particularly in the case of novel substances, whether evidence from the Home Office's commercial testing supplier will be sufficiently robust to ensure convictions. There is also the question of whether the testing will be able to keep pace with the production of new types of substance, which was the essential problem under the pre-PSA 2016 regime, particularly in light of costs constraints.

Offences

14.168 The PSA 2016 creates offences related to the production, supply or offer to supply, possession with intent to supply and importation or exportation of a psychoactive substance for human consumption. There is no possession offence except in the context of possession inside a custodial institution. The government did not want the legislation to lead to the mass criminalisation of young people. It has however been pointed out that 'importing' a psychoactive substance would include buying one from a non-UK based website. This could lead to individual users being prosecuted. In addition to the criminal offences, the Act also creates four civil sanctions: prohibition notices, premises notices, prohibition orders and premises orders. Section 4 makes it an offence to produce a psychoactive substance, either for consumption by the producer himself or by some other person. Section 5 makes it an offence to supply or offer to supply such a substance, and s 6 sets out aggravating factors in relation to supply, including committing the offence near a school, use of couriers who are under 18, and supply within a custodial institution. Section 7 makes it an offence to possess a psychoactive substance with intent to supply. Section 8 makes creates offences relating to the import and export of such substances.

14.169 Possession of a psychoactive substance in a custodial institution will be an offence under s 9. 'Custodial institution' is defined in s 6(10), and includes prisons, young offender institutions, removal centres and service custody premises. Use of 'legal highs' has been a particular problem in such institutions in recent years.

14.170 Section 11 creates 'exceptions to offences'. There will be no offence in relation to the activities prohibited under ss 4 to 9 if 'in the circumstances in which it is carried on by that person, the activity is an exempt activity'. The exempt activities are listed in Schedule 2 to the Act, and relate to healthcare and research.

Powers

14.171 Section 36 confers powers to stop and search persons on a police or customs officer. The power is engaged where the officer has reasonable grounds to suspect that a person has committed, or is likely to commit, an offence under ss 4 to 9 or 26 of the Act. There is no power to stop and search where an officer suspects that a person has in his possession a psychoactive substance intended for personal use, given that there is no possession offence under the PSA 2016. Section 37 provides a similar power to enter and search vehicles.

14.172 Section 39 provides powers to apply to a justice for a warrant to search premises for evidence of an offence under any of ss 4 to 9 and 26. 'Premises' is defined in s 59 to include vehicles or vessels. Applications for a search warrant must be made, in England and Wales and Northern Ireland, by a relevant enforcement officer. Unlike the powers to stop and search persons, vehicles and vessels, the power extends to local authority officers as well as police or customs officers.

14.173 There is a two-stage test for the grant of a search warrant. The first stage is that the court must be satisfied there are reasonable grounds to suspect that evidence of an offence under any of ss 4 to 9 and 26 is to be found on premises. The justice will apply the civil standard of proof. The second element is that any of the conditions in s 39(5) are met. The enforcement officer should only seek a warrant where the co-operation of the occupier of the premises is unlikely to be obtained or where the purpose of the search would be frustrated or seriously prejudiced if immediate entry could not be effected using a warrant. Part 2 of Schedule 3 sets out the procedure for applying for a search warrant under s 39 in England and Wales and provides various safeguards.

14.174   Section 41 enables a relevant enforcement officer searching a vehicle, vessel or premises, to examine anything found, including by testing substances. Section 42 gives a power to require the production of documents and s 43 gives powers of seizure and detention.

Sentencing

14.175   Section 10 sets out penalties for those found guilty of committing the offences in ss 4 to 9 of the PSA 2016. On summary conviction for an offence under ss 4 to 8 a person is liable to a fine and/or a prison sentence of up to 12 months. On conviction on indictment the court can impose a prison sentence of up to 7 years, a fine, or both. Upon summary conviction under s 9, possession in a custodial institution, a person can be fined and/or imprisoned for up to 12 months. Upon conviction on indictment the term can be up to 2 years.

Civil sanctions

14.176   Sections 12 to 35 provide for four civil sanctions – prohibition notices, premises notices, prohibition orders and premises orders. Breach of a prohibition or premises order is a criminal offence. These are intended to enable the police and local authorities to adopt a graded response in appropriate cases.

14.177   According to the Explanatory Notes to the PSA 2016, the use of these powers will enable law enforcement officers 'to take action swiftly to nip a problem in the bud or to adopt a more proportionate approach to low level offending. It will be a matter for the relevant law enforcement agency to determine which approach to adopt in any given circumstances. Where there is evidence of a criminal offence under ss 4 to 8, there is no requirement to apply the civil sanctions in the first instance as a criminal prosecution may be the appropriate action to take'.

14.178   A prohibition notice requires a person to desist from carrying out a prohibited activity. The definition of prohibited activity, set out in s 12, covers the conduct elements of the offences in ss 4, 5 and 8, together with assisting and encouraging those offences. Such a notice may be in general terms or specifically require the recipient to do something, such as stop offering to supply psychoactive substances from a particular website. A prohibition notice will be of indefinite duration unless withdrawn.

14.179   Premises notices provide a means to tackle prohibited activity taking place from premises. These are likely to mainly be used for 'head shops' where NSPs were often sold before the PSA 2016 came into force. If the respondent is the owner of premises being used by a third party for a prohibited activity, a premises notice could be used to compel the owner to take action against the tenant. Unlike prohibition notices a premises notice may only be given to an individual aged 18 or over.

14.180   Prohibition orders can be obtained either on an application to the courts by a relevant law enforcement agency under s 18, or on conviction of a person before the criminal courts for an offence under ss 4 to 8 (or an associated secondary offence). They are similar to prohibition notices in that they can place general or specific requirements on the recipient in relation to prohibited activities, but it is a criminal offence to contravene the order. It is also an offence to contravene a premises order. The requirements for obtaining such an order are set out in s 20. They will probably usually be obtained in cases where a premises notice has already been served and the recipient has failed to comply.

CHAPTER 15

TRAVEL

CONTENTS

INTRODUCTION

15.1   Travel law is an area of law which exists because of a common subject matter, rather than by common legislative provisions or legal concepts. It has contractual, tortious and criminal aspects which are complicated by the inherently international character of the arrangements in question. The common thread is that it governs the arrangements between travellers (in this context, consumers) and travel providers, primarily travel agents, holiday operators and airlines. In addition to the large amount of domestic and European legislation on travel, there is also a vast body of case law interpreting and analysing the various provisions.

15.2   Given the breadth of the subject, an entire textbook could be dedicated to it. This chapter aims to give a practical overview of four of the more important aspects: package travel, timeshare agreements, the role of the CCA and the Air Travel Organiser's Licensing scheme, and compensation for delay, cancellation and damage.

PACKAGE TRAVEL

Introduction

15.3   Package holidays remain one of the most popular ways of travelling for UK consumers, with nearly half of all holidaymakers booking a package trip annually.[1] They are governed by the Package Travel, Package Holidays and Package Tours Regulations 1992[2] ('the PTR') which were made under the European Communities Act 1972. The PTR implement a European Directive[3] and regulate the supply of combinations of travel services when offered for sale at an inclusive price.

15.4   It is impossible to ensure that a consumer's package holiday will be perfect, or even satisfactory. However, the PTR ensure that there are clearly defined consequences in the event of a dispute about the package of goods and services provided within the price. They impose detailed obligations on package travel operators in relation to the information given to consumers prior to purchase, the form and content of package travel contracts, and provide for rights of withdrawal for the consumer and cancellation for the travel operator. They also define terms to be implied into all package travel contracts and impose criminal liability upon operators for failure to comply with certain provisions.

15.5   However, package travel law has been the subject of sweeping reform at European level. The cultural and technological changes during the last 25 years resulted in the EU repealing the PTR' underlying Directive on 31 December

---

1   Association of British Travel Agent's *Consumer Holiday Trends Report 2014*.
2   SI 1992/3288.
3   90/314/EEC on package travel, package holidays and package tours.

2015 and replacing it with a new package travel Directive ('Package Travel Directive').[4] Member States must transpose the Package Travel Directive into domestic law by 1 January 2018, ready for it to come into force from 1 July 2018. At the time of writing there is no indication that implementation will be affected by the result of the referendum on the UK's membership of the EU. This section aims to provide an overview of the PTR and the proposed changes which may occur if the new Package Travel Directive or some form of it is adopted by the UK.

Application of the PTR

15.6 By virtue of reg 3(1), the PTR:

apply to packages sold or offered for sale in the territory of the United Kingdom.

Therefore, consumers purchasing package deals online from overseas suppliers are unlikely to be protected by the PTR, although similar protections will apply throughout the EU by virtue of the underlying Directive. A good example is provided by lowcostholidays.com, a package travel provider based in Spain which marketed itself to UK consumers online. Following its collapse in July 2016, some 77,000 British customers were left without the protections and redress which would have been required to be provided by a UK company.

15.7 A 'package' is defined by reg 2(1) as:

the pre-arranged combination of at least two of the following components when sold or offered for sale at an inclusive price and when the service covers a period of more than twenty-four hours or includes overnight accommodation:

    (a)   transport;

    (b)   accommodation;

    (c)   other tourist services not ancillary to transport or accommodation and accounting for a significant proportion of the package, and

        (i)   the submission of separate accounts for different components shall not cause the arrangements to be other than a package;

        (ii)   the fact that a combination is arranged at the request of the consumer and in accordance with his specified instructions (whether modified or not) shall not of itself cause it to be treated as other than pre-arranged…

15.8 The definition has five primary elements: (1) a pre-arranged combination; (2) of two or more components; (3) sold or offered for sale; (4) at an inclusive price; (5) for a period of more than 24 hours or including overnight accommodation. The definition is a complex one and, if any of the five elements is missing, the deal will not come within the PTR.

15.9 The definition has been considered extensively in case law, much of which is either at county court level (and therefore not binding) or simply complicates matters further. The key aspects of contention however are (1) and

---

4   2015/2302/EU on package travel and linked travel arrangements.

(4), ie whether the deal is 'pre-arranged' and whether the price is 'inclusive'. Guidance has also been given by BERR on the definition.[5]

15.10 In *CAA v Travel Republic Ltd*,[6] Travel Republic Ltd successfully argued that it was merely offering separate services for sale at the same time; the single price charged for all was as a matter of convenience. Elias LJ concluded:

> '…we are dealing with a situation where the customer chooses his or her own combination of services from a wide range of options, in circumstances where [Travel Republic] does not know whether a consumer will select only a single service or a combination. The customer is putting together his own combination for himself…'

This is perhaps a surprising conclusion in light of item (ii) within the definition of 'package', above. Moreover, it apparently conflicts with the guidance of the Court of Appeal in relation to the concept of 'pre-arrangement' in *ABTA v CAA*,[7] where Chadwick LJ noted the width of the definition.[8]

15.11 The *Travel Republic* decision was subsequently considered by the Court of Appeal in *Titshall v Qwerty Travel Ltd*[9] where the question was whether a holiday was a 'package' or a booking of a flight and accommodation separately, albeit paid for together. Tomlinson LJ concluded that it was a 'package' because the consumer had not known the elements could be purchased separately and the price breakdown included 'service fees' presumed to be a charge for the agent putting the deal together.

15.12 In relation to an 'inclusive price' the decision of the ECJ in *Rechberger & Ors v Republic of Austria*[10] should be noted. There, the claimants were newspaper competition winners who had to pay only nominal sums for accommodation and were given 'free' flights. The fact that the price did not reflect the value of the holiday did not matter; the nominal fee was all that was required to constitute an 'inclusive price'. Thus even if one element of the package is free there is still an 'inclusive price' within the meaning of the PTR since the 'free' element is on offer only in combination with the paid-for component(s).

15.13 For the purposes of regs 16–22 of the PTR, a 'contract' is simply 'the agreement linking the consumer to the organiser or to the retailer, or both…'.[11] Unlike in various other European-based legislation considered in this work, no specific definition is provided of consumer other than 'the person who takes or agrees to take the package'.[12] Presumably that is because anyone purchasing a

---

5   *What is a package? A guidance note for organisers* (January 2008).
6   [2010] EWHC 1151 (Admin).
7   [2006] EWCA Civ 1356.
8   At [20].
9   [2011] CTLC 219.
10 [1999] ECR I-3499.
11 PTR, reg 2(1).
12 PTR, reg 2(2).

holiday will inherently be acting outside their business, trade or profession. Regulation 2(1) also defines 'organiser' and 'retailer'. The former is 'the person who, otherwise than occasionally, organises packages and sells or offers them for sale, whether directly or through a retailer'. The latter is 'the person who sells or offers for sale the package put together by the organiser'.

Misleading information

15.14 Regulation 4(1) of the PTR reflects the general law of misrepresentation and provides that no retailer or organiser should supply 'any descriptive matter ... which contains any misleading information.' Breach of the requirement imposes a requirement to compensate the consumer for any loss suffered as a result.[13]

15.15 'Descriptive matter' is an extremely broad category which extends far beyond formal advertising materials. It will certainly include words and photos in brochures, websites, letters, leaflets, and invoices and may include non-written communications, for example, by face-to-face explanation or as shown on radio or television.

15.16 What is or is not misleading is also deliberately broad. As well as obviously false information, it may include information which is literally true but creates a false or misleading impression. For example, a statement that the hotel had a 'rooftop swimming pool' was held to be in breach of reg 4(1) in circumstances where it was, in fact, 400 yards down a busy main road in the hotel's main reception building.[14] The question is to be judged according to the standard of what the consumer might infer, which creates a fine line for retailers and organisers who, inevitably, will want to create a positive impression of the facilities on offer.

15.17 The 'descriptive matter' must be accurate at the time of its supply since reg 4(1) is aimed at preventing the 'supply' of misleading information (as opposed to misleading information per se). Accordingly, a retailer or organiser will not be liable under reg 4(2) if the situation later changes.

15.18 Overall, the provision echoes the law of misrepresentation and, in particular, requires reliance by the consumer in order to claim compensation. For example, if a childless couple booked a package to a resort which was erroneously described as having 'an extensive children's play area', no compensation would be due under reg 4(2).

---

[13] PTR, reg 4(2).
[14] *Minhas v Imperial Travel Ltd* [2003] CLY 2043.

Brochures

15.19   A 'brochure' is defined as 'any brochure in which packages are offered for sale'.[15] That is an obviously unhelpful and circular definition. However, it does mean that the brochure need not exclusively relate to package holidays but could, instead, be more general literature on leisure activities which includes a limited section on packages. Regulations 5 and 6 of the PTR deal with brochures.

Requirements as to brochures

15.20   Regulation 5(1) requires that no organiser should provide a brochure to a possible consumer:

> unless it indicates in a legible, comprehensible and accurate manner the price and adequate information about the matters specified in Schedule 1 to these Regulations... to the extent that those matters are relevant to the packages so offered.

15.21   Schedule 1 lists nine items, including:

- the destination and means, characteristics and categories of transport used;
- the type of accommodation, its location, category or degree of comfort and its main features;
- meals included in the package; and
- the itinerary.

Not all the listed items of information will be relevant to every package. For example, 'the arrangements (if any) which apply if customers are delayed at the outward or homeward points of departure' (paragraph 8). In those cases, it is not necessary to include the information in the brochure.

15.22   In *Inspirations East Ltd v Dudley Metropolitan Borough Council*[16] the parents of a disabled girl booked a package on the basis of a statement that the hotel was fully accessible by ramps. However, there was no access to the pool by ramp and the ramp leading into the hotel was unsuitably steep. Accordingly, a prosecution was brought on the basis that the brochure was not accurate as to the 'main features' of the accommodation under Schedule 1. On appeal it was held that the 'main features' had to be considered in relation to the entire package offered, which would include the wheelchair accessibility of the resort.

15.23   Reg 5(2) provides that 'no retailer shall make available to a consumer a brochure which he knows or has reasonable cause to believe does not comply with paragraph (1).' The obligation to not 'make available' is a continuing one and, therefore, very general. For example, a defendant may be making a

---

[15]   PTR, reg 2(1).
[16]   (1998) 106 ITSA 3 MR 24, QBD.

brochure available if a customer simply handed an out-of-date version to a friend. That would require a retailer or operator to recall all previous editions of a brochure when an updated version is produced. To do so would be nearly impossible. It follows that dating a brochure may be sufficient, eg stating on the front cover that it is applicable only to 'Spring/Summer 2016'.

15.24 In relation to the knowledge required on the part of the retailer, the question is one of fact.[17] However, it is clear that turning a blind eye will cause an offence to be committed. Moreover, it is possible that if an employee of the retailer becomes aware of a breach of reg 5(1) and fails to notify anyone the company will nonetheless be liable by virtue of the doctrine of agency.[18] Breach of the obligation constitutes a triable either way criminal offence.[19]

Particulars of brochure to be binding

15.25 Under reg 6(1) the particulars of a brochure:

> shall constitute implied warranties (or, as regards Scotland, implied terms) for the purposes of any contract to which the particulars relate.

15.26 Again, no definition is given in the PTR of 'particulars', either for the purposes of reg 6(1) or at all. However, it must be the case that particulars can be more than mere written descriptions (eg photographs, symbols or graphs) and must relate to a specific package. The consequence of the provision is that if the package does not comply with the particulars in the brochure, then the consumer will have a claim for breach of contract, sounding in damages. In *Buhus-Orwin v Costa Smeralda Holidays Ltd*[20] the accommodation was described in the brochure as 'opulent luxury in a dramatic landscape ...' whereas, in fact, the villa was found to be rat-infested. Accordingly, the defendant was held to be in breach of the implied warranty and liable in damages for the whole cost of the holiday plus consequential losses.

15.27 However, the provision does not apply to the information in Schedule 1 to the PTR as required by reg 5(1), or where the brochure includes an express statement that changes may be made to the particulars prior to contract and the changes are 'clearly' communicated to the consumer prior to contract.[21] Equally, reg 6(1) does not apply where the parties agree to the contrary.[22] This is a fairly unusual provision in a consumer context which is likely to require clear and express agreement by the consumer. A statement in the small print

---

[17] *Nakkuda Ali v Jayaratne* [1951] AC 66, PC; *Jones v Bertram* (1894) 58 JP 478, 10 TLR 258; *Blaydon Co-op Society v Young* (1916) 86 LJKB, 115 LT 827; *Registrar of Restrictive Trading Agreements v WH Smith & Son Ltd* [1969] 3 All ER 1065 at 1070, [1969] 1 WLR 1460 at 1468, CA; *IRC v Rossminster* [1980] AC 952, [1980] 1 All ER 80, HL.

[18] *Saggerson on Travel Law & Litigation*, 5th edn, para 12.40.

[19] PTR, reg 5(3).

[20] [2001] CLY 4279.

[21] PTR, reg 6(2).

[22] PTR, reg 6(3).

that the parties agree that reg 6(1) of the PTR shall not apply to the particulars in the brochure would not be sufficient.

Information

To be provided before contract is concluded

15.28 Under reg 7(1)–(2), '[b]efore a contract is concluded' the 'intended consumer' must be provided with the following information 'in writing or in some other appropriate form':

- general information about the passport and visa requirements which apply;
- information about health formalities required for the journey and the stay;
- arrangements for security for the money paid over and (where applicable) for repatriation of the consumer in the event of insolvency.

15.29 These obligations overlap to an extent with what must be included pursuant to reg 5(1) and Schedule 1 to the PTR, presumably because some packages will be sold without reference to a brochure. Failure to give the information as required is an either way offence.[23] The imposition of a criminal offence is a harsh one in light of the fairly non-specific requirements, for example to give 'general information' or to provide it in 'some other appropriate form'.

To be provided in good time

15.30 Regulation 8 requires a second set of information to be provided 'in writing or in some other appropriate form'. However, this must be given not before the conclusion of the contract but, rather, 'in good time before the start of the journey ...'.[24] There is no definition of 'good time' but it is likely that it must be enough to enable the customer to digest the information in question and ask any questions they may have. It may also be relevant when the holiday was booked. For example, a last-minute deal may simply require the information to be given as soon as possible.

15.31 The information required is as follows:[25]

- times and places of intermediate stops and transport connection and particulars of the place to be occupied by the traveller (eg seat numbers);
- name, address and telephone number of: (i) representative of retailer/operator in the locality where the consumer is to stay; or, if there is no such representative, (ii) of an agency in the locality which can assist; or,

---

[23] PTR, reg 7(3).
[24] PTR, reg 8(1).
[25] PTR, reg 8(2)(a)–(d).

if there is no such agency, (iii) a phone number or information enable the consumer to contact the retailer/operator during the stay;

- in the case of a trip by a child under 16 years old, information to enable direct contact to be made with the child or the person responsible at the place he is to stay;

- except where the customer is required as a term of the contract to take out insurance for cancellation or assistance in the event of accident or illness, information about such insurance.

Failure to comply with reg 8(1) is a criminal offence, triable either way.[26]

The contract

15.32 Regs 9–15 of the PTR set out in detail the requirements for contracts in respect of packages, including mandating and prohibiting certain categories of term.

Contents and form of contract

15.33 Regulation 9 sets out the general minimum requirements for a package contract:

- depending upon the nature of the package, it must contain at least the 'elements specified in Schedule 2';

- the terms must be in writing 'or such other form as is comprehensible and accessible' and must be communicated to the consumer before the contract is made (unless, per reg 9(2), the time between the contract and departure is so short as to make it impracticable to do so);

- a written copy of the terms must be provided to the consumer.

As to the requirement that the terms are 'comprehensible and accessible' the question is an objective one. Namely, whether they are comprehensible and accessible to the consumer (per HH Judge Graham Jones in *Akehurst & Ors v Thomson Holidays Ltd & Ors*[27]).

15.34 Schedule 2 to the PTR sets out 12 elements to be included in the contract. There is considerable overlap with the information in Schedule 1 which must be provided in the brochure under reg 5(1). In addition:

- the name and address of the organiser, retailer and, where appropriate, the insurer;

- the price and whether it may be revised in accordance with a term of the contract;

- the payment schedule and method of payment;

---

26 PTR, reg 8(3).
27 Unreported, 06/05/03, Cardiff CC.

- special requirements the consumer has communicated to the organiser or retailer;
- the period within which the consumer must make any complaint about the failure to perform or inadequate performance.

Regulation 9 provides for no express sanction in the event of breach. However, reg 9(3) provides that compliance with reg 9(1) is an implied condition of the contract. Accordingly, failure to do so will provide the consumer with a right to treat the other party's failure to comply as a repudiatory breach.

Transfer of booking and price revision

15.35   Reg 10(1) imposes an implied term that:

> where the consumer is prevented from proceeding with the package the consumer may transfer his booking to a person who satisfies all the conditions applicable to the package, provided the consumer gives reasonable notice... of his intention to transfer before the date when departure is due to take place.

If such transfer takes place the transferee (the new party) and the transferor (the consumer) are jointly and severally liable for the price.[28]

15.36   Reg 11 renders 'void and of no effect' any term:

> to the effect that the prices laid down in the contract may be revised... unless the contract provide for the possibility of upward or downward revision and satisfies the conditions laid down in paragraph (2) below.

Reg 11(2) requires that, to validly include such a term, the contract must state 'precisely how the revised price is to be calculated' and can only provide for variations in 'transport costs ... dues, taxes or fees ... or the exchange rates applied ...' In any event, pursuant to reg 11(3), no price increase may be made in the 30 day period before departure or which would result in an increase of less than 2% (so called 'non-eligible variations').

Withdrawal and cancellation

15.37   Regs 12 and 13 both deal with withdrawal by the consumer and cancellation by the organiser. Under reg 12(a), an implied term is imposed into package contracts that where:

> the organiser is constrained before departure to alter significantly an essential term of the contract... he will notify the consumer as quickly as possible to enable him to take appropriate decision and in particular to withdraw from the contract...

The decision to withdraw by the consumer must be informed to the retailer or organiser 'as soon as possible'.[29]

---

[28]   PTR, reg 10(2).
[29]   PTR, reg 12(b).

15.38 The key limitation under reg 12 is that the organiser must be 'constrained' to alter the contract. It has been held that this requires the change to be 'absolutely inevitable' and 'unavoidable'.[30] Accordingly, it was held in two cases that reg 12(a) did not apply to claimants who attempted to withdraw from the contract and claim their money back as a result of the SARS outbreak in China in 2003.[31] That was on the basis that although there had been strong advice from the World Health Organisation and Foreign Office not to travel, there was still a vague possibility that the contract could be performed as originally agreed.

15.39 A submission was rejected in *Wilkinson & Ors v First Choice Holidays & Flights Ltd*[32] to the effect that an organiser was 'constrained' to alter the terms of a package trip to Kenya in circumstances where there was widespread civil unrest and violence. There, during the course of the two week trip, the consumers were confined to the grounds of their resort for the first week but were able to undertake limited excursions during the second.

15.40 Regulation 13 is linked to reg 12 and provides for implied terms if either the consumer withdraws pursuant to reg 12(a) or, for a reason other than the fault of the consumer, the organiser cancels the package. Under reg 13(2) the implied terms are that the consumer is entitled to:

- take advantage of a substitute package of equivalent or superior quality if the other party is able to offer it;
- take advantage of a substitute package of lower quality if the other party is able to offer it and recover the price difference;
- have a refund of all monies paid by him under the contract as soon as possible.

15.41 Pursuant to reg 13(3) the consumer is entitled 'to be compensated by the organiser for non-performance' unless the package is cancelled because:

- the number of persons who agree to it is below the minimum required and the consumer is informed of cancellation in writing in the period indicated in the description of the package; or
- of 'unusual and unforeseeable circumstances'

15.42 The compensation payable under reg 13(3) can work to a consumer's advantage. For example, in *Robson v Thomson Holidays Ltd*[33] the claimant specifically requested direct flights which the tour operator confirmed it had arranged. However, as a result of an administrative error, it had in fact booked indirect flights (albeit these made no difference to travel time or length of holiday). The consumer treated this as a repudiatory breach (admitted by the

---

[30] *Lambert v Travelsphere Ltd*, Unreported, 01/09/04, Peterborough CC.
[31] *Lambert* (ibid) and *Clark & Ors v Travelsphere Ltd*, Unreported, 22/10/04, Leeds CC.
[32] Unreported, 16/09/08, Liverpool CC.
[33] Unreported, 05/04/02, Luton CC.

defendant) and sought a full refund of over £5,000. When the defendant refused, the claimant instead reserved club class seats for a direct flight. Upon her return she sued the defendant for the additional expense of having done so (some £10,000). It was undisputed that the club class seats were the only direct flights available which conformed to the claimant's existing dates and requirements. On appeal it was held that the consumer had, in effect, put together her own package of superior quality, for which she was entitled to be compensated.

15.43 Regulation 14 provides for two alternative implied terms where the organiser becomes aware that it will be unable to procure a 'significant proportion of the services to be provided' under the contract.

Liability for non-performance

15.44 Reg 15 of the PTR is the primary provision through which consumers are able to claim civil compensation. An entire chapter could be dedicated to its provisions and the case law on it.[34] What follows is a brief overview only. It provides for a cause of action against the other party 'for the proper performance of the obligations under the contract ...'[35] and 'any damage caused to [the consumer] by the failure to perform' unless 'the improper performance is due neither to any fault of that other party nor to that of another supplier of services ...'.[36]

15.45 In the case of damages arising from non-performance or improper performance the contract may provide that compensation is to be limited 'in accordance with international conventions which govern such services'.[37] Further for non-personal injury claims, a term may limit the compensation recoverable 'provided the limitation is not unreasonable'.[38] These provisions reflect the mandatory rights created by international conventions and the requirements of the Consumer Rights Act 2015 ('CRA 2015').[39]

15.46 Regulation 15 also implies terms as follows:

- that the other party to the contract 'will give prompt assistance to a consumer in difficulty';[40]
- if the consumer complains of a defect in the performance of the contract, that the other party or his local rep 'will make prompt efforts to find appropriate solutions'.[41]

---

[34] See *Saggerson on Travel Law & Litigation*, Ch 5: 'Liability for Non-performance'.
[35] PTR, reg 15(1).
[36] PTR, reg 15(2).
[37] PTR, reg 15(3).
[38] PTR, reg 15(4).
[39] Section 65(1) (formerly in the Unfair Contract Terms Act 1977).
[40] PTR, reg 15(7).
[41] PTR, reg 15(8).

The contract must also 'clearly and explicitly' oblige the consumer to notify the other party of 'any failure which he perceives at the place where the services are supplied'.[42]

15.47 One of the key issues in relation to reg 15 is the difference between 'strict' and 'fault-based' obligations. It arises from the fact that liability accrues to the other party to the contract irrespective of whether another supplier, further down the chain, had responsibility for the issue in question. The issue was considered at great length and resolved by the Court of Appeal in *Hone v Going Places Leisure Travel Ltd*.[43] In *Hone* the claimant booked a package holiday with the defendant via its Teletext service. On the return flight, the plane had to make an emergency landing and passengers were required to disembark via emergency inflatable chutes. As the claimant descended the chute he saw a 'huge' woman, estimated to weigh around 25 stone, stuck at the bottom and unable to get up. He collided with her and was struck by his wife as she followed him down the chute. As a result, he suffered serious spinal injuries.

15.48 The claimant sued the defendant alleging inadequate supervision of the evacuation and contended that reg 15 imposed absolute liability on the other party for the injuries sustained. At first instance Douglas Brown J. rejected the claim because the claimant had not proven that a party was at fault, for whom the defendant was responsible:

> '...the claimant has wholly failed to establish that this accident was anyone's fault. Before criticising employees of an airline in respect of failure arising in an emergency crash, I would need to know much more than I am told in evidence in this case.'

The claimant then appealed to the Court of Appeal which also rejected the arguments advanced on his behalf. Longmore LJ said:

> 'In the absence of any contrary intention, the normal implication will be that the service contracted for will be rendered with reasonable care and skill. Of course, absolute obligations may be assumed. If the brochure... promises a swimming pool, it will be a term of the contract that a swimming pool will be provided. But in the absence of express wording, there would not be an absolute obligation, for example, to ensure that the holiday-maker catches no infection while swimming in the swimming pool.'

15.49 Thus, following *Hone*, a two stage approach is to be adopted. In the example of a coach which breaks down during an excursion run by a local operator, the first question is whether the local operator acted with all reasonable care and skill. If not, then pursuant to the wording of reg 15(1), it follows that the 'other party to the contract' (ie the retailer or organiser) will be

---

[42]   PTR, reg 15(9).
[43]   [2001] EWCA Civ 947.

strictly liable. If the local operator did act with reasonable care and skill, however, then no liability accrues to the other party to the contract under the PTR.

15.50 As to the relevant standard to be applied, the key authority is *Wilson v Best Travel Ltd*,[44] where it was held that local standards were what the situation had to be benchmarked against:

> 'Save where uniform international Regulations apply, there are bound to be differences in the safety standards applied in respect of many hazards of modern life between one country and another. All civilised countries attempt to cater for those hazards by imposing mandatory Regulations. The duty of care of the tour operator is likely to extend to checking that local safety Regulations are complied with.'

Although this decision related to the law prior to the implementation of the PTR, it has since been affirmed in numerous cases as a generally applicable principle (eg Swinton Thomas LJ in *C (A Child) v Thomson Tour Operations Ltd*[45]).

15.51 Accordingly, if the local supplier has complied with what would be considered reasonable in the locality, the obligation on the retailer or organiser under reg 15 of the PTR will have been discharged. Certainly it is not sufficient simply to say that the failure by the local supplier is obvious from the outcome (see *Hone*). Relevant matters when considering what is reasonable will include local regulations, laws safety standards and customs. The only exception to Philips J's conclusion in *Wilson* is where the local standard is so poor or the absence of a standard so stark that a fully informed and reasonable consumer would decline to stay in the location:

> '...I do not consider that the tour operator owes a duty to boycott a hotel because of the absence of some safety feature which would be found in an English hotel unless the absence of such a feature might leave a reasonable holidaymaker to decline to take a holiday at the hotel in question.'

However, the circumstances in which that might apply are likely to be few and far between.

Ancillary matters

15.52 Regulations 16 to 21 of the PTR set out various obligations on retailers and organisers to ensure that monies paid by the consumer are protected in the event of insolvency. Of particular significance is reg 16, which provides:

> (1) The other party to the contract shall at all times be able to provide sufficient evidence of security for the refund of money paid over and for the repatriation of the consumer in the event of insolvency.

---

44   [1993] 1 All ER 352 (QBD).
45   [2000] CA BS/1999/1321.

(2) Without prejudice to paragraph (1) above, and subject to paragraph (4) below, save to the extent that—

(a) the package is covered by measures adopted or retained by the member State where he is established for the purpose of implementing Article 7 of the Directive; or

(b) the package is one in respect of which he is required to hold a licence under the Civil Aviation (Air Travel Organisers' Licensing) Regulations 1972 or the package is one that is covered by the arrangements he has entered into for the purposes of those Regulations,

the other party to the contract shall at least ensure that there are in force arrangements as described in regulations 17, 18, 19 or 20 or, if that party is acting otherwise than in the course of business, as described in any of those regulations or in regulation 21.

(3) Any person who contravenes paragraph (1) or (2) of this regulation shall be guilty of an offence and liable:—

(a) on summary conviction to a fine not exceeding level 5 on the standard scale; and

(b) on conviction on indictment, to a fine.

15.53 The ECJ considered the meaning and purpose of Art 7 of the implementing directive (from which reg 16 of the PTR derives) in *Verein für Konsumenteninformation v Österreichische Kreditversicherrungs AG*.[46] There, Austrian consumers had booked a package through a travel operator, Karthago-Reisen GmbH, and had paid in full in advance for flights and half-board. However, Karthago-Reisen became insolvent and therefore did not pay the hotel. The hotel owner demanded payment directly from the consumers and refused to allow them to leave the resort in the event that they did not do so. When Karthago-Reisen's insurers refused to compensate the consumers, a claim was brought via the Austrian consumer regulator. The question was whether the payment of sums by the consumers in those circumstances constituted 'security for repatriation' within the meaning of Art 7 of the Directive.

15.54 At paragraph 19, the court held:

'The security for the 'refund of money paid over' covers cases in which the organiser's insolvency becomes known after the contract has been concluded and before it has begun to be performed or cases in which the services are interrupted while the contract is being performed and the consumer must be reimbursed a proportion of the money paid over corresponding to the services which have not been provided. The purpose of the security for the 'repatriation of the consumer' is to ensure that the consumer does not become stranded, during the performance of the contract, at the place where he is staying, through the carrier refusing, on account of the organiser's insolvency, to supply the service of transporting the consumer back to his place of departure.'

---

[46] [1998] ECR I-2949.

Accordingly, it was held that the Austrian consumers' situation was within the scope of Art 7 of the Directive.

15.55 Regulations 17 and 18 both relating to 'bonding'. Regulation 17(1) requires that the other party to the contract ensures that a bond is taken with an authorised institution which will pay 'to an approved body of which the other party [to the contract] is a member' in the event of insolvency.[47] The monies paid must be those 'as may be reasonably expected to enable all monies paid over by consumers ... to be repaid' and must, in any event, be the smaller of either 'not less than 25% of the payments which the other party to the contract estimates he will receive ... or the minimum amount of all the payments which the other party to the contract expects to hold at any one time ...'.[48]

15.56 Where the approved body has a reserve fund or insurance, the amount paid by the bond institution can be reduced to the less of either 'the maximum amount of all the payments which the other party to the contract expects to hold at any one time...' or 'a sum which represents not less than 10% of all the payments which the other party to the contract estimates he will receive...'.[49] Under reg 19(1), the other party to the contract must have insurance under which the consumer is indemnified in the event of insolvency of the contract.

15.57 Regs 20 and 21 relate to monies in trust. The former provides that all monies paid over by the consumer must be held in trust in the UK until the contract has been fully performed or any money paid by the consumer has been returned to him or has been forfeited.[50] Where the other party to acting otherwise than in the course of business, the variation provided for by reg 21 applies. Making certain false statements under regs 20 and 21 constitutes a criminal offence triable either way (reg 22).

Due diligence defence

15.58 All of the criminal offences created by the PTR are subject to the due diligence defence at reg 24(1):

> ...it shall be a defence for that person to show that he took all reasonable steps and exercised all due diligence to avoid committing the offence.

Where the defendant wishes to alleged that '...the offence was due – (a) to the act or default of another; or (b) to reliance on information giving by another' notice must be given identifying the relevant third party not less than 'seven clear days before the hearing of the proceedings...'.[51] A full analysis of the defence of due diligence is to be found in Chapter 3, Criminal Enforcement.[52]

---

[47] PTR, reg 17(1).
[48] PTR, reg 17(3)–(4).
[49] PTR, reg 18(1)–(7).
[50] PTR, reg 20(1).
[51] PTR, reg 24(2)–(3).
[52] See Chapter 3, Criminal Enforcement.

The Package Travel Directive

15.59   The Package Travel Directive was adopted in late 2015 and must be implemented by Member States by 1 January 2018, ready for its coming into force on 1 July 2018. It echoes many of the existing obligations under the PTR as to the provision of information prior to contract, withdrawal and cancellation, liability for non-performance and insolvency. It also includes certain additions. For example, it:

- includes a specific definition of 'unavoidable and extraordinary circumstances' for the purposes of the withdrawal and cancellation provisions (Arts 3 and 12);
- requires a summary of the key rights provided by the Package Travel Directive to be provided prior to contracting (Art 5 and Parts A and B of Annex I);
- increases the threshold for non-eligible variations of price from 2% to 8% (Annex I);
- imposes liability on the trader for booking errors caused by technical defects in the booking system (Art 21).

15.60   However, there are certain criticisms which may be levelled at the draft. Of particular note is the potential confusion which might result from the concept of 'establishment'. As set out above, the PTR apply to any package sold or offered for sale in the UK (reg 3). However, the Package Travel Directive makes reference to the seller's 'Member State of establishment', defined in the Services Directive[53] as that where, through a 'stable infrastructure', its business of providing services is actually carried out. In particular the insolvency protections for consumers are by reference to those available in the operator's 'Member State of establishment'.[54] The ultimate consequence of that change in language may be that UK consumers who book through operators established in other European countries may have a lesser degree of insolvency protection to that provided for by UK law. For example, under the current PTR or ATOL (see below).

15.61   Assuming post-Brexit that it will be adopted in some form or another, it will inevitably be slightly different to the original European text. By way of example, the standard information in Annex I, required to be provided by the trader to the traveller prior to being bound by any package travel contract, refers to and lists the consumer's 'key rights under the Directive'. However, that would make no sense to a consumer in a country which is not a member of the European Union and is therefore not afforded the protections of such legislation.

---

[53]   2006/123/EC.
[54]   Art 18(1).

TIMESHARES

Introduction

15.62 Timeshares have been traditionally controversial products. In theory, they enable a holidaymaker to enjoy the benefits of ownership of a holiday property for a specified period of each year. However, they are often entered into as the result of high pressure selling techniques and misrepresentations, which has previously led to complex litigation under s 75 of the Consumer Credit Act 1974.[55] Timeshare contracts are now governed by the Timeshare, Holiday Products, Resale and Exchange Contracts Regulations 2010[56] (the 'TSR') which came into force from 23 February 2011 and implement EU Directive 2008/122/EC.[57] The TSR repealed the Timeshare Act 1992 and revoked various other secondary legislation made under it.[58] As with the PTR, they include both civil and criminal aspects, all of which are considered below. However, their primary focus is threefold: the provision of information, the control of advertising and the creation of a right of withdrawal.

Scope of the TSR

15.63 In fact the TSR apply not just to timeshares but to any contract which comes within the definition of a 'regulated contract'; that includes any 'holiday accommodation contract' which is not an 'excluded arrangement' (reg 3). A 'holiday accommodation contract' means: a 'timeshare', 'long term holiday product', 'resale' or 'exchange' contract (reg 4). Each of those types of contract is defined in regs 7 to 10 of the TSR.

15.64 Pursuant to reg 7(1)(a) a 'timeshare contract' means a contract 'between a trader and a consumer ... under which the consumer, for consideration, acquires the right to use overnight accommodation for more than one period of occupation ...' Accommodation 'includes a reference to accommodation within a pool of accommodation'.[59] Accordingly, it does not have to be specific accommodation but, rather, can be one allocated from an identified group or 'floating'. This definition of timeshare improves that found in the Timeshare Act 1992. It no longer refers just to agreements relating to 'immoveable property' and decreases the period of agreements caught to those of one year in duration.

15.65 Regulation 8(1)(a) defines 'long-term holiday product contract' as a contract 'the main effect of which is that the consumer, for consideration, acquires the right to obtain discounts or other benefits in respect of accommodation ... irrespective of whether the contract makes provision for the consumer to acquire other services.' Therefore, the difference with a timeshare

---

[55] *Jarrett v Barclays Bank Ltd* [1999] 1 QB 1.
[56] SI 2010/2960.
[57] Directive on the protection of consumers for certain aspects of timeshare, long-term holiday product, resale and exchange contracts.
[58] TSR, reg 36.
[59] TSR, reg 7(2).

is that a long-term holiday product contract gives no definitive right to use accommodation. Both a timeshare and long-term holiday product contracts must have a duration of more than one year or, alternatively, contain a provision allowing for it to be renewed or extended so as to have a duration of more than one year.[60]

15.66 A 'resale contract' is defined by reg 9 as one to assist a consumer in buying or selling rights under either a timeshare or long-term holiday product contract. Resale contracts are where many complaints are made. Often consumers are the subject of an unsolicited telephone call telling them that a 'definite buyer' has been found for their timeshare and a market offer has been made to buy it. They are then required to make an upfront payment of several hundred pounds to cover 'administration costs' or similar. Once payment is made the consumer is then told the sale has fallen through, but that a meeting has been set up with an available corporate buyer. These meetings often take place abroad where the consumer is made to sit through a lengthy high-pressure sale presentation to join a bogus holiday club in exchange for their timeshare contract plus a top-up payment.

15.67 Regulation 10(1) defines an 'exchange contract' as one between a consumer under a timeshare contract and a trader where the consumer joins a 'timeshare exchange system'. A 'timeshare exchange system' is one which allows the consumer to swap with other persons the benefits of other accommodation or services for use of the consumer's timeshare accommodation.[61]

15.68 Under reg 5, the TSR only apply to the above holiday accommodation contracts which also fall within reg 5(2)–(4) being contracts which are governed:

- by the law of the UK or part of the UK;[62]
- by the law of a non-EEA state relating to accommodation which is immovable property in an EEA state, the parties to which are subject to the jurisdiction of the courts of the UK;[63]
- by the law of a non-EEA state not relating to immoveable property but where the trader carries on 'commercial or professional activities' in the UK and the contract falls within those activities.[64]

15.69 The TSR considerably reduce the jurisdictional scope of their protection, in comparison with the old Timeshare Act 1992. Moreover, it is important to consider Regulation 44/2001,[65] which sets out standard rules for determining

---

[60] TSR, regs 7(1)(b) and 8(1)(b).
[61] TSR, reg 10(2).
[62] TSR, reg 5(2).
[63] TSR, reg 5(3).
[64] TSR, reg 5(4).
[65] Council Regulation (EC) No 44/2001 of 22 December 2000 on jurisdiction and the recognition and enforcement of judgments in civil and commercial matters.

which Member State has jurisdiction in cross-border disputes. In particular, it provides for special rules on consumer contracts for goods and services,[66] which may in practice coincide with the above. In addition, the contract in question cannot be regulated by the TSR if it is an 'excluded contract'.[67] These include life insurance investment products that incorporate access to holiday accommodation on a timeshare-like basis, but which are regulated by the Financial Services and Markets Act 2000.

15.70 'Trader' and 'consumer' are defined by reference to whether the party is 'acting for the purposes of a trade, business, craft or profession' (reg 11). These concepts are considered in greater detail in Chapter 2, Interpretation of Consumer Law.

15.71 Accordingly, the TSR treat all holiday accommodation contracts which fall within their scope in the same manner and apply the same rights and protections to consumers under all of them. In particular, consumer under all types of holiday accommodation contracts are given the 14-day cooling-off period during which time the taking of accounts or payments is banned (see below). Further, they are all subject to the specified information to be provided before contracting and to be included in the contract. Finally, the TSR are expressed to be without prejudice to the application of the PTR (reg 37). Accordingly, if a regulated holiday accommodation contract also falls within the scope of the PTR, both sets of regulations apply.

Pre-contract matters

15.72 Pre-contract matters are dealt with by regs 12 to 14 under Part 3 of the TSR.

Key information

15.73 Regulation 12 deals with 'key information' which must be provided to the consumer by the trader 'in good time before entering into the contract.' The 'key information' is defined by reg 12(3) as:

  (a)   the information required by Part 1 of the standard information form ...,
  (b)   the information set out in Part 2 of that form, and
  (c)   any additional information required by Part 2 of that form.

Schedules 1 to 4 to the TSRs set out the 'key information' for timeshare, long-term holiday accommodation, resale and exchange contracts, respectively. Each of the Schedules is divided into three parts.

15.74 Generally-speaking, Part 1 of each Schedule relates to the specifics of the contract. These include:

---

66   Arts 15 and 16.
67   See reg 6.

- identity, place of residence and legal status of the trader(s);
- description of the product or services (as applicable);
- duration of the agreement;
- price (including obligatory costs);
- whether the trader has signed up to a code of conduct and, if so, where it can be found.

15.75 Part 2 then requires what is described as 'general information' relating to the consumer's right to withdraw from and terminate the contract, and that the contract may be governed by the law of another country.

15.76 Finally, Part 3 of each of the Schedules sets out the 'additional information' to which the consumer is entitled. If the trader does not include it within the pre-contract information, it must state 'where it can be obtained specifically (for example, under which chapter of a general brochure) ...' The information under Part 3 includes matters such as:

- information about the rights acquired under the contract, eg conditions governing their exercise;
- information on the properties including details of immovable property and services available, eg refuse collection or water maintenance;
- where applicable, certain information on properties still under construction;
- information on costs and termination of the contract (including the consequences of doing so);
- additional information, eg on maintenance and repairs to the property, languages available for communication and, where available, out-of-court dispute resolution.

15.77 Regard should be had to the relevant Part of the relevant Schedule in any given case to determine what 'key information' ought to have been provided at the pre-contract stage. In any event, the key information must be 'clear, comprehensible and accurate' and 'sufficient to enable the consumer to make an informed decision about whether or not to enter into the contract'.[68] In particular, the latter may present some difficulty since it suggests a subjective test according to the needs of each consumer (by use of the words 'the consumer'). However, it must be the case that the trader needs to simply consider what information would be appropriate for the average consumer in all the circumstances. Further, the 'key information' must be in the standard form in the Schedules (as required by reg 13), in writing, provided free of charge and in a manner which is easily accessible to the consumer.[69]

---

[68] TSR, reg 12(4).
[69] TSR, reg 12(5)(a)–(d).

Marketing and sales

15.78   Regulation 14 governs the marketing and sale of holiday accommodation contracts. All advertising must now 'indicate how the key information ... can be obtained'.[70] Further a trader must not offer a consumer to enter into a contract at a promotional or sales event unless the invitation 'clearly indicates the commercial purpose and nature of the event' and 'the key information ... is made available to the consumer for the duration of the event'.[71] This provision is intended to prevent traders luring in consumers and then applying a hard sell without providing accurate and detailed information on the products being offered for sale.

Criminal liability

15.79   Breach of regs 12 and 14 is a criminal offence.[72] It was the view of the Department for Business that there would be a considerable overlap between these offences and those created by the Consumer Protection from Unfair Trading Regulations 2008 ('CPUTR').[73] Failure to provide the 'key information' or failure to provide it in the language required is likely to impact a consumer's transactional decision thereby creating criminal liability under the CPUTR. However, failure to comply with reg 12(5), ie providing the information but in the wrong format, is where reg 12(8) is likely to have most free-standing relevance because, insofar as they key information is still intelligible and unambiguous, it will not affect the consumer's transaction decision. The same was considered to be true under reg 14: there is likely to be dual liability for breach of the requirements as to marketing and sales under both reg 14(5) of the TSR and the CPUTR.

Regulated contract: formalities

15.80   The formalities for a regulated contract are set out at Part 4 of the TSR in regs 15 to 19. Under reg 15, the contract must be in writing and include:

- the identities, place of residence and signature of the parties;
- the date and place of conclusion of the contract;
- the 'key information' required by reg 12 set out as terms of the contract with no changes other than those communicated to the consumer in writing prior to the conclusion of the contract (aka 'permitted changes');
- the standard withdrawal form set out Schedule 3 to the TSR.

15.81   In order to make the rights of withdrawal effective, the trader is obliged to specifically draw the consumer's attention to the right of withdrawal, the length of the withdrawal period and the prohibition on advance consideration

---

[70]   TSR, reg 14(1).
[71]   TSR, reg 14(2).
[72]   TSR, regs 12(8) and 14(5) triable either way (reg 27).
[73]   See Chapter 7, Unfair Commercial Practices.

during the withdrawal period.[74] Further, the trader must obtain the consumer's signature in each of those sections of the contract[75] and provide the consumer with a copy of the contract at the time of conclusion.[76]

15.82 Regulations 17 and 18 deal with the language of the contract. Similarly in relation to the provision of pre-contract information, the contract must be provided to the consumer in the language of EEA state in which he resides or, if there are two or more official languages, that which is nominated by the consumer.[77] It must also be drawn up in English if the consumer is resident in the UK or the trader carries on sales activities in the UK.[78] In relation to timeshare contracts for immoveable property in an EEA state, the trader 'must not enter into the contract unless the trader has provided the consumer with a certified translation of the contract in the language, or one of the languages, of that State'.[79] Accordingly, if the consumer is based in the UK and the timeshare property is in France, the contract must be provided in both English and a certified translation in French. Finally, under reg 19 'a regulated contract is void to the extent that it purports to allow the consumer to waive the rights conferred on them by these Regulations.'

Sanctions for non-compliance

15.83 Part 4 of the TSR impose both civil and criminal penalties for failures to comply with the obligations. Breach of regs 15, 16 and 17 results in the unenforceability of the contract as against the consumer. In other legal contexts it has been held that such a sanction does not render an agreement void or of no effect. Accordingly, there is no right to the return of payments made by a consumer voluntarily under an enforceable contract.[80] However, it does mean that the trader is prevented from taking court action against the consumer for breach of its terms.[81] Moreover, should be noted that the enforceability is only 'against the consumer.' Accordingly, the consumer could still seek to hold the trader to his contractual obligations under the deal even if no counterclaim would be available to the trader. In addition to those civil sanctions, criminal offences are also created for breaches of regs 15, 16 and 18. Again, these are either way offences pursuant to reg 27.

Termination of regulated contracts

15.84 Regulations 20 to 24 in Part 5 of the TSR deal with rights of withdrawal and termination. They are the key provisions of the legislation and provide

---

74 TSR, reg 16(1).
75 TSR, reg 16(2).
76 TSR, reg 16(3).
77 TSR, reg 17(2)–(3).
78 TSR, reg 17(4).
79 TSR, reg 18(2).
80 *Orakpo v Manson Investments Ltd* [1978] AC 95.
81 *McGuffick v Royal Bank of Scotland plc* [2010] Bus LR 1108.

important protections for consumers to get out of the contract either shortly after its conclusion or at the time of renewal.

Withdrawal

15.85 Under reg 20 all that is necessary for the consumer to withdraw from a regulated contract is that he gives written notice to the trader during the withdrawal period. No reason need be provided. The notice is presumed to have been given by the consumer 'at the time it is sent'. Therefore, so long as the notice is sent during the withdrawal period it will be valid, even if received by the trader outside it.

15.86 Regulation 21(1) to (7) provides:

(1) The withdrawal period for a regulated contract –

    (a)   begins on the start date, and

    (b)   ends on the date which is 14 days after the start date, subject to the following provisions.

(2) The start date is the later of –

    (a)   the date of the conclusion of the contract;

    (b)   the date on which the consumer receives a copy of the contract.

(3) Paragraph (4) applies if the standard withdrawal form is not included in the contract in accordance with regulation 15(7).

(4) The withdrawal period ends –

    (a)   on the date which is one year and 14 days after the start date, or

    (b)   in a case where the standard withdrawal form is provided to the consumer within the period of one year beginning on the start date, which is 14 days after the day on which the consumer receives the form.

(5) Paragraph (6) applies if the key information in relation to the contract is not provided to the consumer in accordance with the requirements in regulation 12(4) to (7).

(6) The withdrawal period ends –

    (a)   on the date which is three months and 14 days after the start date, or

    (b)   in a case where the key information is provided to the consumer within the period of three months beginning with on the start date in accordance with the requirements regulations 12(4) to (7), on the date which is 14 days after the day on which the consumer receives the information.

(7) In a case where both paragraphs (4) and (6) apply, the withdrawal period ends on the later of the dates determined by those paragraphs.

15.87 Accordingly, the standard period for withdrawal is 14 days after the consumer received the agreement (if later than the date of completion). However, failure to properly given notice of rights of withdrawal or key information extends the withdrawal period for up to a further 12 or three months. The purpose of the extension periods is likely to be two-fold. First, they allow for the trader to correct failures to provide the relevant information. Secondly, they ensure that the consumer remains able to take advantage of the key right of withdrawal even if important information about it or the contract itself was not provided when it should have been.

Effect of withdrawal

15.88 The effect of withdrawal is to terminate the consumer's obligations under the contract and, if it is a timeshare or long-term holiday product contract, their obligations under any ancillary contract.[82] Further, upon withdrawal the consumer cannot be liable for any costs or charges in respect the contract or any ancillary contract.[83] Moreover, since no advance payment can be requested in relation to a timeshare, long-term holiday product or exchange contract during the withdrawal period,[84] it means that the consumer can withdraw at no cost to himself.

15.89 Therefore, withdrawal allows the consumer to simply walk away from the contract without any further obligation. In an arena where high-pressure sales tactics may be employed and long-term commitments are entered into as a result, the protection afforded by this right is invaluable. Withdrawal from the contract also results in automatic termination of any related consumer credit agreement 'at no cost to the consumer'.[85] If the trader is not also the creditor, he must inform the creditor of the consumer's withdrawal 'without delay'.[86]

Termination of long-term holiday product contracts

15.90 Regulation 24 deals with termination of long-term holiday product contracts. In effect, this is a repetition of the right to withdraw each time when the consumer receives a request for payment of an instalment under the contract. The consumer may terminate the contract within '14 days after any day on which the consumer receives a request for payment of an instalment …'.[87] For the avoidance of doubt, 'instalment' does not include the first instalment.[88]

Criminal and civil proceedings under TSR

Criminal proceedings

15.91 As set out above, various provisions provide for criminal liability. Regulation 28 permits the prosecution and conviction of any 'director, manager, secretary, or other similar officer' of a company or 'any person who was

---

82   TSR, reg 22(2).
83   TSR, reg 22(4).
84   TSR, reg 25(3).
85   TSR, reg 23(2).
86   TSR, reg 23(3).
87   TSR, reg 24(2).
88   TSR, reg 24(4).

purporting to act in such a capacity' where an offence under the TSR has been committed by the company 'with the consent and connivance' of that person or as a result of that person's neglect. Where the affairs of the body corporate are managed by its members, the provisions apply in relation to the acts and defaults of 'a member in connection with his functions of management as if he were a director of the body corporate'. Regulation 28 also provides for liability where an offence under the TSR is committed by a Scottish partnership in Scotland.

15.92   Regulation 29 provides for the situation where an offence has been committed due to the default of another. In that circumstance, the other person is also guilty of the offence whether or not he is a trader and whether or not proceedings are also taken against the principal.[89]

15.93   Regulations 30 and 31 provide for the two primary defences under the TSR. Regulation 30 provides a defence of due diligence in relation to offences under regs 12, 14, 15, 16, 17, 18, 25 and 26.[90] Regulation 31 also provides a defence for the innocent publication of an advertisement in relation to reg 14(3) (marketing a timeshare or long-term holiday product contract as an investment if it would be a regulated contract).

15.94   Regulation 27 provides that the offences are punishable by fine, not exceeding the statutory maximum on summary conviction and unlimited on indictment. Although prosecutions are rare, sentences in analogous situations have been substantial. In *R v Goddard & Hill*[91] two defendants defrauded £460,000 from over 50 people, having invited victims on a free mini-break on condition they attend a sales presentation. The victims were put under severe pressure to sign up to timeshares on holiday lodges and were not told of their right to cancel. Many were also required to pay £1,000 at point of purchase. The two defendants were sentenced to 2.5 years' imprisonment after guilty pleas were entered.

Obligations as statutory duties

15.95   Regulation 35 has the effect of rendering certain obligations under the TSR duties owed by the trader, so that failure to comply would give the consumer a right to bring an action for breach of statutory duty. Under reg 35(5) liability for breach of such duties 'is not to be limited or excluded by any contractual term, by any notice or by any other provision.' This goes further than is required by the Consumer Rights Act 2015 ('CRA 2015'). Although anything which attempt to exclude statutory duties would certainly constitute an unfair term, there would ordinarily be scope to include a clause limiting the trader's liability for breach, subject to the usual test under s 62 of the CRA. Actions brought pursuant to reg 35 would, however, be subject to the usual requirements for a tortious claim. Namely, a six year

---

[89]   See Chapter 3, Criminal Enforcement.
[90]   Ibid.
[91]   Unreported, November 2009, Mold Crown Court.

limitation period from the date the cause of action accrued[92] and the ordinary rules on causation, remoteness and loss.

Liability for quality of services provided under regulated contracts

15.96 Finally, it should be noted that a question mark remains over what rights a consumer has when the timeshare or holiday accommodation provided under a regulated contract is of a sub-standard quality. The TSR themselves are not concerned with those issues but, instead, focus upon ensuring that the consumer understands the nature of the agreement and has time to reflect upon it and withdraw if appropriate. Where would a consumer direct complaints during the course of the holiday or upon his return? In particular, the structure of timeshare and long-term accommodation product contracts is such that it is often difficult to pinpoint the party who bears responsibility.

15.97 Although the PTR could provide an answer to such difficulties, despite reg 37 of the TSR it is in fact unlikely that a contract will ever be governed by both regimes. Once accommodation has been obtained via contract governed by the TSR, the consumer will probably not purchase other holiday services as part of a bundle for an inclusive price. Usually, transport and other similar matters will be arranged separately and privately by the consumer for each visit to the accommodation.

15.98 Ultimately the consumer is most likely to have to claim for breach of contract. However, where the trader is not UK-based this may give rise to preliminary jurisdictional issues under Regulation 44/2001/EC.[93]

15.99 The solution may be, if the consumer has paid for the timeshare contract (partly or wholly) by credit card, a claim under s 75 of the Consumer Credit Act 1974 against their credit card provider.[94] Such claims may be brought in relation to transactions which occurred with suppliers based outside of the jurisdiction.[95] For example, see *Jarrett v Barclays Bank plc*.[96]

REGULATION OF UK AIR TRAVEL

The Civil Aviation Authority

15.100 In 2015, 75 million passengers either arrived or departed from London Heathrow, the UK's busiest airport.[97] Air travel is now the fastest, and often the

---

[92] Limitation Act 1980, s 2.
[93] Council Regulation (EC) No 44/2001 of 22 December 2000 on jurisdiction and the recognition and enforcement of judgments in civil and commercial matters.
[94] See Chapter 18, Consumer Credit.
[95] *Office of Fair Trading v Lloyds TSB Bank plc* [2008] 1 AC 316.
[96] [1999] 1 QB 1.
[97] www.heathrow.com/company/company-news-and-information/company-information/facts-and-figures

cheapest, way for British holidaymakers reach their destination. As with all major industries, air travel is subject to intervention by a regulatory body, the Civil Aviation Authority ('CAA'). The CAA is a statutory body. It was created in 1972 under the Civil Aviation Act 1971, following the recommendations of a government committee chaired by Sir Ronald Edwards. It is now governed by the Civil Aviation Act 1982 ('1982 Act'), Part I of which deals with the administration of the CAA. It is crucially important in protecting consumers who make use of the UK's airports and travel with the air carriers regulated by it.

Function and purposes of the CAA

Statutory obligations

15.101 Section 3 of the 1982 Act sets out the functions of the CAA. Its functions are any conferred upon it by virtue of:

- the 1982 Act, including 'with respect to the licensing of air transport, the licensing of the provision of accommodation in aircraft, the provision of air navigation services and the provision of assistance and information';
- Air Navigation Orders, including 'with respect to the registration of aircraft, the safety of air navigation and aircraft (including airworthiness), the health of persons on board aircraft, the control of air traffic, the certification of operators of aircraft and the licensing of air crews and aerodromes';
- any other act of Parliament from time-to-time.

15.102 In carrying on those functions, the CAA must work towards the defined purposes as set out in the 1982 Act. The purposes defined by s 4(1) are to ensure that British air transport 'satisfies all substantial categories of demand ... at the lowest charges consistent with a high standard of safety ...' and 'to further the reasonable interest of air transport users.' On its website the CAA interprets its purposes as being to ensure:

- the aviation industry meets the highest safety standards;
- consumers have choice, value for money, are protected and treated fairly when they fly;
- we drive improvements in airlines and airports' environmental performance;
- the aviation industry manages security risks effectively.

15.103 For example, it ensures that all UK airlines comply with the regulations made by the European Aviation Safety Agency, although it does not itself set safety guidelines. Equally, the CCA can take enforcement action against airlines on behalf of consumers and ensure that ticket prices are transparently displayed, but has no power to order airlines to pay compensation or to regulate fares. Thus, the CCA regulates the air transport market to ensure that consumers are protected physically and economically, and to ensure that the industry complies with wider environment and security obligations.

Consumer enforcement action

15.104 In carrying out its functions the CAA comes within the definition of an 'EU Enforcer' under Schedule 5 to the Consumer Rights Act 2015.[98] It may therefore bring proceedings under Part 8 of the Enterprise Act 2002 to protect the collective interest of consumers.

15.105 The CAA's Regulatory Enforcement Policy[99] emphasises that its intention in taking regulatory action is to ensure a 'just culture'. This presumably means that its intention is to ensure that the playing field between airlines and consumers should be levelled insofar as possible. According to its Enforcement Policy, three principles underpin the CAA's approach:

- A 'proportionate and risk based approach': The CAA act proportionately to the evidence of risk to consumers. Accordingly, where there is clear evidence of immediate and substantial risk, enforcement action will follow rapidly. However, where there is a concern which is not supported by evidence, the CAA may simply monitor the situation, ready to take further steps if necessary.

- Taking 'independent evidence-based decisions': This is to be achieved by communication with the airline industry and ensuring that the CAA's enforcement actions are consistent across its areas of control. However, it emphasises that it will take any enforcement action it considers to be appropriate and 'will not alter our course just because we have been challenged, whether through a legal case or other action.' Its view is that such challenges are a natural consequence of its role and ensure that 'any uncertainties or ambiguities in the applicable law are fully tested to the ultimate benefit of consumers ...'

- Publicising enforcement where to do so 'is in the interests of the consumer or the public': The CAA considers that publicising its regulatory actions provides a transparent method to let the public and the industry know what work it is doing. Further it has the benefit of possibly acting as a wider deterrent. Full details of what, when and how the CAA will publish details of enforcement action are set out in the Appendix to the Enforcement Policy.

Examples of enforcement activity

15.106 All enforcement actions taken by the CAA are published on its website in chronological order. The CAA's prosecutions between 1 April 2015 and 31 March 2016 included successfully obtaining fines against defendants causing dangerous goods to be delivered for carriage in an aircraft, negligently causing

---

an aircraft to endanger a person, making flight accommodation available without holiday an air travel organiser's licence, and flying within the Glastonbury Festival restricted airspace.[100]

15.107   A good example of the first of the CAA's principles of enforcement is provided by a recent prosecution of a hot air balloon owner.[101] The individual was registered as the owner of seven hot air balloons who was therefore required to provide evidence of insurance to the CAA. When he did so, the CAA checked with the insurance broker, which confirmed that the certificates were not genuine and that there had been no such insurance in place since 2011. Accordingly, the CAA placed a 'no-fly' direction against the balloons. However, in breach of that direction the balloons were flown on four subsequent occasions including, on one occasion, with passengers. A prosecution was brought under regs 9 and 12(1) of the Civil Aviation (Insurance) Regulations 2005 (knowingly providing the CAA with seven false insurance certificates). The defendant pleaded guilty to three charges and was sentenced to three-months imprisonment on each, suspended for 18 months. Further details on the CAA's approach to criminal enforcement can be found in its 'Code of Practice for the Investigations and Enforcement Team'.[102]

Civil Aviation (Air Travel Organisers' Licensing) Regulations 2012

The 'ATOL' scheme

15.108   The Civil Aviation (Air Travel Organisers' Licensing) Regulations 2012[103] (the 'ATOL Regulations') are perhaps the most important protection for consumers within the remit of the CAA. Their purpose is to enforce the CAA's ATOL scheme which aims to ensure that 'consumers are not stranded abroad or do not lose money paid to the travel organiser for holidays and flights.' In effect the ATOL scheme operates as a form of mandatory insurance for air accommodation providers, to protect consumers against the insolvency of the airline.

15.109   The ATOL scheme was initially developed shortly after the CAA's creation in the 1970s to require airlines to hold a licence. It was then codified into the ATOL Regulations 1995 which were variously amended before being revoked and replaced by the ATOL Regulations 2012.[104] The ATOL Regulations came into force on 29 April 2012 and introduced various new concepts into travel law. The most notable is the concept of 'Flight-Plus' which has had an impact in the realm of package holidays and the PRTs (see below).

---

[100] *Brooks Discount Ltd t/a Top Brand Discounts 4 U*, 09/04/15, Bournemouth Magistrates Ct; *Anderson*, 08/08/15, Bodmin Magistrates Ct; *Ahmed Sajawal t/a Al-Karem Travel*, 03/09/15, Leicester Magistrates Ct; *Hoare*, 21/01/16, Weston-Super-Mare Magistrates Ct.
[101] *R v Nimmo*, 10/12/15, Southwark Crown Ct.
[102] CAP 1422.
[103] SI 2012/1017.
[104] See reg 3 and Schedule to the ATOL Regulations.

15.110 In addition, somewhat unusually, the ATOL Regulations foreshadow their own demise. Regulation 2 requires that 'before the end of the period of five years beginning with the day on which' they came into force (ie by the end of April 2017), the Secretary of State must review the Regulations, reach conclusions and publish them in a report. In particular, he or she must 'so far as is reasonable, have regard to how Council Directive 90/314/EEC of 13 June 1990 on package travel, package holidays and package tours is implemented in other member States'.[105] Thus, the intention is to entirely overhaul the scheme of consumer protection for package and air travel at some point in the future and to introduce a new Civil Aviation Act with its own regulations on subsidiary various matters.

Licensing

15.111 The core part of the ATOL Regulations is Part 4 which covers the licensing provisions. It sets out the process and procedure for applying for and obtaining an ATOL, as well as details on revocation and appeals against CCA decisions. Having an ATOL puts the holder within the direct regulatory control of the CAA and entitles him or her to undertake various other activities regulated by the CAA (see below).

15.112 Under reg 31 the CAA is entitled to publish the requirements for an application for an ATOL. There are six categories of ATOL. Each depends upon the size and nature of the applicant's business and, in some cases, requires a bond to be put up by the licence holder. The purpose of the bond is to meet refund and repatriation costs should the ATOL holder become insolvent. If those costs are greater than the amount of the bond then the shortfall is met by the Air Travel Trust Fund.

15.113 The categories of ATOL are as follows:

- Standard: The Standard ATOL is not subject to any trading restrictions. Accordingly, an applicant may have unlimited employees and turnover. It is, however, subject to a £50,000 bond, a personal fitness and competence test and various financial criteria.

- Small business: Applicants in this category are limited to 500 passengers per year and £1m licensable turnover for the first three years. Again, a £50,000 bond must be paid and the applicant must meet a personal fitness and competence test and various financial criteria. In addition, the applicant must not have been previously involved in a failed licence holder. The latter is clearly aimed at preventing directors and managers of failed entities trading as start-ups and thereby repeating previous mistakes.

- ABTA Joint Administration Scheme: This is available to members of the Association of British Travel Agents ('ABTA') with an estimated licensable turnover of £1.5m or less. The application is via ABTA. Accordingly,

---

[105] Art 2(2).

although there are personal fitness and competence tests, there is no requirement to pay a bond nor any need to satisfy financial criteria.

• Franchise: The Franchise ATOL is restricted to those who have no more than 1,000 passengers per year and is granted on the basis of membership of an approved franchise customer protection scheme. Again, as a result, there is no bond or financial requirement test, although the personal fitness and competence requirements remain in place.

• Trade: A Trade ATOL is restricted to those who wish to only deal with other ATOL holders. It is subject to a £50,000 bond plus personal fitness and competence requirements and meeting the financial requirements.

• Accredited Bodies: In fact, this is not a category of ATOL. Rather, if a person is a member of an accredited body he/she is exempt from the requirement to hold an ATOL and can trade under the body's licence instead.

15.114 Pursuant to reg 32(2) of the ATOL Regulations, upon receipt of an application for any of the categories of ATOL, the CAA 'must' refuse the application if not satisfied of any of the following:

(a) that the applicant is competent to make available flight accommodation;

(b) that the resources of the applicant and the financial arrangements made by the applicant are adequate for discharging the actual and potential obligations in respect of the activities in which the applicant is engaged (if any) and in which the applicant may be expected to engage if granted the ATOL;

(c) that it has appointed a person acceptable to the CAA as its accountable person; or

(d) that the applicant has complied with all or any of regulations 7, 8 and 9 of the Civil Aviation (Contributions to the Air Travel Trust) Regulations 2007 which are applicable to it in the circumstances.

15.115 Equally the CAA has power to revoke, suspend or vary an ATOL under reg 35. It 'must' do so if it becomes satisfied that the licensee is no longer a 'fit person to make available flight accommodation.' Otherwise it 'may' do so if the licensee either no longer meets the reg 32(2) criteria (above) or fails to comply with a term of its licence. In making a decision to grant, revoke, vary or suspend an ATOL, the person affected by the decision may request a hearing within 10 days of the service of notice by the CAA of its proposed decision.

15.116 The procedure for such hearings is set out under Part 5 of the ATOL Regulations. Regulation 56 onwards sets out various procedural requirements for such hearings, including the:

• need for seven days' notice of the time, date and place (reg 57);

• entitlement of the person concerned to be heard (reg 59);

• right to proceed with the hearing in the absence of the person concerned (reg 60);

• right to be represented and present evidence (reg 62);

- procedure during the hearing itself (reg 64).

An appeal from any decision of the CAA lies to the County Court in England and Wales and the Sheriff's Court in Scotland, with the CAA to be named as the respondent to any such appeal (reg 67).

Who is entitled to provide 'flight accommodation'?

15.117 Part II of the ATOL Regulations regulates the provision of accommodation in an aircraft. In effect it ensures that only those who are licensed or exempted by the CAA are able to sell flights. This ensures that the regulator can control who does so and, thereby, protect consumers. The relevant jargon for the sale of air travel is 'flight accommodation'. It is defined by reg 4(1) as 'accommodation for the carriage of persons on flights in any part of the world.'

15.118 Regulation 9 specifies the persons entitled to provide flight accommodation. They are:

- the operator of the aircraft'
- an ATOL holder acting in accordance with the terms of his ATOL'
- a person exempt from holding an ATOL.

15.119 The persons exempted from the requirement to hold an ATOL are set out at reg 10. They include regulatory bodies (such as the CAA), employees and agents of ATOL holders, airline ticket agents and any person making flight accommodation available as part of a Flight-Plus (see below). Under reg 11 it is within the CAA's power to further add to that list provided it is 'satisfied that consumers will receive a level of consumer protection equivalent to that which would otherwise be required under these Regulations.'

15.120 Regulations 12 to 14 then provide further requirements and details on who may come within the scope of some of the categories of exempt person under reg 10. It is a criminal offence to hold one's self out as being able to make flight accommodation available when not permitted to do so (reg 16).

15.121 Under reg 17, when a person provides flight accommodation (whether on its own, as part of a package or as part of a 'Flight-Plus') he must supply the consumer with an ATOL certificate. This must be done when the person:

(a) accepts a first payment, whether in part or in full, for flight accommodation;
(b) makes a booking for the flight accommodation requested by the consumer where payment for such flight accommodation is made by the consumer to the aircraft operator or another ATOL holder; or
(c) accepts a first payment, whether in part or in full, for anything other than the flight accommodation which is or would be a component of a Flight-Plus.

However, a person must not provide an ATOL certificate unless required to do so.[106] The ATOL certificate itself must comply with the form and content of the example published by the CAA.[107]

15.122 Regulation 20 requires:

> Where a person makes available flight accommodation, that person must provide to the consumer—
>
> (a) the name of the person who would be accepting the payment;
> (b) the capacity in which that person is making available the flight accommodation;
> (c) if that person is acting as an agent for an ATOL holder and the flight accommodation is not to form part of a Flight-Plus, the name and ATOL number of that ATOL holder;
> (d) if that person is acting as an agent for an ATOL holder and the flight accommodation is to form part of a Flight-Plus, the agent's name and the agent's ATOL number; and
> (e) if that person is a member of an accredited body, the name and ATOL number of that accredited body.

When issued with an ATOL, a person must not contravene any of the terms or conditions of it or any other accreditation (reg 21). Failure to comply with regs 17, and 21 of the ATOL Regulations also constitute criminal offences.

'Flight-Plus'

15.123 The concept of 'Flight-Plus' under the ATOL Regulations was created in an attempt to bridge the gap between the PTR and the ATOL scheme and to ensure that certain consumers were not left without protection in the event of difficulty. It is dealt with at regs 24 to 30 under Part 3 of the ATOL Regulations.

15.124 A 'Flight-Plus' is defined by reg 24:

> (1) Subject to paragraphs (3), (4) and (5), a Flight-Plus exists when paragraphs (a) to (d) are satisfied—
>
> (a) flight accommodation is made available which includes as a minimum—
>   (i) a flight out of the United Kingdom; or
>   (ii) a flight into the United Kingdom where the consumer has commenced the journey in the United Kingdom and departed the United Kingdom using another means of transport; and
> (b) living accommodation outside the United Kingdom or self-drive car hire outside the United Kingdom or both is requested to be booked and is supplied by any person under or in connection with the contract for such flight accommodation; and

---

[106] Reg 17(3).
[107] Reg 19.

(c)   such living accommodation or self-drive car hire is requested to be booked by or on behalf of the consumer on the same day as the consumer requests to book the flight accommodation, the previous day or the next day;

(d)   the arrangement covers a period of more than twenty-four hours or includes overnight living accommodation.

(2) Where a Flight-Plus exists, any other tourist services will be included in the Flight-Plus if such services—

(a)   are not ancillary to flight accommodation or living accommodation;

(b)   account for a significant proportion of the Flight-Plus;

(c)   were supplied under or in connection with the contract for the flight accommodation; and

(d)   were requested to be booked by or on behalf of the consumer on the same day as the consumer requested to book the flight accommodation, the previous day or the next day.

(3) A package is not a Flight-Plus except—

(a)   where a package does not include flight accommodation, flight accommodation (as described in paragraph (1)(a)) is requested to be booked by or on behalf of the consumer on the same day as the consumer requests to book the package, the previous day or the next day; or

(b)   where a package does include flight accommodation, living accommodation or self-drive car hire outside the United Kingdom is requested to be booked by or on behalf of the consumer on the same day as the consumer requests to book the package, the previous day or the next day.

(4) A flight which begins and ends in the United Kingdom does not form part of a Flight-Plus.

(5) A Flight-Plus will cease to exist if—

(a)   the consumer withdraws from the contract for any component of the Flight-Plus; and

(b)   as a consequence of that withdrawal, the requirements in paragraph (1) are no longer satisfied.'

15.125 The use of the phrase 'requested to be booked' at various points in reg 24 is noteworthy. It implies that it is the consumer's request for (for example) living accommodation or self-drive car hire outside the UK which makes the arrangement a 'Flight-Plus' as opposed to the existence of those elements per se. Moreover, the three day period defined by reg 24(3) is to avoid the arguments in relation to a 'package' that, because certain parts of the deal were not agreed exactly contemporaneously, it is not a 'pre-arranged combination' at an 'inclusive price'.

15.126 Under reg 4, 'consumer' is given a broad interpretation under the ATOL Regulations as a person who makes use of or intends to make use of flight accommodation in person or to provide it to another person:

...but is not a person who procures flight accommodation in the course of business while acting as the agent of another person who uses that flight accommodation for travel in person.

15.127 Thus, booking agents or PAs making travel arrangements would not constitute a 'consumer'. However, a corporate traveller booking for him or herself would not be excluded merely because the trip was not for pleasure. The 'Flight-Plus' arranger (being the person who makes the flight accommodation available to the consumer and has taken any step to including it within the 'Flight-Plus' (reg 25)) has certain defined obligations pursuant to regs 26 to 29. All four provisions operate by making various obligations implied terms of the 'Flight-Plus' arranger's ATOL. Accordingly, failure to comply will be a criminal offence and may justify the revocation, suspension or variation of the ATOL.

15.128 Reg 26(1) provides that where a 'Flight-Plus' arranger becomes aware 'that flight accommodation, living accommodation, self-drive car hire or any combination of these forming part of a Flight-Plus' will not be provided, he 'must make suitable alternative arrangements, at no extra cost to the consumer ...' Alternatively, if to do so is 'impossible' the arranger must 'refund to the consumer the amount paid by the consumer, on their own behalf or on another consumer's behalf' for those elements. For the purposes of reg 26(1) non-provision of a 'Flight-Plus' includes supplying the flight accommodation which 'varies significantly from that contracted for.' (reg 26(2)).

15.129 Reg 27 deals with each of the various elements of the 'Flight-Plus' individually:

- In relation to the flight accommodation, the arranger 'must provide the consumer, at no extra cost, with suitable alternative transport back to the place of departure, or to another return-point to which the consumer has agreed' (reg 27(a)).

- If there is an issue with living accommodation or self-drive car hire discovered 'after departure', the arranger 'must provide the consumer, at no extra cost, with suitable alternative living accommodation or self-drive car hire, as appropriate' (reg 27(b)).

Again, as with reg 26, if those alternative arrangements are 'impossible' the consumer must have his monies refunded (reg 27(c)).

15.130 Both of regs 26 and 27 are supplemented by reg 28. That provides that the arranger must compensate the consumer for the difference between the flight accommodation, living accommodation or self-drive hire contract for and actually provided; such compensation must include 'any incidental expenses reasonably incurred by the consumer including but not limited to additional living accommodation expenses.'

15.131 Finally, reg 29 provides:

... in the case of the non-provision of any tourist service forming part of a Flight-Plus other than flight accommodation, living accommodation or self-drive car hire, the Flight-Plus arranger is liable to refund to the consumer the amount paid by the consumer, on their own behalf or on another consumer's behalf, for that tourist service.

Interaction between 'Flight-Plus' and the PTR

15.132 The obligations at regs 26 to 29 may appear identical to those imposed by regs 13 and 14 of the PTR. However the key difference is the circumstances in which they apply. Under reg 30 of the ATOL Regulations:

A Flight-Plus arranger is not liable to the consumer under regs 26 to 29... except where the reason for the non-availability... is –

(a) the insolvency of any person concerned with its provision; or
(b) the failure of the ATOL holder who made available the flight accommodation.

Accordingly, they are limited to very specific circumstances of insolvency or failure by an ATOL licensee.

Criminal liability

15.133 The criminal liability created by regs 13(2), 17 and 21 are summary only offences punishable by a fine up to the statutory maximum.[108] However, the offences created by regs 9, 15, 16 or 41 are triable either way. On summary conviction they are punishable by a fine up to the statutory maximum and, on indictment, by a fine or imprisonment for a term of not more than two years or both (reg 69(2)). Under regs 9, 13(2) and 15 to 17 a due diligence defence applies (reg 70). A full analysis of the defence of due diligence can be found in Chapter 3, Criminal Enforcement.

15.134 Reg 71 deals with time limits for prosecutions. They are as follows:

- Notwithstanding anything to the contrary in s 127(1) of the Magistrates' Courts Act 1980, an information laid under the ATOL Regulations in England and Wales may be so tried if it is laid 'at any time before the end of the period of twelve months beginning with the date of the commission of the offence.'

- Notwithstanding anything to the contrary in s 136 of the Criminal Procedure (Scotland) Act 1995, summary proceedings in Scotland may be commenced at any time before 'the end of the period of twelve months beginning with the date of the commission of the offence.' For that purpose, s 136(3) of the Criminal Procedure (Scotland) Act 1995 apples.

- Notwithstanding anything to the contrary in Art 19 of the Magistrates' Courts (Northern Ireland) Order 1981, a complaint charging an offence in

---

[108] Reg 69(1).

the Magistrates' Court can be tried if made 'at any time before the end of the period of twelve months beginning with the date of the commission of the offence.'

INTERNATIONAL CONVENTIONS ON CANCELLATION, DELAY AND DAMAGE

Introduction

15.135 In addition to the above regulatory schemes, a major aspect of travel law involves the rules surrounding compensation for incidents which occur in transit, notably in relation to air travel. Such matters are dealt with via international conventions to overcome the complications of cross-border disputes, and have been regulated since the earliest days of air travel. An initial set of rules was drawn up following an international convention in Warsaw in 1929, which were amended in 1955 and further revised in 1963.[109]

15.136 However, the purpose of those rules was undermined by the creation of new diverging rules governing the EU and the United States, which led to travellers either being governed by more than one set of rules or left without protection. Accordingly, the Montreal Convention ('the Convention') was agreed in 1999, and came into force on 4 November 2003. Upon signing the Convention, the US Department of Transport described it as 'a comprehensive and up-to-date set of rules defining and governing the liability of air carriers in relation to passengers, baggage and cargo.' The Convention is given effect in domestic law by the Carriage by Air Acts (Implementation of the Montreal Convention 1999) Order 2002,[110] which came into force on 28 June 2004.

15.137 Much of the Convention is beyond the scope of this work. However, of interest are those aspects relating to passenger compensation for lost baggage and delay, which are considered below. This section will also consider the application of Regulation 261/2004[111] ('the Regulation') which governs EU air travel and deals with the same issues of delay and cancellation from a different perspective.

Position at common law

15.138 The earliest cases on travel compensation in English law relate to the familiar problem of cancelled and delayed trains. The analysis was based upon a contractual offer being contained in the rail operator's timetable with acceptance upon purchase of a ticket. A passenger whose journey was subject

---

[109] Known as the Warsaw Convention as amended at The Hague 1955.
[110] SI 2002/263.
[111] Regulation (EC) No 261/2004 of the European Parliament and of the Council of 11 February 2004 establishing common rules on compensation and assistance to passengers in the event of denied boarding and of cancellation or long delay of flights, and repealing Regulation (EEC) No 295/91.

to delays or cancellation was entitled to compensation for reasonably incurred expenses insofar as the delay was within the control of the train company.

15.139 In *Denton v The Great Northern Railway Co*[112] the defendant's timetable showed a train which left London at 5pm, arrived at Peterborough at 7pm and then proceeded to Hull, arriving at around midnight. The timetable included the following condition: 'The Companies make every exertion that the trains shall be punctual, but their arrival or departure at the times stated will not be guaranteed, nor will the Companies hold themselves responsible for delay or any consequences arising therefrom.' In fact, that part of railway which ran from Peterborough to Hull was not owned by the defendant and the 7pm train to Hull was discontinued by the line operator from 1 March 1855 but no amendment was made to the defendant's timetable.

15.140 The plaintiff had business in Peterborough on 25 March and in Hull on 26 March 1855. In possession of the defendant's timetable, he purchased a ticket from London with the intention that he would travel to Peterborough early on 25 March and then catch the 7pm train from Peterborough to Hull, to be there ready for the following morning. However, as a result of the discontinuation, the plaintiff was unable to make his connection to Hull and issued a writ for damages. Lord Campbell CJ considered that 'timetables cannot be treated as mere waste paper.' He concluded:

> 'It seems to me that, if the Company promised to give tickets for a train, running at a particular hour to a particular place, to any one who would come to the station and tender the price of the ticket, it is a good contract with any one who so comes. I take it to be clear that the issuing of the time tables in this way amounts in fact to such a promise; any one who read them would so understand them. ... the promise is to the public at large, exactly as it is here; it is in effect the same as if made to each individual conditionally; and, on an individual fulfilling the condition, it is an absolute contract with him, and he may sue. That being so, there is, I think, a contract...'

On the basis that the timetable had still been in circulation after the defendant came to know it was no longer accurate, the court held that there had been fraudulent misrepresentation and upheld the plaintiff's claim.

15.141 The authority of *Hamlin v Great Northern Railway Co*[113] again illustrates the apparent difficulty of travelling to Hull by train in the mid-19th century. In *Hamlin*, because the advertised evening train from Grimsby to Hull did not in fact exist, the plaintiff was forced to spend the night at Grimsby and purchase a fresh ticket to continue his journey the following morning. On the basis of breach of contract, he successfully claimed compensation for the price

---

[112] (1856) 5 E&B 860.
[113] (1856) 1 H&N 408.

of the additional ticket and his overnight expenses. However, he was denied anything other than nominal damages for the trouble and inconvenience caused to him.[114]

15.142   A third and final example of the common law approach is *Le Blanche v London & Northwestern Railway Co*,[115] where the plaintiff missed a series of connections from Leeds to Scarborough as a result of delay to his initial train from Liverpool to Leeds. Although the plaintiff had no particular business in Scarborough and no need to arrive at any particular time, he purchased a second ticket for a special train to Scarborough rather than waiting for the next service covered by his ticket. The defendant's timetable included the following statement seeking to limit liability: 'Every attention will be paid to insure punctuality, so far as it is practicable; but the directors give notice that the company do not undertake that the trains shall start or arrive at the time specified in the bills, nor will they be accountable for any loss, inconvenience, or injury which may arise from delays or detention.'

15.143   The court held that the limitation clause meant that the defendant was not liable for delays which were beyond its control. In concluding that the plaintiff's action should fail, Mellish LJ stated:

> 'The question ... is, whether, according to the ordinary habits of society, a gentleman in the position of the plaintiff, who was going to Scarborough for the purpose of amusement, and who missed his train at York, would take a special train from York to Scarborough at his own cost, in order that he might arrive at Scarborough an hour or an hour and a half sooner than he would do if he waited at York for the next ordinary train. This question seems to me to admit of but one answer, namely, that no one but a very exceptionally extravagant person would think of taking a special train under such circumstances.'

15.144   By way of modern contrast to the above case law, the Department for Transport has introduced an enhanced consumer redress scheme, which applies the CRA 2015 to train delays from late 2016. The consequence is that consumers can now claim compensation for delays of even a few minutes, compared to the previous graduated compensation structure which required at least a 30-minute delay. Moreover, from 1 October 2016, Chapters 4 and 5 of the CRA 2015 (relating to 'Services') have now been extended to cover contracts for the supply of consumer transport services.[116] Therefore pre-contract information about timetabling could now justify a claim for breach of contract pursuant to s 50. At the very least it means that consumer transport operators must be more circumspect about how they describe their services. For further information see Chapter 5, Consumer Rights.

---

[114] In relation to the question of general damages for mental distress, *Hamlin* was subsequently overturned by *Jarvis v Swans Tours Ltd* [1973] QB 233.

[115] (1876) 1 CPD 286.

[116] Consumer Rights Act 2015 (Commencement No 3, Transitional Provisions, Savings and Consequential Amendments) (Amendment) Order 2016 (SI 2016/484), Art 2(2).

The Convention

Scope of application

15.145 As of June 2016 there are currently 120 parties to the Convention including the all Member States of the European Union, the USA, China and a substantial number of South American, African and Asian nations. Art 1 of the Convention deals with its scope:

> 1. This Convention applies to all international carriage of persons, baggage and cargo performed by aircraft for reward. It applies equally to gratuitous carriage by aircraft performed by an air transport undertaking.

'International carriage' is defined as any carriage where 'according to the agreement between the parties' the place of departure and destination are 'situated either within the territories of two States Parties, or within the territory of a single State Party if there is an agreement stopping place within the territory of another State, even if that State is not a State Party'.[117]

15.146 Accordingly, one must look at the entire journey in considering whether the Convention applies, rather than merely the leg of the journey during which the mishap occurred. For example, if a person bought a ticket from Edinburgh to Los Angeles via London, and an incident occurred between Edinburgh and London causing them to disembark in London, it would be covered by the Convention. That is because the 'agreement between the parties' provided for departure and arrival in the territories of two State Parties.

15.147 Moreover, carriage by 'several successive carriers is deemed, for the purposes of this Convention, to be one undivided carriage if it has been regarded the parties as a single operation, whether it had been agreed upon under the form of a single contract or of a series of contracts...'.[118] Somewhat unexpectedly 'aircraft' is not defined anywhere in the Convention, although under the General Classification of Aircraft in Air Navigation Order 2000[119] it includes airplanes, gyroplanes, gliders, airships and helicopters. It has been held by the Court of Appeal that a paraglider is not an aircraft[120] but that a hot air balloon is.[121]

Jurisdiction

15.148 Art 33 of the Convention deals with jurisdiction:

> 1. An action for damages must be brought, at the option of the plaintiff, in the territory of one of the State Parties, either before the court of the domicile of the

---

[117] Art 1(2) of the Convention.
[118] Art 1(3) of the Convention.
[119] SI 2000/1562.
[120] *Disley v Levine* [2001] EWCA Civ 1087, [2002] 1 WLR 785.
[121] *Laroche v Spirit of Adventure* [2009] EWCA Civ 12, [2009] 3 WLR 351.

carrier or of its principal place of business, or where it has a place of business through which the contract has been made or before the court at the place of destination.

...

4. Questions of procedure shall be governed by the law of the court seized of that case.

15.149   Thus, putting aside the additional option in cases of damage resulting from death or injury set down by Art 33(2), proceedings may be issued under the Convention where:

- the carrier is ordinarily based;
- the carrier has its principal place of business;
- the carrier has an establishment through which the contract is made; or
- the journey ended.

15.150   Certainly in relation to the previous Warsaw-Hague Convention 1955, the claimant's choice of jurisdiction was held to be final and the doctrine of forum non conveniens was thus inapplicable.[122]

Liability

15.151   The Convention imposes liability in three situations:

- death and injury (Art 17(1));
- damage or loss of baggage (Art 17(2)-(3));
- damage to cargo (Art 18);
- delay to passengers and baggage (Art 19).

As stated above, the focus here is upon Arts 17(2)-(3) and 19.

15.152   In the first instance, damage to baggage is subject to the provisions at Art 17. Art 17(2) provides the carrier is only liable for damage to baggage 'during any period within which the check baggage was in the charge of the carrier.' However, it will not be liable 'to the extent that the damage resulted from the inherent defect, quality or vice of the baggage.' In the case of unchecked baggage the carrier will be liable only if 'the damage resulted from its fault or that of its servants or agents.' In relation to lost checked luggage, Art 17(3) allows passengers to enforce against carriers if 'the carrier admits the loss ... or if the checked baggage has not arrived at the expiration of twenty-one days after the date on which it ought to have arrived'.

15.153   Art 17(2) effectively provides a causation requirement in relation to damaged baggage. The liability of carriers is (understandably) stricter for

---

[122]   *Milor SrL v British Airways* [1996] QB 702.

baggage which has been checked-in. Unchecked bags can only be the subject of claim if the damages was directly the fault of the carrier.

15.154   As to delay, Art 19 provides:

> The carrier is liable for damage occasioned by delay in the carriage by air of passengers, baggage or cargo. Nevertheless, the carrier shall not be liable for damage occasioned by delay if it proves that its servants and agents took all measures that could reasonably be required to avoid the damage or that it was impossible for it or them to take such measures.

Notably, unlike the Regulation (below), the Convention gives no guidance on what constitutes 'delay'. Presumably *de minimis* delays of no more than a few minutes could be excluded under the usual rules of interpretation. However, many other short or medium term delays will cause little or no damage. Thus the question remains as to what 'delay' is.

15.155   The 'reasonable measures' defence in the second sentence of Art 19 echoes the common law test laid down in *Le Blanche*.[123] For example, force majeures such as severe weather or terrorism will exonerate the carrier from Art 19 liability. Moreover, many carriers will include as a standard term a limitation clause stating that timetables are not guaranteed and liability is not accepted for consequential losses (most commonly this protects them against liability for missed connections).

15.156   Over many years 'damage' under the Convention was repeatedly held in domestic first-instance cases not to include non-material damage. For example, compensation for loss of enjoyment, distress, anxiety or inconvenience. These decisions relied upon other foreign cases on the point including substantial authorities from the United States Supreme Court.

15.157   However, the status quo was thrown into doubt by the decision of the ECJ in *Walz v Clickair*.[124] The court, having failed to refer to any of the other relevant authorities on the point, concluded a very broad-brush analysis by stating that damage 'must be construed as including both material and non-material damage.'[125] It entirely failed to consider the importance of consistent interpretation throughout signatory states (which has been emphasised by various other global decisions relating to the Convention) and, instead, focussed exclusively upon the position within the EU.

Limits of liability

15.158   Article 20 of the Convention imposes a fairly standard contributory negligence provision upon which a carrier can rely if it is able to prove 'that the damage was caused or contributed to by the negligence or other wrongful act or omission of the person claiming compensation...' In those circumstances 'the

---

[123]   (1876) 1 CPD 286.
[124]   [2011] Bus LR 855.
[125]   Para 29.

carrier shall be wholly or party exonerated from its liability to the claimant...'. Article 22(1) relates to limits of liability for delay and damage to baggage and cargo.

15.159 Given that the Convention operates globally, it deals with financial limits by reference to 'Special Drawing Rights' ('SDR'). The SDR is a notional international currency created by the International Monetary Fund defined by a weighted average of various convertible currencies. Although secondary legislation has been created for the purposes of determining the domestic value of the SDR,[126] it can now be easily converted online. It is likely that the valuation of the SDR is to be determined as at the date of the damage, rather than the date of issue or judgment.

15.160 Article 22 provides:

> 1. In the case of damage caused by delay as specified in Art 19 in the carriage of persons, the liability of the carrier for each passenger is limited to 4,150 Special Drawing Rights.

> 2. In the carriage of baggage, the liability of the carrier in the case of destruction, loss, damage or delay is limited 1,000 Special Drawing Rights for each passenger unless the passenger has made, at the time when the checked baggage was handed over to the carrier, a special declaration of interest in delivery at destination and has paid a supplementary sum if the case so requires. In that case the carrier will be liable to pay a sum not exceeding the declared sum, unless it proves that the sum is greater than the passenger's actual interest in delivery at destination.

15.161 Article 22(1) therefore limits damages for delay to a value (at the time of writing) of just under £4,500.[127] Article 22(2) provides for a general limit (at the time of writing) of just over £1,000 in respect of damage to baggage unless the passenger declares a special interest and pays a supplement. In that case the carrier will be liable for the declared sum unless it can be proved that the passenger's actual interest was less. In effect, it allows a passenger to purchase a top-up of the carrier's liability to the actual value of the item in question. This is most often done for baggage with a value greater than the limit of 1,000 SDR which are to be checked-in. For example, expensive musical instruments or sports equipment.

15.162 However, per Art 22(5), the limit on liability:

> shall not apply if it is proved that the damage resulted from the act or omission of the carrier, its servants or agents, done with the intent to cause damage or recklessly with the knowledge that damage would probably result; providing that ... it is also proved that such agent or servant was acting within the scope of its employment.

15.163 Under Art 25 a carrier may stipulate that higher limits of liability or no limits apply. However, under Art 26, 'any provision tending to relieve the carrier of liability or to fix a lower limit than that which is laid down in this

---

[126] Carriage by Air (Sterling Equivalents) Order 1999, SI 1998/2881.
[127] As of 15/8/16, the SDR was worth £1.08.

Convention shall be null and void'. Finally, the relevant limitation period under the Convention is 'two years, reckoned from the date of arrival at the destination, or from the date on which the aircraft ought to have arrived, or from the date on which the carriage stopped.'

The Regulation

Scope of the Regulation

15.164 As set out above, the Regulation covers many of the same situations as the Convention, ie for denied boarding, delay and cancellation. In *IATA v Department for Transport*,[128] the ECJ concluded that there was no conflict between the two schemes and that the existence of the Convention did not invalidate the Regulation. The difference was said to be that the Convention provided a mechanism for passengers to bring damages claims, whereas the Regulation introduced a strict liability scheme of standardised, fixed compensation.

15.165 Pursuant to Art 3(1), the Regulation applies only to flights departing from an airport in 'the territory of a Member State' or from a third party country to an airport in 'the territory of a Member State'. To be covered by the Regulation, passengers must:

- have a confirmed reservation and have presented themselves for check-in at the time stipulated by 'the air carrier, the tour operator or an authorised travel agent';
- if no time is indicated, not later than 45 minutes 'before the published departure time'; or
- have been transferred onto the flight 'irrespective of the reason'.

15.166 The Regulation does not cover passengers 'travelling free of charge or at a reduced fare not directly available to the public'.[129] Accordingly, only paying members of the general public are entitled to protection under the Regulation. Cabin crew or travel agents who travel at a discount would not be entitled to compensation. Presumably, however, a passenger travelling at a reduced fare which was available to the public-at-large is covered. For example, under a frequent flyer scheme or flights purchase in the sale.

15.167 Unlike the Convention which does not defined 'aircraft' the Regulation specifically provides that it 'shall only apply to passengers transported by motorised fixed wing aircraft.'[130]

15.168 Three types of event entitle a passenger to compensation under the Regulation:

---

[128] [2006] ECR I-00403.
[129] Art 3(3) of the Convention.
[130] Art 3(4) of the Convention.

- denied boarding (Art 4);
- cancellation (Art 5);
- delay (Art 6).

Denied boarding

15.169 'Denied boarding' is defined under Art 2(j) as:

> a refusal to carry passengers on a flight, although they have presented themselves
> for boarding under the conditions laid down in Article 3(2), except where there
> are reasonable grounds to deny them boarding, such as health, safety or security,
> or inadequate travel documentation.

15.170 Article 4 mandates a three-step process for denied boarding. First,
'where the air carrier reasonably expects to deny boarding on a flight' it must
ask for volunteers to 'surrender their reservations in exchange for benefits to be
agreed…' Secondly, if there are not enough volunteers, 'the operating air carrier
may then deny boarding to passengers against their will.' Thirdly, in the event
that boarding is denied to passengers against their will, the air carrier 'shall
immediately compensate them in accordance with Article 7 and assist them in
accordance with Articles 8 and 9.' The concept most commonly arises as a
result of overbooking although it could also cover broad operational reasons
such as flight rescheduling.[131]

15.171 Under the definition at Art 2(j), an air carrier's defence is that there
were 'reasonable grounds' for denying boarding. Certain concrete examples are
given, which have been given a fairly wide interpretation. For example, in
Limbert v My Travel Group plc,[132] the Limberts were denied boarding when
the original aircraft was damaged in a runway collision such that a smaller
plane had to be employed. They were therefore flown to a different city and put
on a coach to their final destination. It was held that the airline had proven that
the smaller aircraft was necessary for safety reasons such that there were
'reasonable grounds' and Art 4 of the Regulation was inapplicable.

Cancellation

15.172 Cancellation is fairly self-explanatory. Nonetheless it is defined in the
Regulation as 'the non-operation of a flight which was previously planned and
on which at least one place was reserved'.[133] It has been held that
'non-operation' includes not only when a flight fails to operate at all, ie doesn't
take off, but also where it has to return before being abandoned.[134] Thus if a
flight is scheduled to reach a certain destination – say, Rome – but fails to do
so, it is to be considered as non-operational.

---

[131] *Finnair v Lassooy* (Case C-22/11), para 26.
[132] Unreported, 07/06/06, Pontefract CC.
[133] Art 2(l).
[134] *Rodriguez v Air France* [2011] WLR (D) 348 (ECJ).

15.173 Passengers who are subject to cancellations are provided with a variety of rights under Art 5:

- assistance in accordance with Art 8;
- assistance in accordance with Art 9(1)(a) and (2), plus if the replacement flight is more than a day later, assistance in accordance with Art 9(1)(b)-(c);
- to be compensated in accordance with Art 7, unless the passenger is informed of the cancellation:
  - more than two weeks before the scheduled departure;
  - between two weeks and seven days before the scheduled departure and are offered re-routing allowing them to depart no more than two hours before the originally scheduled departure and to arrive no more than four hours after the originally scheduled arrival;
  - less than seven days before the scheduled departure and are offered re-routing allowing departure not more than one hour before the original schedule and arrival not more than two hours after the original arrival.

Article 5(3) provides a key defence for the air carrier 'if it can prove the cancellation is caused by extraordinary circumstances which could not have been avoided even if all reasonable measures had been taken.'

Delay

15.174 Delay is perhaps the most significant basis for compensation under the Regulations. Article 6(1) defines it as when the air carrier 'reasonably expects a flight to be delayed beyond its scheduled time of departure...' Different requirements are imposed upon the air carrier depending upon the length of the delay and the distance to be travelled. The minimum requirements for compensation are a delay of two hours (Art 6(1)(a)).

15.175 On the face of it, Art 6 only refers to air carriers offering assistance to delayed passengers under Arts 8 and 9. Accordingly, it would appear that no compensation was available for delay. As a result, for many years, air carriers sought to argue that what would otherwise might be considered cancellations were, in fact, delays. For example, passengers on a flight scheduled for 20:00hrs on Friday might be told to return to depart at 13:00 on Saturday and, upon re-checking in be allocated different seats etc. On those facts, although an air carrier might present the situation as one of a 17-hour delay so as to avoid compensation, on a true analysis the first flight was cancelled and the second flight scheduled in its place.

15.176 Such attempts were dealt with by the ECJ in *Sturgeon v Condor Flugdienst GmbH*.[135] The court held that cancellation and delay are two distinct concepts; a flight which is cancelled cannot also be delayed and vice

---

[135] [2010] Bus LR 1206 (ECJ).

versa. The relevant test is whether the flight departs with its original planning (ie flight number, crew, itinerary, seat allocation, etc). The ECJ then went considerably further and expanded the Regulation well-beyond its apparent scope by ruling that the right to compensation under Art 7 should also apply to cases of delay for three or more hours. The basis for doing so was that the 'difference in treatment therefore appears to fall foul of the principle of equal treatment.'[136] Further, that the 'primary objective of the Regulation' was 'consumer protection'.[137] While both reasons are commendable and no doubt true, the effect of *Sturgeon* is to expand the Regulation well beyond any justifiable meaning to be derived from its text.

15.177 Nonetheless, the decision was upheld following a challenge by British air carriers in *TUI Travel & Ors v Civil Aviation Authority*.[138] The ECJ again concluded in respect of cancellation and long delays that 'the inconvenience suffered by those two groups of passengers is equivalent.'[139]

'Extraordinary circumstances' defence

15.178 As set out above, Art 5(3) provides for a defence to cancellation claims if the air carrier can provide it was caused 'by extraordinary circumstances which could not have been avoided even if all reasonable measures had been taken.' The effect of the ECJ's decision in *Sturgeon* is that if compensation is also available to delayed passengers, the extraordinary circumstances defence must also be available to air carriers facing such claims.

15.179 The ECJ considered the concept in *Sturgeon* and followed an earlier decision of the Court[140] to the effect that the defence did not apply to a technical problem with the aircraft 'unless that problem stems from events which, by their nature or origin, are not inherent in the normal exercise of the activity of the air carrier concerned and are beyond its actual control.' The ECJ, in effect, acknowledged that dealing with technical difficulties with airplanes is part of the day-to-day operation of an airline and cannot therefore be considered an 'exceptional circumstance' under Art 5(3) either for the purposes of cancellation or delay.

15.180 The authorities on the point have been recently analysed in detail by the Court of Appeal in *Jet2.com Ltd v Huzar*.[141] There, Mr Ronald Huzar and his family were subject to a delay of 27 hours in their flight from Malaga to Manchester and sought compensation under Art 7. The delay had been caused by a fuel advisory light coming on (indicating a possible fault) during the plane's in-bound journey to Malaga. When the plane landed, a spare part was

---

[136] At [62].
[137] At [63].
[138] *TUI Travel & Ors v CAA* (conjoined with *Nelson v Deutsche Lufthansa AG*) [2013] 1 CMLR 42.
[139] At [36].
[140] *Wallentin-Hermann v Alitalia Linee Aeree Italiane SpA* [2009] Bus LR 1016.
[141] [2014] Bus LR 1324.

fitted but the warning light remained on. It was not possible to resolve the problem before the airport shut for the night. Accordingly, further investigations were undertaken the following day which revealed that wiring needed to be replaced. To have done so would have required an engineer and parts to be flown from its hangar in Manchester to Malaga. Instead, the air carrier opted instead to fly a new place into Malaga from Glasgow.

15.181 The air carrier argued that those constituted 'extraordinary circumstances' within the meaning of *Sturgeon*. The district judge at first instance accepted the argument on the basis that the delay was unforeseen and unforeseeable. However, that was overturned by HH Judge Platts, from whom an appeal was made to the Court of Appeal.

15.182 Elias LJ noted that the ECJ in *Sturgeon* had defined the defence by two limbs: first, whether the events which caused the problem were not inherent in the normal exercise of the air carrier's obligations; secondly, if so, whether the events were beyond the air carrier's actual control. He declined to consider how those limbs might interact on the basis that, clearly, the defence here failed on the first alone: the event causing the delay had been a mechanical issue which, even if not foreseen, was something inherent in the normal exercise of Jet2.com Ltd's obligations as an airline.

Compensation

15.183 Compensation under Art 7 is now available for denied board, cancellation and delays. The amount of compensation available is tiered according to the distance of the flight. Under Art 7(1) compensation is available as follows:

- €250 for flights of 1,500km or less;
- €400 for all 'intra-community flights' of more than 1,500 km and for all other flights between 1,500km and 3,500km;
- €600 for all other flights.

The distance is to be determined according to 'the last destination at which the denial of boarding or cancellation will delay the passenger's arrival after the scheduled boarding time.'

15.184 Under Art 7(2) compensation can be reduced by 50% in the event that passengers are offered re-routing under Art 8 (see below), the arrival time of which does not exceed the scheduled arrival time of the original flight by:

- two hours in respect of all flights of 1,500km or less;
- three hours in respect of 'all intra-Community flights' of more than 1,500km and all other flights of between 1,500km and 3,500km;
- four hours in respect of all other flights.

There are also special rules on compensation where a customer has been upgraded or downgraded from the ticket purchased (Art 10).[142]

15.185 Under Art 12 the specific right to compensation under Art 7 is expressly:

> ... without prejudice to a passenger's rights to further compensation. The compensation granted under this Regulation may be deducted from such compensation.
>
> 2. Without prejudice to the relevant principles and rules of national law, including case-law, paragraph 1 shall not apply to passengers who have voluntarily surrendered a reservation under Article 4(1).

Rights to reimbursement, re-routing and care

15.186 Where Art 8 is referred to under Arts 4 to 6, passengers must be offered a choice between:

- reimbursement within seven days of the cost of the ticket or those interrupted parts of the journey and a return flight to the first point of departure at the earliest opportunity;
- re-routing under comparable transport conditions to their final destination at the earliest opportunity;
- re-routing under comparable transport conditions to their final destination at a later date at the passenger's convenience, subject to availability of seats.

15.187 Where Art 9 is referred to under Arts 4 to 6, passengers must be offered free of charge:

- meals and refreshments in a reasonable relating to the waiting time
- hotel accommodation if a stay of one or more nights is necessary or a stay additional to that intended by the passenger is necessary
- transport between the airport and place of accommodation

Limitation

15.188 The Regulation contains nothing in relation to limitation. In a 2011 County Court case[143] it was decided that the limitation period should be the same as the two years that apply under the Convention. That has now been established as wrong by the ECJ decision in *Moré v Koninklijke Lucktvaart Maatschappij*.[144] There the court concluded that the limitation period could not be the same as under the Convention. However, it declined to specify a

---

[142] For useful analysis of the basis of compensation under Art 10 see *Steef Mennens v Emirates Direktion für Deutschland* (CJEU case C-255/15).

[143] *Schreiber v TUI UK Ltd*, unreported. 28/07/11, Clerkenwell CC.

[144] Case C-139/11.

limitation period, stating somewhat unhelpfully that it was to be 'determined in accordance with the rules of each Member State on the limitation of actions.'[145]

15.189 Accordingly, the question remains without a definitive answer for UK passengers. Although there is an argument that it would be a claim on a specialty to which a 12-year limitation period applies,[146] the safer assumption (at least for claimants) is that compensation under the Regulation is a sum due 'under any enactment' to which a six year limitation period applies.[147]

Civil Aviation (Denied Boarding, Compensation and Assistance) Regulations 2005[148]

15.190 These are domestic Regulations which create criminal liability in relation to breaches of Arts 4 to 6, 10, 11 or 14 of the Regulation. Under reg 3(2), such offences are summary only and subject to a fine of not more than the statutory maximum. Under reg 4 there is a due diligence defence, namely for 'the air carrier to show that it took all reasonable steps and exercised all due diligence to avoid committing the offence.'[149] Regulation 5(1) also designates the CAA as the UK enforcer for the purposes of Art 16 of the Regulation, which requires Member States to designate a body for 'the enforcement of this Regulation as regards flights from airports situated on its territory and flights from a third country to such airports.'

---

[145] At [33].
[146] Eg 'Pioneering Passengers rights: legislation and jurisprudence from the aviation sector' (2012) 12(2) *ERA Reform* 301.
[147] Limitation Act 1980, s 9(1).
[148] SI 2005/975.
[149] See Chapter 3, Criminal Enforcement.

CHAPTER 16

AGE RESTRICTED PRODUCTS

INTRODUCTION

16.1 The principal method of control by successive governments to prevent the sale of potentially harmful consumer products to children has been the creation of criminal liability for traders. However, as the first edition of this book commented:

'The law on age-restricted sales is in a lamentable state. There is manifest inconsistency between the elements of the offences, their penalties and the duty of enforcement ...'

and proposed:

'– a single statute containing all of the age-restricted selling offences;
– all offences to be made strict liability offences with a due diligence defence;
– an express power to make test purchases;
– a duty of enforcement should be placed upon trading standards departments.'

16.2 Little has changed in the last decade. In August 2010 the Age-restricted Products Review Group, representing major businesses, trade associations and professional bodies, made twelve recommendations in *Better Regulation of Age-restricted Products: A Retail View*. The recommendations came 'in response to a call from the Local Better Regulation Office for an independent and evidence-based review of the regulation and enforcement of age-restricted products'. They included the suggestions that:

(a) The current piecemeal legislation should be consolidated into a single piece of legislation to provide simplicity and greater consistency across the product categories with standardisation of offences and defences. This would provide a framework by which any new controls can be easily implemented in a consistent way to ensure future coherent development of the law. The legislation should include a binding code of practice.

(b) A simple general due diligence defence should be available for retail employees across all product categories to provide fairness where a genuine and reasonable mistake in judging age has been made.

16.3 Following this, the Better Regulation Delivery Office (BRDO) – which replaced LBRO – held a consultation in September 2012 on a proposed collaborative 'Code of Practice' to be followed by both communities and businesses, as well as regulators and enforcers, in order to better protect children from the hazards of age-restricted products. The consultation framework focused on four areas: prioritisation and targeting of resources to areas which present the most risk, working with businesses and communities to help them fulfill their obligations, the conduct of checks on compliance by local enforcers and how to respond to non-compliance. However, although the (non-statutory) Code of Practice, which was published on 24 January 2013 and only applies to England and Wales, includes the aim that 'an enforcing authority should ensure clear information and guidance on relevant legislation is readily available' the issue of law reform and the need for a more cohesive legislative approach was not addressed at all. The Code was updated in April 2014 to reflect the introduction of the Regulators' Code and changes to Primary Authority that took effect in October 2013. However, its core recommendations were not amended. Thus the law looks set to remain 'piecemeal' in the short term at least.

Test purchases

16.4 The enforcement of age restricted sales offences is particularly reliant upon the power to make test purchases. Test purchases are discussed in Chapter 3, Criminal Enforcement.

TOBACCO

Introduction

16.5 England, Wales and Northern Ireland each have responsibility for their own smoking cessation and health education campaigns. However, UK-wide policy and law applies to taxation, smuggling, advertising and consumer-protection issues such as the provision of health warnings on tobacco packaging.

16.6 The role of Trading Standards in regulating the sale of tobacco is more extensive than age-related sales but it is not possible in a work of this nature to provide detailed reference to all legislative provisions relating to matters such as counterfeit and illicit tobacco, fiscal marks, novel or niche products including tobacco mixtures for use in water pipes (such as shisha) and smokeless tobacco, oral tobacco, smoking accessories and smoke-free places. The types of operational activity undertaken by Trading Standards may be gleaned from a 2011 consultation on the draft Tobacco Control Plan for Wales, which contained the following:

> 'One area of local government activity of particular importance is that of Trading Standards, which extends right throughout the supply chain from manufacture to the various forms of distribution:
>
> • Tobacco manufacture and labelling;
> • Tobacco advertising and promotion;
> • Counterfeit tobacco;
> • Underage sales from shops and vending machines;
> • Niche products; and
> • Associated products, such as electronic cigarettes.
>
> Trading Standards also plays an essential role in advice and education to ensure that the trade understands its responsibilities in law, as well as raising awareness with young people.'

16.7   A raft of initiatives has been introduced by Trading Standards authorities and public health bodies over the last few years. For example, in May 2013, Newcastle City Council passed a declaration committing the council to take comprehensive action to address the harm caused by smoking. This has become known as the 'Local Government Declaration on Tobacco Control' and councils across the UK have been signing up to it. The Declaration commits councils to a number of actions and has been endorsed by a number of organisations, including the Chartered Trading Standards Institute. In August 2014 a sister document, the 'National Statement of Support' was launched by the NHS to allow public health organisations to show their support for tobacco control.

16.8   More recently, the Local Government Association's report 'Tackling Tobacco and Nicotine Dependency' (February 2015) outlined a number of proposals which would enable councils to engage with the problem, for example: allowing Trading Standards teams to do more proactive work with shopkeepers to ensure they understand the law about underage sales; how to avoid illegal sales; and what penalties they could face if they fail to comply with the law.

16.9   There are also a number of recent wider legislative developments in this area. In May 2016, the Tobacco and Related Products Regulations 2016 came into force, enacting Directive 2014/40/EU. The new legislation revises the regime for the manufacture, presentation and sale of tobacco products which existed under the 2001 directive. Amongst other measures, the 2016 Regulations prohibit the sale of cigarettes and tobacco with 'characterising flavours' (such as fruit or chocolate), which might be particularly enticing to children and young people; phases out menthol cigarettes from 2020; and requires stark and sizeable health warnings to appear on tobacco and related products, which must cover 65% of the front and back of cigarette packages.

16.10   Legal challenges to the directive were brought by tobacco companies on the grounds that Art 20 breaches EU law, most notably *Poland v European Parliament and Council of the European Union* (concerning flavoured and menthol cigarettes); *Pillbox 38 (UK) Limited (t/a 'Totally Wicked') v Secretary of State for Health* (concerning e-cigarettes and refills); and *R (on the application of Philip Morris Brands Sarl & Others) v Secretary of State for Health and Others* (concerning the presentation of tobacco products). The CJEU delivered judgment in all three matters on 4 May 2016 and dismissed the challenges in each case.

Scotland, Northern Ireland and Wales

16.11   Legislation relating to the prohibition of sales of tobacco to a person under 18 in Scotland is set out at para 11.3.

16.12   Legislation relating to the prohibition of sales of tobacco and related matters in Northern Ireland is contained in:

- Tobacco Retailers Act (Northern Ireland) 2014 (and associated secondary regulation).
- Children and Young Persons (Sale of Tobacco etc) Regulations (Northern Ireland) 2008.
- Smoking (Northern Ireland) Order 2006.
- Children and Young Persons (Protection from Tobacco) (Northern Ireland) Order 1991.
- Health and Personal Social Services (Northern Ireland) Order 1978.

16.13 Legislation relating to the prohibition of sales of tobacco specifically pertaining to Wales is contained in:

- Proxy Purchasing of Tobacco, Nicotine Products etc (Fixed Penalty Notice) Wales Regulations 2015.

Application and territorial jurisdiction

16.14 The Children and Young Persons Act 1933 (as amended – see the Protection of Children (Tobacco) Act 1986, the Children and Young Persons (Protection from Tobacco) Act 1991, the Tobacco Advertising and Promotion Act 2002, the Health Act 2006 and the Children and Young Persons (Sale of Tobacco etc) Order 2007[1]) contain the main offences relating to the sale of tobacco to a person under 18. To which the Children and Families Act 2014 adds offences relating to the purchase of tobacco on behalf of a person under 18; and (as of October 2015) the sale of 'Nicotine Inhaling Products' (electronic cigarettes) to a person under 18, or on behalf of a person under 18. The Children and Young Persons Act 1933 ('CYPA 1933') extends to England and Wales only.

16.15 For the purposes of s 7 CYPA 1933 the expression 'tobacco' includes cigarettes, any product containing tobacco and intended for oral or nasal use and smoking mixtures intended as a substitute for tobacco, and the expression 'cigarettes' includes cut tobacco rolled up in paper, tobacco leaf, or other material in such form as to be capable of immediate use for smoking.

Offences under the CYPA 1933

16.16 Section 7 CYPA 1933 states:

7 Sale of tobacco, etc, to persons under eighteen

(1) Any person who sells to a person under the age of eighteen years any tobacco or cigarette papers, whether for his own use or not, shall be liable, on summary conviction to a fine not exceeding level 4 on the standard scale.

(2) If on complaint to a court of summary jurisdiction it is proved to the satisfaction of the court that any automatic machine for the sale of tobacco kept

---

[1] SI 2007/767.

on any premises has been used by any person under the age of eighteen years, the court shall order the owner of the machine, or the person on whose premises the machine is kept, to take such precautions to prevent the machine being so used as may be specified in the order or, if necessary, to remove the machine, within such time as may be specified in the order, and if any person against whom such an order has been made fails to comply therewith, he shall be liable, on summary conviction, to a fine not exceeding level 4 on the standard scale.

16.17 In *R (on the application of London Borough of Merton) v Sinclair Collis Ltd*[2] the prosecution's case was that children had made test purchases of a packet of cigarettes from vending machines, each situated in a different public house, and that these were sales of cigarettes to a child – and, so, on each occasion an offence under s 7(1) CYPA 1933 was committed. The defendant's case was that s 7(1) did not apply to purchases from a cigarette vending machine and that the statutory scheme to control the purchase of cigarettes from vending machines was exclusively contained in s 7(2). The district judge accepted the defence contention. On appeal – Mitting J:

> 'Nothing in the legislative history suggests that the current provision should be construed in any way more favourable to the operators of vending machines than the 1908 Act. If, as I am satisfied, the 1908 Act made it an offence to sell cigarettes to someone who was apparently a child or a young person under 16 by a machine, then those provisions in their re-enacted and amended form continue to have that effect.'

> (... 'There is, however, one proviso. I am told that on the machines from which the test purchases were made the statutory notice appeared. D wish to contend that in consequence there could be no sale within the classical definition in section 2 of the Sale of Goods Act: because the transaction effected by the child test purchaser was in breach of the prohibition in the notice it was not the willing transfer of property in cigarettes to a buyer in consideration for payment of a price but, the taking by the child of something which he knew he was not entitled to take in return for something that did not amount to a price. That is an argument which has been canvassed before me but did not form any part of the stated case. It would not be right for me to express any view upon it now, let alone to decide it. It is an argument which remains open.')

16.18 In *Sinclair Collis Ltd v Secretary of State (Interested party – the Members of National Association of Cigarette Machine Operators)*[3] the Administrative Court dismissed judicial review challenges to primary and secondary legislation which bans the sale of tobacco from vending machines.

16.19 A more concerted attempt to use s 2 of the Sale of Goods Act to escape liability under s 7(1) CYPA1933 can be seen in the case of *Wm Morrisons Supermarkets v Reading BC*.[4] In that case a 15-year-old child made a test purchase of 10 cigarettes from a tobacco kiosk in a Morrisons' store, and handed them to an officer of the prosecuting authority, who was waiting

---

2   [2010] EWHC 3089 (Admin).
3   [2010] EWHC 3112 (Admin).
4   [2012] PTSR 1643.

around the corner. It was argued by the defence that since the child was acting at all times on behalf of the local authority, there was no sale for the purposes of the Sale of Goods Act 1979, because the child acquired no rights in or ownership of the cigarettes. It was further argued that the sale was really between the local authority and Morrisons, the child acting merely as an agent, and therefore no sale to a person under 18 had taken place within the meaning of s 7 CYPA 1933. However, the door left somewhat ajar by Mitting J in *R (on the application of London Borough of Merton) v Sinclair Collis Ltd* was firmly closed by Lloyd Jones J, who stated:

> 20 I can see that difficult questions could arise as to whether property passes to the agent or directly to the undisclosed principal. These have not been argued before us. However, it seems clear that property would pass from the seller either to the young person or to his undisclosed principal as a result of entering into this transaction. That the question of criminal liability might turn on such a nice analysis of the transaction in civil law would perhaps be undesirable but certainly a possibility, as is apparent from some of the authorities to which we have referred earlier in this judgment.

> 21 However, I consider that in this instance such an analysis is not called for. I am persuaded that Parliament did not intend to limit the application of this provision to a case where a child or young person acts as principal and therefore property passes to him. On the contrary, I have come to the clear conclusion that section 7(1) of the 1933 Act applies where a child or young person enters into a transaction of sale, whether as a principal or on behalf of someone else, whether disclosed or undisclosed and whether or not property passes to him.

Other offences

Loose cigarettes

16.20 Section 3 of the Children and Young Persons (Protection from Tobacco) Act 1991 creates an offence for any person carrying on a retail business to sell cigarettes to any person other than in pre-packed quantities. (Regulation 4(8) of the Standardised Packaging of Tobacco Products Regulations 2015 provides that a unit packet of cigarettes must now contain a minimum of 20 cigarettes.)

Statutory notice

16.21 Section 4 of the 1991 Act creates an offence for such a person to fail to exhibit, in a prominent position, a notice displaying the statement 'It is illegal to sell tobacco products to anyone under the age of 18', at every premises at which tobacco is sold by retail. The notice must be exhibited where the statement is readily visible to persons at the point of sale of the tobacco. The Protection from Tobacco (Display of Warning Statements) Regulations 1992[5] prescribe the dimensions of the notice and the size of the statement which must be displayed on such a notice.

---

[5]   SI 1992/3228.

Defences

16.22   Section 7(1A) CYPA 1933 provides:

> 7(1A) It shall be a defence for a person charged with an offence under subsection
> (1) above to prove that he took all reasonable precautions and exercised all due
> diligence to avoid the commission of the offence.

16.23   *Tesco Stores Ltd v Norfolk County Council*[6] concerned a case where the
defendant relied on a defence under s 7(1A) CYPA 1933 that he had taken all
reasonable precautions and exercised all due diligence. It was held that in every
case where the statutory defence was raised that the decision would turn on the
specific facts of the case. In the instant case, the trader had put in place a sound
and comprehensive system designed to avoid sales to under age buyers, which
was under continual review, and care had been taken over the selection of staff,
training and supervision by staff. That more could have been done (examples
relied upon by the prosecution being the existence of a till prompt and a
refusals book) did not equate to a lack of reasonable precautions. The appeal
was allowed and the conviction quashed.

16.24   Although not a defence, note that s 7(4) provides:

> 7(4) Nothing in this section shall make it an offence to sell tobacco or cigarette
> papers to, or shall authorise the seizure of tobacco or cigarette papers in the
> possession of, any person who is at the time employed by a manufacturer of or
> dealer in tobacco, either wholesale or retail, for the purposes of his business, or is
> a boy messenger in uniform in the employment of a messenger company and
> employed as such at the time.

Restriction on proceedings

16.25   The offence s 7(1) CYPA 1933 is summary-only – there is therefore a 6
months' time limit, from the time when the offence was committed (see s 127
Magistrates' Courts Act 1980).

Prosecutions

16.26   The offence under s 7(1) CYPA 1933 can be committed by the actual
seller or, where applicable, his employer. In *St Helens MBC v Hill* Lloyd LJ
said:[7]

> 'I have no doubt that the offence of selling cigarettes to a child apparently under
> the age of 16 is an offence of strict liability ... The justices were, therefore, wrong
> to regard the sale as having been a sale by the assistant. In the eye of the law, the
> sale was made by the [owner] of the shop himself.'

The decision in *St Helens MBC v Hill* raises a further question of whether the
sales assistant who actually sold the cigarettes could have been prosecuted? It

---

[6]   [2002] LLR 240.
[7]   (1992) 156 JP 602.

might be argued – on the basis of the comments of Lloyd J – that a mere employee is not in law the seller, and that the concept of selling is limited to the owner of the business who is the likely owner of the cigarettes. It is our view that this interpretation of the law is unhelpful and that the word 'sells' in s 7(1) should not be construed so narrowly. It is not clear from Lloyd LJ's judgment in *St Helens MBC v Hill* that he was attempting to confine liability, however any remarks made about the liability of mere employees are necessarily obiter dicta because it was unnecessary to decide whether the sales assistant was liable to find that the proprietor was liable.

16.27 There are, however several other reasons why such an interpretation is wrong. Firstly, Parliament has not attempted to complicate the notion of selling by reference to ownership, or proprietorship. There will be many occasions when a vendor will sell over-the-counter tobacco goods that he, or his company, does not in law own. Parliament cannot have intended a complex definition of selling, which was attributed only to those who owned the tobacco or premises from which it is sold. Furthermore, other legislation where liability has been restricted to those who own businesses has expressly stated the limitation within the statute.[8]

16.28 In our view there is no reason why there cannot be more than one seller at the same time, so that there would be concurrent liability of both the proprietor of a shop and sales assistant. This is supported by an earlier decision in *Preston v Albuery*[9] which focused upon the meaning of sells (under the Merchandise Marks Act 1887, since repealed). Although *Preston v Albuery* is not in relation to the same statute, it is a decision on the ordinary construction of the word 'sells' and therefore directly relevant.[10] In *Preston v Albuery* the defendant was an employee of a coal merchant who delivered sacks of short weight to a purchaser. The court held that he had sold the goods, finding that the person who passes the property in the goods was a seller. Ashworth J stated that, 'where in order to complete a sale, property has to be transferred or appropriated, the person who does transfer or appropriate is a person who sells'.

16.29 It is submitted that the wider construction of 'sells' attributed by the court in *Preston v Albuery* should be preferred. There is no reason that a rogue employee who sells cigarettes to children should escape sanction. This is even more important when the employer has a due diligence defence because it cannot have been the policy of the legislation that nobody would be liable in such circumstances. In any case that a corporate defendant is likely to raise the due diligence defence and argue that the employee was acting on a frolic of their own, it is submitted that it would be open to the prosecutor to charge both employee and employer at the same time.

---

[8] For example, the Consumer Protection Act 1987, s 20, a business 'of his'.
[9] [1963] 3 All ER 897.
[10] It is also worth noting that *Albuery* was not cited to the court in *Hill*.

Duty to enforce

16.30 Section 5 of the Children and Young Persons (Protection from Tobacco) Act 1991 provides for enforcement action by defined local authorities in England and Wales in relation to s 7 CYPA 1933 (and ss 3 and 4 of the Children and Young Persons (Protection from Tobacco) Act 1991). Section 5 requires councils to carry out a programme of enforcement at least once a year and sets out what the programme must involve.

Sentencing

16.31 A person who commits an offence under s 7(1) or 7(2) CYPA 1933 is liable, on summary conviction to a fine not exceeding level 4 on the standard scale.

Restricted premises orders and restricted sale orders

16.32 Section 143 of the Criminal Justice and Immigration Act 2008:

- Inserts s 12A into CYPA 1933, enabling a magistrates' court to impose restricted premises orders preventing the sale, either in person or by automatic machine, of tobacco products or cigarette papers on certain premises for up to one year. A magistrates' court may make a restricted premises order only if, in addition to the offence on the premises for which the offender has been convicted, the offender has also committed at least two other tobacco offences on the premises within a two-year period (whether or not convicted of those other offences).

- Inserts s 12B into CYPA 1933 enabling a magistrates' court to impose restricted sale orders. A restricted sale order is an order which prohibits a person from making any sale of tobacco or cigarette papers (whether in person or by automatic machine) to any person. It also prohibits the person from having management functions in relation to such sales. A magistrates' court may make a restricted sale order only if, in addition to the offence for which the offender has been convicted, the offender has also committed at least two other tobacco offences within a two-year period (whether or not convicted of those other offences).

16.33 A person found guilty of breaching restricted premises orders or restricted sale orders is liable to a fine of up to £20,000 (which under s 85 of the Legal Aid, Sentencing and Punishment of Offenders Act 2012 would now be an unlimited fine). Section 22(2) of the Health Act 2009 extends the definition of 'tobacco offence' for the purposes of ss 12A and 12B CYPA 1933 to include an offence committed under the s 3A of the Children and Young Persons (Protection from Tobacco) Act 1991 (which provides power for the appropriate national authority to prohibit the sale of tobacco from vending machines).

16.34 The Protection from Tobacco (Sales from Vending Machines) (England) Regulations 2010[11] prohibits the sale of tobacco products from vending machines in England from 1 October 2011. The Regulations state:

Prohibition of the sale of tobacco from vending machines

2(1) The sale of tobacco from an automatic machine is prohibited.

(2) The person who controls, or is concerned with the management of, the premises where the automatic machine is located shall be liable for a breach of paragraph (1).

16.35 The Tobacco (Sales from Vending Machines) (Wales) Regulations 2011 (as from 1 February 2012) and the Protection from Tobacco (Sales from Vending Machines) Regulations (Northern Ireland) 2012 (as from 1 March 2012) and the Tobacco & Primary Medical Services (Scotland) Act 2010 (as from 1 April 2013) are of similar effect.

Offence under s 91 of the CFA 2014

16.36 Section 91(1) of the Children and Families Act 2014 ('CFA 2014') provides:

Purchase of tobacco etc. on behalf of persons under 18

(1) A person aged 18 or over who buys or attempts to buy tobacco or cigarette papers on behalf of an individual aged under 18 commits an offence.

16.37 Regulation 2 of the Nicotine Inhaling Products (Age of Sale and Proxy Purchasing) Regulations 2015 came fully in to force on 1 October 2015. Regulation 2 amends CFA 2014, s 91 so as to make it an offence for a person to purchase relevant nicotine products on behalf of a person under the age of 18. In August 2016 the Chartered Trading Standards Institute ('CTSI') reported that officers had carried out the first national test purchase operation, for the Department of Health, since sales of nicotine e-cigarettes and vaping liquids to under 18s were banned under the Regulations. The operation found compliance was 'disappointingly low, with illegal sales made on 246 occasions', equivalent to 39% of cases, drawn from independent pharmacies, specialist e-cigarette suppliers, discount stores, markets and tobacconists.

Defences

16.38 Section 91(2) provides:

(2) Where a person is charged with an offence under this section it is a defence –

    (a)   that the person had no reason to suspect that the individual concerned was aged under 18, or

---

[11]   SI 2010/864, made under s 3A of the Children and Young Persons (Protection from Tobacco) Act 1991.

(b)   in a case where the person has bought or attempted to buy cigarette papers, that the person had no reason to suspect that the individual concerned intended to use the papers for smoking.

Time limits

16.39   The offence under s 91 is summary only: there is therefore a six-month time limit on bringing proceedings, which runs from the time when the offence was committed (Magistrates' Courts Act 1980, s 127).

Duty to enforce

16.40   Section 91(4) makes it the duty of each local weights and measures authority in England and Wales to enforce the provisions of the section within its area.

Powers of enforcement officers

16.41   Section 91(6) provides that the powers of entry under s 11 and Sch 2 of the Health Act 2006 apply to this section, save that those powers relating to persons authorised by the local weights and measures authority (whether or not an officer of that authority).

Sentencing

16.42   Section 91(3) provides that a person who commits an offence under the section is liable on summary conviction to a fine not exceeding level 4 on the standard scale. Section 91(5) further provides that fixed penalty notices can be issued by a person authorised by the local weights and measures authority. The Proxy Purchasing of Tobacco, Nicotine Products etc. (Fixed Penalty Amount) Regulations 2015 set the amount of the fine at £90.

Offence under Nicotine Inhaling Products (Age of Sale and Proxy Purchasing) Regulations 2015

16.43   Section 92(1) provides that the Secretary of State may make regulations prohibiting the sale of nicotine products to persons aged under 18. Section 92(2) states that a person breaching prohibition in regulations under subsection (1) commits an offence. As stated above, the Nicotine Inhaling Products (Age of Sale and Proxy Purchasing) Regulations 2015 came into force in October 2015. Regulation 3 prohibits the sale of such products to persons under the age of 18. The Regulations also set out exceptions for nicotine inhaling products which are licensed as medicines and set a statutory review of the Regulations within five years of their coming in to force.

Defences

16.44 Section 92(3) provides that no offence is committed where at the time of sale, the person to whom the nicotine product is sold is employed by a manufacturer of or dealer in nicotine products, and the purchase is made for the purpose of that business. Section 92(4) provides a statutory defence where the person took all reasonable precautions and exercised all due diligence to avoid committing the offence.

Time limits

16.45 The offence under s 92 is summary only – there is therefore a six-month time limit on bringing proceedings, which runs from the time when the offence was committed (see s 127 of the Magistrates' Courts Act 1980).

Sentencing

16.46 A person who commits an offence under s 92 is liable on summary conviction to a fine not exceeding level 4 on the standard scale.

Commentary

16.47 Other recent legislative developments, relating to the sale of tobacco, include:

(i)   The implementation of legislation to end tobacco displays in shops. Legislation to end tobacco displays came fully into effect on 6 April 2015.[12]

(ii) Legislative developments relating to the plain packaging of tobacco products. CFA 2014, s 94 provides for the making of regulations relating to the retail packaging of tobacco products in order to reduce the risk of harm to, or to promote, the health and welfare of people under the age of 18. The Standardised Packaging of Tobacco Products Regulations 2015 are made under the CFA 2014 and came into force on 20 May 2016. The Regulations will be enforced by Local Authority Trading Standards (or environmental health officers in Northern Ireland), using their powers under the Consumer Protection Act 1987, s 18. The Regulations relate to packaging of cigarettes and rolling tobacco and cover, *inter alia*, the colour and shade of packaging; the material, shape, opening and unit contents of the packets, the appearance of cigarettes and the scent of the tobacco.

---

[12] Tobacco Advertising and Promotion (Display) (England) Regulations 2010; Tobacco Advertising and Promotion (Specialist Tobacconists) (England) Regulations 2010; Tobacco Advertising and Promotion (Display of Prices) (England) Regulations 2010; Tobacco Advertising and Promotion (Display of Prices) (Wales) Regulations 2012; Tobacco Advertising and Promotion (Specialist Tobacconists) (Wales) Regulations 2012; Tobacco Advertising and Promotion (Display) (Wales) Regulations 2012; Tobacco Advertising and Promotion (Display of Prices) Regulations (Northern Ireland) 2012 and the Tobacco Advertising and Promotion (Display) Regulations (Northern Ireland) 2012.

Regulation 15 creates an either-way offence of breaching any of the requirements in the Regulations, punishable summarily by three months' imprisonment and/or fine; and on indictment by two years' imprisonment and/or fine.

(iii) Legislative developments relating to smoking in cars carrying children. CFA 2015, s 95 amends the Health Act 2006, s 5 which relates to smoke-free vehicles, inserting a subsection (1A) which provides 'Regulations under this section may in particular provide for a private vehicle to be smoke-free where a person under the age of 18 is present in the vehicle'. The Smoke-Free (Private Vehicles) Regulations 2015 come into force in October 2015. They will require private vehicles in England to be smoke free where they are enclosed; there is more than one person present; and one of those present is under the age of 18. They also place a duty on the driver of a vehicle to stop a person smoking in that vehicle in those circumstances. Regulation 4 provides that a Fixed Penalty Notice may be given by an authorised officer of an enforcement authority where there is reason to believe that a person has committed an offence of failing to prevent smoking in a vehicle that is smoke-free by virtue of the Regulations.

TOBACCO (SCOTLAND)

Introduction

16.48 Responsibility for tobacco regulation is devolved to the Scottish Parliament. Legal provisions – brought into force during 2010 and 2011 – relating to the prohibition of sales of tobacco to a person under 18 (and a new offence of purchasing tobacco products by under 18s or by persons aged 18 or over on behalf of under 18s) are contained in the Tobacco and Primary Medical Services (Scotland) Act 2010 ('TPMS(S)A 2010').

16.49 TPMS(S)A 2010 also contains a number of other controls on sales of tobacco, including a ban on the display of tobacco products and on the sale of tobacco products from vending machines, the establishment of a Register of Tobacco Retailers and the introduction of tobacco retailing banning orders. The Act consolidates and updates some tobacco sales legislation (including provisions from the Children and Young Persons (Scotland) Act 1937; the Children and Young Persons (Protection from Tobacco) Act 1991; the Tobacco Advertising and Promotion Act 2002; and the Smoking, Health and Social Care (Scotland) Act 2005).

16.50 In the case of *Petition of Imperial Tobacco Ltd for Judicial Review of sections 1 and 9 of the Tobacco and Primary Medical Services (Scotland) Act 2010*,[13] Imperial Tobacco Ltd brought a judicial review seeking a ruling by the Outer House, Court of Session that s 1 (which prohibits the display of

---

13   [2010] CSOH 134.

tobacco products) and s 9 (which prohibits the use of vending machines) were outside the legislative competence of the Scottish Parliament and therefore were not law. The Court held that ss 1 and 9 were within the competence of the Scottish Parliament and dismissed the petition. This was confirmed by the Supreme Court in *Imperial Tobacco v Lord Advocate*.[14]

16.51 Coinciding with the remainder of the UK, a tobacco display ban in Scotland came into force on 6 April 2015, by virtue of the Sale of Tobacco (Display of Tobacco Products and Prices etc.) (Scotland) Regulations 2013. As from 29 April 2013, the ban only applies to a 'large shop', which means a shop with a relevant floor area exceeding 280 square metres.

16.52 The Smoking Prohibition (Children in Motor Vehicles) (Scotland) Act 2016 received Royal Assent in January 2016, and creates an offence of smoking in a vehicle in which a child is present, bringing it in line with the rest of the UK, where similar legislation has been in force since 2015.[15]

Application

16.53 Section 35 TPMS(S)A 2010 provides that 'tobacco product' means a product consisting wholly or partly of tobacco and intended to be smoked, sniffed, sucked or chewed. Note that s 33 raises a presumption in prosecutions for selling tobacco to persons under the age of 18 that the contents of a container conform to the packaging. The presumption can be rebutted by the accused or other party in a trial.

Offences

16.54 The following offences are created by TPMS(S)A 2010 in relation to persons under the age of 18:

Section 4(1) provides:

> 4(1) A person who sells a tobacco product or cigarette papers to a person under the age of 18 commits an offence.

16.55 Section 5(1) provides:

> 5(1) A person under the age of 18 who buys or attempts to buy a tobacco product or cigarette papers commits an offence.

It is not an offence under subsection (1) for a person under the age of 18 to buy or attempt to buy a tobacco product or cigarette papers if the person is authorised to do so by a council officer or a constable for the purpose of determining whether an offence is being committed under s 4 (s 5(2)). However, a council officer or a constable may only authorise a person under the age of 18

---

[14]   [2013] SLT 2.
[15]   Smoking Prohibition (Children in Motor Vehicles) (Scotland) Act 2016 (Commencement) Regulations 2016.

to buy or attempt to buy a tobacco product or cigarette papers if he is satisfied that all reasonable steps have been or will be taken to avoid any risk to the welfare of the person (s 5(3)).

Avoiding any risk to the welfare of the test-purchaser

16.56 *A Practical Guide to Test Purchasing in Scotland* sets out guidance to be adopted by those authorities and agencies that intend to report criminal offences based on evidence obtained through the use of children (or young people) to test-purchase age-restricted goods. The guide is based on the original LACORS/LGR guidance for England and Wales. It was prepared with the assistance of LACORS, and with advice from Crown Office and the Procurator Fiscal Service (COPFS); by the Scottish Executive Enforcement Advisory Group on Age-restricted Sales in consultation with the Society of Chief Officers of Trading Standards in Scotland ('SCOTSS'); Association of Chief Police Officers in Scotland ('ACPOS'); business representatives; and health interest groups and agencies. The Scottish Commissioner for Children and Young People was consulted about tobacco and alcohol test purchasing.

16.57 Paragraph 4.4.3 indicates that it may be considered good practice:

'to follow the requirements of the Regulation of Investigatory Powers (Juveniles) (Scotland) Order 2002 (SSI 2002/206) to ensure that:

- the safety and welfare of the child or young person has been fully considered;
- the officer is satisfied that any risk has been properly explained to, and understood by the child or young person;
- a risk assessment has been undertaken, covering the physical dangers and the moral and psychological aspect of the child or young person's deployment;
- a record is kept.

In the vast majority of test purchase exercises, it is likely that there will be minimal risk to the young volunteer involved.'

16.58 Section 6(1) provides:

(1) A person aged 18 or over who knowingly buys or attempts to buy a tobacco product or cigarette papers on behalf of a person under the age of 18 commits an offence.

16.59 Section 8 makes it an offence for tobacco retailers, without reasonable cause, not to display a warning statement ('It is illegal to sell tobacco products to anyone under the age of 18'), in accordance with prescribed dimensions, at all points of sale where tobacco products are sold. It is a restatement of the equivalent provision in s 4 of the Children and Young Persons (Protection from Tobacco) Act 1991.

16.60 TPMS(S)A 2010 creates a number of other offences:

- displaying tobacco products and smoking-related products in a place (other than a website) where tobacco products are offered for sale (s 1(1));
- displaying prices of tobacco products or smoking related products that does not comply with regulations (s 3(3));
- a person under 18, who is in possession of tobacco products or cigarette papers in a public place, failing to comply with a request from the police to surrender these items or to supply a name and address (s 7(5));
- selling tobacco products from vending machines (s 9(1));
- carrying on a tobacco business whilst not on the Register of Tobacco Retailers (s 20(1) or carrying on such a business from unregistered premises (s 20(2)). Section 10 requires the Scottish Ministers to keep a register of persons carrying on a tobacco business and s 11(2) of the Act sets out what must be contained in an application to be registered or to add premises to a person's existing entry in the register. The Sale of Tobacco (Register of Tobacco Retailers) Regulations 2010[16] prescribe information which must be contained in such an application;
- a person who is on the register failing to notify certain changes to the Scottish Ministers (s 20(3));
- breaching a tobacco retailing banning order or an ancillary order (s 20(4));
- failing to display a notice relating to a tobacco retailing banning order (s 20(5)).

Defences

16.61 Section 4 restates (with modifications) the offence in s 18 of the Children and Young Persons (Scotland) Act 1937 of selling tobacco products to persons under the age of 18. However, under s 4(2), the accused person has a defence if he/she believed that the customer was over 18 and had taken reasonable steps to establish a customer's age by being shown acceptable proof of identification. Acceptable proof of identification includes a passport, a European Union photo identification card, driving licence, or a document prescribed by Ministers. The Sale of Tobacco (Prescribed Document) Regulations 2010[17] prescribes 'a photographic identity card bearing the national Proof of Age Standards Scheme hologram' as a document to establish a person's age. Whatever document is shown it must have been capable of satisfying a reasonable person as to the customer's age.

Restrictions on proceedings

16.62 As the offences in ss 4–6 can only be tried under summary procedure, the time limits are established under s 136 of the Criminal Procedure (Scotland) Act 1995: within 6 months after the contravention occurred.

---

[16] SSI 2010/407.
[17] SSI 2010/406.

Prosecutions

16.63 The offence under s 4 can be committed by the actual seller or, where applicable, his employer. Section 34 makes provisions where a body corporate, Scottish partnership or other unincorporated association commits an offence under the Act, which is proved to have been committed with the consent or the connivance of a 'relevant individual' or an individual acting as such, or because of neglect by the 'relevant individual'. In these circumstances, the 'relevant individual', as well as the relevant organisation, will be guilty of the offence. The Scottish Government has published *Guidance for Officers in the enforcement of the provisions of Tobacco and Primary Medical Services (Scotland) Act 2010 relating to the sale of tobacco products*. This document states:

> 'The following enforcement action is available to officers:
>
> * written warning
> * Fixed Penalty Notice (FPN)
> * report to the Procurator Fiscal
> * application to the sheriff for a tobacco retailing banning order
>
> All action taken should be fair, proportionate and consistent and in accordance with the local authority's own enforcement policy.
>
> The term "person" covers any person including individuals, partnerships, bodies corporate and unincorporated associations. It is the intent of the legislation that vicarious liability should apply. Accordingly, in section 4(1),
>
> "a person" may be a shop assistant, manager and/or controller or the owner of the business.
>
> "Relevant individuals" as well as bodies corporate, partnerships or unincorporated associations may also be liable to proceedings if the offence was proved to be due to their consent, connivance or neglect.
>
> It is not possible to recommend what course of action should be implemented in any set of circumstances but in normal circumstances officers will consider any mitigating circumstances (e.g. where the retailer has taken all reasonable to steps to prevent a sale but a member of staff ignores their training and company procedures). They will also consider any aggravating circumstances (e.g. where the seller is advised by the attempted purchaser that they are under age but proceeds with the sale so that a warning or FPN may not be appropriate but merits a report to the PF).'

Duty to enforce

16.64 It is the duty of councils[18] to enforce within its area the provisions relating to age-restricted sales and regulations made under them. Section 26

---

[18]   Those constituted under s 2 of the Local Government etc (Scotland) Act 1994.

requires councils to carry out a programme of enforcement at least once a year and sets out what the programme must involve.

Powers of enforcement officers

16.65 Sections 28–32 set out powers of enforcement and related matters. In summary, council officers, in order to establish compliance with requirements set out in the Act, may enter non-residential premises, take possession of documents and records and require other people to provide them with information and assistance (s 28). Police powers to enforce the Act are similar to those provided for council enforcement officers (s 32). Sections 29 and 30 provide for warrants for entry in specific circumstances including when the officer has been refused entry or expects to be refused entry. Section 31 creates offences for obstructing a council officer or making false statements to such an officer. There is a defence to the latter charge if the accused did not know that the information was false and had reasonable grounds to believe it was true.

Sentencing

16.66 TPMS(S)A 2010 sets out different levels of penalty for the offences under ss 4–6, as follows:

- a person guilty of an offence under s 4 (1) – sale of tobacco products to persons under 18 – is liable on summary conviction to a fine not exceeding level 4 on the standard scale (s 4(5)).

- a person guilty of an offence under s 5(1) – purchase of tobacco products by persons under 18 – is liable on summary conviction to a fine not exceeding level 1 on the standard scale (s 5(4)).

- a person guilty of an offence under s 6(1) – purchase of tobacco products on behalf of persons under 18 – is liable on summary conviction to a fine (s 6(2)).

Fixed penalty notices

16.67 Section 27 allows council officers and police constables to issue fixed penalty notices for the above offences. Fixed penalty notices may not be issued to under 16s. Sch 1 to the Act makes further provision in relation to the fixed penalty notice regime.

16.68 The Sale of Tobacco (Registration of Moveable Structures and Fixed Penalty Notices) (Scotland) Regulations 2011[19] prescribe that:

- a fixed penalty notice cannot be given after 7 days from the date of the offence;

---

[19]   SSI 2011/23.

- the amount of the fixed penalty for offences under ss 5 (purchase of tobacco products by persons under 18) and 7 (confiscation of tobacco products from persons under 18) is £50 (and the discounted amount is £30);
- the amount and the discounted amount for all other offences under Chapters 1 and 2 of Part 1 is £200 (and the discounted amount is £150);
- where the person receiving the fixed penalty notice has already had a fixed penalty or a conviction for a tobacco offence under the Act within the previous two years, the amounts are escalated in accordance with the Schedule to the Regulations.

Tobacco retailing banning orders

16.69   Section 15 provides that a council may apply to the sheriff for an order banning a tobacco retailer from selling tobacco from specified premises within the council's area. The conditions are that the retailer has received three or more enforcement actions relating to those premises, at least one of the enforcement actions has been within the two months preceding the application made by the council and the conduct which gave rise to the enforcement actions all took place within a two-year period. Enforcement actions can either be in the form of a fixed penalty notice or a conviction for an offence under Chapters 1 or 2 of the Act. The ban can be for a period up to 24 months.

16.70   Section 16 allows councils to apply to the sheriff for an 'ancillary order' which can be made along with an application for a banning order or at a later date once a banning order is in place. The order can be sought against the person (whom a s 15 order is being sought or has already been made) from being connected to or seeking to control another person carrying on a tobacco business at the specified premises. In addition, where this person is not an individual (eg is a company or partnership), an order can be sought to ban any person connected to the person from carrying on a tobacco business at the specified premises or being connected to any such person.

16.71   An appeals process against a tobacco retailing banning order or an ancillary order is set out in s 17. Section 18 requires the sheriff to notify the Scottish Ministers on making a tobacco banning order or ancillary order. The sheriff principal must also notify the Scottish Ministers of the outcome of any appeal.

16.72   Under s 19, a tobacco retailer, in respect of whom a tobacco retailing banning order has been granted, is required to display a notice in the premises specified in the order if the person continues to carry on a retail business at those premises. The section sets out specific requirements of the notice, including the content of the notice, where it is to be displayed and the period in which the notice has to be displayed. The Sale of Tobacco (Register of Tobacco Retailers) Regulations 2010[20] prescribe information which must be contained in such a notice.

Offences relating to the sale of Nicotine Vapour Product

16.73 The Health (Tobacco, Nicotine etc and Care) (Scotland) Act 2016 recieved Royal Assent on 6 April 2016 and introduces a similar regime of control of the sale of nicotine vapour product (NVP). Chapter 1 of the Act deals with the sale and purchase of NVPs. Section 2 makes it an offence for a person to sell NVP to a person under the age of 18. Section 2(2) provides a statutory defence where the seller believed the customer to be aged 18 or over; and had taken reasonable steps to establish the customer's age. What will amount to 'reasonable steps' is defined by s 2(3): where the seller has been shown a passport; an EU photocard driving licence; or such other document as may be prescribed.

16.74 Section 3 makes it an offence for a person carrying on a tobacco or NVP business to fail to have an age verification policy (unless the business operates by dispatching such products for delivery elsewhere – for example, a fulfillment centre or warehouse run by an online business). Section 4C makes it an offence for a responsible person to all a person under the age of 18 to sell a tobacco product, cigarette papers or an NVP. Section 4D provides a defence of due diligence in relation to the s 4C offence. Section 6A makes it an offence for a person aged 18 or over to knowingly buy or attempt to buy an NVP on behalf of a person who is under the age of 18. Section 7 extends the definition of 'vending machine' in s 9(3) of the 2010 Act to include a prohibition on the sale of NVPs via automatic vending machines.

Commentary

16.75 Almost 13,500 people die in Scotland each year from smoking-related diseases: that makes smoking the most important preventable cause of ill health and premature death in Scotland. It is estimated that 47,000 under-18s smoke. Young people do not find it difficult to buy cigarettes under the legal age. Data indicates that 57 per cent of 15-year-old smokers and 42 per cent of 13-year-old smokers buy their own cigarettes from shops.

16.76 On 27 March 2013, the Scottish Government published its new *Tobacco Control Strategy – Creating a Tobacco-Free Generation*. The new strategy sets out the Scottish Government's ambition for a smoke-free Scotland by 2034. A technical paper accompanies this target. The strategy also sets out a range of actions, many of which have been implemented since the publication of the report, including:

• standardised tobacco packaging;

20 SSI 2010/407.

- smoke-free hospital grounds;
- social marketing campaign on second-hand smoke;
- review of smoking cessation services; and
- a pilot of the ASSIST peer-education programme in schools.

ALCOHOL

Introduction

16.77 'Protection of children from harm' is one of the 'licensing objectives' that underpin the Licensing Act 2003 ('LA 2003') and the Act (in ss 145–154) contains a number of specific offences relating to children. Although the legal drinking age is 18, a 16 or 17-year-old may drink beer, wine or cider with 'a table meal' on licensed premises, where accompanied by an adult aged 18 years or over. The Licensing Act 2003 (Mandatory Licensing Conditions) Order 2010[21] provides that the premises licence holder or club premises certificate holder must ensure that an age verification policy applies to the premises in relation to the sale or supply of alcohol. The policy must require individuals who appear to the responsible person to be under 18 years of age (or such older age as may be specified in the policy) to produce on request, before being served alcohol, identification bearing their photograph, date of birth and a holographic mark. To assist businesses, the Home Office issued in July 2012 a document entitled 'False ID Guidance' to provide better understanding of the issues surrounding false IDs and how to deal with them.

16.78 In Scotland, only the police can deal with the enforcement of the age restrictions applying to the sale of alcohol, in particular, under the Licensing (Scotland) Act 2005. The Act creates a number of offences including: selling alcohol to a 'child' (a person under the age of 16) or a 'young person' (a person aged 16 or 17) under s 102 (subject to the defence under that section); or for a child or young person to buy or attempt to buy alcohol (whether for himself or herself or another person) under s 105. It will not be an offence if the child or young person is authorised to do so by the chief constable for the purpose of determining whether an offence is being committed (but only if the chief constable is satisfied that all reasonable steps have been or will be taken to avoid any risk to the welfare of the child or young person). The Alcohol etc (Scotland) Act 2010 makes a number of provisions regulating the sale of alcohol and, specifically, has the effect of imposing a further mandatory condition in premises licences to ensure that there must be an age-verification policy in relation to the sale of alcohol on the premises.

16.79 Similarly, the Police Service of Northern Ireland (PSNI) enforces the laws on underage drinking primarily through the Licensing (Northern Ireland) Order 1996 (as amended). The legislative scheme in England and Wales does not specifically require premises to display age-related notices but there are

---

[21]   SI 2010/860, Sch 1, para 4.

obligations to do so in Scotland (under s 110 Licensing (Scotland) Act 2005) and in Northern Ireland (under the Licensing (Notice Relating to Age) Regulations (Northern Ireland) 2012 and the Registration of Clubs (Notice Relating to Age) Regulations (Northern Ireland) 2012).

Territorial jurisdiction

16.80   The Licensing Act 2003 extends to England and Wales only.

Offences

Licensing Act 2003

Sale of alcohol to children (s 146)

16.81

146 Sale of alcohol to children

(1) A person commits an offence if he sells alcohol to an individual aged under 18.

(2) A club commits an offence if alcohol is supplied by it or on its behalf –

(a)   to, or to the order of, a member of the club who is aged under 18, or
(b)   to the order of a member of the club, to an individual who is aged under 18.

(3) A person commits an offence if he supplies alcohol on behalf of a club –

(a)   to, or to the order of, a member of the club who is aged under 18, or
(b)   to the order of a member of the club, to an individual who is aged under 18.

Allowing the sale of alcohol to children (s 147)

16.82

147 Allowing the sale of alcohol to children

(1) A person to whom subsection (2) applies commits an offence if he knowingly allows the sale of alcohol on relevant premises to an individual aged under 18.

(2) This subsection applies to a person who works at the premises in a capacity, whether paid or unpaid, which authorises him to prevent the sale.

(3) A person to whom subsection (4) applies commits an offence if he knowingly allows alcohol to be supplied on relevant premises by or on behalf of a club –

(a)   to or to the order of a member of the club who is aged under 18, or
(b)   to the order of a member of the club, to an individual who is aged under 18.

(4) This subsection applies to –

(a) a person who works on the premises in a capacity, whether paid or unpaid, which authorises him to prevent the supply, and (b)	any member or officer of the club who at the time of the supply is present on the relevant premises in a capacity which enables him to prevent it.

Persistently selling alcohol to children (s 147A)[22]

16.83

147A Persistently selling alcohol to children

(1) A person is guilty of an offence if –

(a)	on 2 or more different occasions within a period of 3 consecutive months alcohol is unlawfully sold on the same premises to an individual aged under 18;

(b)	at the time of each sale the premises were either licensed premises or premises authorised to be used for a permitted temporary activity by virtue of Part 5; and

(c)	that person was a responsible person in relation to the premises at each such time.

(2) For the purposes of this section alcohol sold to an individual aged under 18 is unlawfully sold to him if –

(a)	the person making the sale believed the individual to be aged under 18; or

(b)	that person did not have reasonable grounds for believing the individual to be aged 18 or over.

(3) For the purposes of subsection (2) a person has reasonable grounds for believing an individual to be aged 18 or over only if –

(a)	he asked the individual for evidence of his age and that individual produced evidence that would have convinced a reasonable person; or

(b)	nobody could reasonably have suspected from the individual's appearance that he was aged under 18.

(4) A person is, in relation to premises and a time, a responsible person for the purposes of subsection (1) if, at that time, he is –

(a)	the person or one of the persons holding a premises licence in respect of the premises; or

(b)	the person or one of the persons who is the premises user in respect of a temporary event notice by reference to which the premises are authorised to be used for a permitted temporary activity by virtue of Part 5.

(5) The individual to whom the sales mentioned in subsection (1) are made may, but need not be, the same in each case.

(6) The same sale may not be counted in respect of different offences for the purpose –

(a)	of enabling the same person to be convicted of more than one offence under this section; or

---

22	Inserted by s 23 of the Violent Crime Reduction Act 2006 and amended by s 28 of the Policing and Crime Act 2009.

(b)   of enabling the same person to be convicted of both an offence under this section and an offence under section 146 or 147.

(7) In determining whether an offence under this section has been committed, the following shall be admissible as evidence that there has been an unlawful sale of alcohol to an individual aged under 18 on any premises on any occasion –

(a)   the conviction of a person for an offence under section 146 in respect of a sale to that individual on those premises on that occasion;

(b)   the giving to a person of a caution (within the meaning of Part 5 of the Police Act 1997) in respect of such an offence; or

(c)   the payment by a person of a fixed penalty under Part 1 of the Criminal Justice and Police Act 2001 in respect of such a sale.

16.84   There are a number of other offences relating to alcohol and children contained in the LA 2003, which fall outside the ambit of this book by reason of the fact that the relevant prosecuting authorities are either the police or the relevant licensing authority. They are listed below:

- By virtue of s 145 it is an offence to admit children under 16 to certain categories of 'relevant premises' (see s 159) if they are not accompanied by an adult and those premises are open for the supply of alcohol for consumption there.

- There was until May 2015 an offence under s 148 of selling liqueur confectionery to a child under 16. In April 2011 one outcome from the retail sector Red Tape Challenge was a government statement to 'abolish symbolic cases of heavy-handed intervention, such as shops needing an alcohol licence to sell chocolate liqueurs'. By virtue of s 70 of the Deregulation Act 2015 that recommendation was adopted and the offence abolished.

- Section 149 makes it an offence for a person to purchase or attempt to purchase alcohol on behalf of a child but this does not apply where the individual buys or attempts to buy the alcohol at the request of a constable, or a weights and measures inspector, who is acting in the course of his duty.

- Section 150 makes it an offence for a child knowingly to consume alcohol on relevant premises (see the definition in s 159).

- Section 151 sets out offences relating to the delivery of alcohol to children.

- By virtue of s 152 it is an offence for a person to knowingly send an individual aged under 18 to obtain alcohol but this does not apply where the individual buys or attempts to buy the alcohol at the request of a constable, or a weights and measures inspector, who is acting in the course of his duty.

- Section 153 provides for the prohibition of unsupervised sales of alcohol by children.

Defences

Sale of alcohol to children (s 146)

16.85

> (4) Where a person is charged with an offence under this section by reason of his own conduct it is a defence that –
>
> (a)   he believed that the individual was aged 18 or over, and
> (b)   either –
>
> > (i)   he had taken all reasonable steps to establish the individual's age, or
> > (ii)   nobody could reasonably have suspected from the individual's appearance that he was aged under 18.
>
> (5) For the purposes of subsection (4), a person is treated as having taken all reasonable steps to establish an individual's age if –
>
> (a)   he asked the individual for evidence of his age, and
> (b)   the evidence would have convinced a reasonable person.
>
> (6) Where a person ("the accused") is charged with an offence under this section by reason of the act or default of some other person, it is a defence that the accused exercised all due diligence to avoid committing it.

Due diligence is covered in Chapter 3, Criminal Enforcement.

Restrictions on proceedings

16.86   Section 186(2) provides that proceedings for offences under LA 2003 may be instituted:

> (a)   by a licensing authority except in the case of an offence under section 147A,
> (b)   by the Director of Public Prosecutions, or
> (c)   in the case of an offence under section 146, 147 or 147A ..., by a local weights and measures authority ...

Section 186(3) extends the limitation period for bringing summary proceedings in s 127(1) of the Magistrates' Courts Act 1980 from 6 months to a period of 12 months of the offence being committed.

Prosecutions

16.87   Prior to the Licensing Act 2003, there were many cases where the liability of licensees and other persons had been considered and it was conventional wisdom that only a licensee, either directly or by his servant or agent, may sell intoxicating liquor. (However, it is clear from cases such as *Nottingham City Council v Wolverhampton and Dudley Breweries Ltd*,[23] where it was held that the proprietor of alcoholic drink could 'sell' under the

---

[23]   [2003] EWHC 2847 (Admin).

Food Safety Act 1990, in the same way that he could sell any other type of food, that this notion was limited to licensing legislation).

16.88 A case under predecessor legislation, the Licensing Act 1964, *Haringey London Borough Council v Marks & Spencer plc/Liverpool City Council v Somerfield Stores Ltd*,[24] held that a proprietor of intoxicating liquor was not a 'person' under the provisions of that Act which made it an offence to sell intoxicating liquor to a person under eighteen.

16.89 Section 146 LA 2003 represents a departure from the previous offence in the Licensing Act 1964. Original guidance issued under s 182 of LA 2003 (which was approved by Parliament) stated 'It should be noted that a body corporate, partnership or unincorporated association (see s 187 of the 2003 Act) may be the subject of proceedings for an offence under s 146' but subsequent issues do not contain that statement. The opinion of LACORS/LGR is that a corporate body that sells alcohol may commit an offence of selling alcohol to a person under the age of 18 but that a pub-owning company, using tenants, that has no title to the stock, and does not 'sell' cannot, therefore commit an offence under s 146.

Duty to enforce

16.90 Section 154 LA 2003 states:

> **154 Enforcement role for weights and measures authorities**
>
> (1) It is the duty of every local weights and measures authority in England and Wales to enforce within its area the provisions of sections 146 and 147, so far as they apply to sales of alcohol made on or from premises to which the public have access.

Powers of enforcement officers

16.91 Section 154(2) LA 2003 provides:

> (2) A weights and measures inspector may make, or authorise any person to make on his behalf, such purchases of goods as appear expedient for the purpose of determining whether those provisions [sections 146 and 147] are being complied with.

Sentencing

16.92 The offences of selling alcohol to children (s 146) and allowing the sale of alcohol to children (s 147) are now punishable by an unlimited fine.[25] The offence of Persistently selling alcohol to children (s 147A) remains limited to a fine not exceeding £20,000. It should be noted that underage sales do not necessarily lead to the prosecution of individuals or corporate bodies. There are

---

[24] [2004] EWHC 1141 (QBD).
[25] Legal Aid, Sentencing and Punishment of Offenders Act 2012, s 85.

other possible sanctions: the issuing of fixed penalty notices; the issuing of closure notices; and a review of the licence, which could, if evidence of persistent illegal sales were presented, lead to revocation of the licence.

Fixed penalty notices

16.93 Section 15 of the Police and Justice Act 2006 inserts s 41A (Accreditation of weights and measures inspectors) into the Police Reform Act 2002 enabling a chief constable to grant accreditation to a weights and measures inspector for the purpose of carrying out specified powers set out in Sch 5A of the Police Reform Act 2002, including the issuing of fixed penalty notices.

Closure notices

16.94 Section 24 of the Violent Crime Reduction Act 2006 inserted ss 169A and 169B into LA 2003 providing for the issuing of closure notices for persistently selling alcohol to children.[26] Section 169A enables the police and trading standards officers to issue a closure notice to a person in relation to whom there is evidence that he has committed an offence under s 147A LA 2003 and for which there is a reasonable prospect of conviction. The closure notice discharges the person from any further criminal liability but prevents him from selling alcohol for the period specified in the notice.[27]

Licensing reviews (Licensing Act 2003, s 51)

16.95 Amended guidance issued under s 182 of the Licensing Act 2003 on 31 October 2012 stated that where there were persistent sales of alcohol to children occurring at a particular premises, responsible authorities should consider applying for a review of the licence, whatever other steps they were also taking. The following cases all relate to licensing reviews which followed the sale of alcohol to a child as part of test purchasing exercises and/or evidence of underage drinking:

- *R (Bassetlaw District Council) v Worksop Magistrates' Court;*[28]
- *Carmarthenshire County Council v Llanelli Magistrates Court;*[29]
- *Prasannan v Royal Borough of Kensington & Chelsea;*[30]
- *Khan v Coventry City Magistrates' Court and Coventry City Council;*[31]
- *Rertrobars Wales Ltd v Bridgend County Borough Council.*[32]

---

[26] See also the Licensing Act 2003 (Persistent Selling of Alcohol to Children) (Prescribed Form of Closure Notice) Regulations 2007, SI 2007/1183.

[27] The Police Reform and Social Responsibility Act 2011 increased the period from a maximum of 48 hours to a period of between 48 hours and 336 hours.

[28] [2008] EWHC 3530 (Admin).

[29] [2009] EWHC 3016 (Admin).

[30] [2010] EWHC 319 (Admin).

[31] [2011] EWCA Civ 751.

[32] [2012] EWHC 3834 (Admin).

16.96 The case of *LIDL UK GmbH v City of Glasgow Licensing Board* [2013] CSIH 25, is an example of the equivalent procedure in Scotland under s 39(1) of the Licensing (Scotland) Act 2005: a premises licence was suspended for five days following a single sale to a 16-year-old child authorised by the duty manager. Following the incident, the manager was dismissed for failing to comply with the company's policies and staff were given additional training. The company appealed against the suspension of its licence citing lack of evidence that underage sales at the premises were a recurring problem and that that the staff-training programme was of a high standard. The Inner House of the Court of Session held that it was not open to the Board to have found that a ground for review had been established; and that the decision to suspend the licence was unjustified.

16.97 *City of Sunderland Council v Dawson.*[33] A 15-year-old girl made a test purchase of a bottle of 'wine', which looked like alcohol and was labelled as such (with a 7.5% alcohol by volume statement) but there was no evidence, such as a certificate of analysis, to prove that the contents were actually alcohol. The Justices accepted the defendant's submission of no case to answer. On appeal it was held that the court can draw such inferences as it thinks proper from a document – defined as 'anything in which information of any description is recorded' – by s 24(1) of the Criminal Justice Act 1988.[34] The case was remitted for a rehearing.

16.98 *Davies v Carmarthenshire County Council.*[35] The defendant, who was the manageress and joint licensee of a Spar Store was convicted of an offence under s 146 of the Licensing Act 1964 when a sales assistant sold alcohol to a 15-year-old test purchaser. On appeal the court found that justices were not entitled to reject the defence of due diligence in the circumstances of this case.

16.99 *R (on the application of Paul Verma) v Stratford Magistrates' Court.*[36] In this case, involving the sale of alcohol to a 15-year-old test purchaser, a number of issues arose, including the fact that her witness statement had been served under s 9 of the Criminal Justice Act 1967 and a late application was made for the test purchaser to give oral evidence. The justices refused the late application and further declined an application to exclude the evidence under s 78 of the Police and Criminal Evidence Act 1984. The defendant was convicted and an application for judicial review was dismissed.

16.100 *Cambridgeshire County Council v Kama.*[37] The defendant was convicted of an offence under s 146 of the Licensing Act 1964 when an employee sold alcohol to a 15-year-old test purchaser. The Magistrates dismissed the information on the basis of a 'due diligence' defence. The prosecutor's appeal was dismissed. Treacy J:

---

[33]   [2004] EWHC 2796 (Admin).
[34]   See ss 117 and 134 of the Criminal Justice Act 2003.
[35]   [2005] EWHC 464 (Admin).
[36]   [2006] EWHC 715 (Admin).
[37]   [2006] EWHC 3148 (Admin).

'With some hesitation, I have come to the conclusion that the Justices' decision, whilst not one that every court would necessarily have come to, was one to which they were entitled to come in the particular circumstances of this case. This decision is not to be taken as one which gives a licence to small corner shops, for example, not to have refusals book.'

16.101 In *City of Sunderland Council v Dawson* Thomas LJ said:

'It is important that licensees who are found guilty of selling alcohol to those underage are dealt with sternly in the light of the fact that the sale of alcohol to those underage is a serious contributor to many social and criminal problems.'

FIREWORKS

Introduction

16.102 Throughout the year, fireworks are widely used to mark public and private celebrations, as well as traditional events. As explosives, there are strict rules in place in the UK regulating the sale, possession and use of fireworks.[38] From 17 August 2015, the legislative provisions relating to age-restricted are contained in the Pyrotechnic Articles (Safety) Regulations 2015[39] which implement two European Directives.[40] The Regulations revoke and replace the Pyrotechnic Articles (Safety) Regulations 2010.[41]

Territorial jurisdiction

16.103 The Pyrotechnic Articles (Safety) Regulations 2015 ('PA(S)R 2015') are applicable throughout the United Kingdom.

Offences

16.104 Regulations 31 to 38 of PA(S)R 2015 set out obligations that manufacturers, importers and distributors have – in particular, reg 62 provides for offences in relation to a failure to comply with the prohibition, contained in reg 31, on making specified pyrotechnic articles available to persons younger than the minimum age limit. The obligations also include not making category F4 fireworks, category T2 theatrical pyrotechnic articles or category P2 other pyrotechnic articles available to persons without specialist knowledge.

16.105 Schedule 1 defines the categories of pyrotechnic articles:

---

[38] Explosives Act 1875; Fireworks Act 2003; Fireworks Regulations 2004, SI 2004/1836; Explosives (Fireworks) Regulations (Northern Ireland) 2002, SI 2002/147; Fireworks (Scotland) Regulations 2004, SSI 2004/393 and Explosives Regulations 2014, SI 2014/1638.

[39] SI 2015/1553.

[40] Directive 2013/29/EU (which recasts Directive 2007/23/EU and sets harmonised rules relating to the safety of pyrotechnic articles) and Directive 2014/58/EU (on setting up a system for the traceability of pyrotechnic articles).

[41] SI 2010/1554.

Schedule 1

Fireworks

1. Category F1 fireworks are fireworks which present a very low hazard and negligible noise level and which are intended for use in confined areas, including fireworks which are intended for use inside domestic buildings.

2. Category F2 fireworks are fireworks which present a low hazard and low noise level and which are intended for outdoor use in confined areas.

3. Category F3 fireworks are fireworks which present a medium hazard, which are intended for outdoor use in large open areas and whose noise level is not harmful to human health.

4. Category F4 fireworks are fireworks which present a high hazard, which are intended for use only by persons with specialist knowledge and whose noise level is not harmful to human health.

Theatrical pyrotechnic articles

5. Category T1 theatrical pyrotechnic articles are theatrical pyrotechnic articles which present a low hazard.

6. Category T2 theatrical pyrotechnic articles are theatrical pyrotechnic articles which are intended for use only by persons with specialist knowledge.

Other pyrotechnic articles

7. Category P1 other pyrotechnic articles are pyrotechnic articles, other than fireworks and theatrical pyrotechnic articles, which present a low hazard.

8. Category P2 other pyrotechnic articles are pyrotechnic articles, other than fireworks and theatrical pyrotechnic articles, which are intended for handling or use only by persons with specialist knowledge.

16.106 Regulation 2 provides for the interpretation of various terms which are relevant to the prohibition contained in reg 31 and the offences in reg 62:

"economic operator" means a manufacturer, importer or distributor;

"manufacturer" means a person who –

  (a)   manufactures a pyrotechnic article, or has such an article designed or manufactured; and
  (b)   markets that pyrotechnic article under that person's name or trade mark;

"importer" means any person who –

  (a)   is established within the EU; and
  (b)   places a pyrotechnic article from a third country on the EU market;

"distributor" means any person in the supply chain, other than the manufacturer or the importer, who makes a pyrotechnic article available on the market;

"firework" means a pyrotechnic article intended for entertainment purposes;

"Christmas cracker" means a paper or foil tube, crimped at each end, enclosing novelties and with one or more snaps running along the length of the tube;

"snap" means two overlapping strips of cardboard or paper, or two strings, with a friction sensitive pyrotechnic composition in sliding contact with an abrasive surface and designed to be held in the hand.

16.107 Regulation 31 (Prohibition on making available to persons younger than the minimum age limit) provides:

31. An economic operator must not make a pyrotechnic article available on the market in the United Kingdom to a person younger than the following minimum age limits –

(a)   for a Christmas cracker, 12 years;
(b)   for a category F1 firework other than a Christmas cracker, 16 years;
(c)   for a category F2 firework or a category F3 firework, 18 years;
(d)   for a category T1 theatrical pyrotechnic article, 18 years;
(e)   for a category P1 other pyrotechnic article, 18 years.

Regulation 62 provides for offences for a manufacturer, importer or distributor who contravenes reg 31.

16.108 Other firework-related provisions in PA(S)R 2015 include, under reg 62(1)(f), an offence for a manufacturer to contravene or fail to comply with any requirement of reg 11 (which deals with labelling of pyrotechnic articles). The required labelling information (contained in Schedule 3) must include instructions for use and safety information, which must include the minimum age limit for persons to whom the pyrotechnic article can be made available on the market. The labelling of sparklers must also display the words 'Warning: not to be given to children under 5 years of age'.

16.109 Other firework-related provisions of relevance include:

• under s 80 of the Explosives Act 1875 (as amended) it is an offence to throw or discharge a firework in a street or public place (which may be dealt with by the police serving a fixed penalty notice of £80);

• the Fireworks Regulations 2004 make it an offence for persons under 18 to possess adult fireworks in public places (which may be dealt with by the police serving a fixed penalty notice of £80);

• the Fireworks Regulations 2004 require suppliers of fireworks to the public display in a prominent position a notice stating that it is illegal to sell adult fireworks or sparklers to anyone under 18, and that it is also illegal for anyone under 18 to possess adult fireworks in a public place.

Defences

16.110 Regulation 64 provides for a defence of due diligence:

64(1) Subject to paragraph (2), (4) and (6), in proceedings for an offence under regulation 62, it is a defence for a person ("P") to show that P took all reasonable steps and exercised all due diligence to avoid committing the offence.

(2) P may not rely on a defence under paragraph (1) which involves a third party allegation unless P has –

(a) served a notice in accordance with paragraph (3); or
(b) obtained the leave of the court.

(3) The notice must –

(a) give any information in P's possession which identifies or assists in identifying the person who –
(i) committed the act or default; or
(ii) supplied the information on which P relied.
(b) be served on the person bringing the proceedings not less than 7 clear days before –
(i) in England, Wales and Northern Ireland, the hearing of the proceedings;
(ii) in Scotland, the trial diet.

(4) P may not rely on a defence under paragraph (1) which involves an allegation that the commission of the offence was due to reliance on information supplied by another person unless it was reasonable for P to have relied upon the information, having regard in particular –

(a) to the steps that P took, and those which might reasonably have been taken, for the purpose of verifying the information; and
(b) to whether P had any reason to disbelieve the information.

(5) In this regulation, "third party allegation" means an allegation that the commission of the offence was due –

(a) to the act or default of another person; or
(b) to reliance on information supplied by another person.

(6) This regulation does not apply in respect of proceedings for offences under regulation 62(6)."

Due diligence provisions are covered in Chapter 3, Criminal Enforcement.

Time limits

16.111 Regulation 66 provides for the time limit for prosecution of offences:

66(1) Subject to paragraph (4), in England and Wales, an information relating to an offence under regulation 62 that is triable by a magistrates' court may be so tried if it is laid within 12 months after the date on which evidence sufficient in the opinion of the prosecutor to justify the proceedings comes to the knowledge of the prosecutor.

(2) Subject to paragraph (4), in Scotland –

(a) summary proceedings for an offence under regulation 62 may be commenced before the end of 12 months after the date on which evidence sufficient in the Lord Advocate's opinion to justify the proceedings came to the Lord Advocate's knowledge; and
(b) section 136(3) of the Criminal Procedure (Scotland) Act 1995 (time limit for certain offences) applies for the purpose of this paragraph as it applies for the purpose of that section.

(3) Subject to paragraph (4), in Northern Ireland summary proceedings for an offence under regulation 62 may be instituted within 12 months after the date on which evidence sufficient in the opinion of the prosecutor to justify proceedings comes to the knowledge of the prosecutor.

(4) No proceedings may be brought more than 3 years after the commission of the offence.

(5) For the purposes of this regulation a certificate of the prosecutor (or in Scotland, the Lord Advocate) as to the date on which the evidence referred to paragraphs (1), (2) or (3) came to light, is conclusive evidence.

(6) This regulation has effect subject to paragraphs 1(o) and 2(n) of Schedule 8 (enforcement powers of the Health and Safety Executive under the 1974 Act).

Note also that, under reg 62(6) only the Lord Advocate may prosecute an offence under PA(S)R 2015 in Scotland. Time limits are covered generally in Chapter 3, Criminal Enforcement.

Prosecutions

16.112   Regulation 65 provides for liability of persons other than principal offender.

65(1) Where the commission of an offence by one person ("A") under regulation 62 is due to anything which another person ("B") did or failed to do in the course of business, B is guilty of the offence and may be proceeded against and punished, whether or not proceedings are taken against A.

(2) Where a body corporate commits an offence, a relevant person is also guilty of the offence where the body corporate's offence was committed –

    (a)   with the consent or connivance of the relevant person; or
    (b)   as a result of the negligence of the relevant person.

(3) In paragraph (2), "relevant person" means –

    (a)   a director, manager, secretary or other similar officer of the body corporate;
    (b)   in relation to a body corporate managed by its members, a member of that body corporate performing managerial functions;
    (c)   in relation to a Scottish partnership, a partner; or
    (d)   a person purporting to act as a person described in sub-paragraphs (a), (b) or (c).

Duty to enforce

16.113   Part 5 sets out provisions for market surveillance and enforcement. Regulation 52 identifies the market surveillance authority which has an obligation to enforce PA(S)R 2015 in respect of each category of pyrotechnic article. For categories F1, F2 and F3 fireworks the market surveillance authority in Great Britain, is, within its area, the weights and measures authority and, in Northern Ireland, within its area, the district council.

16.114   Regulation 53 provides:

53(1) The market surveillance authority must enforce these Regulations, and RAMS in its application to pyrotechnic articles, or ensure that they are enforced.

(2) In Great Britain, a GB enforcer other than the market surveillance authority may enforce these Regulations and RAMS in its application to pyrotechnic articles.

(3) In Northern Ireland, a NI enforcer other than the market surveillance authority may enforce these Regulations and RAMS in its application to pyrotechnic articles.

(4) Before taking action under paragraphs (2) or (3) a GB enforcer or NI enforcer must notify the market surveillance authority of the proposed action.

(5) The Secretary of State may appoint a person to act on behalf of the Secretary of State for the purposes of enforcing these Regulations and RAMS in its application to pyrotechnic articles.

(6) In Scotland, only the Lord Advocate may prosecute an offence under these Regulations.

(7) In this regulation—

"GB enforcer" means—

(a) a weights and measures authority;
(b) the Health and Safety Executive; or
(c) the Secretary of State;

"NI enforcer" means –

(a) a district council; or
(b) the Secretary of State.

Powers of enforcement officers

16.115 Regulation 54 and Schs 7, 8 and 9 provide for the enforcement powers which the enforcing authorities are to have. When enforcing PA(S)R 2015, the enforcing authority must exercise its powers in a manner which is consistent with the factors set out in regs 55–61. The Schedules to the Regulations set out the various powers available to enforcement authorities. Regulation 54 provides for offences for intentional obstruction of an enforcing authority (or officer of such authority) and for knowingly or recklessly providing any statement, information, document or record which is false or misleading in a material respect in purported compliance with any requirement under PA(S)R 2015. It is also an offence under reg 54 for a person who is not authorised to act on behalf of an enforcing authority to purport to exercise any of the powers of the enforcing authority under PA(S)R 2015.

Sentencing

16.116 Regulation 63 sets out the penalties that are to apply for offences under PA(S)R 2015.

63(1) A person guilty of an offence under regulation 62 in respect of a category F1 firework, a category F2 firework, or a category F3 firework is liable on summary conviction –

(a)   in England and Wales, to a fine or imprisonment for a term not exceeding 3 months or to both;

(b)   in Scotland or Northern Ireland, to a fine not exceeding level 5 on the standard scale or imprisonment for a term not exceeding 3 months or to both.

(2) A person guilty of an offence under regulation 62 in respect of a pyrotechnic article to which paragraph (1) does not apply is liable –

(a)   on summary conviction—
(i)   in England and Wales, to a fine or imprisonment for a term not exceeding 3 months or to both;
(ii)   in Scotland or Northern Ireland, to a fine not exceeding the statutory maximum or imprisonment for a term not exceeding 3 months or to both;

(b)   on conviction on indictment, to a fine or imprisonment for a term not exceeding 2 years or to both.

KNIVES AND OFFENSIVE WEAPONS

Introduction

16.117   The Criminal Justice Act 1988 ('CJA 1988') prohibits the sale of knives and certain articles with blade or point to persons under 18 years of age. Legislation such as the Restriction of Offensive Weapons Act 1959 and the Knives Act 1997 (which are outside of the scope of this work) also create offences in relation to the sale of knives which are completely prohibited and the unlawful marketing of knives.

Territorial jurisdiction

16.118   The offence in s 141A CJA 1988 extends to England, Wales and Scotland.[42] Article 54 of the Criminal Justice (Northern Ireland) Order 1996 makes similar provision to s 141A CJA 1988.

Offence

16.119   Section 141A(1) CJA 1988[43] states:

(1) Any person who sells to a person under the age of eighteen years an article to which this section applies shall be guilty of an offence...

The offence applies[44] to:

---

[42]   Subject to s 141A(3A).
[43]   Inserted by the Offensive Weapons Act 1996 and amended by the Violent Crime Reduction Act 2006.
[44]   Subject to s 141A(3).

(a) any knife, knife blade or razor blade;

(b) any axe; and

(c) any other article which has a blade or which is sharply pointed and which is made or adapted for use for causing injury to the person.

Section 141A CJA 1988 does not apply to any article described in s 1 of the Restriction of Offensive Weapons Act 1959 or an Order made under s 141A or s 141(2) of the Act.

16.120 In *Regina (Windsor and Maidenhead Royal Borough Council) v East Berkshire Magistrates' Court*[45] it was held that whether an article was a 'knife' within the meaning of s 141A(2)(a) CJA 1988 was not a pure question of fact, but a question of mixed fact and law; and the justices had erred in law in finding that s 141A did not apply to a grapefruit knife, notwithstanding that it was a cutting instrument consisting of a blade with a handle. Sir Anthony May stated:

'In my judgment this grapefruit knife is a cutting instrument consisting of a blade with a sharpened longitudinal edge -it has two such edges in fact -fixed in a handle, and in my judgment it is a knife within section 141A(2) of the 1988 Act ... I should add for completeness that there is a definition of "knife" in section 10 of the Knives Act 1997 which is consistent with what I have just held, but that is subsequent legislation. Accordingly, in my judgment this claim for judicial review succeeds and it will be necessary for the matter to be sent back to the magistrates, having quashed their decision, for them to continue to hear the case.'

Defences

16.121 Section 141A(4) CJA 1988 provides:

(4) It shall be a defence for a person charged with an offence under subsection (1) above to prove that he took all reasonable precautions and exercised all due diligence to avoid the commission of the offence.

16.122 Whilst mainly concerned with the general principle of retrospective precautions taken after an offence has been committed, *Enfield London Borough Council v Argos Ltd*[46] featured a case where the defendant's employee sold a six-piece knife block to a test-purchasing child who was under the age of 16 (the statutory age-limit at the time).

16.123 Section 141A CJA 1988 was amended by s 75 of the Police, Public Order and Criminal Justice (Scotland) Act 2006 by inserting:

(3A) It is not an offence under subsection (1) to sell a knife or knife blade to a person if –

(a) the person is aged 16 or over; and

(b) the knife or blade is designed for domestic use.

---

45 [2010] EWHC 3020 (Admin).
46 [2008] EWHC 2597 (Admin).

Note that this provision applies only in Scotland.

16.124   In *London Borough of Croydon v Pinch a Pound (UK) Ltd*[47] trading standards' volunteers test purchased a Rolson utility knife (an item with a retractable blade similar to a Stanley knife) selected from an open display. The till was operated by an employee of the defendant company, who did not challenge the purchase. The company was convicted of an offence under s 141A of the Criminal Justice Act 1988 but successfully appealed to the Crown Court against that conviction. That decision was appealed by way of case stated to the High Court. The issue before the Magistrates, and on appeal, was whether the defendant could avail itself of the statutory defence provided by s 141A(4), which states: 'It shall be a defence for a person charged with an offence under s 141A(1) above to prove that he took all reasonable precautions and exercised all due diligence to avoid the commission of the offence.'

16.125   Roderick Evans J stated:

> 'Although there is no legal requirement to maintain a record of refused sales, the Crown Court concluded that "the refusals register was adhered to in a less than effective way and not implemented fully. The system needed to be considerably strengthened to be a source of assistance to management and staff ..." The Crown Court acknowledged that, on the balance of probabilities, signs were in place at the time of the test purchase, but found that the "signs were homemade, colloquial, with no great base in law and needed to be updated in content and position. The signs needed to be fixed on the till and laminated to make them effective ..." The finding of the Crown Court was that "some training had taken place, but the [Defendant] needed to recognise that managers had to be confident about legislation and to pass this down effectively to staff members, including those who work on Saturdays. Implementation had to be updated regularly so there could be no recurrence." As to the display of restricted items, some of which were kept behind the counter and some on general display, the Crown Court concluded that "all restricted items ... needed to be kept behind the counter rather than displayed in a piecemeal, confused and cavalier way, which had led to confusion in the minds of staff members ..."
>
> The Crown Court identified serious shortcomings in the precautions taken in this case and in the way they were implemented. On a correct application of the test under s 141A(4), the findings of the Crown Court are, in my view, inconsistent with the acquittal of the defendant on the basis that the statutory defence had been proved. Accordingly, I would allow the appeal, and send this case back to the Crown Court with a direction to convict the defendant and to proceed to sentence.'

16.126   Pill LJ stated:

> 'In relation to the refusal register, the Justices found that it was adhered to in a "less than effective way and not implemented fully. The system needed to be considerably strengthened". As to signs, they found that they were displayed in a "piecemeal, confused and cavalier way, which had led to confusion in the minds of

---

[47]   [2010] EWHC 3283 (Admin).

staff members". As to training about legislation, they found that the respondents "needed to recognise" aspects of the matter, indicating that they had not already recognised them. These are serious shortcomings, as Roderick Evans J has found.'

Time limits

16.127 The offence under s 141A CJA 1988 is summary-only. There is therefore a six-month time limit for bringing proceedings, from the time when the offence was committed.[48] In Scotland, as the offence can only be tried under summary procedure, the time limits are established under s 136 of the Criminal Procedure (Scotland) Act 1995 – within six months after the contravention occurred.

Prosecutions

16.128 The offence under s 141A CJA 1988 can be committed by the actual seller or, where applicable, his employer.

Duty to enforce

16.129 There is no duty of enforcement prescribed for s 141A CJA 1988. However, In Scotland, businesses selling non-domestic knives must be registered with the local authority in which the premises are located.[49]

Sentencing

16.130 A person found guilty of an offence under s 141A CJA 1988 is liable on summary conviction to imprisonment for a term not exceeding six months, or a fine not exceeding level 5 on the standard scale, or both.

Commentary

16.131 In September 2009 the Home Office published *Tackling Youth Knife Crime – Practical advice for police*. The advice includes:

'3.1 Trading Standards and Test Purchase Operations. Under the supervision of joint working between the police and Trading Standards officers, it is vital that the law on knife sales is enforced to protect young people. Ensuring responsible retailing and conducting Test Purchase Operations should be a feature of local Basic Command Unit operations.'

---

[48] Magistrates' Courts Act 1980, s 127.
[49] Civic Government (Scotland) Act 1982, s 27A.

VIDEO RECORDINGS

Introduction

16.132 The primary purpose of the Video Recordings Act 1984 ('VRA 1984') is child protection. The Act regulates the supply of films and certain video games in the form of the physical product, such as discs, magnetic tape and other physical storage devices. Some video works are deemed inappropriate for children to view and the Act gives powers to a designated authority to determine the suitability of a video work and classify it accordingly. This suitability ranges from those works which are suitable for general viewing to those which may only be sold in a licensed sex shop (ensuring that the recipient of the video work is verifiably over 18). The scheme introduced by the Act requires that videos should have affixed to them a symbol indicating which of the range of classifications the particular video work belongs to.

16.133 The British Board of Film Classification ('BBFC') is the designated Video Works Authority. Under the Act all *'video works'* (films, TV programmes, video games, etc) which are supplied on a disc, tape or any other device capable of storing data electronically are required to be classified by the BBFC, unless they fall within the definition of an exempted work. This chapter deals with the offences created by ss 9–14 of the Act. The principal offence relating to age-restricted products is contained in s 11 but there are other offences under the Act.

Territorial jurisdiction

16.134 The Act has application throughout the UK.

Offences

Supplying a video recording of unclassified work

16.135 Section 9(1) provides:

> (1) A person who supplies or offers to supply a video recording containing a video work in respect of which no classification certificate has been issued is guilty of an offence unless –
>
> > (a) the supply is, or would if it took place be, an exempted supply, or
> > (b) the video work is an exempted work.

Possession of video recording of unclassified work for the purposes of supply

16.136 Section 10(1) provides:

> (1) Where a video recording contains a video work in respect of which no classification certificate has been issued, a person who has the recording in his possession for the purpose of supplying it is guilty of an offence unless –

(a) he has it in his possession for the purpose only of a supply which, if it took place, would be an exempted supply, or

(b) the video work is an exempted work.

Supplying video recording of classified work in breach of classification

16.137 Section 11(1) provides:

(1) Where a classification certificate issued in respect of a video work states that no video recording, or no video recording described in the certificate, that contains that work is to be supplied to any person who has not attained the age specified in the certificate, a person who supplies or offers to supply such a video recording to a person who has not attained the age so specified is guilty of an offence unless (a) the video work is an exempted work, or(b)the supply is, or would if it took place be, an exempted supply.

16.138 In *Ealing London Borough Council v Woolworths plc*[50] the local authority engaged a child of 11 years to purchase an '18' category video film from the defendant company whilst under the observation of trading standards officers.

Russell LJ:

'The justices in their finding came to the conclusion that the Trading Standards Department's officers had acted in a way that they described as 'ultra vires' by instructing the boy to make the purchase. The justices went on to say that the transaction was contrived and instigated by the Trading Standards Department and that consequently they were at liberty to exclude the evidence under section 78 of the Police and Criminal Evidence Act 1984. I have to say that ... the justices were fundamentally in error in the approach that they made. Entrapment is not a defence known to English law. ... If the process employed, which we understand to be a common practice up and down the country, were to fall foul of section 78, it would ... emasculate the enforcement of a sensible piece of legislation which ... was passed for the express purpose of protecting young people such as the boy employed for the test purchase in this case from being exposed to undesirable influences. I do not accept that what happened was in any sense an entrapment of [Woolworths], or that the boy acted as an agent provocateur, nor, incidentally, did he commit any offence in purchasing the video. He did not incite, aid or abet the commission of an offence by [Woolworths]. By purchasing the video he was simply playing a part in the situation which rendered [Woolworths] culpable. Had there been any element of persuasion of the sales girl by the customer, then perhaps different considerations would have prevailed.'

Certain video recordings only to be supplied in licensed sex shops

16.139 Section 12(1) provides:

---

[50] [1995] Crim LR 58.

(1) Where a classification certificate issued in respect of a video work states that no video recording or no video recording described in the certificate, that contains that work is to be supplied other than in a licensed sex shop, a person who at any place other than in a sex shop for which a licence is in force under the relevant enactment –

(a)   supplies such a video recording, or
(b)   offers to do so,

is guilty of an offence unless the supply is, or would if it took place be, an exempted supply.

16.140   Section 12(3) provides:

(3) Where a classification certificate issued in respect of a video work states that no video recording or no video recording described in the certificate, that contains that work is to be supplied other than in a licensed sex shop, a person who has such a video recording in his possession for the purpose of supplying it at any place other than in such a sex shop is guilty of an offence, unless he has it in his possession for the purpose only of a supply which, if it took place, would be an exempted supply.

16.141   The 'R (Restricted) 18' category '... is a special and legally restricted classification primarily for explicit works of consenting sex between adults ...'. R18 films and videos can only be shown in licensed cinemas, or supplied in licensed sex shops, and then only to persons of not less than 18 years.

16.142   The issue as to whether it is an offence to supply R18 films to customers other than at licensed sex shops in person was considered in *Interfact Ltd* and *Pabo Ltd v Liverpool City Council*.[51] The cases related to test purchases of R18 videos by a trading standards officer, from Pabo Limited and Interfact Limited, which were ordered by post, telephone and online from his office. He subsequently received in the post the videos, accompanied by catalogues advertising R18 videos – which gave rise to charges of offering to supply. The two companies are unconnected. They each operated licensed sex shops – Pabo Limited at premises in Birmingham, Interfact Limited at premises in Bexley. Both companies were convicted of VRA 1984 offences at Liverpool Magistrates' Court and appealed. The questions posed by the case stated in relation to *Interfact Limited* were:

'(1)   Whether a licensed sex shop can supply R18 videos by way of mail or telephone order or whether supply can only be made to a person physically present in the licensed sex shop.
(2)   Whether a licensed sex shop may offer to supply R18 videos by way of mail order or telephone order.'

16.143   The questions in the *Pabo Limited* case raised similar issues. Maurice Kay LJ, giving the judgment of the court rejected the appellants' submissions:

---

[51]   [2005] EWHC 995 (Admin).

'… the requirement that the event of supply is to be confined to a licensed sex shop gives heightened protection, reducing the opportunity for the material to be viewed by children.'

He said that the VRA 1984 restriction is not directed simply to ensure a supply takes place 'by' a licensed sex shop proprietor: the provisions were '… aimed at securing that the supply of a video work so classified is to be *in* a licensed shop' (added emphasis).

'We have no doubt that one of the main reasons for the restriction is to ensure that the customer comes face to face with the supplier so that there is an opportunity for the supplier to assess the age of the customer. It is a disincentive to a visibly under age customer to seek out the forbidden material.'

The defendants' submissions relating to 'offer to supply' failed because the Act expressly provides that there can be a supply where there has been 'no binding contract to supply'… a gratuitous offer to supply without any consideration and therefore not made under a binding contract would equally be an offer to supply a video recording.

16.144 The judgment in the *Liverpool* case therefore clearly establishes that the offence of 'supplying' a R18 video recording, other than in a licensed sex shop, will be committed whenever such videos are ordered by mail, telephone or electronically and delivered to an address which is not a licensed sex shop, and the offence of 'offering to supply' such videos will be committed wherever an offer was made to make such a supply other than in a licensed sex shop.

Supply of video recording not complying with requirements as to labels, etc

16.145 Section 13(1) provides:

(1) A person who supplies or offers to supply a video recording or any spool, case or other thing on or in which the recording is kept which does not satisfy any requirement imposed by regulations under section 8 of this Act is guilty of an offence unless –

    (a) the video work is an exempted work, or
    (b) the supply is, or would if it took place be, an exempted supply.

16.146 The Video Recordings (Labelling) Regulations 2012 came in to force on 30 July 2012. The Regulations, which are made under ss 8 and 22A of the VRA 1984, provide for the labelling of video recordings in the UK – they specify requirements as to the indications of the contents of any classification certificate in the form of labels and markings, and the position in which such labels and markings are to be shown on any video recording containing the video work in respect of which the certificate was issued. The requirements for labelling of video games only apply to those video games for which a classification certificate is issued by the VSC/GRA. The Regulations revoke the Video Recordings (Labelling) Regulations 2010 but the labelling requirements that apply to video works for which a classification certificate is issued by the BBFC (ie other than video games) remain unchanged.

Supply of video recording containing false indication as to classification

16.147   Section 14(1) provides:

(1) A person who supplies or offers to supply a video recording containing a video work in respect of which no classification certificate has been issued is guilty of an offence if the video recording or any spool, case or other thing on or in which the recording is kept contains any indication that a classification certificate has been issued in respect of that work unless –

(a)   the video work is an exempted work, or
(b)   the supply is, or would if it took place be, an exempted supply.

16.148   Section 14(3) provides:

(3) A person who supplies or offers to supply a video recording containing a video work in respect of which a classification certificate has been issued is guilty of an offence if the video recording or any spool, case or other thing on or in which the recording is kept contains any indication that is false in a material particular of any statement falling within section 7(2) of this Act (including any advice falling within paragraph (a) of that subsection) contained in the certificate, unless –

(a)   the video work is an exempted work, or
(b)   the supply is, or would if it took place be, an exempted supply.

The offences created by ss 9–14 VRA 1984 have a number of common ingredients which are examined below.

Video recording

16.149   Section 1(3) of the Act defines a video recording as 'any disc, magnetic tape or any other device capable of storing data electronically containing information by the use of which the whole or part of a video work may be produced'. A video work is defined by s 1(2) of the Act as being 'any series of visual images (with or without sound) produced electronically by the use of information contained on any disc, magnetic tape or any other device capable of storing data electronically and shown as a moving picture'.

16.150   Continuity of images is not the deciding factor in whether a sequence of images constitute a moving picture. Where the sequence is long enough to show continuing movement it can be a moving picture.[52] Both the Home Office and LACOTS[53] have expressed the opinion that images designed to simulate motion by the camera rather than the object viewed constitute a moving

---

[52]   *Kent CC v Multi Media Marketing (Canterbury) Ltd* (1995) *The Times*, 9 May, DC.
[53]   LACOTS Circular CO 14 95 5.

picture, although this would not be the case if the movement of the still image were created only by the end users manipulation of the image, for instance by the use of 'scroll bars'.

16.151 Section 22(2) VRA 1984 provides further interpretation as to the circumstances when a video recording contains a video work: in particular, it states that a video recording contains a video work if it contains information by means of which all or part of the video work can be produced. There is an exception to this: if a video work contains an extract of another video work (for example, a film that includes an extract from another film), the extract is not part of the work of which it is an extract but a part of the video work which contains the extract; and hence the video recording contains that video work including the extract.

16.152 An increasing variety of video recordings are available, some of which contain a mixture of films and video games. Section 22(2A) (inserted by DEA 2010) provides a power for the Secretary of State to make provision about the circumstances in which a video recording does or does not contain a video work for the purposes of the Act. This allows provision to be made to take account of new formats, such as where a video game contains a whole film within it or a film contains a game within it.

16.153 The DEA 2010 extended the statutory classification requirement to video games that are only suitable for viewing by persons aged 12 years and above.

Supply

16.154 Section 1(4) of the Act states that the question of reward is irrelevant to the concept of supply, which includes supply by way of 'sale, letting on hire, exchange or loan'. Supply by a company may be committed vicariously by an employee acting in the course of his employment.[54] Where the supply is to an under-aged person who is buying on behalf of an undisclosed adult principal, the supply is to the under-aged person.[55]

Exempted works

16.155 Section 2 of the Act defines a video work as an exempted work if, taken as a whole, it is either:

- designed to inform, educate or instruct; or
- concerned with sport, religion or music; or
- a video game.

---

[54] *Tesco Stores Ltd v Brent London Borough Council* [1993] 1 WLR 1037, DC.
[55] *Tesco Stores Ltd v Brent London Borough Council* [1993] 1 WLR 1037, DC.

16.156 As a result of a Government consultation on Exemptions to the Video Recordings Act and on Advertising in Cinemas, the Video Recordings Act 1984 (Exempted Video Works) Regulations 2014 were introduced and came in to force in October 2014.

16.157 New categories in which a video work (other than a video game) is not an exempted work are contained in s 2(1ZA), as inserted by the 2014 Regulations, and relate to:

- violence or threats of violence;
- the immediate aftermath of violence on human or animal characters;
- imitable dangerous activity;
- activities involving illegal drugs or misuse of drugs;
- use of alcohol or tobacco;
- suicide or attempted suicide, or the immediate aftermath of such an event;
- an act of scarification or mutilation of a person, or self harm, or the immediate aftermath of such an act;
- techniques likely to be useful in the commission of offences or promotion of such activity;
- words or images intended or likely to convey a sexual message;
- human sexual activity[56] or acts of force or restraint associated with such activity; or
- mutilation or torture of, or other acts of gross violence towards, humans or animals; or
- human genital organs or human urinary or excretory functions;
- swearing (other than mild bad language);
- it includes words or images that are intended or likely to cause offence, whether on the grounds of race, gender, disability, religion or belief or sexual orientation, or otherwise.

16.158 Section 40 DEA 2010 sets out conditions that must be satisfied for a video game to be an exempted work under the Act. The existing statutory exemptions for video games will continue to apply. Those games that, taken as a whole, are designed to inform, educate or instruct, and those concerned with sport, religion or music, will not be required to be classified, provided that they do not depict human sexual activity, gross violence or any of the other matters set out in s 2(1Z) and (3) of the Act. A video game will also be exempted if it satisfies one or more the conditions set out in s 2A of the Act.

---

[56] 'Human sexual activity' need not be intercourse or masturbation if what is depicted is designed to stimulate or encourage such activity: *Kent CC v Multi Media Marketing (Canterbury) Ltd* (1995) *The Times*, 9 May, DC.

Exempted supplies

16.159 Section 3 of the Act sets out the circumstances in which a supply of a video recording is an exempted supply, even if the film or game contained in the video recording is not exempted. The supply of a video recording is an exempted supply if it is neither:

- a supply for reward, nor
- a supply in the course or furtherance of a business.[57]

16.160 Where a video is supplied on premises such as a video shop it is to be treated as having been supplied in the course or furtherance of business.[58] There are other specific instances of exempt supplies which are set out below.

(a) By s 3(4) of the Act, the supply of a video recording to a person in the video trade is exempt unless it is made with a view to the eventual supply of that recording to the general public.

(b) By s 3(5) of the Act (as amended by the 2014 Regulations), the supply of a video work designed to provide a record of an occasion for those who took part or those connected with them, which does not to any significant extent, depict:
  (i) human sexual activity or acts of force or restraint associated with such activity (and is not designed to any significant extent to stimulate or encourage such activity);
  (ii) mutilation or torture of, or other acts of gross violence towards, humans or animals (and is not designed to any extent to stimulate or encourage such activity); or
  (iii) human genital organs or human urinary or excretory functions.

(c) By s 3(6) of the Act the supply of a video recording for the purpose showing it in private or where the public are admitted without payment[59] is an exempted supply.

(d) By s 3(8) of the Act the supply of a video recording with a view only to its use for or in connection with a program service within the meaning of the Broadcasting Act 1990 is an exempted supply.

(e) By s 3(9) of the Act the supply of a video recording for the issue of a classification certificate or other arrangements by the designated authority is an exempted supply.

(f) By s 3(10) and (11) of the Act the supply of a video recording for medical training is an exempted supply.

(g) By s 3(12) of the Act the return, otherwise than for reward, of a video recording to person who had previously made an exempt supply of it is itself an exempted supply.

---

[57] Section 3(2).
[58] Section 3(3).
[59] See s 5 of the Cinematograph Act 1952.

16.161 Section 12(6) provides that where a video recording's classification means that it can only be supplied through a licensed sex shop, it is an exempted supply if it is to an (unlicensed) business that makes video works or supplies video recordings, and it is with a view to an eventual supply in licensed sex shops. DEA 2010 amended s 3 of the Act to secure that the supply of video games by means of amusement arcade machines is exempted (see s 3(8A) and (8B)), unless the game includes any of the matters mentioned in s 2(2) and (3) of the Act.

Classification certificate

16.162 Section 7 of the Act defines a classification certificate as a certificate issued in respect of a video work in pursuance of arrangements made by the designated authority.[60] The certificate must contain the unique title assigned to the video work,[61] and either:

(a) a statement that it is suitable for general viewing and unrestricted supply with or without advice as to the desirability of parental guidance;

(b) a statement that it is suitable for viewing only by those of the age specified in the certificate that it is not to be supplied to any younger person; or

(c) a statement under para (b) above together with a statement that it is only to be supplied in a licensed sex shop.

16.163 Where it is necessary to prove that a particular video work has been issued with a particular classification certificate, or that no such certificate has been issued in respect of the work, or that a particular video work differs from another video work, this may be done by means of a certificate signed by a person authorised to make such a statement by the Secretary of State. Such a certificate is admissible only if a copy of it has been served on the defendant not less than 7 days before the hearing.[62] Where an alteration or addition has been made to a video work in respect of which a classification certificate has been issued, the certificate is not valid for the altered work.[63]

In the course of a business

16.164 It is a requirement of many of the offences under ss 9–14 that the offender be acting 'in the course of a business'. Except in s 3(4) of the Act (exempted supplies) the word business in the Act includes any activity carried on by a club.[64]

In possession

16.165 Many of the offences under the Act involve proof of the possession by the defendant of a video recording. In order for offences of possession to be

---

60 The British Board of Film Classification.
61 Sections 2(2) and 4(1)(b)(ia).
62 Section 19.
63 Section 22(3).
64 Section 22(1).

made good the law requires proof of an element of control over the item in question, although not necessarily of physical proximity.[65] It appears that possession by an employee will be held to be possession by the employer.[66]

Defences

16.166   There are specific defences relating to each of the offences contained in ss 9–14.

Supplying a video recording of unclassified work

16.167   Section 9(2) provides:

(2) It is a defence to a charge of committing an offence under this section to prove that the accused believed on reasonable grounds –

    (a)   that the video work concerned or, if the video recording contained more than one work to which the charge relates, each of those works was either an exempted work or a work in respect of which a classification certificate had been issued, or

    (b)   that the supply was, or would if it took place be, an exempted supply by virtue of section 3(4) or (5) of this Act.

Due diligence defences are now covered in Chapter 3, Criminal Enforcement.

Possession of video recording of unclassified work for the purposes of supply

16.168   Section 10(2) provides:

(2) It is a defence to a charge of committing an offence under this section to prove –

    (a)   that the accused believed on reasonable grounds that the video work concerned or, if the video recording contained more than one work to which the charge relates, each of those works was either an exempted work or a work in respect of which a classification certificate had been issued,

    (b)   that the accused had the video recording in his possession for the purpose only of a supply which he believed on reasonable grounds would, if it took place, be an exempted supply by virtue of section 3(4) or (5) of this Act, or

    (c)   that the accused did not intend to supply the video recording until a classification certificate had been issued in respect of the video work concerned.

---

[65]   See *Warner v Metropolitan Police Commissioner* [1969] 2 AC 256, *Bellerby v Carle* [1983] 2 AC 101, [1983] 1 All ER 1031, HL.
[66]   *Towers & Co v Gray* [1961] 2 QB 351, [1961] 2 All ER 68, DC.

Supplying video recording of classified work in breach of classification

16.169 Section 11(2) provides:

> (2) It is a defence to a charge of committing an offence under this section to prove –
>
> (a) that the accused neither knew nor had reasonable grounds to believe that the classification certificate contained the statement concerned,
>
> (b) that the accused neither knew nor had reasonable grounds to believe that the person concerned had not attained that age,
>
> (ba) that the accused believed on reasonable grounds that the video work concerned or, if the video recording contained more than one work to which the charge relates, each of those works was an exempted work,or
>
> (c) that the accused believed on reasonable grounds that the supply was, or would if it took place be, an exempted supply by virtue of section 3(4) or (5) of this Act.

Certain video recordings only to be supplied in licensed sex shops

16.170 Section 12(2) provides:

> (2) It is a defence to a charge of committing an offence under subsection (1) above to prove –
>
> (a) that the accused neither knew nor had reasonable grounds to believe that the classification certificate contained the statement concerned,
>
> (b) that the accused believed on reasonable grounds that the place concerned was a sex shop for which a licence was in force under the relevant enactment, or
>
> (c) that the accused believed on reasonable grounds that the supply was, or would if it took place be, an exempted supply by virtue of section 3(4) of this Act or subsection (6) below.

16.171 Section 12(4) provides:

> (2) It is a defence to a charge of committing an offence under subsection (3) above to prove –
>
> (a) that the accused neither knew nor had reasonable grounds to believe that the classification certificate contained the statement concerned,
>
> (b) that the accused believed on reasonable grounds that the place concerned was a sex shop for which a licence was in force under the relevant enactment, or
>
> (c) that the accused had the video recording in his possession for the purpose only of a supply which he believed on reasonable grounds would, if it took place, be an exempted supply by virtue of section 3(4) of this Act or subsection (6) below.

Supply of video recording not complying with requirements as to labels, etc

16.172 Section 13(2) provides:

> (2) It is a defence to a charge of committing an offence under this section to prove that the accused –
>
> (za) believed on reasonable grounds that the video work concerned or, if the video recording contained more than one work to which the charge relates, each of those works was an exempted work,
>
> (a) believed on reasonable grounds that the supply was, or would if it took place be, an exempted supply by virtue of section 3(4) or (5) of this Act, or
>
> (b) neither knew nor had reasonable grounds to believe that the recording, spool, case or other thing (as the case may be) did not satisfy the requirement concerned.

Supply of video recording containing false indication as to classification

16.173 Section 14(2) provides:

> (2) It is a defence to a charge of committing an offence under subsection (1) above to prove –
>
> (a) that the accused believed on reasonable grounds –
>   (i) that a classification certificate had been issued in respect of the video work concerned,
>   (ia) that the video work concerned or, if the video recording contained more than one work to which the charge relates, each of those works was an exempted work, or
>   (ii) that the supply was, or would if it took place be, an exempted supply by virtue of section 3(4) or (5) of this Act, or
>
> (b) that the accused neither knew nor had reasonable grounds to believe that the recording, spool, case or other thing (as the case may be) contained the indication concerned.

16.174 Section 14(4) provides:

> (4) It is a defence to a charge of committing an offence under subsection (3) above to prove –
>
> (a) that the accused believed on reasonable grounds –
>   (ai) that the video work concerned or, if the video recording contained more than one work to which the charge relates, each of those works was an exempted work,
>   (i) that the supply was, or would if it took place be, an exempted supply by virtue of section 3(4) or (5) of this Act, or
>   (ii) that the certificate concerned contained the statement indicated, or
>
> (b) that the accused neither knew nor had reasonable grounds to believe that the recording, spool, case or other thing (as the case may be) contained the indication concerned.

Knew or had reasonable grounds to believe

16.175   The specific defences provided by each of the sections creating offences involve a requirement for the defendant to prove that he knew, or had reasonable grounds to believe certain matters. Knowledge includes turning a blind eye to relevant matters,[67] while some authorities suggest that deliberately to refrain from making enquiries where the results may be unwelcome constitutes actual knowledge of the facts concerned.[68] Mere failure to find out what could have been ascertained by reasonable enquiry does not amount to knowledge.[69]

16.176   Where the issue is what the defendant had 'reason to believe' it is arguable that the prosecution must prove what was actually believed, rather than the objective question of whether there was 'reason to believe' something else.[70] The defendant must have knowledge of facts from which a reasonable person would come to the relevant belief and enough time must have elapsed for such a person to convert the facts into the relevant belief before a defendant can be held to have 'reason to believe' something.[71] The question of whether a defendant had reason to believe a particular state of affairs pertained, and the existence of any belief founded on the reason is ultimately a question of fact.[72] Where a person is in possession of credible but contradictory facts it is unlikely that he has sufficient 'reason to believe'.[73]

General defence to offences under this Act

16.177   In addition to the specific defences detailed above, a general defence, applicable to all offences in ss 9–14, is contained in s 14A.

16.178   Section 14A provides:

14A General defence to offences under this Act

Without prejudice to any defence specified in the preceding provisions of this Act in relation to a particular offence, it is a defence to a charge of committing any offence under this Act to prove –

---

67   *James & Son Ltd v Smee* [1955] 1 QB 78, [1954] 3 All ER 273, *ZYX Music Gmbh v King* [1995] 3 All ER 1, [1997] 2 All ER 129, CA, *Westminster City Council v Croyalgrange Ltd* [1986] 2 All ER 353, [1986] 1 WLR 674, HL.

68   *Westminster City Council v Croyalgrange Ltd* [1986] 2 All ER 353, [1986] 1 WLR 674, HL, *Mallon v Allon* [1964] 1 QB 385 at 394, [1963] 3 All ER 843 at 847.

69   *Taylor's Central Garages (Exeter) Ltd v Roper* (1951) 115 JP 445 at 449.

70   *R v Banks* 1916 2 KB 621, [1916–1917] All ER 356, *R v Harrison* [1938] 3 All ER 134, 159 LT 95, *Nakkuda Ali v Jayaratne* [1951] AC 66, PC.

71   *LA Gear Inc v Hi-Tec Sports plc* [1992] FSR 121 at 129.

72   *Nakkuda Ali v Jayaratne* [1951] AC 66, PC, *Jones v Bertram* (1894) 58 JP 478, 10 TLR 285, *Blaydon Co-op Society v Young* (1916) 86 LJKB, 115 LT 827, *Registrar of Restrictive Trading Agreements v WH Smith & Son Ltd* [1969] 3 All ER 1065 at 1070, [1969] 1 WLR 1460 at 1468, CA, *IRC v Rossminster* [1980] AC 952, [1980] 1 All ER 80, HL.

73   *Hutchinson Personal Communications Ltd v Hook Advertising Ltd* [1995] FSR 365.

(a)   that the commission of the offence was due to the act or default of a
      person other than the accused, and
(b)   that the accused took all reasonable precautions and exercised all due
      diligence to avoid the commission of the offence by any person under his
      control.

16.179   Section 14A, added to the original scheme of VRA 1984 by the Video
Recordings Act 1995, provides a defence of the type that the Court of Appeal
were unable to find implicit in the provision of s 11(2) of the Act in *Tesco
Stores Ltd v Brent London Borough Council*,[74] namely a 'due diligence' defence
of the type prescribed in s 24 of the Trade Descriptions Act 1968. The defence
is available where the defendant can show that the offence was caused by the
act or default of some other person and that the defendant took all reasonable
precautions and exercised all due diligence to avoid the commission of the
offence by any person under his control.

16.180   In *Tesco Stores Ltd v Brent London Borough Council* (a case decided
prior to the introduction, by amendment, of the general defence under s 14A)
the Court of Appeal held that the state of mind relevant to establishing the
defence under s 11(2)(b) was that of the employee making the supply rather
than that of her employer, the company. Since the magistrates had found that
she had had reasonable grounds to believe that the purchaser, a 14-year-old
boy, was under the age of 18, the defence was not available and the appeal
dismissed.

The act or default of another person

16.181   Assistance is to be gained from authorities concerned with the similarly
worded defence under s 24 of the Trade Descriptions Act 1968. Thus it seems
that where the defendant is a company the fact that the 'other person' is an
employee of the company (as where a company sold a mislabelled turkey
through the failure of the manager of one of a chain of shops to read his
instructions) does not prevent the company from relying on the statutory
defence.[75] On the other hand it has been held insufficient simply to name all the
persons who might be to blame (for example all the assistants present in the
relevant branch of a chain of shops at the relevant time). The defendant must
establish that he has done everything possible to establish the identity of the
person to blame.[76]

Precautions and due diligence

16.182   Having established the cause of the offence the defendant must go on
to prove that he took all reasonable precautions and exercised all due diligence.
This is, of course, a question of fact and degree to be considered in the light of
the particular circumstances of each case. Particular problems may arise in

---

[74]   [1993] 1 WLR 1037, DC.
[75]   *Barker v Hargreaves* [1981] RTR 197.
[76]   *McGuire v Sittingbourne Co-op* [1976] 140 JP 306, DC.

cases involving very large businesses where the company cannot undertake the detailed supervision of all employees, however junior, and delegates supervisory duties to more senior employees.

16.183   The remarks of Lord Diplock in *Tesco Supermarkets Ltd v Nattrass*[77] are of assistance; 'If the principal has taken all reasonable precautions in the selection and training of servants to perform supervisory duties and has laid down an effective system of supervision and used due diligence to see that it is observed, he is entitled to rely on a default by a superior servant in his supervisory duties as a defence under s 24(1).'

16.184   That case is to be contrasted with *Knowsley Metropolitan Borough Council v Harry Bernard Coburn Cowan*[78] where one of the reasons that the Divisional Court found that the defendant was not entitled to rely upon a similarly worded defence under s 34 of the Weights and Measures Act 1985 was that as the employer he had failed to give any guidance to unit managers as to staff selection procedures or to implement any formal staff training program.

16.185   Where the defendant is the employee, rather than the employer, the case of *Russell v DPP*[79] is of note. In that case the Divisional Court held that where a trainee made a sale under the supervision of an experienced manager, in the context of a company with a proper and normally effective system of preventing under aged sales, it was not a failure to take reasonable precautions to rely upon the assessment the manager made as to the adequacy of a customer's manner of purported proof of age, rather than making inquiries himself.

Restrictions on proceedings

16.186   No prosecutions under VRA 1984 may be brought more than 3 years after the offence was committed or one year after the offence was discovered by the prosecutor, whichever is earlier (s 15(1)).

16.187   In Scotland, the reference to the date of discovery by the prosecutor is construed as a reference to the date on which evidence sufficient in the opinion of the Lord Advocate to warrant proceedings came to his knowledge. A certificate signed by the Lord Advocate or on his behalf and stating the date on which evidence came to his knowledge is conclusive evidence of that fact and other presumptions and deeming provisions apply to this process. Cases such as *Burwell v DPP*[80] and *RSPCA v Ian James King and Kathleen Patricia King*[81] underline the importance of a prosecutor, who wishes to avail himself of the benefits of such a certificate, fully complying with the statutory requirements.

---

[77]   [1972] AC 153.
[78]   Unreported (1991), see *Butterworths Trading and Consumer Law*, para 3[252].
[79]   (1996) 161 JP 185, DC.
[80]   [2009] EWHC 1069 (Admin).
[81]   [2010] EWHC 637 (Admin).

Prosecutions

16.188 Any person (whether an individual or a body corporate), other than the Crown or its servants or agents, can be prosecuted under the Act. Section 16 of the Act permits the prosecution and conviction of any 'director, manager, secretary or other similar officer' of a company or 'any person who was purporting to act in such a capacity' where an offence under the Act has been committed by the company 'with the consent and connivance' of that person or as a result of that person's neglect. Where the affairs of the body corporate are managed by its members, the provisions apply in relation to the acts and defaults of 'a member in connection with his functions of management as if he were a director of the body corporate'. It is normal and advisable (though not strictly necessary) that the company should be a defendant in the same proceedings as the person prosecuted under s 16, since even if it is not, it will be necessary to prove that the company could have been found guilty of the offence. (See also chapter 1 at p 28.)

Duty to enforce

16.189 Section 16A VRA 1984 specifies that the functions of a local weights and measures authority include the enforcement of its provisions. The right to prosecute is not restricted to a member or officer of an enforcement authority. Any person can bring a prosecution under the Act although the rights contained within the Act to facilitate the gathering of evidence may not be exercised by such a private prosecutor.

Powers of enforcement officers

16.190 Section 16A(2) imports into VRA 1984 the powers given to officers of trading standards authorities under ss 27, 28, 29 and 33 of the Trade Descriptions Act 1968, that is powers of test purchase and entry of premises for the purposes of inspection and seizure. Provisions making it an offence to obstruct an authorised officer and providing a right to compensation for goods seized are also imported by the same section. In addition there are specific powers of entry, search and seizure (upon the issue of a warrant by a magistrate or, in Scotland, by a sheriff),[82] which may only be exercised by police officers. Where a person refuses to give a police officer his name and address, or gives details which the officer reasonably believes to be false, he may be arrested.[83]

16.191 VRA 1984 specifically provides that, where offences are suspected to be linked with others committed in the area of another trading standards department, then, provided the consent of the relevant trading standards department has been obtained, investigations and prosecutions may be initiated 'out of area'. The powers of magistrates' courts to issue summonses and

---

[82] Section 17.
[83] Section 18.

warrants in respect of offences under the Act are similarly extended. Under s 16A(4A) offences in another area are 'linked' to the area of a local weights and measures authority if:

(i)   the supply or possession of video recordings in contravention of (the) Act within their area is likely to be or to have been the result of the supply or possession of those recordings in the other area; or

(ii) the supply or possession of video recordings in contravention of (the) Act in the other area is likely to be or to have been the result of the supply or possession of those recordings in their area.

16.192   These provisions are probably superfluous in the light of the comments made by Sweeney J in *R (Donnachie) v Cardiff Magistrates' Court*[84] where, in relation to the District Judge referring to the Trade Descriptions Act 1968:

'as not imposing any geographical restriction he should be taken to be referring to the Council's ability to investigate offences under the Act outside its own area (subject to the usual investigative courtesies), rather than to the Council's ability to prosecute such offences outside its own area ...'.

Sentencing
Maximum sentences
16.193

Section	Brief description	Mode of trial	Maximum on indictment	Maximum summarily
9(1)	Supplying an unclassified video	Either way	2 years and unlimited fine or both	6 months, a fine or both
10(1)	Possession of an unclassified video	Either way	2 years and unlimited fine or both	6 months, a fine or both
11(1)	Supplying a video in breach of classification	Summary only		6 months, a fine or both
12(1)	Supplying a restricted video	Summary only		6 months, a fine or both
12(3)	Possession of a restricted video	Summary only		6 months, a fine or both
13(1)	Supply of wrongly labelled video	Summary only		6 months, a fine or both

---

84   [2009] EWHC 489 (Admin).

Section	Brief description	Mode of trial	Maximum on indictment	Maximum summarily
14(1)	Supply of video wrongly indicating fact of classification	Summary only		6 months, a fine or both
14(3)	Supply of video indicating wrong classification	Summary only		6 months, a fine or both

Forfeiture

16.194 By s 21, following conviction the court may order that any video produced to the court and shown to its satisfaction to relate to the offence be forfeited. Before doing so an opportunity must be given to any person claiming to be interested in the video to show cause why an order of forfeiture should not be made. If an order is made it does not take effect until the expiration of the ordinary time for an appeal to be lodged and, if one is lodged or application is made to appeal, until the appeal is finally decided.

Commentary

16.195 The Digital Economy Bill had its First Reading in the House of Commons on 5 July 2016 (at the time of writing, a date for a Second Reading is yet to be announced). The Bill proposes the introduction of age verification for the supply of online pornography, such that it will be prohibited to make pornographic material available on the internet on a commercial basis without ensuring that the material will not normally be accessible by persons under the age of 18. The Bill seeks to restrict access by young people to the same kinds of material as is covered by the Video Recordings Act 1984, but which is accessed via the internet.

AEROSOL PAINT

Introduction

16.196 Section 54 of the Anti-social Behaviour Act 2003 ('ASBA 2003') makes it an offence to sell aerosol spray paints to persons aged under 16. The objective is to reduce the incidence of criminal damage caused by acts of graffiti. A similar offence is created in Scotland by s 122 of the Antisocial Behaviour etc (Scotland) Act 2004 ('ASB(S)A 2004') and in Northern Ireland by s 37 of the Clean Neighbourhoods and Environment Act (Northern Ireland) 2011.

Territorial jurisdiction

16.197 Section 54 ASBA 2003 extends to England and Wales only. ASB(S)A 2004 applies only to Scotland.

Offence

16.198 Section 54 ASBA 2003 provides:

54 Sale of aerosol paint to children

(1) A person commits an offence if he sells an aerosol paint container to a person under the age of sixteen.

(2) In subsection (1) "aerosol paint container" means a device which –

(a)   contains paint stored under pressure, and
(b)   is designed to permit the release of the paint as a spray.

16.199 In Scotland s 122 of the ASB(S)A 2004 provides an offence in almost identical terms. But the Scottish legislation goes further: s 123 of the ASB(S)A 2004 also requires a notice displaying the statement 'It is illegal to sell a spray paint device to anyone under the age of 16' to be exhibited at an appropriate place (ie a prominent position where the statement is readily visible to persons at the point of sale of spray paint devices) at every retail premises at which spray paint devices are sold. The Sale of Spray Paint (Display of Warning Statement) (Scotland) Regulations 2004[85] prescribe the dimensions of the notice and the size of the statement which must be displayed on such a notice. Section 123(4) provides that, where a person carries on a business involving the retail of spray paint devices at any premises, and no notice is exhibited at those premises, that person shall be guilty of an offence.

Defences

16.200 Section 54(4) ASBA 2003 provides:

(4) It is a defence for a person charged with an offence under this section in respect of a sale to prove that –

(a)   he took all reasonable steps to determine the purchaser's age, and
(b)   he reasonably believed that the purchaser was not under the age of sixteen.

16.201 Section 54(5) ASBA 2003 provides:

(5) It is a defence for a person charged with an offence under this section in respect of a sale effected by another person to prove that he (the defendant) took all reasonable steps to avoid the commission of an offence under this section.

16.202 Section 122(4) ASB(S)A 2004 provides in Scotland that:

---

[85] SSI 2004/419.

(4) It shall be a defence for a person charged with an offence under subsection (1) [*selling spray paint to child*] to show that the person took all reasonable precautions and exercised all due diligence to avoid the commission of the offence.

16.203 Section 123(6) ASB(S)A 2004 provides in Scotland that:

(6) It shall be a defence for a person charged with an offence under subsection (4) [*failure to display notice*] to show that the person took all reasonable precautions and exercised all due diligence to avoid the commission of the offence.

16.204 It is difficult to see the practical difference between the operation of the s 54(4) defence, as applicable in England and Wales, and the s 122(4), as applicable in Scotland, despite the difference in wording. If a defendant (who made the sale) has taken all reasonable steps to determine the purchaser's age, and reasonably believes them to be over 16, this is likely to amount to reasonable precautions to avoid the commission of the offence and *vice versa*.

Restrictions on proceedings

16.205 The offence under s 54 ASBA 2003 is summary-only. There is therefore a six months' time limit on bringing proceedings, running from the time when the offence was committed (see s 127 Magistrates' Courts Act 1980). In Scotland, as the offences in ss 122 and 123 ASB(S)A 2004 can only be tried under summary procedure, the time limits are established under s 136 of the Criminal Procedure (Scotland) Act 1995 and similarly establish a time limit for bringing proceedings of six months after the contravention occurred.

Prosecutions

16.206 The offence under s 54 ASBA 2003 (or, in Scotland, under either s 122 or s 123 ASB(S)A 2004) can be committed by the actual seller or, where applicable, his employer.

Enforcement powers

16.207 There is no specific duty of enforcement nor are there any powers of enforcement (to test purchase etc) in relation to s 54 ASBA 2003. However, s 32 of the Clean Neighbourhoods and Environment Act 2005 adds s 54A to ASBA 2003. Section 54A provides for a duty on local weights and measures authorities to consider, at least once a year, the extent to which it is appropriate to have a programme of enforcement action in relation to s 54 and, to that extent, to carry out such a programme. Such a programme involves all or any of the following:

- the bringing of prosecutions in respect of offences under s 54;
- the investigation of complaints in respect of alleged offences under s 54;
- the taking of other measures intended to reduce the incidence of offences under s 54.

In Scotland, s 124 ASB(S)A 2004 places a duty on local authorities to enforce ss 122 and 123.

Sentencing

16.208 Section 54(3) ASBA 2003 provides:

> A person guilty of an offence under this section shall be liable on summary conviction to a fine not exceeding level 4 on the standard scale.

16.209 In Scotland, a person guilty of an offence under s 122(1) ASB(S)A 2004 is liable on summary conviction to a fine not exceeding level 3 on the standard scale and a person guilty of an offence under s 123(4) is liable on summary conviction to a fine not exceeding level 2 on the standard scale.

Commentary

16.210 Prohibition on the sale of spray paints to children is of course not the only way in which the problem of Graffiti is addressed. Although beyond the scope of this publication, it is worth noting that graffiti is usually regarded as criminal damage under s 1(1) of the Criminal Damage Act 1971. Councils may issue a fixed penalty notice to deal with an offence under s 1(1) 'which involves only the painting or writing on, or the soiling, marking or other defacing of, any property by whatever means' (s 43 of the ASBA 2003). Section 1 of the Criminal Justice Act 2003 extends the definition of prohibited articles under s 1 of the Police and Criminal Evidence Act 1984 ('PACE') so that it includes articles made, adapted or intended for use in causing criminal damage. It does this by amending the list of offences in s 1(8) of PACE to include offences under s 1 of the Criminal Damage Act 1971. The effect is to give police officers power to stop and search where they have reasonable suspicion that a person is carrying, for example, a paint spray can which they intend to use in producing graffiti. The above legal provisions are not applicable in Scotland or Northern Ireland. In Scotland, graffiti may be dealt with either as malicious mischief at common law or under s 52 of the Criminal Law (Consolidation) (Scotland) Act 1995 as a form of vandalism.

CIGARETTE LIGHTER REFILLS

Introduction

16.211 According to NHS statistics, volatile substance abuse ('VSA'), such as the inhalation of solvents and other chemicals, is the most common form of substance misuse amongst 11–13 year olds and is second only to cannabis abuse by those aged 15 (*Smoking, drinking and drug use among people in England in 2012*, NHS, 2013). There were 46 deaths associated with volatile substance abuse in 2009, bringing the cumulative total of VSA deaths in the UK since 1971 to 2,390. In the past decade, VSA has killed more under-15s in the UK than all illegal drugs combined. The single product of butane gas lighter refills is responsible for over one-third of deaths and volatile substance abuse which led to death. Since 1971, butane gas lighter fuel has been associated with a little higher than 80% of fatal abuses of gas fuel, and 38% of all substances fatally abused. (Data from the International Centre for Drug Policy based at St George's, University of London).

16.212 Various legislative initiatives have been instituted to curb the use of volatile substances – including solvents and butane gas. The Intoxicating Substances (Supply) Act 1985 made it an offence to supply or to offer to supply a substance to someone under the age of 18 if the retailer knew or had reasonable cause to believe that the it would be inhaled to cause intoxication. The 1985 Act has been repealed by the Psychoactive Substances Act 2016 ('PSA 2016') which prohibits the supply of any substance 'which is capable of producing a psychoactive effect in a person who consumes it [...] by stimulating or depressing the person's central nervous system', see Chapter 14, Product Safety.[86] It prohibits the supply of such substances not just to those under the age of 18, but to people of any age. However, the Cigarette Lighter Refill (Safety) Regulations are unaffected by the PSA 2016, and remain in force.

Territorial jurisdiction

16.213 The Cigarette Lighter Refill (Safety) Regulations 1999[87] ('CLR(S)R 1999') apply across the United Kingdom.

Offence

16.214 The CLR(S)R 1999 are 'safety regulations' for the purposes of s 11 of the Consumer Protection Act 1987 ('CPA 1987'). Regulation 2 CLR(S)R 1999 states:

> No person shall supply any cigarette lighter refill canister containing butane or a substance with butane as a constituent part to any person under the age of eighteen years.

16.215 Section 12 CPA 1987 provides where safety regulations prohibit a person from supplying or offering or agreeing to supply any goods or from exposing or possessing any goods for supply, that person shall be guilty of an offence if he contravenes the prohibition.

Defences

16.216 There are no statutory defences under the Regulations. Section 39 CPA 1987 provides a defence of due diligence.

---

[86] Section 2 Psychoactive Substances Act 2016.
[87] SI 1994/1844.

Time limits

16.217 The offence under the CLR(S)R 1999 is summary-only: there is therefore a 6 months' time limit to bring proceedings, running from the time when the offence was committed (see s 127 Magistrates' Courts Act 1980). In Scotland, as the offence can only be tried under summary procedure, the time limits are established under s 136 of the Criminal Procedure (Scotland) Act 1995: within 6 months after the contravention occurred.

Prosecutions

16.218 Section 39 (and thus, s 40) CPA 1987 applies to an offence under the CLR(S)R 1999 and action against a person other than the principal offender can only be taken where the commission of the offence is due to an act or default committed of that person 'in the course of any business of his'. The section also permits the prosecution and conviction of any 'director, manager, secretary or other similar officer' of a company or 'any person who was purporting to act in such a capacity' where an offence under the Act has been committed by the company 'with the consent and connivance' of that person or as a result of that person's neglect. Where the affairs of the body corporate are managed by its members, the provisions apply in relation to the acts and defaults of 'a member in connection with his functions of management as if he were a director of the body corporate'. (See also Chapter 1 at p 28.)

Duty to enforce

16.219 Section 27 CPA 1987 provides that:

Enforcement

(1) Subject to the following provisions of this section –

    (a)   it shall be the duty of every weights and measures authority in Great Britain to enforce within their area the safety provisions and the provisions made by or under Part III of this Act; and

    (b)   it shall be the duty of every district council in Northern Ireland to enforce within their area the safety provisions.

Powers of enforcement officers

16.220 Powers for the enforcement of Regulations made under s 11 CPA 1987 are contained in Part IV (ss 27–35) CPA 1987.

Sentencing

16.221 By virtue of s 12 CPA 1987, contravention of the CLR(S)R 1999 constitutes an offence punishable on summary conviction by imprisonment for a term not exceeding 6 months or by an unlimited fine or by both.

PET ANIMALS

Introduction

16.222 The Pet Animals Act 1951 (in Scotland, the Pet Animals Act 1960) provided general protection of the welfare of animals sold as pets and, specifically, created offences for selling an animal as a pet to a person under the age of 12 years. The Animal Welfare Act 2006 and the Animal Health and Welfare (Scotland) Act 2006 repealed these offences and extended their scope.

Territorial jurisdiction

16.223 The Animal Welfare Act 2006 ('AWA 2006') extends to England and Wales. In Scotland the sale of animals to children is governed by the Animal Health and Welfare (Scotland) Act 2006 ('AWA(S)A 2006'). Section 15 of the Welfare of Animals Act (Northern Ireland) 2011 (Transfer of animals by way of sale or prize to persons under 16) is identically worded to the provisions described below. The meaning of 'animals' – throughout all of this legislation – is 'vertebrates other than man', so the provisions are not restricted to 'pet' animals.

Offences

16.224 Section 11(1)–(3) AWA 2006 (Transfer of animals by way of sale or prize to persons under 16) provides:

(1) A person commits an offence if he sells an animal to a person whom he has reasonable cause to believe to be under the age of 16 years.

(2) For the purposes of subsection (1), selling an animal includes transferring, or agreeing to transfer, ownership of the animal in consideration of entry by the transferee into another transaction.

(3) Subject to subsections (4) to (6), a person commits an offence if –

(a)   he enters into an arrangement with a person whom he has reasonable cause to believe to be under the age of 16 years, and

(b)   the arrangement is one under which that person has the chance to win an animal as a prize.

16.225 The offence of selling etc under s 11(1) AWA 2006 applies equally to the direct sale of an animal and to any indirect sale that may accompany an otherwise legal transaction. In Scotland, s 30 of the Animal Health and Welfare (Scotland) Act 2006 (Sale of animals to children) provides:

(1) A person ("person A") commits an offence if person A sells an animal to a person ("person B") who is under 16 years of age.

...

(3) For the purposes of subsection (1), selling an animal includes transferring, or agreeing to transfer, ownership of the animal in consideration of entry by the transferee into another transaction.

It is also an offence under that Act (s 31) for a person to offer or give an animal to another person (of any age) as a prize but this does not apply where the prize is offered or given in a family context.

Defences

16.226 There are no statutory defences in relation to the offences under s 11(1) or 11(3) AWA 2006. However, the offence under s 11(3) is not committed in the circumstances specified in s 11(4)–(6) AWA 2006, which provides:

> (4) A person does not commit an offence under subsection (3) if –
>
> > (a)   he enters into the arrangement in the presence of the person with whom the arrangement is made, and
> >
> > (b)   he has reasonable cause to believe that the person with whom the arrangement is made is accompanied by a person who is not under the age of 16 years.
>
> (5) A person does not commit an offence under subsection (3) if –
>
> > (a)   he enters into the arrangement otherwise than in the presence of the person with whom the arrangement is made, and
> >
> > (b)   he has reasonable cause to believe that a person who has actual care and control of the person with whom the arrangement is made has consented to the arrangement.
>
> (6) A person does not commit an offence under subsection (3) if he enters into the arrangement in a family context.

16.227   In Scotland, s 30 AWA(S)A 2006 provides:

> (2) It is a defence to a charge of an offence under subsection (1) for person A to demonstrate that person A –
>
> > (a)   having been shown convincing evidence (for example, a passport or a photocard driving licence) of person B's identity and age, or
> >
> > (b)   having no reasonable cause to suspect from person B's appearance that person B was under 16 years of age, believed that person B was aged 16 years or over.

Restrictions on proceedings

16.228   Section 31 AWA 2006 details the time limits for prosecutions, which are to be commenced by an information being laid:

(a)   before the end of the period of 3 years beginning with the date of the commission of the offence, and

(b)   before the end of the period of 6 months beginning with the date on which evidence which the prosecutor thinks is sufficient to justify the proceedings comes to his knowledge.

16.229 Section 31(2) AWA 2006 provides that if a prosecutor certifies the date on which he learnt of the relevant evidence, that date shall be the starting point for calculating the period within which proceedings must be commenced. Issues relating to s 31 have arisen in *RSPCA v Johnson*[88] and *RSPCA v Ian James King* and *Kathleen Patricia King*.[89] The latter case underlines the importance of a prosecutor, who wishes to avail himself of the benefits of a certificate under s 31(2), fully complying with the statutory requirements.

16.230 The appellant in *Lamont-Perkins v RSPCA*[90] asserted that the RSPCA could not rely on the time-limits set out in s 31 as it was not a 'prosecutor' within the meaning of the Act, and therefore was subject instead to the time limit of 6 months set by s 127 of the Magistrates Court Act 1980. This was rejected by Wyn Williams MJ who found that the term 'prosecutor' was not limited to local authorities simply because they are given express powers in s 30 of the Act, but rather the term simply referred to any party bringing a prosecution under the Act. The other issue raised in this case was the circumstances in which a certificate under s 31 could be challenged and the court confirmed it could be challenged either on the basis that it constituted a fraud or on the basis that it is plainly wrong.

16.231 The case of *Leatherbarrow v Warwickshire County Council*[91] is authority for the proposition that 'prosecutor' for the purposes of s 31 means the person within the local authority who has the responsibility of deciding whether there is sufficient evidence to prosecute. Time runs from the moment that responsible individual is in a position to make that nuanced decision, and not, for example, from the time the matter is reported to the trading standards department of a local authority. The case also clarified that a s 31 certificate could be issued after a challenge had been raised in court proceedings.

16.232 In Scotland, as the offence under s 30 AWA(S)A 2006 can only be tried under summary procedure, the time limits are established under s 136 of the Criminal Procedure (Scotland) Act 1995 – within 6 months after the contravention occurred.

Prosecutions

16.233 The offences in s 11 AWA 2006 can be committed by any person – whether an individual or a corporate body – and there is no requirement that such offences be committed in the course of a trade or business. Section 57 AWA 2006 permits the prosecution and conviction of any 'director, manager, secretary or other similar officer' of a company or 'any person who was purporting to act in such a capacity' where an offence under the Act has been committed by the company 'with the consent and connivance' of that person or as a result of that person's neglect. Where the affairs of the body corporate are

---

[88]   [2009] EWHC 2702 (Admin).
[89]   [2010] EWHC 637 (Admin).
[90]   [2012] EWHC 1002.
[91]   [2014] EWHC 4820 (Admin).

managed by its members, the provisions apply in relation to the acts and defaults of 'a member in connection with his functions of management as if he were a director of the body corporate'. In Scotland, s 45 AWA(S)A 2006 makes similar provision to s 57 above and in addition, s 45 provides for liability where an offence is committed by a Scottish partnership in Scotland.

Duty to enforce

16.234   There is no prescribed duty of enforcement for AWA 2006. Although s 30 AWA 2006 provides a power for a local authority to prosecute offences (which may be seen as superfluous in the light of s 222 of the Local Government Act 1972) the right to launch private prosecutions derives from the common law and the Act does not limit that right. There is no prescribed duty of enforcement for AWA(S)A 2006.

Powers of enforcement officers

16.235   There are no powers of test purchasing under AWA 2006. General enforcement powers are set out in ss 22–29 (and Sch 2), including powers of entry and search, seizure of animals and inspection under certain conditions. In Scotland, the provisions of s 49 and Sch 1 AWA(S)A 2006 permit a local authority to appoint inspectors and set out the powers of inspectors in respect of entry, inspection, search and the conditions for obtaining warrants.

Sentencing

16.236   Sections 32–45 AWA 2006 set out the penalties available on conviction, which include imprisonment, fine, deprivation, disqualification, destruction, forfeiture of equipment and cancellation of a licence or registration.

16.237   Section 32(4) applies to the offences under s 11 and provides:

> 32(4) A person guilty of any other offence under this Act shall be liable on summary conviction to –
>
> (a)   imprisonment for a term not exceeding 51 weeks, or
> (b)   a fine not exceeding level 4 on the standard scale,
>
> or to both.

OTHER LEGISLATION

Gambling

Gambling Act 2005

16.238   The Gambling Act 2005 introduced a new regulatory system to govern the provision of all gambling in Great Britain, other than the National Lottery and spread betting. In broad terms, people aged under eighteen are not permitted to gamble but, specifically, s 46(1) provides: 'A person commits an offence if he invites, causes or permits a child or young person to gamble.' ('Child' means an individual who is less than 16 years old; 'young person' means an individual who is not a child but who is less than 18 years old.)

16.239 There are a number of exceptions to the general prohibition on gambling by children and young people. Children and young persons may participate in all forms of private or non-commercial gaming and betting. Young persons may participate in lotteries and pool betting on association football. Children and young persons may use the category of gaming machine with the lowest stakes and prizes (Category D). They may also take part in equal chance prize gaming at certain premises, as provided under Part 13 of the Act.

16.240 Children and young persons may not enter a casino, a betting shop or an adult gaming centre at any time when facilities for gambling are being provided on the premises in reliance on the relevant premises licence. This is subject to the exception that children and young persons may enter the non-gambling area of a regional casino, but they may not enter the gambling area. However, a person of any age may enter bingo premises, the betting areas of a horse racecourse or a greyhound track on days on which races are being run, or the non-gambling area of a regional casino. A person of any age may also enter any area of a family entertainment centre where no Category C gaming machines are provided at that place.

16.241 The Gambling Commission supported a test-purchasing operation conducted at Ascot racecourse in June 2014, which found that every track book maker tested served a 16-year-old without asking for proof of age. Further operations in September of that year, carried out jointly with local authorities, found that half of the 40 adult gaming centres and betting shops investigated allowed a test purchaser under the age of 18 to play on gaming machines without being asked their age. Following a public consultation in October 2014, the commission issued an updated code of practice in April 2015 relating to access to gambling by children and young persons. This included requirements that *inter alia*:

- Licensees must have put into effect policies and procedures designed to prevent underage gambling.
- A supervisor of a venue must check the age of customers who appear to be underage; refuse entry to anyone unable to produce an acceptable form of identification; and take action when there are unlawful attempts to enter the premises including removing anyone who cannot produce an acceptable form of identification.
- Licensees must not deliberately provide facilities for gambling in such a way as to appeal to children or young people.

- Licensees must take all reasonable steps to ensure that all staff understand their responsibilities for preventing underage gambling, including appropriate training.
- Licensees must conduct test purchasing or take part in collective test purchasing programmes as a means of providing reasonable assurance that they have effective policies and procedures to prevent under age gambling, and must provide their test-purchase results to the Commission.

Reasonable belief about a person's age

16.242 Where a person is charged with an offence under the Act of doing anything in relation to a child or young person it is a defence (under s 63) for the person to prove that he took all reasonable steps to determine the relevant person's age and he reasonably believed that the person was not a child or a young person.

Use of children in enforcement operations

16.243 Section 64 of the Act enables children and young persons to be used in test purchasing operations for the purpose of assessing whether the provisions in this Part, prohibiting under-age gambling, are being complied with. For example, a constable, enforcement officer or authorised person will not commit an offence under s 46 if, in the course of their duty, they invite a child or young person to gamble. Equally, a young person will not commit an offence under s 48 if he gambles at the request of a constable, enforcement officer or authorised officer who is acting in the course of his functions. In February 2015 the Gambling Commission published an updated advice note setting out its approach to test purchasing for gambling in England and Wales.

National Lottery etc Act 1993

16.244 The National Lottery Regulations 1994[92] were made under s 12 of the National Lottery Act etc 1993. Regulation 3 provides: 'No National Lottery ticket shall be sold by or to a person who has not attained the age of 16 years'. The Regulations also prohibit sales of National Lottery tickets in a street and on certain premises, imposes restrictions on the sales tickets by means of vending machines and on sales of tickets at a person's home.

16.245 Section 13 of the Act provides that contravention of Regulations made under s 12 is an offence. The following persons may be found to be guilty of an offence:

- the promoter of the lottery shall be guilty of an offence, except if the contravention occurred without the consent or connivance of the promoter and the promoter exercised all due diligence to prevent such a contravention;

---

[92]   SI 1994/189.

- any director, manager, secretary or other similar officer of the promoter, or any person purporting to act in such a capacity, shall be guilty of an offence if he consented to or connived at the contravention or if the contravention was attributable to any neglect on his part; and

- any other person who was party to the contravention shall be guilty of an offence.

16.246 The Act has application throughout the UK but the following provisions apply to Scotland. Summary proceedings in Scotland for an offence under s 13 may be commenced within a period of 6 months from the date on which evidence sufficient in the opinion of the procurator fiscal to warrant proceedings came to his knowledge; but no proceedings in Scotland shall be commenced by virtue of this section more than 3 years after the commission of the offence. For the purposes of s 13, a certificate signed by or on behalf of the procurator fiscal and stating the date on which evidence sufficient in his opinion to warrant the proceedings came to his knowledge shall be conclusive evidence of that fact; and a certificate stating that matter and purporting to be so signed shall be taken to be so signed unless the contrary is proved.

16.247 In *Harrow London Borough Council v Shah and another*[93] the defendants were husband and wife who owned a newsagent's shop. An employee, who knew of his obligations not to sell lottery tickets to under 16-year-olds, sold a National Lottery ticket to a 13½-year-old. Mitchell J:

> 'The prosecution does not have to prove, for the purposes of establishing the offence, that the defendant or his agent was either aware of the buyer's age, or reckless as to his age ... This ticket was sold, not by either Mr or Mrs Shah, but by their employee. ... Unfortunately, but inevitably, his offence was, at once, their offence, given the principles of vicarious liability ... applied in *St Helens Metropolitan BC v Hill*.'

Tattoos

Tattooing of Minors Act 1969

16.248 Section 1 of the Act, which applies to Great Britain, provides:

1 Prohibition of tattooing of minors

It shall be an offence to tattoo a person under the age of eighteen except when the tattoo is performed for medical reasons by a duly qualified medical practitioner or by a person working under his direction, but it shall be a defence for a person charged to show that at the time the tattoo was performed he had reasonable cause to believe that the person tattooed was of or over the age of eighteen and did in fact so believe.

'Tattoo' means the insertion into the skin of any colouring material designed to leave a permanent mark.

---

[93]   [1999] 3 All ER 302.

16.249 The Heath and Safety Executive publish Local Authority Circulars to advise and guide local authority health and safety enforcement officers on enforcement, management and technical matters. Local Authority Circular 76/2 provides technical guidance to enforcement officers and others on health, safety and legal issues related to cosmetic piercing, permanent tattooing and scarification. In Scotland, this area is also governed by the Civic Government (Scotland) Act 1982 and, in particular, the Civic Government (Scotland) Act 1982 (Licensing of Skin Piercing and Tattooing) Order 2006[94] which designates the activity of carrying on a business which provides skin-piercing or tattooing as an activity for which a licence is required. (A licence is not required by a member of certain professions that are regulated by law.)

Petroleum

Petroleum (Consolidation) Regulations 2014

16.250 Previously governed by the Petroleum (Consolidation) Act 1928, there was until recently no direct offence of selling petrol to a minor. Sales of petrol to under 16s was dealt with as a breach of licensing conditions established by the Act. The former legislation was abolished by the coming in to force in October 2014 of the Petroleum (Consolidation) Regulations 2014. The Regulations replaced the licensing regime under the 1928 Act with a certification scheme. To store petrol at a filling station a petroleum storage certificate is required, which are issued by the previous licensing authorities (albeit now renamed Petroleum Enforcement Authorities).

16.251 Under-age sales are now expressly prohibited by Regulation 12 which states:

> **12 General prohibitions on dispensing and supply of petrol**
>
> [...]
>
> 12(2) No person under the age of sixteen years is to operate a dispenser on dispensing premises.
>
> (3) No person is to supply, or allow the supply of, petrol to a person under the age of sixteen years.

16.252 However, no offence of breaching the regulations is apparently created, where previously it was an offence to supply petroleum in breach of the conditions of the licence (which would generally include a condition not to supply to persons under 16). It therefore seems that the only penalty open to enforcers faced with a trader supplying petrol to minors would be to refuse future grants of storage certificates.

---

94   SSI 2006/43.

Scrap metal

Scrap Metal Dealers Act 2013

16.253 The Scrap Metal Dealers Act 2013 (SMDA 2013) abolishes the 1964 Act of the same name, which previously applied and introduces a revised regulatory regime for the scrap-metal industry. The previous legislation made it an offence for a scrap metal dealer to *purchase* scrap metal from a person who was apparently under the age of 16 (somewhat of an anomaly in this chapter dealing with the prohibition on *sales* to minors). Presumably the prohibition stemmed from an assumption that scrap metal provided by under 16 would be more likely to come from illegitimate sources.

16.254 There is no directly equivalent offence in the 2013 Act. The new regime's focus is upon due diligence on the part of the dealer: who is now required to verify the supplier's full name and address, from a reliable and independent source, rather than form a view about the supplier's age. Section 11(4) makes it an offence for a scrap metal dealer to receive scrap metal in breach of the requirement. The offence is summary only and punishable by a fine not exceeding level 3 on the standard scale.

Sunbeds

Sunbeds (Regulation) Act 2010

16.255 The Act – which extends to England and Wales – seeks to prevent persons aged under 18 from using sunbeds. With a few exceptions, the Act provides for offences where a person who carries on a sunbed business fails to ensure that a person under 18 uses, or is offered the use of, one of the business's sunbeds on the business premises (an offence is still committed where the person aged under 18 did not go on to use the sunbed because, for example, the sunbed failed to work or the person changed their mind). A duty of enforcement is placed local authorities and powers for authorised officers include provision to make '... such purchases and secure the provision of such services as the officer considers necessary for the purpose of the proper exercise of the officer's functions under this Act'.

16.256 The Sunbeds (Regulation) Act 2010 (Wales) Regulations 2011[95] apply in relation to Wales and have a commencement date of 31 October 2011. The Regulations impose: a duty on a person who carries on a sunbed business on domestic premises to prevent sunbed use on those premises by persons aged under 18; a requirement for a person who carries on a sunbed business to supervise the use of sunbeds on the business's premises; a prohibition on the sale or hire of sunbeds to persons aged under 18; requirements for the provision of information to sunbed users; and requirements relating to the use of protective eyewear by sunbed users.

---

[95] SI 2011/1130.

Scotland

16.257 In Scotland, Part 8 of the Public Health etc (Scotland) Act 2008 regulates the use, sale and hire of sunbeds. The Act prohibits operators from allowing use of sunbeds on their premises by persons under 18; from allowing unsupervised use of sunbeds on their premises; prohibits the sale or hire of sunbeds to persons under 18; places a duty upon operators of sunbed premises to display a public information notice; and requires operators to provide customers with information on the health risks associated with sunbed use each time they intend to use a sunbed. The information to be provided to customers (and the form and manner in which it is to be provided) and the information to be displayed in sunbed premises (and the form and manner of display of the notice) is prescribed in the Public Health etc (Scotland) Act 2008 (Sunbed) Regulations 2009.[96]The Act enables local authority officers – who are given powers of enforcement – to issue a fixed penalty notice to the operator of the premises where the officer has reason to believe an offence has taken place. The fixed penalty notice gives the operator the opportunity of discharging liability to conviction for that offence by payment of the fixed penalty.

Northern Ireland

16.258 The Sunbeds Act (Northern Ireland) 2011 prohibits the use, sale or hire of a sunbed to persons under the age of 18 and provides an exemption for medical treatment. The Act places a duty on operators of sunbed premises to display an information notice. It places a duty on sunbed operators and those who hire or sell sunbeds to provide sunbed users, hirers and buyers with information about the risks associated with sunbed use. It places a duty on operators of sunbed premises and those who hire or sell sunbeds to make protective eyewear available to sunbed users. It also places a duty on sunbed operators and those who hire or sell sunbeds to secure that those who allow people to use sunbeds are trained to a required standard and that all sunbeds for use in sunbeds premises, for hire or for sale meet required standards. The Act sets out the enforcement powers available to authorised officers and provides for fixed penalties for particular offences. The Sunbeds (Information) Regulations (Northern Ireland) 2012 outline the wording to be contained in the information leaflet that must be provided to a person who proposes to use a sunbed on sunbed premises, or is hiring or buying a sunbed. The Regulations also outline the wording to be contained in the display notice that sunbed premises must display in a prominent position and the style and format of this notice. Similar legislation came into force in Scotland on 1 December 2009 and in Wales on 31 October 2011.

---

[96]   SSI 2009/388.

CHAPTER 17

METROLOGY AND HALLMARKING

INTRODUCTION

17.1 The purpose of regulating weights and measures is to ensure that consumers have accurate information in which they can place confidence when making purchasing decisions. However, it is uncontroversial to note that the evolution of the weights and measures regime has been fragmented and complex and it is almost universally recognised that, as a result of this evolution, the present state of the law is convoluted, burdensome for commerce and impenetrable for consumers. Over the years, there have been a number of recommendations and proposals to reform and simplify the law. However, whilst there have been provisions, for example, to deregulate controls on packaged goods, to allow self-verification after adjustment, to remove outdated and obsolete regulations from the statute book[1] and to repeal the fixed sizes that products must be sold in,[2] there are still no substantive proposals for fundamental reform.

17.2 With that in mind, this chapter aims to cut through the complexity and provide practical information on the core elements of the weights and measures regime: the commonly committed offences and associated defences that are set out in ss 28–37 of Part IV of the Weights and Measures Act 1985 ('WMA 1985'). The WMA 1985 consolidated and very largely replaced the previous Acts of the same name of 1963, 1976 and 1979. Its provisions must be complied with whenever weights and measures are 'used for trade',[3] an expression considered in detail below. Whilst the WMA 1985 remains the core piece of legislation that governs the regulation of weights and measures it has been amended in a significant manner on a number of occasions: for example, the WMA was amended in December 2014[4] to align the UK weights and measures regime with the Food Information to Consumers Regulation[5] and in October 2015 to reflect movement of the disparate enforcement powers across the trading standards field into the Consumer Rights Act 2015.[6]

17.3 Other recent changes include the launch of 'Regulated Delivery' on 1 April 2016. Regulated Delivery is part of the Department for Business, Energy and Industrial Strategy and brings together the National Measurement and Regulation Office ('NMRO') and Better Regulation Delivery Office ('BRDO'). Accordingly, the NMRO's role and responsibilities in respect of weights and measures now sit with Regulated Delivery who will work with businesses and Local Weights and Measures Authorities with the intention of reducing burdens on business, saving public money and ensuring the proper protection of

---

[1]   The Weights and Measures (Revocations) Regulations 2015.
[2]   For example, yarn and unwrapped bread: see Deregulation Act 2015, s 16 (c. 20) and the Weights and Measures (Specified Quantities) (Unwrapped Bread and Intoxicating Liquor) Order 2011, SI 2011/2331 respectively.
[3]   WMA 1985, s 7.
[4]   Weights and Measures (Food) (Amendment) Regulations 2014/2975.
[5]   Regulation 1169/2011.
[6]   Consumer Rights Act 2015, Sch 5 (c. 15).

consumers. Whilst the Regulated Delivery website is developed, most of the useful weights and measures resources can still be found on the archived NMRO website.[7]

17.4 Regulated Delivery also has policy (legislative) responsibility for the hallmarking of precious metal articles. The British Hallmarking Council, established and governed by the Hallmarking Act 1973, is an Executive Non-Departmental Public Body established the Hallmarking Act 1973. The Council is funded by the UK's four Assay Offices.

SUMMARY OF THE WMA 1985

17.5 Parts I and II of the WMA 1985 specify the units of measurement and the measures and weights permitted for 'use in trade' as being those set out in Schs 1 and 3 respectively. Weighing and measuring equipment for use for trade must be inspected and passed as fit for such use and be stamped.[8] The forging of, or interference with, official stamps and the possession of false weights are offences.[9] Unjust equipment and the fraudulent use of proper equipment are offences.[10]

17.6 Under Part III of the WMA 1985, operators of public weighing machines are required to hold a certificate[11] and misuse of such equipment is an offence.[12] Part IV of the WMA 1985 contains[13] requirements concerned with the sale of a wide variety of goods and commodities. It grants power to the Secretary of State to make Orders and Regulations as to such matters as to the quantities by which particular goods may be sold, the marking of containers of goods specified within the Schedules to the WMA 1985, the units of measurement to be used in marking such containers and the identification of the packer of pre-packed goods.

17.7 Selling, or offering for sale, goods in breach of the provisions of Part IV is an offence.[14] Certain goods must have their quantity stated in writing.[15] Since 13 December 2014, Part IV of the WMA 1985 also made it an offence for relevant Food Business Operators to fail to comply with certain aspects of the Food Information to Consumers Regulation.[16] The Weights and Measures

---

7 https://www.gov.uk/government/organisations/national-measurement-and-regulation-office.
8 WMA 1985, s 11.
9 WMA 1985, ss 16 and 17.
10 WMA 1985, s 17(3).
11 WMA 1985, s 18.
12 WMA 1985, s 20.
13 WMA 1985, ss 21–24 and Schs 4–7.
14 WMA 1985, s 25.
15 WMA 1985, ss 26 and 27.
16 Arts 8 and 9(1)(e) and WMA 1985, s 31A.

(Packaged Goods) Regulations 2006[17] repealed Part V of the WMA 1985 and set out a complete regime for the average system of quantity control applied to packaged goods.

17.8 Parts VI and VII of the WMA 1985 specify the local weights and measures authorities for England, Wales and Scotland, the requirement on the authorities to appoint inspectors and the duties and powers of these authorities and persons. (No section under the WMA 1985 authorises a local weights and measures authority to institute proceedings in Scotland for an offence.) Since 1 October 2015, the investigatory powers available to local weights and measures authorities have been contained in Schedule 5 to the Consumer Rights Act 2015.

17.9 Whilst only the provisions set out in Sch 10 WMA 1985 extend to Northern Ireland, the legislative position, relating to weights and measures in that country, is reflected by the Explanatory Notes to the Weights and Measures (Amendment) Act (Northern Ireland) 2000. The Notes state: 'The principal policy objective of the Act is to replicate for Northern Ireland those three deregulatory measures contained in the Deregulation (Weights and Measures) Order 1999, which was made by the DTI under the 1994 Act on 1 March 1999. Parity will thus be maintained between the legislative provisions on weights and measures here and those in Great Britain (GB), with Northern Ireland continuing to remain on all fours with the rest of the UK.' Similarly, the Weights and Measures (Packaged Goods) Regulations (Northern Ireland) 2011 and the Weights and Measures (Specified Quantities) (Unwrapped Bread and Intoxicating Liquor) Order (Northern Ireland)[18] – statutory rules made under the Weights and Measures (Northern Ireland) Order 1981 and the European Communities Act 1972 – reformed Northern Ireland legislation in this area in a comparable manner to that adopted in Great Britain by the Weights and Measures (Packaged Goods) Regulations 2006 and the Weights and Measures (Specified Quantities) (Unwrapped Bread and Intoxicating Liquor) Order 2011 respectively.

TIME LIMITS

17.10 By s 83(3) of the WMA 1985 no proceedings for offences under Part IV of the WMA 1985,[19] which include the commonly committed offences contrary to ss 28, 30, 31 and 50 (note that s 29 (Misrepresentation) was repealed by the Consumer Protection from Unfair Trading Regulations 2008[20]) may be instituted:

---

[17] SI 2006/659.
[18] SI 2013/261.
[19] With the exception of offences contrary to ss 33(6), 57(2) or 64, or proceedings by virtue of s 32.
[20] SI 2008/1277.

(a) unless the defendant has been served with a written notice giving the date and nature of the alleged offence; or

(b) unless the notice was served within 30 days of the date when evidence which the prosecutor considers is sufficient to justify a prosecution came to his knowledge; or

(c) more than 12 months after the date given in the notice or more than 3 months after the date in (b) above, whichever first occurs.

17.11 In Scotland, the Crown Office has issued instructions to weights and measures authorities, in relation to s 83(3), the relevant parts of which are as follows:

> 'For the sake of uniformity of practice and to ensure that accused persons receive the notice at the earliest opportunity, the Lord Advocate has instructed that, in future, the notice in terms of Section 83(3) should be served by the enforcement officer of the Weights and Measures Authority and not by the Procurator Fiscal. A copy of the notice and certificate of posting or execution of service, should be attached to any relevant report received by the Procurator Fiscal from the local authority department.
>
> In any case where the Procurator Fiscal discovers that no copy notice accompanies the report he or she should contact the Weights and Measures Authority to give them the opportunity to send a notice provided that 30 days have not expired since the Fiscal has received this report.
>
> Once the notice has been served the Procurator Fiscal will have to consider whether either three months have elapsed from the date of receipt of the report or, whether 12 months have elapsed since the date of the offence. If either period has been overrun, proceedings will be time barred.'

17.12 The notice may be served either in person or by post at the defendant's last known residence or place of business in the UK, or at a company's registered office.[21]

PROSECUTIONS

17.13 Proceedings in respect of offences under the WMA 1985 in England and Wales can only be instituted by or on behalf of a local weights and measures authority[22] or the police.[23] The authority may appear in and prosecute proceedings through any member or officer authorised to represent it, and such a person need not be a solicitor holding a current practising certificate.[24] In

---

[21] WMA 1985, s 83(4).
[22] Defined in WMA 1985, s 69.
[23] WMA 1985, s 83(1).
[24] Local Government Act 1972, s 223.

Scotland, proceedings can only be instituted by the Procurator Fiscal/Crown Office. Any person, other than the Crown or its servants or agents,[25] can be prosecuted under the WMA 1985.

Causal liability

17.14 Section 32 of the WMA 1985 provides for causal liability, which is now covered in Chapter 3, Criminal Enforcement.

Directors' liability

17.15 Section 82 of the WMA 1985 permits the prosecution and conviction of any 'director, manager, secretary or other similar officer' of a company or 'any person who was purporting to act in such a capacity'. Directors' liability provisions are now covered in Chapter 3, Criminal Enforcement.

WEIGHING AND MEASURING FOR TRADE

Units and measures

17.16 Section 8 of the WMA 1985 prescribes the units of measurement which are lawful for use for trade. They are recited in Sch 1 to the WMA 1985. They are now almost all metric, the imperial measures having been deleted from the Schedule by Regulations.[26] Section 8 also prescribes the measures and weights which are lawful for use for trade. The lawful measures are those recited in Sch 3 to the WMA 1985. Thus, for example, cloth may be sold by the metre or the centimetre, but not by the millimetre. There are savings for units and measures set out in s 8(2)(a)–(d) of the WMA 1985 (relating to precious metals and stones and measures of alcohol), but since 1 January 2000[27] the imperial units and measures or weights are unlawful if used as the sole measurement of weight or quantity. Imperial units and measures are, for the present permitted as a 'supplementary indication'[28] provided they accompany an indication of quantity expressed as a metric unit which is the more prominent of the two. The permitted units and measures for 'supplementary' use are set out in Sch 1, Part VI.

Drugs

17.17 The prohibition on the use of units of measurement other than those set out in Sch 1 to the WMA 1985 does not apply to drugs,[29] which may continue to be prescribed and dispensed in the existing, non-metric, units.

---

25   See Chapter 1 on Crown Immunity generally.
26   Units of Measurement Regulations 1994, SI 1994/2867, reg 6(1), (5)(a).
27   Units of Measurement Regulations 1995, SI 1995/1804.
28   WMA 1985, s 8(5A).
29   WMA 1985, s 8(3). The word 'drugs' bears the same meaning as 'controlled drugs' under the Misuse of Drugs Act 1971.

Weighing and measuring equipment

17.18 Offences under the WMA 1985 are frequently concerned with the use or possession of weighing or measuring equipment. This is defined in s 94(1) as 'equipment for measuring in terms of length, area, volume, capacity, weight or number, whether or not the equipment is constructed to give an indication of the measurement made or other information determined by reference to that measurement'.

Use for trade

17.19 Section 7 defines the expression 'use for trade', which is an ingredient of almost all the transaction based offences under the WMA 1985. Only those transactions which involve the transfer of money, or money's worth, in consideration of money, or money's worth, are affected.[30]

17.20 The essential words of s 7 are:

> ... use in connection with, or with a view to a transaction ... where –
>
> (a)   the transaction is by reference to quantity or is a transaction for the purposes of which there is made or implied a statement of the quantity of goods to which the transaction relates and,
>
> (b)   the use is for the purpose of the determination or statement of that quantity.

17.21 The kernel of the definition is that where units of weight or quantity, or equipment for weighing or measuring, are used to determine the quantity of the goods involved in a transaction for value then this will be 'use for trade'. Use includes within its meaning causing or permitting use,[31] and thus an employer is liable for the WMA 1985 actions of his employee even if the employee has been acting contrary to instructions.[32] If the employer can establish that the employee has acted altogether outside the scope of his authority then he may escape liability.[33] It is not only the seller of goods who may be caught by the provisions of the WMA 1985. Where the buyer checks the weight of goods supplied, the equipment he uses is in 'use for trade'[34] and must comply with the WMA 1985. Further, under the Non-automatic Weighing Instruments Regulations 2000,[35] the use and possession for use of non-complying instruments, for the following applications, is prohibited:

(a)   Determination of mass for commercial transactions.

(b)   Determination of mass for the calculation of a toll, tariff, tax, bonus, penalty, remuneration, indemnity or similar type of payment.

---

[30]   WMA 1985, s 7(2).
[31]   *FE Charman Ltd v Clow* [1974] 3 All ER 371, [1974] 1 WLR 1384.
[32]   *Elder v Bishop Auckland Co-op Society* (1917) 86 LJKB 1412, [1910–1917] All ER 961.
[33]   *Navarro v Moregrand* [1951] 2 TLR 674 at 681, 95 Sol Jo 367, CA, per Denning LJ.
[34]   *Crick v Theobald* (1895) 64 LJMC 216, 72 LT 807.
[35]   SI 2000/3236.

(c) Determination of mass for the application of laws or regulations including expert opinions given in court proceedings.

(d) Determination of mass in the practice of medicine for weighing patients for the purpose of monitoring, diagnosis and medical treatment.

(e) Determination of mass for making up medicines on prescription in a pharmacy and determination of mass in analyses carried out in medical and pharmaceutical laboratories.

(f) Determination of price on the basis of mass for the purposes of direct sales to the public and the making up of pre-packages.

Wholesaling goods abroad

17.22 Section 7(3) exempts statements of the quantity of goods for wholesale to destinations abroad from the definition of 'use for trade', while by s 7(4) scales and measuring equipment made available for public use and egg grading equipment are always to be treated as equipment in use for trade.

Presumption of use for trade

17.23 Section 7(5) deems weighing or measuring equipment found on a person carrying out a trade, to be in 'use for trade' unless the contrary is proved and the same subsection applies as against the occupier of premises on which such equipment is found.[36] This 'reverse onus' provision will have to be tested against the 'fair trial' provisions of Art 6(2) of the ECHR.[37] In the opinion of the authors it is likely to survive.[38]

Transaction by reference to quantity

17.24 Goods sold by price alone are outside 'use for trade', because a transaction must bear a reference to quantity to be within s 7. In *Craig v M'Phee*[39] whisky was for sale in three different containers. There was no reference to the quantity which each contained, only to the price. Customers were invited to buy 'a shilling's worth of whisky'. The court found that a transaction concluded under such arrangements was not a transaction 'by reference to quantity', but rather a 'contract by price' and fell outside the legislation. That case is to be contrasted with *Robinson v Golding*,[40] where milk was sold by filling a can which, although unmarked, did in fact have a capacity of a pint. When questioned by investigating officers the defendant said that he had delivered a pint of milk when he left the can on a doorstep. The court rejected the argument that this was a 'contract by price', finding that the evidence showed that the can was being used as a measure. In essence the

---

36 'Occupier' and 'Premises' are defined in WMA 1985, s 94(1).
37 See *R v Lambert & Ors* [2002] QB 1112, [2001] 2 WLR 211.
38 In relation to a reverse onus provision relating to trade marks, see *R v S* [2002] EWCA 2558.
39 (1883) 48 JP 115.
40 (1910) 13 LT 248.

distinction between the two cases is that in *Robinson* there was an implied reference to quantity, whereas in *M'Phee* there was not.[41]

Being 'in possession'

17.25 Offences under ss 8(4), 11(3), 17(1) and 30(1)) of the WMA 1985 may also be committed by a person being 'in possession' of certain items or equipment. In *Bellerby v Carle*[42] the House of Lords ruled on the meaning of the words 'in possession', in the context of a prosecution under the equivalent provisions to s 17(1) of the WMA 1985. It was held that two licensees of a Public House were not in possession of unjust beer measuring equipment owned, supplied and maintained by the brewery under the terms of a contract between the brewery and the licensees' company. In order for the prosecution to make good an offence of 'being in possession' the law requires proof of an element of control over the item in question, although not necessarily of physical proximity.[43] The same case also established that use for trade and possession for use for trade in the circumstances defined in the relevant sections are two distinct offences and should not be charged as alternative wording within the one alleged offence.

PRINCIPAL OFFENCES

Unlawful units and measures

17.26

> **Weights and Measures Act 1985, s 8**
>
> **8 Units of measurement, weights and measures lawful for use for trade**
>
> (1) No person shall –
>
> (a) use for trade any unit of measurement which is not included in Parts I to V of Schedule 1 to this Act, or
>
> (b) use for trade, or have in his possession for use for trade, any linear, square, cubic or capacity measure which is not included in Schedule 3 to this Act, or any weight which is not so included.
>
> (2) No person shall use for trade –
>
> (a) the ounce troy, except for the purposes of transactions in, or in articles made from, gold, silver or other precious metals, including transactions in gold or silver thread, lace or fringe, or
>
> (b) the carat (metric), except for the purposes of transactions in precious stones or pearls, or
>
> (c) a capacity measure of 35, 70, 125, 150 or 175 millilitres, except for the purposes of transactions in intoxicating liquor, or

---

41 See also *Bellamy v Great Western & Metropolitan Dairies* (1908) 98 LT 757.
42 [1983] 2 AC 101, [1983] 1 All ER 1031, HL.
43 See *Warner v Metropolitan Police Commissioner* [1969] 2 AC 256, [1968] 2 WLR 1303.

(d)   the pint except for –
   (i)   the purposes of the sale of draught beer or cider, or
   (ii)   the purposes of the sale of milk in returnable containers.

(3) Subsection (1)(a) above shall not apply to the prescribing of, or the dispensing of a prescription for, drugs.

(4) A person who contravenes subsection (1) or (2) above shall be guilty of an offence, and any measure or weight used, or in any person's possession for use, in contravention of that subsection shall be liable to be forfeited.

(5) The preceding provisions have effect subject to –

(a)   subsection (5A) below, and
(b)   sections 9 and 89 below.

(5A) Nothing in this section precludes the use for trade of any supplementary indication; and for this purpose any indication of quantity ("the imperial indication") is a supplementary indication if –

(a)   it is expressed in a unit of measurement other than a metric unit,
(b)   it accompanies an indication of quantity expressed in a metric unit ("the metric indication") and is not itself authorised for use in the circumstances as a primary indication of quantity, and
(c)   the metric indication is the more prominent, the imperial indication being, in particular, expressed in characters no larger than those of the metric indication.

(6) The Secretary of State may by order –

(a)   amend Schedule 3 to this Act by adding to or removing from it any linear, square, cubic or capacity measure, or any weight;
(b)   add to, vary or remove from subsection (2) above any restriction on the cases or circumstances in which, or the conditions subject to which, a unit of measurement, measure or weight may be used for trade or possessed for use for trade.

(7) An order under subsection (6) above may contain such transitional or her supplemental or incidental provisions as appear to the Secretary of State expedient.

(8) In this section "unit of measurement" means a unit of measurement of length, area, volume, capacity, mass or weight.

Section 8(4) of the WMA 1985 makes it an offence to use for trade any unit of measurement not included in Sch 1 to the WMA 1985. Thus, since 1 January 2000, traders selling loose vegetables by the pound (formerly an exception to the prohibition) are committing an offence. The same section makes it an offence to use for trade a measure or weight not included in Sch 3 to the WMA 1985.

Supplementary indications

17.27 The Units of Measurement Regulations 1986[44] were amended to provide: 'Supplementary indications are authorised to be used in the specified circumstances up to and including 31 December 2009.' Thus, while the use of imperial measures as primary indicators for the sale of loose goods in bulk had ceased to be lawful on 1 January 2000, their use as supplementary indicators was to be permitted until 31 December 2009.

17.28 However, the Weights and Measures (Metrication Amendments) Regulations 2009[45] and Units of Measurement Regulations 2009[46] – which came into force on 1 January 2010 – implemented the major changes made by Directive 2009/3/EC[47] to Directive 80/181/EC, to remove:

- the deadline of 31 December 2009 for the end of supplementary indications (where imperial units are used alongside metric ones); and

- any requirement for the UK to end the use of certain imperial units (the mile, yard and foot for road traffic, the pint for draught beer and cider and bottled milk, the troy ounce for precious metals) that are in use as primary indications. (Although the UK had not in fact set any deadlines to end the use of these units.)

Use of unstamped equipment

17.29

Weights and Measures Act 1985, s 11

11 Certain equipment to be passed and stamped by inspector

(1) The provisions of this section shall apply to the use for trade of weighing or measuring equipment of such classes or descriptions as may be prescribed.

(2) No person shall use any article for trade as equipment to which this section applies, or have any article in his possession for such use, unless that article, or equipment to which this section applies in which that article is incorporated or to the operation of which the use of that article is incidental –

    (a)   has been passed by an inspector or approved verifier as fit for such use, and

    (b)   except as otherwise expressly provided by or under this Act, bears a stamp indicating that it has been so passed which remains undefaced otherwise than by reason of fair wear and tear.

(3) If any person contravenes subsection (2) above, he shall be guilty of an offence and any article in respect of which the offence was committed shall be liable to be forfeited.

---

[44]   SI 1986/1082.
[45]   SI 2009/3045.
[46]   SI 2009/3046.
[47]   OJ L114, 7.5.2009, p 10.

(4) Any person requiring any equipment to which this section applies to be passed by an inspector as fit for use for trade shall submit the equipment, in such manner as the local weights and measures authority may direct, to the inspector who (subject to the provisions of this Act and to any regulations under section 15 below) shall –

    (a)   test the equipment by means of such local or working standards and testing equipment as he considers appropriate or, subject to any conditions which may be prescribed, by means of other equipment which has already been tested and which the inspector considers suitable for the purpose,

    (b)   if the equipment submitted falls within the prescribed limits of error and by virtue of subsection (10) below is not required to be stamped as mentioned in paragraph (c) of this subsection, give to the person submitting it a statement in writing to the effect that it is passed as fit for use for trade, and

    (c)   except as otherwise expressly provided by or under this Act, cause it to be stamped with the prescribed stamp.

(4A) An approved verifier may (subject to the provisions of this Act, to any regulations under section 15 below and to any conditions included in his approval) –

    (a)   test any equipment to which this section applies by means of other equipment which has already been tested and which the verifier considers suitable for the purpose,

    (b)   if the equipment being tested falls within the prescribed limits of error and by virtue of subsection (10) below is not required to be stamped as mentioned in paragraph (c) below, make a statement in writing to the effect that it is passed fit for use for trade, and

    (c)   except as otherwise expressly provided for by or under this Act, stamp it with the prescribed stamp.

(5) There shall be charged in respect of any test carried out under subsection (4) above such reasonable fees as the local weights and measures authority may determine.

(6) An inspector shall keep a record of every test carried out by him under subsection (4) above.

(6A) In this Act "approved verifier", in relation to weighing or measuring equipment of any class or description, means a person who is for the time being approved under section 11A below in relation to the testing, passing and stamping of weighing or measuring equipment of that class or description.

(7) Except as otherwise expressly provided by or under this Act, no weight or measure shall be stamped as mentioned in subsection (4)(c) or (4A)(c) above unless it has been marked in the prescribed manner with its purported value.

(8) Subject to subsection (9) below, where any equipment submitted to an inspector under subsection (4) above is of a pattern in respect of which a certificate of approval granted under section 12 below is for the time being in force, the inspector shall not refuse to pass or stamp the equipment on the ground that it is not suitable for use for trade.

(9) If the inspector is of opinion that the equipment is intended for use for trade for a particular purpose for which it is not suitable, he may refuse to pass or stamp it until the matter has been referred to the Secretary of State, whose decision shall be final.

(10) The requirements of subsections (2), (4), (4A) and (7) above with respect to stamping and marking shall not apply to any weight or measure which is too small to be stamped or marked in accordance with those requirements.

(11) Where a person submits equipment to an inspector under this section, the inspector may require the person to provide the inspector with such assistance in connection with the testing of the equipment as the inspector reasonably considers it necessary for the person to provide and shall not be obliged to proceed with the test until the person provides it; but a failure to provide the assistance shall not constitute an offence under section 81 below.

(12) If an inspector refuses to pass as fit for use for trade any equipment submitted to him under this section and is requested by the person by whom the equipment was submitted to give reasons for the refusal, the inspector shall give to that person a statement of those reasons in writing.

(13) In the case of any equipment which is required by regulations made under section 15 below to be passed and stamped under this section only after it has been installed at the place where it is to be used for trade, if after the equipment has been so passed and stamped it is dismantled and reinstalled, whether in the same or some other place, it shall not be used for trade after being so reinstalled until it has again been passed under this section.

(14) If any person –

   (a)   knowingly uses any equipment in contravention of subsection (13) above, or
   (b)   knowingly causes or permits any other person so to use it, or
   (c)   knowing that the equipment is required by virtue of subsection (13) above to be again passed under this section, disposes of it to some other person without informing him of that requirement,

he shall be guilty of an offence and the equipment shall be liable to be forfeited.

(15) Subject to subsection (13) above, a stamp applied to any equipment under this section shall have the like validity throughout Great Britain as it has in the place in which it was originally applied, and accordingly that equipment shall not be required to be re-stamped because it is used in any other place.

(16) If at any time the Secretary of State is satisfied that, having regard to the law for the time being in force in Northern Ireland, any of the Channel Islands or the Isle of Man, it is proper so to do, he may by order provide for any equipment to which this section applies duly stamped in accordance with that law, or treated for the purposes of that law as if duly stamped in accordance with it, to be treated for the purposes of this Act as if it had been duly stamped in Great Britain under this section.

Section 11(2) and (3) of the WMA 1985 make it an offence to use for trade any weighing or measuring equipment 'as may be prescribed' unless it has been passed by an inspector[48] or an approved verifier[49] as fit for such use and duly stamped with a stamp which remains undefaced save by reason of fair wear and tear. The same section makes it an offence to have possession for use for trade of such equipment. Use or possession of equipment marked with the sign of EC pattern approval and exemption from EC initial verification or marked with EC initial verification is not an offence.[50] This is an offence of strict liability, no *mens rea* is required and mistake is no defence. Note that s 11A(2)(a) permits approved verifiers to be appointed to verify or re-verify equipment which they have manufactured, installed or repaired and the Legislative Reform (Verification of Weighing and Measuring Equipment) Order 2008[51] amended s 11A so as to permit approved verifiers to be approved for the additional purpose of re-verifying equipment which they have adjusted.

17.30 In *Thoburn v Sunderland City Council; Hunt v LB Hackney; Harman/Dove v Cornwall County Council; Collins v LB Sutton*[52] – the 'metric martyrs' case – Thoburn was prosecuted for offences under s 11(2) and (3) WMA 1985. The essence of the cases was that certain Weights and Measures legislation and the Price Marking Order 1999 were unlawful and invalid. It was held that the legislation was lawful and the appeals by all defendants were dismissed. When the matters reached the admissibility stage before the European Court of Human Rights – appeals to the House of Lords having been refused – the Court found that the applicants' complaints '… did not disclose any appearance of a violation of the rights and freedoms set out in the convention or its protocols'. The domestic appeal is, however, an important case on the effect of the EU Treaties and EU legislation on the sovereignty of the British Parliament – Laws LJ said:

> '[T]here is nothing in the [European Communities Act 1972] which allows the [European Court of Justice], or any other institutions of the EU, to touch or qualify the conditions of Parliament's legislative supremacy in the United Kingdom.'

Prescribed equipment

17.31 Section 11, and the offences under it, apply only to such weighing or measuring equipment 'as may be prescribed'. Note that many types of weighing and measuring equipment are now tested, approved and placed on market through Old or New Approach Directives which are independent of s 11. However with the New Approach Directives (such as Directive 2009/23/EC on non-automatic weighing instruments (the 'NAWI Directive') or Directive

---

48   As appointed under WMA 1985, s 72(1).
49   Under the Deregulation (Weights and Measures) Order 1999, SI 1999/503.
50   Measuring Instruments (EEC Requirements) Regulations 1988, SI 1988/186.
51   SI 2008/3262.
52   [2002] EWHC 195 (Admin), [2003] QB 151.

2004/22/EC (the Measuring Instruments Directive) ('MID')[53]), whilst the initial verification must be performed by a Notified Body any subsequent reverification is carried out under s 11.

Using false or unjust equipment

17.32

> Weights and Measures Act 1985, s 17
>
> **17 Offences relating to false or unjust equipment or fraud**
>
> (1) If any person uses for trade, or has in his possession for use for trade, any weighing or measuring equipment which is false or unjust, he shall be guilty of an offence and the equipment shall be liable to be forfeited.
>
> (2) Without prejudice to the liability of any equipment to be forfeited, it shall be a defence for any person charged with an offence under subsection (1) above in respect of the use for trade of any equipment to show –
>
> > (a) that he used the equipment only in the course of his employment by some other person, and
> >
> > (b) that he neither knew, nor might reasonably have been expected to know, nor had any reason to suspect, the equipment to be false or unjust.
>
> (3) If any fraud is committed in the using of any weighing or measuring equipment for trade, the person committing the fraud and any other person party to it shall be guilty of an offence and the equipment shall be liable to be forfeited.

Section 17(1) makes it an offence to use for trade any weighing or measuring equipment which is false or unjust. This is an offence of strict liability, no *mens rea* is required and mistake is no defence, nor does the fact that the offence was an isolated and untypical occurrence assist the defendant.[54] The allegation should specify whether the equipment is alleged to be 'false' or 'unjust'.[55] Falsity and unjustness are questions of fact for the court,[56] but s 85(1) permits any party to proceedings for an offence under the WMA 1985, or the court itself, to refer the question to the Secretary of State, whose decision will be final. Where the equipment is marked with the sign of EC pattern approval and exemption from EC initial verification, or marked with EC initial verification, and the inaccuracy found is within the prescribed limits of error then it cannot be found to be false or unjust for the purposes of s 17(1).[57] The question of whether the falsity or unjustness gives rise to a deficiency or excess is irrelevant,[58] as is the fact that the customer may have requested or acquiesced in the use of the unjust equipment.[59] A weighing machine which, by its

---

[53] OJ L135, 30.4.2004, p 1.
[54] *Percival v Hurst* (1931) 39 Monthly Review 176.
[55] *Moore v Ray* [1951] 1 KB 98, [1950] 2 All ER 561, DC, *Bastin v Davies* [1950] 2 KB 579, [1950] 1 All ER 1095.
[56] *R v Baxendale* (1880) 44 JP 763.
[57] Measuring Instruments (EEC Requirements) Regulations 1988, SI 1988/186, reg 6(3).
[58] *Quality Dairies (York) Ltd v Pedley* [1952] 1 KB 275, [1952] 1 All ER 380, DC.
[59] *LCC v Payne (No 2)* [1905] 1 KB 410, DC.

construction, is liable to variation and needs adjustment, by means of an appliance provided for that purpose, before use is not 'false' or unjust,[60] but the adjustment appliance must be an integral part of the machine rather than an easily detachable device. Where that is the case the machine would be unlawful, even if it were registering correctly at the time of inspection.[61] Thus, even where a machine is inaccurate by an ascertainable amount, and allowance is customarily made for this so that no one has been defrauded, the offence is still committed.[62] Likewise, where an otherwise accurate balance was hung with a four pound weight, so as to deduct that amount from the weight of live pigs sold at market, that being the local custom and no one having been defrauded, an offence was committed.[63] Where a machine used for weighing tea had a piece of paper placed on it to facilitate weighing, thus making it inaccurate by the weight of the paper, the machine was found to be false and unjust;[64] likewise where the pans of a set of scales could be reversed and the weight was inaccurate when this was done,[65] or where the balance was incorrect when the article to be weighed was not placed in the centre of the pan.[66] A modern case where no offence was found is *Makinson v Dewhurst*[67] where a butchers shop had in its possession a self-indicating and price-computing weighing machine which, by its construction had a tendency after a time to give short weight. A mechanism was provided for appropriate adjustment. Test purchases were made and the employee concerned failed to zero the machine when this was done. The Divisional Court held that no offence under s 17(1) was committed since the mechanism provided made the machine a just one. It seems clear that an allegation of an offence of short weight, under s 28, in similar factual circumstances would have succeeded.

Defence

17.33 It is a defence under s 17 for the defendant to prove, on the balance of probabilities, that he used the equipment only in the course of his employment by some other person and that he neither knew, nor might reasonably have been expected to know or have any reason to suspect[68] that the equipment was false or unjust.[69]

Fraudulent use of equipment

17.34 Section 17(3) makes it an offence to commit, or be party to, fraud in the use of weighing or measuring equipment for trade, while s 20(3)(b) creates a similar offence in respect of the use of public weighing or measuring equipment.

---

60   *London and North Western Railway Co v Richards* 121 ER 1094, (1862) 2 B&S 326.
61   *Carr v Stringer* (1868) LR 3 QB 433.
62   *Great Western Railway Co v Bailie* 112 ER 1076, (1864) 5 B & S 928, 34 LJMC 31.
63   *Collins v Denny & Sons* (1897) 31 ILT 167.
64   *Lane v Rendall* [1899] 2 QB 673.
65   *Henton v Radford* (1881) 45 JP 224.
66   *R v Baxendale* (1880) 44 JP 763.
67   Unreported, transcript in (1981) 89 Monthly Review 87.
68   This is a matter of fact for the court, *McArdle v Egan* (1933) 150 LT 412.
69   WMA 1985, s 17(2).

These offences differ from those examined thus far in that they require a *mens rea* on the part of the person committing them, namely an intention to commit the fraud. To defraud is to induce another to take a course of action by deceit.[70] Typically, therefore, a fraud covered by this subsection would be one whereby the customer was induced to buy a quantity of goods less than he believed he was receiving by means of some manipulation of the weighing or measuring equipment. In contrast to the offences under s 17(1), evidence of the consent or acquiescence of the customer to the placing of paper on the pan of a set of scales,[71] or of a particular trade custom in relation to the WMA 1985 on which it is alleged constitutes a fraud[72] may be of great importance in establishing whether or not an offence has been committed, since such matters are likely to go to the heart of whether or not the defendant has been acting deceitfully or dishonestly.

PRINCIPAL OFFENCES UNDER PART IV OF THE WMA 1985

Short weight

Weights and Measures Act 1985, s 28

17.35

> Weights and Measures Act 1985, s 28
>
> **28 Short weight, etc**
>
> (1) Subject to sections 33 to 37 below, any person who, in selling or purporting to sell any goods by weight or other measurement or by number, delivers or causes to be delivered to the buyer –
>
> > (a) a lesser quantity than that purported to be sold, or
> > (b) a lesser quantity than corresponds with the price charged, shall be guilty of an offence.
>
> (2) For the purposes of this section –
>
> > (a) the quantity of the goods in a regulated package (as defined by section 68(1) below) shall be deemed to be the nominal quantity (as so defined) on the package, and
> > (b) any statement, whether oral or in writing, as to the weight of any goods shall be taken, unless otherwise expressed, to be a statement as to the net weight of the goods.
>
> (3) Nothing in this section shall apply in relation to any such goods or sales as are mentioned in section 24(2)(a) or (b) above.

---

70 *Re London and Globe Finance Corporation Ltd* [1903] 1 Ch 728.
71 *Harris v Allwood* (1892) 57 JP 7.
72 *King v Spencer* (1904) 91 LT 470, 68 JP 530.

Section 28 of the WMA 1985 makes it an offence, where goods are sold by weight, or other measurement, or number, to deliver, or cause to be delivered to the buyer, a lesser quantity than that purported to be sold[73] or than corresponds to the price.[74] For the purposes of the section, any statement as to the weight of the goods is to be taken to refer to their net weight,[75] that is their weight without wrapping, containers or any other article.[76] This is an offence of strict liability, no *mens rea* is required and mistake is no defence. Again the question of the purchaser's state of mind is irrelevant.[77] Where an offence of short measure is committed by an employee in the absence of the employer, and without his knowledge, the employer may nevertheless be guilty of causing short measure to be delivered.[78] Thus where a delivery driver had caused short weight deliveries by stealing some coal after leaving his employer's premises it was no defence for the employer that they did not know of the short weight.[79] In the case of the sale of beer the court has held that a reasonable head of froth is an integral part of the measure purported to be sold[80] but only when required in accordance with local customer preference.[81]

Quantity less than stated (pre-packed goods)

17.36

> **Weights and Measures Act 1985, s 30**
>
> **30 Quantity less than stated**
>
> (1) If, in the case of any goods that are pre-packed within the meaning of this Act or are prepacked food within the meaning of the FIC Regulation and (in either case) are in or on a container marked with a statement in writing with respect to the quantity of the goods, the quantity of the goods is at any time found to be less than that stated, then, subject to sections 33 to 37 below –
>
> (a)   any person who has those goods in his possession for sale shall be guilty of an offence, and
>
> (b)   if it is shown, that the deficiency cannot be accounted for by anything occurring after the goods had been sold by retail and delivered to, or to a person nominated in that behalf by, the buyer, any person by whom or on whose behalf those goods have been sold or agreed to be sold at any time while they were pre-packed within the meaning of this Act or were prepacked food within the meaning of the FIC Regulation and (in either case) were in or on the container in question, shall be guilty of an offence.
>
> (2) If –

---

[73]   Section 28(1)(a).
[74]   Section 28(1)(b).
[75]   Section 28(2).
[76]   *Tansley v J Sainsbury & Co Ltd* (1941) 105 JP 337, DC.
[77]   *Sopp v Co-op Retail Services* (1969) 68 LGR 106, DC.
[78]   *Sopp v Long* [1970] 1 QB 518, [1969] 1 All ER 855.
[79]   *Winter v Hinckley and District Co-op Society Ltd* [1959] 1 All ER 403, [1959] 1 WLR 182.
[80]   *Bennett v Markham* [1982] 3 All ER 641, [1982] 1 WLR 1230.
[81]   *Allied Domecq Leisure Ltd v Cooper* (1999) 163 JP 1, [1999] Crim LR 230.

(a) in the case of a sale of or agreement to sell any goods which, not being pre-packed within the meaning of this Act or prepacked food within the meaning of the FIC Regulation, are made up for sale or for delivery after sale in or on a container marked with a statement in writing with respect to the quantity of the goods, or

(b) in the case of any goods which, in connection with their sale or an agreement for their sale, have associated with them a document containing such a statement,

the quantity of the goods is at any time found to be less than that stated, then, if it is shown that the deficiency cannot be accounted for by anything occurring after the goods had been delivered to, or to a person nominated in that behalf by, the buyer, and subject to sections 33 to 37 below and paragraph 10 of Schedule 4 to this Act, the person by whom, and any other person on whose behalf: the goods were sold or agreed to be sold shall be guilty of an offence.

(3) Subsections (1) and (2) above shall have effect notwithstanding that the quantity stated is expressed to be the quantity of the goods at a specified time falling before the time in question, or is expressed with some other qualification of whatever description, except where –

(a) that quantity is so expressed in pursuance of an express requirement of this Part of this Act or any instrument made under this Part, or

(b) the goods, although falling within subsection (1) or subsection (2)(a) above –

(i) are not required by or under this Part of this Act to be pre-packed as mentioned in subsection (1) or required by the FIC Regulation to be prepacked food as mentioned in that subsection or, as the case may be, to be made up for sale or for delivery after sale in or on a container only if the container is marked as mentioned in subsection (2)(a), and

are not goods on a sale of which (whether any sale or a sale of any particular description) the quantity sold is required by or under any provision of this Part, of this Act other than section 26 or required by the FIC Regulation, to be made known to the buyer at or before a particular time, or

(c) the goods, although falling within subsection (2)(b) above, are not required by or under this Part of this Act to have associated with them such a document as is mentioned in that provision.

(4) In any case to which, by virtue of paragraph (a), (b) or (c) of sub- section (3) above, the provisions of subsection (1) or (2) above do not apply, if it is found at any time that the quantity of the goods in question is less than that stated and it is shown that the deficiency is greater than can be reasonably justified on the ground justifying the qualification in question, then, subject to sections 33 to 37 below –

(a) in the case of goods such as are mentioned in subsection (1) above, if it is further shown as mentioned in that subsection, then –

(i) where the container in question was marked in Great Britain, the person by whom, and any other person on whose behalf: the container was marked, or

(ii) where the container in question was marked outside Great Britain, the person by whom, and any other person on whose behalf: the goods were first sold in Great Britain,

shall be guilty of an offence;

(b)   in the case of goods such as are mentioned in subsection (2) above, the person by whom, and any other person on whose behalf: the goods were sold or agreed to be sold shall be guilty of an offence if: but only if: he would, but for paragraph (a), (b) or (c) of subsection (3) above have been guilty of an offence under subsection (2).

(5) Subsection (2) of section 28 above shall have effect for the purposes of this section as it has effect for the purposes of that section.

(6) Nothing in this section shall apply in relation to any such goods or sales as are mentioned in section 24(2)(a) or (b) above.

Section 30 creates offences in relation to goods which have been packaged in two different circumstances. Section 30(1) deals with goods pre-packed[82] in or on a container[83] where the quantity of goods is found to be less than that which is indicated by a statement marked on the container. For the purposes of the section, any statement as to the weight of the goods is to be taken to refer to their net weight,[84] that is their weight without wrapping, containers or any other article.[85] Where goods have been sold or agreed to be sold in a container so marked, or a person has such goods in his possession for sale,[86] and there is a deficiency which can be shown to be not attributable to the buyer, the person who sold or agreed to sell the goods, or any person on whose behalf the goods were sold or agreed to be sold, is guilty of an offence.[87] This is an offence of strict liability, no *mens rea* is required and mistake is no defence. It is generally no defence that the statement of quantity marked on the container relates to a particular time or that it is qualified in some other way[88] save where:

(a)   the quantity is expressed as it is to comply with an express requirement of s 21, or of statutory instruments made under s 22[89] of the WMA 1985, or

(b)   the goods are not required by the WMA 1985 or the Food Information to Consumers Regulation to be pre-packed and are not goods on a sale of which the quantity sold is required by the WMA 1985 (other than by virtue of s 26) or the Food Information to Consumers Regulation to be made known to the buyer.[90]

Where (a) or (b) above apply to render the seller's actions lawful, but the deficiency is greater than can reasonably be justified by reason of the qualification to the statement of quantity marked on the packet, then offences

---

[82]   Defined in s 94(1) as 'Made up in advance ready for retail sale in or on a container'.
[83]   Defined in s 94(1) as including 'Any form of packaging of goods for sale as a single item ...'.
[84]   Section 30(5).
[85]   *Tansley v J Sainsbury & Co Ltd* (1941) 105 JP 337, DC.
[86]   See *Bellerby v Carle* [1983] 2 AC 101, [1983] 1 All ER 1031, HL and the comments in the text above.
[87]   Section 30(1)(b).
[88]   Section 30(3).
[89]   Section 30(3)(a).
[90]   Section 30(3)(b).

may lie against the person who marked the container with the false statement or the first wholesaler to sell the goods in the UK.[91]

Quantity less than stated (goods made up for sale or delivery)

17.37 Section 30(2) deals with non-prepacked goods which are made up, after sale or agreement to sell, in a container marked with a statement with respect to the quantity of the goods. It also deals with statements made in documents associated with the sale of goods. Where there is a deficiency in the quantity of the goods which can be shown to be not attributable to the buyer, the person who sold or agreed to sell the goods, or any person on whose behalf the goods were sold or agreed to be sold, is guilty of an offence.[92] This is an offence of strict liability, no *mens rea* is required and mistake is no defence. There is an exceptional defence to this offence in respect of ballast carried by road.[93] It is generally no defence that the statement of quantity marked on the container, or set out in the associated document, is said to relate to a particular time or that it is qualified in some other way[94] save where:

(a) the quantity is expressed as it is to comply with an express requirement of s 21, or of statutory instruments made under Part IV of the WMA 1985; or

(b) any container in which the goods are made up, after sale or agreement to sell, is not required by the WMA 1985 or the Food Information to Consumers Regulation to be marked with a statement of quantity and the goods are not goods on a sale of which the quantity sold is required by the WMA 1985 to be made known to the buyer (other than by virtue of s 26);[95] or

(c) in the case of a statement in an associated document, the goods are not required by the WMA 1985 to have such a document.[96]

Where (a) or (b) above apply to render the seller's actions prima facie lawful, but the deficiency is greater than can reasonably be justified by reason of the qualification to the statement of quantity marked on the packet, then offences may still lie against the seller.

---

[91] Section 30(4)(a).
[92] Section 30(2).
[93] Sch 4, para 10.
[94] Section 30(3).
[95] Section 30(3)(b).
[96] Section 30(3)(c).

Incorrect statements

17.38

Weights and Measures Act 1985, s 31

31 Incorrect statements

(1) Without prejudice to section 30(2) to (4) above, if in the case of any goods required by or under this Part of this Act to have associated with them a document containing particular statements, that document is found to contain any such statement which is materially incorrect, any person who, knowing or having reasonable cause to suspect that statement to be materially incorrect, inserted it or caused it to be inserted in the document, or used the document for the purposes of this Part of this Act while that statement was contained in the document, shall be guilty of an offence.

(2) Subsection (2) of section 28 above shall have effect for the purposes of this section as it has effect for the purposes of that section.

(3) Nothing in this section shall apply in relation to any such goods or sales as are mentioned in section 24 (2) (a) or (b) above.

Certain goods are required,[97] when delivered in connection with a sale, to have associated with them a document containing particular statements. Sand and other ballast and solid fuel are notable examples. Where such a statement is found to be materially incorrect any person who, knowing or having reasonable cause to suspect (arguably these words require not just reasonable grounds for suspicion but actual suspicion[98]) it to be so, inserted it or caused it to be inserted in the document is guilty of an offence under s 31(1) of the WMA 1985. It is also an offence under s 31(1) knowingly to use such a document for the purposes of compliance with the WMA 1985 while that statement was contained in it. These offences require the offender to have the requisite *mens rea* and are not ones of strict liability.

Failure to comply with Food Information for Consumers Regulation

17.39

Weights and Measures Act 1985, s 31A

31A Non-compliance with certain requirements of the FIC Regulation

(1) Subject to subsection (2) below, a food business operator to which Article 1(3) of the FIC Regulation applies is guilty of an offence if that food business operator fails to comply with –

---

[97] By s 21 and Schs 4 and 5, or statutory instruments made under WMA 1985, s 22.
[98] *R v Banks* [1916] 2 KB 621, [1916–1917] All ER 356, *R v Harrison* [1938] 3 All ER 134, 159 LT 95, *Nakkuda Ali v Jayaratne* [1951] AC 66, PC.

(a) any of the provisions of Article 8 of the FIC Regulation (responsibilities of food business operators) applicable to the food business operator, to the extent that the provisions relate to net quantity;

(b) Article 9(1)(e) of the FIC Regulation (mandatory indication of net quantity of food), except to the extent that it relates to a failure to comply with Article 13(5) of the FIC Regulation; or

(c) Chapter V of the FIC Regulation (voluntary food information), to the extent that it imposes requirements in respect of net quantity.

(2) A food business operator is not guilty of an offence under subsection (1) if the food business operator acts in accordance with any of the following –

(a) an exception contained in Chapter IV of the FIC Regulation;

(b) national measures adopted under Article 40 of the FIC Regulation (milk and milk products);

(c) national measures maintained under Article 42 of the FIC Regulation (measures adopted before 12 December 2011);

(d) transitional measures under Article 54(1) of the FIC Regulation.

(3) In this section "food business operator" and "net quantity" have the same meanings as in the FIC Regulation.

By virtue of the Food Information to Consumers Regulation[99] food business operators whose activities concern the supply of food information to consumers are (subject to certain limited exceptions)[100] required to ensure that the net quantity[101] of the food appears on the food's pre-packaging or the label attached thereto.[102] A failure to comply with these requirements under the Food Information to Consumers Regulation is an offence under s 31A(1).

GENERAL DEFENCES TO PART IV OFFENCES

17.40 As a counterbalance to the strict liability regime within which the majority of the offences created by the WMA 1985 fall, there is an important safeguard in the form of the statutory defences under ss 33–37.

Warranty

17.41

Weights and Measures Act 1985, s 33

33 Warranty

(1) Subject to the following provisions of this section, in any proceedings for an offence under this Part of this Act or any instrument made under this Part, being

---

[99] Implemented into domestic weights and measures law by the Weights and Measures (Food) (Amendment) Regulations 2014, SI 2014/2975.

[100] For example, where the net quantity is less than 5g or 5ml or the food in question is usually sold by quantity.

[101] As set out in Art 23.

[102] Arts 8 and 9(e).

an offence relating to the quantity or pre-packing of any goods, it shall be a defence for the person charged to prove –

(a)　that he bought the goods from some other person –
　　(i)　as being of the quantity which the person charged purported to sell or represented, or which was marked on any container or stated in any document to which the proceedings relate, or
　　(ii)　as conforming with the statement marked on any container to which the proceedings relate, or with the requirements with respect to the pre-packing of goods of this Part of this Act or any instrument made under this Part,
　　as the case may require, and

(b)　that he so bought the goods with a written warranty from that other person that they were of that quantity or, as the case may be, did so conform, and

(c)　that at the time of the commission of the offence he did in fact believe the statement contained in the warranty to be accurate and had no reason to believe it to be inaccurate, and

(d)　if the warranty was given by a person who at the time he gave it was resident outside Great Britain and any designated country, that the person charged had taken reasonable steps, to check the accuracy of the statement contained in the warranty, and

(e)　in the case of proceedings relating to the quantity of any goods, that he took all reasonable steps to ensure that, while in his possession, the quantity of the goods remained unchanged and, in the case of such or any other proceedings, that apart from any change in their quantity the goods were at the time of the commission of the offence in the same state as when he bought them,

(2) A warranty shall not be a defence in any such proceedings as are mentioned in subsection (1) above unless, not later than three days before the date of the hearing, the person charged has sent to the prosecutor a copy of the warranty with a notice stating that he intends to rely on it and specifying the name and address of the person from whom the warranty was received, and has also sent a like notice to that person.

(3) Where the person charged is the employee of a person who, if he had been charged, would have been entitled to plead a warranty as a defence under this section, subsection (1) above shall have effect –

(a)　with the substitution, for any reference (however expressed) in paragraphs (a), (b), (d) and (e) to the person charged, of a reference to his employer, and

(b)　with the substitution for paragraph (c) of the following-
　　"(c)　that at the time of the commission of the offence his employer did in fact believe the statement contained in the warranty to be accurate and the person charged had no reason to believe it to be inaccurate,".

(4) The person by whom the warranty is alleged to have been given shall be entitled to appear at the hearing and to give evidence.

(5) If the person charged in any such proceedings as are mentioned in subsection (1) above wilfully attributes to any goods a warranty given in relation to any other goods, he shall be guilty of an offence.

(6) A person who, in respect of any goods sold by him in respect of which a warranty might be pleaded under this section, gives to the buyer a false warranty in writing shall be guilty of an offence unless he proves that when he gave the warranty he took all reasonable steps to ensure that the statements contained in it were, and would continue at all relevant times to be, accurate.

(7) Where in any such proceedings as are mentioned in subsection (1) above ("the original proceedings") the person charged relies successfully on a warranty given to him or to his employer, any proceedings under subsection (6) above in respect of the warranty may, at the option of the prosecutor, be taken either before a court having jurisdiction in the place where the original proceedings were taken or before a court having jurisdiction in the place where the warranty was given.

(8) For the purposes of this section, any statement with respect to any goods which is contained in any document required by or under this Part of this Act to be associated with the goods or in any invoice, and, in the case of goods made up in or on a container for sale or for delivery after sale, any statement with respect to those goods with which that container is marked, shall be taken to be a written warranty of the accuracy of that statement.

Section 33(1) of the WMA 1985 makes it a defence for a person charged with an offence under Part IV of the WMA 1985, or Regulations made thereunder, relating to the quantity or pre-packing of goods to prove, on the balance of probabilities:[103]

(a) that the goods were bought from another person as being of the quantity represented by that person, or as marked on their container or stated in a document, and

(b) that the goods were bought with a written warranty that they were of the relevant quantity, and

(c) that the warranty was believed to be accurate and that there was no reason to believe the warranty was inaccurate (although it is arguable that it is the subjective question of what was actually believed, rather than the objective question of whether there was 'reason to believe' which should apply here[104]), and

(d) that, if the warranty was given by a person resident outside the United Kingdom or other associated territory, that all reasonable steps were taken to check its accuracy, and

(e) in cases relating to the quantity of goods, that all reasonable steps were taken to ensure that the quantity remained unchanged while it was in the possession of the defendant and that, apart from any change in quantity, they were at the time of the commission of the offence in the same state as when they were bought.[105]

---

[103] *R v Carr-Briant* [1943] KB 607.

[104] *R v Banks* 1916 2 KB 621, [1916–1917] All ER 356, *R v Harrison* [1938] 3 All ER 134, 159 LT 95, *Nakkuda Ali v Jayaratne* [1951] AC 66, PC, *Jones v Bertram* (1894) 58 JP 478, 10 TLR 285, *Blaydon Co-op Society v Young* (1916) 86 LJKB, 115 LT 827.

[105] For a case where a retailer failed in reliance upon a warranty because of failure to comply with this requirement see *FW Woolworth and Co Ltd v Gray* [1970] 1 All ER 953.

17.42 Any alteration of the goods, however harmless, will prevent the warranty applying as a defence.[106] The defence can only be relied upon where, not later than 3 days before the date of the hearing, a copy of the warranty has been sent to the prosecutor with a notice stating the intention to rely on it and specifying the name and address of the person from whom the warranty was received. The same notice must be sent to the alleged warrantor.[107] The person by whom the warranty is alleged to have been given may give evidence at the proceedings.[108] It is an offence both willfully to attribute to goods a warranty given in relation to other goods[109] and to give a false warranty[110] in writing unless the warrantor proves that he took all reasonable steps to ensure that the warranty was and would remain accurate.[111]

Reasonable precautions and due diligence

17.43

> **Weights and Measures Act 1985, s 34**
>
> **34 Reasonable precautions and due diligence**
>
> (1) In any proceedings for an offence under this Part of this Act or any instrument made under this Part, it shall be a defence for the person charged to prove that he took all reasonable precautions and exercised all due diligence to avoid the commission of the offence.
>
> (2) If in any case the defence provided by subsection (1) above involves an allegation that the commission of the offence in question was due to the WMA 1985 or default of another person or due to reliance on information supplied by another person, the person charged shall not, without the leave of the court, be entitled to rely on the defence unless, before the beginning of the period of seven days ending with the date when the hearing of the charge began, he served on the prosecution a notice giving such information identifying or assisting in the identification of the other person as was then in his possession.

It is a defence to offences under Part IV of the WMA 1985 (which include the remaining offences under ss 28–31A) to show that all reasonable precautions were taken and all due diligence exercised to avoid the commission of an offence. The defence of due diligence is considered in detail in Chapter 3, Criminal Enforcement.

---

[106] *Hotchin v Hindmarsh* [1891] 2 QB 181, 60 LJMC 146, *Hennen v Long* (1904) 90 LT 387, 68 JP 237, *Pugh v Williams* (1917) 86 LJKB 1407, 117 LT 191.
[107] Section 33(2).
[108] Section 33(4).
[109] Section 33(5).
[110] *Herman Jennings & Co Ltd v Slatcher* [1942] 2 KB 115, [1942] 2 All ER 1.
[111] Section 33(6).

Subsequent deficiency

17.44

Weights and Measures Act 1985, s 35

35 Subsequent deficiency

(1) This subsection applies to any proceedings for an offence under this Part of this Act, or any instrument made under this Part, by reason of the quantity –

    (a)   of any goods made up for sale or for delivery after sale (whether by way of pre-packing or otherwise) in or on a container marked with an indication of quantity,

    (b)   of any goods which, in connection with their sale or an agreement for their sale, have associated with them a document purporting to state the quantity of the goods, or

    (c)   of any goods required by or under this Part of this Act to be pre-packed, or to be otherwise made up in or on a container for sale or for delivery after sale, or to be made for sale, only in particular quantities,

being less than that marked on the container or stated in the document in question or than the relevant particular quantity, as the case may be.

(2) In any proceedings to which subsection (1) above applies, it shall be a defence for the person charged to prove that the deficiency arose –

    (a)   in a case falling within paragraph (a) of subsection (1) above, after the making up of the goods and the marking of the container,

    (b)   in a case falling within paragraph (b) of that subsection, after the preparation of the goods for delivery in pursuance of the sale or agreement and after the completion of the document,

    (c)   in a case falling within paragraph (c) of that subsection, after the making up or making, as the case may be, of the goods for sale,

and was attributable wholly to factors for which reasonable allowance was made in stating the quantity of the goods in the marking or document or in making up or making the goods for sale, as the case may be.

(3) In the case of a sale by retail of food, other than food pre-packed in a container which is, or is required by or under this Part of this Act or the FIC Regulation to be, marked with an indication of quantity, in any proceedings for an offence under this Part of this Act or any instrument made under this Part, by reason of the quantity delivered to the buyer being less than that purported to be sold, it shall be a defence for the person charged to prove that the deficiency was due wholly to unavoidable evaporation or drainage since the sale and that due care and precaution were taken to minimise any such evaporation or drainage.

(4) If in any proceedings for an offence under this Part of this Act or any instrument made under-this Part, being an offence in respect of any deficiency in the quantity of any goods sold, it is shown that between the sale and the discovery of the deficiency the goods were with the consent of the buyer subjected to treatment which could result in a reduction in the quantity of those goods for delivery to, or to any person nominated in that behalf by, the buyer, the person charged shall not be found guilty of that offence unless it is shown that the deficiency cannot be accounted for by the subjecting of the goods to that

treatment.

Where the offence involves goods in containers marked with incorrect quantities or goods with associated documents stating incorrect quantities (and thus most often offences under ss 30, 31 and 31A) it is a defence that the deficiency arose after the container was marked or the document completed, provided that it is additionally proved that the deficiency was attributable to factors for which reasonable allowance was made at the time the marking or document was made.[112] The defence is available to manufacturers, wholesalers and retailers, as well as the person who actually packed and marked the goods.[113]

17.45   Where non-prepacked food[114] is sold by retail (that is to a person buying for his own use or consumption[115]) and the quantity delivered is less than that purported to be sold, it is a defence to prove that the deficiency was due wholly to unavoidable evaporation or drainage since the sale, provided that it can also be shown that due care and precaution were taken to minimise such a deficiency.[116]

17.46   Where the defendant shows that, between sale and the discovery of any deficiency in the quantity of the goods the goods were, with the consent of the buyer, subjected to treatment which could result in a reduction in quantity of the goods this is a defence unless it shown that the deficiency cannot be accounted for by such treatment.[117]

Excess due to precautions

17.47

Weights and Measures Act 1985, s 36

36 Excess due to precautions

In any proceedings for an offence under this Part of this Act or any instrument made under this Part, being an offence in respect of any excess in the quantity of any goods, it shall be a defence for the person charged to prove that the excess was attributable to the taking of measures reasonably necessary in order to avoid the commission of an offence in respect of a deficiency in those or other goods.

---

[112]   Section 35(1) and (2).
[113]   *FW Woolworth and Co Ltd v Gray* [1970] 1 All ER 953, [1970] 1 WLR 764, DC.
[114]   Food is defined by the Food Safety Act 1990 as including drink, articles and substances of no nutritional value used for human consumption, and articles and substances used as ingredients in the preparation of food, a definition imported into the WMA 1985 by s 94(1).
[115]   *Chappell and Co Ltd v Nestle Co Ltd* [1958] Ch 529, [1958] 2 All ER 155 CA, on appeal [1960] AC 87, [1959] 2 All ER 701, HL.
[116]   Section 35(3).
[117]   Section 35(4).

Where the offence alleges an excess in the quantity of goods, it is a defence to show that the excess was caused by taking measures reasonably necessary to avoid committing an offence in respect of a deficiency in those or other goods.[118]

Reasonable testing

17.48

Weights and Measures Act 1985, s 37

37 Provisions as to testing

(1) If proceedings for an offence under this Part of this Act, or any instrument made under this Part, in respect of any deficiency or excess in the quantity –

(a) of any goods made up for sale (whether by way of pre-packing or otherwise) in or on a container marked with an indication of quantity, or

(b) of any goods which have been pre-packed or otherwise made up in or on a container for sale or for delivery after sale, or which have been made for sale, and which are required by or under this Part of this Act or the FIC Regulation to be pre-packed, or to be otherwise so made up, or to be so made, as the case may be, only in particular quantities,

are brought with respect to any article, and it is proved that, at the time and place at which that article was tested, other articles of the same kind, being articles which, or articles containing goods which, had been sold by the person charged or were in that person's possession for sale or for delivery after sale, were available for testing, the person charged shall not be convicted of such an offence with respect to that article unless a reasonable number of those other articles was also tested.

(2) In any proceedings for such an offence as is mentioned in subsection (1) above, the court –

(a) if the proceedings are with respect to one or more of a number of articles tested on the same occasion, shall have regard to the average quantity in the articles tested,

(b) if the proceedings are with respect to a single article, shall disregard any inconsiderable deficiency or excess, and

(c) shall have regard generally to all the circumstances of the case.

(3) Subsections (1) and (2) above shall apply with the necessary modifications to proceedings for an offence in respect of the size, capacity or contents of a container as they apply to proceedings for an offence in respect of the excess or deficiency in the quantity of certain goods.

(4) Where by virtue of section 32 above a person is charged with an offence with which some other person might have been charged, the reference in subsection (1) above to articles or goods sold by or in the possession of the person charged shall be construed as a reference to articles or goods sold by or in the possession of that other person.

---

[118] Section 36.

Where a test has been conducted on one of a number of articles made up for sale at the same time and place and that article has been found to be deficient, the defendant shall not be convicted unless a reasonable number of the articles available was also tested.[119] If the proceedings are with respect to a single article, the court must also disregard any inconsiderable deficiency or excess[120] and, in all cases, the court must have regard generally to all the circumstances of the case.[121] However, where a person takes an article which he has purchased to an inspector, at some location other than the place of purchase, there is no obligation on the inspector to test other items which were on sale at the same time and place, since 'available' means physically available to the inspector at the time and place of testing.[122]

Average quantity

17.49   Under the average quantity system, packers and importers of packaged goods are responsible for ensuring that their packages meet legislative requirements with regard to quantity control, marking, equipment, checks and documentation. The Weights and Measures (Packaged Goods) Regulations 2006[123] repealed and replaced Part V of the WMA 1985 and the Weights and Measures (Packaged Goods) Regulations 1986[124] as amended. They also removed the statutory effect of provisions contained in the 'Code of Practical Guidance for Packers and Importers' and the 'Manual of Practical Guidance for Inspectors'. The Regulations apply to packages which are packed in constant nominal quantities by weight or volume which are predetermined by the packer and are not less than 5 grams or 5 millilitres and not more than 25 kilograms or 25 litres (reg 3). They also apply to 'outer containers' containing at least one package and to bread which is unwrapped.

17.50   Regulation 4 sets out the three rules with which packers must comply in making up packages. Compliance with the rules is to be determined by the reference test set out in Sch 2. Regulations 5 and 6 set out the information which must be marked on packages and outer containers and the circumstances in which the E-mark (the form of which is shown in Sch 4) may be marked on a package or outer container. Regulation 7 provides that a person other than a packer or importer who marks an indication of nominal quantity on a package will become liable under the Regulations as though he were a packer or importer. Regulation 8 sets out specific requirements as to the marking of weight or volume on packages.

17.51   Regulation 9 imposes duties on packers and importers as to the measurement of the contents of packages, the checking of the contents and keeping of records. Regulation 13 makes it an offence to fail to comply with

---

[119]   Section 37(1).
[120]   Section 37(2)(b).
[121]   Section 37(2)(c).
[122]   *Sears v Smiths Food Group Ltd* [1968] 2 QB 288, [1968] 2 All ER 721, DC.
[123]   SI 2006/659.
[124]   SI 1986/2049.

regs 4–7 and 9 or, with intent to deceive, to alter records or evidence kept for the purposes of these regulations. Regulation 14 lays down offences in respect of the knowing sale of packages containing short measure or of packages which come from a batch that has failed the reference test. Regulation 15 prohibits the marking of the E-mark on packages except as permitted by the Regulations. Regulation 16 makes the unauthorised disclosure of information concerning trade secrets and secret manufacturing processes an offence. Regulations 17–20 contain provisions supplementary to the offence provisions including penalties and defences.

ENFORCEMENT POWERS

17.52 Section 72 deals with the appointment of inspectors of weights and measures. A weights and measures authority must appoint a chief inspector of weights and measures and '... such number of other inspectors of weights and measures, if any ... as may be necessary for the efficient discharge in the authority's area of the functions conferred or imposed on inspectors by or under this Act'.[125]

17.53 Qualification requirements for inspectors first appeared in Weights and Measures Acts of 1889 and 1904. Section 73 currently provides for the granting of a certificate of qualification to act as inspector (by the Secretary of State) for those who pass examinations held '... for the purpose of ascertaining whether persons possess sufficient skill and knowledge for the proper performance of the functions of an inspector ...'. This has been an area considered for change – for example the National Weights and Measures Laboratory commenced a 'Reform Project' in October 2007 and specifically examined the 'Qualification and Appointment of Inspectors of Weights and Measures'. Options put forward included the possibility that '... Heads of Service would wish to see the statutory requirement removed so that they have more flexibility in their resourcing of staff'. To date, no substantive reforms have been introduced.

17.54 Future proposals will need to take account of the fact that the post of 'Inspector of Weights and Measures' has found itself in non-metrological settings such as the Police Reform Act 2002 and the Licensing Act 2003, in relation alcohol sales to children in England and Wales, and under the Glasgow Commonwealth Games Act 2008 (where the power of designating enforcement officers is restricted to inspectors of weights and measures and to other individuals who meet specified criteria).

---

[125] It is worth noting that the number of inspectors actually working in weights and measures fell from 503 in 2011 to 304 in 2013 (NMO Annual Report 2013/2014).

Powers of entry and inspection

17.55 The Consumer Rights Act 2015 omits s 79 (general powers of inspection and entry) and inserts s 79A. The powers of officers are now contained within that Act:

79A Investigatory powers

For the investigatory powers available to a local weights and measures authority for the purposes of the enforcement of this Act, see Schedule 5 to the Consumer Rights Act 2015.

17.56 Note, in particular, that s 79 restricted an inspector to exercise the general powers of inspection and entry only within the area for which he was appointed inspector. Paragraphs 43 to 46 of Sch 5 to the Consumer Rights Act 2015 clarify the law to ensure that Trading Standards Services are able to operate across local authority boundaries. In summary, a local weights and measures authority in England or Wales may:

- exercise their consumer law enforcement function;
- bring civil proceedings in respect of specified conduct/applications for specified forfeiture;
- bring proceedings for a consumer offence allegedly committed in a part of England or Wales which is outside that authority's area.

Powers of seizure

17.57 Powers of entry and associated powers, including powers of seizure, are now contained in Sch 5 to the Consumer Rights Act 2015 (see Chapter 3, Criminal Enforcement).

Offences concerned with officers and their powers

17.58 It is an offence, contrary to s 75(2), to impersonate an 'inspector' or an approved verifier. It is an offence contrary to s 75(1) for an inspector knowingly to commit a breach of duty or otherwise misconduct himself. It is an offence contrary to s 79(7) of the WMA 1985 for any person to disclose information about such secrets obtained as a result of his entry to premises under the powers granted by the WMA 1985, unless the disclosure is in the course of duty. It is an offence contrary to reg 16 of the Weights and Measures (Packaged Goods) Regulations 2006 for an Officer, or any person who accompanies him, to disclose any information which relates to a trade secret or secret manufacturing process, unless the disclosure is in the course of duty.

Obstruction of officers

17.59 It is an offence, contrary to s 80, wilfully to obstruct an Officer acting in pursuance of the WMA 1985. Section 81 creates three offences:

(a) Section 81(1)(a) – wilfully failing to comply with a requirement made under the Officers powers of inspection and seizure under ss 38–40 of the WMA 1985,

(b) Section 81(1)(b) – without reasonable cause failing to give any inspector acting in pursuance of the WMA 1985 any other assistance or information which the inspector may reasonably require of him for the purposes of the performance by the inspector of his statutory functions,

(c) Section 81(2) – in purporting to give information required under 1(a) and (b) above, knowingly giving false information.

17.60 Section 81(3) excuses the person who fails to comply with an Officer's requirements under s 81(1)(a) and (b) above if his failure to answer a question or give information is based on the fear that it might incriminate him. The use of information provided by a Defendant under the compulsion of s 81 in evidence at his trial would, arguably, be a breach of his right to a fair trial.[126]

Test purchases

17.61 The power to make test purchases is now found in Sch 5 to the Consumer Rights Act 2015 (see Chapter 3, Criminal Enforcement).

PENALTIES AND SENTENCING

Imprisonment

17.62 The only offences under the WMA 1985 for which a sentence of imprisonment can be imposed are those relating to the improper disclosure of trade secrets (s 79(7)), fraudulent use of weighing or measuring equipment (s 17(3)), fraud in connection with public weighing machines (s 20(3)(b)) and deceitfully stamping solid fuel (Sch 5, para 10). These are summary offences with a maximum sentence of 6 months' imprisonment.

Financial penalties and forfeiture

17.63 All the other offences under the WMA 1985 carry financial penalties only, and the possible forfeiture of equipment or goods connected with the offences. As most of the commonly committed offences in the WMA are summary only offences it should be noted that, in relation to offences committed after 12 March 2015, the old £5,000 limit on the financial penalty that can be imposed in the magistrates' court has been removed.[127] Where anything other than money is forfeited on a conviction by a magistrates' court it must be sold or otherwise disposed of as the court may direct and the proceeds

---

[126] Art 6 of the ECHR.
[127] Legal Aid, Sentencing and Punishment of Offenders Act 2012, s 85.

applied as if they were a fine.[128] In Scotland anything used or connected with the commission of an offence may be forfeited under s 21 of the Proceeds of Crime (Scotland) Act 1995.

HALLMARKING

Introduction

17.64 When the Hallmarking Act 1973 ('HA 1973') came into force it replaced, in whole or in part some 26 other statutes, many of them dating back to Stuart or Hanoverian times, which were concerned with the regulation of the trade in precious metals. The HA 1973 provides for the composition, assaying, marking and description of articles made from or containing gold, silver and platinum and (since 21 July 2009) palladium.[129] The scheme of criminal liability introduced by the Hallmarking Act 1973 follows the structure of the Trade Descriptions Act 1968 ('TDA') (now largely repealed). The HA 1973 extends to the United Kingdom. Practical guidance in relation to the Hallmarking Act 1973 published by the UK's assay offices was updated in August 2016 to include information on hallmarking Mokume Gane articles containing precious metals.

European hallmarks

17.65 The UK remains a signatory to the Convention on the Control and Marking of Articles of Precious Metals signed in Vienna in 1972.[130] The Convention recognises hallmarks applied in another convention country; and as a consequence articles bearing such marks will be hallmarked for the purposes of the HA 1973 and can therefore be described in the United Kingdom as being of the precious metal (gold, silver, platinum or palladium) of which they are made. The Hallmarking (International Convention) Order 2002 also provides for the application in the United Kingdom of similar marks which will be recognised in other convention countries.[131]

Time limits

17.66 By para 2 of Sch 3 to the HA 1973, no prosecutions under the HA 1973 may be commenced more than 3 years after the offence was committed or one year after the offence was discovered[132] by the prosecutor, whichever is earlier.

---

[128] Magistrates' Courts Act 1980, ss 140 and 148(1).

[129] Hallmarking Act 1973 (Application to Palladium) Order 2009, SI 2009/2040.

[130] This is now under the Hallmarking (International Convention) Order 2002, SI 2002/506.

[131] Articles of fineness of only 830 (accepted by some countries but not by the United Kingdom) may have applied to them marks appropriate to articles of that fineness, but may not be described in the United Kingdom as being of silver unless they are intended for despatch to a destination outside the United Kingdom.

[132] See *Brooks v Club Continental* Transcript DC/345/81 and *R v Beaconsfield JJ, ex p Johnson Sons Ltd* (1985) 149 JP 535.

17.67 Time limits are considered in detail in Chapter 3, Criminal Enforcement.

Prosecutions

17.68 The right to prosecute in England and Wales is not restricted to a member or officer of an enforcement authority – any person can bring a prosecution under the HA 1973. In Scotland proceedings may only be taken by the Procurator Fiscal or Lord Advocate (s 9(5)). Any person (whether an individual or a body corporate), other than the Crown or its servants or agents, can be prosecuted under the HA 1973.

Directors' liability

17.69 Paragraph 3 of Sch 3 to the HA 1973 permits the prosecution and conviction of any 'director, manager, secretary or other similar officer' of a company or 'any person who was purporting to act in such a capacity' where an offence under the HA 1973 has been committed by the company 'with the consent and connivance' of that person or as a result of that person's neglect. The liability of directors etc is considered in detail in Chapter 3, Criminal Enforcement.

Causal liability

17.70 By virtue of para 4 of Sch 3 of the HA 1973, where the prosecution can show that A has committed an offence under the HA 1973 and that the offence has been committed because of the 'act or default' of B, then B may be prosecuted and convicted even if A is not proceeded against. The fact that B is a private individual, and thus otherwise not subject to the legislative scheme of the HA 1973 (which generally requires a defendant to have been acting in the course of a trade or business) is no defence to a prosecution under para 4 of Sch 3. The liability of other persons is considered in detail in Chapter 3, Criminal Enforcement.

Offences

17.71 The HA 1973 creates criminal offences contrary to ss 1, 3, 5, 6, 7, and 11. Those under s 1 are the most important. The ingredients of the offences are examined below. Other words commonly used in the HA 1973 are defined in s 22. The case of *Chilvers v Rayner*[133] established that offences under s 1 are absolute offences for which no *mens rea* is required.

Applying a description

17.72 The only descriptions with which the HA 1973 is concerned are those 'indicating that [an article] is wholly or partly made of gold, silver platinum or palladium': s 1(1)(a). By virtue of s 1(5) of the HA 1973 and Part III of Sch 1 to

---

[133] [1984] 1 WLR 328.

the HA 1973, a description indicating that an article, or the metal in an article, is of so many carats is to be presumed to be an indication that the article or metal is of gold and that its fineness is that specified in the following table:

Number of carats	Indicates gold of a standard of fineness of
9	375 parts per thousand
12	500 parts per thousand
14	585 parts per thousand
15	625 parts per thousand
18	750 parts per thousand
22	916.6 parts per thousand

Applying

17.73   Section 1(7)(b) imports the definition of applying a trade description set out in s 4 TDA into the HA 1973. Section 4 of the TDA has now been largely replaced by the CPUTR; however, it remains of relevance for prosecutions under the HA 1973.

> **Trade Descriptions Act 1968, s 4**
>
> **4 Applying a trade description to goods**
>
> (1) A person applies a trade description to goods if he –
>
> > (a)   affixes or annexes it to or in any manner marks it on or incorporates it with –
> > > (i)   the goods themselves, or
> > > (ii)   anything in, on or with which the goods are supplied; or
> > (b)   places the goods in, on or with anything which the trade description has been affixed or annexed to, marked on or incorporated with, or places any such thing with the goods; or
> > (c)   uses the trade description in any manner likely to taken as referring to the goods.
>
> (2) An oral statement may amount to the use of a trade description.
>
> (3) Where goods are supplied in pursuance of a request in which a trade description is used and the circumstances are such as to make it reasonable to infer that the goods are supplied as goods corresponding to that trade description, the person supplying the goods shall be deemed to have applied that description to the goods.

17.74   Section 4 of the TDA defines 'applying a trade description'. It is drafted very widely, but generally covers five situations that will in practice overlap:

(1) When goods are given a description by physically marking them, or affixing a description to them or material supplied with them, for example packaging or instructions (s 4(1)(a)).

(2) Placing different goods with goods of a particular trade description, for example a steel ring sold in a display of silver rings (s 4(1)(b)).

(3) Using a general trade description in a manner likely to be taken as referring to the goods in question, for example a shop with a hoarding suggesting that it sells only gold, which sells products that look like they are made of gold (s 4(1)(c)).

(4) An oral description of goods (s 4(2)).

It also includes omissions after goods of a particular trade description have been requested. For example a jeweller who is requested to supply an 18 carat gold bracelet, but instead supplies a 9 carat gold bracelet omitting to describe it as such.

The time of application

17.75 The time that a trade description is applied to goods is when one of the acts described in s 4 takes place. This does not need to be part of any contractual negotiations and does not need to take place before the contract is concluded.[134] The time of the application is not when another person sees the trade description or is misled by it. The moment that a false trade description is, for example, affixed to goods, the offence is complete.[135] This accords with logic as the offence is designed to capture those who make it their business to apply false trade descriptions.

17.76 There is limited support for the contention that there is an additional requirement to s 4; that the application of the trade description must be associated with the sale or supply of goods. Under the TDA in *Hall v Wickens Motors (Gloucester) Ltd*,[136] 40 days after the appellant sold a car, he described it as having nothing wrong with it. In a decision that was directed specifically towards the merits of the case, Widgery LCJ allowed the appeal on the basis that the application of a false trade description must be, 'associated with the sale or supply of goods'. However, it is doubtful that this case provides a proposition of universal application.

17.77 In *Fletcher v Sedmore*, a mechanic agreed to sell a motor car to a dealer. While the mechanic was repairing the car, the dealer brought a buyer to view it. The mechanic falsely told the buyer that it had a good engine. The Divisional Court, which included Widgery LCJ,[137] distinguished *Hall v Wickens Motors*

---

[134] *Fletcher v Sledmore* [1973] LGR 179.
[135] *Ex parte Vernon* [1999].
[136] [1972] 3 All ER 759, following his decision in *Wycombe Marsh Garages v Fowler* [1972] 3 All ER 248.
[137] [1973] LGR 179 Widgery LCJ casting doubt over the generality of his words in *Hall v Wickens Motors*.

and held that the representation was associated with the sale or supply of goods. Eveleigh J, in a judgment with which Widgery LCJ agreed, stated:

> 'There are no qualifications in section 1 [of the TDA] as to the time when the representation is to be made; the only qualification ... is that it should be in the course of a trade or business, in other words, should be made as part of the business activities of the person charged ... The question then remains whether or not there is reason to introduce the qualification that the person charged should himself be a contracting party in the matter in which the representation is made. No such limitation appears in the section.'

17.78 In the case of *Telford & Wrekin Council v Jordan*[138] the respondent motor car repairer had replaced the faulty dashboard of a car, with one showing a lower mileage. His contention was that he had not intended to sell the car, but merely use it as a family car. In relation to this point, Wright J stated:

> 'Even if a false odometer reading is applied to a car ... at a time when he has no intention of selling the car on but merely wishes to have it as a family car for his own or his family's use, nevertheless the offence is committed because the mischief against which the Trade Descriptions Act is directed is to prevent vehicles with odometers so altered ultimately finding their way into the market, as is very likely to happen sooner or later, bearing false readings as to the mileage that the vehicle has in fact covered. It follows therefore that even though [the Respondent] may have had no immediate intention of releasing the car into the market when he changed the odometer on this car that did not prevent what he did being an offence under section 1(1)(a).'

It is submitted that the decision in *Wickens Motors* is now of limited importance. The essential question is whether a false trade description has been applied in the course of a trade or business.

Truth and falsity

17.79 The HA 1973, by contrast to the TDA, is not concerned with the question of whether such an indication is true or false, only with the question of whether the article to which the description is applied is hallmarked or not. If such an indication is made, true or false, of an unhallmarked article, an offence is committed.

Unhallmarked

17.80 Section 2(1) sets out the marks which qualify as 'approved hallmarks'. They are marks struck by assay offices in the UK, or marks struck abroad providing equivalent information. Section 3 sets out the marks which qualify as 'sponsors' marks' (which provide information about the manufacturer of the goods). By s 2(4)(a) an article which does not bear both an approved hallmark *and* a sponsor's mark is regarded as unhallmarked for the purposes of the HA

---

[138] DC, 20/6/2000 CO/1282/00.

1973. An article may also become unhallmarked if it has been the subject of an 'improper alteration', as defined by ss 2(5) and 5 of the HA 1973.

17.81 The Hallmarking (Hallmarking Act Amendment) Regulations 1998 amended s 2 in order to make the HA 1973's provisions consistent with Art 30 of the EC Treaty, in relation to the importation by one Member State of articles made of or comprising precious metals from another Member State, as explained by the European Court of Justice in the case of *Houtwipper*.[139] Essentially, an 'approved hallmark' includes a mark struck in an 'EEA State' other than the UK. By virtue of the Hallmarking Act 1973 (Amendment) Regulations 2007, 'EEA State' now has the meaning given to it in Sch 1 to the Interpretation Act 1978 (see also s 22 of the HA 1973).

17.82 The Legislative Reform (Hallmarking) Order 2013 makes a number of amendments to the HA 1973:

- enabling assay offices to strike hallmarks outside the United Kingdom and for items bearing those hallmarks to be treated in the same way as items bearing hallmarks struck in the United Kingdom;
- removing the requirement that a manufacturer's or sponsor's mark, registered under s 3, must include the initial letters of the name or names of the manufacturer or sponsor; and
- allowing articles of silver, gold or platinum bearing a hallmark, to be coated with platinum without having to first obtain the written consent of an assay office.

In the course of a business

17.83 It is a requirement of offences under s 1 of the HA 1973 that the offender be acting 'in the course of a trade or business'.

Possession custody and control

17.84 Sections 1 and 6 of the HA 1973 create offences involving the 'possession' or the 'custody or control' of particular things. It appears that possession by an employee will be held to be possession by the employer.[140] In order for offences of possession to be made good the law requires proof of an element of control over the item in question, although not necessarily of physical proximity[141] and thus the use of the word control rather than possession appears to make little difference. There is no authority on whether the inclusion of the word 'custody' obviates the need for the prosecution to prove an element of control. It is submitted that it should not.

---

[139] Case C-293/93 [1994] ECR 1–4249.
[140] *Towers & Co v Gray* [1961] 2 QB 351, [1961] 2 All ER 68, DC.
[141] See *Warner v Metropolitan Police Commissioner* [1969] 2 AC 256, *Bellerby v Carle* [1983] 2 AC 101, [1983] 1 All ER 1031, HL.

Dealers

17.85   A 'dealer' is defined by s 22 of the HA 1973 as a person engaged in the business of making, supplying, selling (including by auction) or exchanging articles of precious metal, or in other dealings in such articles.

Specific offences

Prohibited descriptions of unhallmarked articles

17.86   Section 1(1)(a) of the HA 1973 makes it an offence for a person, in the course of a trade or business, to apply to an unhallmarked article a description indicating that it is wholly or partly made of gold, silver, platinum or palladium. Section 1(1)(b) creates an offence for such a person to supply or to offer to supply (which includes a person exposing articles for supply, or having articles in his possession for supply – s 1(7)(c)) an unhallmarked article to which such a description is applied.

Striking an article with a mark purporting to be an authorised sponsor's mark

17.87   Section 3 of the HA 1973 requires that, before an article is sent to the Assay Office for hallmarking, a mark must be struck on the article indicating its manufacturer. This is known as the sponsor's mark. Sponsor's mark have to be authorised by and registered with the relevant Assay Office and s 3 sets out how this is to be done and what marks are acceptable. By s 3(6), where the Assay Office in question is of the opinion that it would not be justified in requiring a person submitting an article for hallmarking to register a sponsor's mark, it may strike the article with its own sponsor's mark. It is an offence under s 3(8) without authority to strike an article with a mark purporting to be an authorised sponsor's mark.

Altering a hallmarked article

17.88   Section 5(1) makes it an offence to make an addition, alteration or repair to an article bearing approved hallmarks, except in accordance with the written consent of an assay office. There are four standard consents in writing, made by the Joint Committee of the Assay Offices of Great Britain, which allow specified alterations without further application. The scrapping of articles for remanufacture and the recoating of articles in the same fineness of precious metal (including palladium[142]) as the original are exceptions to these offences by virtue of s 5(3) and 5(5) respectively. Similarly additions to hallmarked articles which do not change their character and purpose and which comply which specified requirements are excepted by virtue of s 5(4).

---

[142] As inserted into s 5 by the Hallmarking Act 1973 (Application to Palladium) Order 2009, SI 2009/2040.

17.89 Section 5(2) makes it an offence to remove, alter or deface any mark struck on an article, except in accordance with the written consent of the assay office.

Counterfeiting

17.90 Section 6(1)(a) makes it an offence to make a counterfeit of any die or mark. This offence requires the prosecution to prove that the defendant acted with 'intent to defraud or deceive'. Section 6(2) defines a die as any plate, tool or instrument by means whereof any mark is struck on any metal and defines a mark as any mark in the nature of a sponsor's mark or hallmark.

Removal of marks

17.91 Section 6(1)(b) makes it an offence to remove a mark from an article of precious metal with intent to transpose it to any other article whether of precious metal or not, or to affix to any article any mark which has been removed from an article of precious metal.

Uttering counterfeits

17.92 Section 6(1)(c) makes it an offence to utter any counterfeit of a die or any article bearing a counterfeit of a mark. 'Uttering' is defined by s 6(3) as the supply, offer to supply or delivery of the die or article, in the knowledge or belief that it is counterfeit. The uttering of counterfeits has been held to include any attempt to pass the counterfeit as genuine, and is thus much wider than the concepts of 'supply' and 'offer to supply' in s 1 of the HA 1973.[143]

Possession of counterfeits

17.93 Section 6(1)(d) makes it an offence, without lawful authority or excuse, for a person to have in his custody or under his control anything which is, and which he knows or believes to be, a counterfeit die or an article bearing a counterfeit mark.

Supply of articles bearing marks likely to be confused with hallmarks

17.94 Section 7 deals with the situation where an article comes into the custody of an assay office bearing a mark likely to be confused with a hallmark, but which is not an approved hallmark because it has not been struck by an assay office according to law or because the article appears to have been the subject of improper alteration. Section 7(1) gives the assay office power to cancel or obliterate such a mark. Section 7(6) makes it an offence for any person knowingly, or for any dealer (without any qualifying *mens rea*) to

---

[143] *Selby v DPP* [1972] AC 515, [1971] 3 All ER 810, and see *R v Walmsley* (1977) 122 Sol Jo 127, CA.

supply or offer to supply an article bearing such a mark, unless the article has first been submitted to an assay office to enable them to cancel, obliterate or deface the mark.

Failure to exhibit a notice as to hallmarks

17.95 Section 11(1) makes it an offence for dealers to fail to keep exhibited in a conspicuous position in the parts of his premises to which those with whom he deals are commonly admitted a notice as to hallmarks in terms approved and in a form supplied by the British Hallmarking Council.

Statutory exceptions

Permitted descriptions

17.96 By virtue of s 1(2) and Part I of Sch 1, the use of the word 'gold' will not constitute an offence under s 1, when used to describe an unhallmarked article, where it is qualified by the words 'plated' or 'rolled'. Thus the description of an unhallmarked fountain pen as 'rolled gold' will not constitute an offence under this legislation (but a plainly and unequivocally false description 'rolled gold' may give rise to action under the CPUTR – see *Kingston-Upon-Thames Royal London BC v FW Woolworth & Co Ltd*.[144] The same section and Schedule make similar exceptions in the case of the descriptions of unhallmarked articles as 'silver plated' and 'platinum plated'.

Exempted articles

17.97 By virtue of s 1 (3) and Part II of Sch 1, the offences created by s 1(1) do not apply to a variety of articles. These are set out in the Schedule. The most noteworthy of the articles completely exempt are those for export, articles in the course of consignment from abroad to an assay office in the UK, current or former coinage, articles used or intended to be used for medical, dental, veterinary, scientific or industrial purposes, raw materials or bullion and uncompleted articles. Other articles, such as those manufactured before, and unaltered since, 1950, the mouthpieces of musical instruments, and articles so small that they cannot be hallmarked are exempt provided that their fineness is not less than 375 parts per thousand in the case of gold and 800 parts per thousand in the case of silver. There are also exemptions for specific articles, such as watch chains, again of minimum fineness, manufactured before 1975. By para 18 of Part II of Sch 1, where exemption depends upon the date of an article's manufacture, the manufacture shall be presumed to be after that date until the contrary is proved.

---

[144] [1968] 1 QB 802.

Statutory defences

Reliance on information as to exemption supplied by another

17.98   Paragraph 6 of Sch 3 provides a defence to offences under s 1 of the HA 1973 where the defendant can show that the offence was caused by reliance on information supplied to him by another person which caused him to believe that the article concerned was one which was exempt from hallmarking by virtue of Part II of Sch 1. The defendant must also satisfy the court that he could not, with reasonable diligence, have ascertained that it was not such an article.

Innocent publication of advertisement

17.99   Paragraph 5 of Sch 3 provides a defence where the allegation is of an offence committed by the publication of an advertisement. It is a defence for the defendant to show that he is a person whose business is to publish or arrange for the publication of advertisements and that the advertisement in question was received in the ordinary course of business and that he did not know and had no reason to suspect that its publication would amount to an offence under the HA 1973.

Duty to enforce

17.100   Under s 9(1) of the HA 1973 it is the duty of every local weights and measures authority to enforce the provisions of this Act within their area. Under this subsection, the British Hallmarking Council and the assay offices may also enforce the provisions of the HA 1973. Schedule 6, para 10 of the Consumer Rights Act 2015 inserts the following subsection into s 9 of the HA 1973:

> (2A) For the investigatory powers available to a local weights and measures authority, the Council and an assay office for the purposes of the duty in subsection (1) and the power in subsection (2), see Schedule 5 to the Consumer Rights Act 2015.

17.101   The powers of enforcement officers and offences related to the enforcement provisions are considered in detail in Chapter 3, Criminal Enforcement.

Delivery of articles to the Assay Office

17.102   Section 10 permits the court, following a person's conviction of an offence under the HA 1973, to order any article the subject of the proceedings to be delivered to an assay office for hallmarking, before it is returned to the person entitled to it.

Maximum sentences

17.103

Section	Brief description	Mode of trial	Maximum on indictment	Maximum summarily
1(1)(a)	Applying a prohibited description to an unhallmarked article	Either way	2 years and unlimited fine	6 months and unlimited fine
1(1)(b)	Supplying an unhallmarked article with a prohibited description	Either way	2 years and unlimited fine	6 months and unlimited fine
3	Striking an article with a purported sponsor's mark	Either way	2 years and unlimited fine	6 months and unlimited fine
5(1)	Altering a hallmarked article	Either way	2 years and unlimited fine	6 months and unlimited fine
5(2)	Altering a hallmark	Either way	2 years and unlimited fine	6 months and unlimited fine
6(1)(a)	Counterfeiting	Either way	10 years and unlimited fine	6 months and unlimited fine
6(1)(b)	Removal of marks	Either way	10 years and unlimited fine	6 months and unlimited fine
6(1)(c)	Uttering counterfeits	Either way	10 years and unlimited fine	6 months and unlimited fine
6(1)(d)	Possession of Counterfeits	Either way	10 years and unlimited fine	6 months and unlimited fine
7	Supply of articles bearing marks likely to be confused with hallmarks	Either way	2 years and unlimited fine	6 months and unlimited fine
11	Failure to exhibit a notice as to Hallmarks	Either way	2 years and unlimited fine	6 months and unlimited fine

CHAPTER 18

CONSUMER CREDIT

CONTENTS

INTRODUCTION

18.1   Recent developments in consumer credit law represent some of the most significant changes to the regulation of the consumer credit industry since the enactment of the Consumer Credit Act ('CCA') in 1974. On 1 April 2014, consumer credit regulated activities came within the ambit of the Financial Services and Markets Act 2000 ('FSMA') and the CCA was amended significantly. The Financial Conduct Authority ('FCA') replaced the Office of Fair Trading ('OFT') as the industry regulator and the established system of consumer credit licensing has been replaced by FCA authorisation for permission to undertake regulated activities. Furthermore, since 21 March 2016, second charge mortgages, which have historically been regulated by the CCA regime, are now regulated by the Mortgages and Home Finance Conduct of Business sourcebook of the FCA handbook, thereby uniting the law relating to first charge and second charge mortgages.

18.2   Often perceived to be complex, the law of consumer credit is arguably now even less accessible following the introduction of additional sources of law, in particular, the FCA handbook Consumer Credit Sourcebook ('CONC'), which sits alongside an amended CCA. Many provisions of the CCA have been retained, in particular provisions governing which agreements are regulated, agreement content and execution, unenforceability provisions, post-contractual notice requirements and unfair relationships. However, advertising rules, licensing (now authorisation) and rules relating to calculating the total charge for credit are now located in the FCA Handbook. OFT guidance on advertising, debt collection and assessment of affordability have been replicated, and in some cases turned into FCA Rules adding further complication.

18.3   Inevitably this chapter cannot contain a detailed analysis of this area of law, but instead offers a basic introduction and guide with footnotes to enable further research. For further detail, Guest and Lloyd's *Encyclopedia of Consumer Credit Law* and *The Law of Consumer Credit and Hire* by *Philpott et al* are recommended.

CONSUMER CREDIT REGULATION

18.4   Historically consumer credit businesses required a licence under the CCA to be able to trade. Now businesses require authorisation under the provisions of the FSMA to carry out activities specified in the Financial Services and Markets Act 2000 (Regulated Activities) Order 2001(as amended) ('the Regulated Activities Order').[1]

18.5   Credit related regulated activities governed by the Regulated Activities Order include: credit broking (Art 36A), operating an electronic system in relation to lending (Art 36H), debt adjusting (Art 39D), debt counselling (Art 39E), debt administration (Art 39G), entering into regulated credit

---

[1]   SI 2001/544.

agreements (Art 60B), entering into a regulated hire agreement (Art 60N), providing credit information services (Art 89A) and providing credit references (Art 89B).

18.6 Firms can apply for either Full Authorisation or Limited Permission. Full Authorisation is required for 'higher risk' activities such as consumer credit lending, credit brokerage as a primary activity, debt adjusting, debt counselling and debt collection. 'Lower risk' activities might include consumer credit lending as a secondary activity on an interest and charges free basis.

18.7 From 1 April 2014, it is an offence to carry on a regulated activity in the UK, or to purport to do so, unless authorised or exempt.[2] Moreover, it is a criminal offence if an authorised person carries on a credit-related activity in the UK otherwise than in accordance with their permission.

18.8 Agreements made by persons in the course of carrying out a regulated activity in contravention of the general prohibition are unenforceable (s 26 of the FSMA). Credit agreements made by an authorised person acting without permission are unenforceable and the other party is entitled to recover any money or property paid or transferred by that party under the agreement and compensation for any loss sustained by that party as a result of having parted with it (s 26A of the FSMA). The FCA may allow such agreements to be enforced but in doing so must consider whether the person carrying on the regulated activity concerned reasonably believed that he was not contravening the general prohibition or acting without permission by making the agreement (s 28A of the FSMA).

18.9 An agreement made by an authorised person in contravention of s 20 (where a person is authorised but for incorrect activities) is unenforceable against the other party if the agreement includes entering into or administering an agreement under which the person provides another person with credit. The borrower would be entitled to recover money or other property paid or transferred under the agreement as well as compensation for any loss sustained as a result of having parted with it.

18.10 An agreement is unenforceable under s 27(1A) where an agreement is made by an authorised person in the course of carrying out a regulated activity as a consequence of something said or done by another person in the course of a regulated activity in contravention of the general prohibition (for example, where a broker is not authorised).

FCA Handbook

18.11 In addition to the Consumer Credit specific chapter: CONC (which is discussed throughout this chapter), the FCA handbook introduces high level principles to the consumer credit industry. The Principles are a general

---

2   FSMA, s 19 contains the general prohibition. Section 23 sets out the offence.

statement of the fundamental obligations of firms under the regulatory system. Therefore, in addition to complying with the rules in CONC and the CCA, firms must comply with the Principles of Business (PRIN):

(1)   A firm must conduct its business with integrity.

(2)   A firm must conduct its business with due skill, care and diligence.

(3)   A firm must take reasonable care to organise and control its affairs responsibly and effectively, with adequate risk management systems.

(4)   A firm must maintain adequate financial resources.

(5)   A firm must observe proper standards of market conduct.

(6)   A firm must pay due regard to the interests of its customers and treat them fairly.

(7)   A firm must pay due regard to the information needs of its clients, and communicate information to them in a way which is clear, fair and not misleading.

(8)   A firm must manage conflicts of interest fairly, both between itself and its customers and between a customer and another client.

(9)   A firm must take reasonable care to ensure the suitability of its advice and discretionary decisions for any customer who is entitled to rely upon its judgment.

(10) A firm must arrange adequate protection for clients' assets when it is responsible for them.

(11) A firm must deal with its regulators in an open and cooperative way, and must disclose to the appropriate regulator appropriately anything relating to the firm of which that regulator would reasonably expect notice.

A contravention of the rules in PRIN does not give rise to a right of action by a private person under s 138D of the Act; however, the FCA may consider disciplinary action (DEPP 6.2.14 G).

CONSUMER CREDIT AGREEMENTS

18.12 A consumer credit agreement is an agreement between an individual ('the debtor') and any other person ('the creditor') by which the creditor provides the debtor with credit of any amount. A consumer credit agreement is a regulated agreement within the meaning of the CCA if it is a regulated credit agreement for the purposes of Chapter 14A of Part 2 of the Regulated Activities Order (s 15(2) CCA 1974). If an agreement is documented as a regulated agreement but as a matter of law it is not, it is not to be treated as a regulated agreement.[3] A regulated credit agreement means any credit agreement which is not an exempt agreement.

---

3   *NRAM v McAdam* [2015] CTLC 169.

18.13 Since 21 March 2016 credit agreements secured on land, both first and second charges, are governed by FSMA and MCOB as a result of the Mortgage Credit Directive.

CATEGORISATION OF AGREEMENTS

18.14 As a starting point, when looking at an agreement, one must classify it within one of the categories provided by the CCA. This is necessary in order to determine which provisions of the CCA are applicable. The RAO also provides for categorisation but often uses different labels for the same thing as the CCA.

'Individual'

18.15 The CCA regulates 'consumer credit agreements', but these are defined to be agreements with an 'individual'.[4] 'Credit agreement' is defined broadly in the Regulated Activities Order Article 60B(3)(a) as an agreement between an individual *or* relevant recipient of credit ('A') and any other person ('B') under which B provides A with credit of any amount. This mirrors s 8(1) of the CCA. An 'individual' includes (i) a consumer, (ii) a sole trader, (iii) joint debtors where only one is an 'individual',[5] (iv) (for agreements entered before 6 April 2007)[6] any partnership not consisting entirely of bodies corporate and/or (v) (a narrower definition for agreements entered on/after 6 April 2007) any such partnership of up to three partners.[7] A limited liability partnership is probably not an 'individual'.[8] There is an exemption for certain agreements made for business purposes.

'Credit'

18.16 'Credit' is defined broadly, to include 'a cash loan, and any other form of financial accommodation'.[9] In *Dimond v Lovell*,[10] the House of Lords gave a well-known gloss on the statutory definition, essentially saying that credit will be provided if the debtor is granted the contractual right to defer payment of a debt.[11] Therefore the crucial question is often whether the debtor is entitled to defer payment from the date it would otherwise be expected.

---

4   CCA, s 8(1).
5   CCA, s 185(5).
6   In general the narrowing of the definition of 'individual' is effective from 6 April 2007, save for the purposes of sections of the CCA which use the word 'debtor' (Consumer Credit Act 2006 (Commencement No 2 and Transitional Provisions and Savings) Order 2007, SI 2007/123, Arts 4–5.
7   CCA, s 189(1).
8   Guest and Lloyd, *Encyclopaedia of Consumer Credit Law*, vol 1, 2010–2011.
9   CCA, s 9(1).
10   [2002] 1 AC 384.
11   So that the 'contract provides for the debtor to pay, or gives him the option to pay, later than the time on which payment would otherwise have been earned under the express or implied terms of the contract' (395).

18.17 The following arrangements have been held on their facts not to be credit:

(i)   monthly payments of estimated minimum commission to an employee, pursuant to an employment contract (this was advance remuneration for services, rather than credit);[12]

(ii)   monthly payments pursuant to a gym membership contract (these payments were made for continuing access to the facilities, in relation to each month);[13]

(iii)   requiring an after-the-event insurance premium to be paid at the conclusion of the litigation (simply because the premium was required to be paid in the future, this was not deferment as there was no established practice requiring such premiums to be paid at the inception of the policy);[14]

(iv)   where any obligation to pay is postponed until a future possible indebtedness arises (which might not ever arise);[15]

(v)   forbearance by the lender to sue on a right to immediate payment (although this has the same result);[16]

(vi)   where payment is postponed as security for the performance of some other obligation by the creditor;[17]

(vii) a future payment to enable a lease to be assigned.[18]

Hire and hire-purchase agreements

18.18   Hire agreements are defined by CCA, s 15. There must be a requirement for the hirer to make payment in exchange for the bailment of the goods: gratuitous payments are not included.[19] Hire agreements are not usually credit agreements, but hire-purchase agreements are a sub-category of credit agreements.[20] However, throughout this chapter 'creditor' is used as shorthand for 'creditor or owner' and 'debtor' as shorthand for 'debtor or hirer'.

Running-account and fixed-sum credit

18.19   Credit must fall into one of these two categories, which are mutually exclusive. Running-account credit (eg credit cards, bank overdrafts and a dealer's stocking plan agreement) is a facility whereby the debtor can receive from time to time cash/goods/services to a value such that, taking into account

---

12   *McMillan Williams v Range* [2004] 1 WLR 1858, CA.
13   *Office of Fair Trading v Ashbourne Management Services Ltd* [2011] EWHC 1237 (Ch); [2011] CTLC 237.
14   *Tilby v Perfect Pizza Ltd* [2003] CCLR 9.
15   *Nejad v City Index Ltd* [2000] CCLR 7.
16   *Aspinall's Club Ltd v Al-Zayat* [2008] EWHC 2101 (Comm).
17   See *Dimond v Lovell* per Lord Hobhouse.
18   *Burrell v Helical (Bramshott Place) Ltd* [2016] CTLC 1.
19   *TRM Copy Centres (UK) Ltd v Lanwell Services Ltd* [2008] 4 All ER 608; [2008] CTLC 182.
20   CCA, s 9(3).

repayments made by him, the credit limit, if any, is never exceeded.[21] Fixed-sum credit (eg loans, hire-purchase, credit sale and conditional sale agreements) is anything else, even if the credit is paid in instalments.

18.20 If an agreement is truly running-account (eg so that repayments 'refresh' or 'top up' drawings, under a single credit facility), individual draw-downs of credit will not be treated as separate fixed-sum credit agreements, even if different repayment terms are applicable to those draw-downs.[22] However, the contractual earmarking of the first draw-down on a running-account for a specific purpose (eg to discharge existing debt, or to purchase an after-the-event insurance premium) may make that draw-down constitute a separate fixed-sum agreement.[23]

Restricted-use and unrestricted-use credit

18.21 Credit must fall into one of these two categories, which are mutually exclusive. Under CCA, s 11(1), there are three sub-categories of restricted-use credit:

(a)   to finance a transaction with the creditor
      (eg hire-purchase, credit sale or conditional sale);
(b)   to finance a transaction with a third party supplier
      (eg loans to finance the purchase of goods; credit cards (which can be used only with a network of suppliers selected by the card issuer); and credit to finance the purchase of payment protection insurance); or
(c)   to refinance existing debt.

'Finance' includes 'partly' financing (CCA, s 189(1)). There must be a contractual restriction (express or implied) on the purpose of the credit – a common intention which falls short of this does not suffice.[24]

18.22 Anything else is unrestricted-use credit (s 11(2)) (eg cash loans and overdrafts). Unrestricted-use credit also includes agreements where the contractual terms require the credit to be used for a restricted purpose, but the credit in fact passes to the debtor's control, so he is free to use it as he chooses, rather than it being paid directly to the supplier unless CCA, s 12(c) applies (s 11(3)).

---

[21]   CCA, s 10(1).
[22]   See Guest and Lloyd, *Encyclopaedia of Consumer Credit Law*, vol 1, 2023.
[23]   See *Goshawk Dedicated (No 2) Ltd v The Governor and Company of the Bank of Scotland* [2006] 2 All ER 610.
[24]   *National Westminster Bank plc v Story* [1999] Lloyd's Rep Bank 261.

Debtor-creditor (DC) and debtor-creditor-supplier (DCS) agreements

18.23   Credit must fall into one of these two categories, which are mutually exclusive. Under CCA, s 12, DCS agreements have three sub-categories:

(a)   a restricted-use credit agreement where the creditor is also the supplier (ie a s 11(1)(a) agreement) (this is a two-party arrangement, but still DCS);

(b)   a restricted-use credit agreement with a third party supplier (ie a s 11(1)(b) agreement) made by the creditor under pre-existing 'arrangements',[25] or in contemplation of future arrangements, between himself and the supplier;[26]

(c)   an unrestricted-use agreement made under pre-existing arrangements between the creditor and the supplier, in the knowledge that the credit is to be used to finance a transaction between the debtor and the supplier
       (eg if a dealer introduces a customer to a finance company, which knows that the loan will be used to purchase a car from the dealer, even though in theory the loan could be used for other purposes).

Article 60L of the RAO describes this category as 'borrower-lender-supplier').

18.24   Under CCA, s 13, DC agreements also have three sub-categories:

(a)   a restricted-use credit agreement with a third party supplier (ie a s 11(1)(b) agreement) not made by the creditor under pre-existing arrangements, or in contemplation of future arrangements, between himself and the supplier
       (eg a loan to finance the purchase of goods where the creditor, at the debtor's request, paid the loan directly to the supplier);

(b)   a restricted-use credit agreement to refinance existing debt (ie a s 11(1)(c) agreement);

(c)   an unrestricted-use agreement not made under pre-existing arrangements between the creditor and the supplier, in the knowledge that the credit is to be used to finance a transaction between the debtor and the supplier
       (eg a cash loan or bank overdraft).

Article 60L of the RAO describes this category as 'borrower-lender'.

---

[25]   CCA, s 187 defines 'future arrangements' and 'pre-existing arrangements' for the purposes of s 12, but there is no definition of the word 'arrangements' itself; in *OFT v Lloyds TSB Bank plc* [2007] QB 1, CA, it was held that where a supplier had been recruited to accept cards of a particular network (eg Visa/Mastercard) by other members of the network (and not by the card issuer in question), there were 'arrangements' between the supplier and the card issuer, because each had agreed (albeit separately) to adhere to the network rules.

[26]   See *Consolidated Finance Ltd v McCluskey* [2012] CTLC 133; *Consolidated Finance Ltd v Collins* [2013] EWCH Civ 475.

EXEMPT AGREEMENTS

18.25 An agreement is not a regulated credit agreement if it is an exempt agreement. An exempt agreement is an agreement falling within one of the exemptions in Arts 60C–60H of the Financial Services and Markets Act 2000 (Regulated Activities) Order 2001. These include the following types of agreement:

(a) a regulated mortgage contract (Art 60C);

(b) where the agreement provides the borrower with credit exceeding £25,000 and the agreement is entered into by the borrower wholly or predominantly for the purposes of a business carried on, or intended to carried on by the borrower (Art 60C);[27]

(c) agreements made in connection with trade in goods or services between the United Kingdom and a country outside of the United Kingdom (Art 60C);

(d) where sums due under the agreement are secured by a legal (or equitable) mortgage on land and less than 40% of the land is used or is intended to be used, as or in connection with a dwelling by the borrower or in the case of credit provided to trustees, by an individual who is a beneficiary of the trust or a related person of a beneficiary (Art 60D);

(e) an agreement relating to the purchase of land where the lender is a local authority or specified, or of a description specified, in rules made by the FCA (such as a charity, friendly society or an organisation of employers) save where the agreement is of a type described in Art 3(2) of the Mortgage Credit Directive (an agreement secured by a mortgage or which is to acquire or retain property rights in land or in an existing or projected building) and is not exempt by virtue of Article 3(2) of the Directive (Art 60E/Art 60HA);

(f) a linked transaction if it is entered into by the borrower under the principal agreement (which must be financing the purchase of land provision of dwellings on land) and it does not relate to the provision of security and does not form part of the principal agreement, and it is either entered into in compliance with a term of the principal agreement or the transaction is financed or to be financed by the principal agreement (Art 60E(8));

(g) where the lender is an investment firm or a credit institution and the agreement is entered into for the purpose of allowing the borrower to carry out a transaction relating to one or more financial instruments (Art 60E(6);

(h) a borrower-lender-supplier agreement (also known as a debtor-creditor-supplier agreement under the CCA) for fixed-sum credit where the number of payments to be made by the borrower is not more than 12 and made within a period of 12 months or less (beginning with the date of the agreement) (Art 60F);

---

[27] See *Wood v Capital Credit* [2015] EWCA Civ 451.

(i)   a running-account credit agreement where the borrower is to make payments in relation to specified periods which must be, unless the agreement is secured on land, of 3 months or less, the number of payments to be made by the borrower in repayment of the whole amount of credit in each such period is not more than one and the credit is secured on land or provided without interest or other significant charges (Art 60F);

(j)   an agreement to finance the purchase of land where the number of payments to be made by the borrower is not more than four, and the credit is secured on land or provided without interest or other charges (Art 60F(4));

(k)   a borrower-lender-supplier agreement for fixed-sum credit to finance a premium under a contract of insurance relating to land or anything on land, where the lender is the lender under a credit agreement secured by a legal or equitable mortgage on that land, the credit is to be repaid within 12 months or less to which the premium relates and there is no charge forming part of the total charge for credit under the agreement other than interest from time to time payable under the agreement; in the case of an agreement which is not secured on land, the credit is provided without interest or other charges, and the number of payments to be made by the borrower is not more than 12 (Art 60F(5));

(l)   as above but the agreement is to finance a premium under a contract of whole life insurance which provides that in the event of the death of the person on whose life the contract is effected before the credit has been repaid, for payment of a sum not exceeding the amount sufficient to meet the amount which, immediately after that credit has been advanced, would be payable to the lender in respect of that credit (including interest from time to time payable under that agreement) (Art 60F(6));

(m)   a borrower-lender agreement where the lender is a credit union and the rate of the total charge for credit does not exceed 42.6% and the agreement is not of a type described in Article 3(1) of the mortgage directive or it is of such a type but the agreement is of such a kind to which the Mortgage Directive does not apply or the agreement is a bridging loan within the meaning of that directive (Art 60G(2));

(n)   a borrower-lender agreement of a kind offered to a particular class of individual or relevant recipient of credit and not offered to the public generally, which provides that the only charge included in the total charge for credit is interest and interest under the agreement may not at any time be more than the sum of 1% and the highest of the base rates published by the Bank of England on the date 28 days before the date on which the interest is charged, and the total amount to be repaid by the borrower to discharge the borrower's indebtedness will not vary according to a formula which is specified in the agreement and which has effect by reference to movements in the level of any index or other factor, or the agreement is secured on land or is offered by a lender to a borrower as an incident of the borrower's employment with the lender or with an undertaking in the same group as the lender; and does not meet the general interest test (Art 60G(3));

(o) a borrower-lender agreement of a kind offered to a particular class of individual or relevant recipient of credit and not offered to the public generally, which does not provide for or permit an increase in the rate or amount of any item which is included in the total charge for credit, and the total charge for credit under the agreement is not more than the sum of 1% and the highest of the base rates published by the Bank of England on the date 28 days before the date on which the charge is imposed, and the total amount to be repaid by the borrower to discharge the borrower's indebtedness will not vary according to a formula which is specified in the agreement and which has effect by reference to movements in the level of any index or other factor, or the agreement is secured on land or is offered by a lender to a borrower as an incident of the borrower's employment with the lender or with an undertaking in the same group as the lender; and does not meet the general interest test (Art 60G(4));

(p) Where the borrower is an individual and the agreement is secured by land, or is for credit which exceeds £60,260, and, if entered into after 21 March 2016, is for a purpose other than the renovation of residential property, or to acquire or retain property rights in land or in an existing building project, and the agreement includes a declaration by the borrower which provides that the borrower agrees to forgo the protection and remedies that would be available to the borrower if the agreement were a regulated credit agreement, and which complies with rules made by the FCA for the purposes of this paragraph, and a statement made in relation to the income or assets of the borrower which complies with rules made by the FCA for the purposes of this paragraph was provided to the lender before the agreement was entered into (Art 60H).

Partially excluded agreements

18.26 'Non-commercial agreements', which are not made by the creditor in a course of a business[28] are excluded by CCA, s 74, from the form and content and cancellation provisions of the CCA. Overdrafts on a current account are also excluded by CCA, s 74, from these requirements.[29]

AGREEMENTS SECURED ON LAND

18.27 Since 21 March 2016 agreements secured on land whether by first, second or subsequent charge will, subject to exemptions, be subject to FSMA and MCOB as a result of the Mortgage Credit Directive. Article 3(1) MCD provides that the Directive applies to:

---

[28] *Hare v Schurek*: one-off or occasional loans by a motor trader were not made in the course of his business and so were 'non-commercial agreements'.

[29] Although s 74(1B)–(1E) provide that certain provisions nevertheless apply, depending on the type of overdraft.

(a)   credit agreements which are secured either by a mortgage or by another comparable security commonly used in a Member State on residential immovable property or secured by a right related to residential immovable property; and

(b)   credit agreements the purpose of which is to acquire or retain property rights in land or in an existing or projected building.

18.28   Article 3(2) sets out exemptions in the case of:

(a)   Equity release credit agreements where the creditor:
   (i)   contributes a lump sum, periodic payments or other forms of credit disbursement in return for a sum deriving from the future sale of a residential immovable property or a right relating to residential immovable property; and
   (ii)   will not seek repayment of the credit until the occurrence of one or more specified life events of the consumer, as defined by Member States, unless the consumer breaches his contractual obligations which allows the creditor to terminate the credit agreement;

(b)   credit agreements where the credit is granted by an employer to his employees as a secondary activity where such a credit agreement is offered free of interest or at an APRC lower than those prevailing on the market and not offered to the public generally;

(c)   credit agreements where the credit is granted free of interest and without any other charges except those that recover costs directly related to the securing of the credit;

(d)   credit agreements in the form of an overdraft facility and where the credit has to be repaid within one month;

(e)   credit agreements which are the outcome of a settlement reached in court or before another statutory authority;

(f)   credit agreements which relate to the deferred payment, free of charge, of an existing debt and which do not fall within the scope of point (a) of paragraph 1.

18.29   Entering a mortgage contract as lender is a specified kind of activity (Art 61(1) of the RAO) provides that entering into a regulated mortgage contract as a lender is a specified kind of activity. Administering a mortgage contract is also a specified kind of activity where the contract was entered into by way of business on or after 31 October 2004; or the contract was entered into before 31 October 2004, and was a regulated credit agreement immediately before 21 March 2016 (Art 61(2) of the RAO).

CHATTEL SECURITY

18.30 The main legislation dealing with consumer credit which was not repealed by the CCA is that dealing with bills of sale.[30] The legislation remains relevant today. It applies, for example, to 'log-book loans' where credit is granted over the security of a motor vehicle.[31] The application of the legislation was considered in a High Court case dealing with an expensive viola.[32] On 9 September 2015 the Law Commission published a Consultation Paper (No 225) on bills of sale.

GREEN DEAL

18.31 Those Green Deal[33] credit agreements which are regulated agreements are subject to the CCA and CONC, but significant exceptions and qualifications have been made to the legislation in respect of such agreements.[34]

ADVERTISING

18.32 As well as having to comply with general advertising rules and codes (which are outside the scope of this chapter) financial promotions which indicate that a business is willing to provide credit are regulated by the FCA. CONC Chapter 3 applies to communications with a customer in relation to a credit agreement, credit broking, debt counselling or debt adjusting, or approval for communication of a financial promotion in relation to the above.

18.33 CONC 3 does not apply to:

(a) A financial promotion that indicates that it is solely for the promotion of credit agreements or consumer hire agreements or P2P agreements for the purposes of a customer's business.

(b) a financial promotion or a communication to the extent that it relates to qualifying credit or an excluded communication.

(c) a financial promotion or communication that consists of only one or more of the following: the name of the firm, a logo, a contact point, a brief, factual description of the type of product or service provided by the firm.

18.34 CONC 3 applies to a communication to a person in the UK. It will also apply to an unsolicited real time financial promotion unless the communication is from a place, and for the purposes of a business that is only carried on outside the UK. It is immaterial whether the credit agreement or the consumer

---

[30] The most important are the Bills of Sale Act 1878 and the Bills of Sale Act (1878) Amendment Act 1882.

[31] Considered in *Log Book Loans Ltd v OFT* [2011] UKUT 280 (AAC).

[32] *Bossano v Toft* [2014] CTLC 117.

[33] See the Energy Act 2011.

[34] CCA, s 189B.

hire agreement to which the financial promotion or communication relates is subject to the law of a country outside of the UK.

General guidance on advertisements

18.35   A firm must ensure that a communication or a financial promotion is clear, fair, and not misleading. A firm must ensure that the communication:

(a)   uses plain and intelligible language;

(b)   is easily legible (or audible as the case may be);

(c)   Specifies the name of the person making the communication or communicating the financial promotion or the person on whose behalf the financial promotion is made; and

(d)   In relation to credit broking, indicates to the customer the identity of the lender (where it is known).

A firm must not suggest or state, expressly or by implication, that credit is available regardless of the customer's financial circumstances or status.

18.36   Practices likely to contravene the clear, fair and not misleading rule in CONC 3.3.1R include:

(a)   stating or implying that a firm is a lender (where that is not the case);

(b)   misleading a customer as to the availability of a particular credit product;

(c)   concealing or misrepresenting the identity or name of the firm;

(d)   using false testimonials, endorsements or case studies;

(e)   using false or unsubstantiated claims as to the firm's size or experience or pre-eminence;

(f)   in relation to debt solutions, claiming or implying that a customer will be free of debt in a specified period of time or that a debt solution is a stress free or immediate solution;

(g)   providing online tools which recommend a particular debt solution as suitable for a customer which do not carry out a sufficiently full assessment of a customer's financial position.

Risk warning for high-cost short-term credit

18.37   A firm must not communicate, or approve for communication, a financial promotion in relation to high-cost short-term credit, unless it contains the following risk warning displayed in a prominent way:

> Warning: Late repayment can cause you serious money problems. For help, go to moneyadviceservice.org.uk.

A firm may include the Money Advice Service's registered logo instead of the website address. A financial promotion must not be communicated where it indicates that a firm is willing to provide credit under a regulated restricted-use credit agreement relating to goods or services to be supplied by any person, when at the time the financial promotion is communicated, the firm or any supplier under such agreement does not hold itself out as prepared to sell the goods or provide the services for cash.

Representative example

18.38 If the promotion includes a rate of interest or an amount relating to the cost of credit, whether expressed as a sum of money or a proportion of a specified amount, the financial promotion must also include a representative example and specify a postal address at which the person making the financial promotion may be contacted (this last point does not apply where the financial promotion is communicated by television or radio).

18.39 The representative example must comprise of the following items of information:

(a)   the rate of interest and whether it is fixed, variable or both;

(b)   the nature and amount of any other charge included in the total charge for credit;

(c)   the total amount of credit;

(d)   the representative APR;

(e)   in the case of credit in the form of a deferred payment for specific goods, services, land or other things, the cash price and the amount of any advance payment;

(f)   the duration of the agreement;

(g)   the total amount payable;

(h)   the amount of each repayment of credit.

18.40 This information must be:

(a)   specified in a clear and concise way;

(b)   accompanied by the words 'representative example';

(c)   presented together with each item of information being given equal prominence; and

(d)   given greater prominence than any other information relating to the cost of credit in the financial promotion, except for any statement relating to an obligation to enter into a contract for an ancillary service referred to in CONC 3.5.10 R and any indication or incentive of a kind referred to in CONC 3.5.7 R.

18.41 A financial promotion for a credit agreement with no fixed duration is not required to include the duration of the agreement. A financial promotion for an authorised non-business overdraft agreement is not required to include a representative APR. A financial promotion must include the representative APR where it indicates that credit is available to persons who might otherwise consider their access to credit restricted; and where the way in which the credit is offered is more favourable than corresponding ways used in any other case.

18.42 The representative APR must be given greater prominence than any indication or incentive. The APR must be shown as %APR. Where it is subject to change it must be accompanied by the word 'variable', and the representative APR must be accompanied by the word 'representative'. The financial promotion must state where a security is required and specify the nature of the security. It must also clearly and concisely state where there is an obligation to enter into a contract for an ancillary service.

18.43 A financial promotion must not use the following words and phrases: overdraft (as describing running-account credit unless it is in relation to a current account overdraft), interest free (except where the total amount payable does not exceed the cash price), no deposit (except where no advance payments are to be made), the expression loan guaranteed or pre-approved/no credit checks (except where the agreement is free of any conditions regarding the credit status of the customer), the expression gift or present (except where there are no conditions which would require the customer to repay the credit or to return the item that is the subject of the claim).

18.44 CONC 3.6.5 provides specific wording that must be included in a financial promotion where security comprises or may comprise a mortgage or charge on the customer's home. Failing to comply with the advertising rules in CONC 3 will not give rise to a right of action under 138D of the FSMA where reasonable steps have been taken to ensure that the financial promotion is clear, fair and not misleading.

FORM AND CONTENT OF AGREEMENTS

18.45 Certain agreements which should not need to comply with extensive formalities requirements are excluded from the entire CCA form and content requirements by CCA, s 74 (eg overdrafts). Otherwise, there are very detailed provisions regulating the drafting of agreements, set out in subordinate regulations. CCA, s 61(1)(a) provides that a regulated agreement is 'not properly executed' unless it conforms to these regulations. The consequences of an agreement being 'improperly executed' are that it is only enforceable against the debtor on an order of the court (CCA, s 65).

18.46 This chapter can only offer a rough guide to the extremely detailed legislative provisions on the drafting of credit and hire agreements. In some cases pre-6 April 2007 the unenforceability can be irredeemable. At the outset, it should be noted that consumer credit agreements are constructed around several basic financial concepts, which include:

- the amount of credit (ie the amount of the advance in a fixed-sum agreement);
- the total charge for credit ('the TCC') (interest and other charges);
- the total amount payable ('the TAP') (the sum total of the amount of credit and TCC).

Whether old regime or 2010 regime applies

18.47 Confusingly, there are now two sets of regulations for drafting agreements: the Consumer Credit (Agreements) Regulations 1983 ('the 1983 Agreements Regulations') and the Consumer Credit (Agreements) Regulations 2010 ('the 2010 Agreements Regulations'). In addition agreements falling within the MCD must comply with the disclosure requirements in MCOB 7.

18.48 The 2010 Agreements Regulations implement the Consumer Credit Directive 2008/48/EC ('the CC Directive') and came into force on 1 February 2011. However, there was an earlier 'opt-in' date from 30 April 2010 for creditors who have got their tackle in order and wish to implement the entire CC Directive regime in advance.[35]

18.49 Some types of credit agreements are outside the scope of the CC Directive. The 2010 regime treats these agreements as excluded agreements. However, there is a second form of 'opt-in': creditors who enter excluded agreements may choose to opt-in to the 2010 regime.

18.50 Accordingly, the old regime (including the 1983 Agreements Regulations)[36] applies to the following agreements:

(i)   all credit agreements made before 30 April 2010;

(ii) credit agreements made between 30 April 2010 and 31 January 2011, unless the creditor has opted to implement the new regime early;

(iii) credit agreements entered on/after 1 February 2011, where the agreements are outside the scope of the 2010 regime (and the creditor has not 'opted in' to the 2010 regime);

(iv) all regulated hire agreements, whenever made.

18.51 The 2010 regime applies in the following situations:

(i)   all credit agreements made on/after 1 February 2011 which are within the scope of the 2010 regime;

(ii) credit agreements made between 30 April 2010 and 31 January 2011, where the creditor has opted to implement the new regime early;

---

[35] The Consumer Credit (EU Directive) Regulations 2010, reg 101: any one of certain conditions must be satisfied in order to opt-in to the new regime early.
[36] See reg 8.

(iii)   credit agreements entered on/after 1 February 2011, where the agreements are outside the scope of the 2010 regime and the creditor chooses to 'opt in' to the 2010 regime.

Agreements outside the scope of the 2010 regime

18.52   The following types of agreements are excluded from the scope of the 2010 Agreements Regulations (reg 2(1A) and (3)):

(i)   agreements secured on land to which CCA, s 58 does apply, where the creditor gives the debtor an advance copy of the agreement containing the prescribed notice of his right to withdraw;

(ii)   agreements secured on land to which CCA, s 58 does not apply (mortgages to finance the purchase of the land and agreements for bridging loans in connection with the purchase of land);

(iii)   agreements for credit exceeding £60,260;

(iv)   'business agreements' (entered wholly/predominantly for the purposes of a business carried on/intended to be carried on by the debtor).

In addition, hire agreements are not covered by the 2010 Agreements Regulations, which only refer to 'credit agreements'.

Means of 'opt-in'

18.53   If an agreement is outside the scope of the 2010 Agreements Regulations, the creditor can nonetheless 'opt-in' (reg 2(2)) by disclosing pre-contract credit information in compliance or purported compliance with the Consumer Credit (Disclosure of Information) Regulations 2010 (rather than in compliance with the predecessor regulations on disclosure). This right to opt-in cannot be exercised for overdraft agreements (reg 2(4)), which broadly only need to comply with the form and content provisions in reg 8.

1983 Agreements Regulations: order and presentation

18.54   The 1983 Agreements Regulations were substantially amended with effect from 31 May 2005. The requirements applicable prior to that date are outside the scope of this chapter.

18.55   Pursuant to reg 2(4),[37] regulated agreements must give fundamental information in a certain order ('the holy ground'), namely:

(i)   a statement of the nature of the agreement and the parties;[38]

---

[37]   See reg 3(4) for hire agreements.
[38]   1983 Agreements Regulations, Sch 1, paras 1–2.

(ii) 'Key Financial Information';[39] (amount of credit; credit limit; term of agreement; total amount payable; timing and amounts of repayments; APR);

(iii) 'Other Financial Information';[40] (not for hire agreements) (description of goods/services/land; cash price; advance payments; total charge for credit/interest rate; appropriation of payments; variable rates/items);

(iv) 'Key Information';[41]

(v) signature box;[42]

(vi) any separate signature box for the financing of insurance;[43]

(vii) information statements of protection and remedy (see below).

Within each of these subheadings, the required information may be shown in any order.

18.56 All of the information within the holy ground must be 'shown together as a whole', not preceded by any other information (except trade names, logos or the agreement number) and not 'interspersed' with any other information (except subtotals of sums and cross-references to terms) (reg 2(4)). Copies of cancellable agreements require special cancellation notices[44] and consideration copies of some agreements secured on land require notices of the right to withdraw.[45] In addition to the information in the 'holy ground', all regulated consumer credit agreements must contain all of the Sch 1 'information' (in so far as it is applicable to the type of agreement in question) (reg 2(1)). Similarly, all regulated consumer hire agreements must contain the Sch 3 'information' (reg 3(1)). The meaning of some of these items of information is discussed below.

18.57 Further, the majority of regulated agreements must contain the 'Forms' of Statements of protection and remedies under the CCA available to debtors/hirers set out in Sch 2 (for credit agreements; reg 2(3)) and Sch 4 (for hire agreements; reg 3(3)). Schedule 5 sets out 'Forms' of signature boxes for various types of agreements. The wording of any of the applicable Forms in Schs 2, 4 and 5 must be reproduced on the agreement 'without any alteration or addition' (reg 5(1)).[46] This is a strict requirement and the *de minimis* principle cannot be applied[47] (although the court will usually have a discretion to enforce the agreement under CCA, s 127(1)).

---

[39] Sch 1, paras 6–8B, 11–14 and 15–17.
[40] Sch 1, paras 3–5, 9, 10, 14A and 18–19A.
[41] Set out items in reg 2(4)(e), include the Sch 2 statements of protection and remedies.
[42] And, if relevant, the additional reg 2(7)(b) boxes, eg for secured/cancellable agreements.
[43] Reg 2(7)(a).
[44] See CCA, s 64.
[45] CCA s 58 and the Consumer Credit (Cancellation Notices and Copies of Documents) Regulations 1983.
[46] Save for the very limited deviations permitted by reg 5(1).
[47] *Rank Xerox Finance Ltd v Hepple & Pennymore* [1994] CCLR 1.

18.58 There is no corresponding requirement to reproduce the exact wording of 'information' in Schs 1 and 3.[48] Where any such Form uses capital lettering, those words must be afforded more prominence than the other words in the Form, and no less prominence than that given to other information in the agreement (except the heading etc) (reg 5(4)). The lettering of the required information and any terms of the agreement must be 'easily legible' and of 'equal prominence' (except the heading etc) (reg 6(2); CCA, s 61(1)). There are special provisions on the drafting of multiple agreements[49] and modifying agreements,[50] which are outside the scope of this chapter.

2010 Agreements Regulations: order and presentation

18.59 All regulated consumer credit agreements must contain all the Sch 1 'information' (in so far as it is applicable to the type of agreement in question) (reg 3(1)). In contrast to the position under the 1983 Agreements Regulations, there is no prescribed order or 'holy ground' within which this information must be set out.

18.60 The Sch 1 information must be presented in a 'clear and concise' manner and 'clear' means inter alia that the wording be 'easily legible' and of a colour which is easily distinguishable from the background (reg 3(2)–(3)). However, there is no express prohibition on interspersing (as under the 1983 Agreements Regulations). Further, the majority[51] of regulated agreements must contain the 'Forms' of Statements of protection and remedies under the CCA available to debtors set out in Sch 2 (reg 3(4)).

18.61 The wording of any of the applicable Forms in Sch 2 must be reproduced on the agreement 'without any alteration' (reg 7(1)).[52] In contrast to the 1983 Agreements Regulations, 'additions' are not expressly prohibited. There is no corresponding requirement to reproduce the exact wording of 'information' in Sch 1.[53] Where any such Form uses capital lettering, those words must be afforded more prominence than the other words in the Form, and no less prominence than that given to other information in the agreement (except the heading etc) (reg 7(4)). There are special provisions on the drafting of multiple agreements[54] and modifying agreements,[55] which are outside the scope of this chapter.

---

[48]   *Wilson v Hurstanger* [2007] CTLC 59: describing the amount of credit as 'net amount of loan' was permissible.

[49]   See eg reg 2(8)–(9).

[50]   Reg 7 and 8(2).

[51]   This requirement does not apply to secured agreements to which CCA, s 58 applies, where there are no charges forming part of the TCC.

[52]   Save for the very limited deviations permitted by reg 7(1).

[53]   *Wilson v Hurstanger* [2007] CTLC 59: describing the amount of credit as 'net amount of loan' was permissible.

[54]   See, eg, reg 3(6)–(7).

[55]   Reg 5.

Both Agreements Regulations: comments on various pieces of information

Amount of credit

18.62 All fixed-sum credit agreements must include a term stating the amount of credit.[56] The amount of credit does not include any item falling within the TCC, even if time is allowed for its payment (CCA, s 9(4)). Therefore, even if a charge is added to the amount of the advance (as a front-loading charge), it will not be part of the amount of credit.

18.63 In *Wilson v First County Trust Ltd (No 1)*,[57] a 'document fee' of £250 was added to the £5,000 advance, as the debtor did not wish to pay it at the outset. The amount of credit was stated to be £5,250, which the Court of Appeal held to be non-compliant, as the document fee was part of the TCC.

18.64 Fees deducted from the amount of the advance should also not be included in the amount of credit: the amount of credit must be the net advance made to the debtor. In agreements secured on land premiums for payment protection insurance should be stated as an amount of credit, where the insurance is not required by the creditor as a condition of the loan.[58] Other insurance premiums will also be part of the amount of credit (but mortgage indemnity fees will not).[59]

18.65 In *McGinn v Grangewood Securities Ltd*[60] the small-print of the agreement required any arrears on the debtor's first mortgage to be discharged on/before completion of the loan. The balance of the advance would then be paid to the debtor. The Court of Appeal held that the amount of the advance used to discharge the arrears was part of the TCC and should not have been included in the amount of credit. The 'purpose' of the loan for the debtor was home improvements, not to clear her arrears (which she was unaware existed).

18.66 *McGinn* was confined to its peculiar facts in the subsequent case of *London North Securities v Meadows*,[61] where the debtors were informed that clearing the arrears on their first mortgage was a condition of the loan. The Court of Appeal held that clearing the arrears was one of the 'objective purposes of the transaction' and therefore that payment was properly treated as part of the amount of credit.[62]

---

[56] 1983 Agreements Regulations, Sch 1, para 2; 2010 Agreements Regulations, Sch 1, paras 5 and 6.

[57] [2001] QB 407.

[58] CONC Appendix 1.1.5(c).

[59] *Griffiths v Welcome Financial Services* [2007] CTLC 37.

[60] [2002] EWCA Civ 522.

[61] [2005] EWCA Civ 956.

[62] See also *Watchtower Investments v Payne* [2001] EWCA Civ 1159: sums advanced to discharge the arrears under a previous agreement were part of the 'credit', as they formed part of the 'objective purpose' of the loan.

18.67 The label 'amount of credit' need not be used. In assessing whether the agreement contains a 'term stating the amount of credit' there is case-law to the effect that the document must be considered as a whole and the constituent information need not be in one place: it suffices if the debtor can calculate the amount of credit from the financial information provided and 'knowledge' that the amount of credit excludes items in the TCC.[63]

18.68 In *Hurstanger Ltd v Wilson*,[64] the Court of Appeal held that it was a matter of construction whether the agreement contained a 'term' stating the amount of credit: this was a term 'which the parties (with the benefit of legal advice if necessary) and/or the court can identify within the four corners of the agreement'. However, in that case the agreement did set out a figure which was the amount of credit (albeit described as 'net amount of loan').

Total charge for credit

18.69 The Total Charge for Credit Regulations have been replaced by CONC Appendix 1. The TCC is the total of the amounts determined as at the date of making the credit agreement of such of the following charges:

(a) the total of the interest on the credit which may be provided under the credit agreement;

(b) other charges at any time payable under the transaction by or on behalf of the borrower or a relative of his whether to the lender or any other person; and

(c) (for land secured agreements) a premium under a contract of insurance, payable under the transaction by the borrower or a relative of his, where the making or maintenance of the contract of insurance is required by the lender as a condition of making the credit agreement, and for the sole purpose of ensuring complete or partial repayment of the credit and complete or partial payment to the lender of such of those charges included in the total charge for credit as are payable to him under the transaction, in the event of the death, invalidity, illness or unemployment or the borrower, notwithstanding that the whole part of the charge may be repayable at any time or that the consideration therefore may include matters not within the transaction or subsisting at a time not within the duration of the credit agreement.

18.70 Items excluded from the TCC include:

(a) any charge payable under the transaction to the lender upon failure by the borrower or a relative of his to do or to refrain from doing anything which he is required to do or to refrain from doing, as the case may be;

---

[63] *Ocwen v Hughes; Igroup UK Loans Ltd v Freel* [2004] CCLR 4; but cf the stricter approach in *Central Trust plc v Spurway* [2005] CCLR 1 where it was thought a lay reader should not have to attempt his own calculation; both were county court decisions.

[64] [2007] 1 WLR 2351; CTLC 59.

(b)   any charge which is payable by the lender to any person upon failure by the borrower or a relative of his to do or to refrain from doing anything which he is required under the transaction to do or to refrain from doing, as the case may be, and which the lender may under the transaction require the borrower or a relative of his to pay to him or to another person on his behalf;

(c)   any charge relating to a credit agreement to finance a transaction of a description referred to in the definition of restricted-use credit agreement, being a charge which would be payable if the transaction were for cash;

(d)   any charge (other than a fee or commission charged by a credit broker) not within (c) above of a description which relates to services or benefits incidental to the credit agreement and also to other services or benefits which may be supplied to the borrower, and which is payable pursuant to an obligation incurred by the borrower under arrangements effected before he applies to enter into the credit agreement, not being arrangements under which the borrower is bound to enter into any credit agreement;

(e)   any charge under arrangements for the care, maintenance or protection of any land or goods where the services are to be performed after the date of making the credit agreement and the condition of the land or goods becomes or is in immediate danger of becoming such that the land or goods cannot reasonably be enjoyed or used and the charge will not accrue unless the services are performed, or such provision is available under comparable arrangements from a person chosen by the borrower, and if the consent of the lender is required, the transaction provides that such consent may not be unreasonably withheld;

(f)   charges for money transmission services relating to an arrangement for a current account, being charges which vary with the use made by the borrower of the arrangement;

(g)   any charge for a guarantee other than a guarantee which is required by the lender as a condition of making the credit agreement, and the purpose of which is to ensure complete or partial repayment of the credit, and complete or partial payment to the lender of such of those charges included in the total charge for credit as are payable to him under the transaction, in the event of the death, invalidity, illness or unemployment of the borrower;

(h)   charges for the transfer of funds (other than charges within (f) above) and charges for keeping an account intended to receive payments towards the repayment of the credit and the payment of interest and other charges, except where the borrower does not have reasonable freedom of choice in the matter and where such charges are abnormally high; but this sub-paragraph does not exclude from the total charge for credit charges for collection of the payments to which it refers, whether such payments are made in cash or otherwise;

(i)   a premium under a contract of insurance other than a contract of insurance referred to in CONC App 1.1.5R(c).

Credit limit

18.71 Agreements for running-account credit do not include any 'amount of credit', but must instead state the credit limit, which may be expressed as:[65]

(a) a sum of money;

(b) a statement that the credit limit will be determined by the creditor from time to time under the agreement (and that notice of it will be given to the debtor);

(c) a sum of money, together with a statement that the creditor may vary the credit limit to such sum as he may from time to time determine under the agreement (and that notice of it will be given to the debtor); or

(d) in a case not within (a), (b) or (c), either a statement indicating the manner in which the credit limit will be determined and that notice of it will be given to the debtor, or a statement indicating that there is no credit limit.

18.72 Under a running-account agreement, the 'credit limit' is the maximum amount up to which the debtor may draw (CCA, s 10(2)). Therefore it is irrelevant for the purposes of determining the credit limit whether the draw-downs include items which are part of the TCC and are not 'credit'.

18.73 The credit limit is also a 'prescribed term', but under the 1983 Agreements Regulations, Sch 6, para 3 is much shorter than Sch 1, para 8 above, and simply states that the agreement must include a 'term stating the credit limit or the manner in which it will be determined or that there is no credit limit'. However, a statement that the credit limit will be determined from time to time and notified to the debtor is in accordance with Sch 1, para 8 and therefore will also satisfy Sch 6 to the 1983 Agreements Regulations.[66]

APR

18.74 The APR is calculated using the equation in CONC App 1.2.6 R which equates, on an annual basis, to the total present value of drawdowns with the total present value of repayments and payments of charges. All regulated agreements must disclose the APR.[67] Under the 1983 Agreements Regulations, the APR must simply be stated as the 'APR' or 'annual percentage rate' and, where it is subject to change, must be described as 'variable' (reg 2(6)). Under the 2010 Agreements Regulations, all the assumptions used to calculate the APR must be specified (Sch 1, para 13).

---

[65] 1983 Agreements Regulations, Sch 1, para 8; 2010 Agreements Regulations, Sch 1, para 7.
[66] *Brophy v HFC Bank Ltd* [2011] EWCA Civ 67.
[67] 1983 Agreements Regulations, Sch 1, para 15; 2010 Agreements Regulations, Sch 1, para 13.

Interest rate

18.75 Under the 1983 Agreements Regulations, all regulated agreements must include the information in Sch 1, para 9 or 10, namely (i) the TCC[68] (with a list of its constituent parts), (ii) the interest rate (or, where more than one rate applies, all the rates in all cases quoted on a p/a basis, with details of when each rate applies), (iii) a statement explaining how and when interest charges are calculated and applied under the agreement and (iv) (in the case of running-account and limited fixed-sum exceptions) a statement whether any interest rate is fixed or variable.

18.76 If a future rate/charge is unknown, then estimated information must be included (reg 2(2)), unless it falls to be described as 'variable' (reg 2(6)). Under the 2010 Agreements Regulations, there is no requirement to state the TCC separately (although the TAP, being the sum of the TCC and the amount of credit, is required information under Sch 1, para 12; charges, the interest rate and APR must also be stated).

18.77 Pursuant to the 2010 Agreements Regulations, Sch 1, para 11, the interest rate and, where available, any reference rate on which that rate is based (eg a base rate) must be stated. Further, in relation to each applicable interest rate, the agreement must set out:

(i)   the conditions governing the application of the rate;

(ii)   the period during which the rate will apply; and

(iii) the conditions and procedure for changing the rate.

18.78 The 1983 and 2010 Agreements Regulations do 'not purport to dictate how the interest rate is to be expressed'[69] (eg flat, 'present value', nominal, simple or compound). In order not to mislead, the type of rate should be carefully selected and identified. A flat rate can be misleading, as it takes no account of the reduction of the outstanding balance through repayments over time. On the other hand, a flat rate is more comprehensible to the average debtor.

18.79 In *Brooks v Northern Rock (Asset Management) plc*,[70] it was held that the 1983 Agreements Regulations left the creditor free to cite either a nominal or effective interest rate 'or indeed some other rate'. The court also held that the interest rate could be cited to any number of decimal places and there was no need to round up (but in the case of agreements not secured on land see CONC App 1.1.2.6(3)(f)).

---

[68] Total charge for credit.
[69] *Sternlight v Barclays Bank plc* [2010] EWHC 1865, [2010] CTLC 115, in relation to the 1983 Agreements Regulations.
[70] Unreported, Oldham County Court, 16 April 2010.

Timings and amounts of repayments

18.80   Under the 1983 Agreements Regulations, regulated agreements must include the information in Sch 1, para 12, namely the timing of repayments expressed by reference to one/more of the following:

(a)   the dates of repayments;

(b)   the frequency and number of repayments and the date of the first repayment (or a statement indicating the manner in which that date will be determined);

(c)   a statement indicating the manner in which the dates of repayments will be determined.

18.81   Under the 2010 Agreements Regulations, Sch 1, para 14 simply requires 'the number (if applicable) and frequency of repayments'. Further, under both the 1983 and 2010 Agreements Regulations,[71] regulated agreements must include the amount of each repayment expressed as:

(a)   a sum of money;

(b)   a specified proportion of a specified amount (including the amount outstanding from time to time);

(c)   a combination of (a) and (b) above; or

(d)   in a case where the amount of any repayment cannot be expressed in accordance with (a), (b) or (c), a statement indicating the manner in which the amount will be determined.

18.82   In *Wilson v Hurstanger Ltd*,[72] the agreement stated that a £295 charge was repayable upon termination, plus 1.29% interest per month on the charge. Since the agreement had a fixed term, the creditor could theoretically have stated the total sum payable in respect of this charge upon termination (and therefore subparagraph (d) above did not apply). The Court of Appeal held that there was a failure to state the information in this paragraph compliantly, as the debtor was left to make the calculation himself.

18.83   If subparagraph (d) does apply, it is arguable that the creditor could simply state that the amount of the repayment will be determined at its discretion and notified to the debtor, without providing any formula.[73]

Variable items/rates

18.84   Under the 1983 Agreements Regulations, agreements under which the rate/amount of any item in the TCC[74] may be varied (except upon an event which is certain to occur) must include two statements: (i) an indication that in

---

71   1983 Agreements Regulations Sch 1, para 13; 2010 Agreements Regulations, Sch 1, para 15.
72   [2007] EWCA Civ 299; [2007] CTLC 59.
73   Guest and Lloyd, *Encyclopaedia of Consumer Credit Law*, vol 1, 3136/8.
74   Total charge for credit.

calculating the APR no account has been taken of any contractual variation which may occur to the rate/amount of any item (Sch 1, para 18) and (ii) any indication of the circumstances in which any such variation may occur and (if this is ascertainable) when (Sch 1, para 19).

18.85 Under the 2010 Agreements Regulations, the paragraphs of Sch 1 relating to the interest rate and charges (paras 11 and 18) both require the agreement to specify the 'conditions' under which a variation may occur. Further, para 13, which relates to the APR, requires the agreement to set out all the assumptions used to calculate that rate.

18.86 The agreement in *Lombard Tricity Finance Ltd v Paton*[75] displayed an asterisk beside certain items indicating that they were 'subject to variation by the creditor from time to time on notification as required by law'. The Court of Appeal held that this satisfied the requirements of para 19 of Sch 1 to the 1983 Agreements Regulations, as the creditor's discretion to vary was genuinely unfettered. This case was disapproved in *Paragon Finance plc v Nash and Staunton*,[76] on the ground that the creditor's discretion to vary an interest rate is subject to an implied term that it will not vary it arbitrarily or in a way no reasonable lender would.

18.87 In *McGinn v Grangewood Securities Ltd*,[77] the agreement stated that the creditor might defer payment of legal fees 'at its discretion'. In fact, payment of the fees was only deferred on condition that contractual interest was payable on the fees. The agreement was held to be non-compliant, as it failed to state that deferment would be made only on condition that interest was paid, and failed to specify the rate of that interest.

Default charges

18.88 Under the 1983 Agreements Regulations, all regulated agreements must contain the information in Sch 1, para 22, namely a list of any default charges and a statement indicating any term which provides for other charges, or charges not included in the TCC. There is no requirement to state the 'amounts' of default charges.

18.89 Default charges are defined in Sch 1, para 22 as 'charges payable under the agreement' upon failure by the debtor/a relative of his to do or not do something required/prohibited. A broad construction of 'charges' was given in *Rank Xerox v Hepple*[78] to include sums payable under an accelerated payment clause and common law damages payable upon default.

---

75   [1989] 1 All ER 918.
76   [2002] 1 WLR 685.
77   [2002] EWCA Civ 522.
78   [1994] CCLR 1.

18.90 Under the 2010 Agreements Regulations, the agreement must identify any 'charges deriving from the credit agreement' (Sch 1, para 18) and any charges and interest applicable upon late payment (Sch 1, para 19).

Both Agreements Regulations: prescribed terms

18.91 Certain terms, namely those specified in Sch 6 are designated 'prescribed terms' by reg 6(1) of the 1983 Agreements Regulations. Those terms are as follows:

(a)   the amount of credit (for fixed-sum credit agreements);

(b)   the credit limit (for running-account credit);

(c)   the interest rate (for running-account credit or limited types of fixed-sum[79] credit);

(d)   a term stating how the repayment obligations must be discharged.

18.92   All of these Sch 6 terms replicate items of information within Sch 1: they are already required to be included as Sch 1 information, but they are repeated in Sch 6 to highlight their status as 'prescribed terms'. In the 2010 Agreements Regulations, reg 4 designates certain items of Sch 1 information as 'prescribed terms'. These are the same terms as those in Sch 6 to the 1983 Agreements Regulations (save that the interest rate is prescribed for all types of regulated credit agreement).

18.93   In respect of agreements entered prior to 6 April 2007, the 'prescribed terms' had enormous significance, as an agreement which failed to contain all the prescribed terms was 'irredeemably unenforceable' under CCA, s 127(3). However, following the repeal of CCA, s 127(3), for agreements entered after 6 April 2007 it appears that 'prescribed terms' have no different status from any other terms of the agreement.

Single document

18.94   There is a practical question as to whether the full terms and conditions may be provided on a separate sheet from the face of the agreement.

18.95   CCA, s 61(1)(a) requires a properly executed agreement to be 'a document ... itself containing all the prescribed terms'. Therefore the prescribed terms must be contained in the same 'document' as the agreement.

18.96   In *Carey v HSBC Bank Plc*,[80] HHJ Waksman QC considered the question of what constituted a single document for the purposes of s 61, and concluded (at paras 171–174) a document need not be a single piece of paper; the question of what constitutes a document is a question of substance and not

---

79   Those falling within the exceptions in Sch 1, para 9(a)–(c).
80   [2009] EWHC 3417 (QB); [2009] CTLC 103.

form; and a physical connection between several pieces of paper is not necessary in order for them to constitute one document.

18.97 In respect of the other terms and conditions (ie terms which are not 'prescribed'), the requirement is only that they be 'embodied' in the agreement, and not necessarily contained in the same 'document' (s 61(1)(b)). Section 189(4) of the CCA provides:

> A document embodies a provision if the provision is set out either in the document itself or in another document referred to in it.

Therefore the agreement may cross-reference a booklet of full terms and conditions.

18.98 All express terms are required by s 61(1)(b) to be 'embodied' by the signed document: this requirement extends to terms which are part of the agreement between the parties, albeit not required by Regulations (eg a term that part of the advance must be used to consolidate existing debt should be embodied in the signed document).[81]

Signing

18.99 The agreement must be signed by the debtor/hirer[82] in the designated signature box (for the 2010 regime 'in the space in the document indicated for the purpose').[83] The requirements are more lax for the creditor: the signature may be inserted on its 'behalf' and may be added anywhere on the agreement (as long as it is outside the debtor's signature box).[84] The creditor's signature is often stamped rather than handwritten.

18.100 For agreements entered prior to 6 April 2007, the agreement will be irredeemably unenforceable if not signed by the debtor in the prescribed manner (CCA, s 127(3) – there is no equivalent effect if the creditor fails to sign). If any agreement is unsigned by the creditor, or if any agreement entered on/after 6 April 2007 is unsigned by the debtor, the agreement will be enforceable only on an order of the court under s 127(1). The date of signature should also be inserted by both parties, but this is not a strict requirement where the agreement is not cancellable and the last party to sign[85] dates his signature.[86]

---

[81] See Guest and Lloyd, *Encyclopaedia of Consumer Credit Law*, vol 1, 2089/90.
[82] Subject to CCA, s 61(4) re partnerships.
[83] Reg 6(3)(a) of the 1983 Agreements Regulations; reg 4(3)(a) of the 2010 Agreements Regulations.
[84] Reg 6(3)(b) of the 1983 Agreements Regulations; reg 4(3)(b) of the 2010 Agreements Regulations.
[85] Ie the party who makes the agreement 'executed' (usually the creditor).
[86] Reg 6(3)(c) of the 1983 Agreements Regulations; reg 4(3)(c) of the 2010 Agreements Regulations.

18.101 An agreement will only be 'executed' under s 61 once it has been signed by both parties, but it may nonetheless be a 'concluded' agreement under the contractual principles of offer and acceptance without the creditor's signature (eg if the creditor has performed some other act such as delivering the subject goods to the customer).[87] Regulated agreements may be signed by electronic means, but there is no statutory guidance on permissible forms of electronic signatures and an online click should suffice.[88]

Copies of agreement: old regime

18.102 Unless the 2010 regime applies, the creditor is obliged:

(a) to supply a CCA, s 62 copy of the unexecuted agreement (unless the agreement is presented personally to the debtor for his signature and the creditor has already signed it, or signs at the same time);

(b) to supply a CCA, s 63 copy of the executed agreement (unless the agreement is sent to the debtor for his signature and the creditor has already signed it).

18.103 If the agreement is presented personally to the debtor for his signature and the creditor will sign later, then at that time the debtor must be given a s 62 unexecuted copy, and within 7 days after the creditor's signature he must be given a s 63 executed copy. If the agreement is presented personally to the debtor for his signature and the creditor has already signed it, or signs at the same time, then a s 63 executed copy must be given to the debtor at that time (s 63(1), (2)(a)). No s 62 copy is required.

18.104 If a copy of the unexecuted agreement is sent/posted to the debtor to sign, a s 62 unexecuted copy must also be sent at the same time. A s 63 executed copy must be sent within 7 days after the creditor's signature (unless the creditor signed first). In the case of a credit card agreement, the s 63 executed copy need not be given within 7 days of the creditor's signature as long as it is given before or at the same time as the credit card is sent (the copy is usually with/on the card carrier) (s 63(4)).

18.105 The ss 62 and 63 copies must include a copy of any other document 'referred to' in the credit agreement (eg a legal charge). The form and content of the ss 62 and 63 copies must comply with the Consumer Credit (Cancellation Notices and Copies of Documents) Regulations 1983. Overdrafts are again exempt (CCA, s 74).

---

[87] *Carlyle Finance Ltd v Pallas Industrial Finance Ltd* [1999] 1 All ER (Comm) 659 (such an analysis may be required in order to determine whether and when title to goods has passed).

[88] See the Consumer Credit Act 1974 (Electronic Communications) Order 2004; the CCA definition of 'document' is now 'information recorded in any form'. Guest and Lloyd, *Encyclopaedia of Consumer Credit Law*, vol 1, 2095 and Philpott 'E-commerce and Consumer Credit' [2001] JLFM 131. See also *Bassano v Toft* [2014] CTLC 117.

18.106 In the case of cancellable agreements, s 64 obliges both the ss 62 and 63 copies to include the prescribed cancellation notice. In situations where only one copy is required (either under s 62 or 63), a cancellation notice must also be sent to the debtor within the seven days after execution (except where a s 63 executed copy must in any case be given within seven days under s 63(2)) (for credit card agreements, this need not be done within seven days, provided the cancellation notice is sent before or together with the credit card).

18.107 Non-compliance with ss 62, 63 or 64 renders the agreement unenforceable save on a court order (ss 62–65). In some pre-6 April 2007 situations for cancellable agreements a failure may result in irredeemable unenforceability under the repealed CCA, s 127(4).[89]

Copies of agreement: 2010 regime

18.108 Under the new regime, CCA, s 61A obliges the creditor to give the debtor a copy of the 'executed agreement' (and any other document referred to in it). This must be done where the agreement 'has been made' (s 61A(1)). There is no prescribed time limit.

18.109 The obligation to provide a copy of the executed agreement does not arise if the debtor has already been given an unexecuted copy, which is in identical terms to the executed agreement (s 61A(2)). In such a case, the creditor must write to the debtor to state this, and inform him of his right to request an executed copy within 14 days (s 61A(3)).

18.110 Where the creditor signs first and then posts the agreement to the debtor to sign, the natural reading of s 61A is that, after the debtor returns the signed agreement, the creditor must then either post an executed copy or write to the debtor under sub-s (3). However, such an interpretation increases the creditor's obligations compared to those under the old regime, where no s 63 executed copy need be provided in this situation.[90] Copies of overdraft agreements are separately dealt with by CCA, s 61B.

18.111 The ss 61A and 61B copies must comply with the Consumer Credit (Cancellation Notices and Copies of Documents) Regulations 1983 (where applicable). Non-compliance with ss 61A and 61B renders the agreement unenforceable save on a court order (ss 61A, 61B and 65). Section 61A does not apply to cancellable agreements; the old ss 62–63 regime applies to such agreements (s 61A(5)).

---

[89] See *Goshawk Dedicated (No 2) v Bank of Scotland* [2006] 2 All ER 610 and *Bank of Scotland v Euclidian Ltd (No 1)* [2007] CTLC 151.

[90] See Guest and Lloyd, *Encyclopaedia of Consumer Credit Law*, vol 1, 2098.

PRE-CONTRACTUAL OBLIGATIONS

Assessment of creditworthiness

18.112 CONC 5.2 provides that before making a regulated credit agreement a firm must undertake an assessment of the creditworthiness of a customer. The firm must consider:

(a) the potential for the commitments under the regulated credit agreement to adversely impact on the customer's financial situation, taking into account the information of which the firm is aware at the time that the regulated credit agreement is to be made;

(b) the ability of the customer to make repayments as and when they fall due over the life of the regulated credit agreement, or for such an agreement which is an open-end agreement, to make repayments within a reasonable period.

A creditworthiness assessment must be based on sufficient information obtained from the customer and a credit reference agency where necessary.

18.113 The rule does not apply to the following agreements:

(a) an agreement secured on land;

(b) a pawn agreement;

(c) a non-commercial agreement;

(d) a borrower-lender agreement enabling the borrower to overdraw on a current account unless the current account is an authorised business overdraft agreement or an authorised non-business overdraft agreement, or would be but for the fact that the credit is not repayable on demand or within 3 months.

Old regime: pre-contract information

18.114 Unless the 2010 regime applies, pre-contract information documents must be drafted in accordance with the Consumer Credit (Disclosure of Information) Regulations 2004 ('the 2004 Disclosure Regulations'). Such documents look very similar to regulated agreements, save that the signature boxes are omitted. Estimated information may be given if the exact information is as yet unknown.[91]

18.115 Secured agreements to which s 58 applies do not attract the requirement to give pre-contract information, as in such cases the debtor must already be given a consideration copy of the agreement pursuant to s 58. Authorised business overdraft agreements are also exempt (CCA, s 74). Regulation 3 of the 2004 Disclosure Regulations merely requires the pre-contract information to be given 'before' the agreement is made.

---

[91] Reg 3(2) of the 2004 Disclosure Regulations.

Theoretically this permits it to be given to the debtor along with the copy of the agreement for him to sign, although this would render the pre-contract information redundant, as the debtor is also given a s 62 copy of the unexecuted agreement at this stage. If there is any non-compliance with the requirements to give pre-contract information, the agreement is only enforceable on a court order (CCA, s 55(2)).

2010 regime: pre-contract information

18.116 Under the 2010 regime, pre-contract information must be drafted in accordance with the Consumer Credit (Disclosure of Information) Regulations 2010 ('the 2010 Disclosure Regulations').[92] Such information must generally be disclosed by means of the Standard European Consumer Credit Information (SECCI) (see reg 8 and Sch 1). The SECCI must be contained in a written form which the debtor can take away. It must include contact details, key features of the credit product, the cost of the credit, other important legal aspects (eg any right of withdrawal) and additional information in the case of distance marketing. Beyond this, any other information must be provided in a separate document, if it relates to the credit (reg 8(4)).

18.117 Regulation 3 sets out the disclosure requirements for all agreements under the 2010 regime except:

- telephone contracts (which are governed by reg 4)
    (in relation to telephone distance contracts, where the debtor explicitly consents, an abridged set of information can be disclosed before the agreement is made; in relation to non-distance contracts, an even more abridged set of information can be disclosed before the agreement is made; in all cases the SECCI must be disclosed immediately after the agreement is made);
- non-telephone distance contracts[93] where pre-contract information cannot be provided before the agreement is made (governed by reg 5: the SECCI must be disclosed immediately after the agreement is made);
- excluded pawn agreements (reg 9); and
- overdraft agreements (regs 10–11).

18.118 If reg 3 applies, the SECCI must be disclosed by the creditor[94] 'in good time before an agreement is made' (cf the wording under the old regime, which simply says 'before'). There are further provisions for 'distance contracts' in reg 7 (requiring the disclosure of the terms and conditions).

18.119 In the case of distance contracts for the purposes of the debtor's 'business' (where the creditor has 'opted-in' to the 2010 regime), the creditor

---

[92] For guidance on interpretation, see the BIS's 'Guidance on the regulations implementing the Consumer Credit Directive', August 2010, URN 10/1053.
[93] Defined in reg 1(2).
[94] Unless it has already been disclosed by an intermediary: reg 3(3).

can choose simply to disclose the pre-contract information 'immediately after' the agreement is entered, rather than before (reg 6). Secured agreements to which s 58 applies do not attract the requirement to give pre-contract information, as in such cases the debtor must already be given a consideration copy of the agreement pursuant to s 58. Authorised business overdraft agreements are also exempt (CCA, s 74). If there is any non-compliance with the requirements to give pre-contract information, the agreement is only enforceable on a court order (CCA, s 55(2)).

2010 regime: additional pre-contract obligations

Pre-contractual explanations

18.120   CONC 4.2.5[95] provides that before making a regulated credit agreement, the firm must place the customer in a position to assess whether the agreement is adapted to the customer's needs and financial situation by providing the customer with an adequate explanation (orally or in writing) of the following:

(a)   the features of the agreement which may make the credit to be provided under the agreement unsuitable for particular types of use;

(b)   how much the customer will have to pay periodically and, where the amount can be determined, in total under the agreement;

(c)   the features of the agreement which may operate in a manner which could have a significant adverse effect on the customer in a way which the customer is unlikely to foresee;

(d)   the principal consequences for the customer arising from a failure to make payments under the agreement at the times required by the agreement including, where applicable and depending on the type and amount of credit and circumstances of the customer the total cost of the debt growing, default charges, interest for late or missed payment, impaired credit rating and its effect on future access to credit, legal proceedings including reference to charging orders and the associated costs of such proceedings, repossession of the customer's home or other property, where an article is taken in pawn, that the article might be sold, if not redeemed;

(e)   the effect of the exercise of any right to withdraw from the agreement and how and when this right may be exercised.

18.121   The firm must also advise the customer to consider the draft credit agreement and where the information is disclosed in person, that the customer is able to take it away. The firm must provide the customer with an opportunity to ask questions about the agreement and advise the customer how to ask for further information and explanation. The option of giving the explanation orally or in writing is qualified by CONC 4.2.5(4) if certain matters are stated orally so that certain other matters must also be stated orally.

---

[95]   Which replaces CCA, s 55A.

18.122 Where a firm is credit broking in relation to a regulated credit agreement the firm must:

(a) disclose to the customer the fee, if any payable by a customer to the firm for its services;

(b) any fee must be agreed between the customer and the firm, and the agreement must be recorded in writing or other durable medium before a regulated credit agreement is entered into;

(c) the firm must disclose the fee to the lender, to enable the lender to calculate the annual percentage rate of charge for the credit agreement;

(d) a firm must disclose to the customer how and when any fee for its service is payable and in what circumstances a refund may be payable.

Section 55C copy of draft agreement

18.123 Before a regulated agreement is made, a creditor is obliged 'if requested' to give the debtor 'without delay' a copy of the prospective agreement (or such of its terms as have at that time been reduced to writing). The obligation does not arise if the creditor is 'unwilling' at the time of the request to proceed with the agreement. In contrast to the other additional pre-contract obligations, it is expressly provided that breach of the s 55C obligation gives rise to an action for breach of statutory duty (s 55C(3)).

Secured agreements: s 58 consideration period

18.124 In the case of regulated agreements secured on land (other than restricted-use credit agreements to finance the purchase of land, or bridging loans relating to the purchase of land), the creditor must give the debtor a 'consideration copy' of the unexecuted agreement pursuant to CCA, s 58. Overdrafts are again exempt from this obligation (CCA, s 74).

18.125 The consideration copy must contain a prescribed notice indicating the debtor's right to withdraw from the prospective agreement. The creditor must also provide a copy of any other document 'referred to' in the unexecuted agreement, such as a legal charge. Following the provision of the consideration documents, there follows a 'consideration period' of 7–14 days during which the creditor must not contact the debtor except in response to a specific request by him (CCA, s 61(2)). On/after the first 7 days of the consideration period, the creditor must send the debtor a copy of the unexecuted agreement for his signature, presuming no notice of withdrawal has been received (s 61(2)(b) and (d)). The consideration period then expires when the debtor returns the signed agreement or 7 days after the signature copy was sent, whichever is sooner (s 61(3)).

18.126 In the event of non-compliance with these provisions, the agreement is only enforceable on a court order (ss 61(2) and 65).

Pre-contract documentation for first and second charge mortgages

18.127 MCOB, as amended, requires consumer credit lenders to provide customers with a European Standard Information Sheet (ESIS) (MCOB 5A), and a 'binding offer letter' (MCOB 6A). The ESIS is an information document designed to ensure that customers are given information about the mortgage product and to have 'the opportunity to satisfy themselves that it is suitable for them' (MCOB 5A.2.2G). It must be provided in a 'durable medium', with a clear statement (orally or written) about the importance of carefully considering its contents. The ESIS must be provided before any formal application is made for the product in question (MCOB 5A.4.1(1)R) and an ESIS must be provided whenever any of the following occur:

(a) A particular consumer is advised to enter into an MCD regulated mortgage contract.

(b) If the consumer specifically requests an ESIS.

(c) In certain circumstances during the course of the sale of an 'execution-only' mortgage (as defined within the FCA Handbook Glossary).

18.128 In general, the ESIS must be provided 'without undue delay' once the consumer has given the necessary information about his needs, financial situation and preferences at the stage of the affordability assessment or, in any event, in good time before the consumer becomes bound by an offer or contract (MCOB 5A.4.1R). Where an ESIS is not provided, the consumer may not proceed to make a formal application for the MCD regulated mortgage contract. The template format for the ESIS is to be found in the Annex to MCOB 5A.

18.129 Whenever an offer is made with a view to entering into an MCD regulated mortgage contract, following the provision of the ESIS and a customer's application, a firm must provide a 'binding offer letter'. The purpose of the letter is to ensure that the consumer is 'able to check the features and price of the MCD regulated mortgage contract before they enter into it' (MCOB 6A.1.3G). It also provides consumers with a seven day period to consider the proposed terms of a deal, during which the lender is bound by the offer and the consumer may accept at any time.

18.130 The content of the binding offer letter is addressed in MCOB 6A.3, it must include 'a prominent statement' explaining the period of the offer, when any interest rate change might take effect, the consequences of not entering into the agreement (including non-reimbursable fees and charges) and state that, once the offer is accepted, there is no withdrawal period. Moreover, the binding offer must be accompanied by a draft credit agreement, details of how to complain about the firm and a tariff of charges that could be incurred. The letter must be provided in a durable medium.

CONNECTED LIABILITY: S 75 AND S 75A

Section 75

18.131 CCA, s 75(1) makes the creditor liable in certain circumstances for breaches by the supplier.

Which agreements are covered

18.132 Section 75 only applies to debtor-creditor-supplier (DCS) agreements falling within CCA, s 12(b) or (c). Therefore it applies, for instance, to:

• credit card transactions to purchase goods/services; and

• loans to purchase goods under pre-existing arrangements (or in contemplation of future arrangements) between the creditor and the supplier.

However, these agreements are only covered subject to the exceptions.

18.133 Where credit cards operate under a 'network' (eg Visa/MasterCard), the creditor's liability under s 75 is not limited to cover only breaches by suppliers which the creditor has itself enrolled into the network, and with whom the creditor has direct contractual arrangements. There will be sufficient 'arrangements' between the creditor and the supplier if they are both members of the same network.[96] Section 75 will still apply even if the debtor has exceeded the credit limit, or breached another term of the credit agreement (s 75(4)).

Agreements which are not covered

18.134 Section 75 does not apply to debtor-creditor agreements, hire agreements, exempt agreements or CCA, s 12(a) agreements where the creditor itself is the supplier. For CCA, s 12(a) agreements (eg hire-purchase, conditional sale or credit-sale), the contract for the supply of goods will be directly between the creditor and the debtor. In these situations, the creditor is also acting as the supplier and therefore if there is any breach of the supply contract, the debtor can sue the creditor directly (eg for breach of the implied terms as to title, satisfactory quality or correspondence with description: for hire-purchase, under the Supply of Goods (Implied Terms) Act 1973, or in a sale, under the Consumer Rights Act 2015). In addition, under such agreements, the deemed agency provisions for credit-brokers apply (s 56).

18.135 Section 75 does not cover electronic funds transfer at place of sale (EFTPOS) transactions (see s 187(3A)). Even if the agreement is of a type which would usually be covered by s 75, it is excepted if (i) it is a 'non-commercial'

---

[96] *Office of Fair Trading v Lloyds TSB Bank plc* [2006] EWCA Civ 268; [2007] QB 1.

agreement,[97] (ii) the claim relates to any single item to which the supplier has attached a cash price not exceeding £100, or over £30,000, or (iii) it is a charge card agreement (s 75(3)).

Other pre-conditions

18.136   Once it is established that the credit agreement is covered by s 75, there are four pre-conditions in order for s 75 to apply:

(i)   there is a 'claim' against the supplier;

(ii)   that claim is by the 'debtor';

(iii)   that claim is either for breach of contract or misrepresentation;

(iv)   that claim relates to a transaction financed by the credit agreement.

(i)   'Claim' against supplier

18.137   In *Durkin v DSG Retail Limited*,[98] the Supreme Court held that the law implied a term into a restricted use debtor-creditor-supplier agreement, making it conditional upon the survival of the supply agreement. A debtor, on rescinding the supply agreement for breach of contract, could also rescind the credit agreement by invoking that condition. The debtor would then be under an obligation to repay the borrowed funds that he has recovered from the supplier.

18.138   If the supplier has inserted a valid exclusion or limitation clause in the supply contract, then the debtor's claim against the creditor will suffer from the same exclusion or limitation. If the debtor has settled his claim against the supplier, then the creditor's liability will also be extinguished.

18.139   Section 75 covers overseas transactions (ie where a UK credit agreement is used to finance a supply transaction which is made or performed abroad and/or governed by foreign law).[99] Section 75 claims may also be brought in respect of the financing of timeshare agreements concerning properties abroad.[100]

18.140   In some circumstances, the 'supplier' (who must be the other contractual party to the transaction financed by the credit)[101] may not be the

---

[97]   Defined in s 189.

[98]   [2014] 1 WLR 1148.

[99]   *Office of Fair Trading v Lloyds TSB Bank plc* [2007] UKHL 48; [2008] 1 AC 316.

[100]   *Jarrett v Barclays Bank plc* [1999] QB 1, which held that Art 16 of the Brussels Convention (which confers exclusive jurisdiction over disputes over property in rem on the courts of the place where the property is situated) did not apply. See now Art 4.4(c) of Rome I.

[101]   CCA, s 11(1)(b) and s 189.

obvious person. For instance, if a debtor has a complaint against a hotel, he may find that he has no recourse under s 75, as the 'supplier' to whom he paid the monies was a travel agent.[102]

(ii) Claim by the 'debtor'

18.141 In the context of credit cards, s 75 probably only gives the account-holder a claim against the creditor, and not additional card-holders (who are not 'debtors', unless they are joint borrowers under the credit agreement).[103] Claims by family members against the supplier are excluded.

(iii) Claim for breach of contract or misrepresentation

18.142 The claim against the supplier must be for breach of contract (which includes breach of terms implied into the contract by consumer protection legislation) or misrepresentation. It follows that s 75 will not apply if the debtor's sole claim against the supplier is for negligence, or for breach of statutory duty for non-compliance with consumer protection legislation.

(iv) Relates to transaction financed

18.143 'Financed' means financed either wholly or in part (CCA, s 189). Therefore s 75 will apply even where a credit card has only been used to pay part of the purchase price, and the rest has been paid in cash. The claim must 'relate' to the transaction financed by the credit: the connection must not be too remote.

Claim against creditor

18.144 Where s 75 applies, the debtor is given a 'like claim' against the creditor, who is made jointly and severally liable with the supplier. Since liability is joint and several, the creditor cannot require the debtor to exhaust all avenues of redress against the supplier first, before it becomes liable (in contrast to a limited duty to do so under s 75A). The debtor may choose to pursue the creditor instead of the supplier.

18.145 In general, the debtor's claim against both supplier and creditor will be monetary. Nevertheless, the words 'a like claim' could indicate that if the debtor has a claim to rescind the supply contract, or treat it as repudiated, he should also be entitled to rescission of the credit agreement, or to treat it as repudiated by the creditor. However, this interpretation has its difficulties, and has been rejected by the Scottish courts; whilst agreeing that s 75 did not give a right to rescind the credit agreement, the Supreme Court held that such a right was derived from an implied term of the credit agreement that it is conditional

---

[102] However, the debtor may be assisted in such a situation by the Package Travel, Package Holidays and Package Tours Regulations 1992.

[103] See definition of 'debtor' in CCA, s 189; see also Guest and Lloyd, *Encyclopaedia of Consumer Credit Law*, vol 1, 2140: however, it is possible that an additional card-holder may be acting as agent for the account-holder, who will then have a s 75 claim in his capacity as principal.

on the survival of the supply contract.[104] The limitation period for a s 75 claim against the creditor will normally be 6 years (Limitation Act 1980, s 9).

18.146   There is a tricky question of what happens if the credit agreement has been assigned. Guest and Lloyd[105] are of the view that the original creditor would remain liable under s 75(1), but that if the debtor was sued for the outstanding balance by the assignee, he could still plead a counterclaim under s 75(1) by way of set off.

Creditor's indemnity against supplier

18.147   Section 75(2) grants the creditor a right of indemnity against the supplier (subject to any agreement between them). The indemnity covers loss in satisfying its s 75(1) liability[106] to the debtor and any legal costs reasonably incurred by the creditor in defending those proceedings. When the debtor issues a s 75(1) claim against the creditor, the creditor will usually issue a Part 20 claim against the supplier for a s 75(2) indemnity. Section 75(2) does not impose any obligation on foreign suppliers to indemnify the creditor.[107]

Section 75A

18.148   A separate provision for connected lender liability was added on 1 February 2011 to ensure compliance with the CC Directive. This provision applies from 1 February 2011 to credit agreements made on/after 11 June 2010.[108] If the creditor has chosen to implement the new regime early, then it applies from the date of that implementation to credit agreements made on/after 30 April 2010.

18.149   Section 75A is narrower than s 75, and only applies in restricted circumstances. In particular:

- s 75A only applies to transactions where the cash value of the goods/services exceeds £30,000;[109]

- s 75A only applies where the credit agreement 'serves exclusively' to finance an agreement for the supply of 'specific' goods/services;[110]

- s 75A only applies where either the credit agreement expressly identifies the specific goods/services, or the creditor uses the supplier's services in connection with the preparation or making of the credit agreement;

---

[104]   *Durkin v DSG Retail Ltd and HFC Bank plc* [2014] 1 WLR 1148; see also Guest and Lloyd, *Encyclopaedia of Consumer Credit Law*, vol 1, 2142 for further analysis.

[105]   *Encyclopaedia of Consumer Credit Law*, vol 1, 2144.

[106]   Either pursuant to a judgment, or a settlement of the claim; the supplier may, however, contest the question of liability, or dispute the quantum.

[107]   *Office of Fair Trading v Lloyds TSB Bank plc* [2007] UKHL 48, [2008] 1 AC 316.

[108]   Consumer Credit (EU Directive) Regulations 2010, reg 100(3)(a) and (4)(a).

[109]   CCA, s 75A(6)(a).

[110]   CCA, s 75A(5): it seems the credit agreement must not be used to finance anything else.

- s 75A does not apply to agreements outside the scope of the CC Directive (where the amount of credit exceeds £60,260, or the credit agreement is secured on land, or the credit agreement is wholly/predominantly for business purposes).[111]

18.150 Where s 75A does apply, it provides that if the debtor has a claim against the supplier for breach of contract, he may pursue that claim against the creditor. Section 75A only covers claims for breach of contract, and does not extend to misrepresentation.

18.151 In contrast to the position under s 75, before the creditor becomes liable under s 75A, the debtor must in some way be unable to obtain satisfaction from the supplier: either (i) the supplier cannot be traced or is insolvent, (ii) the debtor has contacted the supplier but it has not responded, or (iii) the debtor has taken reasonable steps to pursue his claim against the supplier (which need not include litigation) but has not obtained satisfaction (s 75A(2) and (3)).

DEFAULT NOTICES
When required

18.152 Under CCA, s 87, a creditor must serve a default notice before becoming entitled, by reason of any breach of a regulated agreement by the debtor, to:

- terminate the agreement;
- demand earlier payment of any sum;
- recover possession of any goods/land;
- treat any right conferred on the debtor by the agreement as terminated, restricted or deferred; or
- enforce any security.

18.153 Most credit agreements include an acceleration clause, so that if there is a serious breach by the debtor (eg two or more missed repayments), the creditor will immediately become entitled to the entire outstanding balance. If the creditor issues proceedings to recover the outstanding balance in these circumstances, this will amount to 'demanding earlier payment of any sum' and so a valid default notice will need to have been served. However, a default notice need not be served in order to obtain a money judgment solely for arrears (as such a judgment does not compel 'earlier payment' of any sum). Neither is a default notice required in order for the creditor to sue the debtor for damages for breach of the credit agreement.

---

[111] CCA, s 75A(6)(b) and (c) and (8).

18.154   Immediately after the debtor's breach, without the need for any default notice, the creditor may take steps to prevent the debtor making further drawings of credit (s 87(2): eg the creditor may warn suppliers not to accept a credit card where the credit limit has been exceeded).

Form and content

18.155   In order to be a valid default notice for the purposes of s 87, the notice must be compliant with s 88 and the associated Consumer Credit (Enforcement, Default and Termination Notices) Regulations 1983 ('the Notices Regulations'), which prescribe the form and content of default notices.

18.156   The default notice must specify (i) the nature of the alleged breach (eg missing monthly instalments), (ii) if the breach is capable of remedy, what action is required to remedy it (eg payment of the arrears), by which date and (iii) if the breach is not capable of remedy,[112] the sum (if any) required to be paid as compensation, by which date. It must also state what action is intended to be taken by the creditor such as demanding earlier payment of any sum or enforcing any security.

18.157   Where the debtor has missed repayment(s) and, pursuant to an acceleration clause, the entire outstanding balance has become due, when identifying the 'breach', the default notice should only refer to the missed repayments, and not refer to the failure to pay the entire balance. However, if the default notice is not complied with and the arrears are not cleared, the creditor may treat non-payment under the acceleration clause as a breach and need not serve a further default notice before seeking to enforce that clause (s 88(3)). The same is true of any obligation to pay default interest: the default notice should not treat this as part of the breach, but if the original breach is not remedied, the creditor need not serve a further default notice in relation to the failure to pay default interest (s 88(3)).

18.158   Certain statements must be set out in the notice, using prescribed forms of wording.[113] The lettering of each prescribed form of statement must be afforded more prominence than any other lettering in the notice. Any words shown in capital letters and underlined in the prescribed forms must be afforded yet more prominence.[114] The wording of the statements in the prescribed form must generally be reproduced without alteration or addition.[115]

18.159   The default notice must allow the debtor at least 14 days to take the specified action. There has been a considerable amount of litigation concerning whether the full 14 days have been provided. Since s 88 refers to 14 days 'after the date of service', it is uncontroversial that the date on which the default notice is served should be excluded in counting the 14 days. However, on one

---

[112]   Eg where the breach is bankruptcy, or the sale of goods let under a hire-purchase agreement.
[113]   Notices Regulations, reg 2 and Sch 2.
[114]   Notices Regulations, reg 2(5).
[115]   Notices Regulations, reg 2(6) and (7).

view, 14 days also means 14 'clear' days, so that the day on which the prescribed steps must be taken should also be excluded from the count.[116]

18.160 Each default notice must include a copy of the current FCA default information sheet (s 88(4A)). The default notice must be given in paper form, so may not be sent by email.[117] Its lettering must be easily legible and of a colour that is readily distinguishable from the paper.[118] A default notice sent by post may be validly 'served' even though it is never received.[119]

Obtaining judgment

18.161 If the creditor issues proceedings to recover the outstanding balance before expiry of the term of the agreement, without serving a compliant default notice, the Court may refuse to grant judgment, on the basis that there is no valid cause of action. There is some rather dubious case-law[120] to the effect that even if a default notice fails to allow 14 days after service to remedy the breach and so is technically defective, this is not relevant if the debtor has suffered no 'prejudice' as a result. The debtor will have suffered no prejudice if (i) he did not attempt to comply with the default notice anyway and (ii) the creditor did not take any enforcement action within 14 days.

18.162 Generally, however, all the prescribed information must be accurately stated in order for the notice to be compliant. If the arrears figure is overstated on the notice (and the error is not *de minimis*) then the notice will be defective. In *Woodchester Lease Management Services Ltd v Swain & Co*,[121] the Court of Appeal refused to grant judgment for the outstanding balance in these circumstances (although it did grant judgment for the arrears). It held that s 88 required a precise statement of the remedial action to correct the breach.

18.163 Where a default notice is required to obtain judgment, it is questionable whether it needs to have been served prior to the creditor's issue of proceedings (in order to found the cause of action), or whether it can be served during the course of proceedings (provided that the 14-day period for compliance has expired by the time judgment is entered).[122]

---

[116] 'Goode: Consumer Credit Law and Practice' to CCA, s 88 (vol 2, para 5.168).
[117] Notices Regulations, reg 2(4A).
[118] Notices Regulations, reg 2(4).
[119] CCA, s 176(2); *Lombard North Central v Power-Hines* [1994] 8 CL 57.
[120] *Brandon v American Express Services Europe PE Ltd* [2010] CTLC 139 Bristol County Court, the Court of Appeal ([2011] EWCA Civ 1187); [2011] CTLC 177 declined to comment on the merits of this argument save to say that it was not appropriate for a summary judgment application to be decided on that basis (at para 30).
[121] [1999] 1 WLR 263.
[122] See Guest and Lloyd, *Encyclopaedia of Consumer Credit Law*, vol 1, 2205 for the view that a default notice may be served during the course of proceedings.

Sanctions

18.164 Apart from the consequences for obtaining judgment (above), there is no sanction under the CCA against a creditor who fails to serve a default notice when required, or serves a defective notice, or enforces it before the 14 days have expired. Nonetheless, such failures may be relevant to authorization considerations, especially if persistent (s 170(2)), or contribute towards an 'unfair relationship'. Failures to serve statutory notices may also constitute offences under the Consumer Protection from Unfair Trading Regulations 2008 (eg as an 'unfair commercial practice' or a 'misleading omission').

18.165 It is possible that the debtor may be able to obtain an injunction prohibiting the creditor from enforcing the agreement without serving a valid default notice (s 170(3)). There may be remedies outside the CCA: for instance, a creditor who recovers possession of goods under a hire-purchase or conditional sale agreement without serving a compliant default notice can be sued in conversion.[123] However, there can be no damages claim by a debtor for loss caused by failure to serve a default notice (or service of a defective notice).[124]

18.166 There is nothing to prevent the creditor from serving multiple default notices before deciding to issue proceedings. However, in such a case it can be difficult to ascertain when the agreement was 'terminated' by the creditor (where no termination notice is served, the agreement may simply terminate upon expiry of the 14-day period specified in the default notice).

Running-account agreements

18.167 There is some authority[125] that where a credit card agreement gives the creditor the contractual right to terminate without relying on the debtor's breach, it is irrelevant if the default notice is defective. In these circumstances the creditor does not need to rely on the debtor's default in order to terminate, and so any default notice complying with CCA, s 88 is redundant. The rationale for this is that a credit card agreement (as opposed to a fixed-sum loan) is open-ended, and so the creditor needs to have a contractual right to terminate at any time, without relying upon the debtor's breach. However, the creditor will still need to have fulfilled any contractual pre-conditions on its right to terminate (which may include serving a notice, albeit that this does not need to comply with s 88). It is possible that contractual notice of non-default termination and s 87 notice of default can be combined within a single

---

123 *Eshun v Moorgate Mercantile Co Ltd* [1971] 1 WLR 722.
124 CCA, s 170(1); enforcement without serving a valid default notice would not amount to a breach of contract (unless it is required by a clause in the credit agreement).
125 *American Express Services Europe Ltd v Harrison*, unreported, Exeter County Court, 18 February 2009; approved by the Court of Appeal in *Brandon v American Express Services Europe Ltd* [2011] EWCA Civ 1187, at paras 35–36; [2011] CTLC 177.

notice.[126] It should be noted that the CCA, s 98A requirements for termination notices must now also be complied with, as regards running-account credit agreements.

INFORMATION AND NOTICES

18.168 There are a considerable number of statutory notices and pieces of information which are obliged to be supplied in certain circumstances. This is an important, developing area of law, as the failure to comply with these obligations can have severe consequences, and the requirements are detailed. These were introduced by CCA 2006. In December 2012, it was announced that Northern Rock (Asset Management) plc would be refunding its customers £270m for interest which it was not entitled to charge due to defects in annual statements. Most of the obligations to supply statements and notices do not apply to 'non-commercial' agreements and 'small' agreements.[127]

Assignees

18.169 When credit agreements have been assigned, it is often unclear whether the duties under the CCA to supply information and notices are imposed on the original creditor, or on the assignee. These duties are stated to be imposed on 'the creditor'. CCA, s 189(1) defines 'the creditor' to mean, unless the context otherwise requires, 'the person providing credit under a consumer credit agreement *or* the person to whom his *rights and duties* under the agreement have passed by assignment or operation of law' (emphasis added). The difficulty is that in an ordinary legal assignment, only the 'rights' of the original creditor are transferred to the assignee, and not the duties. Therefore, on the face of it, most assignees will not be obliged to comply with the duties to supply information and notices.

18.170 For a comprehensive analysis of the question, see *The Law of Consumer Credit and Hire* by Philpott et al.[128] The author's view is that it is probable that legal assignees are not subject to the duties to supply information and notices, which can only be transferred from the original creditor if there is a novation. However, it was the OFT's view that legal assignees have a duty to comply with requests for copies of the agreement under ss 77–79.[129]

---

[126] *Brandon* at paras 34–37.
[127] See the relevant sections imposing the duties to give statements and notices; a 'non-commercial' agreement is not made by the creditor in the course of a business carried on by him (CCA, s 189); a 'small' agreement is for under £50 – see s 17.
[128] At para 8.145 *et seq*.
[129] CONC 13 Guidance on the duty to give information under the CCA 1974, ss 77–79 (OFT 1272, October 2010).

Joint debtors

18.171 Where there are joint debtors, the creditor must give the required statement/notice to each of them (CCA, s 185). One joint debtor may give the creditor a 'dispensing notice' authorising the creditor only to send periodic statements[130] to his co-debtor (s 185(2) and (2B)).

Enforcement notices

18.172 Where the duration of a regulated agreement is specified[131] in the agreement and has not yet expired, CCA, s 76 requires the creditor to give the debtor at least 7 days' written notice[132] before becoming entitled to take certain enforcement action. That enforcement action comprises steps to 'enforce'[133] a contractual term by (i) demanding earlier payment of any sum,[134] (ii) recover possession of goods/land, or (iii) treat any right conferred on the debtor as terminated, restricted or deferred.

18.173 Section 76 does not apply where the right to enforce arises by reason of any 'breach' of the debtor (s 76(6)). In this situation, see the requirements for a default notice under s 87 instead. A s 76 enforcement notice does not need to be served before terminating the agreement (in such a case, not based on default, see s 98). A debtor's right to draw credit may be restricted or deferred (but not terminated) without having to serve an enforcement notice (s 76(4)).

18.174 The form and content requirements are similar to those for default notices. As for default notices, there is no express sanction for failure to serve a valid enforcement notice when required.

Non-default termination notices

18.175 Contrary to popular belief, a termination notice does not need to be served in every case. For instance, where the agreement is terminated upon non-compliance with a default notice, no further notice need be served. CCA, ss 98 and 98A only regulate termination in non-default cases. As for default notices, there is no express sanction for failure to serve a valid termination notice when required.

---

[130] Under CCA, s 77A or s 78(4).

[131] An agreement still has a 'specified' duration even if a party can terminate early: s 76(2).

[132] The notice must be in the form prescribed by the Consumer Credit (Enforcement, Default and Termination Notices) Regulations 1983, and must be in paper format.

[133] 'Enforcement' does not include the mere commencement of proceedings: see p 660 below.

[134] A creditor whose loan is repayable on demand is not required to serve an enforcement notice prior to demanding payment: *Barclays Bank plc v Brillouet* [1999] GCCR 1541, CA.

Agreements of specified duration: s 98

18.176 Section 98 applies where the agreement is terminated for a reason other than the debtor's breach[135] (so no default notice has been served). Where the agreement is one of a specified duration, if the creditor wishes to terminate it before the end of that duration, it must give the debtor at least 7 days' written notice. A debtor's right to draw further credit may be restricted or deferred (but not terminated) without having to serve a termination notice (s 98(4)). The form and content requirements are similar to those for default notices. The form and content is prescribed by reg 2(3) and Sch 3 to the Notices Regulations. A s 98 termination notice and a s 76 enforcement notice may be combined within a single document.[136] A s 98 termination notice may also incorporate the s 86E notice of default sums and/or the s 130A notice of post-judgment interest.[137]

Indefinite duration agreements: s 98A

18.177 As of 1 February 2011,[138] s 98A applies to 'open-ended' credit agreements (ie agreements of indefinite duration, which includes most credit card agreements). Agreements secured on land and overdrafts are excluded.[139] Section 98A(3) limits the creditor's contractual right to terminate such agreements in non-default[140] cases as follows:

(i) the creditor must terminate the agreement by serving the debtor with written notice (there are no form and content requirements);

(ii) the termination can only take effect after 2 months, beginning with the day after the day of service of the notice.[141]

18.178 Alternatively, where the creditor wishes to terminate/suspend the debtor's right to draw on credit (whether or not due to default), there are special provisions in s 98A(4)–(6) (generally, the creditor must serve a notice with objectively justified reasons for taking the step, such as the unauthorised use of credit, or a significantly increased risk of the debtor being unable to repay). If a debtor wishes to terminate an agreement of indefinite duration, he may do so at any time, simply by giving notice (which need not be in writing, unless the creditor requires) (s 98A(2)). The debtor's right of termination is subject to any contractual notice period, which cannot exceed one month (s 98A(1)).

---

135 CCA, s 98(6).
136 Notices Regulations, reg 2(8).
137 CCA, s 86E(3); s 130A(5).
138 CCA, s 98A applies as of 1 February 2011 to agreements made at any time.
139 CCA, s 98A(8).
140 CCA, s 98A(7).
141 Or such longer period as the credit agreement stipulates.

Information and copies to be provided on request

Sections 77, 78 and 79: request for copies of agreements

18.179 CCA, s 77 applies to fixed-sum agreements, s 78 applies to running-account agreements and s 79 applies to hire agreements. All three sections require the creditor/owner to provide certain information within 12 working days[142] after receiving payment of a £1 fee and a written request. In response to a s 77/s 78/s 79 request, the creditor must provide:

(a)   a copy of the executed agreement (if any);[143]

(b)   a copy of any other document referred to in the credit agreement; and

(c)   a statement signed by or on behalf of the creditor/owner showing (according to the information to which it is practicable for him to refer):

    (i)   in the case of a fixed-sum agreement: (i) the total sum paid under the agreement, (ii) the total sum which has become payable but which remains unpaid, the various amounts comprised in that total sum, and the date when each became due and (iii) the total sum which is to become payable, the various amounts comprised in that total sum, and the date (or the means of determining the date) when each becomes due;[144]

    (ii)   in the case of a running-account agreement: (i) the state of the account, (ii) the amount, if any, currently payable under the agreement and (iii) the amounts and the due dates of any payments which, if there are no further drawings on the account, will later become payable under the agreement;

    (iii)   in the case of a hire agreement: the total sum which has become payable but remains unpaid and the various amounts comprised in that total sum, with the date when each became due.

18.180   The 'copies' of the documents in (a) and (b) above must be 'true copies' and comply with the requirements in reg 3 of the Consumer Credit (Cancellation Notices and Copies of Documents) Regulations 1983 ('the Copies Regulations') (see CCA, s 180(2)). In particular, the copy of the executed agreement need not include the signature boxes. It follows from this that the copy of the executed agreement need not be a photocopy or microfiche copy of the original document which the debtor signed. A 'reconstituted' copy of the credit agreement is permissible. Moreover, the agreement may be reconstituted from sources other[145] than the actual document which the debtor signed.[146]

---

[142] 'Working days' is defined in s 189.

[143] 'If any' appears to cover agreements which are exempt under s 74 from the CCA form and content requirements; if the creditor has lost its copy of the agreement it is still 'obliged' to provide a copy.

[144] If the creditor has insufficient information to ascertain the amounts and dates of payments which are yet to become payable (eg because there is a variable interest rate), it may instead state the basis on which they will be ascertained (s 77(2); s 78(2)).

[145] Eg the creditor's database of templates used for different periods.

[146] *Carey v HSBC Bank Plc & ors* [2009] EWHC 3417 (QB); [2009] CTLC 103: the primary

18.181 If the terms of the credit agreement have subsequently been varied, the creditor must supply copies of both the original and the current terms and conditions.¹⁴⁷ The creditor/owner need not respond if the agreement is one under which 'no sum is or will or may become payable by the debtor/hirer' (s 77(3); s 78(3); s 79(2)).¹⁴⁸ In addition, the creditor/owner need not respond if the request was made less than 1 month after it complied with a previous such request relating to the same agreement (s 77(3); s 78(3); s 79(2)).

18.182 If the creditor/owner fails to comply with the request, then the agreement is temporarily unenforceable until a compliant response is sent (s 77(4); s 78(6); s 79(3)). There is no scope for any discretionary enforcement. An agreement may effectively become irredeemably unenforceable if the request can never be complied with. While the agreement is temporarily unenforceable, the creditor/owner is prevented from taking any steps that amount to 'enforcement'. However, the debtor's repayment obligations remain valid, albeit temporarily unenforceable. Failure to comply with a s 77/s 78/s 79 request will not, without more, give rise to an 'unfair relationship'.¹⁴⁹ The debtor may seek a declaration from the court that the agreement is temporarily unenforceable. The court may only order such declaratory relief under its general jurisdiction, and not under CCA, s 142.¹⁵⁰ A s 77/78/79 response may incorporate the s 86E notice of default sums and/or the s 130A notice of post-judgment interest.¹⁵¹

Statement of account

18.183 As of 1 February 2011, there is a further obligation under CCA, s 77B to supply debtors with statements of account upon request. The obligation only applies to fixed-sum agreements of a fixed duration, where the credit is repayable in instalments. Agreements outside the scope of the CC Directive are excluded (agreements secured on land, agreements for credit exceeding £60,260 and 'business' agreements). The creditor must, upon request, send the debtor a written statement of account complying with s 77B(3)–(5). The statement must be sent 'as soon as reasonably practicable', without charge. The debtor may not request a statement of account if the agreement has terminated, or if the creditor has already complied with a previous request made less than a month before (s 77B(6)). There is an express sanction: the creditor's non-compliance is actionable as a breach of statutory duty (s 77B(8)). In addition, breach could be relevant to fitness and/or contribute towards an 'unfair relationship'.

---

purpose of the obligations under ss 77–79 is to provide the debtor with information about the terms of the agreement, not to enable him to prove whether or not he signed a properly executed agreement.

¹⁴⁷ *Carey v HSBC*; Copies Regulations regs 7–9.

¹⁴⁸ It was also held by the High Court in *Rankine v Halifax plc* [2009] CCLR 3 that the duty is only imposed on a creditor 'under an agreement' and therefore the duty ceases once the agreement has been terminated.

¹⁴⁹ *McGuffick v RBS plc* [2009] EWHC 2386 on s 77; [2010] 1 All ER 634, *Carey v HSBC Bank plc* [2009] EWHC 3417 QB on s 78; [2009] CTLC 103.

¹⁵⁰ *Carey v HSBC* [2009] EWHC 3417 QB on s 78; [2009] CTLC 103.

¹⁵¹ CCA, s 86E(3); s 130A(5).

Other requests

18.184 For the obligation to give 'surety' copies of documents, see CCA s 107 (in relation to fixed-sum agreements), s 108 (in relation to running-account agreements) and s 109 (in relation to hire agreements). For requests by the debtor for a copy of the 'security instrument', see s 110. For requests by the debtor for early settlement information, see s 97. For requests by the debtor for a termination statement (confirming that he has discharged his indebtedness) see s 103.

Periodic statements

18.185 There are separate obligations to provide periodic statements for both fixed-sum and running-account credit agreements. The form and content of periodic statements is prescribed by the Consumer Credit (Information Requirements and Duration of Licences and Charges) Regulations 2007 ('the Information Regulations 2007'). In light of the very detailed provisions, it is fortunate that reg 41 of the Information Regulations 2007 provides that an error or omission which does not affect the 'substance' of the information or wording in a periodic statement will not itself constitute a breach.

18.186 The prescribed information must be easily legible and no less prominent than any other information in the document (except names of parties, headings etc).[152] There are only minor restrictions (regs 37–38) on the ordering and interspersing of information. There are some additional requirements for periodic statements relating to running-account agreements in the Consumer Credit (Running-Account Credit Information) Regulations 1983 ('the Running-Account Information Regulations'). A periodic statement may incorporate the s 86E notice of default sums and/or the s 130A notice of post-judgment interest.[153]

Fixed-sum agreements

18.187 The obligation to provide periodic statements in respect of regulated agreements is contained in CCA, s 77A. The statements must relate to consecutive periods, each of which must not exceed 1 year. The first period must commence either with the day the agreement was made, or the day the first movement occurs on the debtor's account.[154] Each statement must be given to the debtor within 30 days, beginning with the day after the end of the period to which the statement relates (s 77A(1E)).

---

[152] Information Regulations 2007, regs 39–40.

[153] CCA, s 86E(3); s 130A(5).

[154] CCA, s 77A(1B); but see transitional provisions for agreements made before 1 October 2008 (Art 5(2) of the Legislative Reform (Consumer Credit) Order 2008 and Information Regulations 2007, regs 36 and 45–49). There is no obligation to give a statement under s 77A if the agreement was written as if it was a regulated agreement but in fact it was not (*NRAM v McAdam* [2015] CTLC 169).

18.188 In *JP Morgan Chase Bank v Northern Rock (Asset Management) plc*,[155] the court found that where a debtor has been provided with a non-compliant s 77A statement, the period of non-compliance commences on a date to be calculated as if no statement had been served at all (the day following the last day on which a compliant statement could have been given).

18.189 Under the Information Regulations 2007, periodic statements must contain a range of information, including the amount of credit, the opening balance at the beginning of the statement period and the amounts and dates of payments. Prescribed statements about early settlement[156] and paying less than the agreed sum must be included. Where any interest rates are 'applicable on a per annum basis',[157] the statement must specify those rates, the periods during which they applied and (if applicable) the element of the credit to which each such rate applied. The amounts and dates of any interest which became due during the statement period must be separately stated.

18.190 Otherwise, where the interest rates are not 'applicable on a per annum basis', the statement must quote the interest rates on a per annum basis and explain how and when interest charges are calculated. There need be no separate statement of the amounts and dates of any interest which became due during the statement period (unless any movement on the account consisted solely of interest becoming due). The obligation to provide periodic statements ends when the debtor has no further liability under the agreement (s 77A(4)).

18.191 There are three express sanctions for non-compliance (s 77A(6)):

(i) the agreement is temporarily unenforceable during the 'period of non-compliance';

(ii) the debtor will not be liable to pay any interest calculated by reference to all/part of the 'period of non-compliance';

(iii) the debtor will not be liable to pay any default sum which would have become payable during the 'period of non-compliance', or would have become payable after the end of that period in connection with a breach which occurred during the period.[158]

---

[155] [2014] 1 WLR 2197, [2014] CTLC 33.

[156] If the agreement is a hire-purchase/conditional sale, the form of wording about early settlement must be shown together as a whole with a form of wording about termination rights (Information Regulations 2007, reg 37).

[157] For the uncertain meaning of this expression, see *The Law of Consumer Credit and Hire* by Philpott et al, paras 8.07–8.11: it is likely that it only includes rates applied so as to oblige the debtor to make one interest payment each year (and possibly rates that are compounded annually).

[158] The debtor is not liable to pay the default sum even if his breach continues after the end of the period of non-compliance.

The 'period of non-compliance' begins on the 31st day after the end of the period to which the notice should have related (s 77A(1E), (5) and (7)). It ends once a compliant statement is given (or, if earlier, when the debtor has no further liability under the agreement).

Running-account agreements

18.192 The obligation to provide periodic statements is contained in CCA, s 78(4). The statements must show the state of the account at regular intervals of not more than 12 months. Where the agreement provides for repayments in relation to specified periods[159] (or for the applying of interest/charges in relation to specified periods), the periodic statement must also show the state of the account at the end of each such period during which there is a movement in the account (s 78(4)(b)).

18.193 The first periodic statement must relate to a period starting on/before the date of the first movement on the account, and each subsequent statement is consecutive.[160] Each statement must be given within a prescribed time after the end of the period to which the statement relates, namely:[161]

(i)   1 month after the end of the period (if the statement includes a demand for payment);

(ii)   12 months after the end of the period (if there is no demand for payment and the statement indicates there is no credit/debit balance at the end of the period);

(iii)   12 months after the date of the first credit/debit balance on the account following the end of the period if there has been no credit/debit balance on the account at any time during the period); or

(iv)   6 months after the end of the period (in any other case).

18.194 The periodic statement must contain the information prescribed by reg 2(1) and the Schedule to the Running-Account Information Regulations (eg the opening and closing balances for the period, the date of any movement on the account, the amounts of payments/drawings, any interest/charges applied during the period and information about the calculation of interest and any variation in the rate).

18.195 In addition, the periodic statement must contain the forms of wording prescribed by the Information Regulations 2007. Importantly, where the agreement requires the payment each month of a minimum sum (as for most credit card agreements), the notice must include a form of wording as follows:

---

[159] As, eg, on a credit card.

[160] Regulation 2 of the Running-Account Information Regulations; there are no transitional provisions for pre-1 October 2008 agreements (as there are for periodic statements relating to fixed-sum agreements).

[161] See CCA, s 78(5) and reg 3 of the Running-Account Information Regulations.

Minimum payments

If you make only the minimum payment each month, it will take you longer and cost you more to clear your balance.

If you do not pay off the full amount outstanding, we will allocate your payment to the outstanding balance in a specific order, which is set out [...]. The way in which payments are allocated can make a significant difference to the amount of interest you will pay until the balance is cleared completely.[162]

18.196 This form of wording must be shown 'together as a whole' with the closing balance for the end of the period.[163] It must be more prominent than any other information/wording in the periodic statement.[164] There is a separate, additional form of wording if the debtor has failed to make the minimum payment.

18.197 There is no express provision as to when the obligation to provide periodic statements ends (as there is for fixed-sum agreements), but the obligation is stated only to apply where 'credit is provided' under an agreement. Therefore it is unclear whether the obligation ceases (i) upon withdrawal of the credit facility, (ii) upon termination of the credit agreement, or (iii) when no sums remain payable by the debtor. Further, there is no express sanction for non-compliance (as there is for fixed-sum agreements). However, there may be indirect sanctions: failures to serve statutory notices may be relevant to authorisation considerations, especially if persistent (s 170(2)), or contribute towards an 'unfair relationship'. Such failures may also constitute offences under the Consumer Protection from Unfair Trading Regulations 2008 (eg as an 'unfair commercial practice' or a 'misleading omission').

Interest rate change

18.198 CCA, s 78A imposes a duty to give debtors written information before a change in interest rate can take effect. As from 1 February 2011, this obligation applies to agreements of indefinite duration whenever made. For agreements of fixed duration, the obligation only applies to agreements made on/after 1 February 2011, unless the creditor has chosen to implement the new regime early. Agreements secured on land are excluded.[165] For agreements to which s 78A does not apply, see the more general 'variation' provisions in CCA, s 82(1).

18.199 The information which must be supplied is set out in s 78A(3) and comprises the rate variation, the new payment amount (if different) and the new number or frequency of payments (if different). However, the obligation to provide the s 78A information does not arise where the rate varies according to

---

[162] Information Regulations 2007, reg 14 and Sch 2.
[163] Information Regulations 2007, reg 38.
[164] Information Regulations 2007, reg 40.
[165] Consumer Credit (EU Directive) Regulations 2010; regs 27, 100; CCA, s 78A(6).

a publicly available reference rate and the creditor is contractually obliged to inform the debtor periodically in writing of the information in s 78A(3). There is a more limited obligation in respect of overdrafts (the creditor need only send information of an increase, and can restrict the information to the variation) (s 78A(4)). There is no express sanction for non-compliance.

Arrears notices

18.200   There are separate obligations to provide arrears notices for both fixed-sum and running-account credit agreements. The form and content of arrears notices is prescribed by the Information Regulations 2007. In particular, an arrears notice must state that the debtor is behind with the sums payable under the agreement, and encourage him to discuss the state of his account with the creditor. The arrears notice must include a copy of the FCA information sheet on arrears. Again, it should be noted that reg 41 of the Information Regulations 2007 provides that an error or omission which does not affect the 'substance' of the information or wording in a periodic statement will not itself constitute a breach.

18.201   The prescribed information must be easily legible and no less prominent than any other information in the document (except names of parties, headings etc).[166] An arrears notice may incorporate the s 86E notice of default sums and/or the s 130A notice of post-judgment interest.[167] Arrears notices need not be issued where there is an outstanding judgment debt in relation to the agreement.[168] There are transitional provisions for agreements entered before 1 October 2008.[169]

18.202   There are three express sanctions for non-compliance (s 86D):

(i)   the agreement is temporarily unenforceable during the 'period of non-compliance';

(ii)   the debtor will not be liable to pay any interest calculated by reference to all/part of the 'period of non-compliance';

(iii) the debtor will not be liable to pay any default sum which would have become payable during the 'period of non-compliance', or would have become payable after the end of that period in connection with a breach which occurred during the period.[170]

18.203   The 'period of non-compliance' begins on the day after the end of the period within which the arrears notice should have been given (s 86D(5)). Where the agreement is for running-account credit, the 'period of non-compliance' ends on the day the arrears notice is given. Where the

---

166   Information Regulations 2007, regs 39–40.
167   CCA, s 86E(3); s 130A(5).
168   CCA, s 86B(1)(e); s 86C(1)(d).
169   See CCA 2006, Sch 3 paras 6–7.
170   The debtor is not liable to pay the default sum even if his breach continues after the end of the period of non-compliance.

agreement is for fixed-sum credit or hire, the 'period of non-compliance' ends, in the case of a first arrears notice, on the day that notice is given, and in the case of a subsequent notice, on the day that notice is given, or, if earlier, when the debtor 'ceases to be in arrears'.[171]

Fixed-sum credit and hire agreements

18.204 Section 86B obliges creditors/owners to send arrears notices whenever at least two payments have fallen due, the amount of the shortfall equals or exceeds the sum of the most recent two payments[172] to have fallen due, and the creditor is not already obliged to provide an arrears notice relating to the agreement. Where repayments are due weekly (or more frequently), arrears notices need only be given when there are four missed payments (s 86B(9)).[173]

18.205 The first arrears notice must be given within 14 days of the date the conditions for service of an arrears notice are met (unless arrears notices are already being given, due to the conditions being met previously). After the first notice, subsequent arrears notices must be given at intervals of not more than 6 months, until the customer 'ceases to be in arrears'[174] (or a judgment is given requiring him to pay a sum).

18.206 Since subsequent arrears notices must be given at intervals of not more than 6 months, the period to which each notice relates should be 5 months or less (in order that they can be served on the debtor in time). If the customer ceases to be in arrears during the 14 days within which the first arrears notice is to be given, that notice must still be sent (s 86B(3)). The arrears notice must quote the opening balance at the date when the duty to give the notice arose,[175] and set out various other financial figures. The first arrears notice must either supply broken down information about the shortfall, or inform the debtor that he can request further information about which payments he failed to make. If such a request is made, the creditor must respond within 15 working days.[176]

---

[171] 'Ceases to be in arrears' is defined by s 86B(5) to include the case where a default sum payable in respect of a breach other than non-payment remains outstanding.

[172] 'Payments' does not include default charges, unless (possibly) they can be said to be payable 'at predetermined intervals' (s 86B(13)).

[173] Further, where such an agreement was made more than 20 weeks before the date the most recent payment fell due, see s 86B(10) and (11).

[174] 'Ceases to be in arrears' is defined by s 86B(5) to exclude most cases where interest and default charges remain 'owing'; it is unclear whether a customer will be in arrears where interest or default charges have accrued, but are not yet due and payable; it also unclear what the effect of any repayment arrangement will be, where the creditor has agreed to waive its contractual rights to the full repayments.

[175] For subsequent arrears notices, it seems that the part of the opening balance which comprises any sum not paid when due (para 7 of Sch 3 to the Information Regulations 2007) must be taken from the balance on the day after the previous notice was given; the part of the closing balance which comprises any sum not paid when due (para 12) must be taken from the balance on the last day of the period to which the notice relates (see *The Law of Consumer Credit and Hire* by Philpott et al, para 8.62).

[176] Information Regulations 2007, reg 19(2).

18.207 There is much scope for error in the drafting of arrears notices, due to the ambiguous language used in the Information Regulations 2007 to describe various pieces of financial information which must be included. For instance, 'balance' could refer either to the balance on which interest is accruing, or to the total outstanding balance including accrued daily interest which has not yet been debited.

Running-account agreements

18.208 Section 86C obliges creditors to send arrears notices whenever at least two payments have fallen due, the most recent two payments[177] to have fallen due have not been made,[178] and the creditor has not already become obliged to give an arrears notice in relation to either of those two payments. The arrears notice must be given no later than the end of the period within which the creditor is next obliged[179] to give a periodic statement.

18.209 The arrears notice may be incorporated into the periodic statement, or into any other CCA statement/notice relating to the agreement (s 86C(4)). In accordance with the Information Regulations 2007, the arrears notice must set out various pieces of financial information (unless the two missed payments are minimum monthly payments which do not exceed £2).[180]

Notice of default sums

18.210 CCA, s 86E imposes a duty to issue notices of any default sums that become payable, within 35 days of the sum becoming payable. A 'default sum' is any sum[181] (other than interest) payable by the debtor in connection with a breach by him of the agreement (s 187A). It only includes sums 'payable' as a result of a breach, not sums where the obligation to pay is merely accelerated due to breach.

18.211 The form and content of notices of default sums is prescribed by the Information Regulations 2007. In particular, the notice must state that it relates to default sums and set out the amount, nature and date of each default sum (and the total amount). The notice must state that it does not take account of default sums which were the subject of a previous notice, whether or not they remain unpaid.

18.212 There is a special form of wording where interest is payable in connection with the default sums (referring to the fact that interest on default

---

177 'Payments' does not include default charges, unless (possibly) they can be said to be payable 'at predetermined intervals' (s 86C(8)).

178 It is unclear whether 'not been made' encompasses the situation where, although the payments have not been made on time, there are no arrears, because of the way subsequent payments are appropriated to the outstanding balance.

179 Under CCA, s 78(4).

180 Information Regulations 2007, reg 26.

181 Potentially including legal costs.

sums may not be charged for the first 28 days after the notice is given – s 86E(4)). It should also be noted that a creditor can only charge simple interest on default sums (s 86F). Again, it should be noted that reg 41 of the Information Regulations 2007 provides that an error or omission which does not affect the 'substance' of the information or wording in a periodic statement will not itself constitute a breach.

18.213 The prescribed information must be easily legible and no less prominent than any other information in the document (except names of parties, headings etc).[182] There are transitional provisions for agreements entered before 1 October 2008.[183]

18.214 A notice of default sums may incorporate the s 130A notice of post-judgment interest.[184] The notice of default sums may itself be incorporated into a periodic statement, or into any other CCA statement/notice relating to the agreement (s 86E(3)). There are two express sanctions for non-compliance (s 86E(4) and (5)):

(i) the agreement is temporarily unenforceable until the notice is given; and

(ii) no interest is recoverable on a default sum until 28 days have elapsed after the sending of a compliant notice.

Current account overdrafts

18.215 Where the account-holder may be allowed to incur an overdraft that is not pre-arranged, or to exceed a pre-arranged overdraft limit ('overrunning'), the current account agreement must provide the information listed in CONC 4.7.2R(2). Unless this overrunning would be secured on land, the creditor must also inform the account-holder of this information annually (CONC 6.3.3R). Where the account-holder overdraws on the current account without a pre-arranged overdraft, or exceeds a pre-arranged overdraft limit, for a period exceeding 1 month; and the amount of that overdraft or excess is significant throughout that period; the overdraft or excess is a regulated credit agreement and a firm must inform the account holder in writing of the matters in CONC 6.3.4 R(2) without delay.

18.216 The matters in CONC 6.3.4 R(2) are:

(a) the fact that the account is overdrawn or the overdraft limit has been exceeded;

(b) the amount of that overdraft or excess;

(c) the rate of interest charged on it; and

(d) any other charges payable by the customer in relation to it (including any penalties and any interest on those charges).

---

[182] Information Regulations 2007, regs 39–40.
[183] See CCA, Sch 3, paras 8–9.
[184] CCA, s 130A(5).

Notices of post-judgment interest

18.217 No statutory interest is payable on a judgment given in proceedings to recover money due under a regulated agreement.[185] However, contractual interest may be payable. CCA, s 130A obliges notice to be given if the creditor wishes to recover post-judgment contractual interest.

18.218 The first notice must be given after the judgment (no time limit is imposed, but post-judgment interest is irrecoverable until it is given) and subsequent notices must be given at intervals of no more than 6 months. The form and content of notices of post-judgment interest is prescribed by the Information Regulations 2007. In particular, the notice must set out the amount on which post-judgment interest is being charged and the rate of that interest. It must include special forms of wording. Subsequent notices must set out the total amount of interest charged since the date of the last notice. Again, it should be noted that reg 41 of the Information Regulations 2007 provides that an error or omission which does not affect the 'substance' of the information or wording in a periodic statement will not itself constitute a breach.

18.219 The prescribed information must be easily legible and no less prominent than any other information in the document (except names of parties, headings etc).[186] There are transitional provisions for agreements entered before 1 October 2008.[187] The notice of post-judgment interest may be incorporated into a periodic statement, or into any other CCA statement/notice relating to the agreement (s 130A(5)). If the notices are not given, the debtor is not liable to pay any post-judgment interest for any period when the creditor has not complied with the s 130A requirements (s 130A(2) and (3)).

ENFORCEABILITY OF AGREEMENT

18.220 In default of many of the CCA obligations imposed on a creditor, the agreement is 'improperly executed'. CCA, s 65 provides that an 'improperly executed' agreement is enforceable against the debtor only on an order of the court. Applications for enforcement orders are dealt with in accordance with CCA, s 127. Alternatively, a debtor may consent to enforcement under CCA, s 173(3).

Effect of unenforceability

18.221 Where an agreement is unenforceable, the debtor's repayment obligations remain valid contractual obligations, and are not void.[188] Letters sent by a creditor requesting payment in such circumstances would not result in

---

[185] Art 2(3) of the County Court (Interest on Judgment Debts) Order 1991.
[186] Information Regulations 2007, regs 39–40.
[187] See CCA, Sch 3, para 13.
[188] *Wilson v First County Trust Ltd (No 2)* [2003] UKHL 40; [2004] 1 AC 816.

an unfair relationship between the creditor and the debtor.[189] Accordingly, default will still affect the debtor's credit rating (even if the creditor cannot obtain judgment for the outstanding balance without the granting of an enforcement order). There is no provision in the CCA for the debtor to recover payments made pursuant to an unenforceable agreement.[190]

18.222 Where the creditor has not applied for an enforcement order (or its application has been dismissed), the court may grant a CCA, s 142 declaration that the agreement should not be enforced. In relation to a secured agreement, where a s 142 declaration has been granted, or the creditor's application for an enforcement order has been dismissed,[191] the security shall be treated as never having effect.[192] The creditor must ensure any registered charge is removed.[193] Further, any amount received by the creditor on 'realisation' of the security shall (so far as referable to the agreement) be repaid.[194]

18.223 Enforcement of an improperly executed agreement by the creditor without a court order (ie in breach of s 65) does not incur any sanction, but may be taken into consideration by the FCA when exercising their powers under CCA (s 170(2)). Further, where goods are wrongfully repossessed without a court order, the debtor/hirer may have a cause of action against the creditor for wrongful interference, or may be able to apply for a mandatory injunction.[195]

What constitutes enforcement

18.224 In *McGuffick v RBS plc*,[196] a narrow interpretation was given to the concept of 'enforcement' for which an enforcement order was required. It was held that the following steps did not amount to 'enforcement':

(i) making adverse reports to credit reference agencies, without explaining that the agreement was temporarily unenforceable;

(ii) disseminating information about the agreement to third parties;

---

[189] *Re London Scottish Finance Ltd (In Administration)* [2014] Bus LR 424, [2013] CTLC 231.

[190] *Barclays Bank plc v Lee* [1993] CLY 474: payments made under an unenforceable credit agreement are not recoverable unless there has been a total failure of consideration. Cf *Wilson v Howard Pawnbrokers* [2005] EWCA Civ 147 and the possibility of an unjust enrichment claim. The issue of recoverability was considered in *Re London Scottish Finance Ltd* [2013] CTLC 231. When dealing with unenforceable agreements under the Money Lenders Act 1927, Lord Diplock in *Orakpo v Manson Investments Ltd* [1978] AC 95 said that they were not devoid of all legal effect. Payments made voluntarily pursuant to their terms are not recoverable.

[191] Except on technical grounds only.

[192] CCA, ss 113 and 106(a); see also s 177 (saving for proprietor of charge for valuable consideration, without notice of the defect).

[193] CCA, s 106(c).

[194] CCA, s 106(d): in *Wilson v Howard Pawnbrokers* [2005] All ER (D) 61 the Court of Appeal held (dubiously) that 'realisation' of the security included sums paid by the debtor by way of instalments, as well as the proceeds of sale of the security.

[195] See CCA, s 170(3).

[196] [2009] EWHC 2386; [2010] 1 All ER 634.

(iii) issuing demands for payment;

(iv) issuing default notices;

(v) threatening legal action or issuing proceedings;

(vi) instructing a debt collection agency.

18.225 Obtaining judgment for the outstanding balance will amount to 'enforcement' of the agreement, and therefore judgment cannot be obtained where the agreement is improperly executed unless an enforcement order is also granted. It is expressly provided by s 65(2) that repossession of goods/land to which the agreement relates amounts to 'enforcement'. However, in the case of live hire-purchase, conditional sale and hire agreements, ownership of goods will not yet have passed to the debtor/hirer. Accordingly, it seems that if the debtor/hirer under such an improperly executed agreement wrongfully sells the goods, the creditor/owner may still sue him for conversion without this amounting to 'enforcement' for which a court order is required. Further, if the term of a hire or hire-purchase agreement has expired, the creditor/owner does not need to 'enforce' the agreement in order to repossess the goods, but can rely on its ownership rights.[197]

18.226 However, where an improperly executed agreement remains live, the creditor/owner will need an enforcement order to obtain an order for delivery-up of the goods from the debtor/hirer (eg where there has been no wrongful onward sale).

Applying for an enforcement order

18.227 The granting of an enforcement order is discretionary. CCA, s 127(1) provides that the court shall dismiss an application by the creditor for an enforcement order only if it considers it 'just' to do so, having regard to:

(i) the 'prejudice'[198] caused to any person 'by the contravention in question';[199]

(ii) the degree of 'culpability'[200] for the contravention; and

(iii) the court's powers under s 127(2)[201] and ss 135–136.[202]

---

[197] See further Guest and Lloyd, *Encyclopaedia of Consumer Credit Law*, vol 1, 2108.

[198] Eg if the debtor would not otherwise have entered the agreement (see *PB Leasing Ltd v Patel and Patel* [1995] CCLR 82: financial figures not inserted prior to signature and no s 62 copy).

[199] Ie by the defect which made the agreement improperly executed.

[200] Eg deliberate misstating of the APR in order to attract more custom.

[201] To reduce/discharge any sum payable by the debtor, to compensate him for the prejudice (see *National Guardian Mortgage Corp v Wilkes* [1993] CCLR 1: interest rate reduced where consideration copy of secured agreement not provided, depriving debtor of opportunity to borrow at lower rate elsewhere; *Rank Xerox v Hepple* [1994] CCLR 1: reduction in amount of accelerated payment due to absence of information).

[202] CCA, s 135 empowers the court to make the operation of a term conditional upon some act, or to suspend a provision of an order; s 136 empowers the court to amend agreements.

The starting point is that an enforcement order will be granted, so the burden is on the debtor to show that it would be 'just' to dismiss the application. It is rare that an enforcement order is not granted: the debtor can be compensated for any prejudice by the court exercising its powers under s 127(2), to reduce/discharge any sum payable by him.[203]

Irredeemably unenforceable agreements

18.228   An agreement may be irredeemably unenforceable (ie the court can make no enforcement order in respect of it) if it was entered before 6 April 2007[204] and:

(i)   the agreement omits or misstates a 'prescribed term';

(ii)   the agreement was not signed by the debtor;[205] or

(iii) the agreement was cancellable and no notice of cancellation rights was given (or no s 62/63 copy was given).[206]

18.229   Where an agreement is irredeemably unenforceable, there will be no prospect of the creditor ever being able to 'enforce' the agreement (eg by obtaining judgment for the outstanding balance). However, the debtor's repayment obligations remain valid (albeit unenforceable). There is no provision in the CCA for the debtor to recover payments made pursuant to an irredeemably unenforceable agreement. However, the debtor could conceivably sue at common law for restitution of payments, on the grounds of mistake at law.[207]

18.230   In *Grace & Anr v Black Horse Limited*[208] the Court of Appeal held that it would not be accurate to describe a person as a defaulter (to a credit reference agency) once a competent court has decided that the agreement is irremediably unenforceable against him.

---

[203] *National Guardian Mortgage Corp v Wilkes* [1993] CCLR 1: interest rate reduced where consideration copy of secured agreement not provided, depriving debtor of opportunity to borrow at lower rate elsewhere; *Rank Xerox v Hepple* [1994] CCLR 1: reduction in amount of accelerated payment due to absence of information about that payment; *Wilson v Hurstanger* [2007] EWCA Civ 299 [2007] CTLC 59: debtor discharged from liability to pay administration fee plus interest thereon.

[204] When s 127(3) and (4) were repealed.

[205] Failure to sign by the creditor cannot give rise to irredeemable unenforceability.

[206] The creditor could remedy this defect by giving the debtor a copy of the executed agreement before the proceedings commenced (s 127(4)); the debtor could then exercise his cancellation rights.

[207] This being a unilateral mistake that the agreement was enforceable.

[208] [2015] 3 All ER 223, [2014] CTLC 312.

UNFAIR RELATIONSHIPS

Which regime applies

18.231 Some credit agreements will still be governed by the predecessor 'extortionate credit bargain' ('E-C-B') regime, rather than the new 'unfair relationship' ('U-R') regime. There are detailed transitional provisions,[209] but the principal rules are:

(i)   if the agreement was redeemed/settled before 6 April 2008: E-C-B regime;

(ii)   if the agreement was entered before 6 April 2007, but not redeemed/settled before 6 April 2008: U-R regime (provided legal proceedings were issued on/after 6 April 2008);

(iii) if the agreement was entered on/after 6 April 2007: U-R regime.

There is a more tricky situation where a credit agreement was entered on/after 6 April 2007 (and so falls under the U-R regime), but consolidates an earlier agreement with the same creditor[210] which would otherwise fall under the E-C-B regime.

18.232 The High Court has held[211] that although the earlier agreement is a 'related agreement',[212] that does not entitle the Court to make it the subject of a U-R order if the earlier agreement does not itself fall within the transitional provisions (ie because it was redeemed before 6 April 2008) – the two regimes are mutually exclusive. However, there is contrasting authority[213] that an order may be made that there is a U-R arising out of the later agreement 'taking into account' the earlier agreement. It may, therefore, resolve to a pleading point.

Extortionate credit bargains

18.233 The old E-C-B regime can be found in CCA, ss 137–140. An E-C-B was defined as a 'credit bargain'[214] which required the debtor to make 'grossly exorbitant' payments, or otherwise 'grossly contravened ordinary principles of fair dealing'. There was a indicative list of relevant factors, which included prevailing interest rates,[215] the debtor's personal characteristics, any financial

---

[209] CCA 2006, s 22(3) and Sch 3, paras 1 and 14–16.

[210] Or an 'associate' of the creditor as defined by s 184.

[211] *Soulsby v Firstplus Financial Group plc* [2010] CTLC 177.

[212] Under CCA, s 140C(4): this would include an agreement wholly or partly refinanced by the subsequent agreement (s 140C(7)).

[213] *Barnes v Black Horse Ltd* [2011] EWHC 1416 (QB).

[214] 'Credit bargain' was defined by s 137(2) to include the credit agreement and any other transaction to be taken into account in computing the total charge for credit; in *Paragon Finance v Nash* [2001] EWCA Civ 1466, [2002] 1 WLR 685 this definition was used to exclude from consideration interest rate variations occurring after the credit agreement was entered.

[215] The case-law makes clear that like for like must be compared: sub-prime interest rates cannot be compared with prevailing high street lending rates.

pressure the debtor was under, the value of any security provided[216] and whether a 'colourable cash price'[217] was quoted for any goods/services included in the credit bargain.

18.234 Most E-C-B cases were unsuccessful attempts by consumers to challenge high interest rates. The High Court held that an interest rate of 48% pa on a short-term bridging loan was not extortionate,[218] and neither was an interest rate of 12% pa on a mortgage for buy-to-let domestic property.[219] Contraventions of the former OFT's Non-Status Guidelines (failures by the lender to enquire as to the purpose of the loan or check the information provided by the broker, and the processing of the loan without a signed application form) were also held not to 'grossly contravene the ordinary principles of fair dealing'.[220] The threshold was generally recognised to be very high.

Scope of the regime

18.235 The U-R provisions apply to 'credit agreements'[221] rather than 'regulated agreements'. Therefore exempt agreements may fall within the U-R regime, unless they are exempt because they are FSMA regulated agreements.[222] For the uncertain position of assignees, see CCA, s 140C(2) (on a strict interpretation, legal assignees are not covered). Any acts or omissions by 'associates' and 'former associates' of the creditor are deemed by s 140A(3) to have been acts or omissions by the creditor (in so far as this is 'appropriate'). 'Associates' are defined broadly in CCA, s 184 to include certain companies with shared directors.

Ways in which unfair relationship may arise

18.236 Section 140A(1)–(2) of the CCA provides:

> (1) The court may make an order under section 140B in connection with a credit agreement if it determines that the relationship between the creditor and the debtor arising out of the agreement (or the agreement taken with any related agreement) is unfair to the debtor because of one or more of the following –
>
> > (a) any of the terms of the agreement or any related agreement;
> > (b) the way in which the creditor has exercised or enforced any of his rights under the agreement or any related agreement;

---

[216] What would be considered an extortionate rate for an unsecured advance is very different from what would be considered extortionate in secured lending.

[217] Ie where an inflated cash price for goods/services is quoted so as to artificially reduce the interest rate.

[218] *A Ketley Ltd v Scott* [1981] ICR 241.

[219] *Davies v Directloans Ltd* [1986] 1 WLR 823; see also *Wills v Wood* [1984] CCLR 7 where the CA overturned an E-C-B finding on a 12% pa loan from a solicitors' firm to an inexperienced borrower.

[220] *Broadwick Financial Services Ltd v Spencer* [2002] EWCA Civ 35.

[221] Defined in CCA, s 140C: the debtor must be an 'individual'.

[222] Ie the U-R provisions do not apply to agreements which are exempt under RAO Article 60C(2); see CCA, s 140A(5).

(c)   any other thing done (or not done) by, or on behalf of, the creditor (either before or after the making of the agreement or any related agreement).

(2) In deciding whether to make a determination under this section the court shall have regard to all matters it thinks relevant (including matters relating to the creditor and matters relating to the debtor).'

Therefore there are three ways in which a U-R can arise, which are listed in s 140(1)(a)–(c).

Terms of the agreement

18.237 The first limb deals with unfairness arising from contractual terms. There is no exclusion for 'core terms', as under the Unfair Terms in Consumer Contracts Regulations 1999. Therefore a U-R can arise due to a high interest rate,[223] or cost. However, whether a term is 'unfair' under the UTCCRs is likely to be 'relevant'. It should be noted that there can also be a U-R arising from the terms of any 'related agreement'.[224] This would not only include an earlier consolidated credit agreement, but would also cover a supply contract for goods/services, or a Payment Protection Insurance (PPI) policy.[225] Therefore there could be a U-R because the price of such items is unfairly high.

Way rights are exercised/enforced

18.238 The post-contract exercise of the creditor's 'rights' is covered by the second limb, eg the amount of any variation to the interest rate, or the manner in which debt-collection activity is undertaken. Unsolicited increases in the credit limit under a credit card agreement could also be covered, in cases where this can be criticised as irresponsible lending. An unsolicited extension in the repayment term could also be described as unfair, where this results in additional interest being payable. Any act or omission which does not literally amount to an exercise of the creditor's 'rights' will fall within the third limb. The steps the creditor takes in relation to unenforceable agreements could also give rise to a U-R, although in *McGuffick v RBS plc*,[226] the High Court held that, in the context of a temporarily unenforceable agreement, taking steps which did not actually amount to 'enforcement' did not give rise to a U-R.

---

[223] See *Patel v Patel* [2009] EWHC 3264: U-R where interest rate charged by a friend was three times that of retail banks, and was compounded monthly.

[224] Defined in s 140C(4).

[225] Provided that the supply contract/PPI policy falls within the s 19 definition of a 'linked transaction'.

[226] [2009] EWHC 2386, [2010] 1 All ER 634.

Any act or omission 'by or on behalf of the creditor'

18.239 The third way in which a U-R can arise is because of something 'done (or not done) by, or on behalf of the creditor' (s 140A(1)). Debtors often seek to argue that conduct by a credit broker or motor dealer should be taken into account under this subsection.

18.240 In *Plevin v Paragon Personal Finance Ltd*,[227] the Supreme Court held that 'by or on behalf of' should be confined to common law agency and deemed agency. The broker in this case was not acting as Paragon's agent (indeed it was the debtor's agent) and therefore it was not acting 'on behalf of' Paragon for the purposes of the Unfair Relationships test. This is an important limitation on the breadth of s 140A. Restricting 'on behalf of' to agency follows the ordinary meaning of the statutory words, and is supported by cross-referencing other CCA provisions.

> 'The practice by which the agent of a consumer of financial services is remunerated by the supplier of those services has often been criticised. It is, however, an almost universal feature of the business, and it is of the utmost legal and commercial importance to maintain the principle that the source of the commission has no bearing on the identity of the person for whom the intermediary is acting or the nature of his functions.'[228]

18.241 It is made explicit in CCA, s 140A(1) that acts/omissions occurring at any time are covered. For instance, the third limb encompasses irresponsible lending decisions,[229] any failure to issue statutory notices (or the issue of non-compliant notices), misleading advertising and non-compliance with any other statutory provisions (whether or not express sanctions are also provided in relation to those provisions). In *Carey v HSBC Bank plc*,[230] the High Court held that breach of CCA, s 78 (duty to provide information on request) did not, without more, give rise to a U-R.

Unfairness and relevant matters

18.242 There is no indicative list of relevant matters (as there is under the E-C-B provisions). The former OFT guidance 'Unfair Relationships – Enforcement Action under Part 8 of the Enterprise Act 2002'[231] may be considered by the court although it does not appear to have any statutory basis.[232] Matters 'relating to the creditor' will include the scope and content of

---

[227] [2014] 1 WLR 4222.
[228] *Plevin v Paragon Personal Finance Limited* [2014] 1 WLR 4222 at para 33.
[229] Eg where the creditor fails to take reasonable steps to check that the repayments are affordable, or where an interest-only loan is sold without checking that the debtor has a repayment vehicle in place; however an argument by the debtor that 'you should not have given me the loan I requested' is not attractive.
[230] [2009] EWHC 3417, [2009] CTLC 103.
[231] OFT 854 rev, May 2008 (updated August 2011).
[232] Section 140D has been repealed see SI 2013/1881.

any regulatory obligations imposed on the creditor. If there has been full compliance with detailed rules specifically governing the area in question, there is unlikely to be a U-R.

18.243 In *Harrison v Black Horse Ltd*,[233] the lender selling single premium PPI had failed to disclose to the debtor that it would retain some 87% of the premium as commission. There was no obligation to disclose commission under the Insurance (Conduct of Business) Rules (ICOB). The Court of Appeal held (at para 58) that the 'touchstone' for whether there was a U-R must be the standard imposed by the FSA (now FCA) through ICOB, rather than a 'visceral instinct that the relevant conduct is beyond the pale'. It would be 'anomalous' if a creditor was obliged to disclose commission in order to escape a finding of a U-R, yet not obliged to disclose it under ICOB. However, this decision was disapproved in the Supreme Court in the case of *Plevin*.

18.244 In *Tamimi v Khodari*,[234] the Court of Appeal held that there was no U-R in a context where a 'very large' 10% charge had been imposed on a wealthy compulsive gambler for short-term loans. The credit risk was high, and the gambler 'wanted these loans and could well afford to repay them'. Although the U-R provisions do not explicitly incorporate any causation test, it was noted by the High Court in *Harrison v Black Horse Ltd*[235] that 'the test is still whether there is unfairness as a result'.

Gateways to make application

18.245 There are three gateways to make an application for relief (s 140B(2)):

(a)   on an application made[236] by the debtor/a surety;

(b)   at the instance of the debtor/surety in any enforcement proceedings[237] in any Court to which the debtor and creditor are parties;

(c)   in any other proceedings in any court where the amount paid/payable under the agreement (or any related agreement) is relevant.

Burden of proof

18.246 Section 140B(9) provides for a reverse burden of proof: once the debtor alleges an U-R, the creditor bears the burden of proving that there is not a U-R. It is likely that the burden on the creditor is a 'persuasive' burden, which only arises once the 'evidential' burden of proof has been discharged by the debtor.[238]

---

[233] [2011] EWCA Civ 1128; [2011] CTLC 103.
[234] [2009] EWCA Civ 1109; [2009] CTLC 208.
[235] [2010] EWHC 3152 (QB) at para 61; [2011] CTLC 103.
[236] This must be in the county court: s 140B(4).
[237] To enforce the agreement or any related agreement.
[238] This was the case under the old E-C-B regime: see Guest and Lloyd, *Encyclopaedia of Consumer Credit Law*, vol 1, 2222/83-84, see *Carey v HSBC Bank Plc* [2009] EWHC 3417 (QB); [2010] Bus LR 1142; [2009] CTLC 103.

Powers of the court to order relief

18.247 If the court makes a U-R finding, there are seven categories of powers it has to order relief (s 140B(1)). Any such order must be with regard to the agreement or any related agreement. Whether to order any relief, and which form of relief to grant is discretionary.[239] The seven categories of relief are:

(i) an order requiring the creditor[240] to repay (in whole/part) any sum paid[241] by the debtor/surety by virtue of the agreement (or any related agreement);

(ii) an injunction requiring the creditor[242] to do/not do/cease doing something[243] in connection with the agreement (or any related agreement);

(iii) reduction/discharge[244] of any sum payable by the debtor/surety by virtue of the agreement (or any related agreement);

(iv) return to surety[245] of any property provided by him for security;

(v) setting aside (in whole/part) any duty[246] imposed on the debtor/surety by virtue of the agreement (or any related agreement);

(vi) alteration of the terms[247] of the agreement (or any related agreement);

(vii) directing accounts to be taken.[248]

Limitation

18.248 The leading authority on limitation periods in relation to the old E-C-B provisions is *Rahman v Sterling Credit*.[249] The Court of Appeal held that the limitation period for an E-C-B claim for declaratory relief, or relief from future liability to make payments was 12 years (Limitation Act 1980, s 8). However, the limitation period for an E-C-B claim for repayment of sums already paid was 6 years (Limitation Act 1980, s 9). It was stated obiter in *Rahman* that the 6-year period begins to run from the date of the agreement. However, it is arguable that the 6 years should instead run from the date of the last payment.[250]

---

[239] See the word 'may' in s 140B(1).
[240] Or any associate/former associate of the creditor.
[241] Whether or not paid to the creditor, eg sums paid to insurers/ brokers (see also s 140B(3)).
[242] Or any associate/former associate of the creditor.
[243] Eg an order requiring the cessation of debt collection activities, or requiring the creditor to respond to a request for information/documents.
[244] Eg by reducing the interest rate under the agreement.
[245] Defined by s 189 to include the debtor: therefore the court could order that a mortgage be discharged.
[246] Other than repayment duties (which are covered by (iii)), eg insurance and maintenance obligations.
[247] Eg extension of the repayment period.
[248] Eg if the interest rate is reduced after an agreement has been terminated, an account may be needed to determine how much one party should pay the other.
[249] [2001] 1 WLR 496.
[250] See Guest and Lloyd, *Encyclopaedia of Consumer Credit Law*, vol 1, 2222/84-85.

18.249 Under the U-R provisions, the date from when the 6-year limitation period starts to run may be different. In *Patel v Patel*[251] it was held that the Court must take account of unfairness throughout the 'relationship'. Therefore time only started to run when the 'relationship' ended (usually this will be when the credit agreement is redeemed).

PPI MISSELLING

18.250 From 2009 onwards, there was a wave of litigation about payment protection insurance (PPI) 'misselling'. PPI is insurance to cover the debtor's credit repayments in the event of death, accident, sickness and/or unemployment. The PPI insurance policy is a separate contract between the debtor and the insurer, but it will usually fall within the CCA, s 19 definition of a 'linked transaction' to the credit agreement.[252] Factually, the most common allegations are:

(i) the debtor was told he 'had to' purchase the PPI in order to get the loan;

(ii) PPI was not discussed at all, or inadequately discussed (eg the debtor was not orally informed that it was optional);

(iii) the PPI was unsuitable (eg because the debtor had generous employee benefits, existing insurance, or a pre-existing illness which would have been excluded);

(iv) the required documents were not provided;

(v) Non-disclosure of commission;[253]

(vi) Failure to adequately assess a customer's demands and needs.[254]

As a matter of law, the usual causes of action are:

(i) breach of the FSA's rules (ICOB[255] or ICOBS)[256] giving rise to damages under s 138D of the FSMA;[257]

(ii) an 'unfair relationship' under CCA, s 140A;

(iii) negligence or misrepresentation;[258]

---

[251] [2009] EWHC 3264 (QB).

[252] Single premium PPI financed on credit will fall within s 19(1)(b); monthly premium PPI may fall within s 19(1)(c); being a 'linked transaction' will make it a 'related agreement' for the purposes of the unfair relationship test (s 140C(4)(b)).

[253] In *Plevin v Paragon Personal Finance Limited* [2014] UKSC 61, [2014] 1 WLR 4222 the Supreme Court found that the non-disclosure of commission may render a lenders relationship with a borrower unfair (see para 18).

[254] *Saville v Central Capital Ltd* [2014] CTLC 97.

[255] Insurance (Conduct of Business) Rules, in force from 14 January 2005 until 5 January 2008.

[256] Insurance (Conduct of Business) Sourcebook, in force from 6 January 2008.

[257] The Financial Services and Markets Act 2000.

[258] Usually pleaded where the agreement pre-dates the coming into force of ICOB/ICOBS, or (in the case of negligence) where there are limitation difficulties and the 'unfair relationship' regime does not apply (the debtor has a weak argument that the 'date of knowledge' provisions in the Limitation Act 1980, s 14A apply).

(iv) misstatement of the amount of credit, rendering the agreement irredeemably unenforceable (only for pre-6 April 2007 agreements, where it can be said that the PPI was 'required by the creditor as a condition' of the loan).[259]

18.251 Whether there is an 'unfair relationship' will usually be tied to whether there has been a breach of ICOB/ICOBS, but the ss 140A–140D cause of action offers the debtors the added advantage of a reversed burden of proof and more favourable limitation provisions. In *Scotland v British Credit Trust Ltd*,[260] a misrepresentation by a double-glazing salesmen about the need to purchase PPI when taking out a loan was taken into account by the court as something 'done by, or on behalf of, the creditor' when determining whether the relationship between the creditor and the debtor was unfair under the CCA, s 140A.

18.252 In *Figurasin v Central Capital Limited*,[261] the court held that each communication made to a customer must be clear, fair and not misleading (see ICOBS 2.3.3). Therefore, the fact that an agreement contains all of the necessary details did not mitigate against a company that had failed to properly mention the cost of the PPI on a prior telephone call with the customer.

SECRET COMMISSIONS

18.253 In *Hurstanger Ltd v Wilson & anor*,[262] the Court of Appeal held that the creditor had procured the broker's breach of fiduciary duty by paying it an undisclosed commission, in circumstances where the debtor had also paid the broker a substantial fee. This was a 'half secret' commission (the fact of the possible commission payment was disclosed, but not the amount). The creditor was held to be liable to make equitable compensation to the debtor in the amount of the commission. However, *Hurstanger* has been distinguished in the subsequent case-law, where the courts have found on the facts that there was no fiduciary relationship between the broker and the debtor, and therefore no cause of action.

18.254 This is particularly so where the debtor himself does not pay any fee to the broker. In *Bowstead & Reynolds on Agency*[263] at 6–086 it is said:

> 'where [the borrower] leaves [the broker] to look to the other party for his remuneration or knows that he will receive something from the other party, he cannot object on the ground that he did not know the precise particulars of the amount paid.'

---

[259] The PPI must have been required 'by the creditor', so it seems the amount of credit cannot be misstated where it was a separate party (eg a broker/dealer) who sold the PPI and wrongly told the debtor that it was compulsory.

[260] [2015] 1 All ER 708.

[261] [2014] 2 All ER (Comm) 257.

[262] [2007] 1 WLR 2351; [2007] CTLC 59.

[263] (20th edn) Sweet and Maxwell Common Law Library.

18.255   Even where a fee has been paid by the debtor, allegations of secret commission have recently been dismissed on the basis that no fiduciary duty was owed by the broker.[264] However, in *McWilliam v Norton Finance (UK) Limited*,[265] the court held that a credit broker providing its services on an information only basis was acting in a capacity which involved the repose of trust and confidence and accordingly owed its consumer clients a fiduciary duty such that it was liable to account to them for commissions it had received without their informed consent. In *Nelmes v NRAM*,[266] the court found that non-disclosure of a broker's procuration fee, could amount to an unfair relationship. Such a payment deprived the borrower of the disinterested advice of his broker.

SECTION 56 DEEMED AGENCY

18.256   CCA, s 56(2) provides that certain 'antecedent negotiations' with the debtor are deemed to have been conducted by the negotiator (the credit broker/supplier) as agent of the creditor. Section 56 deemed agency only arises in the context of DCS agreements: it is inapplicable to DC agreements and hire agreements. In the case of DC agreements and hire agreements, the debtor must rely on common law agency.[267] Section 56(3) prevents the creditor from contracting out of the deemed agency.

Credit brokers

18.257   Section 56(1)(b) covers negotiations conducted by a credit-broker 'in relation to goods' sold (or proposed to be sold) by the credit-broker to the creditor before forming the subject matter of a s 12(a) DCS agreement. This would cover, for instance, negotiations conducted by a motor dealer in relation to a vehicle which will become the subject of a hire-purchase, conditional sale or credit sale agreement. If the dealer first sells the goods to another intermediary, who then sells them on to the creditor, the High Court has held that s 56(1)(b) does not apply to representations by the dealer.[268]

18.258   Only negotiations 'in relation to goods' are covered. Representations about the terms of the hire-purchase or credit agreement itself are not

---

[264]   *Yates and Lorenzelli v Nemo Personal Finance & anor*, unreported, Manchester County Court, 14 May 2010, HHJ Platts; *Flanagan v Nemo Personal Finance*, unreported, Manchester County Court, 5 August 2011, HHJ Stephen Stewart QC; *Sealey and Winfield v Loans.co.uk and GE Money Ltd*, unreported, Mold County Court, 15 August 2011, HHJ Jarman QC.

[265]   [2015] 1 All ER (Comm) 1026, [2015] CTLC 60.

[266]   [2016] EWCA Civ 491.

[267]   At common law, a dealer is not normally an agent of the creditor in respect of representations, even if it receives commission from the creditor (*Branwhite v Worcester Works Finance Ltd* [1969] 1 AC 552), but the creditor may occasionally be held to have held the dealer out as its agent or be estopped from denying representations were made on its behalf (*Lease Management Services Ltd v Purnell Secretarial Services Ltd* [1994] CCLR 127).

[268]   *Black Horse Ltd v Langford* [2007] EWHC 907; [2007] CTLC 75.

covered.[269] However, the Court of Appeal gave a broad interpretation to the phrase 'in relation to goods' in *Forthright Finance Ltd v Ingate*,[270] extending it in the context of hire-purchase to cover discussions about the discharge of an old agreement (even though the value of the old car was equal to the outstanding balance under the old agreement), as 'all the negotiations form part of the one transaction' to acquire the new car.[271] If *Ingate* is followed, representations about any linked insurance product could also be covered, in the face of the natural meaning of s 56(1)(b).

Suppliers

18.259 Section 56(1) covers negotiations conducted by the supplier 'in relation to a transaction financed' (or proposed to be financed) by a s 12(b) or (c) DCS agreement. This would cover, for instance, negotiations conducted by a supplier before the debtor enters a loan agreement with a finance company to finance the purchase of goods/services. Again, representations about the credit agreement itself will not be covered.[272]

Effect of deemed agency

18.260 Where a credit-broker/supplier is deemed to have made certain representations as the agent of the creditor (eg representations that the goods are of satisfactory quality), then the debtor may have a cause of action against the creditor for misrepresentation or (if the representations were incorporated as terms) breach of contract. The creditor could also be liable in tort (eg for negligent misstatement by the negotiator). A cause of action for misrepresentation, tort or breach of contract may entitle the debtor to rescission/repudiation of the credit agreement, or damages. The creditor could also be guilty of a statutory offence committed by the negotiator, in contravention of consumer protection legislation. Section 56 claims may also be brought in respect of the financing of timeshare agreements concerning properties abroad.[273]

18.261 Section 56 does not confer on the creditor a right to an indemnity from the credit-broker/supplier for any liability it incurs as deemed principal. However, the creditor may be able to rely upon the Civil Liability (Contribution) Act 1978. There is a tricky question of what happens if the credit agreement has been assigned. Guest and Lloyd[274] are of the view that the

---

[269] Contrast the wording in s 56(1)(a).
[270] [1997] 4 All ER 99.
[271] See also *UDT v Whitfield and First National Securities* [1987] CCLR 60: dealer's representation that he would discharge the outstanding balance under the old agreement fell within s 56(1)(b), as it was an integral part of the transaction to purchase the new car.
[272] Contrast the wording in s 56(1)(a).
[273] *Jarrett v Barclays Bank plc* [1999] QB 1, which held that Art 16 of the Brussels Convention (which confers exclusive jurisdiction over actions in rem under the timeshare agreement on the courts of the place where the property is situated) did not apply. See now Art 4.1(c) of Rome I.
[274] Guest and Lloyd, *Encyclopaedia of Consumer Credit Law*, vol 1, 2076 and 2080.

original creditor would remain liable under s 56, but that if the debtor was sued for the outstanding balance by the assignee, he could still plead a counterclaim under s 56 by way of set off.

WITHDRAWAL AND CANCELLATION

Section 66A withdrawal

18.262   Section 66A applies from 1 February 2011 to all credit agreements except 'excluded agreements'.[275] It provides a 14-day right of 'withdrawal' to debtors. In order to exercise this right, the debtor must give the creditor oral[276] or written notice of withdrawal within the 14 days beginning with the day after 'the relevant day'. 'The relevant day' is whichever is the latest of (a) the day the agreement is made, (b) the day the creditor first informs the debtor of the credit limit[277] or (c) the day the debtor receives a s 61A/s 63 copy of the executed agreement, or receives the written s 61A(3) information.[278]

18.263   If the debtor exercises his right to withdraw, the credit agreement (and any ancillary service contract)[279] is treated as never having been entered (s 66A(7)). Crucially, the debtor must repay any advance (plus accrued interest at the contractual rate); this must be repaid within 30 days of giving notice of withdrawal (s 66A(9) and (10)). Only the credit agreement is erased: if the credit was extended to finance a sale/supply contract, then that contract will remain valid and the purchase price will have to be paid to the supplier by the debtor.

18.264   Section 66A(11) expressly provides that in the case of hire-purchase, conditional sale or credit sale, the debtor who chooses to withdraw and repay the advance (effectively the purchase price) will gain title to the goods 'on the same terms as would have applied had the debtor not withdrawn'. If the debtor fails to repay the credit within 30 days, it is unclear whether (i) the debtor is entitled to retain possession of any goods and (ii) when title will pass to the debtor (eg may title only pass if he makes payment within 30 days, or will title pass whenever payment is finally made?).[280]

---

[275]   Agreements for credit exceeding £60,260; agreements secured on land; hire agreements; restricted-use credit agreements to finance the purchase of land and agreements for bridging loans in connection with the purchase of land (s 66A(14)).

[276]   Oral notice must be given in any manner specified by the agreement: s 61A(4).

[277]   Where the creditor is required to inform the debtor of the credit limit.

[278]   If s 61A/s 63 respectively applies.

[279]   Eg a PPI policy.

[280]   For an analysis of this uncertainty, see Guest and Lloyd, *Encyclopaedia of Consumer Credit Law*, vol 1, 2113.

Section 67 cancellable agreements

18.265 From 1 February 2011 (when s 66A came into effect), the s 67 cancellation rights only[281] apply to:

- regulated agreements where the amount of credit exceeds £60,620; and
- regulated hire agreements.

Even within these two categories, s 67 does not apply to overdrafts,[282] or in cases where the agreement is signed on trade premises.[283] Additionally, s 67 does not apply to agreements secured on land or to restricted-use agreements to finance the purchase of land or bridging loans to purchase land (s 67(1)(a)).

18.266 Where s 67 does apply, the agreement is only cancellable if the 'antecedent negotiations'[284] included 'oral representations[285] made when in the presence of the debtor/hirer' by an 'individual acting as, or on behalf of the negotiator' (ie face-to-face negotiations). The main situations in which an agreement will be cancellable are therefore doorstep sales and where the negotiations occur on trade premises, but the debtor takes the agreement home to sign.

18.267 Agreements are only cancellable if the face-to-face negotiations were conducted by the 'negotiator'. Following the definition of 'negotiator' in s 56(1), this can generally only include a dealer or credit-broker where the agreement is DCS. In the case of DC or hire agreements, only the creditor or its employee can be the 'negotiator' (unless, unusually, the dealer or credit-broker has actual/ostensible authority to act as the agent of the creditor).[286]

18.268 Where an agreement is cancellable, the debtor must be given a pre-contract document in accordance with the 2010 or 2004 Disclosure Regulations. The agreement itself must include the prescribed[287] notice of cancellation rights and this notice must also be included in the ss 62–63 copies of the unexecuted and executed agreements given to the debtor (s 64).[288]

---

[281] See CCA, s 66A(14) and s 67(1)(a) and (2).

[282] Section 67 does not apply to agreements listed in s 74, which includes overdrafts and non-commercial agreements.

[283] Section 67(1)(b): s 67 does not apply where the agreement is signed at premises where any of the following is carrying on business: the creditor/owner, any party to a linked transaction, or the negotiator in antecedent negotiations.

[284] 'Antecedent negotiations' is defined in s 56(1).

[285] See *Moorgate Services Ltd v Kabir* [1995] CCLR 74, where the Court of Appeal narrowed the definition of 'representation' to a statement of fact/opinion, or an undertaking as to the future, which was capable of inducing the debtor/hirer to enter the agreement.

[286] See *Woodchester Leasing Equipment v Clayton (RM) and Clayton (DM) (t/a Sudbury Sports)* [1994] 4 CLY 506: held supplier was acting as agent of hire company when making representations, so agreement was cancellable.

[287] See the Consumer Credit (Cancellation Notices and Copies of Documents) Regulations 1983.

[288] Where s 63(2) does not apply (only one copy of the agreement is required), the cancellation notice must also be sent to the debtor within 7 days after the agreement is entered (s 64(1)(b)); in the case of credit-token agreements see s 64(2).

18.269   A cancellable agreement is 'improperly executed' if the requirements for the notice in s 64 are not complied with. Prior to 6 April 2007, cancellable agreements where the creditor had failed to give notice of cancellation rights (or any s 62/63 copy) were irredeemably unenforceable (s 127(4)). The cooling-off period starts when the debtor signs the unexecuted agreement and ends at the end of the 5th day following the day on which he received the s 63 executed copy, or (if there is no s 63 copy) a s 64(1)(b) cancellation notice (s 68).[289] The debtor may give the creditor written notice of cancellation in any form (see s 69). The credit agreement will then be treated as if it had never been entered, and linked transactions[290] will also be cancelled (s 69(1)(i) and (4)).

18.270   Sometimes credit agreements are drafted in the form of cancellable agreements (in case there happen to be face-to-face negotiations, causing s 67 to apply). In such a case, the debtor will have contractual cancellation rights, but the agreement will not be treated as 'cancellable' under the CCA when it comes to sanctions.[291]

Distance marketing

18.271   The Financial Services (Distance Marketing) Regulations 2004 apply to credit agreements with consumers which are concluded at a distance. The cancellation rights do not apply to credit agreements secured on land or if there is a right to withdraw under s 66A.[292] The cooling-off period is 14 days, either from the time the contract is concluded or (if later) from the time the prescribed information[293] is provided.[294] Where an agreement is cancellable under these Regulations, the debtor will need to be given a pre-contract document in accordance with Sch 1. Agreements may also be cancellable under other legislation.[295]

MISCELLANEOUS

Unilateral variation of agreements

18.272   Most credit agreements will give the creditor the contractual power to unilaterally vary any term of the agreement. Where this power is exercised, then s 82(1) comes into effect and the variation will not take effect until notice of it

---

[289]   If s 64(1)(b) does not apply, the cooling-off period ends at the end of the 14th day following signing (s 68(b)).

[290]   Eg an agreement to purchase goods/services; but some linked transactions (eg insurance contracts) are exempted from automatic cancellation by the Consumer Credit (Linked Transactions) (Exemptions) Regulations 1983.

[291]   *Rankine v MBNA Europe Bank Ltd* [2007] EWCA Civ 1273; [2007] CTLC 241.

[292]   See reg 11.

[293]   Reg 8.

[294]   Reg 10.

[295]   Eg the Consumer Contracts (Information, Cancellation and Additional Charges) Regulations 2013; the Timeshare, Holiday Products, Resale and Exchange Contracts Regulations 2010; the Package Travel, Package Holidays and Package Tour Regulations 1992.

has been given to the debtor in the prescribed[296] manner. The general rule is that notice of variation must be served 7 days before the variation takes effect. Section 78A imposes a duty to give notice of variations in the interest rate under certain types of agreements. For agreements which are outside the scope of s 78A (eg agreements secured on land), s 82(1) only applies where the interest rate is varied by the creditor pursuant to a contractual power. This may exclude some automatic changes in interest rate by reference to external factors.

18.273 In *Paragon Finance plc v Nash and Staunton*,[297] it was held that the creditor's discretion to vary an interest rate is subject to an implied term that it will not vary it arbitrarily or in a way no reasonable lender would. Variations in rate (or a failure to vary the rate) could now be the basis of an alleged unfair relationship.

Modifying agreements

18.274 A full analysis of this area is outside the scope of this chapter. Section 82(2) introduces the concept of a 'modifying agreement', which is a subsequent agreement which varies or supplements an earlier agreement by mutual consent (in contrast to a unilateral variation under s 82(1)). It is provided that a modifying agreement shall be treated as revoking the earlier agreement and containing provisions reproducing the combined effect of the two agreements (s 82(2)). There are special form and content requirements for modifying agreements in the 1983 and 2010 Agreements Regulations.

18.275 Examples of situations where modifying agreements will have to be drafted are where a further advance is made under a loan agreement, where the term of a fixed-term agreement is extended,[298] where there is a substitution in the security, or where the goods which are the subject of a hire agreement are changed.

18.276 There is often an alteration in the amount/number of repayments, or repayment term. In order for there to be a contractual modification of the agreement under s 82(2), as opposed to a mere concession by the creditor, there must be some consideration provided by the debtor (eg additional payment obligations). Further, there will not be a s 82(2) modification of the agreement where the changes involve a termination of the earlier agreement and its replacement by a new, separate agreement – that is a novation.

Multiple agreements

18.277 A full analysis of this difficult area is outside the scope of this chapter. A multiple agreement is defined by CCA, s 18(1), as an agreement where:

---

[296] Consumer Credit (Notice of Variation of Agreements) Regulations 1977.

[297] [2002] 1 WLR 685.

[298] Unless this is simply by way of waiver or forbearance in allowing further time to pay, rather than a contractual variation (*Broadwick Financial Services Ltd v Spencer* [2002] EWCA Civ 35); [2002] CCLR 5.

its terms are such as:

    (a)   to place a part of it within one category of agreement mentioned in [the CCA] and another part of it within a different category of agreement so mentioned, or within a category of agreement not so mentioned, or

    (b)   To place it, or a part of it, within two or more categories of agreement so mentioned.

Section 18(1)(a) applies to agreements in 'parts' (where the parts fall within different categories).

18.278   Section 18(1)(b) uses the words 'it, or a part of it' and therefore applies both to (i) agreements in 'parts' (where one part falls within more than one category) and (ii) 'unitary' agreements (which fall within more than one category). Where there is an agreement in 'parts', the part within the s 18(1)(a) or (b) must be treated as a separate agreement (s 18(2)). Where there is a unitary agreement which falls within s 18(1)(b), it must be treated as an agreement in each of the relevant categories (s 18(3)). Whether a 'part' is treated as a separate agreement affects the applicable form and content requirements and compliance with other CCA obligations.

18.279   In *Southern Pacific Mortgage Ltd v Heath*,[299] the Court of Appeal dismissed the argument that a credit agreement was a multiple agreement where part of the advance was s 11(2) unrestricted-use credit paid directly to the borrowers, and part was s 11(1)(c) restricted-use credit used to redeem a prior mortgage. The Court of Appeal held (at para 41) that: 'It is not correct to start from the proposition that more than one disparate category is concerned, and to conclude from this that the agreement must fall into two or more parts.' The correct approach was set out by the Court of Appeal as follows:

'the starting point is that it is from the terms of the agreement that one must find out whether the agreement is one under which there are two or more parts.

It is significant that it is the agreement which is to be placed in one or more categories, not the credit provided under the agreement.'

On the facts in *Heath*, the Court of Appeal found that the credit agreement was a single agreement, saying:

'It is a single agreement which cannot be dissected into separate parts ... it is not possible to collect from the document as a whole what amount to the respective terms of two or more separate agreements.'

Retaking of protected hire-purchase goods

18.280   Under a hire-purchase or conditional sale agreement, s 90 provides that where the debtor is in breach of the agreement, but has paid 'one third or more of the total price of the goods', the creditor can only recover possession of the

---

[299] [2009] EWCA Civ 1135; [2009] CTLC 20.

goods on a court order. The 'total price' means the total sum payable by the debtor under the agreement (including contractual interest on the credit for the goods, but excluding any payment protection premium or default interest). If the creditor proceeds, in breach of s 90, to recover the goods without a court order, there is a drastic sanction: the agreement will terminate and the debtor may recover all sums he has paid under the agreement (s 91).

Termination of hire-purchase and hire agreements

Hire-purchase agreements

18.281 Section 99 gives the debtor the right to terminate a hire-purchase agreement at any time before the final payment falls due, by giving notice. If the creditor terminates the agreement (with the requisite notice) and the outstanding balance thereupon becomes due (under an acceleration clause), it is likely that this will amount to the 'final payment' falling due, so that the debtor cannot thereafter terminate under s 99.[300]

18.282 Section 99 termination by the debtor will not affect any liability under the agreement which has already accrued (s 99(2)). Further, upon termination, the debtor must pay 'the amount (if any) by which half of the total price exceeds the aggregate of the sums paid and the sums due in respect of the total price' (s 100(1)). The court has the power to make an order that the debtor pay a lesser amount (s 100(3)).[301] Of course, the debtor must also return the goods.

Section 93: increasing interest rate on default

18.283 CCA, s 93 prevents a creditor charging default interest (interest on 'sums which, in breach of the agreement, are unpaid')[302] at a higher rate than the contractual interest rate. However, it seems s 93 may be circumvented by drafting the agreement so as to stipulate a certain level of repayments, then sending the debtor a 'concession letter' offering a reduced level of repayments if he makes timely payments (and making clear that such a concession is not contractually binding, or a variation of the agreement).[303]

Time orders

18.284 If it considers it 'just', the court may make a 'time order' under CCA, s 129, providing that a debt be paid by reasonably affordable instalments. The court must have regard to the means of the debtor. Time orders are often made in the context of enforcement actions by the creditor, but may also be made in applications by the creditor for an enforcement order, or specific s 129

---

[300] See *Wadham Stringer Finance Ltd v Meaney* [1981] 1 WLR 39.
[301] If the actual loss sustained by the creditor as a result of the termination is less than the sum payable under (1).
[302] This does not include default charges, provided they are paid on time.
[303] *Broadwick v Spencer* [2002] CCLR 5.

applications by the debtor following receipt of a default/enforcement/ termination notice, or a notice of sums in arrears.[304]

18.285 A time order can only be made in respect of sums which are already due and payable (unless the agreement is for hire-purchase or conditional sale – s 130(2)). Therefore a time order can deal with arrears and, if an acceleration clause has been triggered due to default, the accelerated outstanding balance. A time order should usually be made for a fixed period, to accommodate temporary financial difficulty. If the debtor is unlikely to be able to resume the contractual instalments within time, it is more equitable to permit enforcement.[305] Upon the making of a time order, consequential orders may also be made under s 136 (eg reducing the interest rate).

No contracting out

18.286 Section 173(1) provides that a contractual term will be void if, and to the extent that, it is inconsistent with the consumer protection provided by the CCA. This could, for instance, render void clauses stipulating that foreign law applies, or imposing a fee payable upon early settlement. However, s 173(3) adds that if the CCA provides that an act may be done in relation to any person only on an order of the court/the FCA, that does not preclude that person from consenting to the act, without needing an order. The consent must be given at the time, and cannot be retrospective.

Jurisdiction

18.287 Pursuant to s 141, the county court has exclusive jurisdiction over actions by the creditor to enforce regulated agreements or linked transactions.

CRIMINAL ENFORCEMENT

Offences

18.288 A large number of offences created by the CCA, as originally drafted, have subsequently been repealed. Most of these offences related to obligations on the part of the creditor/owner to supply appropriate documentation and/or information to the debtor/hirer and were repealed by the Consumer Protection from Unfair Trading Regulations 2008, Sch 4, para 1. Breach of the FCA Handbook rules does not give rise to criminal sanctions but may give rise to civil remedies under FSMA, s 138D. In relation to financial promotions, provided that reasonable care is taken to ensure that the promotion is clear, fair and not misleading, a consumer will not have a right to damages under s 138D (CONC 3.3.1R).

---

[304] If the debtor applies for a time order after receipt of a notice of sums in arrears, he must first give the creditor a s 129A notice of intent, then wait for 14 days.

[305] *Southern and District Finance plc v Barnes* [1995] CLY 724; [1995] CCLR 62.

Directors' liability

18.289 Section 169 of CCA permits the prosecution and conviction of any director, manager, secretary or other similar officer of the company, or any person who was purporting to act in such capacity. These provisions are now covered in Chapter 3, Criminal Enforcement.

Statutory defence

18.290 Section 168 of CCA provides a due diligence defence. This is now covered in Chapter 3, Criminal Enforcement.

DUTY TO ENFORCE

18.291 In Great Britain, Trading Standards Departments, as the local weights and measures authorities, have a duty – alongside the FCA – to enforce the CCA; in Northern Ireland it is the duty of the Department of Enterprise, Trade and Investment (DETI) (s 161).

18.292 Section 6 of the Financial Services Act 2012 replaces the provisions in Part 1 of the Financial Services and Markets Act 2000 ('FSMA'). New s 3R FSMA enables the FCA to enter into arrangements with local weights and measures authorities or DETI for the provision of services in relation certain types of regulated activity (for example, consumer credit). This would allow the FCA to enter into a contract with a local weights and measures authority or DETI so that those authorities carry out compliance checks on behalf of the FCA. Further, the Order-making powers of the Treasury in s 107 of the Financial Services Act 2012 include provision for local weights and measures authorities or DETI to exercise investigative powers under the CCA in relation to the commission or suspected commission of an offence under FSMA in relation to activities relating to consumer credit, which are regulated under FSMA. Those enforcers would be able to institute proceedings, without obtaining the consent of the Director of Public Prosecutions, for such offences.

18.293 Section 230 of the Enterprise Act 2002 requires local weights and measures authorities in England and Wales to give notice to the CMA of intended prosecutions and their outcome under specified enactments and secondary legislation. The Enterprise Act 2002 (Part 8 Notice to OFT of Intended Prosecution Specified Enactments, Revocation and Transitional Provision) Order 2003[306] provides that all offences under CCA 1974 are specified for the purposes of s 230 of the Enterprise Act 2002 – but proceedings are not invalid by reason only of the failure of the authority to comply with this section.

---

[306] SI 2003/1376.

Enforcement powers

18.294   Enforcement powers specified in CCA, ss 162–165, including: powers of entry and inspection and the power to make test purchases have been replaced by Sch 5 to the Consumer Rights Act 2015.

CHAPTER 19

FOOD STANDARDS AND INFORMATION

INTRODUCTION

19.1   The safety and composition of food is a matter of public importance, and a series of laws have been passed to ensure consumers can have confidence that the food they buy and eat is safe and is accurately described so that they know what they are eating. Most UK food legislation is now derived from European Union law, with domestic legislation generally only providing for its enforcement. EU Regulations apply directly in all Member States. (There remain a few instances of 'domestic' food law – notable examples being the ban, since 1982, of the sale of raw milk in Scotland and the Food Hygiene Rating (Wales) Act 2013, which was passed by the National Assembly for Wales on 22 January 2013 and received Royal Assent on 4 March 2013.)

19.2   Following the process of devolution, food legislation is now commonly made on a separate parallel basis in England, Scotland and Wales (and has been traditionally transferred in Northern Ireland) so that, for example, the Official Feed and Food Controls (England) Regulations 2009,[1] the Official Feed and Food Controls (Scotland) Regulations 2009[2] and the Official Feed and Food Controls (Wales) Regulations 2009[3] each provide for the execution and enforcement of the feed and food elements of Regulation (EC) No 882/2004 – amongst other matters – in the respective countries of Great Britain. Food legislation is enforced, in Northern Ireland, by district councils and, in Scotland, principally by local councils (and delegated to directors/heads of environmental health to manage local service delivery arrangements). In a work of this nature it is not possible to list all parallel provisions that are connected with the transposition of an EU Directive or Regulation into domestic legislation.

19.3   The primary legislation presently in force in England and Wales is the Food Safety Act 1990, supported by regulations dealing with the specific and technical details of the various food industries. Since the Food Safety Act 1990 was passed there have been significant changes to food safety law in the United Kingdom, as a result principally of European Union legislation. In particular, the General Food Law Regulation, Regulation (EC) 178/2002,[4] which was adopted by the European Union, and which was put into effect in England and Wales by the General Food Regulations 2004,[5] effected significant amendments to the Food Safety Act 1990 itself.

19.4   Alongside the Food Safety Act 1990 are two important statutory instruments of general application in England, each coming into effect as a result of European legislation. This chapter concentrates on the provisions of

---

[1]   SI 2009/3255.
[2]   SI 2009/446.
[3]   SI 2009/3376.
[4]   Regulation (EC) No 178/2002 of the European Parliament and of the Council of 28 January 2002 laying down the general principles and requirements of food law, establishing the European Food Safety Authority and laying down procedures in matters of food safety (OJ L31, 1.2.2002, p 1).
[5]   SI 2004/3279.

the Food Safety Act 1990, together with the Food Safety and Hygiene Regulations (England) Regulations 2013[6] (replacing the offences formerly contained in the General Food Regulations 2004 in England,[7] and the Food Hygiene (England) Regulations 2006,[8] which are repealed in their entirety), and the Food Information Regulations 2014.[9] The scope of this work does not permit detailed analysis of the considerable body of other specific legislation covering the composition and safety of food, which are often limited to particular foods or categories of foods and are often highly specific and technical.

19.5 The Food Information to Consumers Regulation, Regulation (EC) 1169/2011 (the FIC Regulation),[10] entered into force on 13 December 2011. The provisions of the FIC Regulation in respect of the labelling requirements have applied since 13 December 2014 and will come into force on 13 December 2016 in respect of the mandatory nutrition declaration requirements. The FIC Regulation modifies the previous legislation in relation to food labelling, and establishes the general principles of, and the requirements and responsibilities of food business operators governing, the provision of food information to consumers, and in particular in relation to food labelling.

19.6 There is increased recognition of the role that animal feed plays in the safety of the food chain, having implications for the composition and quality of products such as milk, meat and eggs. EU legislation applies principally to feed for food-producing animals (ie farmed livestock) but also covers feed for pet animals, farmed and ornamental fish, zoo and circus animals and, in certain circumstances, creatures living freely in the wild. The Directives on the labelling and composition of animal feed cover declarations of the ingredients used (including the additives and the GM varieties which have been authorised for use in feed – but note that the requirement for the ingredients of compound feeds to be declared by their percentage weight of inclusion has been abolished), analytical declarations for protein, fibre, ash, etc, the name and address of the business, the batch number and shelf-life of the feed product, and certain allowable claims.

19.7 EU feed legislation also specifies the maximum permitted levels of certain undesirable substances (contaminants), lays down a list of prohibited ingredients which must never be used in feed, and provides a list of permitted dietetic purposes for which certain feeds may be promoted. These provisions

---

6 SI 2013/2996.
7 The provisions of the General Food Regulations 2004 continue to apply in Scotland and Wales.
8 SI 2006/14.
9 SI 2014/1855.
10 Regulation (EU) No 1169/2011 of the European Parliament and of the Council of 25 October 2011 on the provision of food information to consumers, amending Regulations (EC) No 1924/2006 and (EC) No 1925/2006 of the European Parliament and of the Council, and repealing Commission Directive 87/250/EEC, Council Directive 90/496/EEC, Commission Directive 1999/10/EC, Directive 2000/13/EC of the European Parliament and of the Council, Commission Directives 2002/67/EC and 2008/5/EC and Commission Regulation (EC) No 608/2004 (OJ L304, 22.11.2011, p 18).

are contained in a number of EU measures which are given force in England by the Animal Feed (England) Regulations 2010[11] which were made under the Agriculture Act 1970 and the European Communities Act 1972. The Regulations also link provisions to the powers already available to local authority enforcement officers under the Feed (Hygiene and Enforcement) (England) Regulations 2005.[12] Separate but parallel legislation applies in Wales – the Animal Feed (Wales) Regulations 2010[13] – in Scotland – the Animal Feed (Scotland) Regulations 2010[14] and in Northern Ireland – the Animal Feed Regulations (Northern Ireland) 2010.[15]

FOOD SAFETY ACT 1990

Introduction and application

19.8   The Food Safety Act 1990 ('FSA 1990'), as amended, provides the overall legislative framework for food safety in the United Kingdom and operates alongside regulations setting out the detailed and specific requirements for particular industries. The FSA 1990 was amended in significant respects following the adoption into UK law of the European Union General Food Law Regulation – Regulation (EC) 178/2002.

19.9   Enforcement of the provisions of the Act is the duty of the relevant food authority,[16] unless a particular duty is imposed expressly or by necessary implication upon another authority. The Food Authorities in England are the London Borough Councils, District Councils and Non-metropolitan County Councils, the Common Council for the City of London, the Treasurers of the Inner and Middle Temples and the council of the Isles of Scilly.[17] In Wales, the Food Authorities are the County Councils or County Borough Councils, as the case may be.[18]

19.10   The effect of the definition of a food authority in the Act gives rise to situations in which two different food authorities have responsibility for enforcing provisions of the Act, and therefore to concurrent responsibilities. Where enforcement falls concurrently on both the county council and the district council, the Secretary of State may, by statutory instrument, specify which of the authorities has responsibility for enforcement of any particular power.[19]

---

[11]   SI 2010/2503.
[12]   SI 2005/3280.
[13]   SI 2010/2652.
[14]   SSI 2010/373.
[15]   SR 2010 No 355.
[16]   Food Safety Act 1990, s 6, as amended.
[17]   Food Safety Act 1990, s 5(1), as amended.
[18]   Food Safety Act 1990, s 5(1A), as amended.
[19]   Food Safety Act 1990, s 5(4), as amended.

19.11 The Food Safety (Enforcement Authority) (England and Wales) Order 1990[20] provides that the responsibility for issuing emergency prohibition notices and orders shall be exercised solely by the district council, and that responsibility for enforcing the provisions of s 15 of the Act, relating to the false description and presentation of food, shall be the preserve of the county council.[21]

19.12 The Secretary of State may also direct that certain duties of food authorities shall be exercised either by the Secretary of State or by the Food Standards Agency, rather than by the relevant food authority,[22] or to take over the conduct of proceedings instituted by a food authority,[23] or to direct that the Food Standards Agency shall take over the conduct of proceedings instituted by a food authority.[24] The Food Standards Agency may also take over the conduct of proceedings without being directed so to do by the Secretary of State, but in those circumstances only with the consent of the person instituting them.[25]

Key concepts and definitions

'Food'

19.13 'Food' for the purposes of the FSA 1990 has the same meaning as in Regulation (EC) No 178/2002.[26] Article 2 of Regulation (EC) 178/2002 defines food as 'any substance or product, whether processed, partially processed or unprocessed, intended to be, or reasonably expected to be ingested by humans'. The definition includes drink (including alcoholic drinks), chewing gum and any substance, including water, intentionally incorporated into the food during manufacture, preparation or treatment. 'Food' does not however include animal feed, live animals (unless prepared for placing on the market for human consumption – for example, oysters), plants prior to harvesting, cosmetics, medicinal products, narcotics, tobacco and tobacco products or residues or contaminants.[27] A 'food source' is any growing crop or live animal, bird or fish from which food is intended to be derived (including by harvesting, slaughtering, milking, collecting eggs or by other means).[28]

---

20 SI 1990/2462.
21 Food Safety (Enforcement Authority) (England and Wales) Order 1990, SI 1990/2462, Art 2. Of less general application, Art 2 also provides that the Treasurers of the Middle and Inner Temples shall have responsibility for emergency prohibition notices and orders, and that the Common Council of the City of London shall have responsibility for the enforcement of the provisions of s 15 of the Act.
22 Food Safety Act 1990, s 6(3), as amended.
23 Food Safety Act 1990, s 6(5A), as amended.
24 Food Safety Act 1990, s 6(5B), as amended.
25 Food Safety Act 1990, s 6(5C), as amended.
26 Food Safety Act 1990, s 1, as amended.
27 Regulation (EC) 178/2002 of the European Parliament and of the Council of 28 January 2002 laying down the general principles and requirements of food law, establishing the European Food Safety Authority, and laying down procedures in matters of food safety, Art 2.
28 Food Safety Act 1990, s 1(3), as amended.

'Food business'

19.14   Certain provisions of the FSA 1990 apply only to 'food businesses'. A food business is defined as any business in the course of which commercial operations with respect to food or food sources are carried out. The definition of a business includes the operation of canteens, clubs, schools, hospitals or institutions and the undertakings and activities carried on by public or local authorities, whether carried out for profit or not, in addition to commercial enterprises.

19.15   A commercial operation is defined as selling, possessing for sale, offering exposing or advertising for sale; consigning, delivering or serving by way of sale; preparing for sale or presenting, labelling or wrapping for the purpose of sale; storing or transporting for the purpose of sale; importing or exporting; or deriving food from a food source for the purpose of sale or for purposes connected with sale.[29]

'Sale'

19.16   Where the word 'sale' is used in provisions of the FSA 1990, it bears an extended meaning. 'Sale' includes the supply of food otherwise than on sale in the course of a business,[30] *Swain v Old Kentucky Restaurants Ltd.*[31] Food offered as a prize or reward or given away, either in connection with any social gathering, amusement, exhibition, performance, game, sport, or trial of skill, or for the purpose of advertisement or in furtherance of business, shall be treated as being exposed for sale by the person concerned in the organisation of the entertainment or by the person offering or giving away the food as the case may be.[32] In *Haringey London Borough Council v Tshilumbe*[33] the magistrates' court had concluded there had not been a breach of an Emergency Prohibition Order under the Food Hygiene (England) Regulations 2006, because food, cans of drink, had allegedly been supplied free of charge. On appeal, Pill LJ said:

> 'It may be that their apparent unawareness of s 2(1) FSA1990 which provides that the sale of food in s 1 extends to the supply of food, otherwise than on sale, in the course of a business, contributed to their error.'

This case reinforced the decision in *Graff v Evans*,[34] where it was held that no monetary consideration was needed if the supply is in the course of a business.

19.17   'Sale' also includes exposure for sale and possession for sale. In relation to food law, case law has stated that it is not necessary for the purchaser to see the product for there to be an exposure for sale (*Wheat v Brown*,[35] where a

---

[29]   Food Safety Act 1990, s 1(3), as amended.
[30]   Food Safety Act 1990, s 2(1), as amended.
[31]   *Swain v Old Kentucky Restaurants Ltd* (1973) 138 JP JO 84.
[32]   Food Safety Act 1990, s 2(2), as amended.
[33]   [2009] EWHC 2820 (Admin).
[34]   (1882) 8 QBD 373.
[35]   [1892] 1 QB 418.

product wrapped in paper was still deemed to have been exposed for sale), and goods already sold and in the course of delivery to a purchaser are not in possession for sale (*Rye v Collip Ltd*[36]).

Presumption that food intended for human consumption

19.18 Where food is commonly used for human consumption, there is a presumption that where it is sold, offered, exposed or kept for sale that the food was intended for human consumption. The presumption applies until the contrary is proven by the party seeking to establish that the presumption does not apply.[37]

19.19 Similarly:

- where food commonly used for human consumption is found on premises used for the preparation, storage or sale of that food, it is presumed that the food was intended for sale for human consumption;[38]
- where an article or substance commonly used in the manufacture of food for human consumption is found on such premises, it is presumed that the article or substance is intended for manufacturing food for sale for human consumption;[39]
- where an article or substance capable of being used in the composition or preparation of food commonly used for human consumption is found on premises on which that food is prepared it is presumed that the article or substance is intended for such use.[40]

Offences

Rendering food injurious to health

19.20 Section 7 of the FSA 1990 creates the offence of rendering food injurious to health. Section 7(1) provides as follows:

> **7 Rendering food injurious to health**
>
> (1) Any person who renders any food injurious to health by means of any of the following operations, namely –
>
> (a) adding any article or substance to the food;
> (b) using any article or substance as an ingredient in the preparation of the food;
> (c) abstracting any constituent from the food; and
> (d) subjecting the food to any other process or treatment, with intent that it shall be sold for human consumption, shall be guilty of an offence.

---

36 *Rye v Collip Ltd* (1957) unreported.
37 Food Safety Act 1990, s 3(2).
38 Food Safety Act 1990, s 3(3).
39 Food Safety Act 1990, s 3(3).
40 Food Safety Act 1990, s 3(4).

19.21   It must be proved to the criminal standard that the offender:

(a)   either added an article or substance to the food, used an article or substance as an ingredient in its preparation, abstracted a constituent from the food, or otherwise subjected the food to some other process or treatment;

(b)   which had the effect of rendering the food injurious to health; and

(c)   intended that the food should be sold for human consumption.

19.22   The phrase 'injurious to health' is not further defined, but in determining whether the food in question is injurious to health, the court will have regard to certain considerations set out in paras 14(4)(a)–(c) of Regulation (EC) 178/2002.[41] Regard shall be had:

(a)   not only to the probable immediate and/or short-term and/or long-term effects of that food on the health of a person consuming it, but also on subsequent generations;

(b)   to the probable cumulative toxic effects;

(c)   to the particular health sensitivities of a specific category of consumers where the food is intended for that category of consumers.[42]

Selling food not of the nature or substance or quality demanded

19.23   It is an offence to sell food not of the nature or substance or quality demanded by the purchaser, to the purchaser's prejudice.[43] Section 14(1) of the FSA 1990 provides as follows:

> **14 Selling food not of the nature or substance or quality demanded**
>
> (1) Any person who sells to the purchaser's prejudice any food which is not of the nature or substance or quality demanded by the purchaser shall be guilty of an offence.
>
> (2) In subsection (1) above the reference to sale shall be construed as a reference to sale for human consumption; and in proceedings under that subsection it shall not be a defence that the purchaser was not prejudiced because he bought for analysis or examination.

19.24   It must be proved to the criminal standard that the offender:

(a)   sold food for human consumption;[44]

(b)   to the purchaser's prejudice;

(c)   which was not of the nature or substance or quality demanded.

---

[41]   Food Safety Act 1990, s 7(2), as amended.
[42]   Regulation (EC) 178/2002, Art 14(4).
[43]   Food Safety Act 1990, s 14(1), as amended.
[44]   Sale is to be construed as sale for human consumption – Food Safety Act 1990, s 14(2), as amended.

It is no defence to proceedings under that section that the purchaser was not prejudiced because the purchase was for analysis or examination, as in circumstances where an authorised officer makes a test purchase of food.[45]

Falsely describing or presenting food

19.25 Where food is sold, offered or exposed for sale with a label, whether or not that label is attached to or printed on the packaging which either falsely describes the food or is likely to mislead as to the nature or quality of the food, the person selling, offering or exposing the food for sale is guilty of an offence under s 15 of the FSA 1990.[46] Further offences are created in respect of the publication of advertisements falsely describing food[47] and in respect of selling, offering or exposing for sale food the presentation of which is likely to mislead as to the nature or substance or quality of the food.[48] The offences are created by s 15(1), (2) and (3), which provide as follows:

> **15 Falsely describing or presenting food**
>
> (1) Any person who gives with any food sold by him, or displays with any food offered or exposed by him for sale or in his possession for the purpose of sale, a label, whether or not attached to or printed on the wrapper or container, which –
>
> > (a)   falsely describes the food; or
> > (b)   is likely to mislead as to the nature or substance or quality of the food,
>
> shall be guilty of an offence.
>
> (2) Any person who publishes, or is a party to the publication of, an advertisement (not being such a label given or displayed by him as mentioned in subsection (1) above) which –
>
> > (a)   falsely describes any food; or
> > (b)   is likely to mislead as to the nature or substance or quality of any food,
>
> shall be guilty of an offence.
>
> (3) Any person who sells, or offers or exposes for sale, or has in his possession for the purpose of sale, any food the presentation of which is likely to mislead as to the nature or substance or quality of the food shall be guilty of an offence.

19.26 In relation to the offence contrary to s 15(1), it must be proved to the criminal standard that the offender:

(a)   sold, offered or exposed for sale, or had in his possession for the purposes of sale, food for human consumption;[49]

(b)   with a label;

---

45   Food Safety Act 1990, s 14(2), as amended.
46   Food Safety Act 1990, s 15(1), as amended.
47   Food Safety Act 1990, s 15(2), as amended.
48   Food Safety Act 1990, s 15(3), as amended.
49   References to sale are to be construed as references to sale for human consumption – Food Safety Act 1990, s 15(5), as amended.

(c)   which either falsely describes the food, or is likely to mislead as to the nature or substance or quality of the food.

19.27   In relation to offences contrary to s 15(2), it must be proved to the criminal standard that the offender:

(a)   either published or was party to the publication of an advertisement;
(b)   which either falsely describes the food, or is likely to mislead as to the nature or substance or quality of the food.

19.28   In relation to offences contrary to s 15(1) or (2), the fact that the label or advertisement carried an accurate statement of the composition of the food does not automatically provide a defence. The question remains whether the label or advertisement either falsely describes the food or is likely to mislead as to nature, substance or quality.[50]

19.29   In relation to offences contrary to s 15(3), it must be proved to the criminal standard that the offender:

(a)   sold, offered or exposed for sale, or had in his possession for the purpose of sale any food;
(b)   the presentation of which is likely to mislead as to the nature, substance or quality of the food.

Obstruction of officers

19.30   The intentional obstruction of officers or other persons acting in the execution of their duties under the Act is an offence contrary to s 33. That section also creates offences relating to the failure without reasonable excuse to provide such information or assistance as may be reasonably required of a person by an officer acting in execution of his duties under the Act, or by the furnishing of false information, either knowingly or recklessly.

19.31   Section 33 provides as follows:

> **33 Obstruction etc. of officers**
>
> (1) Any person who –
>
> > (a)   intentionally obstructs any person acting in the execution of this Act; or
> > (b)   without reasonable cause, fails to give to any person acting in the execution of this Act any assistance or information which that person may reasonably require of him for the performance of his functions under this Act,
>
> shall be guilty of an offence.
>
> (2) Any person who, in purported compliance with any such requirement as is mentioned in subsection (1)(b) above –

---

[50]   Food Safety Act 1990, s 15(4), as amended.

(a) furnishes information which he knows to be false or misleading in a material particular; or

(b) recklessly furnishes information which is false or misleading in a material particular,

shall be guilty of an offence.

(3) Nothing in subsection (1)(b) above shall be construed as requiring any person to answer any question or give any information if to do so might incriminate him.

19.32 Three offences are created: intentional obstruction of a person acting in execution of the FSA 1990;[51] failing without reasonable cause to provide such information or assistance as is reasonably requested by a person acting in execution of the Act;[52] and furnishing information to a person acting in execution of the Act which he either knows to be false or misleading in a material particular, or which is false or misleading in a material particular and such information is provided recklessly.[53]

19.33 In relation to offences contrary to s 33(1)(a) it must be proved to the criminal standard that the offender:

(a) intentionally;

(b) obstructed;

(c) a person acting in execution of the Act.

19.34 In relation to offences contrary to s 33(1)(b) it must be proved to the criminal standard that the offender:

(a) failed to give information or assistance;

(b) to a person acting in execution of the Act;

(c) which had been requested by that person;

(d) that the request was a reasonable request;

(e) that the failure was without reasonable cause.

19.35 It should be noted that s 33(3) provides that the right against self-incrimination is expressly preserved. If therefore the request of information or assistance is such as would tend to incriminate the person to whom the request is made, then the person is entitled to refuse to provide such information and assistance, and would have a defence to any charge under s 33(1)(b). The right is a right against self-incrimination, however – it does not extend the right to a representative of a company refusing to provide information on the grounds that it might incriminate the company,[54] nor indeed

---

[51] An offence contrary to the Food Safety Act 1990, s 33(1)(a).
[52] An offence contrary to the Food Safety Act 1990, s 33(1)(b).
[53] An offence contrary to the Food Safety Act 1990, s 33(2).
[54] *Walkers Snack Foods Ltd v Coventry City Council* [1998] 3 All ER 163, [1998] EHLR 260, (1998) *Times*, April 9, DC.

on that analysis to an employee on the grounds that it might incriminate his employer or anyone else, whether that employer or other person is a company or an individual.

19.36 In relation to offences contrary to s 33(2), it must be proved to the criminal standard that the offender, having been requested to provide information or assistance by a person acting in execution of the FSA 1990, either:

(a) provides information which he knows is untrue or misleading in a material particular; or

(b) recklessly provides information which is untrue or misleading in a material particular.

Penalties

19.37 Under s 35, offences under ss 7, 14 and 15 of the FSA 1990 are triable either way.[55] The maximum sentence on indictment for each of the offences is 2 years' imprisonment, a fine or both.[56] Where an offender is sentenced in the Magistrates' Court, the maximum sentence is 6 months' imprisonment, a fine or both.[57] The offence contrary to s 33 of obstruction of an officer is a summary only offence, and carries a maximum sentence of 3 months' imprisonment, a fine or both.[58]

Time limits

19.38 Offences contrary to ss 7, 14 and 15 are subject to specific time limits under s 34 of the Act. By virtue of that section, no prosecution may be commenced in relation to those offences later than 3 years from the commission of the offence, or one year after its discovery by the prosecutor, whichever is the earlier. Time limits are now covered in Chapter 3, Criminal Enforcement.

Causal liability

19.39 Section 20 of the FSA 1990 provides that:

> 20 Where the commission by any person of an offence under any of the preceding provisions of this Part is due to the act or default of some other person, that other person commits the offence; and a person may be convicted of the offence by virtue of this section whether or not proceedings are taken against the first-mentioned person.

Causal liability is now covered in detail in Chapter 3, Criminal Enforcement.

---

[55] Food Safety Act 1990, s 35, as amended.
[56] Food Safety Act 1990, s 35(2)(a), as amended.
[57] Food Safety Act 1990, s 35(2)(b), as amended.
[58] Food Safety Act 1990, s 35(1), as amended.

Defences

The due diligence defence

19.40 In relation to all offences under the FSA 1990, a defence of due diligence applies under s 21. The due diligence defence are now generally considered in Chapter 3, Criminal Enforcement. In relation to offences under s 14 (selling food not of the nature or substance or quality demanded) or s 15 (falsely describing food), if the accused neither prepared the food nor imported it into Great Britain, then the due diligence defence can be established by an accused who satisfies specified requirements under s 21(3) or (4). In either case, it is for the accused to prove those facts under s 21(3) or (4) as the case may be. The particular requirements do not supersede the general due diligence defence, but provide that a person who establishes those requirements shall be deemed to have made out the due diligence defence.[59]

Defence of publication in the course of business

19.41 A further specific defence is provided where the allegation involves the advertising for sale of any food. In those circumstances, it shall be a defence for the accused to prove (to the civil standard) that he is a person whose business it is to publish advertisements, that he had received the advertisement in the ordinary course of business, and that he had no reason to suspect that its publication would amount to an offence under the Act.[60]

Powers of enforcement authorities

Inspection and seizure of suspected food

19.42 Under s 9 authorised officers of an enforcement authority have powers to inspect food intended for human consumption which has been sold, or is offered or exposed for sale, or is in the possession of a person for sale or preparation for sale or which is otherwise placed on the market within the meaning of Regulation (EC) 178/2002.[61]

19.43 Where it appears to the officer that any food fails to comply with food safety requirements,[62] or to be likely to cause food poisoning or any communicable disease in humans,[63] then such an authorised officer has the power to seize the food and remove it, so that it can be dealt with by a justice of the peace by way of an application for its condemnation, or to issue a notice specifying that it must not be used for human consumption and must not be removed except as specified in the notice.[64]

---

[59] Food Safety Act 1990, s 21(2), as amended.
[60] Food Safety Act 1990, s 22, as amended.
[61] Food Safety Act 1990, s 9(1), as amended.
[62] Food Safety Act 1990, s 9(1), as amended.
[63] Food Safety Act 1990, s 9(2), as amended.
[64] Food Safety Act 1990, s 9(3), as amended.

19.44   The issue of a notice under s 9(3)(a) allows an enforcement authority 21 days to determine whether or not the food contravenes food safety requirements. As soon as is practicable, an in any event within 21 days, the notice must either be withdrawn, or the food seized in order for it to be dealt with by a justice of the peace.[65] Knowingly contravening a notice issued under s 9(3)(a) is a criminal offence.[66]

19.45   If it appears to a justice of the peace upon application by the authorised officer that food contravenes food safety requirements, the food will be ordered to be destroyed or otherwise disposed of to prevent it being used for human consumption, with the expenses of such destruction or disposal to be met by the owner of the food.[67] Once a justice of the peace is satisfied that the food contravenes food safety requirements, there is no discretion not to order destruction of the food – such an order is mandatory.[68] Should he not be so satisfied, or should a notice under s 9(3)(a) be withdrawn, then the enforcement authority is liable to compensate the owner of the food for losses incurred.[69]

Procurement and analysis of samples

19.46   Authorised officers of enforcement agencies have powers to take samples of foods pursuant to powers contained within s 29 of the FSA 1990. That section permits an authorised officer to purchase a sample of any food or substance capable of being used in the preparation of food, to take samples of any food which appears to him to be intended for sale, or to have been sold, for human consumption, or which is found by him in premises entered under his powers of entry under s 32 of the Act. An officer is also entitled to take samples from any food source or contact material from such premises, or from any substance within such premises which may be required as evidence.

19.47   If considered appropriate by the officer, such a sample may be submitted for analysis or examination. If it is to be analysed, then the sample should be submitted to the public analyst for the area covered by the enforcement authority, or for the area in which the sample was obtained. If it is to be examined, then the sample should be submitted to a food examiner.[70] In either case, the analyst or examiner should provide to the officer a certificate setting out the results of the analysis or examination.[71] Such a certificate is sufficient evidence within subsequent proceedings under the Act of the facts stated within it unless the other party to the proceedings requires the analyst or examiner to give live evidence.[72]

---

[65]   Food Safety Act 1990, s 9(4), as amended.
[66]   Food Safety Act 1990, s 9(3), as amended.
[67]   Food Safety Act 1990, s 9(6), as amended.
[68]   *R (on the application of the Food Standards Agency) v Brent Justices* [2004] EWHC 459 (Admin), (2004) 168 JP 241, (2004) 168 JPN 380.
[69]   Food Safety Act 1990, s 9(7), as amended.
[70]   Food Safety Act 1990, s 30(1), as amended.
[71]   Food Safety Act 1990, s 30(6), as amended.
[72]   Food Safety Act 1990, s 30(8), as amended.

Powers of entry

19.48 Specific powers of entry are given to authorised officers of an enforcement authority by s 32 of the FSA 1990. Upon production of official identification showing their authority, such officers are entitled to enter premises at all reasonable hours in the circumstances specified and for the purposes specified in s 32.

19.49 Under that section, authorised officers have the right to enter premises within their own authority's area for the purposes of ascertaining whether there is or has been on the premises any contravention of the provisions of the FSA 1990, or of any regulations made under the Act.[73] Authorised officers also have the right to enter business premises, whether within or outside their own area for the purpose of ascertaining whether there is on those premises evidence of a contravention within the enforcement authority's jurisdiction.[74] Where the officer is an authorised officer of a food authority, he has, in addition, the power to enter any premises for the purpose of the performance of the food authority of their functions under the Act.[75]

19.50 In relation to business premises, no prior warning of the proposed exercise of the rights of entry in s 32 need be given. Where the premises sought to be entered is used only as a private dwelling house, then entry as of right under s 32 shall not be demanded unless at least 24 hours' notice has been given to the occupier.[76]

19.51 The right of entry includes the right to inspect any records held relating to a food business, including records held on computer, and to take copies of such records where he has reason to believe that they are required as evidence. Where records are held on computer, the officer may require the assistance of the person having control of that computer, and for the records to be made available to him in a suitable format to be taken away.[77]

19.52 In certain circumstances, officers may apply to a magistrate for a warrant to enter premises. Such a warrant may authorise the use of reasonable force to effect entry. In order for a warrant to be issued, a justice of the peace must be satisfied on sworn evidence that there are reasonable grounds for the entry, and either:

(a) that admission has been refused, or a refusal is anticipated, and notice of an intention to apply for a warrant has been given;

(b) that either a request for admission or notice of intention to apply would defeat the purpose of the warrant;

(c) that the case is one of urgency; or

---

[73] Food Safety Act 1990, s 32(1)(a), as amended.
[74] Food Safety Act 1990, s 32(1)(b), as amended.
[75] Food Safety Act 1990, s 32(1)(c), as amended.
[76] Food Safety Act 1990, s 32(1), as amended.
[77] Food Safety Act 1990, s 32(5) and s 32(6), as amended.

(d)   that the premises are unoccupied or the occupier is temporarily absent.

Prohibition orders

19.53   Under s 11, where the proprietor of a food business is convicted of an offence under regulations made under the FSA 1990 which make provision for requiring, prohibiting or regulating the use of any process or treatment in the preparation of food; or for securing the observance of hygienic conditions and practices in connection with the carrying out of commercial operations with respect to food or food sources, and the court is satisfied that the health risk requirement is made out, then the court shall (in addition to sentencing the defendant) make a prohibition order.[78]

19.54   The health risk requirement is satisfied if there is a risk of injury to health owing to:

(a)   the use, for the purposes of the business, of any process or treatment;

(b)   the construction of any premises used for the purposes of the business, or the use for those purposes of any equipment; and

(c)   the state or condition of any premises or equipment used for the purposes of the business.[79]

'Injury' includes any impairment whether temporary or permanent.[80]

19.55   In those circumstances, the court must make the appropriate order for prohibition:

(a)   in a case falling within para (a) of s 11(2), as set out above, a prohibition on the use of the process or treatment for the purposes of the business;

(b)   in a case falling within para (b) of that subsection, a prohibition on the use of the premises or equipment for the purposes of the business or any other food business of the same class or description;

(c)   in a case falling within para (c) of that subsection, a prohibition on the use of the premises or equipment for the purposes of any food business.[81]

19.56   A prohibition order in those terms continues until the enforcement authority issue a certificate, certifying that the proprietor has taken sufficient measures such that the health risk condition was no longer fulfilled.[82]

19.57   Where the breach of the regulations relate to securing the observance of hygienic conditions and practices in connection with the carrying out of commercial operations with respect to food or food sources, then the court has

---

[78]   Food Safety Act 1990, s 11, as amended.
[79]   Food Safety Act 1990, s 11(2), as amended.
[80]   Food Safety Act 1990, s 11(2A), as amended.
[81]   Food Safety Act 1990, s 11(3), as amended.
[82]   Food Safety Act 1990, s 11(6), as amended.

a discretionary power 'where the court thinks it proper to do so in all the circumstances of the case' to impose a prohibition on the proprietor, or a manager of a food business, participating in the management of any food business, or any food business of a class or description specified in the order.[83]

19.58 A prohibition order prohibiting a proprietor from participating in the management of a food business continues until a court directs that it shall cease to have effect. A person affected by such an order may apply to the court no sooner than 6 months after the making of such an order for a direction that the prohibition order shall cease to have effect. Such a direction will be made if the court thinks it proper to do so having regard to all the circumstances of the case, including in particular the conduct of the proprietor since the making of the order. If the application is refused no further application can be made within 3 months.[84]

19.59 In *R v Crestdane Ltd*,[85] the Court of Appeal considered the circumstances in which it would be appropriate for a court to exercise its discretion where it thinks it proper to do so in all the circumstances of the case to impose a hygiene prohibition order under reg 7(4) of the Food Hygiene (England) Regulations 2006 prohibiting a food business owner or manager from participating in the management of a food business.

19.60 The exercise of the discretion to make a hygiene prohibition order was not limited to circumstances in which the immediate closure of the premises was necessary to safeguard public health. The exercise of the discretion to make a hygiene prohibition order was not limited to circumstances in which the immediate closure of the premises was necessary to safeguard public health, such as would give rise to a hygiene emergency prohibition notice, although the protection of the public from a future risk of harm is clearly a relevant consideration. Where there is an immediate risk to public health that would be a powerful consideration in favour of making such an order, but even if there has been an improvement in conditions such that a hygiene emergency prohibition notice is no longer necessary, it does not follow that a hygiene prohibition order ought not to be made. It would be open to the court to conclude that notwithstanding the present improvement that there remained a sufficient future risk that a hygiene prohibition order ought to be made.

19.61 The number and nature of the breaches in the present case, particularly where they are numerous and long-standing, might give rise to such a concern, although a single breach might also be of such severity that it required the making of a hygiene prohibition order. Previous convictions and failures to heed warnings were also clearly relevant in assessing the level of future risk. Improvements made after the event were relevant, but a court was entitled to view protestations of future good conduct with a degree of scepticism where there was a history of failures to comply. Deterrence too was an important

---

[83] Food Safety Act 1990, s 11(4), as amended.
[84] Food Safety Act 1990, s 11(8), as amended.
[85] *R v Crestdane Limited* [2012] EWCA Crim 958.

consideration. The imposition of an order was a powerful message to the food industry that strict compliance with rigorous food hygiene regulations was vital.

19.62 In any event, the future risk to human health was but one consideration. The facts of any particular offence might alone justify the imposition of a hygiene prohibition order – whilst the considerations set out above will be relevant, the discretion remains a wide one, and the test remained whether it was proper to impose such an order in all the circumstances of the case. It is likely that similar considerations will apply to the exercise of the court's discretion to make a prohibition order under s 11 of the FSA 1990.

Improvement notices

19.63 Where an officer has reasonable grounds for believing that the proprietor of a food business is failing to comply with certain regulations to which the section applies, he may issue an improvement notice under s 10 of the FSA 1990. Such notice should set out the grounds for believing that there is a failure to comply, the matters constituting the failure to comply and the measures necessary to secure compliance. The effect of such a notice is to require those measures to be taken within a specified period, which shall be not less than 14 days. Strict compliance with the requirements of s 10 is necessary in order for an improvement notice to be enforceable.[86] Failure to comply with an improvement notice constitutes a criminal offence.[87]

Emergency prohibition notices and orders

19.64 Where an authorised officer is satisfied that the health risk condition[88] is fulfilled in respect of a food business, an emergency prohibition notice may be issued in respect of that business under s 12 of the FSA 1990. The risk of injury to health must be 'imminent' for an emergency notice to be issued. Knowingly contravening an emergency prohibition notice constitutes a criminal offence.[89]

19.65 An emergency prohibition notice expires after 3 days unless an application is made to the Magistrates' Court for an emergency prohibition order. If such an application is made within 3 days, then the notice continues until the conclusion of such an application.[90] The proprietor of a food business must be given one day's notice of the intention of the officer to apply for such an order.[91] If a magistrates' court is satisfied, on the application of such an officer, that the health risk condition is fulfilled with respect to any food

---

86 *Bexley LBC v Gardiner Merchant* [1993] COD 383.
87 Food Safety Act 1990, s 10, as amended.
88 Food Safety Act 1990, s 11.
89 Food Safety Act 1990, s 12(6), as amended.
90 Food Safety Act 1990, s 12(7), as amended.
91 Food Safety Act 1990, s 12(3), as amended.

business, the court shall impose the appropriate prohibition.[92] Knowingly contravening an emergency prohibition order is a criminal offence.[93]

19.66 An emergency prohibition notice or emergency prohibition order shall cease to have effect on the issue by the enforcement authority of a certificate to the effect that they are satisfied that the proprietor has taken sufficient measures to secure that the health risk condition is no longer fulfilled with respect to the business.[94] Should no application for an order be made, or the application fail then compensation for the loss caused as a result of the emergency prohibition notice is payable to the proprietor of the food business.[95]

FOOD SAFETY AND HYGIENE (ENGLAND) REGULATIONS 2013

Introduction and application

19.67 The Food Safety and Hygiene (England) Regulations 2013[96] revoke and re-enact with some minor changes the Food Hygiene (England) Regulations 2006[97] and certain provisions of the General Food Regulations 2004[98] in relation to England.[99] The Regulations provide for the enforcement of certain European Regulations, namely the General Food Law Regulation (Regulation (EC) 178/2002)[100] and a number of other regulations, defined in reg 2 of the 2013 Regulations as 'the EU Hygiene Regulations'.[101]

19.68 The General Food Law Regulation (Regulation (EC) 178/2002) is the European legislation laying down the general principles of food law, creating

---

[92] Food Safety Act 1990, s 12(2), as amended.
[93] Food Safety Act 1990, s 12(6), as amended.
[94] Food Safety Act 1990, s 12(8), as amended.
[95] Food Safety Act 1990, s 12(10), as amended.
[96] SI 2013/2996.
[97] SI 2006/14.
[98] SI 2004/3279.
[99] In Scotland and Wales the relevant provisions of the General Food Regulations 2004 remain in force, as do the Food Hygiene (Wales) Regulations 2006 and the Food Hygiene (Scotland) Regulations 2006.
[100] Regulation (EC) No 178/2002 of the European Parliament and of the Council of 28 January 2002 laying down the general principles and requirements of food law, establishing the European Food Safety Authority and laying down procedures in matters of food safety (OJ L31, 1.2.2002, p 1).
[101] Namely Regulation (EC) No 852/2004 of the European Parliament and of the Council on the hygiene of foodstuffs (OJ L139, 30.4.2004, p 1), Regulation (EC) 853/2004 of the European Parliament and of the Council laying down specific hygiene rules for food of animal origin (OJ L139, 30.4.2004, p 55), Regulation (EC) No 854/2004 of the European Parliament and of the Council laying down specific rules for the organisation of official controls on products of animal origin intended for human consumption (OJ L139, 30.4.2004, p 206), Commission Regulation (EC) No 2073/2005 on microbiological criteria for foodstuffs (OJ L338, 22.12.2005, p 1) and Commission Regulation (EC) 2075/2005 laying down specific rules on official controls for Trichinella in meat (OJ L338, 22.12.2005, p 60).

the European Food Safety Authority and laying down procedures in matters of food safety, with the aim of protecting human health and the interests of consumers in respect of food. The Regulation applies at all stages of the commercial production, processing and distribution of food. The provisions of the General Food Regulation had previously been brought into effect in England by the General Food Regulations 2004, now repealed in relation to England and replaced by the provisions of the 2013 Regulations.

19.69 Enforcement of the provisions of the 2013 Regulations is governed by reg 5, setting out the areas of responsibility of the food authorities and the Food Standards Agency.

Key concepts and definitions

'Food'

19.70 The definition of 'food' in s 1 of the Food Safety Act 1990, taken from the definition in Regulation (EC) 178/2002, applies under the 2013 Regulations as it does under the Act.

Presumption that food is intended for human consumption

19.71 Under Regulation 3, where food is commonly used for human consumption, there is a presumption that where it is placed on the market, or offered, exposed or kept for placing on the market, the food was intended for human consumption. The presumption applies until the contrary is proven by the party seeking to establish that the presumption does not apply.[102] For further details in relation to the presumption that food is intended for human consumption (see above) relating to the presumption in s 3 of the Food Safety Act 1990, which is in identical terms save for references to 'sale' being replaced by references to 'placing on the market'.

'Food business'

19.72 A food business is defined as any undertaking, whether for profit or not, and whether public or private, carrying out any of the activities related to any stage of production, processing and distribution of food.[103]

'Food business operator'

19.73 A food business operator is defined as the natural or legal persons responsible for ensuring compliance with food law in the food business under their control.[104]

---

[102] Reg 3(2).
[103] Regulation (EC) 178/2002, Art 3.
[104] Regulation (EC) 178/2002, Art 3.

Offences

19.74 Regulation 19 of the 2013 Regulations provides that contravention of the EU provisions specified in Sch 2 to the Regulations constitutes a criminal offence under the law of England. The provisions specified in Sch 2 are as follows:

(1) Article 12 of Regulation 178/2002, as it relates to food;

(2) Article 14(1) of Regulation 178/2002;

(3) Article 16 of Regulation 178/2002, as it relates to food;

(4) Article 18(2) and (3) of Regulation 178/2002, as it relates to food business operators;

(5) Article 19 of Regulation 178/2002;

(6) The provisions of the EU Hygiene Regulations specified in the Schedule.

Exporting in contravention of requirements of food law

19.75 Article 12 of Regulation (EC) 178/2002 provides that:

> 1. Food and feed exported or re-exported from the Community for placing on the market of a third country shall comply with the relevant requirements of food law, unless otherwise requested by the authorities of the importing country or established by the laws, regulations, standards, codes of practice and other legal and administrative procedures as may be in force in the importing country.
>
> In other circumstances, except in the case where foods are injurious to health or feeds are unsafe, food and feed can only be exported or re-exported if the competent authorities of the country of destination have expressly agreed, after having been fully informed of the reasons for which and the circumstances in which the food or feed concerned could not be placed on the market in the Community.
>
> 2. Where the provisions of a bilateral agreement concluded between the Community or one of its Member States and a third country are applicable, food and feed exported from the Community or that Member State to that third country shall comply with the said provisions.

19.76 It is an offence therefore to export or re-export food from the EU which does not comply with the requirements of food law. It must be proved to the criminal standard that the offender:

(a) exported or re-exported food from the EU to a third country;

(b) which failed to comply with the relevant requirements of food law, unless:
   (i)   the export is in accordance with the law, regulations, standards etc. of the importing country; or
   (ii) the export is with the express agreement of the importing country, having been fully informed of the circumstances of non-compliance with EU Food Law.

Contravention of food safety requirements

19.77   Article 14 of Regulation (EC) 178/2002 provides that:

> 1. Food shall not be placed on the market if it is unsafe.
>
> 2. Food shall be deemed to be unsafe if it is considered to be:
>
>   (a)   injurious to health;
>   (b)   unfit for human consumption.

19.78   It is an offence therefore to place food on the market which is unsafe. It must be proved to the criminal standard that the offender:

(a)   placed food on the market;

(b)   which is unsafe, in that it is either:
   (i)   injurious to health; or
   (ii)   unfit for human consumption.

19.79   The question of whether food is unsafe is a question of fact in each case. Further assistance is given in determining that issue in Art 14. In considering whether food is unsafe, regard is to be had to the normal conditions of use of the food by the consumer and at each stage of production, processing and distribution and to any information provided to the consumer concerning the avoidance of specific adverse health effects from a particular food or foods.[105]

19.80   Specific guidance as to whether a food is injurious to health can be found in Art 14 of Regulation (EC) 178/2002. Regulation 14 is discussed in relation to the offence contrary to s 7 of the Food Safety Act 1990 (see above).

19.81   In considering whether food is unfit for human consumption, regard is to be had to whether the food is unfit for human consumption according to its intended use, as a result of contamination or through putrefaction, deterioration or decay.[106] Where, however, there are specific Community provisions concerning food safety applicable to the food in question, then compliance with those provisions will mean that the food is deemed to be safe insofar as the aspects covered by the provisions are concerned.[107] A finding that food is unsafe in respect of food which forms part of a batch, lot or consignment will give rise to a presumption that the remainder of the batch, lot or consignment is also unsafe, unless on detailed analysis of the remainder there is no evidence that the remainder is unsafe.[108]

Presentation of food

19.82   Article 16 of Regulation (EC) 178/2002 reads as follows:

---

[105]   Regulation (EC) 178/2002, Art 14(3).
[106]   Regulation (EC) 178/2002, Art 14(5).
[107]   Regulation (EC) 178/2002, Art 14(7).
[108]   Regulation (EC) 178/2002, Art 14(6).

Presentation

Without prejudice to more specific provisions of food law, the labelling, advertising and presentation of food or feed, including their shape, appearance or packaging, the packaging materials used, the manner in which they are arranged and the setting in which they are displayed, and the information which is made available about them through whatever medium, shall not mislead consumers.

19.83 It must be proved to the criminal standard that the offender has:

(a) misled consumers;

(b) by way of the labelling, advertising or presentation of food.

Traceability of food

19.84 Article 18 imposes obligations upon food business operators to ensure that traceability of all food, feed, food-producing animals and other substances can be established in respect of food. Obligations are imposed upon food and feed business operators to ensure that proper records are kept, both of food and other substances supplied to them, and food and other substances supplied by them to others. The relevant Article reads as follows:

Traceability

1. The traceability of food, feed, food-producing animals, and any other substance intended to be, or expected to be, incorporated into a food or feed shall be established at all stages of production, processing and distribution.

2. Food and feed business operators shall be able to identify any person from whom they have been supplied with a food, a feed, a food-producing animal, or any substance intended to be, or expected to be, incorporated into a food or feed. To this end, such operators shall have in place systems and procedures which allow for this information to be made available to the competent authorities on demand.

3. Food and feed business operators shall have in place systems and procedures to identify the other businesses to which their products have been supplied. This information shall be made available to the competent authorities on demand.

4. Food or feed which is placed on the market or is likely to be placed on the market in the Community shall be adequately labelled or identified to facilitate its traceability, through relevant documentation or information in accordance with the relevant requirements of more specific provisions.

5. Provisions for the purpose of applying the requirements of this Article in respect of specific sectors may be adopted in accordance with the procedure laid down in Article 58(2).

Breach of any of the obligations imposed by Art 14 is, if proved to the criminal standard, an offence.

Withdrawal, recall and notification

19.85 Article 19 of Regulation (EC) 178/2002 covers the responsibilities of food business operators in a situation in which the food business operator considers or has reason to believe that food for which it bears responsibility is unsafe. In those circumstances, the food business operator has a duty to initiate proceedings to withdraw the food and inform the authorities, and to recall the food where the food may have reached consumers. Article 19 provides:

> **Responsibilities for food: food business operators**
>
> 1. If a food business operator considers or has reason to believe that a food which it has imported, produced, processed, manufactured or distributed is not in compliance with the food safety requirements, it shall immediately initiate procedures to withdraw the food in question from the market where the food has left the immediate control of that initial food business operator and inform the competent authorities thereof. Where the product may have reached the consumer, the operator shall effectively and accurately inform the consumers of the reason for its withdrawal, and if necessary, recall from consumers products already supplied to them when other measures are not sufficient to achieve a high level of health protection.
>
> 2. A food business operator responsible for retail or distribution activities which do not affect the packaging, labelling, safety or integrity of the food shall, within the limits of its respective activities, initiate procedures to withdraw from the market products not in compliance with the food-safety requirements and shall participate in contributing to the safety of the food by passing on relevant information necessary to trace a food, cooperating in the action taken by producers, processors, manufacturers and/or the competent authorities.
>
> 3. A food business operator shall immediately inform the competent authorities if it considers or has reason to believe that a food which it has placed on the market may be injurious to human health. Operators shall inform the competent authorities of the action taken to prevent risks to the final consumer and shall not prevent or discourage any person from cooperating, in accordance with national law and legal practice, with the competent authorities, where this may prevent, reduce or eliminate a risk arising from a food.
>
> 4. Food business operators shall collaborate with the competent authorities on action taken to avoid or reduce risks posed by a food which they supply or have supplied.

19.86 Failure to comply with those duties is a criminal offence. In the case of a breach of Art 19(1), it must be proved to the criminal standard that the offender:

(a) was the operator of food business;

(b) who considered, or had reason to believe, that food which the business had imported, produced, processed, manufactured or distributed is not in compliance with the food safety requirements;

(c) failed to fulfil his responsibilities under Art 14 in respect of withdrawal, recall and/or notification as the case may be.

Failure to comply with hygiene regulations

19.87 It is an offence contrary to reg 19 of the 2013 Regulations to contravene or to fail to comply with specified provisions of Regulation (EC) 852/2004,[109] Regulation (EC) 853/2004,[110] Regulation (EC) 2073/2005[111] and Regulation (EC) 2075/2005. It must be proved to the criminal standard that the offender:

(a) was subject to a provision of the EU Hygiene Regulations specified in Sch 2; and

(b) contravened or failed to comply with the requirements of that provision.

Obstruction of officers

19.88 Like offences to those created by s 33 of the Food Safety Act 1990 are created by reg 17 of the 2013 Regulations, which provides as follows:

> **17. Obstruction etc. of officers**
>
> (1) Any person who –
>
> (a) intentionally obstructs a person acting in the execution of the Hygiene Regulations or Regulation 178/2002; or
>
> (b) without reasonable cause, fails to give to any person acting in the execution of the Hygiene Regulations or Regulation 178/2002 any assistance or information which that person may reasonably require of them for the performance of their functions under the Hygiene Regulations,
>
> commits an offence.
>
> (2) Any person who, in purported compliance with any such requirement as is mentioned in sub-paragraph (b) of paragraph (1) –
>
> (a) furnishes information which they know to be false or misleading in a material particular; or
>
> (b) recklessly furnishes information which is false or misleading in a material particular,
>
> commits an offence.
>
> (3) Nothing in sub-paragraph (b) of paragraph (1) is to be construed as requiring any person to answer any question or give any information if to do so might incriminate them.

The considerations in relation to obstruction of officers under regulation 17 are identical to those set out in relation to s 33 of the Food Safety Act 1990 – see para **19.30**.

---

[109] OJ L139, 30.4.2004, p 1.
[110] OJ L139, 30.4.2004, p 55.
[111] OJ L139, 30.4.2004, p 206.

Penalties

19.89   Under reg 19 offences contrary to the Regulations (save contrary to reg 17 and paras 1A and B of Sch 6) are offences which are triable either way. The maximum sentence on indictment is a term of imprisonment not exceeding 2 years, a fine, or both.[112] Where an offender is sentenced in the magistrates' court, the maximum sentence is a fine.[113]

19.90   For offences contrary to reg 19 which fall to be sentenced on or after 1 February 2016, regard must be had to the Sentencing Council's Definitive Guideline for Health and Safety Offences, Corporate Manslaughter and Food Safety and Hygiene Offences. Separate guidelines are included within the Definitive Guideline for offences committed by corporate defendants and by individuals. The Definitive Guideline is published on the Sentencing Council's website.[114]

19.91   Offences contrary to reg 17 (obstruction of officers) are summary-only offences. The maximum sentence is 3 months' imprisonment, a fine or both.[115]

Hygiene prohibition orders

19.92   Where the proprietor of a food business is convicted of an offence under the 2013 Regulations then, under reg 7 of the Regulations, the sentencing court has the power to make a hygiene prohibition order. Where the court is satisfied that the health risk requirement is made out, then the court shall (in addition to sentencing the defendant) make a hygiene prohibition order in the appropriate terms.[116] In addition, a hygiene prohibition order may be made at the discretion of the court where 'it thinks it proper to do so in all the circumstances of the case' prohibiting a food business owner or manager from participating in the management of any food business, or any food business of a particular class.[117]

19.93   The health risk requirement is satisfied if there is a risk of injury to health owing to:

(a)   the use for the purposes of the business of any process or treatment;

(b)   the construction of any premises used for the purposes of the business, or the use for those purposes of any equipment; and

(c)   the state or condition of any premises or equipment used for the purposes of the business.[118]

---

112   Reg 19(2)(b).
113   Reg 19(2)(a).
114   www.sentencingcouncil.org.uk
115   Reg 19(3).
116   Reg 7(1).
117   Reg 7(4).
118   Reg 7(2).

'Injury' includes any impairment whether temporary or permanent.[119]

19.94 In those circumstances, the court must make the appropriate order for prohibition:

(a) in a case falling within para (a) of reg 7(2) above, a prohibition on the use of the process or treatment for the purposes of the business;

(b) in a case falling within para (b) of reg 7(2), a prohibition on the use of the premises or equipment for the purposes of the business or any other food business of the same class or description;

(c) in a case falling within para (c) of reg 7(2), a prohibition on the use of the premises or equipment for the purposes of any food business.[120]

19.95 A prohibition order in those terms continues until the enforcement authority issue a certificate, certifying that the proprietor has taken sufficient measures such that the health risk condition was no longer fulfilled.[121] In addition to cases in which the health risk condition is fulfilled, the court has a discretionary power to impose a prohibition on the proprietor, or a manager of a food business, participating in the management of any food business, or any food business of a class or description specified in the order. Such an order may be made by the court if it 'thinks it proper to do so in all the circumstances of the case'.[122]

19.96 The circumstances in which the court ought to exercise its discretion under reg 7(4) were considered by the Court of Appeal in *R v Crestdane Ltd*.[123] The exercise of the discretion to make a hygiene prohibition order was not limited to circumstances in which the immediate closure of the premises was necessary to safeguard public health, such as would give rise to a Hygiene Emergency Prohibition Notice, although the protection of the public from a future risk of harm is clearly a relevant consideration. Where there is an immediate risk to public health that would be a powerful consideration in favour of making such an order, but even if there has been an improvement in conditions such that a Hygiene Emergency Prohibition Notice is no longer necessary, it does not follow that a Hygiene Prohibition Order ought not to be made. It would be open to the court to conclude, notwithstanding the present improvement, that there remained a sufficient future risk that a Hygiene Prohibition Order ought to be made.

19.97 The number and nature of the breaches in the present case, particularly where they are numerous and long-standing, might give rise to such a concern, although a single breach might also be of such severity that it required the

---

[119] Reg 7(2).
[120] Reg 7(3).
[121] Reg 7(6)(a).
[122] Reg 7(4).
[123] *R v Crestdane Ltd* [2012] EWCA Crim 958.

making of a Hygiene Prohibition Order. Previous convictions and failures to heed warnings were also clearly relevant in assessing the level of future risk.

19.98 Improvements made after the event were relevant, but a court was entitled to view protestations of future good conduct with a degree of scepticism where there was a history of failures to comply. Deterrence too was an important consideration. The imposition of an order was a powerful message to the food industry that strict compliance with rigorous food hygiene regulations was vital.

19.99 In any event, the future risk to human health was but one consideration. The facts of any particular offence might alone justify the imposition of a Hygiene Prohibition Order – whilst the considerations set out above will be relevant, the discretion remains a wide one, and the test remained whether it was proper to impose such an order in all the circumstances of the case.

19.100 A prohibition order prohibiting a proprietor from participating in the management of a food business continues until a court directs that it shall cease to have effect.[124] A person affected by such an order may apply to the court no sooner than 6 months after the making of such an order for a direction that the prohibition order shall cease to have effect. Such a direction will be made if the court thinks it proper to do so having regard to all the circumstances of the case, including in particular the conduct of the proprietor since the making of the order. If the application is refused, no further application can be made within 3 months.[125]

Time limits for prosecutions

19.101 Offences contrary to the 2013 Regulations are subject to specific time limits under reg 18. By virtue of that regulation, no prosecution may be commenced in relation to those offences later than 3 years from the commission of the offence, or 1 year after its discovery by the prosecutor, whichever is the earlier. Time limits are now covered in Chapter 3, Criminal Enforcement.

Directors' liability

19.102 Regulation 20 provides for individual responsibility where an offence is committed by a body corporate with the consent or connivance of a director, manager, secretary or similar officer, or the offence is attributable to their neglect. The Regulation is in identical terms to s 36 of the Food Safety Act 1990. Directors' liability is now covered in Chapter 3, Criminal Enforcement.

---

[124] Reg 7(6)(b).
[125] Reg 7(8).

Causal liability

19.103 Regulation 11 provides that:

> Where the commission by any person of an offence under these Regulations is due to the act or default of some other person, that other person commits the offence; and a person may be convicted of the offence by virtue of this regulation whether or not proceedings are taken against the first-mentioned person.

19.104 The provision is in effectively the same terms as s 20 of the Food Safety Act 1990 and applies to offences under the 2013 regulations as it does under the Act. Causal liability is now dealt with in detail in Chapter 3, Criminal Enforcement.

Defences

Due diligence

19.105 The general defence of due diligence applies under reg 12 of the 2013 Regulations as under s 21 of the Food Safety Act 1990. Due diligence defences are now covered generally in Chapter 3, Criminal Enforcement. In relation to offences under Art 12 or Art 14, if the accused neither prepared the food nor imported it into the UK, then the due diligence defence can be established by an accused who satisfies specified requirements under reg 12(3) or (4). In either case, it is for the accused to prove those facts under reg 12(3) or (4) as the case may be. The particular requirements do not supersede the general due diligence defence, but provide that a person who establishes those requirements shall be deemed to have made out the due diligence defence.[126]

Defence in relation to exports

19.106 Under reg 13 it is a defence to an offence of contravening or failing to comply with food law for the accused to prove that:

(a) the item in respect of which the offence is alleged to have been committed was intended for export to a country that is not a Member State and that the item could lawfully be exported there under Art 12 of Regulation 178/2002; or

(b) the item in respect of which the offence is alleged to have been committed was intended for export to a Member State and that:
  (i) the legislation applicable to that item in that Member State is compatible with the relevant provisions of food law (except in so far as it relates to feed produced for or fed to food producing animals) at EU level, and
  (ii) the item complies with that legislation.

---

126 Reg 12(2).

Powers of enforcement authorities

Inspection and seizure of suspected food

19.107   The provisions of s 9 of the Food Safety Act 1990 applies for the purpose of the 2013 Regulations to authorised officers of an enforcement authority under the Regulations as to authorised officers of a food authority under the Act.[127]

Procurement and analysis of samples

19.108   Equivalent powers in respect of the procurement (in reg 14) and analysis (in reg 15) of samples are given to authorised officers enforcing the food hygiene legislation as are contained within ss 29 and 30 of the Food Safety Act 1990. Save for references to the Act being replaced by references to the Regulations, regs 14 and 15 are in identical terms to ss 29 and 30.

Powers of entry

19.109   Regulation 16 of the 2013 Regulations provides authorised officers of an enforcement authority in relation to Regulation (EC) 178/2002 or the EU Hygiene Regulations with comparable powers of entry to those exercised by authorised officers of a food authority under s 32 of the Food Safety Act 1990. Save for references to the Act being replaced by references to the EU Regulations and other minor modifications, reg 16 is in identical terms to s 32 of the Food Safety Act 1990, and extends identical powers of entry including in relation to the applications for warrants to authorised officers enforcing the provisions of the General Food Law Regulation and the EU Hygiene Regulations.

Hygiene improvement notices

19.110   Where an officer has reasonable grounds for believing that the food business operator is failing to comply with the Hygiene Regulations, he may issue an improvement notice under reg 6. Such notice should set out the officer's grounds for believing that there is a failure to comply, the matters constituting the failure to comply and the measures necessary to secure compliance. The effect of such a notice is to require those measures to be taken within a specified period, which shall be not less than 14 days. Failure to comply with a hygiene improvement notice constitutes a criminal offence.[128]

---

[127]   Reg 25.
[128]   Reg 6(2).

Hygiene emergency prohibition notices and orders

19.111 The considerations in relation to hygiene emergency prohibition notices and orders are identical to those set out in the section detailing emergency prohibition notices and orders under the Food Safety Act 1990 (see above).

Remedial Action Notices

19.112 Where it appears to an authorised officer that[129] any of the requirements of the Hygiene Regulations is being breached or inspection under the Hygiene Regulations is being hampered, the officer may serve on the food business operator or duly authorised representative a remedial action notice. A remedial action notice may prohibit the use of any equipment or any part of the establishment specified in the notice; impose conditions upon or prohibit the carrying out of any process; or require the rate of operation to be reduced to such extent as is specified in the notice, or to be stopped completely.

19.113 The notice must be served as soon as practicable, and state why it is being served, and if it is served as a result of alleged breaches of the Hygiene Regulations, it must specify the breach and the action needed to remedy it. As soon as the enforcement authority is satisfied that such remedial action has been taken, a further notice should be served, withdrawing the remedial action notice. Any person who fails to comply with a remedial action notice commits an offence.

Detention Notices

19.114 An authorised officer may in relation to an establishment requiring approval under Art 4(2) of Regulation 853/2004 serve on the food business operator a detention notice, requiring the detention of any animal or food for the purpose of examination or the taking of samples. As soon as the enforcement authority is satisfied that detention is no longer required, a further notice should be served, withdrawing the detention notice. Any person who fails to comply with a detention notice commits an offence.

Rights of appeal

19.115 There is a right of appeal against a decision of an authorised officer of an enforcement authority to serve a hygiene improvement notice, a decision of an enforcement authority to refuse to issue a certificate that the health risk condition is no longer fulfilled under para (6) of reg 7 or para (8) of reg 8; or a decision of an authorised officer of an enforcement authority to serve a remedial action notice by way of complaint to a magistrates' court.[130] On

---

[129] In relation to an establishment requiring approval under Art 4(2) of Regulation 853/2004.
[130] Reg 22.

appeal, the court may cancel the notice, or affirm it, either in its original form or with such modifications as the court thinks fit.[131]

19.116   There is a further right of appeal to the Crown Court following either the dismissal of an appeal under reg 22, or the making of a Hygiene Prohibition Order or Emergency Hygiene Prohibition Order by the magistrates' court.[132]

THE EU FOOD INFORMATION REGULATION

Introduction and application

19.117   On 25 October 2011, the European Parliament and the Council adopted the Regulation on the Provision of Food Information to Consumers (Regulation (EU) 1169/2011) (the 'FIC Regulation').[133] The FIC Regulation came into force on 12 December 2011, and enacts significant changes to the existing EU law on the labelling of food.

19.118   The requirements of the FIC Regulation apply from 1 January 2014 in respect of the provisions relating to the composition of and labelling of minced meat, from 13 December 2014 in respect of the general food labelling requirements, and from 13 December 2016 in respect of the provisions relating to the mandatory provision of nutrition information.

19.119   The FIC Regulation required national legislation in order for its provisions to be brought into effect in the UK, and the Food Information Regulations 2014 were implemented in England on 14 July 2014. Equivalent legislation exists in Wales, Scotland and Northern Ireland. The provisions of the FIC Regulation replaced the labelling requirements of the FLR 1996 from 13 December 2014. After that date only remaining stocks of foods labelled to comply with the FLR 1996 may be sold.

19.120   The FIC Regulation repealed most of the FLR 1996 with effect from 13 December 2014, although some provisions remain in place until 13 December 2018. The Food Information Regulations 2014 do not contain equivalent offences to many of the specific offences contained in the FLR 1996, and the initial frontline measure will be the issuing of an improvement notice under s 10 of the Food Safety Act 1990. Failure to comply with such a notice constitutes a criminal offence. Such an approach marked a radical departure from the regime which had applied previously.

---

[131]   Reg 24.
[132]   Reg 23.
[133]   Regulation (EU) No 1169/2011 of the European Parliament and of the Council of 25 October 2011 on the provision of food information to consumers, amending Regulations (EC) No 1924/2006 and (EC) No 1925/2006 of the European Parliament and of the Council, and repealing Commission Directive 87/250/EEC, Council Directive 90/496/EEC, Commission Directive 1999/10/EC, Directive 2000/13/EC of the European Parliament and of the Council, Commission Directives 2002/67/EC and 2008/5/EC and Commission Regulation (EC) No 608/2004 (OJ L304, 22.11.2011, p 18).

19.121 Sections 10 (Improvement Notices), 20 (offences due to fault of another), 21 (due diligence defence), 35 (punishment of offences) and 37 (appeals) of the Food Safety Act 1990 apply with modifications, as do the powers of entry under s 32.[134] Sections 3 (presumptions that food is intended for human consumption), 20 (offences due to fault of another person), 21 (defence of due diligence), 22 (defence of publication in the course of business), 30(8) (which relates to documentary evidence), 33 (obstruction etc of officers), and 36 (offences by bodies corporate) also apply.[135]

19.122 Failure to comply with certain articles of the FIC Regulation relating to the provision of information in respect of ingredients causing allergies or intolerances is a separate offence, triable summarily with a fine.[136]

19.123 In appropriate cases, prosecutions may be brought under other legislation – for example, where the labelling of the food is misleading, a prosecution may be brought under reg 19 of the Food Safety and Hygiene (England) Regulations 2013 and Art 16 of the General Food Law Regulation (EC).

19.124 Specific provision is also made in respect of food sold after the expiry of a 'use by' date, which by virtue of Art 24(1) is deemed to be unsafe for the purposes of reg 14 of the General Food Law Regulation. Accordingly a prosecution can be brought under reg 19 of the Food Safety and Hygiene (England) Regulations 2013, without further proof being required that the food is unsafe.

19.125 The provisions of the FIC Regulation apply to any food intended for supply to the final consumer or to mass caterers. In such a case, the food must be accompanied by food information complying with the FIC Regulation.[137] The responsibility for compliance lies with food business operator under whose name or business name the food is marketed or, if that operator is not established in the Union, the importer into the Union market.[138] Guidance was produced by Defra in relation to the Food Information Regulations 2014 in October 2014.

Key provisions of the FIC Regulation

Fair information practices

19.126 Article 7 specifies fair information practices in respect of food. It provides that food information must not be misleading, particularly as to the characteristics of the food, by attributing to food properties which it does not possess, by suggesting that the food has some special characteristic where all

---

[134] Food Information Regulations 2014, Sch 4, Parts 1 and 2, 3 and 5.
[135] Food Information Regulations 2014, Sch 4, Part 5.
[136] Reg 10 of the Food Information Regulations 2014.
[137] Regulation (EU) No 1169/2011, Art 6.
[138] Regulation (EU) No 1169/2011, Art 8.

similar foods possess those characteristics (such as the presence or absence of an ingredient which is common to all similar foods) or by suggesting the presence of a particular ingredient which is not present.

19.127 Food information must be clear, accurate and easy to understand for the consumer. Fair information practices extend to advertising of food, and to the presentation of food.

19.128 Subject to derogations applicable to natural mineral waters and foods for particular nutritional uses, food information must not attribute to any food the property of preventing, treating or curing a human disease, nor refer to such properties.

General labelling requirements

19.129 The general requirements in respect of food labelling of pre-packed goods are contained in Art 9. The food must be labelled with the name of the food, an ingredients list, information in relation to the use of certain foods causing allergies or intolerances, the quantity of certain ingredients, the net quantity of the food, a date mark, any special storage conditions, the name or business name and address of the food business operator under whose name the food is being marketed, the country of origin or place of provenance where required, instructions for use, the alcoholic strength by volume where applicable and, from 13 December 2016, a nutrition declaration.[139]

19.130 In the case of pre-packed food, the mandatory food information must appear on the package or on a label attached thereto,[140] and be prominently displayed so as to be easily visible, clearly legible and, where appropriate, indelible.[141] The provisions of Art 9(1) will not apply to milk or milk products when sold in a glass bottle which is intended for re-use.[142] Articles 17 to 28 provide detailed particulars in relation to the mandatory information specified in Art 9.

The name of the food

19.131 The food must be marked with the name of the food. The name of the food shall be its legal name, where such a name exists. In the absence of such a name, the name of the food shall be its customary name, or, if there is no customary name or the customary name is not used, a descriptive name of the food shall be provided. A brand name, trade mark or fancy name cannot be used as the name of the food.

---

[139] Regulation (EU) No 1169/2011, Art 9.
[140] Regulation (EU) No 1169/2011, Art 12(2).
[141] Regulation (EU) No 1169/2011, Art 13(1).
[142] Reg 3 of the Food Information Regulations 2014.

Allergen listing

19.132 Annex II of the FIC Regulation specifies a number of allergens or ingredients giving rise to intolerances which must be specified in the list of ingredients. Where it is not obvious from the name of the ingredient, it is necessary to identify the allergen clearly by reference to the particular ingredient, and highlighted by the use of font, style or background colour so as to stand out from the list of ingredients.

Date of minimum durability

19.133 All foods, other than those listed in Annex X 1(d) of the FIC Regulation, must be marked with a date of minimum durability. In the case of foods which are, from a microbiological point of view, highly perishable and which are therefore likely after a short period to constitute an immediate danger to human health, the food must be marked with a 'use by' date. In other cases, the food should be marked with a 'best before' date.

19.134 After the 'use by' date a food shall be deemed to be unsafe in accordance with Art 14(2) to (5) of Regulation (EC) No 178/2002. Accordingly a prosecution can be brought under reg 19 of the Food Safety and Hygiene (England) Regulations 2013 where food is sold (within the extended definition of sale) after the 'use by' date. By virtue of Art 24, the food shall be deemed to be unsafe, without further proof being required.

Mandatory nutrition labelling

19.135 From 13 December 2016, food business operators will need to provide mandatory 'back of the pack' nutritional information on all pre-packed food. The mandatory nutritional information required is a declaration of the energy value in kilojoules and kilocalories, together with the amount in grams of fat, saturates, carbohydrates, sugars, protein and salt which the food contains. If nutritional information is given voluntarily as 'front of the pack' nutritional information, it must comprise either the energy value alone, or the energy value with the amounts of fat, saturates, sugars and salt in the food. No other combination of nutritional information is permitted. The nutritional information must be expressed per 100g, or per 100ml.[143] Food business operators may also include in addition to per 100g or per 100ml an expression of the nutritional information by reference to the pack or portion size.[144]

Allergen information in food which is not pre-packed

19.136 In general, foods which are not pre-packed are not subject to the labelling requirements of the FIC. In the case of the information regarding allergens required by Art 9(1)(c), FBOs will need to provide information if any

---

[143] Regulation (EU) No 1169/2011, Art 32.
[144] Regulation (EU) No 1169/2011, Art 33.

of the foods/ingredients listed in Annex II of the EU FIC are used in the preparation of foods which they supply which are not in a pre-packed form by virtue of Art 44.

19.137 In such cases, rather than requiring the use of an attached label, the information can be provided in such manner as the FBO may choose, including orally by a member of staff.[145] Where it is intended that the information be provided orally, it must be indicated to the consumer either by a label attached to the food or by a notice, such as on a menu, indicating that the allergen information can be obtained by asking a member of staff.[146]

Offences

19.138 Regulation 10 of the Food Information Regulations 2014 provides as follows:

> Offence
>
> 10(1) A person is guilty of an offence if the person fails to comply with –
>
> (a)   any provision of FIC specified in paragraph (2), as read with Articles 1(3) and 6 and the first subparagraph of Article 54(1), or
> (b)   regulation 5(5).
>
> (2) The provisions of FIC are –
>
> (a)   Article 9(1)(c), as also read with Annex II;
> (b)   Article 21(1)(a), as also read with Articles 9(1)(c) and 18(1) and Annex II;
> (c)   the second subparagraph of Article 21(1), as also read with Articles 9(1)(c) and 19(1) and Annex II; and
> (d)   Article 44(1)(a), as also read with Article 9(1)(c) and regulation 5.

Failing to comply with the specified provisions of the Food Information Regulations

19.139 It is an offence for a food business operator to fail to comply with Arts 9(1)(c), 21(1)(a), the second sub-paragraph of Art 21(1) or Art 44(1)(a). It must be proved to the criminal standard that the offender:

(a)   was a food business operator;
(b)   who failed to comply with the specified provisions.

19.140 Article 9(1)(c) requires a food business operator to provide particulars of any ingredient or processing aid listed in Annex II or derived from a substance or product listed in Annex II causing allergies or intolerances used in the manufacture or preparation of a food and still present in the finished product, even if in an altered form.

---

[145] Reg 5(1) of the Food Information Regulations 2014.
[146] Reg 5(3) of the Food Information Regulations 2014.

19.141 Article 21(1)(a) requires a food business operator to indicate the particulars of any ingredient or processing aid listed in Annex II causing allergies or intolerances within the list of ingredients. The second sub-paragraph of Art 21(1) requires a food business operator to specify the particulars of any ingredient or processing aid listed in Annex II causing allergies or intolerances by stating that the product contains that ingredient where there is no list of ingredients on the label.

19.142 Article 44(1)(a) provides that where a food business operator offers food for sale to the final consumer or to mass caterers without pre-packaging, or where foods are packed on the sales premises at the consumer's request or pre-packed for direct sale, the provision of the particulars specified in Art 9(1)(c) above is mandatory.

Failing to comply with reg 5(5)

19.143 It is an offence to fail to comply with reg 5(5) of the Food Information Regulations 2014. It must be proved to the criminal standard that the offender:

(a) offered food for sale to the final consumer, or to a mass caterer, otherwise than by means of distance communication, which was either not pre-packed, was packed on the operator's premises at the consumer's request or was pre-packed for direct sale;

(b) in respect of which he did not give particulars of any ingredient or processing aid listed in Annex II or derived from a substance or product listed in Annex II causing allergies or intolerances used in the manufacture or preparation of a food and still present in the finished product, even if in an altered form.

Penalties

19.144 Offences of failing to comply with the provisions of the FIR are offences which are triable summarily. The maximum sentence in the magistrates' court is a fine.

Failure to comply with an Improvement Notice

19.145 The initial frontline measure for the enforcement of the other aspects of the FIC Regulation is the issuing of an Improvement Notice under s 10 of the Food Safety Act 1990. Failure to comply with such a notice will constitute a criminal offence. The maximum penalty for failing to comply with an Improvement Notice where it relates to a breach of the FIR 2014 is a fine. The offence is triable summarily.[147]

---

[147] Food Information Regulations 2014, Sch 4, Part 1.

CHAPTER 20

ENVIRONMENTAL TRADING STANDARDS

CONTENTS

INTRODUCTION

20.1 Successive governments of the United Kingdom have indicated their commitment to reducing waste and greenhouse gas emissions, whilst emphasising the economic, scientific, and legislative realities that must come with achieving this aim. This chapter outlines the roles that environmental legislation and the work of Trading Standards both play in achieving these aims. Trading Standards authorities are responsible for enforcing regulations concerning both the quantity and nature of the packaging used for consumer products. They are responsible for enforcing consumer products energy consumption labelling requirements. Trading Standards are also concerned with the energy consumption of buildings, both public and private. The role of Trading Standards in enforcing these important regulations is considered below. Other areas of environmental legislation that concern Trading Standards authorities are also outlined. Finally, mention is made of the Energy Act 2011 and the Green Deal.

The Packaging and Waste Directive

20.2 The Packaging and Waste Directive 94/62/EC requires:[1]

- packaging to be minimised;
- packaging to be designed for recovery and re-use;
- recovery targets for waste packaging to be met by the UK; and
- heavy metals in packaging to be restricted.

20.3 Launching the Government's review of waste policies in November 2010, Environment Secretary Caroline Spelman said:

> 'We are committed to working towards a zero waste economy because it makes environmental and economic sense. Reducing waste needs to be made as easy as possible for people; it should be driven by incentives not penalties and common sense rather than coercion.'

20.4 The Directive has been transposed into UK law by two regulations:

- the Packaging (Essential Requirements) Regulations 2015 ('PERR 2015');[2]
- the Producer Responsibility Obligations (Packaging Waste) Regulations 2007 (as amended) ('PROPWR 2007').[3]

20.5 The PERR 2015 are enforced by the Trading Standards Departments of local weights and measures authorities in Great Britain and by the Department of Enterprise, Trade and Investment ('DETI') in Northern Ireland. The PERR are examined in detail below. The PROPWR 2007 are the responsibility of the

---

[1]   Directive 94/62/EC, Arts 9 and 11.
[2]   SI 2015/1640.
[3]   SI 2007/871.

Department for Environment, Food and Rural Affairs ('DEFRA') and are enforced by the Environment Agency ('EA') in England and Wales, the Scottish Environment Protection Agency, and the Northern Ireland Environment Agency. The most significant provisions may be summarised as follows:

- the Directive imposes recycling and recovery targets for packaging waste on the UK and the aim of the PROPWR 2007 is to meet those targets through the principle of producer responsibility;

- companies with an annual turnover of £2m and handling more than 50 tonnes of packaging a year must pay for a certain amount of the UK obligation to recycle packaging;

- companies' obligations are met by purchasing Packaging Waste Recovery Notes ('PRNs') or Packaging Waste Export Recovery Notes ('PERNs');

- companies can either join a compliance scheme to deal with their obligations for them or register directly with enforcement authorities.

20.6 The EA is also responsible for enforcing specific obligations regarding electrical or electronic equipment imposed by the Waste Electronic and Electrical Equipment Regulations 2013 ('WEEE 2013').[4] Scotland's first Zero Waste Plan was published in June 2010.

PACKAGING (ESSENTIAL REQUIREMENTS) REGULATIONS 2015

20.7 The PERR 2015[5] came into force on 1 October 2015. They replace the Packaging (Essential Requirements) Regulations 2003 which implemented the Packaging and Waste Directive.[6] They define a 'responsible person' in respect of the packaging of products and place upon that person a duty to satisfy essential requirements as to the manufacturing and composition of the packaging, its reusability, and its suitability for recycling, energy recovery, or composting. Further duties are placed upon the responsible person in respect of the presence of heavy metals in packaging and the production of technical documentation. Contravention of these duties is an offence under PERR 2015.

20.8 In June 2009, a new Government strategy published by Defra, with input from BIS and the Devolved Administrations – *Making the Most of Packaging, A strategy for a low-carbon economy* – considered the direction for packaging policy for the next 10 years and acknowledged the enforcement difficulties for Trading Standards in proving that the amount of packaging used is excessive under PERR 2003:

---

4   SI 2013/3113.
5   SI 2015/1640.
6   94/62/EC, Arts 9 and 11.

'The UK would like to see clearer language on this in the Directive to aid enforcement. We have already raised this formally with the Commission, and intend to continue pressing them for a review of this wording.'

Despite this, the wording remains the same in the PERR 2015.

Regulatory framework

20.9 The PERR 2015 include derogations for the heavy metals limits in respect of certain glass packaging and plastic pallets and crates, as set out in Commission Decisions 1999/177/EC and 2001/171/EC. They also maintain a set time frame for producing technical documentation, requiring compliance within 28 days.

Prosecutions

The duty to enforce

20.10 Regulation 7 imposes a duty upon every local weights and measures authority[7] in Great Britain (and DfE in Northern Ireland) to enforce the Regulations within their areas. The Regulations do not authorise any enforcement authority to bring proceedings in Scotland for an offence (Sch 4, para 2) – only the Crown Office and Procurator Fiscal Service ('COPFS') may do so.

The right to prosecute

20.11 The right to prosecute is not restricted to enforcement authorities. Any person can bring a prosecution under the Regulations, although the rights contained within the PERR 2015 to facilitate the gathering of evidence may not be exercised by such a private prosecutor.

Time limits

20.12 Schedule 4, para 1(c) provides that, in England and Wales, and Northern Ireland, a magistrates' court may try an information in respect of an offence committed under the PERR 2015 if the information is laid within 12 months from the time when the offence is committed. In Scotland, summary proceedings for such an offence may be commenced at any time within 12 months from the time when the offence is committed. Time limits are now covered generally in Chapter 3, Criminal Enforcement.

---

7   Defined in s 69(1) of the Weights and Measures Act 1985.

Defendants

Causal liability

20.13 Regulation 8 provides causal liability. This is now covered in Chapter 3, Criminal Enforcement.

Directors' liability

20.14 Regulation 11(2) permits the prosecution and conviction of any 'director, manager, secretary or other similar officer' of a company or 'any person who was purporting to act in such a capacity'. Directors' liability provisions are now covered in Chapter 3, Criminal Enforcement.

Offences: definitions

20.15 By virtue of reg 8 it is an offence to contravene, or fail to comply with, regs 4 and 5. It is also an offence not to supply or retain technical documentation or other information as required by reg 6(1) and (2). The definitions of terms used in the offences under the PERR 2015 are to be found in reg 2 and the more frequently used of those are summarised below. The definition of 'packaging' (originally introduced by the 2013 Amendment Regulations) is reproduced in full below, along with the illustrative guide contained within Sch 5.

Packaging

20.16

Packaging (Essential Requirements) Regulations 2015, reg 3

Packaging

(2) In these Regulations "packaging" means all products made of any materials of any nature to be used for the containment, protection, handling, delivery and presentation of goods, from raw materials to processed goods, from the producer to the user or the consumer, including non-returnable items used for the same purposes, but only where the products are –

    (a)   sales packaging or primary packaging, that is to say packaging conceived so as to constitute a sales unit to the final user or consumer at the point of purchase;

    (b)   grouped packaging or secondary packaging, that is to say packaging conceived so as to constitute at the point of purchase a grouping of a certain number of sales units whether the latter is sold as such to the final user or consumer or whether it serves only as a means to replenish the shelves at the point of sale, and which can be removed from the product without affecting its characteristics; or

    (c)   transport packaging or tertiary packaging, that is to say packaging conceived so as to facilitate handling and transport of a number of sales units or grouped packagings in order to prevent physical handling and transport damage; for the purposes of these Regulations transport packaging does not include road, rail, ship and air containers.

(3) The following items must also be considered to be packaging on the basis of the criteria set out below –

(a)   items that fulfil the above definition without prejudice to other functions which the packaging might also perform, unless the item is an integral part of a product and it is necessary to contain, support or preserve that product throughout its lifetime and all elements are intended to be used, consumed and disposed of together.

(b)   items designed and intended to be filled at the point of sale and disposable items sold, filled or designed and intended to be filled at the point of sale provided they fulfil a packaging function.

(c)   packaging components and ancillary elements integrated into packaging and ancillary elements hung directly on, or attached to, a product and which perform a packaging function unless they are an integral part of that product and all elements are intended to be consumed or disposed of together.

(4) Schedule V to these Regulations lists the illustrative examples of packaging referred to in paragraph (3) and set out in Annex 1 of the Directive as amended by Commission Directive 2013/2/EU amending Annex I to Directive 94/62/EC of the European Parliament and of the Council on packaging and packaging waste

SCHEDULE 5

ILLUSTRATIVE EXAMPLES OF PACKAGING REFERRED TO IN THE DEFINITION OF PACKAGING IN REGULATION 3(2)

Illustrative examples for criterion in regulation 3(3)(a) –

Packaging

Sweet boxes
Film overwrap around a CD case
Mailing pouches for catalogues and magazines (with a magazine inside)
Cake dollies sold with a cake
Rolls, tubes and cylinders around which flexible material (e.g. plastic film, aluminium, paper) is wound, except rolls, tubes and cylinders intended as parts of production machinery and not used to present a product as a sales unit
Flower pots intended to be used only for the selling and transporting of plants and not intended to stay with the plant throughout its life time
Glass bottles for injection solutions
CD spindles (sold with CDs, not intended to be used as storage)
Clothes hangers (sold with a clothing item)
Matchboxes
Sterile barrier systems (pouches, trays and materials necessary to preserve the sterility of the product)
Beverage system capsules (e.g. coffee, cacao, milk) which are left empty after use
Refillable steel cylinders used for various kinds of gas, excluding fire extinguishers

Non-packaging
Flower pots intended to stay with the plant throughout its lifetime
Tool boxes
Tea bags
Wax layers around cheese
Sausage skins
Clothes hangers (sold separately)
Beverage system coffee capsules, coffee foil pouches, and filter paper coffee pods disposed together with the used coffee product
Cartridges for printers
CD, DVD and video cases (sold together with a CD, DVD or video inside)
CD spindles (sold empty, intended to be used as storage)
Soluble bags for detergents
Graveside lights (containers for candles)
Mechanical quern (integrated in a refillable recipient, e.g. refillable pepper mill)

Illustrative examples for criterion in regulation 3(3)(b) –

Packaging, if designed and intended to be filled at the point of sale
Paper or plastic carrier bags
Disposable plates and cups
Cling film
Sandwich bags
Aluminium foil
Plastic foil for cleaned clothes in laundries

Non-packaging
Stirrer
Disposable cutlery
Wrapping paper (sold separately)
Paper baking cases (sold empty)
Cake dollies sold without a cake

Illustrative examples for criterion in regulation 3(3)(c)

Packaging
Labels hung directly on or attached to a product

Part of packaging
Mascara brush which forms part of the container closure
Sticky labels attached to another packaging item
Staples
Plastic sleeves
Device for measuring dosage which forms part of the container closure for

detergents
Mechanical quern (integrated in a non-refillable recipient, filled with a product,
e.g. pepper mill filled with pepper)

Non-packaging
Radio frequency identification (RFID) tags

Reuse

20.17 'Reuse' (the word is used as noun) means any operation by which
packaging, which has been designed to accomplish a number of rotations
during its life cycle, is refilled or used for the same purpose. The reuse of
packaging will not constitute 'placing on the market'.[8]

Responsible person

20.18 The 'responsible person' is defined in four ways. First, it is the person
responsible for packing of filling products into packaging. Second, it is any
person presenting himself as being so responsible by affixing to the packaging
his name or mark. Third, it is the person who reconditions the packaging for
reuse. Fourth, it is the importer. For the purposes of reg 6(2) the responsible
person only includes the manufacturer or his authorised representative in the
Community. It seems from these multiple definitions that there may be more
than one responsible person in respect of any packaging. The responsible
person can, of course, be a company.

The essential requirements

20.19 The 'essential requirements' are those set out in the Sch 1, which
reproduces Annex II of the Directive.

Packaging (Essential Requirements) Regulations 2015

SCHEDULE 1 (Annex II of the Directive)

**ESSENTIAL REQUIREMENTS ON THE COMPOSITION AND THE
REUSABLE AND RECOVERABLE, INCLUDING RECYCLABLE, NATURE
OF PACKAGING**

(Regulation 2(1))

1. Requirements specific to the manufacturing and composition of packaging

    (1)   Packaging must be so manufactured that the packaging volume and
weight is limited to the minimum adequate amount to maintain the
necessary level of safety, hygiene and acceptance for the packed product
and for the consumer;

    (2)   Packaging must be designed, produced and commercialised in such a way
as to permit its reuse or recovery, including recycling, and to minimise its

---

[8]   Regulation 5(1).

impact on the environment when packaging waste or residues from packaging waste management operations are disposed of; and

(3)   Packaging must be so manufactured that the presence of noxious and other hazardous substances and materials as constituents of the packaging material or of any of the packaging components is minimised with regard to their presence in emissions, ash or leachate when packaging or residues from management operations or packaging waste are incinerated or landfilled.

2. Requirements specific to reusable packaging

The following requirements must be simultaneously satisfied:

(a)   the physical properties and characteristics of the packaging must enable a number of trips or rotations in normally predictable conditions of use,

(b)   it must be possible to process the used packaging in order to meet health and safety requirements for the workforce,

(c)   the requirements specific to recoverable packaging must be fulfilled when the packaging is no longer reused and thus becomes waste.

3. Requirements specific to the recoverable nature of packaging

Packaging recoverable in the form of material recycling

(1)   Packaging must be manufactured in such a way as to enable the recycling of a certain percentage by weight of the materials used into the manufacture of marketable products, in compliance with current standards in the European Union. The establishment of this percentage may vary, depending on the type of material of which the packaging is composed.

Packaging recoverable in the form of energy recovery

(2)   Packaging waste processed for the purpose of energy recovery shall have a minimum inferior calorific value to allow optimisation of energy recovery.

Packaging recoverable in the form of composting

(3)   Packaging waste processed for the purpose of composting must be of such a biodegradable nature that it should not hinder the separate collection and the composting process or activity into which it is introduced.

Biodegradable packaging

(4)   Biodegradable packaging waste must be of such a nature that it is capable of undergoing physical, chemical, thermal or biological decomposition such that most of the finished compost ultimately decomposes into carbon dioxide, biomass and water.

20.20 The essential requirements set out in Sch 1 can be summarised as follows.

Requirements specific to the manufacture and composition of packaging

20.21   All packaging must satisfy all of the following requirements:

–   The weight and volume of packaging shall be the minimum amount adequate to maintain the necessary level of safety for the consumer and acceptance for the packed product. The amount of packaging 'necessary' for it to be accepted by the consumer is likely to be highly subjective and will no doubt be relied upon by those providing luxury or gift wrapped goods;

–   Packaging shall be designed and produced so as to permit its reuse or recovery, and to minimise its impact on the environment on disposal;

–   Packaging shall be manufactured so that when it is incinerated or landfilled the presence of any noxious or hazardous substances in emissions, ash, or leachate is minimised.

Requirements specific to the reusable nature of packaging

20.22   In order to be declared 'reusable', packaging must satisfy all of the following requirements:

–   The packaging must be robust enough to survive a number of trips;

–   It must be possible to process the used packaging in order to meet the health and safety requirements of the workforce;

–   The requirements specific to the recoverable nature of packaging (set out below) must be fulfilled.

Requirements specific to the recoverable nature of packaging

20.23   All packaging must satisfy one of the following requirements:

–   Where the packaging is designed to be recyclable, it must be possible to recycle a certain percentage of the weight of materials used into marketable products (in compliance with current standards in the EU). This percentage may vary depending on the type of material used in the packaging.

–   Where the packaging is designed to be incinerated, it must be reasonably combustible.

–   Where the packaging is recoverable in the form of composting, it must be reasonably biodegradable and must ultimately decompose into carbon dioxide, biomass, and water.

20.24   A series of standards covering the essential requirements and containing details of the minimum recyclable weight and minimum recoverable inferior calorific values have been published by the European Committee for Standardisation (CEN). These provide framework methodologies for considering reduction, reuse, recyclability, and recovery. These provide guidance when considering packaging minimisation and are available from the British Standards Institute.

Requirements for exemptions – plastic crates and pallets

20.25 The requirements for exemption for plastic crates and pallets from the heavy metal concentration levels specified in reg 5(1) are contained in Sch 2 to the Regulations. Commission Decision 1999/177/EC established the conditions for a derogation for plastic crates and plastic pallets in relation to the heavy metals concentration limits in the Directive. This derogation was replaced by Commission Decision 2001/171/EC. This has the same effect as the original derogation but without a time limit and provides for a further review of the functioning of the system and the progress made in phasing out these plastic crates and pallets containing heavy metals after 5 years.

SCHEDULE 2

REQUIREMENTS FOR EXEMPTION FOR PLASTIC CRATES AND PALLETS FROM HEAVY METAL CONCENTRATION LEVELS SPECIFIED IN REGULATION 5(1)

(Regulation 5(3)(a))

1 (1) The plastic crate or plastic pallet must be, or must have been, manufactured in a controlled recycling process, that is to say a process in which the recycled material originates only from other plastic crates or plastic pallets and in which the introduction of external materials is the minimum which is technically feasible but in any event does not exceed 20 per cent by weight.

(2) No regulated metal must be intentionally introduced as an element during the manufacture or distribution of the plastic crate or plastic pallet provided always that the incidental presence of any of these elements must be permitted.

(3) The concentration levels of regulated metals in the plastic crate or plastic pallet may only exceed the levels referred to in regulation 5 as a result of the addition of recycled materials.

2 (1) The plastic crate or plastic pallet must be introduced in a controlled distribution and reuse system and the following requirements must be complied with –

    (a)   the plastic crate or plastic pallet containing regulated metals must be identified in a permanent and visible way;

    (b)   a system of inventory and record keeping must be established, which must include a method of regulatory and financial accountability, to document the compliance with the requirements set out in this Schedule including the return rates. The return rates are the percentage of returnable entities which are not discarded after use but are returned to the manufacturer of the packaging or the responsible person or an authorised representative established in the European Union of the said manufacturer or the responsible person, as the case may be. The said return rates shall be as high as possible but in no case lower than 90 per cent over the lifetime of the said crate or pallet;

(c)   in addition the system must account for all the reusable entities put into, and removed from, service; and

(d)   all returned plastic crates or plastic pallets that are no longer reusable must be either disposed of by a procedure specifically authorised by the Environment Agency in England, the Natural Resources Body for Wales in Wales, the Environment and Heritage Service in Northern Ireland and the Scottish Environment and Protection Agency in Scotland or be recycled in a recycling process in which the recycled material is made up of plastic crates or plastic pallets in the circuit and the introduction of external material is the minimum which is technically feasible but in any event does not exceed 20 per cent by weight.

(2) The manufacturer or his authorised representative established in the European Union must –

(a)   draw up on an annual basis a written declaration of conformity, including an annual report demonstrating how the conditions in this Schedule have been complied with; the declaration of conformity must contain a list of any changes to the system and the manufacturer's authorised representatives; and

(b)   retain the documentation referred to in paragraph (a) at the disposal of the enforcement authority for inspection purposes for a period of four years from the date of its drawing up;

provided always that where neither the manufacturer nor his authorised representative is established within the EU, the responsible person who places the product on the market must keep and, upon request, make available to the enforcement authority, the documentation referred to in paragraph (a).

20.26   The requirements can be summarised as follows.

The derogation allows plastic pallets and crates with heavy metals concentrations greater than those permitted by PERR 2015 to be placed on the market if they fulfil a number of conditions, namely:

–   the plastic pallet or crate concerned must have been manufactured in a controlled recycling process, involving a maximum of 20% virgin material, and for which the remaining material was other plastic pallets and crates;

–   none of the identified heavy metals are intentionally added during the production process;

–   the plastic pallet or crate may only exceed the heavy metal limits as a result of the addition of recycled materials.

20.27   Further to this, the crates and pallets must be introduced in a controlled distribution and reuse system in which:

–   new plastic pallets and crates containing the regulated metals are marked in a permanent and visible way;

–   a system of inventory and record-keeping is established;

– the return rate of the pallets and crates over their lifetime is not less than 90%;

– an annual declaration of conformity is drawn up by the responsible party, which must be made available on request for 4 years.

Requirements for exemptions – glass packaging

20.28 The requirements for exemption for glass packaging from the heavy metal concentration levels specified in reg 5(1) are contained in Sch 3. Commission Decision 2006/340/EC indefinitely extended the derogation in relation to the heavy metals concentration limits in glass packaging. Heavy metal concentration limits do not apply to lead crystal glass packaging.

SCHEDULE 3

REQUIREMENTS FOR EXEMPTION FOR GLASS PACKAGING FROM HEAVY METAL CONCENTRATION LEVELS SPECIFIED IN REGULATION 5(1)

(Regulation 5(3)(b))

1 (1) No regulated metals must be intentionally introduced during the manufacturing process of glass packaging.

(2) The concentration levels of regulated metals in glass packaging may only exceed the level referred to in regulation 5 as a result of the addition of recycled materials.

2 (1) The manufacturer or the manufacturer's authorised representative, or, where neither the manufacturer nor the manufacturer's authorised representative is established within the EU, the responsible person who places the product on the market, must submit a report in accordance with sub-paragraph (2) to the enforcement authority, where the average heavy metals concentration levels on any twelve consecutive monthly controls made from the production of each individual glass furnace, representative of normal and regular production activity, exceeds a concentration level of 200 ppm.

(2) The report must include as a minimum the following information –

– measures values;
– description of measurement methods employed;
– suspected sources for the presence of heavy metals concentration levels; and
– detailed description of the measures taken to reduce the heavy metals concentration levels.

(3) Measurement results from production sites and measurement methods employed must be made available at any time to the enforcement authority, if requested.

20.29 The requirements can be summarised as follows.

The derogation allows glass packaging heavy metals concentration limits greater than those permitted by the Regulations to be placed on the market if they fulfil a number of conditions, namely:

–   no regulated metals have been intentionally introduced during the manufacturing process of glass packaging;

–   the limits are exceeded only as a result of the addition of recycled materials containing heavy metals;

–   that the manufacturer or, if the manufacturer is outside the EU, the responsible person placing the product on the market must submit a report to the enforcement authority in the event that the average heavy metals concentration level over 12 months' production from an individual glass furnace exceeds a 200 ppm limit.

Place on the market

20.30   The expression 'place on the market' is crucial to the commission of the offences under the PERR 2015. It is at the moment that non-compliant packaging is placed on the market that the offence will be committed. The PERR 2015 do not define the expression, but it is generally taken to refer to the when a product is made available for the first time. This is considered to take place when the assembled (ie packed/filled) packaging is first transferred from the stage of manufacture with the intention of sale, distribution, or use on the Community market (including the EEA market).

Particular offences

General packaging duty when placing on the market

20.31

Packaging (Essential Requirements) Regulations 2015, reg 4

General duty relating to the placing on the market of packaging

4(1) A responsible person must not place any packaging on the EU market unless it complies with the essential requirements.

(2) Reused packaging is not considered to be placed on the market for the purposes of this regulation.

(3) Packaging complies with the essential requirements –

(a)   if it satisfies national standards which implement the relevant harmonised standards; or

(b)   where there are no relevant harmonised standards, if it satisfies national standards of which the texts are communicated to the Commission pursuant to Article 9(3) of the Directive and which are notified by the Commission to the member States as being deemed to comply with the essential requirements.

(4) In paragraph (3) above, "harmonised standards" means the standards the reference number of which is published in the Official Journal of the European Communities in accordance with Article 9(2)(a) of the Directive.

Failing to comply with the essential requirements

20.32 Regulation 8(a) makes it an offence to contravene reg 4, which forbids a responsible person from placing packaging on the market which does not comply with the essential requirements. There is a presumption in reg 4(3) that packaging which satisfies the relevant harmonised standards also satisfies the essential requirements.

Exceeding concentration levels of heavy metals

20.33

Packaging (Essential Requirements) Regulations 2015, reg 5

Concentration levels of regulated metals present in packaging

5(1) A responsible person must not place any packaging on the EU market if the sum of the concentration levels of regulated metals either in the packaging or in any of its packaging components exceeds 100 ppm.

(2) Paragraph (1) does not apply to packaging which is made entirely of lead crystal glass as defined in Council Directive 69/493/EEC on the approximation of the laws of the Member States relating to crystal glass.

(3) The concentration levels of regulated metals in paragraph (1) do not apply –

(a) to plastic crates or plastic pallets used in product loops which are in a closed and controlled chain provided the requirements set out in Schedule 2 to these Regulations are complied with in relation to that packaging;

(b) to glass packaging provided the requirements set out in Schedule 3 to these Regulations are complied with in relation to that packaging.

Regulation 8(a) makes it an offence to contravene reg 5(1) which in turn limits the concentrations of lead, cadmium, mercury, and hexavalent chromium in packaging. The limit is expressed in parts per million (ppm) and two separate tests are applied. Neither the packaging as a whole nor any individual 'packaging component' may exceed the relevant limits. A 'packaging component' is defined in reg 2 as being any part of packaging that can be separated by hand or by using simple physical means.

Failing to keep and supply technical documentation
20.34

> **Packaging (Essential Requirements) Regulations 2015, reg 6**
>
> **Requirement for technical documentation**
>
> 6(1) The responsible person must –
>
> (a) at the request of the enforcement authority submit within twenty-eight days of the date of the request technical documentation or other information showing that the packaging complies with the essential requirements and the regulated metals concentration limits set out in regulation 5;
>
> (b) retain the technical documentation or other information referred to in paragraph (1)(a) for a period of four years from the date that the responsible person places the packaging on the market.
>
> (2) The responsible person must –
>
> (a) submit a report as required under paragraphs 2(1) and (2) of Schedule 3 to these Regulations to the enforcement authority; and
>
> (b) at the request of the enforcement authority, submit within twenty-eight days of the date of the request, the annual declaration of conformity and other information set out in paragraphs 2(1) and (2) of Schedule 2 and paragraph 2(3) of Schedule 3 to these Regulations.

It is an offence under reg 8(b) for a responsible person to fail to submit within 28 days technical documentation or other information requested by the enforcement authority to show that it complies with the essential requirements and the heavy metal concentration limits. In light of reg 6(1)(b), outlined below, it would seem that any request made more than four years after the relevant packaging is placed on the market is unreasonable.

Failing to keep information

20.35   It is an offence under reg 8(b) to fail to retain technical documentation or other information as required by reg 6(1)(b). It is worth noting that this is not a 'generic' requirement, but one which bites in respect of each item of packaging. Thus, the fact that the same type of packaging, manufactured in exactly the same way and with the same constituents, has been on the market for over 4 years will not remove the need for the information to be kept. The time limit will expire only 4 years after the last item of such packaging is placed on the market.

Defence of due diligence

20.36   Regulation 10(1) establishes a defence for any person prosecuted under reg 8 who can show that he took all reasonable steps and exercised all due diligence to avoid committing the offence. By reg 10(2), where reliance upon the defence involves an allegation that the commission of the offence was due to another person or reliance on information given by another, notice must be served on the prosecution not less than 7 clear days before the hearing of the proceedings. Failure to do so prevents the defendant from relying on the due diligence defence without leave from the court. Regulation 10(3) requires such a notice to contain what information the defendant possesses that identifies the other person (ie the person whom the defendant blames for the offence under reg 10(2)).

20.37 If reliance on the defence involves an allegation that the commission of the relevant offence was due to reliance on information supplied by another person, the defendant must show under reg 10(4) that it was reasonable in all the circumstances for him to have relied upon the information, having regard in particular to:

(a) the steps which he took, and those which might reasonably have been taken, for the purposes of verifying the information; and

(b) whether he had any reason to disbelieve the information.

Due diligence defences are considered in detail in Chapter 3, Criminal Enforcement.

Trading standards officers' powers

20.38 Regulation 7 and Sch 4 provide for certain aspects of the enforcement of the PERR 2015 by importing most of the provisions of ss 14, 15, 31–32, 37, 44 and 47 of the Consumer Protection Act 1987 ('CPA 1987') into the Regulations with appropriate modification. The provisions of Sch 5 to the Consumer Rights Act 2015 apply to main powers of enforcement of the PERR 2015. These powers are discussed in Chapter 3, Criminal Enforcement.

Suspension notices

20.39 By virtue of s 14(1) CPA 1987, an enforcement authority may serve a suspension notice where it has reasonable grounds for suspecting that a regulation has been contravened in relation to any packaging. This can prohibit the person on whom it is served from supplying, offering to supply, agreeing to supply, or exposing for supply the packaging in question for a period of no more than 6 months. By s 14(2), the notice must describe the packaging sufficiently to identify it, set out the grounds for suspecting a contravention of the regulations, and provide information on how to appeal against the notice. By s 14(3), the notice may also require the person on whom it is served to keep the authority informed as to the whereabouts of the relevant packaging. A suspension notice may only be renewed if, on its expiry, proceedings for an offence under the regulations have been commenced: s 14(4). Contravention of a suspension notice is an offence: s 14(6). By s 14(7) and (8), where the service of the notice causes loss and there has, in fact, been no contravention of the Regulations or any negligence or default on the part of the person affected, compensation is payable by the enforcement authority.

20.40 The procedure for appealing a suspension notice is set out in s 15. In essence, it is an application to the magistrates' court (or in Scotland, to a sheriff) where the burden is on the appellant to show that there has been no contravention of the Regulations. In England and Wales, there is a right of appeal from the magistrates' court to the Crown Court. Section 44 sets out the means by which proper service of the suspension notice may be effected. The Consumer Rights Act 2015 has not affected suspension notices.

Powers of test purchase, entry, search and seizure

20.41 These powers are contained in Sch 5 to the Consumer Rights Act 2015, along with an offence to obstruct an authorised officer and a right to compensation for goods seized; see Chapter 3, Criminal Enforcement.

Sentencing

Maximum sentences

20.42

Provision	Description	Mode of Trial	Maximum Penalty on Indictment	Maximum Penalty on Summary Conviction[9]
reg 4	Failing to comply with the essential requirements	Summary only (England and Wales) Either way (Scotland and Northern Ireland)	Unlimited fine	Unlimited fine (England and Wales) Level 5 fine (Scotland and Northern Ireland)
reg 5	Exceeding concentration levels of heavy metals	Summary only (England and Wales) Either way (Scotland and Northern Ireland)	Unlimited fine	Unlimited fine

---

[9] The statutory maximum fine (previously £5,000) on summary conviction was revoked by s 85 of the Legal Aid, Sentencing and Punishment of Offenders Act 2012, which came into force on 12 March 2015. Magistrates may now impose unlimited fines in sentencing most offences.

Provision	Description	Mode of Trial	Maximum Penalty on Indictment	Maximum Penalty on Summary Conviction[9]
reg 6(1)	Failing to supply/keep technical documentation	Summary only		Unlimited fine (England and Wales Level 5 fine (Scotland and Northern Ireland)
reg 6(2)	Failing to submit a report/annual declaration	Summary only		Unlimited fine (England and Wales) Level 5 fine (Scotland and Northern Ireland)
s 14 CPA 1987	Contravening a suspension notice	Summary only		Six months imprisonment and/or unlimited fine

ENERGY INFORMATION REGULATIONS 2011

20.43 The aim of the Energy Information Regulations 2011 (EIR 2011) is to facilitate the labelling of energy-related products (such as washing machines and televisions) so that the power consumption of one model can be easily compared to another, allowing consumers to make informed purchasing decisions. The Regulations introduced a new enforcement regime of civil sanctions, as well as cost sharing.

Regulatory framework

20.44 The EIR 2011 transposes European Directive 2010/30/EU (on the indication by labelling and standard product information of the consumption of energy and other resources by energy-related products). The Regulations apply to products that have a significant direct or indirect impact on energy consumption and other resources (reg 3).

20.45 Schedule 1 lists those products[10] and the dates from which the EU measures apply:

---

[10] The Ecodesign for Energy-Related Products and Energy Information (Amendment) Regulations 2015 amend the EIR 2011 to include residential ventilation units as of 1 January 2016. The Ecodesign for Energy-Related Products and Energy Information (Amendment) Regulations 2016 amend the EIR 2011 to include: (i) professional refrigerated storage cabinets, blast cabinets, condensing units and process chillers; (ii) local space heaters; (iii) solid fuel boilers and packages of a solid fuel boiler, supplementary heaters, temperature controls and solar devices.

Schedule 1 EU measures

In relation to a product identified in column 1 of the following table, the requirements set out in the EU measure in column 2 apply from the date in column 3.

Column 1	Column 2	Column 3
Product	EU measure	Date from which EU measure applies
Household tumble driers	Commission Delegated Regulation (EU) No 392/2012 supplementing Directive 2010/30/EU of the European Parliament and of the Council with regard to energy labelling of household tumble driers	29th September 2013
Household combined washer-driers	Commission Directive 96/60/EC implementing Council Directive 92/75/EEC with regard to energy labelling of household combined washer-driers	20th July 2011
Household lamps	Commission Directive 98/11/EC implementing Council Directive 92/75/EEC with regard to energy labelling of household lamps	20th July 2011
Household electric ovens	Commission Directive 2002/40/EC implementing Council Directive 92/75/EEC with regard to energy labelling of household electric ovens	20th July 2011
Air-conditioners	Commission Delegated Regulation (EU) No 626/2011 supplementing Directive 2010/30/EU of the European Parliament and of the Council with regard to energy labelling of air conditioners	1st January 2013
Household washing machines	Commission Directive 95/12/EEC implementing Council Directive 92/75/EEC with regard to energy labelling of household washing machines	20th July 2011
	Commission Delegated Regulation (EU) No1061/2010 supplementing Directive 2010/30 of the European Parliament and of the Council with regard to energy labelling of household washing machines	20th December 2011
Household dishwashers	Commission Directive 97/17/EC implementing Council Directive 92/75/EEC with regard to energy labelling of household dishwashers	20th July 2011
	Commission Delegated Regulation (EU) No 1059/2010 supplementing Directive 2010/30/EU of the European Parliament and of the Council with regard to energy labelling of household dishwashers	20th December 2011

Column 1	Column 2	Column 3
Product	EU measure	Date from which EU measure applies
Household refrigerators, freezers and their combinations	Commission Directive 94/2/EC implementing Council Directive 92/75/EEC with regard to energy labelling of household refrigerators, freezers and their combinations	20th July 2011
	Commission Delegated Regulation (EU) No 1060/2010 supplementing Directive 2010/30/EU of the European Parliament and of the Council with regard to energy labelling of household refrigerating appliances	30th November 2011
Televisions	Commission Delegated Regulation (EU) No 1062/2010 supplementing Directive 2010/30/EU of the European Parliament and of the Council with regard to energy labelling of televisions	30th November 2011
Electrical lamps and luminaires	Commission Delegated Regulation (EU) No 874/2012 supplementing Directive 2010/30/EU of the European Parliament and of the Council with regard to energy labelling of electrical lamps and luminaires	1st September 2013
Vacuum cleaners	Commission Delegated Regulation (EU) No 665/2013 supplementing Directive 2010/30/EU of the European Parliament and of the Council with regard to energy labelling of vacuum cleaners	The dates set out in Articles 3, 4 and 8 of Commission Delegated Regulation (EU) No 665/2013
Water heaters, hot water storage tanks and packages of water heater and solar device	Commission Delegated Regulation (EU) No 812/2013 supplementing Directive 2010/30/EU of the European Parliament and of the Council with regard to the energy labelling of water heaters, hot water storage tanks and packages of water heater and solar device	The dates set out in Article 3 of Commission Delegated Regulation (EU) No 812/2013
Space heaters, combination heaters, packages of space heater, temperature control and solar device and packages of combination heater, temperature control and solar device	Commission Delegated Regulation (EU) No 811/2013 supplementing Directive 2010/30/EU of the European Parliament and of the Council with regard to the energy labelling of space heaters, combination heaters, packages of space heater, temperature control and solar device and packages of combination heater, temperature control and solar device	The dates set out in Article 3 of Commission Delegated Regulation (EU) No 811/2013

Column 1	Column 2	Column 3
Product	EU measure	Date from which EU measure applies
Domestic ovens and range hoods	Commission Delegated Regulation (EU) No 65/2014 supplementing Directive 2010/30/EU of the European Parliament and of the Council with regard to the energy labelling of domestic ovens and range hoods	The dates set out in Article 10 of Commission Delegated Regulation (EU) No 65/2014

The numerous Regulations that applied to individual energy-related products (and outlined in previous editions of this book) have been revoked. It should be noted that the EIR 2011 do not apply to: (1) second-hand products, (2) any means of transport for persons or goods, or (3) the rating plate or its equivalent affixed for safety purposes to products (reg 3(2)).

Prosecutions

20.46   Regulation 4 provides:

4. Enforcement

(1) The local weights and measures authority, and in relation to Northern Ireland the Department of Enterprise Trade and Investment, enforce regulation 8 (responsibilities of dealers), regulation 9 (information requirements) and RAMS.[11]

(2) The Secretary of State enforces regulation 7 (responsibilities of suppliers), regulation 9, regulation 10 (misleading information) and RAMS.

(3) Each of these is referred to as a "market surveillance authority".

(4) The Secretary of State may delegate to the Director of Public Prosecutions functions in relation to the prosecution of an offence under these Regulations.

20.47   In summary, the 'market surveillance authorities' responsible for the enforcement of EIR 2011 are:

- the Trading Standards Departments and, in relation to Northern Ireland, the Department of Enterprise Trade and Investment – (reg 8 (responsibilities of dealers) and reg 9 (information requirements)); and
- the National Measurement Office – (reg 7 (responsibilities of suppliers), reg 9, reg 10 (misleading information)).

20.48   Following consultation, the Advertising Standards Authority (ASA) has signed a Memorandum of Understanding with the Secretary of State for Environment Food and Rural Affairs (DEFRA) to monitor and use a self-regulatory means to enforce the rules of the advertising codes, which cover

---

[11]   RAMS refers to Regulation (EC) No 765/2008 of the European Parliament and of the Council setting out the requirements for accreditation and market surveillance relating to the marketing of products and repealing Regulation (EEC) No 339/93.

the information requirements within EIR 2011. NMO, Defra and Trading Standards will, if appropriate, pass complaints relating to the presence of a product's energy efficiency class rating or fiche in an advertisement to the ASA.

Offences

20.49 The responsibilities of suppliers and dealers are set out in regs 7–10. The offences, penalties and related matters are contained in regs 11–15.

Suppliers' duties

20.50 Regulation 7 provides:

7. **Responsibilities of suppliers**

(1) When placing on the market or putting into service products regulated by an EU measure, suppliers must –

(a) supply a label and a fiche which comply with these Regulations and the EU measure;
(b) produce technical documentation which is sufficient to enable the accuracy of the information contained in the label and the fiche to be assessed.

(2) The documentation in paragraph (1)(b) must include –

(a) a general description of the product;
(b) if relevant, the results of design calculations;
(c) if available, test reports including those carried out by the relevant notified organisations;
(d) if values are used for similar models, the references allowing identification of those models.

(3) Suppliers must –

(a) make the documentation available for inspection purposes when placing a product on the market or putting it into service, and keep the documentation available until at least 5 years after the date the last product concerned was manufactured;
(b) make available an electronic version of the documentation on request to the market surveillance authority and to the European Commission within 10 working days of receipt of a request by the market surveillance authority or the Commission;
(c) provide the labels free of charge to dealers;
(d) deliver labels promptly upon request from dealers;
(e) provide the fiche free of charge; and
(f) include a fiche in any product brochure.

(4) If the product brochures in paragraph (3)(f) are not provided by the supplier, the supplier must provide fiches in any literature provided with the product.

(5) A supplier must ensure that any information contained on any label or in any fiche is accurate.

(6) Suppliers are deemed to consent to the publication of the information provided on any label or fiche.

20.51 Suppliers must supply a label and a fiche that complies with the requirements set out in the Regulations and the *relevant EU measure for the product type* as stated in the Schedule. It is the responsibility of the National Measurement Office to enforce the above requirements.

Dealers' duties

20.52 Regulation 8 provides:

8. Responsibilities of dealers

(1) Dealers must make the fiche available in the product brochure or any literature which accompanies the product when sold to end-users.

(2) When a product is displayed, dealers must attach the label in the clearly visible position specified in the EU measure.

20.53 Trading Standards officers are responsible for enforcing dealers' duties for point of sale display of the label, in addition to reg 9 of the information requirements outlined below.

Information requirements

20.54 When products are offered for sale or hire directly or indirectly, information regarding energy consumption must be brought to the attention of the user and made available. It is clear that these requirements also apply to any means of distance selling including the internet (reg 9(1)).

20.55 Regulation 9 provides:

9. Information requirements

(1) Any person who offers any products regulated by an EU measure for sale, hire or hire-purchase or displays to end-users directly or indirectly by any means of distance selling, including the internet must bring to the attention of end-users information relating to the consumption of electric energy, and where relevant other essential resources during use, and any other supplementary information, by means of –

    (a) the fiche; and
    (b) the label related to the products,
    in accordance with the EU measure.

(2) A person who builds in or installs a product must display such information if required by the EU measure.

(3) Any person who advertises a specific model of a product regulated by an EU measure must, when energy-related or price information is disclosed, include a reference to the energy efficiency class of the product as set out in the EU measure.

(4) Any person who provides technical promotional material to end-users which describes the specific technical parameters of a product regulated by an EU measure including technical manuals and manufacturers' brochures whether printed or online must –

(a) provide end-users with information regarding the energy consumption of that product; or

(b) include a reference to the energy efficiency class of that product as set out in the EU measure.

20.56 Duties also exist for those who build or install products (reg 9(2)), those who advertise products (reg 9(3)), and those who provide technical or promotional material to end users which describes the specific technical parameters of a product regulated by an EU measure (reg 9(4)). Reg 10 bans the display of labels, marks, symbols or inscriptions that do not comply with the Regulations and that would mislead or cause confusion to users.

Offences and penalties

20.57 Regulation 11 provides:

> **11. Offences and penalties**
>
> (1) It is an offence for any person to contravene any of regulations 7 to 10.
>
> (2) Any person guilty of an offence under paragraph (1) is liable –
>
>> (a) on summary conviction, to a fine not exceeding the statutory maximum;
>> (b) on conviction on indictment, to a fine.

20.58 Offences under the Regulations are therefore triable either way, with both summary conviction[12] and conviction on indictment carrying an unlimited fine.

20.59 An additional offence of obstruction is also created under reg 12, which provides:

> **12. Obstruction etc.**
>
> (1) It is an offence for any person –
>
>> (a) intentionally to fail to comply with any instruction given by an authorised person acting in pursuance of their powers or duties under these Regulations or RAMS;
>> (b) intentionally to obstruct an authorised person acting in pursuance of their powers or duties under these Regulations or RAMS;
>> (c) knowingly or recklessly to make a statement which is false or misleading in purported compliance with any requirement imposed under these Regulations or RAMS;
>> (d) without reasonable cause fail to give an authorised person any other assistance or information which that authorised person may reasonably require for the purposes of the exercise of their powers or duties under these Regulations or RAMS.
>
> (2) Any person guilty of an offence under paragraph (1) is liable on summary conviction to a fine not exceeding level 5 on the standard scale.

---

[12] Magistrates may now impose unlimited fines in sentencing most offences by virtue of s 85 of the Legal Aid, Sentencing and Punishment of Offenders Act 2012.

(3) In this regulation, 'powers or duties' includes powers or duties exercisable by virtue of a warrant under Schedule 2.

To be guilty of an offence under reg 12(1)(a) and (b) of the Regulations a person must *intentionally* fail to comply with or obstruct an authorised person. The offence under reg 12(1)(c) can be committed either knowingly or recklessly and under (d) the failure (under this broad provision) must be without reasonable cause. All of the offences are summary only and are now punishable by an unlimited fine. Schedule 2 of the Regulations outlines in detail the powers of entry, inspection, seizure and detention of products, available to an authorised person enforcing these regulations and the conditions that apply to the use of warrants.

Defendants

Suppliers and dealers

20.60 A person who is a supplier or dealer of any of the product types as listed in Sch 1 of the Regulations can be prosecuted for contravention of, or failure to comply with, the Energy Information Regulations 2011.

20.61 In Art 2 of Directive 2010/30/EU the following definitions are provided:

'dealer' means a retailer or other person who sells, hires, offers for hire-purchase or displays products to end users;

'supplier' means the manufacturer or its authorised representative in the Union or the importer who places or puts into service the product on the Union market. In their absence, any natural or legal person who places on the market or puts into service products covered by this Directive shall be considered a supplier;

'placing on the market' means making a product available for the first time on the Union market with a view to its distribution or use within the Union, whether for reward or free of charge and irrespective of selling technique;

'putting into service' means the first use of a product for its intended purpose in the Union.

'Place on the Community market'

20.62 There is some guidance from Defra in respect of this phrase.[13] The Defra *Guidance notes* state:

'8.1 This relates to the initial action of *making* a product available for the first time on the market. The intention is clearly that all relevant product types should be labelled. So somebody must take responsibility for supplying the information required. This responsibility would normally lie with either the original manufacturer or an importer – who may be a retailer.

8.2 A product is considered to be made available when it is transferred or offered to be transferred from the stage of manufacture with the intention of distribution

---

[13] This guidance relates to the various previous regulations and was published in 2008.

to and/or use by consumers. Moreover, the "place on the market" concept refers to each individual product (in other words not to a product type) and whether it was manufactured as an individual unit or in series.

8.3 The transfer of the product takes place from the manufacturer, or his authorised representative, to the importer or person responsible for distributing the product to the final consumer or user, including the manufacturer's or authorised representative's own commercial distribution chain. The transfer may also take place directly from the manufacturer, or his authorised representative, to the final consumer or user.

8.4 A product is considered to be transferred when either the physical hand-over or the transfer of ownership has taken place. This transfer can be for payment or free of charge, and it can be based on any type of legal instrument. Thus, a transfer of a product is considered to have taken place, for instance, in the circumstances of sale, loan, hire, leasing, and gift.'

Directors' liability

20.63 Regulation 14 provides:

14. Bodies corporate

(1) If an offence under these Regulations committed by a body corporate is proved –

(a) to have been committed with the consent or connivance of an officer, or
(b) to be attributable to any neglect on the part of the officer,

the officer, as well as the body corporate, is guilty of the offence and liable to be proceeded against and punished accordingly.

(2) "*Officer*", in relation to a body corporate, means –

(a) a director, manager, secretary or other similar officer of the body, or
(b) a person purporting to act in any such capacity.

(3) If the affairs of the body corporate are managed by its members, paragraph (1) applies in relation to the acts and defaults of a member in connection with the member's functions of management as it applies to an officer of a body corporate.

(4) If an offence under these Regulations committed by a partnership in Scotland is proved –

(a) to have been committed with the consent or connivance of a partner, or
(b) to be attributable to any neglect on the part of the partner,

the partner as well as the partnership is guilty of the offence and liable to be proceeded against and punished accordingly.

(5) In paragraph (4) "*partner*" includes a person purporting to act as a partner.

Directors' liability is now covered in Chapter 3, Criminal Enforcement.

Time limits

20.64   Regulation 13(1) of the EIR 2011 provides that:

> An offence under these Regulations may be tried by summary proceedings if:
>
> (a)   in England and Wales, the information is laid;
> (b)   in Northern Ireland, the complaint is made; or
> (c)   in Scotland, the proceedings are begun;
>
> before the end of the period of 12 months beginning on the day after the date on which evidence which the enforcement authority thinks is sufficient to justify the proceedings comes to the enforcement authority's knowledge.
>
> (In Scotland this will be evidence sufficient in the opinion of the procurator fiscal to justify proceedings came to his knowledge).

In Scotland, the relevant time will be when such evidence comes to the knowledge of the procurator fiscal. Regulation 13(2) states that a certificate signed by, or on behalf of, the prosecutor and stating the date on which such evidence came to the market surveillance authority's knowledge is to be conclusive evidence of that fact; and a certificate stating that matter and purporting to be so signed is to be treated as so signed unless the contrary is proved. Time limits are covered generally in Chapter 3, Criminal Enforcement.

Enforcement authorities – powers

20.65   The Schedules to the Regulations set out the various powers available to the enforcement authorities in order to assist in the enforcement of the EIR 2011, and should be exercised having regard to the Home Office Powers of Entry Code (see Chapter 3, Criminal Enforcement). An overview of these powers is given below.

Schedule 2 – Powers of entry and warrants

20.66   Provides authorised persons enforcing the Regulations with the power to:

- enter premises;
- inspect, seize, and detain products or goods;
- inspect, seize, and detain records, documents and information;
- take copies of any document or record or any entry in any document or record.

Procedures for gaining and executing a warrant to enforce the Regulations are also outlined.

Schedule 3 – Testing

20.67 Schedule 3 empowers the market surveillance authority to purchase and test products so as to ensure compliance, and to recover from the supplier, the cost of testing products that do not comply with the Regulations. A person on whom a notice has been served may make representations and objections under para 4. The procedure for making an appeal is detailed at para 7. Any such appeal must be made to the First-tier Tribunal General Regulatory Chamber (Environment).

Schedule 4 – Civil sanctions

Parts 1–3

20.68 These parts provide for civil sanctions which the market surveillance authority may impose in relation to an offence committed under reg 11. These powers allow the authority to require compliance with:

- a compliance notice;
- a stop notice;
- an enforcement undertaking; or
- payment of a variable monetary penalty or non-compliance penalty.

Para 6 enables a person to make representations and objections to the authority in respect of a proposed compliance notice or variable monetary penalty. Grounds for appeal in respect of a stop notice are found at para 15(2). The requirement to compensate a person for loss suffered as a result of a stop notice that has been withdrawn or successfully appealed is detailed at para 17(1). Failure to comply with a stop notice within the time limit is an offence punishable on summary conviction with an unlimited fine (para 18). Non-compliance with an enforcement undertaking also allows the authority to bring criminal proceedings at any time up to 6 months from the date of notification of failure to comply.

Part 4

20.69 If a person fails to comply with a compliance notice, stop notice, third party undertaking or enforcement undertaking then the authority may serve a notice on that person imposing a monetary penalty (a 'non-compliance penalty' – para 25(1)). The penalty amount is determined by the authority and must be a percentage (up to 100%, if appropriate) of the costs of fulfilling the remaining requirements of the notice, third party undertaking or enforcement undertaking (para 25(2) and (3)). Grounds of appeal are set out at para 25(7).

Parts 5–7

20.70 Part 5 of the Schedule enables the withdrawal of the various notices available to the authority. Under Part 6, any appeal under the Schedule must be made to the First-tier Tribunal General Regulatory Chamber (Environment) and must be made within 28 days of the date on which the notice or decision is received. Part 7 imposes an obligation on the authority to publish guidance about its use of civil sanctions.

Sentencing

20.71   Offences under reg 11 of the EIR 2011 can be dealt with summarily in the magistrates' court or by indictment in the Crown Court. In either case, the maximum sentence is an unlimited fine.[14] The offence of obstruction under reg 12 is a summary only offence punishable by an unlimited fine. Provisions relating to civil sanctions are contained in Schedule 4.

Recovery of expenses of enforcement

20.72   Regulation 15 provides that where a court convicts a person of an offence under these Regulations, the court may (in addition to any other order it may make as to costs or expenses) order the person convicted to reimburse the market surveillance authority for any expenditure which it or any authorised person has reasonably incurred in investigating the offence. This includes costs incurred in purchasing, testing or examining any product in respect of which the offence was committed. In Scotland, it is likely that these offences will be dealt with in the Sheriff Court.

THE ENERGY PERFORMANCE OF BUILDINGS – GENERAL

20.73   On 19 May 2010 the European Parliament and Council published Directive 2010/31/EU[15] on the energy performance of buildings (EPBD). The EPBD is a recast version of the old Directive 2002/91/EC, which had been transposed into English law by the (now repealed) Energy Performance of Buildings (Certificates and Inspections) (England and Wales) Regulations 2007 (as amended).

20.74   The broad terms of the EPBD, amongst other matters, require that Member States:

- ensure that when buildings are constructed, sold or rented out, an energy performance certificate is made available to the owner or by the owner to the prospective buyer or tenant (Art 11);
- ensure that an energy certificate is prominently displayed in buildings with a total useful floor area over 250m² occupied by public authorities and frequently visited by the public (Art 13);

---

[14]   Legal Aid, Sentencing and Punishment of Offenders Act 2012, s 85.
[15]   OJ L153, 18.6.2010, p 13.

- regularly inspect air-conditioning systems with an effective rated output of more than 12 kW (Art 15). An inspection report must be issued after each inspection (Art 16);
- ensure that the certification of buildings, drafting of recommendations, and the inspection of air-conditioning systems are carried out in an independent manner by qualified experts (Art 17).

England and Wales

20.75 This has been implemented in England and Wales by the Energy Performance of Buildings (England and Wales) Regulations 2012. The Energy Performance of Buildings (England and Wales) (Amendment) Regulations 2016 make a number of changes to the principal regulations, consolidate existing requirements, and make amendments to the existing domestic arrangements and processes for lodging and accessing energy performance of buildings data on the registers. The Energy Performance of Buildings (England and Wales) (Amendment) (No 2) Regulations 2016 update certain references that were overlooked in earlier amendments; make provision for the disclosure from the register of energy performance certificates of data used to prepare certificates to stated persons and bodies for purposes related to Government policy to promote the energy efficiency of buildings; and amend the lists of data items from the register that may be published on a website.

Scotland

20.76 In Scotland, implementation of the EPBD has been made through the Building (Scotland) Act 2003, legislation made under that Act, and the Energy Performance of Buildings (Scotland) Regulations 2008 (as amended). The Building (Energy Performance of Buildings) (Scotland) Amendment Regulations 2016 amend the Building (Scotland) Regulations 2004 to insert requirements in relation to the inspection of air-conditioning systems in buildings and nearly zero-energy buildings. The Assessment of Energy Performance of Non-domestic Buildings (Scotland) Regulations 2016 which make provision for the assessment of the energy performance of non-domestic buildings and of the emission of greenhouse gases from such buildings. The Regulations also provide for the circumstances in which the owners of non-domestic buildings are required to take steps to improve the energy performance of such buildings and reduce such emissions.

Northern Ireland

20.77 The EPBD is implemented in Northern Ireland by the Energy Performance of Buildings (Certificates and Inspections) Regulations (Northern Ireland) 2008 (as amended). The 2008 Regulations implement Arts 11 (energy performance certificate), 15 (inspection of air-conditioning systems) and 17 (independent experts) of the EPBD. The enforcement authority is the relevant district council.

ENERGY PERFORMANCE OF BUILDINGS (ENGLAND AND WALES) REGULATIONS 2012

20.78 The Energy Performance of Buildings (England and Wales) Regulations 2012 (EPBR 2012), which extend to England and Wales, came into force on 9 January 2013. The recast EPBD (2010/31/EU) is transposed in the EPBR 2012.

Regulatory framework

20.79 The effect of the EPBR 2012 is to require:

- Energy Performance Certificates (EPCs) and recommendations for improvement of the energy performance of the building to be produced when buildings are constructed sold, rented out or marketed;

- property advertisements to include details of the EPC rating where available;

- commercial premises larger that 500m² that are frequently visited by the public to display an EPC (where an EPC has been previously issued on sale, rent or construction);

- Display Energy Certificates (DECs) to be displayed in public buildings larger than 250m² that are frequently visited by the public; and the production of reports with recommendations for improvement of the energy performance of the building;

- air-conditioning systems to be inspected at regular intervals not exceeding 5 years; and

- energy assessors producing the certificates or carrying out the inspections to be accredited.

Duty to enforce

20.80 Regulation 34(2) imposes a duty upon every local weights and measures authority[16] to enforce the duties that relate to:

- EPCs: under regs 6(2), 6(5), 7(2)–(5), 7A(2), 10(2), and 11(2);
- DECs: under reg 14(3);
- Inspection of Air Conditioning Systems: under regs 18(1), 20, 21;
- Production of documents under: reg 35(5).

Regulation 7A consolidates the old reg 29 of the Building Regulations 2010. This provision imposes a duty on the person responsible for carrying out the construction work of any newly constructed Crown or statutory undertakers' buildings to provide the new owner with an EPC, no later than 5 days after the construction work has finished.

---

[16] Defined in s 69(1) of the Weights and Measures Act 1985.

Duties on relevant persons

20.81 The duties under regs 6(2), 6(5), 7(2)–(5), 10(2), 11(2), 14(3), 18(1), 20, 21 or 35(5) are summarised below.

Energy performance certificates

20.82 Regulation 6(2) – the relevant person must make available free of charge a valid EPC to any prospective buyer or tenant at the earliest opportunity. Regulation 6(5) – the relevant person must ensure that a valid EPC has been given free of charge to the person who ultimately becomes the buyer or tenant. Regulation 7(2) – where a building is to be sold or rented out and no valid EPC is available, the relevant person must secure that an EPC is commissioned for the building. Regulation 7(3) – before marketing the building, a person acting on behalf of the relevant person must be satisfied that an EPC has been commissioned for the building. Regulation 7(4) – where a building is to be sold or rented out and no valid EPC is available, the relevant person and a person acting on behalf of the relevant person must use all reasonable efforts to secure that a valid EPC is obtained for the property before the end of a period of 7 days starting with the day on which the property was first put on the market or if unable to do so despite using all reasonable efforts secure that certificate within 21 days following that 7-day period (reg 7(5)).

20.83 In this Regulation, the following definitions apply:

(a) 'the market' means the property market in England and Wales;

(b) a building is put on the market when the fact that it is or may become available for sale or rent is, with the intention of marketing the building, first made public in England and Wales by or on behalf of the relevant person;

(c) a fact is made public when it is advertised or otherwise communicated (in whatever form and by whatever means) to the public or to a section of the public;

(d) an energy performance certificate is commissioned when a request is made –

    (i) which is properly addressed to an energy assessor who is accredited to produce energy performance certificates for the category of building in question; and

    (ii) which is in such form, contains all such information and is accompanied by such payment or undertaking to make such payment as is usually necessary to obtain a certificate.

Notes

20.84   An EPC means a certificate which:

(a)   in the case of a certificate entered on the register before 9 January 2013, complied with the requirements of reg 11(1) of the Energy Performance of Buildings (Certificates and Inspections) (England and Wales) Regulations 2007;

(b)   in the case of a certificate entered on the register on or after 9 January 2013, complies with the requirements of reg 9(1) of the Regulations;

(c)   in the case of a certificate issued in respect of an excluded building under regulation 9A, complies with the requirements of regulation 9A(2) of the Regulations; or

(d)   in the case of a certificate entered on the register before 6 April 2016, complies with the requirements of reg 29 of the Building Regulations 2010.

20.85   An 'excluded building' is one owned, occupied or used by or for the purposes of:

(a)   the Security Service, the Secret Intelligence Service or the Government Communications Headquarters;

(b)   any of the armed forces;

(c)   the Royal Family;

(d)   a prison;

(e)   a contracted out prison within the meaning of the Criminal Justice Act 1991; or

(f)   a young offender institution.

The period of validity of all EPCs is 10 years.

20.86   The duties imposed in Part 2 of the Regulations in relation to EPCs do not apply to the buildings listed in reg 5. These include places of worship, buildings of special historical or architectural merit where energy performance requirements would harm their character or appearance, temporary buildings, some non-residential agricultural buildings, and stand-alone buildings of less than 50m². Regulation 8 outlines the circumstances where buildings to be demolished are not subject to the duties imposed under ss 6 and 7 – different conditions apply to dwellings and non-dwellings.

20.87   The 2012 Regulations introduce additional requirements from the EPBD. The requirement to display a valid EPC in a non-dwelling building with a total useful floor area of more than 500m² – where an EPC has previously been issued on its sale, rent or construction – and that is frequently visited by the public is outlined in reg 10. Property advertisements must include details of the EPC rating where available (reg 11). The content of the EPC subject to detailed regulation (reg 9).

20.88 Regulation 12 provides that where the relevant person is required to give, or make available, a valid EPC to any person, it is sufficient to use a copy of the certificate. Regulation 13 allows for an EPC to be provided electronically if the intended recipient consents.

Defences available in respect of breaches of the duty imposed by reg 6

20.89 Regulation 37(1)(a) allows for a defence if the relevant person is not a person to whom the duty under reg 7(2) previously applied and he can show that a request was made for an EPC as soon as possible after he became subject to the duty, and despite all reasonable efforts and enquiries he did not have in his possession or control a valid EPC at the relevant time. Regulation 37(1)(b) affords a defence to the relevant person if when renting to a tenant in urgent need of relocation there is no valid EPC, where there was insufficient time reasonably to obtain one before the building was rented out. The landlord must nonetheless give an EPC to the tenant as soon as is practicable. Regulation 37(2) affords a defence where the relevant person has complied with his duty under reg 7(2), and despite all reasonable efforts and enquiries by the relevant person he did not have in his possession or control a valid EPC at the relevant time.

Display energy certificates

20.90 Regulation 14 provides that every occupier of a building with a total useful floor area over 250m² occupied by public authorities and frequently visited by the public, must have in its possession or control at all times a valid 'recommendation report' (unless there is no reasonable potential for energy performance improvements) and display at all times a valid DEC in a prominent place clearly visible to the public (reg 14(3)).

Notes

20.91 A DEC means a certificate which complies with reg 15 and is valid for 12 months in respect of buildings with a total useful floor area of over 1,000m² and 10 years in the case of any other building (reg 14(4)).

20.92 Regulation 4 provides that a 'recommendation report' is a report made by an energy assessor for the cost-effective improvement of the energy performance of a building.

Inspections of air-conditioning systems

20.93 Regulation 18(1) – the person who has control of the operation of an air-conditioning system with an effective rated output of more than 12kW must ensure that accessible parts of the system are inspected by an energy assessor at regular intervals not exceeding 5 years.

20.94 Regulation 20 – the person who has control of the operation of such an air-conditioning system must keep the most recent inspection report made by an energy assessor (who, under reg 19(1), must give the person in control the report as soon as practicable, after completing the inspection). If a person who has control of the operation changes, the previous person must give to the new person any inspection report kept by him (reg 20(2)).

20.95 Regulation 21 – where the person who has control of the operation of the system changes and the new person is not given any inspection report, the new person must ensure that the system is inspected within 3 months of the day on which he becomes in control of the operation.

Enforcement

20.96 Regulation 35(1) – an enforcement officer may require the production of relevant documents for (ie a copy of a valid EPC, inspection report, or recommendation report – as dictated by regs 6, 7A, 14(3),18(1), 20, or the EPC Construction duty). Such documents must be provided within 7 days, beginning with the day after it the requirement was imposed (reg 35(5).

20.97 Regulations 34A–34C came into force on 9 October 2015. Regulation 34A imposes a requirement on local authorities to arrange for the enforcement of their obligations under the Regulations by the local weights and measures authority. Agreements were to be made by 9 January 2016. Regulation 34B enables enforcement authorities to collect sufficient information concerning buildings to enable them to plan effective enforcement action. Regulation 34C requires enforcement authorities to make annual reports to the Secretary of State of action taken in relation to enforcement of the Regulations.

Notes

20.98 The power under reg 35(1) to require the production of a document for inspection also permits the enforcing officer to take copies of any document produced (reg 35(3)). The requirements under reg 35 may not be imposed more than 6 months after the last day on which the person concerned was subject to such a duty in relation to the building (reg 35(4)). Regulation 35(6) provides that a person is not required to comply with any of the requirements under reg 35 if he has a reasonable excuse for not complying with the requirement.

Breaches

20.99 By virtue of reg 36, an enforcement officer may give a penalty charge notice if he believes that a person has committed a breach of any duty under regs 6(2), 6(5), 7(2)–(5), 10(2), 11(2), 14(3), 18(1), 20, 21 or 35(5) or the EPC construction duty. A person in breach of these Regulations will be liable to a civil penalty; breach of these provisions is not a criminal offence. By virtue of reg 43, a person who obstructs an enforcement officer or who, not being an enforcement officer, purports to act as one, commits a criminal offence and is liable on summary conviction to an unlimited fine.[17]

Penalty charge notices

20.100 Regulation 36(2) provides that a penalty charge notice may not be given after the end of the period of 6 months beginning with the day on which the breach was committed (or, in the case of a continuing breach, the last day). Reg 36(3) lists the information that must be included in a penalty charge notice. This includes the requirement that the recipient respond by either (i) paying the charge, or (ii) requesting a review by the enforcement authority. Either way, the response must be given within 28 days beginning with the day after the penalty charge notice (reg 36(4)) – although this period can be extended at the discretion of the enforcement authority if it considers it appropriate to do so (reg 36(5)).

20.102 The enforcement authority

- may withdraw the penalty charge notice, if the authority considers that the notice ought not to have been given (reg 36(6));

- must withdraw a penalty charge notice where the recipient can demonstrate that he took all reasonable steps and exercised all due diligence to avoid breaching the duty (reg 36(7) or a reg 37 defence applies).

20.103 The receipt of a penalty charge does not remove the need to comply with the duty in respect of which it was given. If a penalty notice is withdrawn, the enforcement authority must refund any charge already paid. A pro-forma penalty charge notice is given in Appendix C of the Communities and Local Government fact sheet *Advice to Local Weights and Measures Authorities on Enforcement of Energy Certificates and Air-Conditioning Inspections for Buildings*.

Penalty amount

20.104 Regulation 38(1) sets out the penalty charge to be specified in the notice:

    (a)   in relation to a breach of a duty under regulation 6(2), 6(5), 7(2), 7(3), 7(4), 7A(2) or 7A(3) –
        (i)   where the building is a dwelling, £200;
        (ii)   where the building is not a dwelling, calculated in accordance with the formula in paragraph (2);
    (b)   in relation to a breach of a duty under regulation 14(3)(a), £1000;
    (c)   in relation to a breach of a duty under regulation 10(2) or 14(3)(b), £500;

---

[17] Legal Aid, Sentencing and Punishment of Offenders Act 2012, s 85.

(d)   in relation to a breach of a duty under regulation 18(1), 20(1), 20(2) or 21, £300; and

(e)   in relation to a breach of a duty under regulation 11(2) or 35(5), £200.

The penalty charge amount is recoverable as a debt (reg 41).

Reviews and appeals

20.105   Regulation 39 provides that, when the recipient of a penalty charge notice has asked the notice authority to review the decision to issue it, the authority must consider any representations etc and withdraw the notice if it is not satisfied that:

(a)   the recipient committed the breach of duty specified in the notice; or

(b)   the notice was issued within time (allowed by reg 36(2)) and contained the necessary particulars; or

(c)   in the circumstances of the case it was appropriate for the notice to be given to the recipient.

20.106   If the recipient of the penalty notice is not satisfied with the review, he may appeal to the County Court under reg 40 within 28 days after having the penalty charge confirmed. Such an appeal can only be made on one or more of the following grounds:

(a)   the recipient did not commit the breach of duty specified in the penalty charge notice;

(b)   the notice was not given within the period specified (by reg 36(2)), or did not contain the necessary particulars;

(c)   in the circumstances of the case it was inappropriate for the notice to be given to the recipient.

Energy assessors

20.107   Part 5 (regs 22–26) implements Art 17 of the EPBD and provides for the accreditation of energy assessors and associated matters. Energy assessors who produce certificates or inspect air-conditioning systems must be members of an accreditation scheme approved by the Secretary of State.

Register of certificates, recommendation reports, and inspection reports

20.108   All energy certificates (EPCs and DECs) and associated recommendation reports must be entered into a central register maintained on behalf of the Secretary of State (Part 6 regs 27–33). There is also a duty upon the energy assessor to enter air-conditioning inspection reports on this central register (reg 27(3)). Regulation 29(1) imposes a general obligation on the keeper of the register not to disclose data that has been entered on the register unless the criteria in regs 30, 31, or 32 are made out. In practice, the data relating to many buildings is available to the general public if the proper form of request is made to the register. Regulation 32(1)(a) grants unfettered disclosure to enforcement officers acting under reg 34(4). A person disclosing or permitting the disclosure of this information in breach of reg 29(1) is guilty of an offence (reg 29(2)) and liable on summary conviction to an unlimited fine.

ENERGY PERFORMANCE OF BUILDINGS (SCOTLAND) REGULATIONS 2008

Regulatory framework

20.109 The recast European Directive 2010/31/EU ('EPBD') on the energy performance of buildings is implemented in Scotland primarily through the Building (Scotland) Act 2003. Certain Articles of the EPBD relating to energy performance certificates for buildings and inspection of air-conditioning systems have been introduced through amendments to the Building (Scotland) Regulations 2004. The Energy Performance of Buildings (Scotland) Regulations 2008 ('EPB(S)R 2008')[18] transpose Art 11 EPBD (energy performance certificates) and also provide for the display of certificates in public buildings.

Application

20.110 In broad terms, the EPB(S)R 2008 impose a duty on the owner of a building to make an EPC available to prospective buyers or tenants where the building is to be sold or let. Under reg 4, the EPB(S)R 2008 do not apply to:

(a) temporary buildings with a planned time of use of 2 years or less, workshops and non-residential agricultural buildings with low energy demand; and

(b) stand-alone buildings with a total useful floor area of less than 50m² which are not dwellings.

Unless otherwise defined in the EPB(S) Regulations 2008, terms used have the same meaning as in the EPBD.

Duty to enforce

20.111 Regulation 15 provides that a 'local authority' (a council constituted under s 2 of the Local Government etc (Scotland) Act 1994) is an enforcement authority for the purposes of the EPB(S) Regulations 2008 and have the duty to enforce the Regulations in its area. An enforcement authority may require an owner, who appears to it to be or to have been subject to the duty under reg 5 in relation to a building, to produce for inspection a copy of the EPC for that

---

[18] SSI 2008/309.

building (reg 16). The power under reg 16 includes power to require the production in a legible documentary form of any EPC which is held in electronic form *and* to take copies of any EPC produced for inspection. The requirements under reg 16 may not be made more than 6 months after the last day on which the owner concerned was subject to a duty under reg 5 in relation to the building. An owner is not required to comply with the requirement if the owner has a reasonable excuse for not complying.

20.112 By virtue of reg 23, a person who obstructs an enforcement officer or who, not being an enforcement officer, purports to act as one under reg 16 or 17 (giving penalty charge), commits an offence and is liable on summary conviction to a fine.

Duty to provide EPC

20.113 The EPB(S) Regulations 2008 prescribe a duty, where a building is to be sold or let, on the owner to make a copy of the most recent, valid EPC (including a recommendations report) for the building, available free of charge, to a 'prospective buyer or prospective tenant' (reg 5). The meaning of prospective buyer or prospective tenant in relation to a building is given in reg 3. Regulation 5 does not apply at any time before the construction of a building has been completed. However, an 'energy performance indicator' must be included in any advertisement in commercial media offering a building for sale (reg 5A).

20.114 The requirements of an EPC are set out in reg 6. An EPC for a building is valid for a period of ten years from the date on which it was issued – unless it is issued under the 'green deal', in which case it is only valid for one year (reg 6(2)). The requirements of a recommendations report are set out in reg 6A.

20.115 Section 98 of the Housing (Scotland) Act 2006 requires that a person responsible for marketing a house which is on the market must possess the prescribed documents in relation to the house. The Housing (Scotland) Act 2006 (Prescribed Documents) Regulations 2008[19] prescribe the documents which a seller or a selling agent must possess and provide in response to a request from potential buyers. The documents, which are prescribed in reg 4, include a survey report which contains information on energy efficiency (including a list of measures to improve the energy efficiency of the dwelling) as set out in Part 2 of Sch 1. Regulation 13 provides an exception for properties to be demolished.

20.116 In Scotland, Display Energy Certificates (DECs) do not exist as such. Instead, under reg 9 of the EPB(S)R 2008, the 'owner' (or, where the owner is not the occupier, the occupier) of 'a building which is frequently visited by the public' must ensure that an EPC for that building is displayed within the building in a prominent place clearly visible to visiting members of the public.

The requirement only applies to (i) buildings occupied by a public authority with a floor area greater than 250m2 and (ii) other buildings with a floor area greater than 500m2 in respect of which an EPC as been issued (reg 9(2)).

20.117   For the purposes of reg 9:

"owner" means a person who has right to the building whether or not that person has completed title, but if, in relation to the building more than one person comes within that description of owner, then "owner" means such person as has most recently acquired such right; and

"building which is frequently visited by the public" means a building into which members of the public have an express or implied licence to enter and which is visited by members of the public on at least a weekly basis.

Breaches

20.118   A person who fails to comply with the duty under reg 5 will be liable to a civil penalty. By virtue of regs 17, 17A, and 17B, an enforcement officer may give a penalty charge notice to a person he believes has breached regs 5, 5A, or 9. Breach of these regulations is not a criminal offence.

Defences

20.119   Regulation 18(1)(a) sets out a defence to a breach of reg 5 and the imposition of a penalty charge if the owner can show that they made a request to an energy assessor to obtain an EPC at least 14 days before it was needed and that, despite all reasonable efforts and enquiries, they have not been able to obtain it. Regulation 18(1)(b) sets out a defence for failing to make available an energy performance certificate to a prospective tenant. The defence is restricted to emergency relocation cases where there is insufficient time to obtain an EPC. Even so, an EPC must be presented to the tenant as soon as reasonably practicable. Regulation 18A also creates a defence for failing to place an energy performance indicator in commercial advertising (contrary to reg 5A). This applies where the recipient of the penalty charge can prove that (i) he instructed the advertisers to include an energy performance indicator for the building, and (ii) he provided sufficient information for the energy performance indicator to be stated in the advertisement.

Penalty charge notices

20.120   Regulation 17(2) provides that a penalty charge notice may not be given:

    (a)   unless the owner has failed to make an energy performance certificate available to a prospective buyer or tenant within a period of 9 days after a request for such a certificate was made to the owner; and

    (b)   after the end of the period of 6 months beginning with the day on which it appeared to the enforcement authority that the duty under regulation 5 was breached.

The information that penalty charge notice must state is set out in reg 17(3). In particular, the notice must direct the recipient to either pay the penalty or request a review by the enforcement authority. Payment or a request for review must be made within the period specified in the notice (which must not be less than 28 days – reg 17(5)). Time runs from the day after that on which the penalty charge notice was given. The enforcement authority:

- may, if it considers that the penalty charge notice ought not to have been given, give the recipient a notice withdrawing the penalty charge notice (reg 17(6));
- must withdraw a penalty charge notice where reg 18 (defence where energy performance certificate unobtainable) applies (reg 17(7)).

20.130   In addition, reg 17(2) prevents a penalty charge notice being given in respect of a breach of reg 5:

(a)   unless the owner has failed to make an energy performance certificate available to a prospective buyer or tenant within a period of 9 days after a request for such a certificate was made to the owner; and

(b)   after the end of the period of 6 months beginning with the day on which it appeared to the enforcement authority that the duty under regulation 5 was breached.

Penalty amount

20.131   The amount payable as a penalty charge is £500 for dwellings or building units that are ancillary to dwellings or £1,000 in any other case (reg 17(4)). Any sum received by a local authority under reg 17 shall accrue to that authority (reg 17(8)).

Reviews and appeals

Reviews

20.132   Regulation 19 provides that if the recipient gives notice in time to the enforcement authority requesting a review, the authority must consider any representations and all the circumstances of the case. Having done so, the authority must decide whether to confirm or withdraw the notice.

20.133   Under reg 19(3), the authority *must* withdraw the penalty charge notice if it is satisfied that:

(a)   the recipient did not commit the breach of duty specified in the notice; or

(b)   the notice was not given within the time allowed by regulation 17(2)(b) [after the end of the period of 6 months beginning with the day on which it appeared to the enforcement authority that the duty under regulation 5 was breached]; or

(c)   the notice did not comply with any other requirements imposed by these Regulations; or

(d)   in the circumstances of the case it was not reasonable for a penalty charge notice to be given to the recipient.

Having made its decision, the authority must serve notice of its decision on the recipient. The decision notice must state the reasons for it and the effect of regs 20 (appeal to the Sheriff Court) and 21 (recovery of penalty charges).

Appeals

20.134 A recipient of a penalty charge notice may not appeal until after it has been reviewed and confirmed by the issuing authority. After the authority has given its decision notice, the recipient may appeal against it to the Sheriff Court of the sheriffdom in which the building is situated (reg 20). Any such appeal must be made by summary application within 28 days of the decision notice being given (reg 20(2)). However, a sheriff may extend the period for appealing on cause shown. Any appeal must be made on one or more of the grounds listed in reg 20(4), which are substantively the same as the grounds for review listed above. If the penalty charge notice is withdrawn or quashed, the enforcement authority must repay any amount already paid.

Register of energy performance certificates

20.135 Regulation 10 provides for the keeping of a register of EPCs. Regulations 11–14A provide for disclosure and use of information from the register.

Independent expert energy assessors

20.136 EPCs must be issued by a qualified member of an approved organisation for that category of building, or accepted by a verifier following submission of a completion certificate in accordance with reg 41 of the Building (Procedure) (Scotland) Regulations 2004.[20] Where the EPC is issued by a qualified member of an approved organisation, the name of the approved organisation must be included in the EPC (reg 6(1)(d)(ii)). Regulation 8 provides for the Scottish Ministers to approve the organisations whose members may issue EPCs.

Air conditioning systems

20.137 Regulation 17 of the Building (Scotland) Regulations 2004[21] implements Art 15 of the recast EPBD regarding the inspection of air conditioning systems.

> **Continuing requirements**
>
> 17(1) Subject to paragraph (2), the owners of buildings shall ensure that –
>
> > (a) every air conditioning system within a building is inspected at regular intervals; and

---

20   SSI 2004/428.
21   SSI 2004/406.

(b)   following each inspection of that system the owner of the building or, where the owner is not the occupier, the occupier is given a report containing the result of the inspection and including recommendations for the cost-effective improvement of the energy performance of that system.

(2) This regulation shall not apply to –

(a)   air conditioning systems with a total effective output rating of less than 12 kW; or

(b)   air conditioning systems solely for processes within a building.

(3) In terms of section 2 of the Building (Scotland) Act 2003 the provisions of paragraph (1) are a designated provision in respect of which there is a continuing requirement imposed on the owners of buildings.

OTHER ENVIRONMENTAL LEGISLATION

20.138   The following legislation has relevance to local authority enforcement.

Passenger Car (Fuel Consumption and CO_2 Emissions Information) Regulations 2001[22]

20.139   In order to contribute to the reduction of greenhouse gas emissions from the transport sector, the EU has set target values for CO_2 emissions from new passenger cars and made efforts to ensure that information on the CO_2 performance of new passenger cars is readily available to its citizens. The Regulations were subject to minor amendments in 2004 and 2013. The Regulations implement Council Directive 1999/94 which relates to the availability of consumer information on fuel economy and CO_2 emissions in respect of the marketing of new passenger cars. Such information is measured in accordance with Regulation (EC) 715/2007 and is referred to in the Regulations as the 'official fuel consumption' and 'official specific emissions of CO_2' figures.

20.140   Duties are imposed on suppliers of and dealers in passenger cars to which the Regulations apply. These include a requirement that suppliers provide the relevant information to dealers (reg 5), as well as a requirement that dealers of new passenger cars display a label specifying fuel economy and CO_2 emissions at the point of sale (reg 6). Regulation 7 provides that a guide covering fuel economy and CO_2 emissions must also be available free of charge to consumers who request one, and reg 8 provides that a poster or display incorporating the relevant information must be exhibited in a prominent position at the point of sale. Regulation 9 provides that the relevant information must also be included in promotional literature relating to new passenger cars. Schedules 1–4 of the Regulations prescribe the form which the guide, label, poster, and promotional material should take. The inclusion of

---

[22]   SI 2001/3523.

misleading or confusing information in the material relating to fuel economy and specific emissions of CO_2 is prohibited under reg 10.

20.141 Regulation 11 and Sch 5 provide for offences and enforcement. Offences exist for failure to comply with the duties under the Regulations. These are enforced by weights and measures authorities in Great Britain. Under para 1 of Sch 5 it is an offence to contravene any of the duties specified in regs 5–10. It is also an offence to obstruct enforcement officers, make false statements, or to make unauthorised searches or seizures. Paragraph 2 of the Schedule provides for the bringing of criminal proceedings, para 3 of the Schedule establishes certain defences and paras 4–8 contain provisions (including powers of entry and seizure) aimed at assisting enforcement.

20.142 The Passenger Car (Fuel Consumption and CO2 Emissions Information) (Amendment) Regulations 2013 extend the scope of the 2001 Regulations to cars which do not emit CO2, hydrocarbons or carbon monoxide while being driven, enabling consumers considering buying battery electric or hydrogen fuel cell electric cars to have the same access to information as those buying traditional vehicles. The Regulations also reduce the minimum area required to be set aside on the new car fuel economy label for specified mandatory text.

Biofuel (Labelling) Regulations 2004[23]

20.143 The Renewable Transport Fuel Obligation, implemented through the Renewable Transport Fuel Obligations Order 2007[24] (as amended), places requirements on fuel suppliers to supply 5% biofuel by volume as an average across all fuel supplied. The overall aim is to reduce greenhouse gas emissions from road transport and contribute to UK targets for such reductions.[25]

20.144 The Regulations, which extend to the United Kingdom, transpose Art 3.5 of Directive 2003/30/EC on the promotion of the use of biofuels or other renewable fuels for transport. The Regulations require retailers to label pumps dispensing petrol or diesel containing more than 5% bioethanol or biodiesel by volume with the following text: 'Not suitable for all vehicles: consult vehicle manufacturer before use.' This text reflects the fact that, until recently, most vehicle manufacturers only warranted their vehicles to run on blends of up to 5% biofuel content. The effect of the Biofuel (Labelling) (Amendment) Regulations 2009[26] was to remove the requirement for retailers to label pumps dispensing diesel containing between 5% and 7% biodiesel, as

---

[23] SI 2004/3349.
[24] SI 2007/3072.
[25] Note also the Motor Fuel (Composition and Content) (Amendment) Regulations 2013 which extend the period – from 1 January 2014 to 31 December 2016 – that the ethanol and oxygen content of super unleaded petrol sold at larger filling stations (those where the total amount of petrol and diesel fuel sold was not less than three million litres in the calendar year prior to sale) must be no more than 5% and 2.7% by volume respectively.
[26] SI 2009/3277.

from 1 April 2010. Therefore, the label is only now required for petrol containing more than 5% bioethanol and diesel containing more than 7% biodiesel by volume. Fuels with 5% biofuel content or less remain free of any labelling requirement.

20.145 Regulation 4 creates an offence for a person who contravenes a provision of the Regulations (punishable on summary conviction with an unlimited fine) and provides that it is the duty of local weights and measures authorities in the UK (outside of Scotland) to enforce the Regulations within their areas. The Schedule to the Regulations establishes a due diligence defence and provides for other matters relating to enforcement.

Volatile Organic Compounds in Paints, Varnishes and Vehicle Refinishing Products Regulations 2012[27]

20.146 The Regulations implement Council Directive 2004/42/EC on the limitation of emissions of volatile organic compounds due to the use of organic solvents in certain paints, varnishes, and vehicle refinishing products. They also set maximum levels of organic solvents in paints, varnishes, and products such as such as cleaners, primers, and fillers. The Regulations extend to the UK. Regulation 6 deals with enforcement and Sch 4 contains specific provisions regarding enforcement in Northern Ireland. Where a local authority in England enforces these regulations, ss 108 and 110 of the Environment Act 1995 apply as if that local authority were an enforcing authority for the purposes of s 108. Regulation 8 creates an offence of failing to comply with reg 4 – which in turn prohibits the marketing of certain products (listed in Schedule 1) with a VOC content above certain limits (listed in Sch 2). The offence is triable either-way and is punishable with an unlimited fine.

Detergents Regulations 2010[28]

20.147 The 2010 Regulations prevent controlled products that do not conform with Regulation 648/2004 being placed on the market. Reg 7 creates the following offences for manufacturers:

- placement of a product on the market which fails to comply with Art 3(1) (required characteristics of detergents and surfactants) and Art 3(2) (requirement that manufacturers be established within the European Community);
- placement of a consumer laundry detergent on the market in contravention of Art 4a (limitations on the content of phosphates and other phosphorous compounds);
- failure to comply with Art 9 (information to be provided by manufacturers to enforcement authorities);

---

[27]   SI 2012/1715.
[28]   SI 2010/740.

- failure to comply with a request under Art 9(3) (requirement to provide an ingredient datasheet to medical personnel on request); and

- placement of a product on the market which does not conform with Art 11 (packaging and labelling requirements).

20.148 Under reg 7(4), a distributer may also be guilty of an offence for failure to comply with Arts 11(3) or (4) (packaging and labelling requirements). All of the above offences are triable either-way. They are punishable on summary conviction by an unlimited fine, a term of imprisonment not exceeding 3 months, or both. On indictment, they are punishable by an unlimited fine, a term of imprisonment not exceeding 2 years, or both. The Regulations also contain the usual enforcement provisions and offences, as well as a due diligence defence. The Detergents (Amendment) Regulations 2013 brought forward the date on which inorganic phosphates in domestic laundry cleaning products are banned – from 1 January 2015 to 30 June 2013.

Chemical hazard labelling and packaging[29]

20.149 The labelling and packaging of hazardous chemicals and other hazardous substances was previously primarily enforced by Trading Standards under the Chemicals (Hazard Information and Packaging for Supply) Regulations 2009 (known as 'CHIP'). However, this has changed with the gradual introduction of measures implementing Regulation (EC) 1272/2008 on classification, labelling and packaging of substances and mixtures ('the CLP Regulation'). Primary responsibility for enforcing the CLP Regulation now rests with the Health and Safety Executive following partial repeal of CHIP by the Biocidal Products and Chemicals (Appointment of Authorities and Enforcement) Regulations 2013 ('the 2013 Regulations').[30]

20.150 Although the HSE has primary responsibility for enforcing the 2013 Regulations, Trading Standards authorities remain responsible for enforcing the CLP Regulation in certain circumstances:

> **18 Allocation of enforcement responsibility**
>
> (2) The enforcing authority for the CLP Regulation is the local weights and measures authority –
>
>   (a)   where a substance, mixture or article is placed on the market within the meaning of the CLP Regulation (other than in the circumstances referred to in paragraph (3)) –
>
>   (i) in or from any shop, mobile vehicle, market stall or other retail outlet; or
>
>   (ii)   otherwise to members of the public, including by way of free sample, prize or by mail order; and
>
>   (b)   for Articles 35(2) and 48 of the CLP Regulation.

---

[29] SI 2009/716.
[30] SI 2013/1506.

(3) Subject to paragraph (4), where a substance, mixture or article is placed on the market in or from premises which are registered under sections 74A to 74L of the Medicines Act 1968, the enforcing authority shall be the General Pharmaceutical Council.

(4) In every case where, by virtue of this regulation and the CLP Regulation, the CLP Regulation is enforced by the General Pharmaceutical Council or the local weights and measures authority, it shall be enforced as if it were a safety regulation made under section 11 of the Consumer Protection Act 1987.

Sections 74A to 74L of the Medicines Act 1968 relate to pharmacies.

REACH

20.151   REACH is Regulation (EC) 1907/2006 concerning the Registration, Evaluation, Authorisation and Restriction of Chemicals. The main aim of REACH is to improve the protection of human health and the environment through the better and earlier identification of the intrinsic properties of over 30,000 chemical substances. It makes those who place chemicals in any form on the market responsible for providing information about them so that any hazards are understood and the risks associated with their use are properly managed. REACH came into force on 1 June 2007 and will be implemented in stages up to 1 June 2018. The REACH Enforcement Regulations 2008[31] create an enforcement regime which includes 'a local (consumer safety) authority' and 'a local (health and safety) authority'.

Plastic carrier bags

20.152   Section 77 and Sch 6 of the Climate Change Act 2008 provide for the making of Regulations about charges for single-use carrier bags in England and Wales, and carrier bags in Northern Ireland. Similar provisions are contained in s 88 of the Climate Change (Scotland) Act 2009. On 1 October 2011, Wales became the first UK country to introduce a charge for single use carrier bags. Under the Single Use Carrier Bags Charge (Wales) Regulations 2010[32] a seller must charge a minimum of 5p for every single-use carrier bag supplied new. Some key points on the legislation – contained in *Guidance on the Single Use Carrier Bags Charge (Wales) Regulations 2010* issued by the Welsh Government – are:

- Single-use carrier bags include those made from plastic, paper, plant-based material or natural starch that are not intended for multiple reuse.

- Some single-use carrier bags – listed in Sch 1 – are exempt from the requirement to charge.

- The minimum charge applies to sales in-store and distance selling. If a person sells goods in Wales or sells goods that are delivered in Wales they need to charge for single-use carrier bags.

---

[31]   SI 2008/2852.
[32]   SI 2010/2880 (W 238) (as amended).

- Civil sanctions, including monetary penalties of up to £5,000 (or £20,000 in cases of obstructing or misleading an administrator), may be imposed by administrators where there are breaches of the Regulations. A duty of 'administration' of the Regulations is placed on county and county borough councils.

- The Regulations impose record-keeping requirements on the number of bags sold, the disposal of the proceeds from the charge etc. The Welsh Government expects retailers to pass on the proceeds from the charge to good causes in Wales.

20.153 The Single Use Carrier Bags Charge Regulations (Northern Ireland) 2013[33] partially replicate the relevant Welsh provisions. The key differences relate to the exemptions from the levy and the requirement for sellers to pay the proceeds of the levy to the Department of Environment instead of distributing them to good causes. In Scotland, the requirement to impose a charge of 5p for each single use carrier bag has been introduced by the Single Use Carrier Bags Charge (Scotland) Regulations 2014.[34] In England, a similar 5p charge was introduced on single use carrier bags on 5 October 2015. This was introduced by the Single Use Carrier Bags Charges (England) Order 2015.[35]

20.154 The Order, which ceases to have effect on 5 October 2022, requires retailers with 250 or more employees to charge a minimum amount (5 pence including any VAT) for unused single use plastic bags used for taking goods out of shops or for delivering them. Exemptions to the charge are based on bag size, thickness, intended use, cost or combination of those factors. The Government expects that (as in Wales) retailers after deducting reasonable costs will donate the rest to good causes. The Explanatory Notes to the Order state that the:

> 'charge will be enforced by local authority trading standards officers. We are expecting the enforcement to be light touch, pragmatic and complaints led. We are introducing two types of civil sanctions (1) Fixed Monetary Penalties or (2) Discretionary Requirements (DR). Provisions for appeals are included in the Order.'

GREEN CLAIMS GUIDANCE

20.155 Defra has published a guide entitled *Green Claims Guidance* (2011). The Guidance states:

> 'This guidance is aimed at anyone producing, selling, marketing or advertising products or services in the UK and who:
>
> - Currently makes environmental claims about their products, services or organisation;

---

[33] SR 2013/4.
[34] SSI 2014/161.
[35] SI 2015/776.

- Is considering how to market their environmental attributes;
- Receives queries from customers about the environmental attributes of their products, services or organisation and is considering how to respond.

The guidance will also be useful for:

- Regulatory bodies that assess environmental claims; and
- Non-profit organisations or consumers with an interest in environmental claims.'

ENERGY ACT 2011 AND THE GREEN DEAL

20.156 The Energy Act 2011 ('the Act') included provision for the 'Green Deal' which establishes a framework enabling private firms to offer consumers energy efficiency improvements to their homes and businesses at no upfront cost. The cost of these improvements is then recouped through a charge paid in instalments on the energy bill. However, on the 23 July 2015 the Government announced 'In light of low take-up and concerns about industry standards there will be no further funding to the Green Deal Finance Company ...' and that the Government will stop any future funding releases of the Green Deal Home Improvement Fund.

CHAPTER 21

ANIMAL HEALTH AND WELFARE

CONTENTS

INTRODUCTION

21.1 This chapter concentrates principally on the domestic and farmed animal health and welfare laws that are designed to:

- prevent, control and eradicate farm animal diseases;
- safeguard human health from transmitted diseases;
- protect the welfare of farm animals in transit and at markets.

ANIMAL HEALTH

21.2 Animal health is concerned with preventing the spread of disease among animals. Human health is affected where animal diseases pass through to humans. A report from the Department of Environment, Farming and Rural Affairs ('DEFRA') in 2011 noted:

> 'The health and welfare of animals concerns not just livestock owners or government, but all of us. There have been over 14 exotic disease outbreaks in the last 10 years including foot and mouth disease, avian influenza and bluetongue. The costs of disease outbreaks range from £2 million to over £3 billion with knock-on effects in other economic sectors.'[1]

21.3 The regulation of animal health in Great Britain is part of an international and European framework. Internationally, the UK is one of 178 members of the World Organisation for Animal Health – the Office International des Epizooties (OIE). The OIE develops and regularly updates standards for the animal health services of its members. The Community Animal Health Policy covers the health of all animals in the EU kept for food, farming, sport, companionship, entertainment and in zoos. The vision of the EU Animal Health Strategy (2007–13) is to work in partnership to increase the prevention of animal health related problems before they happen: 'Prevention is better than cure.'

21.4 In March 2016 a new Regulation[2] on transmissible animal diseases was introduced. The Regulation was published in the Official Journal on 31 March but will not be applicable for 5 years. The new law is designed to consolidate and simplify a vast number of separate provisions. It also provides for the use of new technologies, the early detection, monitoring and control of animal diseases. Every local authority must appoint as many inspectors and other officers as they think necessary for the execution and enforcement of the Act.[3]

21.5 The National Animal Health and Welfare Panel ('NAHWP') is a national[4] public body that provides technical and operational policy support to

---

[1]   See www.defra.gov.uk/consult/files/110318-animal-disease-plan-condoc.pdf.
[2]   Regulation (EU) 2016/429.
[3]   Animal Health Act 1981, s 52(1).
[4]   The NAHWP does not represent authorities in Scotland or Northern Ireland.

local authorities by helping to co-ordinate good practice. The NAHWP provides expert advice on animal health and welfare matters and enforcement. In 2015 the NAHWP agreed and promoted the use of the term 'local authority animal health function' ('LAAHF'). The purpose of the LAAHF is to work 'in partnership with all relevant government agencies and Animal Health and welfare organisations to provide pro-active support to the local farming community with the aim of ensuring compliance with the statutory rules.'

Animal Health Act 1981

21.6 The main legislation governing animal health in Great Britain is the Animal Health Act 1981 ('AHA 1981'), as amended by:

- the Animal Health and Welfare Act 1984, which amongst other matters, relates to the seizure of things for the purpose of preventing the spread of disease, powers of entry and declarations as to places infected with a disease;

- the Animal Health (Amendment) Act 1998, which relates to improving the welfare of animals in quarantine;

- the Animal Health Act 2002 which, amongst other matters, provides additional powers to tackle foot and mouth disease and for these powers to be extendable to other animal diseases;

- the Animal Health and Welfare (Scotland) Act 2006, which makes provisions for both the health and welfare of animals in Scotland.

21.7 In addition there around 200 statutory instruments applying to animal health issues – either made under the AHA 1981 or under the European Communities Act 1972 in order to transpose an EU Directive or Regulation into domestic legislation (for example the Animal By-Products (Enforcement) (England) Regulations 2013[5] and the African Horse Sickness (England) Regulations 2012[6]). The following list is illustrative of the wide range of diseases etc which are subject to legislative control (it is not intended to be comprehensive and it should be emphasised that some diseases have never occurred in Great Britain).

African Swine Fever	Infectious Diseases of Horses
Anthrax	Pleuro-Pneumonia
Aujesky's Disease	Psittacosis or Ornithosis
Avian Influenza and Newcastle Disease	Rabies
Bluetongue	Salmonella
Cattle Plague	Sheep Scab
Classical Swine Fever	Swine Vesicular Disease

---

5   SI 2013/2952.
6   SI 2012/2629.

Enzootic Bovine Leukosis	Transmissible Spongiform Encephalopathies
Equine Viral Arteritis	Tuberculosis
Equine Infectious Anaemia	Warble Fly
Foot and Mouth Disease	Zoonoses

21.8 In a work of this nature it is not possible to provide a complete analysis of the legislative requirements relating to animal health matters and an attempt has therefore been made to focus on those areas which have most significance to local authority trading standards departments. Nor is it possible to list all parallel provisions which are connected with the transposition of an EU Directive or Regulation into domestic legislation within England, Wales, Scotland and Northern Ireland.

Territorial jurisdiction

21.9 Unless otherwise specified the parts of the AHA 1981 referred to in this work apply to Great Britain.

Northern Ireland

21.10 The principal legislation relating to Northern Ireland is the Welfare of Animals Act (Northern Ireland) 2011 and the Diseases of Animals (Northern Ireland) Order 1981,[7] which has been amended considerably, most recently by the Disease of Animals Act (Northern Ireland) 2010. The Department of Agriculture and Rural Development (DARD) has the enforcement responsibility in respect of farmed animals (defined as any animal bred or kept for the production of food, wool or skin or for other farming purposes), licensing of riding establishments, boarding kennels, pet shops and zoos and enforcement of any welfare issues within these premises. District councils have responsibility for enforcement in respect of other (non-farmed) animals, ie domestic pets of any vertebrate species and equines (eg horses and donkeys etc). The All-Island Animal Health and Welfare Strategy – formally agreed in 2010 – enhances North-South co-operation on animal health and welfare issues and has the potential to help reduce and prevent the spread of animal disease.

Application

21.11 Animals are defined under s 87 of the AHA 1981 as being (unless the context otherwise requires): (a) cattle, sheep and goats and (b) all other ruminating animals and swine. The AHA 1981 has effect in relation to poultry as it does in relation to animals. Poultry being defined under s 87(4) as being: (a) domestic fowls, turkeys, geese, ducks, guineafowls and pigeons, and (b) pheasants and partridges. Ministers by Order may extend the definition of the term 'animals' for all or any of the purposes of the AHA 1981 to include any

---

[7]   SI 1981/1115 (NI 22).

mammal except man and any four footed beast which is not a mammal.[8] Similarly under s 87(4) the definition of poultry may by Order be extended to include any other species of bird. So for example in the Foot and Mouth Disease (England) Order 2006,[9] the definition of animals is extended to include 'all four footed beasts' and the definition of poultry to include 'all birds', within the terms of that order.

21.12   The AHA 1981 provides a definition of the term 'disease' under s 88:

> **88. Meaning of "disease".**
>
> (1) In this Act, unless the context otherwise requires, "disease" means cattle plague, pleuro-pneumonia, foot-and-mouth disease, sheep-pox, sheep scab, or swine fever, subject to subsection (2) below.
>
> (2) The Ministers may by order for all or any of the purposes of this Act extend the definition of "disease" in subsection (1) above so that it shall for those or any of those purposes comprise any other disease of animals.
>
> (3) In this Act, in so far as it applies to poultry, and unless the context otherwise requires, "disease" means –
>
> (a)   fowl pest in any of its forms, including Newcastle disease and fowl plague; and
>
> (b)   fowl cholera, infectious bronchitis, infectious laryngotracheitis, pullorum disease, fowl typhoid, fowl pox and fowl paralysis,
>
> subject to subsection (4) below.
>
> (4)   The Ministers may by order for all or any of the purposes of this Act –
>
> (a)   extend the definition of "disease" in subsection (3) above so that it shall for those or any of those purposes comprise any other disease of birds; or
>
> (b)   restrict that definition so that it shall for those or any of those purposes exclude any of the diseases mentioned in paragraph (b) of subsection (3).

There are numerous statutory instruments made under s 88(2) and (4) of the AHA 1981, examples being, Disease of Poultry (England) Order 2003,[10] the Specified Animal Pathogens Order 2008[11] and the African Horse Sickness (Scotland) Order 2012.[12]

Offences

21.13 The main offence provisions are contained in ss 72 and 73 and, for practical enforcement purposes, relate to breaches of Orders made under the AHA 1981.

21.14   Section 72 provides:

---

[8]   Section 87(2).
[9]   SI 2006/182.
[10]   SI 2003/1078.
[11]   SI 2008/944.
[12]   SSI 2012/178.

72 Offences made and declared by and under this Act

A person is guilty of an offence against this Act who, without lawful authority or excuse, proof of which shall lie on him –

(a) does or omits anything the doing or omission of which is declared by this Act or by an order of the Minister to be an offence by that person against this Act; or

(b) does anything which by this Act or such an order is made or declared to be not lawful.

21.15 Within the AHA 1981 itself, there are a number of acts or omissions declared as being 'offences against the Act' or other matters referred to simply as offences. The offences referred to in the AHA 1981 include:

- obstructing or impeding inspectors;
- refusing access or failing to assist when required to do so (see for example ss 4(2), 16, 36G, 66);
- failing to keep diseased animals separate and notifying the authorities promptly (s 15(7));
- disposal in watercourses or on the foreshore of diseased animal carcasses (s 35(4));
- offences relating to equine exports (ss 40, 41, 42 and 45); and
- offences relating to the falsification, use or improper obtaining of licences under the Act (ss 66–71).

This list is not exhaustive and it should be noted that the Animal Health and Welfare (Scotland) Act 2006 amends the AHA 1981, to create different definitions and separate offences applicable in Scotland.

21.16 A general power for Ministers to make orders is expressed under s 1 for the better execution of the AHA 1981 and for the purpose of preventing the spread of disease. Other specific powers for Ministers to regulate exist under the AHA 1981, an example being s 8 which provides the power for Ministers to make orders regulating the movement of animals. Under this section the Welfare of Animals (Transport) (England) Order 2006[13] was enabled which creates a series of offences against the AHA 1981 relating to the transport of animals, enforceable under s 72(a).

21.17 In an example of proceedings brought under s 72(a), *R (Clement) v Durham County Magistrates' Court*,[14] which related to breaches of the Pigs (Records, Identification and Movement) Order 1995,[15] Silber J said:

---

[13] SI 2006/3260.
[14] [2003] EWHC 1154 (Admin).
[15] SI 1995/11 (now repealed).

'Before turning to the questions for the opinion of this court, it is necessary to point out that the Order is a complicated Order and so I have great sympathy with the magistrates when considering the task that confronted them when dealing with this case.'

21.18 As if to demonstrate the complexities of this area of law, that order (which specifically stated that breaches of the order are offences against the AHA 1981), has been repealed and now stands replaced with the Pigs (Records, Identification and Movement) Order 2011.[16] This later order is made under the AHA 1981 but no longer specifies offences as being against the AHA 1981 and anticipates prosecutions being brought under s 73.

21.19 Section 79 deals with certain aspects of evidence and procedure, including:

79 Evidence and procedure

(2) Where the owner or person in charge of an animal is charged with an offence against this Act relative to disease or to any illness of the animal, he shall be presumed to have known of the existence of the disease or illness unless and until he shows to the court's satisfaction that –

(a)   he had no knowledge of the existence of that disease or illness, and

(b)   he could not with reasonable diligence have obtained that knowledge.

(3) Where a person –

(a)   is charged with an offence against this Act in not having duly cleansed or disinfected any place, vessel, aircraft, vehicle or thing belonging to him or under his charge, and

(b)   a presumption against him on the part of the prosecution is raised,

it shall lie on him to prove the due cleansing and disinfection mentioned in paragraph (a).[17]

General offences

21.20 Section 73 provides:

73 General offences

73 A person is guilty of an offence against this Act who, without lawful authority or excuse, proof of which shall lie on him –

(a)   does anything in contravention of this Act, or of an order of the Minister, or of a regulation of a local authority; or

(b)   fails to give, produce, observe or do any notice, licence, rule or thing which by this Act or such an order or regulation he is required to give, produce, observe or do.

---

[16]   SI 2011/2154.
[17]   The section as reproduced applies in England and Wales. An alternative s 79 applies in Scotland, as amended by the Animal Health and Welfare (Scotland) Act 2006.

Care should be taken to establish under which Act the secondary legislation was made. For example the Animal By-Products (Enforcement) (England) Regulations 2011[18] and the African Horse Sickness (England) Regulations 2012[19] are both made under s 2(2) of the European Communities Act 1972 and both contain specific self-contained offence provisions, not invoking the Animal Health Act 1981. Previously, secondary legislation on Animal By-Products had been created under the powers granted by the AHA 1981 (see, for example, the Animal By-Products Order 1999, breach of which formed the basis of a prosecution under s 73(b) in *R (North Yorkshire Trading Standards) v Nicholson*[20]).

Time limits

21.21 Section 71A provides:

> **71A Prosecutions: time limit**
>
> (1) Despite anything in section 127(1) of the Magistrates' Courts Act 1980 an information relating to an offence under this Act which is triable by a magistrates' court in England and Wales may be so tried if it is laid at any time –
>
> > (a) within the period of three years starting with the date of the commission of the offence, and
> >
> > (b) within the period of six months starting with the day on which evidence which the prosecutor thinks is sufficient to justify the proceedings comes to his knowledge.
>
> (2) A certificate by the prosecutor as to the date on which such evidence came to his knowledge is conclusive evidence of that fact.

Note the commentary (below) on time limits under s 31 of the Animal Welfare Act 2006, which is drafted in similar terms. Time limits are dealt with generally in Chapter 3, Criminal Enforcement.

Enforcement

21.22 Sections 60–66A deal extensively with enforcement and s 52 provides that every local authority 'shall appoint as many inspectors and other officers as the local authority think necessary for the execution and enforcement of this Act'. Sections 60–62 provide enforcement powers under the Act for police officers (including under ss 61–62 as regards rabies). Section 63 of the Act provides an inspector with all the powers afforded to a police officer in the place where the inspector is acting, save for the powers under ss 61 and 62 (powers of entry and arrest as regards rabies). In addition, relevant officers should have regard to the Home Office Powers of Entry Code; see Chapter 3, Criminal Enforcement.

---

18 SI 2011/881.
19 SI 2012/2629.
20 [2003] EWHC 1022 (Admin).

Penalties

21.23 The penalties for offences committed under ss 72 and 73 are contained in s 75:

> 75(2) A person guilty of an offence to which this section applies is liable on summary conviction to imprisonment for a term not exceeding six months or to a fine or to both.

ANIMAL WELFARE

Introduction

21.24 The United Kingdom has a long history of protecting animals from cruelty. In 1822, Richard Martin MP piloted the first parliamentary legislation for animal welfare in the world, making it an offence to 'beat, abuse, or ill-treat any horse, mare, gelding, mule, ass, ox, cow, heifer, steer, sheep or other cattle'. The current general principles of animal welfare were set out in the Protection of Animals Acts, the first of which was passed in 1911, which made it an offence to cause any unnecessary suffering to an animal. In June 2004, DEFRA, the Scottish Executive and the Welsh Assembly Government published 'Animal Health and Welfare Strategy for Great Britain'. The aim of the strategy was to 'develop a new partnership in which we can make a lasting and continuous improvement in the health and welfare of kept animals while protecting society, the economy, and the environment from the effect of animal disease'. The strategy has as its scope all animals which are under people's control, but did not address angling, hunting or the use of animals in science.

21.25 The strategic outcomes included 'Promoting the benefits of animal health and welfare: Prevention is better than cure' which has at its heart an understanding that animals that are cared for appropriately and in accordance with existing welfare standards are more likely to be healthy, and less likely to contract or spread disease. A further strategic outcome was for 'Understanding and accepting roles and responsibilities', calling for individuals to understand and accept the duty they have to provide an acceptable standard of health and welfare for the animals in their care.

21.26 The Animal Welfare Act 2006 (AWA 2006) supports the implementation of that strategy as regards welfare of animals in England and Wales. It replaced the Protection of Animals Act 1911, the welfare provisions of the Animal Health Act 1981 and consolidated more than 20 other pieces of legislation. The Animal Health and Welfare (Scotland) Act 2006 (AHWSA 2006) also supports the 2004 Strategy. Part 1 of the AHWSA 2006 amends the Animal Health Act 1981 to provide additional powers to prevent the spread of animal diseases whilst Part 2 of the Act addresses animal welfare.

21.27 Within the EU, following the signing of the Lisbon Treaty, acknowledgement of animals as sentient beings and the need to take regard of their welfare requirements, has been enshrined as a governing principle when formulating and implementing EU policies. Article 13 TFEU (2009) reads:

> 'In formulating and implementing the Union's agriculture, fisheries, transport, internal market, research and technological development and space policies, the Union and the Member States shall, since animals are sentient beings, pay full regard to the welfare requirements of animals, while respecting the legislative or administrative provisions and customs of the Member States relating in particular to religious rites, cultural traditions and regional heritage.'

21.28   In January 2012, the EU issued the 'Strategy for the Protection and Welfare of Animals' (2012–15). With its guiding principle of 'Everyone is responsible', the strategy proposes a single simplified legislative framework to promote animal welfare strategy, together with an emphasis on seeing enhanced compliance with EU rules by Member States. In November 2015 the European Parliament adopted a Resolution calling on the European Commission to formulate a new Animal Welfare Strategy for 2016–2020.

Animal Welfare Act 2006

21.29   The welfare provisions of the Animal Welfare Act 2006 ('AWA 2006') and the Animal Health and Welfare (Scotland) Act 2006 ('AHWSA 2006') are drafted in broadly similar terms. Equivalent sections (and differences) under AHWSA 2006 are indicated as applicable.

Territorial jurisdiction

21.30   The AWA 2006 extends to England and Wales. It extends to Scotland only in respect of s 46, enabling disqualification orders made in England and Wales to have force in Scotland, ss 47–50, making provision for Scottish courts to enforce disqualification orders made under the AWA 2006, the repeal of certain legislation and commencement orders. Section 1 of the AWA 2006, provides that the Act applies only to vertebrate animals, being the only demonstrably sentient animals. Provision is made under s 1(3) for the appropriate national authority[21] to extend cover for invertebrates in the future if satisfied on the basis of scientific evidence that these too are capable of experiencing pain and suffering. The equivalent provision under AHWSA 2006 is contained in s 16(1) and (3) empowering Scottish Ministers to extend by regulation the Act in similar terms.

'Protected animal'

21.31   Section 2 of the AWA 2006 provides that an animal is a 'protected animal' if:

> (a)   it is of a kind which is commonly domesticated in the British Islands,

---

21   Defined in s 62(1) as being the Secretary of State as regards England and the Welsh National Assembly as regards Wales.

(b)   it is under the control of man whether on a permanent or temporary basis, or

(c)   it is not living in a wild state.

Section 17 of the AHWSA 2006 is framed in virtually identical terms. Animals of a kind not commonly domesticated in the British Islands are only 'protected animals' to the extent that they are under the control of man or are not living independently in the wild. 'Under control' is intended to be a broader expression than 'captive animal' under the Protection of Animals Act 1911, which had been narrowly interpreted by the courts.

'Responsibility for animals'

21.32 Certain offences under AWA 2006[22] and AHWSA 2006[23] can only be committed by persons who are 'responsible for an animal'. Section 3 of the AWA 2006 (and s 18 of the AHWSA 2006) provide that references to a person responsible for an animal under the AWA 2006 are to a person responsible on a permanent or temporary basis and references to being responsible include being in charge. The owner of an animal shall always be regarded as being responsible under the AWA 2006 and a person will be treated as responsible for any animal for which a child under the age of 16 of which he has care and control is responsible.

21.33 Responsibility for an animal is only intended to arise where a person can be said to have assumed responsibility for its day-to-day care or for its care for a specific purpose or by virtue of owning it. This includes a person taking responsibility for an animal temporarily, for example a veterinary surgeon taking responsibility for animals kept in the surgery overnight or staff at boarding premises or animal sanctuaries. Section 18(5) of the AHWSA 2006 adds that 'a person does not relinquish responsibility for an animal by reason only of abandoning it'.

Offences

21.34 Sections 4–8 of the AWA 2006 and ss 19–23 of the AHWSA 2006 address the prevention of harm by setting out offences relating to cruelty and animal fighting. Section 9 of the AWA 2006 and s 24 of the AHWSA 2006 create offences where a person responsible for an animal does not ensure its welfare. In a work of this nature it is not possible to cover all offences arising under the Acts or the secondary legislation, so an attempt is made to address the areas of most significance.

Unnecessary suffering

21.35 Section 4 of the AWA 2006 sets out offences relating to unnecessary suffering, but provides, in s 4(4), that nothing in the section applies to the

---

[22]   Sections 4(2), 5(2), 6(2), 7(2) and 9.

[23]   Sections 19(2), 20(2), 21(2), 22(2) and 24.

destruction of an animal in an appropriate and humane manner. Also s 59 of the AWA 2006 states: 'Nothing in this Act applies in relation to anything which occurs in the normal course of fishing.' Under the Protection of Animals Act 1911, it had been an offence to cause unnecessary suffering to any domestic or captive animal, with limited exceptions (for example suffering caused under the Animals (Scientific Procedures) Act 1986). Section 4 of the AWA 2006 seeks to replicate the protection under the 1911 Act, but to simplify and update the legislation. 'Suffering' means physical or mental suffering – s 62 of the AWA 2006 (s 48 of the AHWSA 2006 states: 'In this Part, references to suffering include physical or mental suffering').

21.36   The offence under s 4(1) of AWA 2006 is applicable to any person and applies to acts and omissions.

> 4(1) A person commits an offence if –
>
> > (a)   an act of his, or a failure of his to act, causes an animal to suffer,
> > (b)   he knew, or ought reasonably to have known, that the act, or failure to act, would have that effect or be likely to do so,
> > (c)   the animal is a protected animal, and
> > (d)   the suffering is unnecessary.

The inclusion of the phrase 'ought reasonably to have known', introduces an objective mental element, such that it is not necessary to prove whether the person actually knew his act or failure to act would cause suffering.

21.37   In *Gray v Aylesbury Crown Court*,[24] Toulson LJ in considering this section stated that 'knew or ought reasonably to have known' is a common expression in English law and does not require to be glossed. He rejected the argument that there needed to be some form of actual or constructive knowledge on the part of the defendant and that negligence was not sufficient, stating:[25]

> 'That submission does not accord with a natural reading of the subsection. Its plain effect is to impose criminal liability for unnecessary suffering caused to an animal either by an act or omission which the person responsible knew would, or was likely to, cause unnecessary suffering, or by a negligent act or omission'[26]

21.38   The offence under s 4(2) of AWA 2006:

> 4(2) A person commits an offence if –
>
> > (a)   he is responsible for an animal,
> > (b)   an act, or failure to act, of another person causes the animal to suffer,

---

[24]   [2013] EWHC 500 (Admin).
[25]   At para 26.
[26]   The judge also rejected use of previous reported cases under the Protection of Animals Act 1911, stating (at para 28): 'It would be wrong in principle to construe the provisions of the 2006 Act by reference to differently worded provisions of the repealed legislation'.

(c)   he permitted that to happen or failed to take such steps (whether by way of supervising the other person or otherwise) as were reasonable in all the circumstances to prevent that happening, and

(d)   the suffering is unnecessary.

21.39 In *Riley v Crown Prosecution Service*[27] partners in a slaughterhouse business appealed against their convictions under s 4(2)(c) AWA 2006 for 'failing to take such steps as were reasonable in all the circumstances to prevent an animal ... from suffering unnecessarily by failing to stop the continued handling and movement of the said bovine using ropes'. The High Court rejected the prosecution argument that the offences were of strict liability. A mental element (mens rea) must be proven that of the circumstances which determined what steps would be reasonable.

21.40 The AHWSA 2006 offences relating to unnecessary suffering are contained in s 19 and include an exception for the humane destruction of an animal.[28] Fishing is also excluded from applying to this part of the Act.[29]

21.41 The offence under s 19(1) applies to any person but is restricted to positive acts and not a failure to act as covered under the AWA 2006. This is addressed under s 19(2) but only as against a person responsible for an animal (as to which see s 18). The objective mental element under the AWA 2006 is replicated.

(1) A person commits an offence if –

(a)   the person causes a protected animal unnecessary suffering by an act, and

(b)   the person knew, or ought reasonably to have known, that the act would have caused the suffering or be likely to do so.

(2) A person who is responsible for an animal commits an offence if –

(a)   the person causes the animal unnecessary suffering by an act or omission, and

(b)   the person knew, or ought reasonably to have known, that the act or omission would have caused the suffering or be likely to do so.

Unnecessary

21.42 Section 4(3) of the AWA 2006 sets out the considerations to which the courts should have regard in determining whether the suffering is unnecessary, these include:

(a)   whether the suffering could reasonably have been avoided or reduced;

(b)   whether the conduct which caused the suffering was in compliance with any relevant enactment or any relevant provisions of a licence or code of practice issued under an enactment;

(c)   whether the conduct which caused the suffering was for a legitimate purpose, such as –

---

27   [2016] EWHC 2531 (Admin).
28   AHWSA 2006, s 19(5).
29   AHWSA 2006, s 47(b).

(i)   the purpose of benefiting the animal, or
(ii)   the purpose of protecting a person, property or another animal;
(d)   whether the suffering was proportionate to the purpose of the conduct concerned;
(e)   whether the conduct concerned was in all the circumstances that of a reasonably competent and humane person.

21.43   Section 19(4) of the AHWSA 2006 sets out, in identical terms to s 4(3) of the AWA 2006 above, the considerations to which regard is to be had in determining, for the purposes of s 19(1)–(3) of the AHWSA 2006, whether suffering is unnecessary.

Other offences of unnecessary suffering

21.44   Section 4(2) of the AWA 2006 and s 19(3) of the AHWSA 2006, create offences where people responsible for animals permit or fail to intervene where another person causes an animal to suffer. Section 4(2) of the AWA 2006 states:

4(2) A person commits an offence if –

(a)   he is responsible for an animal,
(b)   an act, or failure to act, of another person causes the animal to suffer,
(c)   he permitted that to happen or failed to take such steps (whether by way of supervising the other person or otherwise) as were reasonable in all the circumstances to prevent that happening, and
(d)   the suffering is unnecessary.

21.45   Section 19(3) of the AHWSA 2006 states:

19(3) A person ("person A") who is responsible for an animal commits an offence if –

(a)   another person causes the animal unnecessary suffering by an act or omission, and
(b)   person A –
(i)   permits that to happen, or
(ii)   fails to take such steps (whether by way of supervising the other person or otherwise) as are reasonable in the circumstances to prevent that happening.

Suffering is as defined under s 62 of the AWA 2006 and s 48 of the AHWSA 2006 and the courts in both jurisdictions are to have regard to the same factors as under the primary offences. No interpretation of the words 'permitted' or 'permits' appears under either the AWA 2006 or AHWSA 2006.

Other cruelty offences

Mutilation

21.46   Section 5(1) of the AWA 2006 makes it an offence for a person to carry out or cause to be carried out a prohibited procedure on a protected animal save as specified under regulations under s 5(4).[30] The carrying out of a prohibited procedure is a procedure which interferes with the sensitive tissues or bone structure of the animal, otherwise than for the purposes of its medical treatment.

21.47 Section 20(1) and (2) of the AHWSA 2006 create like offences, and there is a further offence under s 20(3) of taking (or causing to be taken) an animal from Scotland to have a prohibited procedure carried out outwith Scotland. There is a similar power under s 20(5)[31] to exempt by regulation specified procedures from falling under s 20(1)–(3). Section 21 of the AHWSA 2006 also creates an offence of performing an operation on a protected animal without due care and humanity.

Docking of dogs tails

21.48 Section 6(1) of the AWA 2006 makes it an offence for a person to remove (or cause to be removed by another person) the whole or any part of a dog's tail, otherwise than for the purpose of its medical treatment. Section 6(2) creates an offence for a person responsible for a dog to permit or fail to take such steps as are reasonable to prevent another from removing the whole or part of the dog's tail, otherwise than for the purpose of its medical treatment. The offence is not committed where the dog is a certified working dog (as specified under regulations[32]) not more than 5 days old.[33]

21.49 There is no like offence under the AHWSA 2006, but docking of dog's tails is not preserved under s 20 of the AHWSA 2006 as under s 5 of the AWA 2006, and so would amount to an offence under that section unless permitted by regulation made under s 20(5).[34]

Administration of poisons

21.50 Section 7(1) of the AWA 2006 and s 22(1) of the AHWSA 2006 are similarly drafted and create an offence where a person, without lawful authority or reasonable excuse, administers to or causes to be taken by a protected animal any poisonous or injurious drug or substance, knowing it to be poisonous or injurious. Section 7(2) of the AWA 2006 and s 22(2) create offences where a person responsible for an animal permits another to administer poison, in similar terms as to the foregoing sections. Reference to a poisonous or injurious drug or substance includes where a drug or substance

---

[30] See Mutilation (Permitted Procedures) (England) Regulations 2007, SI 2007/1100 (as amended by SIs 2008/1426 and 2010/3034) and Mutilation (Permitted Procedures) (Wales) Regulations 2007, SI 2007/1029 (as amended by SIs 2008/3094 and 2010/2712).

[31] See the Prohibited Procedures on Protected Animals (Exemptions) (Scotland) Regulations 2010, SSI 2010/387 (as amended by SSIs 2011/164 and 2012/40).

[32] AWA 2006, s 6(4), see the Docking of Working Dogs' Tails (England) Regulations 2007, SI 2007/1120 and Docking of Working Dogs' Tails (Wales) Regulations 2007, SI 2007/1028.

[33] AWA 2006, s 6(3).

[34] See the Prohibited Procedures On Protected Animals (Exemptions) (Scotland) Regulations 2010, SSI 2010/387 (as amended by SSIs 2011/164 and 2012/40).

either through the quantity taken or the manner in which it is administered, has the effect of being poisonous or injurious.[35] Neither provision requires that it be shown that the animal actually suffered as a result of having received a poisonous drug or substance.

Animal fights

21.51   Section 8(1) of the AWA 2006 creates a series of offences regarding animal fighting, from keeping or training an animal to fight, causing an animal to fight, keeping premises for animal fights through to publicising proposed fights, providing information about animal fights to encourage attendance and betting on animal fights. Under s 8(2) it is an offence simply to attend an animal fight. An animal fight is defined[36] as an occasion on which a protected animal is placed with an animal, or with a human, for the purpose of fighting, wrestling or baiting.

21.52   In *RSPCA v McCormick*[37] the defendants went into the countryside at night with lurcher-type dogs with the intention of seeking out wild animals, including deer, foxes and badgers. They set their dogs free and allowed them to pursue, attack and kill wild animals. It was held that this did not amount to the offence because the animal, with which a protected animal is placed, must be the subject of some control or restraint by a person connected with that activity or some other artificial constraint so that its ability to escape is prevented. The court observed that s 8 is aimed at organised and controlled animal fights, such as dog fights. Section 23 of the AHWSA 2006, whilst drafted in different terms, creates similar offences in relation to animal fights.

Welfare offences

21.53   The 2004 Animal Health and Welfare Strategy document stated:

> 'This strategy is not simply concerned with ensuring the absence of cruelty and disease. Quite often problems are caused by complacency, lack of skills or knowledge, or a failure to treat animals humanely and as sentient beings for which we have an ethical responsibility. Anyone who takes ownership of an animal, whether for food, farming, sport, companionship, entertainment or zoos, has a duty of care to meet acceptable animal health and welfare standards.'[38]:

Sections 9–12 of the AWA 2006 set out specific offences which relate to the promotion of welfare. Foremost of these is s 9 which sets out the duty of a person responsible for an animal to ensure its welfare.

21.54   Section 9(1) states:

---

[35]   AWA 2006, s 7(3) and AHWSA 2006, s 22(3).
[36]   AWA 2006, s 8(7).
[37]   [2016] EWHC 928 (Admin).
[38]   Paragraph 31, p 16 of the Animal Health and Welfare Strategy for Great Britain http://archive.defra.gov.uk/foodfarm/policy/animalhealth/strategy/ahws.pdf.

(1) A person commits an offence if he does not take such steps as are reasonable in all the circumstances to ensure that the needs of an animal for which he is responsible are met to the extent required by good practice.

21.55 In *Gray v Aylesbury Crown Court*,[39] this section was considered and it was stated that the section sets 'a purely objective standard of care which a person responsible for an animal is required to provide'.[40] The court also confirmed that an indictment would not be bad for duplicity where a person was charged with the s 4 and s 9 offences arising out of the same facts, given that the offence under s 4 needs proof of unnecessary suffering, which is not required for proving the offence under s 9.

21.56 Under s 9(3), the circumstances which it is relevant to have regard to under s 9(1) include in particular any lawful purpose for which the animal is kept and any lawful activity undertaken in relation to the animal. As to good practice, regard should be had to codes of practice issued under s 14(1).

21.57 The Act sets out in s 9(2) what an animal's needs[41] shall be taken to include, being:

(a)   its need for a suitable environment;

(b)   its need for a suitable diet;

(c)   its need to be able to exhibit normal behaviour patterns;

(d)   any need it has to be housed with, or apart from, other animals;

(e)   its need to be protected from suffering, injury and disease.

21.58 The AWA 2006 repeals the Abandonment of Animals Act 1960[42] and it is intended that this offence applies where a person abandons an animal for which they are responsible without taking reasonable steps to ensure that it is capable of fending for itself and living independently. Should the animal suffer unnecessarily through abandonment, then it is likely that an offence under s 4 will have been committed.[43]

21.59 The AHWSA 2006, s 24, creates a like offence in virtually identical terms. Neither section applies to the destruction of animals in an appropriate and humane manner.[44] Section 10 of the AWA 2006 provides an inspector with the power to issue improvement notices where he is of the opinion that a person is failing to comply with s 9(1). Section 11 of the AWA 2006 and s 30 of the AHWSA 2006 create offences with regard to the sale of animals to persons under the age of 16.

---

[39]   [2013] EWHC 500 (Admin).
[40]   Paragraph 31.
[41]   These needs are derived from the five freedoms for animals referred to in the 2004 Strategy document.
[42]   See s 65 and Sch 4 to the Act.
[43]   Note the AHSWA 2006 has a specific offence of abandonment of animals at s 29.
[44]   AWA 2006, s 9(4) and AHWSA 2006, s 24(4).

Regulations

21.60 The appropriate national authority[45] is given a general power under s 12(1) to, by regulation, make such provision for the purpose of promoting the welfare of animals for which a person is responsible, or the progeny of such animals, including the creation of non-indictable offences arising out of the breach of regulations.[46] Section 26 of the AHWSA 2006 provides for making of regulations to secure the welfare of animals for which a person is responsible. Section 13 of the AWA 2006 provides powers for the making of regulations regarding the licensing and registration of activities involving animals.[47]

Codes of practice

21.61 AWA 2006 provides that codes of practice may be issued (or revised) by an appropriate national authority for the purpose of providing practical guidance in respect of any provision made by or under the Act (s 14(1)).[48] A failure to comply with a code of practice does not of itself render a person liable to any proceedings of any kind (s 14(3)).

21.62 Codes of practice had been issued previously in relation to farmed animals (cattle, sheep, pigs, poultry, goats, rabbits, deer, turkeys and ratites), which have not been replaced and continue to apply in England, with the caveat that references to legislation within them are now out of date.[49] In 2013 DEFRA consulted on replacing statutory based farming welfare codes of practice with industry led drafted guidance, The Government's interim response to the consultation was that it needed further time to consider the responses provided but, in April 2016, a decision was made to retain them in their current statutory format.

21.63 Following commencement of Section 14, codes of practice for England have been issued with effect from 6 April 2010 for dogs,[50] cats,[51] privately kept non-human primates and horses, ponies and donkeys[52] (Wales and Scotland have equivalent codes). A code of practice relating to gamebirds was issued in January 2011.[53]

21.64 Regard should be had to s 14(4) which reads:

> (4) In any proceedings against a person for an offence under this Act or an offence under regulations under section 12 or 13 –

---

[45] The Secretary of State as regards England, the Welsh National Assembly as regards Wales.
[46] Punishable by no more than 51 weeks' custody or a fine not exceeding Level 5 on the standard scale (AWA 2006, s 12(3)(a)).
[47] AHSWA 2006, s 27.
[48] The equivalent power is found at s 37 of the AHWSA 2006.
[49] These can be found on the DEFRA website.
[50] See www.defra.gov.uk/publications/files/pb13333-cop-dogs-091204.pdf
[51] See www.defra.gov.uk/publications/files/pb13332-cop-cats-091204.pdf
[52] See www.defra.gov.uk/publications/files/pb13334-cop-horse-091204.pdf
[53] See www.defra.gov.uk/publications/files/pb13356-game-birds-100720.pdf

(a) failure to comply with a relevant provision of a code of practice issued under this section may be relied upon as tending to establish liability, and

(b) compliance with a relevant provision of such a code of practice may be relied upon as tending to negative liability.

Time limits for prosecutions

21.65 Section 31 of the AWA 2006 sets out the time limits for prosecutions being brought (and is in similar terms to s 71A of the Animal Health Act 1981).

31 Time limits for prosecutions

(1) Notwithstanding anything in section 127(1) of the Magistrates' Courts Act 1980 (c. 43), a magistrates' court may try an information relating to an offence under this Act if the information is laid –

(a) before the end of the period of three years beginning with the date of the commission of the offence, and

(b) before the end of the period of six months beginning with the date on which evidence which the prosecutor thinks is sufficient to justify the proceedings comes to his knowledge.

(2) For the purposes of subsection (1)(b) –

(a) a certificate signed by or on behalf of the prosecutor and stating the date on which such evidence came to his knowledge shall be conclusive evidence of that fact, and

(b) a certificate stating that matter and purporting to be so signed shall be treated as so signed unless the contrary is proved.

For commentary about time limits in general see Chapter 3, Criminal Enforcement.

21.66 In *R v King & King*,[54] the RSPCA were unsuccessful in seeking to rely on a certificate purporting to be issued under s 31(2), but which in fact was unsigned. Dismissing the appeal, Toulson LJ stated:

'Given that a certificate in proper form is conclusive, subject to limited qualifications recognized in the case-law, the court should not adopt a loose approach to the formal requirements of the subsection.'

There is no requirement under s 31 for the certificate to be dated or served at the same time as the information is laid or the summons issued.[55]

21.67 In *RSPCA v Johnson*,[56] the defendant challenged the validity of the date of information coming into the knowledge of the prosecutor, arguing that an earlier date applied thus rendering the information invalid as not properly laid

---

[54] [2010] EWHC 637 (Admin).

[55] *Browning v Lewes Crown Court* [2012] EWHC 1003 (Admin), per Wynn Williams J at para 12, approved in *Letherbarrow v Warwickshire County Council* [2015] EWHC 4820 (Admin).

[56] [2009] EWHC 2702.

within the 6-month time limit of s 31(1)(b). In allowing an appeal against the District Judge's decision to dismiss the information as being out of time, Pill LJ stated:

> 'In my judgment ... the prosecutor is the RSPCA ... (but) It appears to be clear ... that Mr Fletcher was signing on behalf of the RSPCA ... There is no principle of law that knowledge in a prosecutor begins immediately any employee of that prosecutor has the relevant knowledge ... It is right that prosecutors are not entitled to shuffle papers between officers or sit on information so as to extend a time limit. There is, however, a degree of judgment involved in bringing a prosecution, and knowledge, in my judgment, involves an opportunity for those with appropriate skills to consider whether there is sufficient information to justify a prosecution.'[57]

21.68   The appropriateness of the time taken to issue proceedings in this case was influenced by the actions of the defendant, 'the respondent made concerted efforts to avoid and hide from Mr Jackman [the RSPCA investigator] ... the more elusive someone is, the more likely an Inspector is want (sic) to have the clearest evidence in case some point is taken – an unforeseen point – by the elusive person when charged. Mr Jackman made very considerable efforts to get to the bottom of things.'

21.69   This approach was followed in *Letherbarrow v Warwickshire County Council*[58] where Bean LJ commented:

> 'What the section does show is that Parliament expected the consideration of a prosecution under this section to be the subject of careful consideration. The decision which the prosecutor has to make under this subsection is not whether there is a prima facie case but whether the evidence is sufficient to justify a prosecution.'[59]

Thus it was said that the test is not simply the time at which investigations are concluded, but rather the test as set out in the legislation.

21.70   In *Lamont-Perkins v RSPCA*,[60] the Divisional Court confirmed that s 31 applies to all prosecutors whether by a public body or private prosecutors. Moving to consider challenges that could be made to certificates Wyn Williams J stated:

> 'It seems to me to be clear that a certificate issued under section 31(2) of the 2006 Act and which conforms to the criteria specified in section 31(2) can be challenged on two bases alone. First, it can be challenged on the basis that it constitutes a fraud; second, it can be challenged on the basis that it is plainly wrong.'

---

[57]   See also *Letherbarrow v Warwickshire County Council* [2015] EWHC 4820 (Admin), where it was said that the prosecuting authority was the county council but that it is the individual with responsibility for deciding whether a prosecution should go forward whose thoughts and beliefs are relevant.
[58]   [2015] EWHC 4820 (Admin).
[59]   At para 17.
[60]   [2012] EWHC 1002 (Admin).

21.71 The court was asked to consider the procedure that should be adopted where the certificate is 'plainly wrong' (even where this has occurred innocently). Having concluded that the magistrates have no jurisdiction to hear a summons laid out of time (absent a valid certificate under s 31(2)), Wynn Williams J stated:

'A certificate under section 31(2) is conclusive evidence of the facts stated therein unless it is demonstrated that the certificate is plainly wrong. If the certificate is plainly wrong it has no effect and the magistrates must disregard it. They will then be left to determine whether or not the prosecutor has initiated proceedings within the time limit permitted by section 31(1) and if he has not the magistrates will have no jurisdiction to hear the summons in question.'

21.72 A challenge to the jurisdiction of the court would be normally decided as a preliminary issue. In Scotland, the time limits for offences under the AHWSA 2006 (except for proceedings for animal fighting offences committed under s 23) are established under s 136 of the Criminal Procedure (Scotland) Act 1995 – within 6 months after the contravention occurred.

Enforcement

21.73 There is no prescribed duty of enforcement for the AWA 2006 or AHWSA 2006.

21.74 Although s 30 of the AWA 2006 provides a power for a local authority in England Wales to prosecute offences (which may be seen as superfluous in the light of s 222 of the Local Government Act 1972) the right to launch private prosecutions derives from the common law and the AWA 2006 does not limit that right. Powers can be exercised by a constable or an inspector. An inspector is a person appointed either by the appropriate national authority (either the Secretary of State or the National Assembly for Wales, for the AWA 2006, or the Scottish Ministers for the AHWSA 2006) or by a local authority for AWA/AHWSA.

21.75 The enforcement powers available to constables/inspectors are found in ss 18–29, 51–56 and Sch 2 to the AWA 2006 (ss 32, 49(7) and Sch 1 to the AHWSA 2006); they include emergency powers in relation to animals in distress, powers of entry and search, seizure of animals and inspection under certain conditions. In regard to the powers of entry and search, the court in *R (on the application of the RSPCA) v Colchester Magistrates Court*[61] admonished the use of a warrant granted to enter under the Environmental Protection Act 1990 to effectively establish a case of animal cruelty, even though the application for a warrant under the AWA 2006 had been refused.

21.76 Section 51(5) of the AWA 2006 provides immunity for inspectors for actions taken outside their powers, so long as in purporting to act under their powers, they acted reasonably and in good faith:

---

61   [2015] EWHC 1418 (Admin).

(5) An inspector shall not be liable in any civil or criminal proceedings for anything done in the purported performance of his functions under this Act if the court is satisfied that the act was done in good faith and that there were reasonable grounds for doing it.

21.77 Section 49(4) of the AHWSA 2006 is framed in similar terms:

(4) An inspector incurs no civil or criminal liability for anything which the inspector does in purported exercise of any functions conferred on the inspector by a provision of this Part, or by regulations made under this Part, where the inspector acts on reasonable grounds and in good faith.

Sentencing

21.78 Sections 32–45 of the AWA 2006 set out the penalties available on conviction, which include imprisonment, fine, deprivation, disqualification, destruction, forfeiture of equipment and cancellation of a licence or registration.

21.79 Section 32(1) provides that for the offences under ss 4–8 of the AWA 2006:[62]

(1) A person guilty of an offence ... shall be liable on summary conviction to –

    (a)   imprisonment for a term not exceeding 51 weeks, or
    (b)   a fine,

or to both.

For an offence under s 9 of the AWA 2006, the sentence on summary conviction is imprisonment not exceeding 51 weeks or an unlimited fine or both.[63]

21.80 Section 34 provides the power to disqualify following conviction under the Act:

34 Disqualification

(1) If a person is convicted of an offence to which this section applies, the court by or before which he is convicted may, instead of or in addition to dealing with him in any other way, make an order disqualifying him under any one or more of subsections (2) to (4) for such period as it thinks fit.

(2) Disqualification under this subsection disqualifies a person –

    (a)   from owning animals,
    (b)   from keeping animals,
    (c)   from participating in the keeping of animals, and
    (d)   from being party to an arrangement under which he is entitled to control or influence the way in which animals are kept.

---

[62]   Not including s 6(8), (9) or (12).
[63]   References to 51 weeks should be read as 6 months pending the implementation of s 281(5) of the Criminal Justice Act 2003.

(3) Disqualification under this subsection disqualifies a person from dealing in animals.

(4) Disqualification under this subsection disqualifies a person –

  (a)   from transporting animals, and
  (b)   from arranging for the transport of animals.

(5) Disqualification under subsection (2), (3) or (4) may be imposed in relation to animals generally, or in relation to animals of one or more kinds.

21.81   In *R (on the application of the RSPCA) v Guildford Crown Court*,[64] the RSPCA sought judicial review of the decision of a Crown Court judge to vary the terms of a disqualification under s 34(2) so as to not disqualify him from the participation in the keeping of animals under s 34(2)(c). The Divisional Court found that in imposing a disqualification under subss (2), (3) or (4), the sentencing judge has no discretion to relax or vary any of the statutory terms of that disqualification. In *R (on the application of Patterson & Patterson) v RSPCA*,[65] Blake J considered that the prohibition under s 34(2) was not 'so wide as preventing any form of contact with a dog or with an animal or control of an animal'. For there to be a breach of a disqualification order:

> 'it is not sufficient that you are able to control or influence the way in which animals are kept, you must be entitled to control or influence the way in which they are kept under an arrangement to which you are party.'[66]

21.82   Sections 39–43 of the AHWSA 2006 prescribe for post-conviction deprivation and disqualification orders for relevant offences (which include s 19 of the AHWSA 2006). Section 46 of the AHWSA 2006 provides that a person who commits an offence under s 19 of the AHWSA 2006 is liable on summary conviction to imprisonment for a term not exceeding 12 months or to a fine not exceeding £20,000 or to both.

Commentary

21.83   In December 2010 the Memorandum to Environment, Food and Rural Affairs Committee Post-Legislative Assessment of the Animal Welfare Act 2006 was published as part of the process set out in the document Post-Legislative Scrutiny.[67] The Conclusions of the Memorandum noted that the main criticisms of the 2006 Act focused on three specific issues: the way in which it has been enforced, the delay in introducing the secondary legislation that had originally been envisaged and the lack of public awareness surrounding the new responsibilities for pet owners and the functions of the AWA 2006. The report concluded that whilst there was still more to do to achieve higher standards of

---

[64]   [2012] EWHC 3392 (Admin).
[65]   [2013] EWHC 4531 (Admin).
[66]   Blake J at paras 24–25.
[67]   Cm 7320.

animal welfare, improvements had occurred and the objectives of harmonising farm and companion welfare and consolidating and simplifying animal welfare legislation had been met.

WELFARE OFFENCES CREATED UNDER REGULATIONS

21.84   It is not intended to provide an exhaustive list of all offences created under secondary legislation, but rather to highlight regulations of note.

Welfare of farmed animals

21.85   The Welfare of Farmed Animals (England) Regulations 2007[68] is made under s 12 of the AWA 2006, replacing the 2000 Regulation[69] of the same name. The order implements EU directives on the protection of animals for farming purposes and those setting minimum standards for the protection of laying hens, calves and pigs.[70]

21.86   Under reg 3, a 'farmed animal' means an animal bred or kept for the production of food, wool or skin or other farming purposes, but does not include:

(a)   a fish, reptile or amphibian;

(b)   an animal whilst at, or solely intended for use in, a competition, show or cultural or sporting event or activity;

(c)   an experimental or laboratory animal; or

(d)   an animal living in the wild.

21.87   Regulation 4(1) imposes a duty upon a person responsible for a farmed animal to take all reasonable steps to ensure that the conditions under which it is bred or kept comply with specified standards set out at Sch 1 of the Regulations. Further specific duties lie under reg 5 for poultry, laying hens, calves, cattle, pigs, rabbits. Under reg 6, a person responsible for a farmed animal must not attend to the animal unless he is acquainted with any relevant code of practice and has access to the code while attending to the animal and must take all reasonable steps to ensure that a person employed or engaged by him does not attend to the animal unless that other person is acquainted with any relevant code of practice, has access to the code while attending to the

---

[68]   SI 2007/2078, amended by Welfare of Farmed Animals (England) (Amendment) Regulations 2010, SI 2010/3033.

[69]   SI 2000/1870.

[70]   Council Directive 98/58/EC concerning the protection of animals kept for farming purposes, Council Directive 99/74/EC laying down minimum standards for the protection of laying hens, Council Directive 91/629/EEC laying down minimum standards for the protection of calves, as amended by Council Directive 97/2/EC and Commission decision 97/182/EC, and Council Directive 91/630/EEC laying down minimum standards for the protection of pigs, as amended by Council Directive 2001/88/EC and Council Directive 2001/93/EC.

animal and has received instruction and guidance on the code.[71] By reg 7 it is an offence for a person without lawful authority or excuse to contravene or fail to comply with a duty in regs 4, 5 or 6. The local authority is prescribed the power to prosecute under reg 8(1). Equivalent regulations exist for Wales and Scotland.

Welfare of animals in transport

21.88 Notwithstanding the repeal of the welfare provisions under the Animal Health Act 1981, some secondary legislation made under that Act continues to apply to welfare issues in England and Wales (and offences are created under that Act for breaches). The Welfare of Animals (Transport) (England) Order 2006[72] and the Welfare of Animals (Transport) (Wales) Order 2007[73] are created under the Animal Health Act 1981 and breach of the regulations are offences under s 73 of the Act. Each create under reg 4(1) offences of transporting any animal in a way which causes, or is likely to cause, injury or unnecessary suffering to that animal.

21.89 Amongst other offences under the Orders:

'A person who fails to comply with any of the following provisions of Council Regulation (EC) No 1/2005 is guilty of an offence against the Act –

(a)   Article 3 (general conditions for the transport of animals) ...'

21.90 Council Regulation (EC) No 1/2005 applies to the transport of animals taking place in connection with an economic activity but not where the transport of animals relates to veterinary treatment. Article 3 states:

General conditions for the transport of animals

No person shall transport animals or cause animals to be transported in a way likely to cause injury or undue suffering to them.

In addition, the following conditions shall be complied with:

(a)   all necessary arrangements have been made in advance to minimise the length of the journey and meet animals' needs during the journey;
(b)   the animals are fit for the journey;
(c)   the means of transport are designed, constructed, maintained and operated so as to avoid injury and suffering and ensure the safety of the animals;
(d)   the loading and unloading facilities are adequately designed, constructed, maintained and operated so as to avoid injury and suffering and ensure the safety of the animals;
(e)   the personnel handling animals are trained or competent as appropriate for this purpose and carry out their tasks without using violence or any method likely to cause unnecessary fear, injury or suffering;

---

[71]   Regulation 6.
[72]   SI 2006/3260.
[73]   SI 2007/1047.

(f)   the transport is carried out without delay to the place of destination and the welfare conditions of the animals are regularly checked and appropriately maintained;

(g)   sufficient floor area and height is provided for the animals, appropriate to their size and the intended journey;

(h)   water, feed and rest are offered to the animals at suitable intervals and are appropriate in quality and quantity to their species and size.

The Welfare of Animals (Transport) (Scotland) Regulations 2006[74] were made under the European Communities Act 1972 and a person who fails to comply with, for example, Art 3 (general conditions for the transport of animals) of Council Regulation (EC) No 1/2005, as set out above, is guilty of an offence under the Animal Health Act 1981. Enforcement under the orders is expressed for the local authority.

Welfare of animals at markets

21.91   The welfare of animals at markets is regulated by the Welfare of Animals at Markets Order 1990[75] and make it an offence against the Animal Health Act 1981 to contravene any provision of the Order including:[76]

- permitting an unfit animal to be exposed for sale (Art 5);[77]
- being party to injury or unnecessary suffering to an animal, including the exposure to adverse weather conditions (Art 6);
- mishandling animals at market, prohibiting lifting, dragging or inappropriate tying of an animal (Art 7);
- using excessive force to control an animal; the use of sticks, whips, crops and goads are also restricted (Art 8).

Welfare of animals at the time of killing

21.92   Hitherto the welfare of animals at the point of slaughter has been governed by the Welfare of Animals (Slaughter or Killing) Regulations 1995.[78] This legislation makes it an offence to cause or permit an animal avoidable excitement, pain or suffering. There are also specific rules on handling, stunning, slaughter or killing of animals.

21.93   This was replaced by EU Regulation from 1 January 2013,[79] which applies to the killing of all animals bred and kept for the production of food, wool, skin, fur or other products in slaughterhouses or on farms as well as the killing of animals for disease control purposes. The Regulation applies to all

---

[74]   SSI 2006/606.

[75]   SI 1990/2628, made under the Animal Health Act 1981.

[76]   Article 20(c).

[77]   The prosecution must prove the animal is unfit and that the defendant knowingly allowed that unfit animal to be exposed for sale, *Davidson v Strong* (1997) *The Times*, 20 March.

[78]   SI 1995/731.

[79]   EU Council Regulation (EC) No 1099/2009 on the protection of animals at the time of killing.

vertebrate animals including poultry and fish, but excluding reptiles and amphibians. All animals must be spared avoidable pain, distress or suffering during killing and related operations. For all animals (other than fish) specific requirements apply requiring them to be killed by a method that leads to instant death or death after stunning.

21.94 The Regulation places a responsibility on the business operator not to permit welfare abuses and stipulates that animals are to be 'spared any avoidable pain, distress or suffering during killing and related operations'. The key requirements include:

- With the exception of certain low throughput businesses, business operators must have suitably trained and qualified animal welfare officers to ensure that standard operating procedures are developed and implemented, and animal welfare rules are properly understood, applied and reviewed.

- Standard operating procedures are explicitly required for stunning, killing, and all related operations – such as the restraint or handling of animals.

- Individuals carrying out slaughter operations must hold a Certificate of Competence for the operations they perform.

- Animal Welfare Officers are required to hold a Certificate of Competence for all the tasks they are responsible for.

- The keeping of records of maintenance and also routine checks for one year.

The Regulation also encourages the development of guides to good practice.

21.95 In England DEFRA consulted on implementing the Regulation during 2012 on what became the Welfare of Animals at the Time of Killing Regulations 2014.[80] These regulations were revoked on 19 May 2014,[81] the day they were due to come into force as it was decided that the potential impact on some aspects of religious slaughter needed further consideration. The Welfare of Animals at the Time of Killing (England) Regulations 2015[82] came into force on 5 November 2015.

21.96 In August 2016, the Bureau of Investigative Journalism published an article stating that '... vets and meat hygiene inspectors working for the FSA inside abattoirs reported a total of 9,511 animal welfare breaches between July 2014 and June 2016 ...' according to data released by the Food Standards Agency under the Freedom of Information Act 2000. Subsequently, the Food Standards Agency Board Meeting, on 21 September 2016, received a paper setting out its current and proposed activities in England and Wales as part of its ongoing programme to 'Deter, Prevent, Detect and Enforce' animal welfare breaches.

---

[80] SI 2014/1240.
[81] Welfare of Animals at the Time of Killing (Revocation) Regulations 2014, SI 2014/1258.
[82] SI 2015/1782.

21.97　In Scotland, the Regulation is implemented as from 22 November 2012 through the Welfare of Animals at the Time of Killing (Scotland) Regulations 2012,[83] in Wales it is implemented under the Welfare of Animals at the Time of Killing (Wales) Regulations 2014[84] and in Northern Ireland, Welfare of Animals at the Time of Killing (Northern Ireland) Regulations 2014[85] Each of these regulations were made under s 2(2) of the European Communities Act 1972.

OTHER ANIMAL WELFARE LEGISLATION

21.98　Note that, in Scotland, the following Acts were repealed by the Animal Health and Welfare (Scotland) Act 2006.

Performing Animals (Regulation) Act 1925

21.99　The welfare of performing animals is provided for in the general provisions of the Animal Welfare Act 2006. In addition, trainers and exhibitors of performing animals must be registered with the local authority under this Act. Offences are created, including where a person:

- not being registered under the Act, exhibits or trains any performing animal; or
- being registered under the Act, exhibits or trains any performing animal with respect to which or in a manner with respect to which he is not registered.

21.100　Under the Act, police officers and officers of local authorities, have power to enter premises where animals are being trained and exhibited, and if cruelty and neglect is detected, magistrates' courts can prohibit or restrict the training or exhibition of the animals and suspend or cancel the registration granted under the Act.

21.101　Note that the Welfare of Wild Animals in Travelling Circuses (England) Regulations 2012 require all operators of travelling circuses in England that use wild animals to be licensed. In April 2013 the Government proposed a draft Wild Animals in Circuses Bill that would prohibit the use of wild animals in travelling circuses in England. Although introduced before Parliament in 2014, the Bill did not become law before the end of the Parliamentary session. It remains to be seen whether it will be re-introduced in the course of the present parliament.

---

[83]　SSI 2012/321.
[84]　SI 2014/951.
[85]　SI 2014/107.

Pet Animals Act 1951

21.102 The Act requires any person keeping a pet shop (carrying on at premises of any nature – including a private dwelling – of a business of selling animals as pets) to be licensed by the local authority. Before granting a licence the local authority must be satisfied that the animals are kept in accommodation that is suitable as respects size, temperature, lighting, ventilation and cleaniness; that they are supplied with appropriate food and drink; and are adequately protected from disease and fire. The local authority may attach any conditions to the licence, may inspect the licensed premises at all reasonable times and may refuse a licence if the conditions at the premises are unsatisfactory or if the terms of the licence are not being complied with. Offences are created for persons who trade without a licence or in breach of licensing conditions.[86]

Animal Boarding Establishments Act 1963

21.103 The Act requires any person keeping a boarding establishment for animals (carrying on at premises of any nature – including a private dwelling – of a business of providing accommodation for other people's cats or dogs) to be licensed by the local authority. The licence is granted at the discretion of the local authority which may take into account the suitability of the accommodation and whether the animals are well fed, exercised and protected from disease and fire. The local authority may attach any conditions to the licence, may inspect the licensed premises at all reasonable times and may refuse a licence if the conditions at the premises are unsatisfactory. Offences are created for persons who trade without a licence or in breach of licensing conditions.

Riding Establishments Act 1964 and 1970

21.104 The 1964 Act requires any person keeping a riding establishment (carrying on of a business of keeping horses for prescribed purposes) to be licensed by the local authority. The local authority can impose conditions on the licence. The local authority, in the exercise of its discretion, may take into account the suitability of the applicant/manager, the accommodation and pasture, adequacy of the provision for the horses' health, welfare and exercise, precautions against fire and disease and the suitability of the horses as regards the reasons for which they are kept. (Under the 1970 Act – which also amends the 1964 Act – if the local authority is not satisfied that, having regard to all the circumstances they would be justified in granting a licence, they may grant a provisional licence.) Offences are committed where persons trade without a licence, in breach of licensing conditions and also hiring out or uses for the purposes of instruction, a horse where its condition is such that its riding is likely to cause it suffering.

---

[86] Pet Animals Act 1951, s 1(7).

Breeding of Dogs Acts

21.105   The 1973 Act requires any person keeping a breeding establishment for dogs (which is defined) to be licensed by the local authority. The local authority has discretion whether to grant a licence and must ensure that the animals will be suitably accommodated, fed, exercised and protected from disease and fire. The 1973 Act, as amended by the 1999 Act, requires a local authority to have regard to certain matters in determining whether to grant a licence and about which conditions must be included in the licence. (One such matter is that accurate records should be kept at the premises of the establishment and made available for inspection. The Breeding of Dogs (Licensing Records) Regulations 1999,[87] which apply in England and Wales, and the Breeding of Dogs (Licensing Records) (Scotland) Regulations 1999,[88] which apply to Scotland only, prescribe the form in which those records must be kept.) The 1991 Act extended the powers of local authorities to obtain a warrant to enter premises not covered by a licence under the 1973 Act, excluding a private dwelling house, in which it is believed that a dog breeding business is being carried out. All outbuildings, garages and sheds are open to inspection. Previously local authority inspectors could enter and inspect only premises which were already licensed.

Control of horses

21.106   The Control of Horses Act 2015 applies only in England and has been introduced to tackle the problem of 'fly-grazing', namely the practice of deliberately leaving horses to graze on land without the landowner's permission. The Act, which came into force on 26 May 2015, amends the Animals Act 1971 to provide as s 7A of that Act for the power of local authorities to detain a horse which is in any public place within its area, providing that (a) the local authority has reasonable grounds for believing the horse is there without lawful authority, and (b) where the land is lawfully occupied by a person, that person consents to the detention of the horse or the local authority has reasonable grounds for believing that the person would consent to the detention of the horse. If the prescribed notice provisions have been complied with, then under s 7C of the amended Act, the local authority has the power to dispose of the horse in whatever way it sees fit including by selling it or having it destroyed.

Wales

21.107   The Control of Horses (Wales) Act 2014 became law in Wales on 27 January 2014. The Act provides local authorities with the powers to:

- seize and impound horses which are on land without consent;

---

[87]   SI 1999/3192.
[88]   SI 1999/176.

- sell the horses or dispose of them, including destruction by humane means if appropriate;

- recover costs reasonably incurred from the owners of horses in such circumstance.

Microchipping of Dogs (England) Regulations 2015[89]

21.108 These regulations provide for the compulsory microchipping of dogs and the recording of each dog's identity and its keeper's contact details on a database. Local authorities have the power under reg 11(2) to authorise in writing any person to act for the purpose of enforcing the regulations. The authorised person may under reg 12 serve a notice on a keeper to microchip their dog, to microchip a dog and recover the cost of doing so from the keeper and to take possession of a dog for the purpose of microchipping it.

---

[89] SI 2015/108.

INDEX

References are to paragraph numbers.